Salt Lake City

street guide

TELL US WHAT YOU THINK
comment card on last page

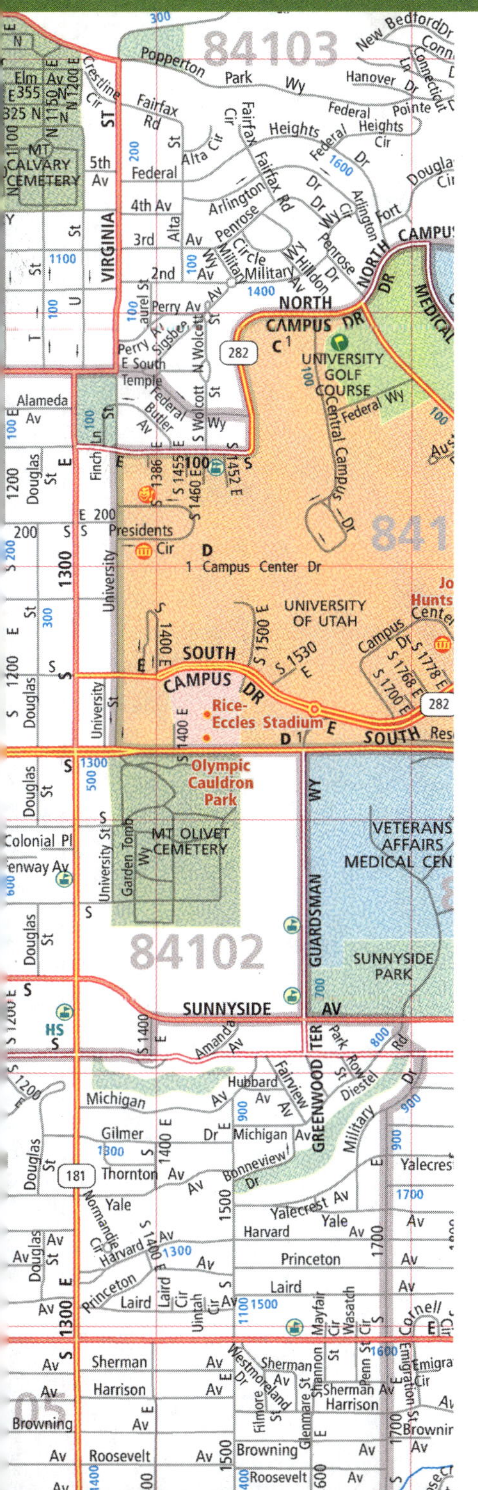

Contents

Introduction

Using Your Street Guide	A
PageFinder™ Map	B
Legend	D
We've Got You Covered	E

Maps

Street Guide Detail Maps	398-3568
Vicinity Map	Inside back cover

Lists and Indexes

Cities & Communities Index	1
List of Abbreviations	2
Street Index and Points of Interest Index	3
Comment Card	Last page

Rand McNally Consumer Affairs
P.O. Box 7600
Chicago, IL 60680-9915
randmcnally.com
For comments or suggestions, please call
(800) 777-MAPS (-6277)
or email us at:
consumeraffairs@randmcnally.com

PAGE
D

Legend

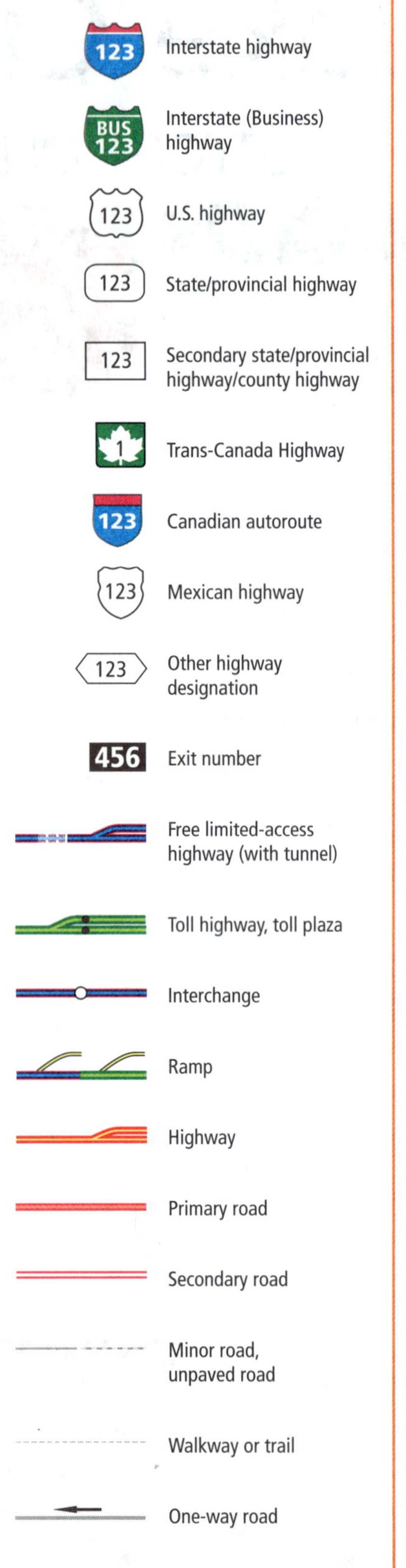
123
Interstate highway
BUS 123
Interstate (Business) highway
123
U.S. highway
123
State/provincial highway
123
Secondary state/provincial highway/county highway
1
Trans-Canada Highway
123
Canadian autoroute
123
Mexican highway
123
Other highway designation
456
Exit number
Free limited-access highway (with tunnel)
Toll highway, toll plaza
Interchange
Ramp
Highway
Primary road
Secondary road
Minor road, unpaved road
Walkway or trail
One-way road

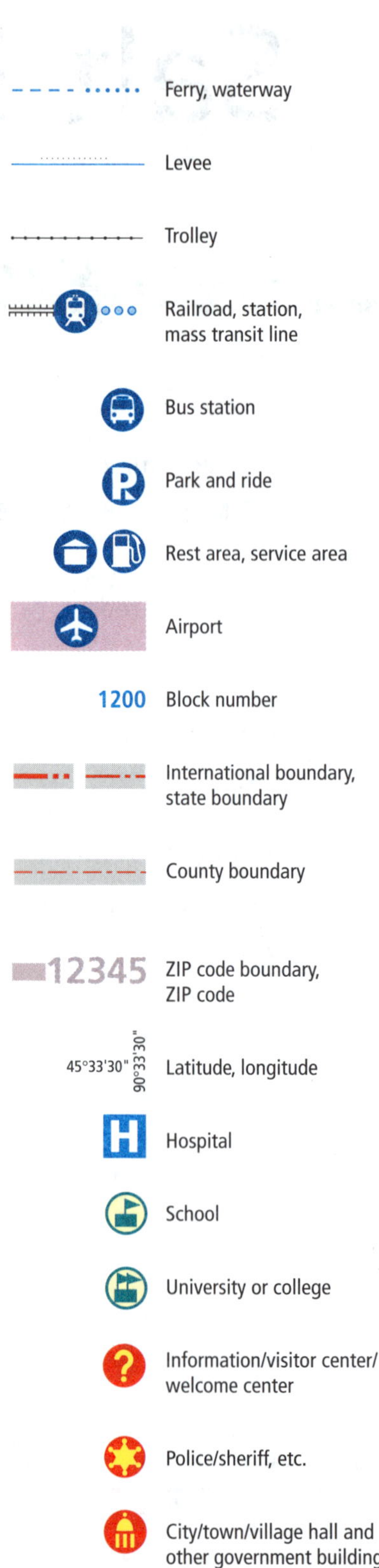
Ferry, waterway
Levee
Trolley
Railroad, station, mass transit line
Bus station
Park and ride
Rest area, service area
Airport
1200
Block number
International boundary, state boundary
County boundary
12345
ZIP code boundary, ZIP code
45°33'30"
90°33'30"
Latitude, longitude
Hospital
School
University or college
Information/visitor center/ welcome center
Police/sheriff, etc.
City/town/village hall and other government buildings

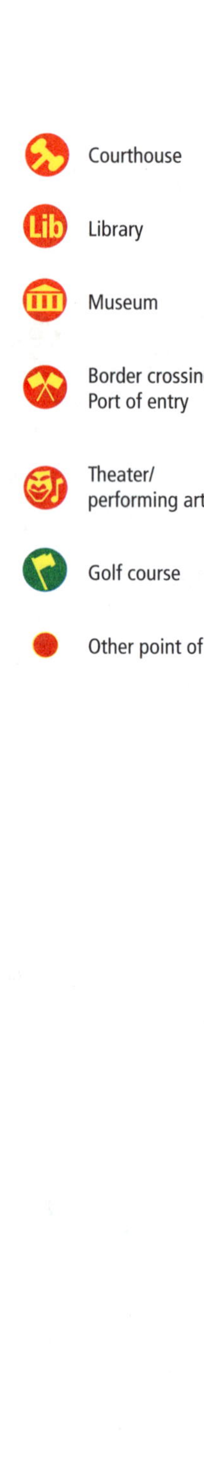
Courthouse
Lib
Library
Museum
Border crossing/ Port of entry
Theater/ performing arts center
Golf course
Other point of interest

we've got you COVERED

Rand McNally's broad selection of products is perfect for your every need. Whether you're looking for the convenience of write-on wipe-off laminated maps, extra maps for every car, or a Road Atlas to plan your next vacation or to use as a reference, Rand McNally has you covered.

Street Guides

Salt Lake City including Logan, Ogden, and Provo

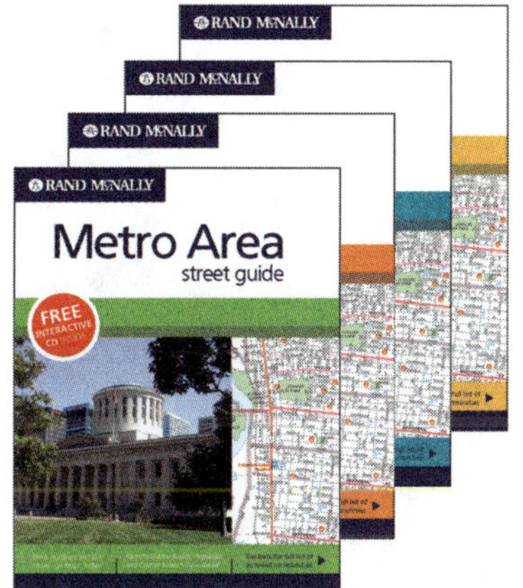

Folded Maps

EasyFinder® Laminated Maps

Nevada/ Utah

Salt Lake City

Paper Maps

Ogden/ Logan/ Brigham City

Salt Lake City/ Park City

Sandy/ Orem/ Provo

Utah

Road Atlases

Road Atlas

Road Atlas & Travel Guide

Large Scale Road Atlas

Midsize Road Atlas

Deluxe Midsize Road Atlas

Pocket Road Atlas

Wherever Rand McNally products are sold or at
www.randmcnally.com

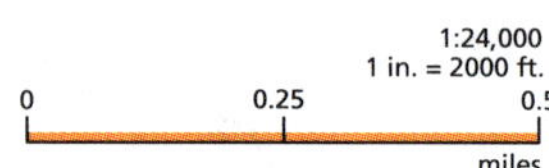

SEE B MAP

Amalga

84335

84341

W 6200 N
218
N 2400 ST W
W 6200 N
2150
6100
W 5900 N
2800
5900
2400
W 5800 N
3100
W 5400 N
5400
Bear River
Summit Creek
Coleman Rd
1600
1700
2000
5400
2000
W 5300 N
5300
BEAR RIVER
N 3200 W
5100
W 4800 N
W 4700 N
4700
W 4600 N
W 4600 N
N 2400 W
4600
2300
W 4600 N
1600
W 5000 N
5000
W 4400 N
4400
4000
W 4200 N
2000
N 2000 W
1200
W 4000 N
4000
W 3800 ST
W 3800 N
N 3200 ST W
3400

41°51'03"
41°50'37"
41°50'11"
41°49'44"
41°49'18"
41°48'52"
41°48'26"
41°48'00"
111°55'00"
111°54'25"
111°53'51"
111°53'16"
111°52'41"
111°52'06"

1 2 3 4 5 6 7
A B C D E

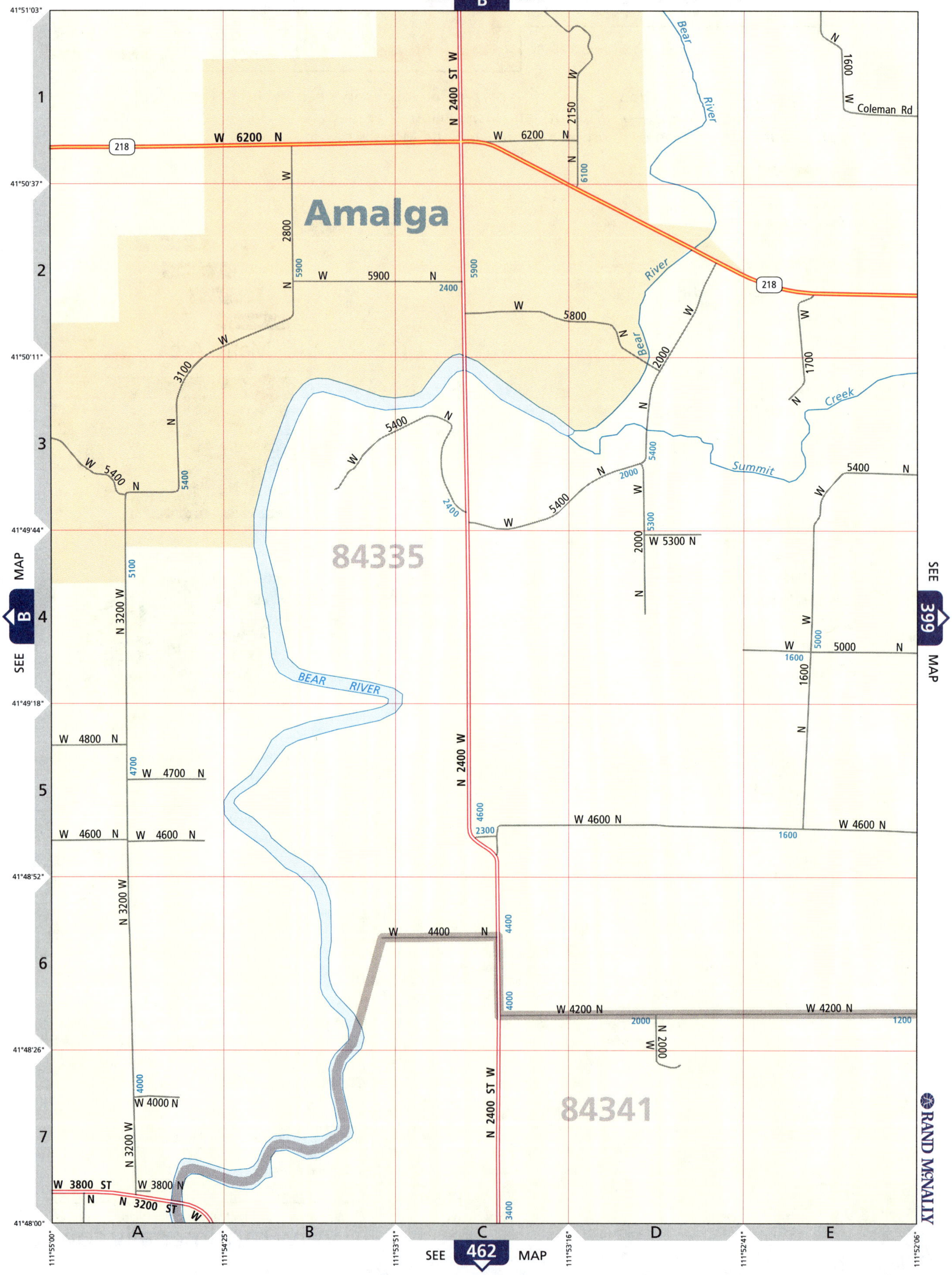

SEE B MAP

SEE 399 MAP

SEE 462 MAP

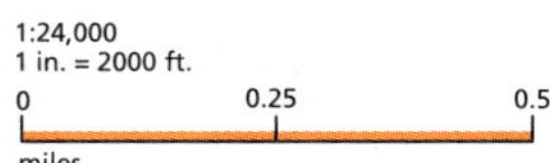

SEE B MAP

Smithfield

Hyde Park

84335

84318

84341

SMITHFIELD CITY CEMETERY

Summit Creek

Coleman Rd

Saddleback Rd

Upper Canyon Rd

Cottonwood Rd

Summit Creek Rd

Canyon Rd

Center St

MAIN ST

Maple Dr

Chestnut Ln

Juniper

Wasatch Blvd

Elm St

W 4600 N

W 5000 N

W 4200 N

E 4400 N

E 4800

E 4100 N

W 3700 N

1

2

3

4

5

6

7

A

B

C

D

E

41°51'02"

41°50'36"

41°50'10"

41°49'44"

41°49'18"

41°48'52"

41°48'26"

41°48'00"

111°52'06"

111°51'31"

111°50'56"

111°50'21"

111°49'47"

111°49'12"

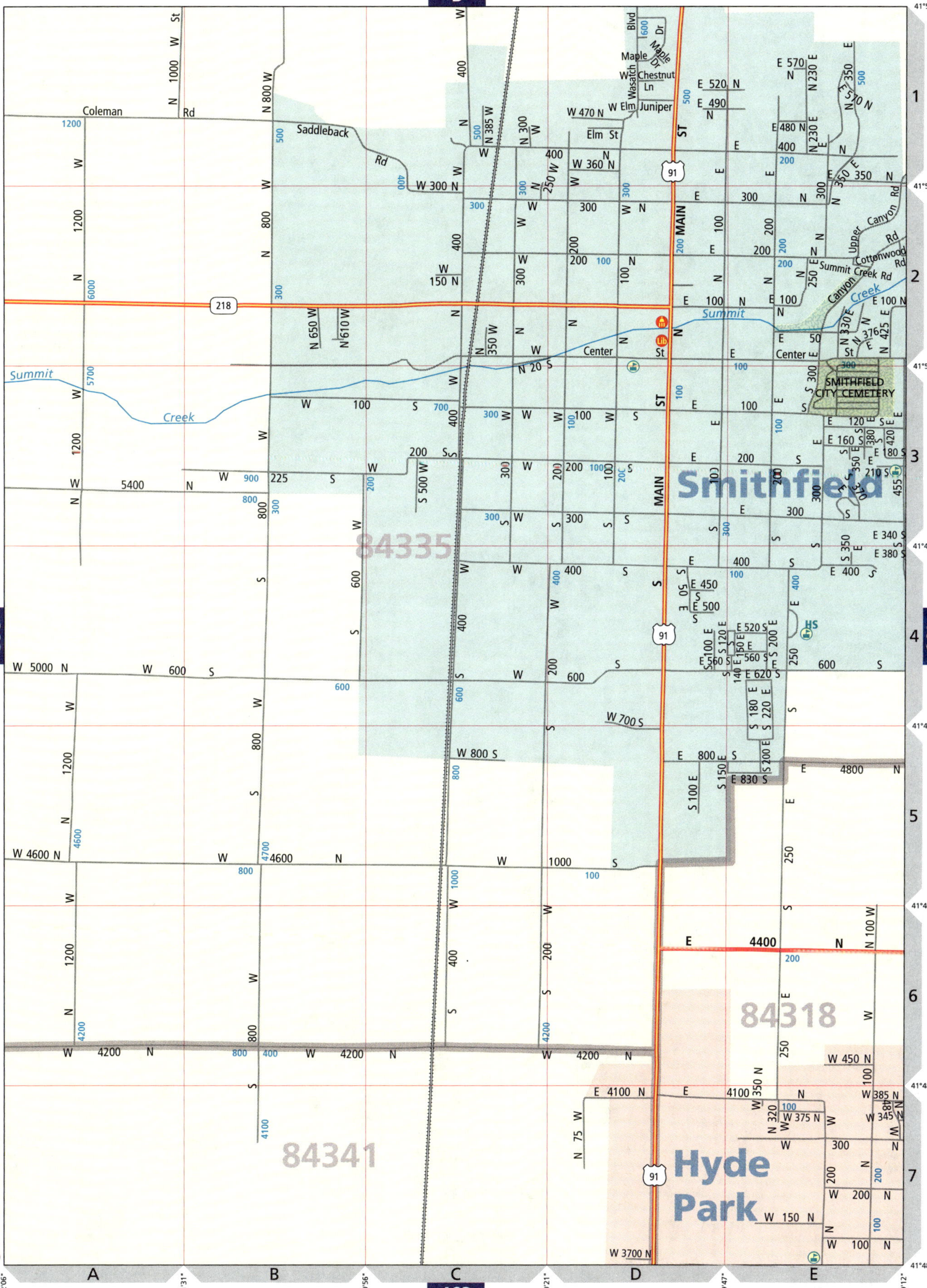

SEE 398 MAP

SEE 400 MAP

SEE 463 MAP

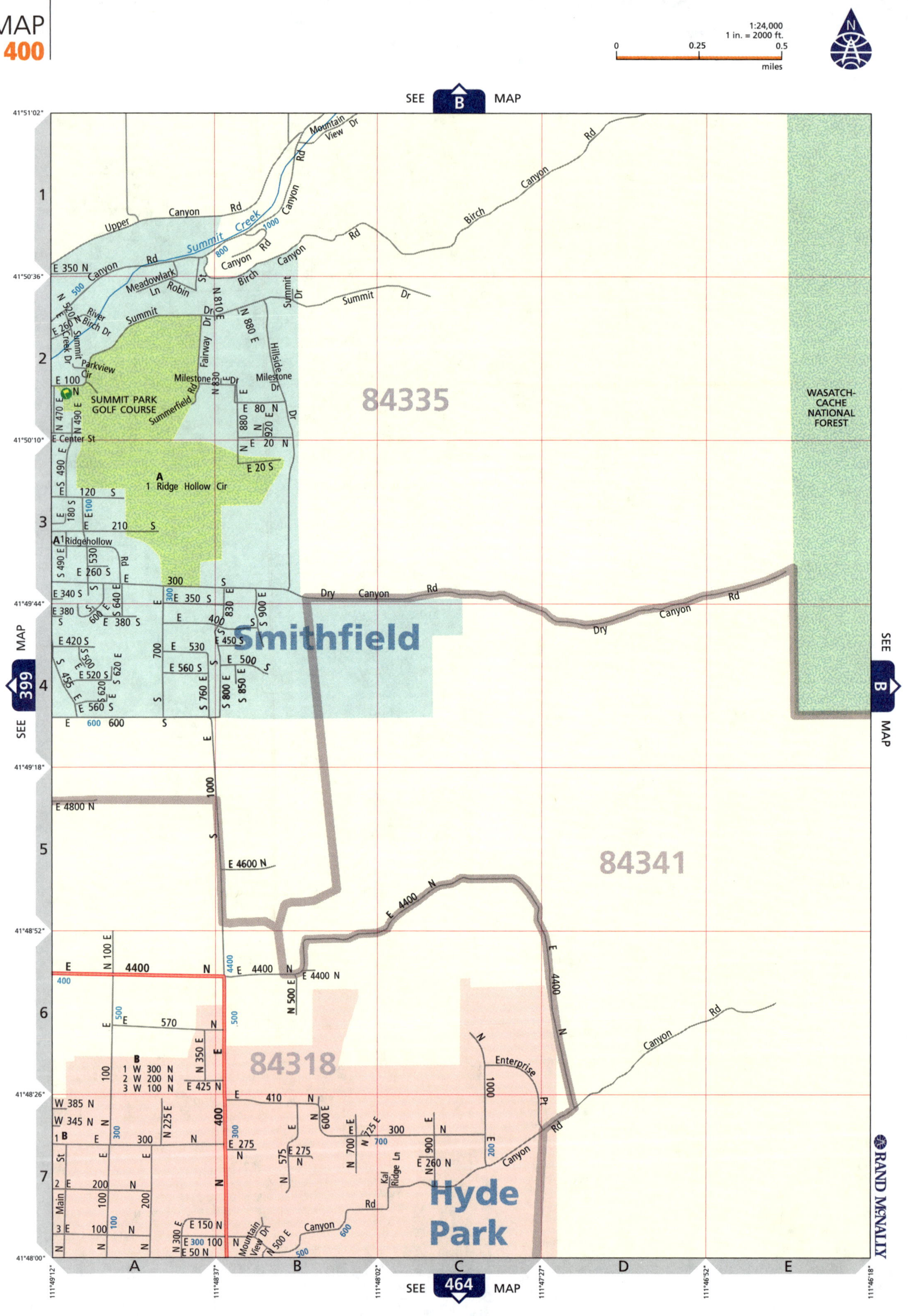
1:24,000
1 in. = 2000 ft.
0
0.25
0.5
miles
N
SEE B MAP
SEE 464 MAP
SEE 399 MAP
SEE B MAP
1
2
3
4
5
6
7
A
B
C
D
E
41°51'02"
41°50'36"
41°50'10"
41°49'44"
41°49'18"
41°48'52"
41°48'26"
41°48'00"
111°49'12"
111°48'37"
111°48'02"
111°47'27"
111°46'52"
111°46'18"
Smithfield
Hyde Park
84335
84341
84318
WASATCH-CACHE NATIONAL FOREST
SUMMIT PARK GOLF COURSE
Upper Canyon Rd
Summit Creek
Birch Canyon Rd
Mountain View Dr
Summit Dr
Summit Canyon Rd
Dry Canyon Rd
Canyon Rd
E 350 N
Meadowlark Ln
Robin St
River Birch Dr
Summit Creek Dr
Parkview Cir
Fairway Dr
Milestone Dr
Summerfield Rd
Hillside Dr
E Center St
A 1 Ridge Hollow Cir
1 Ridgehollow Rd
E 4800 N
E 4600 N
E 4400 N
N 500 E
N 100 E
Enterprise Pt
Kal Ridge Ln
Mountain View Dr
Main St
B 1 W 300 N 2 W 200 N 3 W 100 N
E 425 N
E 410 N
E 275 N
E 260 N
E 150 N
E 50 N
W 385 N
W 345 N
RAND McNALLY

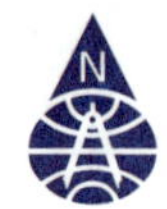

1:24,000
1 in. = 2000 ft.
0 0.25 0.5
miles

SEE 398 MAP

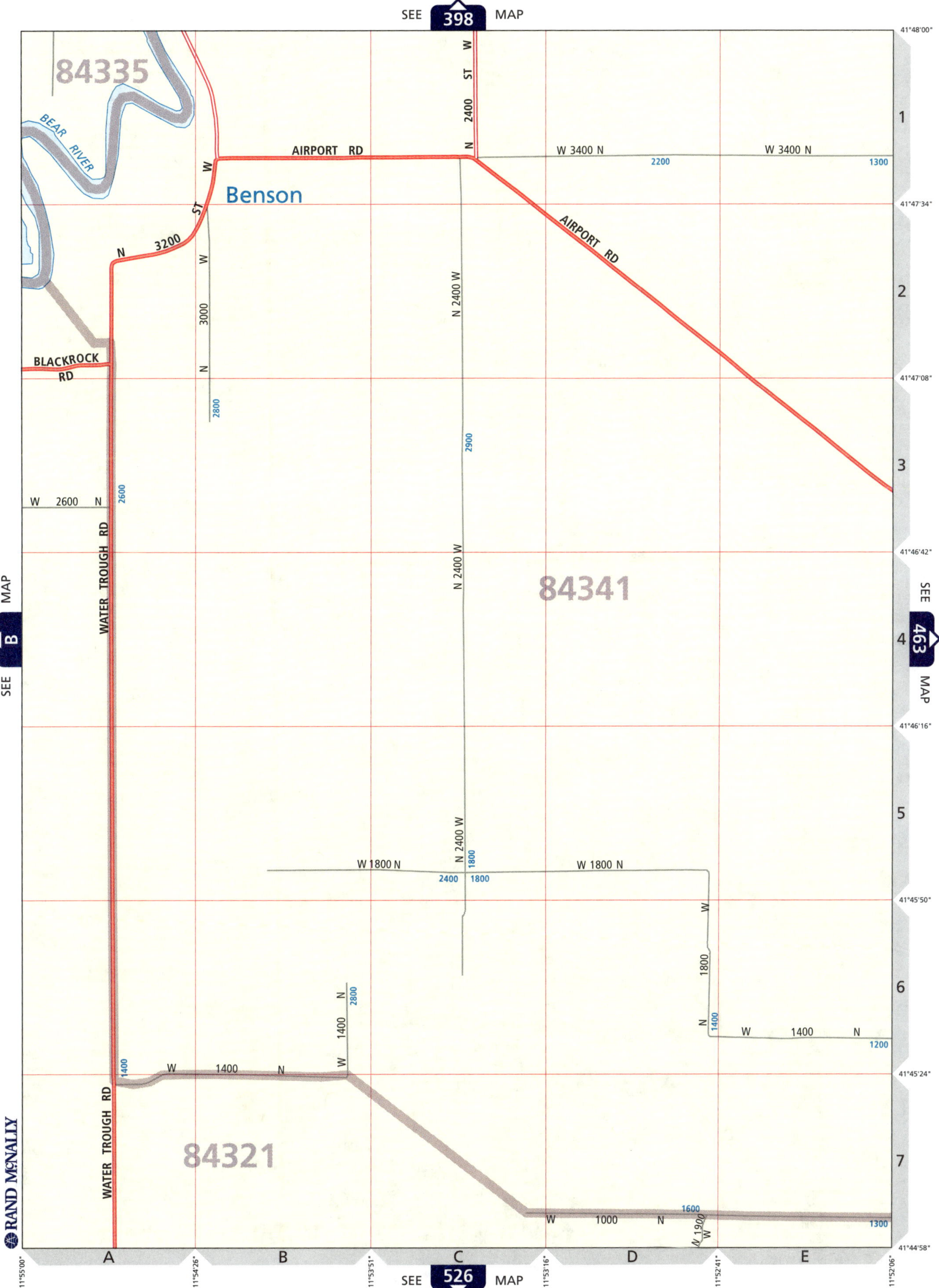

SEE B MAP

SEE 463 MAP

SEE 526 MAP

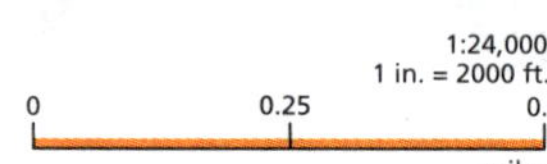

SEE 399 MAP

SEE 462 MAP

SEE 464 MAP

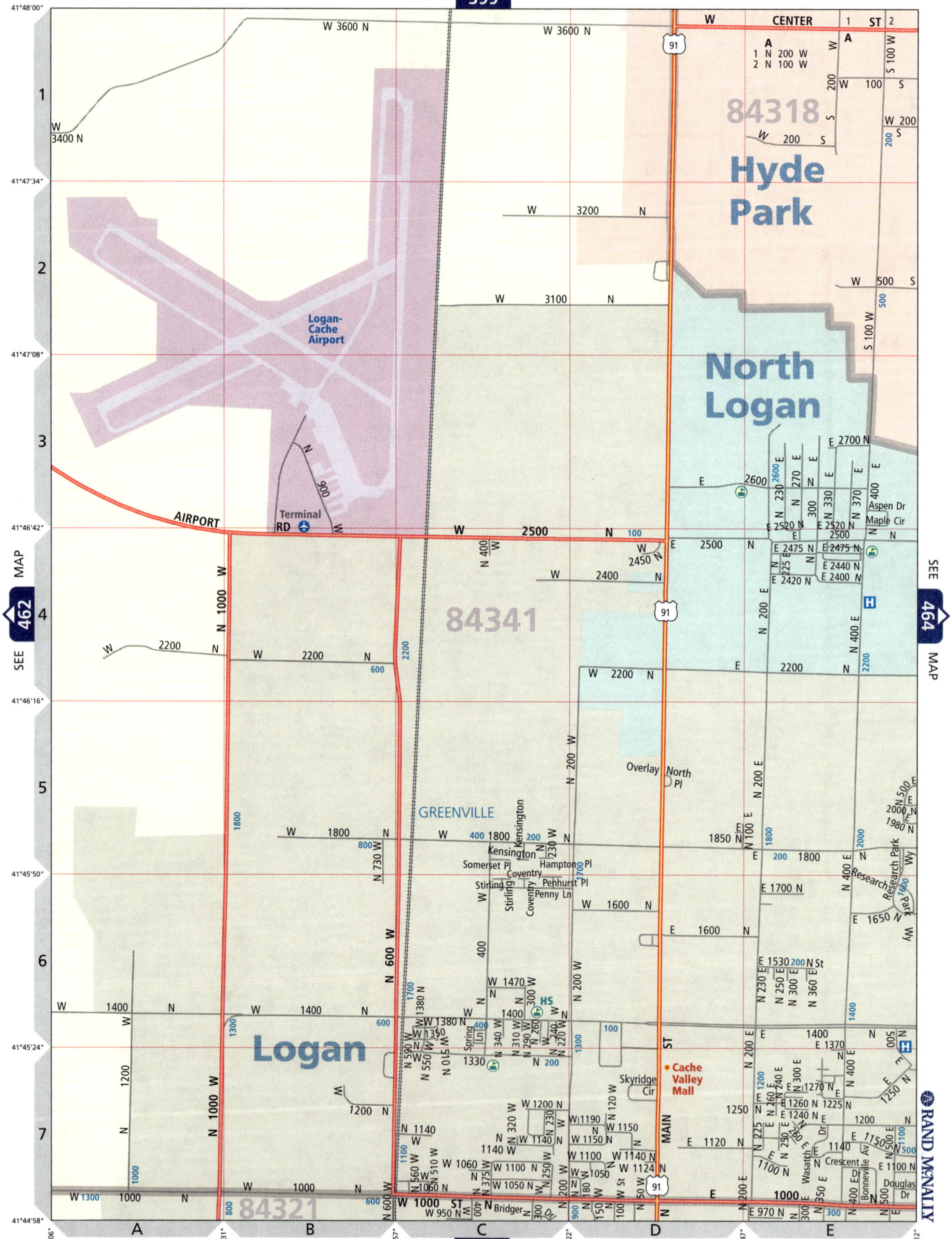

Hyde Park

84318

North Logan

Logan-Cache Airport

Terminal

AIRPORT RD

84341

GREENVILLE

Logan

Cache Valley Mall

Overlay

North Pl

Skyridge Cir

84321

W CENTER ST

W 3600 N

W 3400 N

W 3200 N

W 3100 N

W 2500 N

E 2500 N

E 2700 N

E 2600 N

W 2400 N

W 2450 N

W 2200 N

E 2200 N

W 1800 N

E 1800 N

1850 N

E 1700 N

W 1600 N

E 1600 N

E 1650 N

E 1530 N

W 1470 N

W 1400 N

E 1400 N

E 1370 N

W 1380 N

1330 N

W 1200 N

1250 N

E 1260 N

E 1240 N

E 1270 N

1225 N

1200 N

E 1120 N

1140 N

1100 N

W 1000 N

W 1000 ST

E 1000 N

E 970 N

W 950 N

N 1000 W

N 600 W

N 200 W

N 730 W

MAIN ST

N 200 E

N 100 E

N 400 E

N 1380 N

Kensington

Somerset Pl

Coventry

Stirling

Hampton Pl

Penhurst Pl

Penny Ln

Spring Ln

Aspen Dr

Maple Cir

Research Park Wy

Wasatch Dr

Crescent

Bonneville Av

Douglas Dr

Bridger Dr

HS

91

SEE 527 MAP

41°48'00"
41°47'34"
41°47'08"
41°46'42"
41°46'16"
41°45'50"
41°45'24"
41°44'58"
111°52'06"
111°51'31"
111°50'57"
111°50'22"
111°49'47"
111°49'12"

A B C D E

1 2 3 4 5 6 7

1:24,000
1 in. = 2000 ft.
0 0.25 0.5
miles

SEE 400 MAP

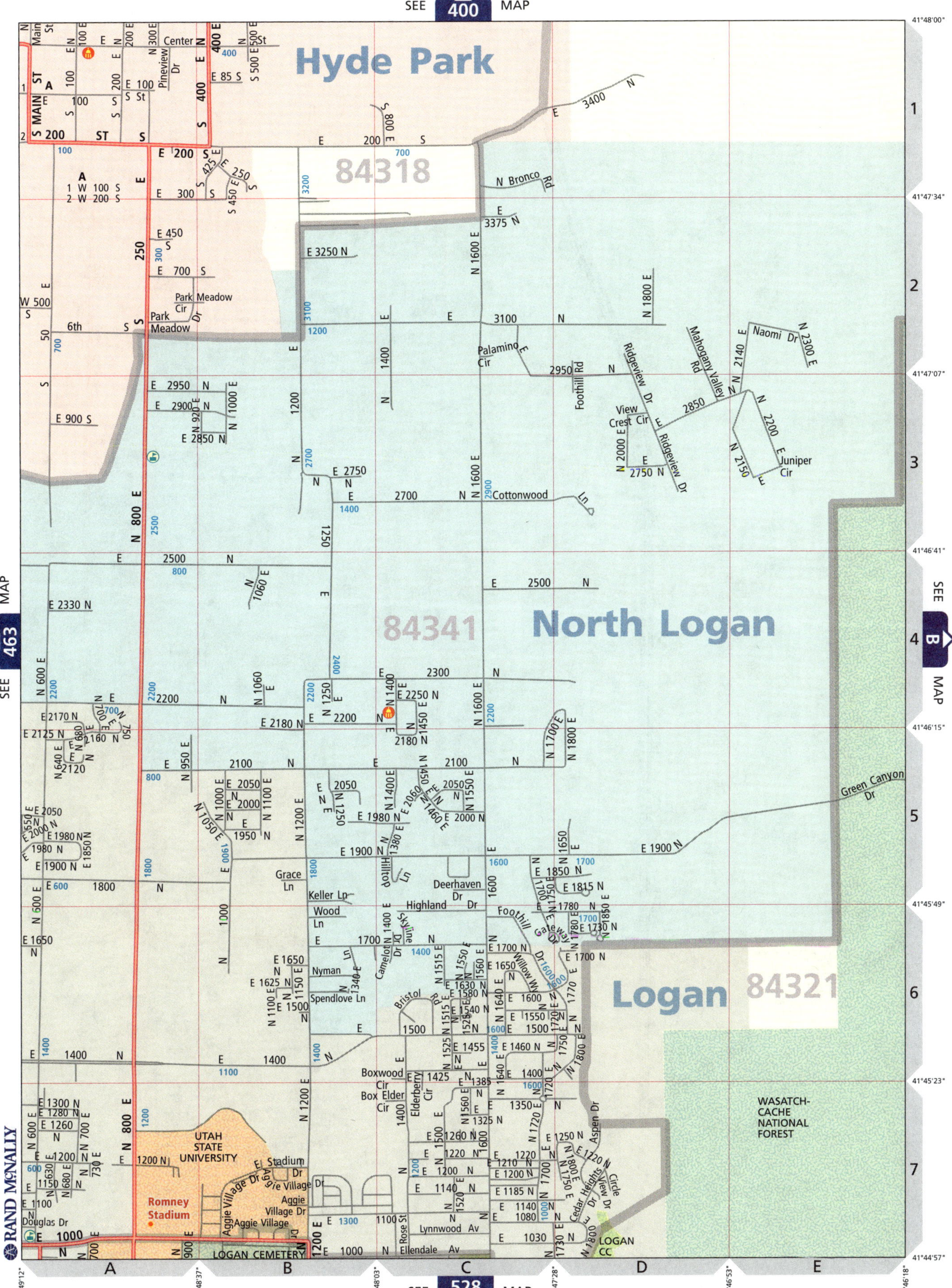

SEE 463 MAP

SEE B MAP

SEE 528 MAP

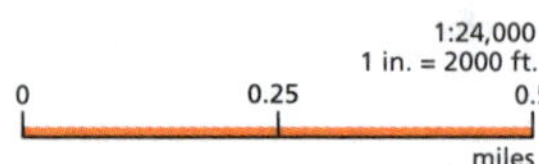

SEE B MAP

SEE B MAP

SEE 521 MAP

Garland

Tremonton

Elwood

84312

84336

84337

SKYWAY GOLF COURSE

Tremonton Municipal Airport

Terminal

VETERANS MEMORIAL HWY

MEMORIAL VETERANS HWY

W FACTORY ST

W 1000 N

W MAIN ST

11200 RD

1400 W ST

1000 W

IOWA STRING RD

MAIN ST

TREMONT ST

300 E

NORTH ST

Canal Bank Rd

Malad River

SEE 584 MAP

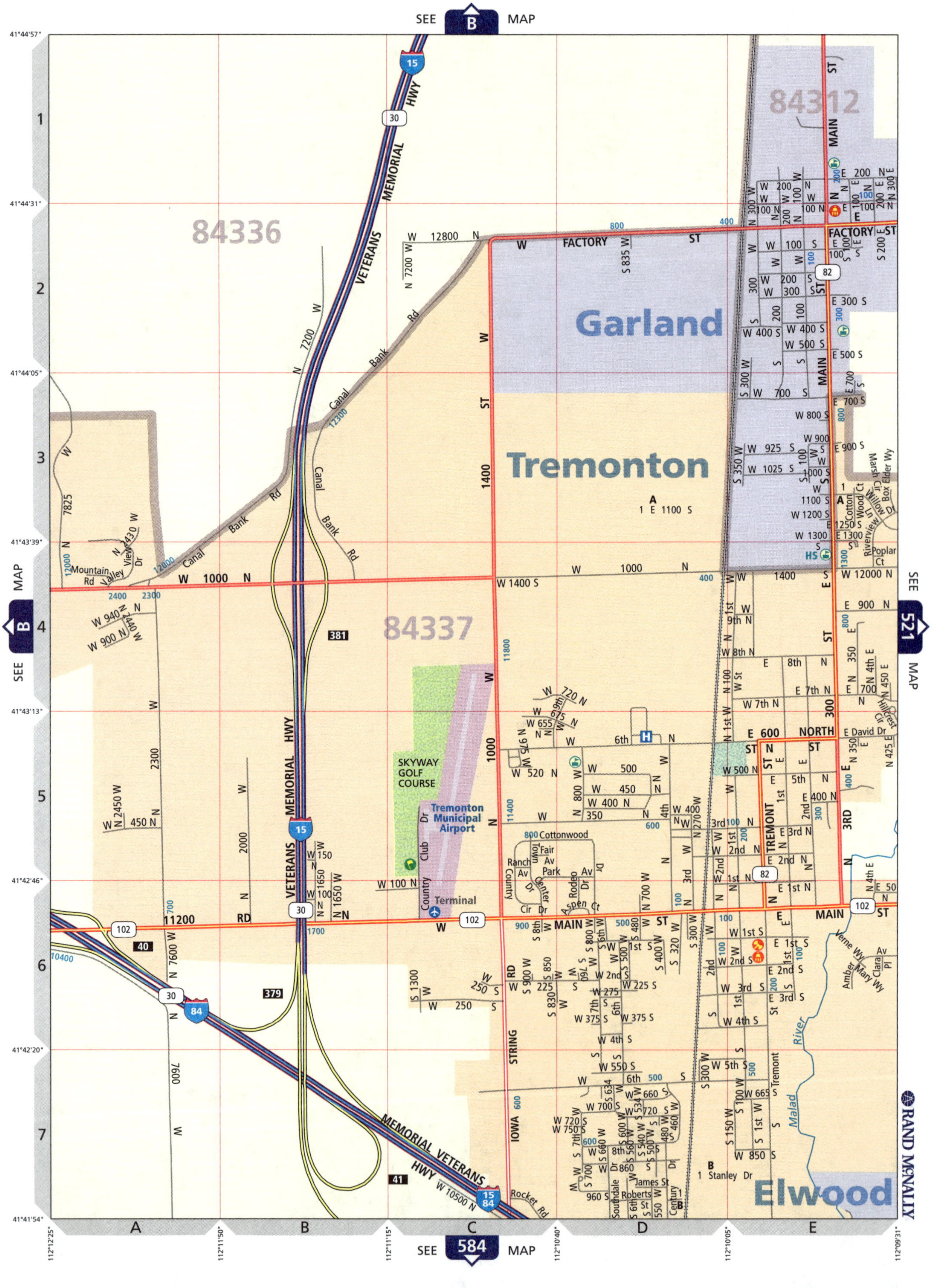

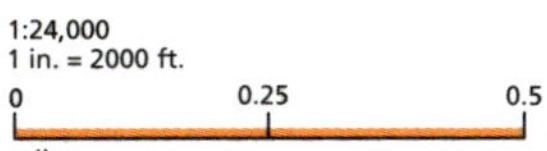
1:24,000
1 in. = 2000 ft.
0
0.25
0.5
miles

SEE B MAP 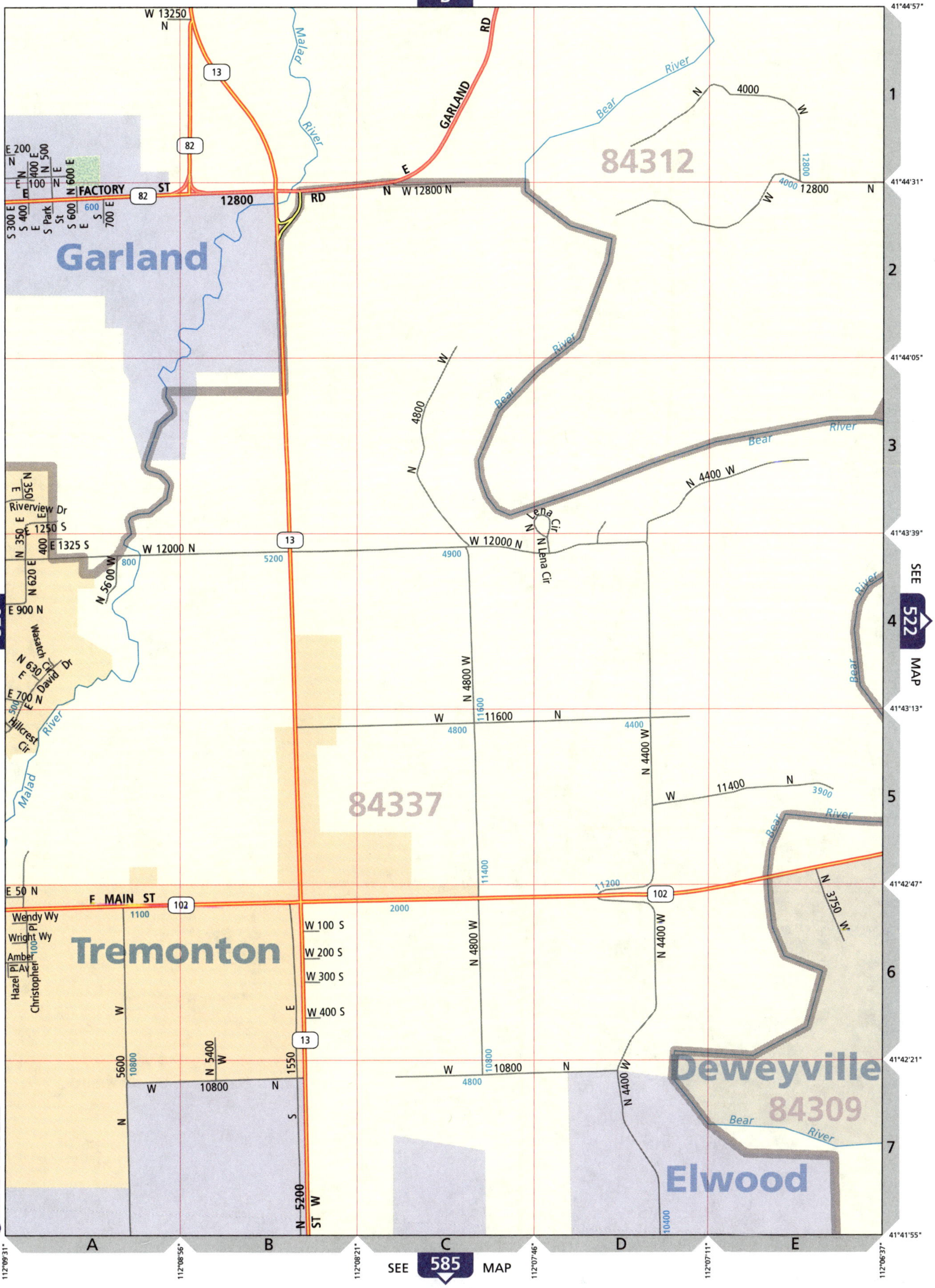
SEE 520 MAP
SEE 522 MAP
SEE 585 MAP
Garland
Tremonton
Deweyville
Elwood
84312
84337
84309
Bear River
Malad River
GARLAND RD
FACTORY ST
E MAIN ST
W 12000 N
W 11600 N
W 11400 N
W 10800 N
W 12800 N
N 4800 W
N 4400 W
N 5200 W
N 5600 W
N Lena Cir
Riverview Dr
Wasatch Cir
David Dr
Hillcrest Cir
Wendy Wy
Wright Wy
Amber Av
Hazel Pl
Christopher Pl
W 100 S
W 200 S
W 300 S
W 400 S
41°44'57"
41°44'31"
41°44'05"
41°43'39"
41°43'13"
41°42'47"
41°42'21"
41°41'55"
112°09'31"
112°08'56"
112°08'21"
112°07'46"
112°07'11"
112°06'37"

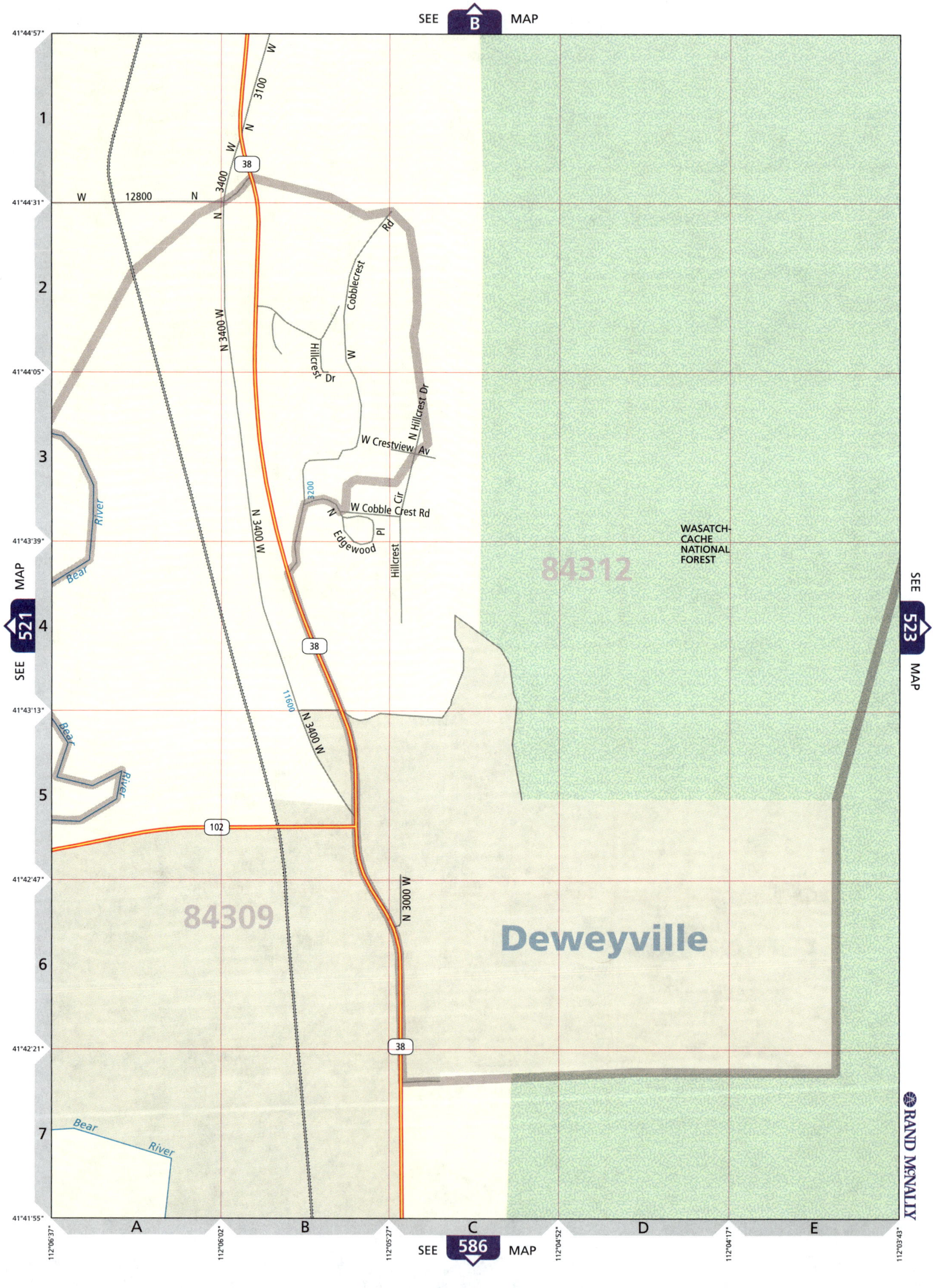
1:24,000
1 in. = 2000 ft.
0
0.25
0.5
miles
N
SEE B MAP
SEE 521 MAP
SEE 523 MAP
SEE 586 MAP
A
B
C
D
E
1
2
3
4
5
6
7
41°44'57"
41°44'31"
41°44'05"
41°43'39"
41°43'13"
41°42'47"
41°42'21"
41°41'55"
112°06'37"
112°06'02"
112°05'27"
112°04'52"
112°04'17"
112°03'43"
N 3100 W
N 3400 W
W 12800 N
38
102
Cobblecrest Rd
Hillcrest Dr
N Hillcrest Dr
W Crestview Av
3200
W Cobble Crest Rd
N Edgewood
Cir
Pl
Hillcrest
11600
N 3000 W
Bear River
Bear
River
WASATCH-CACHE NATIONAL FOREST
84312
84309
Deweyville

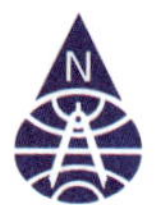

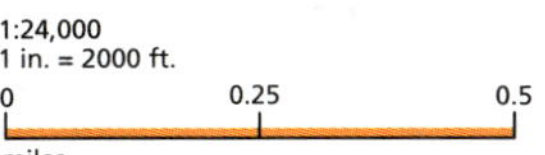

SEE B MAP

84312

BOX ELDER CO

CACHE CO

14000

N 400 W

W 600 N

7100

W 300 N

WASATCH-
CACHE
NATIONAL
FOREST

84325

W 1000 S

84309

SEE 522 MAP

SEE 524 MAP

41°44'58"
1
41°44'32"
2
41°44'06"
3
41°43'39"
4
41°43'13"
5
41°42'47"
6
41°42'21"
7
41°41'55"

A B C D E

112°03'43" 112°03'08" 112°02'33" 112°01'58" 112°01'23" 112°00'49"

SEE 587 MAP

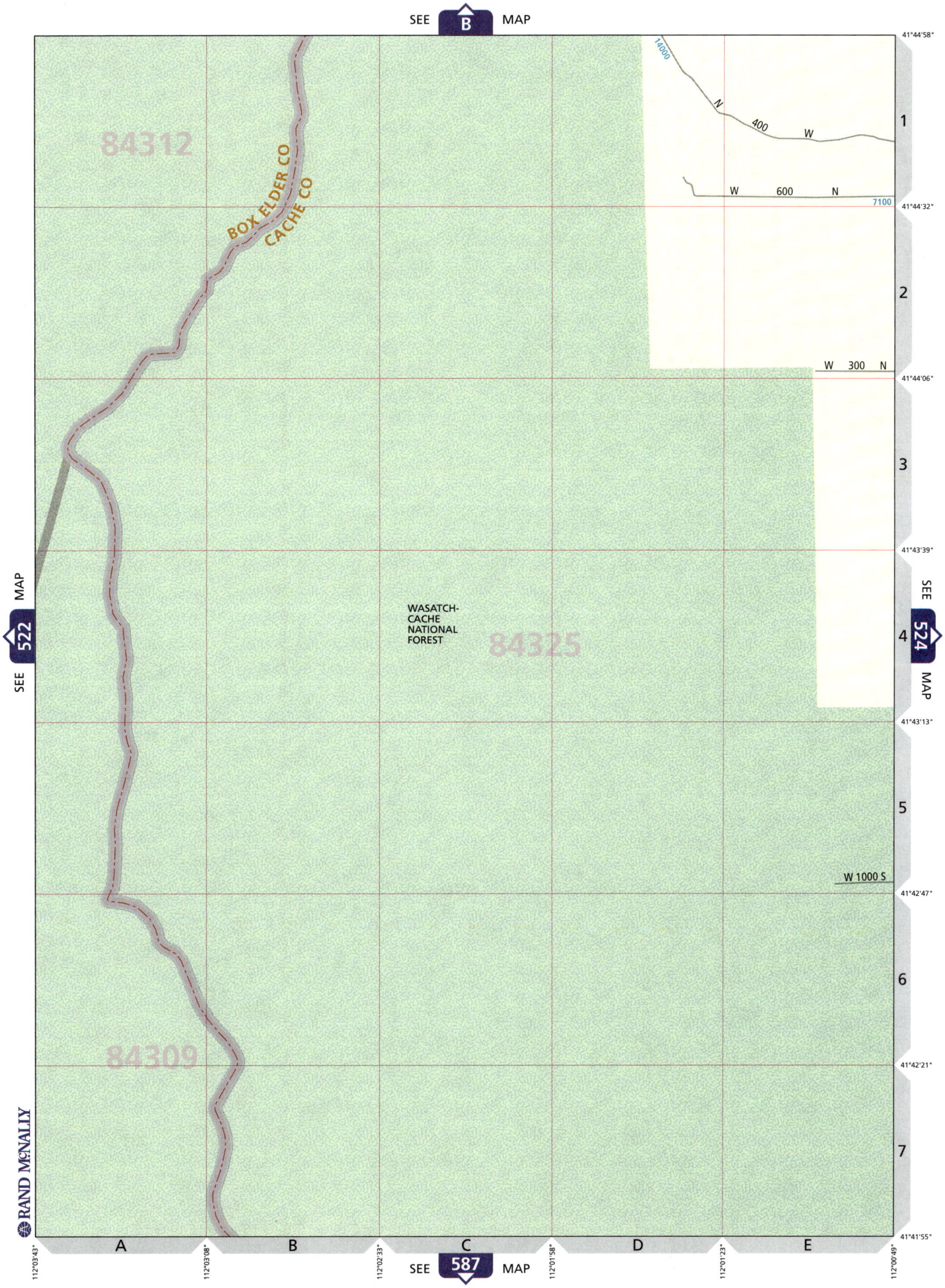

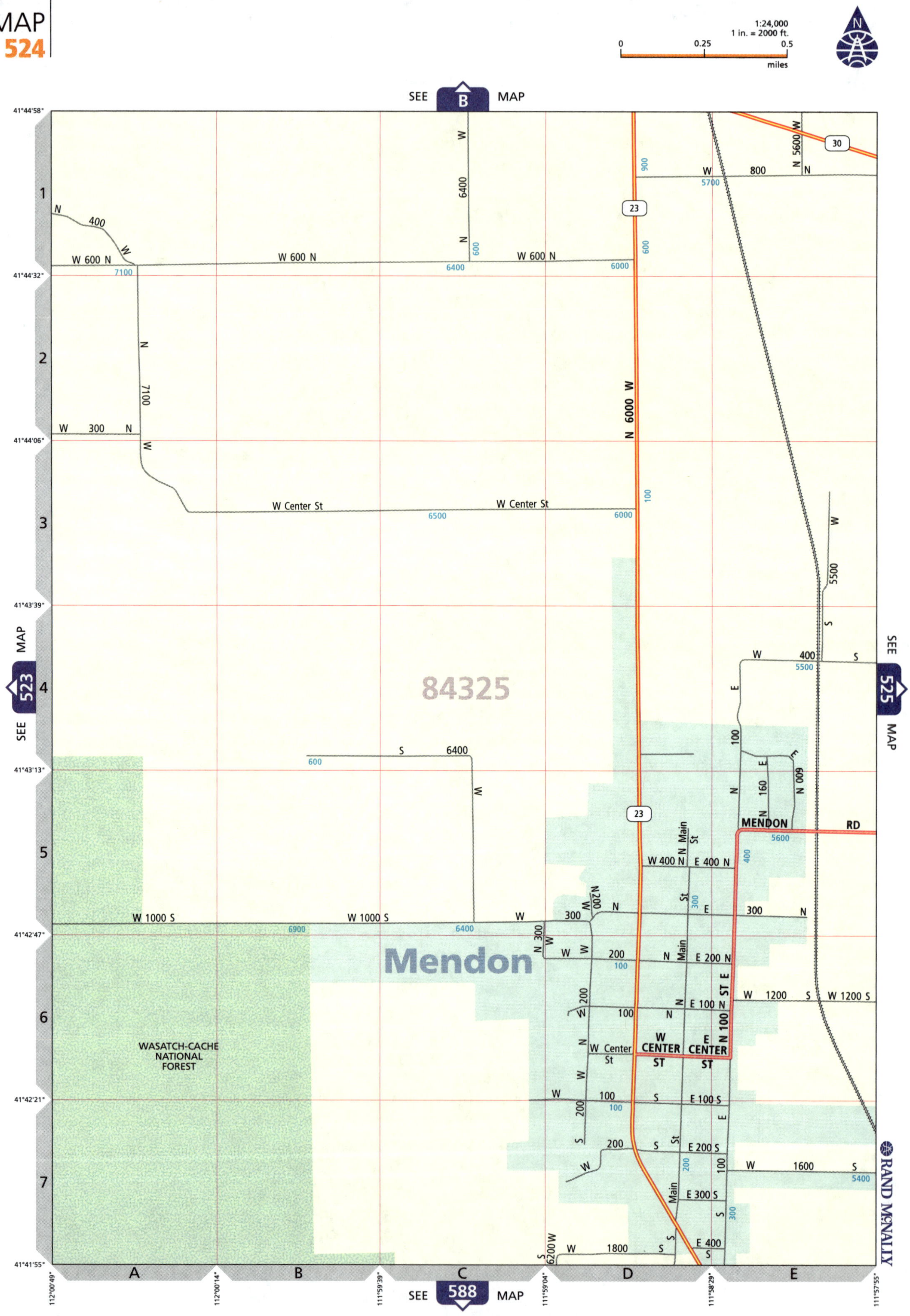

1:24,000
1 in. = 2000 ft.
0 0.25 0.5
miles

SEE B MAP

SEE 523 MAP

SEE 525 MAP

SEE 588 MAP

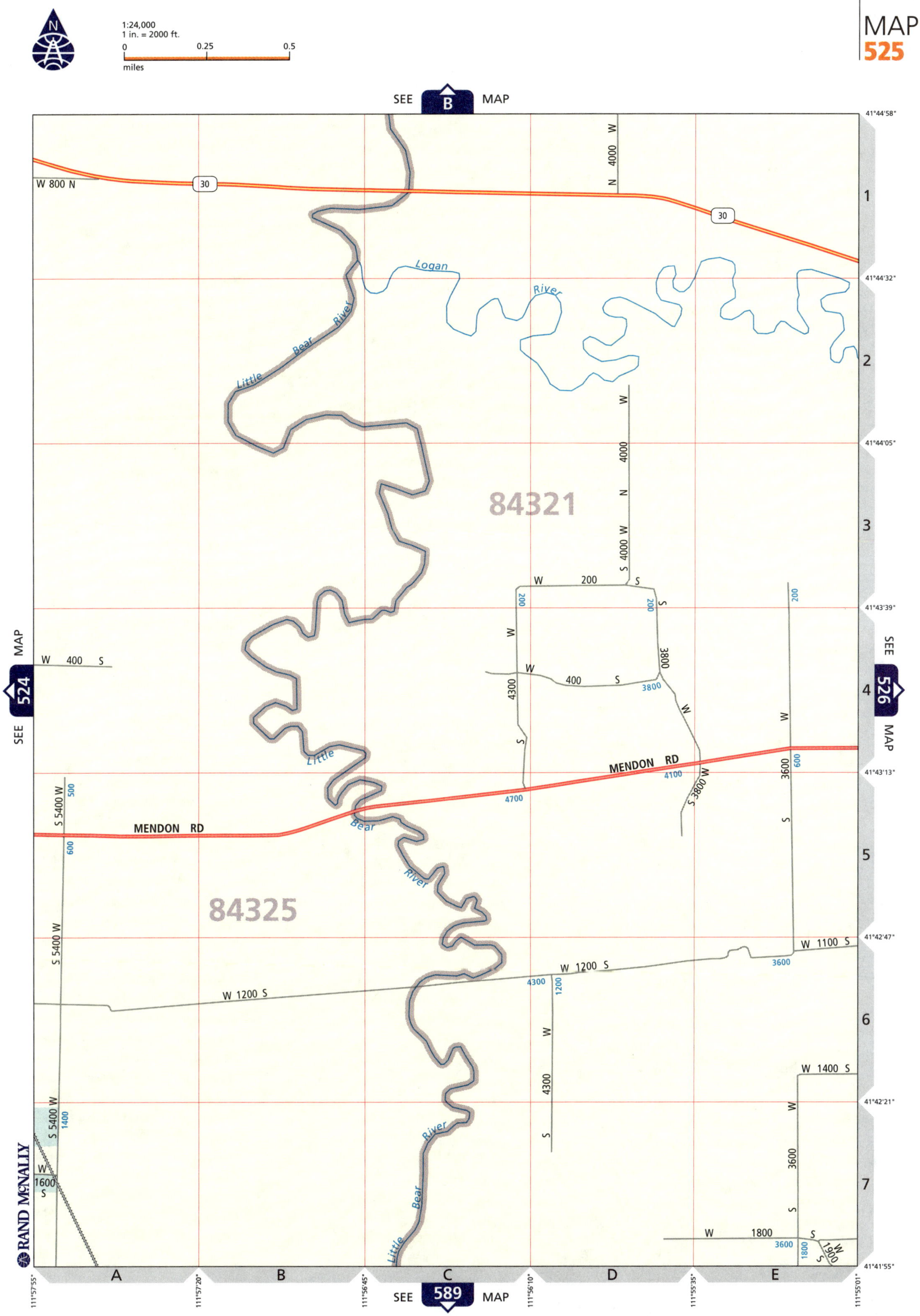

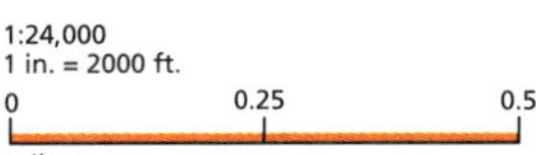

SEE B MAP

SEE 524 MAP

SEE 526 MAP

W 800 N
30
N 4000 W
Logan
River
Little Bear River
84321
W 4000 N
S 4000 W
W 200 S
200
200 S
W 400 S
W
4300
S
W 400 S
3800
3800
W
MENDON RD
4100
S 3800 W
4700
W 3600 S
600
200
S 5400 W
500
MENDON RD
600
Little
Bear
River
84325
S 5400 W
W 1100 S
3600
W 1200 S
4300
1200
W 1200 S
W 4300 S
W 1400 S
S 5400 W
1400
W 1600 S
River
Bear
Little
W 3600 S
W 1800 S
3600
1800
W 1900 S

1
2
3
4
5
6
7
A
B
C
D
E

41°44'58"
41°44'32"
41°44'05"
41°43'39"
41°43'13"
41°42'47"
41°42'21"
41°41'55"
111°57'55"
111°57'20"
111°56'45"
111°56'10"
111°55'35"
111°55'01"

SEE 589 MAP

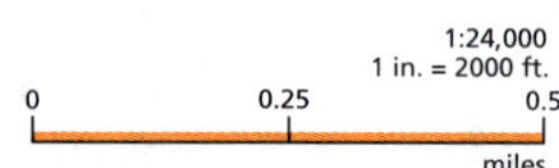

SEE 462 MAP

Logan

84321

84339

WATER TROUGH RD

W 200 N

30

MENDON RD

Logan River

W 600 N

N 1900 W

N 2600 W

W 2600 N

N 2300 W

S 1500 W

W 200 S

S 1900 W

S 1500 W

S 3200 W

S 2800 W

S 2400 W

S 2000 W

W 620 S

W 660 S

S 1530 W

W 1000 S

W 1100 S

W 1200 S

W 1400 S

W 1800 S

S 3400 W

S 1600 W

S 1380 W

500 1100 400 2400 2100 1500 300 1900 3400 3000 2800 600 1800 1100 1400 3200 2400 2000 1600 1700

1 2 3 4 5 6 7

A B C D E

41°44'58" 41°44'32" 41°44'06" 41°43'39" 41°43'13" 41°42'47" 41°42'21" 41°41'55"

111°55'01" 111°54'26" 111°53'51" 111°53'16" 111°52'41" 111°52'07"

SEE 525 MAP

SEE 527 MAP

SEE 590 MAP

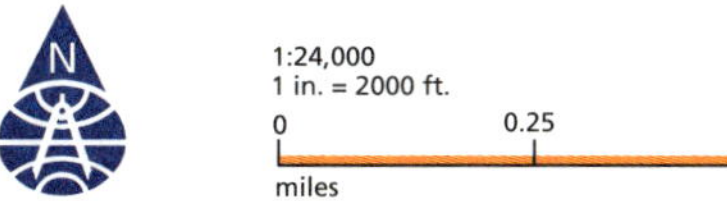

SEE 463 MAP

SEE 526 MAP

SEE 528 MAP

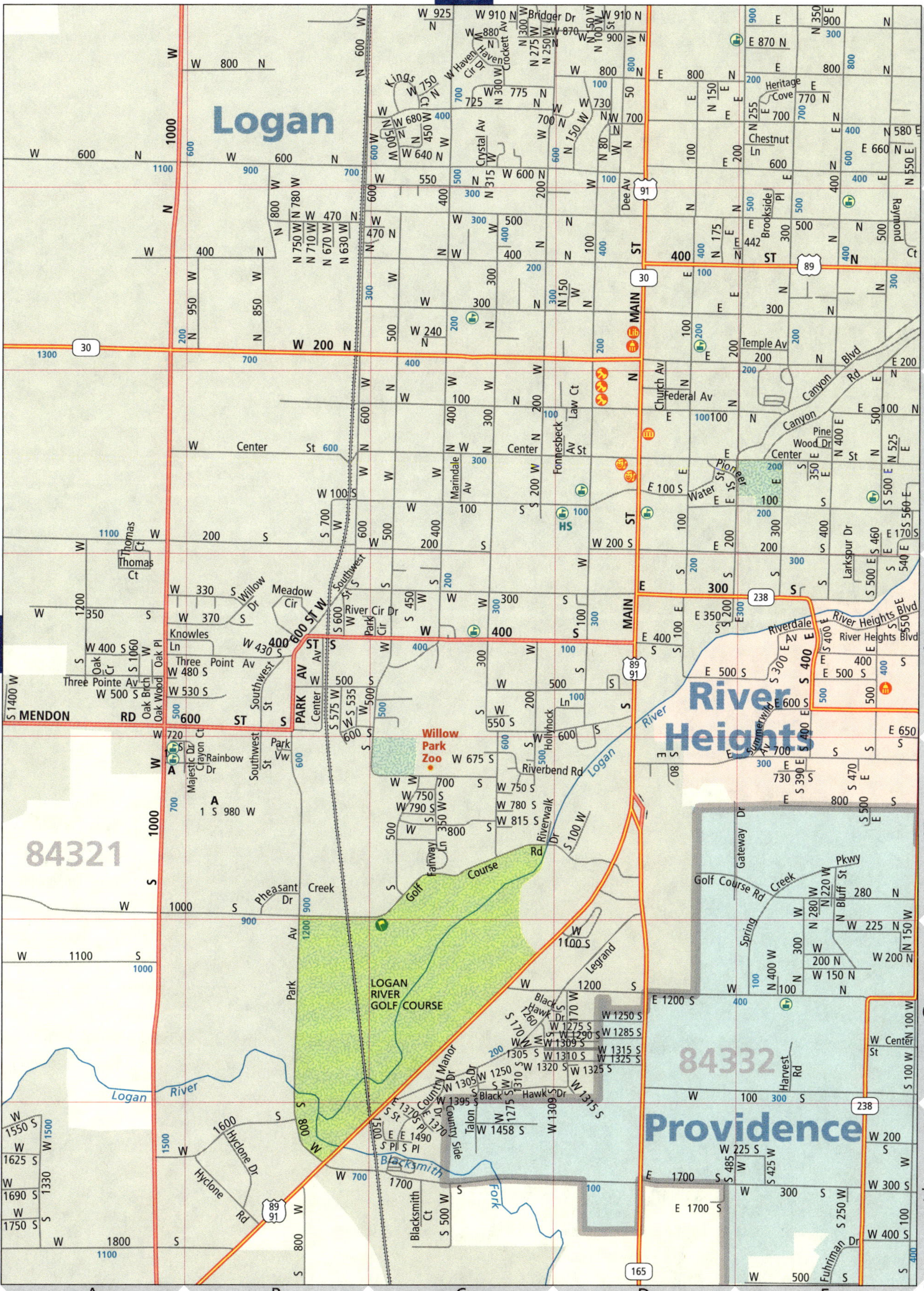

Logan

River Heights

Providence

84321

84332

Willow Park Zoo

LOGAN RIVER GOLF COURSE

Logan River

Blacksmith Fork

MENDON RD

MAIN ST

W 200 N

400 N ST

E 300 S

W 400 S

600 ST

PARK AV

600 ST W

Golf Course Rd

Canyon Rd

Canyon Blvd

River Heights Blvd

Riverdale Av

Riverbend Rd

Legrand

Hyclone Dr

Harvest Rd

Fuhriman Dr

Gateway Dr

Spring Creek Pkwy

Pheasant Creek Dr

Three Point Av

Temple Av

Federal Av

Church Av

Fonnesbeck Av

Marindale Av

Crystal Av

Chestnut Ln

Heritage Cove

Brookside Pl

Raymond Ct

Larkspur Dr

Pine Wood Dr

Water St

Pioneer St

Summerwind Av

Riverwalk Dr

Hollyhock Ln

Fairway Ln

Country Manor Dr

Country Side

Talon Dr

Black Hawk Dr

Blacksmith Ct

Southwest St

Meadow Cir

River Cir Dr

Park Cir

Willow Dr

Knowles Ln

Thomas Ct

Oak Cr

Oak Birch

Oak Wood

Oak Pl

Majestic Dr

Clayton Ct

Rainbow Dr

Park Vw

Kings Ct

Haven Cir Dr

Crockett Av

Bridger Dr

Dee Av

Law Ct

Bluff St

1 2 3 4 5 6 7

A B C D E

SEE 591 MAP

1:24,000
1 in. = 2000 ft.
0 0.25 0.5
miles

SEE 464 MAP

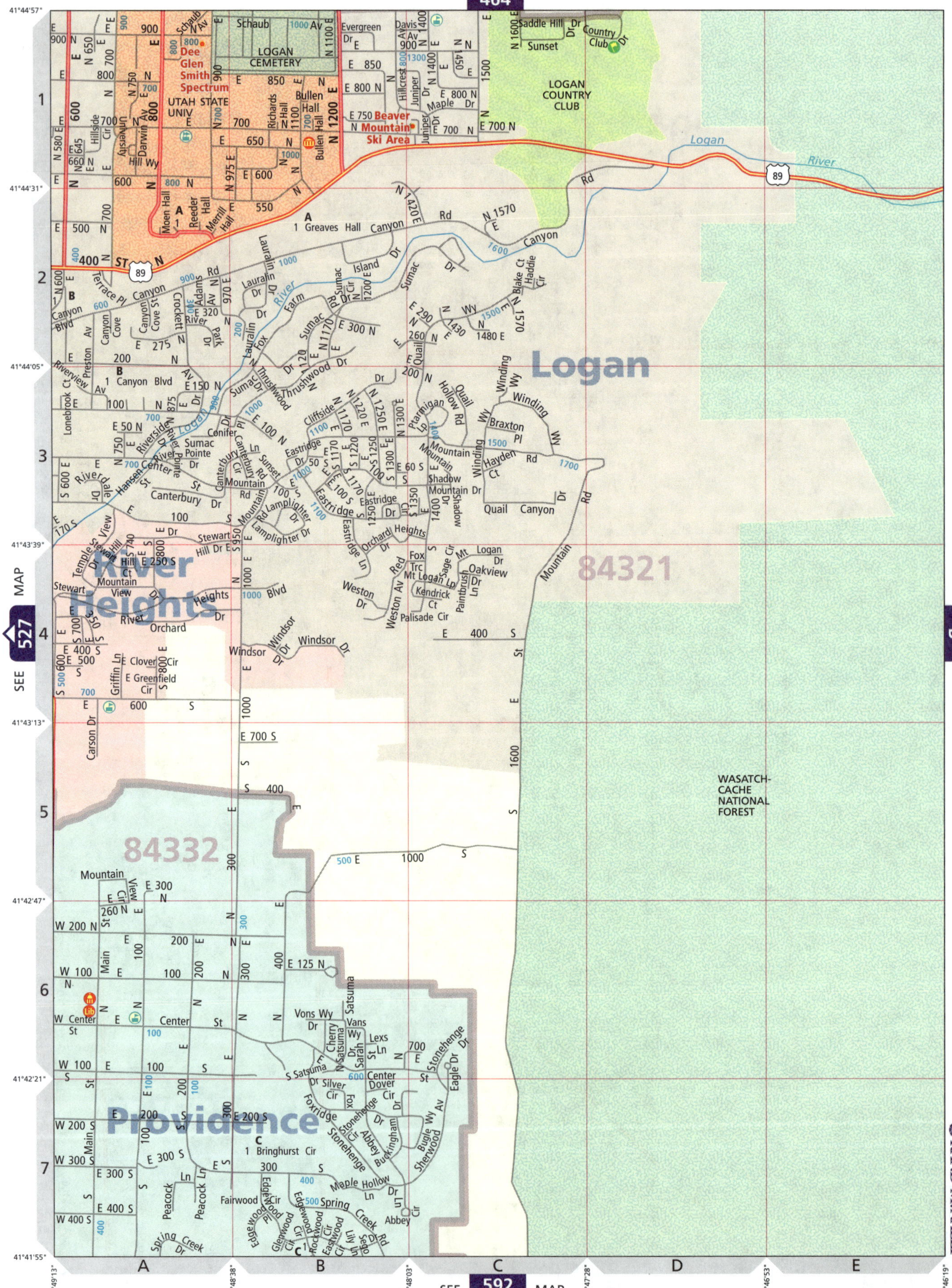

Logan
River Heights
Providence
LOGAN CEMETERY
UTAH STATE UNIV
Dee Glen Smith Spectrum
Beaver Mountain Ski Area
LOGAN COUNTRY CLUB
Logan River
WASATCH-CACHE NATIONAL FOREST
84321
84332

41°44'57"
41°44'31"
41°44'05"
41°43'39"
41°43'13"
41°42'47"
41°42'21"
41°41'55"

111°49'13"
111°48'38"
111°48'03"
111°47'28"
111°46'53"
111°46'19"

1 2 3 4 5 6 7
A B C D E

SEE 527 MAP

SEE B MAP

SEE 592 MAP

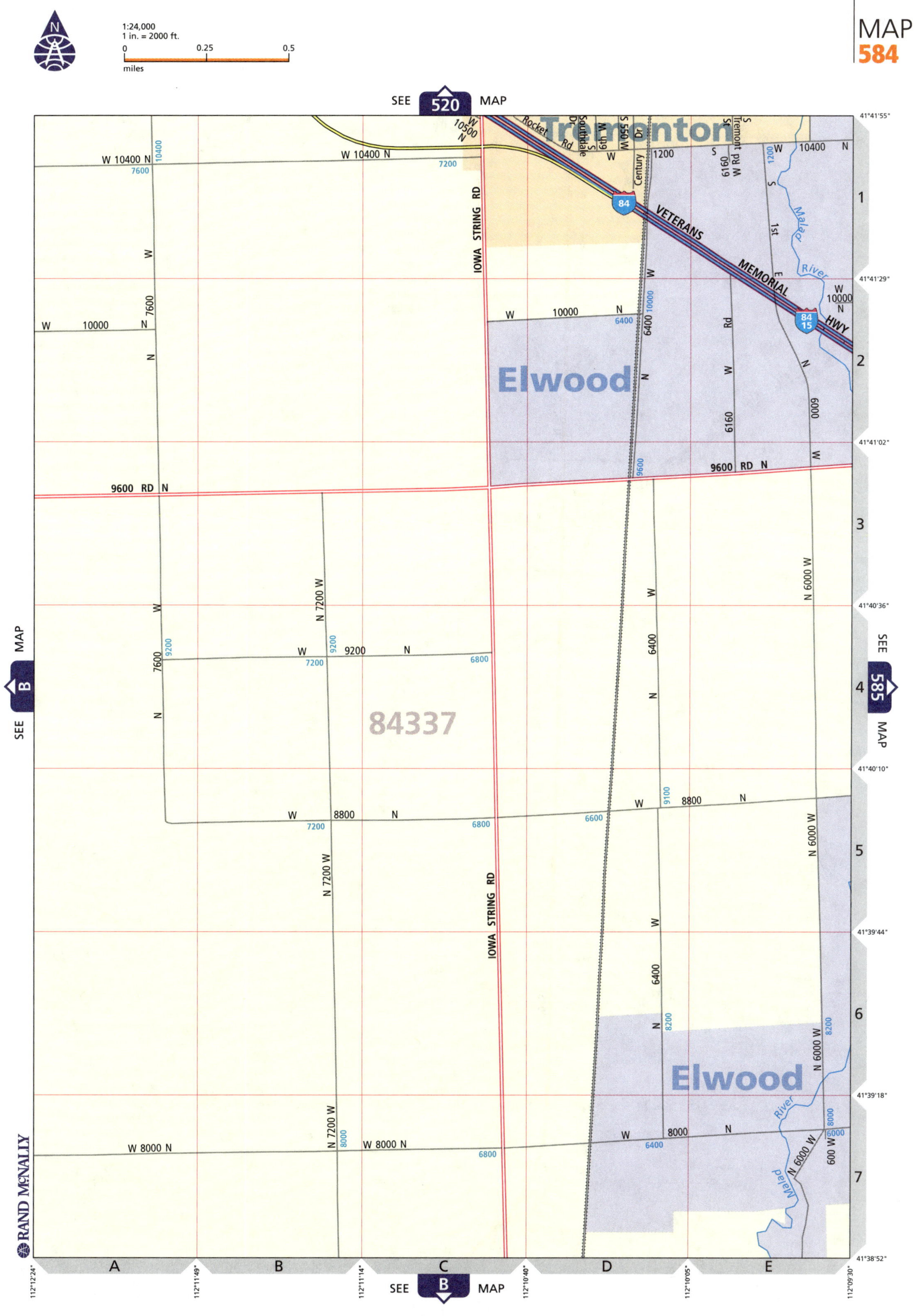

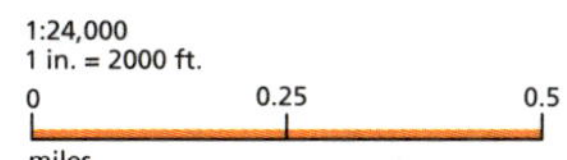

SEE 520 MAP
SEE B MAP
SEE 585 MAP
SEE B MAP

1:24,000
1 in. = 2000 ft.
0 0.25 0.5
miles

SEE 521 MAP

SEE 584 MAP

SEE 586 MAP

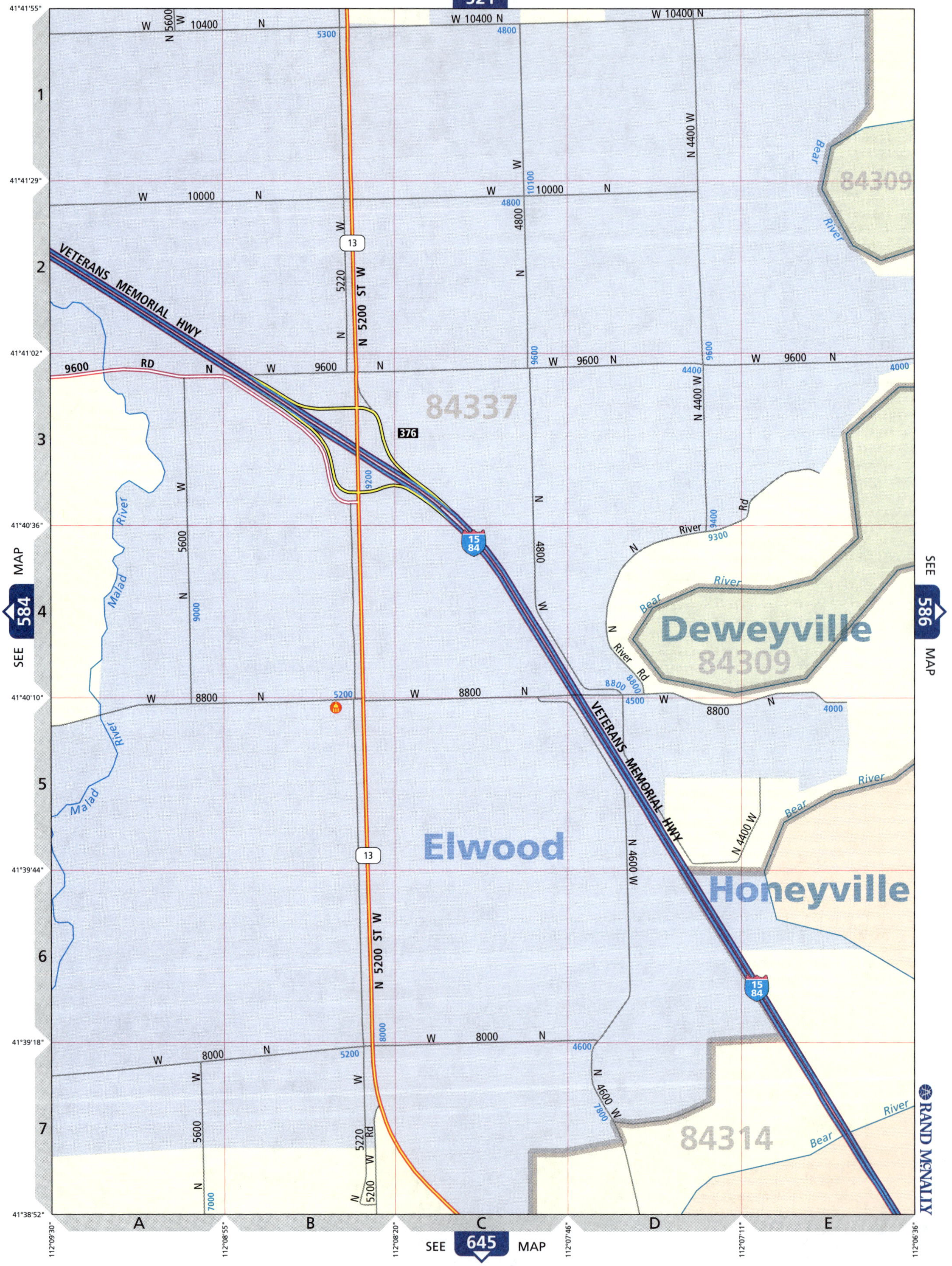

SEE 645 MAP

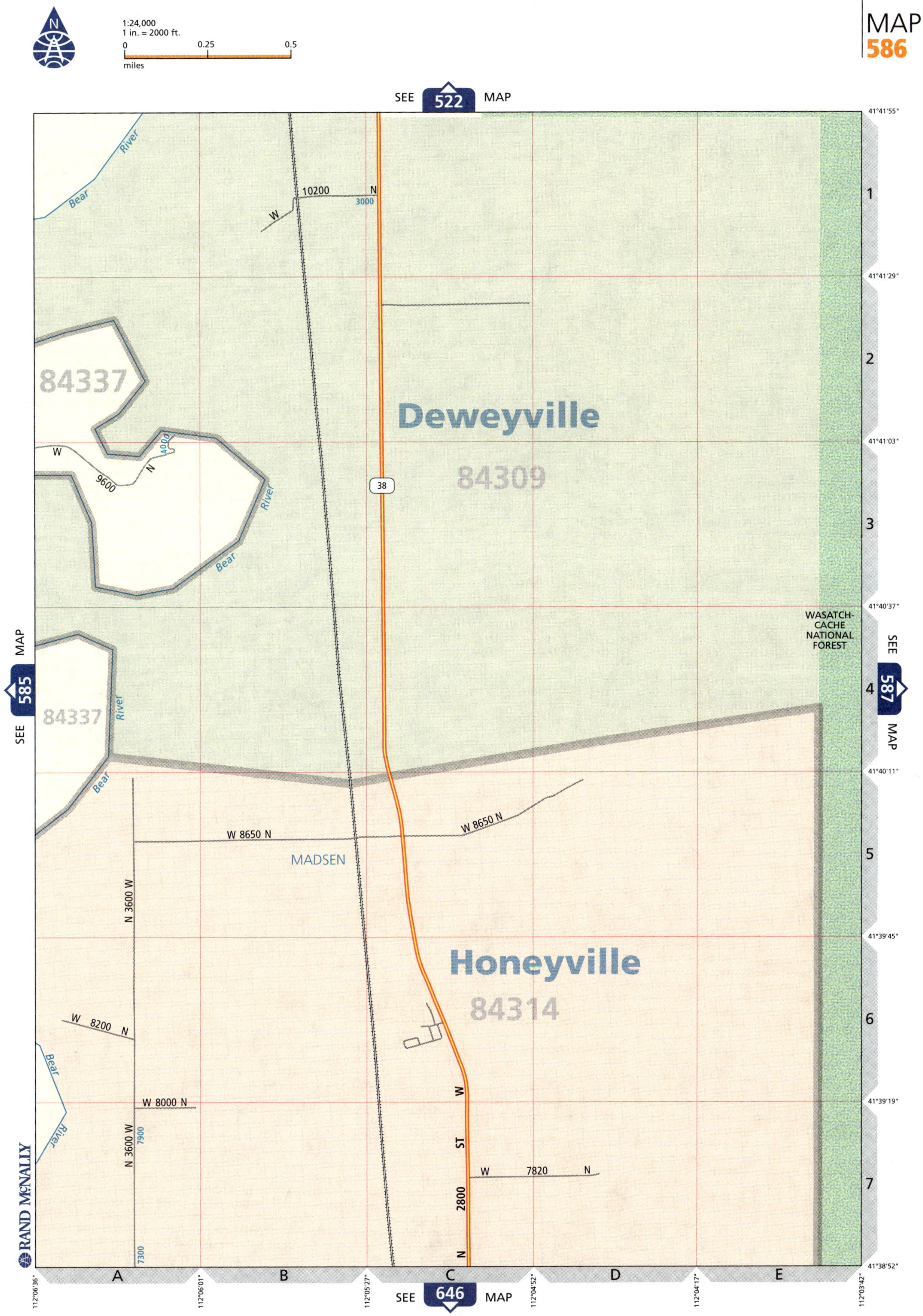

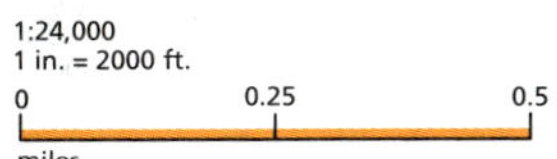

SEE 522 MAP
SEE 585 MAP
SEE 587 MAP
SEE 646 MAP

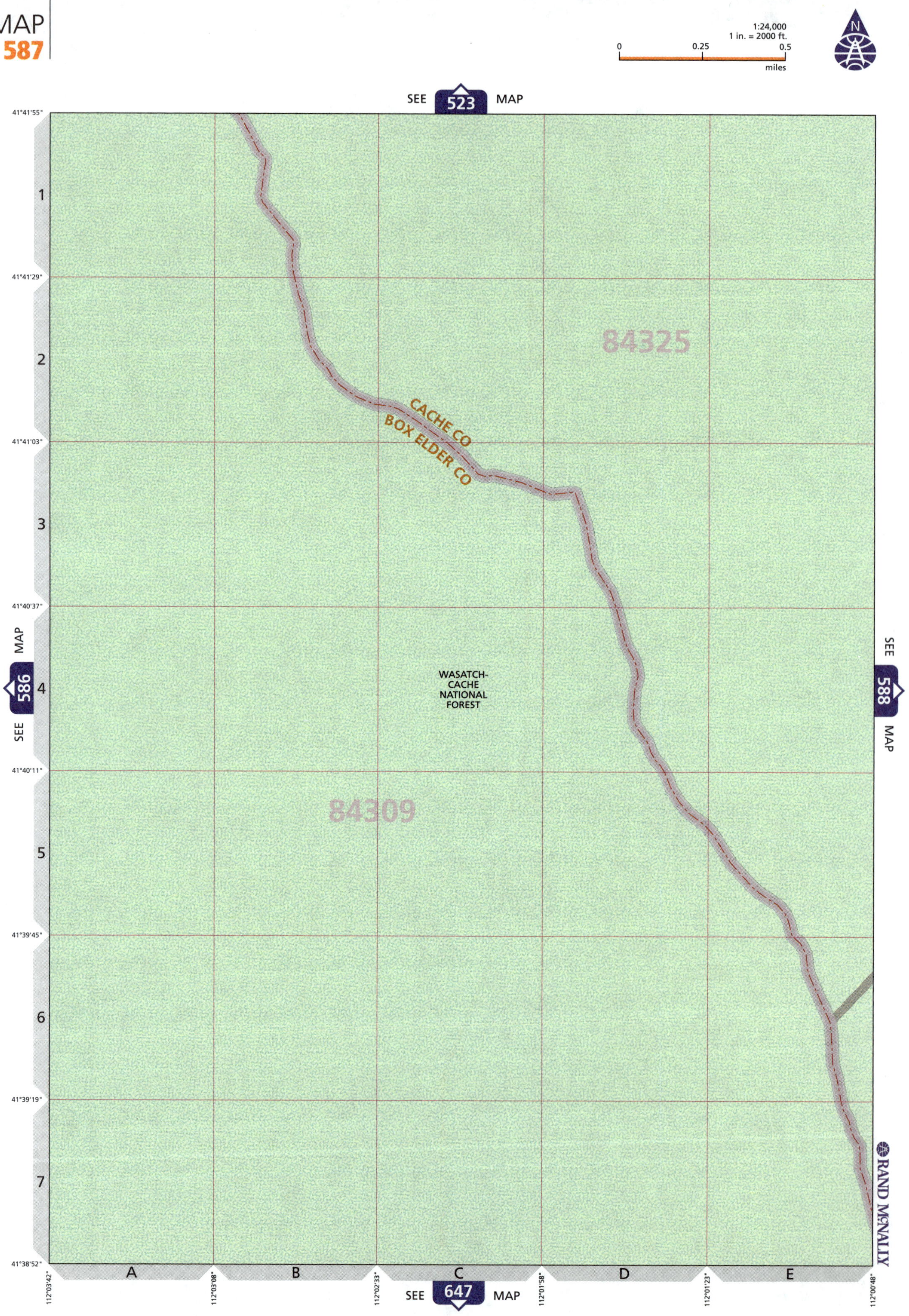

1:24,000
1 in. = 2000 ft.
0 0.25 0.5
miles

SEE 523 MAP

SEE 586 MAP

SEE 588 MAP

41°41'55"
41°41'29"
41°41'03"
41°40'37"
41°40'11"
41°39'45"
41°39'19"
41°38'52"

1
2
3
4
5
6
7

84325

CACHE CO
BOX ELDER CO

WASATCH-
CACHE
NATIONAL
FOREST

84309

RAND McNALLY

A B C D E

112°03'42" 112°03'08" 112°02'33" 112°01'58" 112°01'23" 112°00'48"

SEE 647 MAP

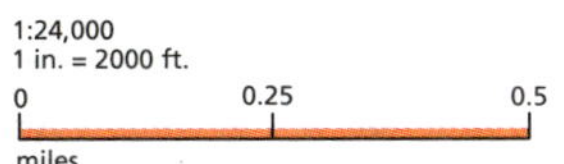

SEE 524 MAP

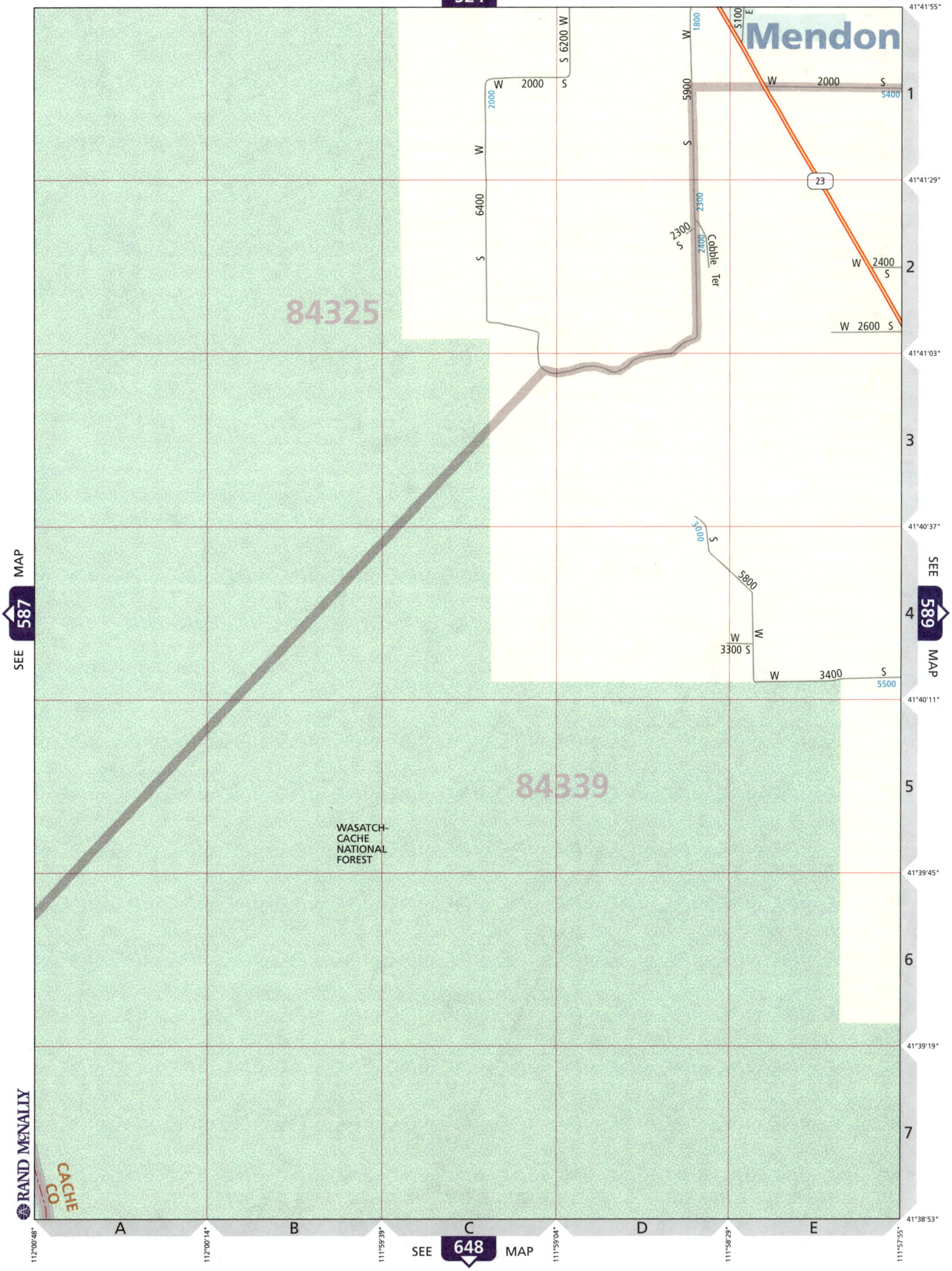

SEE 587 MAP

SEE 589 MAP

Mendon

84325

84339

WASATCH-
CACHE
NATIONAL
FOREST

CACHE
CO

W 2000 S
S 6200 W
W 6400 S
W 5900 S
W 2000 S
23
2300 S
Cobble Ter
W 2400 S
W 2600 S
5800
W 3300 S
W 3400 S

A B C D E

1 2 3 4 5 6 7

41°41'55" 41°41'29" 41°41'03" 41°40'37" 41°40'11" 41°39'45" 41°39'19" 41°38'53"

112°00'48" 112°00'14" 111°59'39" 111°59'04" 111°58'29" 111°57'55"

SEE 648 MAP

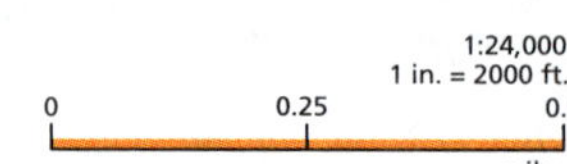

SEE 525 MAP
SEE MAP 588
SEE 590 MAP
SEE 649 MAP

84325
84321
84339
PELICAN POND
Wellsville
WASATCH-CACHE NATIONAL FOREST
Little Bear River
W 2200 S
W 2400 S
W 2600 S
W 2900 S
W 3200 S
W 3400 S
W 3500 S
W 3800 S
W 500 N
Pelican Pond Rd
23

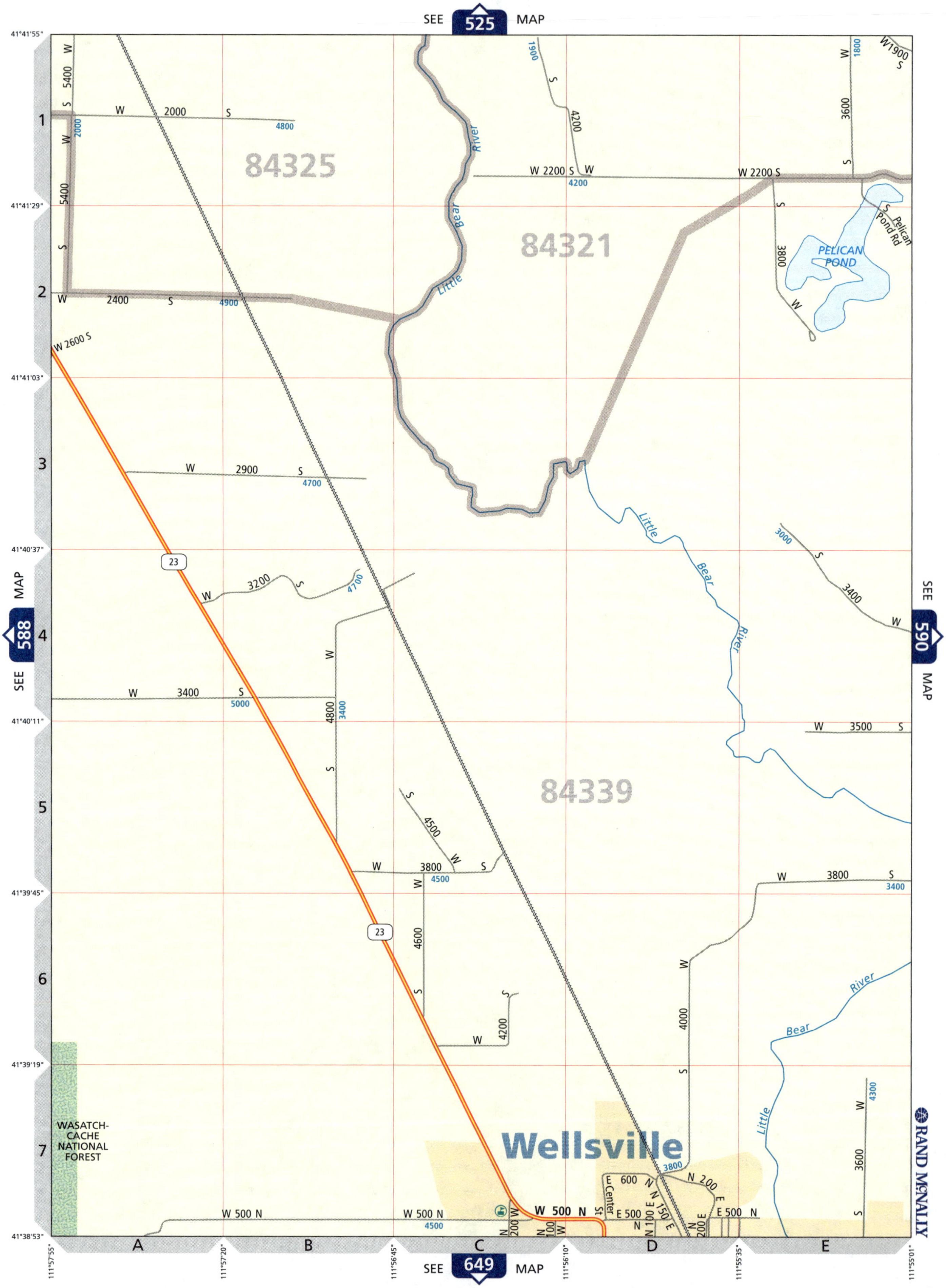

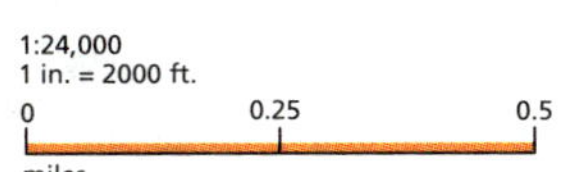

SEE 526 MAP

Logan

84321

84339

Nibley

College Ward

84321

American West Heritage Center

84319

Wellsville

W 1900 S
W 2000 S
W 2200 S
W 2600 S
W 3000 S
W 3200 S
W 3400 S
W 3500 S
W 3600 S
W 3800 S
W 3900 S
W 4200 S
W 4300 S
W 4400 S
W 4600 S
S 1500 W
S 1600 W
S 1900 W
S 2000 W
S 2400 W
S 2500 W
S 2650 W
S 2800 W
S 2900 W
S 3000 W
S 3100 W
S 3200 W
S 3400 W

Little Bear River

91
89

1 2 3 4 5 6 7

A B C D E

41°41'55" 41°41'29" 41°41'03" 41°40'37" 41°40'11" 41°39'45" 41°39'19" 41°38'52"

111°55'01" 111°54'26" 111°53'51" 111°53'16" 111°52'42" 111°52'07"

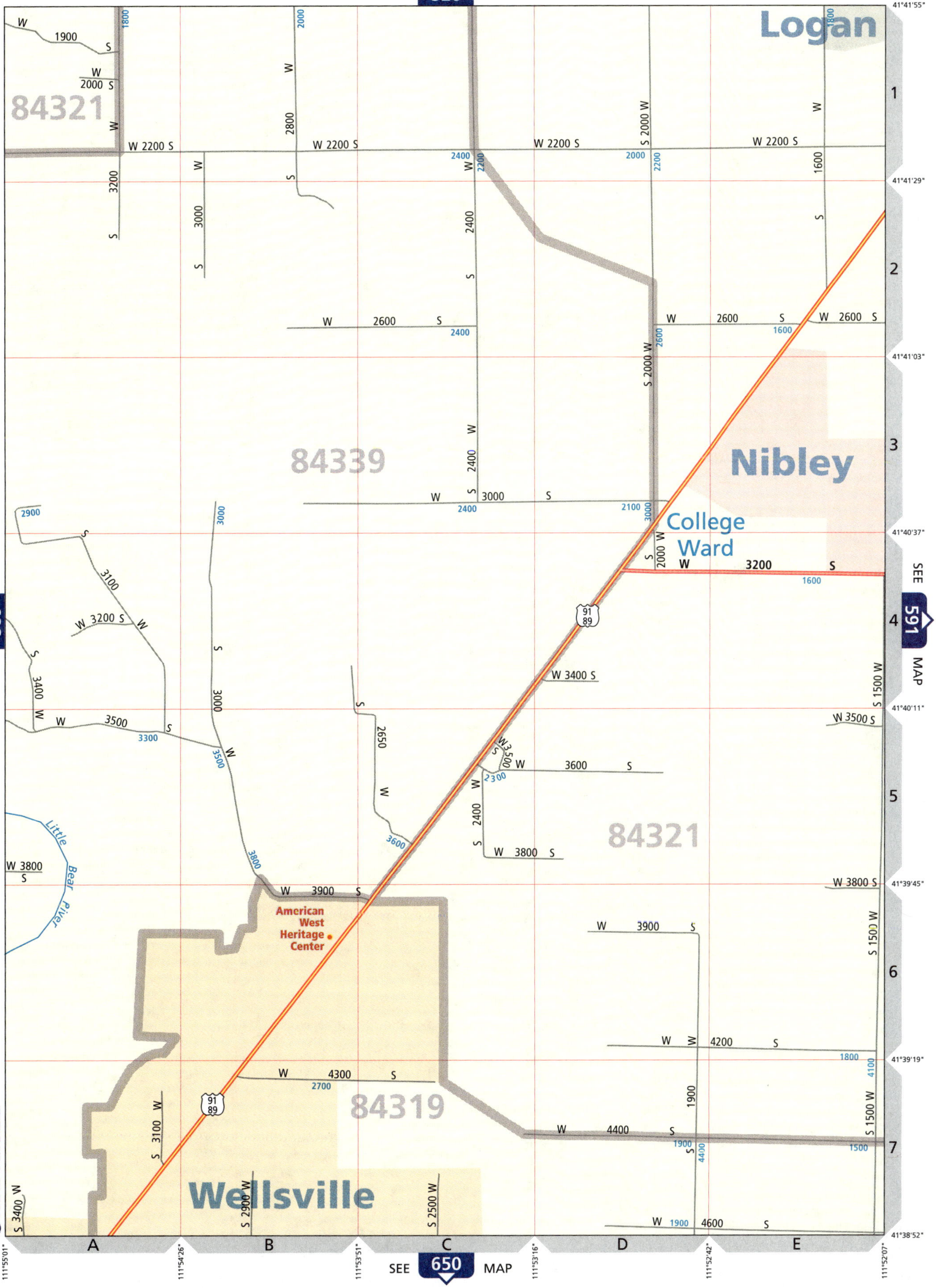

SEE 589 MAP

SEE 591 MAP

SEE 650 MAP

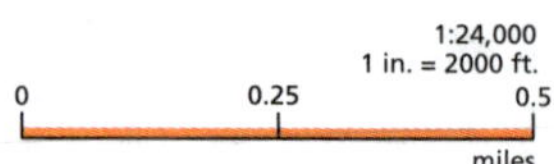

SEE 527 MAP

Logan
Providence
Millville
84332
Nibley
84321
84319

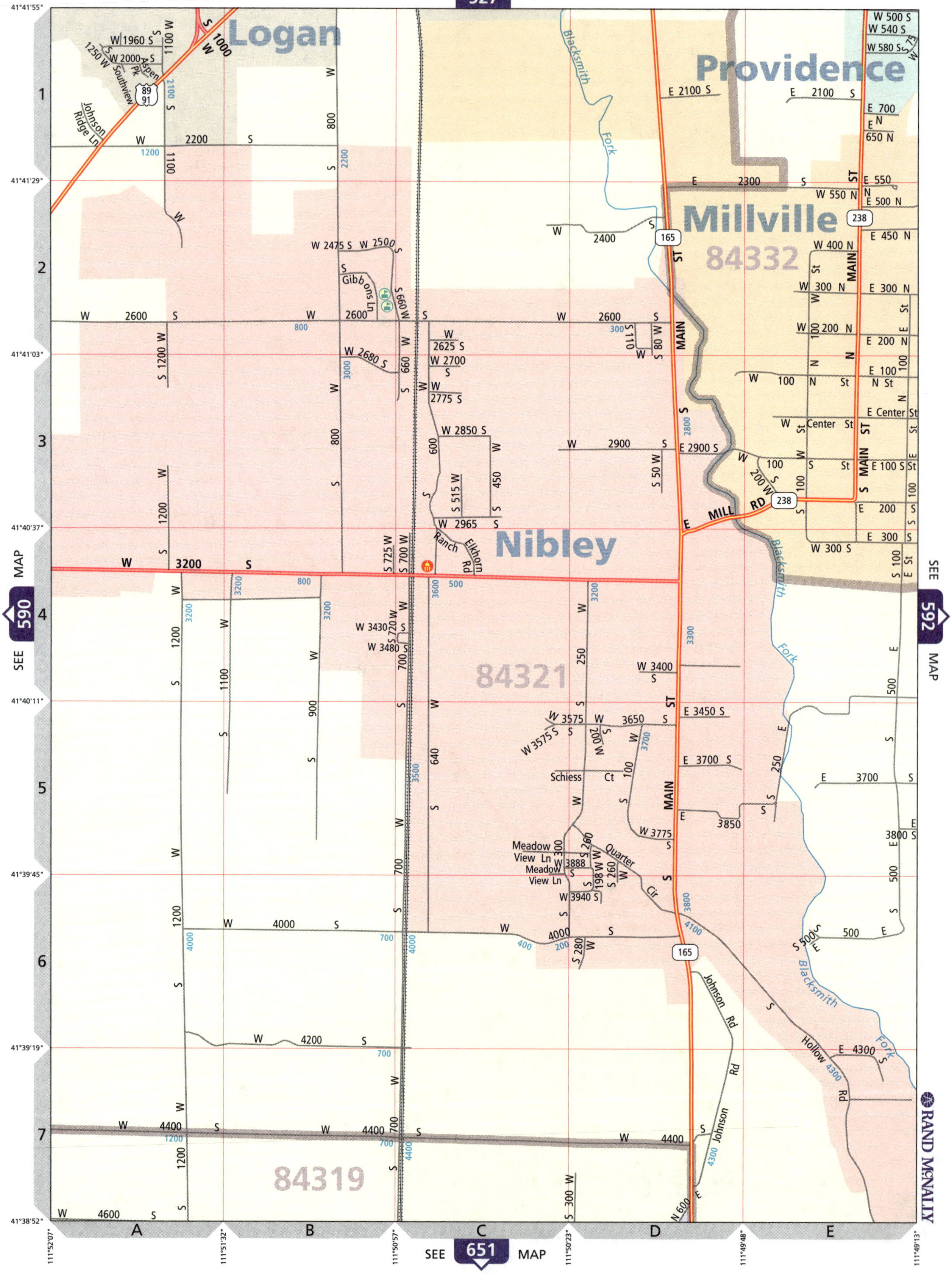

SEE 590 MAP

SEE 592 MAP

SEE 651 MAP

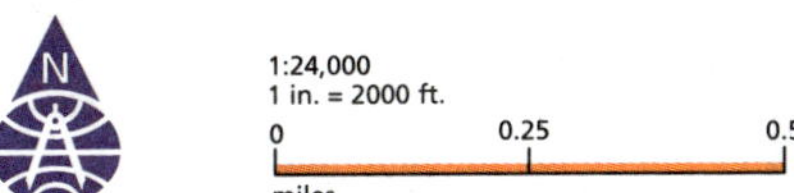

SEE 528 MAP
SEE 591 MAP
SEE B MAP
SEE 652 MAP

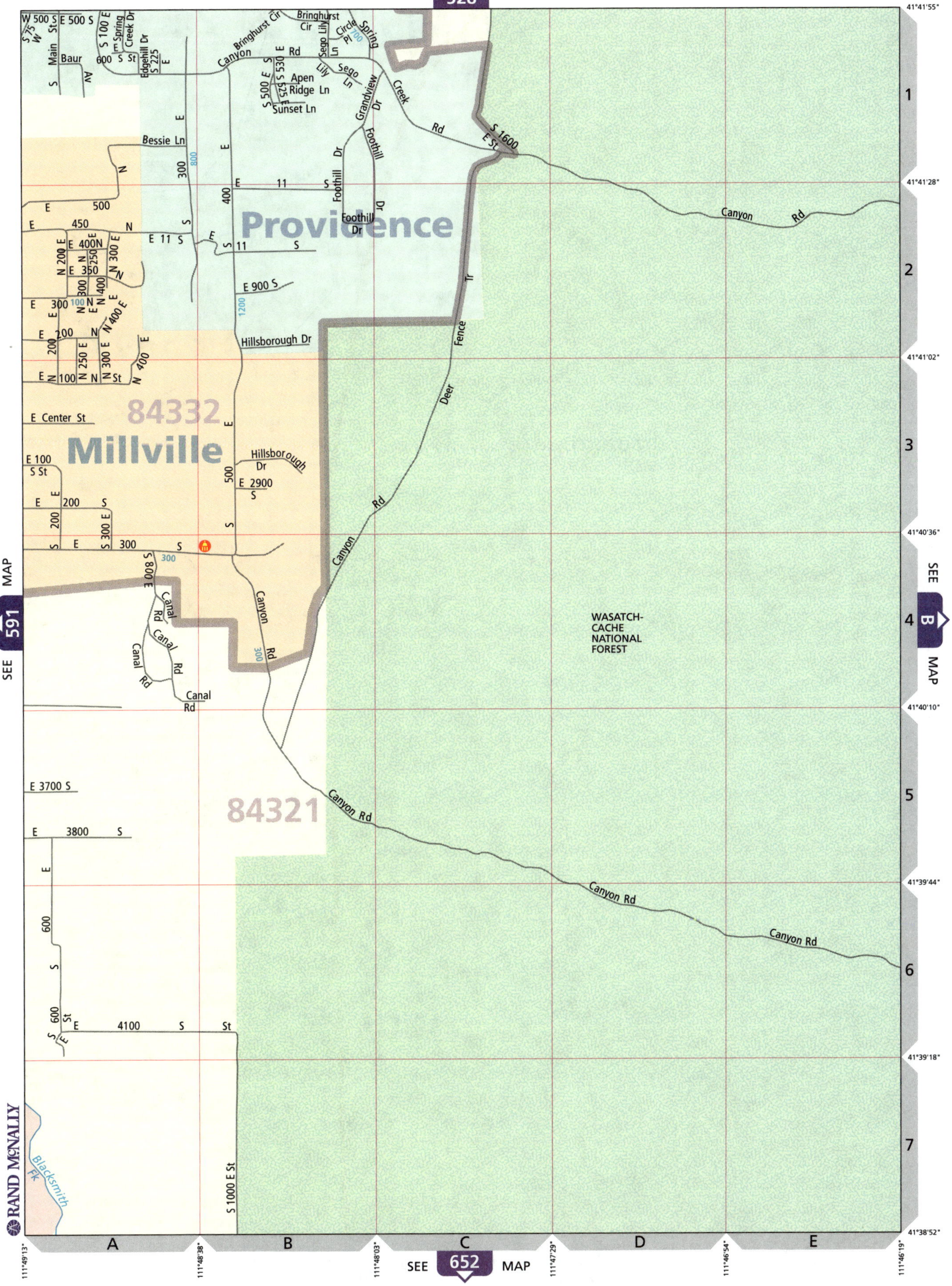

Providence
Millville
84332
84321
WASATCH-CACHE NATIONAL FOREST
Canyon Rd
Deer Fence Tr
Hillsborough Dr
Foothill Dr
Grandview Dr
Bessie Ln
Canal Rd
E Center St
E 3700 S
E 3800 S
E 4100 S St
S 1000 E St
S 1600 E St
Blacksmith Fk

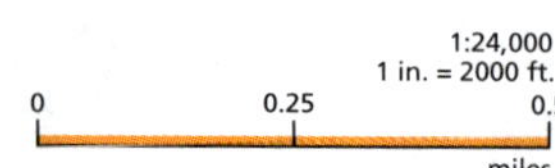

SEE 585 MAP

Elwood
Honeyville
Bradford
Bear River City
84314
84337
84301
84302
Bear River
Malad River
BEAR RIVER
BEAR RIVER CITY PARK
6400 RD N
5600 N Rd
5200 W Rd
N 4700 W
W 6900 ST N
Wakegan Rd
13

SEE B MAP

SEE 646 MAP

SEE 704 MAP

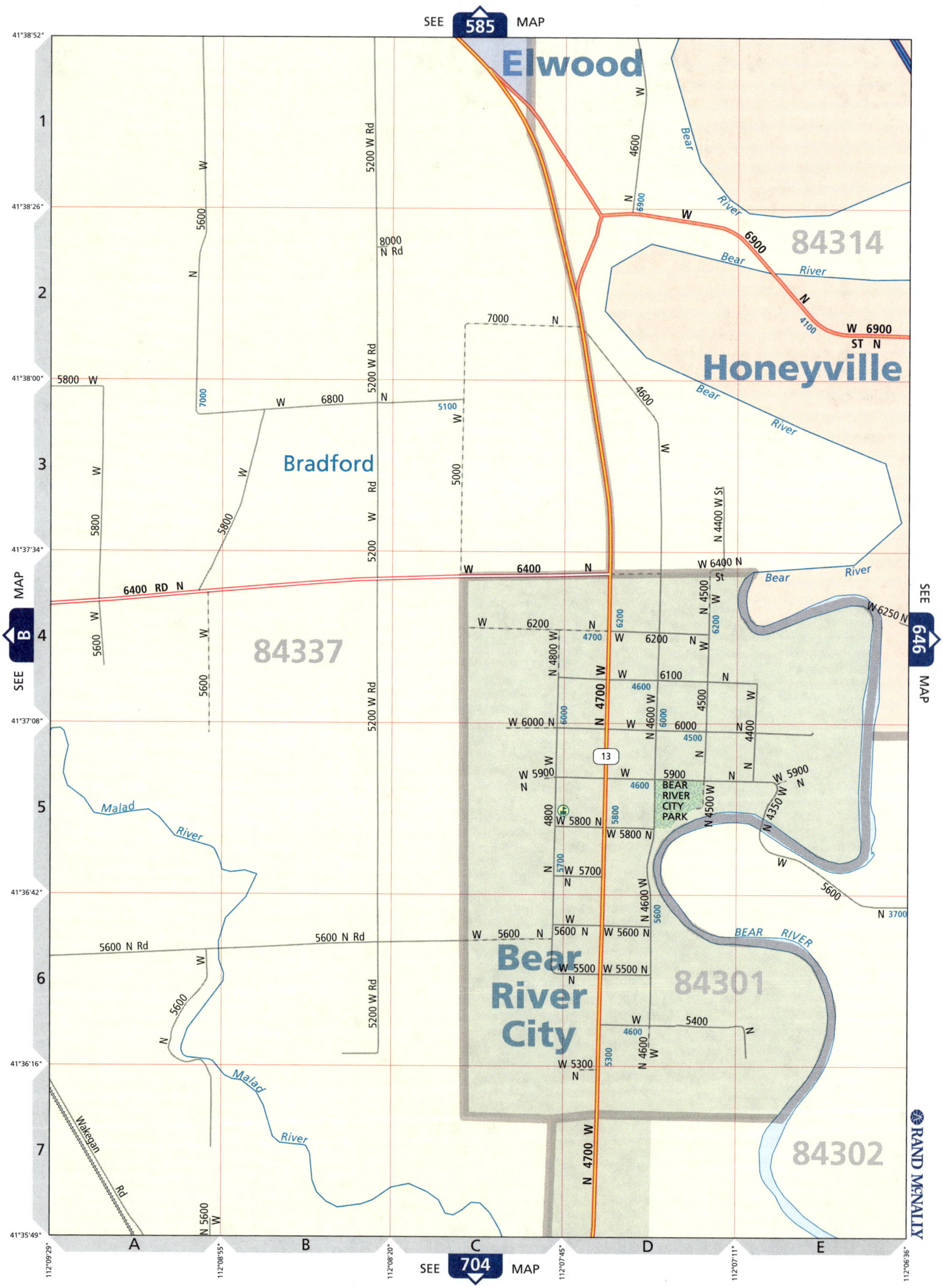

RAND McNALLY

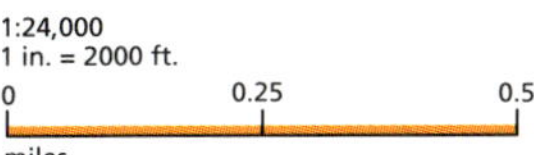

SEE 586 MAP

SEE 645 MAP

SEE 647 MAP

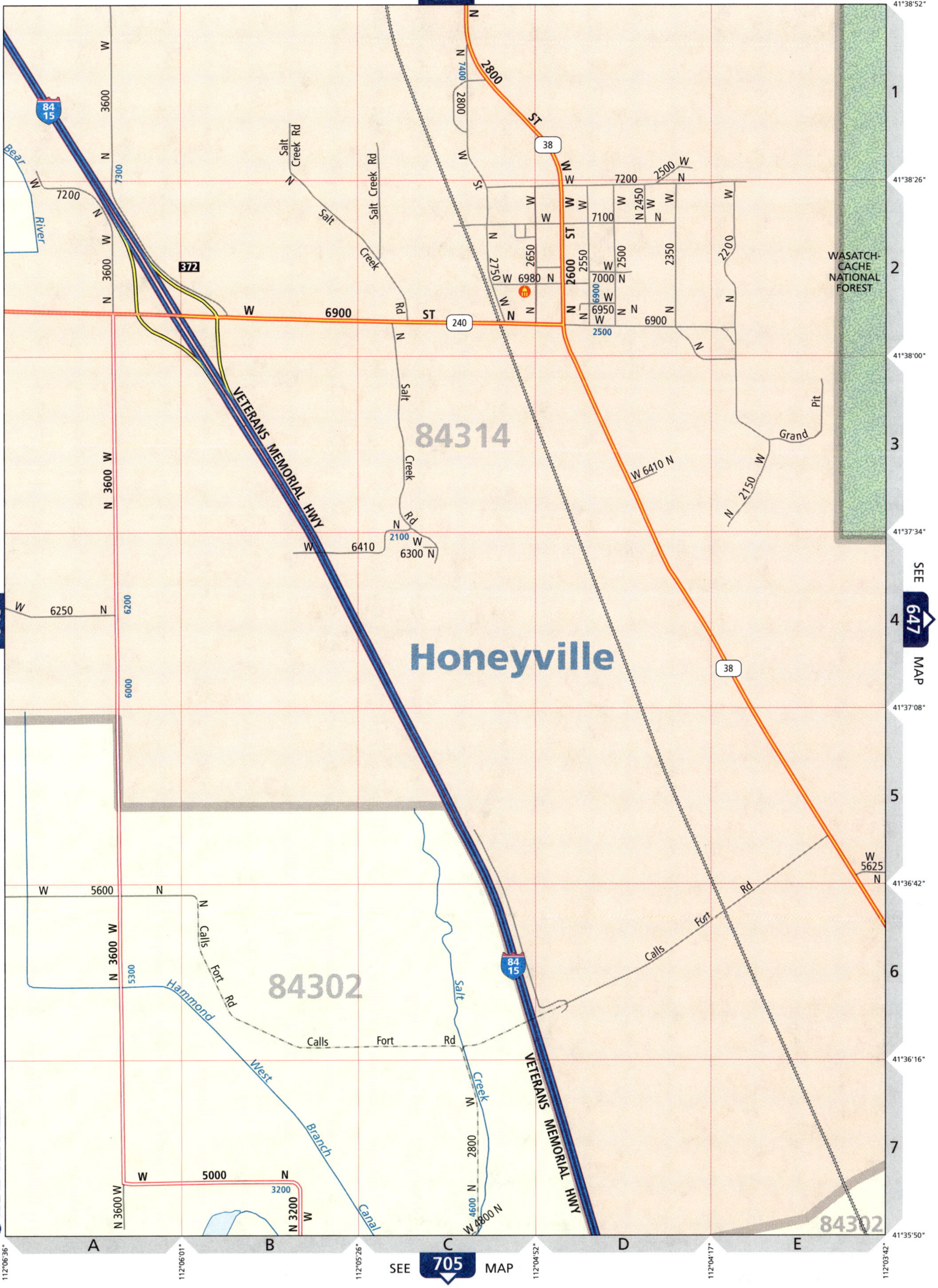

Honeyville

84314

84302

WASATCH-CACHE NATIONAL FOREST

VETERANS MEMORIAL HWY

W 6900 ST

N 2800 W ST

N 3600 W

Salt Creek Rd

Calls Fort Rd

Hammond West Branch Canal

Salt Creek

Bear River

Grand Pit

W 7200 N

W 7100 N

W 7000 N

W 6980 N

W 6950 N

W 6410 N

W 6300 N

W 6250 N

W 5625 N

W 5600 N

W 5000 N

W 4800 N

W 2500 N

N 2750 W

N 2650 W

N 2600 W

N 2550 W

N 2500 W

N 2450 W

N 2350 W

N 2200 W

N 2150 W

N 2100 W

N 3200 W

84 15

38

240

372

7400

7300

6900

6200

6000

5300

3200

4600

2500

2100

1 2 3 4 5 6 7

A B C D E

41°38'52"
41°38'26"
41°38'00"
41°37'34"
41°37'08"
41°36'42"
41°36'16"
41°35'50"

112°06'36"
112°06'01"
112°05'26"
112°04'52"
112°04'17"
112°03'42"

SEE 705 MAP

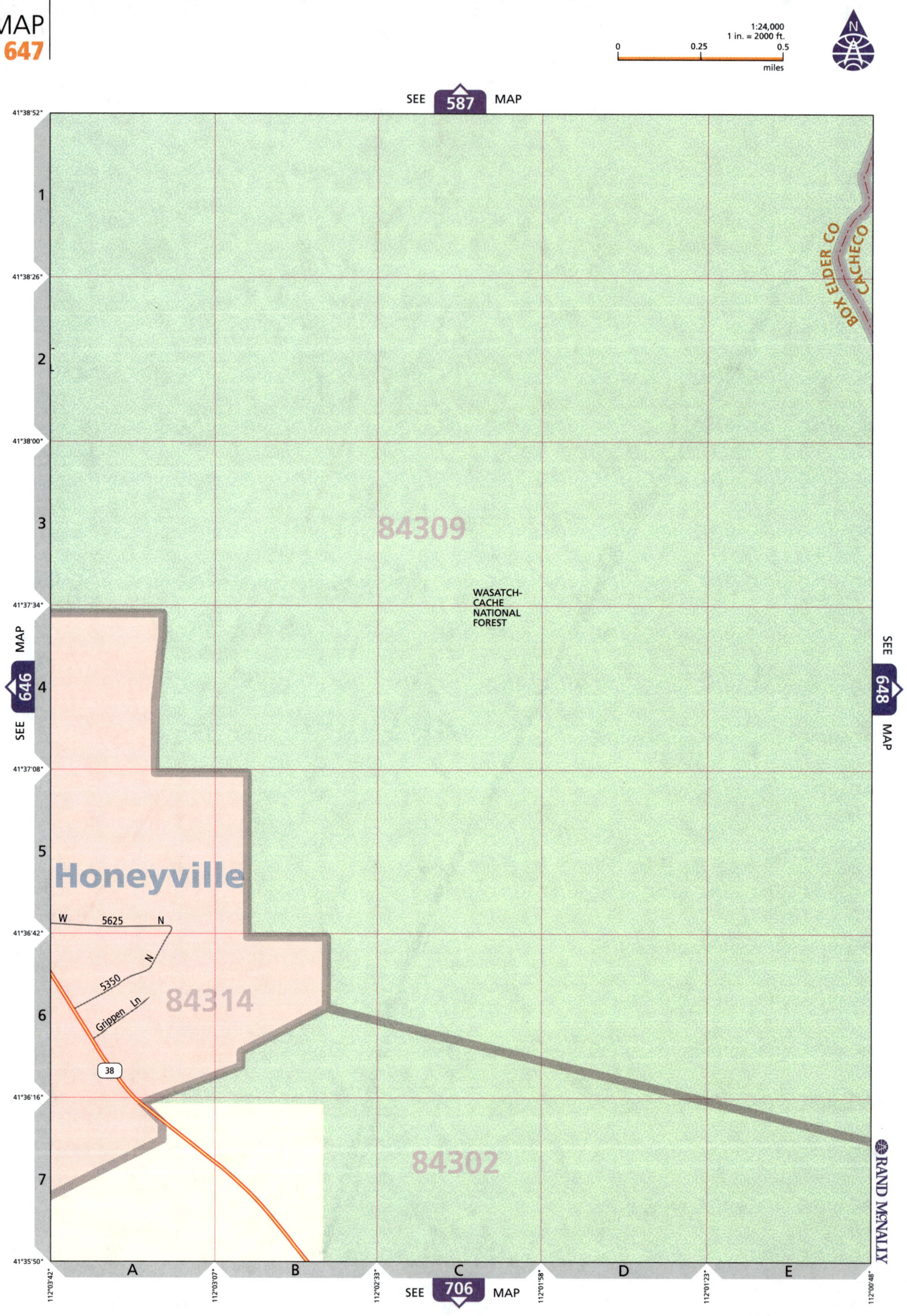

1:24,000
1 in. = 2000 ft.
0 0.25 0.5
miles

SEE 587 MAP

SEE 646 MAP

SEE 648 MAP

SEE 706 MAP

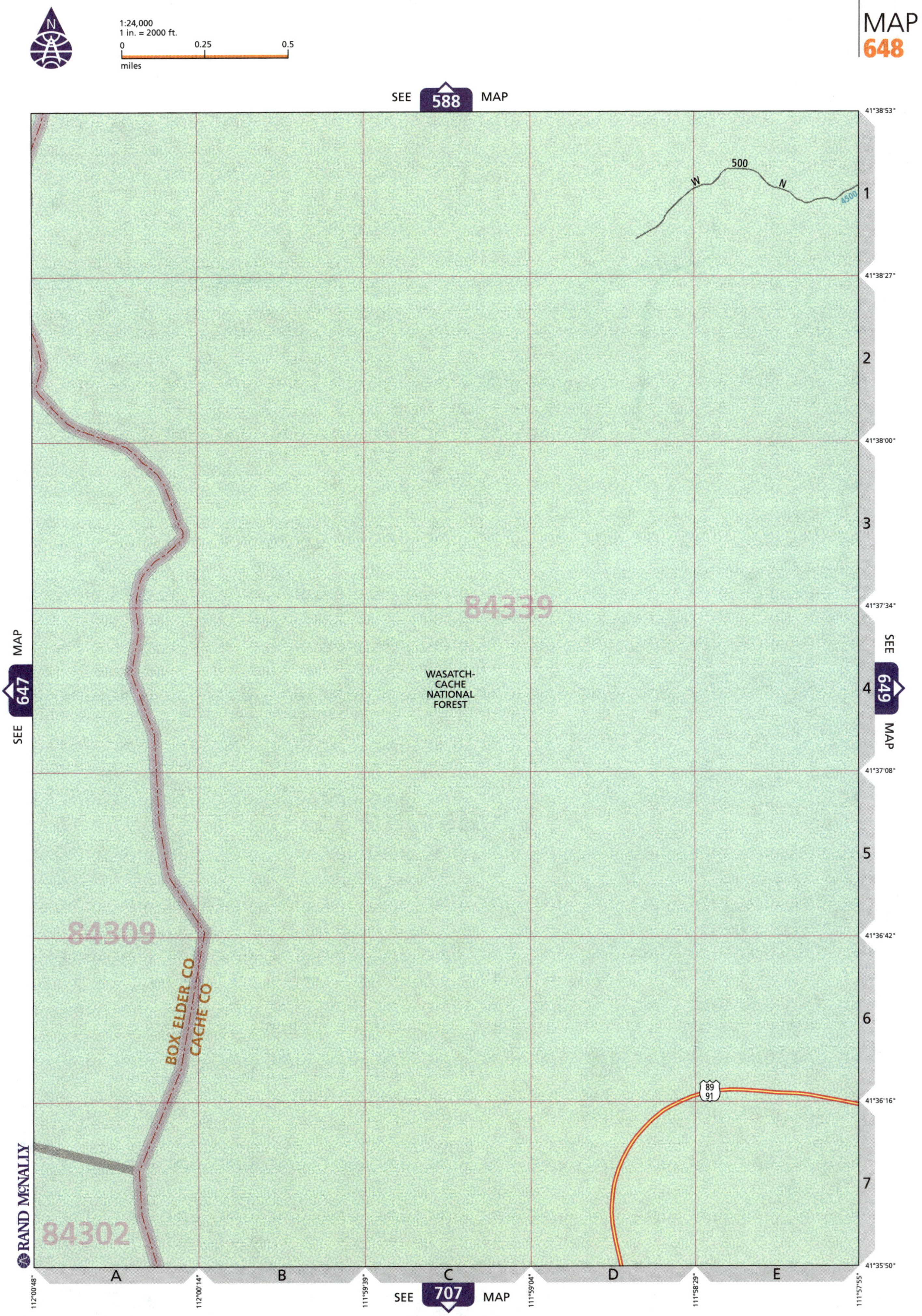

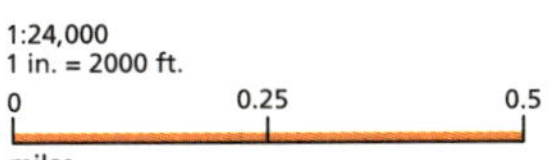

SEE 588 MAP

SEE 647 MAP

SEE 649 MAP

500
W
N
4500

84339

WASATCH-
CACHE
NATIONAL
FOREST

84309

BOX ELDER CO
CACHE CO

89
91

84302

41°38'53"
41°38'27"
41°38'00"
41°37'34"
41°37'08"
41°36'42"
41°36'16"
41°35'50"

1
2
3
4
5
6
7

A
B
C
D
E

112°00'48"
112°00'14"
111°59'39"
111°59'04"
111°58'29"
111°57'55"

SEE 707 MAP

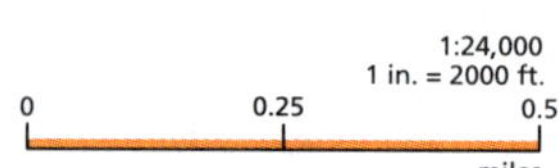

SEE 589 MAP

SEE 648 MAP

SEE 650 MAP

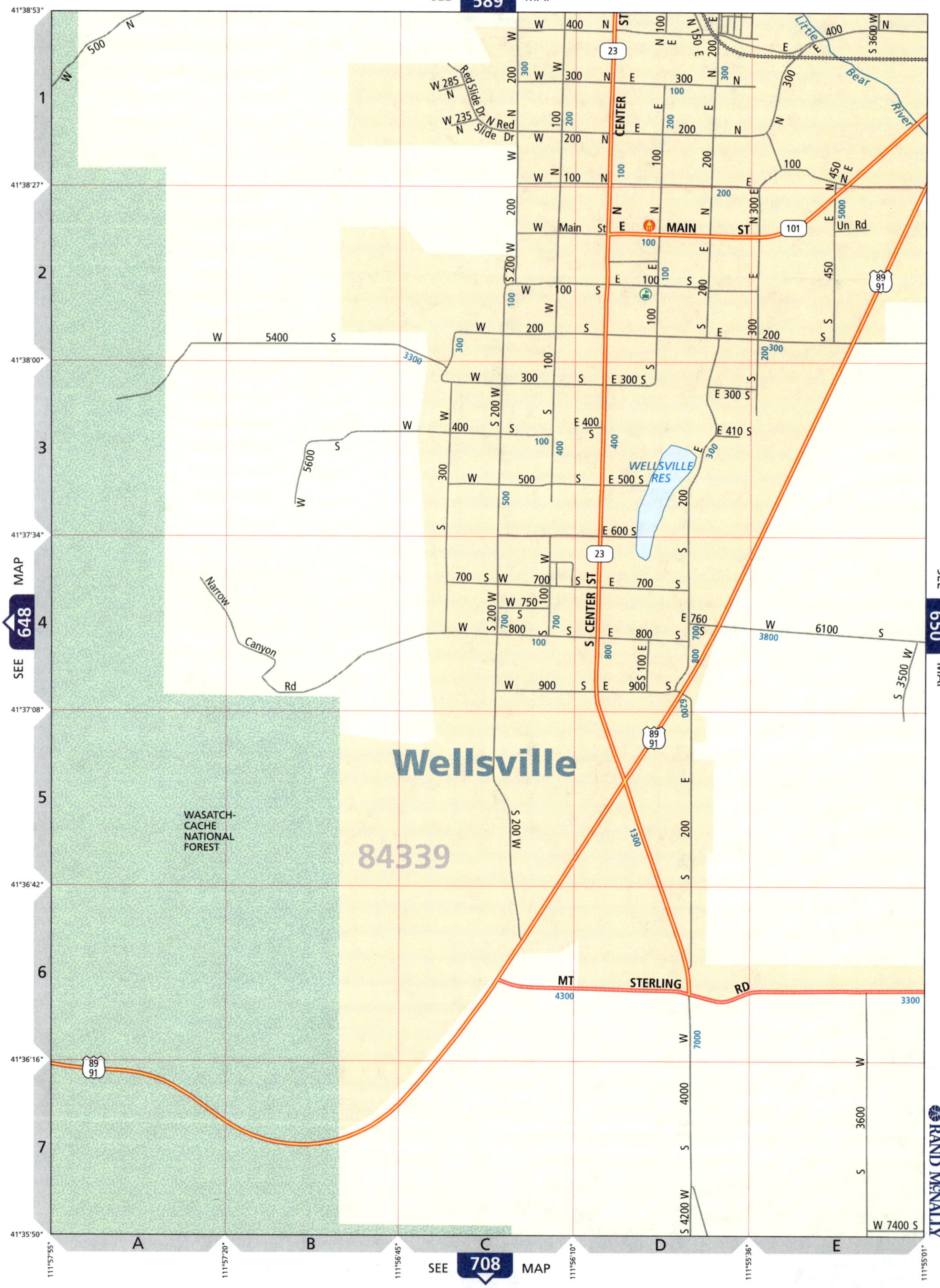

Wellsville

84339

WASATCH-
CACHE
NATIONAL
FOREST

WELLSVILLE
RES

N CENTER ST

S CENTER ST

E MAIN ST

W Main St

MT STERLING RD

Narrow Canyon Rd

Red Slide Dr

N Red Slide Dr

Little Bear River

W 5400 S

W 6100 S

W 500 N

W 400 N

W 300 N

W 200 N

W 100 N

W 200 S

W 300 S

W 400 S

W 500 S

W 700 S

W 750 S

W 800 S

W 900 S

E 300 S

E 400 S

E 410 S

E 500 S

E 600 S

E 700 S

E 760 S

E 800 S

E 900 S

S 200 W

W 5600 S

W 3500 S

W 3600 S

S 4200 W

W 7400 S

Un Rd

23

101

89
91

41°38'53"
41°38'27"
41°38'00"
41°37'34"
41°37'08"
41°36'42"
41°36'16"
41°35'50"

111°57'55"
111°57'20"
111°56'45"
111°56'10"
111°55'36"
111°55'01"

A B C D E

1 2 3 4 5 6 7

SEE 708 MAP

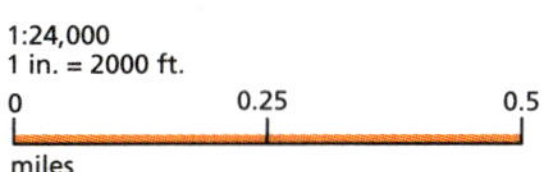

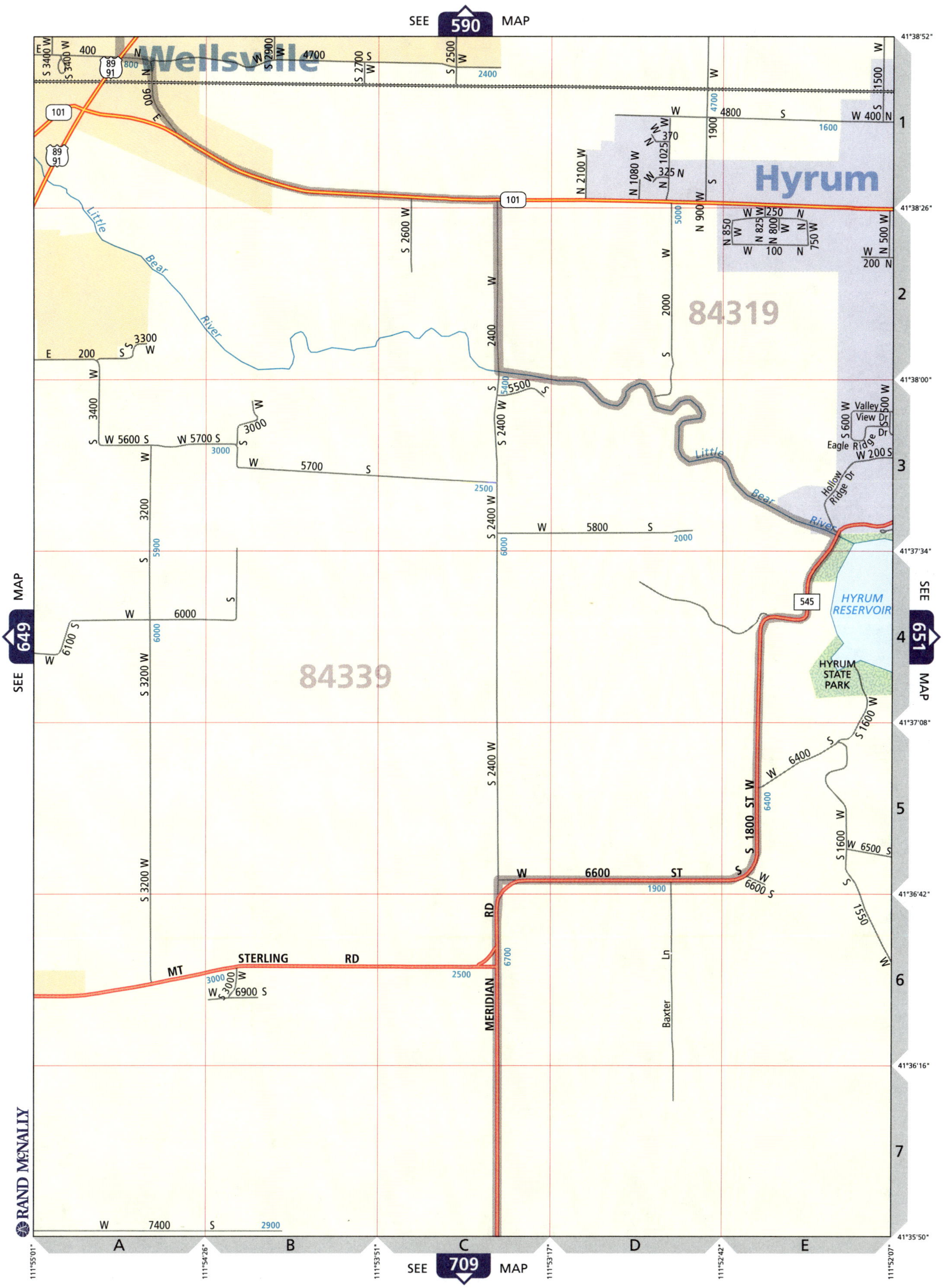

SEE 590 MAP

SEE 649 MAP

SEE 651 MAP

SEE 709 MAP

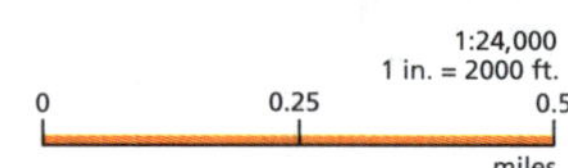

SEE 591 MAP

HYRUM RESERVOIR

HYRUM STATE PARK

HYRUM CITY CEMETERY

EAST PARK

Hyrum

84321

84319

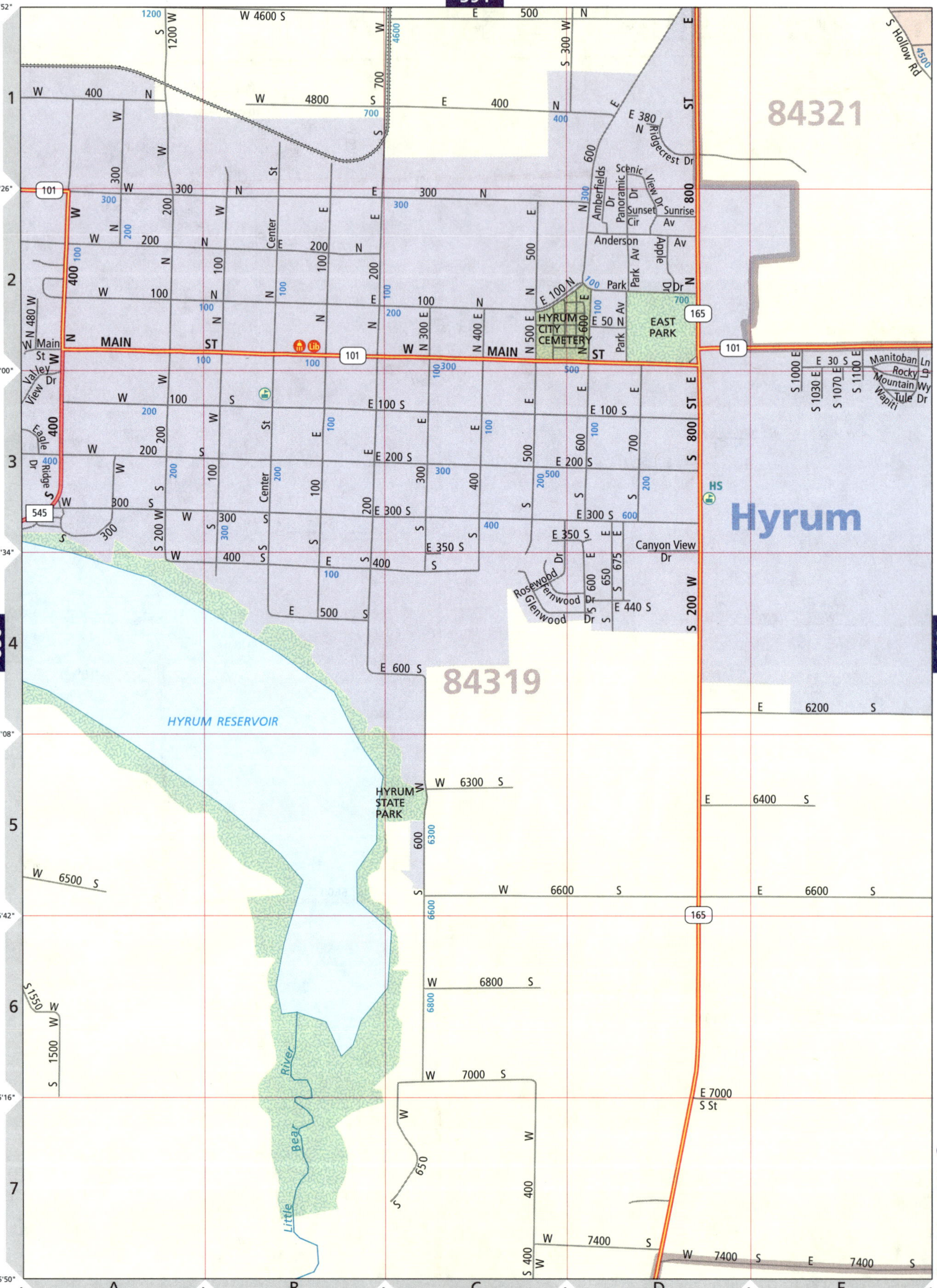

SEE 650 MAP

SEE 652 MAP

SEE 710 MAP

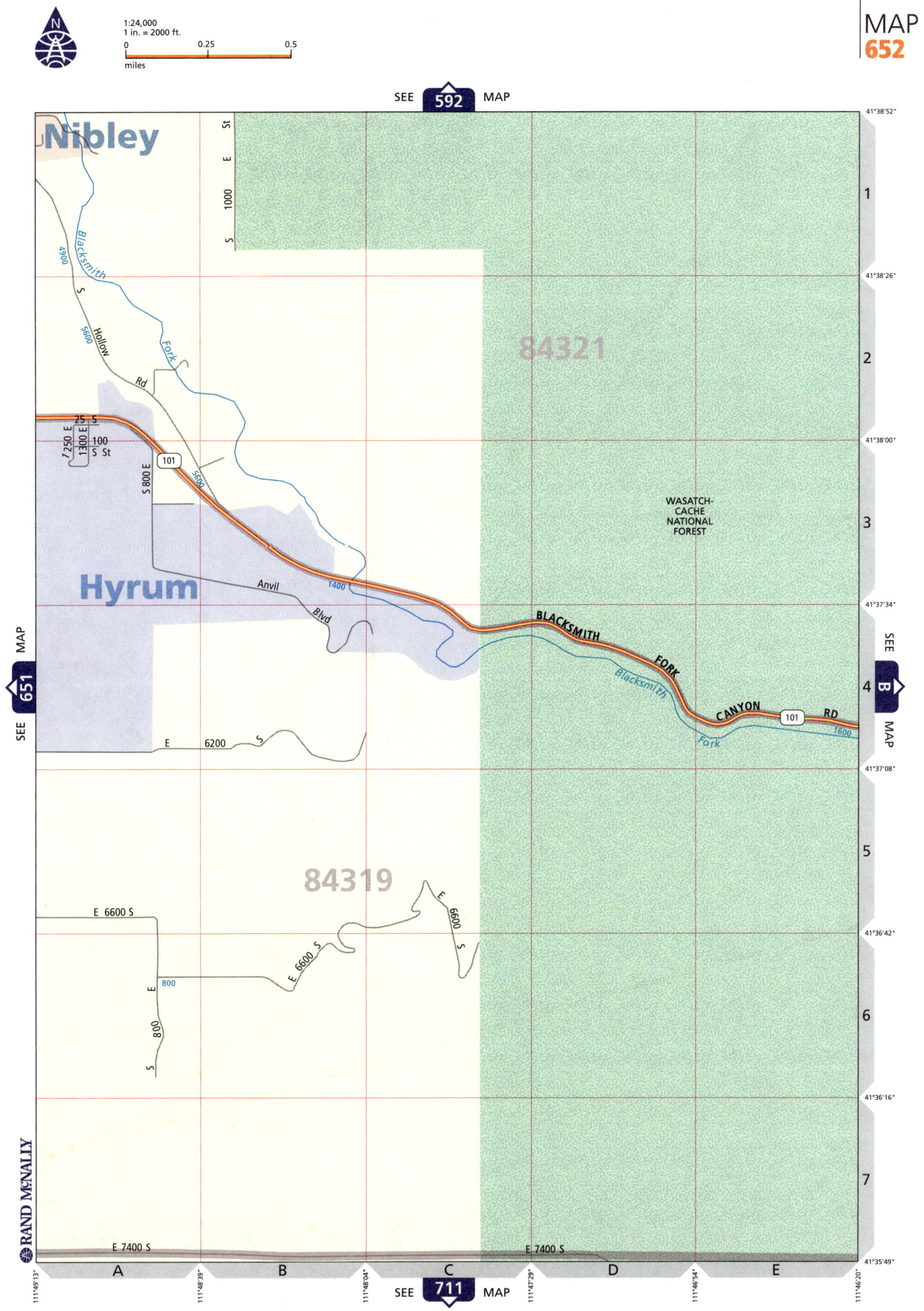

1:24,000
1 in. = 2000 ft.
0 0.25 0.5
miles

SEE 592 MAP

SEE MAP 651

SEE MAP B

SEE 711 MAP

1:24,000
1 in. = 2000 ft.
0 0.25 0.5
miles

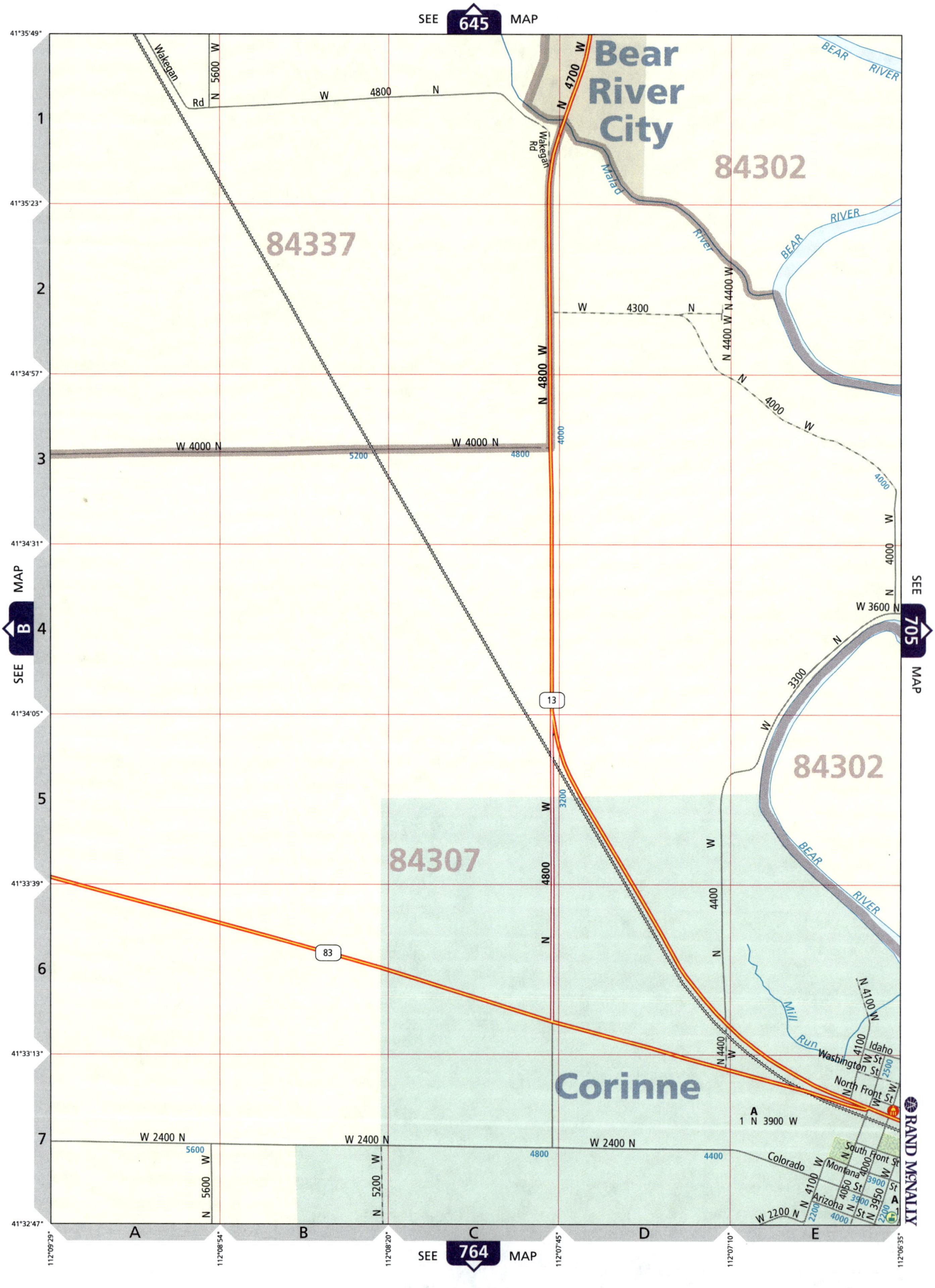

SEE 645 MAP

41°35'49"
41°35'23"
41°34'57"
41°34'31"
41°34'05"
41°33'39"
41°33'13"
41°32'47"

1
2
3
4
5
6
7

A B C D E

112°09'29" 112°08'54" 112°08'20" 112°07'45" 112°07'10" 112°06'35"

Bear River City

84302

84337

84307

84302

Corinne

Wakegan Rd

N 5600 W

W 4800 N

N 4700 W

Wakegan Rd

Malad River

BEAR RIVER

W 4300 N

N 4400 W

N 4000 W

N 4800 W

W 4000 N

5200

4800

4000

N 4000 W

W 3600 N

W 3300 N

13

83

N 4800 W

3200

N 4400 W

Mill Run

N 4100 W

Idaho St

Washington St

North Front St

2500

A

1 N 3900 W

W 2400 N

5600

N 5600 W

N 5200 W

4800

4400

Colorado

South Front St

Montana

4050 St

3900 St

3950

Arizona St

W 2200 N

4100

2200

4000

SEE B MAP

SEE 705 MAP

SEE 764 MAP

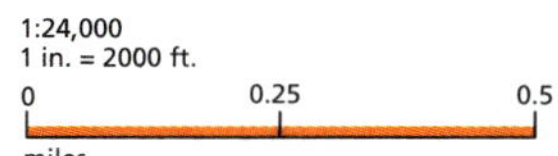

SEE 646 MAP

SEE 704 MAP

SEE 706 MAP

SEE 765 MAP

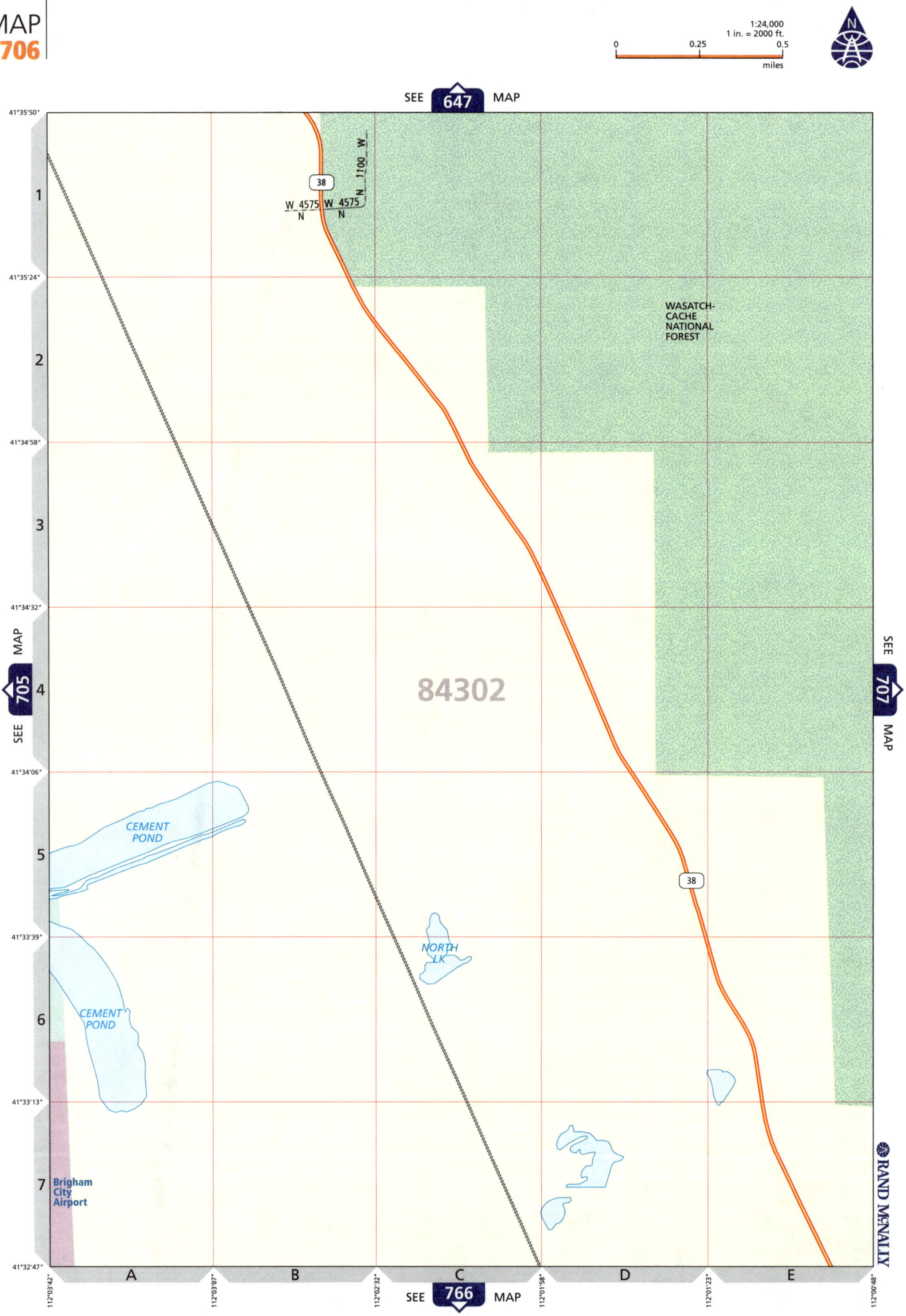

1:24,000
1 in. = 2000 ft.
0 0.25 0.5
miles

SEE 647 MAP

41°35'50"
41°35'24"
41°34'58"
41°34'32"
41°34'06"
41°33'39"
41°33'13"
41°32'47"

38
W 4575 N
W 4575 N
N 1100 W

WASATCH-
CACHE
NATIONAL
FOREST

84302

CEMENT POND

CEMENT POND

NORTH LK

38

Brigham City Airport

1 2 3 4 5 6 7

SEE 705 MAP

SEE 707 MAP

A B C D E

112°03'42" 112°03'07" 112°02'32" 112°01'58" 112°01'23" 112°00'48"

SEE 766 MAP

1:24,000
1 in. = 2000 ft.
0 0.25 0.5
miles

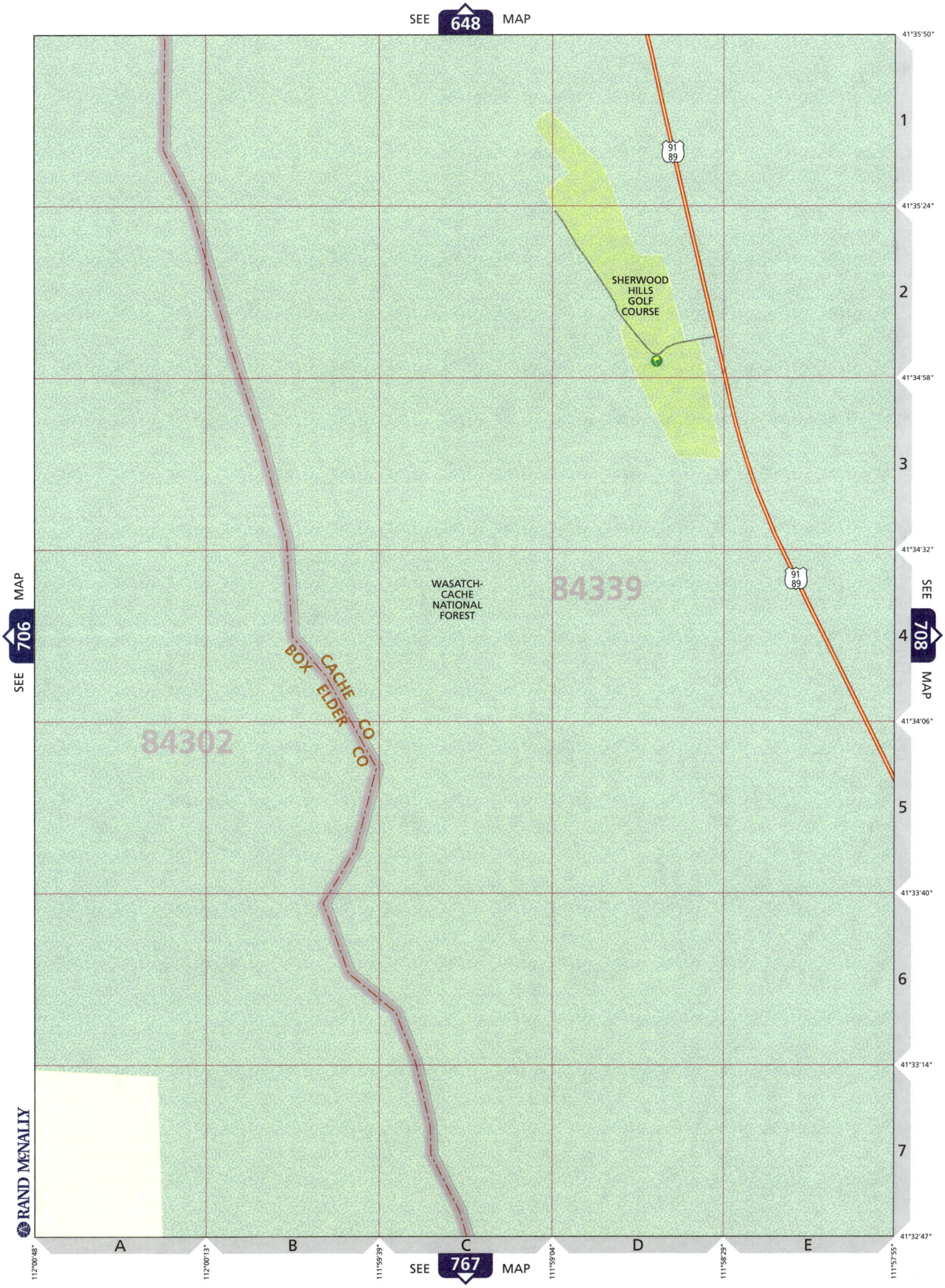

SEE 648 MAP

SEE 706 MAP

SEE 708 MAP

SEE 767 MAP

1:24,000
1 in. = 2000 ft.
0 0.25 0.5
miles

SEE 649 MAP

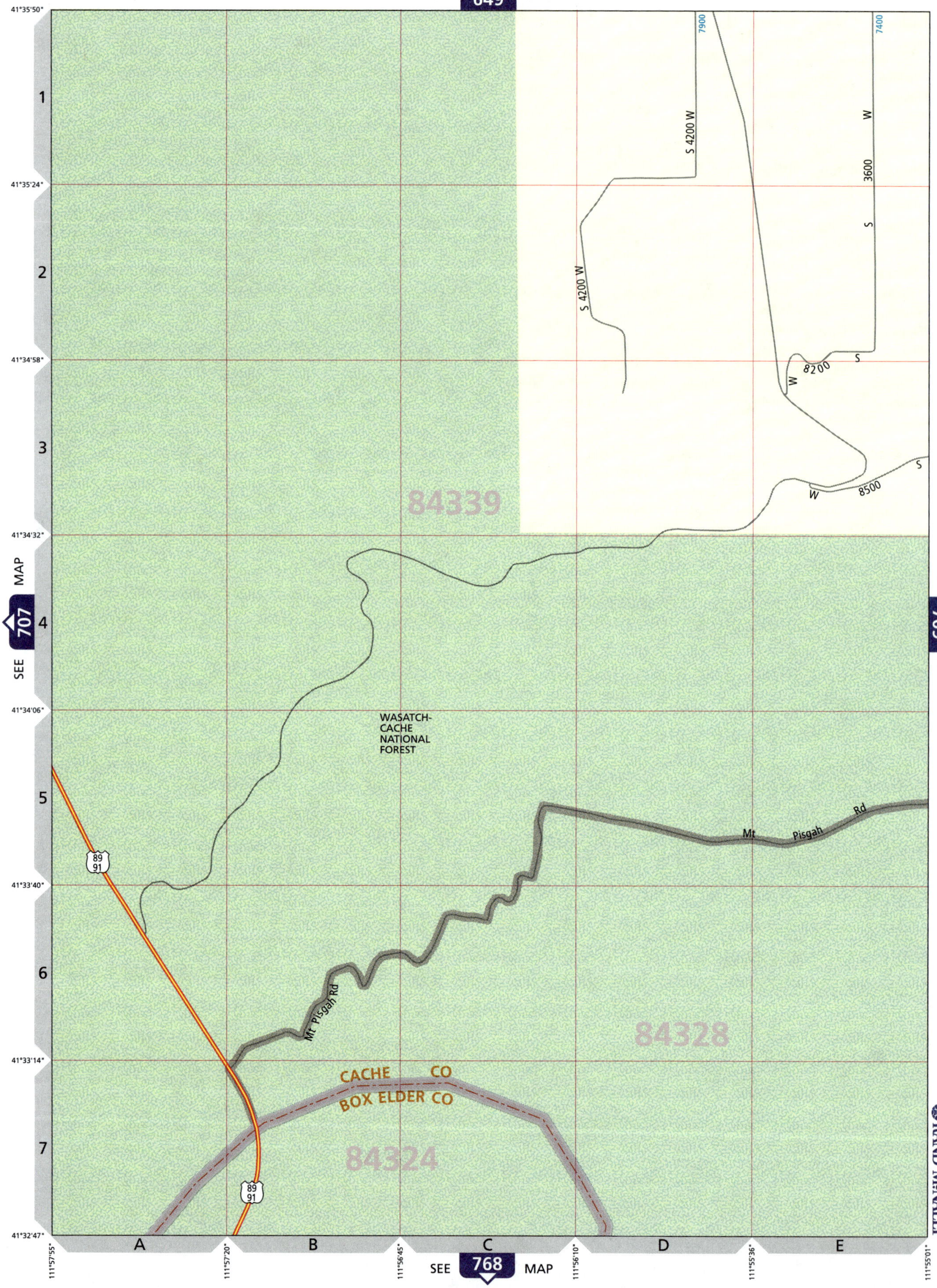

41°35'50"
1
41°35'24"
2
41°34'58"
3
41°34'32"
4
41°34'06"
5
41°33'40"
6
41°33'14"
7
41°32'47"

7900
7400
S 4200 W
S 3600 W
S 4200 W
S 8200 W
S 8500 W
84339
WASATCH-
CACHE
NATIONAL
FOREST
Mt Pisgah Rd
Mt Pisgah Rd
89
91
84328
CACHE CO
BOX ELDER CO
84324
89
91

SEE 707 MAP

SEE 709 MAP

A B C D E

111°57'55" 111°57'20" 111°56'45" 111°56'10" 111°55'36" 111°55'01"

SEE 768 MAP

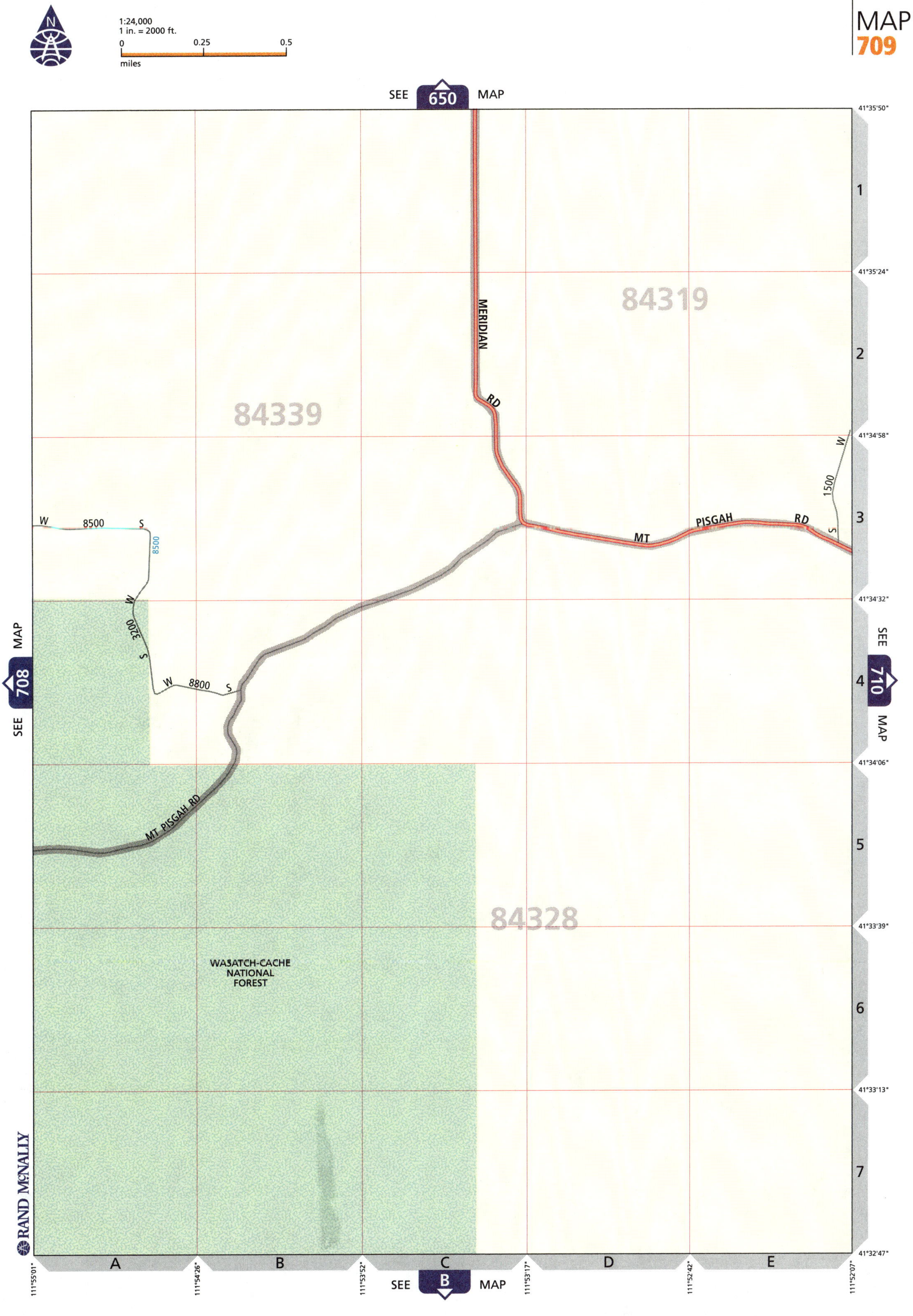

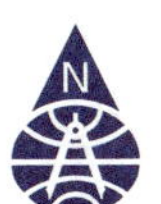

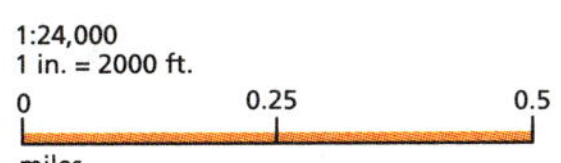

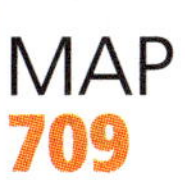

1:24,000
1 in. = 2000 ft.
0
0.25
0.5
miles
SEE 650 MAP
SEE 708 MAP
SEE 710 MAP
SEE B MAP
MERIDIAN RD
MT PISGAH RD
W 8500 S
8500
W 3200 S
W 8800 S
W 1500 S
84319
84339
84328
WASATCH-CACHE NATIONAL FOREST
41°35'50"
41°35'24"
41°34'58"
41°34'32"
41°34'06"
41°33'39"
41°33'13"
41°32'47"
111°55'01"
111°54'26"
111°53'52"
111°53'17"
111°52'42"
111°52'07"
A
B
C
D
E
1
2
3
4
5
6
7
RAND McNALLY

1:24,000
1 in. = 2000 ft.
0 0.25 0.5
miles

SEE 651 MAP

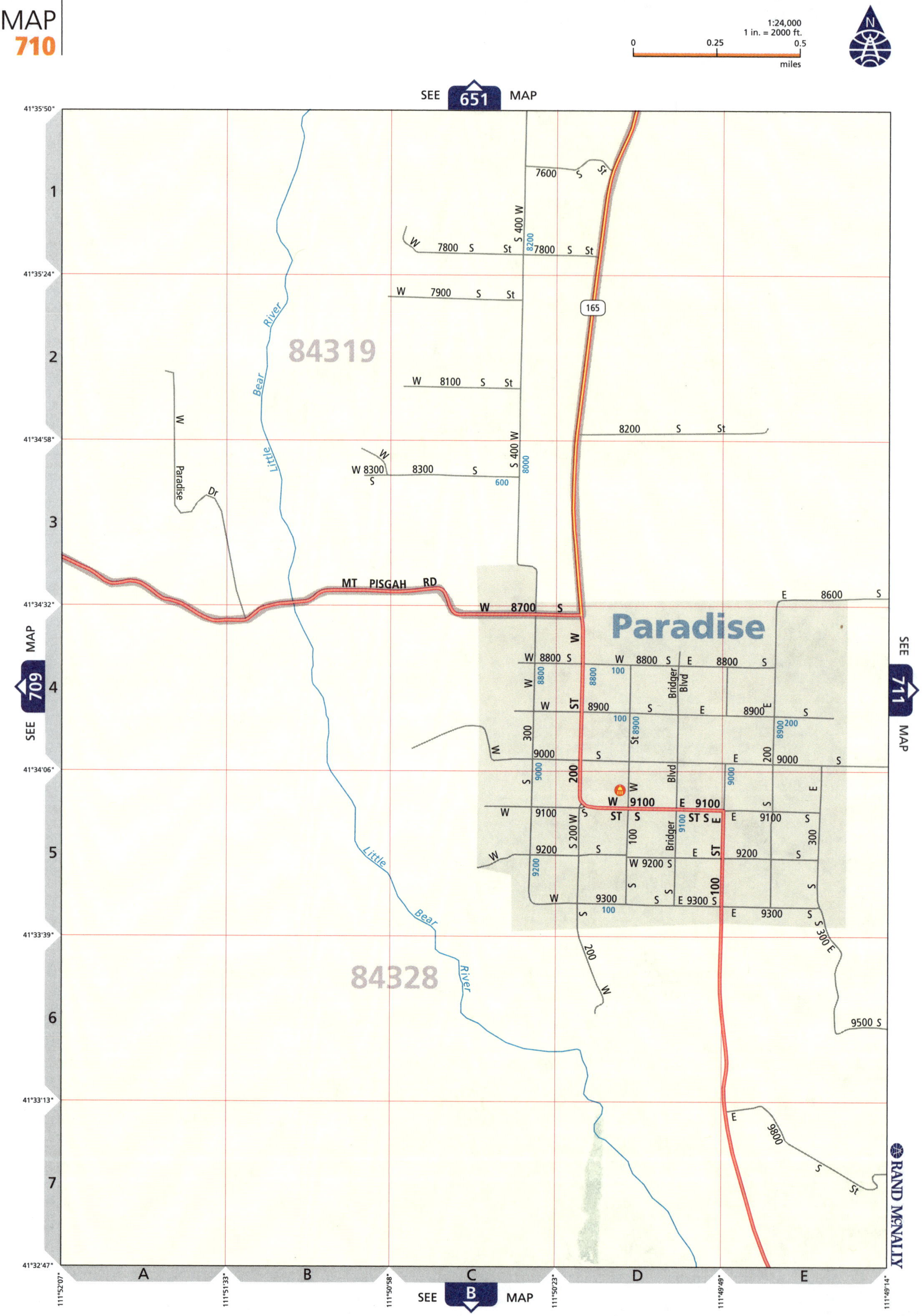

SEE 709 MAP

SEE 711 MAP

SEE B MAP

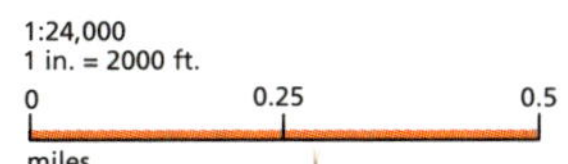

SEE 652 MAP

8100 S
900 E
875 E
875 E
700 E
981 E
980 E
Shelton Dr
S
8560
8560 S
E 8600 S St
900
E 8800 S
200
8800 S
E
E 8800 S
E 8800 S
E 8600 S St
E 8600 S
S 1200 E St
S1200 E St
84328
WASATCH-CACHE NATIONAL FOREST
E 9000 S
400
E 7400 S
9500 S
E 9800 S St
S1500 E St
Paradise Dry Canyon

1
2
3
4
5
6
7
A B C D E

41°35'49"
41°35'23"
41°34'57"
41°34'31"
41°34'05"
41°33'39"
41°33'13"
41°32'47"
111°49'14"
111°48'39"
111°48'04"
111°47'30"
111°46'55"
111°46'20"

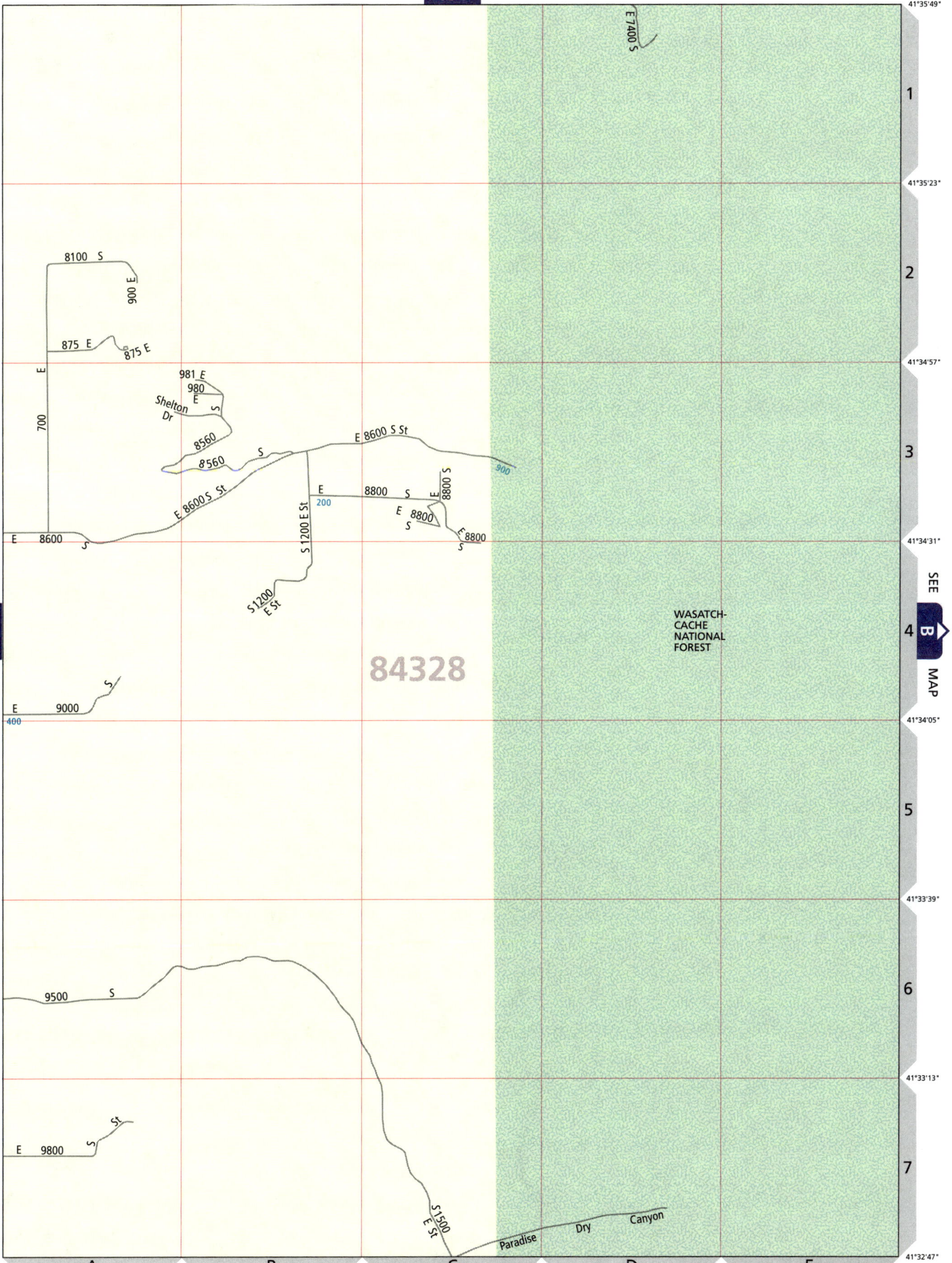

SEE 710 MAP

SEE B MAP

SEE B MAP

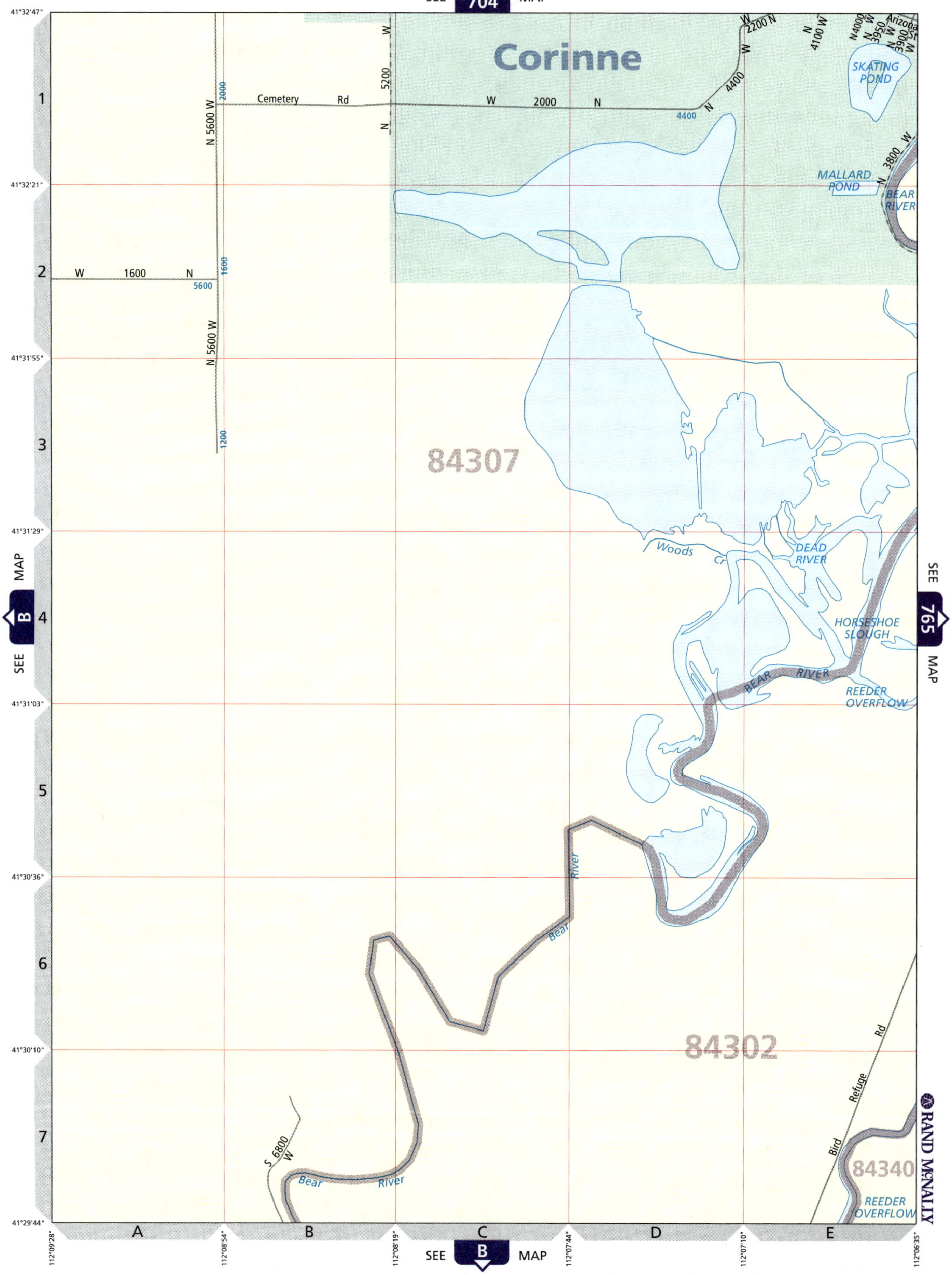

1:24,000
1 in. = 2000 ft.
0 0.25 0.5
miles

SEE 704 MAP

SEE B MAP

SEE 765 MAP

SEE B MAP

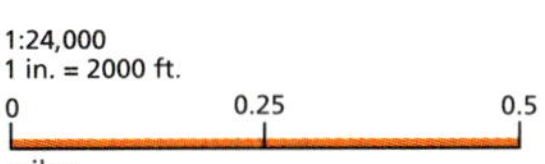

SEE 705 MAP

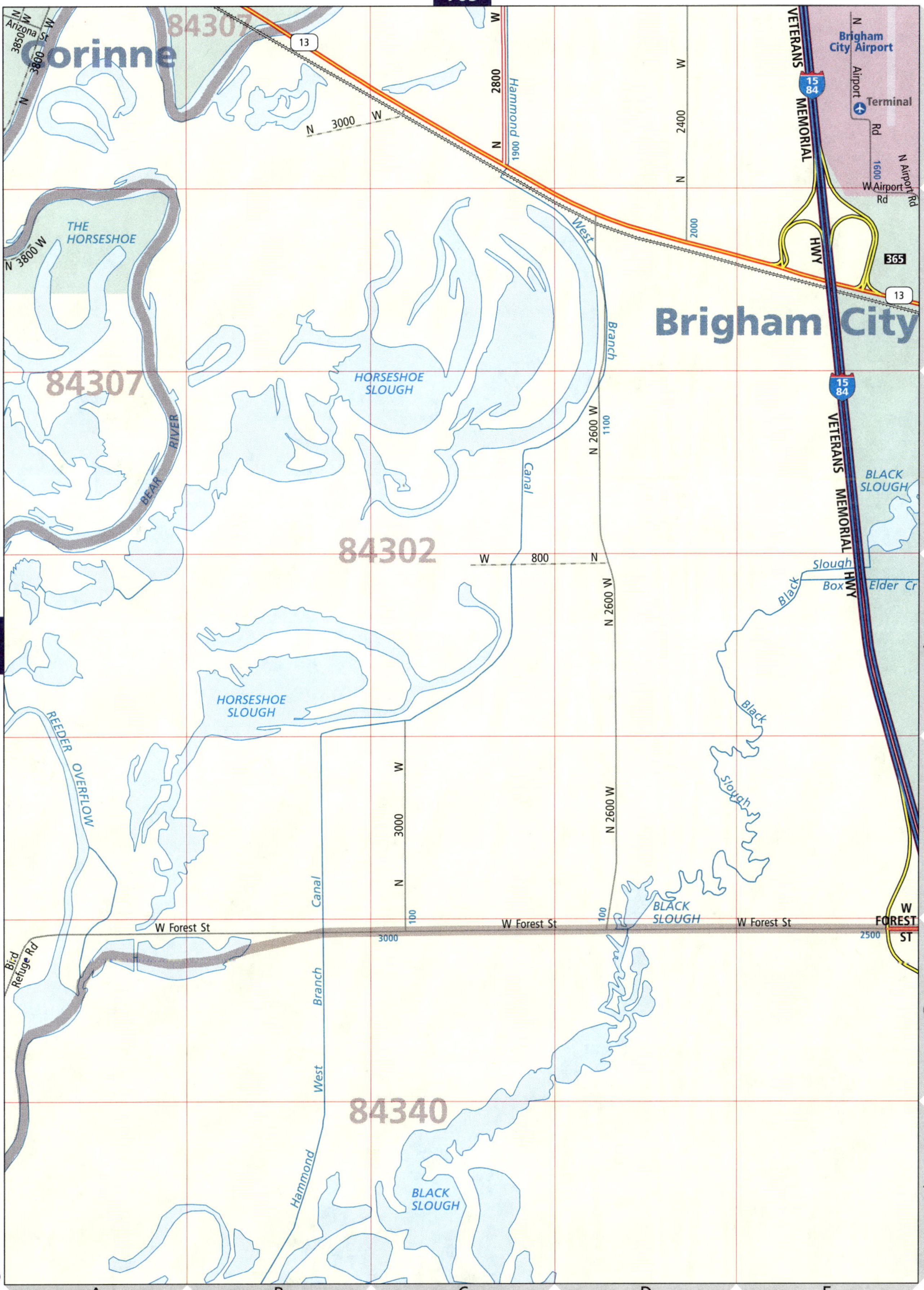

SEE 764 MAP

SEE 766 MAP

SEE B MAP

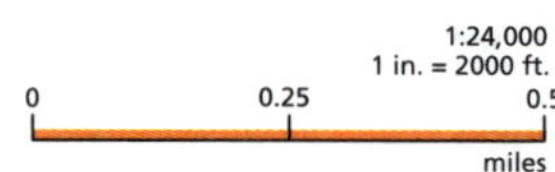

SEE 706 MAP
SEE 765 MAP
SEE 767 MAP
SEE 827 MAP

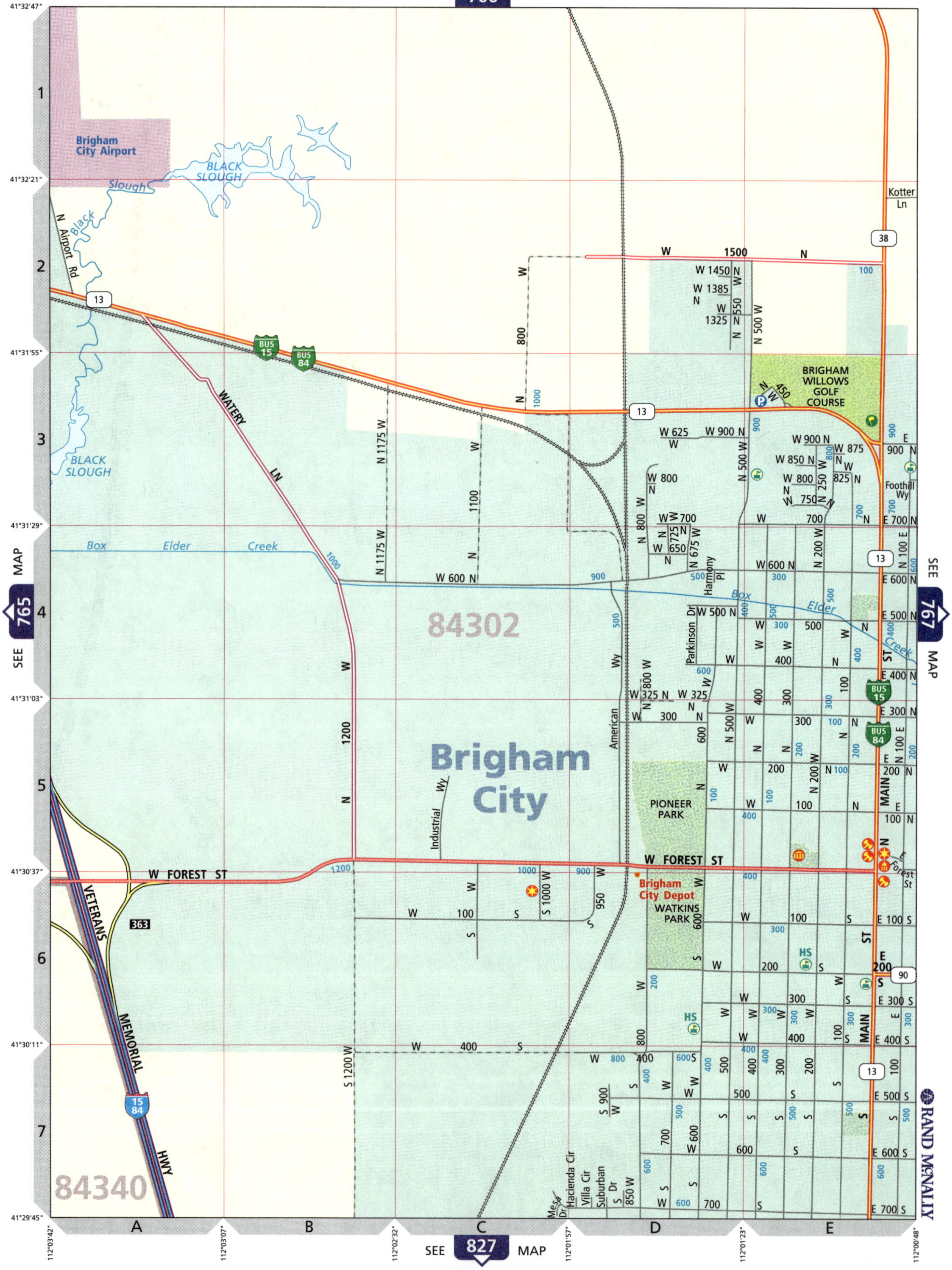

Brigham City Airport
BLACK SLOUGH
Black Slough
Box Elder Creek
84302
Brigham City
84340
BRIGHAM WILLOWS GOLF COURSE
PIONEER PARK
WATKINS PARK
Brigham City Depot
W FOREST ST
WATERY LN
N MAIN ST
S MAIN ST
VETERANS MEMORIAL HWY
W 1500 N
Kotter Ln
N Airport Rd
American Wy
Industrial Wy
Harmony Pl
Parkinson Dr
Foothill Wy
Hacienda Cir
Villa Cir
Suburban Dr
Mesa Dr

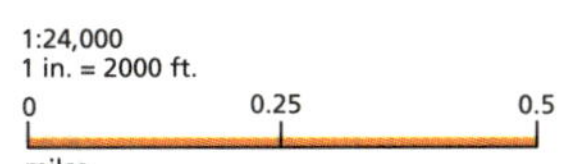

SEE 707 MAP

SEE 766 MAP

SEE 768 MAP

41°32'47"
41°32'21"
41°31'55"
41°31'29"
41°31'03"
41°30'37"
41°30'11"
41°29'45"

1 2 3 4 5 6 7

84339
CACHE CO
BOX ELDER CO
WASATCH-CACHE NATIONAL FOREST
84324
84302
Brigham City

Kotter Ln
N 170 E
E 900 N
Griffin Dr
N 325 E
Peck Cir
Foothill Wy
N 300 E
E 765 N
E 700 N
Medoland Dr
Edgehill Dr
E Highland Blvd
Kingston Pl
Shamrock Dr
Medoland Pl
Deer Haven Dr
Highland Blvd
Anderson Dr
Cherry Dr
Wade Pl
Holiday Dr
Canton Pl
E 600 N
Sunset E 500 N
Fairview Dr
Hawthorne Dr
Aspen Dr
Carolyn Pl
Belmont Dr
Orchard Pl
Oak Pl
Lindon Dr
Crestview Dr
Mountain View Dr
E 400 N
Orchard Dr
Oak Dr
Bott
1000 N
Av
N 950 E
E 300 N
Elm Av
Sycamore Av
Sycamore Dr
Sycamore Cir
E 200 N
Maple Dr
Ashe Dr
Smith Cir
N Eliason Av
Sheri Cir
Poplar Cir
Ashe Cir
Beecher
E 100 N
N 800 E
N 900 E
N 1000 E
Eliason Av
Marie Dr
Karleen Cir
Kaylynne Wy
Karleen Dr
Bywater Cir
JOHN ADAMS PARK
Box Elder Creek
N 500 E
N 700 E
E Forest St
Cathedral Church of St. Mark
E 100 S
Box Elder Canal
Cottonwood Cir
E 200 S
Jones Dr
S 700 E
90
E 300 S
North St
West St
A St
B St
C St
D St
E St
E 350 S
E 400 S
Center St
BRIGHAM CITY CEM
E 500 S
Maclane
E 600 S
E 650 S
E 675 S
S 900 E
S 850 E
E 700 S
Ogden-Brigham Canal
EAGLE MTN GC
89
91
RAND McNALLY

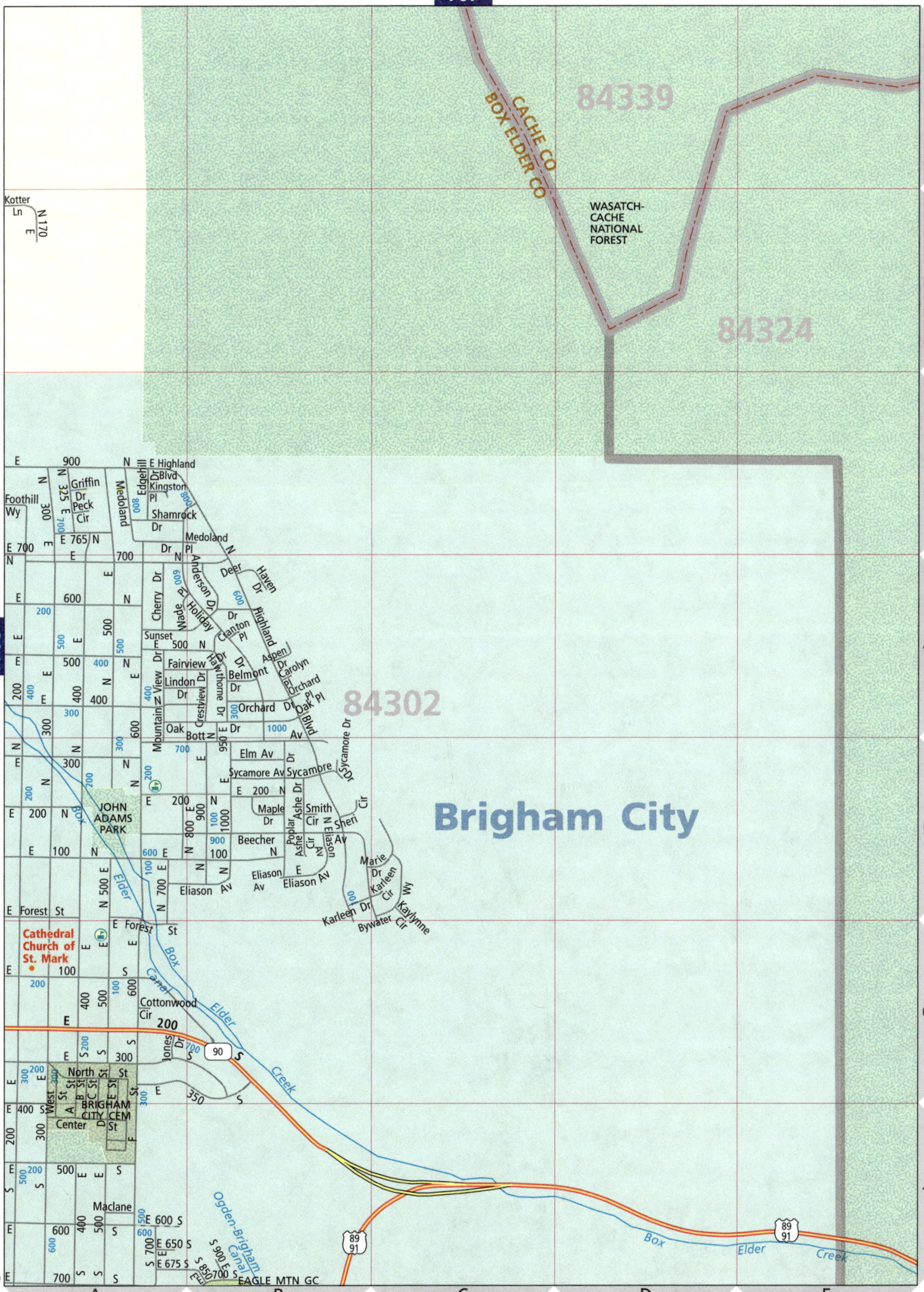

A B C D E

112°00'48"
112°00'13"
111°59'39"
111°59'04"
111°58'29"
111°57'55"

SEE 828 MAP

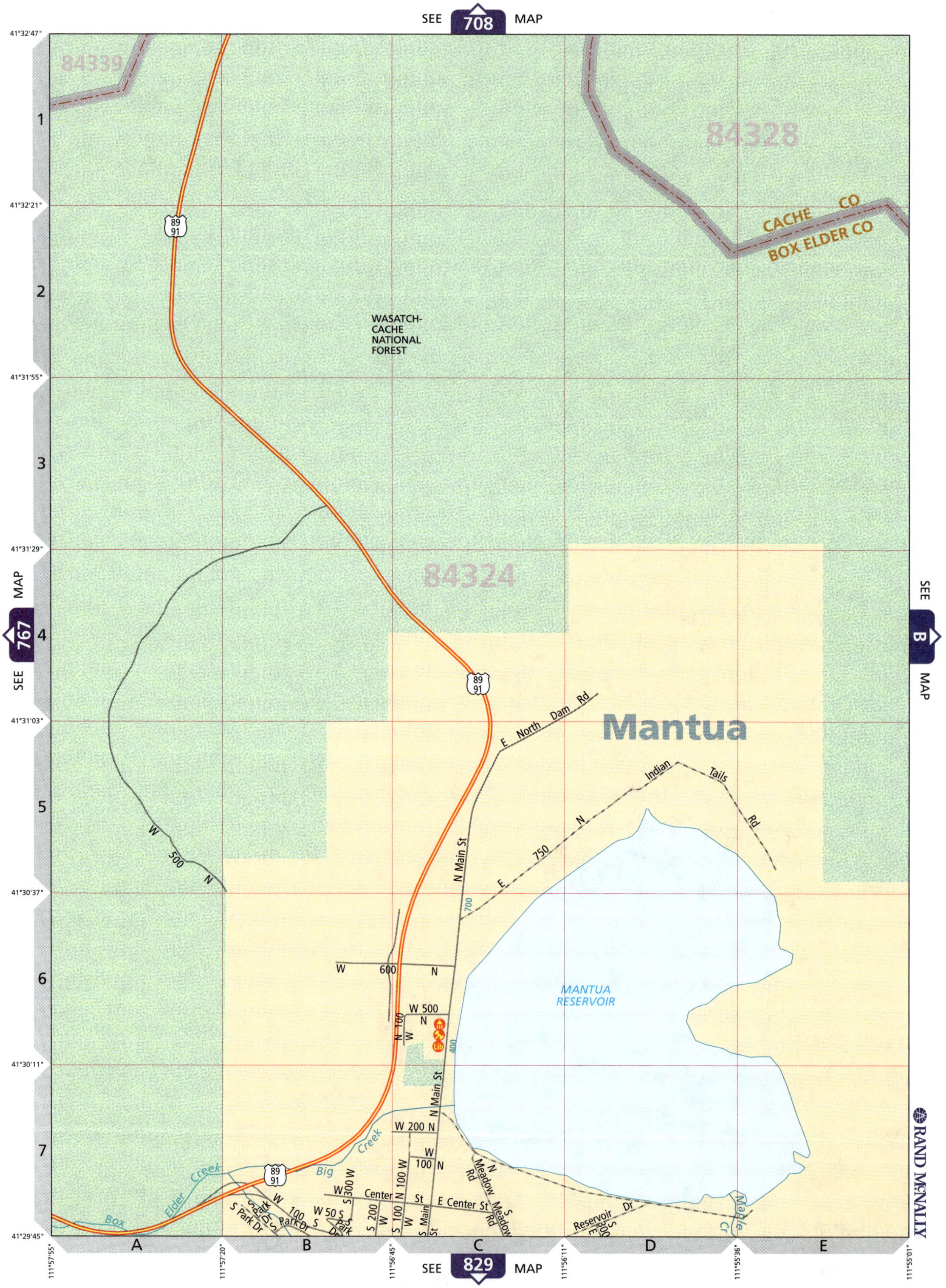
1:24,000
1 in. = 2000 ft.
0
0.25
0.5
miles
SEE 708 MAP
SEE 767 MAP
SEE B MAP
SEE 829 MAP
84339
84328
84324
CACHE CO
BOX ELDER CO
WASATCH-CACHE NATIONAL FOREST
Mantua
MANTUA RESERVOIR
89 91
E North Dam Rd
Indian Tails Rd
E 750 N
N Main St
W 500 N
W 600 N
W 500 N
N 100 W
W 200 N
W 100 N
Big Creek
Box Elder Creek
N Meadow Rd
S Meadow Rd
E Center St
W Center St
S Main St
S 100 W
S 200 W
S 300 W
W 50 S
W 100 S
S Park Dr
Reservoir Dr
Maple Cr
RAND McNALLY

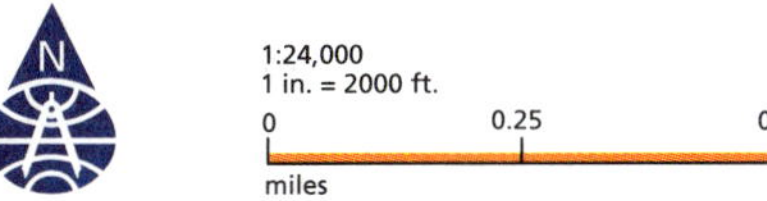

SEE 766 MAP

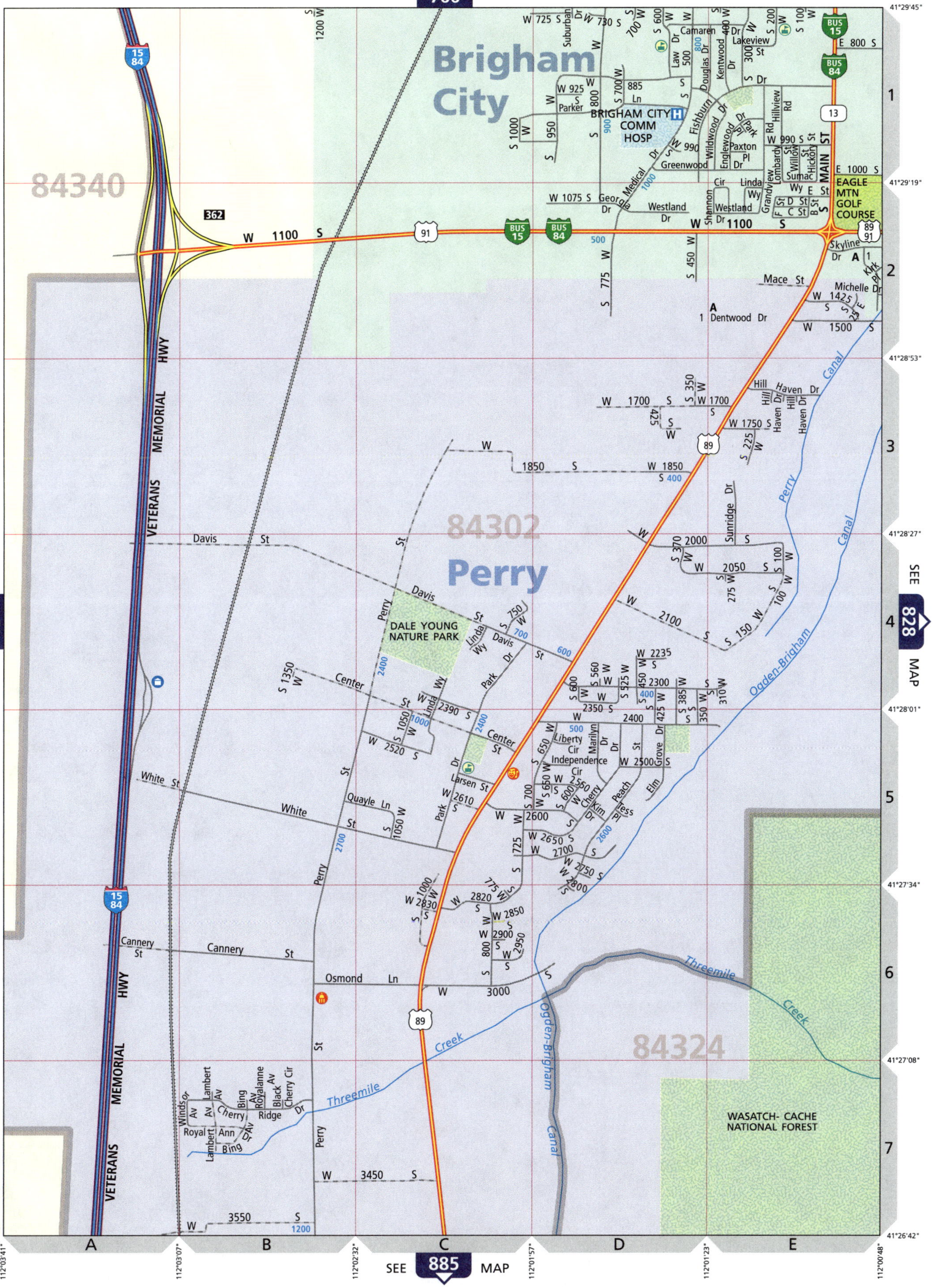

SEE B MAP

SEE 828 MAP

SEE 885 MAP

1:24,000
1 in. = 2000 ft.
0 0.25 0.5
miles

SEE 767 MAP

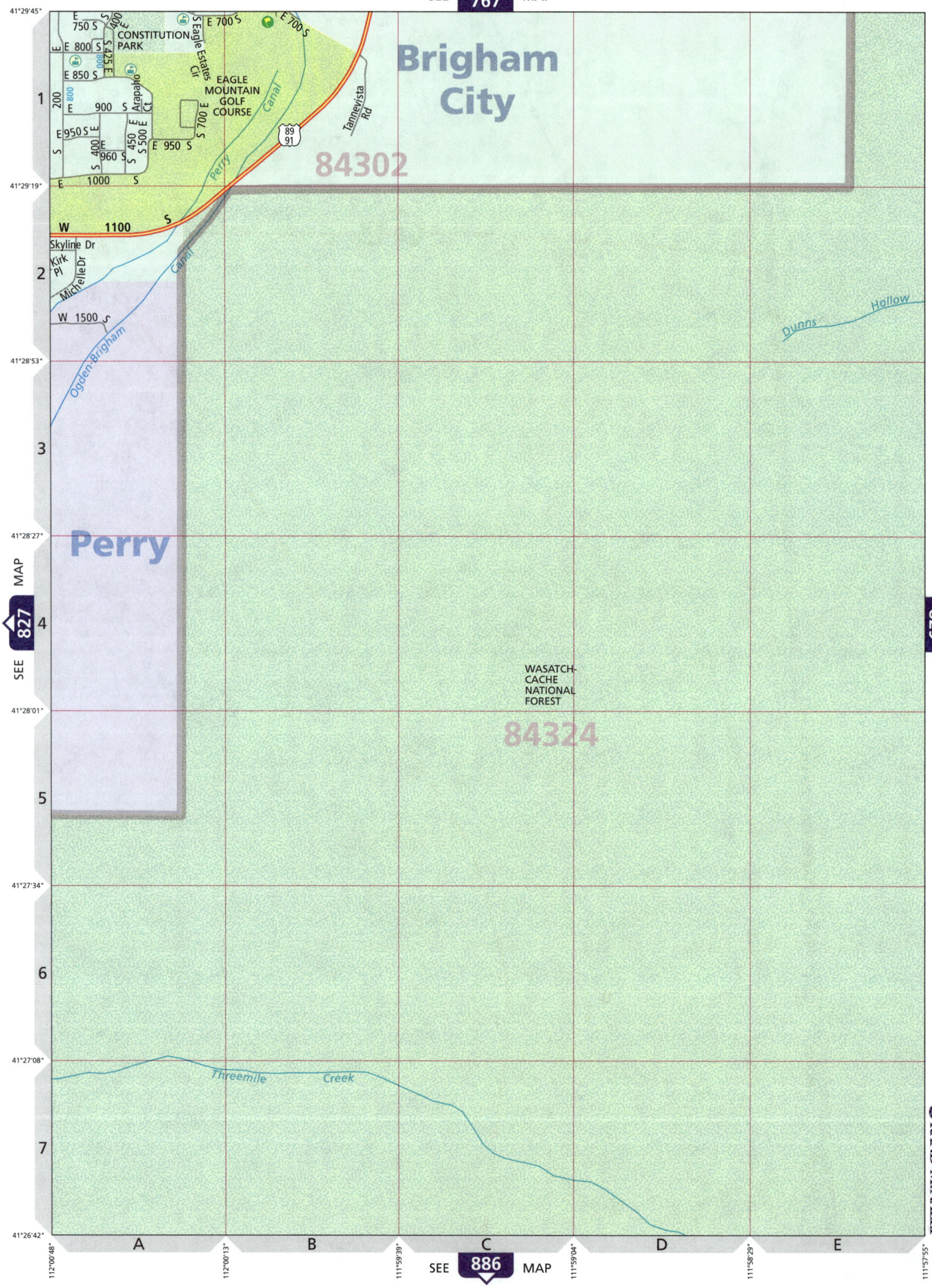

Brigham City
84302
Perry
84324
WASATCH-CACHE NATIONAL FOREST
CONSTITUTION PARK
EAGLE MOUNTAIN GOLF COURSE
E 750 S
E 800 S
E 850 S
E 900 S
E 950 S
E 960 S
E 1000 S
W 1100 S
W 1500 S
E 700 S
S 425 E
S 450 E
S 500 E
S 700 E
S 200 E
S 400 E
Arapaho Ct
Eagle Estates Cir
Tannevista Rd
Skyline Dr
Kirk Pl
Michelle Dr
89
91
800
Perry Canal
Ogden-Brigham Canal
Dunns Hollow
Threemile Creek

41°29'45" 41°29'19" 41°28'53" 41°28'27" 41°28'01" 41°27'34" 41°27'08" 41°26'42"
112°00'48" 112°00'13" 111°59'39" 111°59'04" 111°58'29" 111°57'55"

1 2 3 4 5 6 7
A B C D E

SEE MAP 827
SEE MAP 829
SEE 886 MAP

1:24,000
1 in. = 2000 ft.
0 0.25 0.5
miles

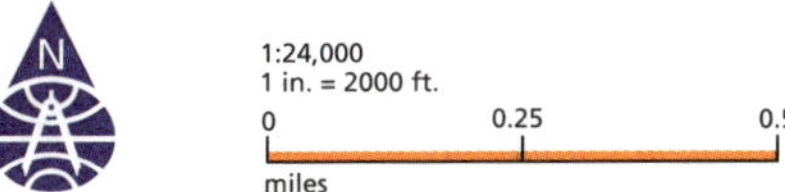

SEE 768 MAP

Mantua
84324
WASATCH-
CACHE
NATIONAL
FOREST
S Park Dr
S Park Dr W
S 200 W
100
S 100 W
S Main St
Reservoir Dr
S Meadow Rd
E 135 S
S 80 E
E 100 Fish
E 300 S
Willard Peak Rd
S 100 E
300 S
E Rocky Dugway Rd
200 E Hatchery Rd
500 E Fish Hatchery Rd
Girls Home Rd
S Park Dr
Maple Creek
Dunns Hollow
Box Elder Creek
1500
1600
1900
Flume Hollow
Devils Hole Canyon
Willard Peak Rd
41°29'45"
41°29'19"
41°28'53"
41°28'27"
41°28'00"
41°27'34"
41°27'08"
41°26'42"
111°57'55"
111°57'20"
111°56'45"
111°56'11"
111°55'36"
111°55'01"
1
2
3
4
5
6
7
A
B
C
D
E

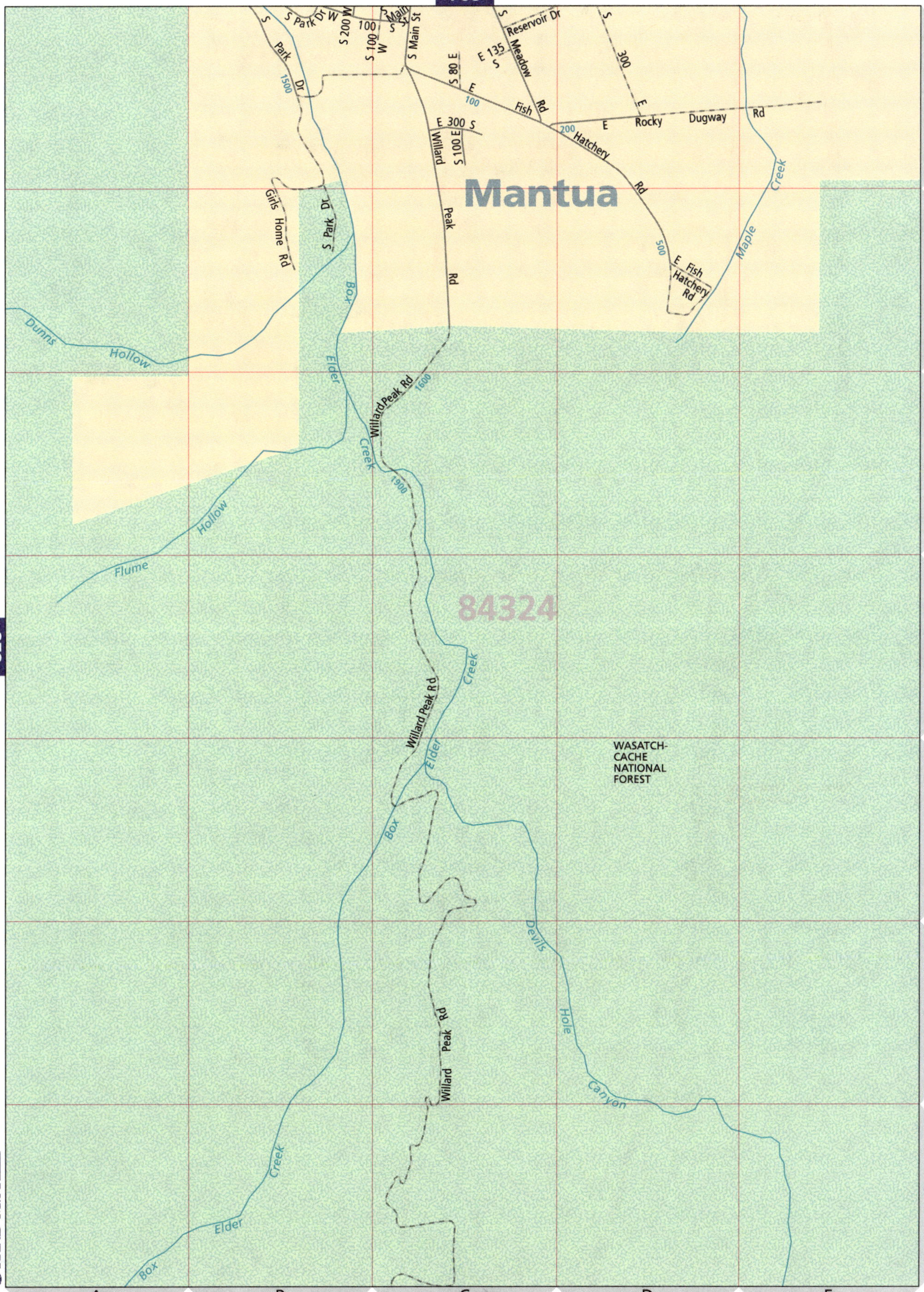

SEE 828 MAP

SEE B MAP

SEE B MAP

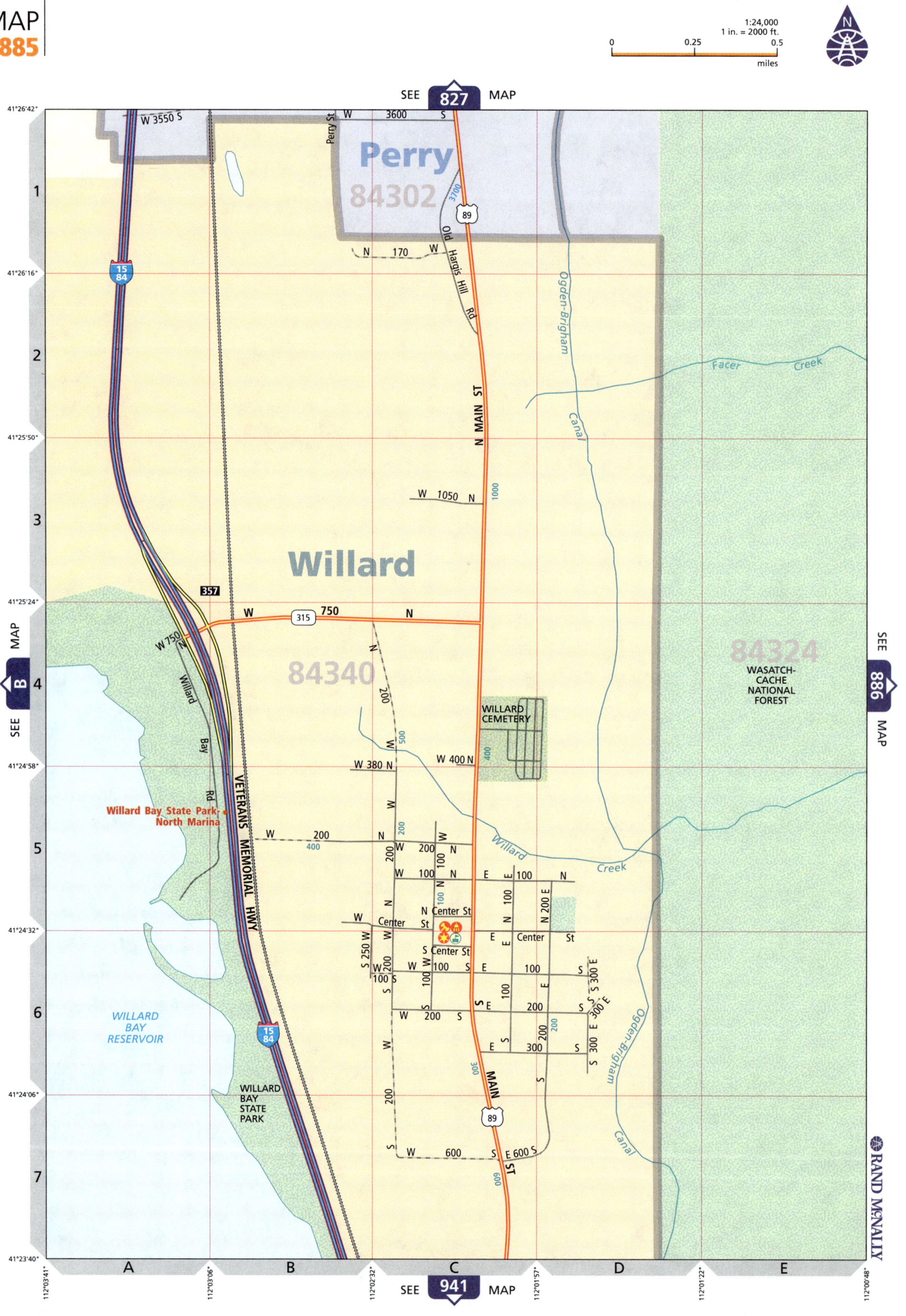

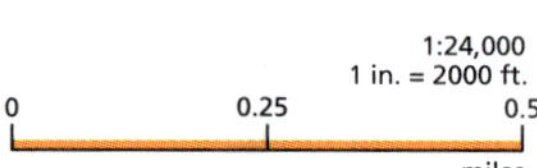

SEE 827 MAP

SEE MAP B

SEE 886 MAP

Perry
84302
Willard
84340
84324
WASATCH-
CACHE
NATIONAL
FOREST
W 3550 S
W 3600 S
Perry St
3700
89
N 170 W
Old Hargis Hill Rd
15
84
Ogden-Brigham Canal
Facer Creek
N MAIN ST
W 1050 N
1000
357
W 315 750 N
W 750 N
Willard Bay Rd
N 200 W
500
W 380 N
W 400 N
400
WILLARD
CEMETERY
VETERANS MEMORIAL HWY
Willard Bay State Park-North Marina
W 200 N
400
200
W 200 N
200 W
100 W
W 100 N
E 100 N
Willard Creek
100
N 100 E
N 200 E
N Center St
W Center St
E Center St
S Center St
S 250 W
W 200 W
100 S
W 100 S
E 100 S
S 100 W
100 E
S 300 E
S 300 E
W 200 S
S 200 E
E 200 S
200
E 300 S
S 200 E
S 300 E
WILLARD
BAY
RESERVOIR
WILLARD
BAY
STATE
PARK
W 200 W
MAIN
300
89
S W 600 S
E 600 S
ST
600
RAND McNALLY

41°26'42"
41°26'16"
41°25'50"
41°25'24"
41°24'58"
41°24'32"
41°24'06"
41°23'40"
112°03'41"
112°03'06"
112°02'32"
112°01'57"
112°01'22"
112°00'48"

1
2
3
4
5
6
7

A
B
C
D
E

SEE 941 MAP

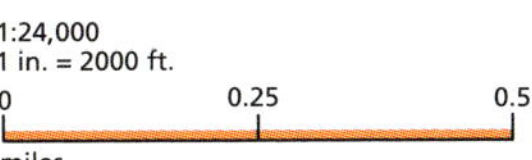

SEE 828 MAP

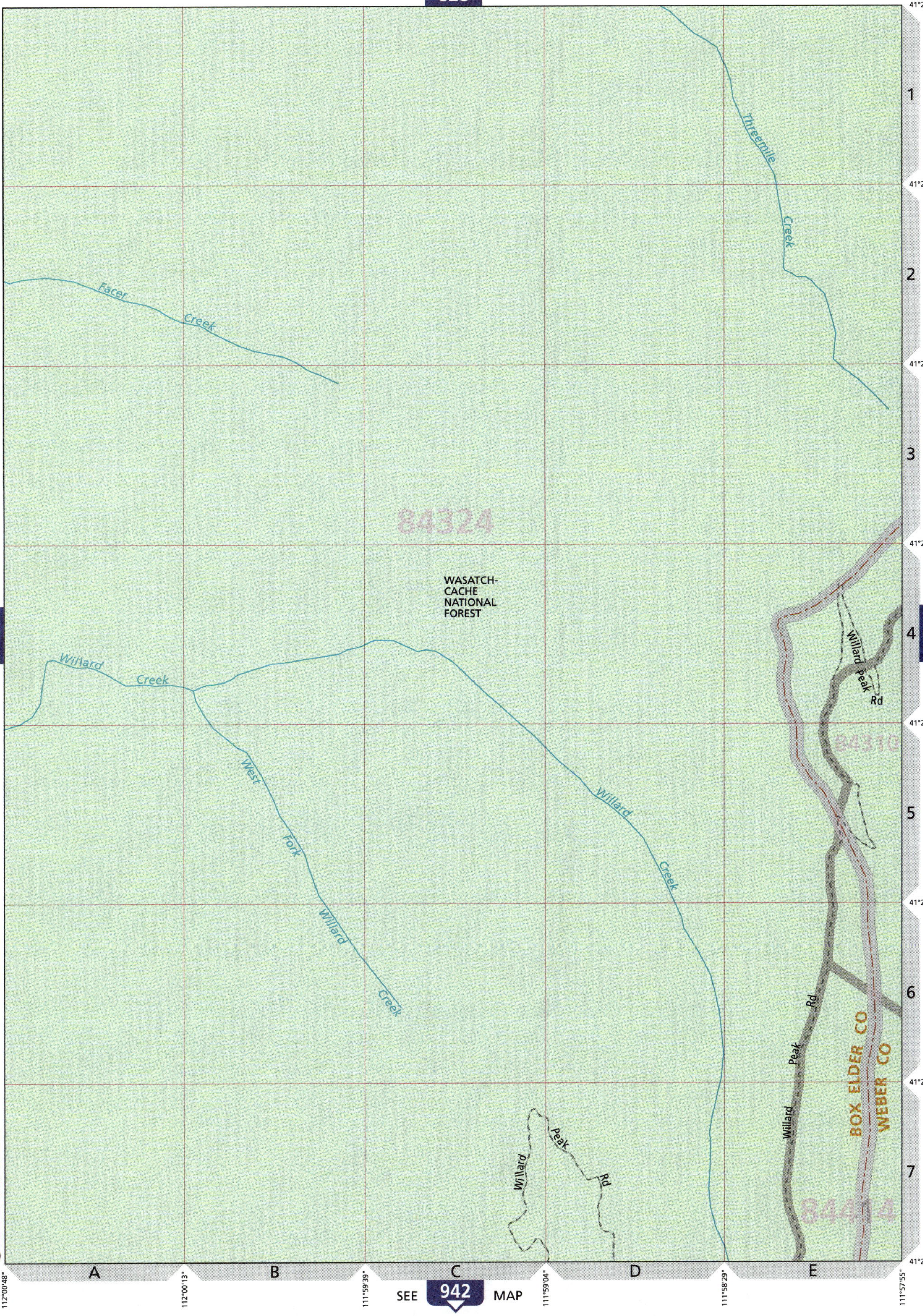

SEE 885 MAP

SEE B MAP

SEE 942 MAP

1:24,000
1 in. = 2000 ft.
0 0.25 0.5
miles

SEE 885 MAP

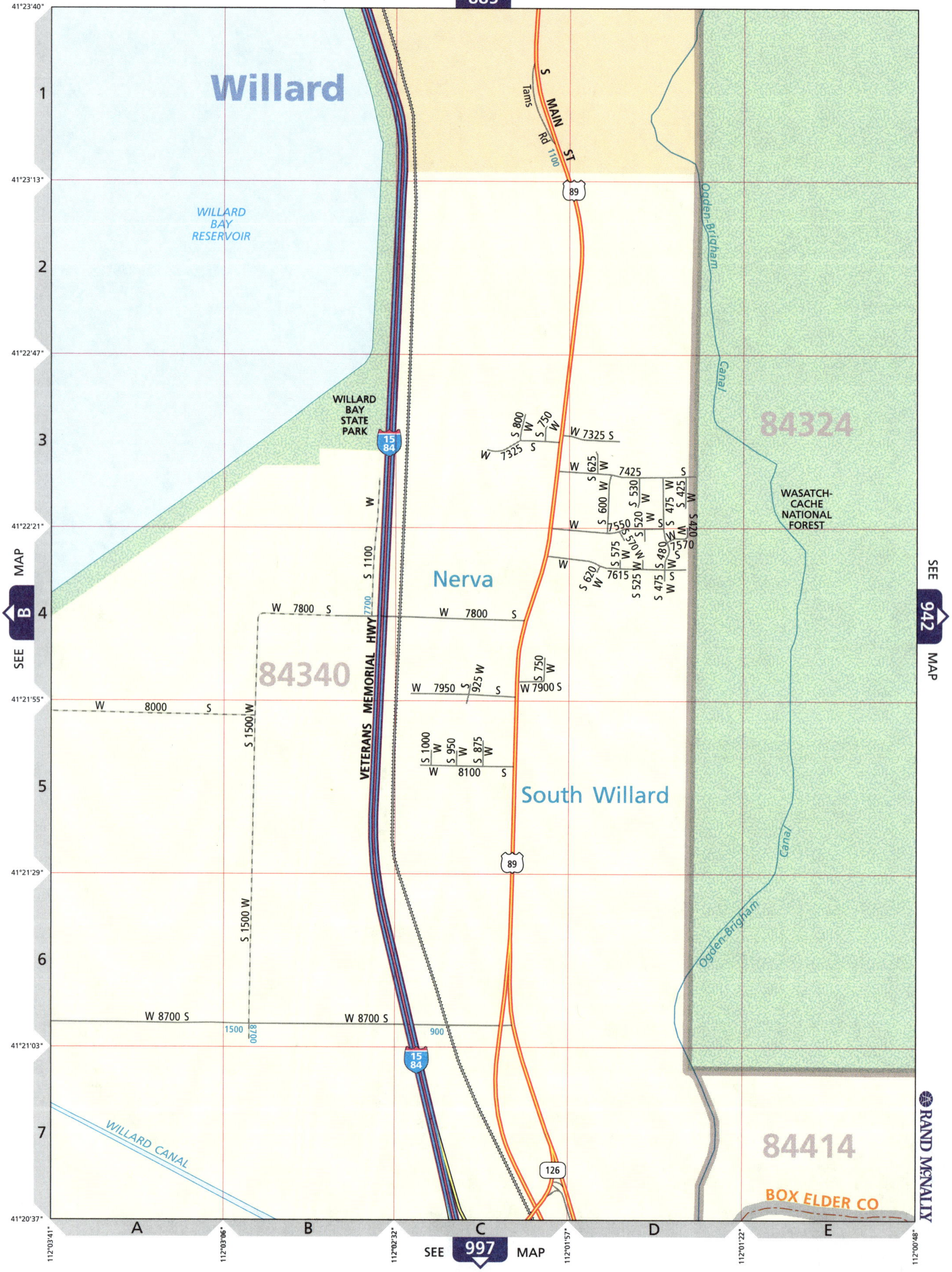

Willard

WILLARD BAY RESERVOIR

WILLARD BAY STATE PARK

S MAIN ST

Tams Rd

1100

89

Ogden-Brigham Canal

84324

WASATCH-CACHE NATIONAL FOREST

W 7325 S

W 7425 S

W 7550 S

W 7615 S

Nerva

W 7800 S

VETERANS MEMORIAL HWY

84340

W 7950 S

W 7900 S

W 8000 S

S 1500 W

W 8100 S

South Willard

W 8700 S

15 84

126

WILLARD CANAL

84414

BOX ELDER CO

RAND McNALLY

SEE B MAP

SEE 942 MAP

SEE 997 MAP

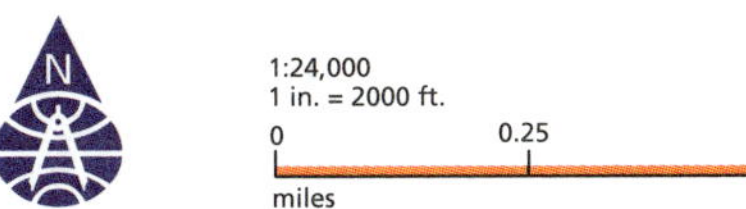

SEE 886 MAP

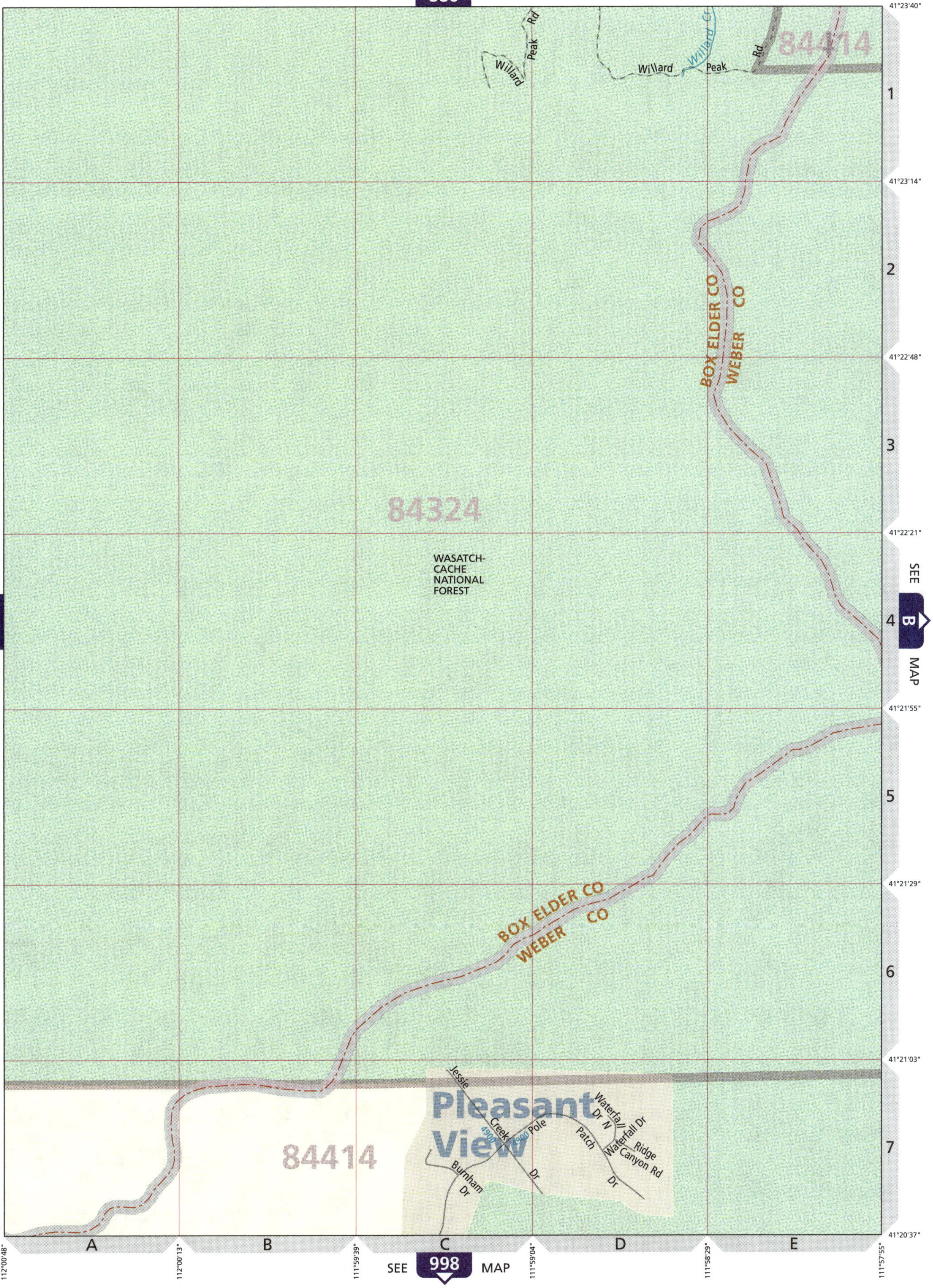

SEE 941 MAP

SEE B MAP

SEE 998 MAP

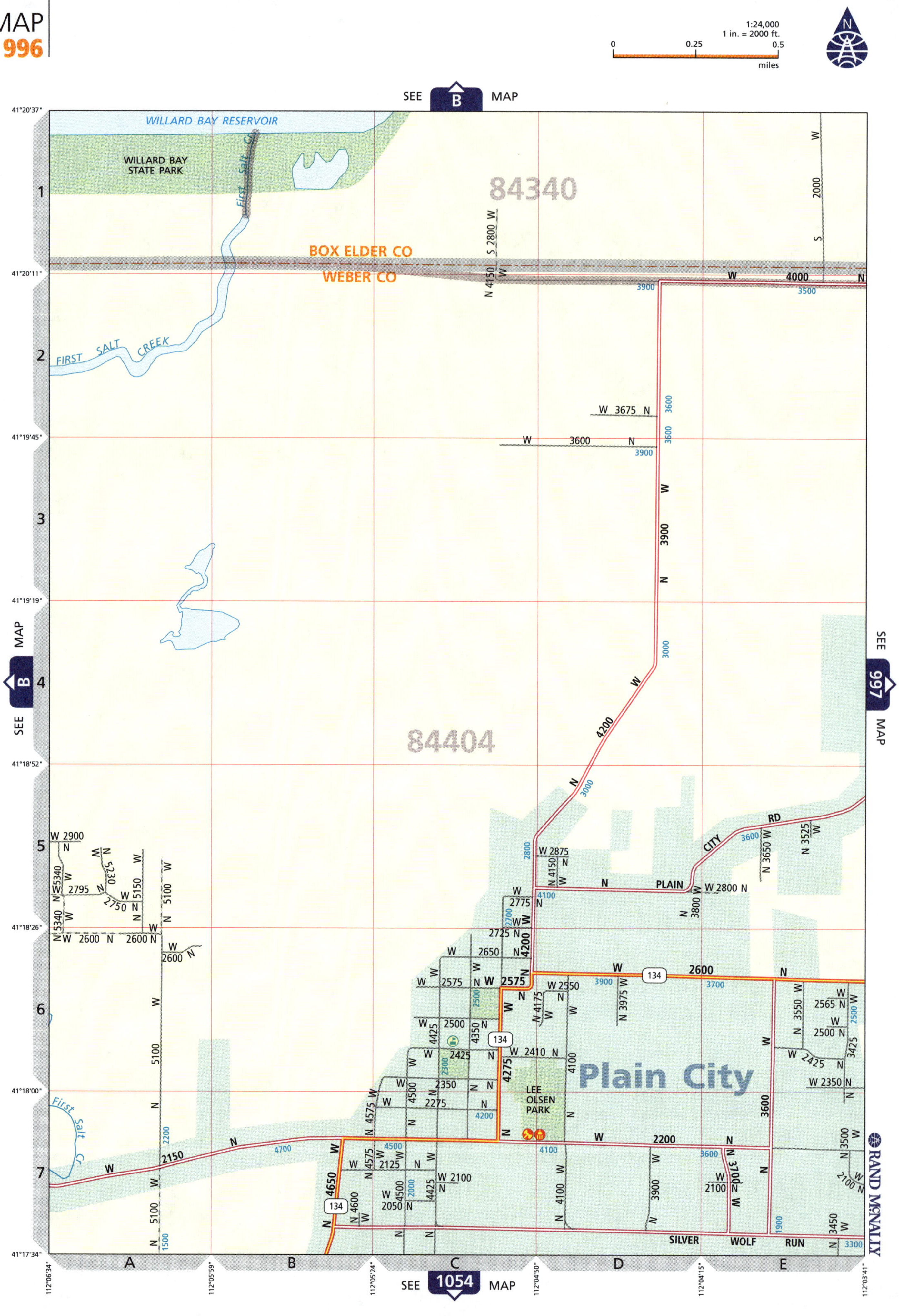

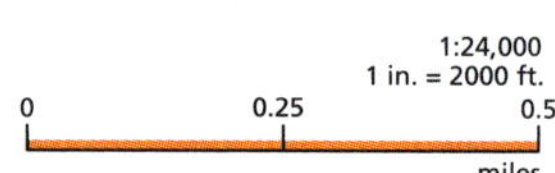

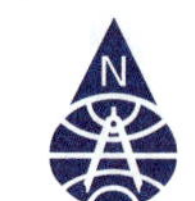

1:24,000
1 in. = 2000 ft.
0 0.25 0.5
miles
N
SEE B MAP
SEE B MAP
SEE 997 MAP
SEE 1054 MAP
WILLARD BAY RESERVOIR
WILLARD BAY STATE PARK
First Salt Cr
FIRST SALT CREEK
84340
84404
BOX ELDER CO
WEBER CO
Plain City
LEE OLSEN PARK
PLAIN CITY RD
SILVER WOLF RUN
W 2200 N
W 2600 N
W 4000 N
W 2150 N
N 3900 W
N 4200 W
N 4275 W
N 4650 W
N 3600 W
N 5100 W
S 2800 W
S 2000 W
W 3675 N
W 3600 N
W 2900 N
W 2875 N
W 2800 N
W 2775 N
W 2725 N
W 2650 N
W 2575 N
W 2550 N
W 2500 N
W 2425 N
W 2410 N
W 2350 N
W 2275 N
W 2125 N
W 2100 N
W 2050 N
W 2795 N
W 2750 N
W 2565 N
134
1
2
3
4
5
6
7
A
B
C
D
E
41°20'37"
41°20'11"
41°19'45"
41°19'19"
41°18'52"
41°18'26"
41°18'00"
41°17'34"
112°06'34"
112°05'59"
112°05'24"
112°04'50"
112°04'15"
112°03'41"
RAND McNALLY

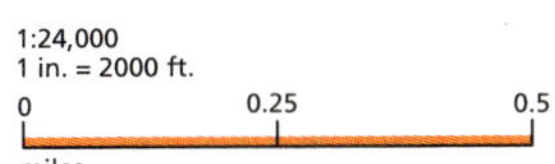

SEE 941 MAP

Farr West

Pleasant View

Plain City

84340 84414 84404

BOX ELDER CO
WEBER CO

REMUDA GOLF COURSE

WILLARD CANAL

Ogden-Brigham Canal

VETERANS MEMORIAL HWY

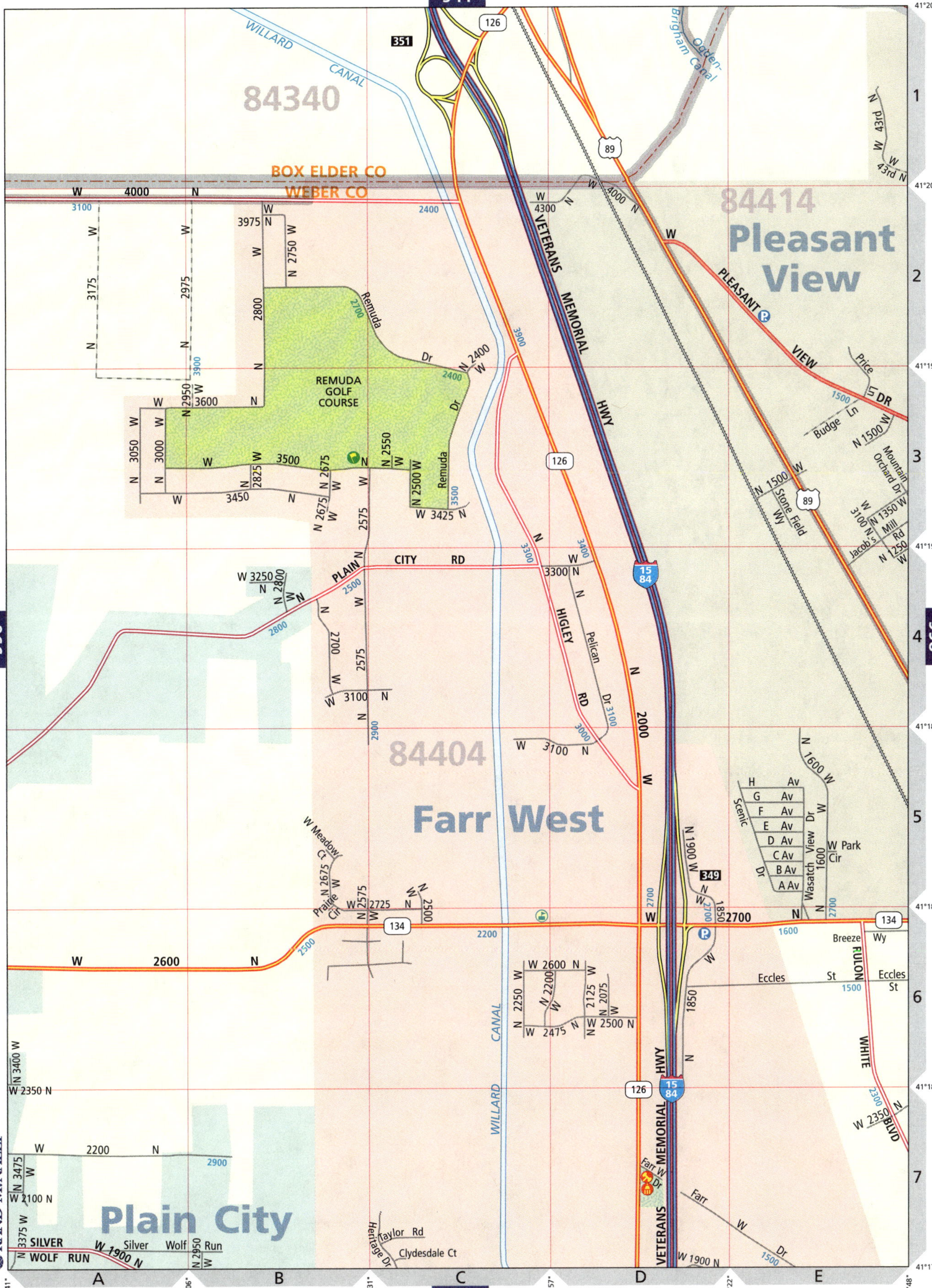

SEE 996 MAP

SEE 998 MAP

SEE 1055 MAP

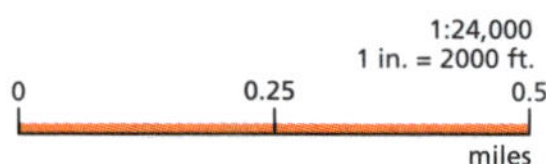

SEE 942 MAP

SEE 997 MAP

SEE 999 MAP

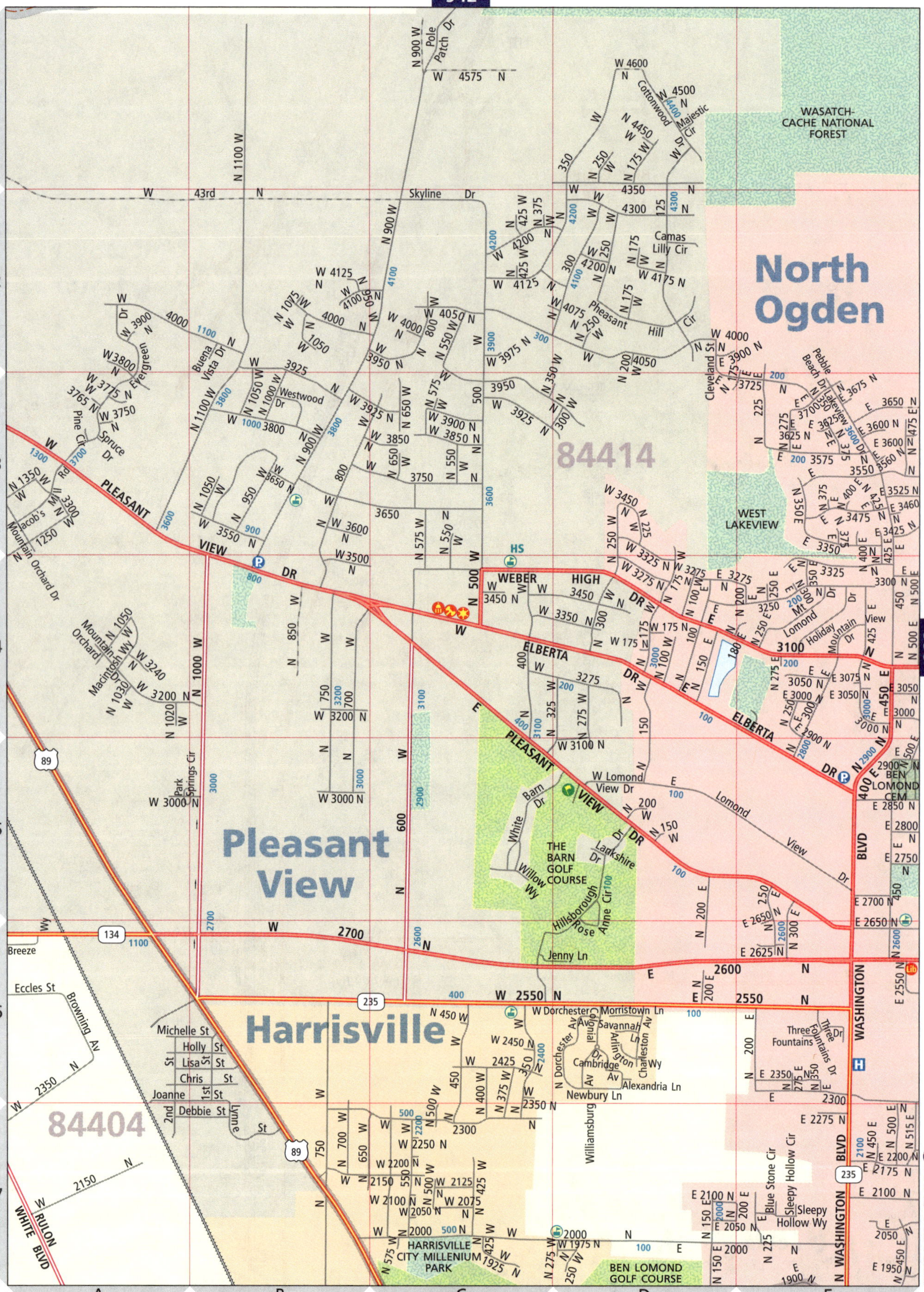

North Ogden

Pleasant View

Harrisville

WASATCH-CACHE NATIONAL FOREST

WEST LAKEVIEW

THE BARN GOLF COURSE

HARRISVILLE CITY MILLENIUM PARK

BEN LOMOND GOLF COURSE

BEN LOMOND CEM

84414

84404

PLEASANT VIEW DR

ELBERTA DR

WEBER HIGH DR

WASHINGTON BLVD

Skyline Dr

W 2700 N

W 2550 N

SEE 1056 MAP

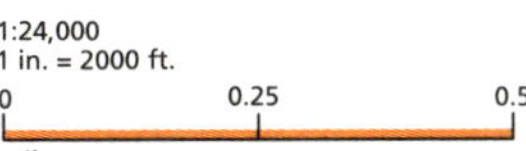

SEE B MAP

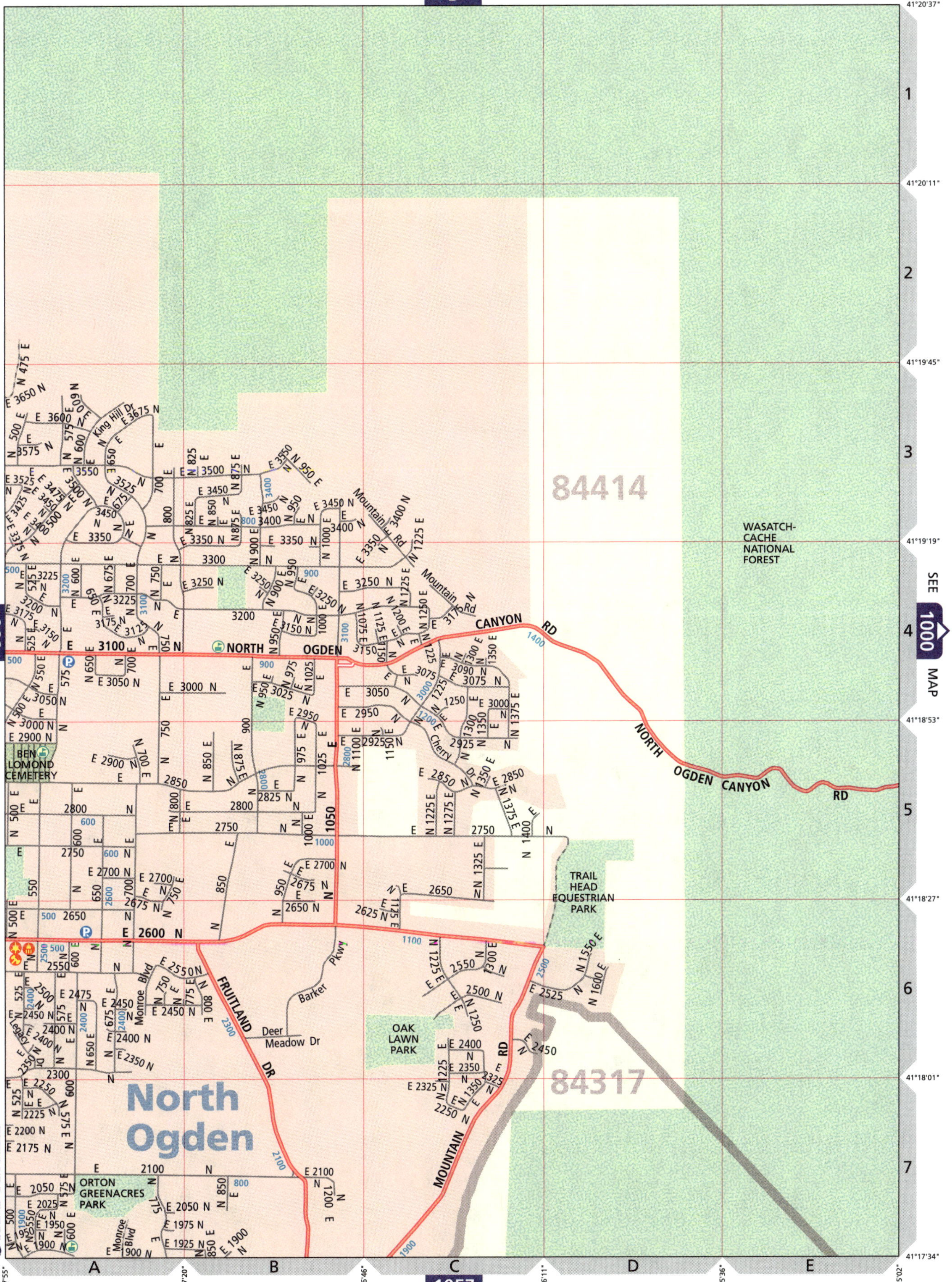

SEE 998 MAP

SEE 1000 MAP

SEE 1057 MAP

A B C D E

1 2 3 4 5 6 7

41°20'37" 41°20'11" 41°19'45" 41°19'19" 41°18'53" 41°18'27" 41°18'01" 41°17'34"

111°57'55" 111°57'20" 111°56'46" 111°56'11" 111°55'36" 111°55'02"

84414

84317

WASATCH-CACHE NATIONAL FOREST

North Ogden

NORTH OGDEN

NORTH OGDEN CANYON RD

CANYON RD

MOUNTAIN RD

FRUITLAND DR

Barker Pkwy

Deer Meadow Dr

Mountain Rd

Cherry Dr

Monroe Blvd

King Hill Dr

Legacy Dr

E 3100 N

E 2600 N

1050 E

BEN LOMOND CEMETERY

TRAIL HEAD EQUESTRIAN PARK

OAK LAWN PARK

ORTON GREENACRES PARK

RAND McNALLY

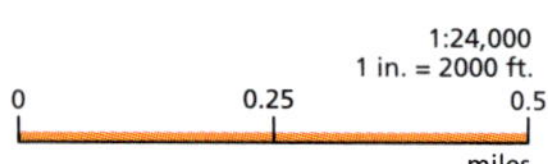

SEE B MAP

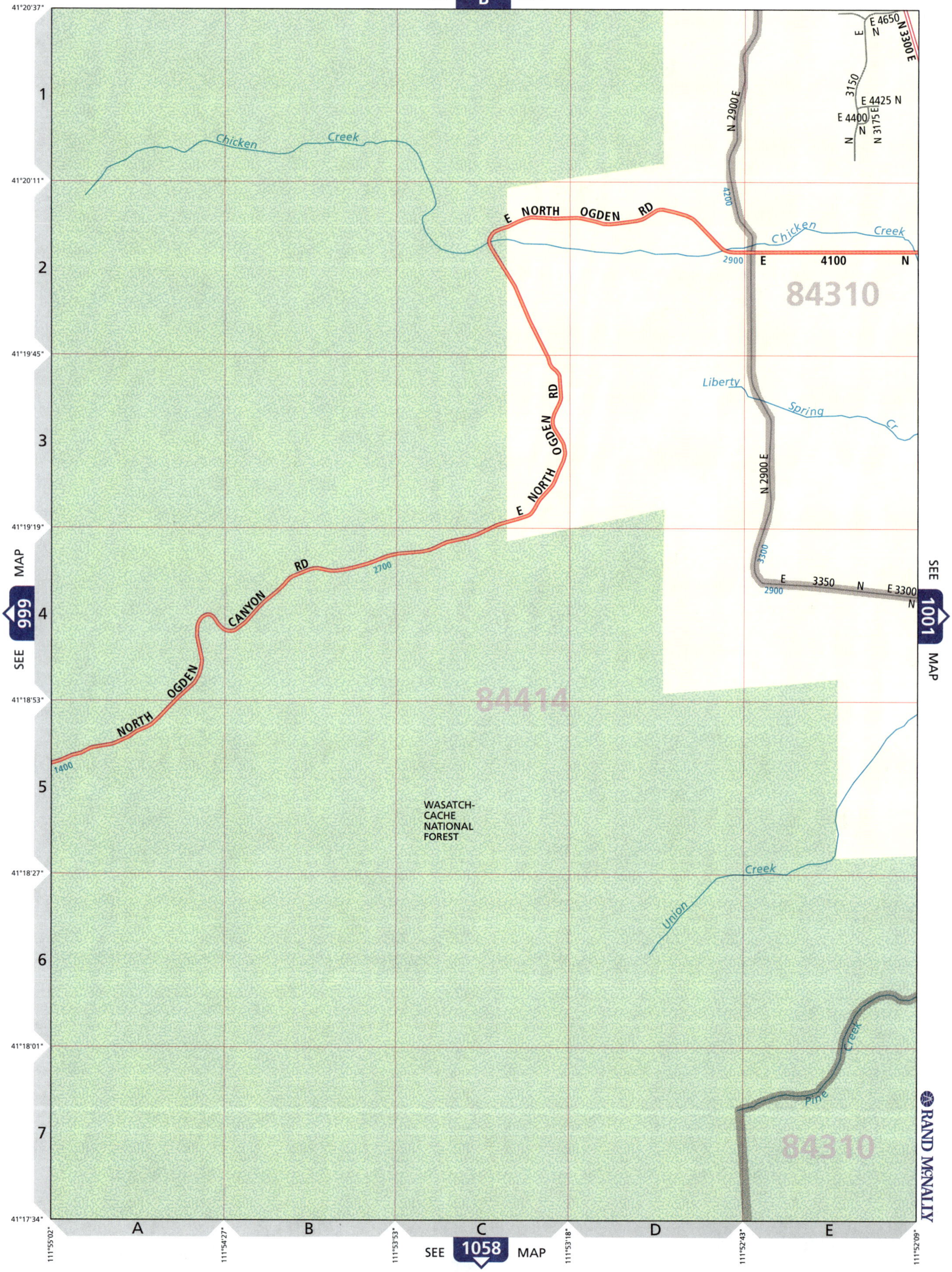

SEE 999 MAP

SEE 1001 MAP

SEE 1058 MAP

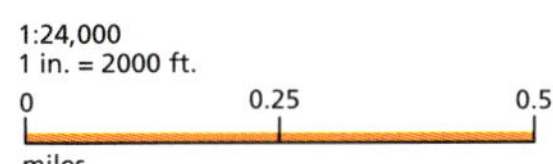

SEE B MAP

WASATCH- CACHE NATIONAL FOREST

Liberty

WOLF CREEK GOLF COURSE

POWDER MOUNTAIN RD

WOLF CREEK DR

158

A
1 Silverado Dr

B
1 Village Wy
2 Creekside Wy
3 Willow Creek Lp

North Fork Ogden River

Sheep Creek

Chicken Creek

Liberty Spring Creek

Union Creek

Pine Creek

Wolf Creek

Ogden Valley Canal

E 4100 N

3300 E

3500 E

E 4500 N

E 4475 N

N 4150 E

E 4350 N

E 4325 N

3800 E

4100 E

River Dr

N River Dr

E 3600 N

E 3300 N

3775 E

E 3950 N

Snowflake Dr

Snowflake Cir

Fairways Dr

Sunrise Dr

Eagle Ridge Dr

Aspen Ln

Juniper Ln

Wolf Ridge Cir

Pinehurst Dr

E Elkhorn Dr

Elkhorn Cir

Tanglewood Ct

Family Oaks Dr

Patiosprings Cir

Patiosprings Dr

N Mountainoak Dr

N 4800 E

N 4825 E

Creek View Dr

E 3650 N

Lakeview Ln

Willowbrook Ln

Willowbrooke Cir

Wolf Creek Dr

Willow Creek Ln

Moose Hollow Dr

Huntsman Pth

Fox Run Dr

Hill Ln

E 3450 N

Eden Hills Dr

Foot Hills Dr

Leonard Dr

Fuller Dr

N 4512 E

E 3050 N

E 2875 N

Jones Dr

E Staples Dr

Clarke St

E 2725 N

N 4950 E

Clarke Ln

N 2600 W

W 2550 N

Valley Junction Dr

84414

84310

Nordic Valley Ski Area

Nordic Valley Hwy

Nordic Valley Rd

Abbeyon Dr

Nordic Valley Dr

E 3750 N

E 2650 N

Nordic Valley Wy

Viking Dr

Somerset Dr

Shady Ln

Panorama Cir

E Big Sky Dr

Blue Beu Dr

Blue Bell Dr N

Big Sky Dr

3850 E

E 2050 N

N 3775 E

E 1950 N

WASATCH-CACHE NATIONAL FOREST

E 2275 N

E 2200 N

WASATCH-CACHE NATIONAL FOREST

41°20'37"
41°20'11"
41°19'45"
41°19'18"
41°18'52"
41°18'26"
41°18'00"
41°17'34"

111°52'09"
111°51'34"
111°51'00"
111°50'25"
111°49'50"
111°49'16"

1 2 3 4 5 6 7

A B C D E

SEE 1000 MAP

SEE 1002 MAP

SEE 1059 MAP

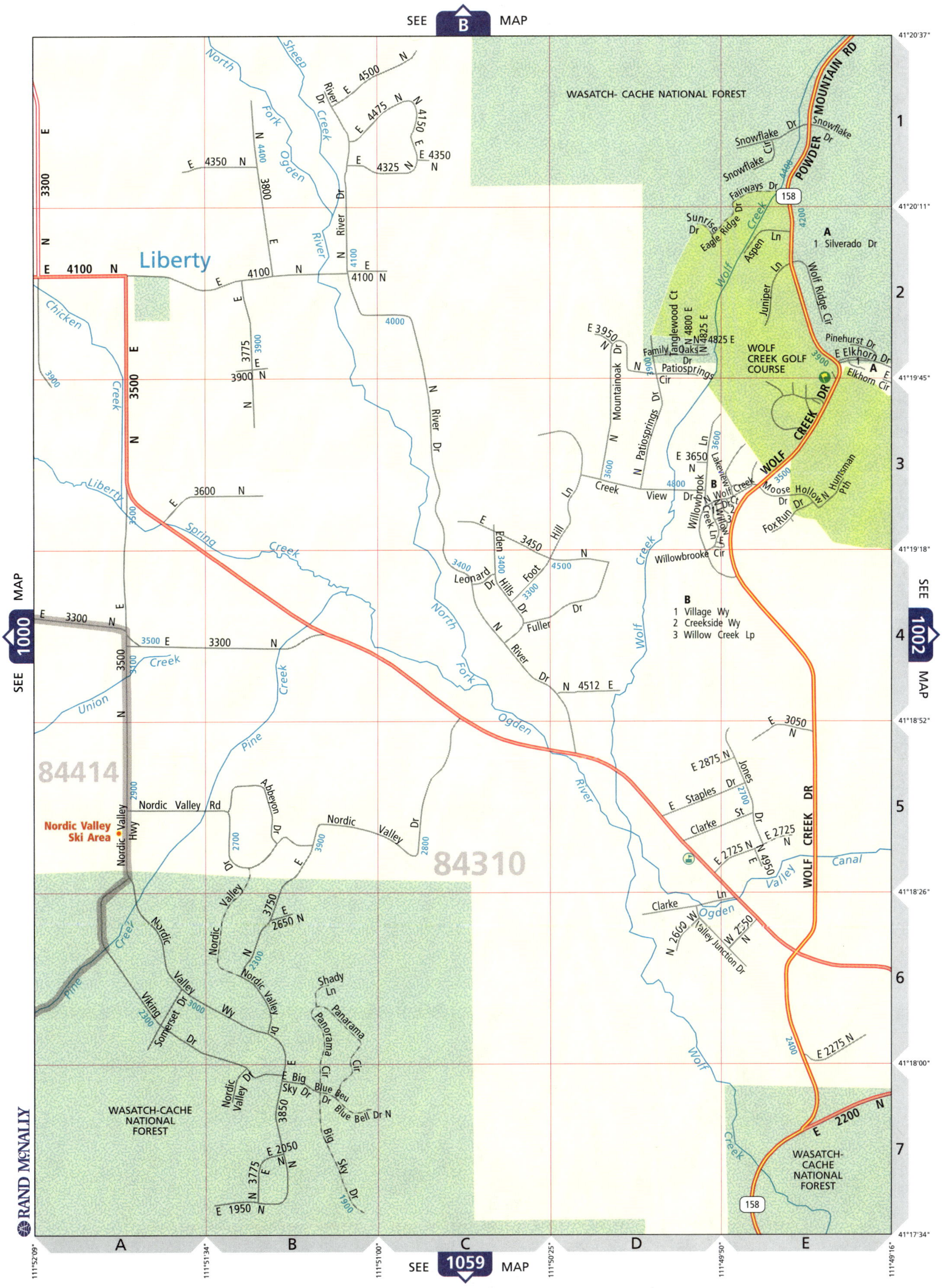

1:24,000
1 in. = 2000 ft.
0 0.25 0.5
miles

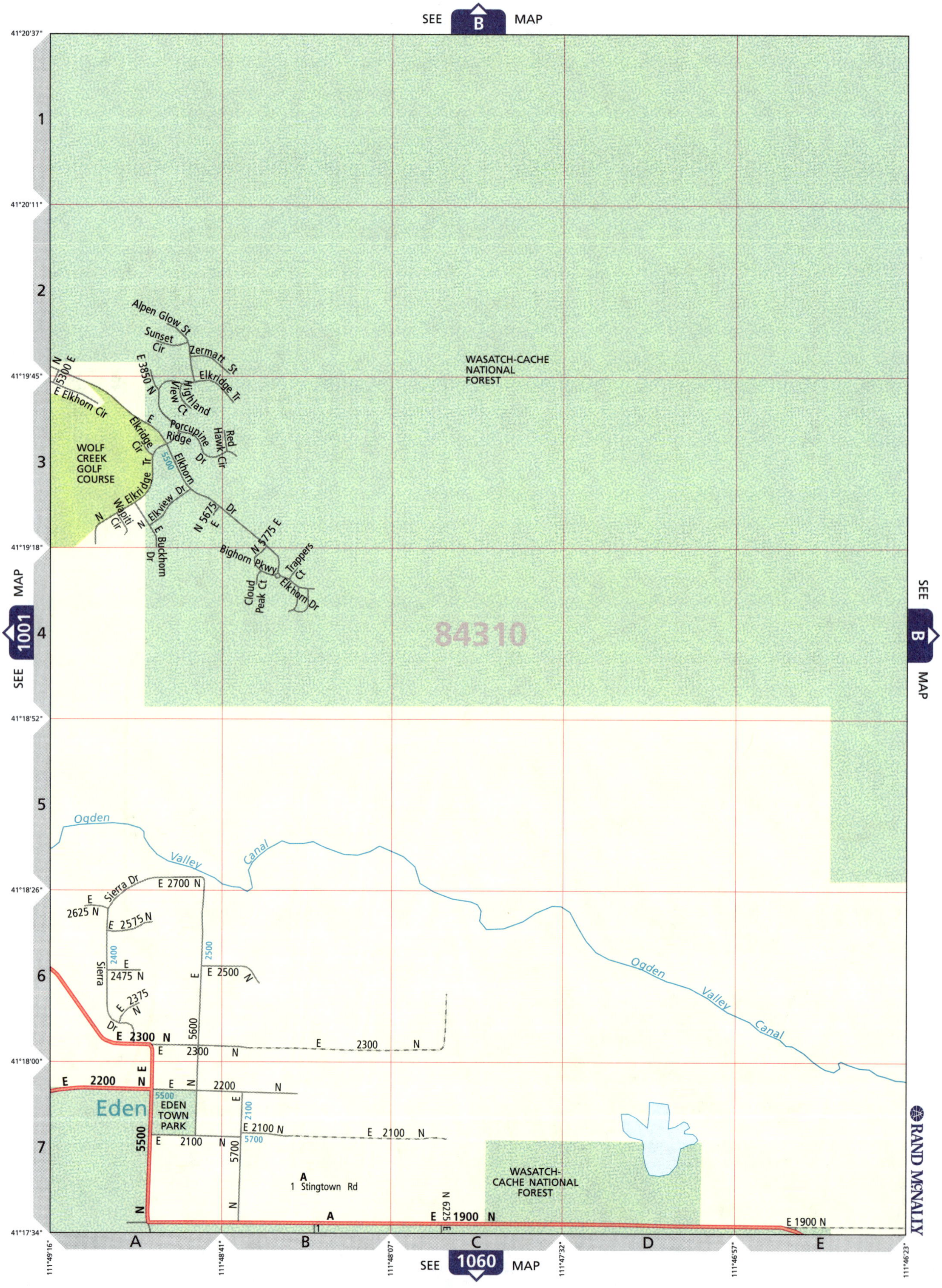

SEE B MAP

SEE 1001 MAP

SEE B MAP

SEE 1060 MAP

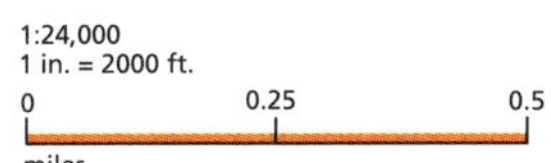

SEE 996 MAP

Plain City

Marriott-Slaterville

West Weber

84404

84401

WEBER RIVER

Warren Canal

Fourmile Creek

Mill Creek

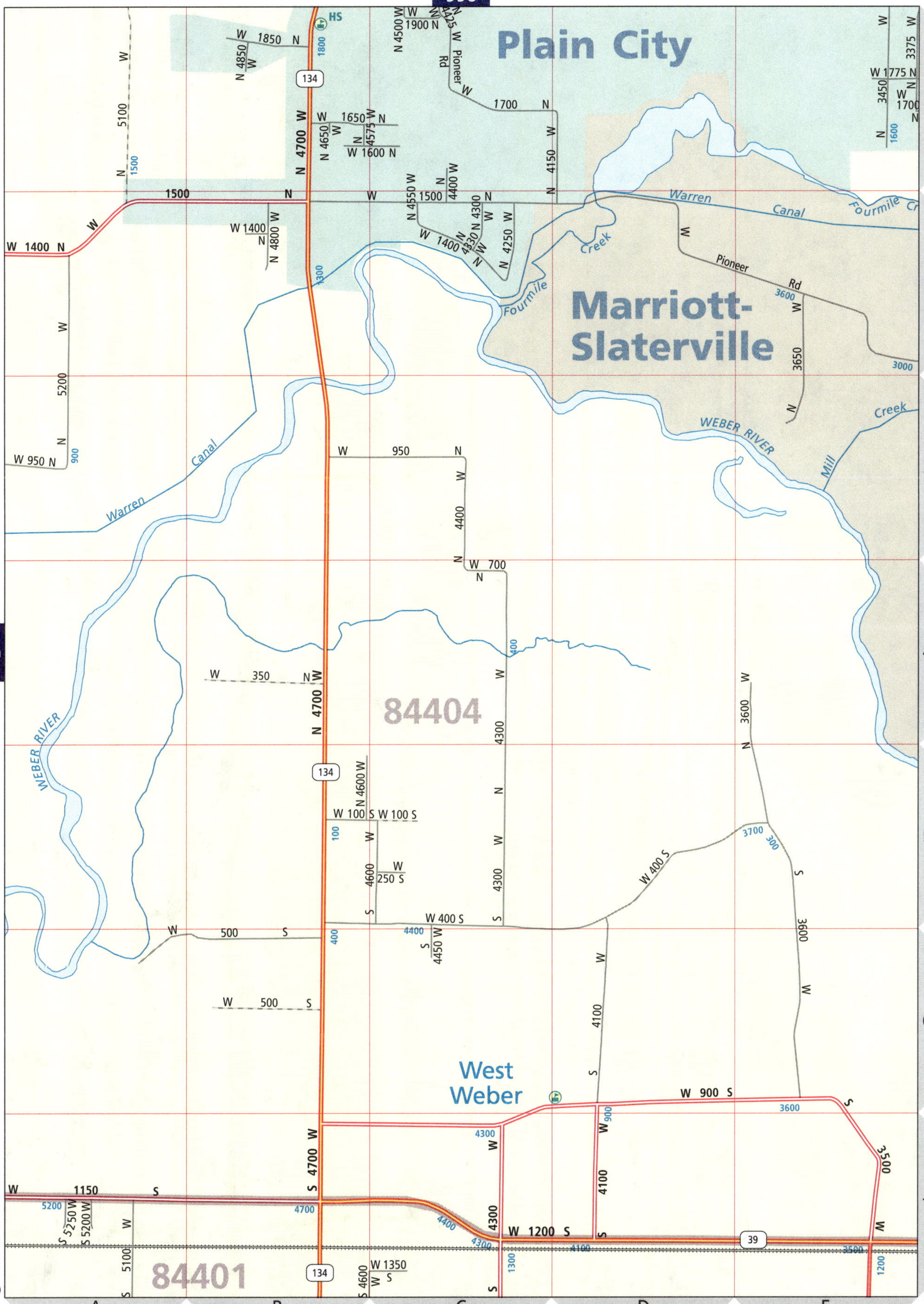

SEE B MAP

SEE 1055 MAP

SEE 1113 MAP

1:24,000
1 in. = 2000 ft.
0 0.25 0.5
miles

SEE 997 MAP

SEE 1054 MAP

SEE 1056 MAP

SEE 1114 MAP

RAND McNALLY

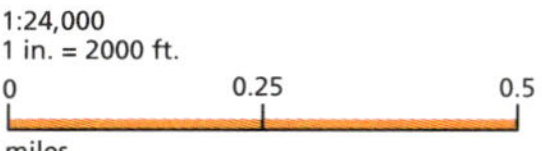

SEE 998 MAP

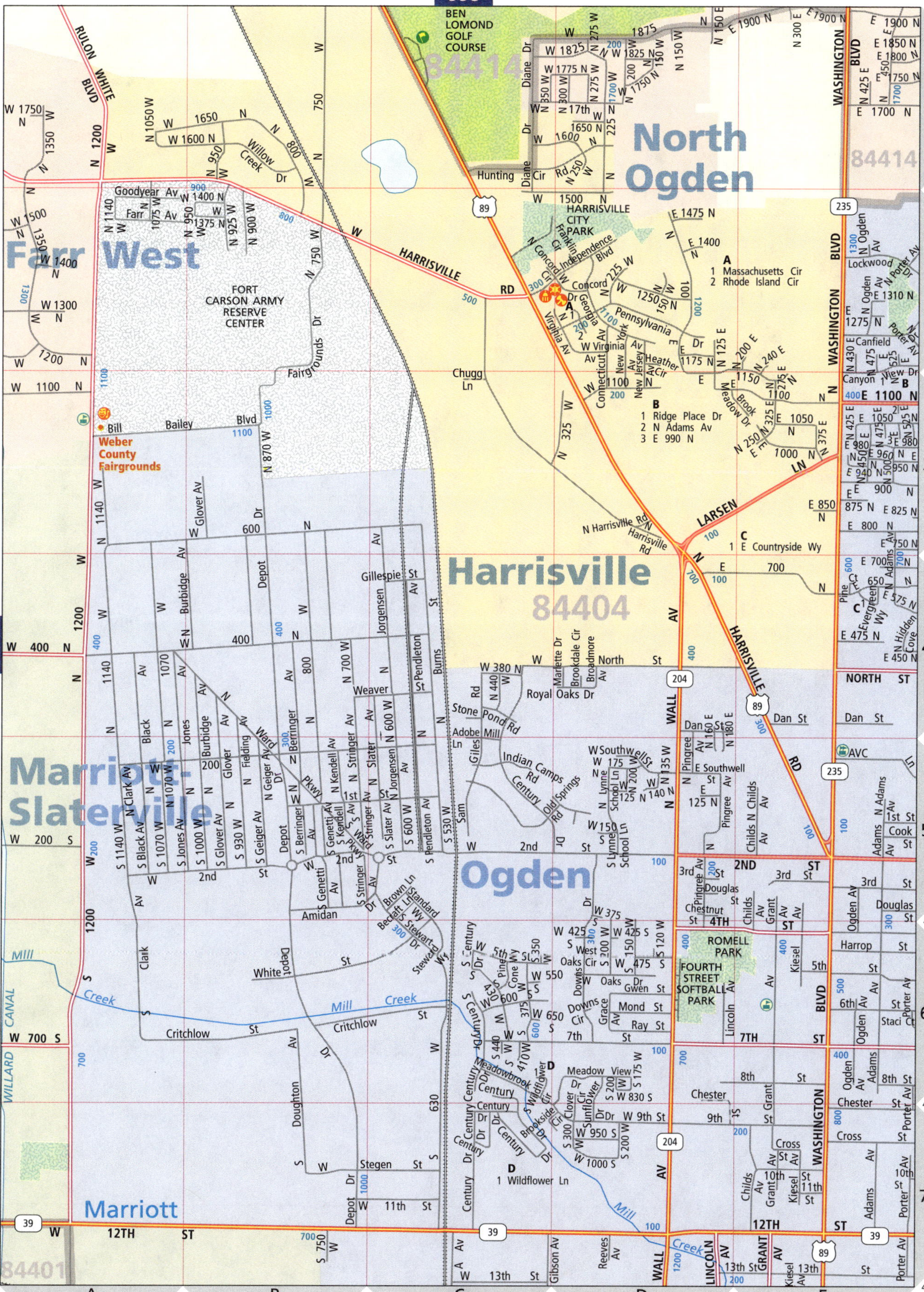

SEE 1055 MAP

SEE 1057 MAP

North Ogden

84414

Farr West

Harrisville

84404

Marriott-Slaterville

Ogden

Marriott

84401

BEN LOMOND GOLF COURSE

HARRISVILLE CITY PARK

FORT CARSON ARMY RESERVE CENTER

Weber County Fairgrounds

ROMELL PARK

FOURTH STREET SOFTBALL PARK

A
1 Massachusetts Cir
2 Rhode Island Cir

B
1 Ridge Place Dr
2 N Adams Av
3 E 990 N

C
1 E Countryside Wy

D
1 Wildflower Ln

HARRISVILLE RD

WASHINGTON BLVD

WALL AV

12TH ST

2ND ST

NORTH ST

LARSEN LN

Bill Bailey Blvd

Critchlow St

Mill Creek

WILLARD CANAL

SEE 1115 MAP

1:24,000
1 in. = 2000 ft.
0 0.25 0.5
miles

SEE 999 MAP

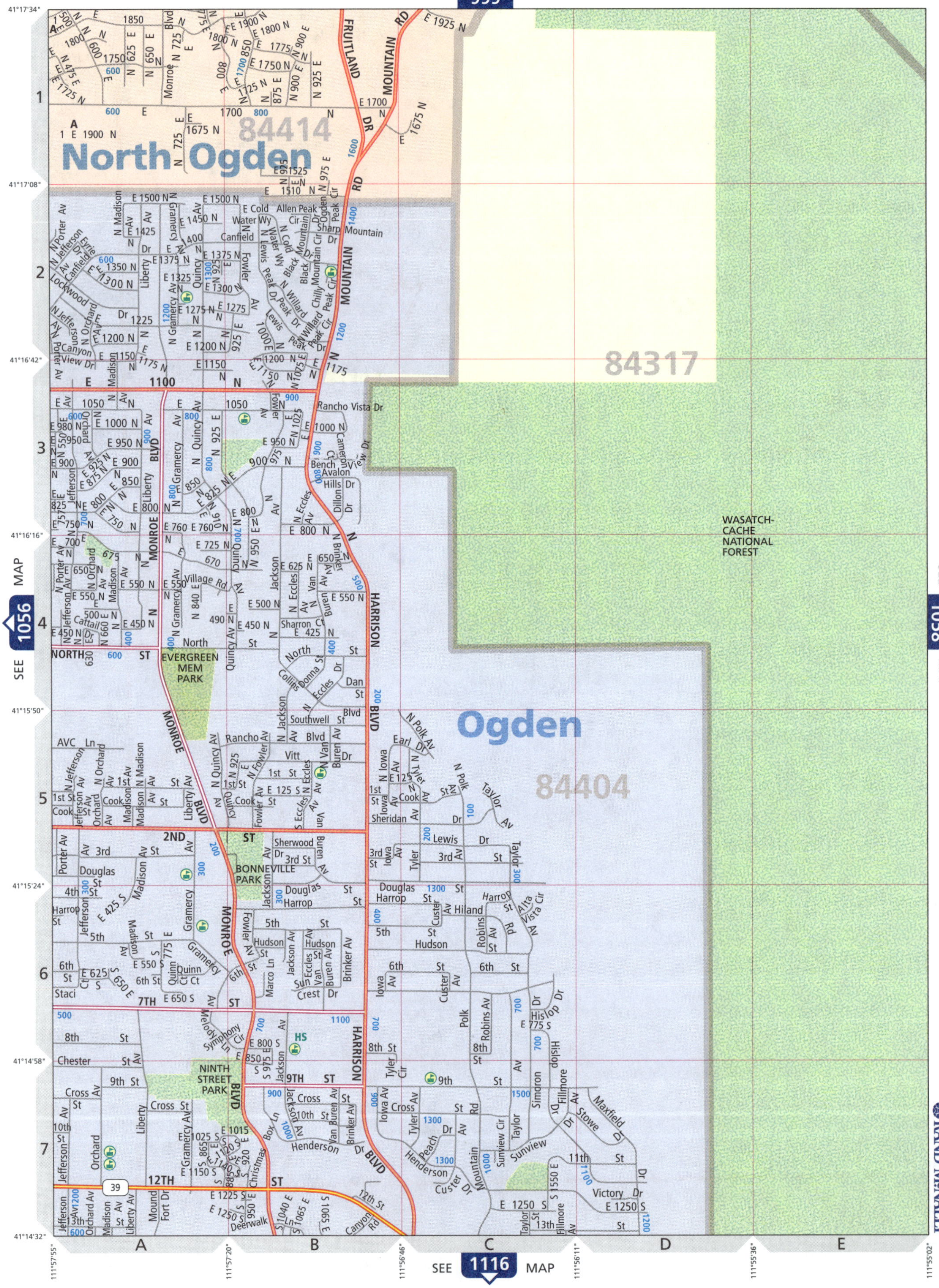

North Ogden
84414
84317
Ogden
84404
WASATCH-CACHE NATIONAL FOREST
EVERGREEN MEM PARK
BONNEVILLE PARK
NINTH STREET PARK
HS

FRUITLAND DR
MOUNTAIN RD
HARRISON BLVD
MONROE BLVD
NORTH ST
2ND ST
7TH ST
9TH ST
12TH ST
E 1100 N
39

SEE 1056 MAP

SEE 1058 MAP

SEE 1116 MAP

41°17'34" 41°17'08" 41°16'42" 41°16'16" 41°15'50" 41°15'24" 41°14'58" 41°14'32"
111°57'55" 111°57'20" 111°56'46" 111°56'11" 111°55'36" 111°55'02"

A B C D E
1 2 3 4 5 6 7

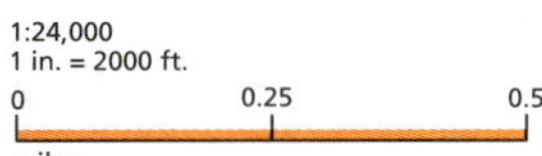

SEE 1000 MAP

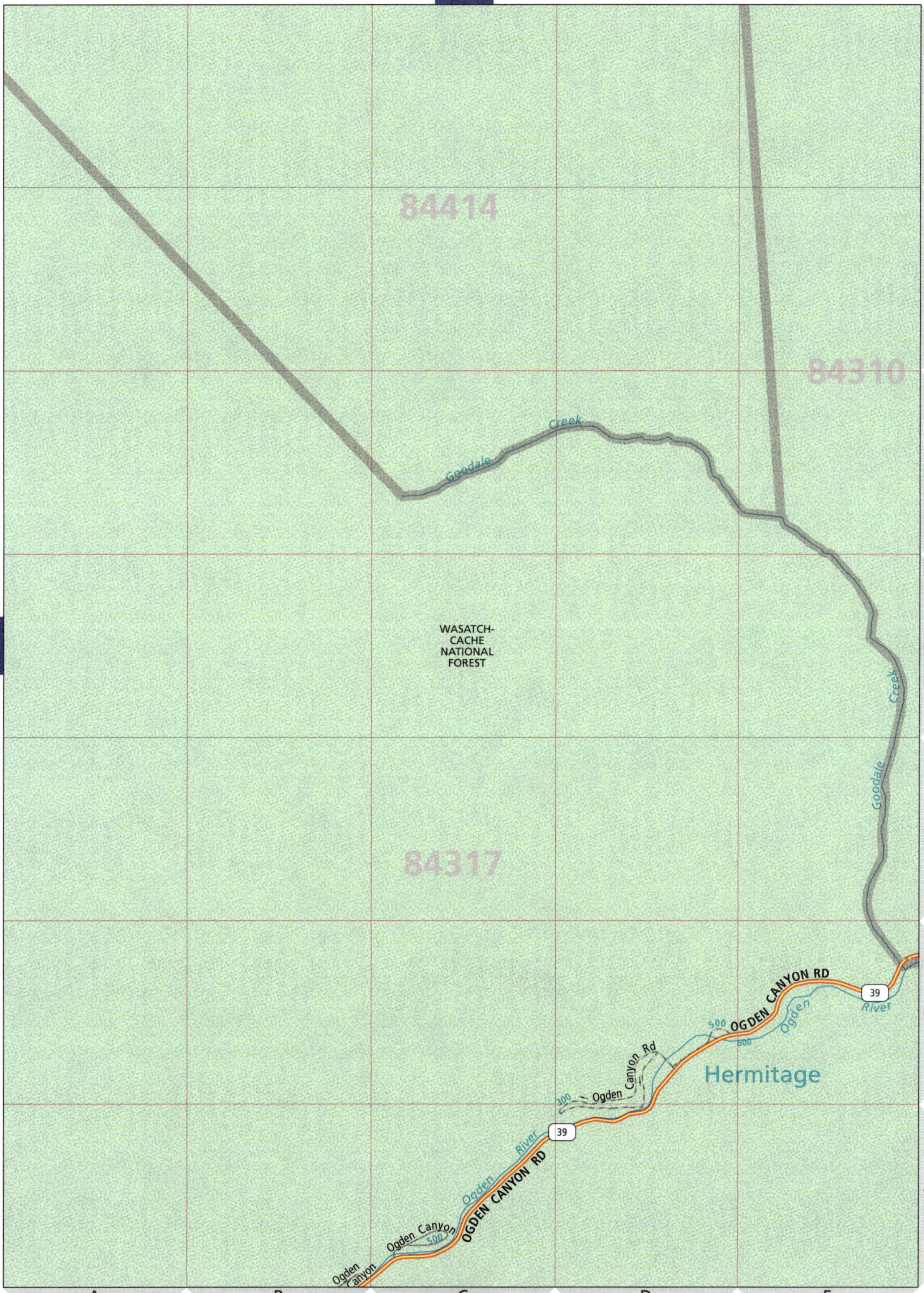

84414

84310

Goodale Creek

WASATCH-
CACHE
NATIONAL
FOREST

84317

OGDEN CANYON RD

39

Ogden River

500

600

Ogden Canyon Rd

Hermitage

300

Ogden Canyon

Ogden Canyon

SEE 1057 MAP

SEE 1059 MAP

41°17'34"
41°17'08"
41°16'42"
41°16'16"
41°15'50"
41°15'24"
41°14'58"
41°14'32"

1
2
3
4
5
6
7

A B C D E

111°55'02"
111°54'27"
111°53'53"
111°53'18"
111°52'44"
111°52'09"

SEE 1117 MAP

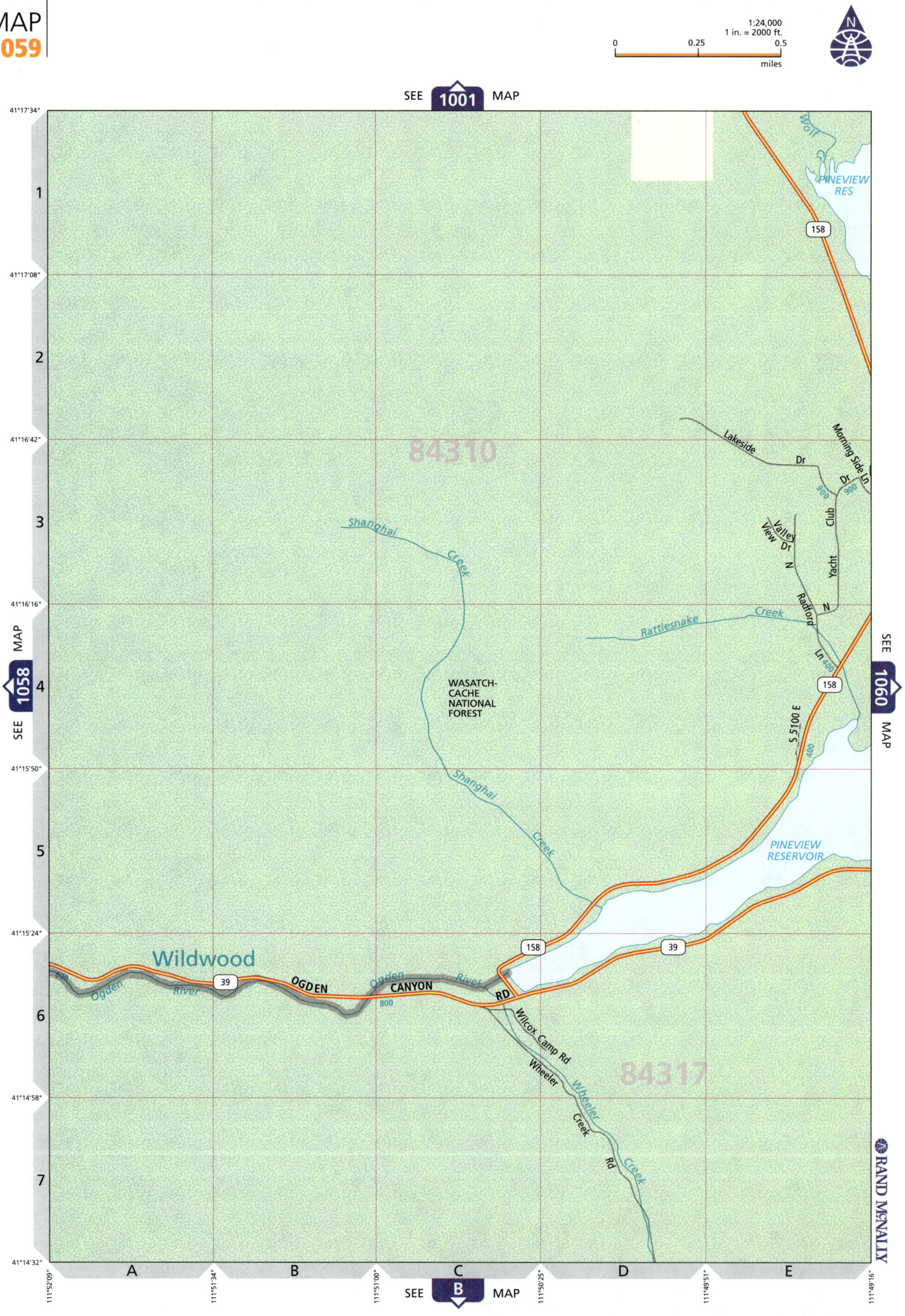

1:24,000
1 in. = 2000 ft.
0 0.25 0.5
miles

SEE 1001 MAP

SEE 1058 MAP

SEE 1060 MAP

SEE B MAP

RAND McNALLY

1:24,000
1 in. = 2000 ft.
0 0.25 0.5
miles

SEE 1002 MAP

SEE 1059 MAP
SEE 1061 MAP
SEE B MAP

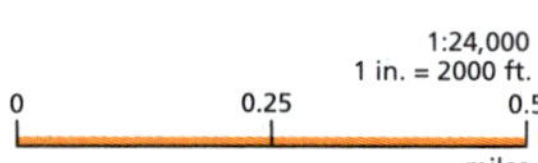

SEE B MAP

SEE 1060 MAP

SEE B MAP

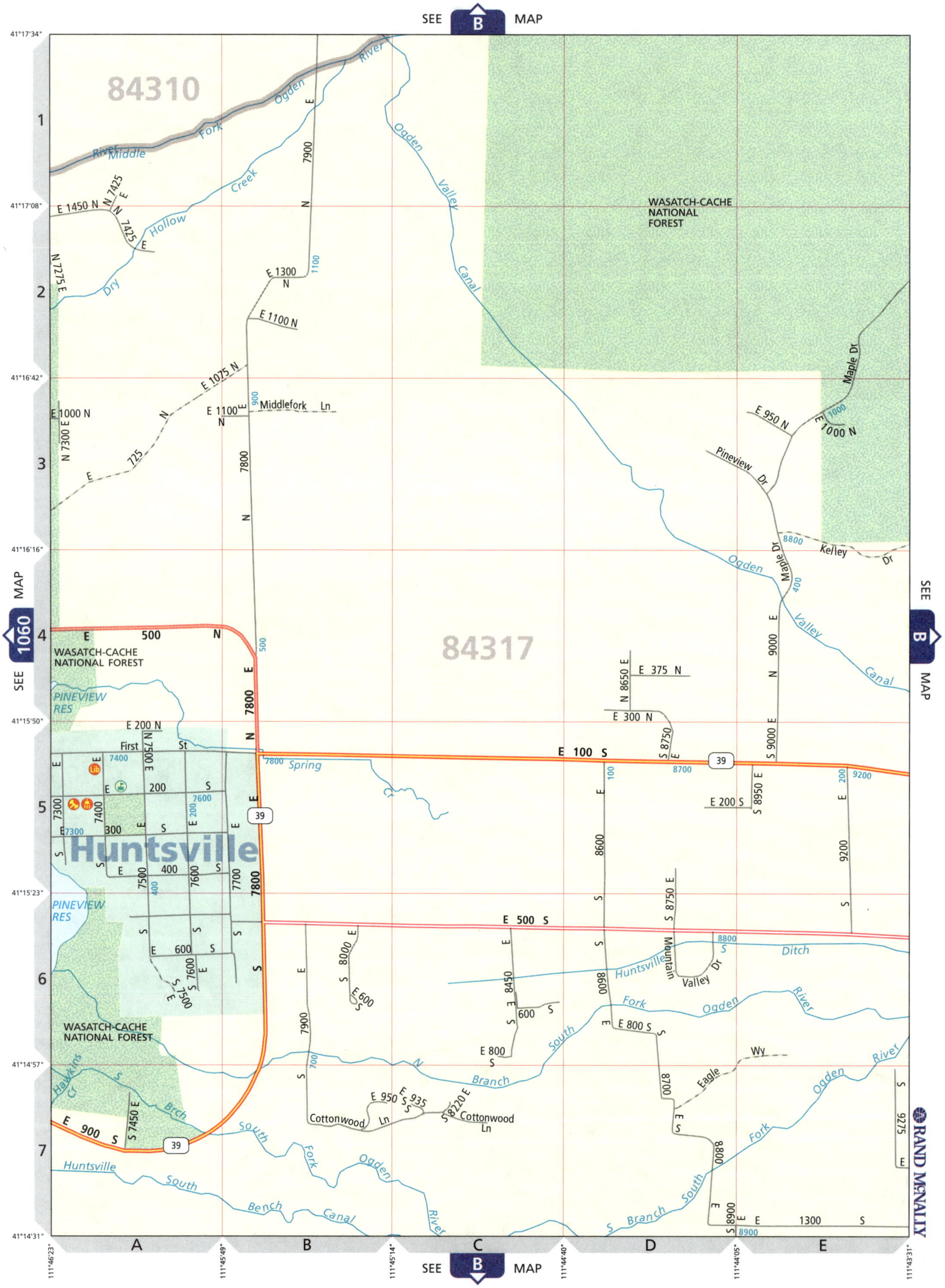

84310

84317

Huntsville

WASATCH-CACHE
NATIONAL
FOREST

WASATCH-CACHE
NATIONAL FOREST

WASATCH-CACHE
NATIONAL FOREST

PINEVIEW
RES

PINEVIEW
RES

Middle Fork Ogden River

Dry Hollow Creek

Ogden Valley Canal

Spring Cr

Huntsville Ditch

South Fork Ogden River

N Branch

S Branch

Hawkins Cr

S Brch

Huntsville South Bench Canal

E 1450 N

N 7425 E

N 7425 E

N 7275 E

7900 N

1100

E 1300 N

E 1100 N

E 1075 N

N 725 E

E 1000 N

N 7300 E

E 1100 N

900

Middlefork Ln

7800 N

E 500 N

500

N 7800 E

E 200 N

First St

N 7500 E

7400

E 200 S

7600

7300

7400

E 300 S

E 200

7300

E 400 S

7500

400

7600

7700

7800

E 600 S

S 7600 E

S 7500 E

S 7800

39

7800 Spring

E 100 S

39

8700

100

9200

200

E 375 N

N 8650 E

E 300 N

S 8750 E

E 950 N

1000

E 1000 N

Pineview Dr

Maple Dr

8800

Kelley Dr

Maple Dr

400

N 9000 E

S 9000 E

E 200 S

S 8950 E

S 9200 E

S 8600 E

E 500 S

S 8750 E

8800 S

Mountain Valley Dr

S 8000 E

E 600 S

S 7900 E

700

E 8450 S

600 S

E 800 S

E 800 S

S 8700 E

Eagle Wy

8800

S 8900 E

8900

E 1300 S

S 9275 E

E 950 S

S 935 S

S 8220 E

Cottonwood Ln

Cottonwood Ln

E 900 S

S 7450 E

39

41°17'34"

41°17'08"

41°16'42"

41°16'16"

41°15'50"

41°15'23"

41°14'57"

41°14'31"

111°46'23"

111°45'49"

111°45'14"

111°44'40"

111°44'05"

111°43'31"

1

2

3

4

5

6

7

A

B

C

D

E

1:24,000
1 in. = 2000 ft.
0 0.25 0.5
miles

SEE 1054 MAP

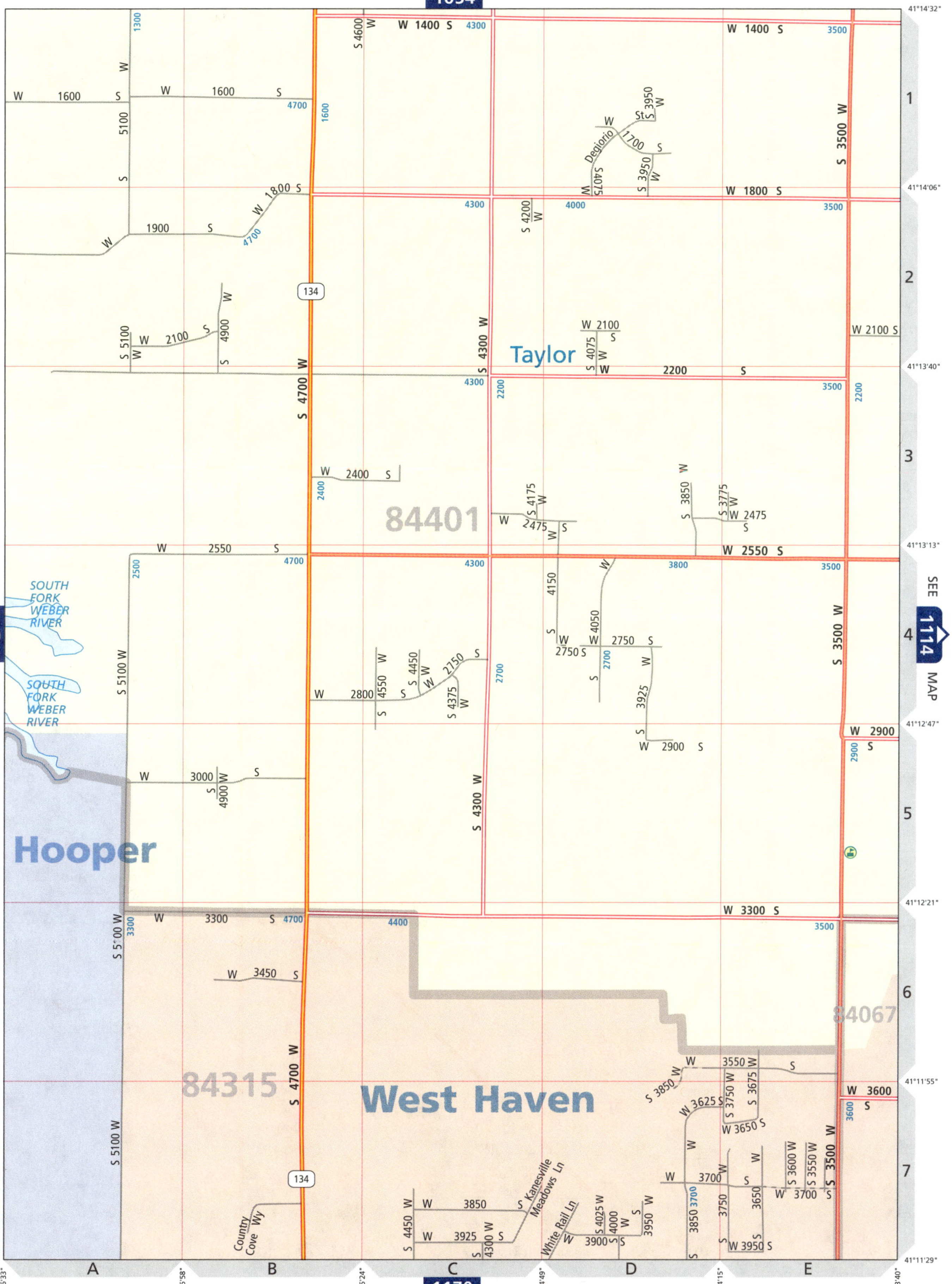

Taylor

84401

Hooper

West Haven

84315

84067

SOUTH FORK WEBER RIVER

SOUTH FORK WEBER RIVER

W 1400 S

W 1600 S

W 1800 S

W 1900 S

W 2100 S

W 2200 S

W 2400 S

W 2475 S

W 2550 S

W 2750 S

W 2800 S

W 2900 S

W 3000 S

W 3300 S

W 3450 S

W 3550 W

W 3600 S

W 3625 S

W 3650 S

W 3700 S

W 3850 S

W 3900 S

W 3925 S

W 3950 S

W Degiorio St

W 1700 S

S 5100 W

S 4900 W

S 4700 W

S 4600 W

S 4550 W

S 4450 W

S 4375 W

S 4300 W

S 4200 W

S 4175 W

S 4150 W

S 4075 W

S 4050 W

S 4025 W

S 4000 W

S 3950 W

S 3925 W

S 3850 W

S 3775 W

S 3750 W

S 3700 W

S 3675 W

S 3650 W

S 3600 W

S 3550 W

S 3500 W

S 5'00 W

Kanesville Meadows Ln

White Rail Ln

Country Cove Wy

134

SEE B MAP

SEE 1114 MAP

SEE 1170 MAP

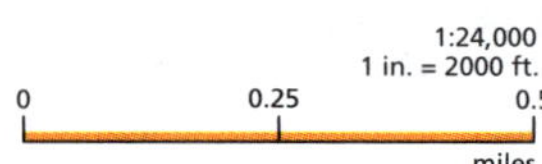

SEE 1055 MAP

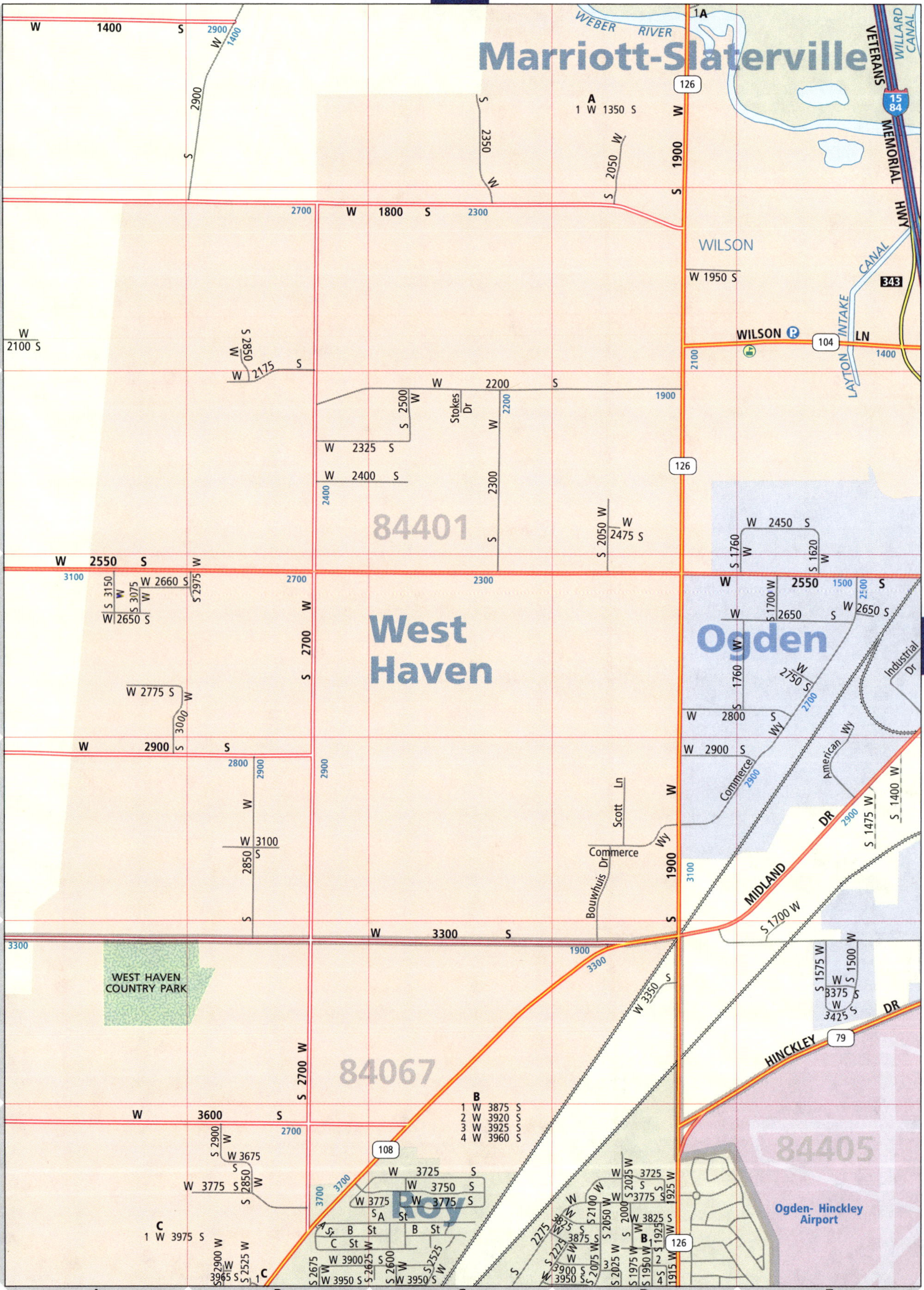

Marriott-Slaterville

WEBER RIVER

WILLARD CANAL

VETERANS MEMORIAL HWY

WILSON

WILSON LN

LAYTON INTAKE CANAL

West Haven

Ogden

Roy

84401

84067

84405

WEST HAVEN COUNTRY PARK

Ogden- Hinckley Airport

MIDLAND DR

HINCKLEY DR

Industrial Dr

American Wy

Commerce Wy

Scott Ln

Bouwhuis Dr

Stokes Dr

W 1400 S

W 1800 S

W 2100 S

W 2175 S

W 2200 S

W 2325 S

W 2400 S

W 2550 S

W 2900 S

W 3300 S

W 3600 S

S 1900 W

S 2700 W

A
1 W 1350 S

B
1 W 3875 S
2 W 3920 S
3 W 3925 S
4 W 3960 S

C
1 W 3975 S

SEE 1113 MAP

SEE 1115 MAP

SEE 1171 MAP

RAND McNALLY

1:24,000
1 in. = 2000 ft.

0 0.25 0.5
miles

SEE 1056 MAP

SEE MAP 1114

SEE MAP 1116

SEE 1172 MAP

1:24,000
1 in. = 2000 ft.
0 0.25 0.5
miles

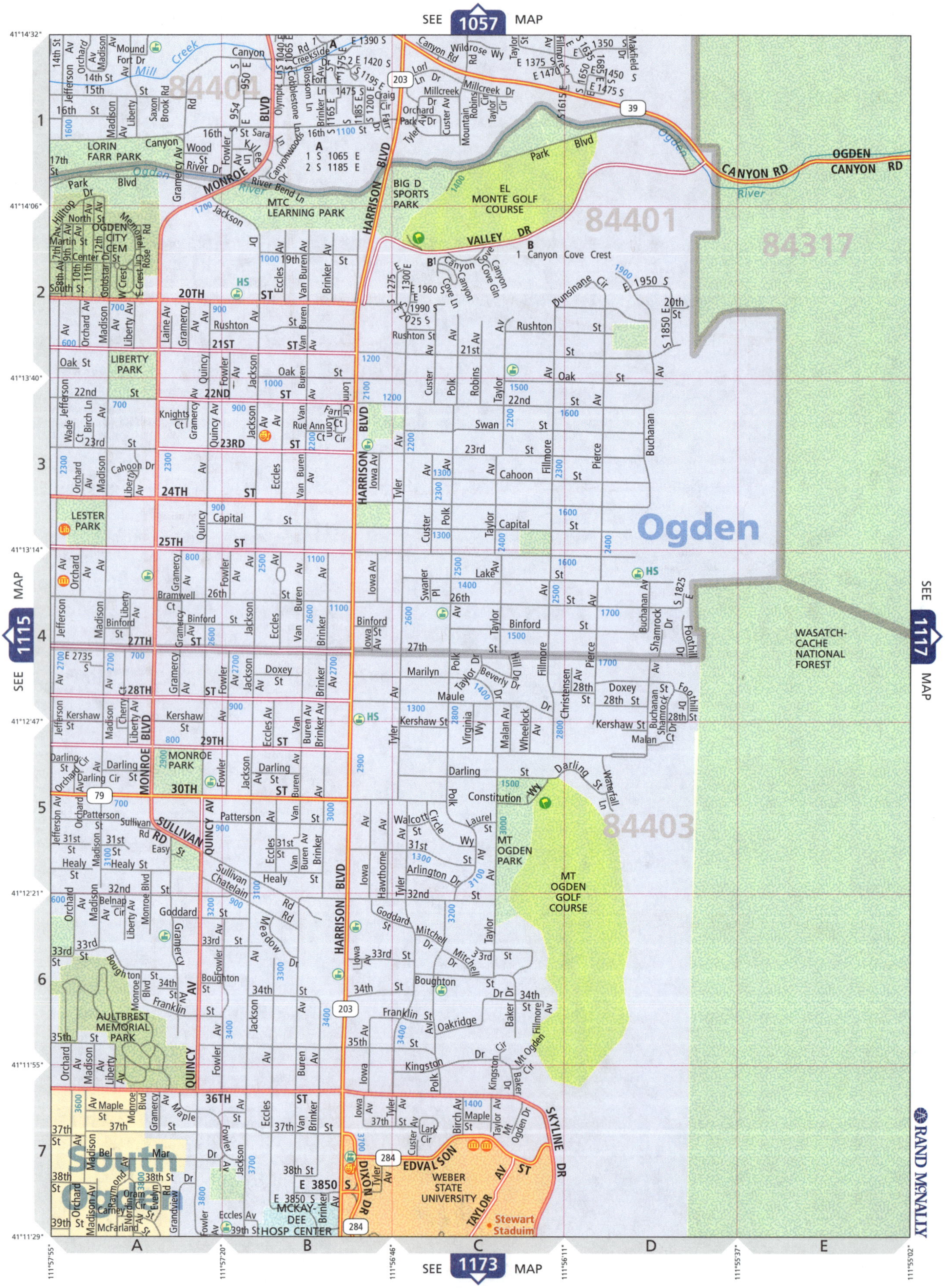

SEE 1057 MAP

SEE 1115 MAP

SEE 1117 MAP

Ogden

84401
84403
84404
84317

LORIN FARR PARK
MTC LEARNING PARK
BIG D SPORTS PARK
EL MONTE GOLF COURSE
OGDEN CITY CEM
LIBERTY PARK
LESTER PARK
MONROE PARK
MT OGDEN PARK
MT OGDEN GOLF COURSE
AULTBREST MEMORIAL PARK
WASATCH-CACHE NATIONAL FOREST
WEBER STATE UNIVERSITY
Stewart Stadium
MCKAY-DEE HOSP CENTER
South Ogden

OGDEN CANYON RD
CANYON RD
HARRISON BLVD
MONROE BLVD
VALLEY DR
20TH ST
21ST ST
22ND ST
23RD ST
24TH ST
25TH ST
27TH ST
28TH ST
29TH ST
30TH ST
36TH ST
QUINCY AV
SULLIVAN RD
SKYLINE DR
EDVALSON ST
DIXON DR
TAYLOR AV

A B C D E
1 2 3 4 5 6 7

SEE 1173 MAP

RAND McNALLY

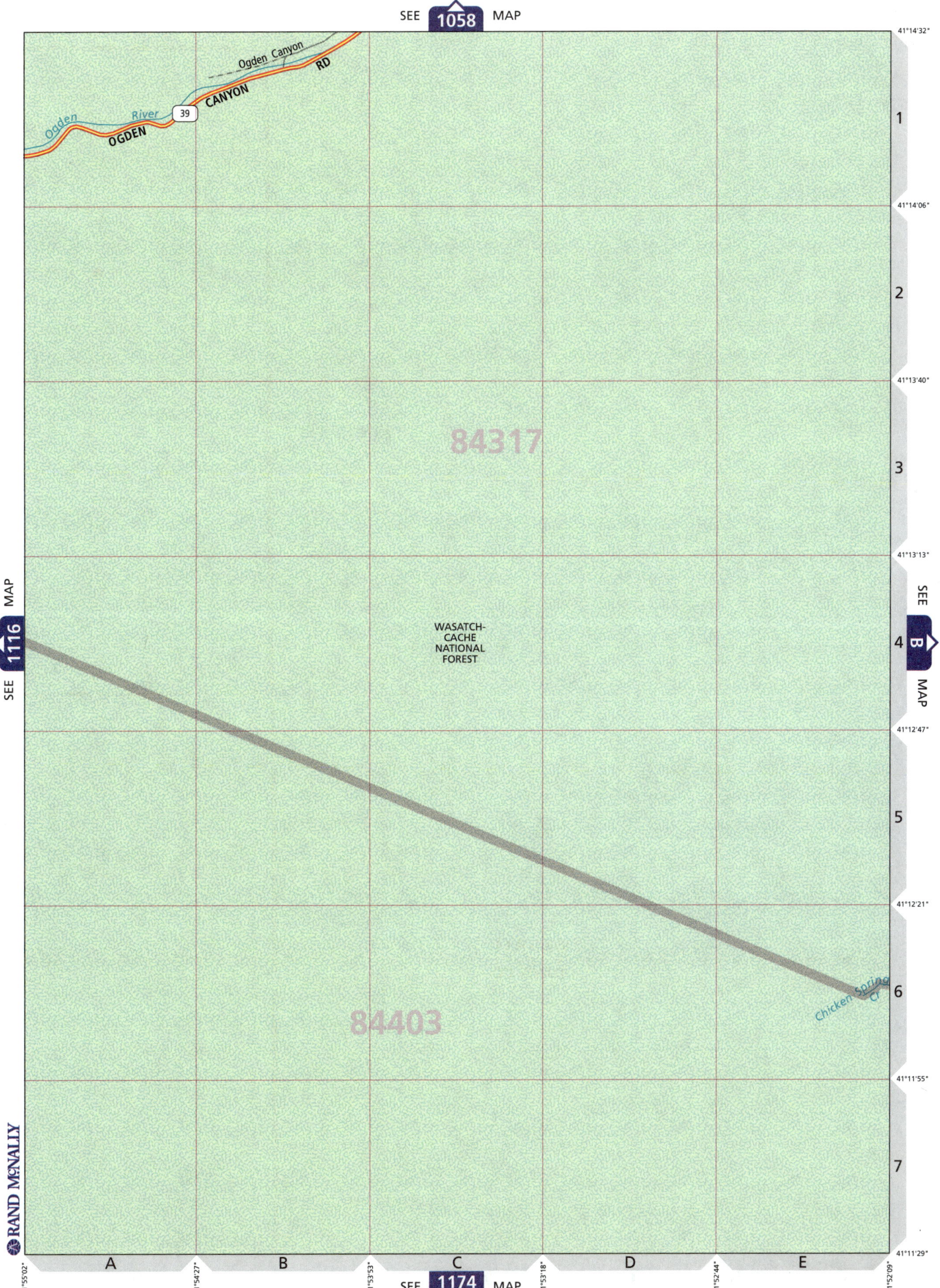
1:24,000
1 in. = 2000 ft.
0
0.25
0.5
miles
SEE 1058 MAP
Ogden Canyon
RD
CANYON
39
River
Ogden
OGDEN
84317
WASATCH-
CACHE
NATIONAL
FOREST
SEE 1116 MAP
SEE B MAP
Chicken Spring Cr
84403
SEE 1174 MAP
A
B
C
D
E
1
2
3
4
5
6
7
41°14'32"
41°14'06"
41°13'40"
41°13'13"
41°12'47"
41°12'21"
41°11'55"
41°11'29"
111°55'02"
111°54'27"
111°53'53"
111°53'18"
111°52'44"
111°52'09"

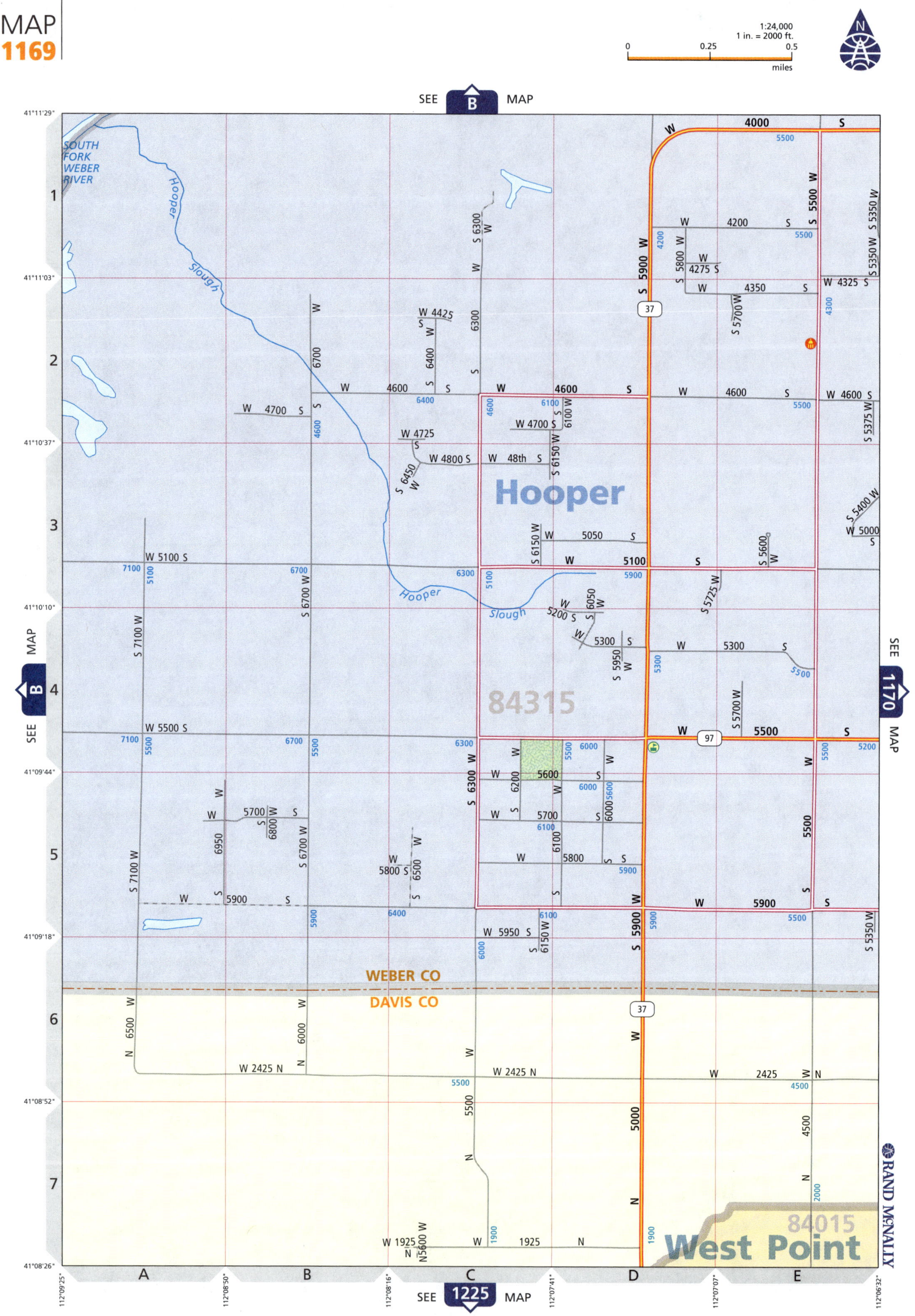

1:24,000
1 in. = 2000 ft.
0 0.25 0.5
miles

SEE B MAP

SEE B MAP

SEE 1170 MAP

SOUTH FORK WEBER RIVER

Hooper Slough

Hooper

84315

WEBER CO

DAVIS CO

West Point

84015

W 4000 S

W 4200 S

W 4275 S

W 4325 S

W 4350 S

W 4425 S

W 4600 S

W 4700 S

W 4725 S

W 4800 S

W 48th S

W 5000 S

W 5050 S

W 5100 S

W 5200 S

W 5300 S

W 5500 S

W 5600 S

W 5700 S

W 5800 S

W 5900 S

W 5950 S

W 2425 N

W 1925 N

S 5350 W

S 5375 W

S 5400 W

S 5500 W

S 5600 W

S 5700 W

S 5725 W

S 5800 W

S 5900 W

S 5950 W

S 6000 W

S 6050 W

S 6100 W

S 6150 W

S 6200 W

S 6300 W

S 6400 W

S 6450 W

S 6500 W

S 6700 W

S 6800 W

S 6950 W

S 7100 W

N 4500 W

N 5000 W

N 5500 W

N 5600 W

N 6000 W

N 6500 W

37

97

A B C D E

1 2 3 4 5 6 7

41°11'29" 41°11'03" 41°10'37" 41°10'10" 41°09'44" 41°09'18" 41°08'52" 41°08'26"

112°09'25" 112°08'50" 112°08'16" 112°07'41" 112°07'07" 112°06'32"

RAND McNALLY

SEE 1225 MAP

1:24,000
1 in. = 2000 ft.
0 0.25 0.5
miles

SEE 1113 MAP

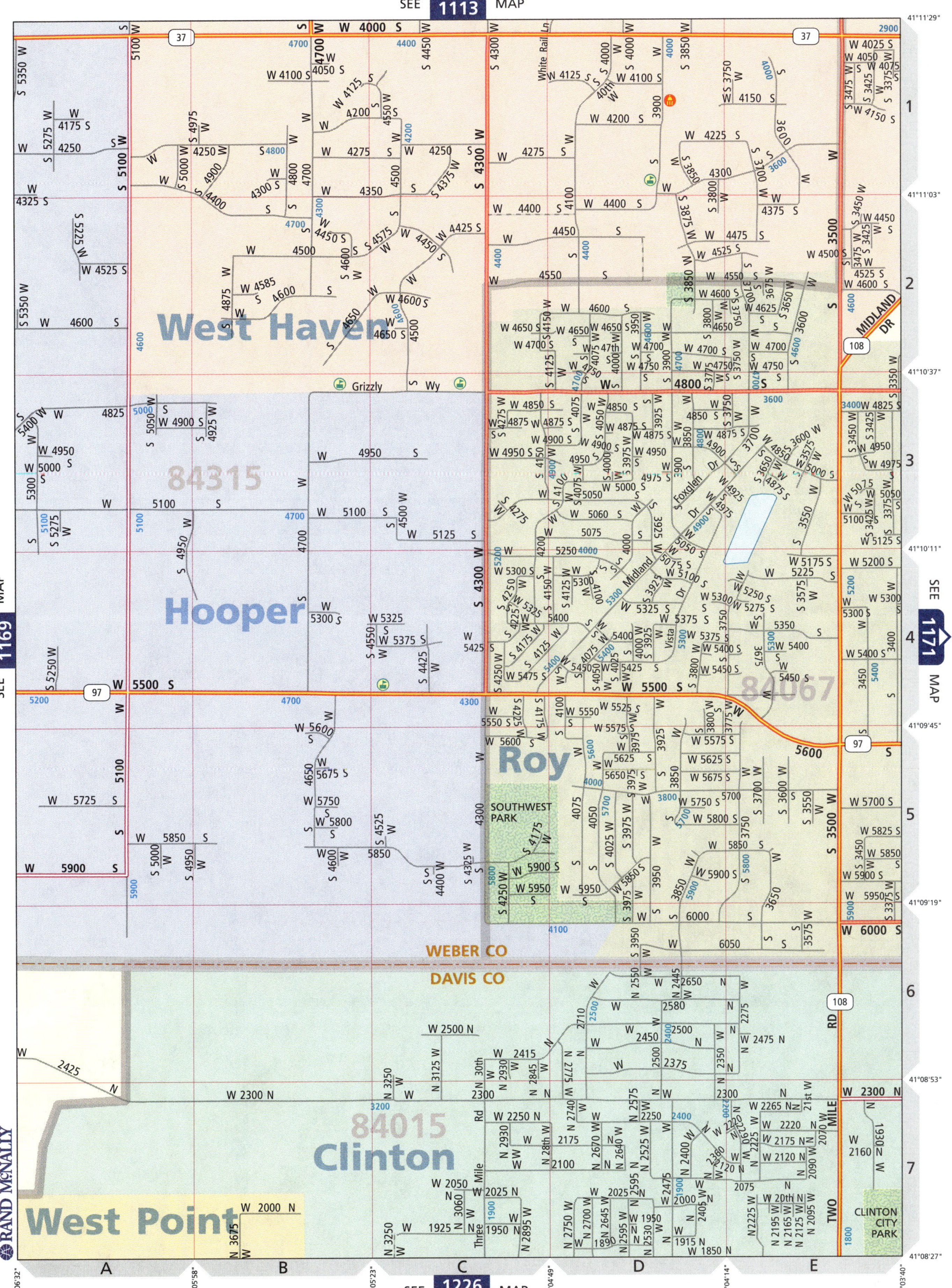

SEE 1169 MAP

SEE 1171 MAP

SEE 1226 MAP

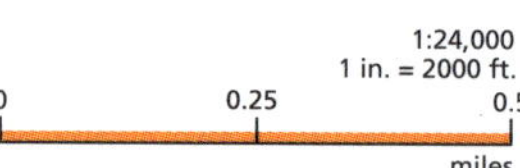

SEE 1114 MAP

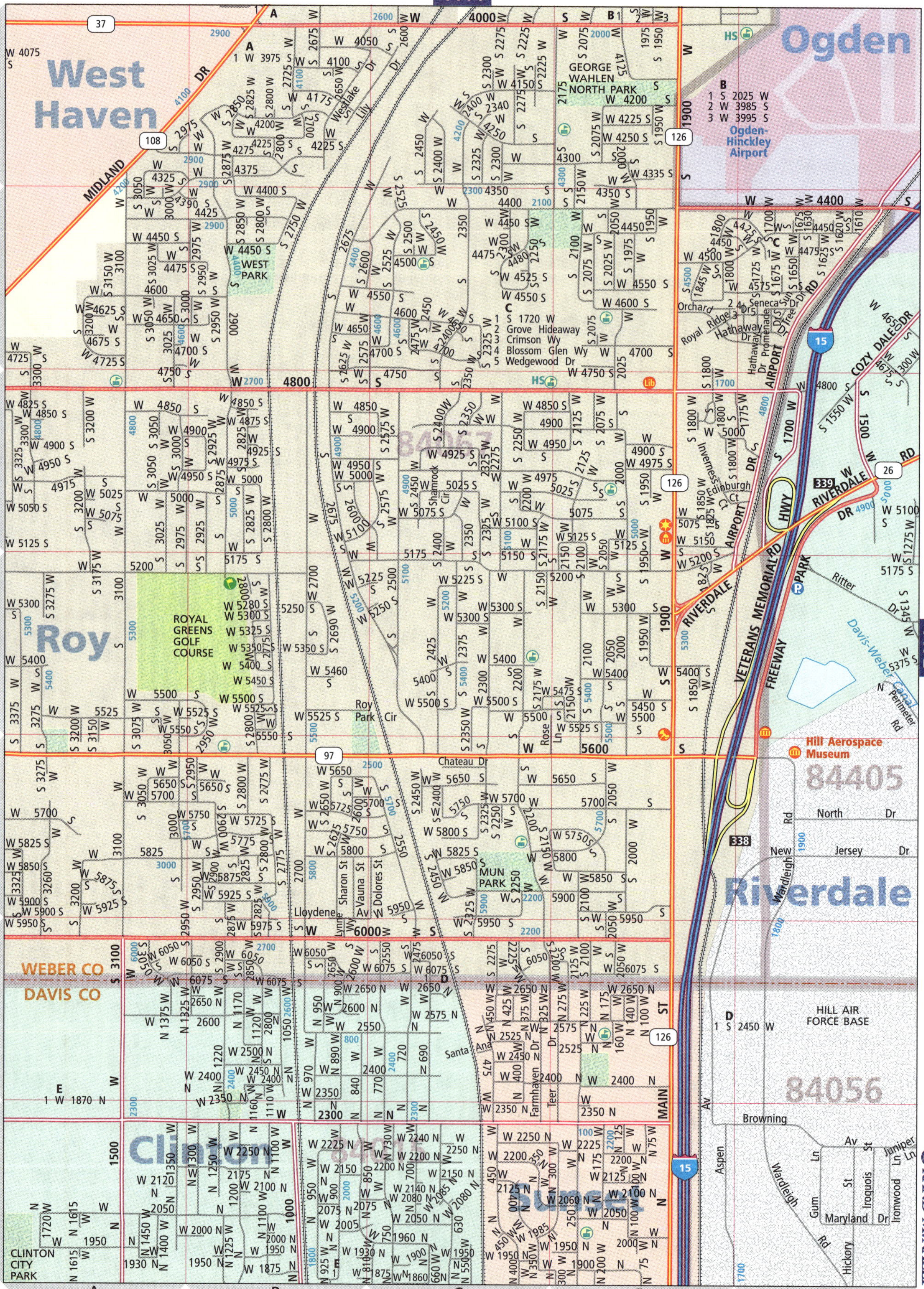

SEE 1170 MAP

SEE 1172 MAP

West Haven

Ogden

Ogden-Hinckley Airport

GEORGE WAHLEN NORTH PARK

WEST PARK

Roy

84067

ROYAL GREENS GOLF COURSE

Roy Park Cir

MUN PARK

Hill Aerospace Museum

84405

Riverdale

WEBER CO

DAVIS CO

HILL AIR FORCE BASE

84056

Clinton

84015

Sunset

CLINTON CITY PARK

MIDLAND DR

VETERANS MEMORIAL FREEWAY

RIVERDALE RD

AIRPORT RD

Davis-Weber Canal

MAIN ST

B
1 S 2025 W
2 W 3985 S
3 W 3995 S

C
1 S 1720 W
2 Grove Hideaway
3 Crimson Wy
4 Blossom Glen Wy
5 Wedgewood Dr

D
1 S 2450 W

E
1 W 1870 N

SEE 1227 MAP

A B C D E

1 2 3 4 5 6 7

1:24,000
1 in. = 2000 ft.
0 0.25 0.5
miles

SEE 1115 MAP

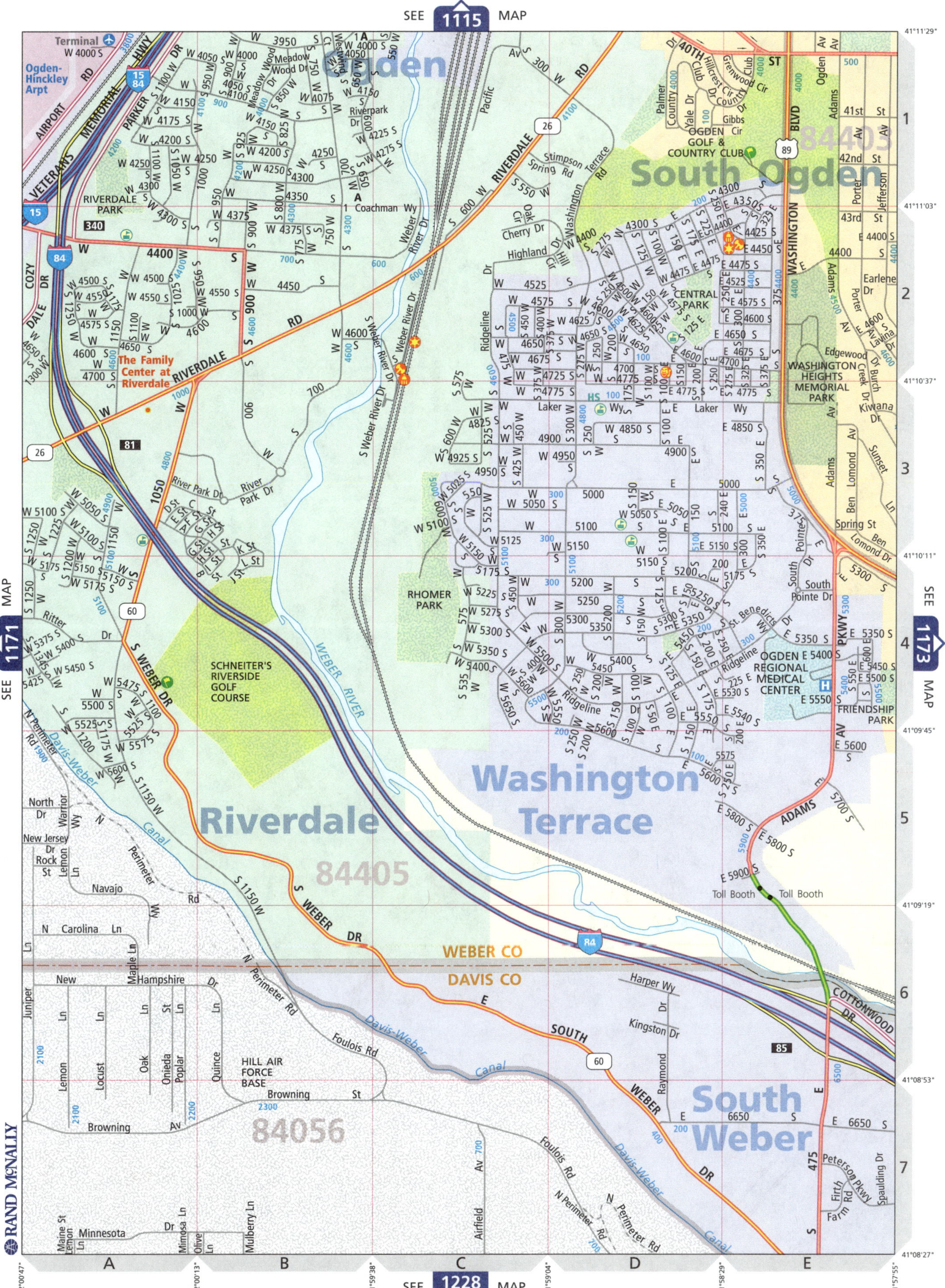

SEE 1171 MAP

SEE 1173 MAP

SEE 1228 MAP

1:24,000
1 in. = 2000 ft.
0 0.25 0.5
miles

SEE 1116 MAP

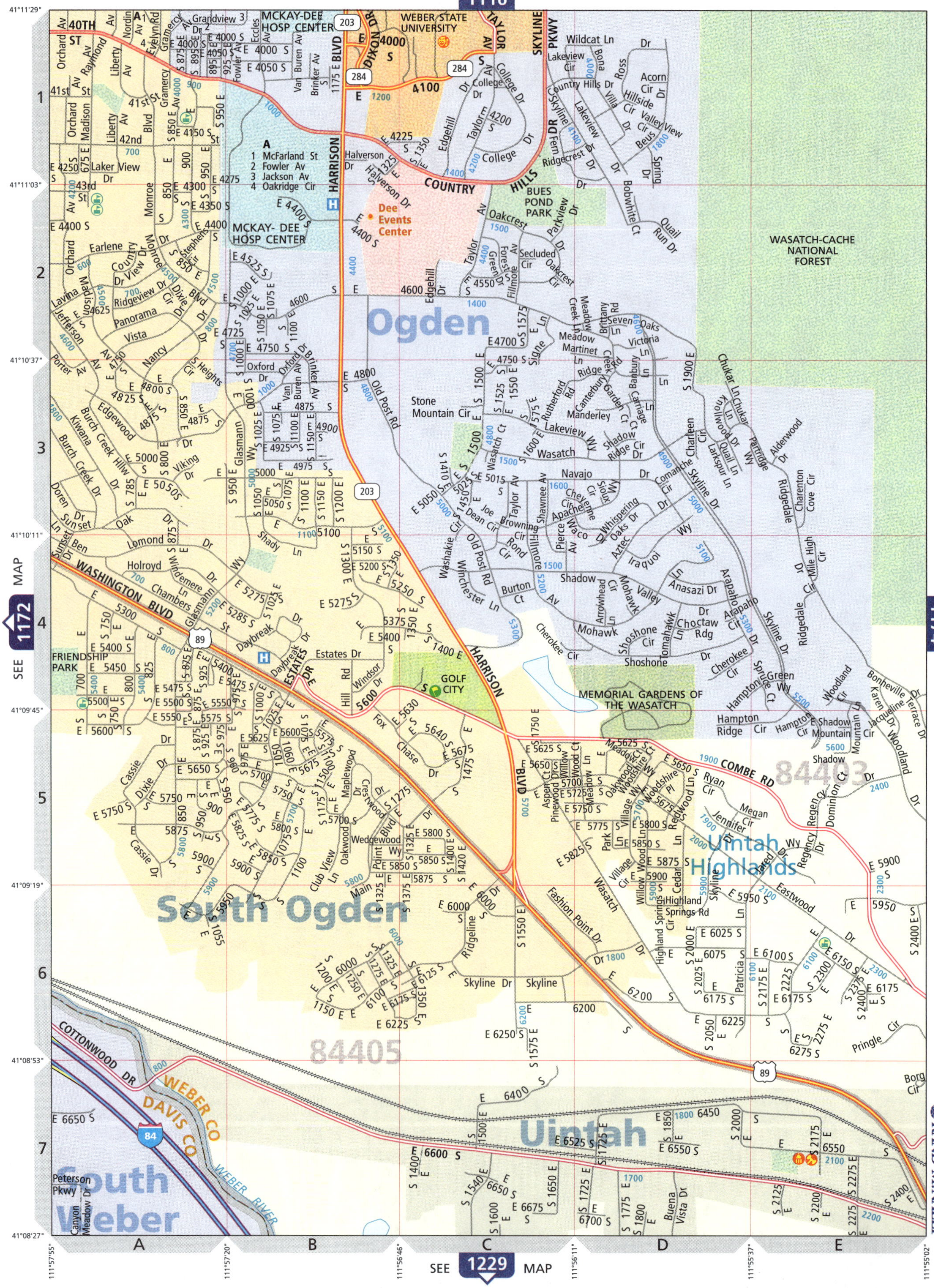

SEE 1172 MAP

SEE 1174 MAP

Ogden

South Ogden

Uintah Highlands

Uintah

South Weber

WASATCH-CACHE NATIONAL FOREST

WEBER STATE UNIVERSITY

MCKAY-DEE HOSP CENTER

Dee Events Center

BUES POND PARK

FRIENDSHIP PARK

GOLF CITY

MEMORIAL GARDENS OF THE WASATCH

WEBER CO

DAVIS CO

WEBER RIVER

84403

84405

SEE 1229 MAP

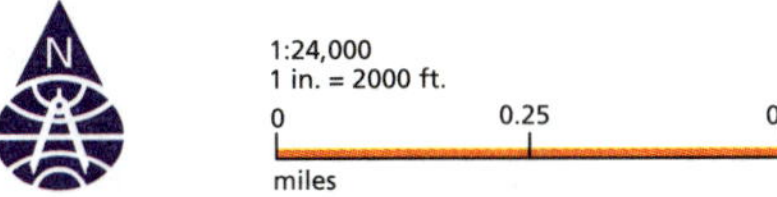

SEE 1117 MAP

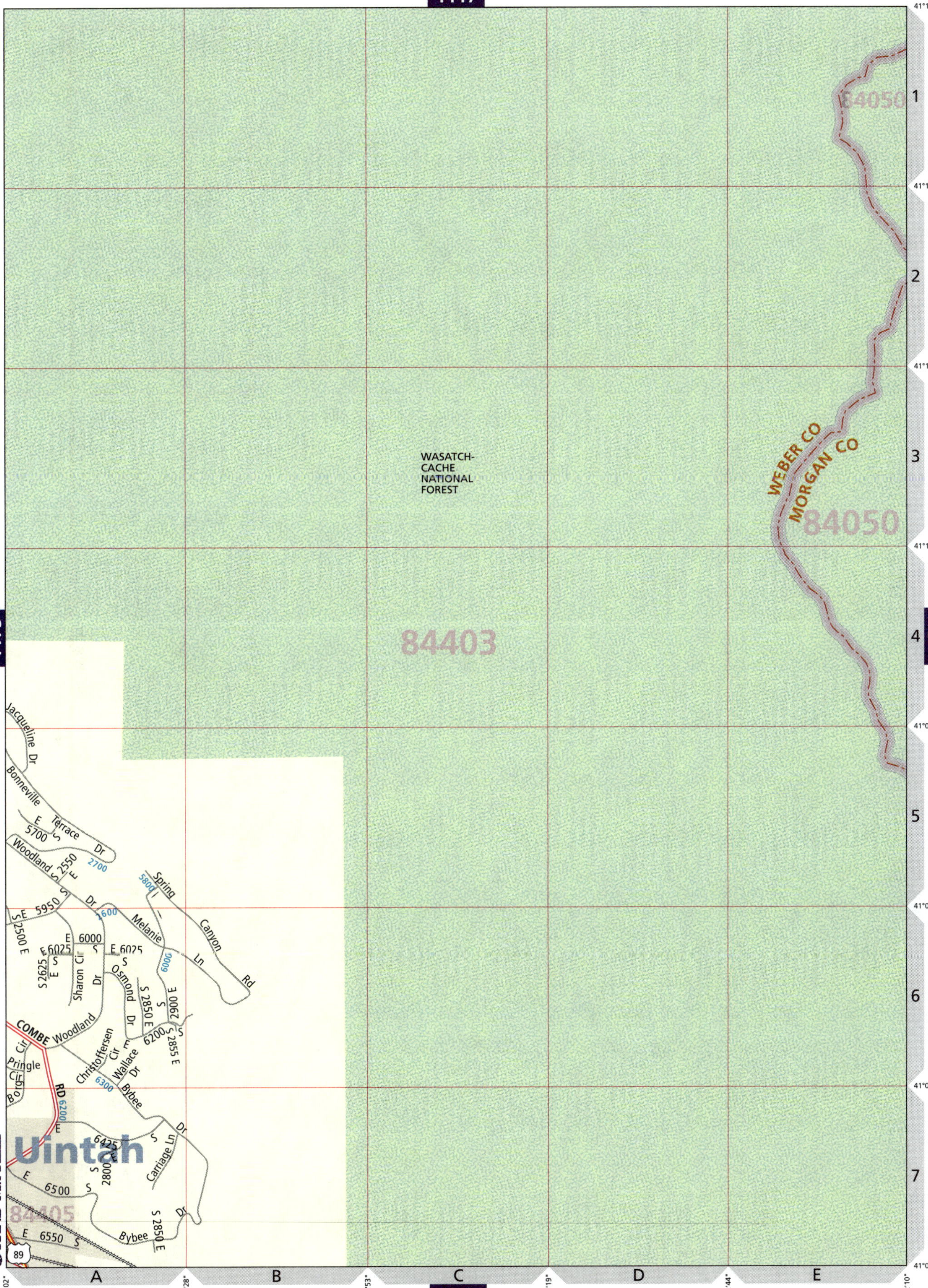

SEE 1173 MAP

SEE B MAP

SEE 1230 MAP

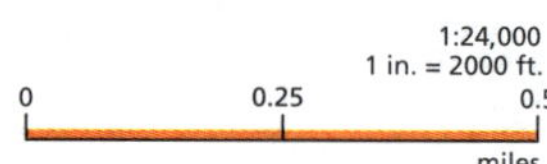

SEE 1169 MAP

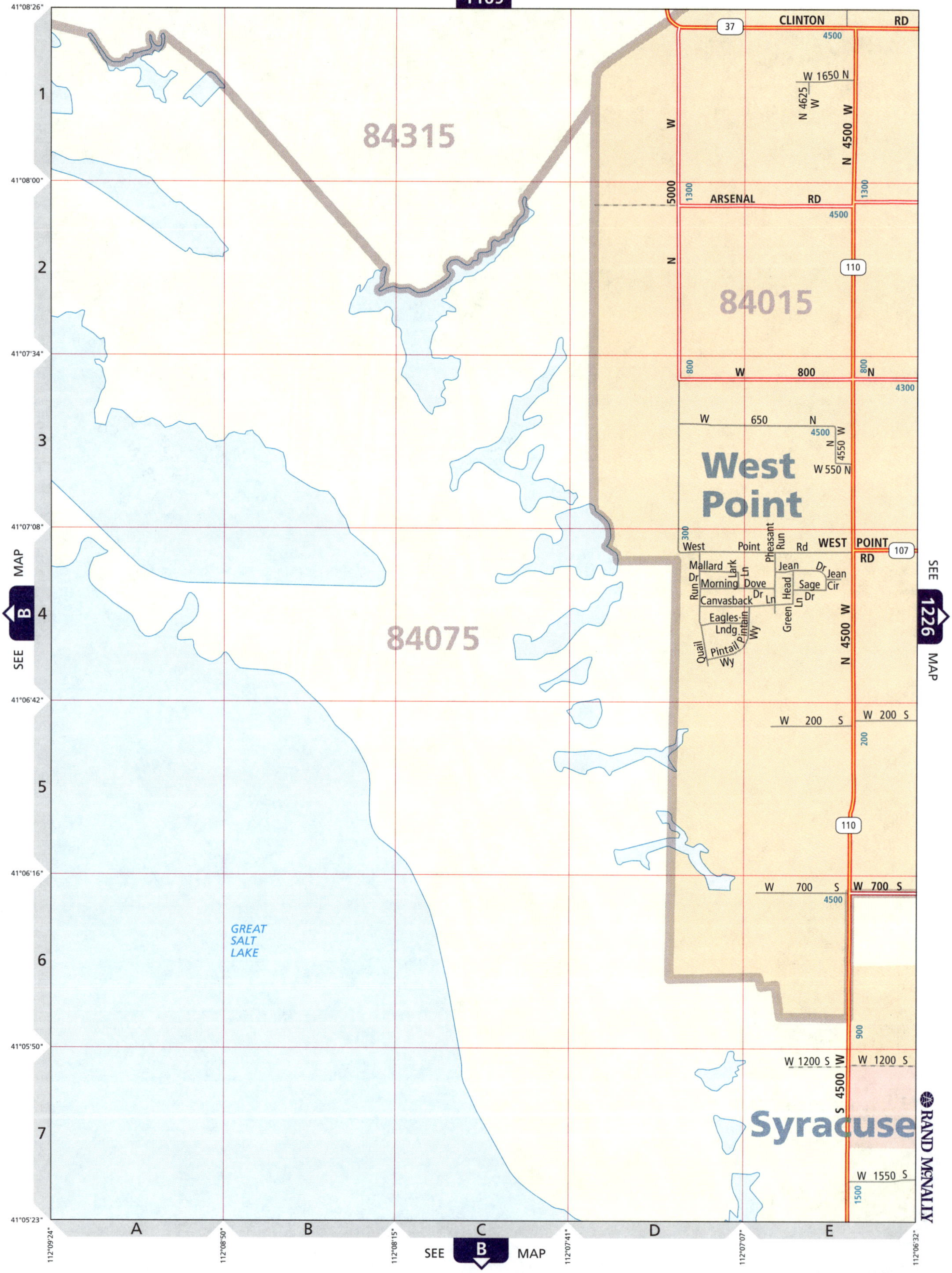

SEE B MAP

SEE 1226 MAP

SEE B MAP

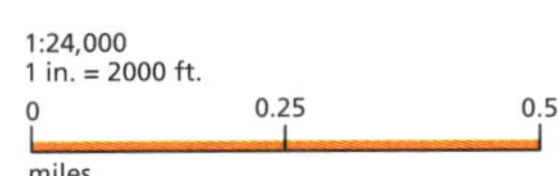

SEE 1170 MAP

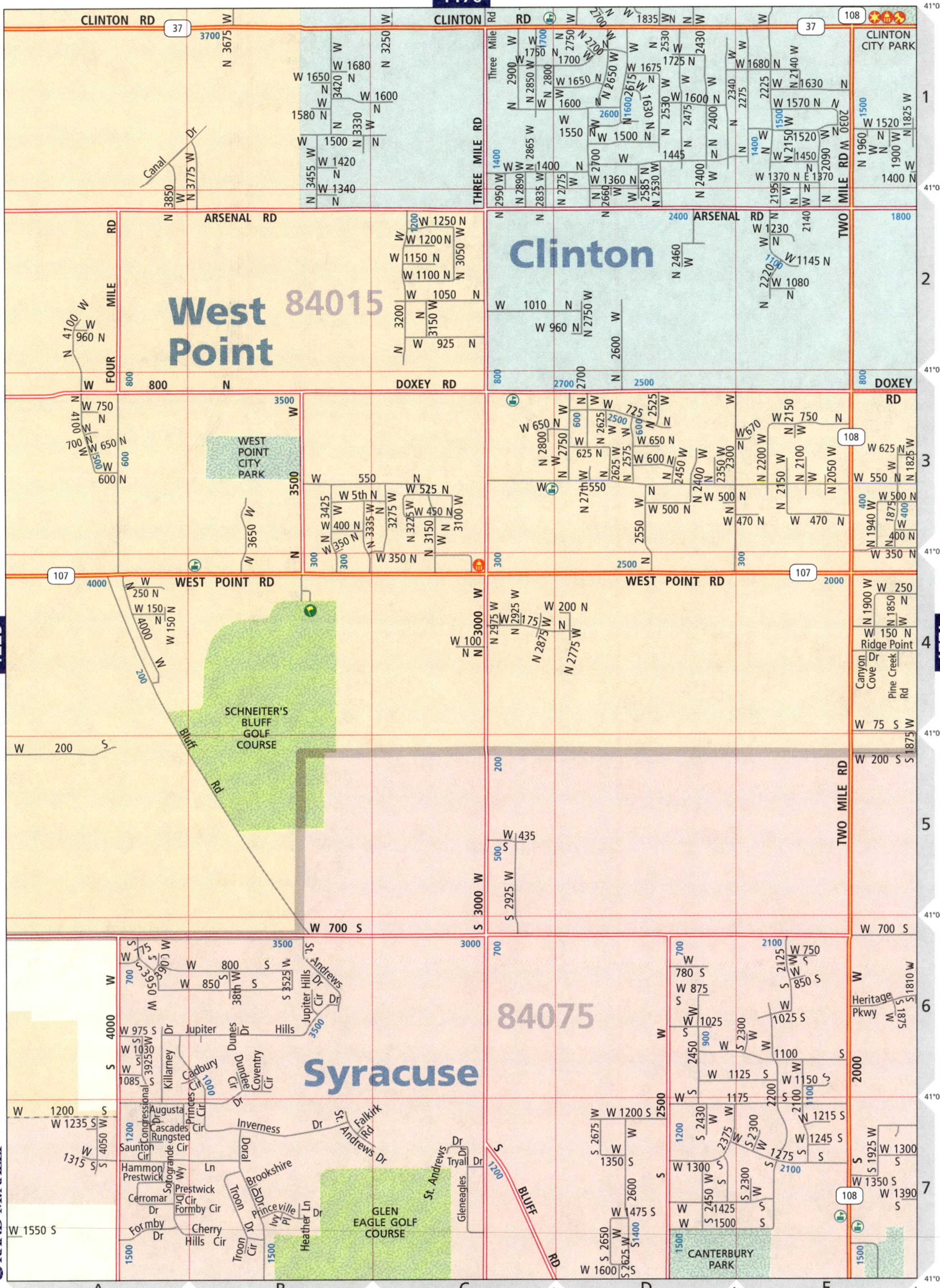

SEE 1225 MAP

SEE 1227 MAP

West Point
84015
Clinton
Syracuse
84075

CLINTON RD
ARSENAL RD
DOXEY RD
WEST POINT RD
THREE MILE RD
TWO MILE RD
FOUR MILE RD
BLUFF RD
W 700 S
W 200 S
S 3000 W
S 2000 W
S 4000 W

CLINTON CITY PARK
WEST POINT CITY PARK
SCHNEITER'S BLUFF GOLF COURSE
GLEN EAGLE GOLF COURSE
CANTERBURY PARK

Jupiter Hills Dr
St. Andrews Dr
Inverness Dr
Brookshire
Princeville
Heather Ln
Gleneagles
Tryall Dr
Augusta
Cascades Cir
Rungsted
Saunton Cir
Hammon Prestwick
Prestwick Cir
Formby Cir
Formby Dr
Cherry Hills Cir
Troon Dr
Troon Cir
Doral
Dundee Cir
Coventry Cir
Cadbury Cir
Killarney
Dunes
Congressional
Sotogrande Cir
Cerromar Dr
Falkirk Rd
Heritage Pkwy
Ridge Point
Canyon Cove Dr
Pine Creek Rd
Canal Dr

41°08'26"
41°08'00"
41°07'34"
41°07'08"
41°06'42"
41°06'16"
41°05'50"
41°05'24"
112°06'32"
112°05'58"
112°05'23"
112°04'49"
112°04'14"
112°03'40"

A B C D E
1 2 3 4 5 6 7

SEE 1280 MAP

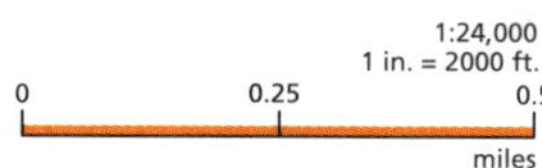

SEE 1171 MAP

Clinton

Sunset

West Point

Syracuse

Clearfield

HILL AIR FORCE BASE

84056

84015

84075

84016

CLINTON CITY PARK

SUNSET CENTRAL PARK

CHARLES E STEED MEMORIAL PARK

CLINTON RD

ARSENAL RD

DOXEY RD

DOXEY ST

WEST POINT RD

MAIN ST

STATE ST

VETERANS MEMORIAL HWY

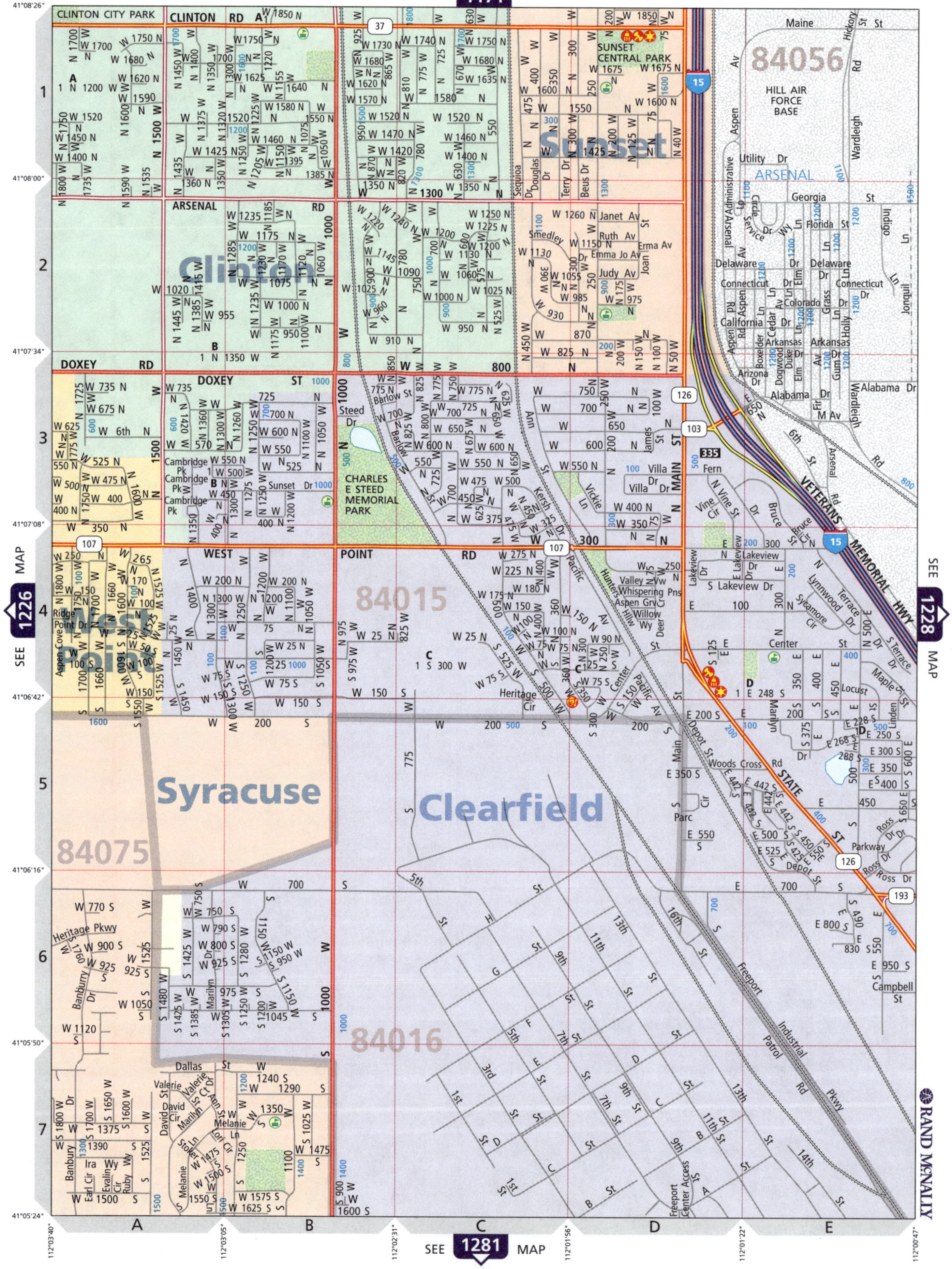

SEE 1226 MAP

SEE 1228 MAP

SEE 1281 MAP

1:24,000
1 in. = 2000 ft.
0 0.25 0.5
miles

SEE 1172 MAP

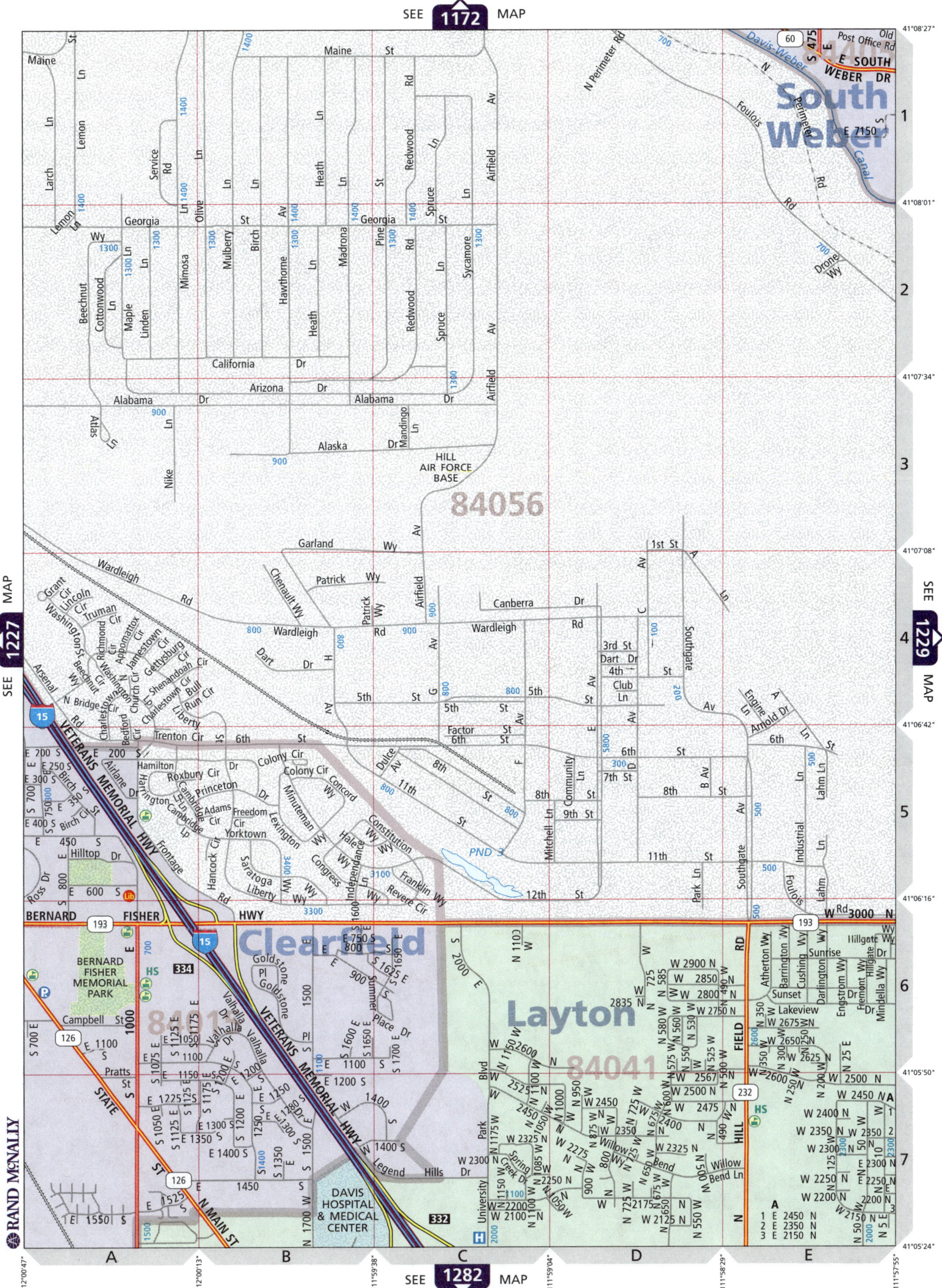

SEE 1227 MAP
SEE 1229 MAP
SEE 1282 MAP

1:24,000
1 in. = 2000 ft.
0 0.25 0.5
miles

SEE 1173 MAP

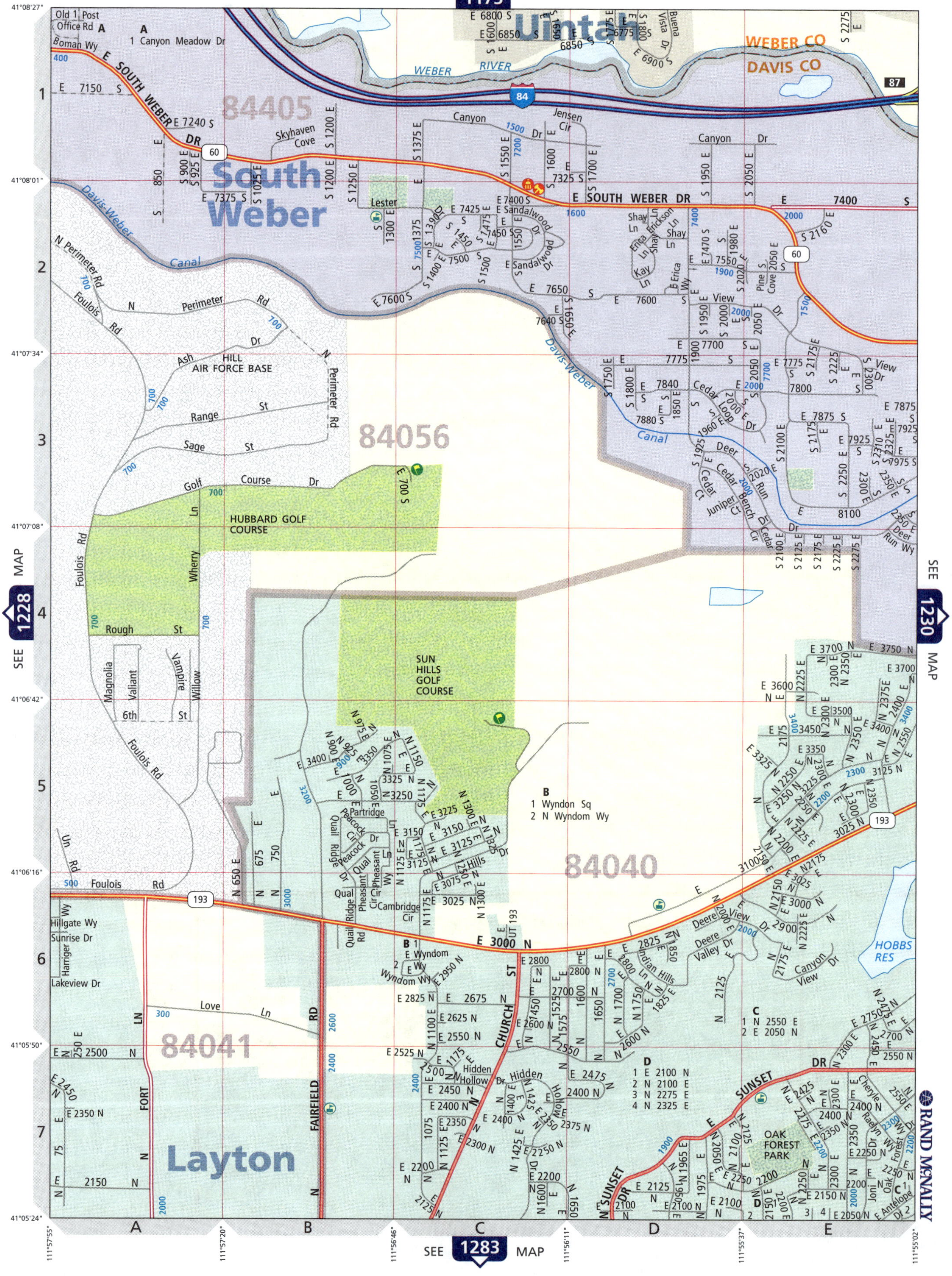

SEE 1228 MAP

SEE 1230 MAP

A
1 Canyon Meadow Dr

B
1 Wyndon Sq
2 N Wyndom Wy

C
1 N 2550 E
2 E 2050 N

D
1 E 2100 N
2 N 2100 E
3 N 2275 E
4 N 2325 E

Uintah
South Weber
Layton
WEBER CO
DAVIS CO
WEBER RIVER
Davis-Weber Canal
HILL AIR FORCE BASE
HUBBARD GOLF COURSE
SUN HILLS GOLF COURSE
OAK FOREST PARK
HOBBS RES
84405
84056
84040
84041

SEE 1283 MAP

RAND McNALLY

1:24,000
1 in. = 2000 ft.
0 0.25 0.5
miles

SEE 1174 MAP

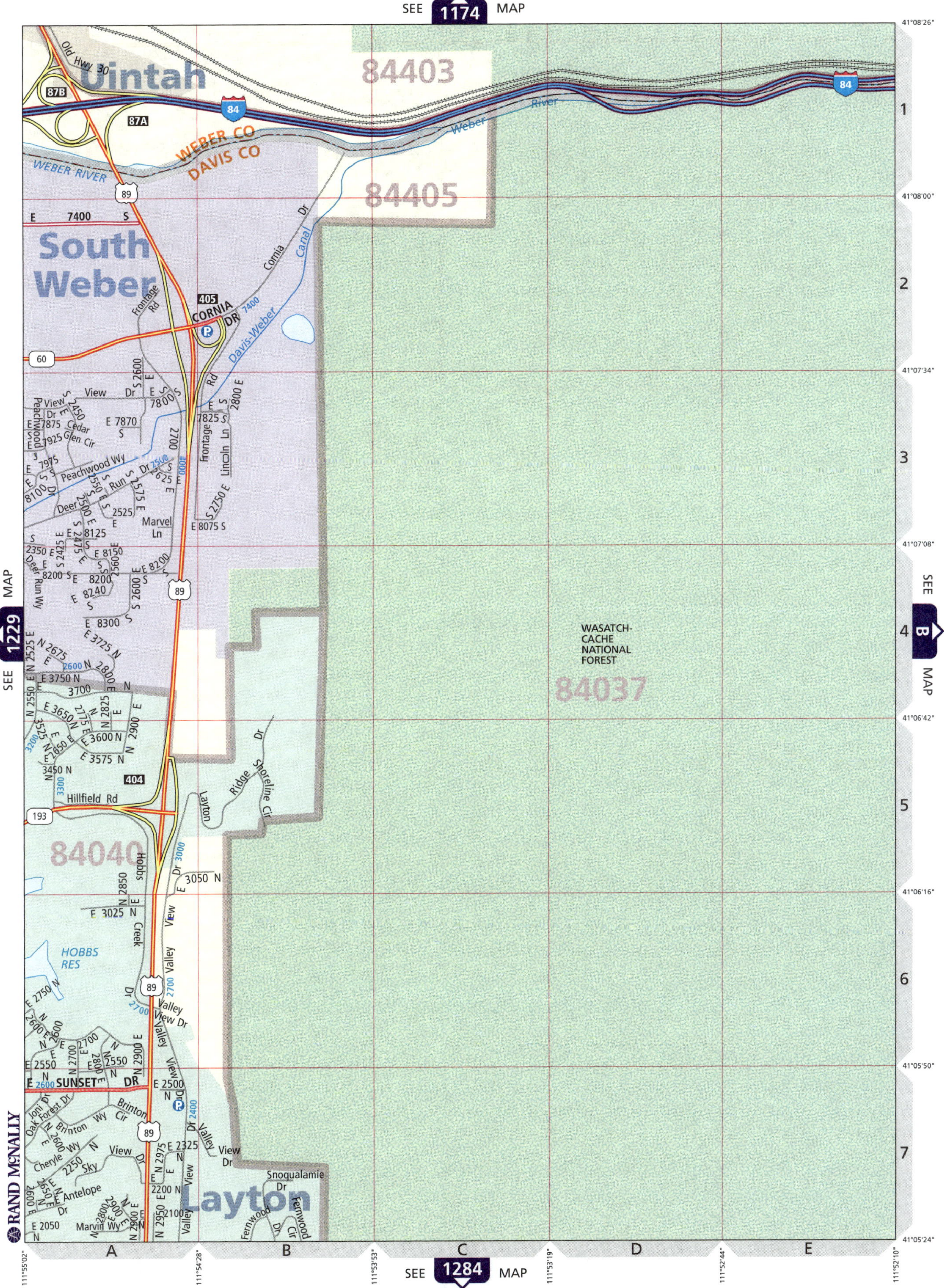

SEE 1229 MAP

SEE B MAP

SEE 1284 MAP

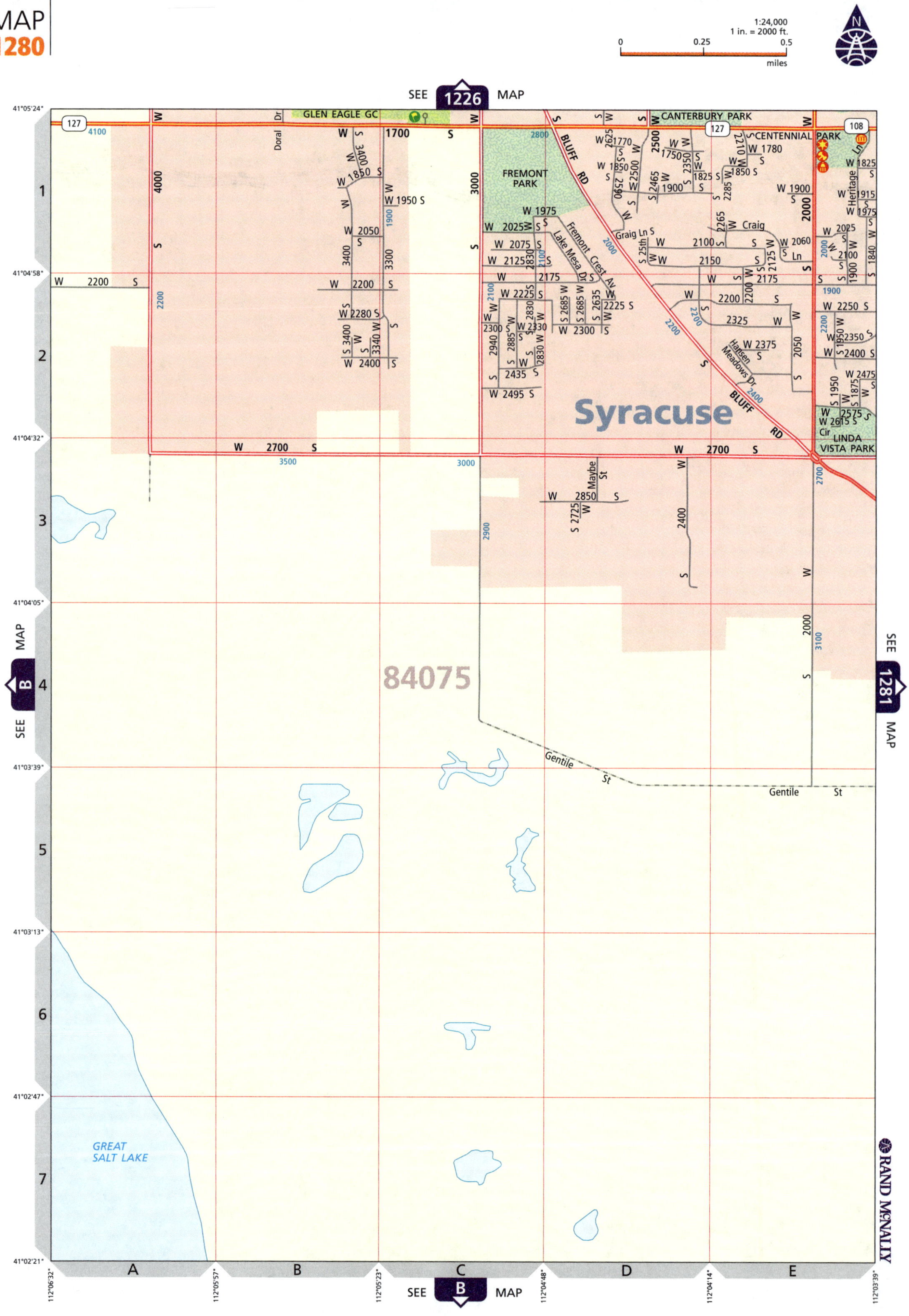

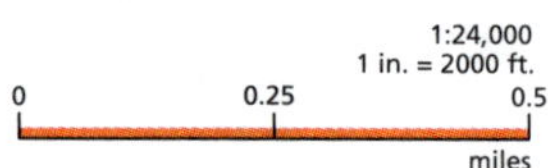

SEE 1226 MAP

Syracuse

84075

GLEN EAGLE GC

CANTERBURY PARK

CENTENNIAL PARK

FREMONT PARK

LINDA VISTA PARK

BLUFF RD

W 2700 S

W 1700 S

W 4000 S

W 3000 S

W 2000 S

Gentile St

GREAT SALT LAKE

SEE B MAP

SEE 1281 MAP

SEE B MAP

1:24,000
1 in. = 2000 ft.
0 0.25 0.5
miles

SEE 1227 MAP

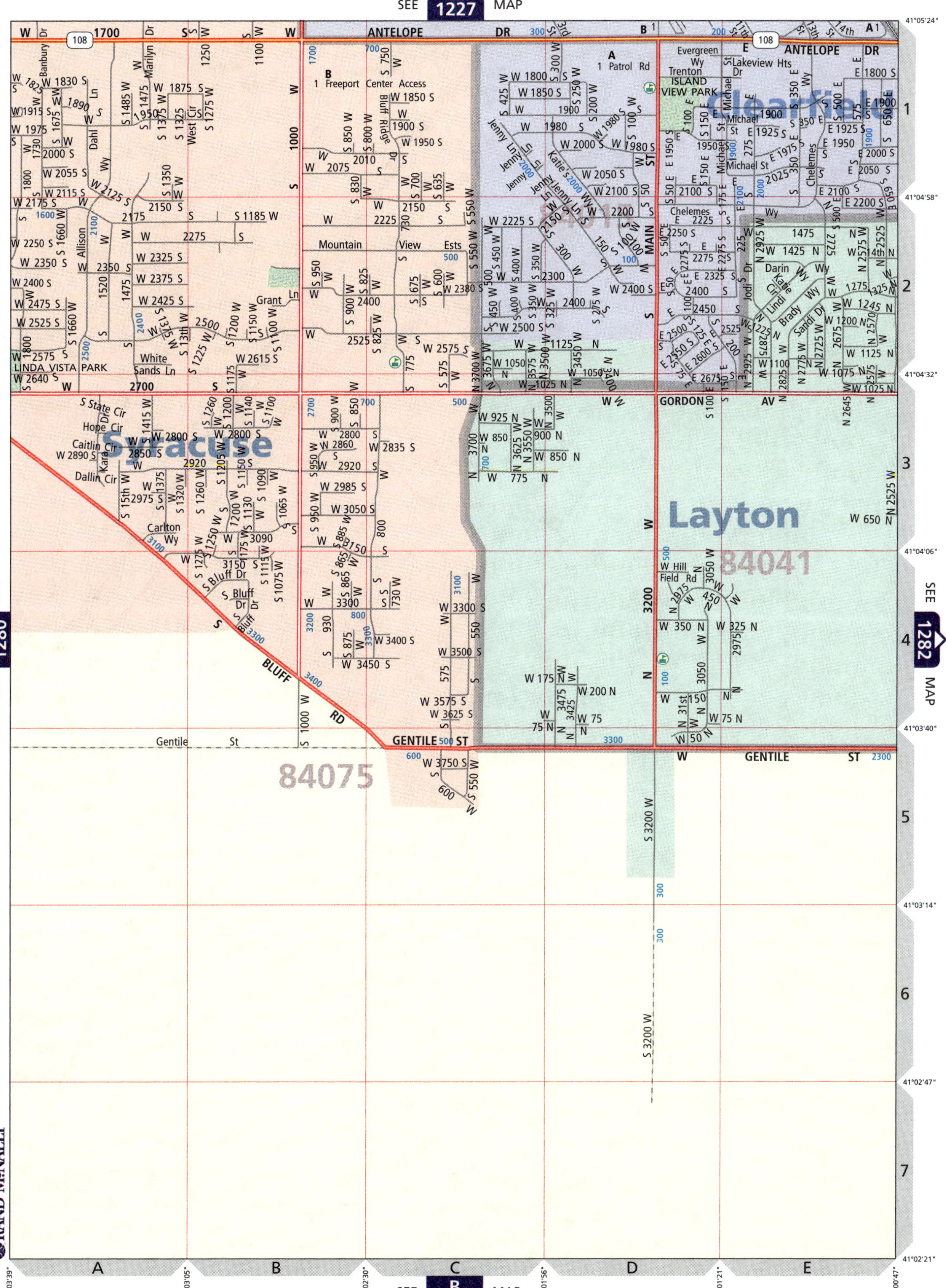

SEE 1280 MAP

SEE 1282 MAP

SEE B MAP

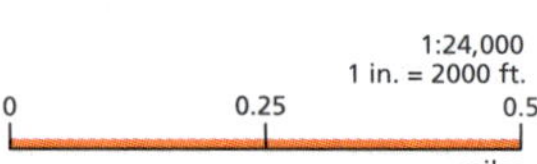

SEE 1228 MAP

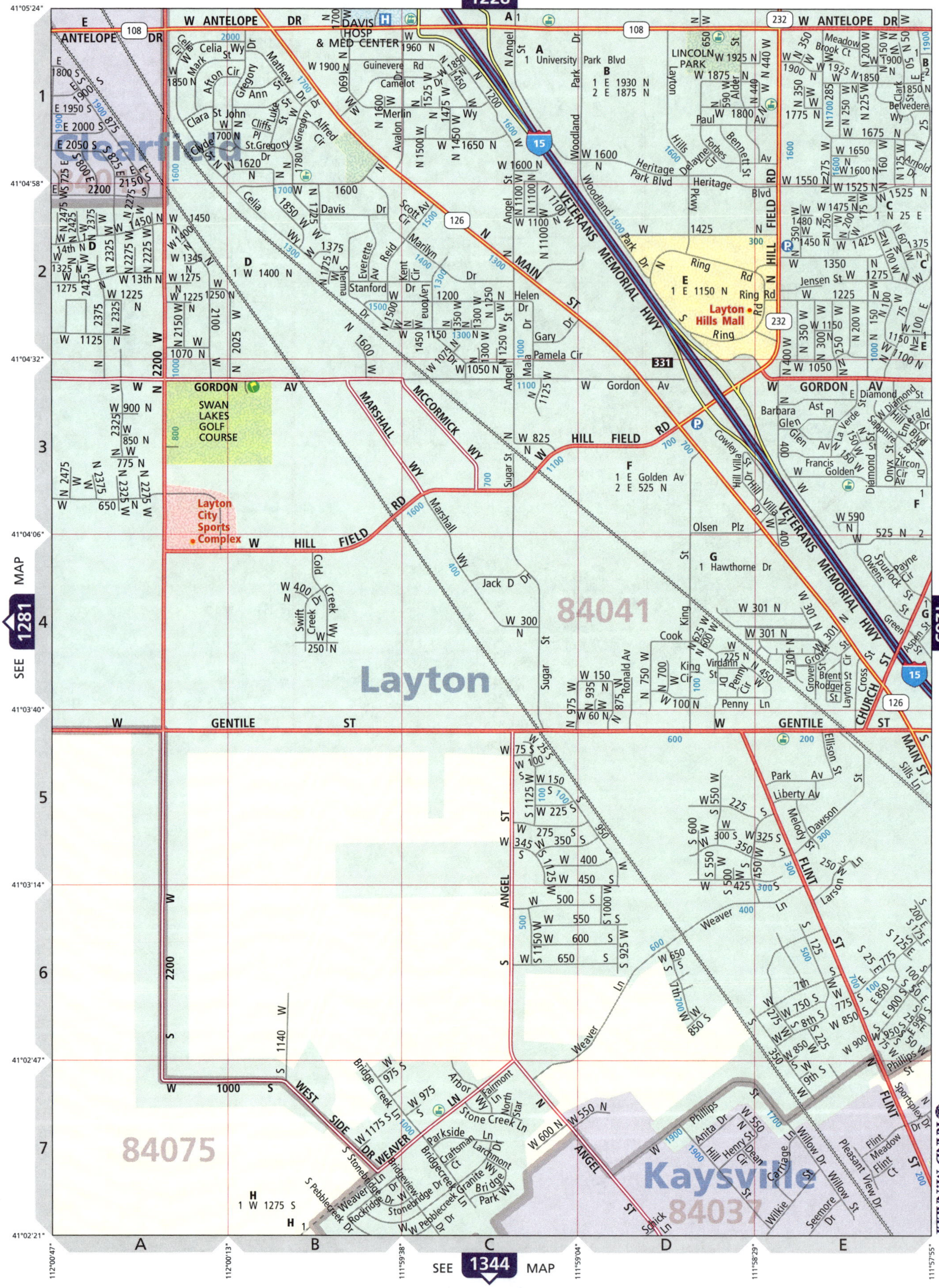

SEE 1281 MAP

SEE 1283 MAP

Layton

Clearfield

Kaysville

84041

84075

84037

Layton Hills Mall

Layton City Sports Complex

SWAN LAKES GOLF COURSE

DAVIS HOSP & MED CENTER

LINCOLN PARK

VETERANS MEMORIAL HWY

W ANTELOPE DR

W GORDON AV

W HILL FIELD RD

W GENTILE ST

N MAIN ST

S ANGEL ST

FLINT ST

WEST SIDE DR

SEE 1344 MAP

1:24,000
1 in. = 2000 ft.
0 0.25 0.5
miles

SEE 1229 MAP

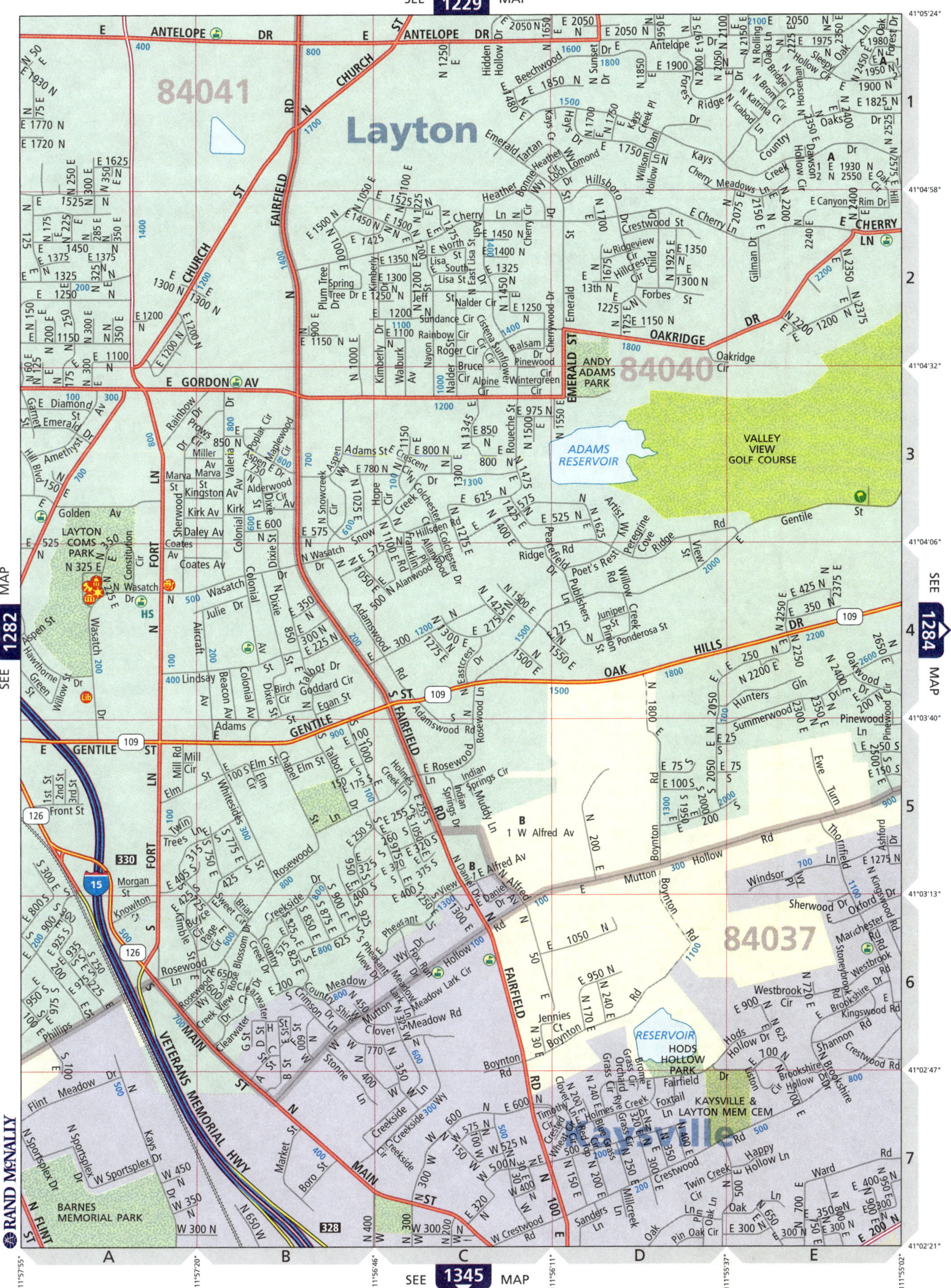

SEE 1282 MAP
SEE 1284 MAP
SEE 1345 MAP

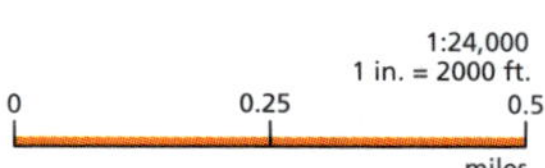

SEE 1230 MAP

SEE 1283 MAP

SEE B MAP

SEE 1346 MAP

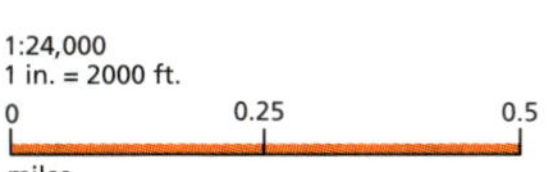

SEE 1282 MAP

Layton

Kaysville

84037

84075

GREAT SALT LAKE

A
1 S Pebblecreek Dr
2 W Pebblecreek Dr

B
1 Country Spring Cir
2 Whispering Breeze Cir
3 W Whispering Meadow Ln
4 Saddlehorn Cir

C
1 Suncrest Ln

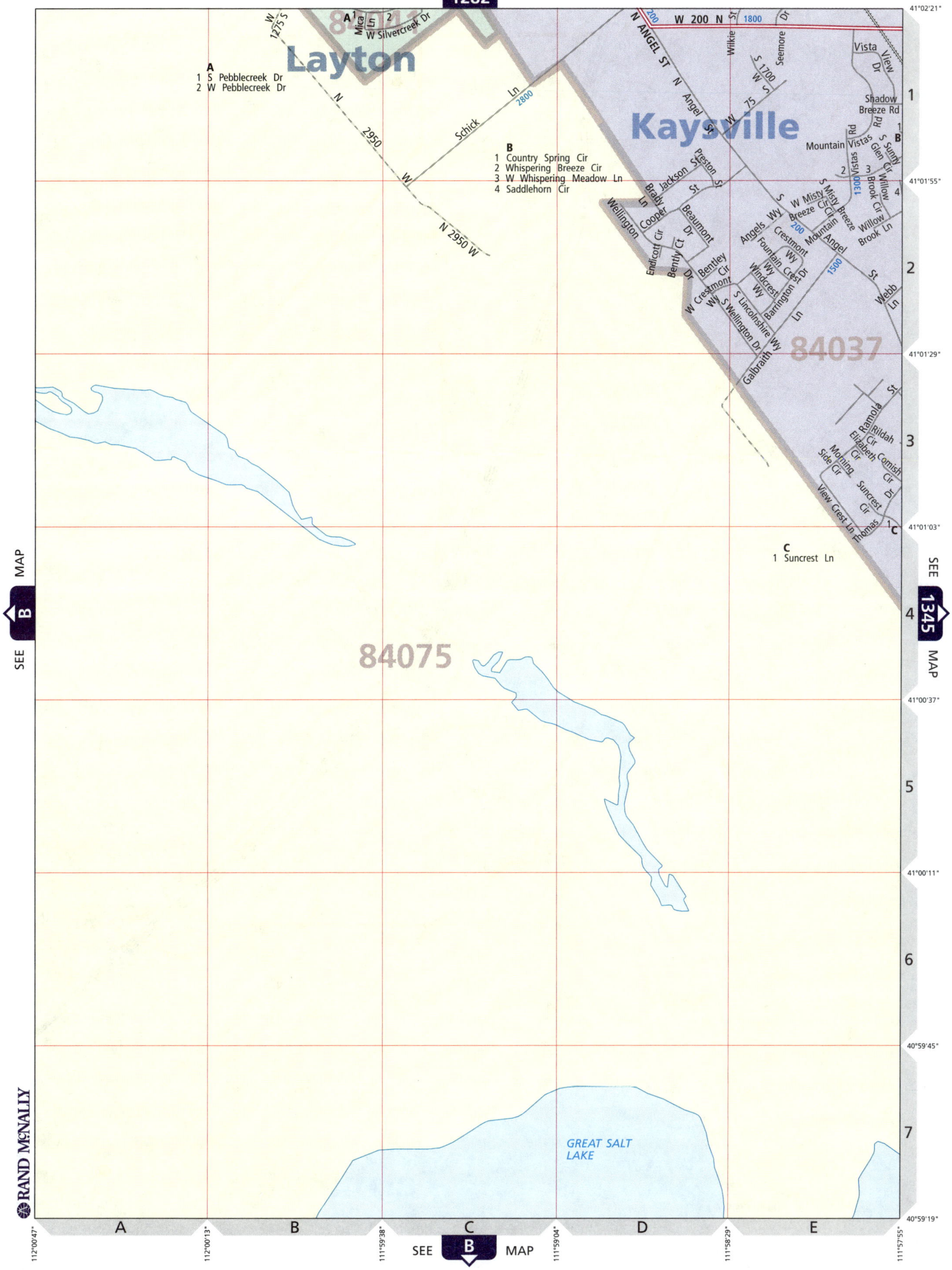

SEE B MAP

SEE 1345 MAP

SEE B MAP

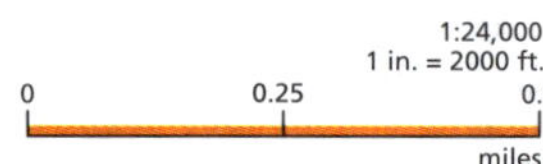

SEE 1283 MAP

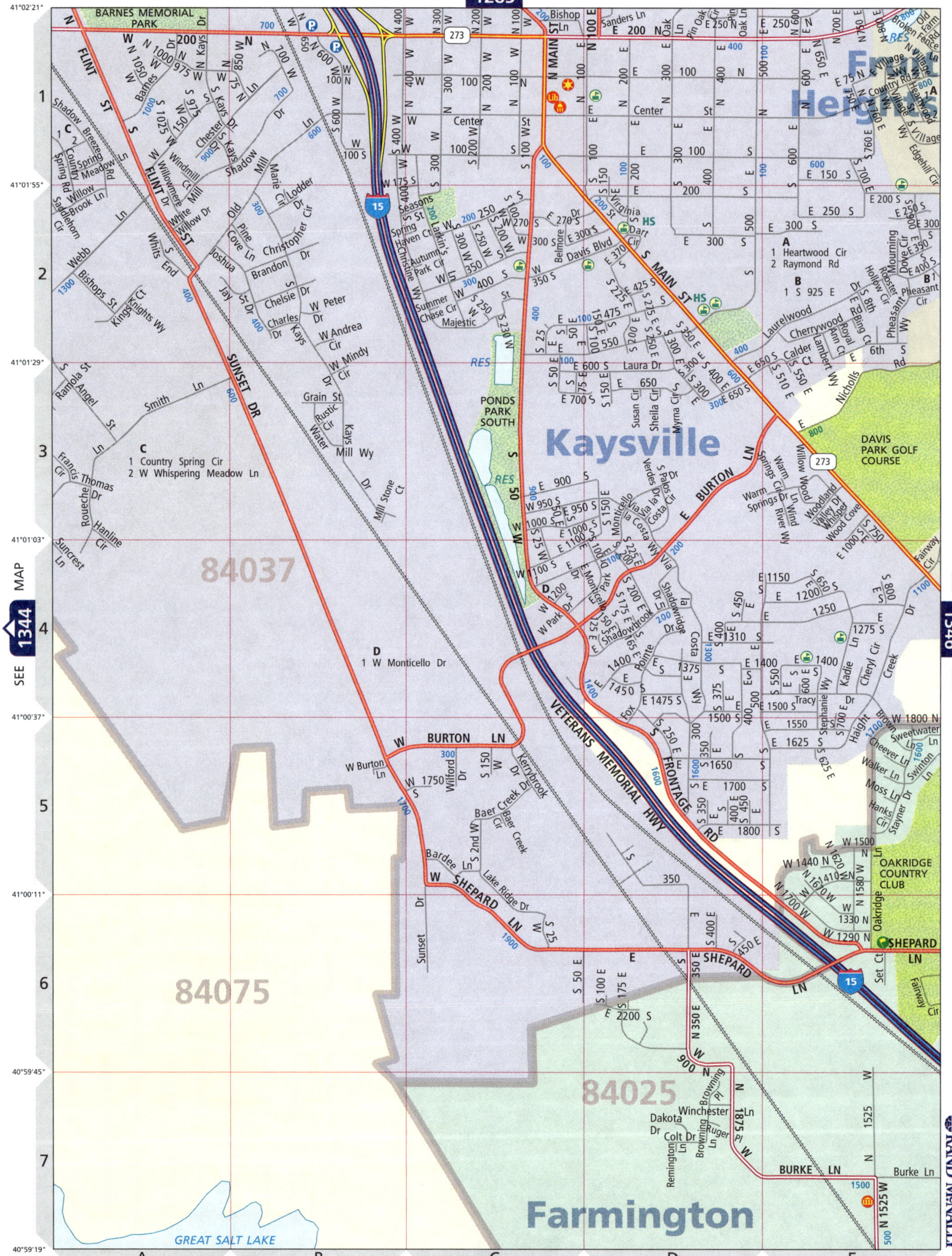

SEE 1344 MAP

SEE 1346 MAP

Kaysville

Fruit Heights

Farmington

BARNES MEMORIAL PARK

PONDS PARK SOUTH

DAVIS PARK GOLF COURSE

OAKRIDGE COUNTRY CLUB

GREAT SALT LAKE

84037

84075

84025

SUNSET DR

FLINT ST

N MAIN ST

S MAIN ST

E BURTON LN

W BURTON LN

W SHEPARD LN

SHEPARD LN

VETERANS MEMORIAL HWY

S FRONTAGE RD

BURKE LN

A
1 Heartwood Cir
2 Raymond Rd

B
1 S 925 E

C
1 Country Spring Cir
2 W Whispering Meadow Ln

D
1 W Monticello Dr

41°02'21"
41°01'55"
41°01'29"
41°01'03"
41°00'37"
41°00'11"
40°59'45"
40°59'19"

111°57'55"
111°57'20"
111°56'46"
111°56'11"
111°55'37"
111°55'03"

SEE 1447 MAP

1:24,000
1 in. = 2000 ft.
0 0.25 0.5
miles

SEE 1284 MAP

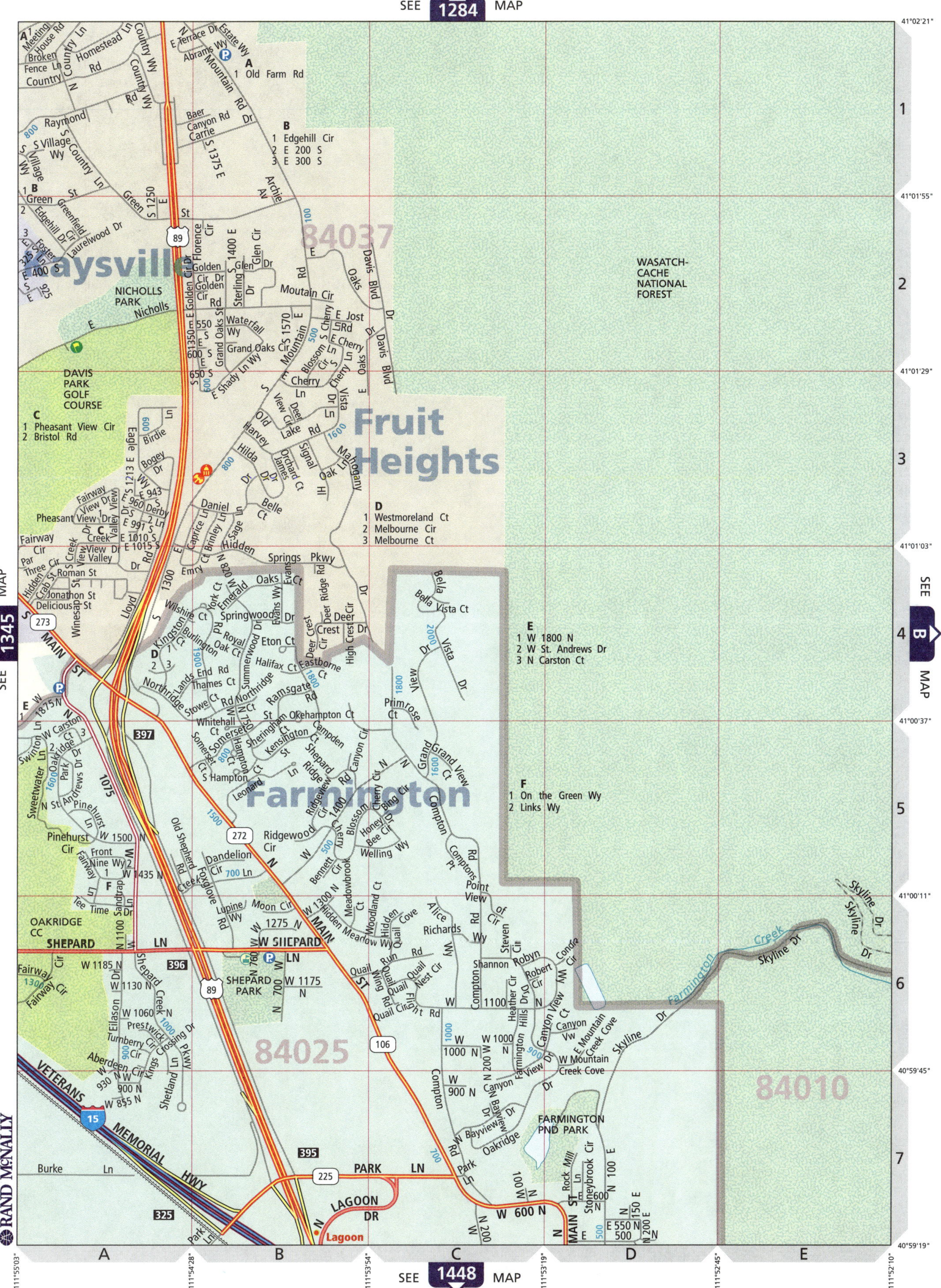

SEE 1345 MAP
SEE B MAP
SEE 1448 MAP

RAND McNALLY

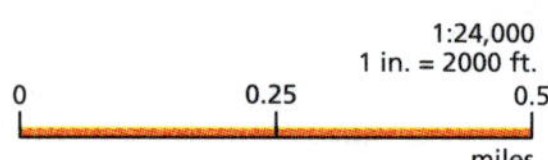

SEE 1345 MAP

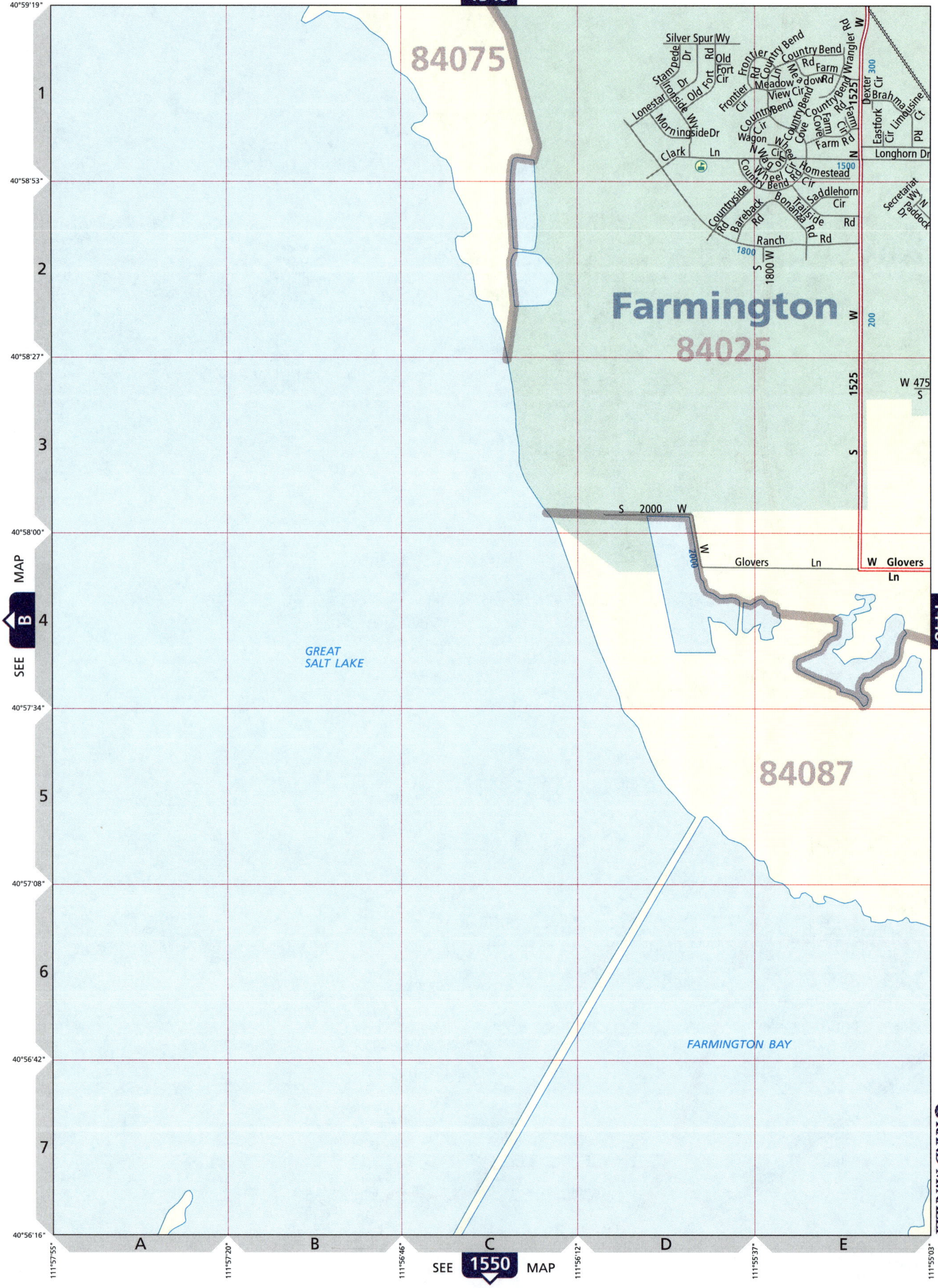

1:24,000
1 in. = 2000 ft.
0 0.25 0.5
miles
N
84075
84025
84087
Farmington
GREAT SALT LAKE
FARMINGTON BAY
Silver Spur Wy
Stampede Dr
Dr
Rd
Old Fort Cir
Old Fort
Ironside Wy
Lonestar
Morningside Dr
Clark Ln
Frontier Rd
Frontier Cir
Country Bend
Country Bend Rd
Country Ln
Meadow Rd
Farm Rd
Meadow View Cir
Wrangler Rd
Country Bend
Country Cir
Wagon Wheel Cir
N Wagon Wheel Cir
Country Bend Cove
Country Bend Rd
Farm Cove
Farm Cir
Farm Rd
Homestead Cir
Country Bend
Countryside Rd
Bareback Rd
Bonanza Rd
Trailside Rd
Saddlehorn Cir
Ranch Rd
1800
S 1800 W
1500
N 1525 W
300
Dexter Cir
Brahma Rd
Eastfork Cir
Limousine Ct
Longhorn Dr
Secretariat Wy
N Paddock Dr
200
S 1525 W
W 475 S
S 2000 W
W 2000
Glovers Ln
W Glovers Ln
A
B
C
D
E
1
2
3
4
5
6
7
40°59'19"
40°58'53"
40°58'27"
40°58'00"
40°57'34"
40°57'08"
40°56'42"
40°56'16"
111°57'55"
111°57'20"
111°56'46"
111°56'12"
111°55'37"
111°55'03"

SEE B MAP

SEE 1448 MAP

SEE 1550 MAP

1:24,000
1 in. = 2000 ft.
0 0.25 0.5
miles

SEE 1346 MAP

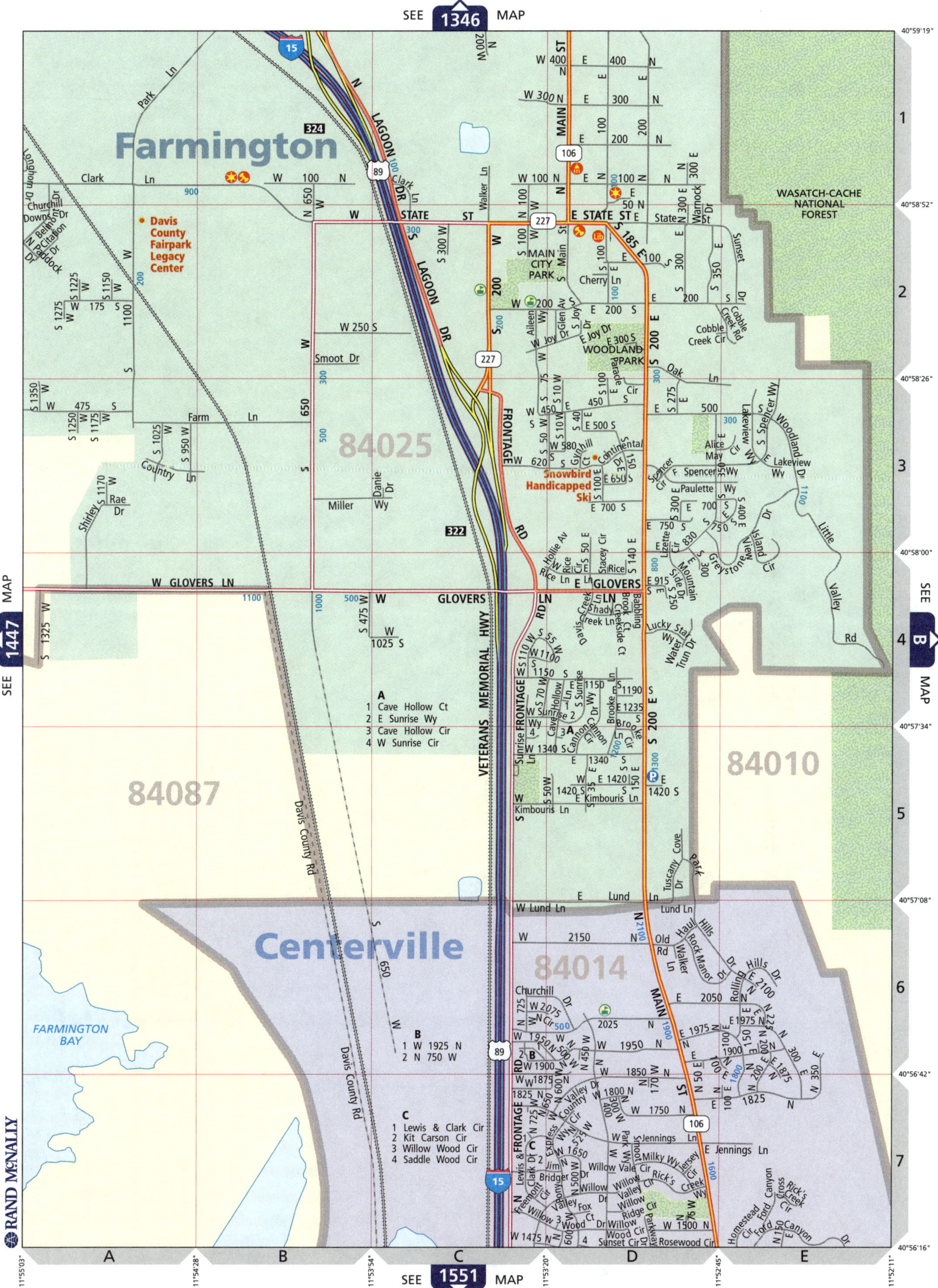

SEE 1447 MAP

SEE B MAP

SEE 1551 MAP

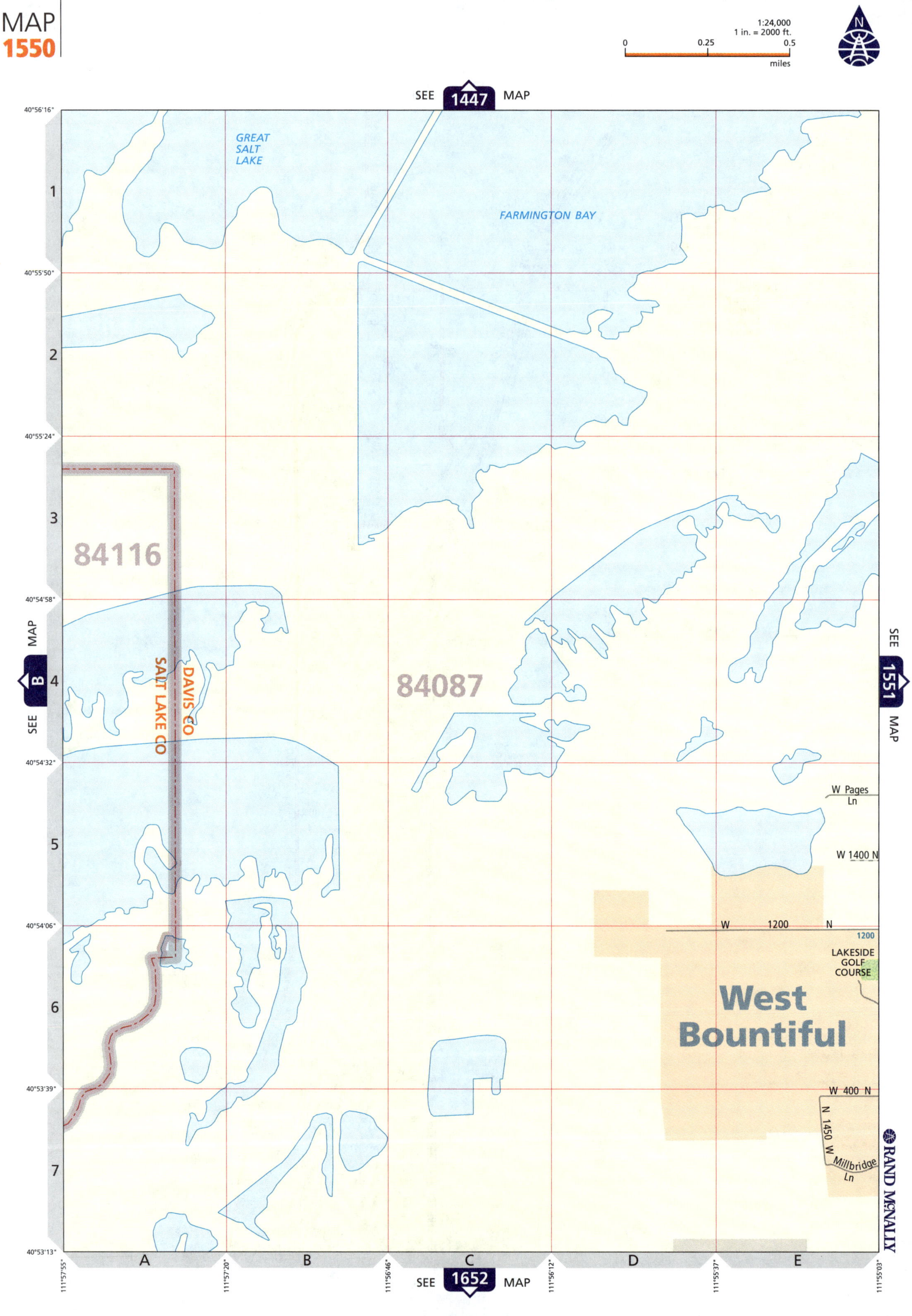

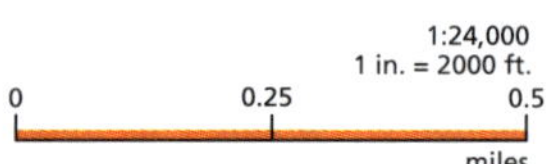

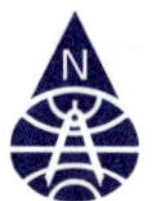

1:24,000
1 in. = 2000 ft.
0 0.25 0.5
miles
N
SEE 1447 MAP
GREAT SALT LAKE
FARMINGTON BAY
84116
84087
DAVIS CO
SALT LAKE CO
SEE B MAP
SEE 1551 MAP
W Pages Ln
W 1400 N
W 1200 N
1200
LAKESIDE GOLF COURSE
West Bountiful
W 400 N
N 1450 W
Millbridge Ln
40°56'16"
40°55'50"
40°55'24"
40°54'58"
40°54'32"
40°54'06"
40°53'39"
40°53'13"
111°57'55"
111°57'20"
111°56'46"
111°56'12"
111°55'37"
111°55'03"
1
2
3
4
5
6
7
A
B
C
D
E
SEE 1652 MAP

1:24,000
1 in. = 2000 ft.
0 0.25 0.5
miles

SEE 1448 MAP

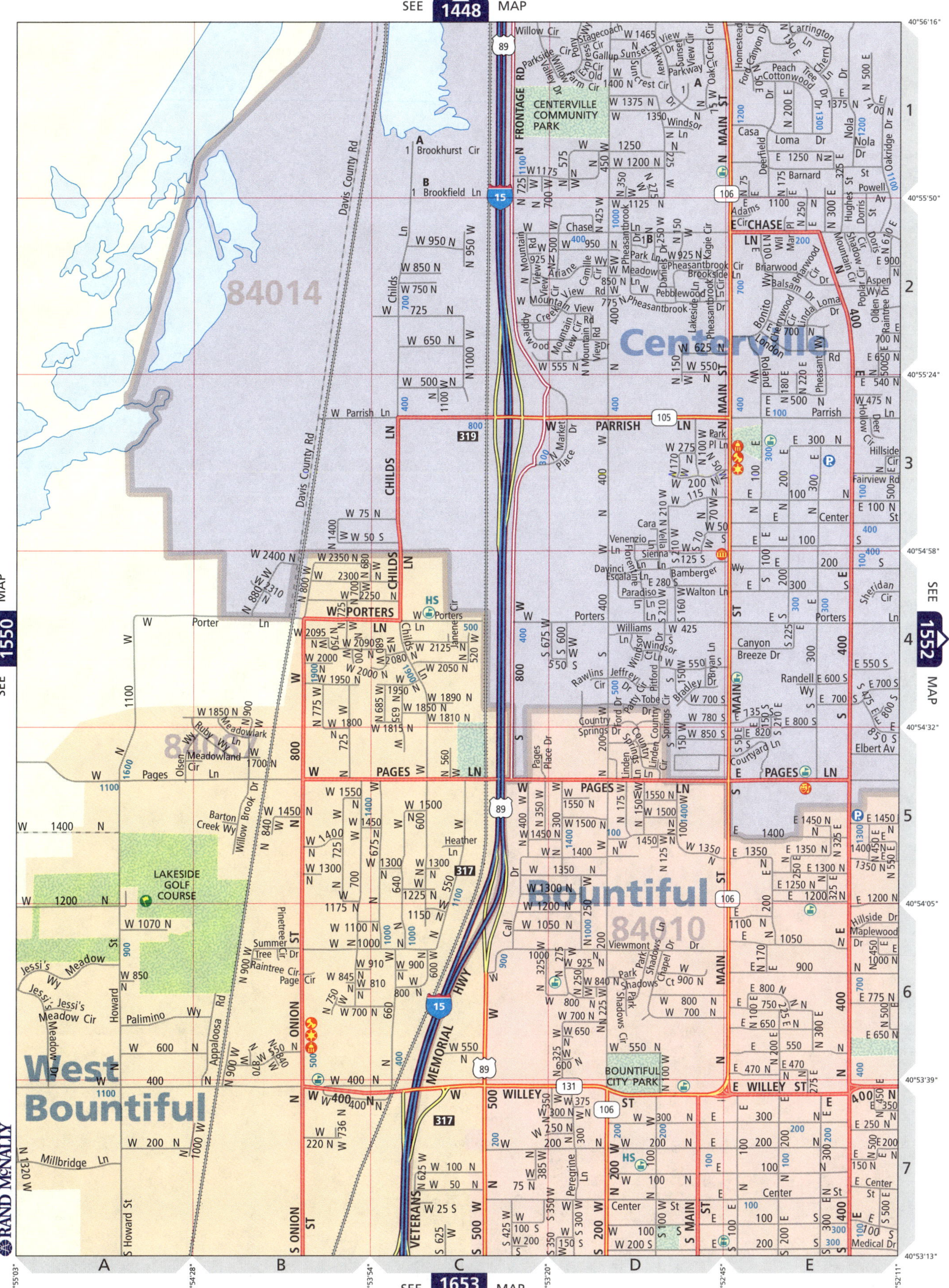

SEE 1550 MAP
SEE 1552 MAP
SEE 1653 MAP

A B C D E
1 2 3 4 5 6 7

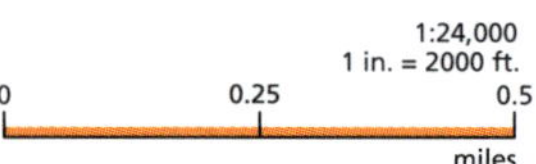

SEE B MAP

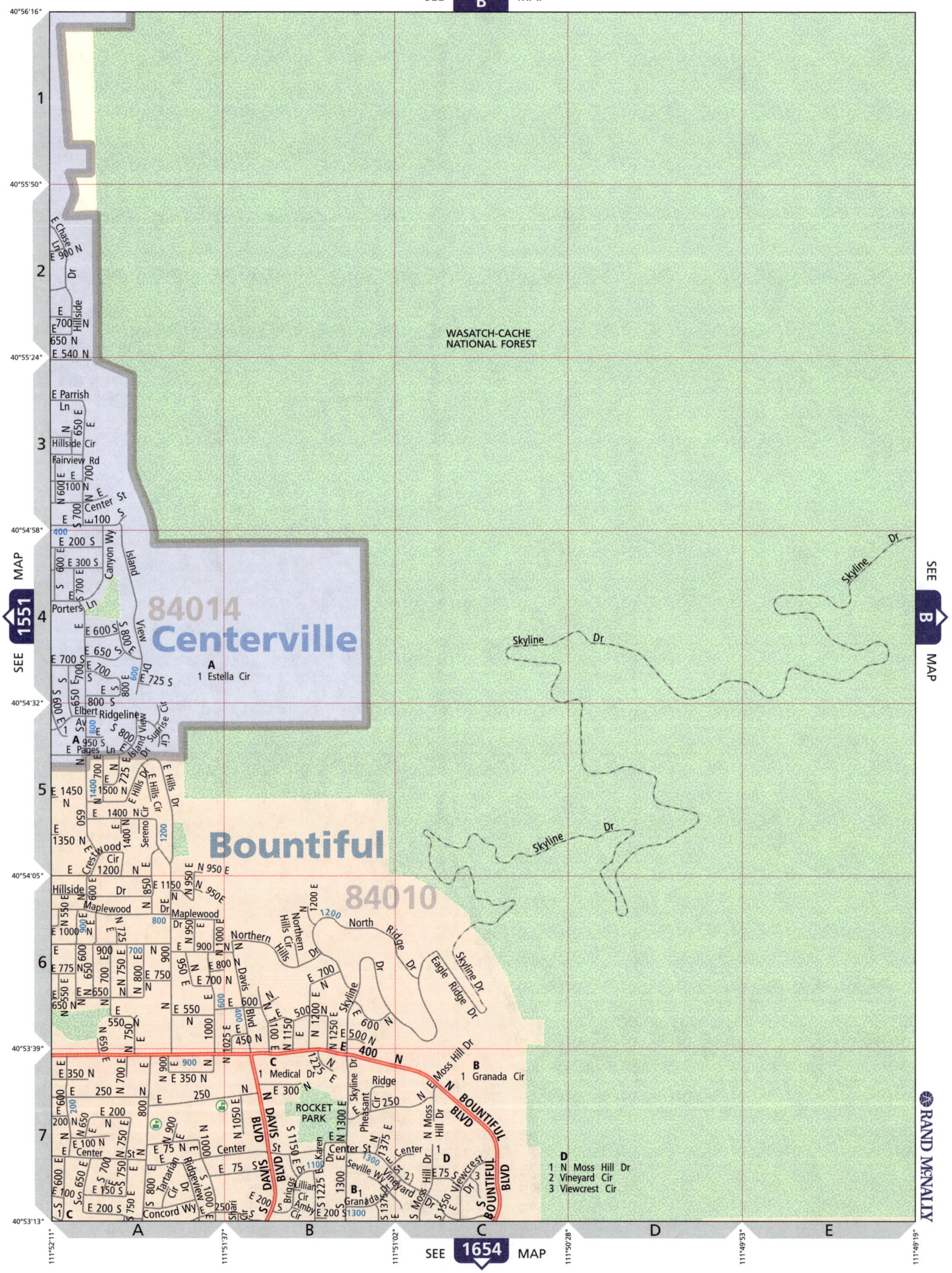

WASATCH-CACHE NATIONAL FOREST

84014
Centerville

Bountiful
84010

A
1 Estella Cir

B
1 Granada Cir

C
1 Medical Dr

D
1 N Moss Hill Dr
2 Vineyard Cir
3 Viewcrest Cir

ROCKET PARK

Skyline Dr

SEE 1551 MAP

SEE B MAP

SEE 1654 MAP

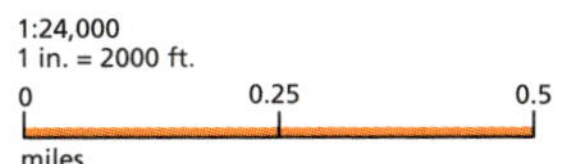

SEE 1550 MAP

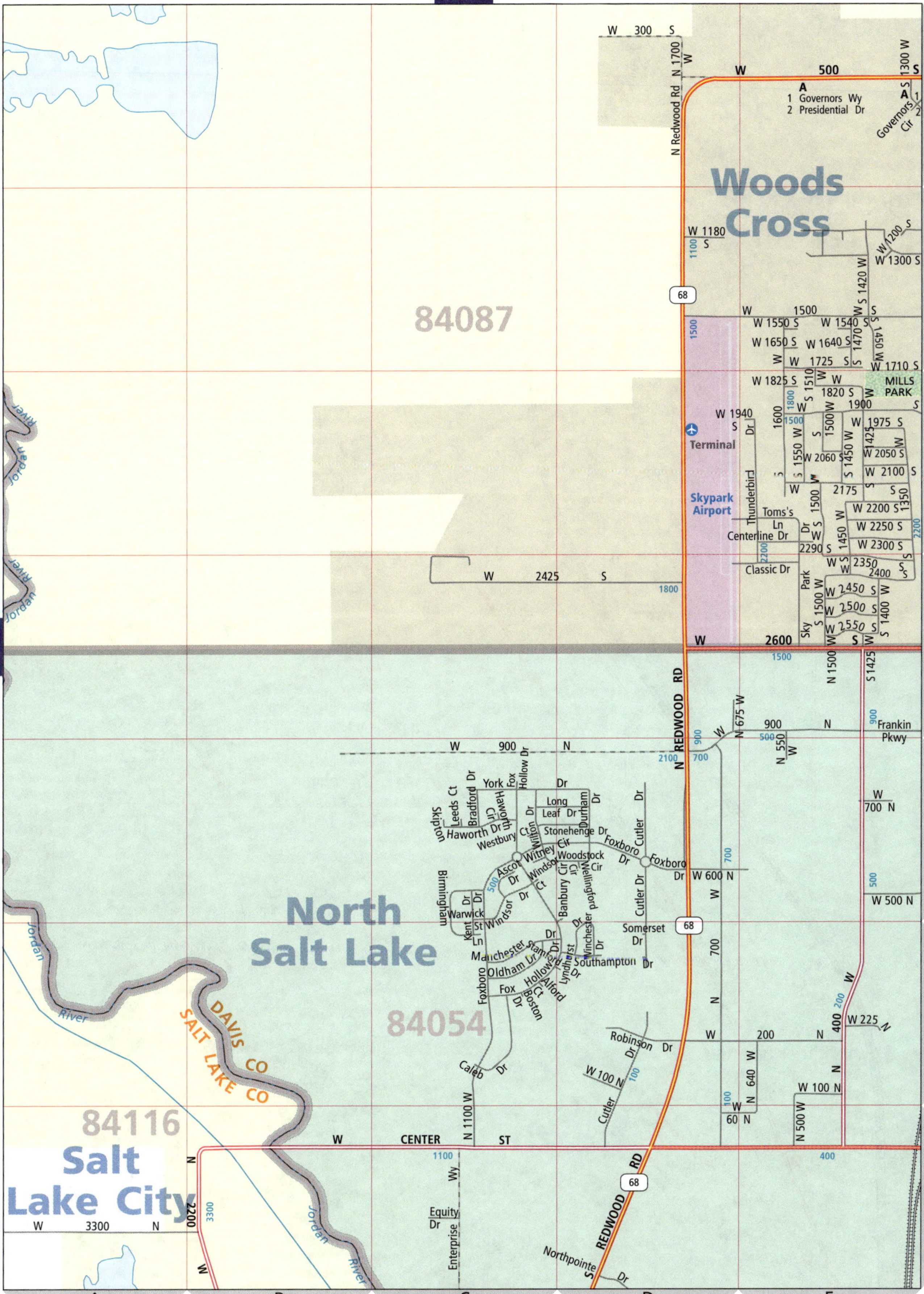

SEE 1653 MAP

SEE B MAP

SEE 1753 MAP

1:24,000
1 in. = 2000 ft.
0 0.25 0.5
miles

SEE 1551 MAP

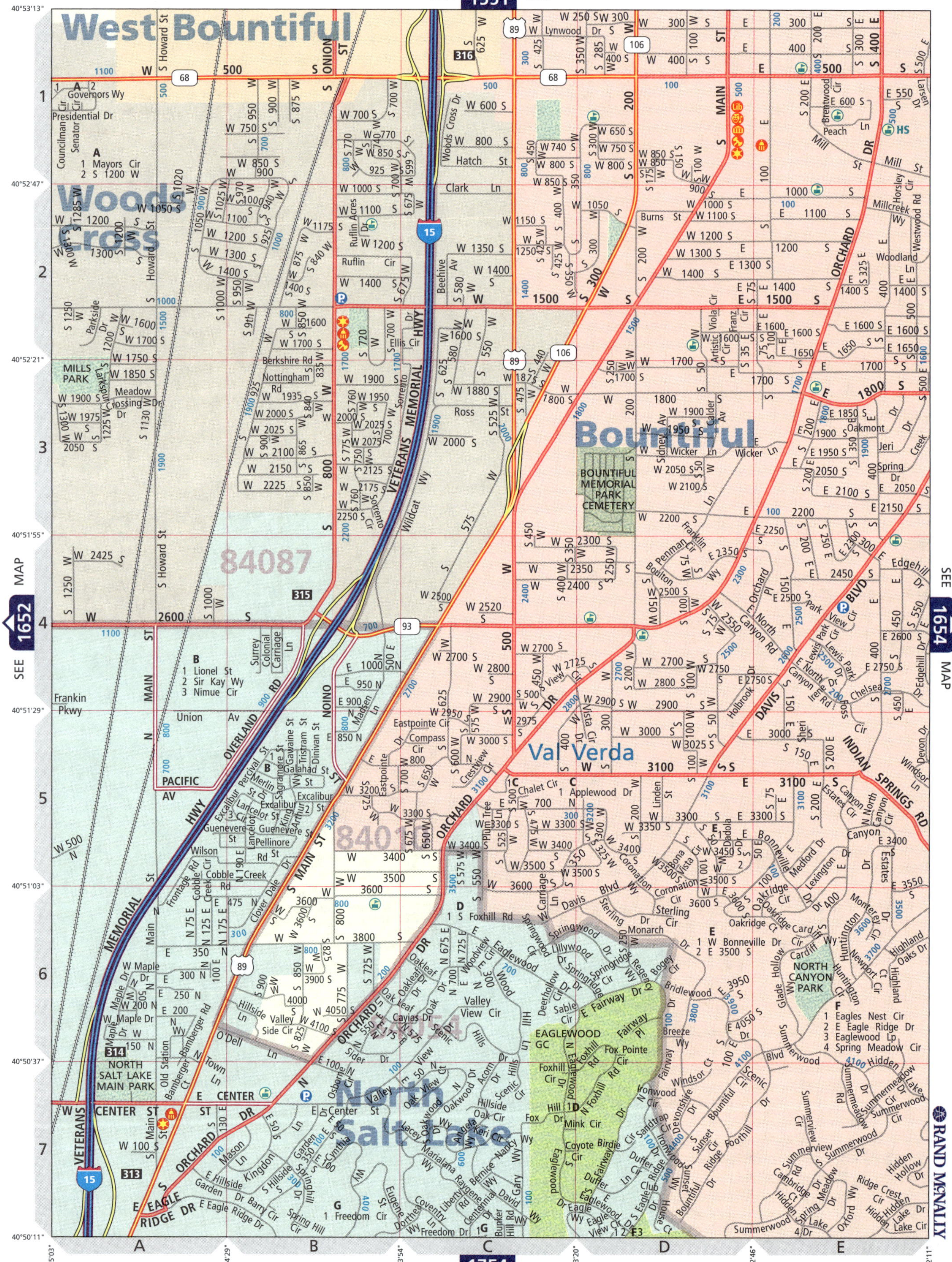

West Bountiful

Woods Cross

Bountiful

Val Verda

North Salt Lake

84087

84010

84054

MILLS PARK

BOUNTIFUL MEMORIAL PARK CEMETERY

NORTH CANYON PARK

EAGLEWOOD GC

NORTH SALT LAKE MAIN PARK

VETERANS MEMORIAL HWY

OVERLAND RD

ORCHARD DR

DAVIS BLVD

INDIAN SPRINGS RD

MAIN ST

ONION ST

PACIFIC AV

A
1 Mayors Cir
2 S 1200 W

B
1 Lionel St
2 Sir Kay Wy
3 Nimue Cir

E
1 W Bonneville Dr
2 E 3500 S

F
1 Eagles Nest Cir
2 E Eagle Ridge Dr
3 Eaglewood Lp
4 Spring Meadow Cir

G
1 Freedom Cir

SEE 1652 MAP

SEE 1654 MAP

SEE 1754 MAP

40°53'13"
40°52'47"
40°52'21"
40°51'55"
40°51'29"
40°51'03"
40°50'37"
40°50'11"

111°55'03"
111°54'29"
111°53'54"
111°53'20"
111°52'46"
111°52'11"

1:24,000
1 in. = 2000 ft.
0 0.25 0.5
miles

SEE 1552 MAP

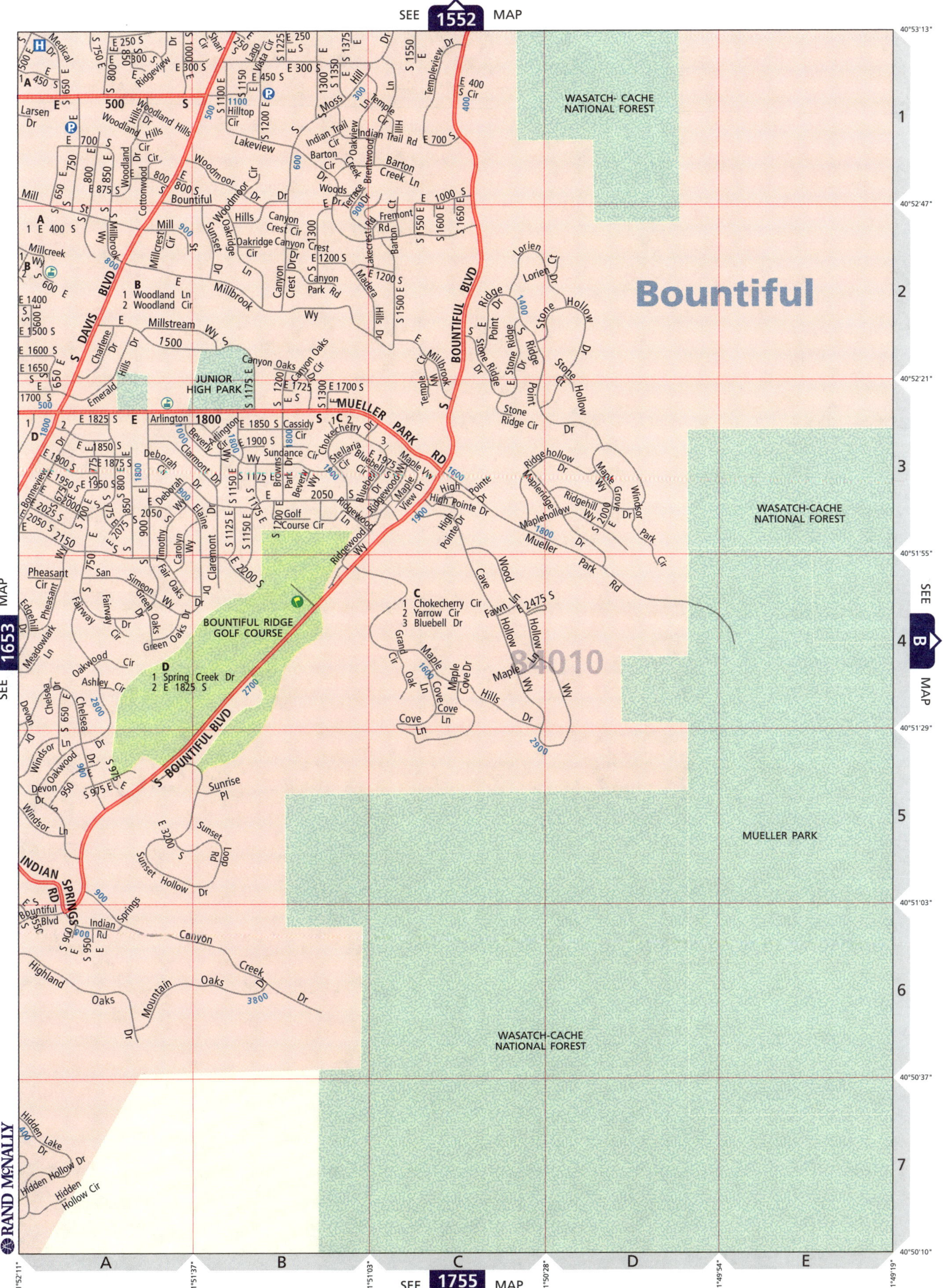

SEE 1653 MAP

SEE B MAP

SEE 1755 MAP

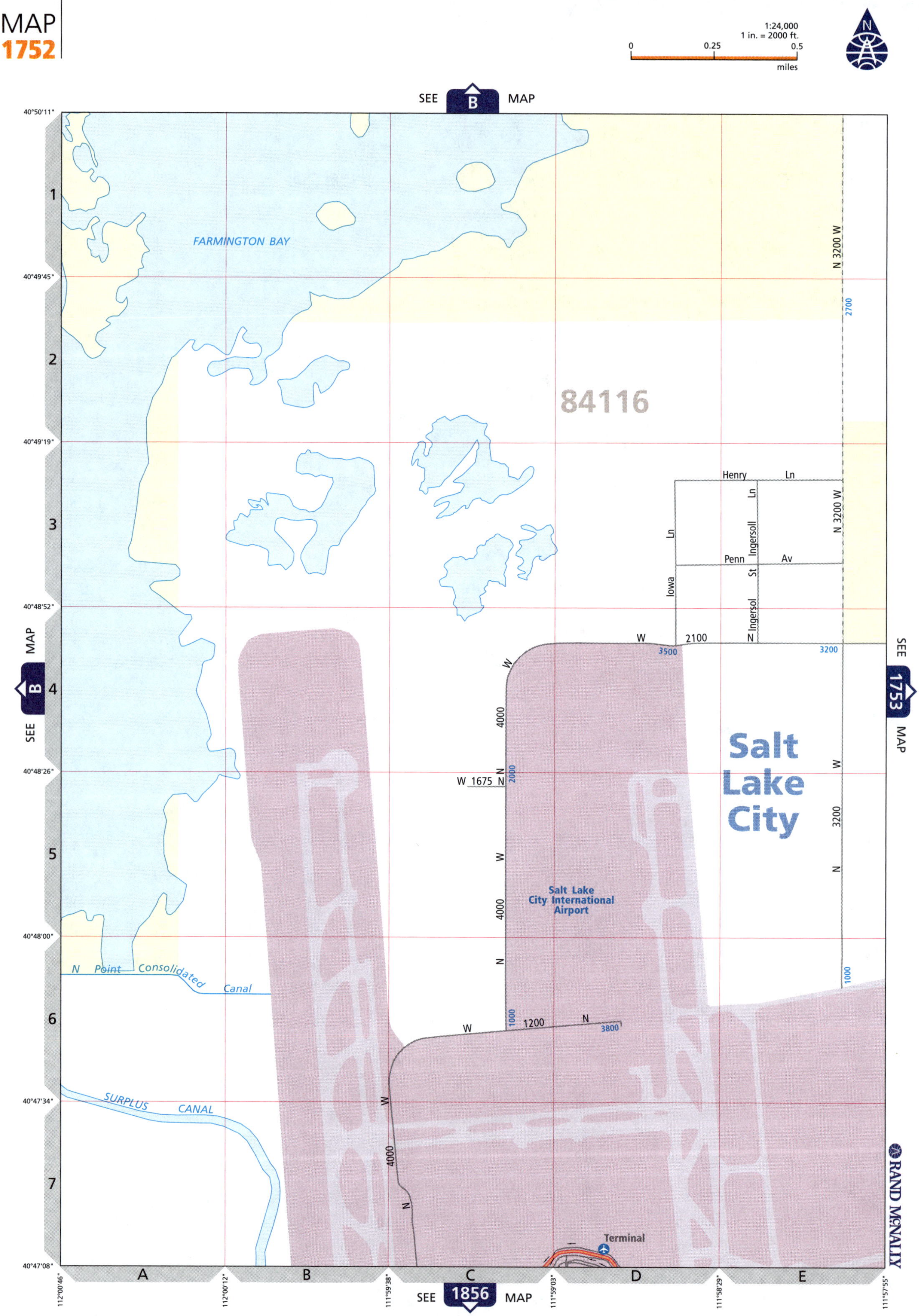

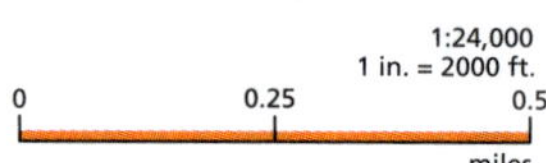

SEE B MAP

SEE B MAP

SEE 1753 MAP

SEE 1856 MAP

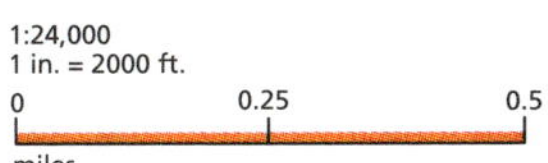

SEE 1652 MAP

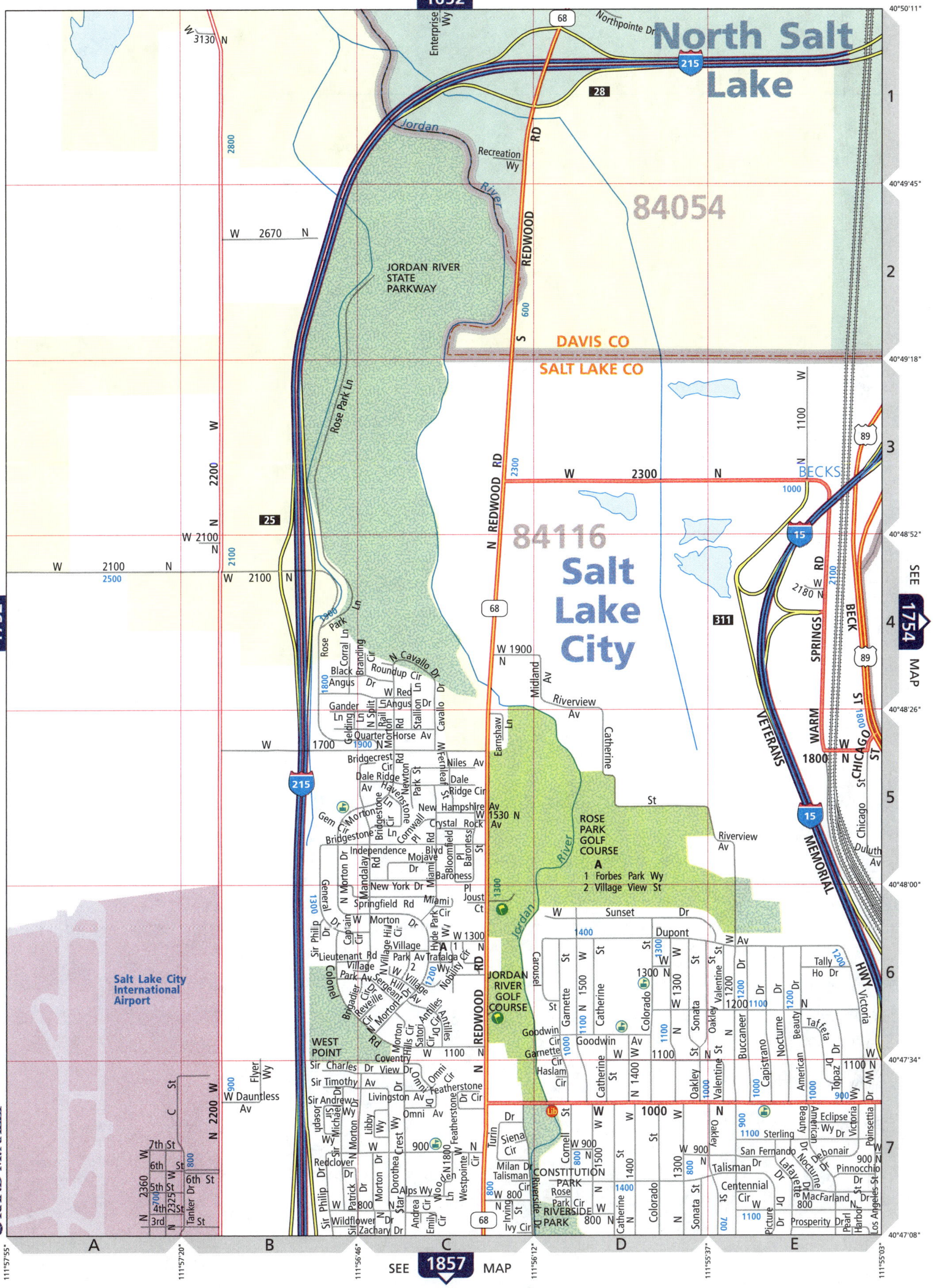

SEE 1752 MAP

SEE 1754 MAP

SEE 1857 MAP

North Salt Lake

84054

DAVIS CO

SALT LAKE CO

84116

Salt Lake City

JORDAN RIVER STATE PARKWAY

ROSE PARK GOLF COURSE

JORDAN RIVER GOLF COURSE

CONSTITUTION PARK

RIVERSIDE PARK

WEST POINT

Salt Lake City International Airport

BECKS

Jordan River

REDWOOD RD

VETERANS MEMORIAL HWY

WARM SPRINGS RD

BECK ST

CHICAGO ST

W 2300 N

W 2100 N

W 1700 N

N 2200 W

W 2670 N

W 3130 N

W 1100 N

W 1000 N

W 1800 N

1 Forbes Park Wy
2 Village View St

40°50'11"
40°49'45"
40°49'18"
40°48'52"
40°48'26"
40°48'00"
40°47'34"
40°47'08"

111°57'55"
111°57'20"
111°56'46"
111°56'12"
111°55'37"
111°55'03"

1
2
3
4
5
6
7

A B C D E

1:24,000
1 in. = 2000 ft.
0 0.25 0.5
miles

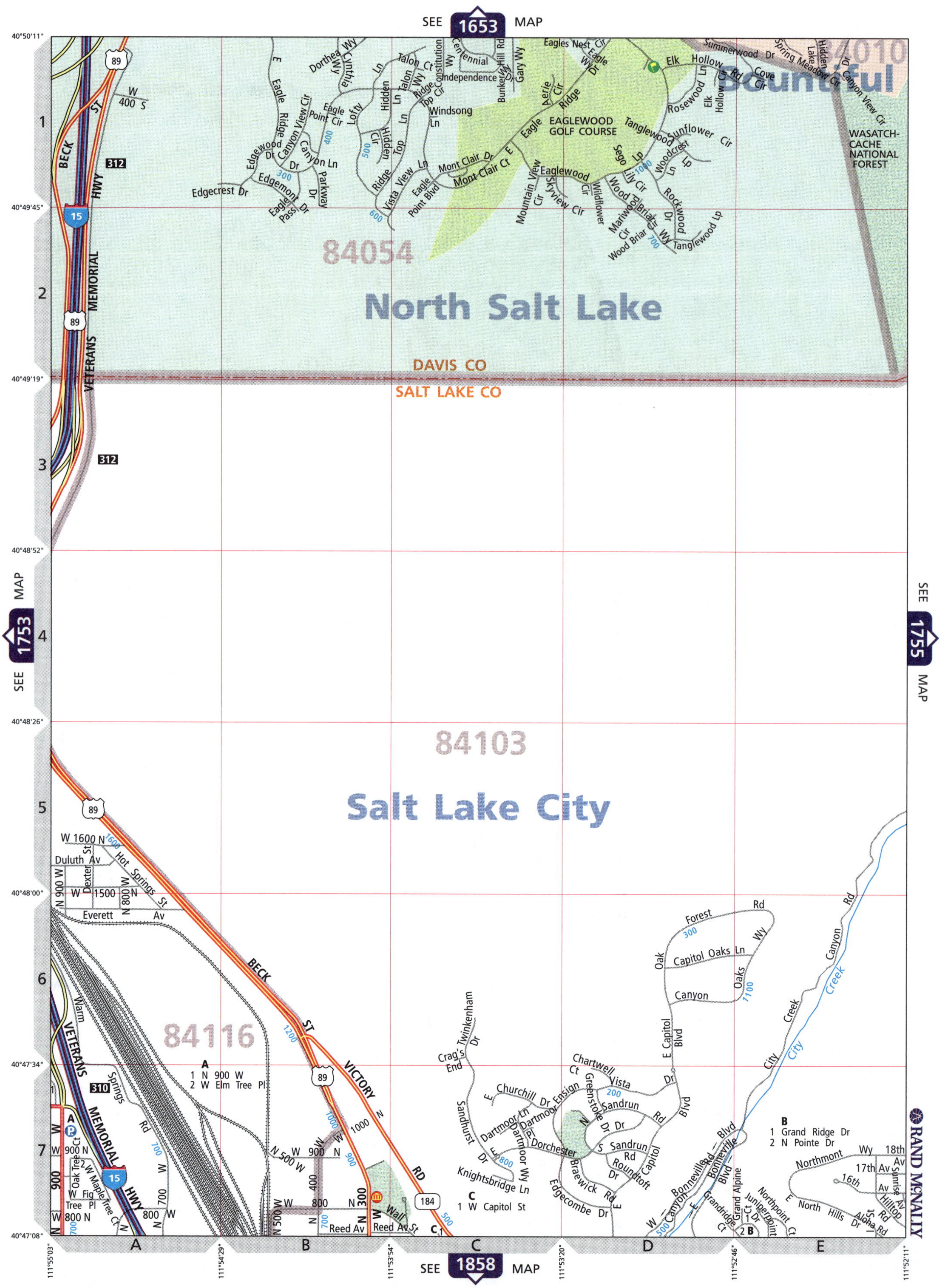

SEE 1653 MAP

SEE 1753 MAP

SEE 1755 MAP

SEE 1858 MAP

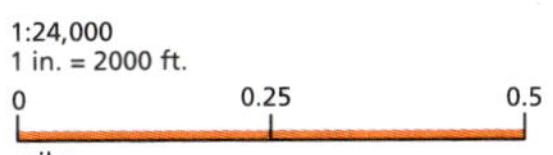

SEE 1654 MAP
SEE 1754 MAP
SEE B MAP
SEE 1859 MAP

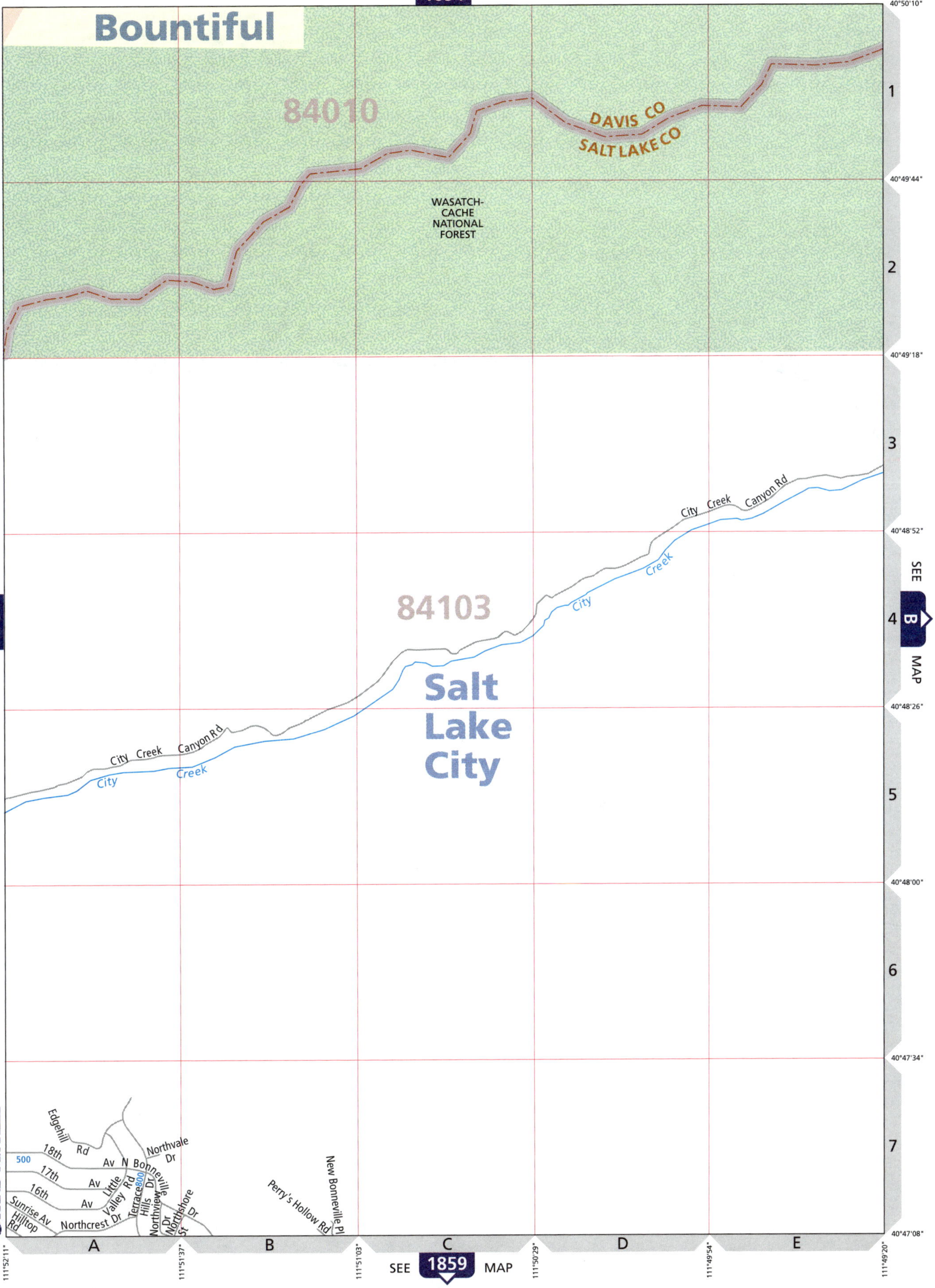

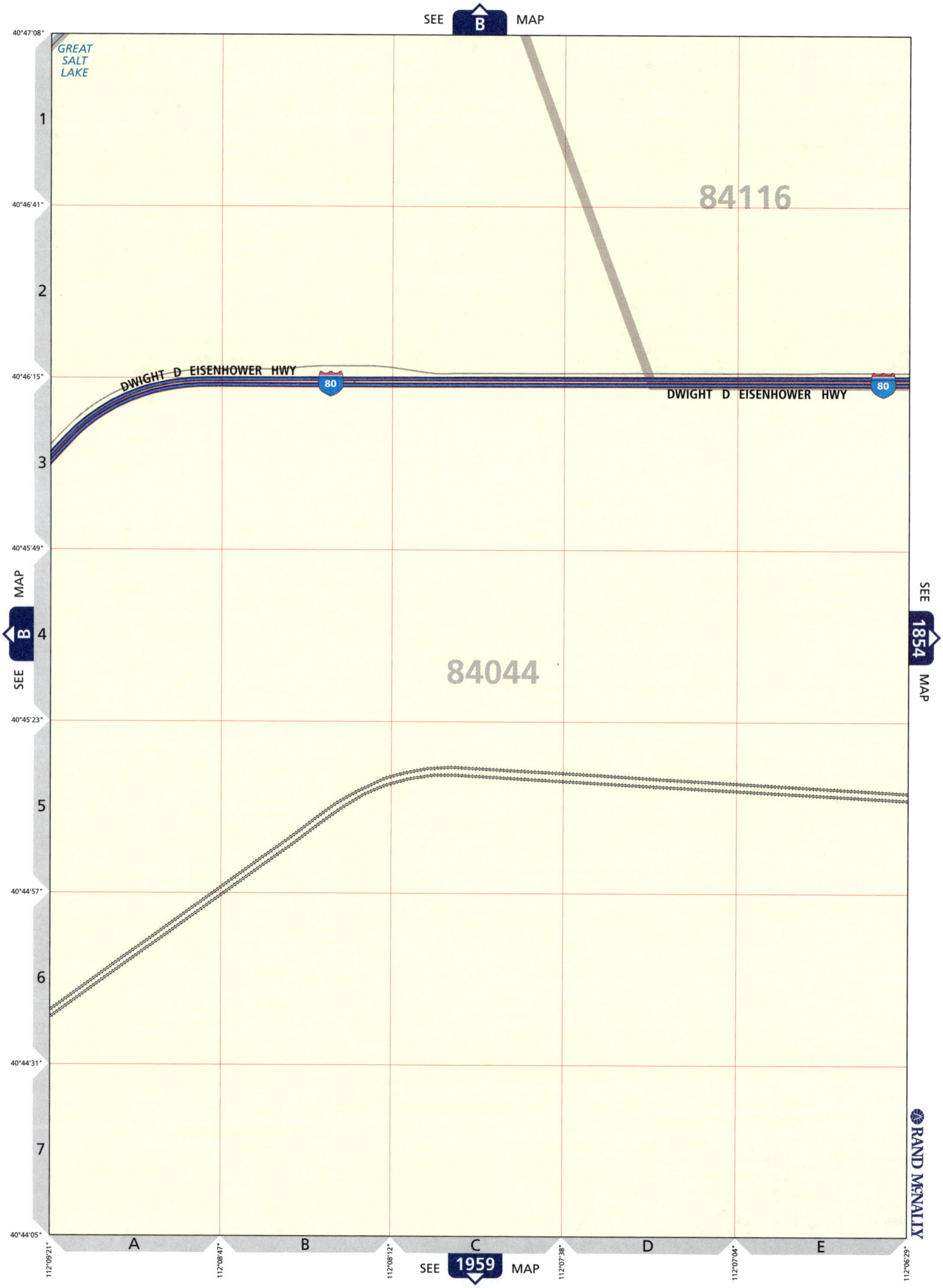

1:24,000
1 in. = 2000 ft.
0 0.25 0.5
miles

SEE B MAP

40°47'08"

GREAT SALT LAKE

1

84116

40°46'41"

2

DWIGHT D EISENHOWER HWY

80

40°46'15"

DWIGHT D EISENHOWER HWY

80

3

40°45'49"

SEE B MAP

4

84044

SEE 1854 MAP

40°45'23"

5

40°44'57"

6

40°44'31"

7

40°44'05"

A B C D E

112°09'21" 112°08'47" 112°08'12" 112°07'38" 112°07'04" 112°06'29"

SEE 1959 MAP

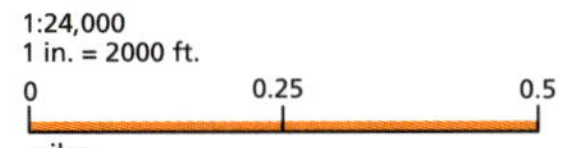

SEE B MAP

84116

Salt Lake City

80

DWIGHT D EISENHOWER HWY

111

S 7200 W

84044

W 1300 St

W 1300 S

W St St St

Garfield Av

S 8000 Arthur Busby Columbia

84104

S 7200 W

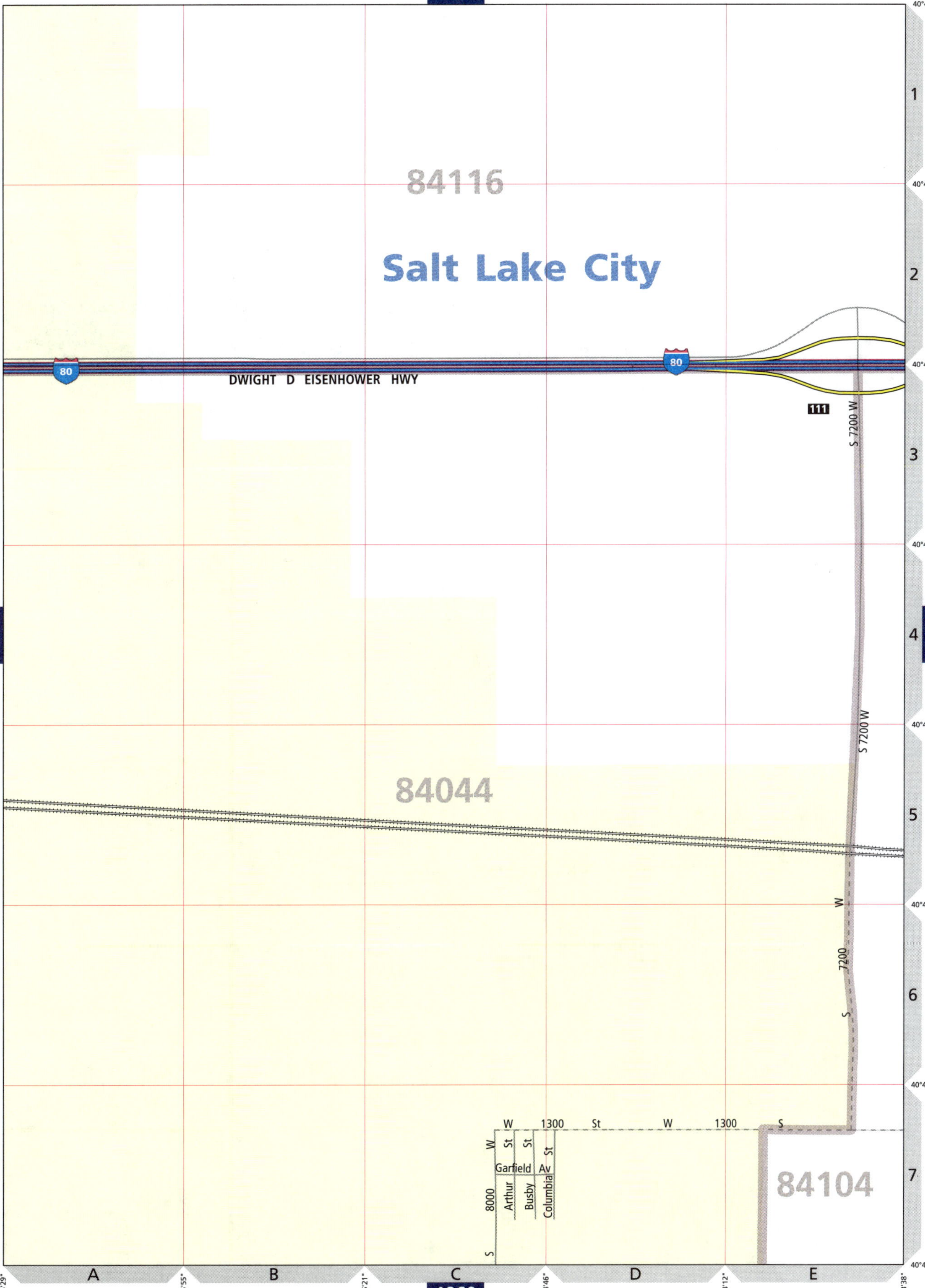

SEE 1853 MAP

SEE 1855 MAP

SEE 1960 MAP

40°47'08"
40°46'42"
40°46'16"
40°45'50"
40°45'24"
40°44'57"
40°44'31"
40°44'05"

112°06'29" 112°05'55" 112°05'21" 112°04'46" 112°04'12" 112°03'38"

A B C D E

1 2 3 4 5 6 7

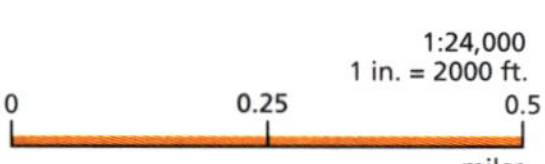

SEE B MAP

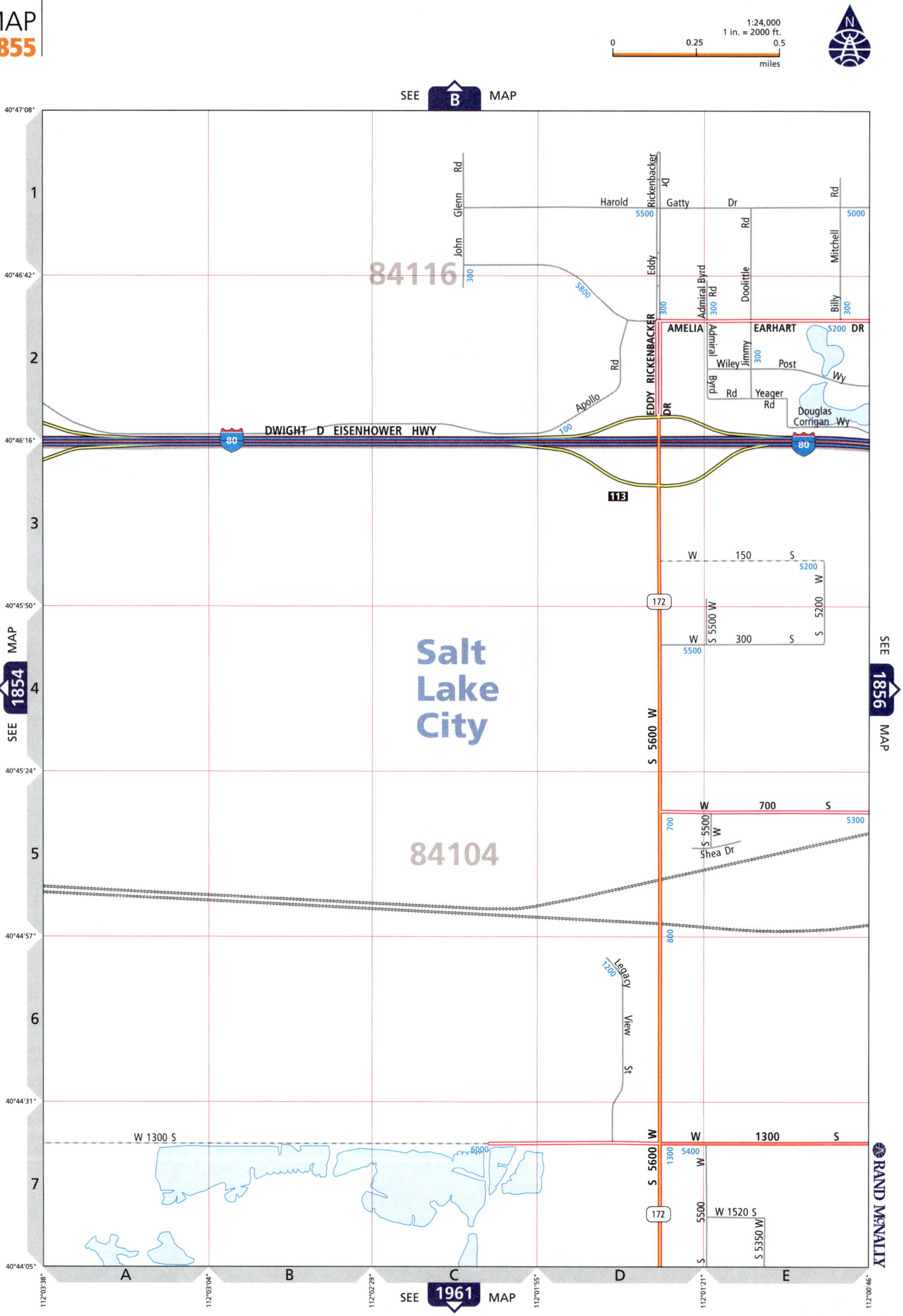

SEE 1854 MAP

SEE 1856 MAP

Salt Lake City

84116

84104

DWIGHT D EISENHOWER HWY

EDDY RICKENBACKER DR

S 5600 W

W 1300 S

SEE 1961 MAP

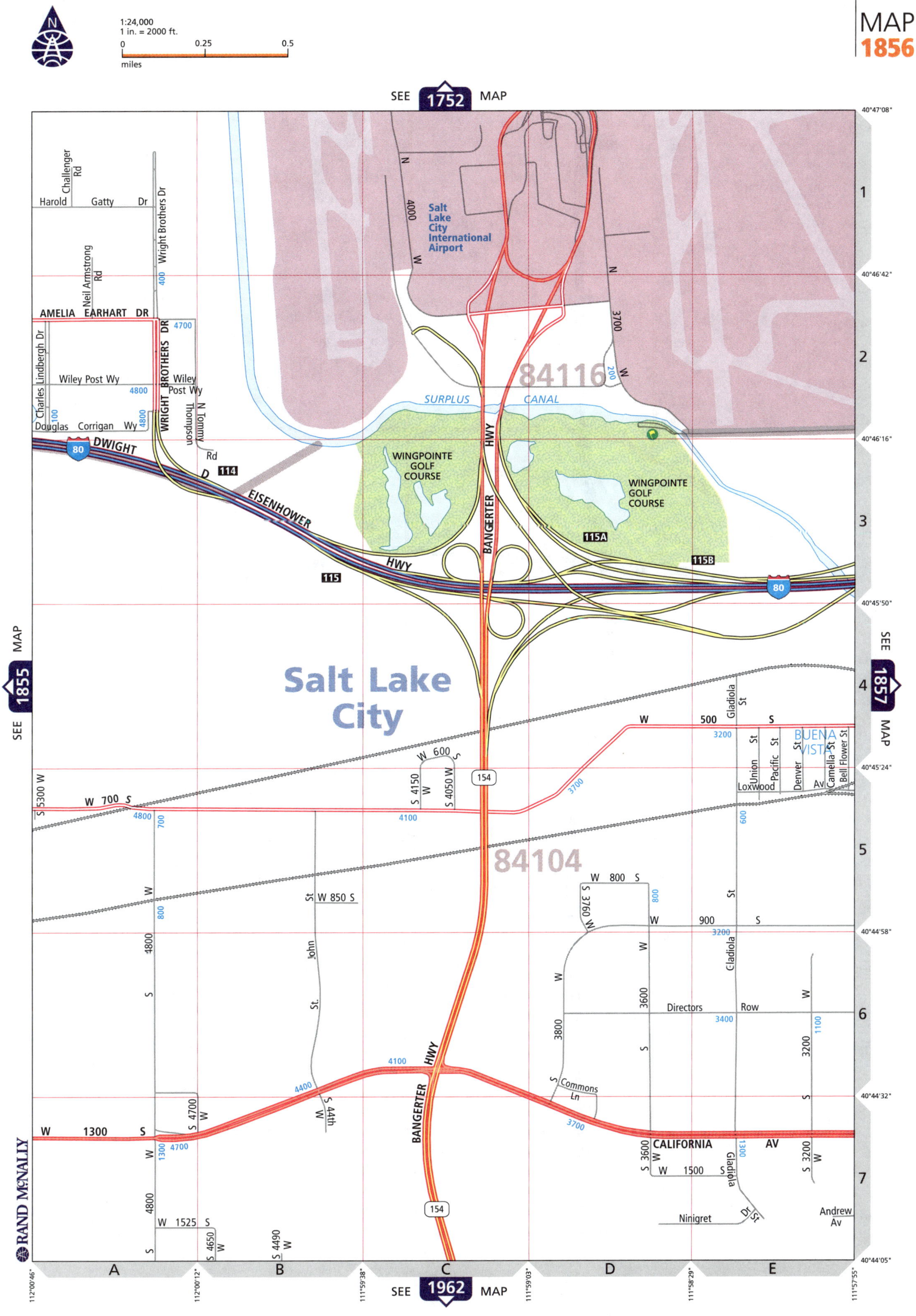

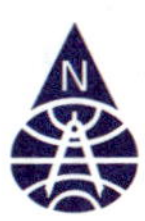

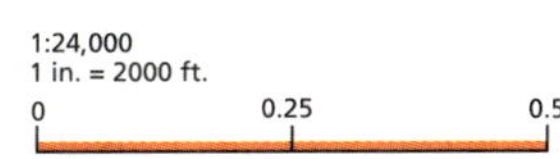

1:24,000
1 in. = 2000 ft.
0 0.25 0.5
miles
SEE 1752 MAP
SEE 1962 MAP
SEE 1855 MAP
SEE 1857 MAP
Salt Lake City International Airport
Salt Lake City
84116
84104
SURPLUS CANAL
WINGPOINTE GOLF COURSE
WINGPOINTE GOLF COURSE
BUENA VISTA
DWIGHT D EISENHOWER HWY
BANGERTER HWY
80
154
114
115
115A
115B
Challenger Rd
Harold Gatty Dr
Wright Brothers Dr
Neil Armstrong Rd
AMELIA EARHART DR
WRIGHT BROTHERS DR
Charles Lindbergh Dr
Wiley Post Wy
Douglas Corrigan Wy
N Tommy Thompson Rd
N 4000 W
N 3700 W
W 500 S
W 600 S
S 4150 W
S 4050 W
W 700 S
S 5300 W
W 800 S
S 3760 W
W 850 S
John St.
W 900 S
Gladiola St
Union St
Pacific St
Denver St
Camella St
Bell Flower St
Loxwood Av
W 4800 S
W 3800 S
W 3600 S
Directors Row
W 3200 S
S Commons Ln
W 1300 S
S 4700 W
S 44th W
CALIFORNIA AV
S 3600 W
W 1500 S
Gladiola
S 3200 W
Ninigret Dr St
Andrew Av
W 1525 S
S 4650 W
S 4490 W
4700
4800
400
100
200
3200
3700
4100
4400
700
800
600
1300
3400
1100
A B C D E
1 2 3 4 5 6 7
40°47'08"
40°46'42"
40°46'16"
40°45'50"
40°45'24"
40°44'58"
40°44'32"
40°44'05"
112°00'46"
112°00'12"
111°59'38"
111°59'03"
111°58'29"
111°57'55"
RAND McNALLY

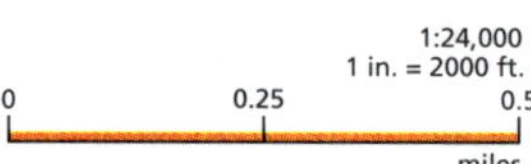

SEE 1753 MAP

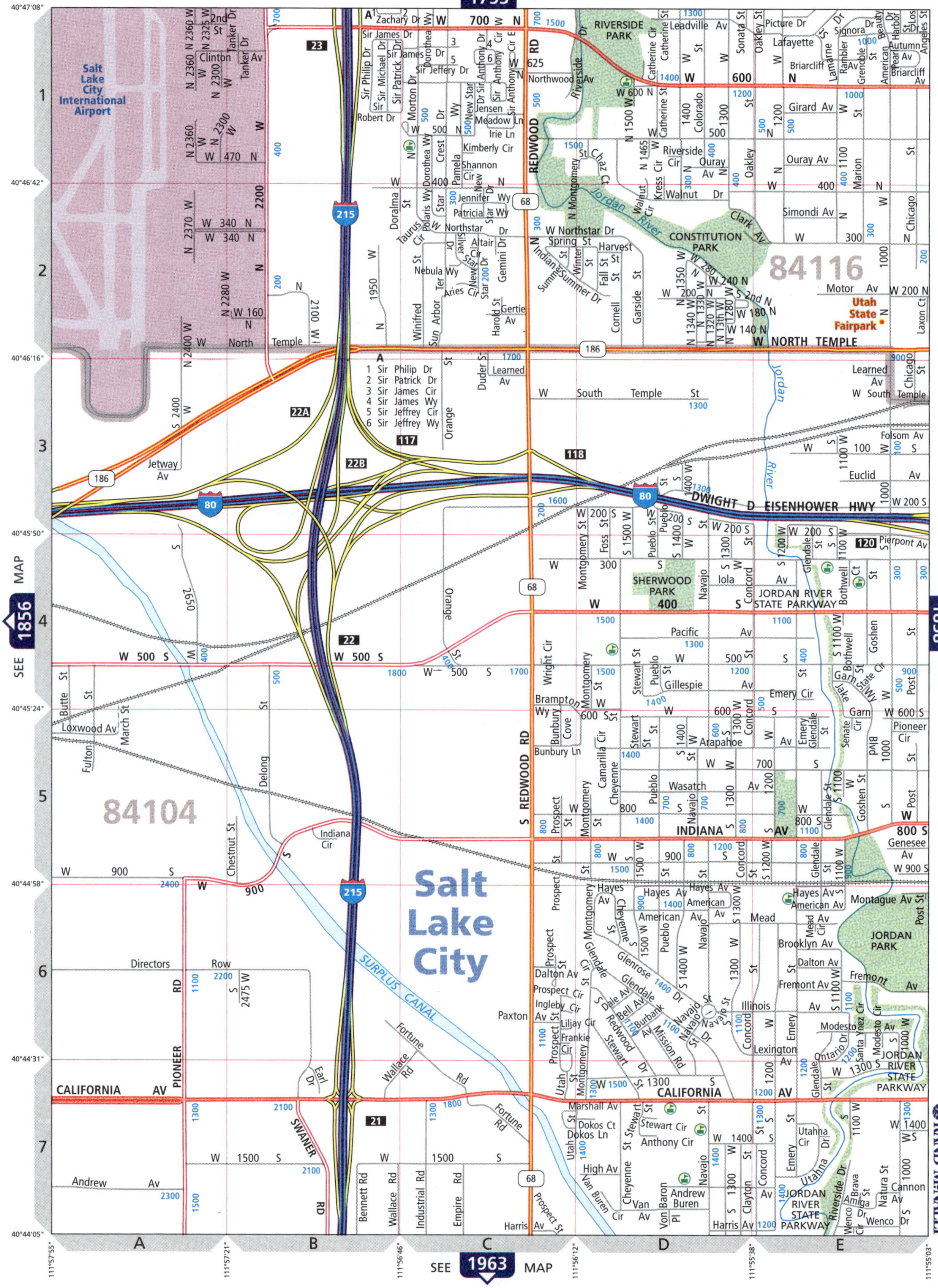

SEE 1856 MAP

SEE 1858 MAP

SEE 1963 MAP

Salt Lake City International Airport

Salt Lake City

84104

84116

RIVERSIDE PARK

CONSTITUTION PARK

SHERWOOD PARK

JORDAN PARK

JORDAN RIVER STATE PARKWAY

Utah State Fairpark

SURPLUS CANAL

Jordan River

DWIGHT D EISENHOWER HWY

W NORTH TEMPLE

W 700 N

W 600 N

W 400 S

W 500 S

INDIANA AV

W 800 S

W 900 S

CALIFORNIA AV

REDWOOD RD

S REDWOOD RD

PIONEER RD

SWANER RD

215

80

186

68

23

22A

22B

22

21

117

118

120

A
1 Sir Philip Dr
2 Sir Patrick Dr
3 Sir James Cir
4 Sir James Wy
5 Sir Jeffrey Cir
6 Sir Jeffrey Wy

1 2 3 4 5 6 7

A B C D E

40°47'08"
40°46'42"
40°46'16"
40°45'50"
40°45'24"
40°44'58"
40°44'31"
40°44'05"

111°57'55"
111°57'21"
111°56'46"
111°56'12"
111°55'38"
111°55'03"

1:24,000
1 in. = 2000 ft.
0 0.25 0.5
miles

SEE 1754 MAP

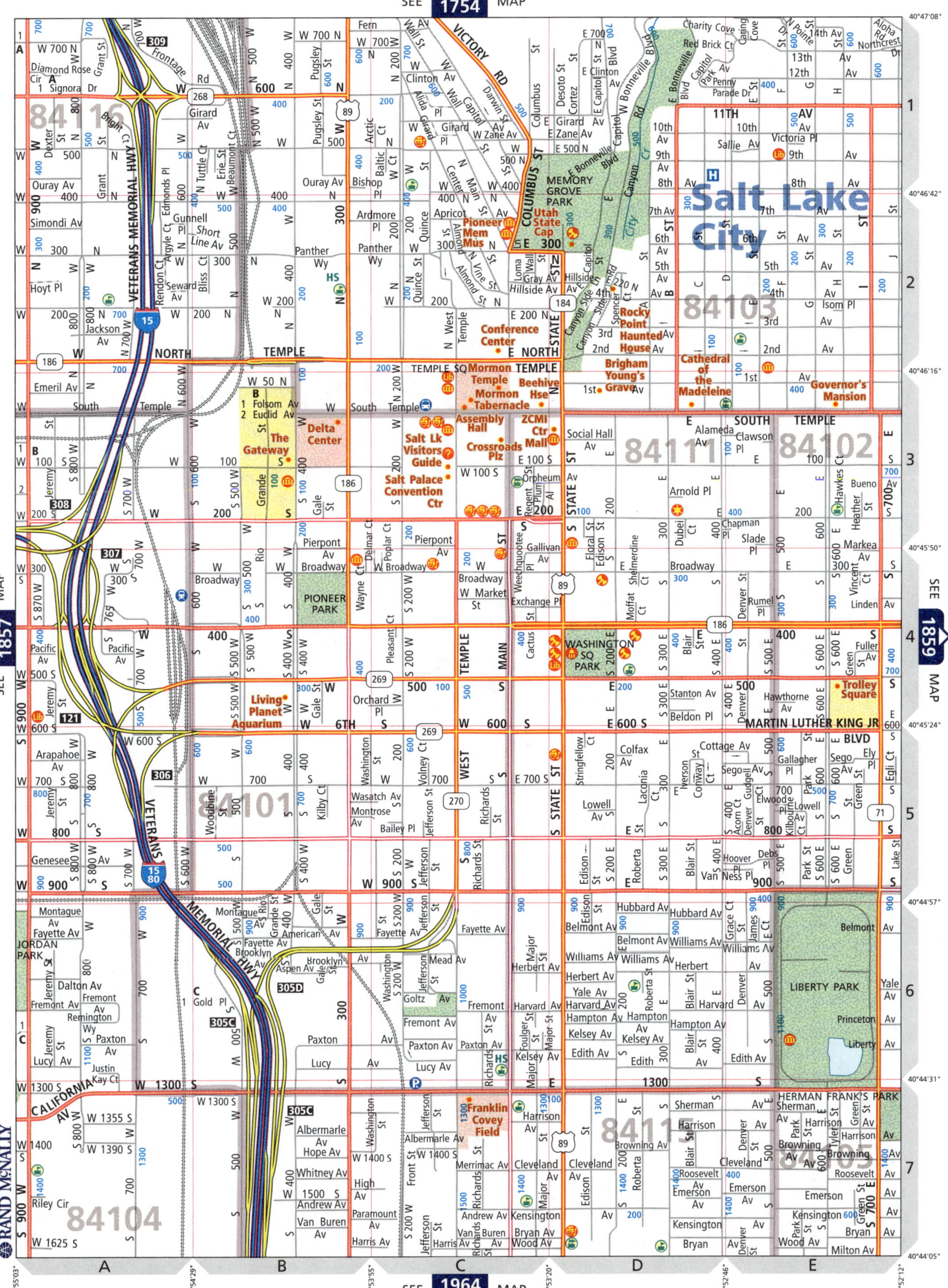

SEE 1857 MAP

SEE 1859 MAP

SEE 1964 MAP

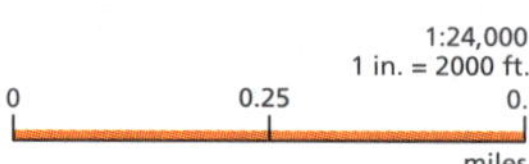

SEE 1755 MAP

Salt Lake City

A
1 New Bonneville Pl

B
1 E 415 N
2 E 385 N
3 E 335 N
4 N 930 E

C
1 S 1560 E

D
1 Campus Center Dr

E
1 Monument Park Cir

F
1 Claremont Wy

84103
84113
84112
84102
84108
84105

11TH AVENUE PARK
LINDSEY PARK
CITY CEMETERY
MT CALVARY CEMETERY
PRIMARY CHILDREN'S MED CTR
UNIVERSITY HOSP
UNIV OF UTAH
SALT LAKE REGIONAL MEDICAL CENTER
UNIVERSITY GOLF COURSE
UNIVERSITY OF UTAH
Jon M Huntsman Center
Rice-Eccles Stadium
Olympic Cauldron Park
MT OLIVET CEMETERY
VETERANS AFFAIRS MEDICAL CENTER
SUNNYSIDE PARK
THIS IS THE PLACE STATE PARK
BONNEVILLE GOLF COURSE
HERMAN FRANK'S PARK
FOOTHILL
DOUGLAS
CEM

11TH AV
SOUTH TEMPLE
VIRGINIA ST
NORTH CAMPUS DR
WASATCH DR
MEDICAL DR
CAMPUS DR
SOUTH CAMPUS DR
FOOTHILL BLVD
FOOTHILL DR
GUARDSMAN WY
SUNNYSIDE AV

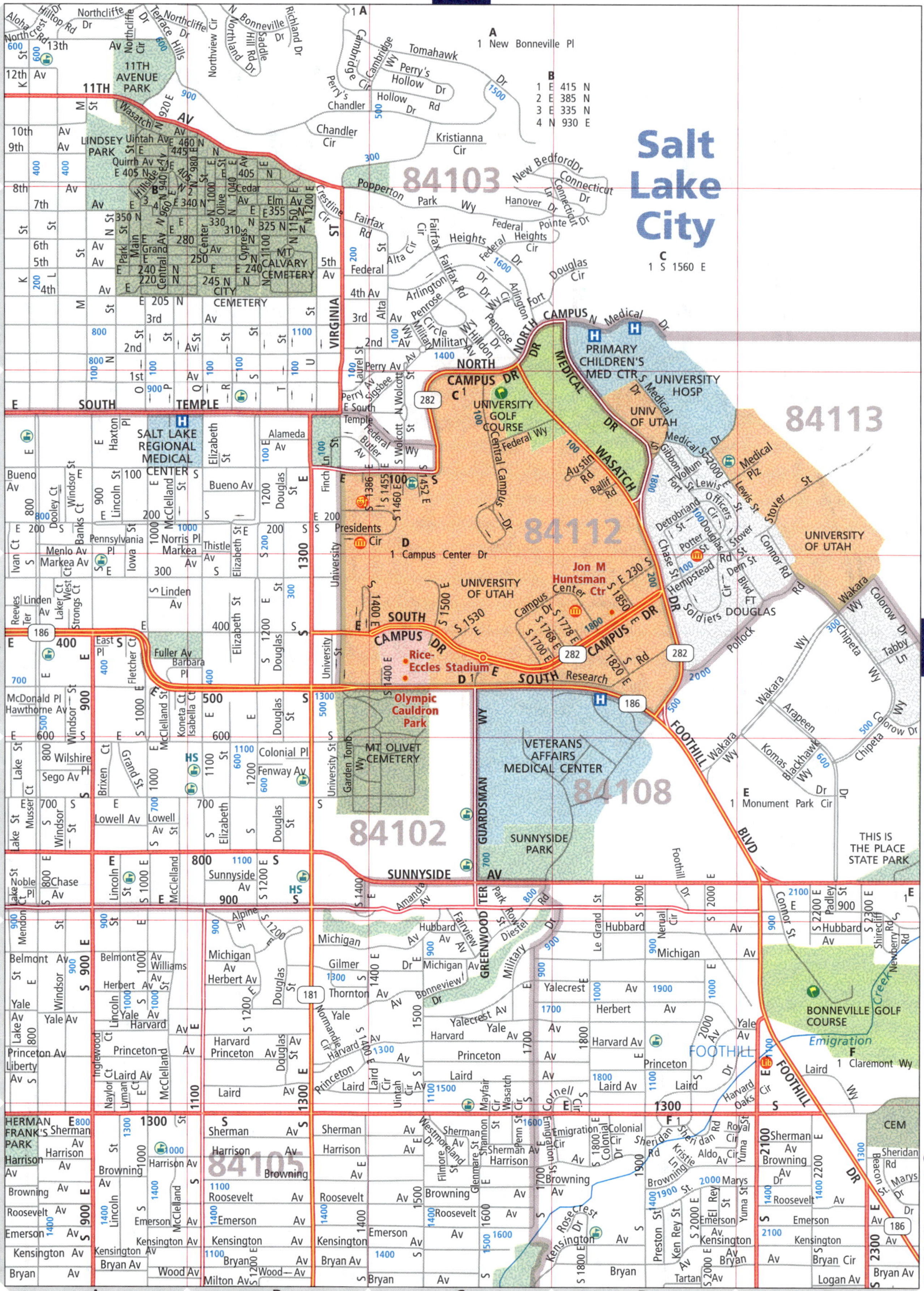

SEE 1858 MAP

SEE 1860 MAP

SEE 1965 MAP

1:24,000
1 in. = 2000 ft.
0 0.25 0.5
miles

SEE B MAP

SEE 1859 MAP

SEE B MAP

SEE 1966 MAP

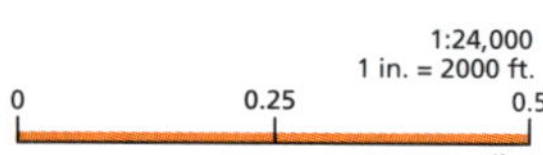

SEE B MAP

SEE B MAP

SEE 1865 MAP

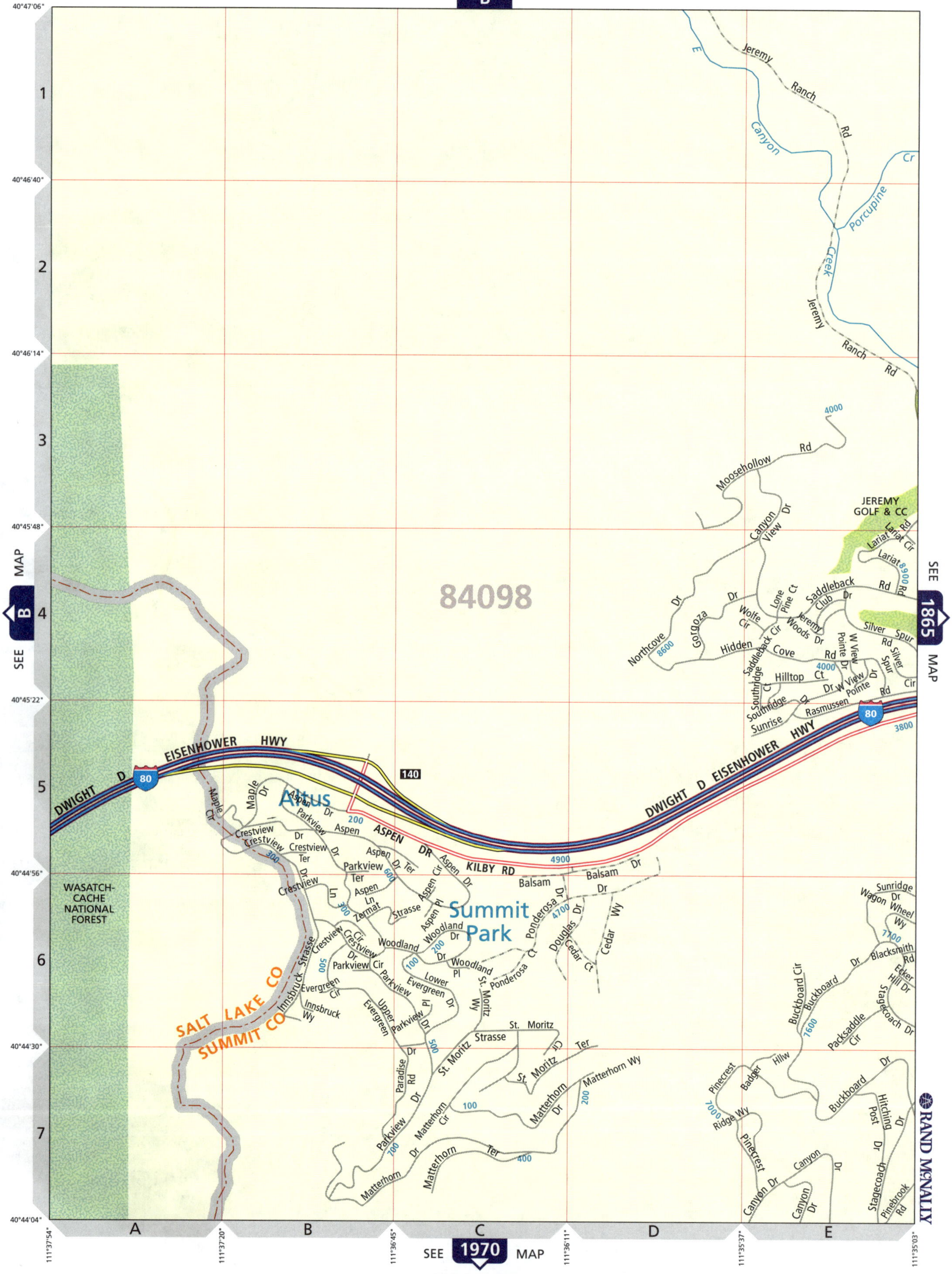

84098

Altus

Summit Park

WASATCH-CACHE NATIONAL FOREST

SALT LAKE CO
SUMMIT CO

JEREMY GOLF & CC

DWIGHT D EISENHOWER HWY

ASPEN DR

KILBY RD

Jeremy Ranch Rd
Canyon Creek
Porcupine Creek
Moosehollow Rd
Canyon View Dr
Northcove Dr
Gorgoza Dr
Saddleback Rd
Lariat Rd
Lariat Cir
Silver Spur Rd
Silver Spur Cir
Hidden Cove Rd
Hilltop Ct
Southridge Ct
Southridge Dr
Sunrise
Rasmussen Rd
W View Dr
W View Pointe Dr
Wolfe Cir
Lone Pine Ct
Club Dr
Jeremy Woods Dr
Saddleback Cir
Maple Dr
Maple Cir
Crestview Dr
Crestview Ter
Crestview Cir
Parkview Dr
Parkview Ter
Parkview Cir
Aspen Dr
Aspen Ter
Aspen Cir
Aspen Pl
Aspen Ln
Zermat Strasse
Woodland Dr
Woodland Pl
Balsam Dr
Ponderosa Dr
Ponderosa Ct
Douglas Dr
Cedar Ct
Cedar Wy
Innsbruck Strasse
Innsbruck Wy
Evergreen Cir
Lower Evergreen Dr
Upper Evergreen Dr
St. Moritz Wy
St. Moritz Strasse
St. Moritz Cir
Matterhorn Wy
Matterhorn Dr
Matterhorn Cir
Matterhorn Ter
Paradise Rd
Sunridge Dr
Wagon Wheel Wy
Blacksmith Rd
Ecker Hill Dr
Stagecoach Dr
Packsaddle Cir
Buckboard Cir
Buckboard Dr
Hitching Post Dr
Pinecrest Ridge Wy
Badger Hllw
Canyon Dr
Pinebrook Rd

SEE 1970 MAP

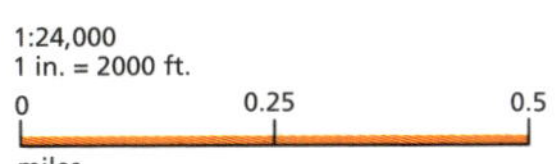

SEE B MAP

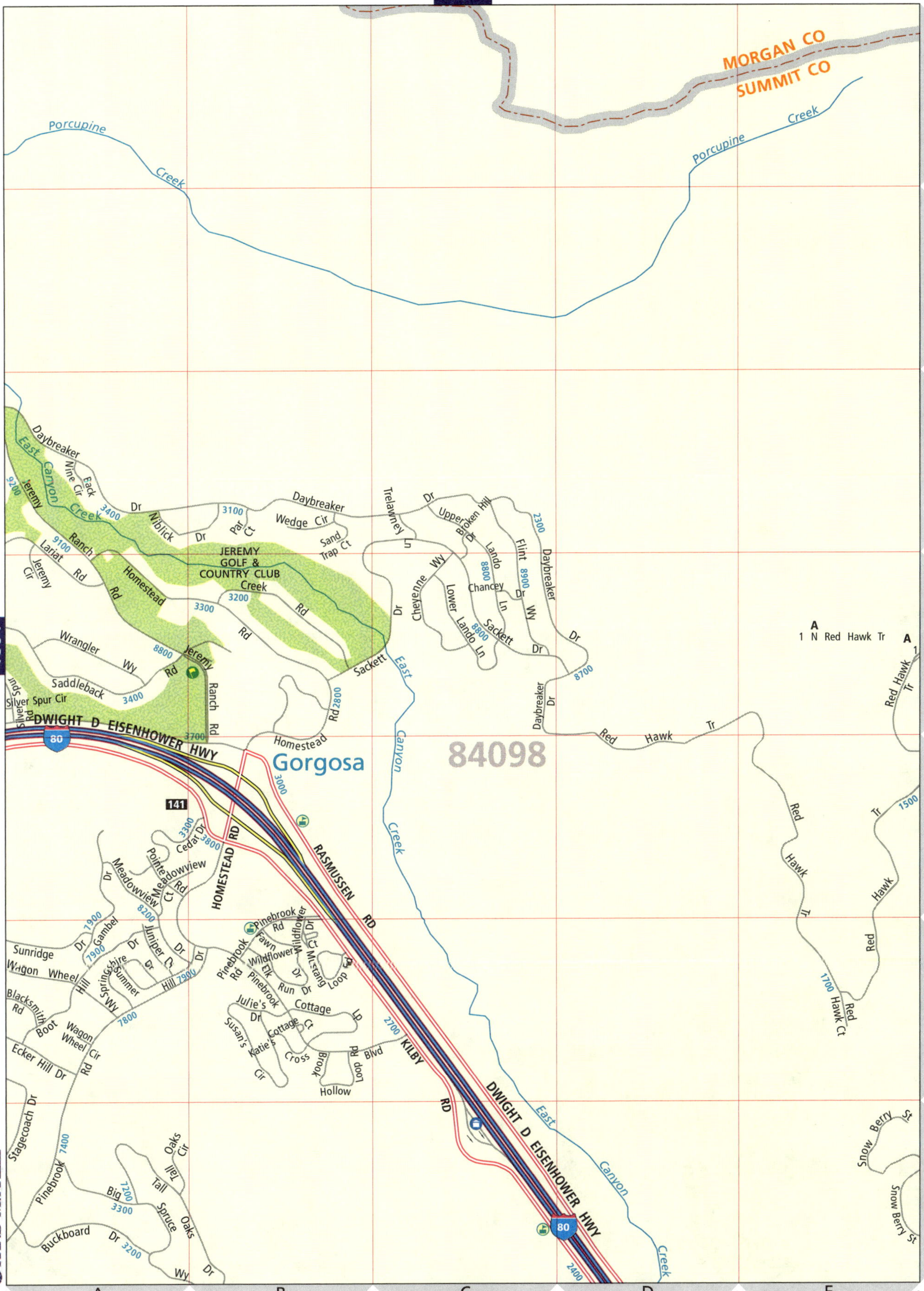

SEE 1864 MAP

SEE 1866 MAP

SEE 1971 MAP

MORGAN CO
SUMMIT CO
Porcupine Creek
East Canyon Creek
JEREMY GOLF & COUNTRY CLUB
Gorgosa
84098
DWIGHT D EISENHOWER HWY
80
141
HOMESTEAD RD
RASMUSSEN RD
KILBY RD
Daybreaker Dr
Nine Cir
Eack
Jeremy Ranch Rd
Lariat Rd
Jeremy Cir
Niblick Dr
Par Ct
Wedge Cir
Sand Trap Ct
Homestead Rd
Creek Rd
Sackett Dr
Trelawney Ln
Upper Lando Ln
Broken Hill Dr
Flint Wy
Cheyenne Wy
Chancey Dr
Lower Lando Ln
Wrangler Wy
Saddleback Rd
Silver Spur Cir
Silver Spur Rd
Red Hawk Tr
1 N Red Hawk Tr
Red Hawk Ct
Cedar Dr
Meadowview Dr
Pointe Meadowview Rd
Meadowview Ct
Gambel Dr
Sunridge Dr
Wagon Wheel Hill Dr
Juniper Ct
Springshire Wy
Summer Dr
Blacksmith Rd
Boot Rd
Wagon Wheel Cir
Ecker Hill Dr
Pinebrook Rd
Fawn Dr
Wildflower Ct
Mustang Loop
Elk Run Dr
Julie's Dr
Cottage Ct
Cottage Loop
Susan's Cir
Katie's Cir
Cross Brook Rd
Hollow Loop
Brook Blvd
Stagecoach Dr
Pinebrook Blvd
Big Spruce Wy
Tall Oaks Cir
Tall Oaks Dr
Buckboard Dr
Snow Berry St
9200
9100
3400
3100
3300
3200
8800
8900
2300
8700
3400
3700
2800
3000
3300
3800
8200
1900
7900
7800
2700
1500
1700
7400
7200
3300
3200
2400

1 2 3 4 5 6 7
A B C D E

40°47'05"
40°46'39"
40°46'13"
40°45'47"
40°45'21"
40°44'55"
40°44'29"
40°44'03"
111°35'03"
111°34'28"
111°33'54"
111°33'20"
111°32'45"
111°32'11"

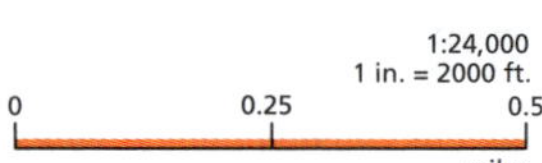

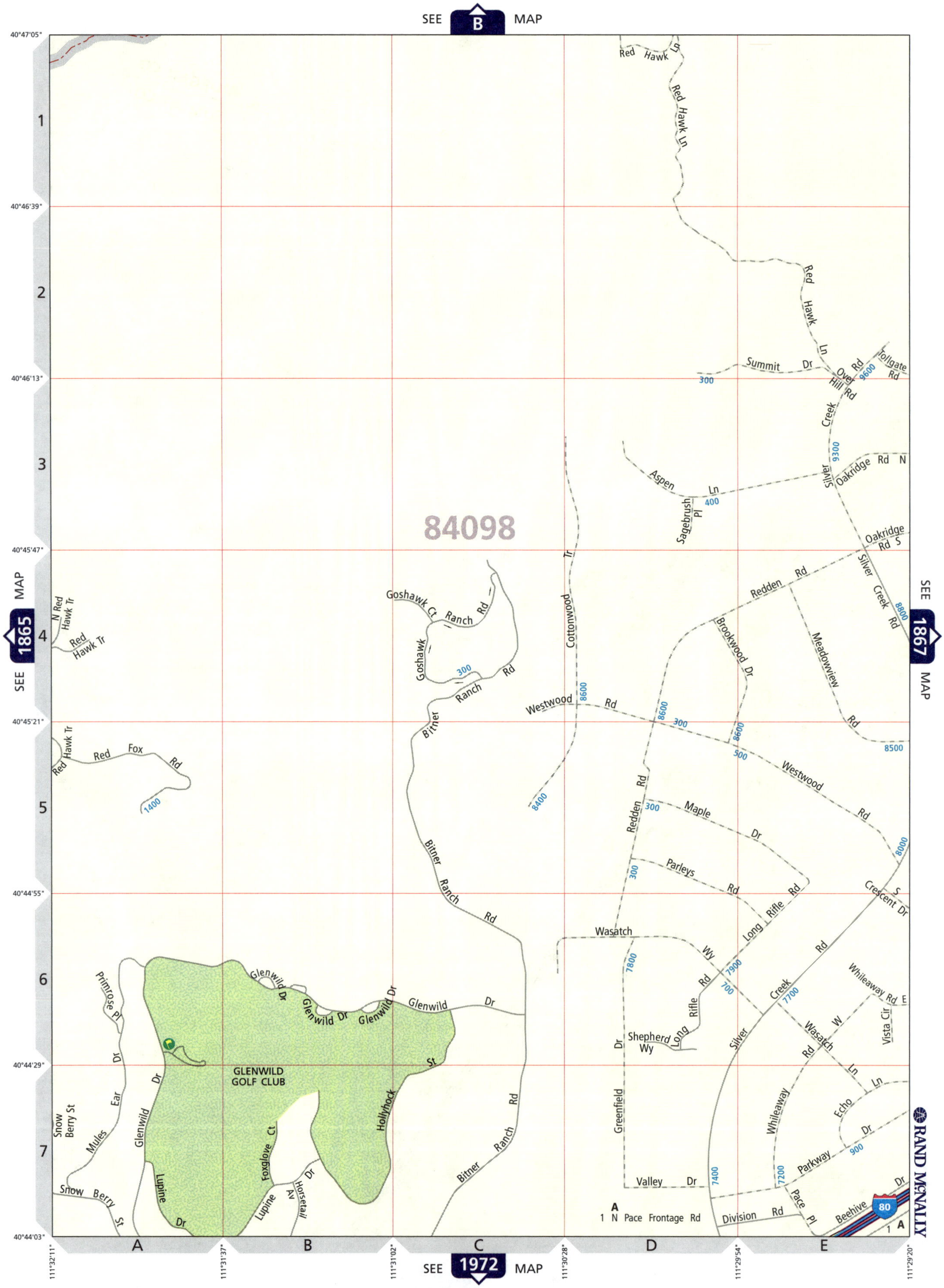

SEE B MAP

SEE 1865 MAP

SEE 1867 MAP

40°47'05"
40°46'39"
40°46'13"
40°45'47"
40°45'21"
40°44'55"
40°44'29"
40°44'03"

1
2
3
4
5
6
7

84098

Red Hawk Ln
Red Hawk Ln
Red Hawk Ln
Summit Dr
300
Over Hill Rd
9600
Tollgate Rd
Silver Creek Rd
9300
Oakridge Rd N
Aspen Ln
400
Sagebrush Pl
Oakridge Rd S
Silver Creek Rd
8800
Redden Rd
Brookwood Dr
Meadowview Rd
8500
Cottonwood Tr
8600
Westwood Rd
8600
300
8600
300
Westwood Rd
8400
Goshawk Ct
Ranch Rd
Goshawk
300
Ranch Rd
Bitner
N Red Hawk Tr
Red Hawk Tr
Red Hawk Tr
Red Fox Rd
1400
Redden Rd
300
Maple Dr
300
Parleys Rd
Long Rifle Rd
8000
Crescent Dr S
Bitner Ranch Rd
Wasatch Wy
7800
7900
700
Long Rifle Rd
Shepherd Wy
Dr
Silver Creek Rd
7700
Whileaway Rd E
Vista Cir
Wasatch W
Rd
Echo Ln
Whileaway
Parkway Dr
900
7200
7400
Greenfield
Valley Dr
Pace Pl
Division Rd
Beehive Dr
80
1 A
A
1 N Pace Frontage Rd
Primrose Pl
Dr
Mules Ear
Glenwild Dr
Snow Berry St
Snow Berry St
Glenwild Dr
Glenwild Dr
Glenwild Dr
Glenwild Dr
GLENWILD GOLF CLUB
St
Hollyhock
Foxglove Ct
Lupine Dr
Lupine
Horsetail Av
Dr
Bitner Ranch Rd

A
B
C
D
E

111°32'11"
111°31'37"
111°31'02"
111°30'28"
111°29'54"
111°29'20"

SEE 1972 MAP

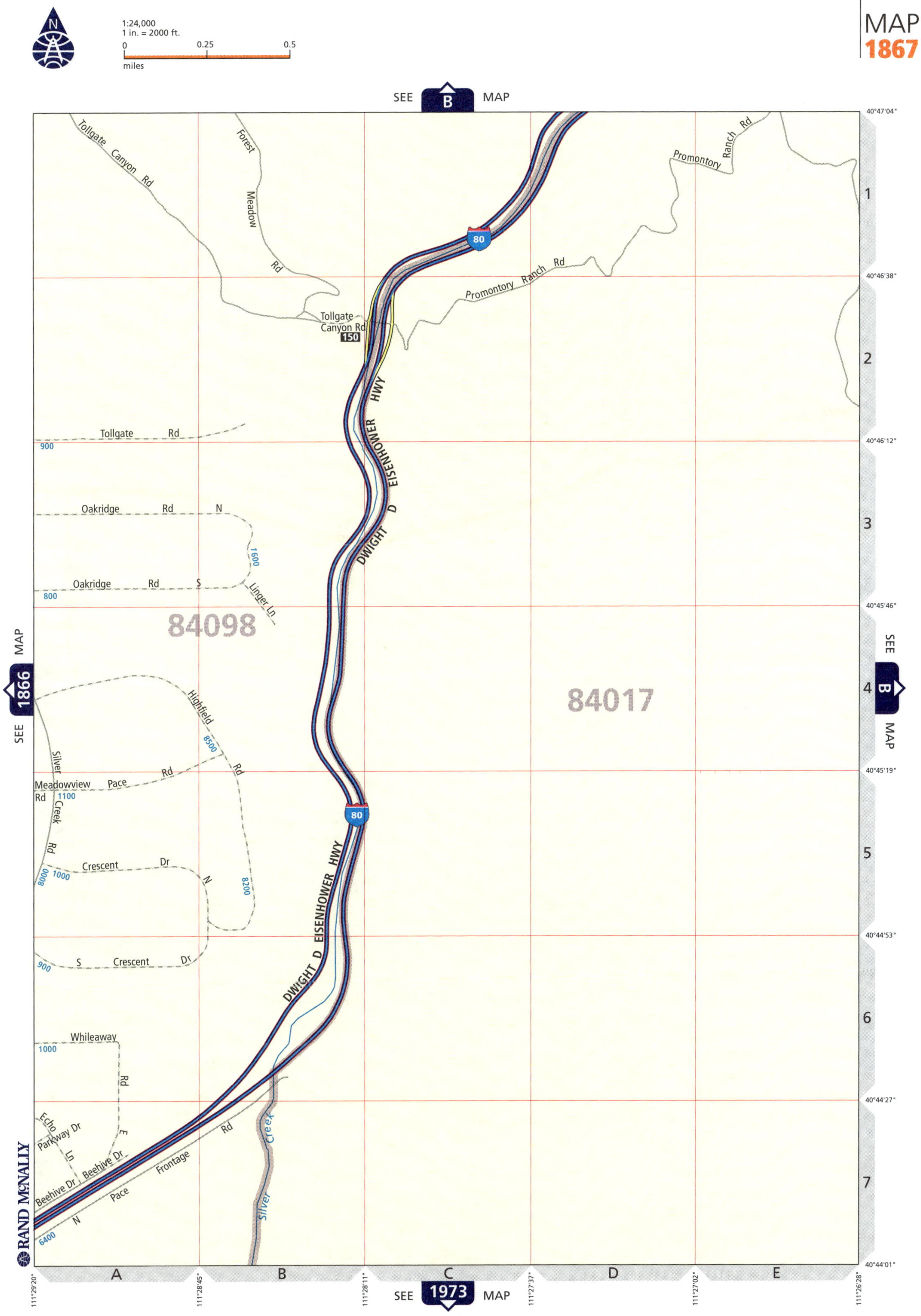

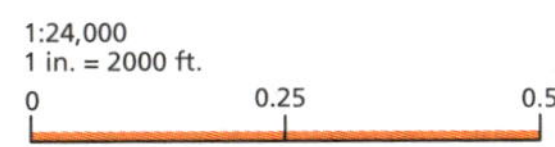

SEE B MAP

SEE 1866 MAP

SEE B MAP

SEE 1973 MAP

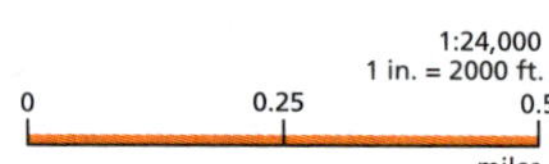

SEE 1853 MAP

84044

84006

W 2400 S
201
9400
9300
W 9180 S
2400
W 2600 S
W 2700 S
W 2760 S
W 2800 S
W 2820 S
W 2880 S
W 2900 S
W 3000 S
W 3100 S
Copper Cove Cir
W 3200 S
W 3500 S
Standard Ct
S Weir Dr
W 9200 S
S 9150 W
S 9100 W
S 9130 W
3000

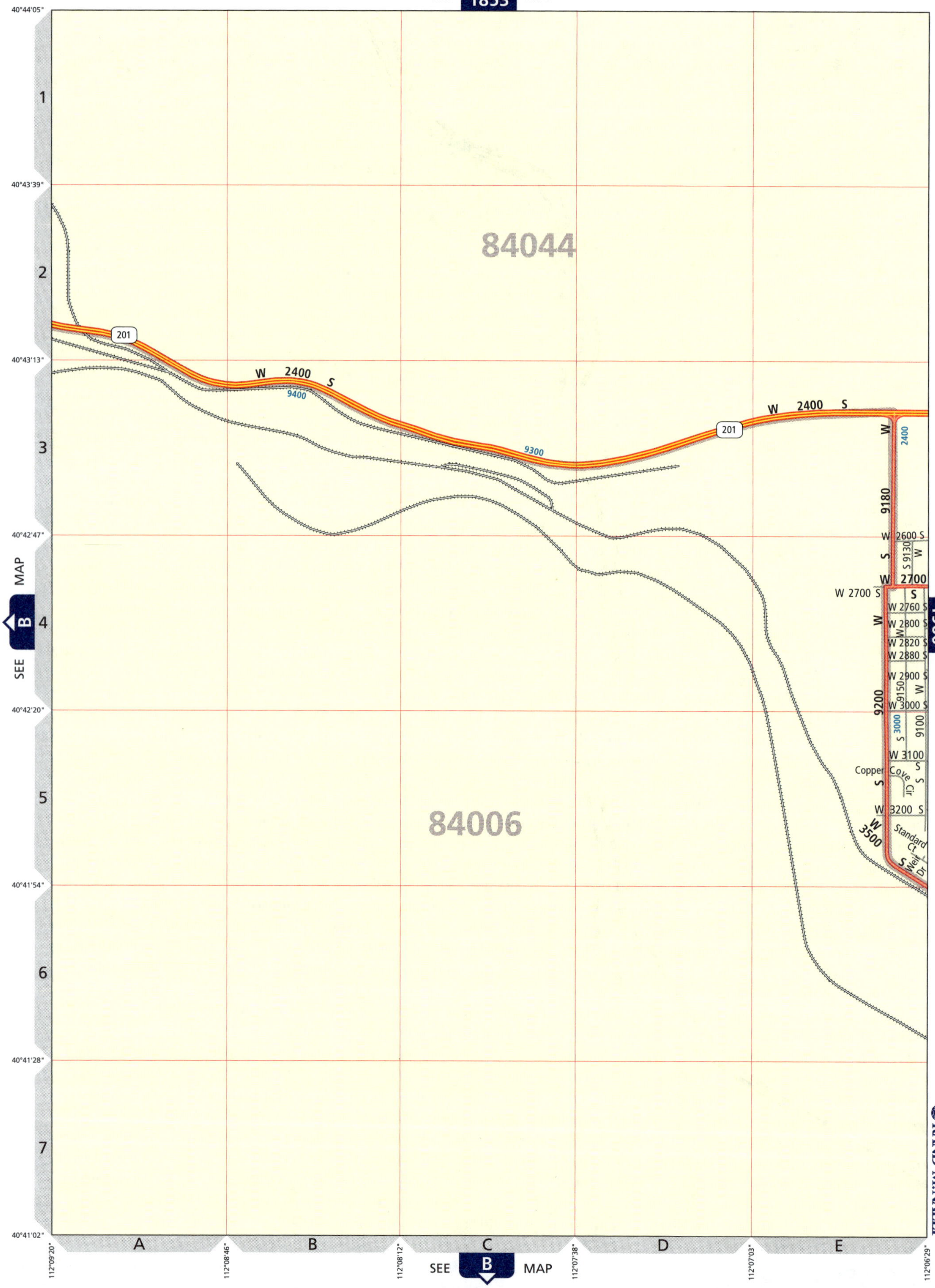

SEE B MAP

SEE 1960 MAP

SEE B MAP

1 2 3 4 5 6 7
A B C D E

40°44'05" 40°43'39" 40°43'13" 40°42'47" 40°42'20" 40°41'54" 40°41'28" 40°41'02"

112°09'20" 112°08'46" 112°08'12" 112°07'38" 112°07'03" 112°06'29"

1:24,000
1 in. = 2000 ft.
0 0.25 0.5
miles

SEE 1854 MAP

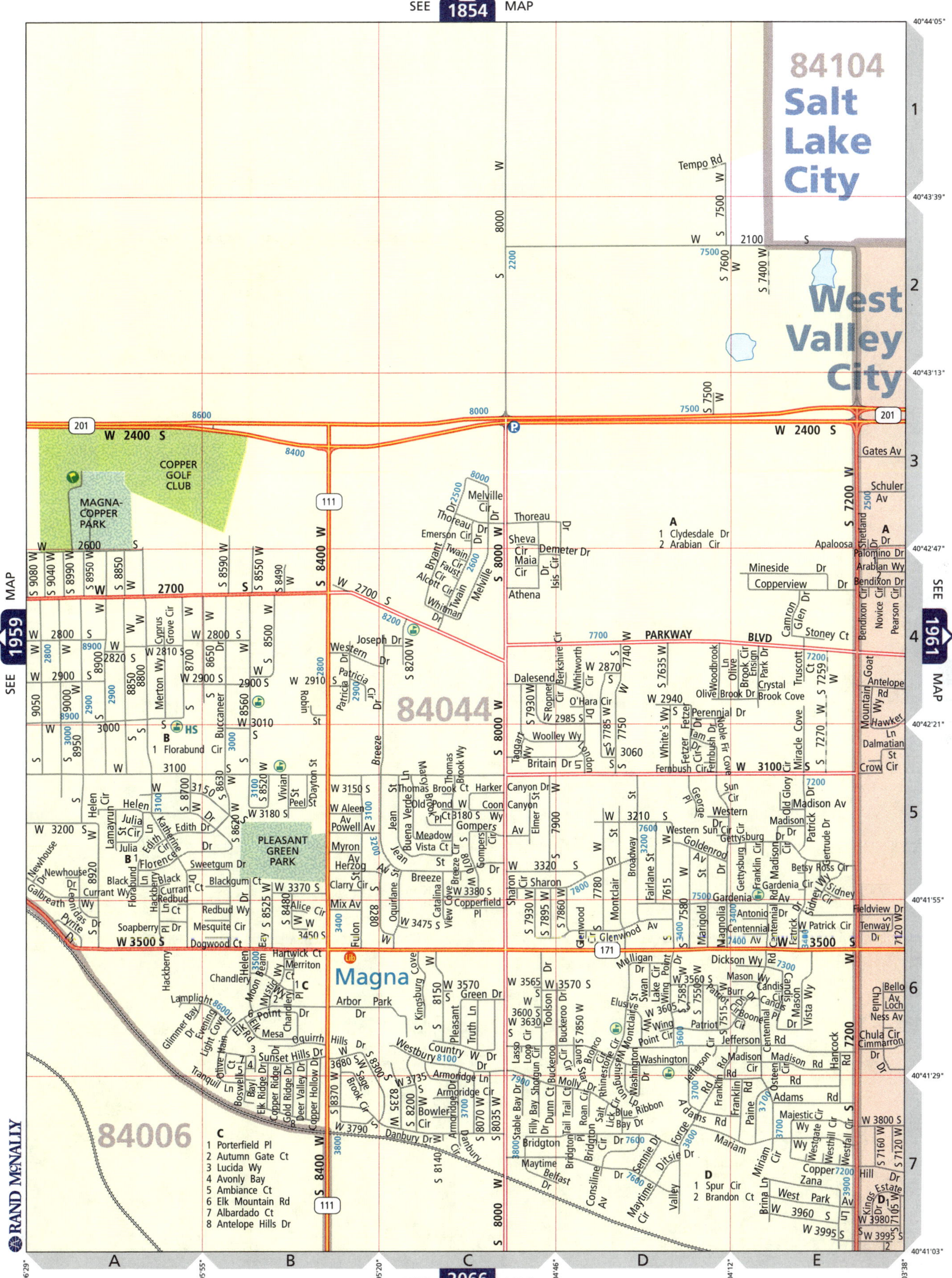

SEE 1959 MAP

SEE 1961 MAP

SEE 2066 MAP

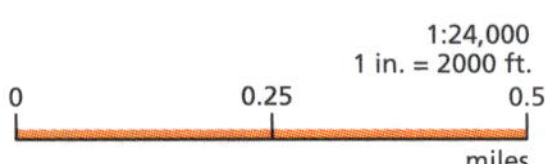

SEE 1855 MAP

Salt Lake City

West Valley City

84104

84128

84120

Rocky Mountain Raceway

CENTENNIAL PARK

HUNTER PARK

Brigham Young Mon

A
1 White Cony Cir
2 Meadow Point Ct

B
1 Summit Trail Dr
2 Summer Trail Dr
3 Lemar Wy

C
1 Ashby Dr
2 Marin Cove
3 Crichton Cove

D
1 Parkbrook Ct
2 Moshier View Cir
3 Pavant Cir
4 Stonecam Av
5 Wood Village Ct
6 Elma St
7 Markwood Ct
8 Boothill Dr

E
1 Davis View Ln

F
1 S 6880 W
2 Kings Estate Ct

G
1 S 5675 W

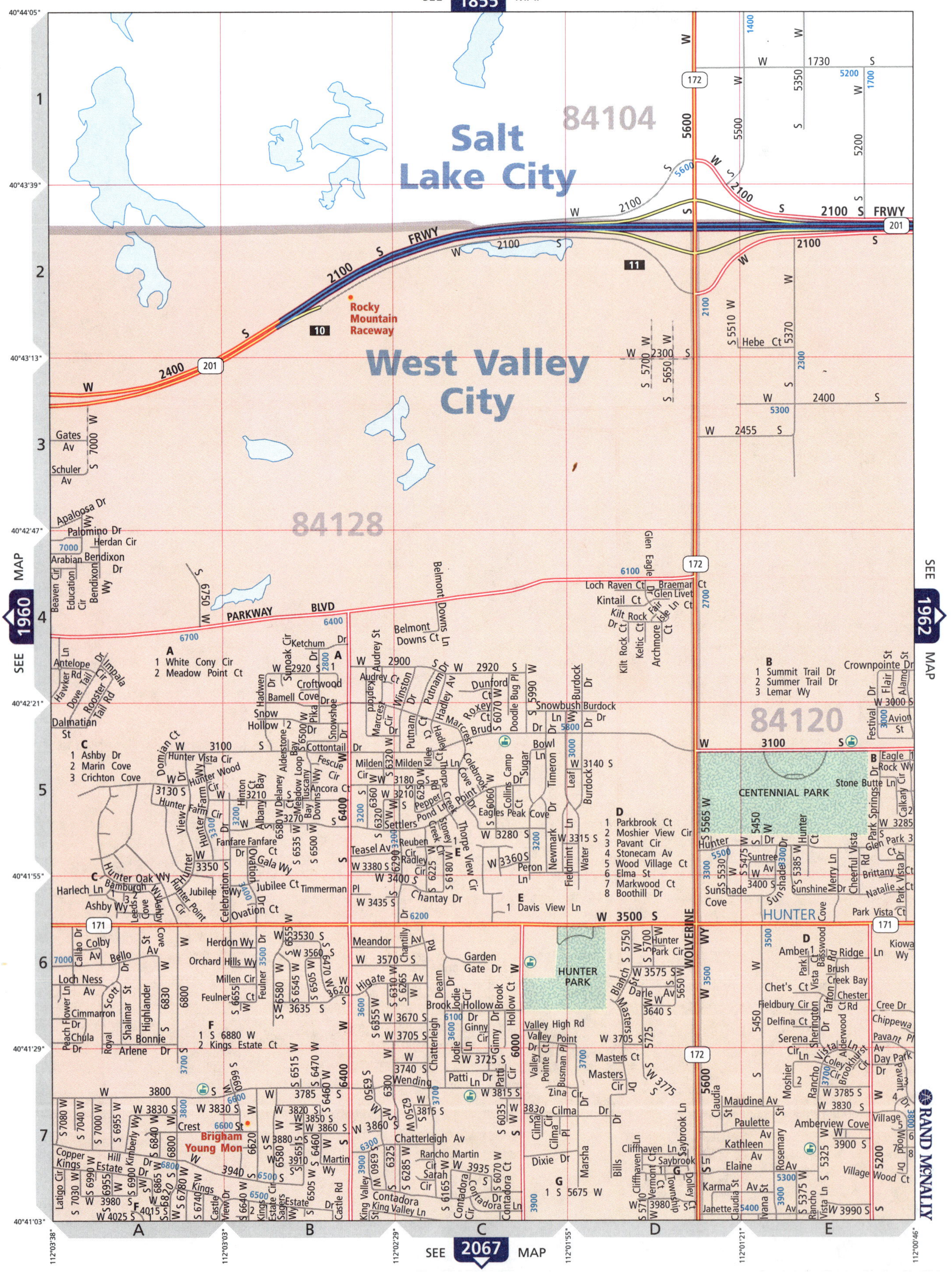

SEE 1960 MAP

SEE 1962 MAP

SEE 2067 MAP

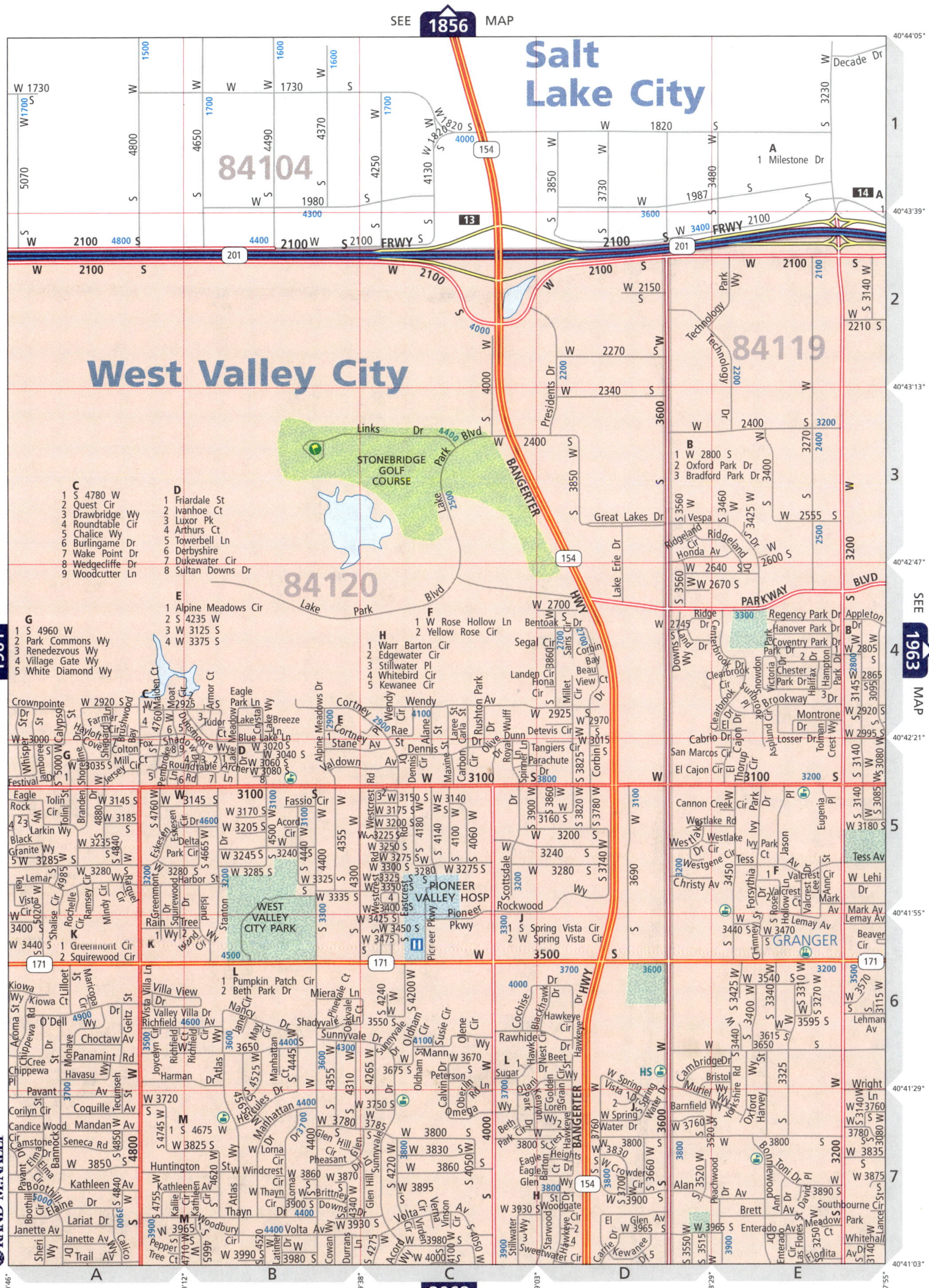
1:24,000
1 in. = 2000 ft.
0 0.25 0.5
miles
SEE 1856 MAP
Salt Lake City
West Valley City
84104
84119
84120
STONEBRIDGE GOLF COURSE
WEST VALLEY CITY PARK
PIONEER VALLEY HOSP
GRANGER
BANGERTER HWY
PARKWAY BLVD
C
1 S 4780 W
2 Quest Cir
3 Drawbridge Wy
4 Roundtable Cir
5 Chalice Wy
6 Burlingame Dr
7 Wake Point Dr
8 Wedgecliffe Dr
9 Woodcutter Ln
D
1 Friardale St
2 Ivanhoe Ct
3 Luxor Pk
4 Arthurs Ct
5 Towerbell Ln
6 Derbyshire
7 Dukewater Cir
8 Sultan Downs Dr
E
1 Alpine Meadows Cir
2 S 4235 W
3 W 3125 S
4 W 3375 S
F
1 W Rose Hollow Ln
2 Yellow Rose Cir
G
1 S 4960 W
2 Park Commons Wy
3 Renedezvous Wy
4 Village Gate Wy
5 White Diamond Wy
H
1 Warr Barton Cir
2 Edgewater Cir
3 Stillwater Pl
4 Whitebird Cir
5 Kewanee Cir
A
1 Milestone Dr
B
1 W 2800 S
2 Oxford Park Dr
3 Bradford Park Dr
J
1 S Spring Vista Cir
2 W Spring Vista Cir
K
1 Greenmont Cir
2 Squirewood Cir
L
1 Pumpkin Patch Cir
2 Beth Park Dr
SEE 1961 MAP
SEE 1963 MAP
SEE 2068 MAP
RAND McNALLY

1:24,000
1 in. = 2000 ft.
0 0.25 0.5
miles

SEE 1857 MAP

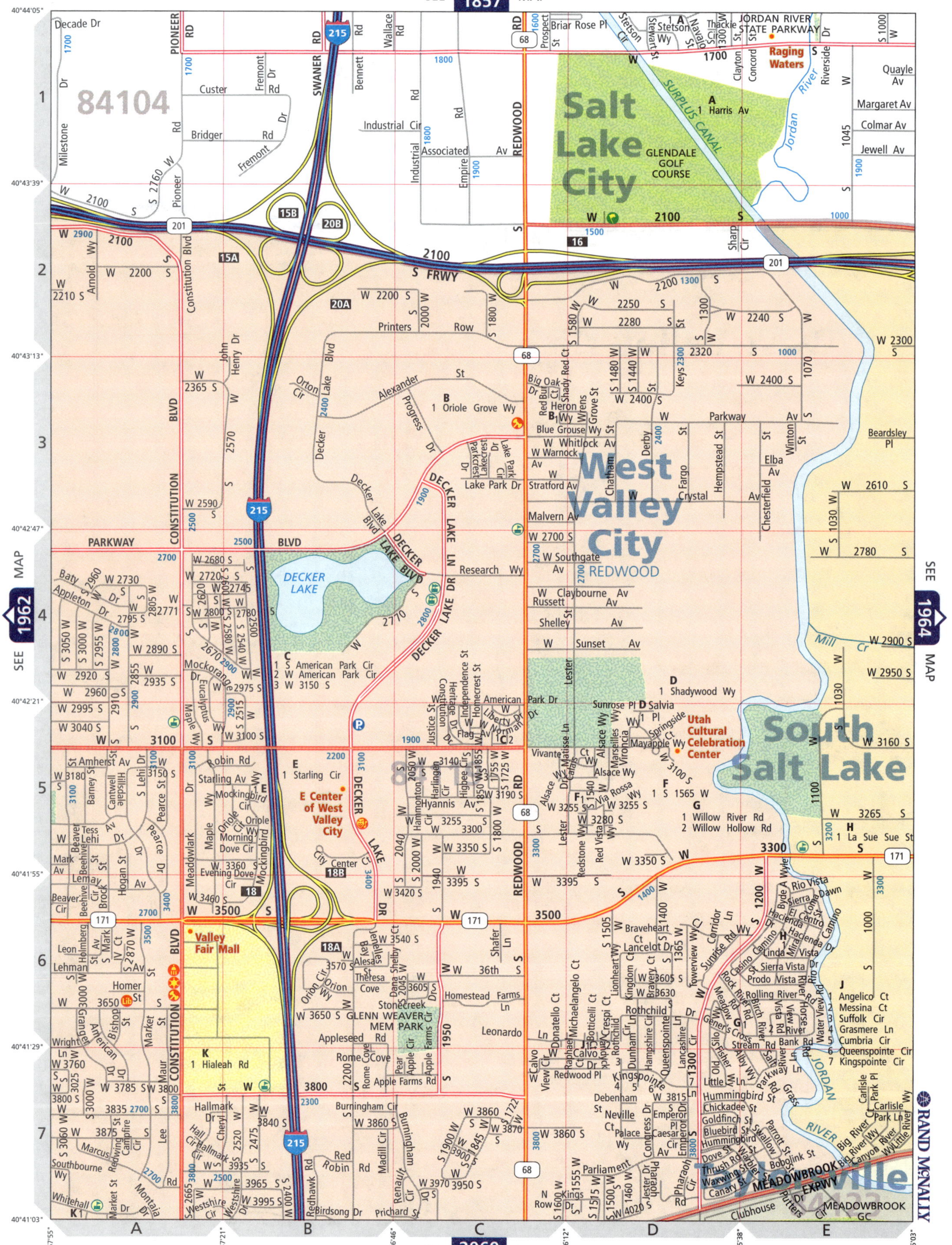

SEE 1962 MAP

SEE 1964 MAP

SEE 2069 MAP

Salt Lake City

West Valley City

South Salt Lake

84104

GLENDALE GOLF COURSE

DECKER LAKE

REDWOOD

Raging Waters

Utah Cultural Celebration Center

E Center of West Valley City

Valley Fair Mall

GLENN WEAVER MEM PARK

JORDAN RIVER STATE PARKWAY

SURPLUS CANAL

MEADOWBROOK EXPWY

MEADOWBROOK GC

A 1 Harris Av

B 1 Oriole Grove Wy

C 1 S American Park Cir
2 W American Park Cir
3 W 3150 S

D 1 Shadywood Wy

E 1 Starling Cir

F 1 S 1565 W

G 1 Willow River Rd
2 Willow Hollow Rd

H 1 La Sue Sue St

J 1 Angelico Ct
2 Messina Ct
3 Suffolk Cir
4 Grasmere Ln
5 Cumbria Cir
6 Queenspointe Cir
7 Kingspointe Cir

K 1 Hialeah Rd

1:24,000
1 in. = 2000 ft.
0 0.25 0.5
miles

SEE 1858 MAP

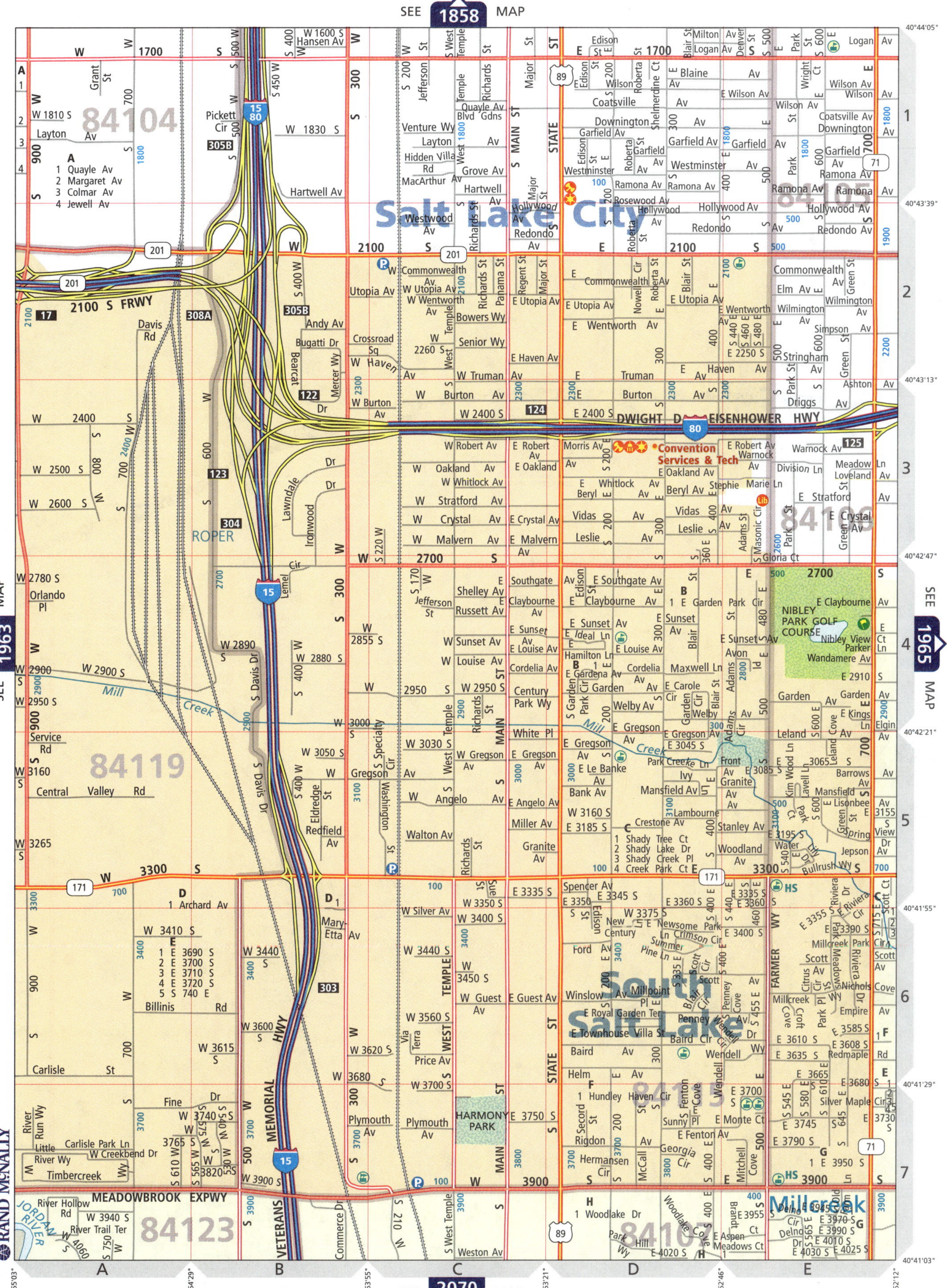

40°44'05"
40°43'39"
40°43'13"
40°42'47"
40°42'21"
40°41'55"
40°41'29"
40°41'03"
111°55'03"
111°54'29"
111°53'55"
111°53'21"
111°52'46"
111°52'12"

SEE 1963 MAP

SEE 1965 MAP

SEE 2070 MAP

1:24,000
1 in. = 2000 ft.
0 0.25 0.5
miles

SEE 1859 MAP

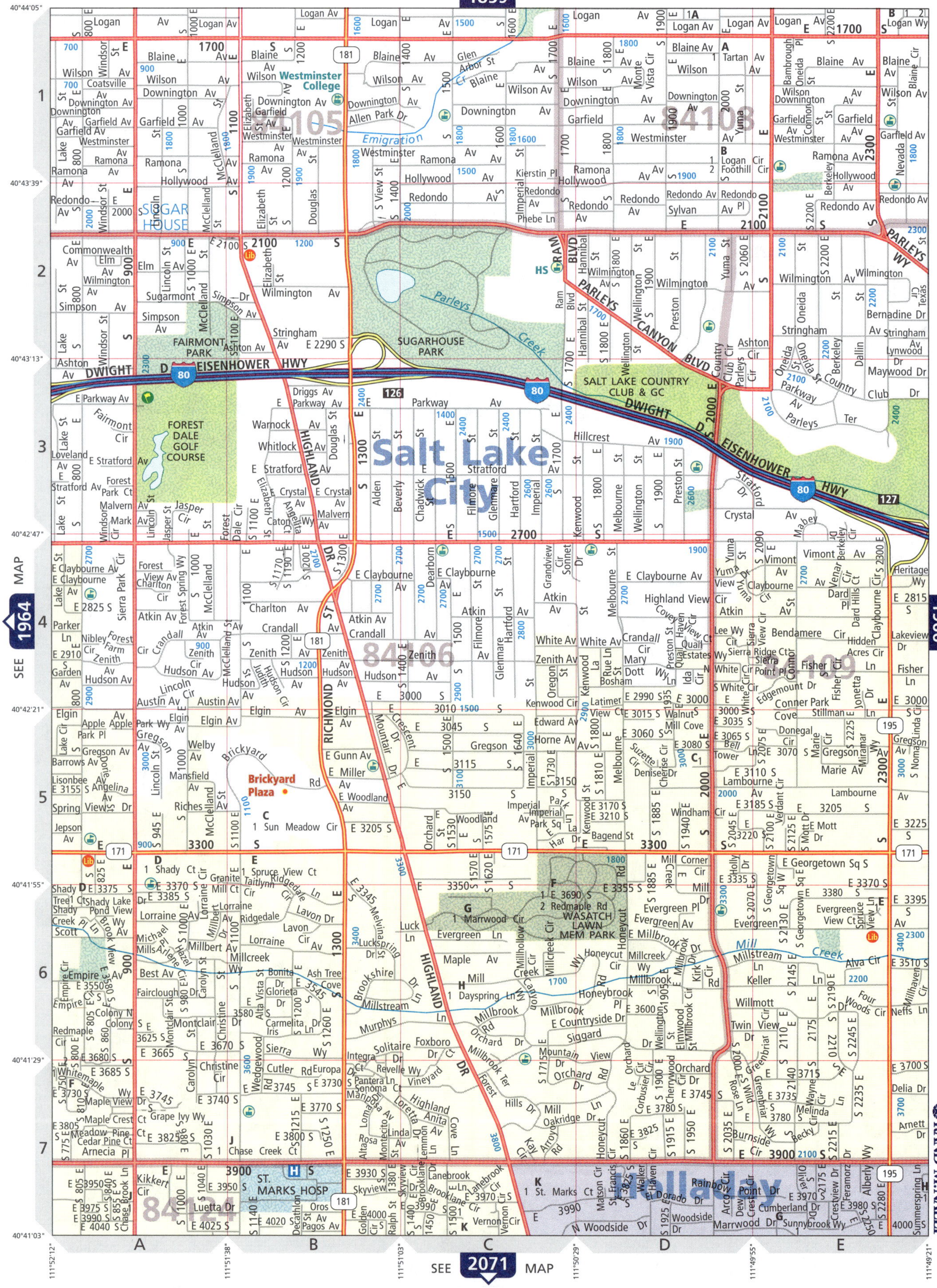

40°44'05" 40°43'39" 40°43'13" 40°42'47" 40°42'21" 40°41'55" 40°41'29" 40°41'03"

1 2 3 4 5 6 7

Westminster College
SUGAR HOUSE
FAIRMONT PARK
SUGARHOUSE PARK
DWIGHT D EISENHOWER HWY
SALT LAKE COUNTRY CLUB & GC
FOREST DALE GOLF COURSE
Salt Lake City
HIGHLAND DR
RICHMOND ST
PARLEYS CANYON BLVD
Brickyard Plaza
WASATCH LAWN MEM PARK
Mill Creek
Parleys Creek
Emigration
ST. MARKS HOSP
Holladay
84105 84108 84106 84109 84124

SEE 1964 MAP

SEE 1966 MAP

A B C D E

111°52'12" 111°51'38" 111°51'03" 111°50'29" 111°49'55" 111°49'21"

SEE 2071 MAP

1:24,000
1 in. = 2000 ft.
0 0.25 0.5
miles

SEE 1860 MAP

SEE 1965 MAP
SEE B MAP
SEE 2072 MAP

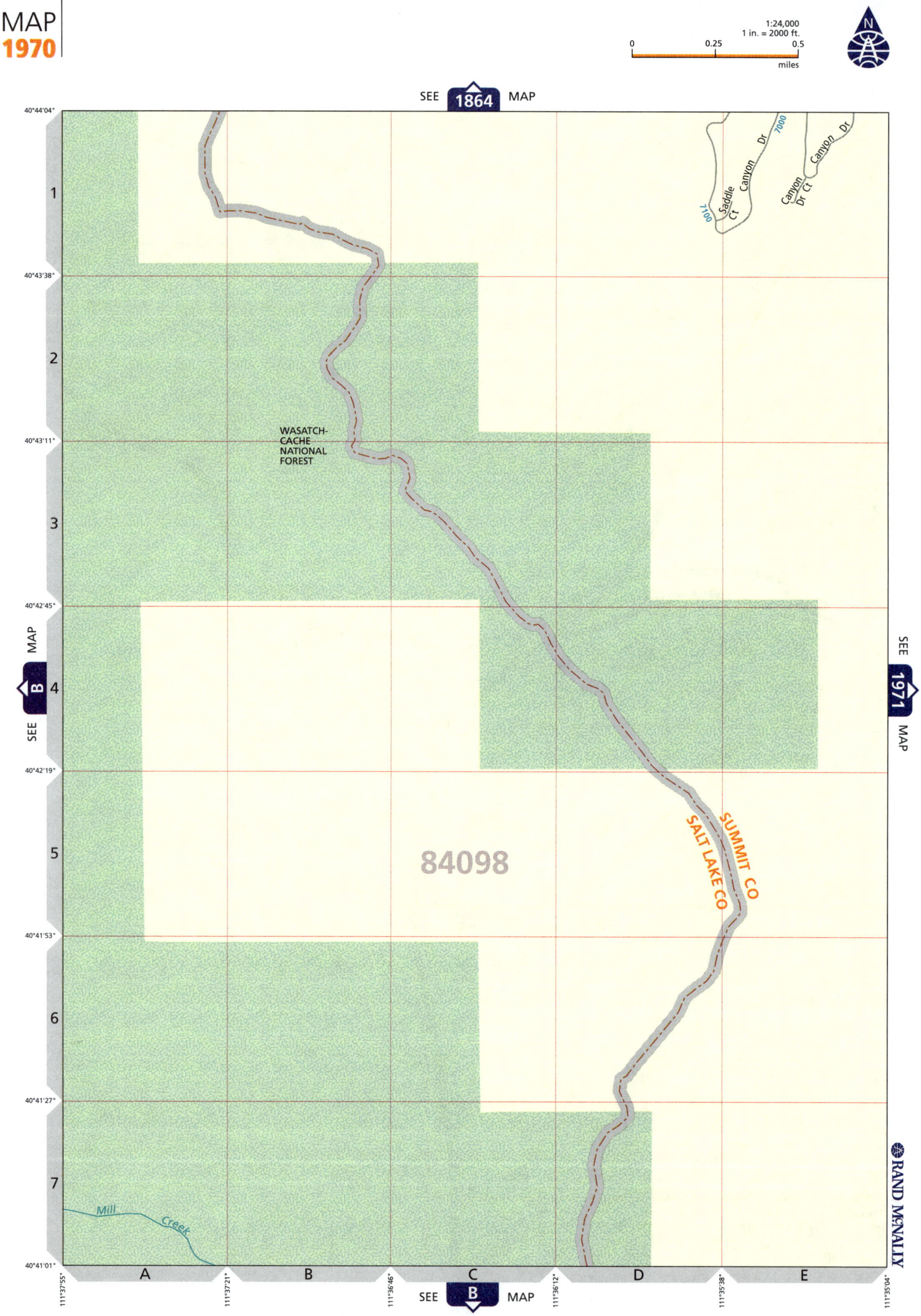

1:24,000
1 in. = 2000 ft.
0 0.25 0.5
miles

SEE 1864 MAP

SEE B MAP

SEE 1971 MAP

SEE B MAP

1:24,000
1 in. = 2000 ft.
0 0.25 0.5
miles

SEE 1865 MAP

SEE 1970 MAP

SEE 1972 MAP

Kimball Junction

Snyderville

84098

Utah Olympic Park

Canyons Ski Resort

A
1 N Meadow Loop Rd
2 Ptarmigan Ct
3 Ptarmigan Lp
4 Quail Meadow Rd

B
1 Brookside Ct
2 White Pine Canyon Rd

SEE 2077 MAP

1:24,000
1 in. = 2000 ft.
0 0.25 0.5
miles

SEE 1866 MAP

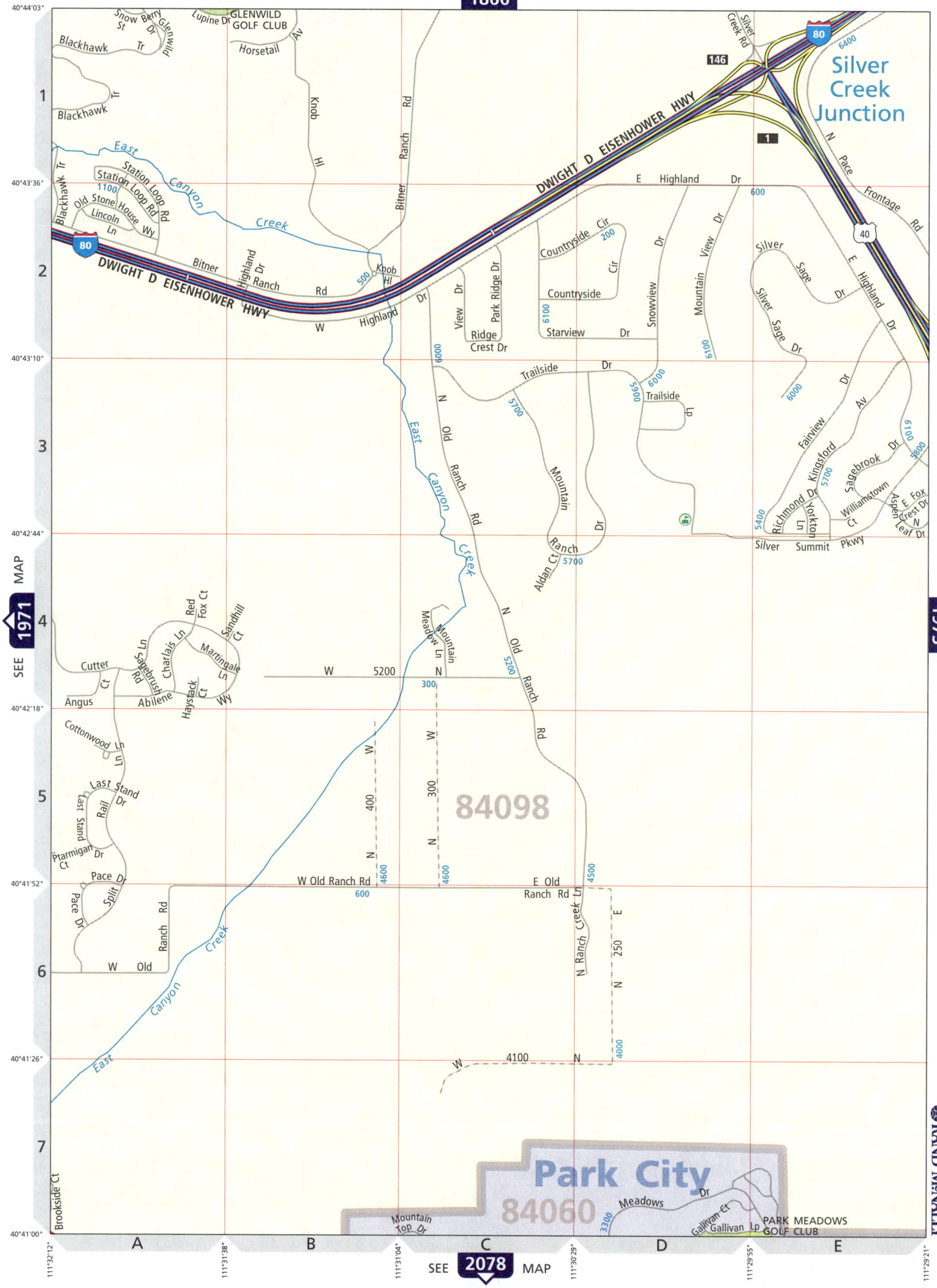

Silver Creek Junction

DWIGHT D EISENHOWER HWY

84098

Park City
84060

PARK MEADOWS GOLF CLUB

GLENWILD GOLF CLUB

SEE 1971 MAP

SEE 1973 MAP

SEE 2078 MAP

1:24,000
1 in. = 2000 ft.
0 0.25 0.5
miles

SEE 1867 MAP

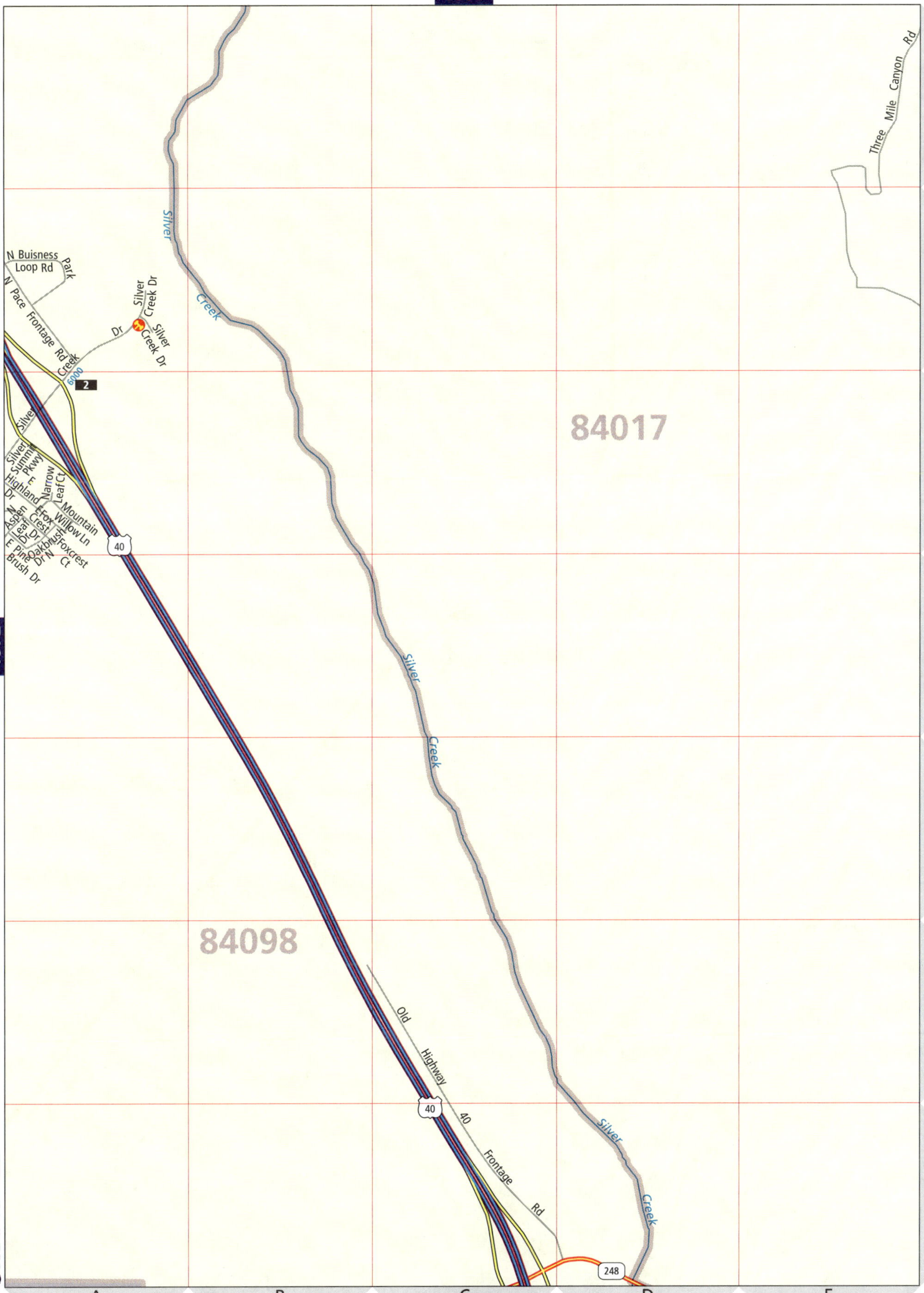

SEE 1972 MAP

SEE B MAP

SEE 2079 MAP

1:24,000
1 in. = 2000 ft.
0 0.25 0.5
miles

SEE 1960 MAP

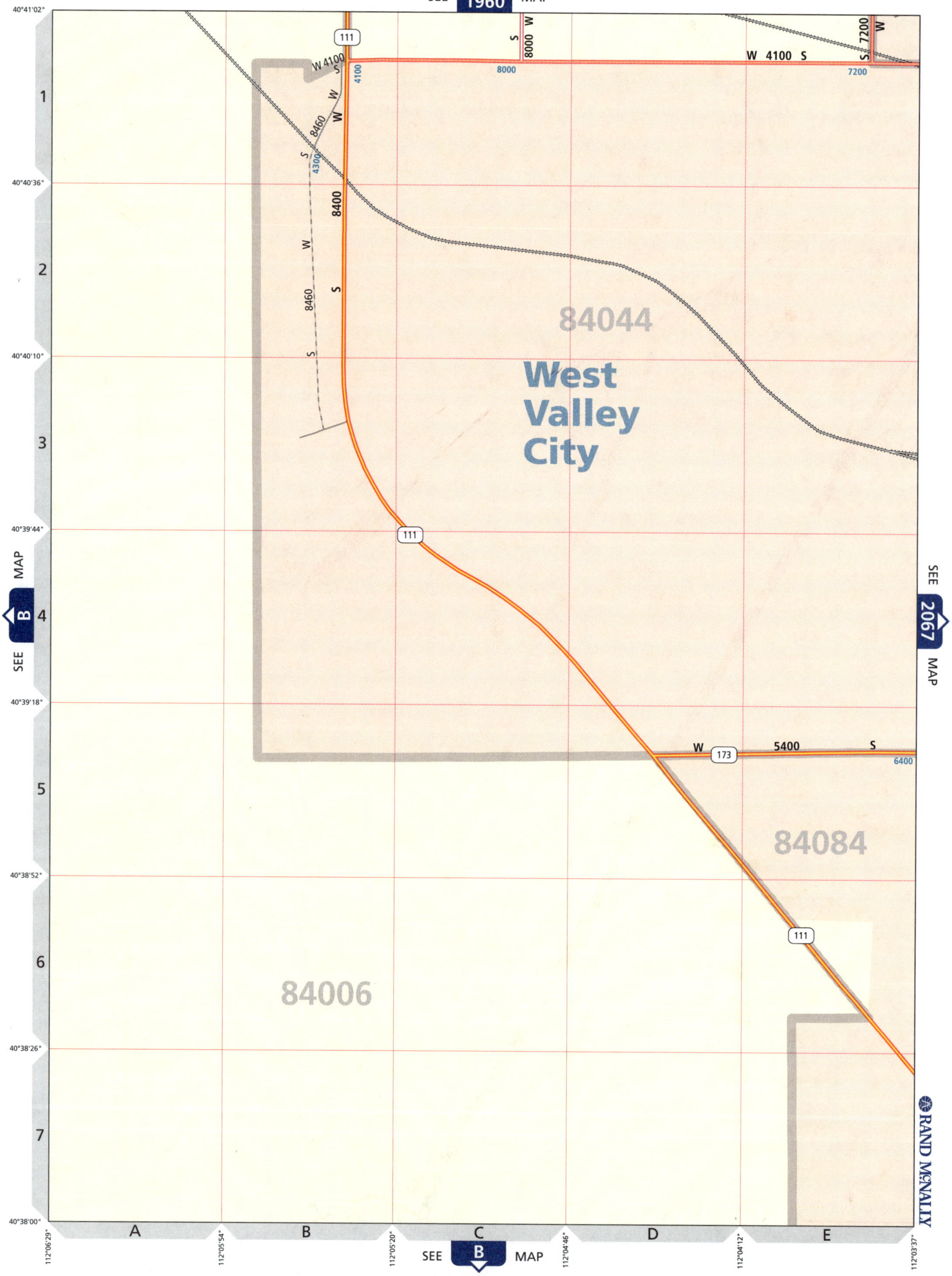

SEE B MAP

SEE 2067 MAP

SEE B MAP

1:24,000
1 in. = 2000 ft.
0 0.25 0.5
miles

SEE 1961 MAP

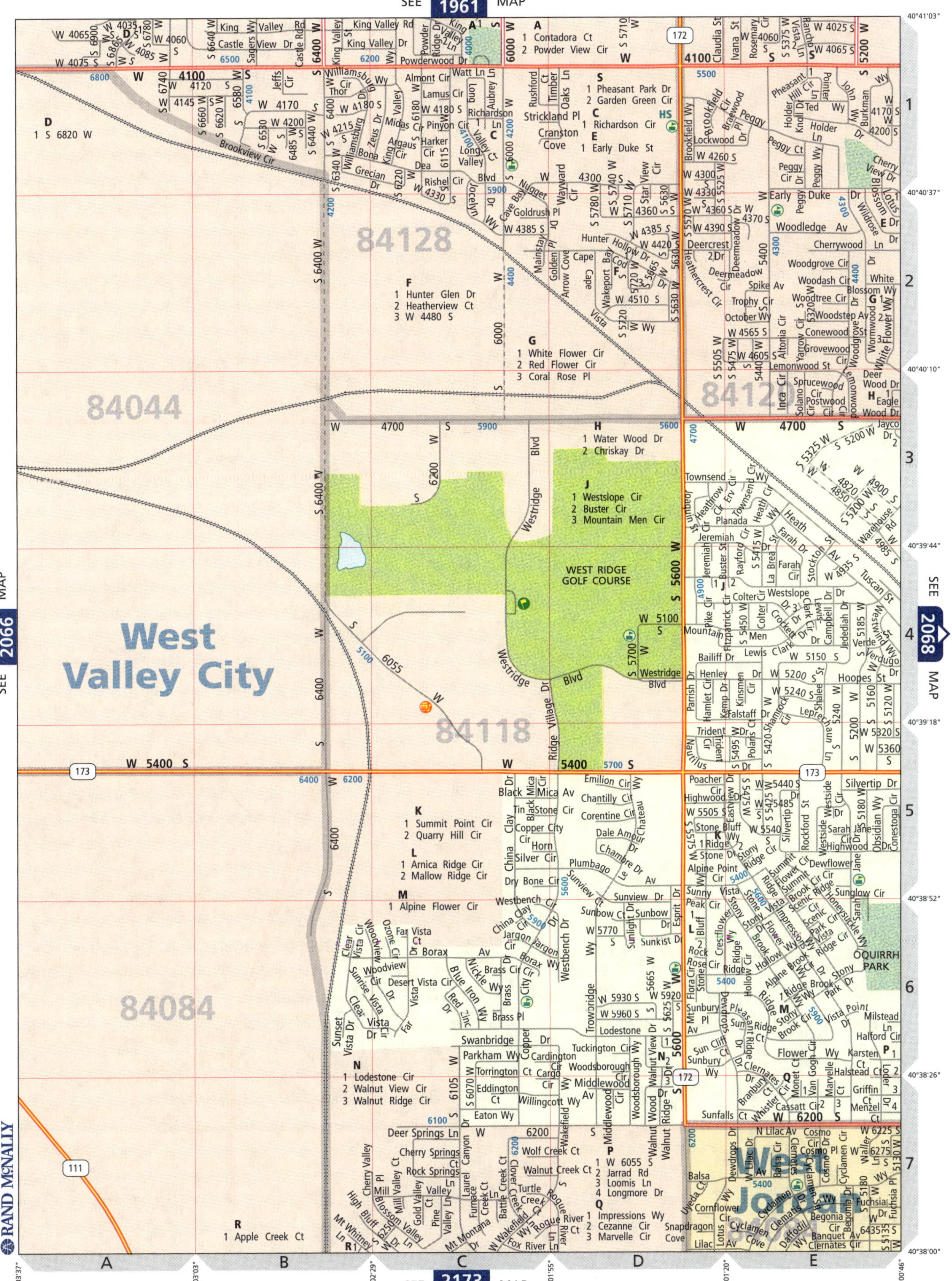

SEE 2066 MAP

SEE 2068 MAP

SEE 2173 MAP

1:24,000
1 in. = 2000 ft.
0 0.25 0.5
miles

SEE 1962 MAP

SEE 2067 MAP

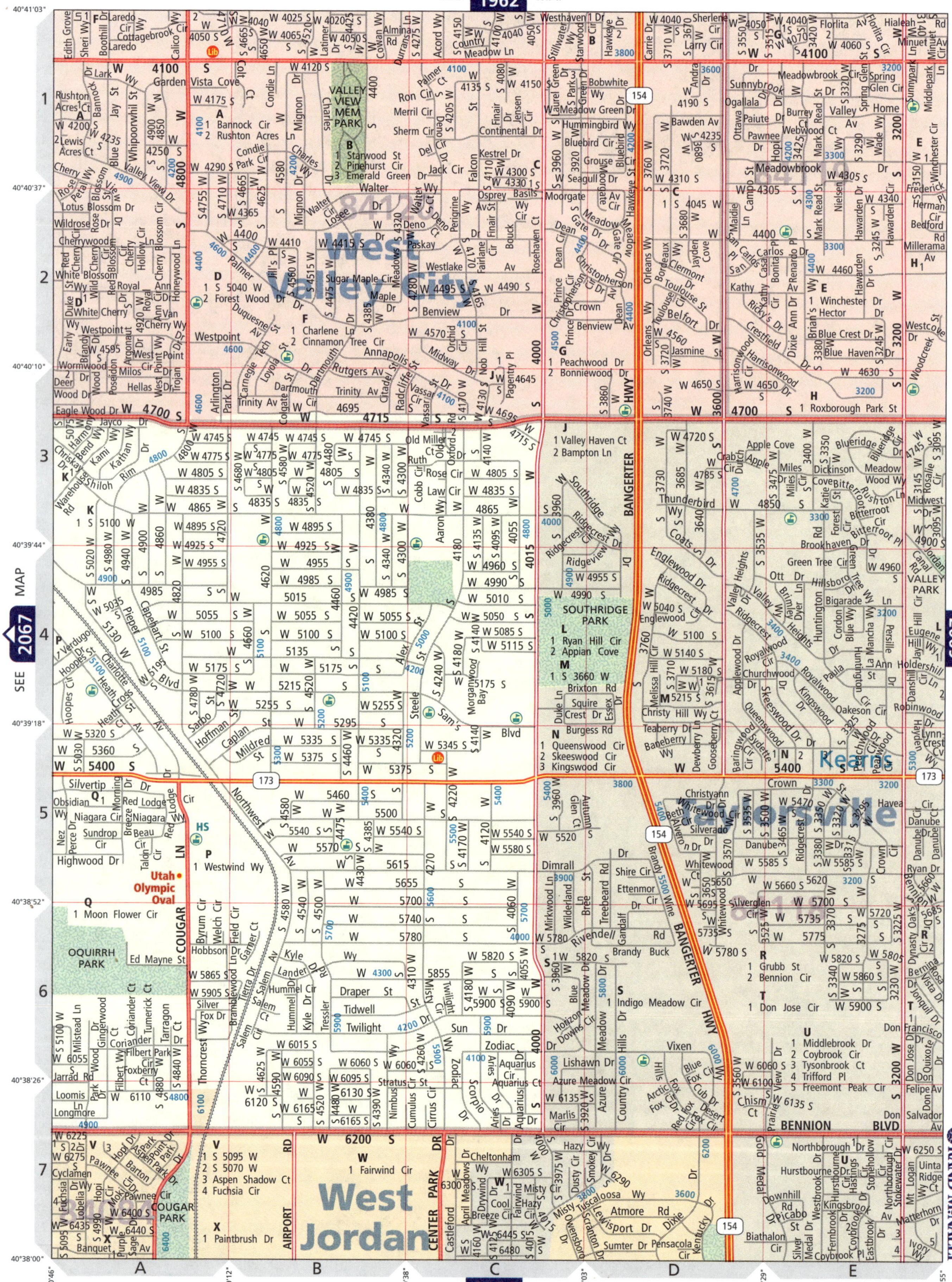

SEE 2069 MAP

West Valley City

84120

Kearns

Taylorsville

84118

West Jordan

84084

VALLEY VIEW MEM PARK

SOUTHRIDGE PARK

VALLEY PARK

OQUIRRH PARK

COUGAR PARK

Utah Olympic Oval

BANGERTER HWY

W 4100 S

W 4700 S

W 5400 S

W 6200 S

BENNION BLVD

A B C D E

1 2 3 4 5 6 7

SEE 2174 MAP

RAND McNALLY

N

1:24,000
1 in. = 2000 ft.
0 0.25 0.5
miles

SEE 1963 MAP

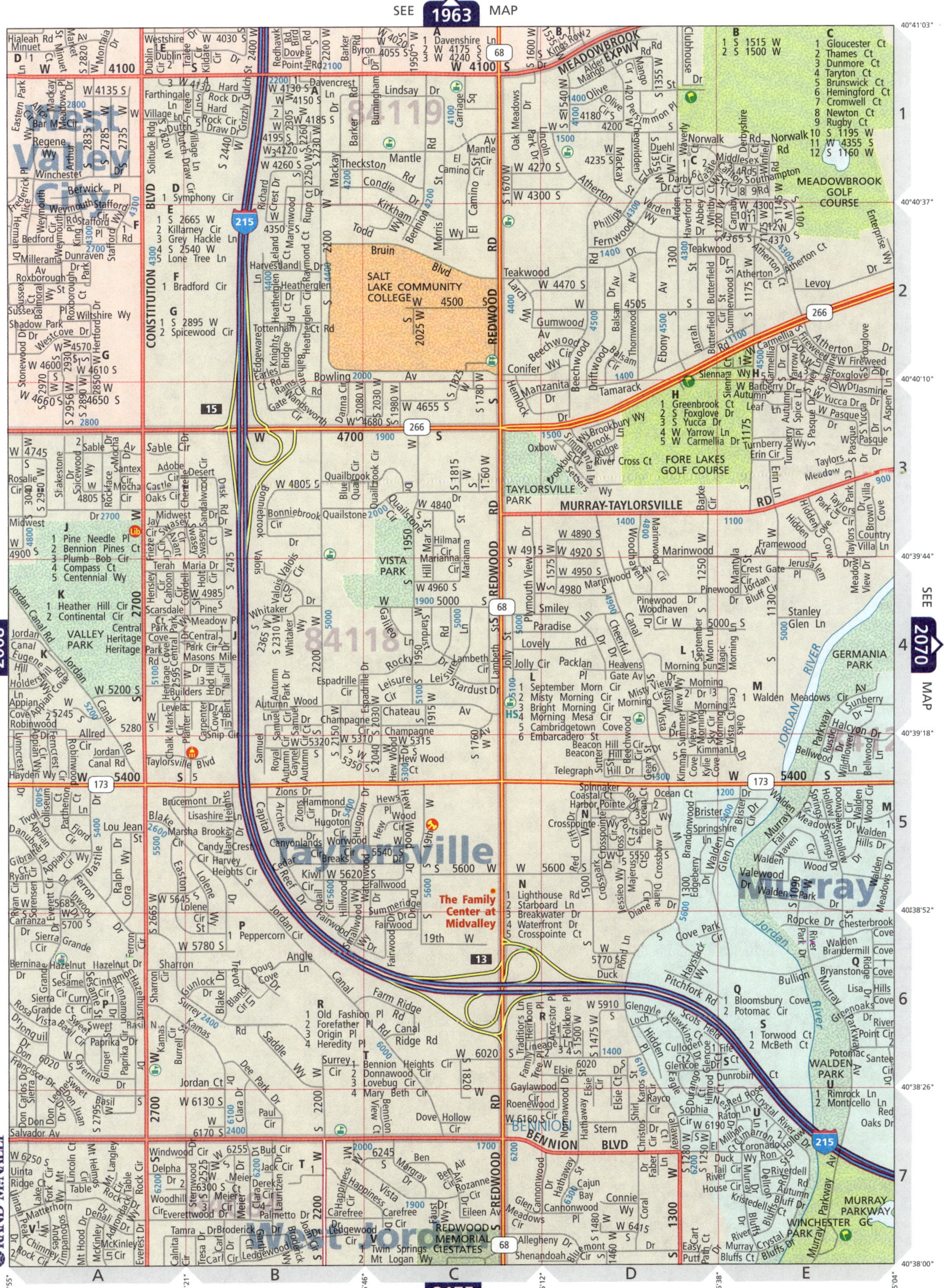

SEE 2068 MAP

SEE 2070 MAP

SEE 2175 MAP

1:24,000
1 in. = 2000 ft.
0 0.25 0.5
miles

SEE 1964 MAP

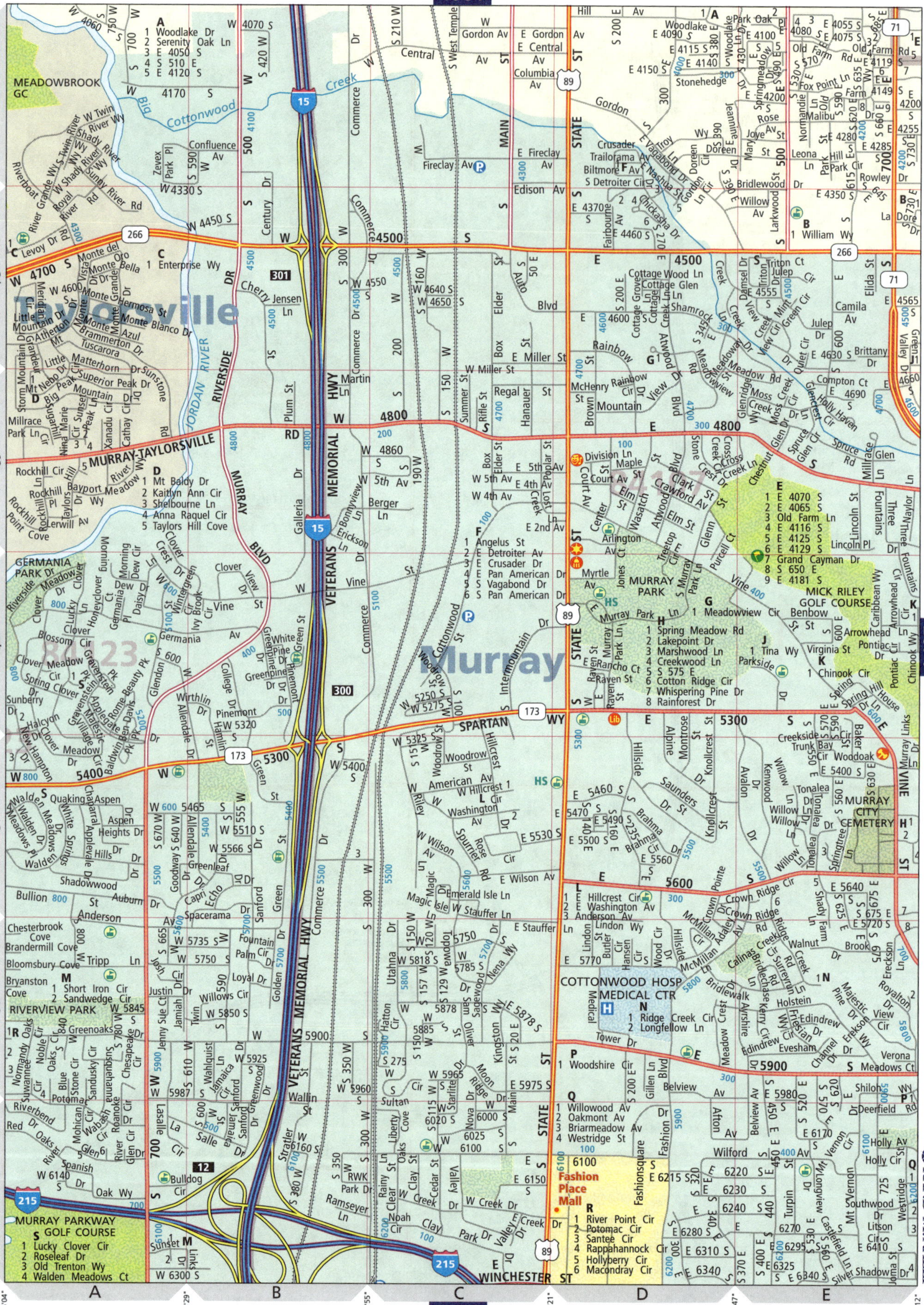

SEE 2069 MAP

SEE 2071 MAP

SEE 2176 MAP

Taylorsville

Murray

MEADOWBROOK GC

GERMANIA PARK

RIVERVIEW PARK

MURRAY PARKWAY GOLF COURSE

MURRAY PARK

MICK RILEY GOLF COURSE

MURRAY CITY CEMETERY

COTTONWOOD HOSP MEDICAL CTR

Fashion Place Mall

VETERANS MEMORIAL HWY

MURRAY-TAYLORSVILLE RD

STATE ST

SPARTAN WY

WINCHESTER ST

JORDAN RIVER

Big Cottonwood Creek

A
1 Woodlake Dr
2 Serenity Oak Ln
3 E 4050 S
4 S 510 E
5 E 4120 S

D
1 Mt Baldy Dr
2 Kaitlyn Ann Cir
3 Shelbourne Ln
4 Anna Raquel Cir
5 Taylors Hill Cove

F
1 Angelus St
2 E Detroiter Av
3 E Crusader Dr
4 E Pan American Dr
5 S Vagabond Dr
6 S Pan American Dr

E
1 E 4070 S
2 E 4065 S
3 Old Farm Ln
4 E 4116 S
5 E 4125 S
6 E 4129 S
7 Grand Cayman Dr
8 S 650 E
9 E 4181 S

G
1 Meadowview Cir

H
1 Spring Meadow Rd
2 Lakepoint Dr
3 Marshwood Ln
4 Creekwood Ln
5 S 575 E
6 Cotton Ridge Cir
7 Whispering Pine Dr
8 Rainforest Dr

J
1 Tina Wy

K
1 Chinook Cir

L
1 Hillcrest Cir
2 E Washington Av
3 Anderson Av

M
1 Short Iron Cir
2 Sandwedge Cir

N
1 Ridge Creek Cir
2 Longfellow Ln

P
1 Woodshire Cir

Q
1 Willowood Av
2 Oakmont Av
3 Briarmeadow Av
4 Westridge St

R
1 River Point Cir
2 Potomac Cir
3 Santee Cir
4 Rappahannock Cir
5 Hollyberry Cir
6 Macondray Cir

S
1 Lucky Clover Cir
2 Roseleaf Dr
3 Old Trenton Wy
4 Walden Meadows Ct

40°41'03" 40°40'37" 40°40'10" 40°39'44" 40°39'18" 40°38'52" 40°38'26" 40°38'00"

111°55'04" 111°54'29" 111°53'55" 111°53'21" 111°52'47" 111°52'12"

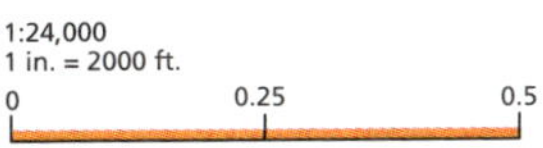

SEE 1965 MAP

40°41'02"

40°40'36"

40°40'10"

40°39'44"

40°39'18"

40°38'52"

40°38'26"

40°38'00"

1 2 3 4 5 6 7

Holladay

Cottonwood Meadows

Cottonwood

Murray

Cottonwood Mall

Walker Lane Reception Ctr

BIG COTTONWOOD PARK

CREEKSIDE PARK

ALYSIAN BURIAL GARDENS

MICK RILEY GOLF COURSE

COTTONWOOD COUNTRY CLUB

WHEELER HISTORIC FARM

84124 84117 84107 84121

HIGHLAND DR

VAN WINKLE EXPWY

MURRAY-HOLLADAY RD

HOLLADAY BLVD

4500 S

5600 S

VINE ST

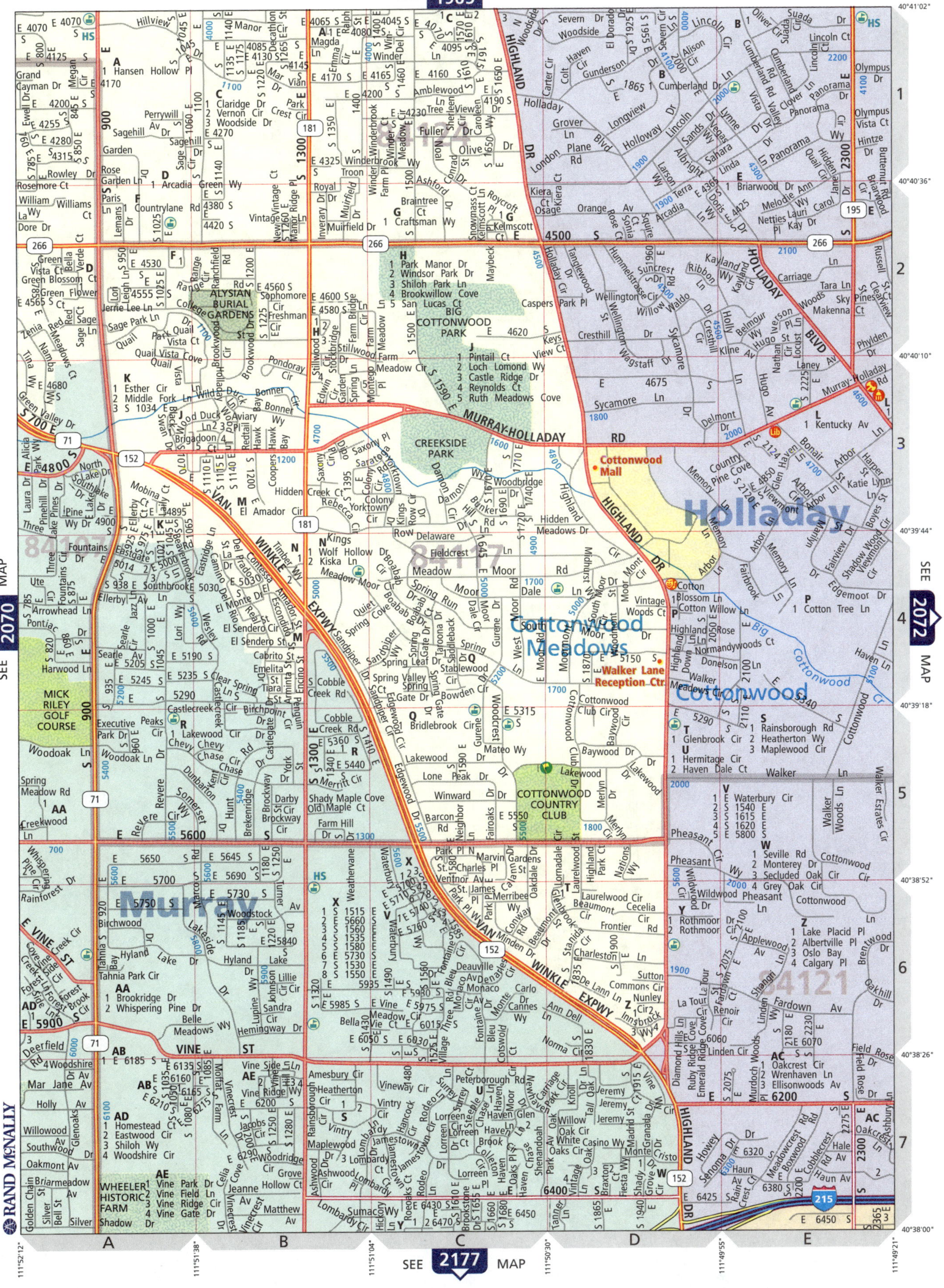

SEE 2070 MAP

SEE 2072 MAP

RAND McNALLY

A B C D E

111°52'12" 111°51'38" 111°51'04" 111°50'30" 111°49'55" 111°49'21"

SEE 2177 MAP

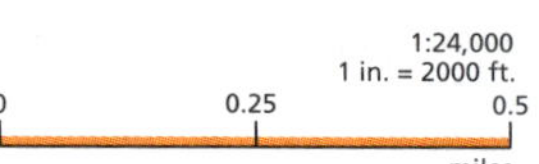

SEE 1966 MAP

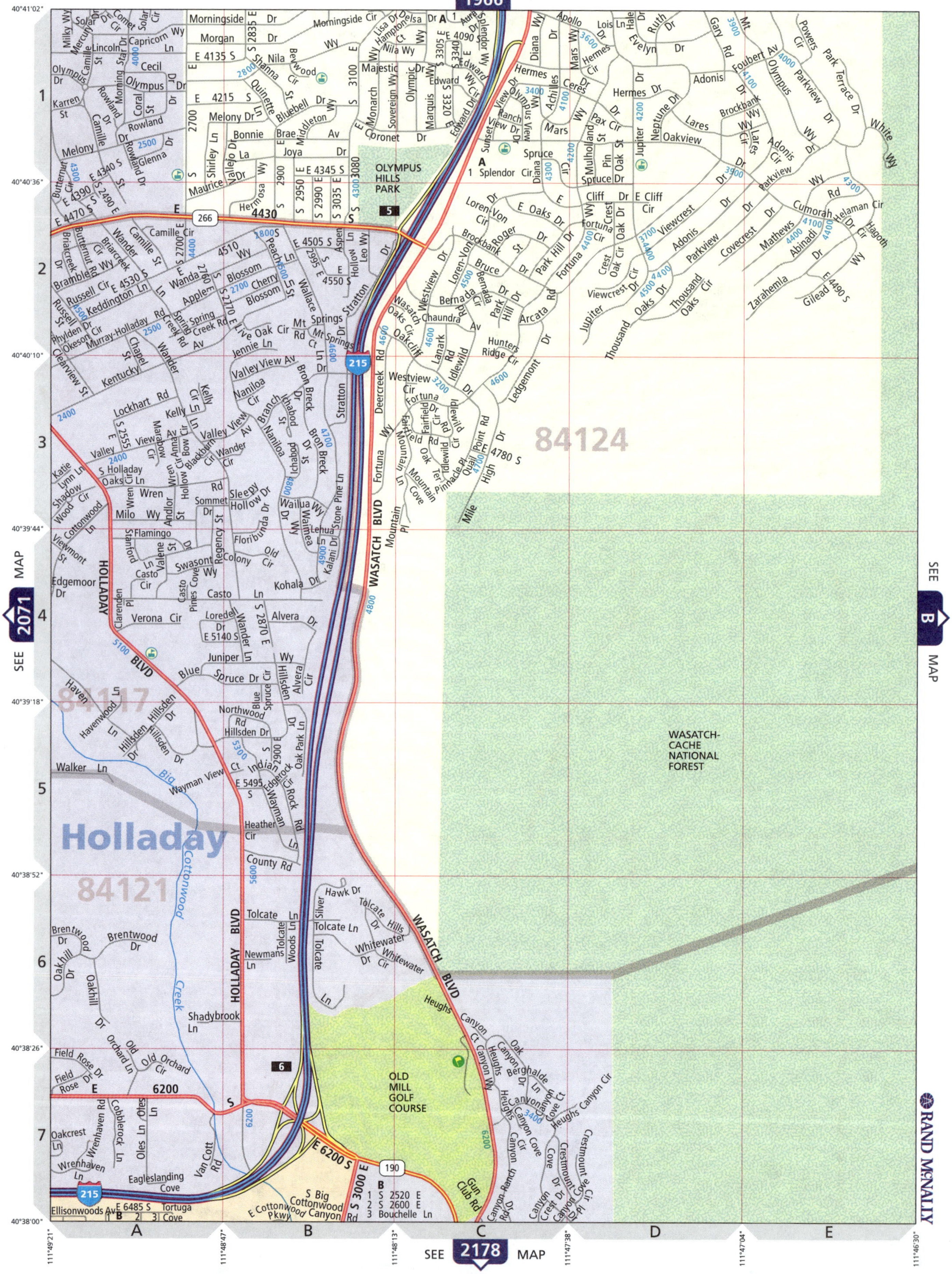

SEE 2071 MAP

SEE B MAP

SEE 2178 MAP

OLYMPUS HILLS PARK

84124

WASATCH-CACHE NATIONAL FOREST

84117

Holladay

84121

OLD MILL GOLF COURSE

WASATCH BLVD

HOLLADAY BLVD

E 4430 S

E 6200 S

E 6200 S

S 3000 E

215

266

190

A
1 Splendor Cir

B
1 S 2520 E
2 S 2600 E
3 Bouchelle Ln

1 2 3 4 5 6 7

A B C D E

40°41'02" 40°40'36" 40°40'10" 40°39'44" 40°39'18" 40°38'52" 40°38'26" 40°38'00"

111°49'21" 111°48'47" 111°48'13" 111°47'38" 111°47'04" 111°46'30"

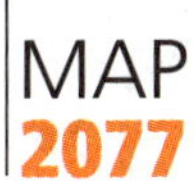

1:24,000
1 in. = 2000 ft.
0 0.25 0.5
miles

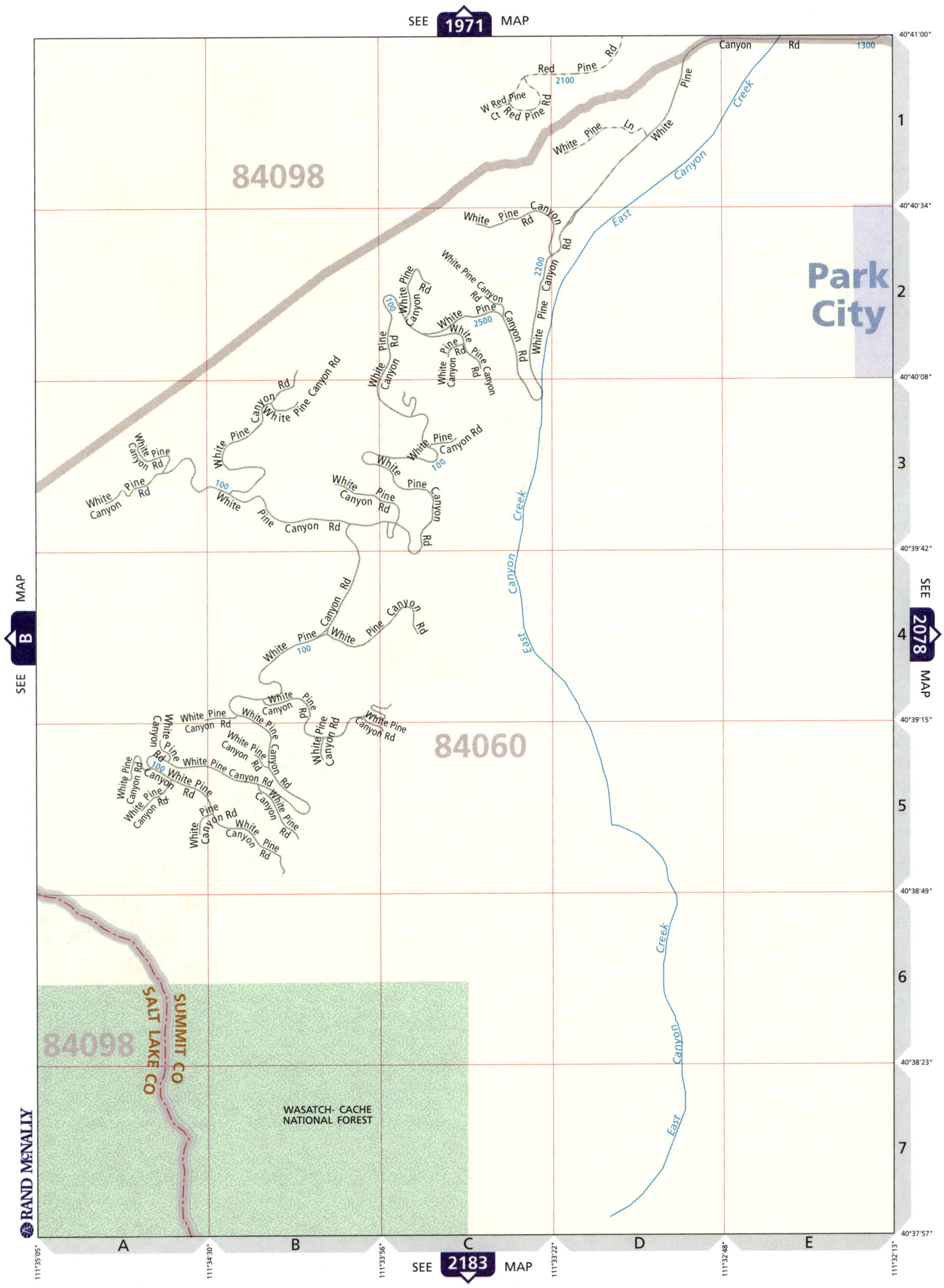

SEE 1971 MAP

84098

Park City

84060

84098

SUMMIT CO
SALT LAKE CO

WASATCH- CACHE NATIONAL FOREST

White Pine Canyon Rd

Red Pine Rd

W Red Pine Ct

White Pine Ln

East Canyon Creek

SEE B MAP

SEE 2078 MAP

SEE 2183 MAP

1:24,000
1 in. = 2000 ft.
0 0.25 0.5
miles

SEE 1972 MAP 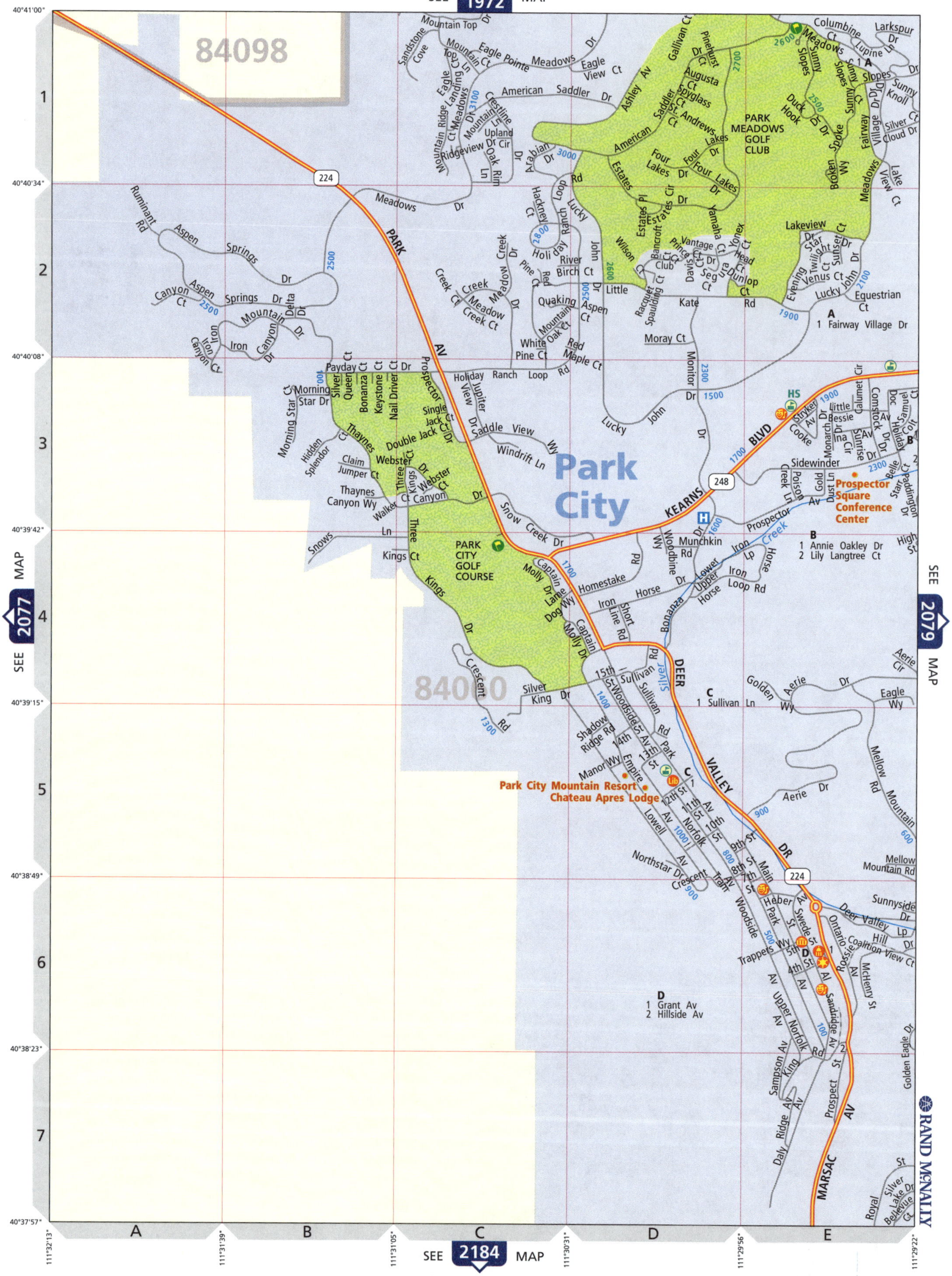
SEE 2077 MAP
SEE 2079 MAP
SEE 2184 MAP

Park City

84098

84060

PARK MEADOWS GOLF CLUB

PARK CITY GOLF COURSE

Prospector Square Conference Center

Park City Mountain Resort

Chateau Apres Lodge

PARK AV

KEARNS BLVD

DEER VALLEY DR

MARSAC AV

A
1 Fairway Village Dr

B
1 Annie Oakley Dr
2 Lily Langtree Ct

C
1 Sullivan Ln

D
1 Grant Av
2 Hillside Av

40°41'00"
40°40'34"
40°40'08"
40°39'42"
40°39'15"
40°38'49"
40°38'23"
40°37'57"

111°32'13"
111°31'39"
111°31'05"
111°30'31"
111°29'56"
111°29'22"

A B C D E

1 2 3 4 5 6 7

1:24,000
1 in. = 2000 ft.
0 0.25 0.5
miles

SEE 1973 MAP

SEE 2078 MAP
SEE B MAP
SEE 2185 MAP

1:24,000
1 in. = 2000 ft.
0 0.25 0.5
miles

SEE 2067 MAP

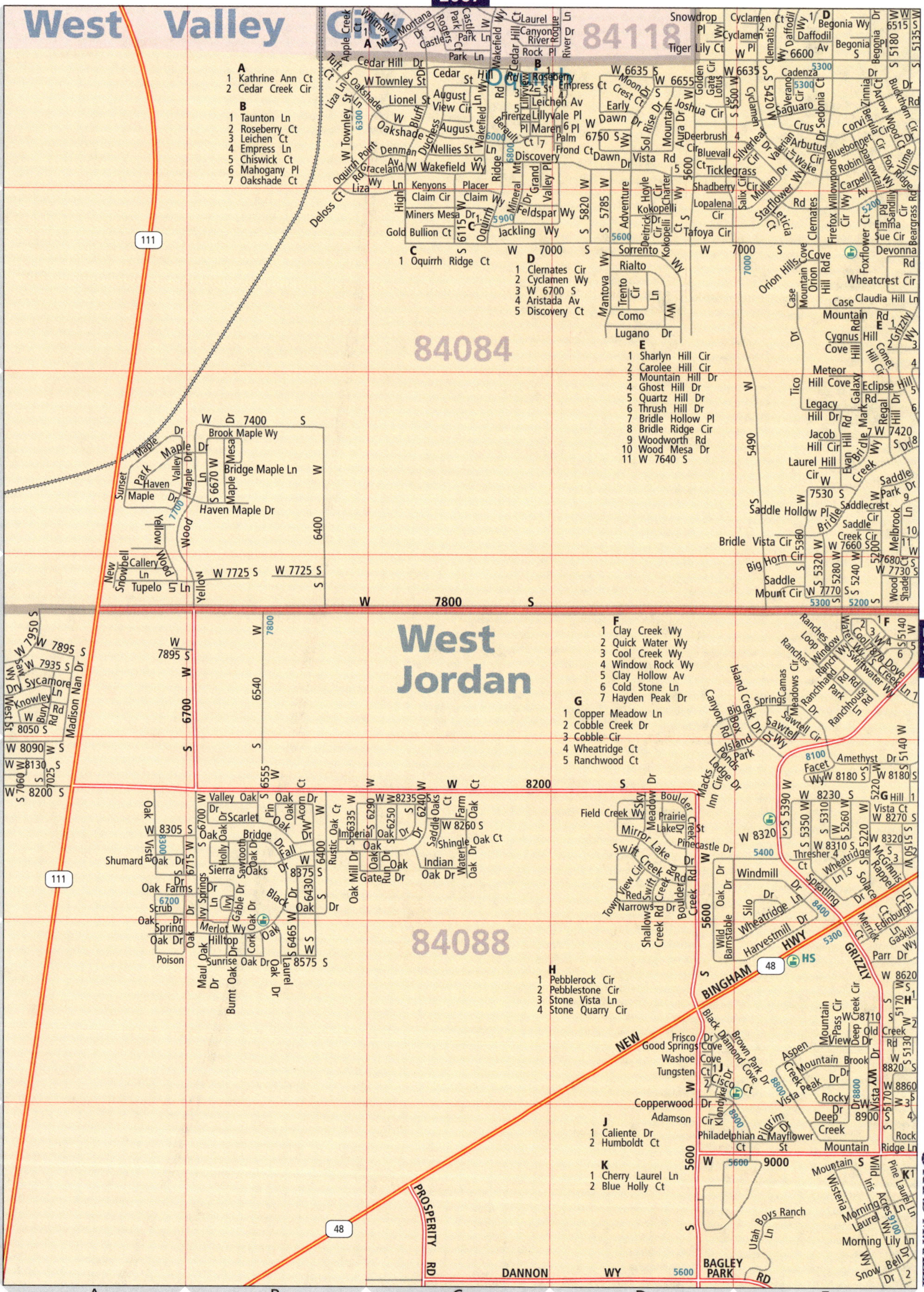

West Valley City

84118

West Jordan

84084

84088

Oquirrh

A
1 Kathrine Ann Ct
2 Cedar Creek Cir

B
1 Taunton Ln
2 Roseberry Ct
3 Leichen Ct
4 Empress Ln
5 Chiswick Ct
6 Mahogany Pl
7 Oakshade Ct

C
1 Oquirrh Ridge Ct

D
1 Clematis Cir
2 Cyclamen Wy
3 W 6700 S
4 Aristada Av
5 Discovery Ct

E
1 Sharlyn Hill Cir
2 Carolee Hill Cir
3 Mountain Hill Dr
4 Ghost Hill Dr
5 Quartz Hill Dr
6 Thrush Hill Dr
7 Bridle Hollow Pl
8 Bridle Ridge Cir
9 Woodworth Rd
10 Wood Mesa Dr
11 W 7640 S

F
1 Clay Creek Wy
2 Quick Water Wy
3 Cool Creek Wy
4 Window Rock Wy
5 Clay Hollow Av
6 Cold Stone Ln
7 Hayden Peak Dr

G
1 Copper Meadow Ln
2 Cobble Creek Dr
3 Cobble Cir
4 Wheatridge Ct
5 Ranchwood Ct

H
1 Pebblerock Cir
2 Pebblestone Cir
3 Stone Vista Ln
4 Stone Quarry Cir

J
1 Caliente Dr
2 Humboldt Ct

K
1 Cherry Laurel Ln
2 Blue Holly Ct

W 7800 S

W 8200 S

NEW BINGHAM HWY

PROSPERITY RD

DANNON WY

BAGLEY PARK RD

SEE B MAP

SEE 2174 MAP

SEE 2279 MAP

1:24,000
1 in. = 2000 ft.
0 0.25 0.5
miles

SEE 2068 MAP

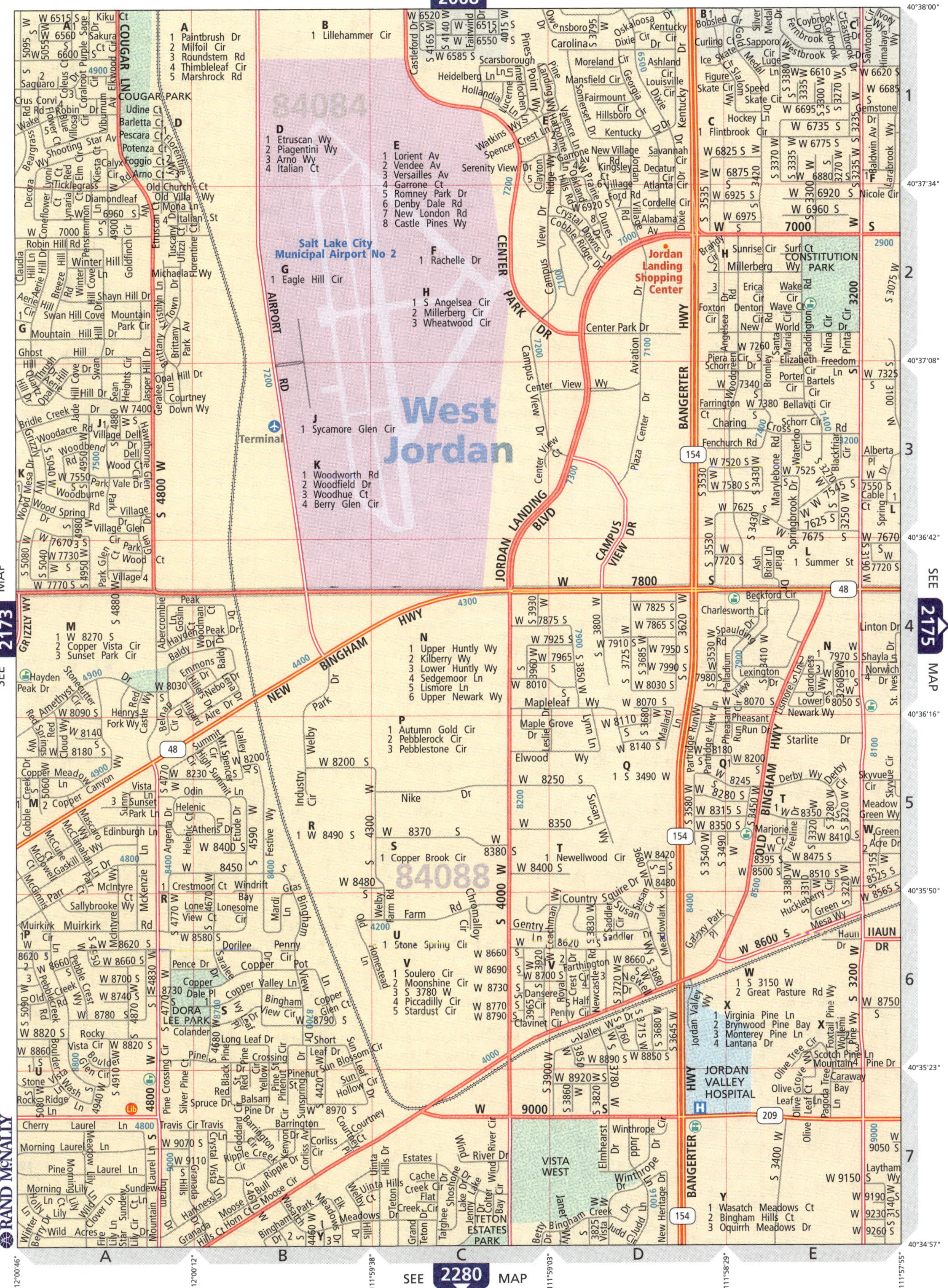

1:24,000
1 in. = 2000 ft.
0 0.25 0.5
miles

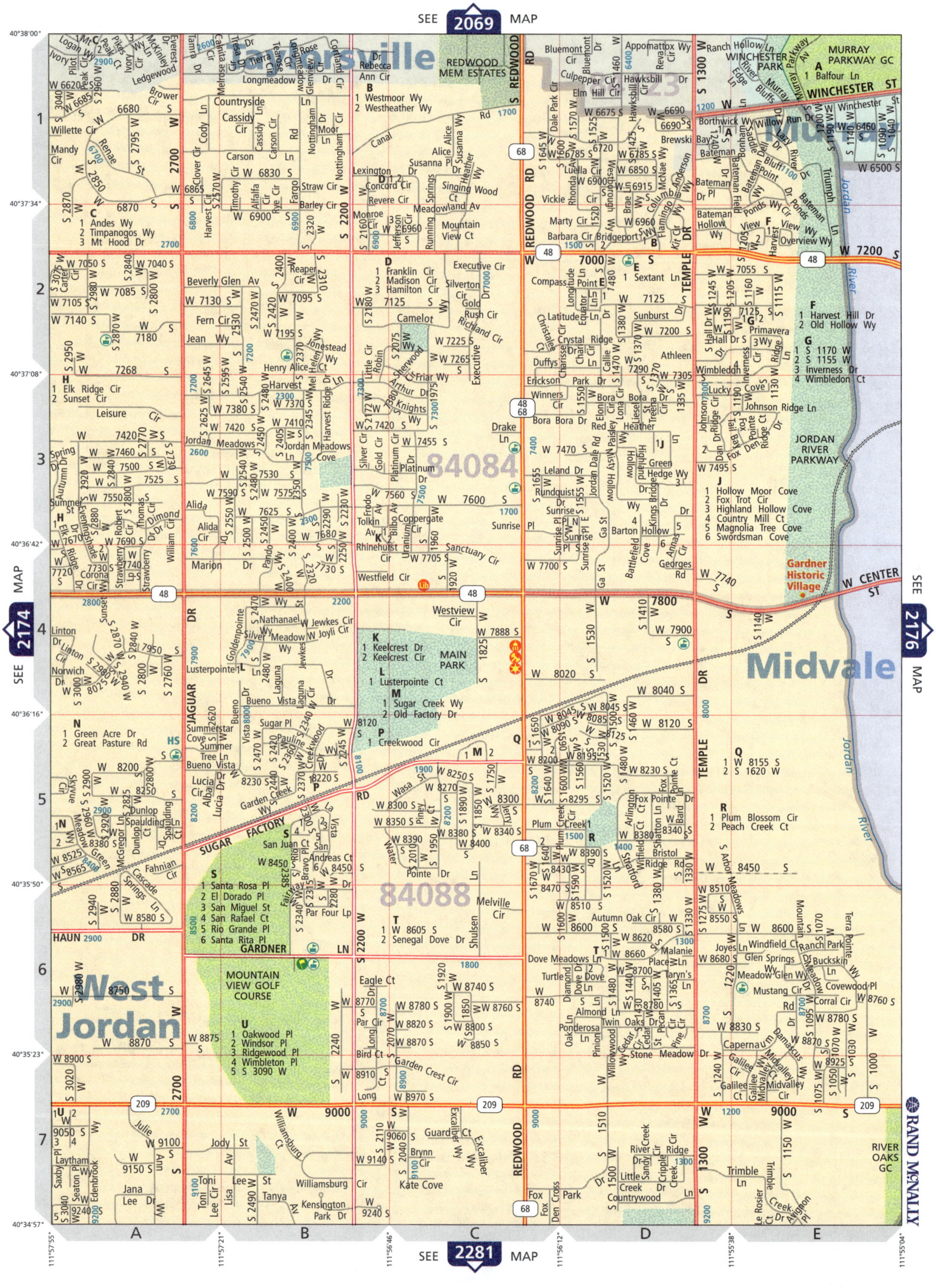

SEE 2069 MAP

Taylorsville
Murray
Midvale
West Jordan

REDWOOD MEM ESTATES
MURRAY PARKWAY GC
WINCHESTER PARK
JORDAN RIVER PARKWAY
Gardner Historic Village
MAIN PARK
MOUNTAIN VIEW GOLF COURSE
RIVER OAKS GC

84084
84088

A
1 Balfour Ln

B
1 Westmoor Wy
2 Westheather Wy

C
1 Andes Wy
2 Timpanogos Wy
3 Mt Hood Dr

D
1 Franklin Cir
2 Madison Cir
3 Hamilton Cir

E
1 Sextant Ln

F
1 Harvest Hill Dr
2 Old Hollow Wy

G
1 S 1170 W
2 S 1155 W
3 Inverness Dr
4 Wimbledon Ct

H
1 Elk Ridge Cir
2 Sunset Cir

J
1 Hollow Moor Cove
2 Fox Trot Cir
3 Highland Hollow Cove
4 Country Mill Ct
5 Magnolia Tree Cove
6 Swordsman Cove

K
1 Keelcrest Dr
2 Keelcrest Cir

L
1 Lusterpointe Ct

M
1 Sugar Creek Wy
2 Old Factory Dr

N
1 Green Acre Dr
2 Great Pasture Rd

P
1 Creekwood Cir

Q
1 W 8155 S
2 S 1620 W

R
1 Plum Blossom Cir
2 Peach Creek Ct

S
1 Santa Rosa Pl
2 El Dorado Pl
3 San Miguel St
4 San Rafael Ct
5 Rio Grande Pl
6 Santa Rita Pl

T
1 W 8605 S
2 Senegal Dove Dr

U
1 Oakwood Pl
2 Windsor Pl
3 Ridgewood Pl
4 Wimbleton Pl
5 S 3090 W

SEE 2174 MAP

SEE 2176 MAP

SEE 2281 MAP

1:24,000
1 in. = 2000 ft.
0 0.25 0.5
miles

SEE 2070 MAP

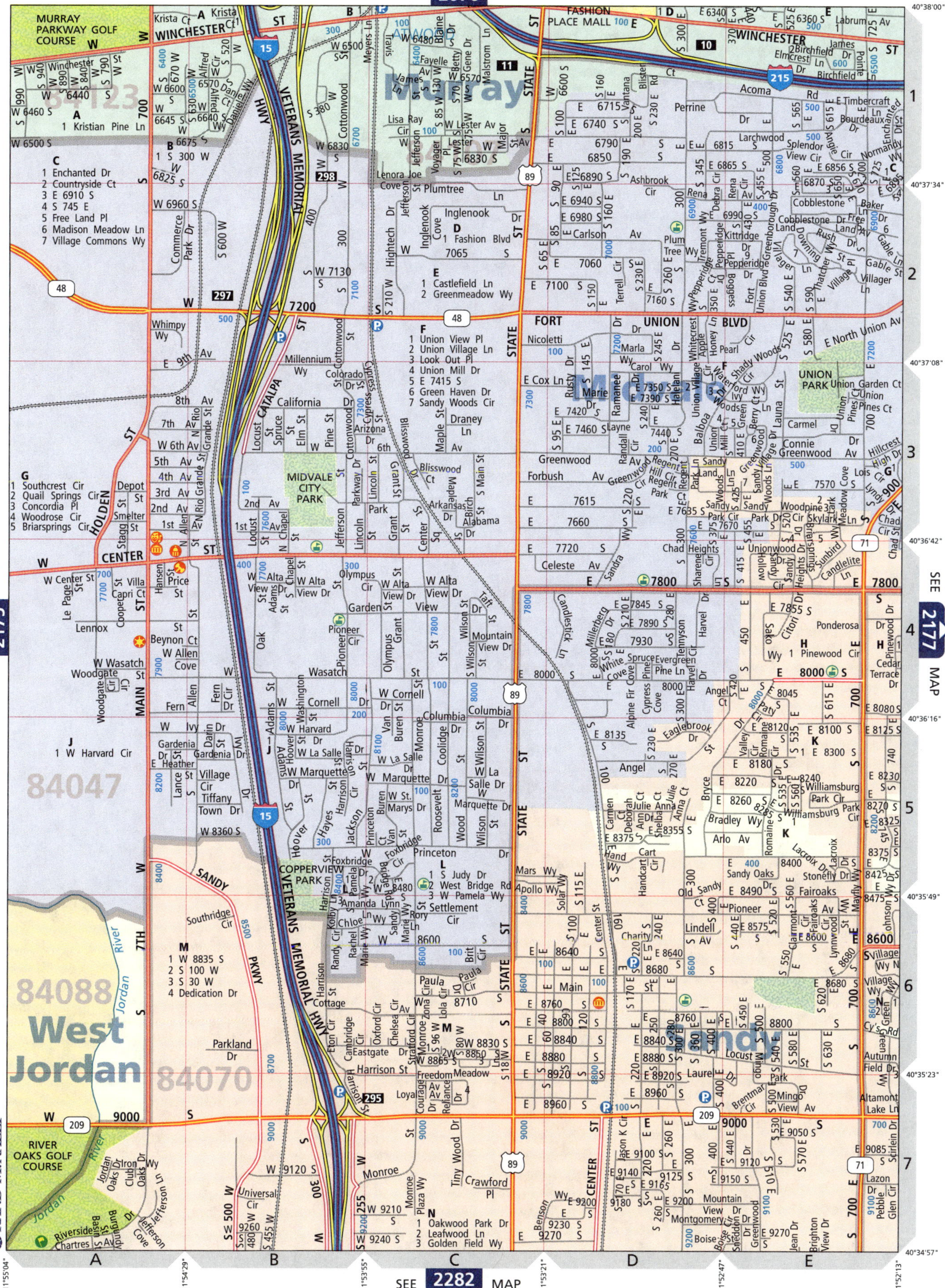

SEE 2175 MAP
SEE 2177 MAP
SEE 2282 MAP

1:24,000
1 in. = 2000 ft.

0 0.25 0.5
miles

SEE 2071 MAP

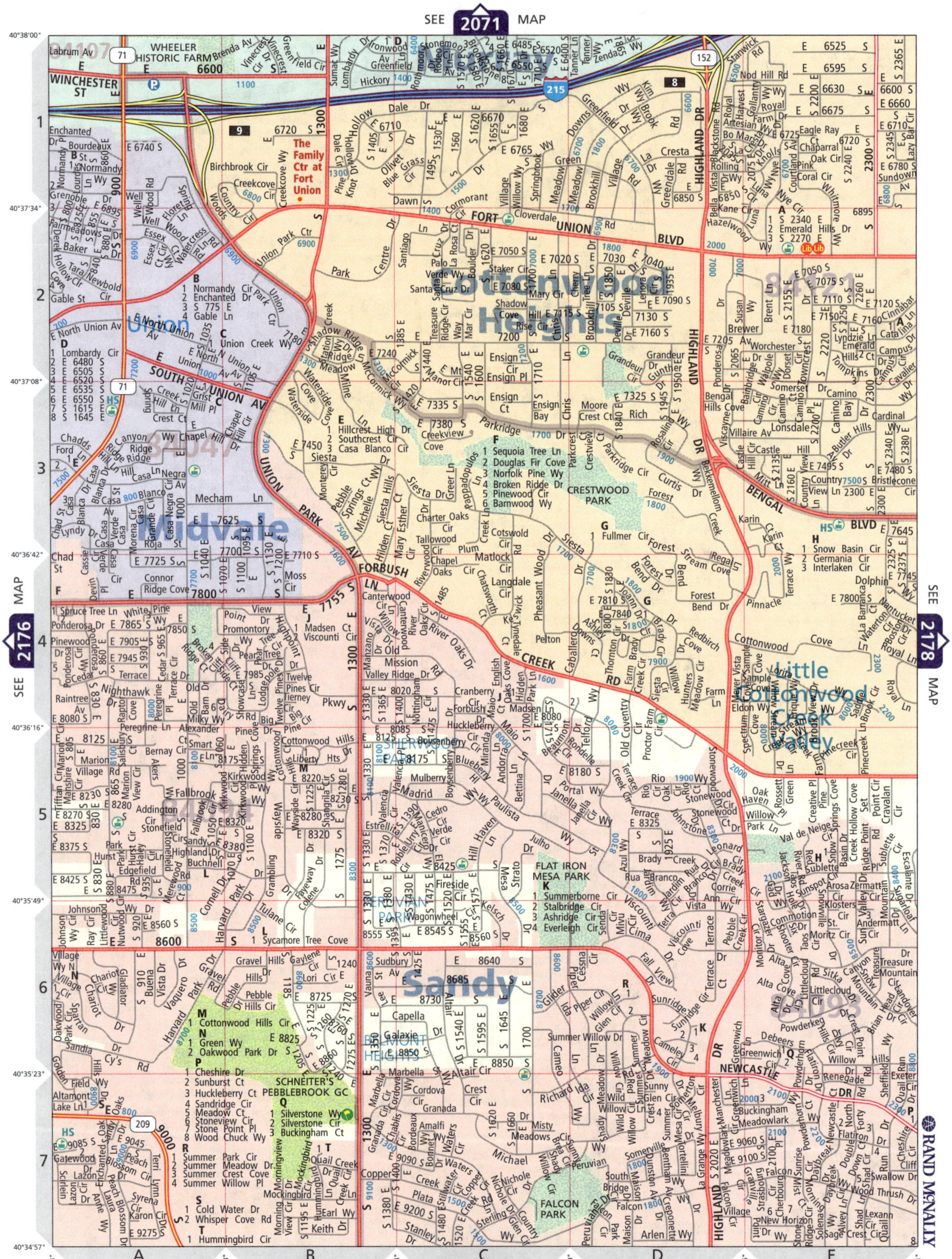

Cottonwood Heights

Union

Midvale

Sandy

Little Cottonwood Creek Valley

WHEELER HISTORIC FARM

The Family Ctr at Fort Union

CRESTWOOD PARK

FLAT IRON MESA PARK

SCHNEITER'S PEBBLEBROOK GC

FALCON PARK

SHERWOOD PARK

PERUVIAN PARK

BELMONT HEIGHTS

FORT UNION BLVD

HIGHLAND DR

UNION PARK AV

FORBUSH LN

CREEK RD

BENGAL BLVD

NEWCASTLE DR

WINCHESTER ST

SOUTH UNION AV

A
1 Normandy Cir
2 Enchanted Dr
3 S 775 E
4 Gable Ln

B
1 Normandy Cir
2 Enchanted Dr
3 S 775 E
4 Gable Ln

C
1 Union Creek Wy

D
1 Lombardy Cir
2 E 6480 S
3 E 6505 S
4 E 6520 S
5 E 6535 S
6 E 6550 S
7 S 1615 E
8 S 1645 E

E
1 Hillcrest High Dr
2 Southcrest Cir
3 Casa Blanco Cir

F
1 Sequoia Tree Ln
2 Douglas Fir Cove
3 Norfolk Pine Wy
4 Broken Ridge Dr
5 Pinewood Cir
6 Barnwood Wy

G
1 Fullmer Cir

H
1 Snow Basin Cir
2 Germania Cir
3 Interlaken Cir

J
1 Madsen Ct
2 Viscounti Cir

K
1 Summerborne Cir
2 Stalbridge Cir
3 Ashridge Cir
4 Everleigh Cir

L
1 Sycamore Tree Cove

M
1 Cottonwood Hills Cir

N
1 Green Wy
2 Oakwood Park Dr

P
1 Cheshire Dr
2 Sunburst Ct
3 Huckleberry Ct
4 Sandridge Cir
5 Meadow Ct
6 Stoneview Cir
7 Stone Point Pl
8 Wood Chuck Wy

Q
1 Silverstone Wy
2 Silverstone Cir
3 Buckingham Ct

R
1 Summer Park Cir
2 Summer Meadow Dr
3 Summer Crest Cove
4 Summer Willow Pl

S
1 Cold Water Dr
2 Whisper Cove Rd

T
1 Hummingbird Cir

40°38'00" 40°37'34" 40°37'08" 40°36'42" 40°36'16" 40°35'49" 40°35'23" 40°34'57"

111°52'13" 111°51'38" 111°51'04" 111°50'30" 111°49'56" 111°49'21"

A B C D E

1 2 3 4 5 6 7

SEE 2176 MAP

SEE 2178 MAP

SEE 2283 MAP

N

1:24,000
1 in. = 2000 ft.
0 0.25 0.5
miles

SEE 2072 MAP

SEE 2177 MAP

SEE B MAP

SEE 2284 MAP

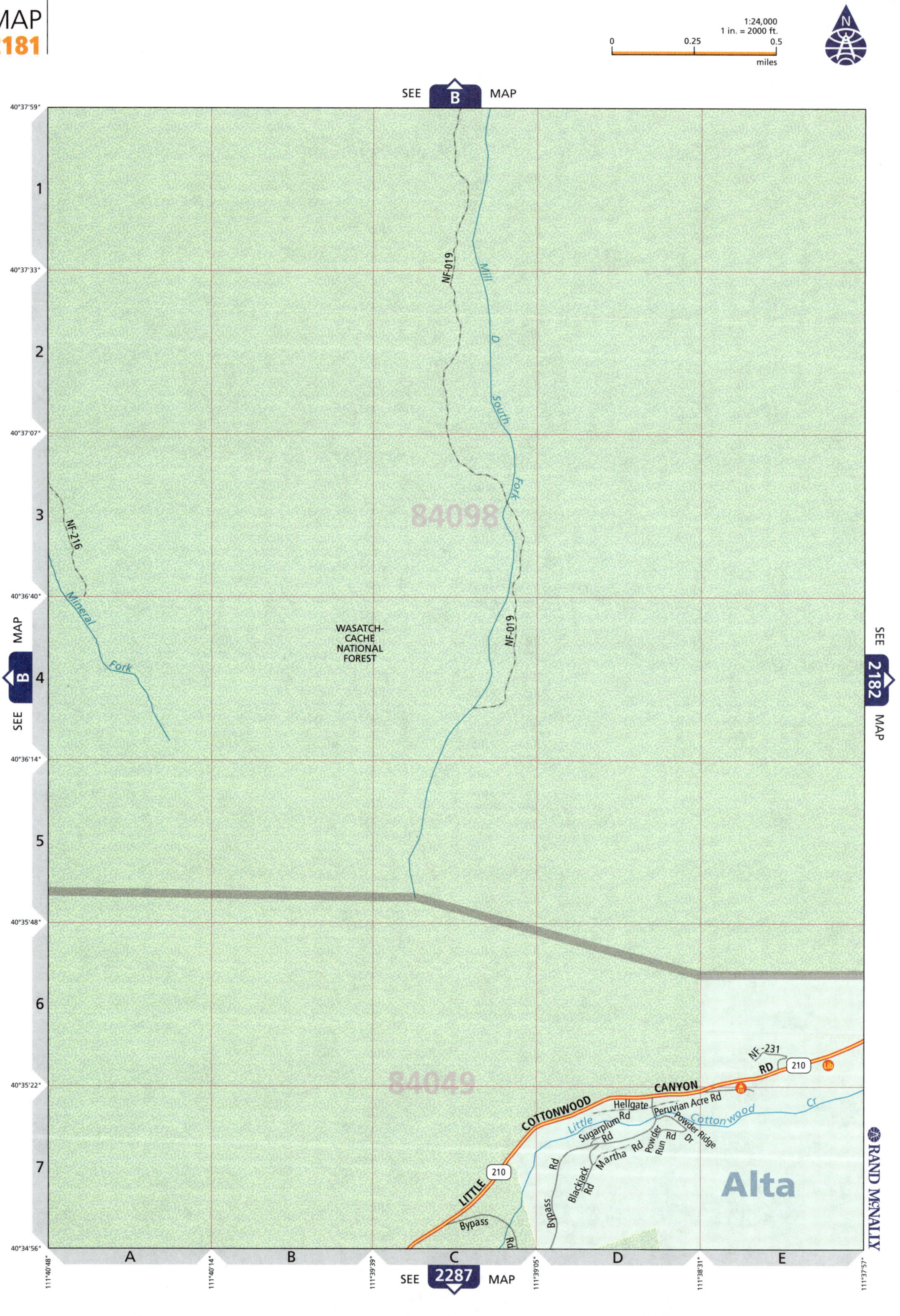

1:24,000
1 in. = 2000 ft.
0 0.25 0.5
miles

SEE B MAP

SEE B MAP

SEE 2182 MAP

SEE 2287 MAP

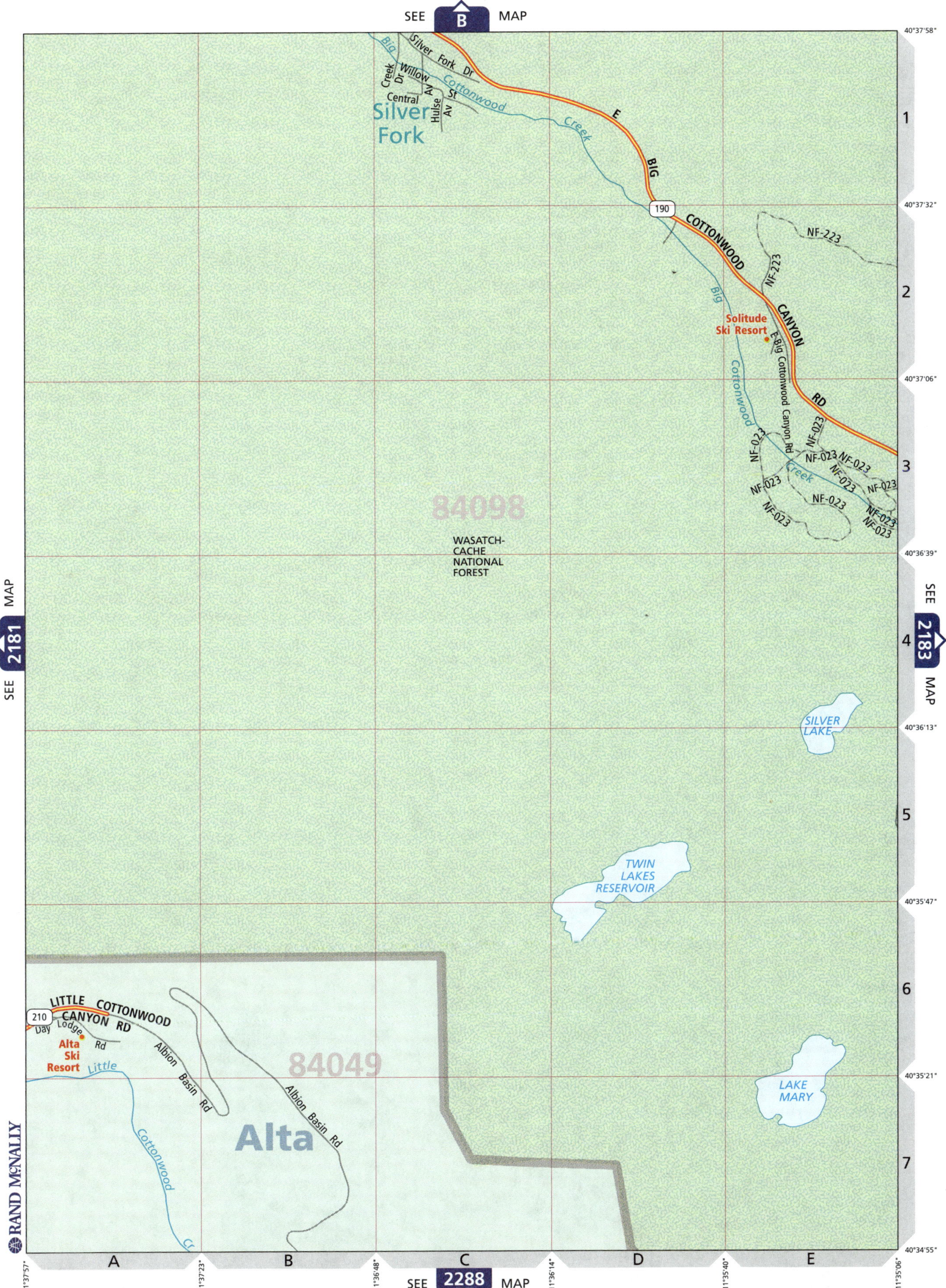

1:24,000
1 in. = 2000 ft.
0
0.25
0.5
miles
SEE B MAP
SEE 2181 MAP
SEE 2183 MAP
SEE 2288 MAP
Silver Fork
Silver Fork Dr
Willow St
Creek Dr
Central Av
Hulse Av
Big Cottonwood Creek
E BIG COTTONWOOD CANYON RD
190
NF-223
Solitude Ski Resort
E Big Cottonwood Canyon Rd
NF-023
84098
WASATCH-CACHE NATIONAL FOREST
SILVER LAKE
TWIN LAKES RESERVOIR
LAKE MARY
LITTLE COTTONWOOD CANYON RD
210
Day Lodge Rd
Alta Ski Resort
Albion Basin Rd
84049
Alta
Little Cottonwood Cr
A
B
C
D
E
1
2
3
4
5
6
7
40°37'58"
40°37'32"
40°37'06"
40°36'39"
40°36'13"
40°35'47"
40°35'21"
40°34'55"
111°37'57"
111°37'23"
111°36'48"
111°36'14"
111°35'40"
111°35'06"

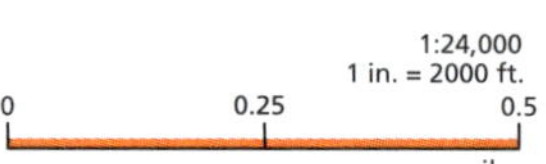

SEE 2077 MAP

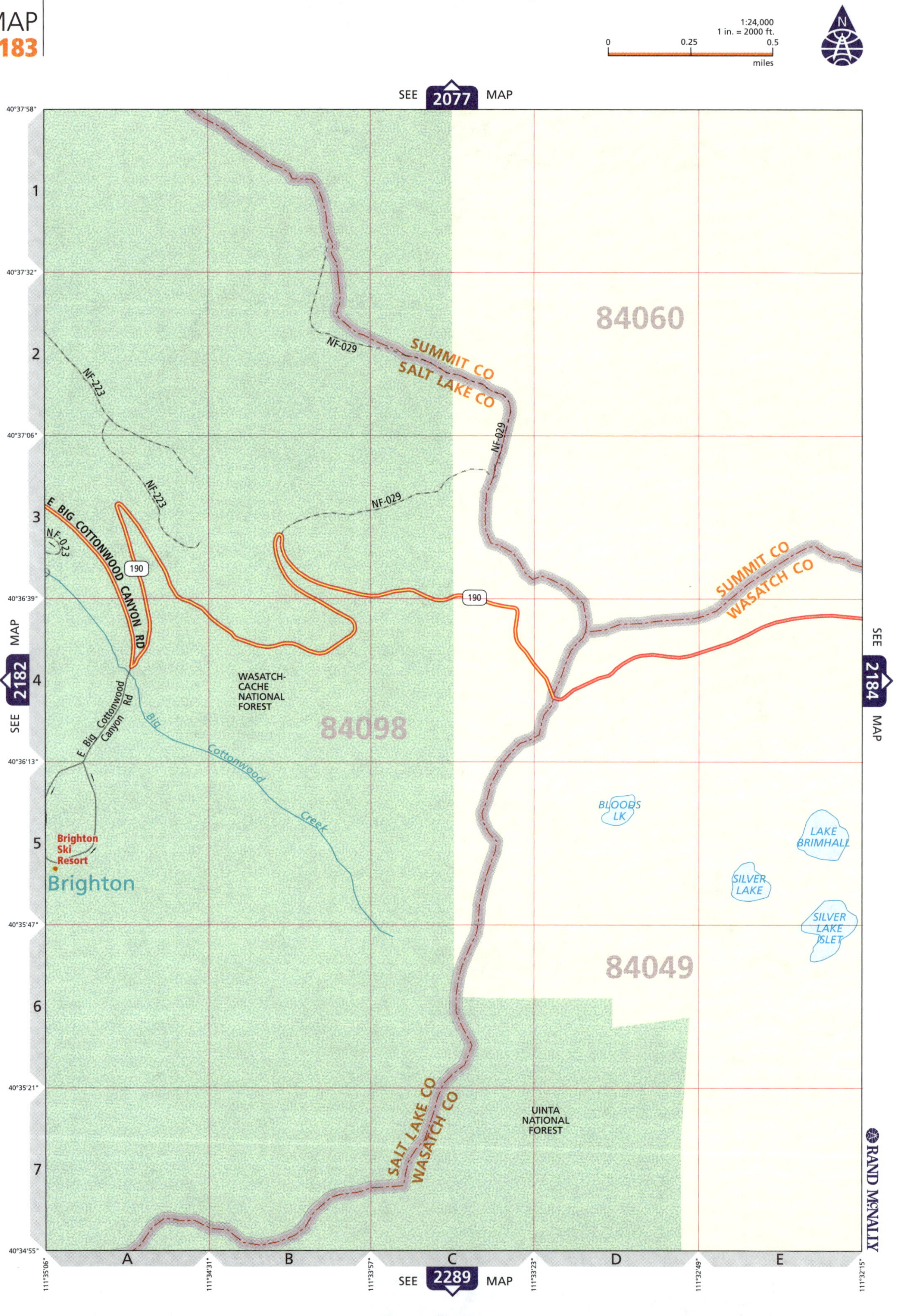

SEE 2182 MAP

SEE 2184 MAP

SEE 2289 MAP

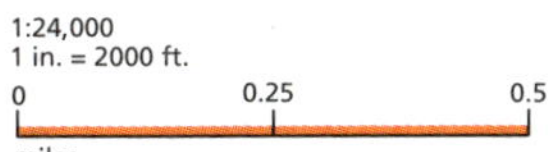

SEE 2078 MAP

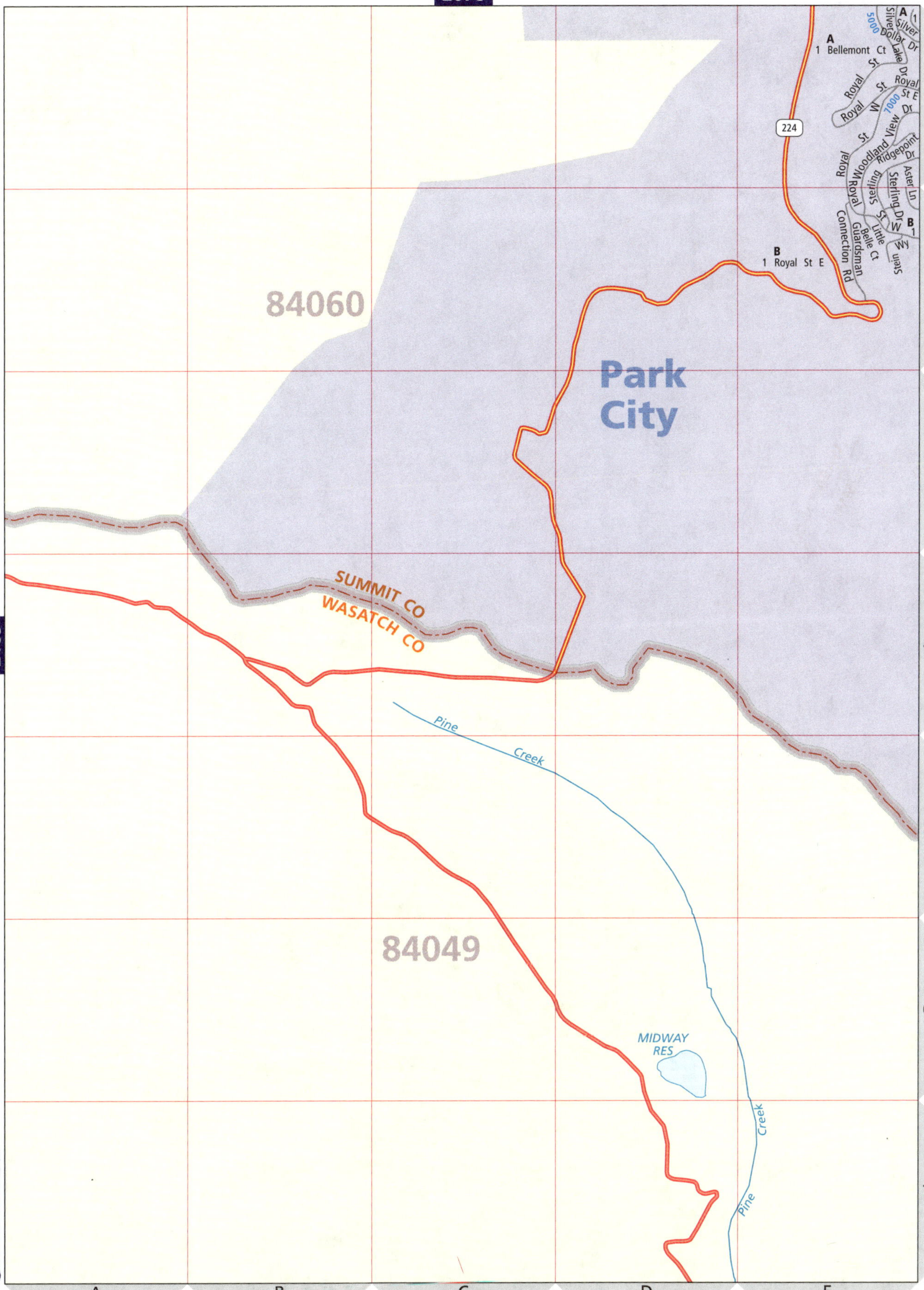

SEE 2183 MAP

SEE 2185 MAP

SEE 2290 MAP

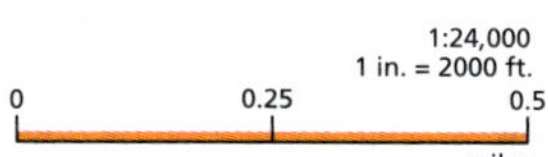

SEE 2079 MAP

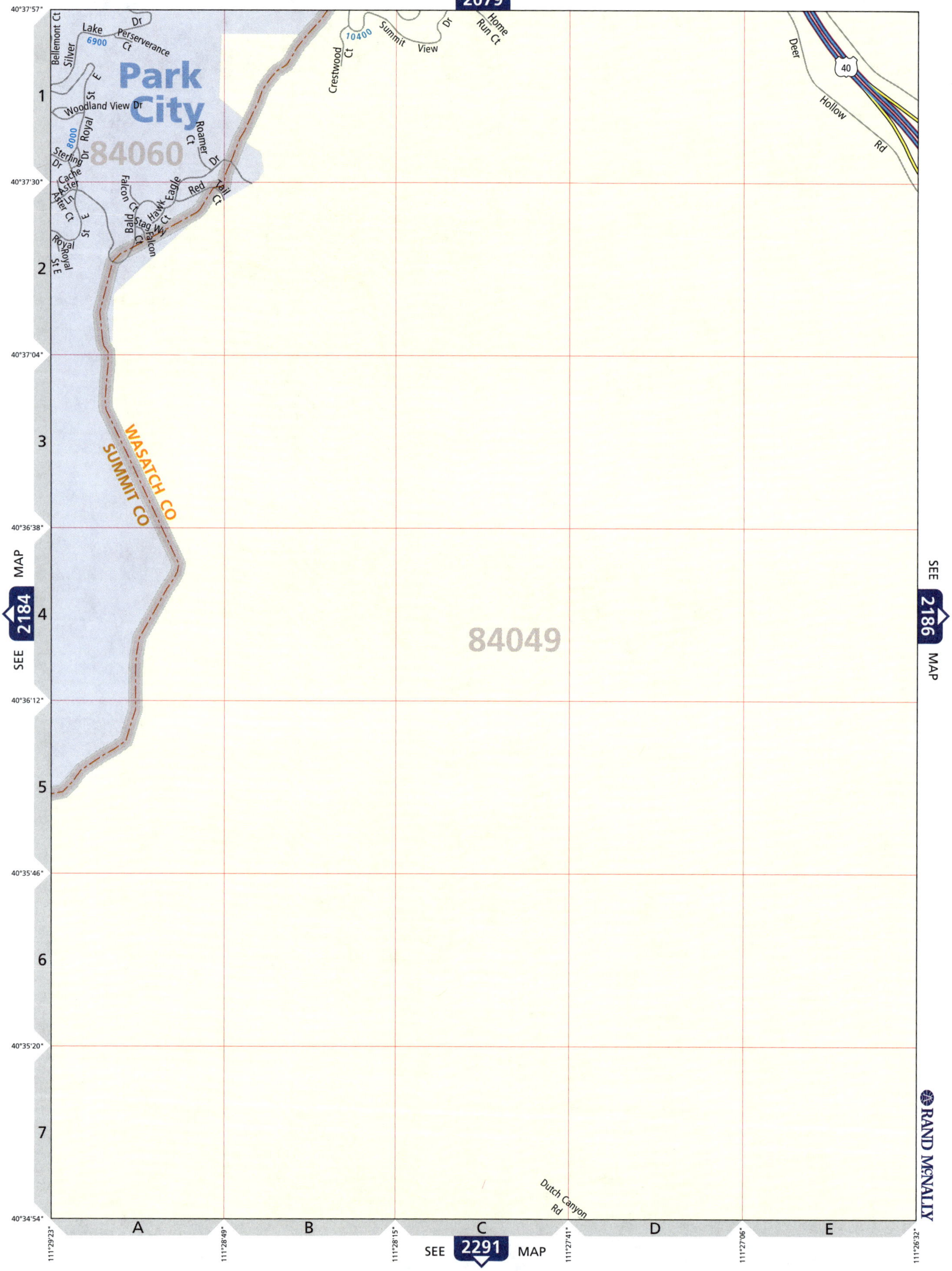

SEE 2184 MAP

SEE 2186 MAP

SEE 2291 MAP

SEE B MAP
SEE 2185 MAP
SEE B MAP
SEE 2292 MAP

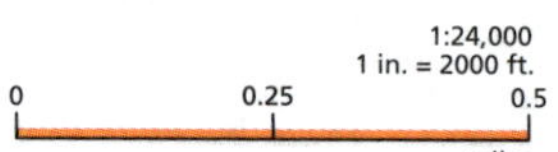

SEE 2173 MAP

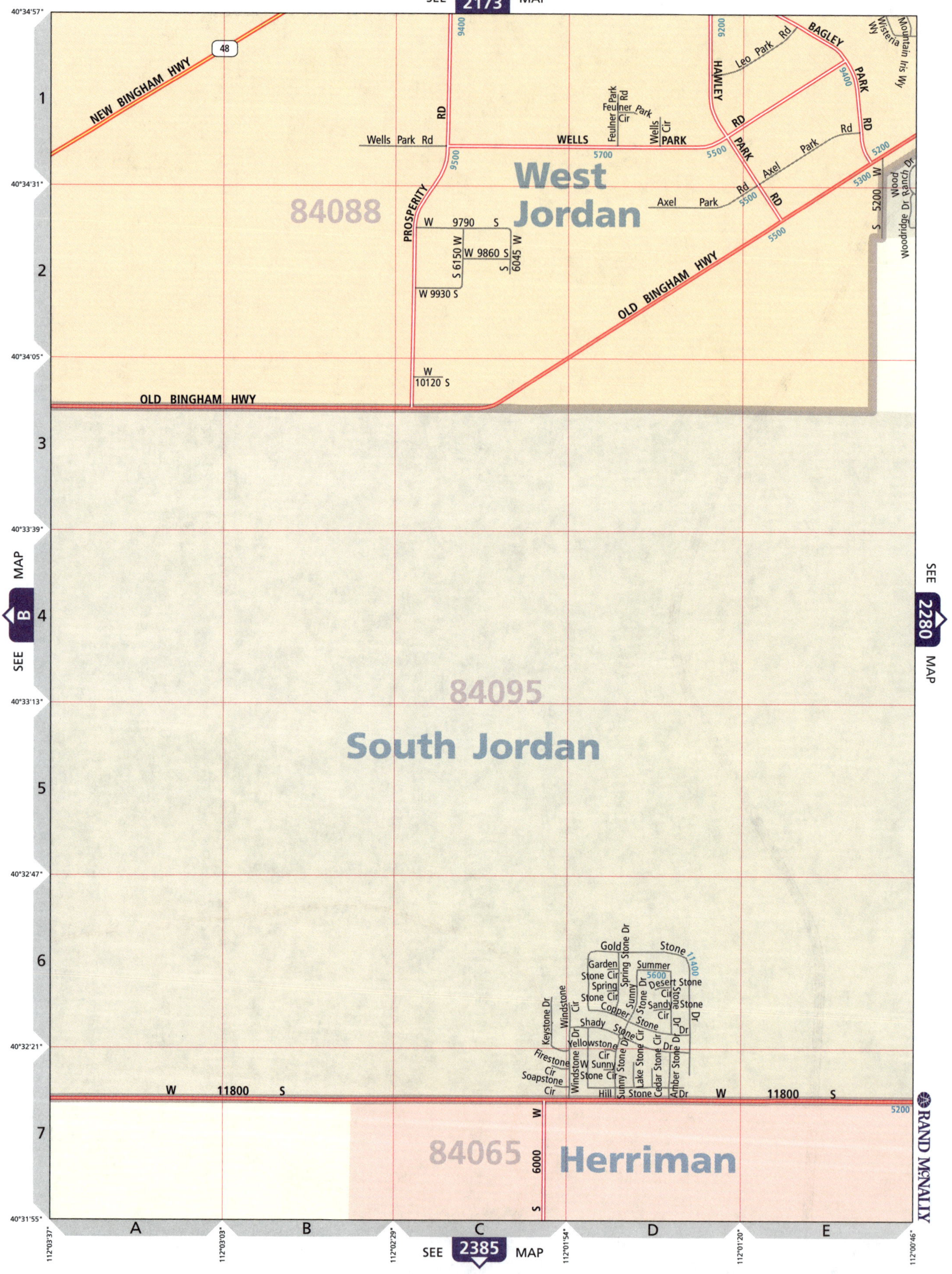

SEE B MAP

SEE 2280 MAP

SEE 2385 MAP

1:24,000
1 in. = 2000 ft.
0 0.25 0.5
miles

SEE 2174 MAP

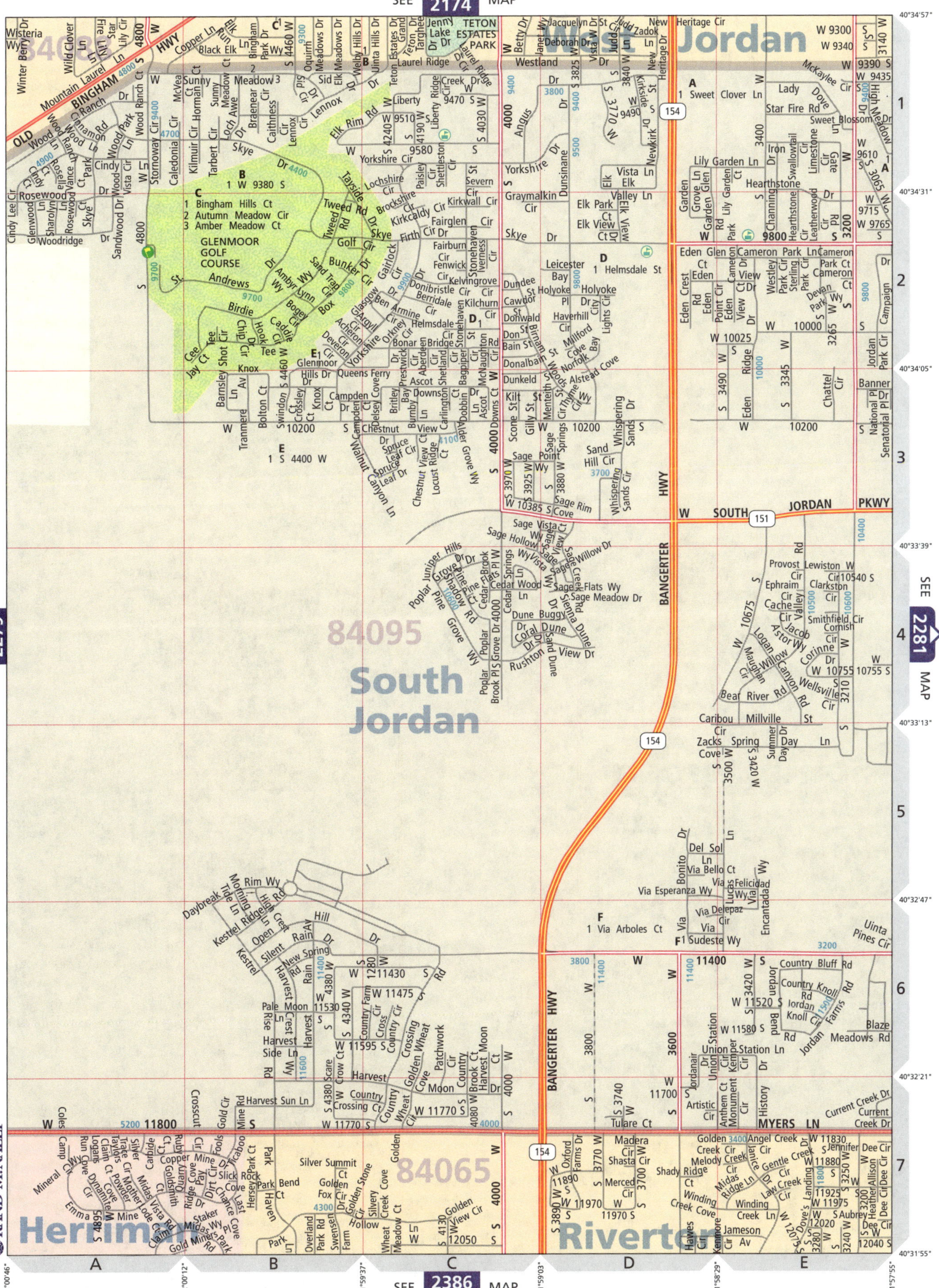

SEE 2279 MAP

SEE 2281 MAP

SEE 2386 MAP

RAND McNALLY

1:24,000
1 in. = 2000 ft.
0 0.25 0.5
miles

SEE 2175 MAP

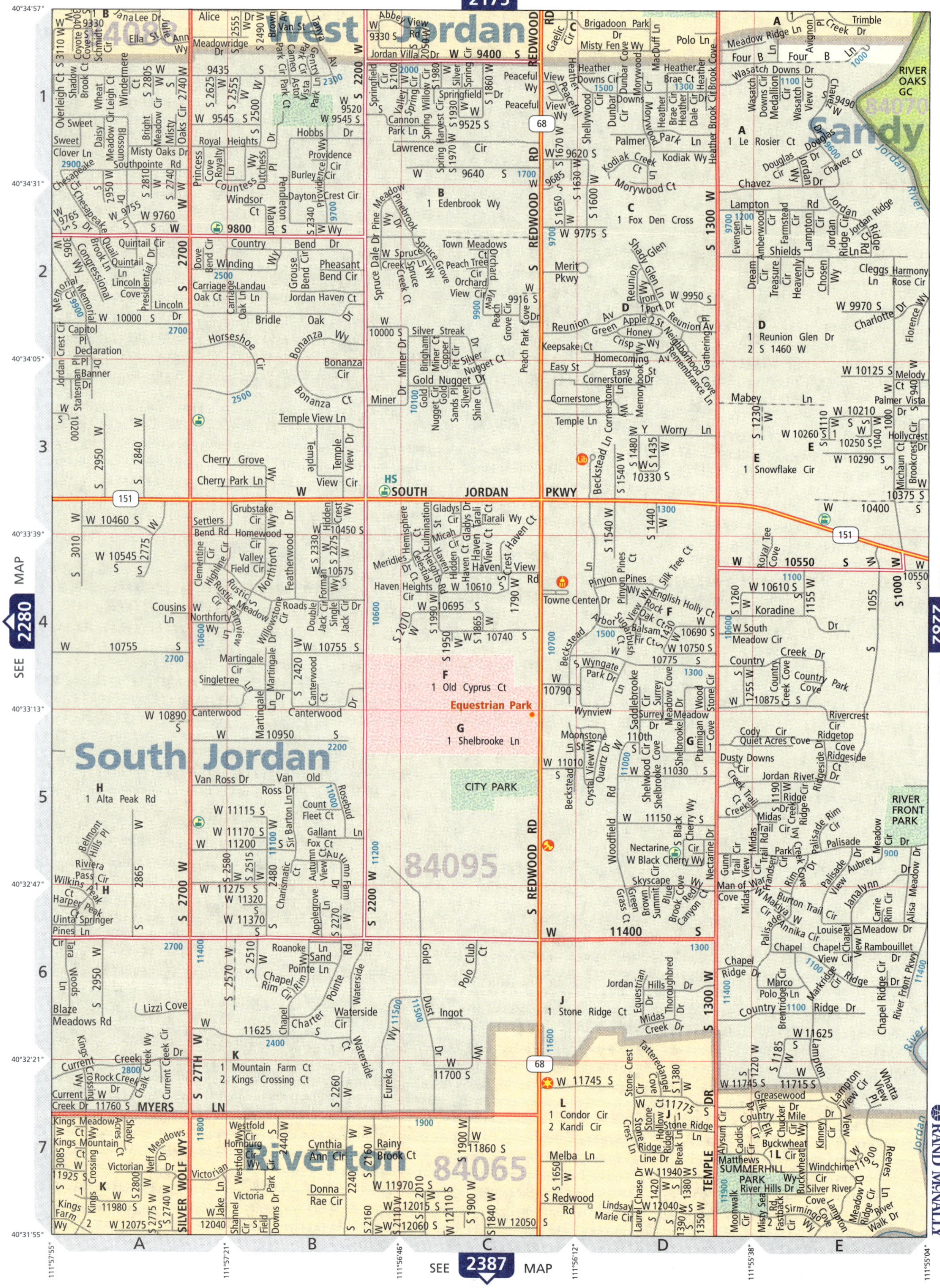

West Jordan

Sandy

South Jordan

Riverton

84095

84065

84070

84088

RIVER OAKS GC

RIVER FRONT PARK

CITY PARK

Equestrian Park

SOUTH JORDAN PKWY

REDWOOD RD

S 1300 W

S 2700 W

S 2200 W

W 9400 S

W 9800 S

W 10000 S

W 10550 S

W 11400 S

MYERS LN

S 27TH W

SILVER WOLF WY

TEMPLE DR

SUMMERHILL PARK

A 1 Le Rosier Ct

B 1 Edenbrook Wy

C 1 Fox Den Cross

D 1 Reunion Glen Dr 2 S 1460 W

E 1 Snowflake Cir

F 1 Old Cyprus Ct

G 1 Shelbrooke Ln

H 1 Alta Peak Rd

J 1 Stone Ridge Ct

K 1 Mountain Farm Ct 2 Kings Crossing Ct

L 1 Condor Cir 2 Kandi Cir

SEE 2280 MAP

SEE 2282 MAP

SEE 2387 MAP

A B C D E

1 2 3 4 5 6 7

40°34'57" 40°34'31" 40°34'05" 40°33'39" 40°33'13" 40°32'47" 40°32'21" 40°31'55"

111°57'55" 111°57'21" 111°56'46" 111°56'12" 111°55'38" 111°55'04"

1:24,000
1 in. = 2000 ft.
0 0.25 0.5
miles

SEE 2176 MAP

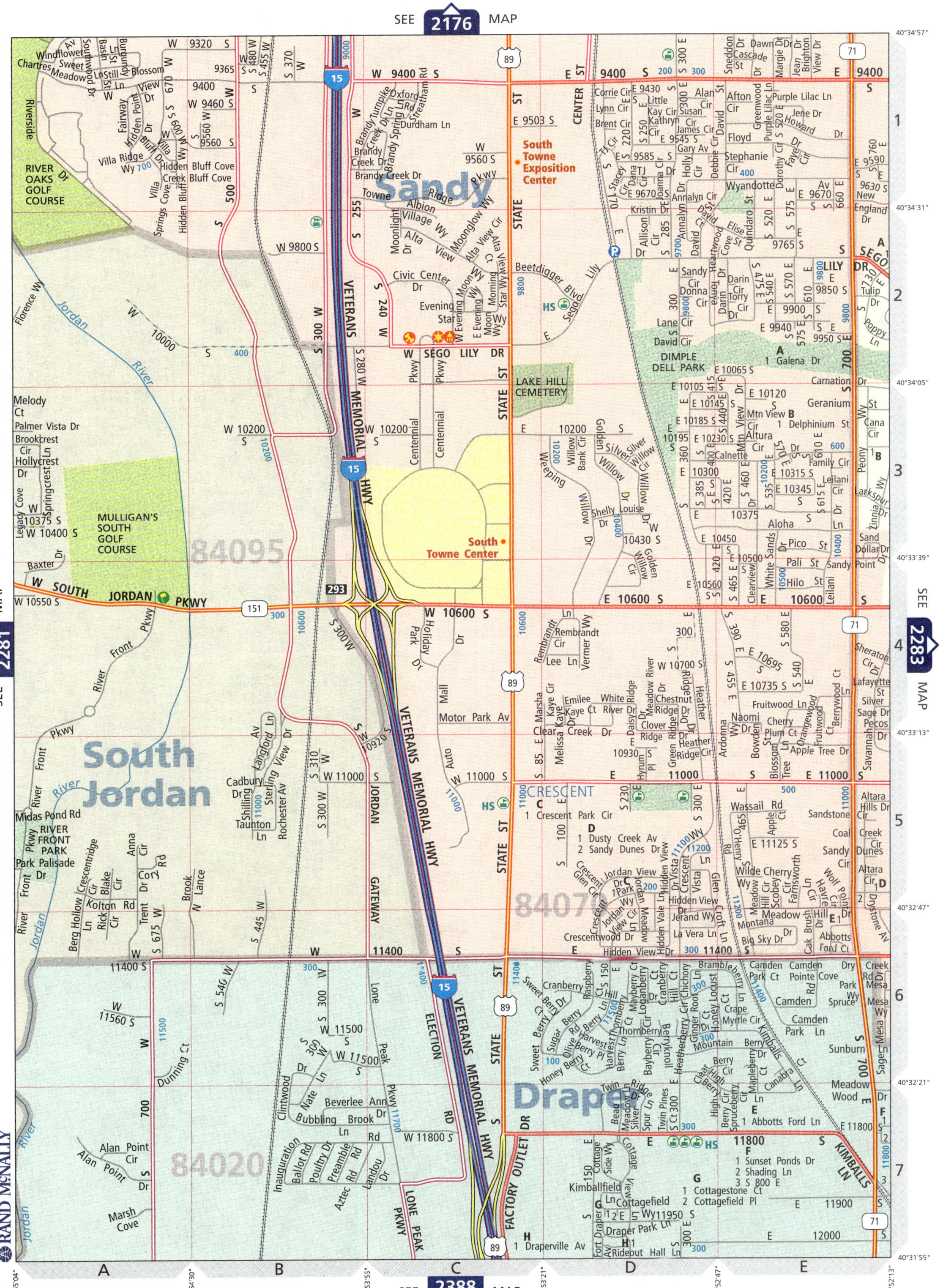

SEE 2281 MAP

SEE 2283 MAP

SEE 2388 MAP

1:24,000
1 in. = 2000 ft.
0 0.25 0.5
miles

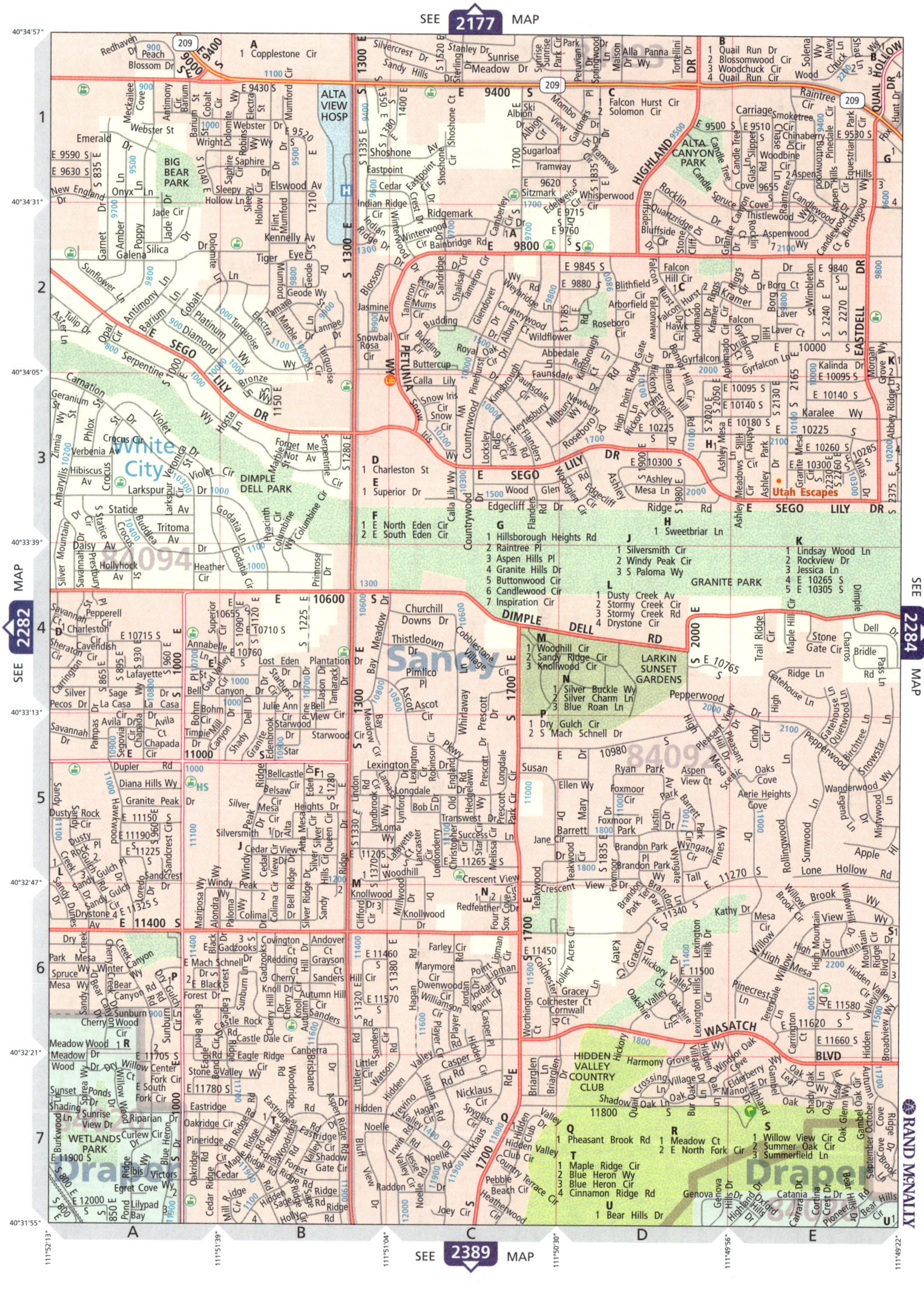

SEE 2177 MAP

A
1 Copplestone Cir

B
1 Quail Run Dr
2 Blossomwood Cir
3 Woodchuck Cir
4 Quail Run Cir

C
1 Falcon Hurst Cir
2 Solomon Cir

D
1 Charleston St

E
1 Superior Dr

F
1 E North Eden Cir
2 E South Eden Cir

G
1 Hillsborough Heights Rd
2 Raintree Pl
3 Aspen Hills Pl
4 Granite Hills Dr
5 Buttonwood Cir
6 Candlewood Cir
7 Inspiration Cir

H
1 Sweetbriar Ln

J
1 Silversmith Cir
2 Windy Peak Cir
3 S Paloma Wy

K
1 Lindsay Wood Ln
2 Rockview Dr
3 Jessica Ln
4 E 10265 S
5 E 10305 S

L
1 Dusty Creek Av
2 Stormy Creek Cir
3 Stormy Creek Rd
4 Drystone Cir

M
1 Woodhill Cir
2 Sandy Ridge Cir
3 Knollwood Cir

N
1 Silver Buckle Wy
2 Silver Charm Ln
3 Blue Roan Ln

P
1 Dry Gulch Cir
2 S Mach Schnell Dr

Q
1 Pheasant Brook Rd

R
1 Meadow Ct
2 E North Fork Cir

S
1 Willow View Cir
2 Summer Oak Cir
3 Summerfield Ln

T
1 Maple Ridge Cir
2 Blue Heron Wy
3 Blue Heron Cir
4 Cinnamon Ridge Rd

U
1 Bear Hills Dr

ALTA VIEW HOSP
BIG BEAR PARK
ALTA CANYON PARK
White City
DIMPLE DELL PARK
GRANITE PARK
84094
Sandy
LARKIN SUNSET GARDENS
84092
HIDDEN VALLEY COUNTRY CLUB
WETLANDS PARK
Draper
Utah Escapes

SEE 2282 MAP

SEE 2284 MAP

SEE 2389 MAP

1:24,000
1 in. = 2000 ft.
0 0.25 0.5
miles

SEE 2178 MAP

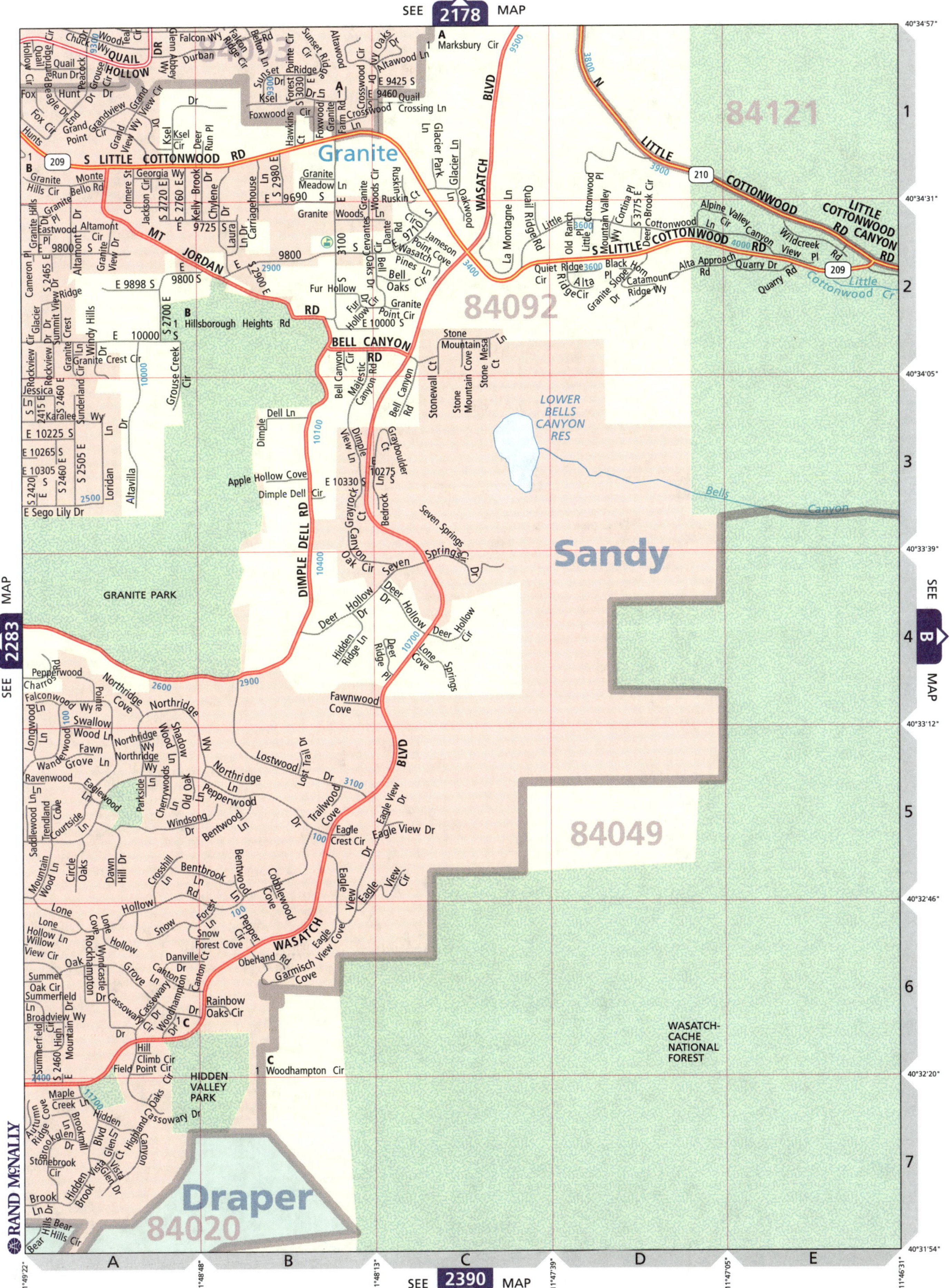

SEE 2283 MAP
SEE B MAP
SEE 2390 MAP

1:24,000
1 in. = 2000 ft.
0 0.25 0.5
miles

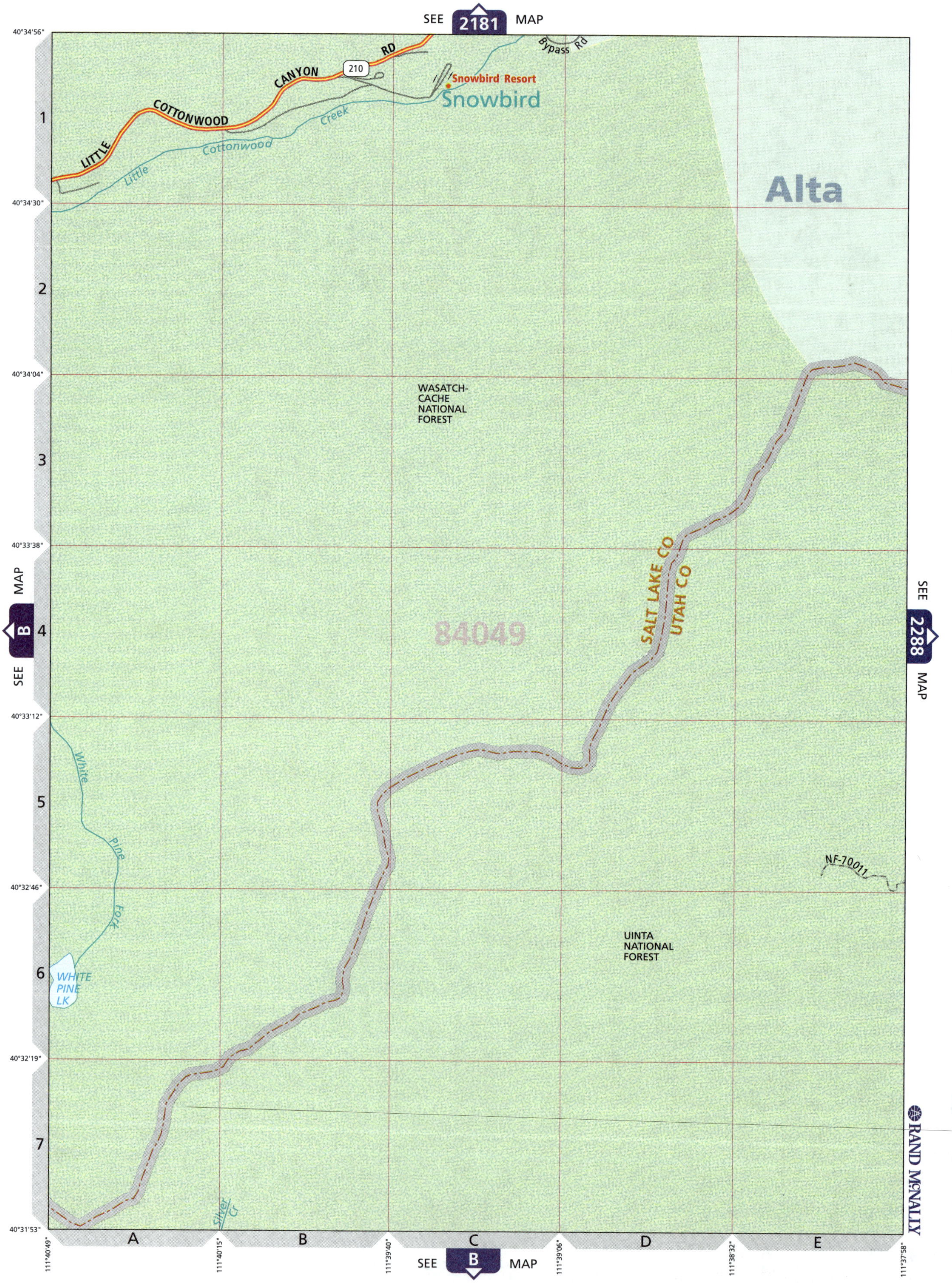

SEE 2181 MAP

SEE B MAP

SEE 2288 MAP

SEE B MAP

1:24,000
1 in. = 2000 ft.
0 0.25 0.5
miles

SEE 2182 MAP

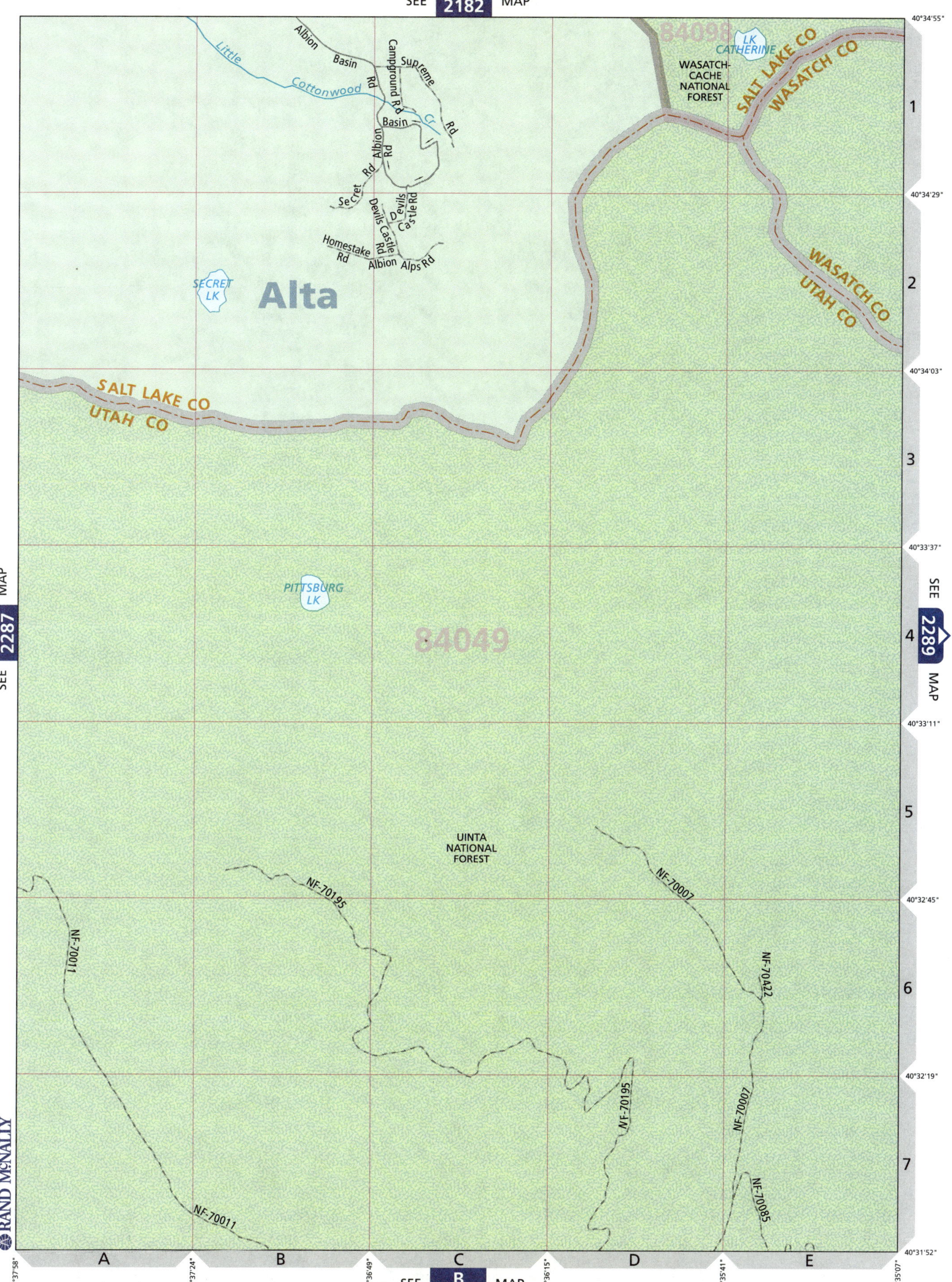

SEE 2287 MAP

SEE 2289 MAP

SEE B MAP

1:24,000
1 in. = 2000 ft.
0 0.25 0.5
miles

SEE 2183 MAP

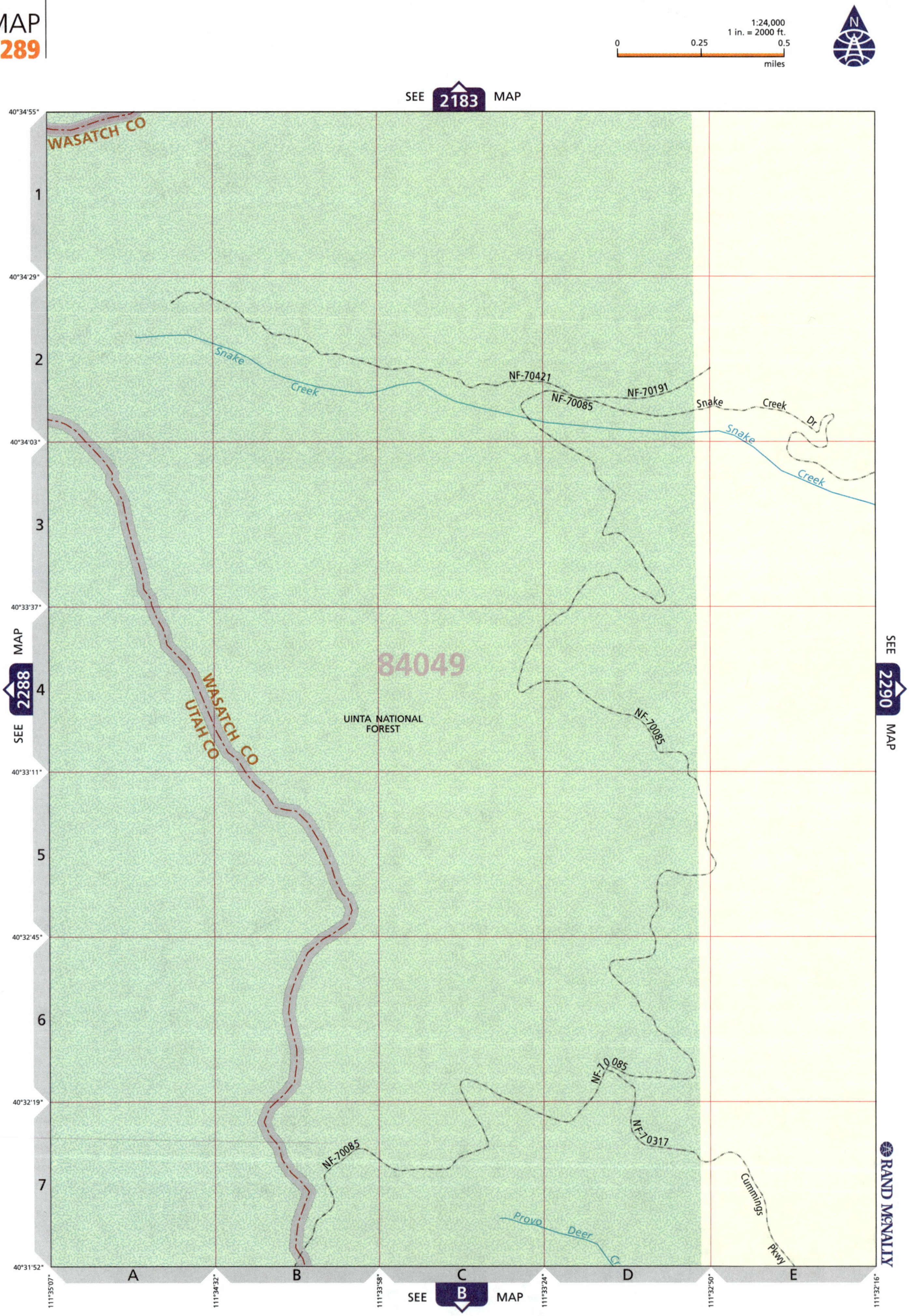

SEE 2288 MAP

SEE 2290 MAP

SEE B MAP

1:24,000
1 in. = 2000 ft.
0 0.25 0.5
miles

SEE 2184 MAP

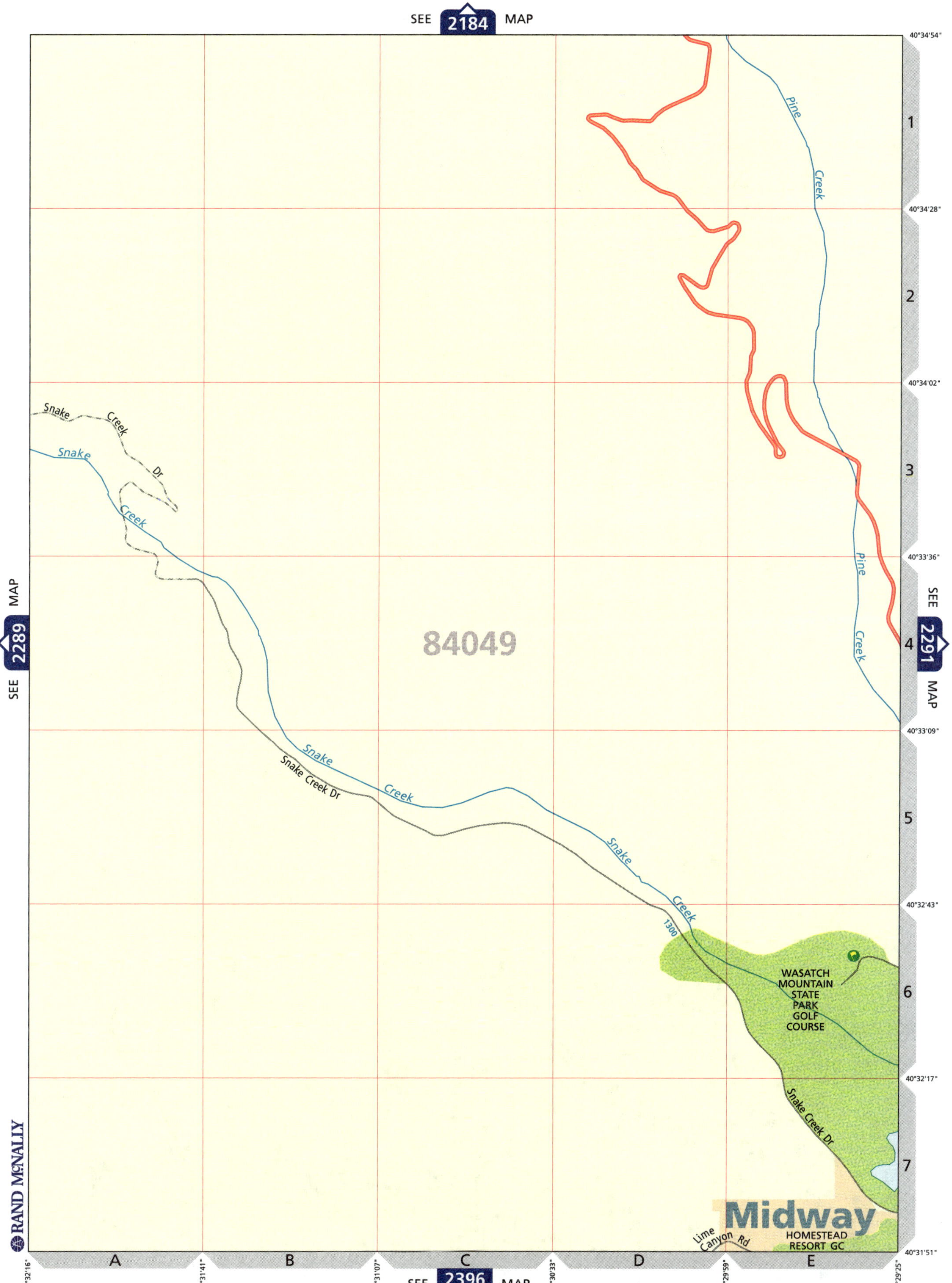

SEE 2289 MAP

SEE 2291 MAP

SEE 2396 MAP

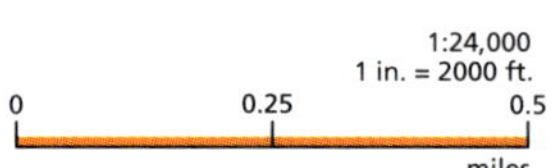

SEE 2185 MAP

SEE 2290 MAP

SEE 2292 MAP

40°34'54"
40°34'28"
40°34'02"
40°33'36"
40°33'09"
40°32'43"
40°32'17"
40°31'51"

1
2
3
4
5
6
7

84049

Dutch Canyon Rd

Pine Creek

WASATCH MTN STATE PARK GC

Snake Cr

Eiger Pt
Jungfrau Hl
300
200
Matterhorn Wy
Moritz Rd
St.
Interlaken Rd
200
300
Wy
Rd
Bern
Luzern
Edelweiss Ln
1200
Interlaken Rd

PINE CANYON RD
1100

A
1 Snake Creek Dr
2 Warm Springs Rd

A
1
2
HOMESTEAD RD
Cottage Wy

Canyon View Rd
Village Ct
W Village Cir
W Oberland Ct
Village Cir
Valais Pkwy

Midway

N RIVER RD
1500
1700

PROVO RIVER

84032

RAND McNALLY

A
B
C
D
E

111°29'25"
111°28'50"
111°28'16"
111°27'42"
111°27'08"
111°26'34"

SEE 2397 MAP

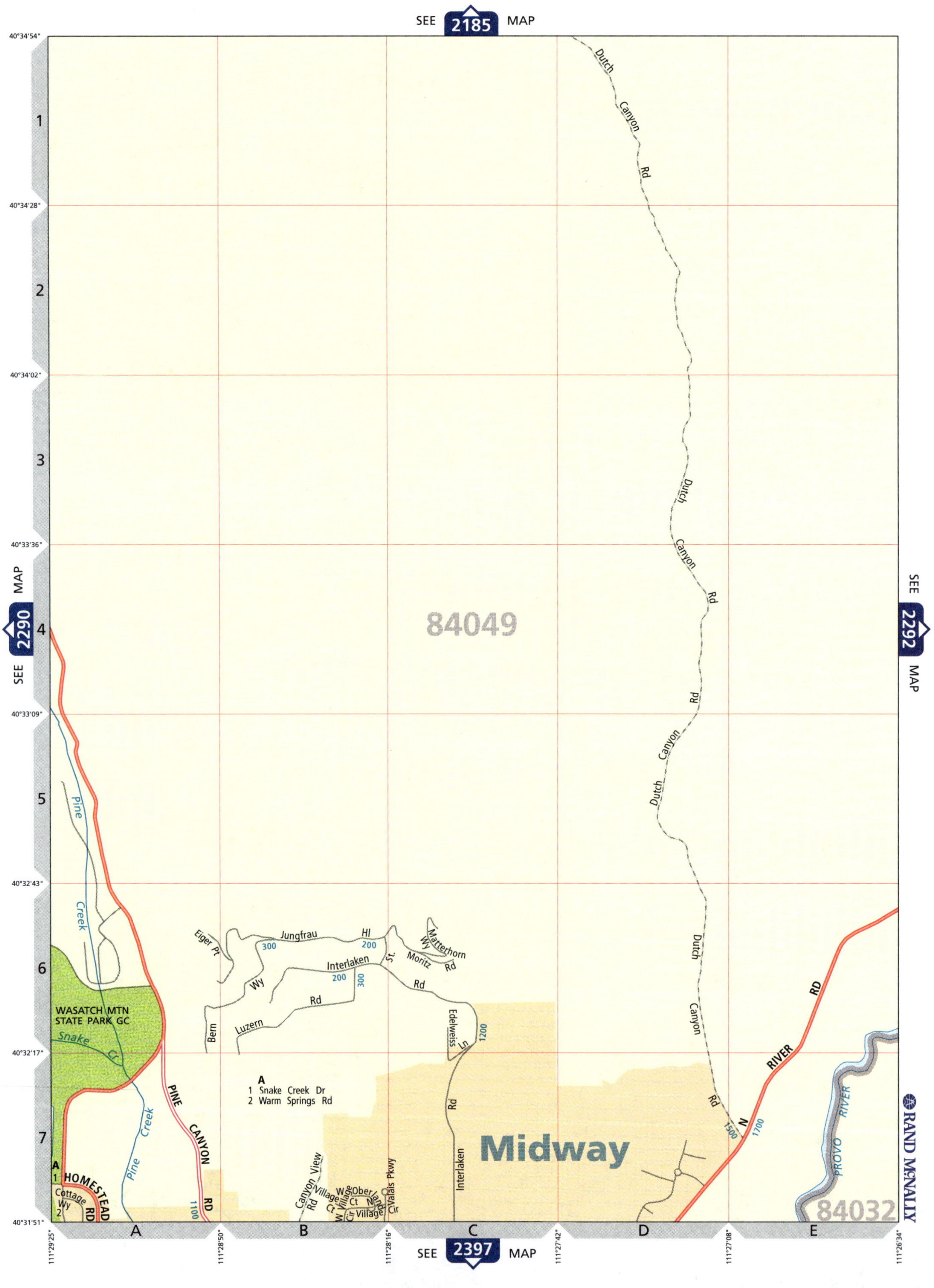

1:24,000
1 in. = 2000 ft.
0 0.25 0.5
miles

SEE 2186 MAP

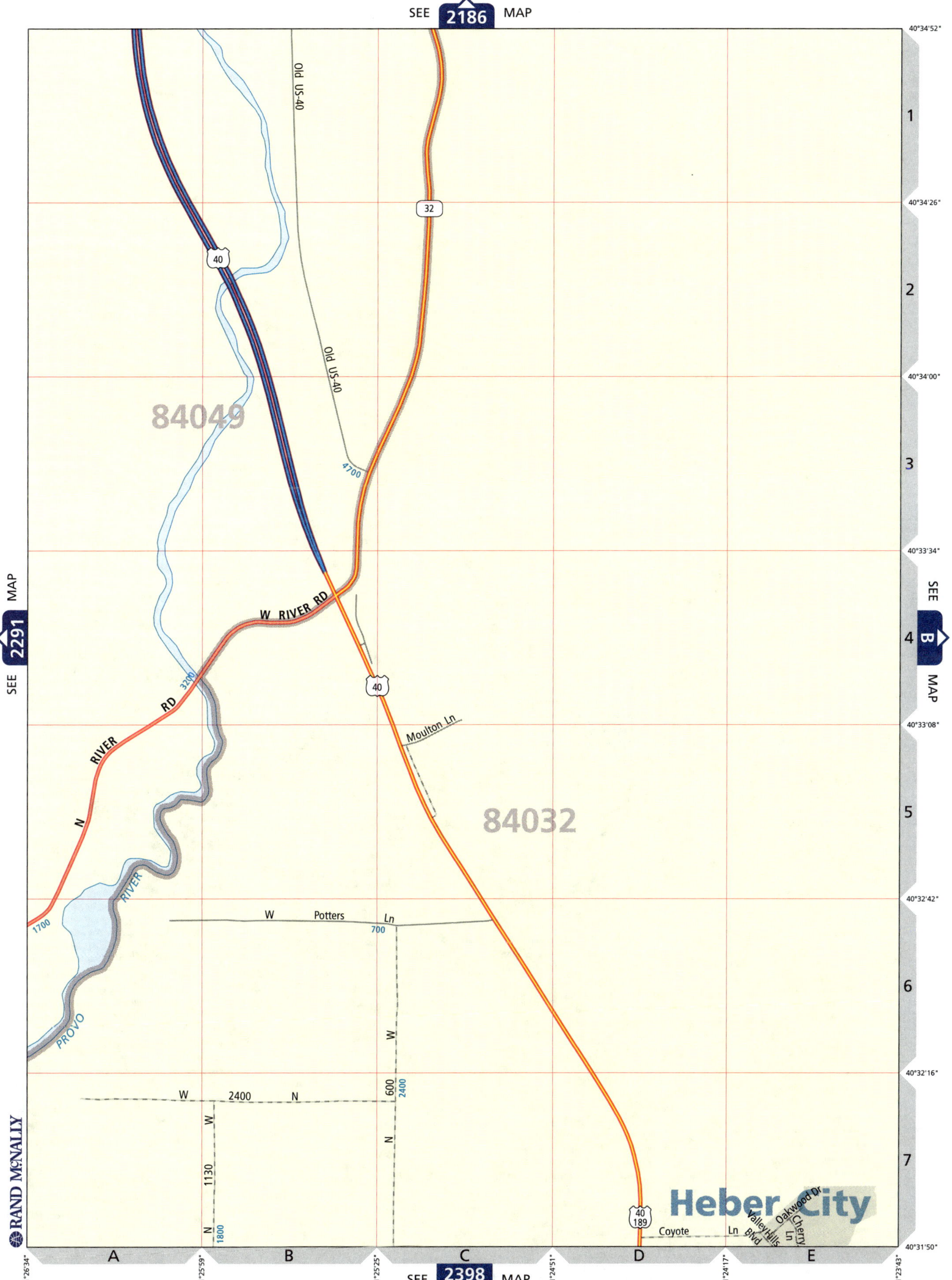

SEE 2291 MAP

SEE B MAP

SEE 2398 MAP

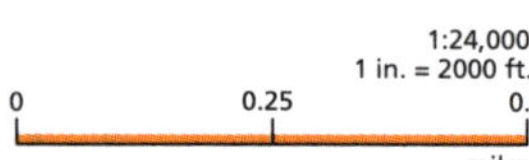

SEE 2279 MAP

SEE B MAP

SEE 2386 MAP

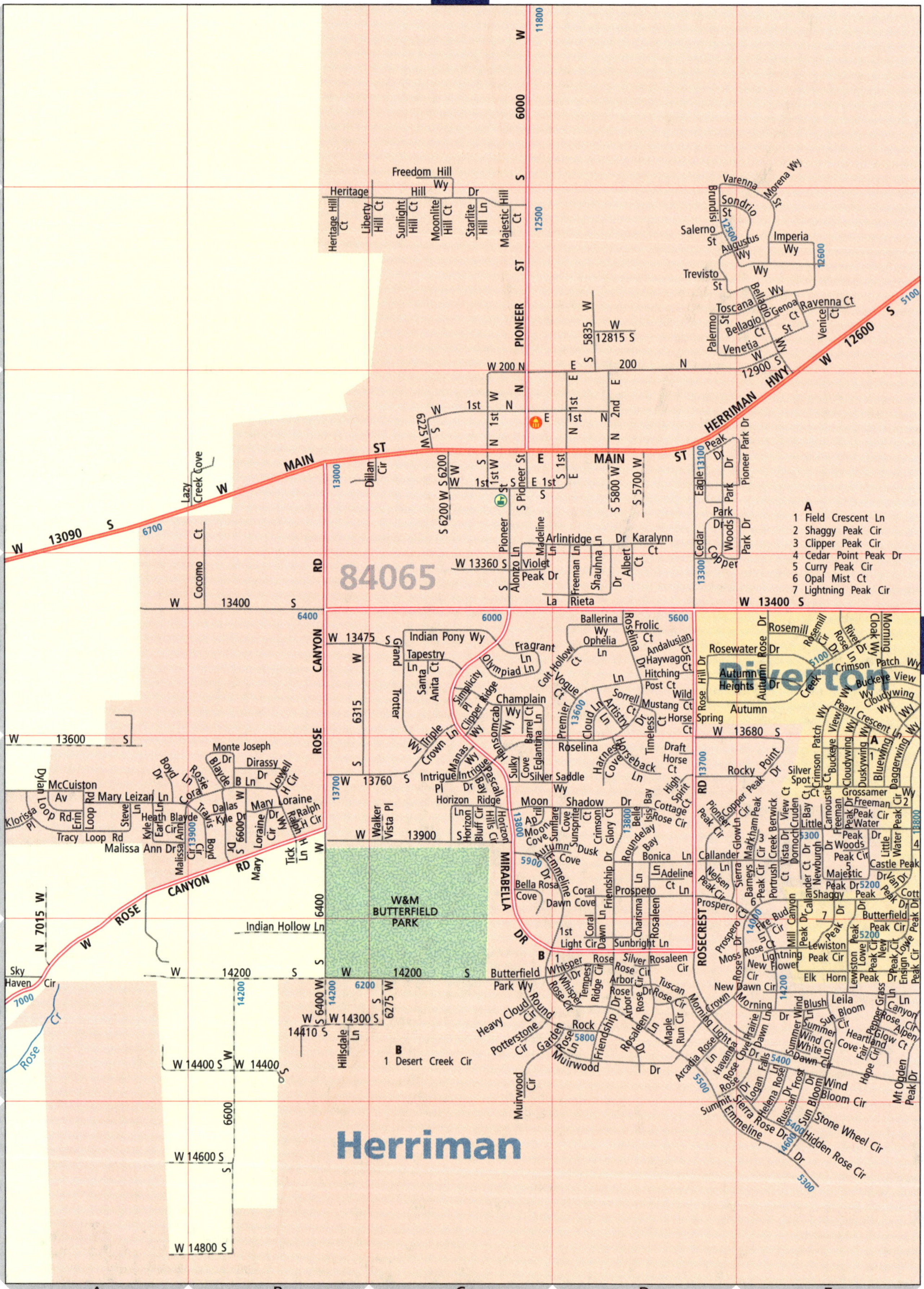

Herriman

Riverton

84065

W&M BUTTERFIELD PARK

MAIN ST

HERRIMAN HWY

PIONEER ST

ROSE CANYON RD

ROSECREST RD

MIRABELLA DR

A
1 Field Crescent Ln
2 Shaggy Peak Cir
3 Clipper Peak Cir
4 Cedar Point Peak Dr
5 Curry Peak Cir
6 Opal Mist Ct
7 Lightning Peak Cir

B
1 Desert Creek Cir

40°31'55"
40°31'28"
40°31'02"
40°30'36"
40°30'10"
40°29'44"
40°29'18"
40°28'52"

112°03'37"
112°03'03"
112°02'28"
112°01'54"
112°01'20"
112°00'46"

A B C D E

1 2 3 4 5 6 7

SEE B MAP

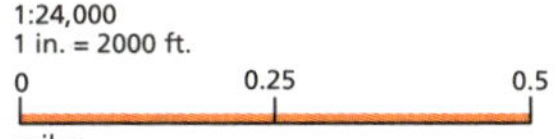

SEE 2280 MAP

Herriman

Riverton

Bluffdale

84065

BANGERTER HWY

A
1 Gold Miners Pl
2 Claim Staker Wy
3 Silver Reef Ct
4 Midas Park Rd

B
1 Overland Park Rd

C
1 Legacy Point Dr

D
1 Timber River Dr
2 Flatbush Cove
3 Aspen Springs Dr
4 Cedar Hollow Ct
5 Stormy Meadow Dr
6 Timber Run Dr

E
1 Whirlabout Ln
2 Dartwhite Ln
3 Skipperling Ln
4 Crimson Patch Wy
5 Buckeye View Wy
6 Daggerwing Wy

F
1 Deer View Pl

G
1 Mt Olympus Peak Dr
2 Vice Admiral Dr
3 Blue Admiral Ct

H
1 Cedar Point Peak Cir
2 Haystack Peak Cir

J
1 Amber Rose Ln
2 Yellow Sage Ct
3 Hearthstone Cir
4 Winterbrook Cir

W 12600 S

W 13400 S

W 13800 S

W 14400 S

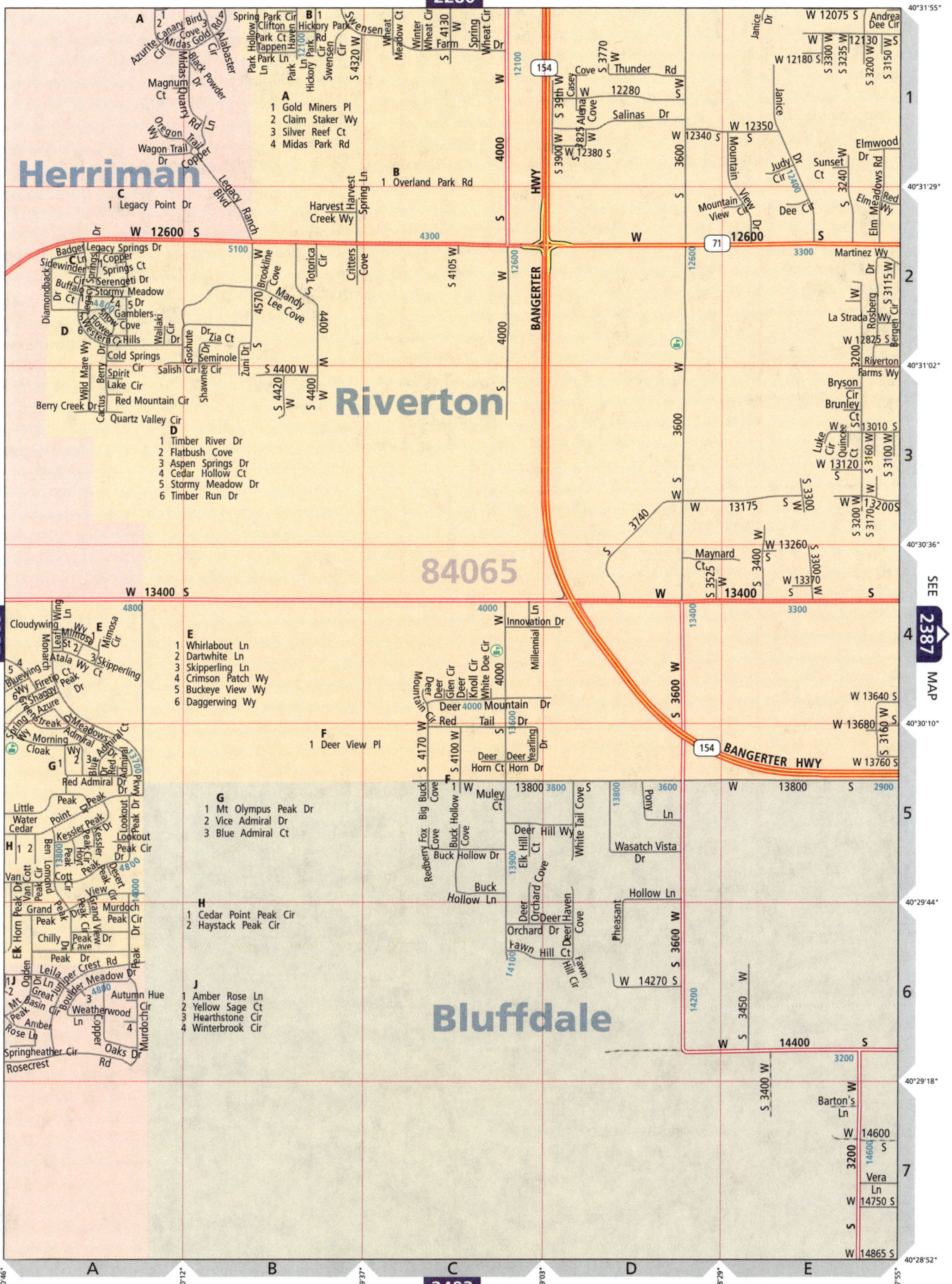

SEE 2385 MAP

SEE 2387 MAP

SEE 2493 MAP

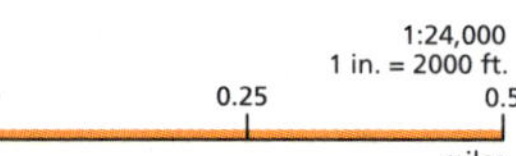

SEE 2281 MAP

SEE 2386 MAP

SEE 2388 MAP

Draper
84020
Riverton
84065
Bluffdale

SOUTH CO PARK
MAIN PARK
CENTENNIAL PARK
RIVERTON CEMETERY
RIVERBEND GOLF COURSE
Jordan River

BANGERTER HWY
REDWOOD RD
WOLF
SILVER
TEMPLE
CAMP WILLIAMS
W 12600 S
W 13400 S
W 14400 S
W 14600 S
71
68
154
140

1
2
3
4
5
6
7

A B C D E

40°31'55"
40°31'29"
40°31'02"
40°30'36"
40°30'10"
40°29'44"
40°29'18"
40°28'52"

111°57'55"
111°57'21"
111°56'47"
111°56'12"
111°55'38"
111°55'04"

SEE 2494 MAP

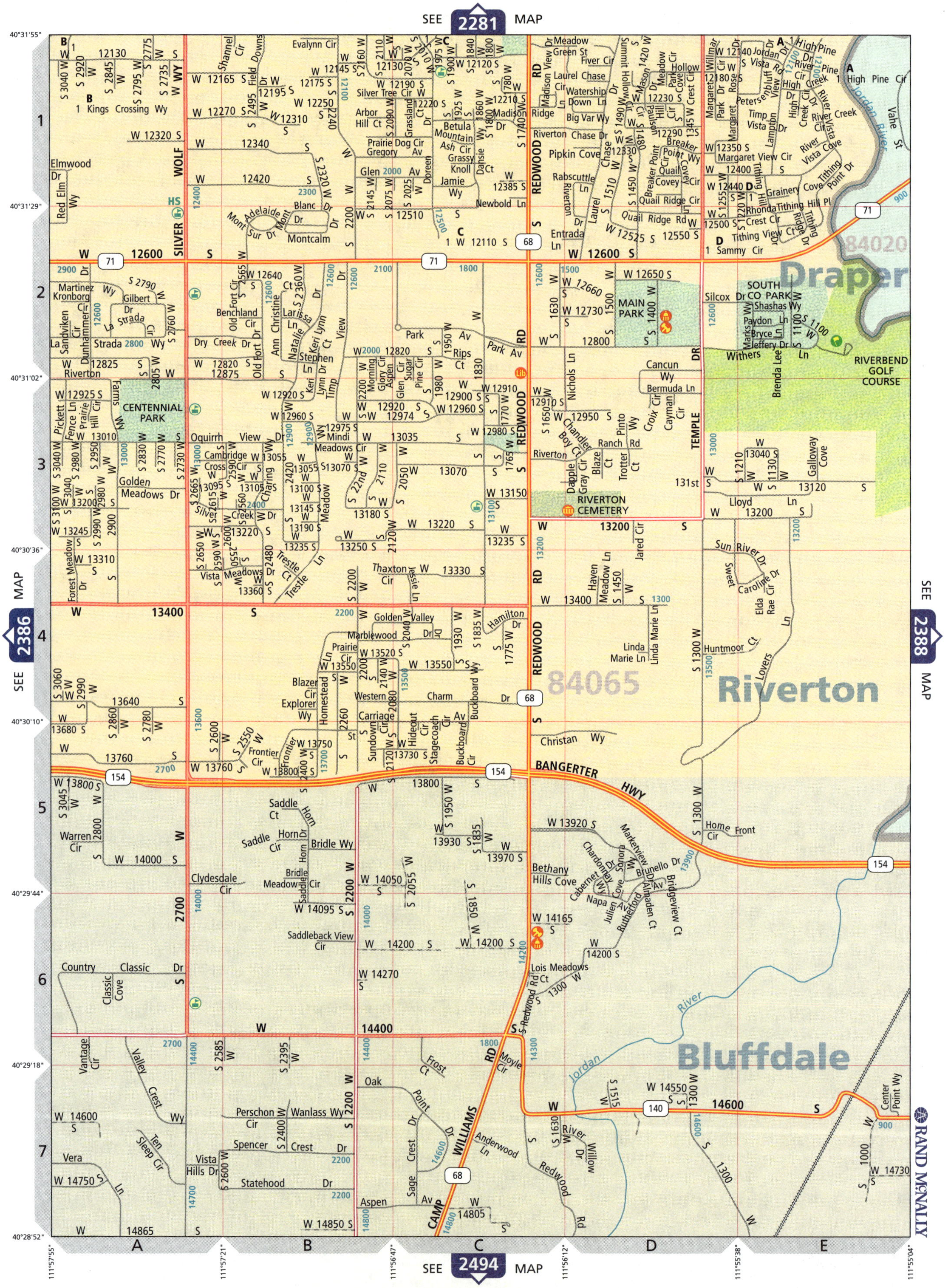

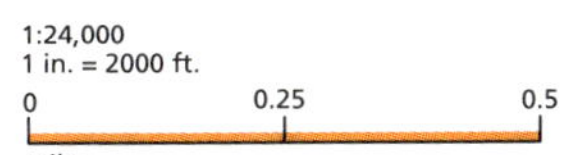

SEE 2282 MAP

SEE 2387 MAP

SEE 2389 MAP

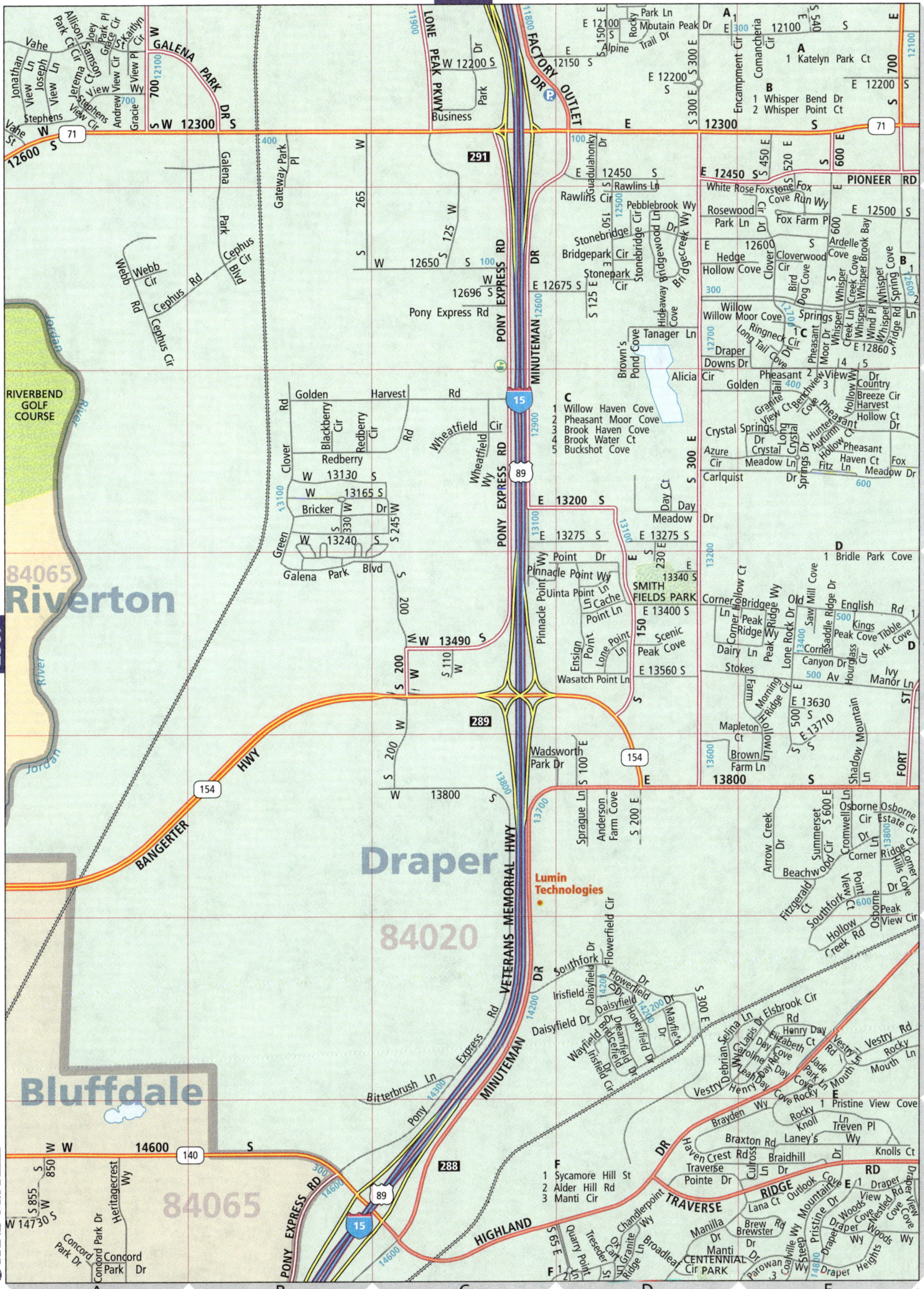

Riverton
84065
Draper
84020
Bluffdale
84065
RIVERBEND GOLF COURSE
Jordan River
SMITH FIELDS PARK
CENTENNIAL PARK
Lumin Technologies

BANGERTER HWY
VETERANS MEMORIAL HWY
MINUTEMAN DR
PONY EXPRESS RD
FACTORY OUTLET DR
LONE PEAK PKWY
GALENA PARK DR
HIGHLAND DR
TRAVERSE RIDGE RD
PIONEER RD
FORT ST
W 12300 S
E 12300 S
W 14600 S
E 13800 S
W 13800 S
E 13200 S
W 13490 S
E 12450 S
W 12650 S
W 13130 S
W 13165 S
W 13240 S
E 13275 S
E 13400 S
E 13560 S
Galena Park Blvd
Golden Harvest Rd
Redberry
Wheatfield Cir
Cephus Rd
Webb Rd
Bitterbrush Ln
Pony Express Rd
Wadsworth Park Dr
Southfork Dr
Daisyfield Dr
Stokes Av
English Rd
Vestry Rd
Braxton Rd
Brayden Wy
Heritagecrest Wy
Concord Park Dr

A
1 Katelyn Park Ct
B
1 Whisper Bend Dr
2 Whisper Point Ct
C
1 Willow Haven Cove
2 Pheasant Moor Cove
3 Brook Haven Cove
4 Brook Water Ct
5 Buckshot Cove
D
1 Bridle Park Cove
E
1 Pristine View Cove
F
1 Sycamore Hill St
2 Alder Hill Rd
3 Manti Cir

RAND McNALLY

A B C D E
1 2 3 4 5 6 7
40°31'55" 40°31'28" 40°31'02" 40°30'36" 40°30'10" 40°29'44" 40°29'18" 40°28'52"
111°55'04" 111°54'30" 111°53'56" 111°53'21" 111°52'47" 111°52'13"

SEE 2495 MAP

1:24,000
1 in. = 2000 ft.
0 0.25 0.5
miles

SEE 2283 MAP

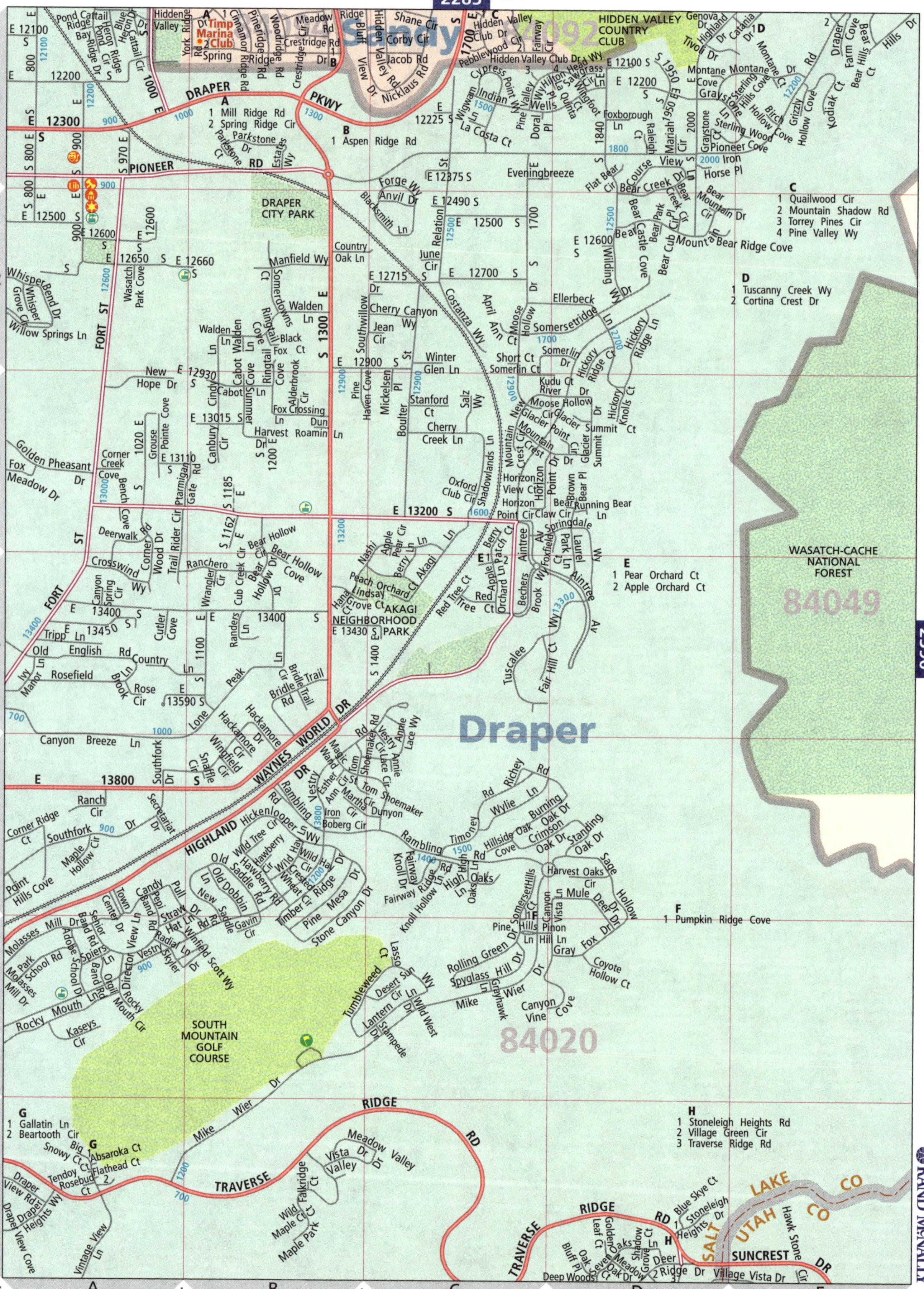

A
1 Mill Ridge Rd
2 Spring Ridge Cir

B
1 Aspen Ridge Rd

C
1 Quailwood Cir
2 Mountain Shadow Rd
3 Torrey Pines Cir
4 Pine Valley Wy

D
1 Tuscanny Creek Wy
2 Cortina Crest Dr

E
1 Pear Orchard Ct
2 Apple Orchard Ct

F
1 Pumpkin Ridge Cove

G
1 Gallatin Ln
2 Beartooth Cir

H
1 Stoneleigh Heights Rd
2 Village Green Cir
3 Traverse Ridge Rd

Sandy
Draper
HIDDEN VALLEY COUNTRY CLUB
DRAPER CITY PARK
AKAGI NEIGHBORHOOD PARK
SOUTH MOUNTAIN GOLF COURSE
WASATCH-CACHE NATIONAL FOREST
84092
84049
84020
Timp Marina Club
SALT LAKE CO
UTAH CO

SEE 2388 MAP

SEE 2390 MAP

SEE 2496 MAP

1:24,000
1 in. = 2000 ft.
0 0.25 0.5
miles

SEE 2284 MAP

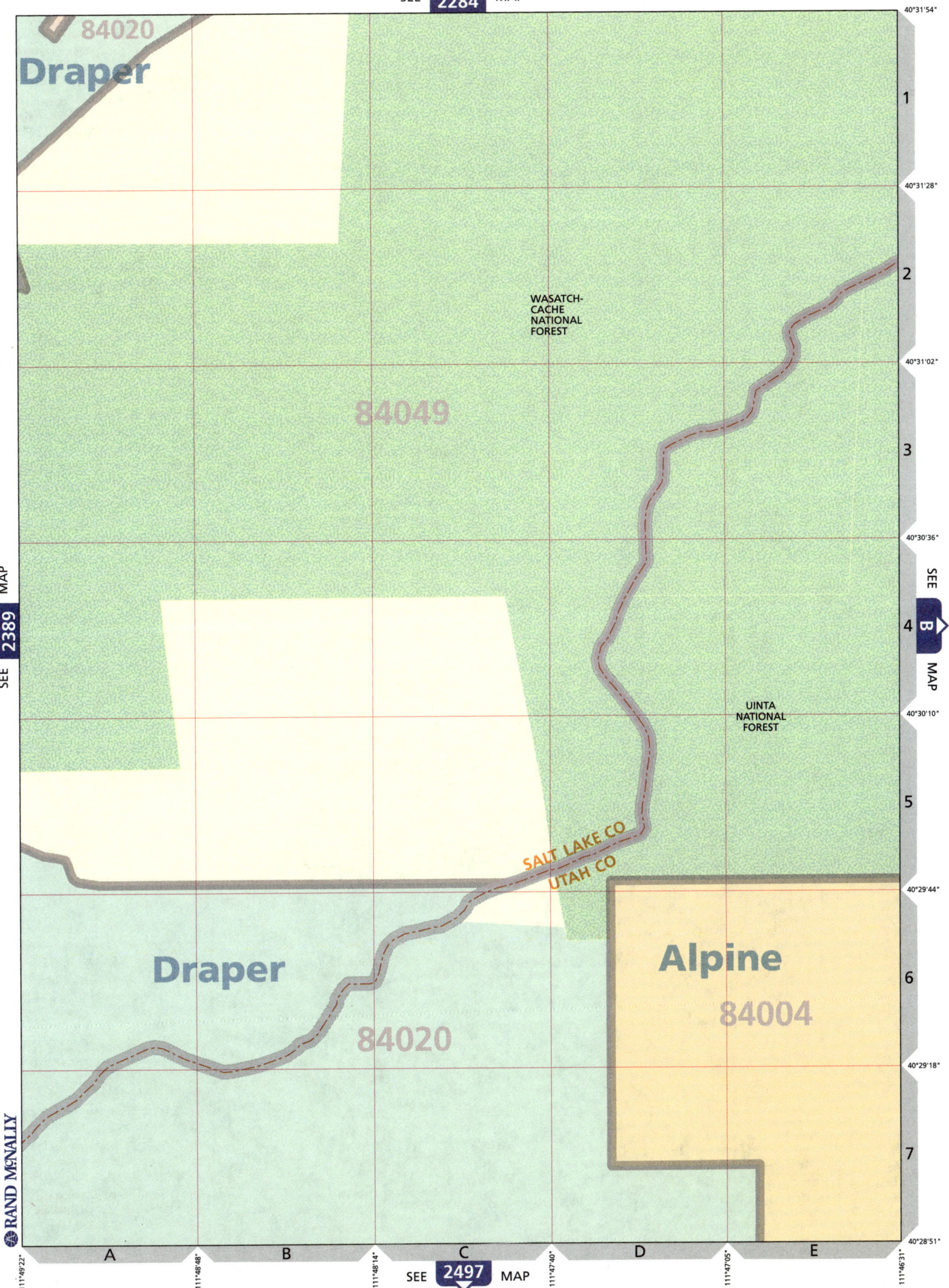

SEE 2389 MAP

SEE B MAP

SEE 2497 MAP

1:24,000
1 in. = 2000 ft.
0 0.25 0.5
miles

SEE 2290 MAP

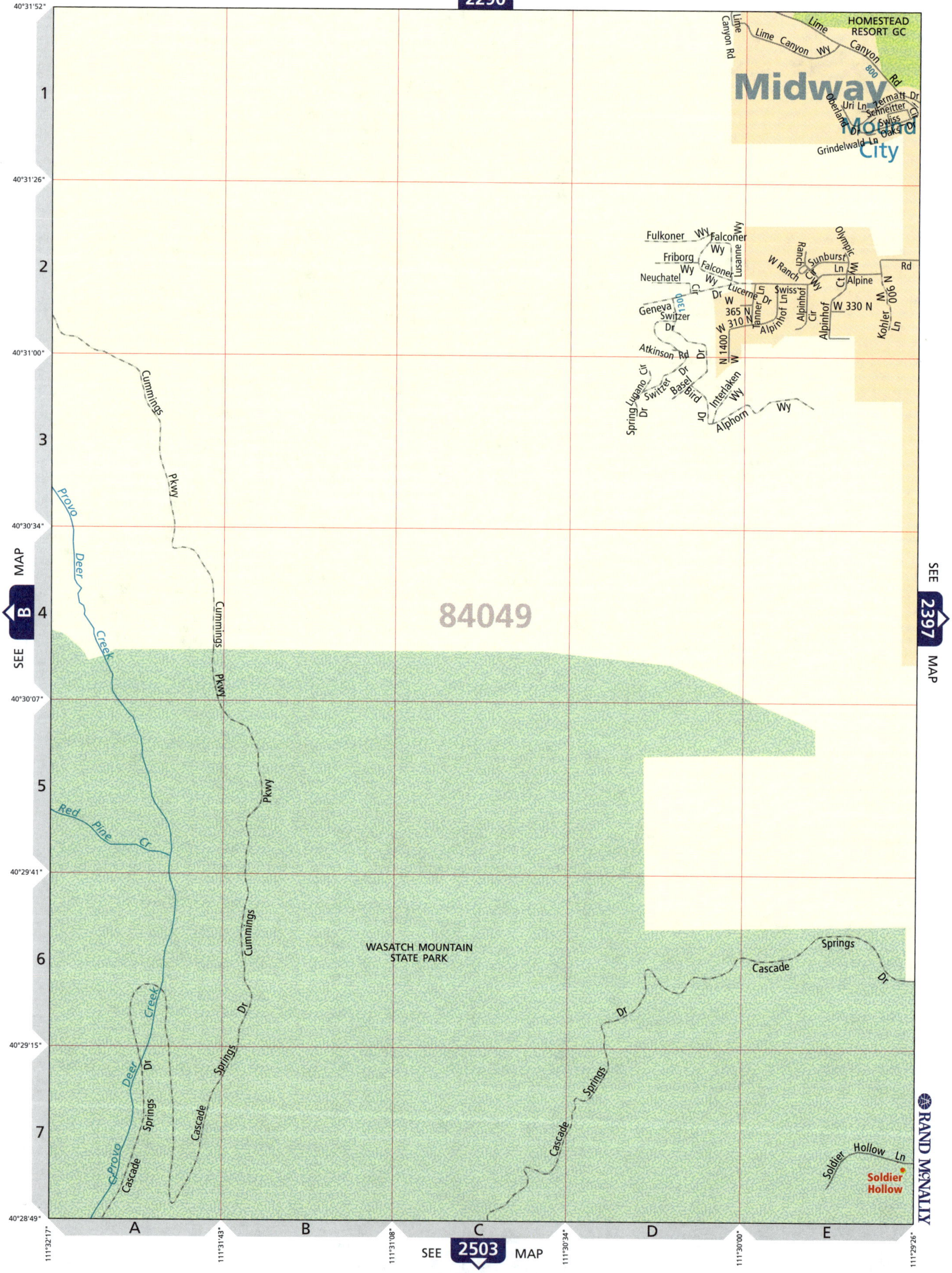

SEE B MAP

SEE 2397 MAP

1 2 3 4 5 6 7
A B C D E

40°31'52" 40°31'26" 40°31'00" 40°30'34" 40°30'07" 40°29'41" 40°29'15" 40°28'49"
111°32'17" 111°31'43" 111°31'08" 111°30'34" 111°30'00" 111°29'26"

SEE 2503 MAP

1:24,000
1 in. = 2000 ft.
0 0.25 0.5
miles

SEE 2291 MAP

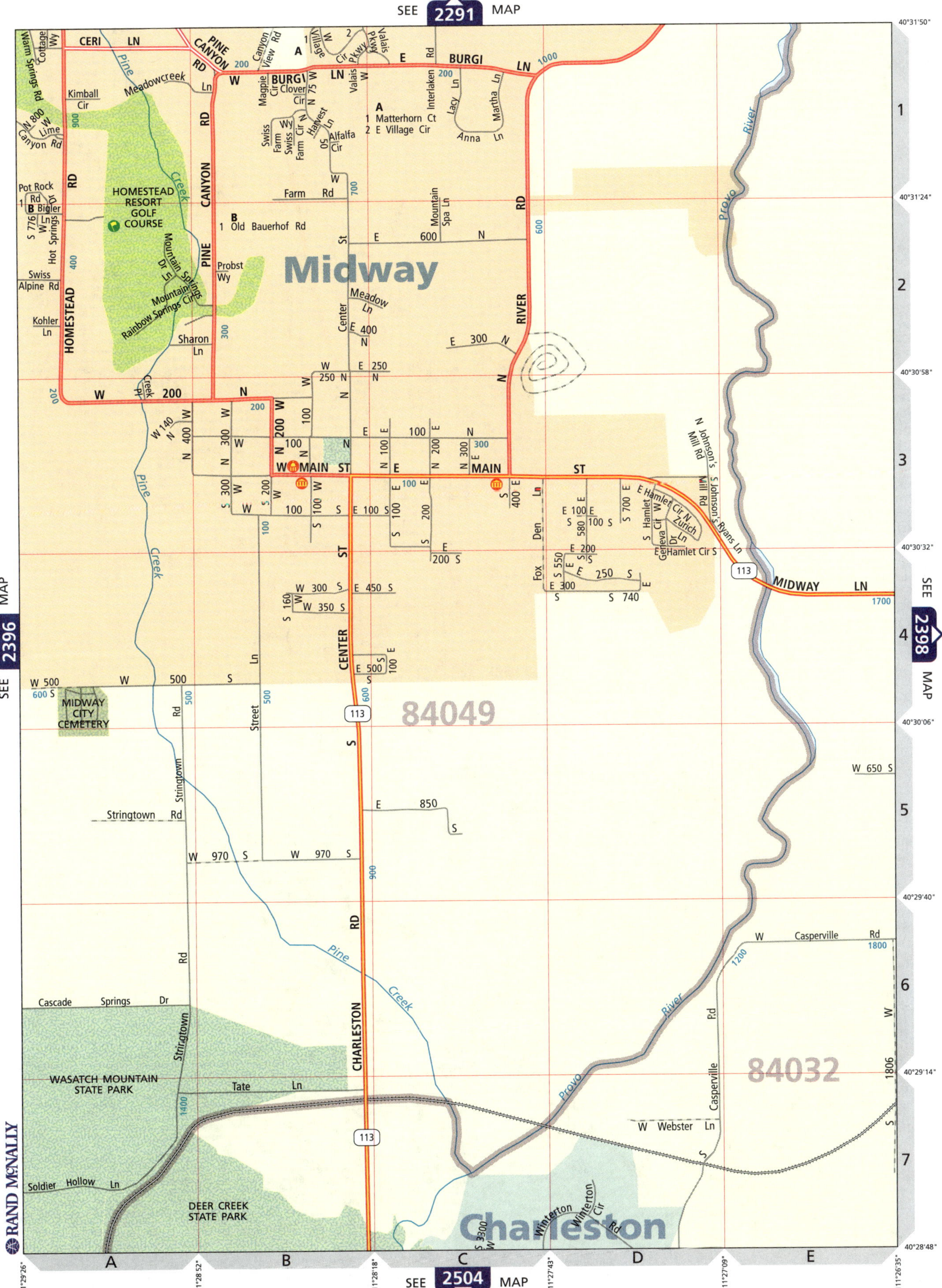

SEE 2396 MAP
SEE 2398 MAP
SEE 2504 MAP

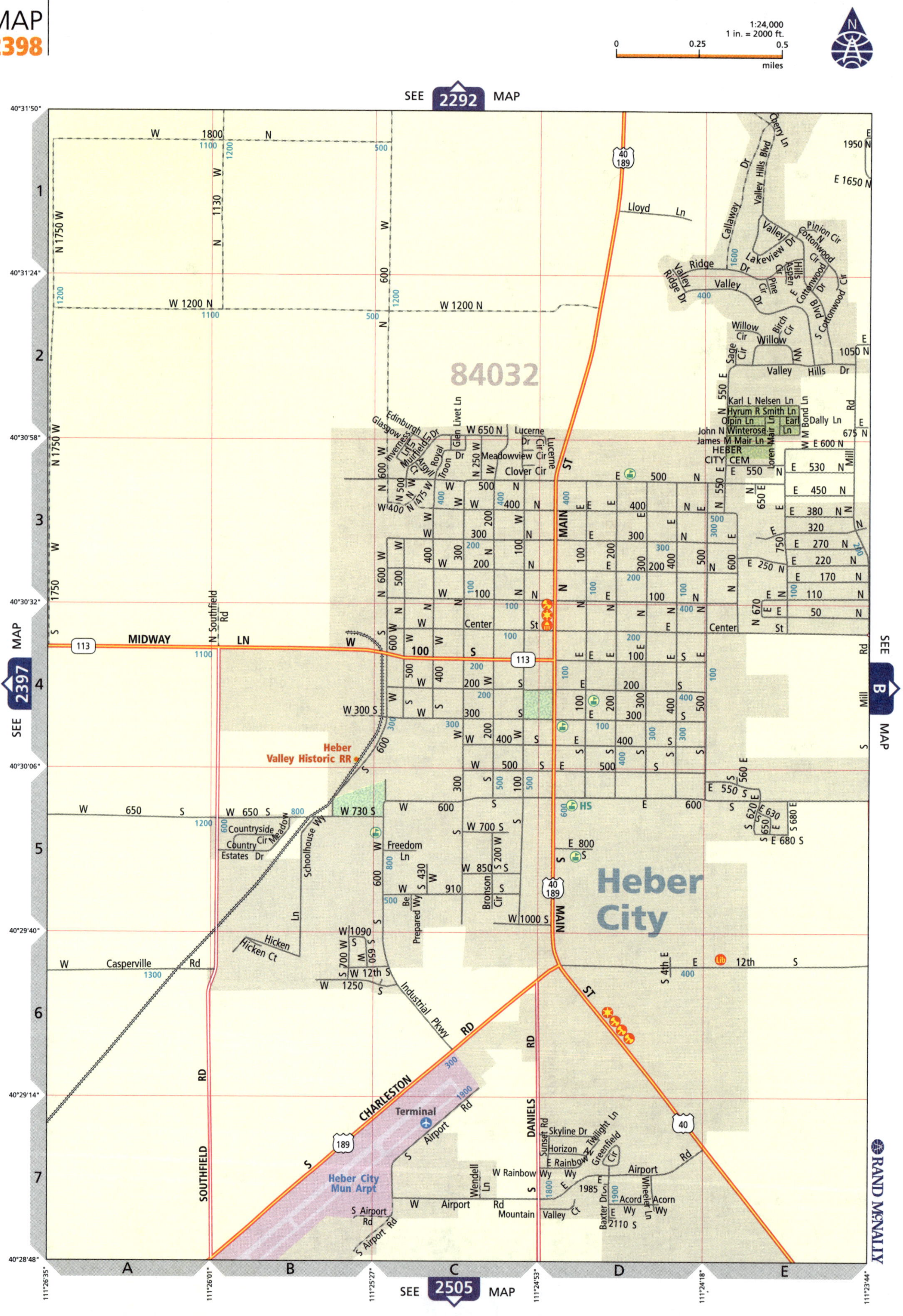

1:24,000
1 in. = 2000 ft.
0 0.25 0.5
miles

SEE 2292 MAP

SEE 2397 MAP

SEE B MAP

SEE 2505 MAP

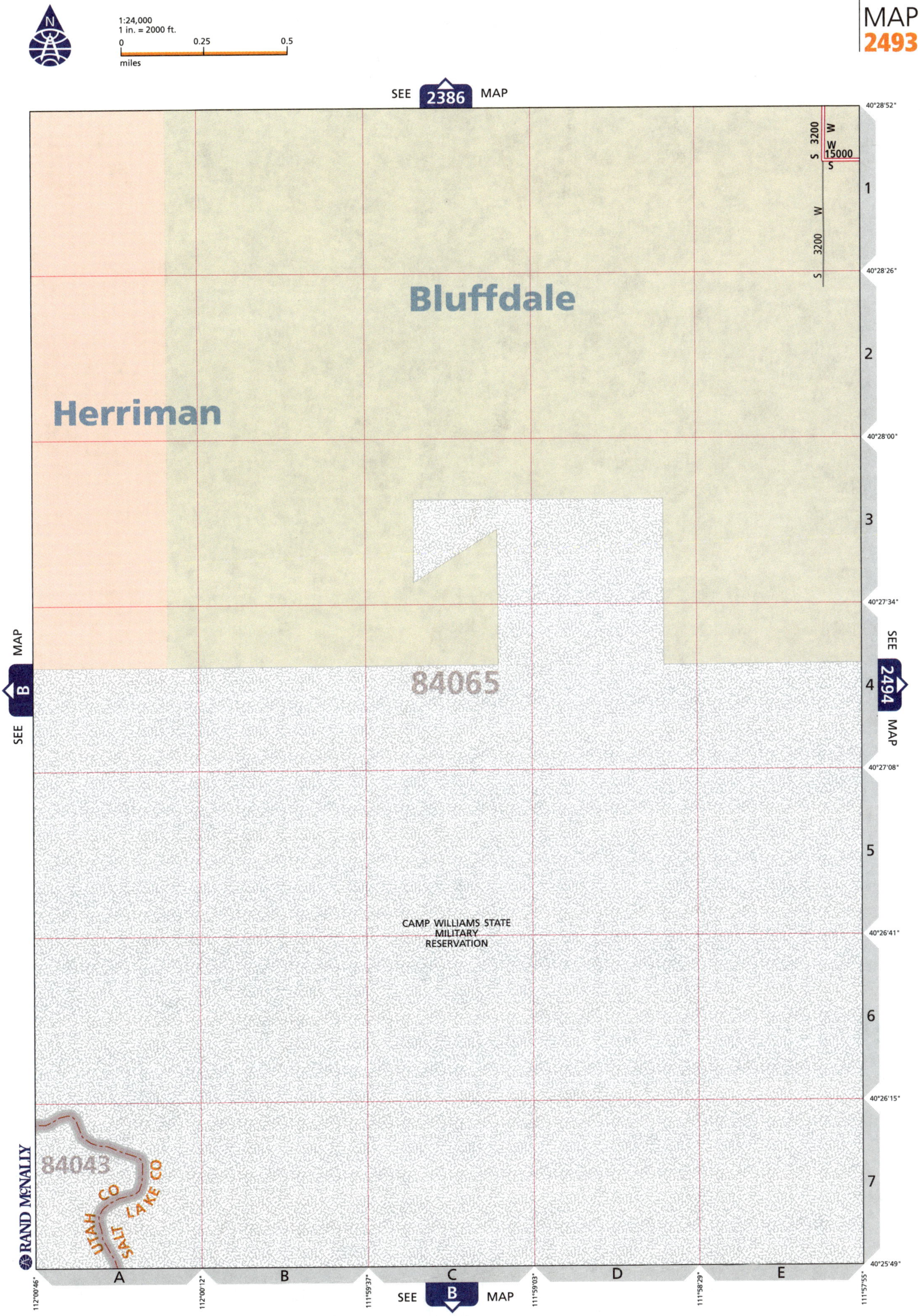

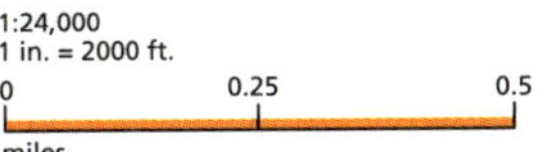

SEE 2386 MAP

SEE B MAP

SEE 2494 MAP

SEE B MAP

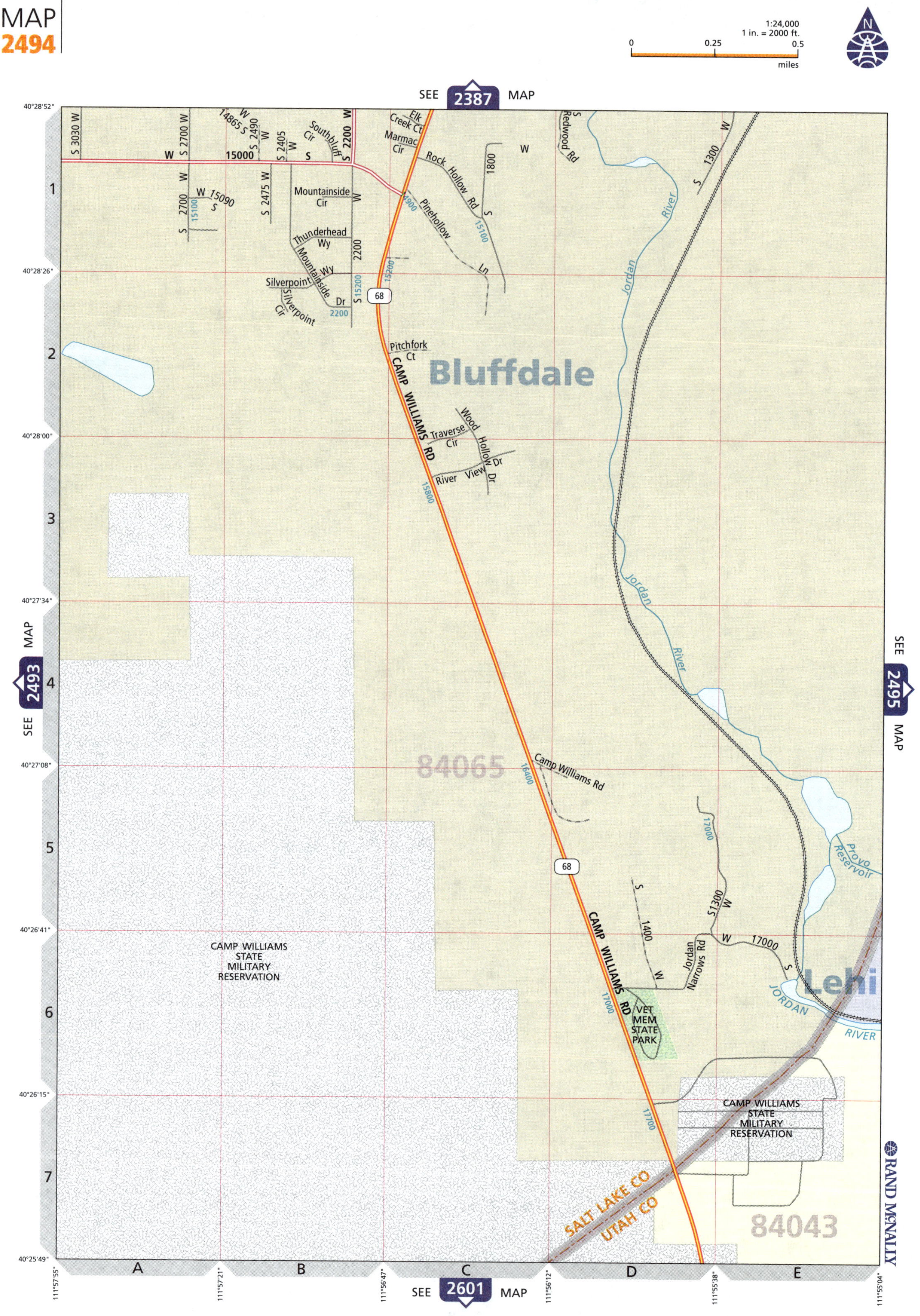

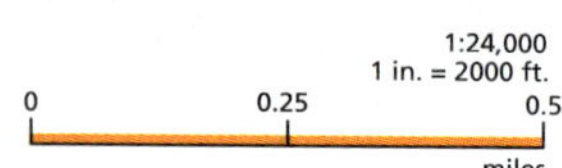

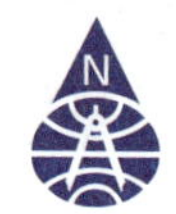

1:24,000
1 in. = 2000 ft.
0
0.25
0.5
miles
N
SEE 2387 MAP
SEE 2601 MAP
SEE 2493 MAP
SEE 2495 MAP
40°28'52"
40°28'26"
40°28'00"
40°27'34"
40°27'08"
40°26'41"
40°26'15"
40°25'49"
111°57'55"
111°57'21"
111°56'47"
111°56'12"
111°55'38"
111°55'04"
A
B
C
D
E
1
2
3
4
5
6
7
Bluffdale
84065
84043
Lehi
CAMP WILLIAMS RD
Camp Williams Rd
68
W 15000 S
S 3030 W
S 2700 W
W 14865 S
S 2490 W
S 2405 W
Southbluff Cir
S 2200 W
Elk Creek Ct
Marmac Cir
Rock Hollow Rd
S 1800 W
Redwood Rd
S 1300 W
W 15090 S
15100
S 2475 W
Mountainside Cir
Thunderhead Wy
Mountainside Dr
Silverpoint Wy
Silverpoint Cir
2200
S 2200 W
15200
14900
Pinehollow Ln
15100
Pitchfork Ct
Wood Hollow Dr
Traverse Cir
River View Dr
15800
16400
17000
S 1300 W
W 17000 S
S 1400 W
Jordan Narrows Rd
17000
17700
Jordan River
Provo Reservoir
JORDAN RIVER
VET MEM STATE PARK
CAMP WILLIAMS STATE MILITARY RESERVATION
CAMP WILLIAMS STATE MILITARY RESERVATION
SALT LAKE CO
UTAH CO
RAND McNALLY

1:24,000
1 in. = 2000 ft.
0 0.25 0.5
miles

SEE 2388 MAP

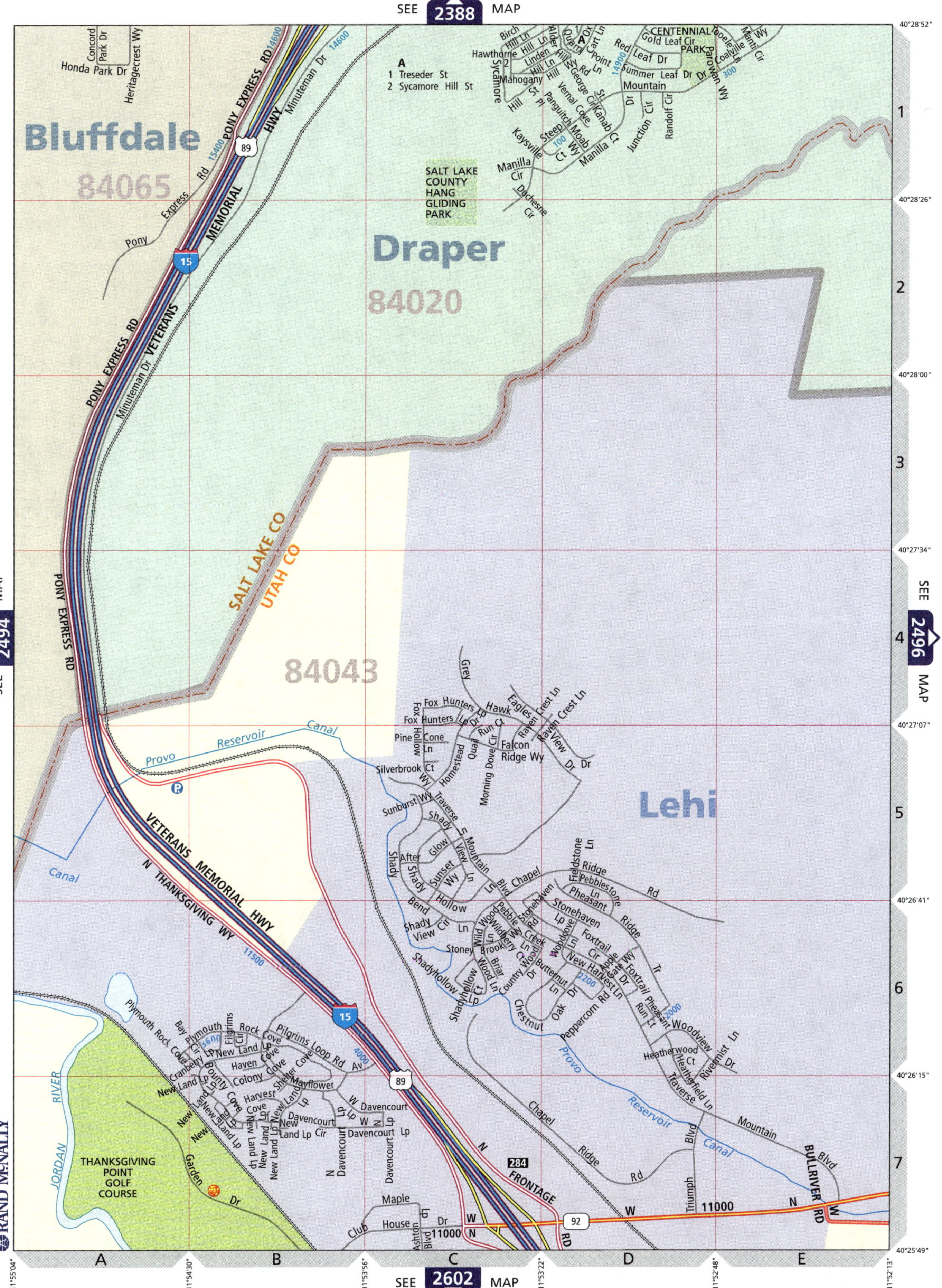

SEE 2494 MAP
SEE 2496 MAP
SEE 2602 MAP

1:24,000
1 in. = 2000 ft.
0 0.25 0.5
miles

SEE 2389 MAP

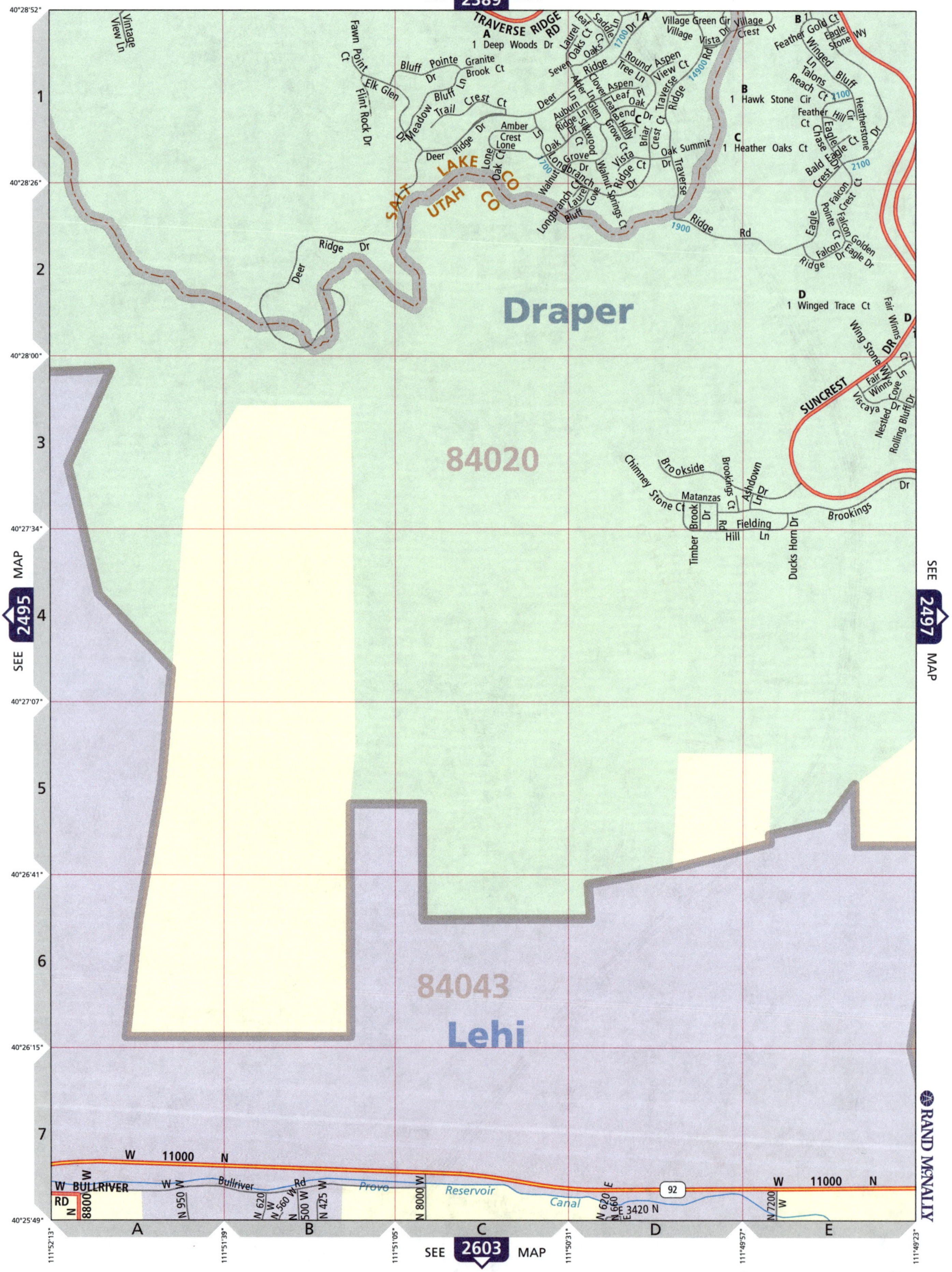

SEE 2495 MAP

SEE 2497 MAP

Draper

84020

84043

Lehi

TRAVERSE RIDGE RD

SALT LAKE CO

UTAH CO

SUNCREST DR

W 11000 N

W BULLRIVER RD

Provo Reservoir Canal

92

A
1 Deep Woods Dr

B
1 Hawk Stone Cir

C
1 Heather Oaks Ct

D
1 Winged Trace Ct

SEE 2603 MAP

1:24,000
1 in. = 2000 ft.
0 0.25 0.5
miles

SEE 2390 MAP
SEE 2496 MAP
SEE 2498 MAP
SEE 2604 MAP

Draper
84020
Alpine
84004
Lehi
Highland
84003

SUNCREST DR
WESTFIELD RD
ALPINE HWY
HIGHLAND HWY
CANYON CREST RD
MAIN ST
Fort Canyon Rd
ALPINE CEM
BECKS HILL PARK
ALPINE COUNTRY CLUB

A 1 Maple Bluff Rd
A Brookings Dr
B 1 Paradise Ln
C 1 Sunset Cir

40°28'51"
40°28'25"
40°27'59"
40°27'33"
40°27'07"
40°26'41"
40°26'15"
40°25'49"
111°49'23"
111°48'48"
111°48'14"
111°47'40"
111°47'06"
111°46'32"

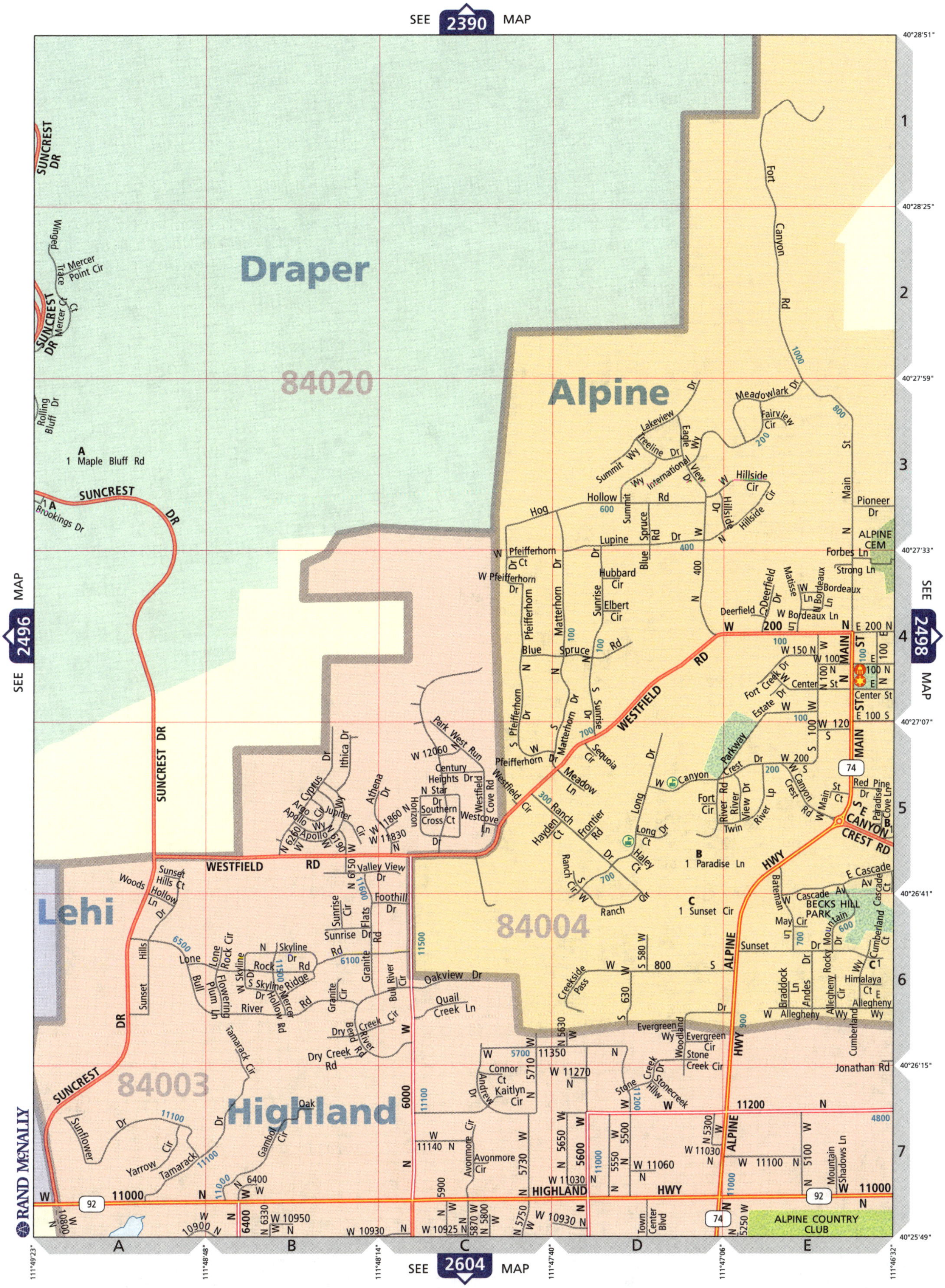

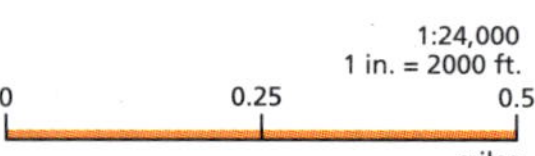

SEE B MAP

LAMBERT PARK

UINTA NATIONAL FOREST

84004

Alpine

84003

Highland

Cedar Hills

ALPINE CEM

PETERSEN PARK

BECKS HILL PARK

ALPINE CC

AMERICAN FORK CANYON RD

ALPINE LOOP RD

CANYON CREST RD

CANYON RD

W 11000 N

W 11200 N

48TH W

92

146

Stoney Brook Cir
Aspen Dr
Cove Dr
Oakridge Dr
Alpine Cove Cir
Juniper Cir
Oakview Dr
Alpine Cir
Oakview Cir
Silver Sage Cir
Bayberry Cir
Grove Dr
Box Elder Ln
Rosanna Dr
Rosanna Cir
Prospect Ln
Box Elder Tr
Box Elder Cir
Cottonwood Dr
Moyle Cir
Moyle Cir
Cottonwood Ln
Birch Cir
Alpine Blvd
Orchard Cir
Sunbrook Cir
Elk Ridge Ln
Eastview Ln
E Eastview Dr
Eastview Dr
Appletree Dr
N Grove Cir
Eastridge Cir
Peach Tree Cir
Moyle Pk
Sunburst Ln
E Eastview Dr
N Coventry Ct
Quincy Ct
E 770 N
N 610 E
Stamford Ct
N Patterson Ln
Pioneer Dr
Lamar Cir
Quail Hollow Cir
Hampton Ct
Quail Hollow Ln
Windsor Ct
Coventry Ln
Knight Cir
Wilderness Dr
Grove Dr
Mountainville Cir
Mountainville Dr
Wintergreen Ct
McDaniel Cir
Aspen Ridge Ln
Country Manor Cir
Mountain Dr
Bald Mountain Cir
Golden Eagle Cir
Bristol Ct
Canterbury Ln
E 426 N
N 425 E
E 350 N
E 300 N
E 300 N
Willow Springs Cir
E Field Cir
Manor Ln
E 200 N
Applewood Dr
Alpine Dr
Brook Cir
Meadowbrook Dr
Meadow Cir
N Lone Peak Dr
Country Cir
E Pine Ridge Cir
S Preston Dr
Drycreek Ln
E 100 N
E Center St
N Meadowbrook Dr
Village Ct
E Lone Peak Dr
Mountain Oaks Cir
Wild Flower Dr
Center St
Village Wy
S Bald Mountain Dr
Holly Dr
E Preston Dr
Holly Cir
Wild Flower Cir
S Country Ln
Alpine Dr
Oakwood Cir
River Meadows Dr
Red Pine Dr
Silver Leaf Dr
Wood Dr
Silver Cir
Ridge Crest Ct
Flannery Dr
Silver Ridge Ln
S Alpine Cir
Pineview Dr
Scenic Dr
Oakhill Cir
Oakhill Dr
E 480 S
Paradise Ln
Ponderosa Dr
Maple Dr
Country Meadow Ln
Oak Ln
High Ct
Arnold Ct
Watkins Ln
E Cascade Av
Sierra Av
Sierra Cir
Pheasant Ridge Dr
Carlisle Av
Pheasant Ridge Cir
Pheasant Ridge Ct
High Ridge Ln
High Ridge Dr
High Ridge Cir
Ostler Ct
E Mountain Dr
Stonehedge Rd
Stonehedge Cir
E Mountain Cir
Bench Rd
E 810 S
Pyreness Dr
Blue Ridge Ln
Healey Dr
Healey Ct
Blvd
Kavin Spring Cir
Healey Cir
Homestead Cir
E Round Mountain Rd
S Country Manor Ln
Cedar Mountain Cir
Allegheny Wy
Sampson Dr
Joey Ct
Elk Cove Cir
Park View Pointe Dr
Shoreline Dr
Park Cir
Manor Dr
Manor Cir
Wasatch Dr
W Panorama Dr
Country Club Dr

A
1 Sampson Ct
2 Jonathan Rd

B
1 N Panorama Dr
2 Canyon View Dr

RAND McNALLY

SEE 2497 MAP

SEE B MAP

SEE 2605 MAP

A B C D E

1 2 3 4 5 6 7

40°28'51" 40°28'25" 40°27'59" 40°27'33" 40°27'07" 40°26'41" 40°26'15" 40°25'49"

111°46'32" 111°45'58" 111°45'24" 111°44'49" 111°44'15" 111°43'41"

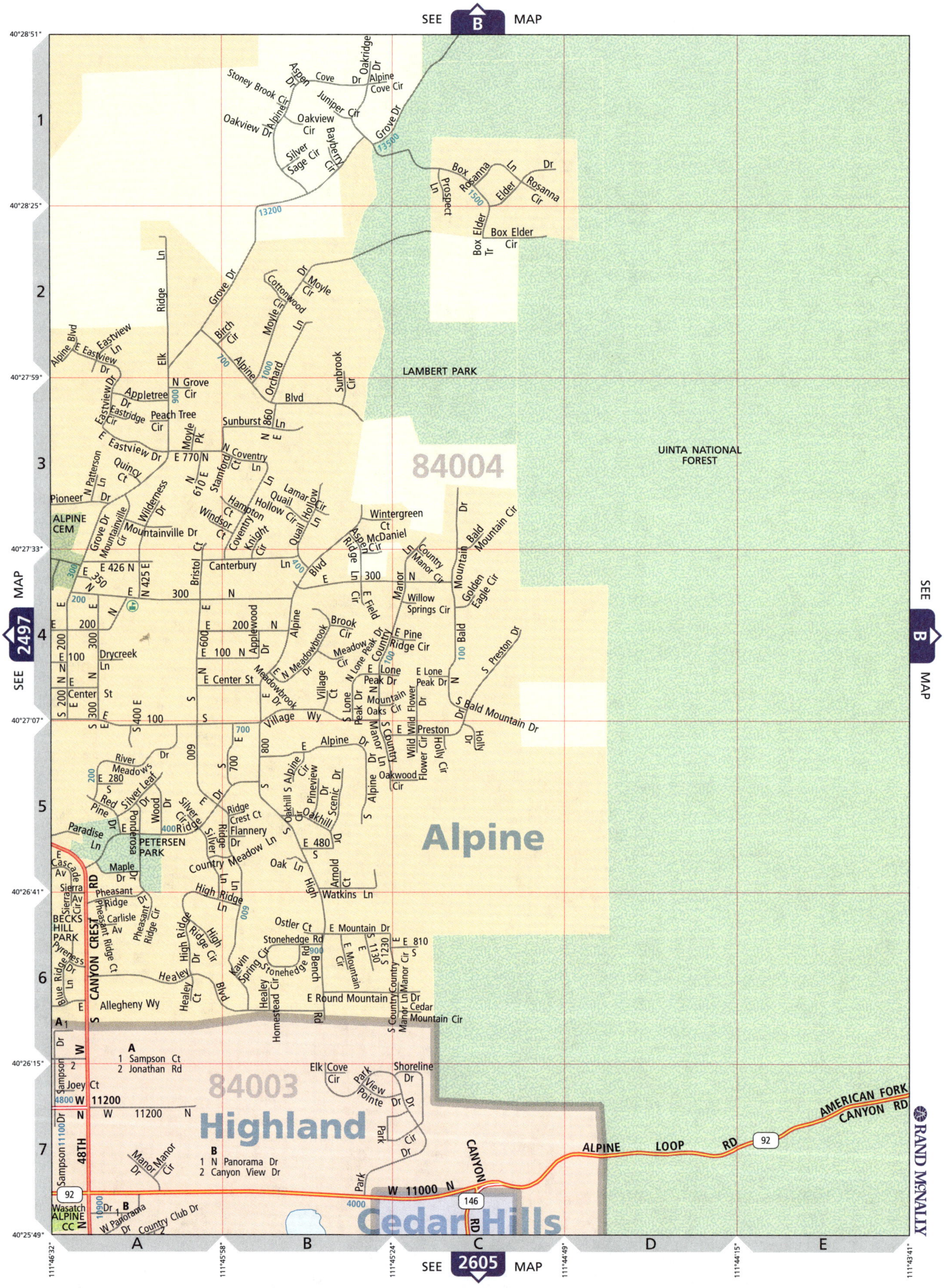

1:24,000
1 in. = 2000 ft.
0 0.25 0.5
miles

SEE 2396 MAP

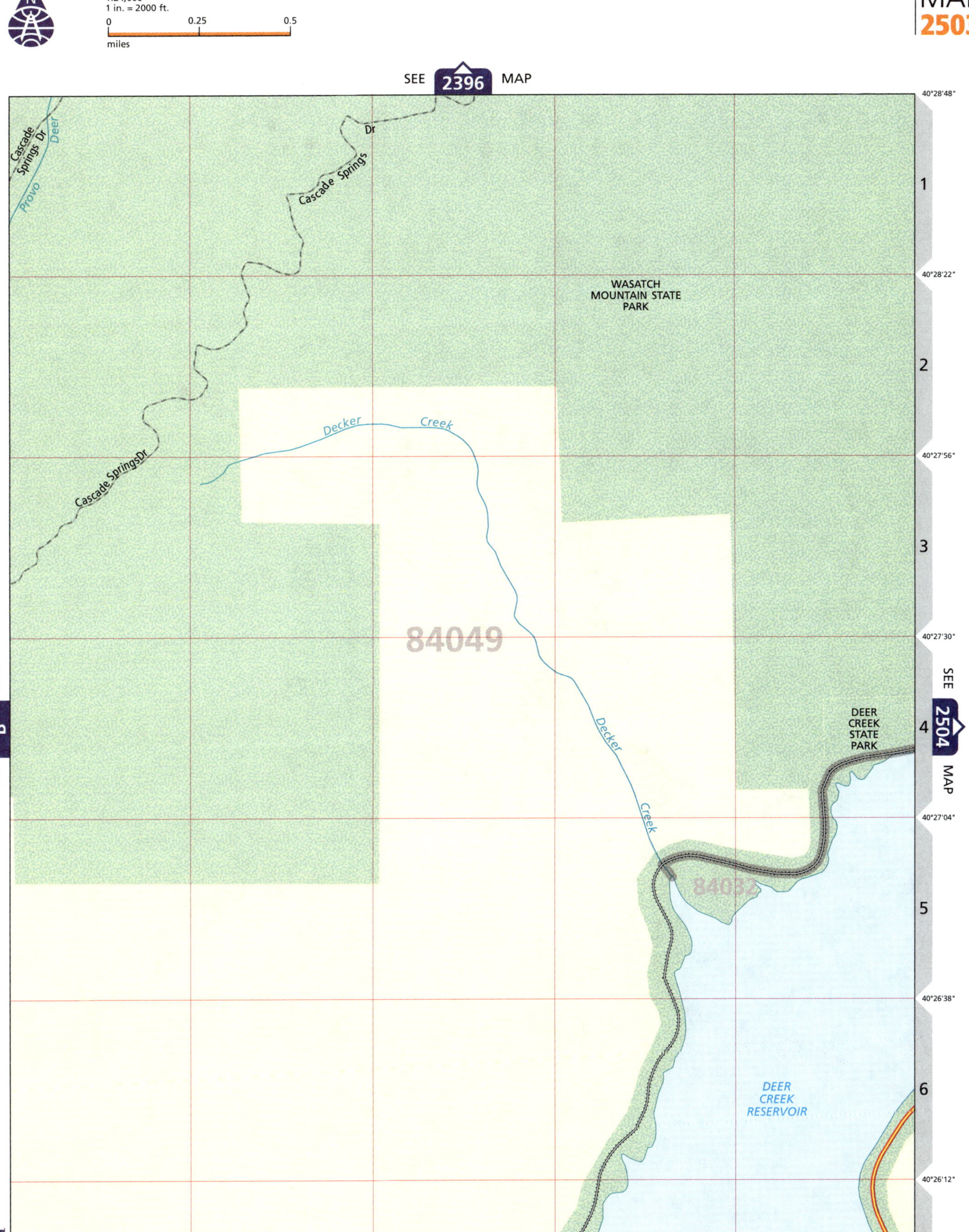

SEE B MAP

SEE 2504 MAP

SEE B MAP

1:24,000
1 in. = 2000 ft.
0 0.25 0.5
miles

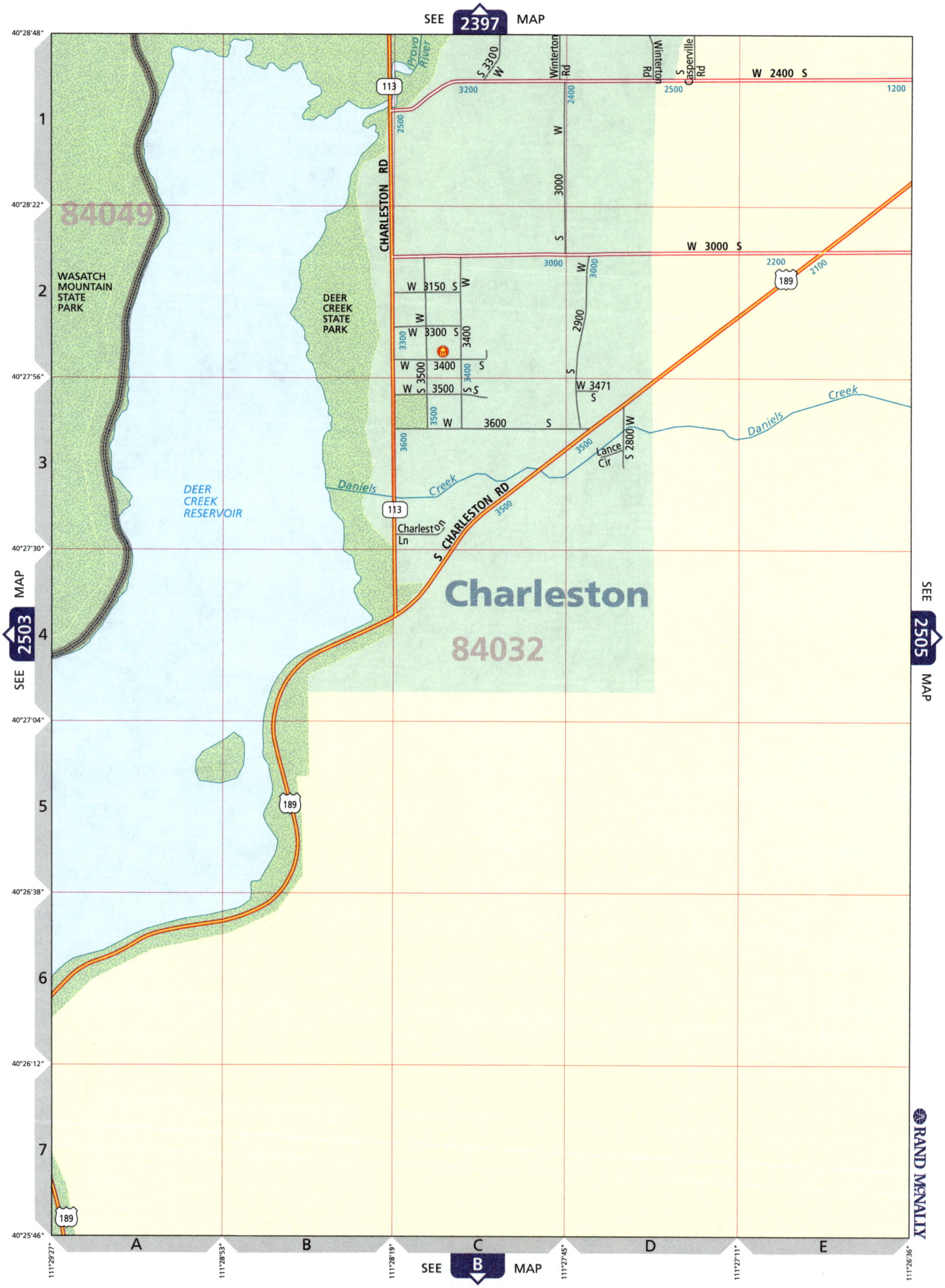

SEE 2397 MAP

SEE 2503 MAP

SEE 2505 MAP

WASATCH MOUNTAIN STATE PARK

DEER CREEK STATE PARK

DEER CREEK RESERVOIR

Provo River

Daniels Creek

Charleston

84049

84032

CHARLESTON RD

S CHARLESTON RD

W 2400 S

W 3000 S

W 3150 S

W 3300 S

W 3400 S

W 3500 S

W 3600 S

W 3471 S

S 3300 W

S 3400 W

S 3500 W

S 2800 W

S 2900 W

S 3000 W

Winterton Rd

S Casperville Rd

Charleston Ln

Lance Cir

113

189

40°28'48" 40°28'22" 40°27'56" 40°27'30" 40°27'04" 40°26'38" 40°26'12" 40°25'46"

111°29'27" 111°28'53" 111°28'19" 111°27'45" 111°27'11" 111°26'36"

1 2 3 4 5 6 7

A B C D E

SEE B MAP

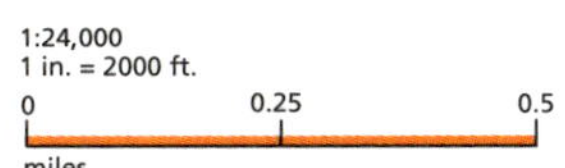

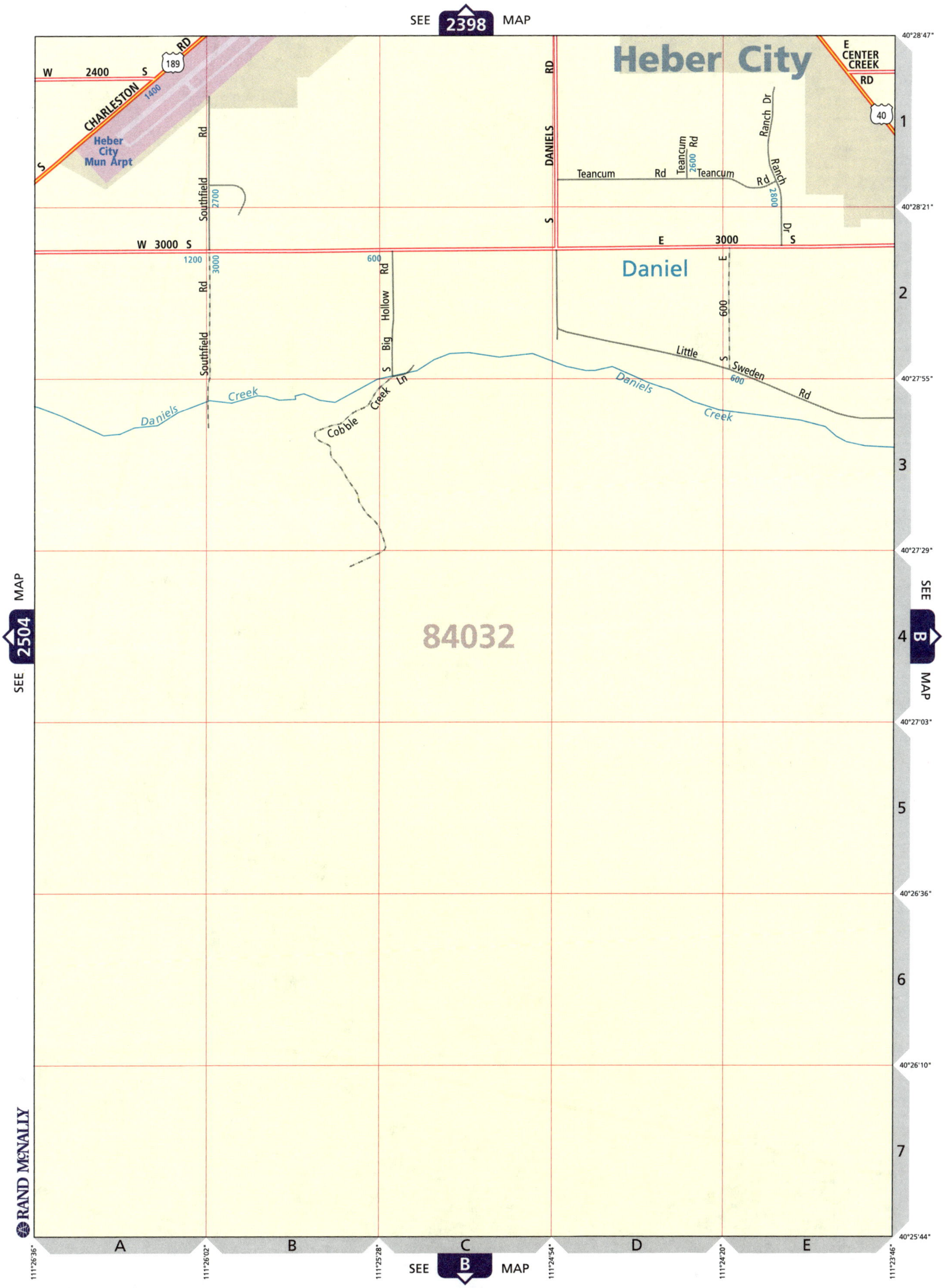

SEE 2398 MAP

SEE 2504 MAP

SEE B MAP

SEE B MAP

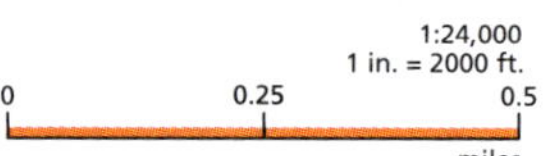

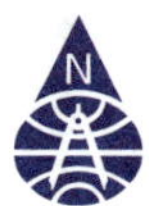

1:24,000
1 in. = 2000 ft.
0 0.25 0.5
miles

SEE 2494 MAP
SEE 2602 MAP
SEE B MAP
SEE B MAP
84065
84043
SALT LAKE CO
UTAH CO
CAMP WILLIAMS
STATE
MILITARY
RESERVATION
Saratoga
Springs
Eagle
Mountain
68
73
W 10400 N
W 10000 N
W 8570 N
10800
11600
W 8350 N
CEDAR
FORT
RD
Country Rd
W 1200 N
Hillside Dr
Sage Hill Dr
Coyote Run
Red Hen Rd
Mustang Ln
Mustang Cir
Jack Rabbit Run
W Buffalo Dr
Rattler Rd
N Buffalo Dr
8300
Goldenrod
Sego Lily Dr
N 660 W
Harvest Wy
Providence
Hills
Granary
Pumpkin Patch Dr
Winter Wheat Wy
Harvest Moon Dr
Harvest Hills Blvd
Jonathan Pl
Apricot Pl
Pearl Pl
Nectar Wy
Apple Ct
Cedar Pl
Peach Pl
Blossom Ct
Cherry Cir
Apple Av
Plum Pl
Harvest Moon
Orchard Dr
Millet Dr
Flax Dr
Barley Wy
Sweet Corn Dr
Strawberry Pl
Raspberry Dr
Boysenberry Dr
Morning Star Dr
Suncrest Ln
Sunlight Wy
Aurora Ln
Daybreak Wy
Berry Patch Wy
Blackberry Dr
Concord Pl
Vineyard Wy
Trellis Cir
Thompson Pl
Moon Dr
Napa Dr
Arbor Dr
Vineyard Pl
Tuscany
Peppermint Cir
Peppermint Ct
Peppermint Pl
Ginger Pl
Bay Leaf Dr
Parsley Ct
Rosemary Ln
Rosemary Pl
Andrews Dr
Cinnamon Dr
Providence Dr
Floribunda Dr
Tea Rose Dr
Rose Garden Ct
Rose Bud Ct
Bountiful Wy
Jacobs Wy
100
2200
A B C D E
1 2 3 4 5 6 7
40°25'49"
40°25'23"
40°24'57"
40°24'31"
40°24'05"
40°23'39"
40°23'13"
40°22'47"
111°57'55"
111°57'21"
111°56'47"
111°56'13"
111°55'38"
111°55'04"

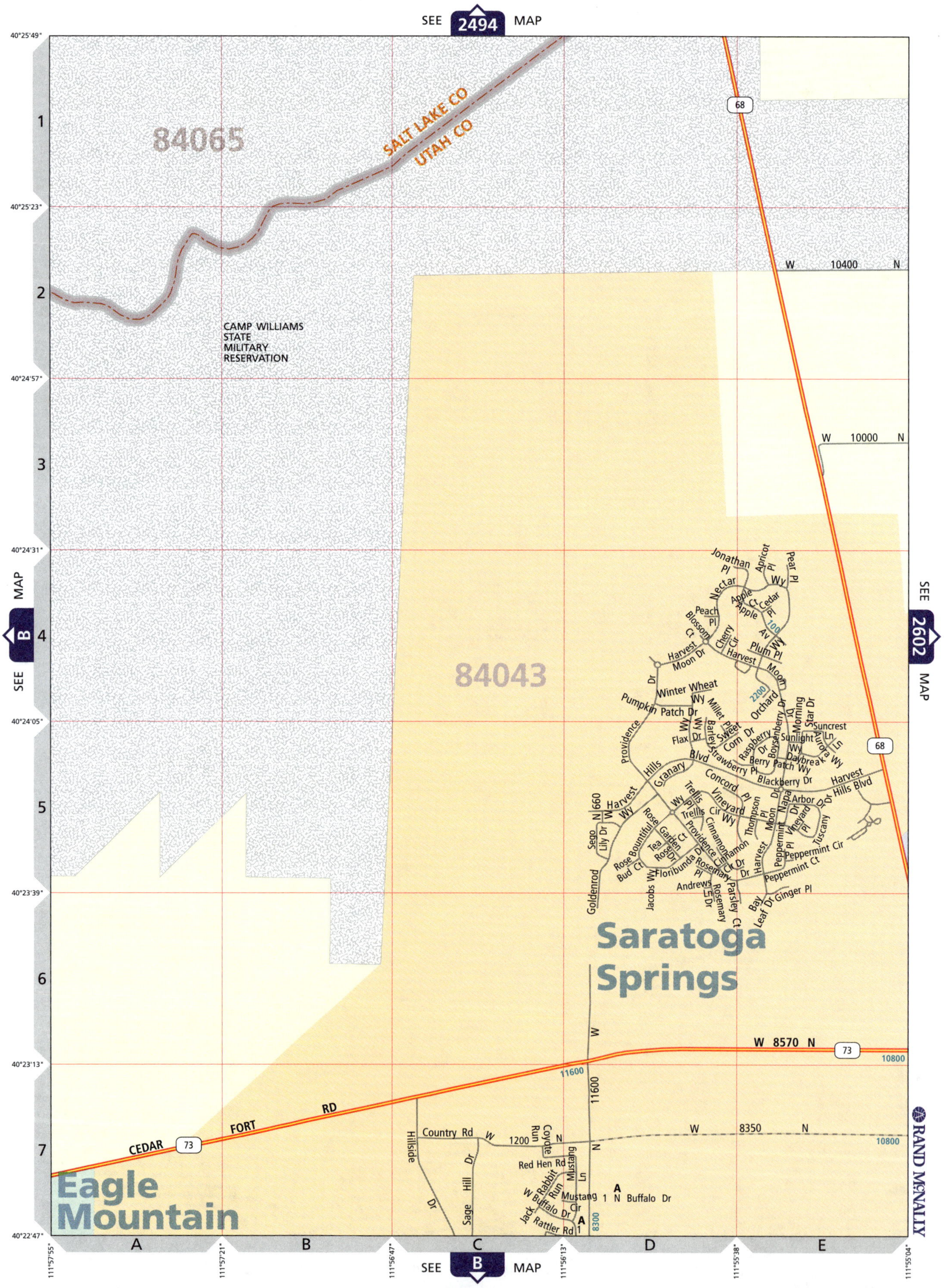

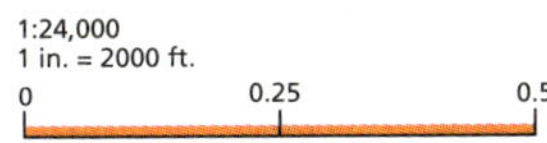

SEE 2495 MAP

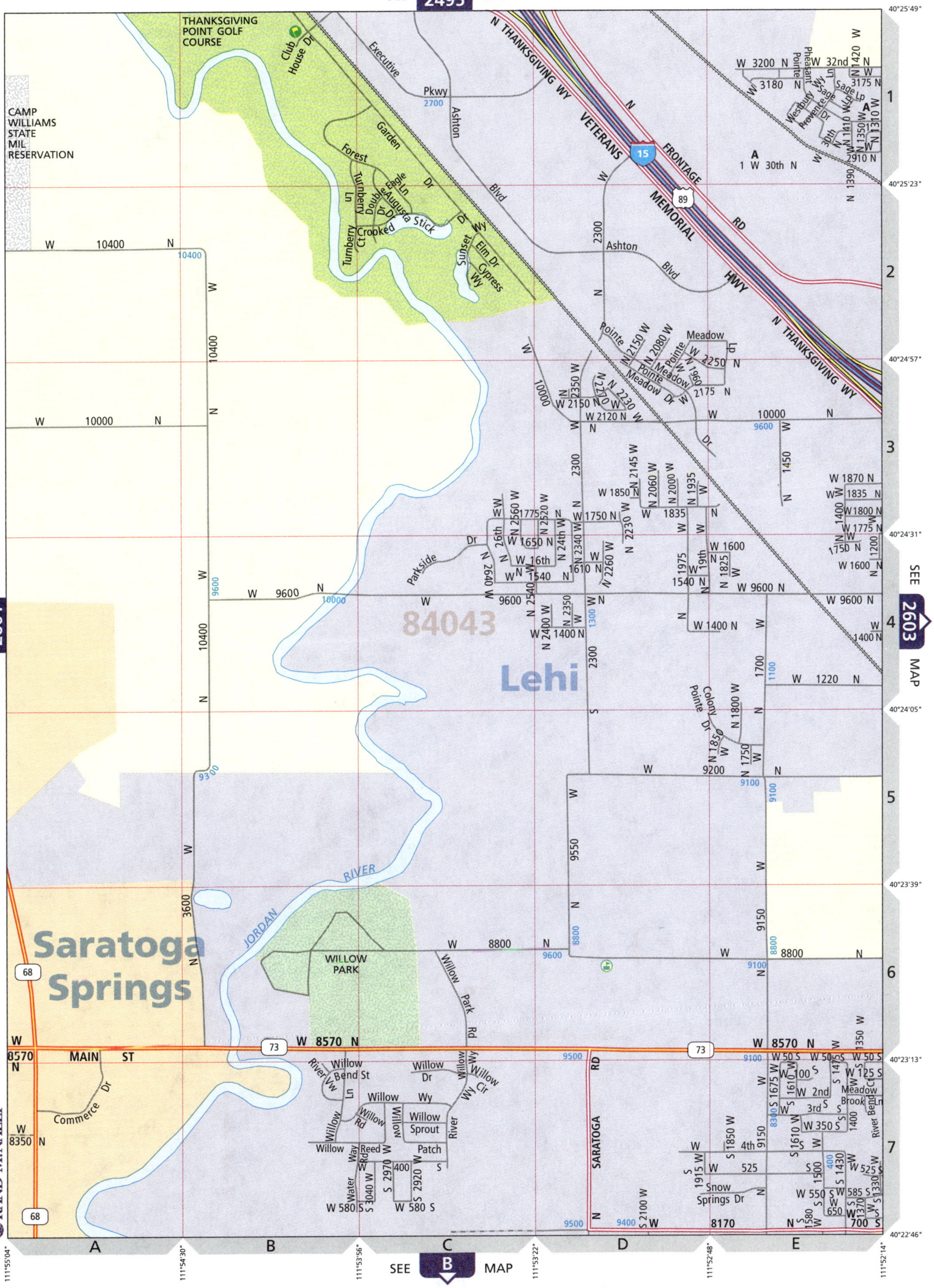

SEE 2601 MAP

SEE 2603 MAP

THANKSGIVING POINT GOLF COURSE

CAMP WILLIAMS STATE MIL RESERVATION

Lehi

84043

Saratoga Springs

WILLOW PARK

JORDAN RIVER

N THANKSGIVING WY

VETERANS MEMORIAL HWY

FRONTAGE RD

MAIN ST

SARATOGA RD

SEE B MAP

1:24,000
1 in. = 2000 ft.
0 0.25 0.5
miles

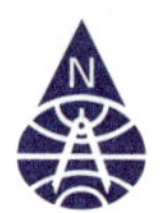

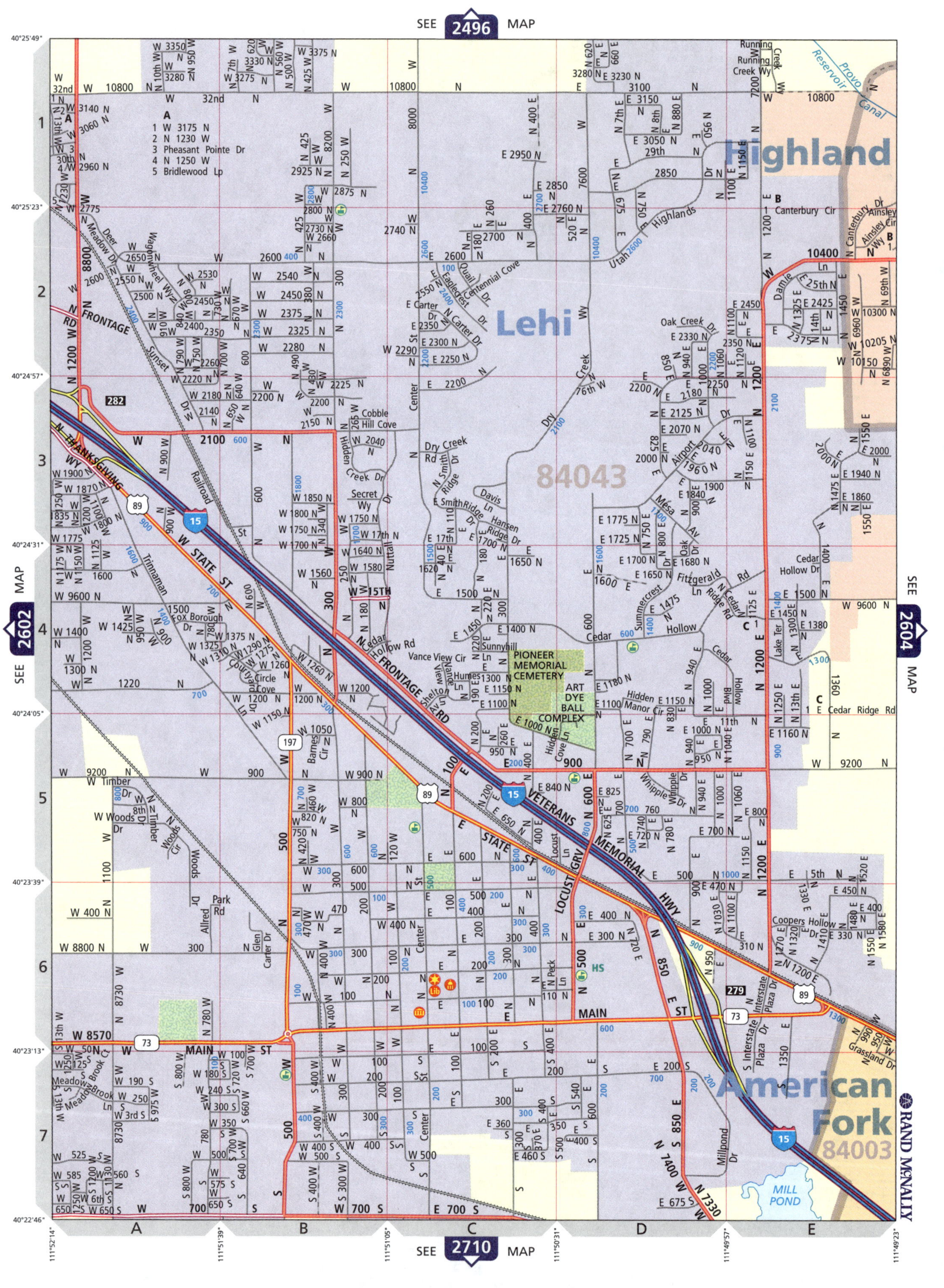
SEE 2496 MAP
SEE 2602 MAP
SEE 2604 MAP
SEE 2710 MAP
Highland
Lehi
84043
American Fork
84003
Provo Reservoir Canal
PIONEER MEMORIAL CEMETERY
ART DYE BALL COMPLEX
MILL POND
Lib
HS
W STATE ST
N FRONTAGE RD
FRONTAGE RD
VETERANS MEMORIAL HWY
W MAIN ST
MAIN
E STATE ST
LOCUST GRV
THANKSGIVING WY
Railroad
Trinnaman
Sunset Dr
Dry Creek
Cedar Hollow Rd
Highlands
Airport
Fitzgerald Ln
Canterbury Cir
Cedar Ridge Rd
Coopers Hollow Dr
Interstate Plaza Dr
Grassland Dr
Millpond Dr
10800
10400
9600
9200
8800
8570
15
89
73
197
279
282
A B C D E
1 2 3 4 5 6 7
40°25'49"
40°25'23"
40°24'57"
40°24'31"
40°24'05"
40°23'39"
40°23'13"
40°22'46"
111°52'14"
111°51'39"
111°51'05"
111°50'31"
111°49'57"
111°49'23"
A
1 W 3175 N
2 N 1230 W
3 Pheasant Pointe Dr
4 N 1250 W
5 Bridlewood Lp
B
1 Canterbury Cir
C
1 E Cedar Ridge Rd
RAND McNALLY

1:24,000
1 in. = 2000 ft.
0 0.25 0.5
miles

SEE 2497 MAP

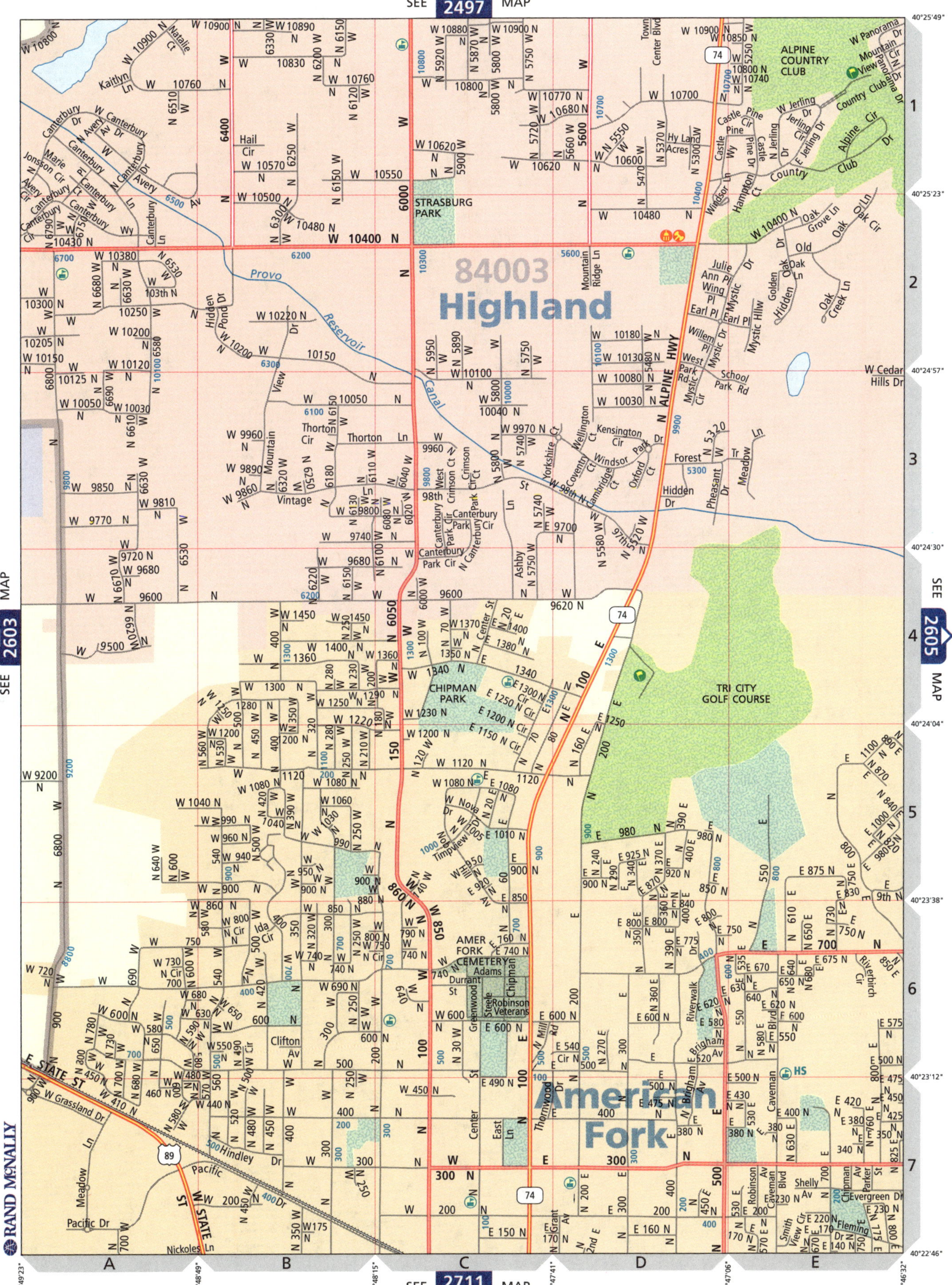

SEE 2603 MAP

SEE 2605 MAP

SEE 2711 MAP

1:24,000
1 in. = 2000 ft.
0 0.25 0.5
miles

SEE 2498 MAP

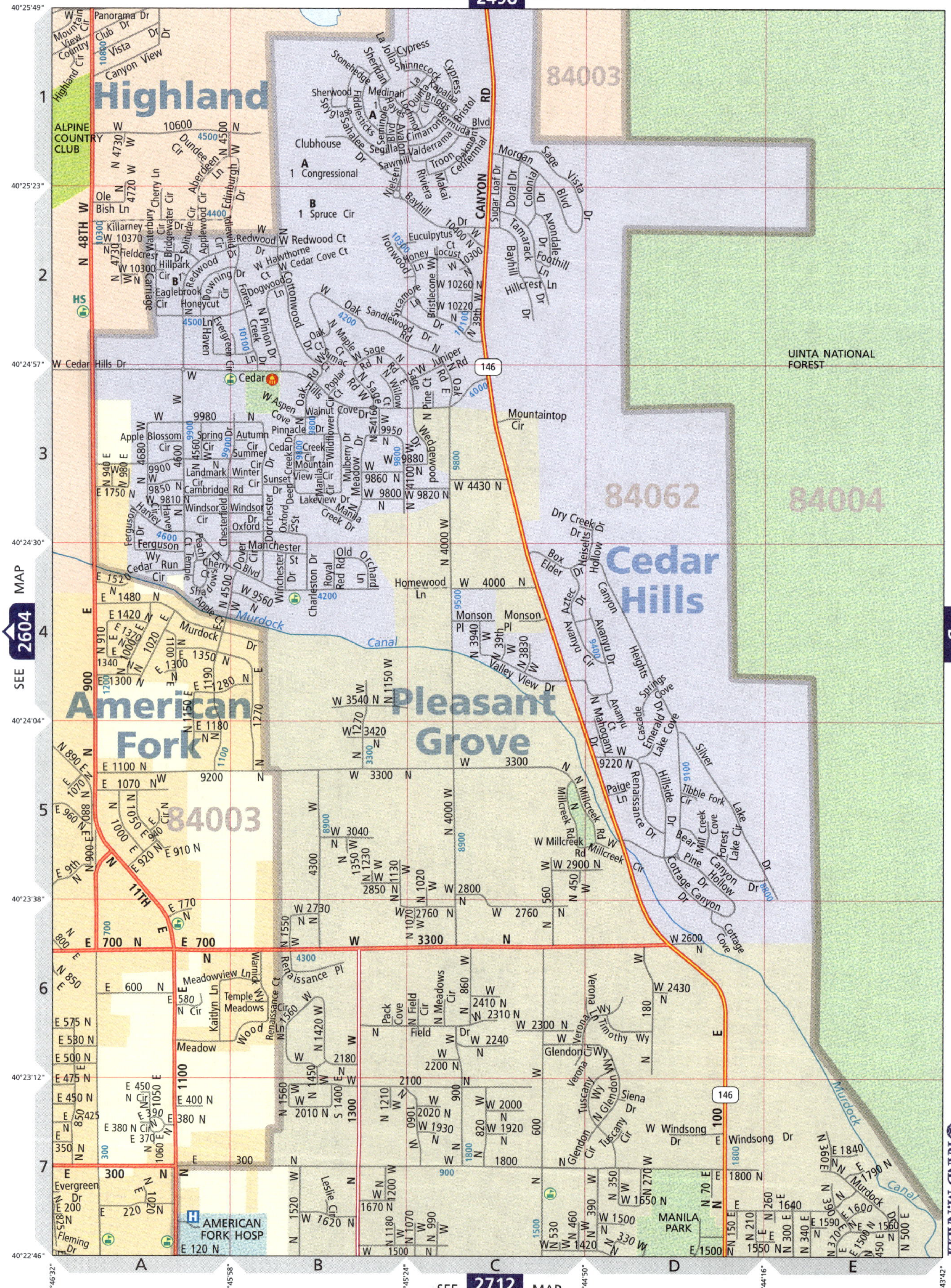

Highland

ALPINE COUNTRY CLUB

Cedar Hills

American Fork

Pleasant Grove

UINTA NATIONAL FOREST

84003

84062

84004

AMERICAN FORK HOSP

MANILA PARK

Murdock Canal

CANYON RD

N 48TH W

W Cedar Hills Dr

W 3300 N

E 700 N

146

40°25'49"
40°25'23"
40°24'57"
40°24'30"
40°24'04"
40°23'38"
40°23'12"
40°22'46"

111°46'32"
111°45'58"
111°45'24"
111°44'50"
111°44'16"
111°43'42"

SEE 2604 MAP

SEE B MAP

SEE 2712 MAP

1:24,000
1 in. = 2000 ft.
0 0.25 0.5
miles

SEE 2603 MAP

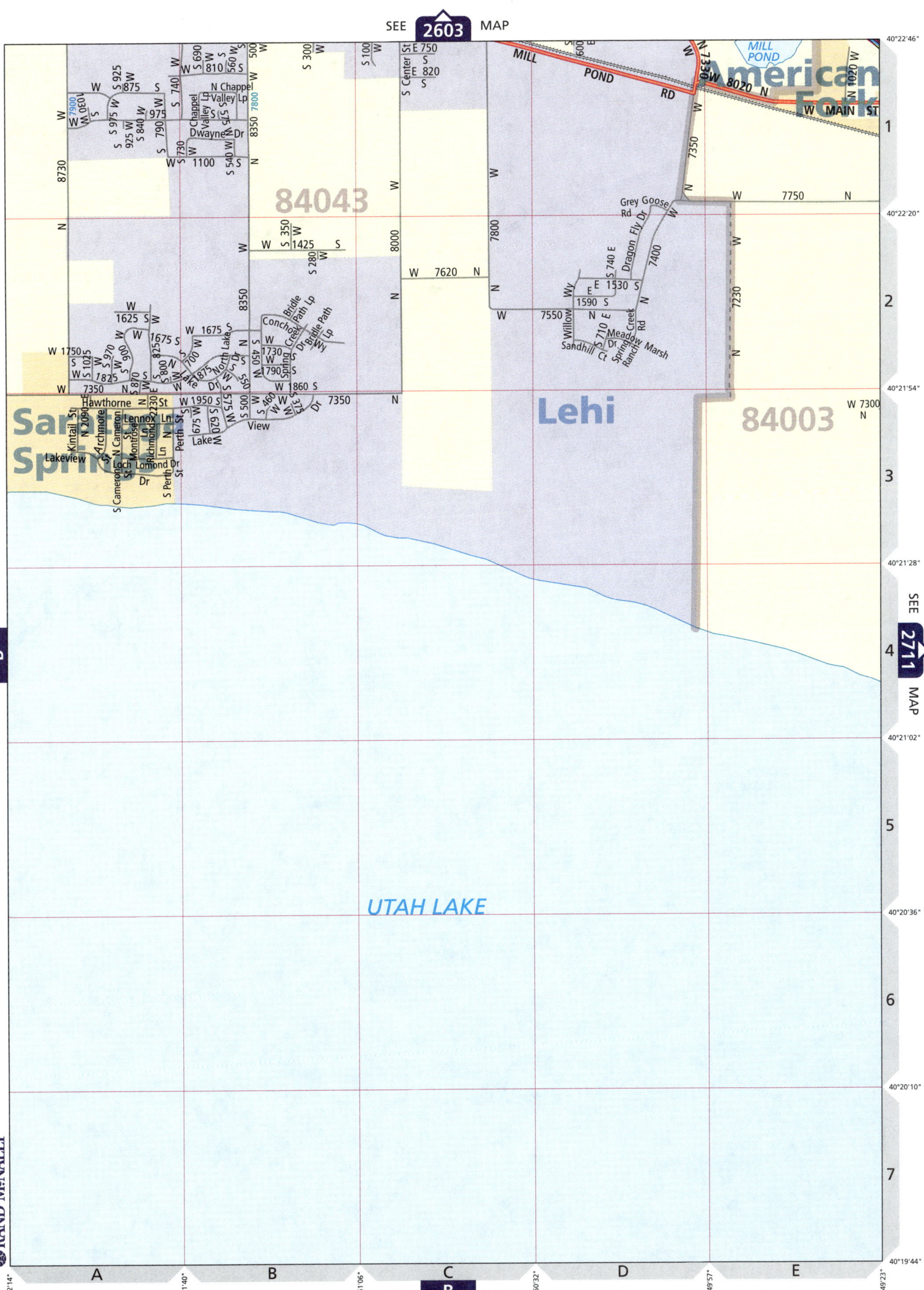

SEE B MAP

SEE 2711 MAP

SEE B MAP

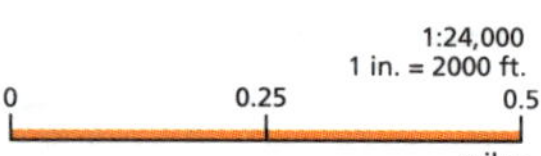

SEE 2604 MAP

SEE 2710 MAP

SEE 2712 MAP

American Fork

84003

UTAH LAKE

BICENTENNIAL PARK

ROTARY PARK

MTN MEADOWS PARK

GREENWOOD PARK

VETERANS MEMORIAL HWY

MAIN ST

STATE ST

STATE RD

W 7750 N

W 7300 N

W 6800 N

W 6400 N

N 6500 W

N 6000 W

N 5750 W

N 5300 W

E 1000 S

E 1300 S

E 1700 S

Bromley Dr

Quality Dr

E Utah Valley Dr

Mahogany Dr

W Frontage Rd

Washington Av

Jefferson Av

Harrison Av

Nickoles Ln

Bamberger Dr

40°22'46"
40°22'20"
40°21'54"
40°21'28"
40°21'02"
40°20'36"
40°20'10"
40°19'44"

111°49'23"
111°48'49"
111°48'15"
111°47'41"
111°47'07"
111°46'33"

A B C D E

1 2 3 4 5 6 7

SEE B MAP

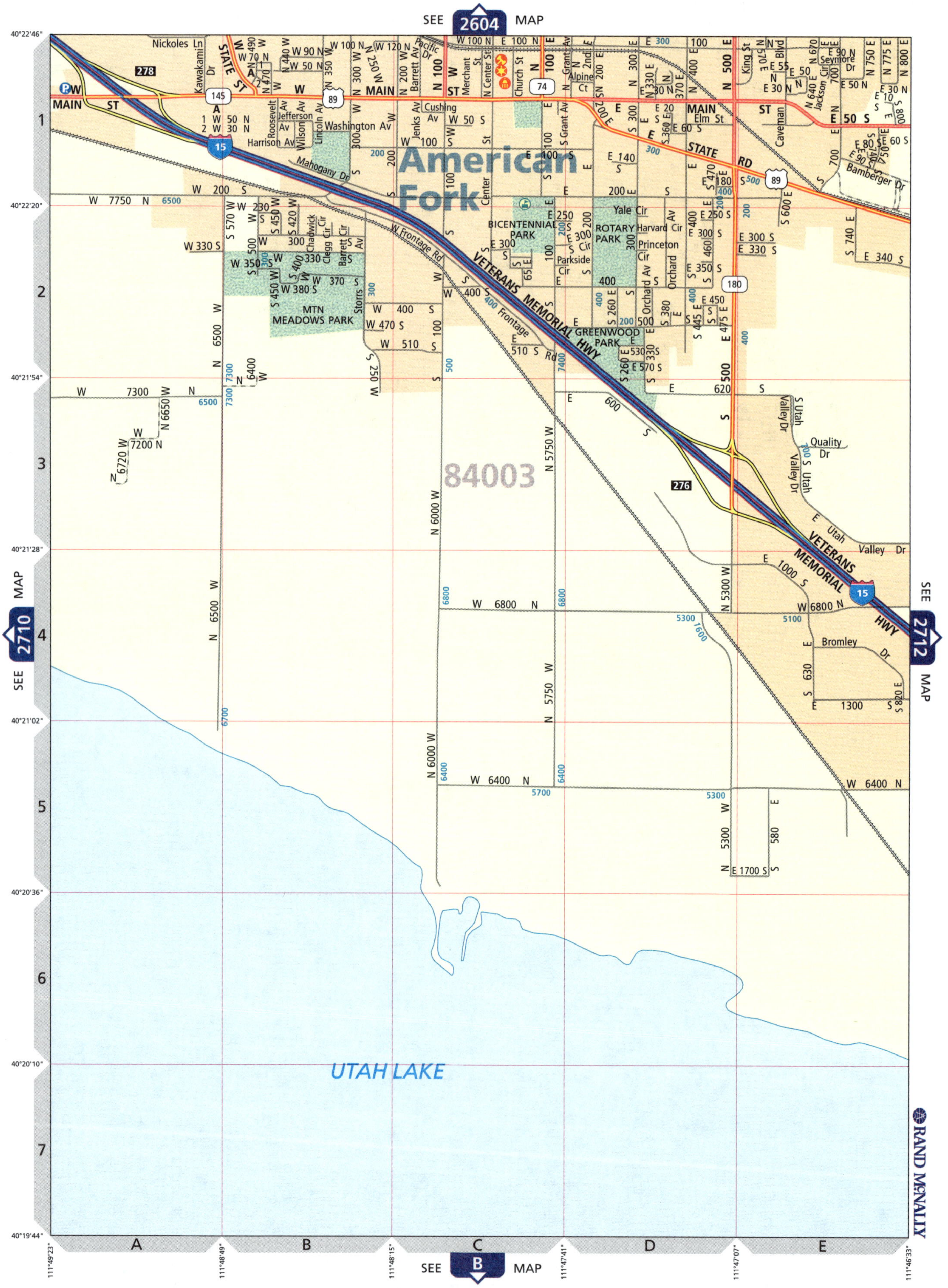

1:24,000
1 in. = 2000 ft.
0 0.25 0.5
miles

SEE 2605 MAP

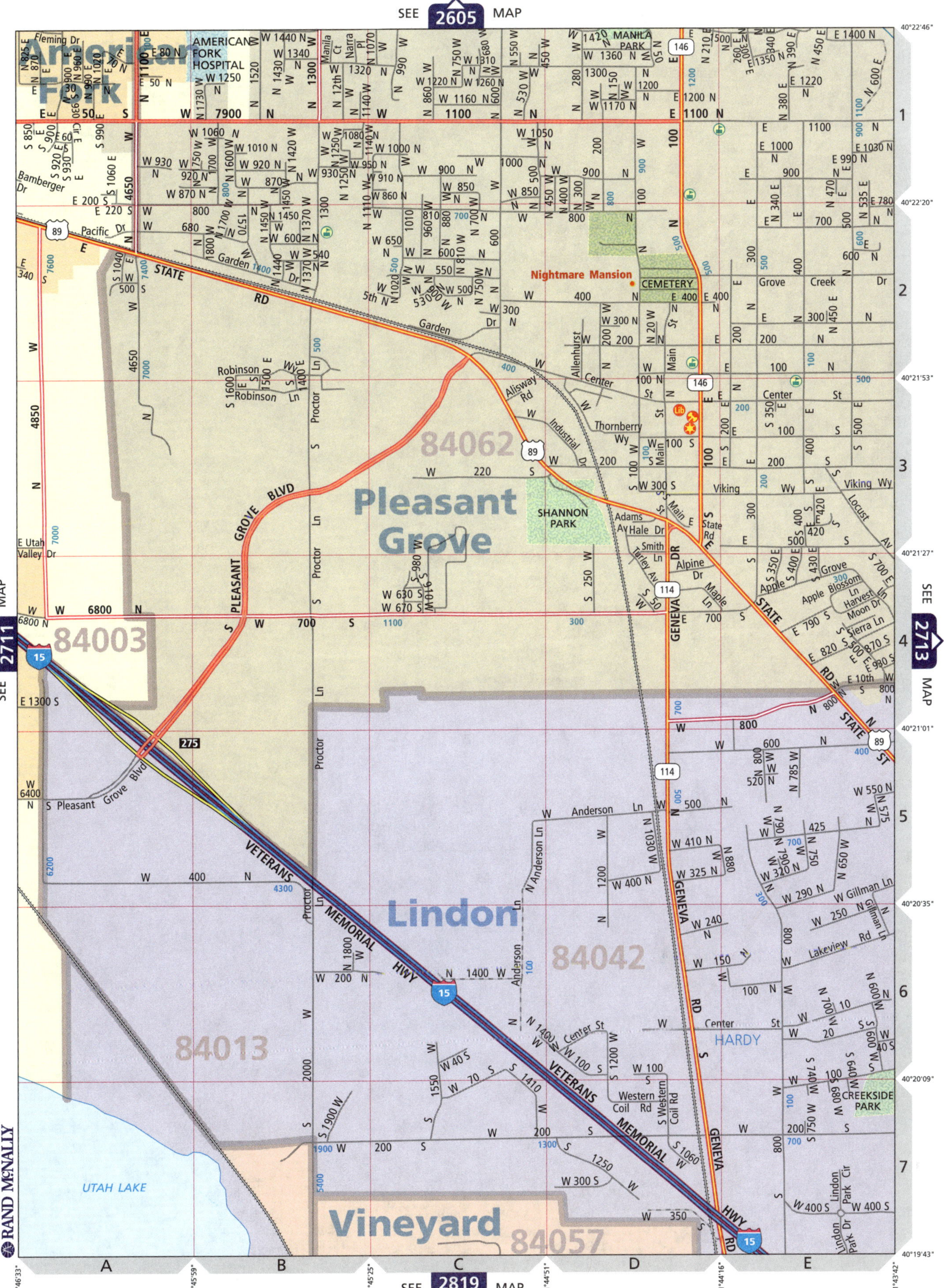

SEE 2711 MAP

SEE 2713 MAP

SEE 2819 MAP

1:24,000
1 in. = 2000 ft.
0 0.25 0.5
miles

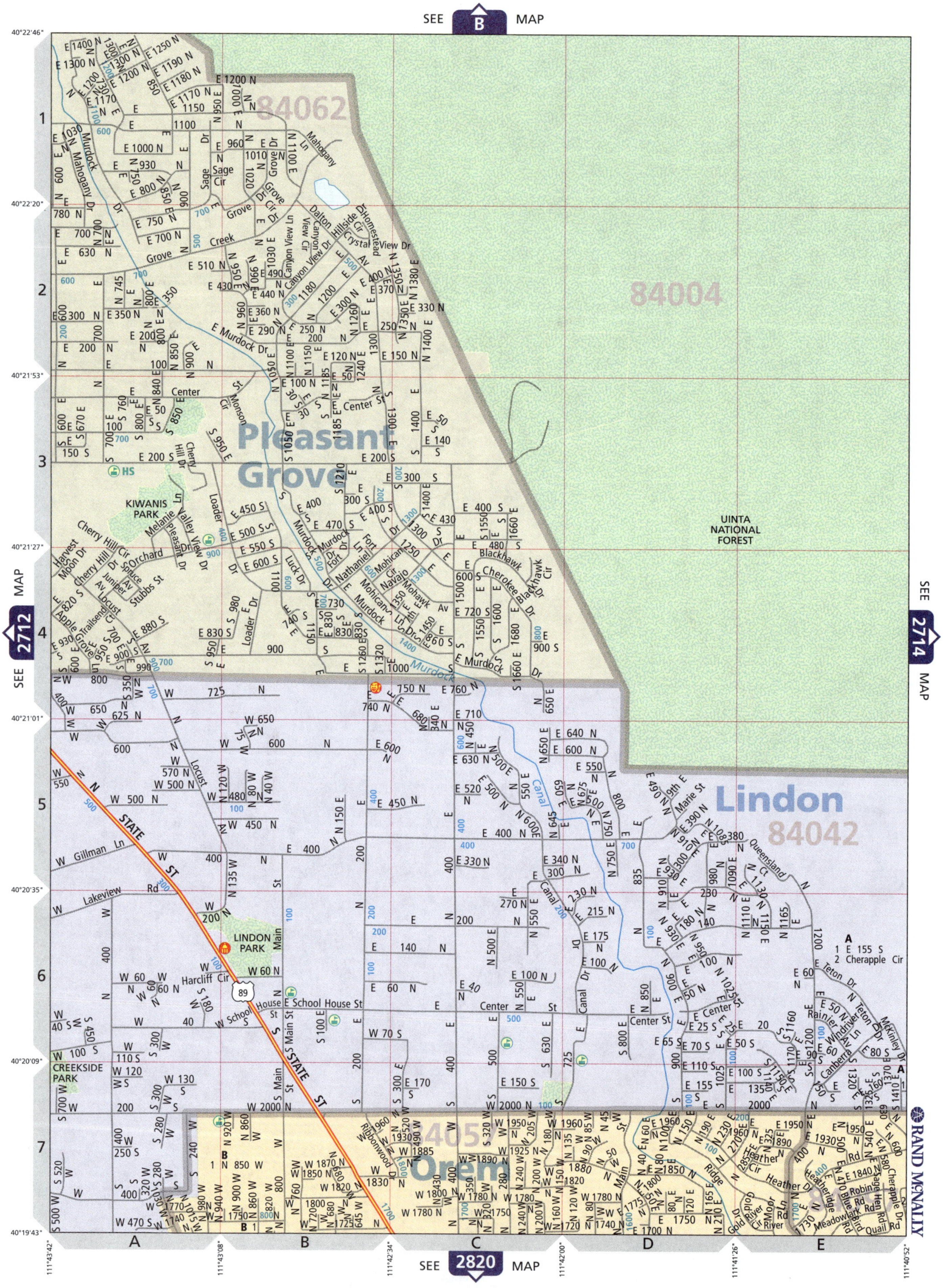

SEE B MAP

SEE 2712 MAP

SEE 2714 MAP

Pleasant Grove

84062

84004

UINTA NATIONAL FOREST

KIWANIS PARK

Lindon

84042

LINDON PARK

CREEKSIDE PARK

Orem

N STATE ST

89

Murdock

Canal

A
1 E 155 S
2 Cherapple Cir

40°22'46"
40°22'20"
40°21'53"
40°21'27"
40°21'01"
40°20'35"
40°20'09"
40°19'43"

111°43'42" 111°43'08" 111°42'34" 111°42'00" 111°41'26" 111°40'52"

A B C D E

1 2 3 4 5 6 7

SEE 2820 MAP

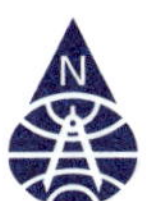

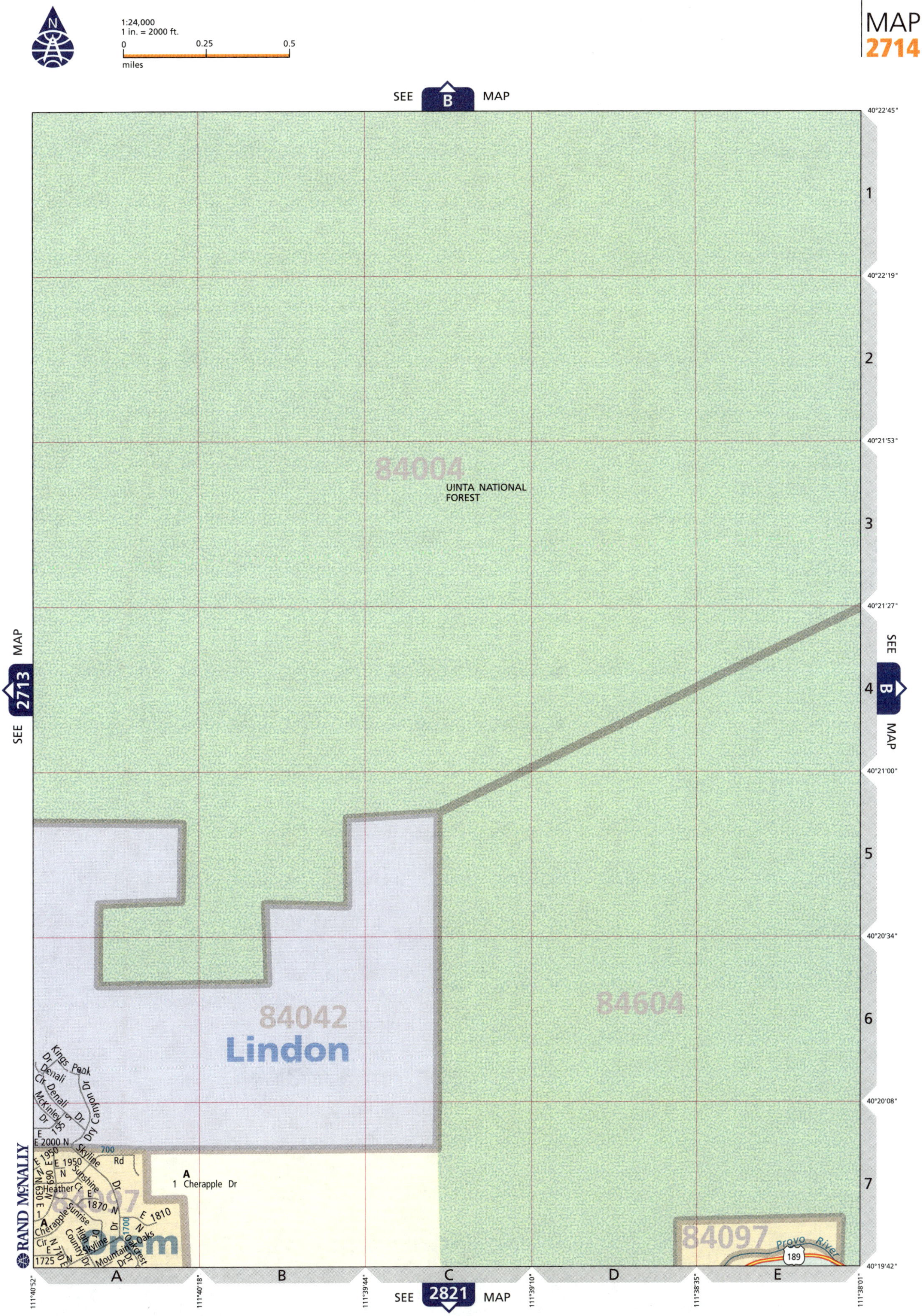
1:24,000
1 in. = 2000 ft.
0
0.25
0.5
miles
SEE B MAP
SEE 2713 MAP
SEE B MAP
SEE 2821 MAP
40°22'45"
40°22'19"
40°21'53"
40°21'27"
40°21'00"
40°20'34"
40°20'08"
40°19'42"
111°40'52"
111°40'18"
111°39'44"
111°39'10"
111°38'35"
111°38'01"
1
2
3
4
5
6
7
A
B
C
D
E
84004
UINTA NATIONAL FOREST
84042
Lindon
84604
84097
Orem
Provo River
189
Kings Peak Dr
Denali Cir
Denali Dr
McKinley Dr
Dry Canyon Dr
155 S
E 2000 N
Skyline Dr
700
Rd
E 1950 N
690 E
630 E
Heather Ct
Sunshine
E 1870 N
E 1810 N
1700
Sunrise Dr
Cherapple Cir
A
1 Cherapple Dr
High Country Dr
Skyline
Mountain Oaks Dr
Oakcrest Dr
710 E
1725 N
RAND McNALLY

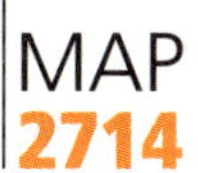

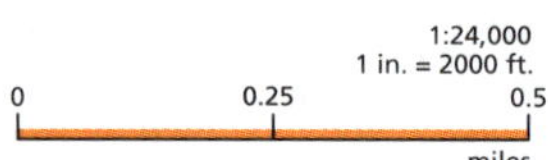

SEE 2712 MAP

UTAH LAKE

Vineyard

Orem

Lindon

84013

84057

84058

84601

84042

COOLING POND

N West Geneva Rd

W Vineyard Rd

N Vineyard Rd

W Gammon Rd

E Gammon Rd

S Holdaway Rd

E Holdaway Rd

S GENEVA RD

N GENEVA RD

W 1600 N

W CENTER ST

W 800 N

W 400 N

W 1200 N

VETERANS MEMORIAL HWY

S Sleepy Ridge Dr

Springwater

W 600 S

S 2000 W

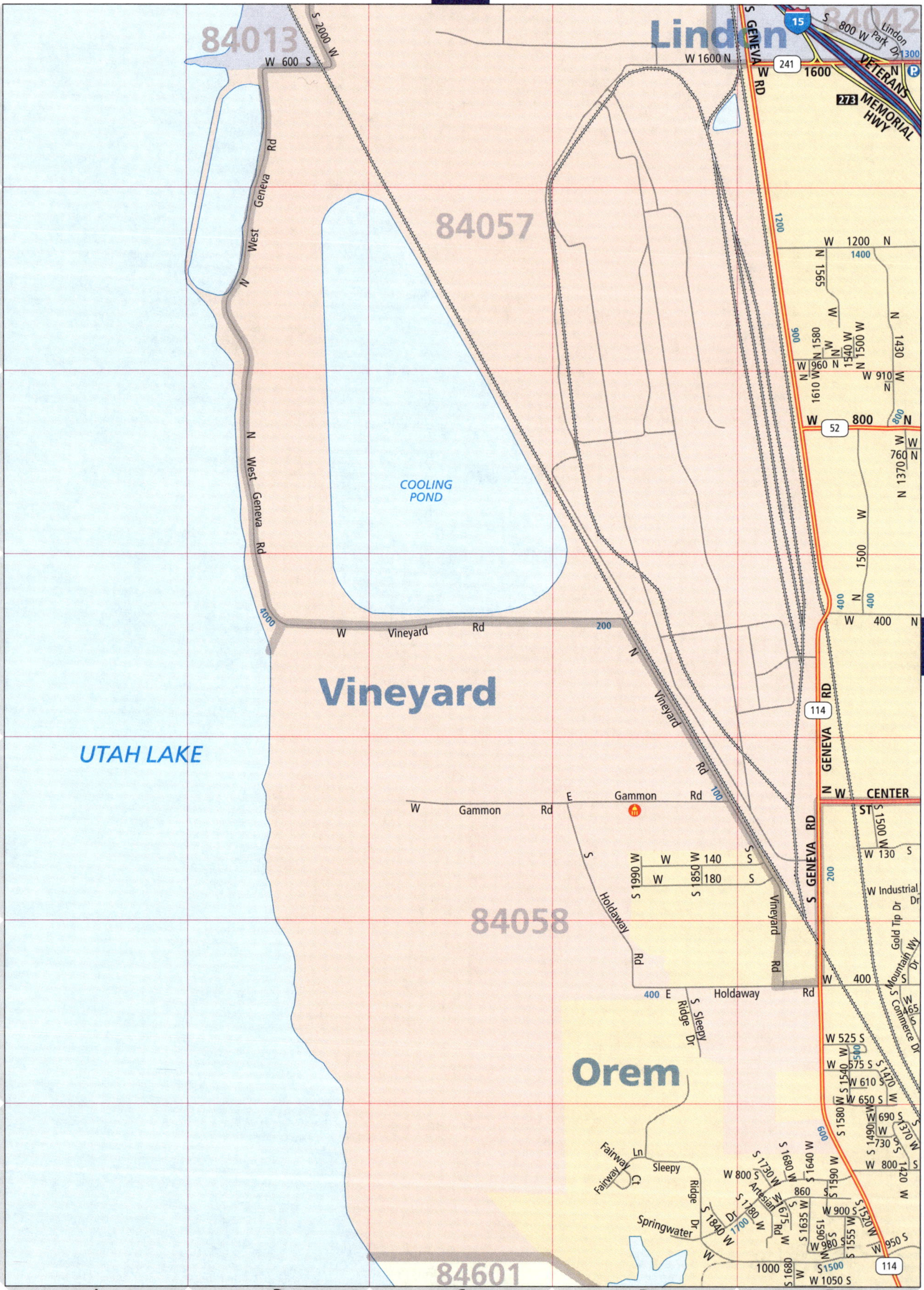

SEE B MAP

SEE 2820 MAP

SEE 2926 MAP

RAND McNALLY

1:24,000
1 in. = 2000 ft.
0 0.25 0.5
miles

SEE 2713 MAP

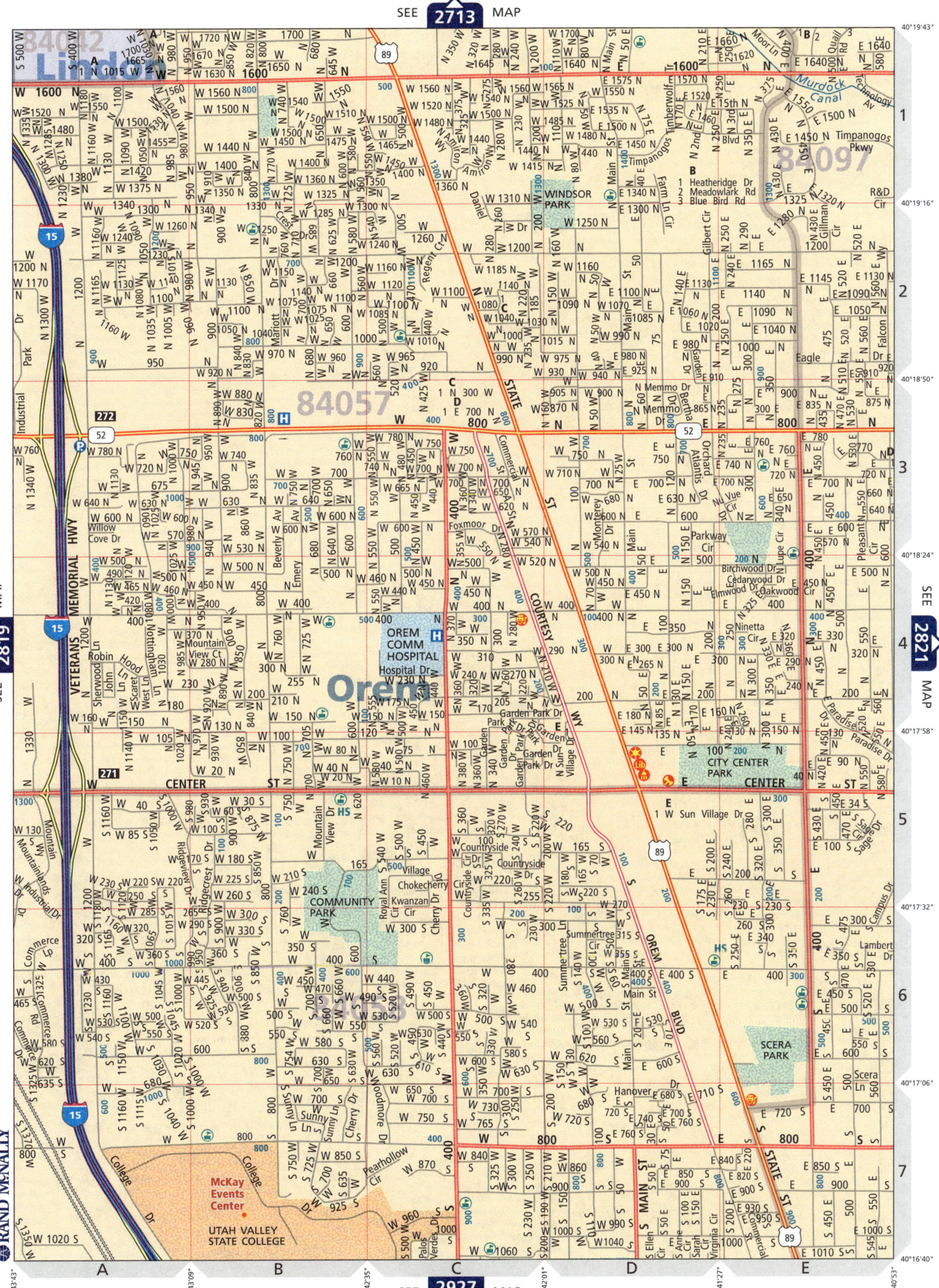

SEE 2819 MAP

SEE 2821 MAP

SEE 2927 MAP

1:24,000
1 in. = 2000 ft.
0 0.25 0.5
miles

SEE 2714 MAP

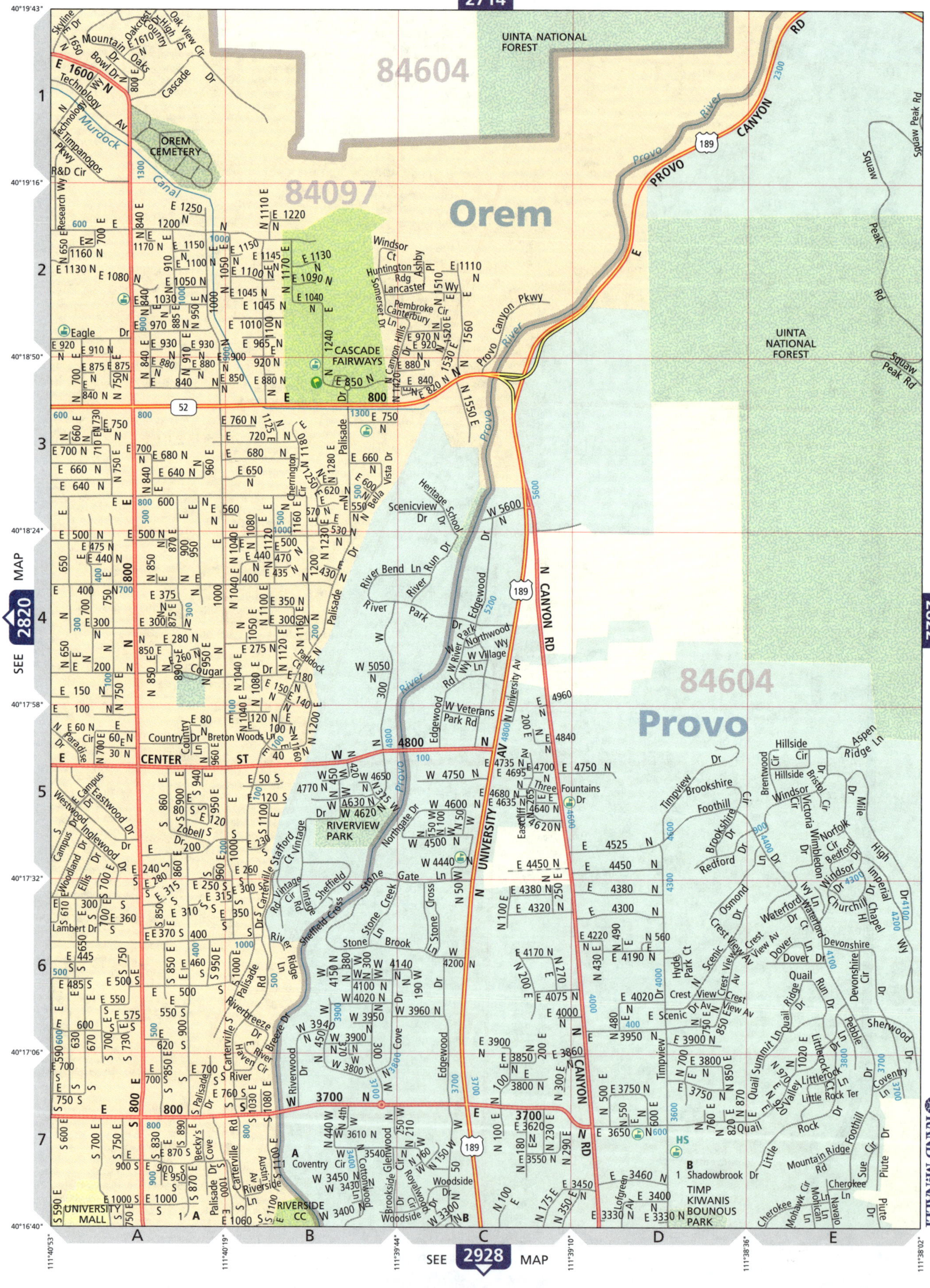

SEE 2820 MAP

SEE 2822 MAP

Orem

Provo

84604

84097

UINTA NATIONAL FOREST

OREM CEMETERY

CASCADE FAIRWAYS

RIVERVIEW PARK

UNIVERSITY MALL

RIVERSIDE CC

TIMP KIWANIS BOUNOUS PARK

PROVO CANYON RD

N CANYON RD

N UNIVERSITY AV

E CENTER ST

W 4800 N

E 800 N

W 3700 N

E 1600 N

Murdock Canal

Provo River

Squaw Peak Rd

A B C D E

1 2 3 4 5 6 7

40°19'43" 40°19'16" 40°18'50" 40°18'24" 40°17'58" 40°17'32" 40°17'06" 40°16'40"

111°40'53" 111°40'19" 111°39'44" 111°39'10" 111°38'36" 111°38'02"

RAND McNALLY

SEE 2928 MAP

1:24,000
1 in. = 2000 ft.
0 0.25 0.5
miles

SEE B MAP

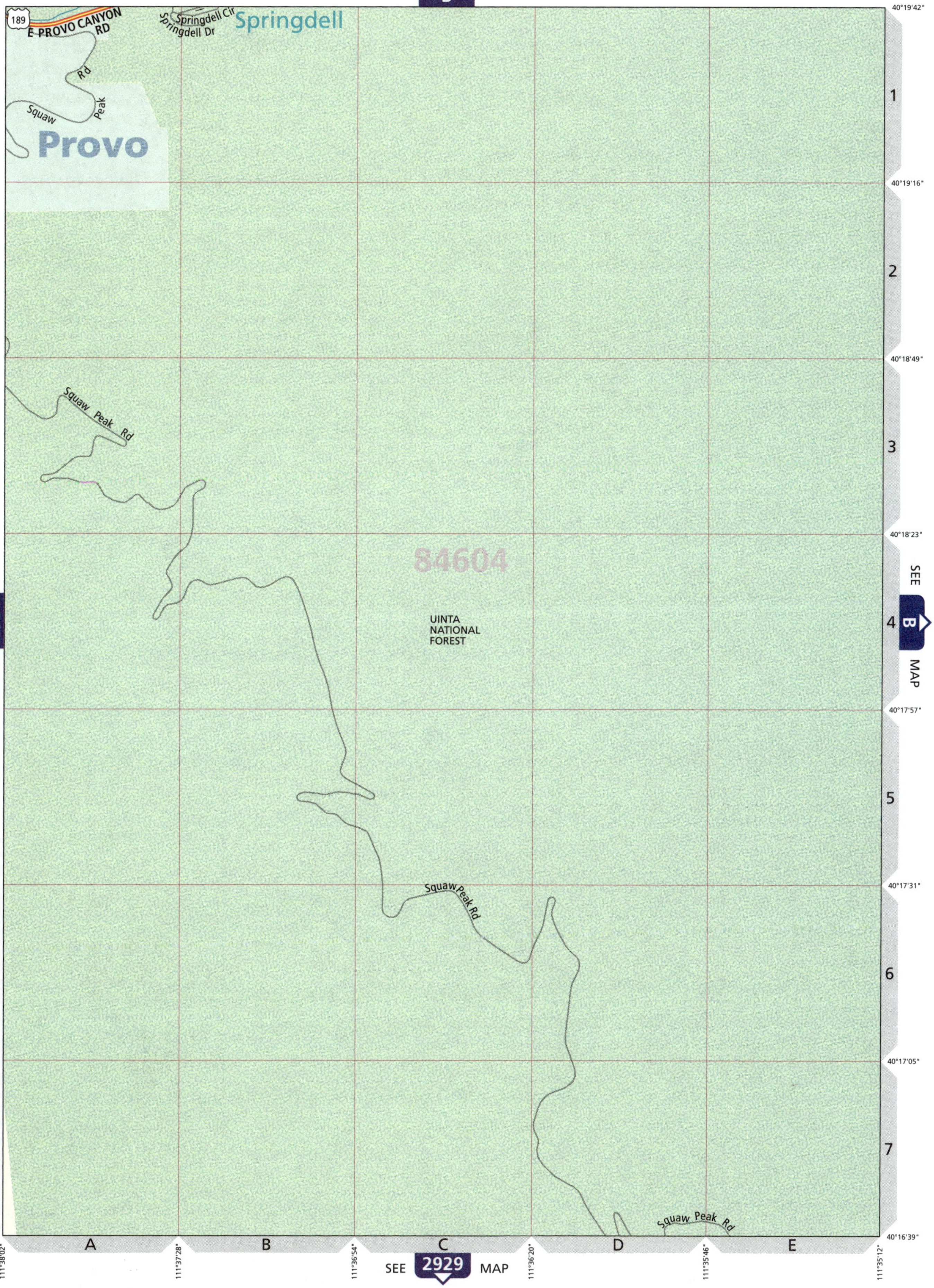

SEE 2821 MAP

SEE B MAP

SEE 2929 MAP

1:24,000
1 in. = 2000 ft.
0 0.25 0.5
miles

SEE 2819 MAP

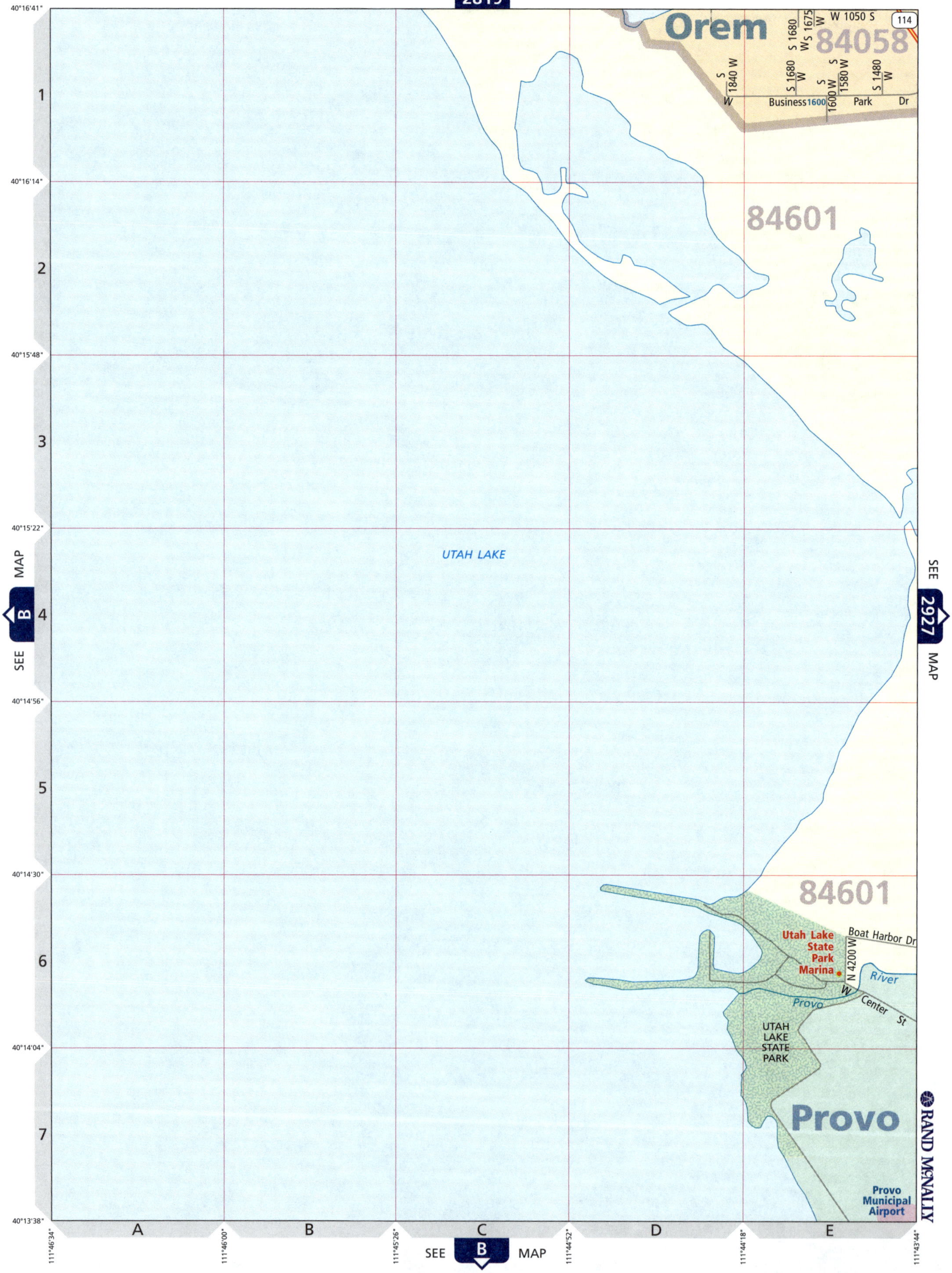

SEE B MAP

SEE 2927 MAP

SEE B MAP

1:24,000
1 in. = 2000 ft.
0 0.25 0.5
miles

SEE 2820 MAP

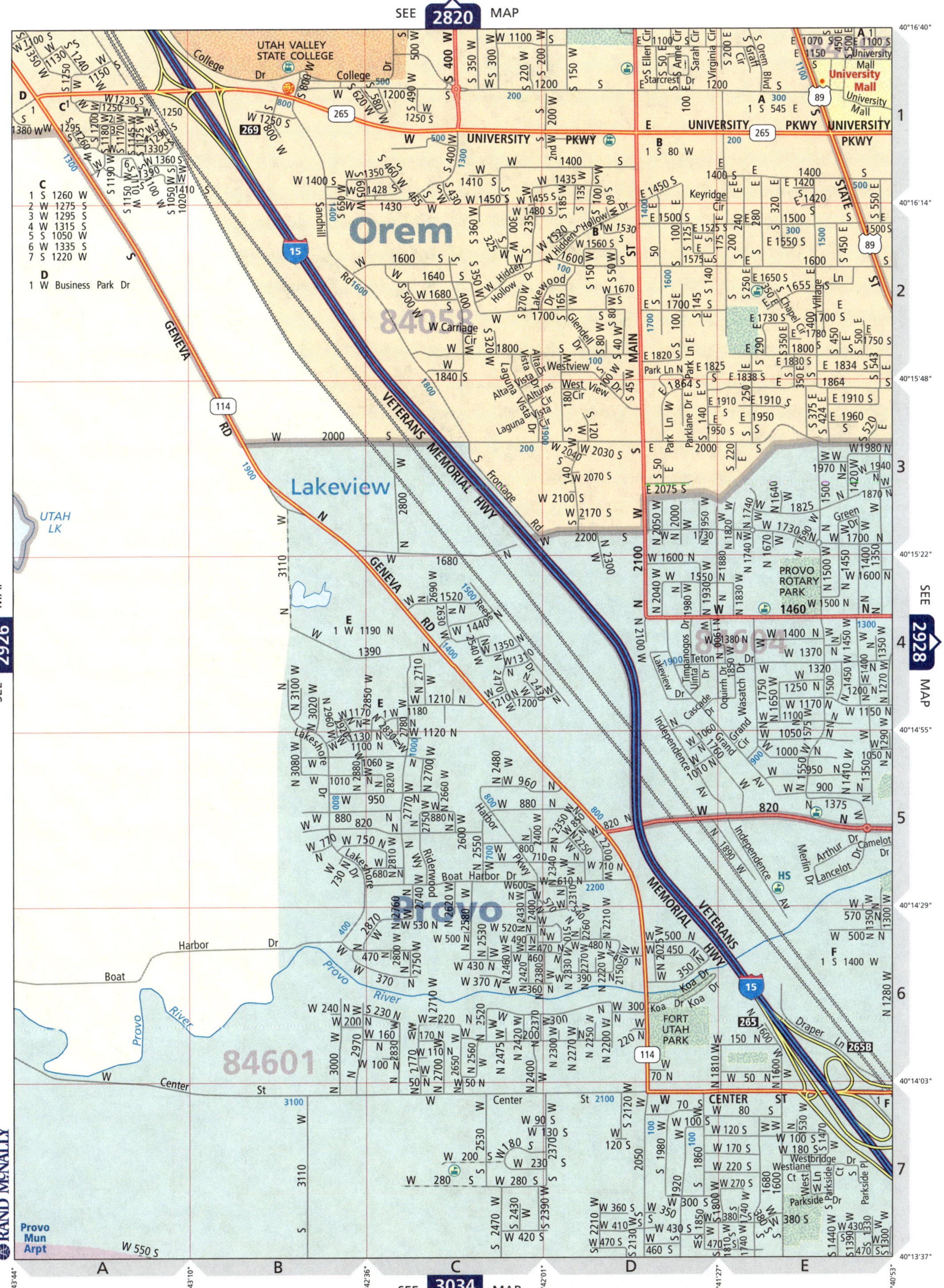

SEE 2926 MAP

SEE 2928 MAP

SEE 3034 MAP

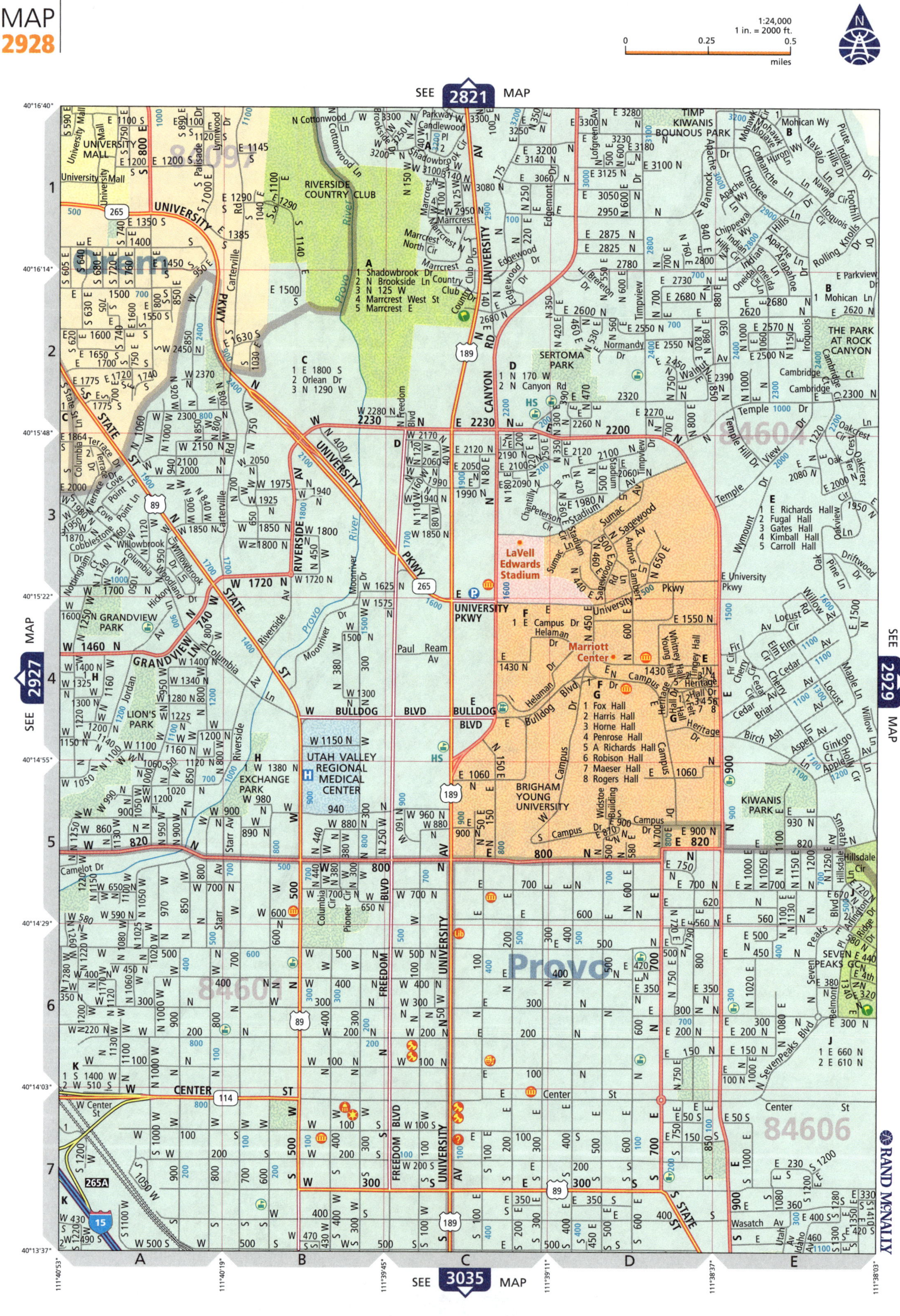

1:24,000
1 in. = 2000 ft.
0 0.25 0.5
miles

SEE 2821 MAP

SEE 2927 MAP

SEE 2929 MAP

Orem
Provo
UNIVERSITY MALL
RIVERSIDE COUNTRY CLUB
TIMP KIWANIS BOUNOUS PARK
THE PARK AT ROCK CANYON
SERTOMA PARK
GRANDVIEW PARK
LION'S PARK
EXCHANGE PARK
UTAH VALLEY REGIONAL MEDICAL CENTER
LaVell Edwards Stadium
Marriott Center
BRIGHAM YOUNG UNIVERSITY
KIWANIS PARK
SEVEN PEAKS GC
84097
84604
84601
84606

A
1 Shadowbrook Dr
2 N Brookside Ln
3 N 125 W
4 Marrcrest West St
5 Marrcrest E

B
1 Mohican Ln
2 E 2620 N

C
1 E 1800 S
2 Orlean Dr
3 N 1290 W

D
1 N 170 W
2 N Canyon Rd

E
1 E Richards Hall
2 Fugal Hall
3 Gates Hall
4 Kimball Hall
5 Carroll Hall

F
1 E Campus Dr

G
1 Fox Hall
2 Harris Hall
3 Horne Hall
4 Penrose Hall
5 A Richards Hall
6 Robison Hall
7 Maeser Hall
8 Rogers Hall

H
1 W 1380 N

J
1 E 660 N
2 E 610 N

K
1 S 1400 W
2 W 510 S

40°16'40" 40°16'14" 40°15'48" 40°15'22" 40°14'55" 40°14'29" 40°14'03" 40°13'37"

111°40'53" 111°40'19" 111°39'45" 111°39'11" 111°38'37" 111°38'03"

A B C D E

1 2 3 4 5 6 7

SEE 3035 MAP

1:24,000
1 in. = 2000 ft.
0 0.25 0.5
miles

SEE 2822 MAP

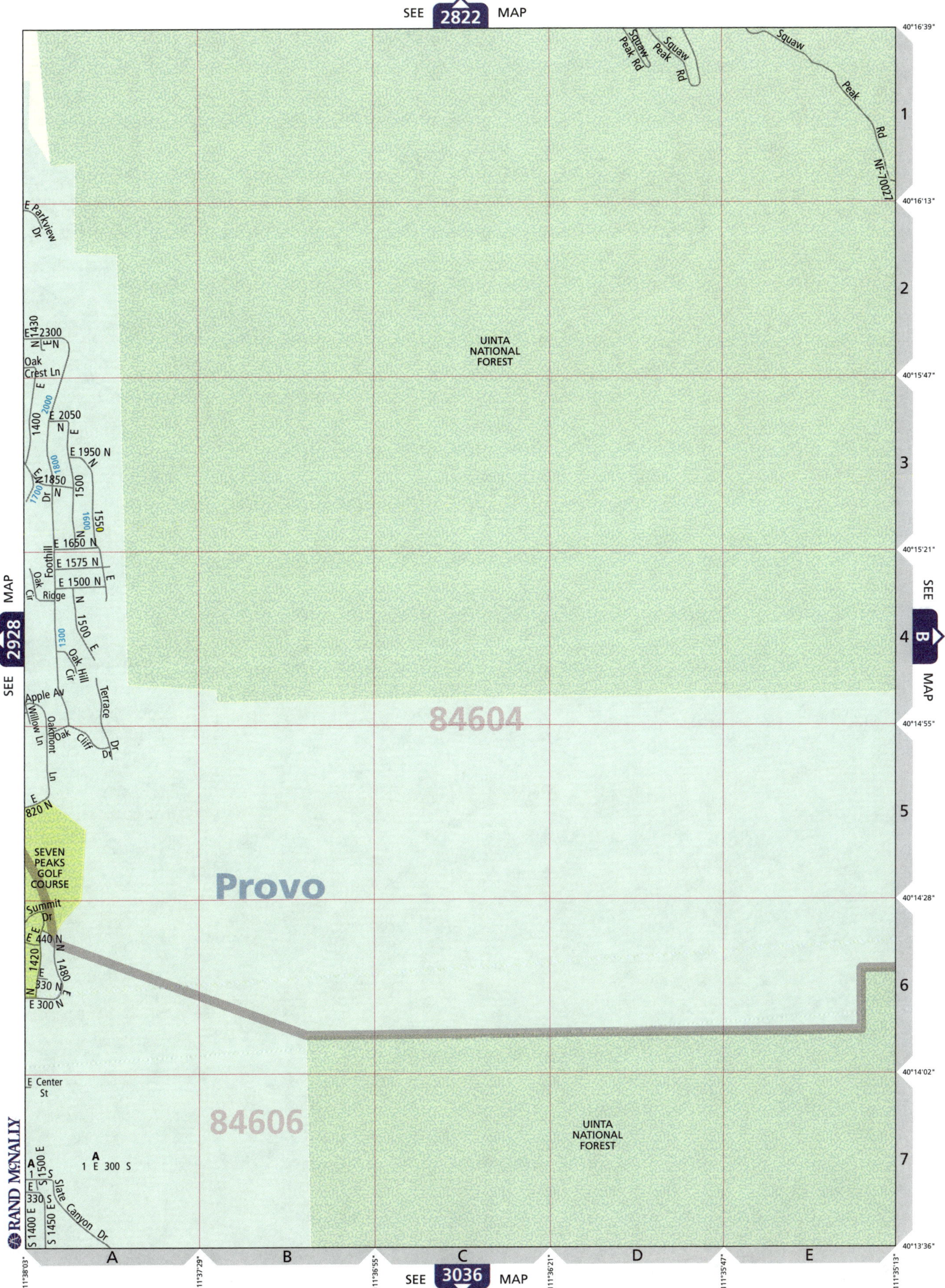

SEE 2928 MAP

SEE B MAP

SEE 3036 MAP

1:24,000
1 in. = 2000 ft.
0 0.25 0.5
miles

SEE 2927 MAP

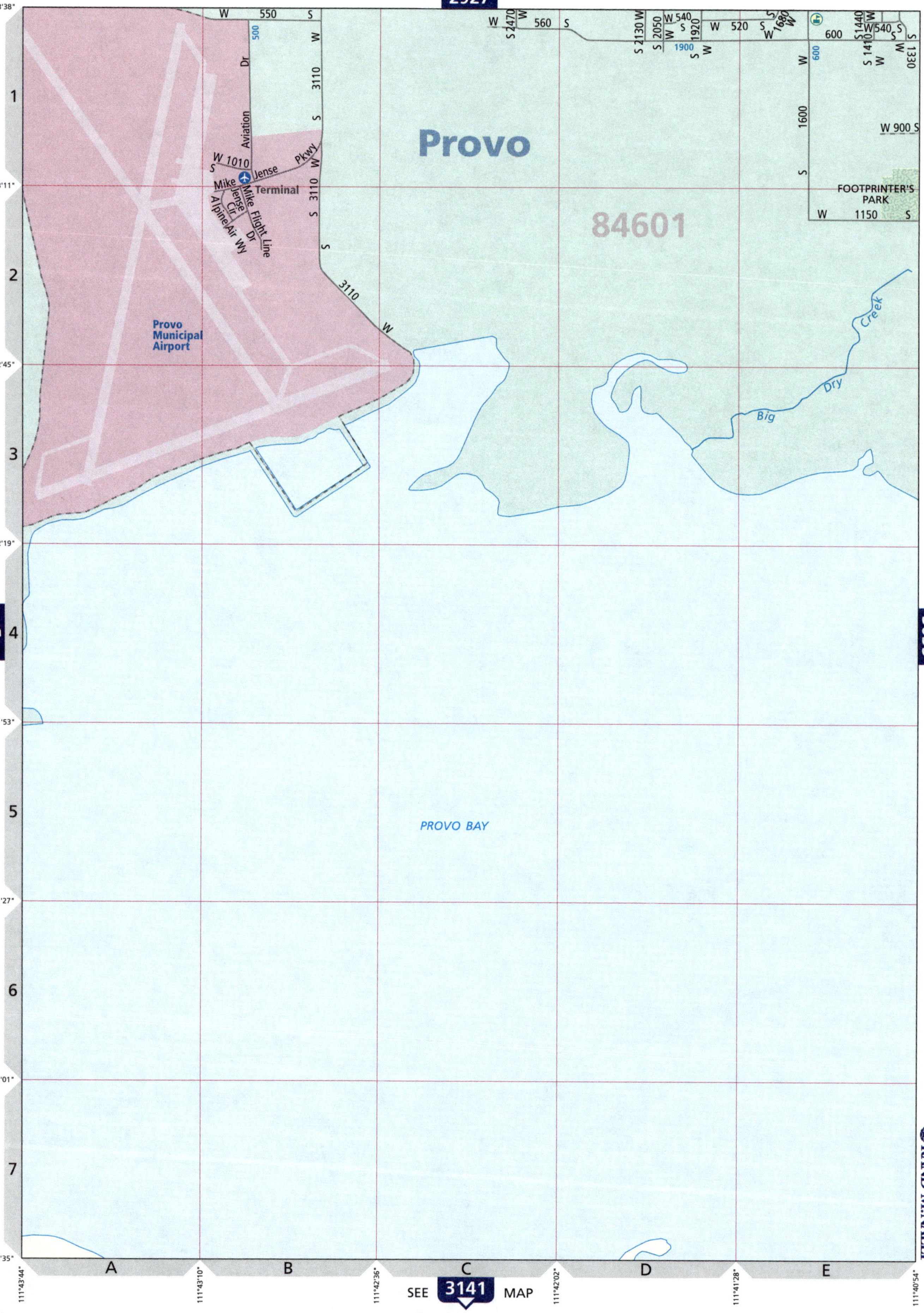

1 2 3 4 5 6 7

A B C D E

40°13'38" 40°13'11" 40°12'45" 40°12'19" 40°11'53" 40°11'27" 40°11'01" 40°10'35"

111°43'44" 111°43'10" 111°42'36" 111°42'02" 111°41'28" 111°40'54"

SEE B MAP

SEE 3035 MAP

SEE 3141 MAP

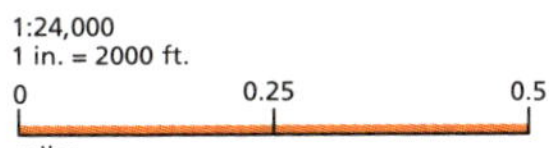

SEE 2928 MAP

Provo

Springville

84601

84606

84663

PROVO BAY

EAST BAY

EAST BAY GOLF COURSE

Provo Towne Center

FOOTPRINTER'S PARK

PROVO CITY PIONEER CEM

VETERANS MEMORIAL HWY

UNIVERSITY AV

EASTBAY BLVD

STATE ST

Industrial Pkwy

Kuhni Rd

Colorado Av

Towne Centre Blvd

Mountain Pkwy N

Hobble Creek

A
1 Meadow Birch Ct

B
1 Nevada Av

15

189

89

75

263

261

40°13'37"

40°13'11"

40°12'45"

40°12'18"

40°11'52"

40°11'26"

40°11'00"

40°10'34"

111°40'54"

111°40'20"

111°39'46"

111°39'12"

111°38'38"

111°38'04"

A B C D E

1 2 3 4 5 6 7

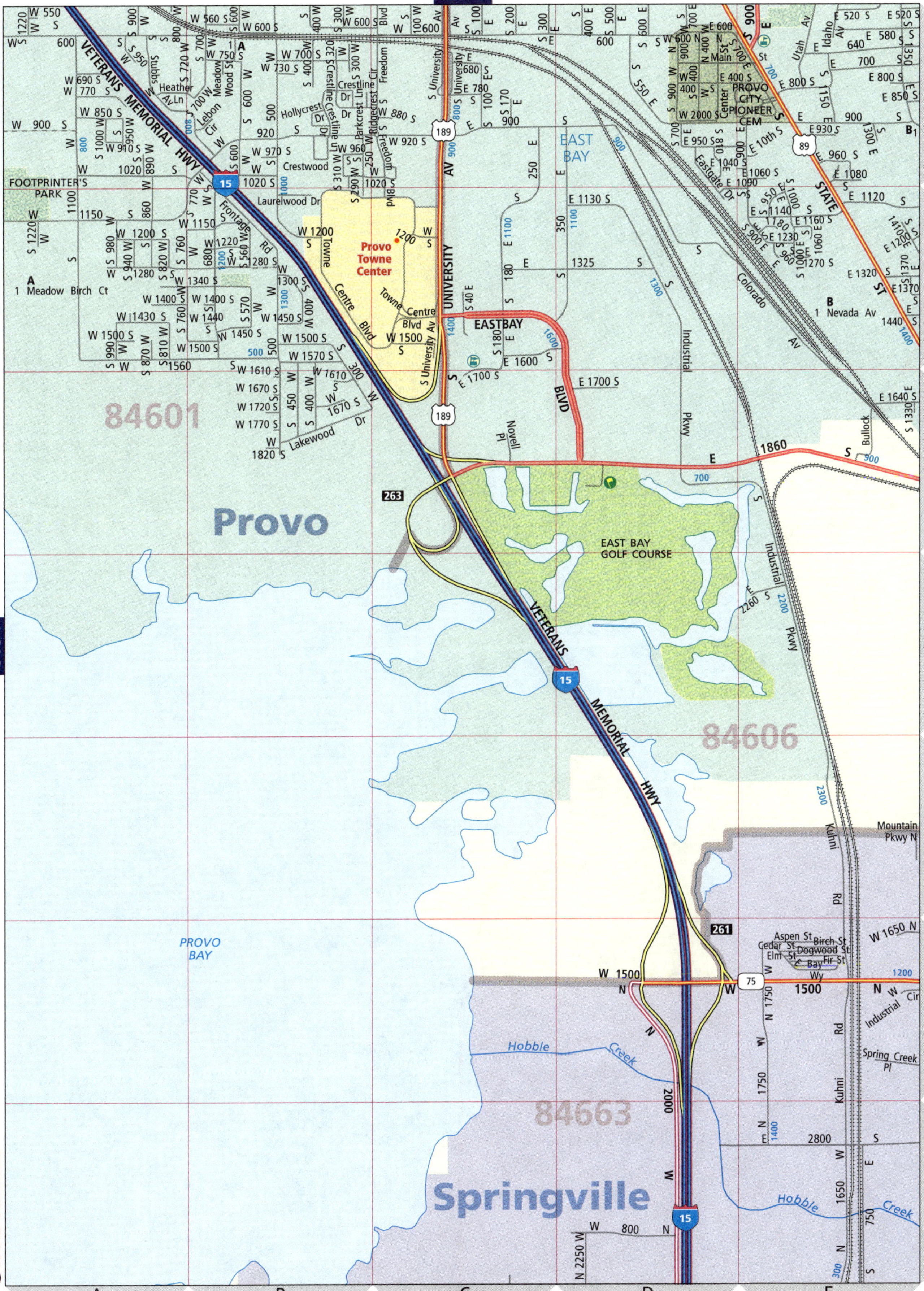

SEE 3034 MAP

SEE 3036 MAP

SEE 3142 MAP

1:24,000
1 in. = 2000 ft.
0 0.25 0.5
miles

SEE 2929 MAP

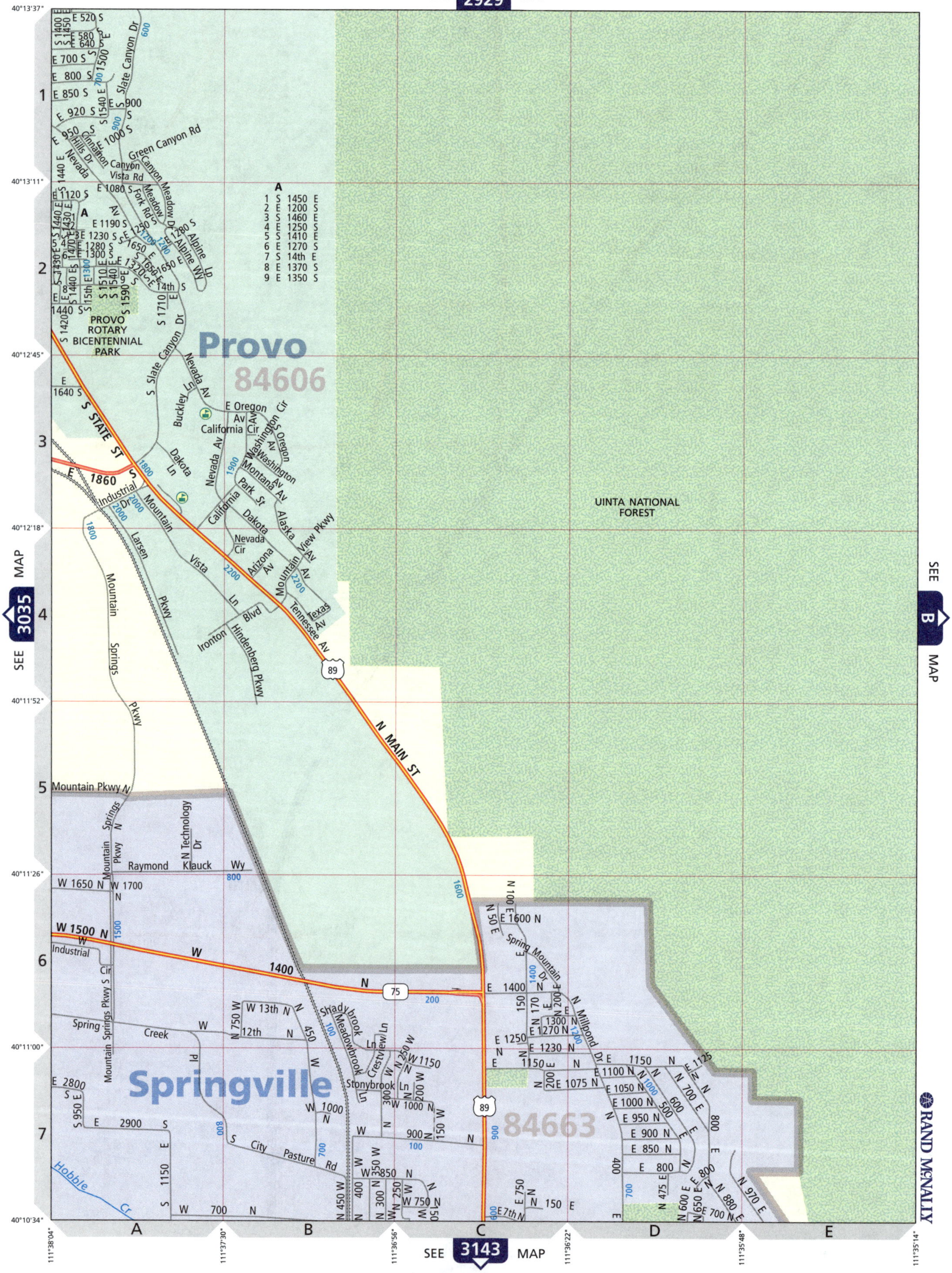

SEE 3035 MAP

SEE B MAP

SEE 3143 MAP

A

1 S 1450 E
2 E 1200 S
3 S 1460 E
4 E 1250 S
5 S 1410 E
6 E 1270 S
7 S 14th E
8 E 1370 S
9 E 1350 S

Provo
84606

PROVO ROTARY BICENTENNIAL PARK

UINTA NATIONAL FOREST

Springville
84663

S STATE ST
N MAIN ST
Mountain Springs Pkwy
W 1400 N
W 1500 N
E 1860 S
Slate Canyon Dr
Green Canyon Rd
Canyon Vista Rd
Canyon Meadow Dr
Alpine Lp
Alpine Wy
Nevada Av
California Cir
E Oregon Av
Washington Av
Montana Av
Dakota Ln
Industrial Dr
Mountain Vista Ln
Mountain View Pkwy
Larsen Pkwy
Ironton Blvd
Hindenberg Pkwy
Tennessee Av
Texas Av
Alaska Av
Arizona Av
Raymond Klauck Wy
N Technology Dr
Spring Creek
W Industrial Cir
S City Pasture Rd
Shadybrook Ln
Meadowbrook Ln
Crestview Ln
Stonybrook Ln
Spring Mountain Dr
N Millpond Dr
Hobble Cr

89
75

A B C D E
1 2 3 4 5 6 7

40°13'37" 40°13'11" 40°12'45" 40°12'18" 40°11'52" 40°11'26" 40°11'00" 40°10'34"
111°38'04" 111°37'30" 111°36'56" 111°36'22" 111°35'48" 111°35'14"

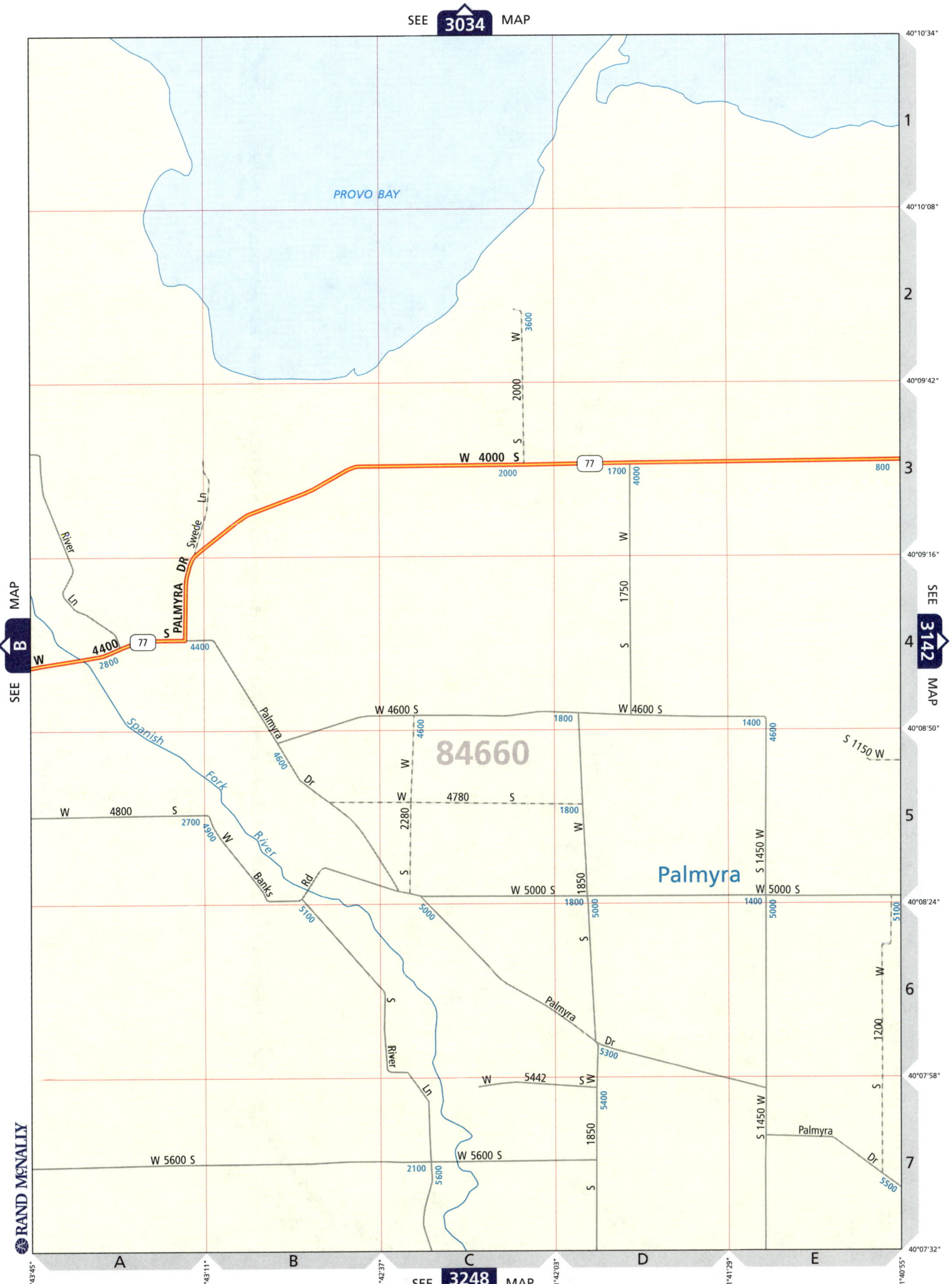
1:24,000
1 in. = 2000 ft.
0
0.25
0.5
miles
SEE 3034 MAP
SEE 3248 MAP
SEE B MAP
SEE 3142 MAP
PROVO BAY
84660
Palmyra
W 4000 S
77
W 4400
PALMYRA DR
Swede Ln
River Ln
Spanish Fork River
Palmyra Dr
W 4600 S
W 4780 S
W 4800 S
W Banks Rd
W 5000 S
S 1450 W
S 1150 W
W 1750 S
W 2000 S
W 2280 S
W 1850 S
S River Ln
W 5442 S
W 5600 S
S 1200 W
Palmyra Dr
RAND McNALLY
40°10'34"
40°10'08"
40°09'42"
40°09'16"
40°08'50"
40°08'24"
40°07'58"
40°07'32"
111°43'45"
111°43'11"
111°42'37"
111°42'03"
111°41'29"
111°40'55"

1:24,000
1 in. = 2000 ft.
0 0.25 0.5
miles

SEE 3035 MAP

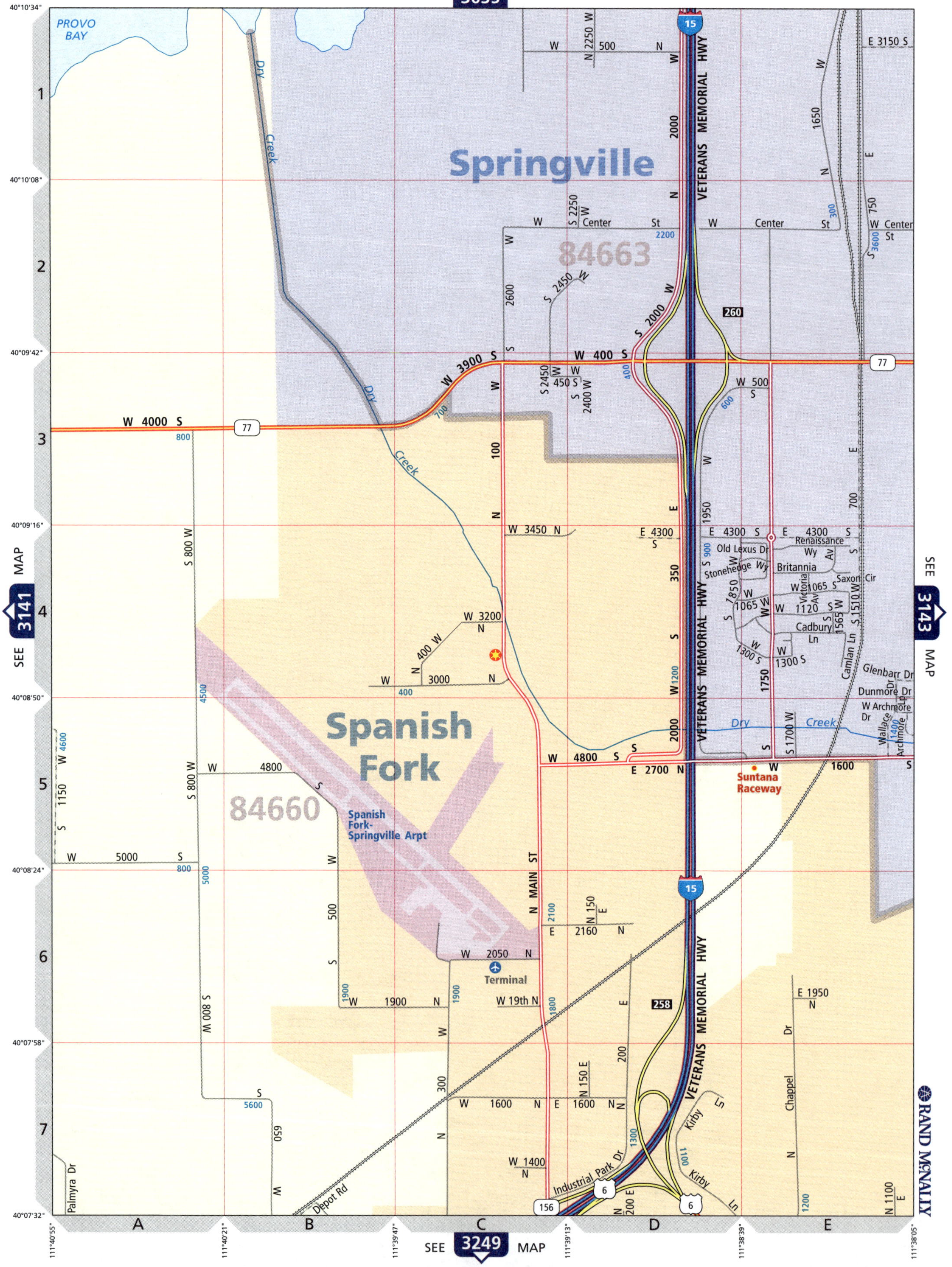

PROVO BAY

Springville

84663

Spanish Fork

84660

Spanish Fork-Springville Arpt

Terminal

Suntana Raceway

VETERANS MEMORIAL HWY

W 4000 S

W 3900 S

W 400 S

W Center St

W 4800 S

E 2700 N

W 5000 S

N MAIN ST

Dry Creek

Industrial Park Dr

Depot Rd

Palmyra Dr

Chappel Dr

Kirby Ln

Old Lexus Dr

Stonehedge Wy

Renaissance Wy

Britannia

Saxon Cir

Cadbury Ln

Camlan Ln

Glenbarr Dr

Dunmore Dr

W Archmore Dr

Wallace Dr

Archmore Lp

SEE 3141 MAP

SEE 3143 MAP

SEE 3249 MAP

RAND McNALLY

1:24,000
1 in. = 2000 ft.
0 0.25 0.5
miles

SEE 3036 MAP

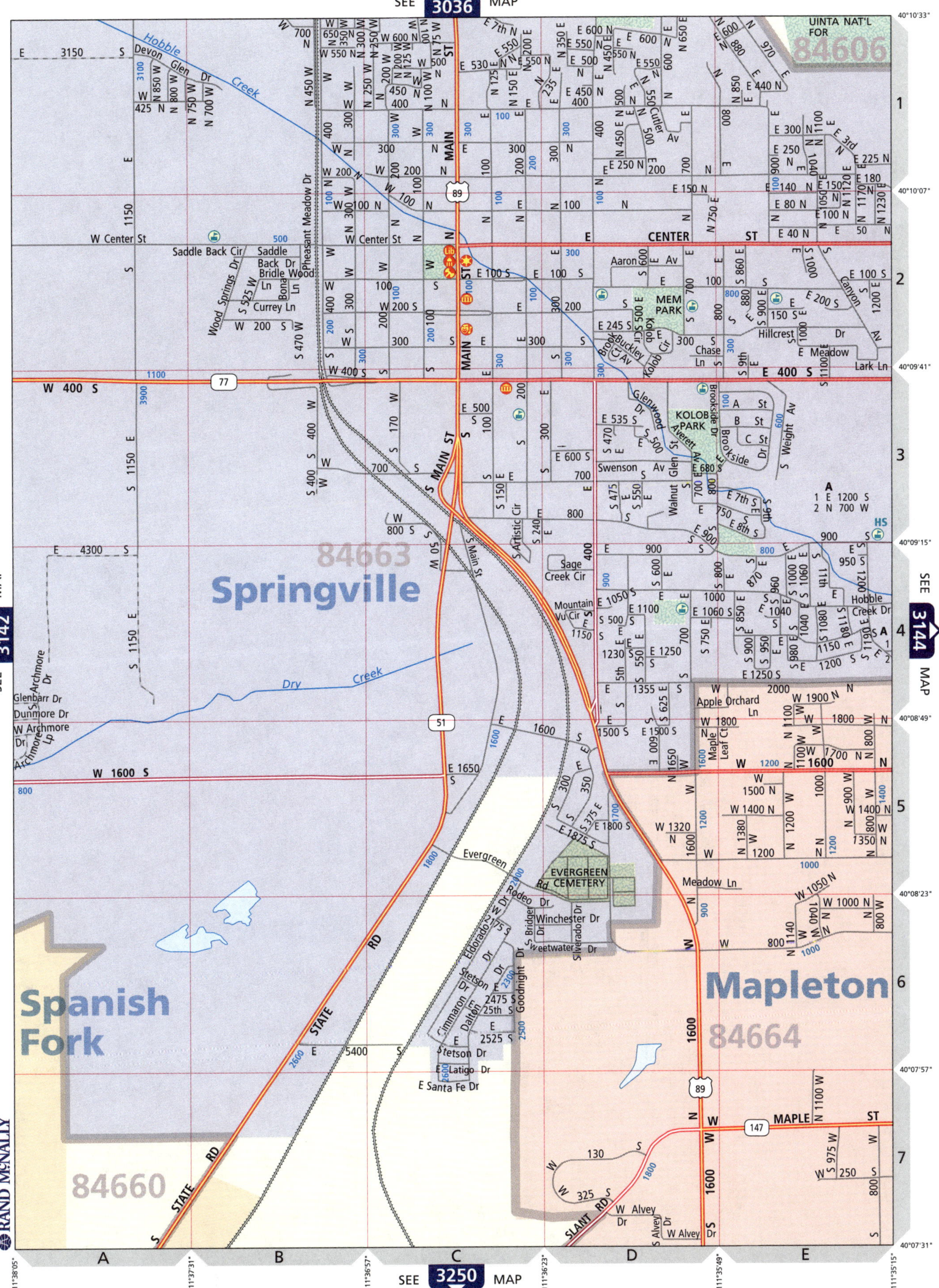

SEE 3142 MAP
SEE 3144 MAP
SEE 3250 MAP

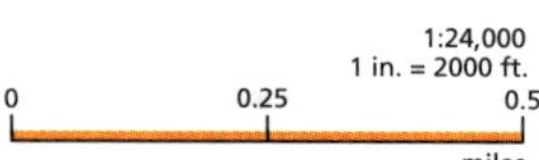

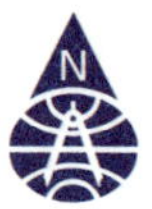

1:24,000
1 in. = 2000 ft.
0 0.25 0.5
miles

SEE B MAP
SEE 3143 MAP
SEE B MAP
SEE 3251 MAP
84606
84663
84664
UINTA NATIONAL FOREST
Springville
Mapleton
Spring Creek
Hobble Creek
HOBBLE CANYON
CANYON RD
CANYON DR
MAIN ST
MAPLE ST
147
NF-70025
1300 E
400 S
1700 E
1600 N
1200 N
2000 W
Thirty Oaks Dr
Meadow Ln
Quiet
Vineyard Wy
Dogwood
Aspen Dr
Eagle Dr
Sierra Bonita
Cobblestone
Flower Wy
Thistle Tree Dr
Willowbrook Ln
Pebble Creek Dr
Red Barn Rd
Town & Country Rd
Bottom Rd
Deer Creek Wy
Cove Dr
Stonebury Rd
Loop
Pheasant Run
Hobble Creek Dr
Eastridge Dr
Houtz Av
Anderson Av
Crandall
Brandon Dr
Oakwood Cir
Center St
Spring Oaks Dr
Canyon Av
Terrace
40°10'33"
40°10'07"
40°09'41"
40°09'15"
40°08'49"
40°08'23"
40°07'57"
40°07'31"
111°35'15"
111°34'41"
111°34'07"
111°33'33"
111°32'59"
111°32'25"
1
2
3
4
5
6
7
A
B
C
D
E
RAND McNALLY

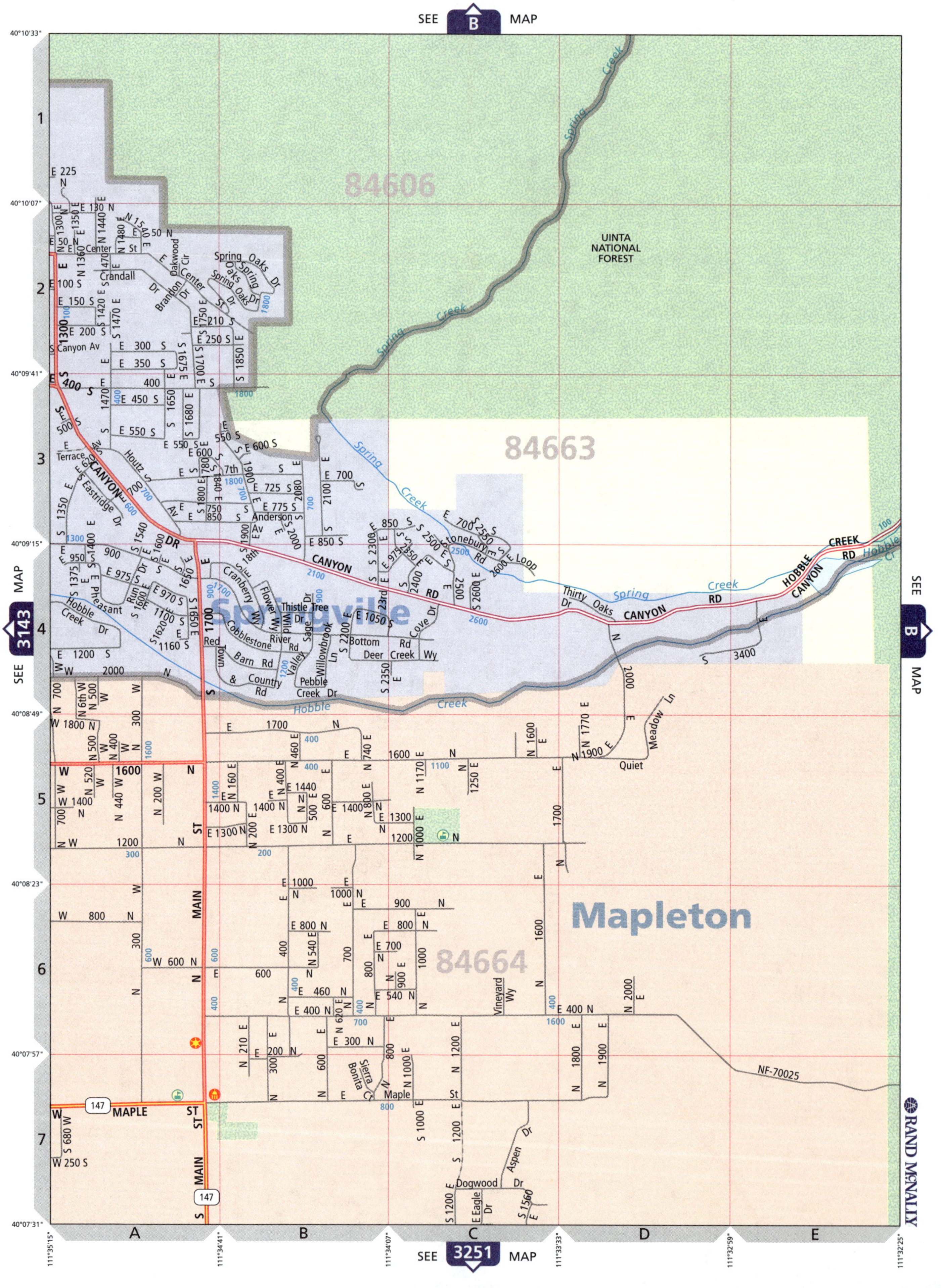

1:24,000
1 in. = 2000 ft.
0 0.25 0.5 miles

SEE 3141 MAP

SEE B MAP

SEE 3249 MAP

SEE 3355 MAP

1:24,000
1 in. = 2000 ft.
0 0.25 0.5
miles

SEE 3142 MAP

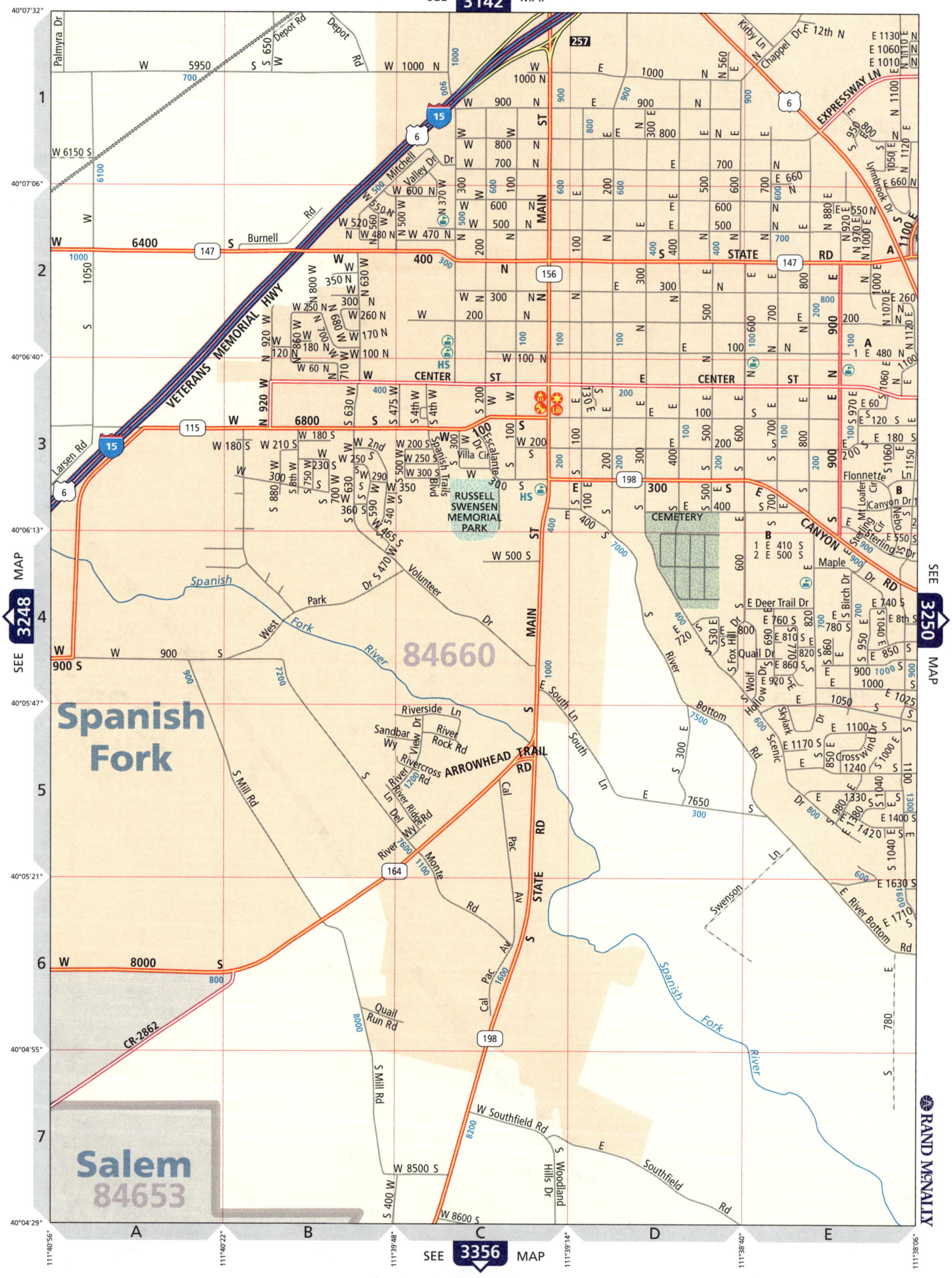

SEE 3248 MAP

SEE 3250 MAP

40°07'32" 40°07'06" 40°06'40" 40°06'13" 40°05'47" 40°05'21" 40°04'55" 40°04'29"

1 2 3 4 5 6 7

Spanish Fork
84660

Salem
84653

VETERANS MEMORIAL HWY
MAIN ST
STATE RD
CENTER ST
CANYON RD
EXPRESSWAY LN
ARROWHEAD TRAIL RD
RUSSELL SWENSEN MEMORIAL PARK
CEMETERY
Spanish Fork River
W 6400 S
W 900 S
W 8000 S
W 6800 S
E 1000 N
S Mill Rd
W Southfield Rd
E Southfield Rd
E River Bottom Rd
CR-2862

A B C D E

111°40'56" 111°40'22" 111°39'48" 111°39'14" 111°38'40" 111°38'06"

SEE 3356 MAP

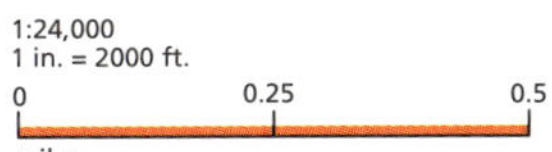

SEE 3143 MAP

Mapleton

Spanish Fork

Sutro

84660

84663

84664

SPANISH OAKS GOLF COURSE

CANYON VIEW PARK

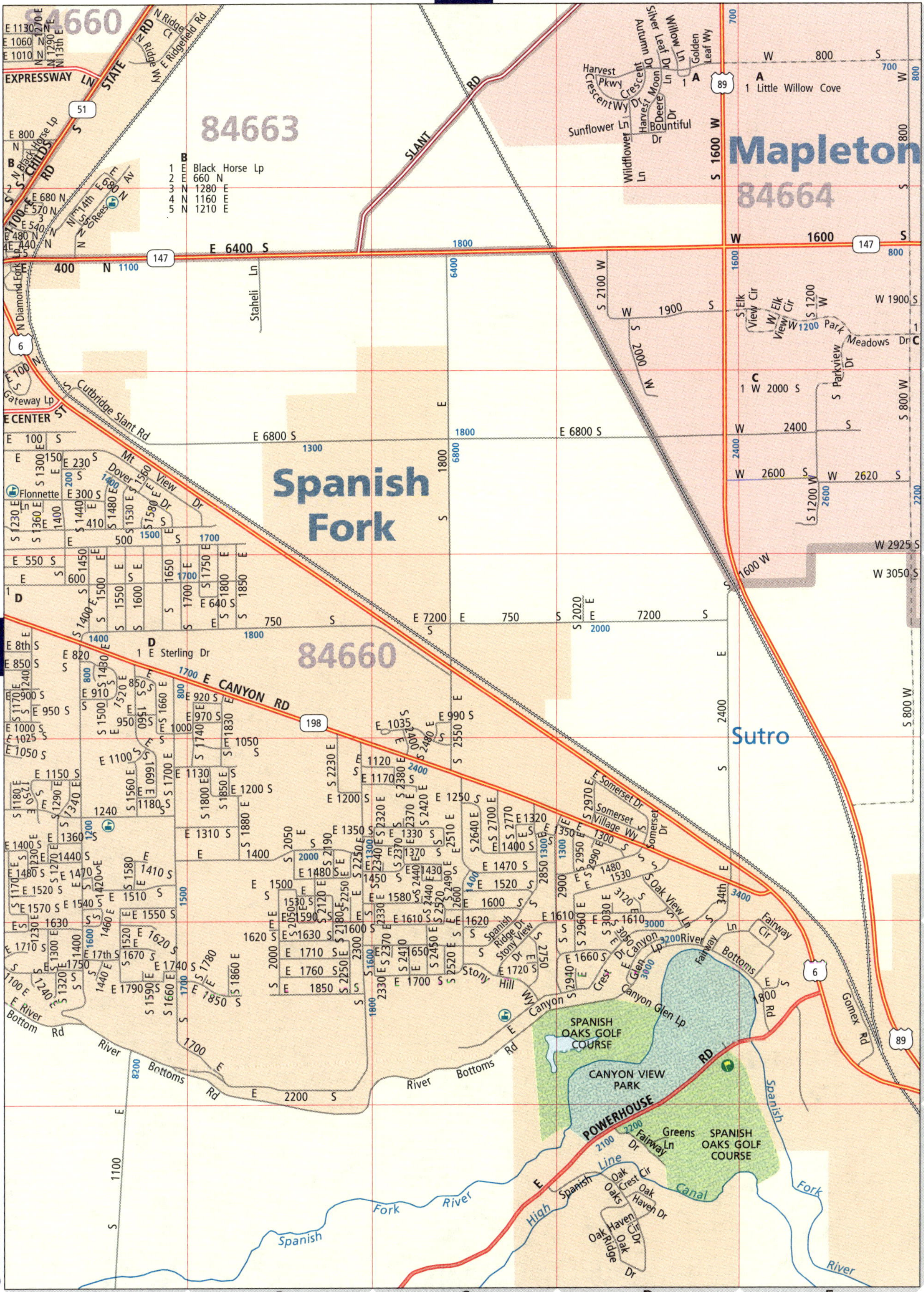

SEE 3249 MAP

SEE 3251 MAP

SEE B MAP

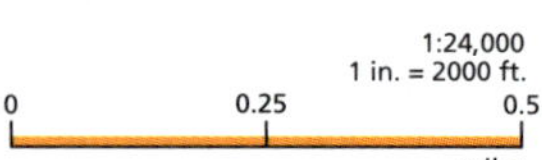

SEE 3144 MAP

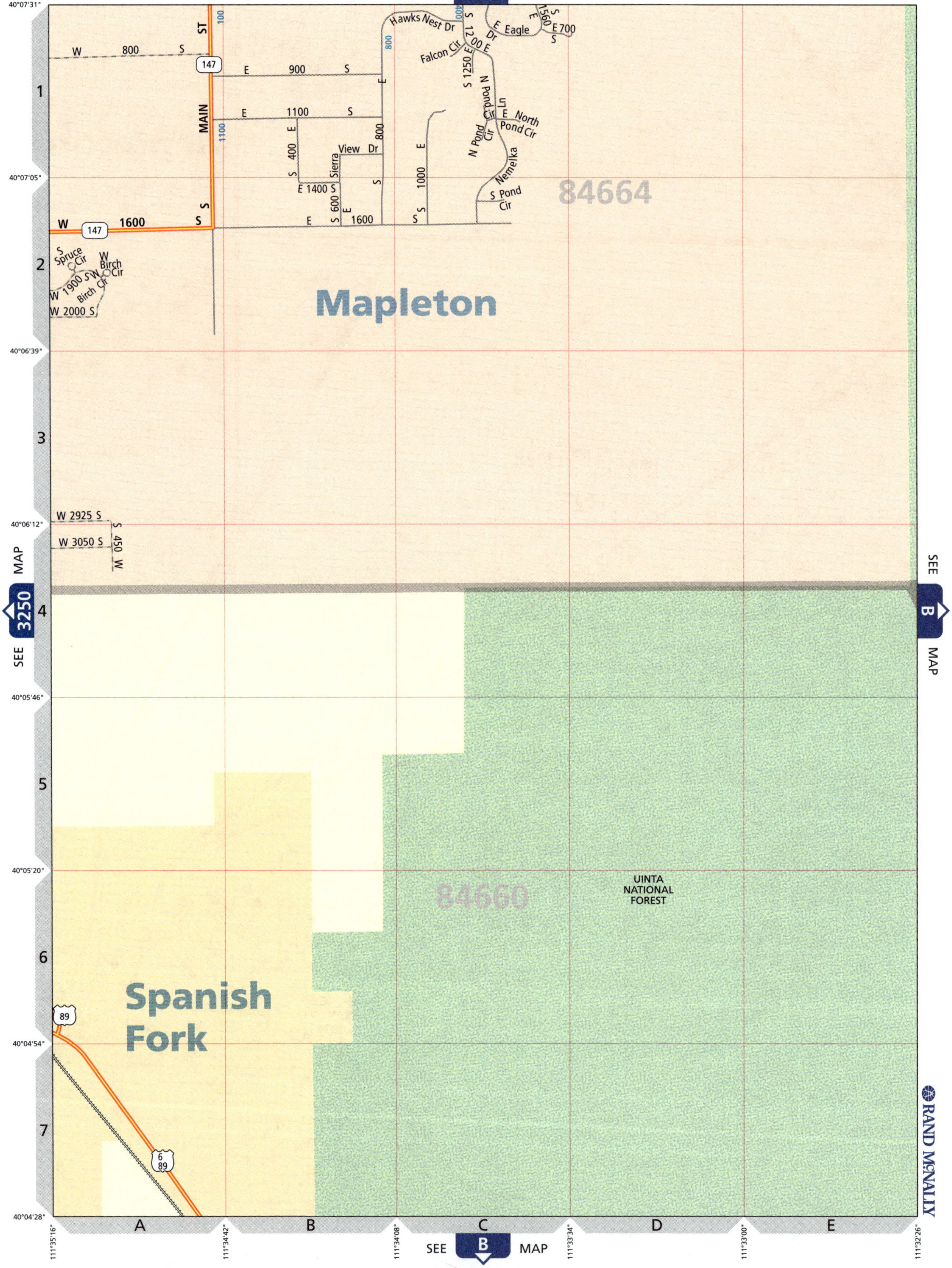

SEE 3250 MAP

SEE B MAP

SEE B MAP

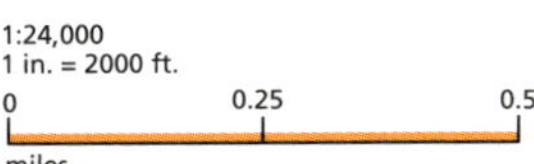

SEE B MAP

84651

Payson

HILLMAN PARK

SEE B MAP

SEE 3355 MAP

SEE 3461 MAP

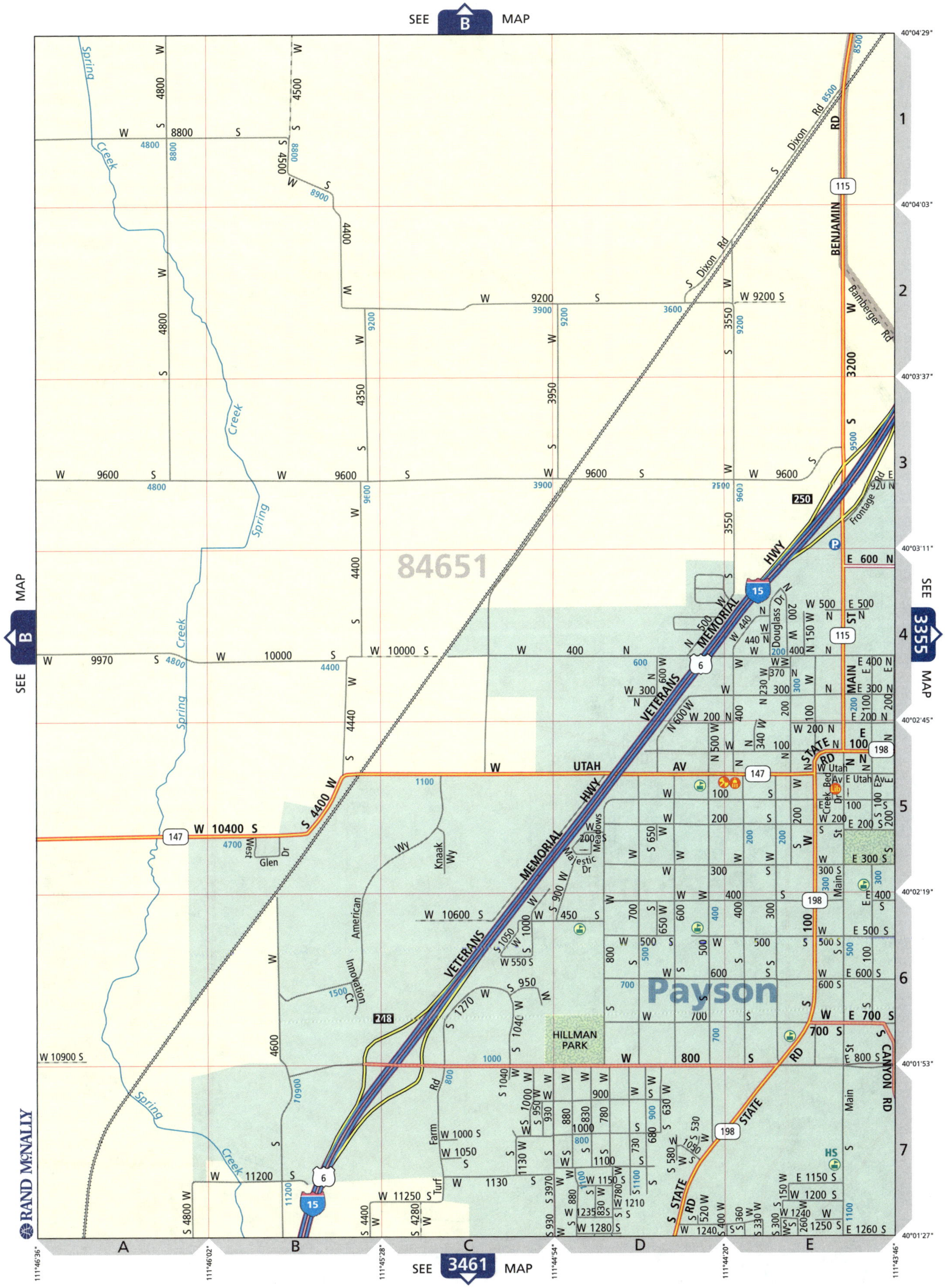

RAND McNALLY

1:24,000
1 in. = 2000 ft.
0 0.25 0.5
miles

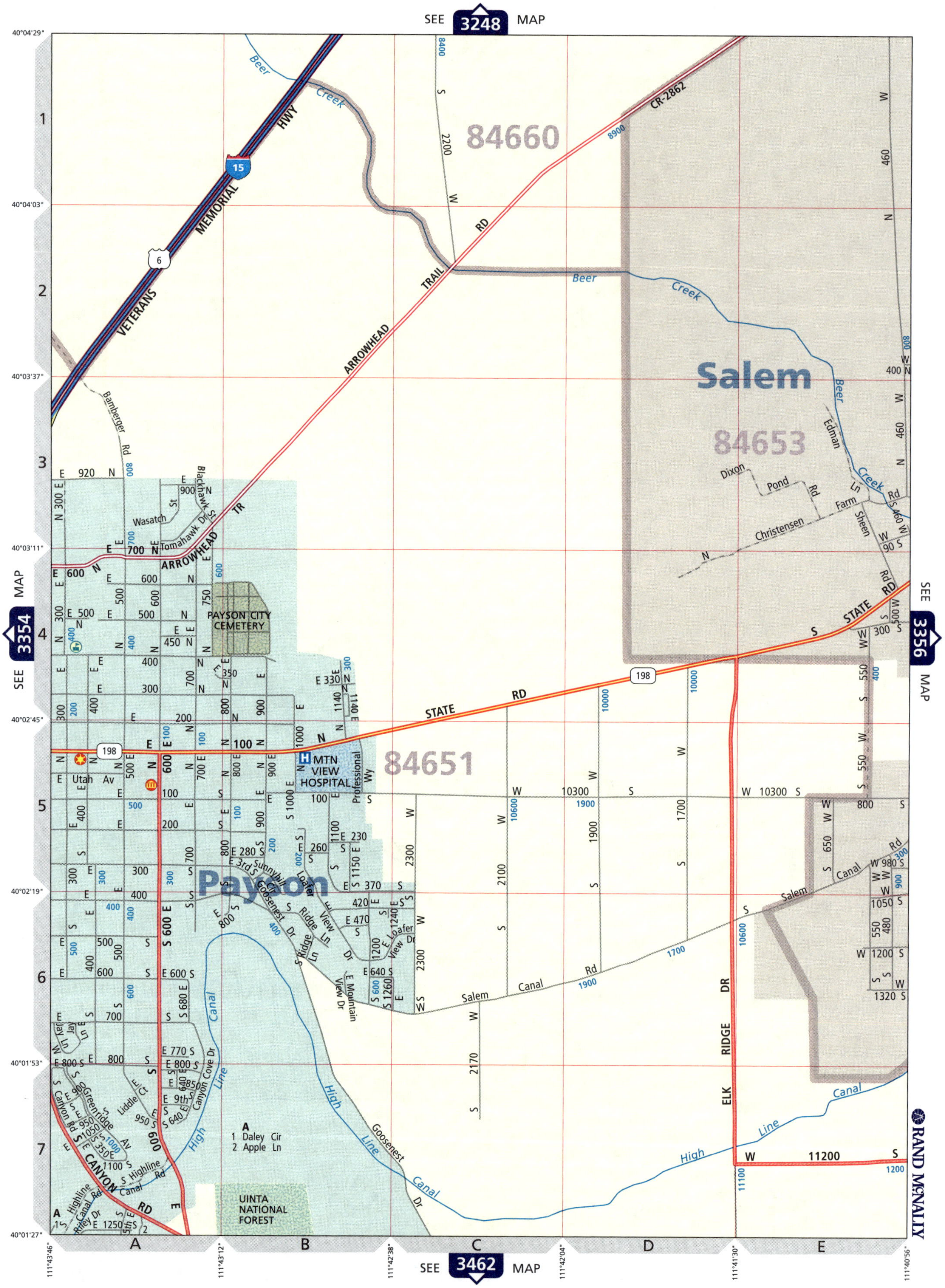

SEE 3248 MAP

SEE 3354 MAP

SEE 3356 MAP

SEE 3462 MAP

40°04'29"
40°04'03"
40°03'37"
40°03'11"
40°02'45"
40°02'19"
40°01'53"
40°01'27"

111°43'46" 111°43'12" 111°42'38" 111°42'04" 111°41'30" 111°40'56"

1 2 3 4 5 6 7
A B C D E

84660
84653
84651

Salem
Payson

15
6
198

VETERANS MEMORIAL HWY
ARROWHEAD TRAIL RD
CR-2862
STATE RD
ELK RIDGE DR
CANYON RD
Beer Creek
High Line Canal
Goosenest Dr
Salem Canal Rd
Bamberger Rd
Dixon Pond Rd
Christensen
Sheen Farm Ln
Edman
W 10300 S
W 11200 S
E 920 N
E 700 N
E 600 N
E 500 N
E 400 N
E 300 N
E 200 N
E 100 N
Utah Av
E 100 S
E 200 S
E 300 S
E 400 S
E 500 S
E 600 S
E 700 S
E 800 S
S 600 E
Wasatch St
Tomahawk Dr
Blackhawk St
Sunnyhill Cir
Goosenest Ridge Dr
Loafer View Ln
E Loafer View Dr
E Mountain View Dr
Professional Wy
Greenridge Av
Liddle Ct
Canyon Cove Dr
S Highline Rd
Highline Canal Rd
Riley Dr
Jay Ln

PAYSON CITY CEMETERY
MTN VIEW HOSPITAL
UINTA NATIONAL FOREST

A
1 Daley Cir
2 Apple Ln

1:24,000
1 in. = 2000 ft.
0 0.25 0.5
miles

SEE 3249 MAP

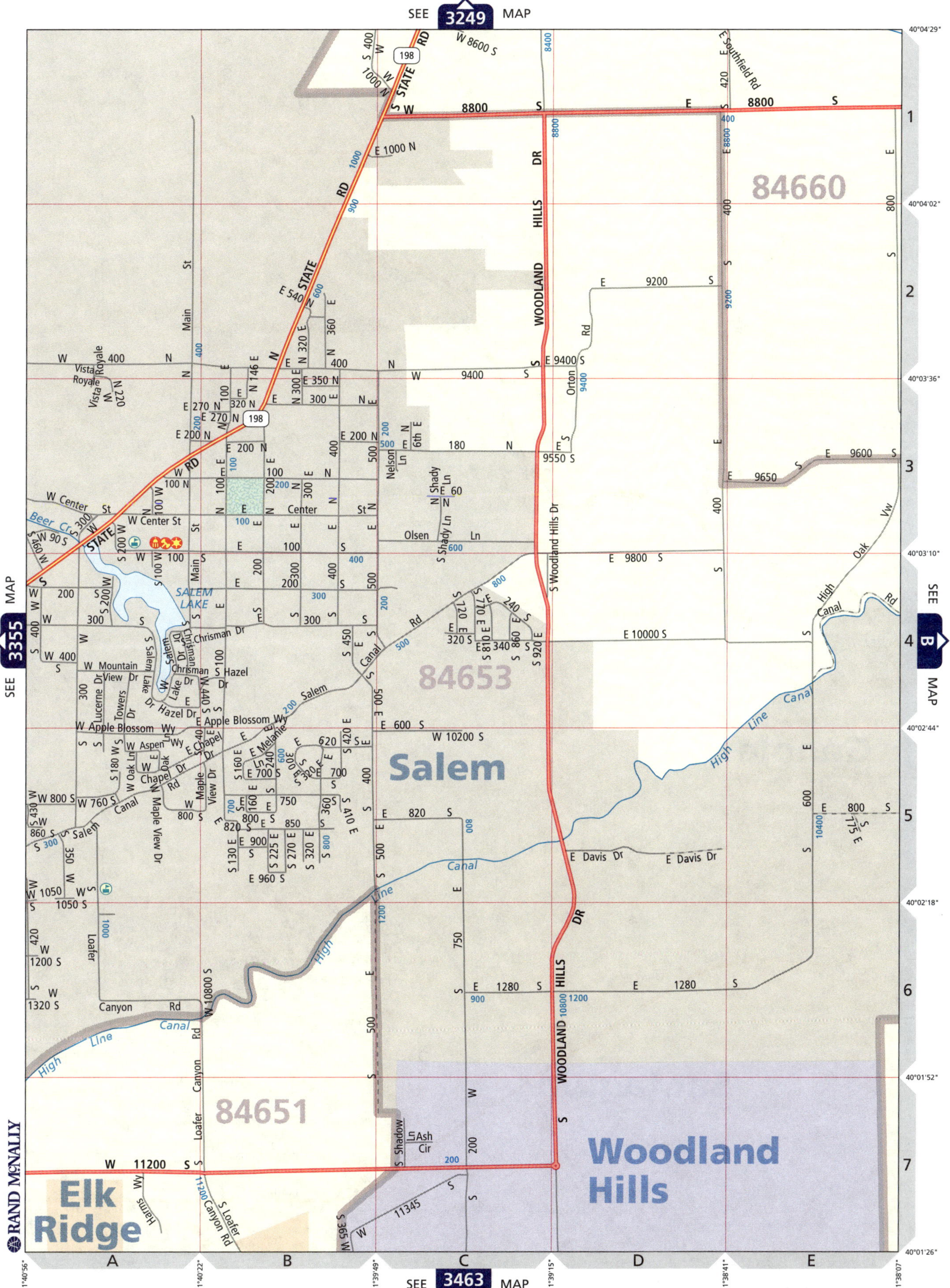

SEE 3355 MAP

SEE B MAP

SEE 3463 MAP

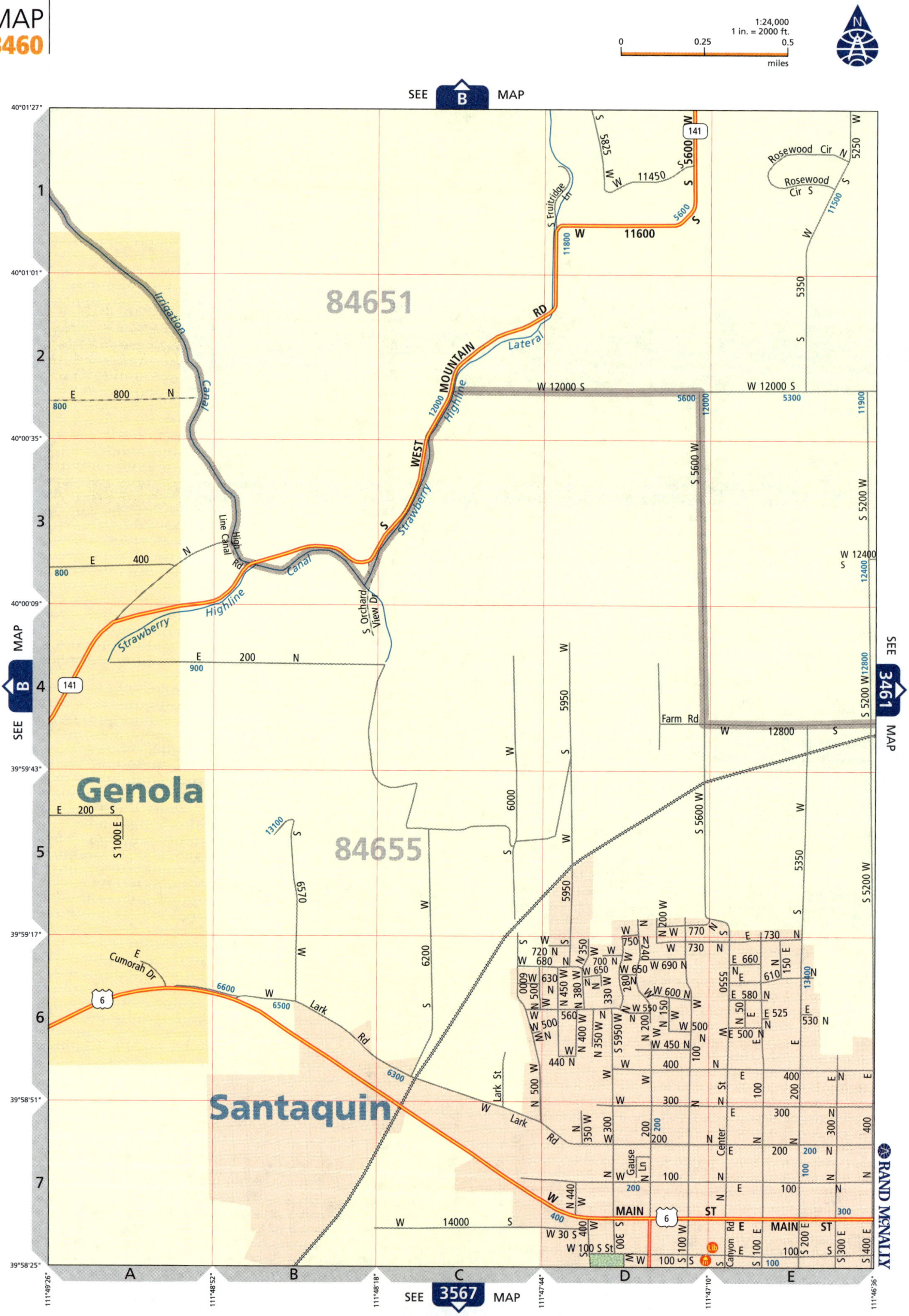

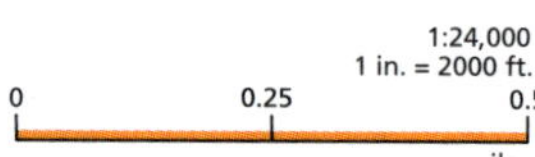

SEE B MAP

SEE B MAP

SEE 3461 MAP

Genola

Santaquin

84651

84655

West Mountain Rd

W 12000 S

W 12800 S

W 11600

W 14000 S

Main St

Highline Canal

Irrigation Canal

Strawberry Highline Canal

W Lark Rd

141

6

SEE 3567 MAP

1:24,000
1 in. = 2000 ft.
0 0.25 0.5
miles

SEE 3354 MAP

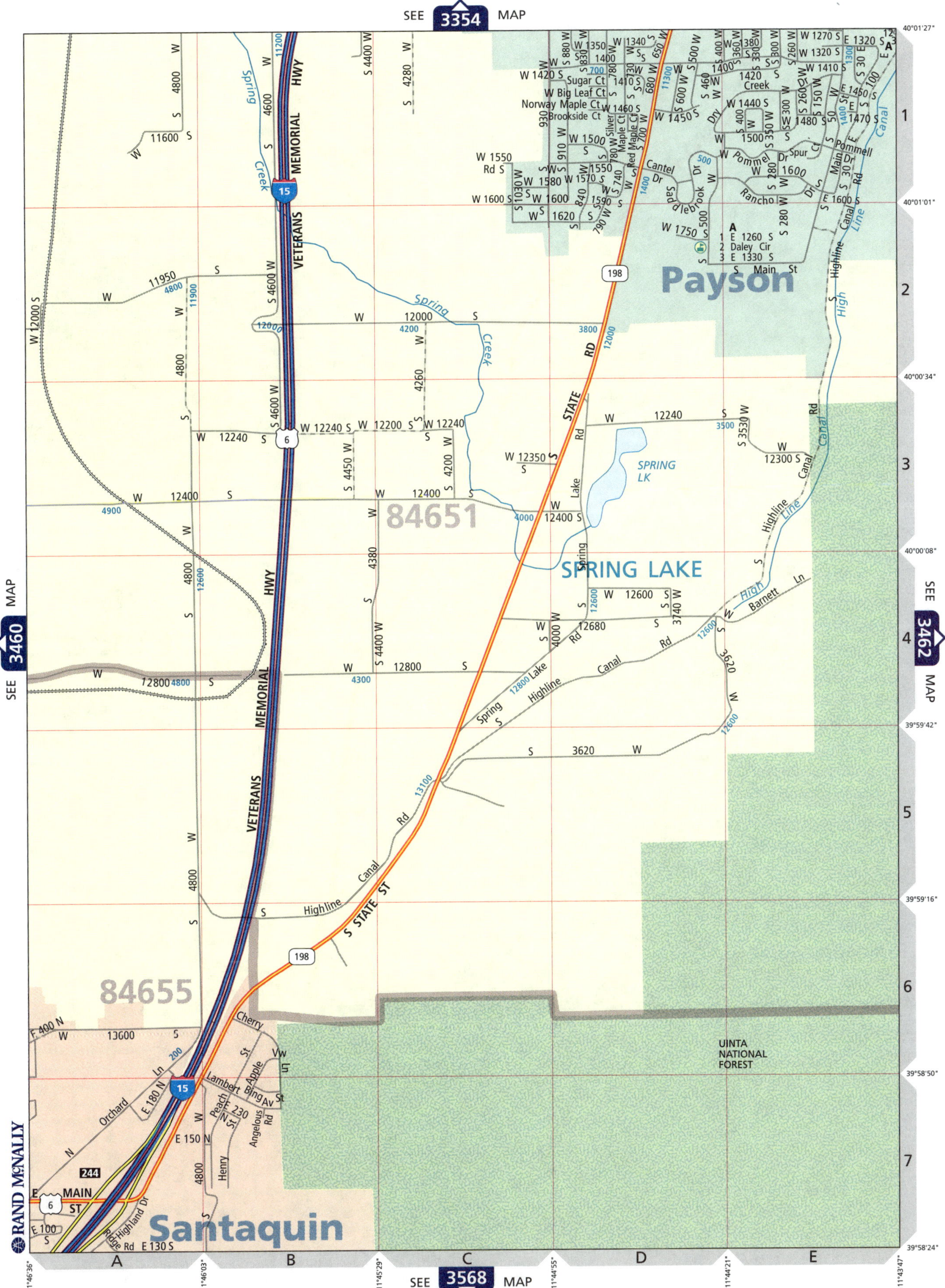

SEE 3460 MAP
SEE 3462 MAP
SEE 3568 MAP

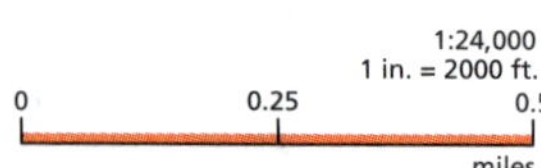

SEE 3355 MAP

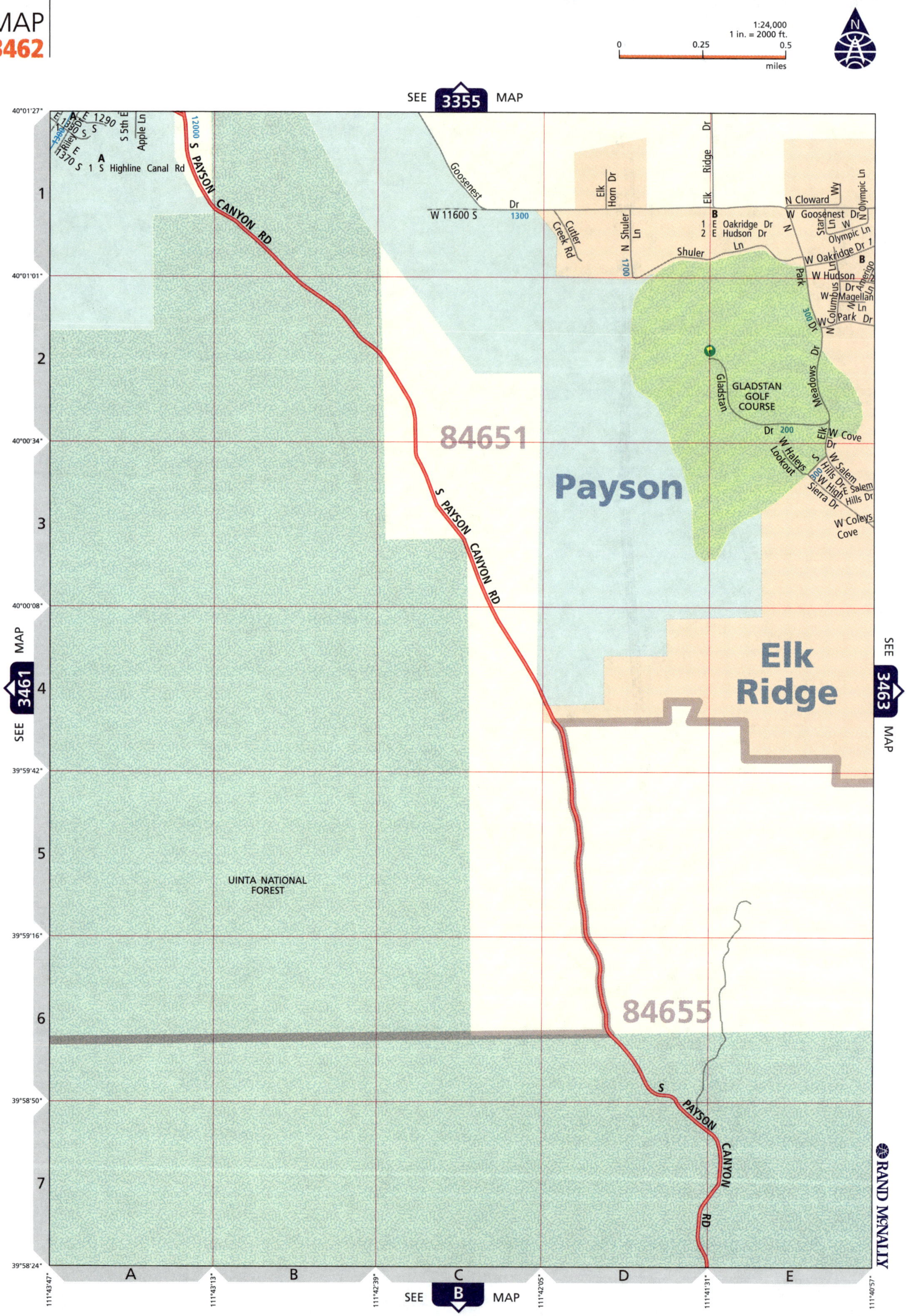

Payson

Elk Ridge

84651

84655

S PAYSON CANYON RD

UINTA NATIONAL FOREST

GLADSTAN GOLF COURSE

Goosenest Dr

W 11600 S

1300

12000

S Highline Canal Rd

Apple Ln

S 5th E

Cutler Creek Rd

Elk Horn Dr

N Shuler Ln

1700

Shuler Ln

Elk Ridge Dr

E Oakridge Dr

E Hudson Dr

N Cloward Wy

W Goosenest Dr

N Olympic Ln

Olympic Ln

W Oakridge Dr

W Hudson Dr

W Magellan Ln

N Columbus Ln

W Park Dr

Park

300

Meadows Dr

Gladstan Dr

200

W Cove Dr

W Haleys Lookout

W Salem Hills Dr

E Salem Hills Dr

W High Sierra Dr

800

W Coleys Cove

SEE 3461 MAP

SEE 3463 MAP

SEE B MAP

RAND McNALLY

1:24,000
1 in. = 2000 ft.
0 0.25 0.5
miles

SEE 3356 MAP

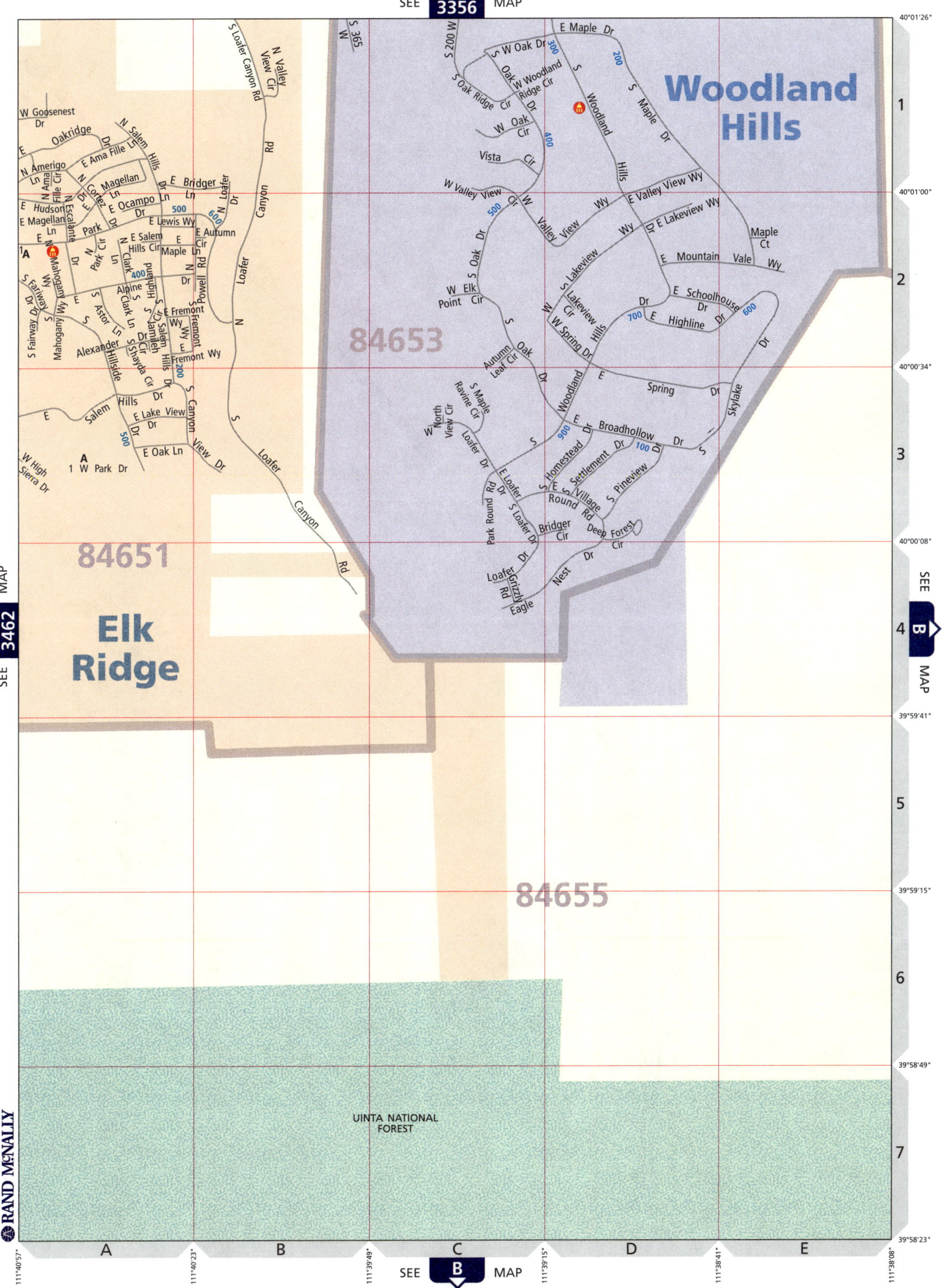

SEE 3462 MAP
SEE B MAP
SEE B MAP

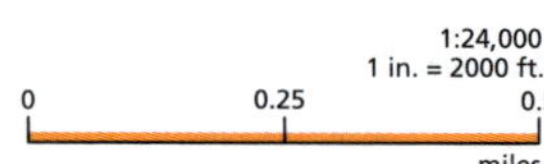

SEE 3460 MAP

Santaquin

84655

84645

UINTA NATIONAL FOREST

UTAH CO
JUAB CO

VETERANS MEMORIAL HWY

GOSHEN CANYON RD

SEE B MAP

SEE 3568 MAP

SEE B MAP

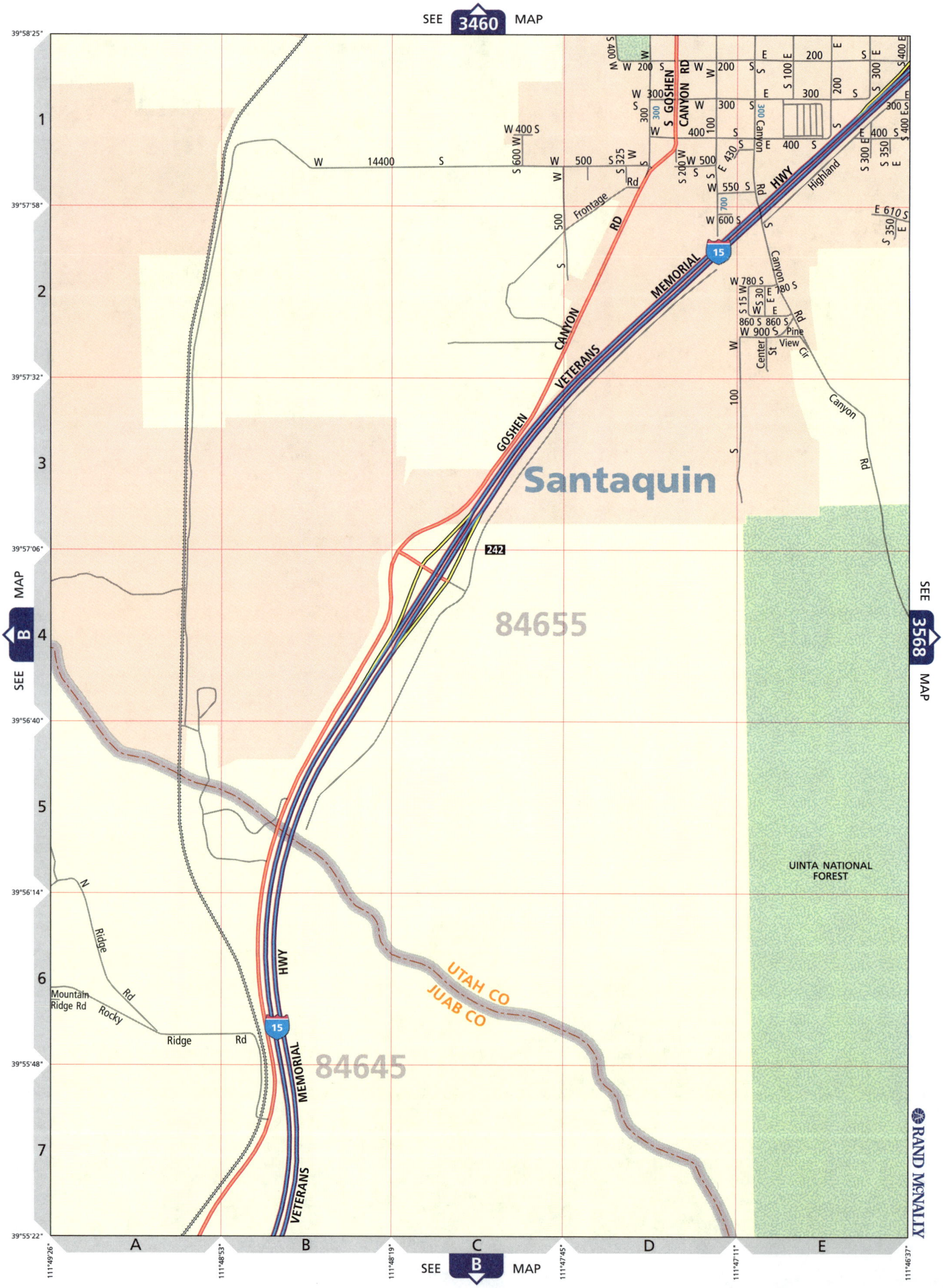

RAND McNALLY

1:24,000
1 in. = 2000 ft.
0 0.25 0.5
miles

SEE 3461 MAP

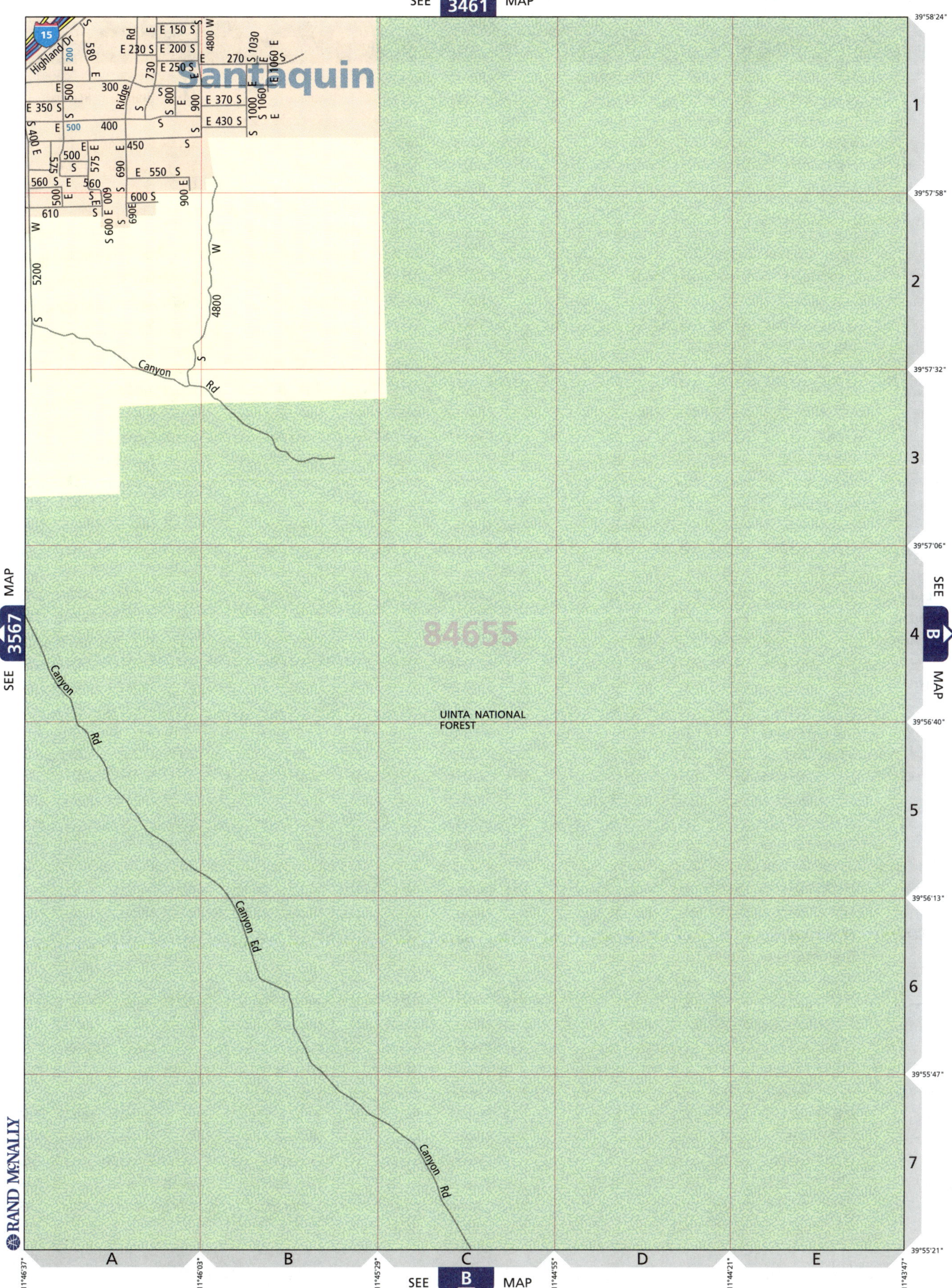

SEE 3567 MAP

SEE B MAP

SEE B MAP

Cities and Communities

Community Name	Abbr.	County	ZIP Code	Map Page
*Alpine	ALPN	Utah	84004	2497
*Alta	ALTA	Salt Lake	84049	2181
Altus		Summit	84098	1864
*Amalga	AMGA	Cache	84335	398
*American Fork	ANFK	Utah	84003	2711
*Bear River City	BRCY	Box Elder	84301	645
Benjamin		Utah	84660	3248
Benson		Cache	84341	462
*Bluffdale	BFDL	Salt Lake	84065	2387
*Bountiful	BNFL	Davis	84010	1653
--Box Elder County	BxEC			
Bradford		Box Elder	84337	645
*Brigham City	BMCY	Box Elder	84302	766
Brighton		Salt Lake	84098	2183
--Cache County	CchC			
Canyon Rim		Salt Lake	84109	1966
*Cedar Hills	CRHL	Utah	84062	2605
*Centerville	CTRV	Davis	84014	1551
*Charleston	CSTN	Wasatch	84032	2504
*Clearfield	CRFD	Davis	84015	1227
*Clinton	CLTN	Davis	84015	1226
College Ward		Cache	84321	590
*Corinne	CRNN	Box Elder	84307	704
Cottonwood		Salt Lake	84117	2071
*Cottonwood Heights	CDHT	Salt Lake	84093	2178
Cottonwd Meadows		Salt Lake	84117	2071
Daniel		Wasatch	84032	2505
*Deweyville	DWVL	Box Elder	84309	586
*Draper	DRPR	Utah	84020	2389
*Draper	DRPR	Salt Lake	84020	2389
*Eagle Mountain	EGMN	Utah	84043	2601
East Millcreek		Salt Lake	84109	1966
Eden		Weber	84310	1002
*Elk Ridge	EKMT	Utah	84651	3463
*Elwood	ELWD	Box Elder	84337	585
Emigration Canyon		Salt Lake	84108	1860
*Farmington	FMTN	Davis	84025	1448
*Farr West	FRWT	Weber	84404	997
*Fruit Heights	FTHT	Davis	84037	1346
*Garland	GRLD	Box Elder	84312	520
*Genola	GNLA	Utah	84655	3460
Gorgosa		Summit	84098	1865
Granite		Salt Lake	84092	2284
*Harrisville	HARR	Weber	84404	1056
*Heber City	HRCY	Wasatch	84032	2398
Hermitage		Weber	84317	1058
*Herriman	HRMN	Salt Lake	84065	2385
*Highland	HILD	Utah	84003	2604
*Holladay	HLDY	Salt Lake	84117	2071
*Honeyville	HYVL	Box Elder	84314	646
*Hooper	HOPR	Weber	84315	1169
*Huntsville	HTVL	Weber	84317	1061
*Hyde Park	HDPK	Cache	84318	464
*Hyrum	HYRM	Cache	84319	651
--Juab County	JubC			
*Kaysville	KYVL	Davis	84037	1345
Kearns		Salt Lake	84118	2068
Kimball Junction		Summit	84098	1971
Lake Shore		Utah	84660	3248
Lakeview		Utah	84601	2927
*Layton	LYTN	Davis	84041	1283
*Lehi	LEHI	Utah	84043	2603
Leland		Utah	84660	3248
Liberty		Weber	84310	1001
*Lindon	LNDN	Utah	84042	2713
Little Cttnwd Cr Vly		Salt Lake	84093	2177
*Logan	LOGN	Cache	84321	527
Magna		Salt Lake	84044	1960
*Mantua	MNTU	Box Elder	84324	768
*Mapleton	MPTN	Utah	84664	3144
Marriott		Weber	84404	1056
*Marriott-Slaterville	MTSV	Weber	84404	1055
*Mendon	MNDN	Cache	84325	524
*Midvale	MDVL	Salt Lake	84047	2176
*Midway	MIDW	Wasatch	84049	2397
Millcreek		Salt Lake	84107	1964
*Millville	MLVI	Cache	84332	592
--Morgan County	MgnC			
Mound City		Wasatch	84049	2396
Mt Olympus		Salt Lake	84124	1966
*Murray	MRRY	Salt Lake	84107	2070
Nerva		Box Elder	84340	941
*Nibley	NBLY	Cache	84321	591
*North Logan	NHLN	Cache	84341	464
*North Ogden	NHON	Weber	84414	999
*North Salt Lake	NSLK	Davis	84054	1653
*Ogden	OGDN	Weber	84401	1115
Oquirrh		Salt Lake	84084	2173
*Orem	OREM	Utah	84057	2820
Palmyra		Utah	84660	3141
*Paradise	PARA	Cache	84328	710
*Park City	PKCY	Wasatch	84049	2185
*Park City	PKCY	Summit	84060	2078
*Payson	PYSN	Utah	84651	3354
*Perry	PRRY	Box Elder	84302	827
*Plain City	PNCY	Weber	84404	996
*Pleasant Grove	PTGV	Utah	84062	2712
*Pleasant View	PTVW	Weber	84414	998
*Providence	PVDN	Cache	84332	528
*Provo	PRVO	Utah	84601	2928
Relico		Weber	84401	1115
*River Heights	RVHT	Cache	84321	527
*Riverdale	RVDL	Weber	84405	1172
*Riverton	RIVN	Salt Lake	84065	2387
*Roy	ROY	Weber	84067	1171
*Salem	SALM	Utah	84653	3356
--Salt Lake County	SLkC			
*Salt Lake City	SLCY	Salt Lake	84111	1858
*Sandy	SNDY	Salt Lake	84070	2282
*Santaquin	SNQN	Utah	84655	3460
*Saratoga Springs	SRSP	Utah	84043	2601
Silver Creek Jct		Summit	84098	1972
Silver Fork		Salt Lake	84098	2182
Slaterville		Weber	84404	1055
*Smithfield	SHFD	Cache	84335	399
Snowbird		Salt Lake	84049	2287
Snyderville		Summit	84098	1971
*South Jordan	SJDN	Salt Lake	84095	2281
*South Ogden	SOGN	Weber	84403	1115
*South Salt Lake	SSLK	Salt Lake	84115	1964
*South Weber	SWBR	Davis	84405	1229
South Willard		Box Elder	84340	941
*Spanish Fork	SPFK	Utah	84660	3249
Spring Lake		Utah	84651	3461
Springdell		Utah	84604	2822
*Springville	SGVL	Utah	84663	3143
--Summit County	SmtC			
Summit Park		Summit	84098	1864
*Sunset	SNST	Davis	84015	1227
Sutro		Utah	84660	3250
*Syracuse	SRCS	Davis	84075	1280
Taylor		Weber	84401	1113
*Taylorsville	TYVL	Salt Lake	84118	2069
*Tremonton	TMTN	Box Elder	84337	520
*Uintah	UNTH	Weber	84405	1173
Uintah Highlands		Weber	84403	1173
Union		Salt Lake	84047	2177
--Utah County	UthC			
Val Verda		Davis	84010	1653
*Vineyard	VNYD	Utah	84058	2819
--Wasatch County	WshC			
*Washington Terrace	WSTR	Weber	84405	1172
--Weber County	WbrC			
*Wellsville	WELV	Cache	84339	649
*West Bountiful	WBNF	Davis	84087	1551
*West Haven	WHVN	Weber	84315	1170
*West Jordan	WJDN	Salt Lake	84088	2175
*West Point	WPT	Davis	84015	1226
*West Valley City	WVCY	Salt Lake	84119	1963
West Weber		Weber	84404	1054
White City		Salt Lake	84094	2283
Wildwood		Weber	84310	1059
*Willard	WLRD	Box Elder	84340	885
*Woodland Hills	WDHL	Utah	84653	3463
*Woods Cross	WDCR	Davis	84087	1653

*Indicates incorporated city

List of Abbreviations

Admin	Administration
Agri	Agricultural
Ag	Agriculture
AFB	Air Force Base
Arpt	Airport
Al	Alley
Amer	American
Anx	Annex
Arc	Arcade
Arch	Archaeological
Aud	Auditorium
Avd	Avenida
Av	Avenue
Bfld	Battlefield
Bch	Beach
Bnd	Bend
Bio	Biological
Blf	Bluff
Blvd	Boulevard
Brch	Branch
Br	Bridge
Brk	Brook
Bldg	Building
Bur	Bureau
Byp	Bypass
Bywy	Byway
Cl	Calle
Cljn	Callejon
Cmto	Caminito
Cm	Camino
Cap	Capitol
Cath	Cathedral
Cswy	Causeway
Cem	Cemetery
Ctr	Center
Ctr	Centre
Cir	Circle
Crlo	Circulo
CH	City Hall
Clf	Cliff
Clfs	Cliffs
Clb	Club
Cltr	Cluster
Col	Coliseum
Coll	College
Com	Common
Coms	Commons
Comm	Community
Co.	Company
Cons	Conservation
Conv & Vis Bur	Convention and Visitors Bureau
Cor	Corner
Cors	Corners
Corp	Corporation
Corr	Corridor
Cte	Corte
CC	Country Club
Co	County
Ct	Court
Ct Hse	Court House
Cts	Courts
Cr	Creek
Cres	Crescent
Cross	Crossing
Curv	Curve
Cto	Cut Off
Dept	Department
Dev	Development
Diag	Diagonal
Div	Division
Dr	Drive
Drwy	Driveway
E	East
El	Elevation
Env	Environmental
Est	Estate
Ests	Estates
Exh	Exhibition
Expm	Experimental
Expo	Exposition
Expwy	Expressway
Ext	Extension
Frgds	Fairgrounds
ft	Feet
Fy	Ferry
Fld	Field
Flds	Fields
Flt	Flat
Flts	Flats
For	Forest
Fk	Fork
Ft	Fort
Found	Foundation
Frwy	Freeway
Gdn	Garden
Gdns	Gardens
Gen Hosp	General Hospital
Gln	Glen
GC	Golf Course
Grn	Green
Grds	Grounds
Grv	Grove
Hbr	Harbor/Harbour
Hvn	Haven
HQs	Headquarters
Ht	Height
Hts	Heights
HS	High School
Hwy	Highway
Hl	Hill
Hls	Hills
Hist	Historical
Hllw	Hollow
Hosp	Hospital
Hse	House
Ind Res	Indian Reservation
Info	Information
Inst	Institute
Int'l	International
I	Island
Is	Islands
Isl	Isle
Jct	Junction
Knl	Knoll
Knls	Knolls
Lk	Lake
Lndg	Landing
Ln	Lane
Lib	Library
Ldg	Lodge
Lp	Loop
Mnr	Manor
Mkt	Market
Mdw	Meadow
Mdws	Meadows
Med	Medical
Mem	Memorial
Metro	Metropolitan
Mw	Mews
Mil	Military
Ml	Mill
Mls	Mills
Mon	Monument
Mtwy	Motorway
Mnd	Mound
Mnds	Mounds
Mt	Mount
Mtn	Mountain
Mtns	Mountains
Mun	Municipal
Mus	Museum
Nat'l	National
Nat'l For	National Forest
Nat'l Hist Pk	National Historic Park
Nat'l Hist Site	National Historic Site
Nat'l Mon	National Monument
Nat'l Park	National Park
Nat'l Rec Area	National Recreation Area
Nat'l Wld Ref	National Wildlife Refuge
Nat	Natural
NAS	Naval Air Station
Nk	Nook
N	North
Orch	Orchard
Ohwy	Outer Highway
Ovl	Oval
Ovlk	Overlook
Ovps	Overpass
Pk	Park
Pkwy	Parkway
Pas	Paseo
Psg	Passage
Pass	Passenger
Pth	Path
Pn	Pine
Pns	Pines
Pl	Place
Pln	Plain
Plns	Plains
Plgnd	Playground
Plz	Plaza
Pt	Point
Pnd	Pond
PO	Post Office
Pres	Preserve
Prov	Provincial
Rwy	Railway
Rec	Recreation
Reg	Regional
Res	Reservoir
Rst	Rest
Rdg	Ridge
Rd	Road
Rds	Roads
St.	Saint
Ste.	Sainte
Sci	Science
Sci	Sciences
Sci	Scientific
Shop Ctr	Shopping Center
Shr	Shore
Shrs	Shores
Skwy	Skyway
S	South
Spr	Spring
Sprs	Springs
Sq	Square
Stad	Stadium
St For	State Forest
St Hist Site	State Historic Site
St Nat Area	State Natural Area
St Pk	State Park
St Rec Area	State Recreation Area
Sta	Station
St	Street
Smt	Summit
Sys	Systems
Tech	Technical
Tech	Technological
Tech	Technology
Ter	Terrace
Terr	Territory
Theol	Theological
Thwy	Throughway
Toll Fy	Toll Ferry
TIC	Tourist Information Center
Trc	Trace
Trfwy	Trafficway
Tr	Trail
Tun	Tunnel
Tpk	Turnpike
Unps	Underpass
Univ	University
Vly	Valley
Vet	Veterans
Vw	View
Vil	Village
Wk	Walk
Wall	Wall
Wy	Way
W	West
WMA	Wildlife Management Area

HIGHWAYS

ALT - Alternate Route
BUS - Business Route
CO - County Highway/Road
FM - Farm To Market Road
HIST - Historic Highway
I - Interstate Highway
LP - State Loop
P - Provincial Highway
PK - Park & Recreation Road
RTE - Other Route
SPR - State Spur
SR - State Route/Highway
US - United States Highway

Block	City	ZIP	Map#	Grid
CO-545				
-	CchC	84319	650	E4
-	CchC	84339	650	E4
-	HYRM	84319	650	E4
-	HYRM	84319	651	A3
I-15				
-	ANFK	-	2603	E7
-	ANFK	-	2711	A1
-	ANFK	-	2712	C6
-	BMCY	-	705	E6
-	BMCY	-	765	E1
-	BMCY	-	766	A7
-	BNFL	-	1551	C6
-	BNFL	-	1653	C2
-	BxEC	-	520	C7
-	BxEC	-	585	E6
-	BxEC	-	646	C6
-	BxEC	-	705	D1
-	BxEC	-	765	E3
-	BxEC	-	766	A7
-	BxEC	-	827	A6
-	BxEC	-	885	A1
-	BxEC	-	941	B3
-	BxEC	-	997	D4
-	CRFD	-	1227	E4
-	CRFD	-	1228	A4
-	CTRV	-	1448	C7
-	CTRV	-	1551	C6
-	DRPR	-	2282	C6
-	DRPR	-	2388	B7
-	DRPR	-	2495	B6
-	DvsC	-	1227	E4
-	DvsC	-	1228	B6
-	DvsC	-	1283	A5
-	DvsC	-	1345	E6
-	ELWD	-	584	E2
-	ELWD	-	585	E6
-	FMTN	-	1345	E6
-	FMTN	-	1346	A7
-	FMTN	-	1448	C7
-	FRWT	-	997	D4
-	FRWT	-	1055	D1
-	HYVL	-	585	E6
-	HYVL	-	645	E1
-	HYVL	-	646	C6
-	HYVL	-	705	D1
-	JubC	-	3567	B6
-	KYVL	-	1283	A5
-	KYVL	-	1345	E6
-	LEHI	-	2495	B6
-	LEHI	-	2602	D1
-	LEHI	-	2603	E7
-	LNDN	-	2712	A4
-	LNDN	-	2819	E1
-	LYTN	-	1228	B6
-	LYTN	-	1282	E4
-	LYTN	-	1283	A5
-	MDVL	-	2176	B1
-	MRRY	-	2070	B1
-	MRRY	-	2176	B5
-	MTSV	-	1055	D1
-	MTSV	-	1114	E1
-	NSLK	-	1653	C2
-	NSLK	-	1754	A2
-	OGDN	-	1115	A2
-	OGDN	-	1171	D7
-	OGDN	-	1172	A2
-	OREM	-	2819	E1
-	OREM	-	2820	A2
-	OREM	-	2927	E6
-	PRRY	-	827	A1
-	PRRY	-	885	B6
-	PRVO	-	2927	B2
-	PRVO	-	2928	A7
-	PRVO	-	3035	B1
-	PTGV	-	2712	A4
-	PTVW	-	997	D4
-	PYSN	-	3354	E4
-	ROY	-	1171	E2
-	RVDL	-	1115	B7
-	RVDL	-	1171	E2
-	RVDL	-	1172	A1
-	SGVL	-	3035	D7
-	SGVL	-	3142	D6
-	SLCY	-	1753	E4
-	SLCY	-	1754	A2
-	SLCY	-	1858	A5
-	SLCY	-	1964	B1
-	SLkC	-	1964	B7
-	SLkC	-	2070	B1
-	SNDY	-	2176	B5
-	SNDY	-	2282	B1
-	SNQN	-	3461	A7
-	SNQN	-	3567	B6
-	SNQN	-	3568	A1
-	SNST	-	1171	D7
-	SNST	-	1227	D1
-	SPFK	-	3142	D6
-	SPFK	-	3248	B7
-	SPFK	-	3249	A3
-	SSLK	-	1964	B4
-	TMTN	-	520	C1
-	TMTN	-	584	E2
-	UthC	-	2495	B6
-	UthC	-	2603	E7
-	UthC	-	2711	E4
-	UthC	-	2712	A4
-	UthC	-	3035	D4
-	UthC	-	3142	D6
-	UthC	-	3248	E4
-	UthC	-	3249	C1
-	UthC	-	3354	B7
-	UthC	-	3355	B1
-	UthC	-	3461	B1
-	UthC	-	3567	D2
-	WBNF	-	1551	C6
-	WBNF	-	1653	C2
-	WbrC	-	1115	A2
-	WDCR	-	1653	C2
-	WHVN	-	1114	E1
-	WHVN	-	1115	A2
-	WLRD	-	885	A1
-	WLRD	-	941	B3
I-15 BUS				
-	BMCY	84302	765	E2
-	BxEC	84302	765	E2
-	BxEC	84302	766	B3
-	BxEC	84302	827	C2
-	BxEC	84340	827	C2
10	BMCY	84302	766	E5
10	BMCY	84302	827	C2
I-15 BUS W 1100 S				
-	BxEC	84302	827	C2
-	BxEC	84340	827	C2
10	BMCY	84302	827	C2
I-15 BUS N Main St				
10	BMCY	84302	766	E5
I-15 BUS S Main St				
10	BMCY	84302	766	E6
700	BMCY	84302	827	E1
I-15 Veterans Memorial Hwy				
-	ANFK	-	2603	E7
-	ANFK	-	2711	A1
-	ANFK	-	2712	C6
-	BMCY	-	705	E6
-	BMCY	-	765	E1
-	BMCY	-	766	A7
-	BNFL	-	1551	C6
-	BNFL	-	1653	C2
-	BxEC	-	520	B5
-	BxEC	-	585	E6
-	BxEC	-	646	C6
-	BxEC	-	705	D1
-	BxEC	-	765	E3
-	BxEC	-	766	A7
-	BxEC	-	827	A6
-	BxEC	-	885	A1
-	BxEC	-	941	B3
-	BxEC	-	997	D4
-	CRFD	-	1227	E4
-	CRFD	-	1228	A4
-	CTRV	-	1448	C7
-	CTRV	-	1551	C2
-	DRPR	-	2282	C6
-	DRPR	-	2388	B7
-	DRPR	-	2495	B6
-	DvsC	-	1227	E4
-	DvsC	-	1228	B6
-	DvsC	-	1283	A5
-	DvsC	-	1345	E6
-	ELWD	-	584	E2
-	ELWD	-	585	C4
-	FMTN	-	1345	E6
-	FMTN	-	1346	A7
-	FMTN	-	1448	C7
-	FRWT	-	997	D4
-	FRWT	-	1055	D1
-	HYVL	-	585	E6
-	HYVL	-	645	E1
-	HYVL	-	646	A1
-	HYVL	-	705	D1
-	JubC	-	3567	B6
-	KYVL	-	1283	A5
-	KYVL	-	1345	E6
-	LEHI	-	2495	B6
-	LEHI	-	2602	D1
-	LEHI	-	2603	E7
-	LNDN	-	2712	A4
-	LNDN	-	2819	E1
-	LYTN	-	1228	B6
-	LYTN	-	1282	E4
-	LYTN	-	1283	A5
-	MDVL	-	2176	B1
-	MRRY	-	2070	B1
-	MRRY	-	2176	B5
-	MTSV	-	1055	D1
-	MTSV	-	1114	E1
-	NSLK	-	1653	C2
-	NSLK	-	1754	A2
-	OGDN	-	1115	A2
-	OGDN	-	1171	E2
-	OGDN	-	1172	A2
-	OREM	-	2819	E1
-	OREM	-	2820	A4
-	OREM	-	2927	E6
-	PRRY	-	827	A1
-	PRRY	-	885	B6
-	PRVO	-	2927	B2
-	PRVO	-	2928	A7
-	PRVO	-	3035	B1
-	PTGV	-	2712	A4
-	PTVW	-	997	D4
-	PYSN	-	3354	E4
-	ROY	-	1171	D7
-	RVDL	-	1115	B7
-	RVDL	-	1171	E2
-	RVDL	-	1172	A1
-	SGVL	-	3035	D7
-	SGVL	-	3142	D6
-	SLCY	-	1753	E4
-	SLCY	-	1754	A2
-	SLCY	-	1858	A2
-	SLCY	-	1964	B1
-	SLkC	-	1964	B7
-	SLkC	-	2070	B1
-	SNDY	-	2176	B5
-	SNDY	-	2282	B1
-	SNQN	-	3461	A7
-	SNQN	-	3567	B6
-	SNQN	-	3568	A1
-	SNST	-	1171	D7
-	SNST	-	1227	E4
-	SPFK	-	3142	D6
-	SPFK	-	3248	B7
-	SPFK	-	3249	A3
-	SSLK	-	1964	B1
-	TMTN	-	520	C1
-	TMTN	-	584	E2
-	UthC	-	2495	B6
-	UthC	-	2603	E7
-	UthC	-	2711	E4
-	UthC	-	2712	C6
-	UthC	-	3035	D4
-	UthC	-	3142	D6
-	UthC	-	3248	E4
-	UthC	-	3249	C1
-	UthC	-	3354	B7
-	UthC	-	3355	B1
-	UthC	-	3461	B1
-	UthC	-	3567	D2
-	WBNF	-	1551	C6
-	WBNF	-	1653	C2
-	WbrC	-	1115	A2
-	WDCR	-	1653	C2
-	WHVN	-	1114	E1
-	WHVN	-	1115	A2
-	WLRD	-	885	A1
-	WLRD	-	941	B3
I-80				
-	SLCY	-	1854	A3
-	SLCY	-	1855	B3
-	SLCY	-	1856	E3
-	SLCY	-	1857	D3
-	SLCY	-	1858	A5
-	SLCY	-	1964	D3
-	SLCY	-	1965	A3
-	SLCY	-	1966	A4
-	SLkC	-	1853	B3
-	SLkC	-	1854	A3
-	SLkC	-	1864	A5
-	SLkC	-	1966	A4
-	SmtC	-	1865	D7
-	SmtC	-	1866	E7
-	SmtC	-	1867	C1
-	SmtC	-	1971	D1
-	SmtC	-	1972	E1
-	SSLK	-	1964	B1
I-80 Dwight D Eisenhower Hwy				
-	SLCY	-	1854	D3
-	SLCY	-	1855	E3
-	SLCY	-	1856	A3
-	SLCY	-	1857	D3
-	SLCY	-	1964	D3
-	SLCY	-	1965	E3
-	SLCY	-	1966	A4
-	SLkC	-	1853	E3
-	SLkC	-	1854	A3
-	SLkC	-	1864	A5
-	SLkC	-	1966	A4
-	SmtC	-	1865	D7
-	SmtC	-	1866	E7
-	SmtC	-	1867	C1
-	SmtC	-	1971	D1
-	SmtC	-	1972	E1
-	SSLK	-	1964	D3
I-80 Veterans Memorial Hwy				
-	SLCY	-	1858	A5
-	SLCY	-	1964	B1
-	SSLK	-	1964	B1
I-84				
-	BMCY	-	705	E6
-	BMCY	-	765	E1
-	BMCY	-	766	A7
-	BxEC	-	520	A6
-	BxEC	-	585	E6
-	BxEC	-	646	C6
-	BxEC	-	705	D1
-	BxEC	-	765	E3
-	BxEC	-	766	A7
-	BxEC	-	827	A1
-	BxEC	-	885	A2
-	BxEC	-	941	B3
-	BxEC	-	997	D4
-	DvsC	-	1230	E1
-	ELWD	-	584	E2
-	ELWD	-	585	C4
-	FRWT	-	997	D4
-	FRWT	-	1055	E6
-	HYVL	-	585	E6
-	HYVL	-	645	E1
-	HYVL	-	646	A1
-	HYVL	-	705	D1
-	MTSV	-	1055	D1
-	MTSV	-	1114	E1
-	OGDN	-	1115	A3
-	PRRY	-	827	A1
-	PRRY	-	885	B6
-	PTVW	-	997	D4
-	RVDL	-	1115	B7
-	RVDL	-	1172	A2
-	SWBR	-	1172	D6
-	SWBR	-	1173	A7
-	SWBR	-	1229	C1
-	TMTN	-	520	A6
-	TMTN	-	584	D1
-	UNTH	-	1230	B1
-	WbrC	-	1115	A3
-	WbrC	-	1172	D6
-	WbrC	-	1229	C1
-	WbrC	-	1230	B1
-	WHVN	-	1114	E1
-	WHVN	-	1115	A3
-	WLRD	-	885	A2
-	WLRD	-	941	B3
I-84 BUS				
-	BMCY	84302	765	E2
-	BxEC	84302	765	E2
-	BxEC	84302	766	B3
-	BxEC	84302	827	D2
-	BxEC	84340	827	D2
10	BMCY	84302	766	E5
10	BMCY	84302	827	D2
I-84 BUS W 1100 S				
-	BxEC	84302	827	D2
-	BxEC	84340	827	D2
10	BMCY	84302	827	D2
I-84 BUS N Main St				
10	BMCY	84302	766	E5
I-84 BUS S Main St				
10	BMCY	84302	766	E6
700	BMCY	84302	827	E1
I-84 Veterans Memorial Hwy				
-	BMCY	-	705	E6
-	BMCY	-	765	E1
-	BMCY	-	766	A7
-	BxEC	-	520	C7
-	BxEC	-	585	E6
-	BxEC	-	646	C6
-	BxEC	-	705	D1
-	BxEC	-	765	E3
-	BxEC	-	766	A7
-	BxEC	-	827	A1
-	BxEC	-	885	A2
-	BxEC	-	941	B3
-	BxEC	-	997	D4
-	ELWD	-	584	E2
-	ELWD	-	585	E6
-	FRWT	-	997	D4
-	FRWT	-	1055	D1
-	HYVL	-	585	E6
-	HYVL	-	645	E1
-	HYVL	-	646	C6
-	HYVL	-	705	D1
-	MTSV	-	1055	D1
-	MTSV	-	1114	E1
-	OGDN	-	1115	B7
-	PRRY	-	827	A1
-	PRRY	-	885	B6
-	PTVW	-	997	D4
-	RVDL	-	1115	B7
-	RVDL	-	1172	A1
-	TMTN	-	520	C7
-	TMTN	-	584	E2
-	WbrC	-	1115	A3
-	WHVN	-	1114	E1
-	WHVN	-	1115	A3
-	WLRD	-	885	A2
-	WLRD	-	941	B3
I-215				
-	CDHT	-	2071	E7
-	CDHT	-	2072	A7
-	CDHT	-	2177	C1
-	DvsC	-	1753	D1
-	HLDY	-	2071	E7
-	HLDY	-	2072	A7
-	HLDY	-	2177	C1
-	MDVL	-	2176	E1
-	MRRY	-	2069	E7
-	MRRY	-	2070	C7
-	MRRY	-	2176	E1
-	MRRY	-	2177	C1
-	NSLK	-	1753	D1
-	SLCY	-	1753	D1
-	SLCY	-	1857	B2
-	SLCY	-	1963	B1
-	SLCY	-	1966	B4
-	SLkC	-	1753	D1
-	SLkC	-	1966	C5
-	SLkC	-	2072	B3
-	TYVL	-	2069	E7
-	WVCY	-	1963	B3
-	WVCY	-	2069	B2
SR-13				
-	BMCY	84302	765	B1
-	BMCY	84302	766	D3
-	BxEC	84302	765	B1
-	BxEC	84302	766	D3
-	BxEC	84307	765	B1
-	BxEC	84312	521	B4
-	BxEC	84314	645	D5
-	BxEC	84337	645	D5
-	CRNN	84307	704	C4
-	CRNN	84307	705	A7
-	CRNN	84307	765	B1
-	ELWD	84337	645	D5
-	GRLD	84312	521	B1
-	TMTN	84337	521	B6
700	BMCY	84302	827	E1
3300	BxEC	84307	704	C4
4000	BxEC	84337	704	C4
4600	BRCY	84302	704	C4
4600	BRCY	84307	704	C4
4600	BRCY	84337	704	C4
5000	BRCY	84302	645	D5
5200	BRCY	84301	645	D5
8000	ELWD	84337	585	B5
10400	BxEC	84337	521	B7
10400	BxEC	84337	585	B2
10400	ELWD	84337	521	B6
SR-13 N 4700 W				
-	BRCY	84302	704	C4
-	BRCY	84307	704	C4
-	BRCY	84337	704	C4
5000	BRCY	84302	645	D7
5200	BRCY	84301	645	D7
SR-13 N 4800 W				
3300	BxEC	84307	704	C4
4000	BxEC	84337	704	C3
4600	BRCY	84302	704	D1
4600	BRCY	84307	704	D1
4600	BRCY	84337	704	D1
SR-13 N 5200 St W				
8000	ELWD	84337	585	B5
10400	BxEC	84337	521	B7
10400	BxEC	84337	585	B2
10400	ELWD	84337	521	B7
SR-13 N Main St				
10	BMCY	84302	766	E4
SR-13 S Main St				
10	BMCY	84302	766	E6
700	BMCY	84302	827	E1
SR-23				
-	CchC	84325	588	E2
-	CchC	84339	588	E2
-	CchC	84339	589	A4
-	MNDN	84325	524	D5
-	MNDN	84325	588	E2
-	WELV	84339	589	B6
10	WELV	84339	649	D1
100	CchC	84325	524	D1
SR-23 W 500 N				
-	CchC	84339	589	C7
-	WELV	84339	589	C7
SR-23 N 6000 W				
100	CchC	84325	524	D2
SR-23 N Center St				
10	WELV	84339	649	D2
SR-23 S Center St				
10	WELV	84339	649	D1
SR-26				
600	RVDL	84405	1172	C1
1200	RVDL	84405	1171	E3
1600	ROY	84067	1171	E3
3400	OGDN	84401	1115	D7
3500	SOGN	84405	1115	D7
4000	RVDL	84405	1115	D7
SR-26 Riverdale Rd				
1600	ROY	84067	1171	E4
1600	RVDL	84405	1171	E3
3400	OGDN	84401	1115	D7
3500	SOGN	84405	1115	D7
4000	RVDL	84405	1115	D7
4000	RVDL	84405	1172	C1
SR-26 W Riverdale Rd				
-	ROY	84067	1171	E3
600	RVDL	84405	1172	C2
1200	RVDL	84405	1171	E3
SR-30				
-	CchC	84325	525	B1
-	BxEC	-	520	A6
-	CchC	84321	525	E1
-	CchC	84325	524	E1
-	BxEC	-	520	B6
-	TMTN	-	520	C1
10	LOGN	84321	527	D2
1300	LOGN	84321	526	E2
2100	CchC	84321	526	E2
SR-30 W 200 N				
10	LOGN	84321	527	D2
1300	LOGN	84321	526	E2
2100	CchC	84321	526	D2
SR-30 N Main St				
200	LOGN	84321	527	D2
SR-30 Veterans Memorial Hwy				
-	BxEC	-	520	B6
-	TMTN	-	520	C1
SR-32				
-	WshC	84032	2186	E6
-	WshC	84032	2292	C2
-	WshC	84049	2186	E6
-	WshC	84049	2292	C2
SR-37				
-	ROY	84067	1171	A1
10	SNST	84015	1227	B1
500	CLTN	84015	1227	B1
1700	CLTN	84015	1226	E1
1800	DvsC	84315	1169	D6
1800	DvsC	84315	1225	D1
1800	WPT	84015	1225	D1
2400	HOPR	84315	1169	D6
2900	WHVN	84067	1170	E1
2900	WHVN	84067	1171	A1
3500	WHVN	84315	1170	E1
3500	WPT	84015	1226	A1
5100	HOPR	84315	1170	A1
SR-37 W 4000 S				
-	ROY	84067	1171	A1
2900	WHVN	84067	1170	E1
2900	WHVN	84067	1171	A1
3500	WHVN	84315	1170	E1
5100	HOPR	84315	1170	A1
5300	HOPR	84315	1169	D2
SR-37 N 5000 W				
1800	DvsC	84315	1169	D7
1800	DvsC	84315	1225	D1
1800	WPT	84015	1225	D1
2400	HOPR	84315	1169	D6
SR-37 S 5900 W				
4100	HOPR	84315	1169	D1
SR-37 Clinton Rd				
10	SNST	84015	1227	B1
500	CLTN	84015	1227	B1
1700	CLTN	84015	1226	E1
3500	WPT	84015	1226	A1
3700	WPT	84015	1225	E1
SR-38				
-	BxEC	84302	647	A6
-	BxEC	84302	706	B1
-	BxEC	84309	522	B4
-	BxEC	84309	586	C3
-	BxEC	84312	522	B1
-	BxEC	84314	647	A6
-	DWVL	84309	522	C7
-	DWVL	84309	586	C3
-	DWVL	84312	522	C7
-	HYVL	84302	647	A6
-	HYVL	84314	586	C3
-	HYVL	84314	646	D1
-	HYVL	84314	647	A6
900	BMCY	84302	766	E2
1300	BxEC	84302	766	E2
SR-38 N 2600 St W				
-	HYVL	84314	646	D2
SR-38 N 2800 St W				
-	HYVL	84314	586	C7
-	HYVL	84314	646	D1
SR-38 N Main St				
900	BMCY	84302	766	E3
1300	BxEC	84302	766	E2
SR-39				
-	OGDN	84401	1116	D1
-	OGDN	84404	1116	D1
-	WbrC	84317	1116	D1
-	WbrC	84317	1117	A1
100	OGDN	84404	1056	E7
500	HTVL	84317	1061	B5
500	OGDN	84404	1057	A7
500	WbrC	84317	1061	B5
600	WbrC	84310	1058	E6
600	WbrC	84310	1059	B6
600	WbrC	84317	1058	E6
600	WbrC	84317	1059	B6
700	MTSV	84404	1056	A7
1200	MTSV	84401	1056	A7
1500	MTSV	84401	1055	D7
1500	MTSV	84404	1055	D7
2300	MTSV	84401	1055	D7
2300	WbrC	84404	1055	D7
2800	WbrC	84401	1054	E7
2800	WbrC	84404	1054	E7
6500	WbrC	84317	1060	E7
SR-39 12th St				
100	OGDN	84404	1056	D7
500	OGDN	84404	1057	A7
SR-39 W 12th St				
100	OGDN	84404	1056	C7
700	MTSV	84404	1056	A7
1200	MTSV	84401	1056	A7
1500	MTSV	84401	1055	E7
1500	MTSV	84404	1055	E7
SR-39 E 100 S				
7800	WbrC	84317	1061	B5
SR-39 E 900 S				
6500	WbrC	84317	1060	E7
7400	WbrC	84317	1061	A7
SR-39 W 1150 S				
4400	WbrC	84401	1054	C7
4400	WbrC	84404	1054	C7
SR-39 W 1200 S				
2000	MTSV	84401	1055	D7
2000	MTSV	84404	1055	D7
2300	WbrC	84401	1055	D7
2300	WbrC	84404	1055	D7
2800	WbrC	84401	1054	E7
2800	WbrC	84404	1054	E7
SR-39 S 7800 E				
500	HTVL	84317	1061	B5
500	WbrC	84317	1061	B5
SR-39 Canyon Rd				
-	OGDN	84401	1116	D1
-	WbrC	84317	1116	E1
SR-39 Ogden Canyon Rd				
-	OGDN	84401	1116	D1
-	WbrC	84317	1116	D1
-	WbrC	84317	1117	A1
600	WbrC	84310	1058	E6
600	WbrC	84310	1059	B6
600	WbrC	84317	1058	E6
600	WbrC	84317	1059	B6
SR-48				
-	MDVL	84047	2175	E2
-	WJDN	84084	2175	E2
-	WJDN	84088	2279	B1
10	MDVL	84047	2176	C2
1700	WJDN	84088	2175	C4
3000	WJDN	84084	2174	E4
3000	WJDN	84088	2174	E4
5300	WJDN	84088	2173	E6
SR-48 W 7000 S				
1300	WJDN	84084	2175	C2
SR-48 W 7200 S				
-	MDVL	84047	2175	E2
10	MDVL	84047	2176	C2
SR-48 W 7800 S				
1700	WJDN	84084	2175	C4
1700	WJDN	84088	2175	C4
3000	WJDN	84084	2174	E4
3000	WJDN	84088	2174	E4
SR-48 New Bingham Hwy				
-	WJDN	84088	2279	B1
4300	WJDN	84084	2174	C4
4300	WJDN	84088	2174	C4
5300	WJDN	84088	2173	E6
SR-48 Redwood Rd				
7000	WJDN	84084	2175	C3
SR-51				
-	SPFK	84660	3143	C5
-	SPFK	84663	3143	C5
-	UthC	84660	3143	C5
400	SPFK	84660	3249	E2
400	SPFK	84660	3250	A1
400	SPFK	84663	3249	E2
400	SPFK	84663	3250	A1
600	SGVL	84663	3143	C5
2600	UthC	84663	3143	C5
3400	UthC	84660	3250	A1
3400	UthC	84663	3250	A1
SR-51 S 1100 E				
400	SPFK	84660	3249	E2
400	SPFK	84660	3250	A2
400	SPFK	84663	3249	E2
400	SPFK	84663	3250	A2
SR-51 S Childs Rd				
500	SPFK	84660	3250	A1
500	SPFK	84663	3250	A1
SR-51 S Main St				
600	SGVL	84663	3143	C5
SR-51 State Rd				
1800	SGVL	84663	3143	B6
2600	UthC	84663	3143	B7
SR-51 S State Rd				
-	SGVL	84663	3143	B7
-	SPFK	84660	3143	B7
-	SPFK	84660	3250	A1
-	SPFK	84663	3143	A7
-	UthC	84660	3143	B7
-	UthC	84663	3143	B7
3400	SPFK	84663	3250	A1
3400	UthC	84660	3250	A1
3400	UthC	84663	3250	A1
SR-52				
-	OREM	84604	2821	A3
10	OREM	84057	2820	D3
400	OREM	84097	2820	D3
600	OREM	84097	2821	A3
1400	OREM	84057	2819	E3
SR-52 E 800 N				
-	OREM	84604	2821	A3
10	OREM	84057	2820	D3
400	OREM	84097	2820	E3
600	OREM	84097	2821	A3
SR-52 W 800 N				
10	OREM	84057	2820	D3
1400	OREM	84057	2819	E3
SR-53				
-	WbrC	84401	1115	D3
100	OGDN	84401	1115	D3
SR-53 Martin Luther King Jr St				
300	OGDN	84401	1115	D3
SR-53 W Martin L King Jr St				
300	OGDN	84401	1115	D3
SR-53 Pennsylvania Av				
-	WbrC	84401	1115	A4
2400	OGDN	84401	1115	B3
SR-60				
-	SWBR	84405	1230	A2
10	RVDL	84405	1172	D6
10	SWBR	84405	1172	D6
400	SWBR	84405	1228	E1
400	SWBR	84405	1229	A1
SR-60 S 1050 W				
4700	RVDL	84405	1172	A4
SR-60 E South Weber Dr				
10	RVDL	84405	1172	C6
10	SWBR	84405	1172	C6
400	SWBR	84405	1228	E1
400	SWBR	84405	1229	A1
SR-60 S Weber Dr				
5400	RVDL	84405	1172	A4
5500	SWBR	84405	1172	C6
SR-68				
-	BNFL	84087	1653	C1
-	LEHI	84043	2601	E5
-	LEHI	84043	2602	A6
-	SLkC	84065	2494	D5
-	SRSP	84043	2601	E5
-	SRSP	84043	2602	A6
-	UthC	84043	2494	D5
-	UthC	84043	2601	E1
10	NSLK	84054	1652	D7
10	SLCY	84104	1857	C2
100	SLCY	84116	1857	C2
200	BNFL	84010	1653	C1
300	NSLK	84054	1753	D1
500	WBNF	84010	1653	C1
500	WDCR	84087	1652	D2
600	DvsC	84054	1753	D1
600	SLkC	84116	1753	D1
600	WBNF	84087	1653	C1
600	WDCR	84087	1653	C1
700	DvsC	84087	1652	D2
700	SLCY	84116	1753	C7
1600	SLCY	84104	1963	C1
2100	WVCY	84119	1963	C3
3900	WVCY	84119	2069	C1
4100	TYVL	84119	2069	C1
4100	TYVL	84123	2069	C1
4700	TYVL	84118	2069	C4
6200	TYVL	84084	2069	C7
6200	WJDN	84084	2069	C7
6400	TYVL	84123	2175	C1
6400	WJDN	84084	2175	C1
7800	WJDN	84088	2175	C5
9300	WJDN	84088	2281	C1
9400	SJDN	84095	2281	C1
11600	RIVN	84065	2281	C7
12100	RIVN	84065	2387	C2
13800	BFDL	84065	2387	C4
14900	BFDL	84065	2494	B2
SR-68 W 500 S				
-	BNFL	84087	1653	C1
200	BNFL	84010	1653	C1
500	WBNF	84010	1653	C1
600	WBNF	84087	1653	C1
600	WDCR	84087	1653	C1
1300	WDCR	84087	1652	E1
SR-68 Camp Williams Rd				
-	SLkC	84065	2494	D7
-	UthC	84043	2494	D7
14400	BFDL	84065	2387	C6
14900	BFDL	84065	2494	C1
SR-68 Redwood Rd				
6600	WJDN	84084	2175	C3
7800	WJDN	84088	2175	C5
9300	WJDN	84088	2281	C1
SR-68 N Redwood Rd				
10	NSLK	84054	1652	D7
10	SLCY	84104	1857	C2
100	SLCY	84116	1857	C2
500	WDCR	84087	1652	D2
700	DvsC	84087	1652	D2
700	SLCY	84116	1753	C7
1700	SLkC	84116	1753	C4
SR-68 S Redwood Rd				
10	NSLK	84054	1652	D7
10	SLCY	84104	1857	C3
300	NSLK	84054	1753	D1
600	DvsC	84054	1753	C2
600	SLkC	84116	1753	C2
1600	SLCY	84104	1963	C1
2100	WVCY	84119	1963	C3
3900	WVCY	84119	2069	C1
4100	TYVL	84119	2069	C1
4100	TYVL	84123	2069	C1
4700	TYVL	84118	2069	C4
6200	TYVL	84084	2069	C7
6200	WJDN	84084	2069	C7
6400	TYVL	84123	2175	C1
6400	WJDN	84084	2175	C1
9400	SJDN	84095	2281	C1
11600	RIVN	84065	2281	C7
12100	RIVN	84065	2387	C2
13800	BFDL	84065	2387	C4
SR-71				
10	DRPR	84020	2388	E1
400	SLCY	84102	1858	E5
900	DRPR	84020	2387	E2
900	SLCY	84105	1858	E5
1200	RIVN	84065	2387	E2
1600	SLCY	84105	1964	E1
2100	SLCY	84106	1964	E1
2700	SLkC	84106	1964	E1
2800	SSLK	84106	1964	E7
2900	RIVN	84065	2386	D2
3900	SLkC	84107	1964	E7
3900	SLkC	84124	1964	E7
4000	SLkC	84107	2070	E1
4000	SLkC	84124	2070	E1
4500	MRRY	84107	2070	E1
4600	MRRY	84107	2071	A3
4600	SLkC	84107	2071	A3
4800	SLkC	84117	2071	A3
4900	MRRY	84117	2071	A3
5600	MRRY	84121	2071	A5
6400	MRRY	84047	2177	A1
6400	MRRY	84107	2177	A1
6400	MRRY	84121	2177	A1
6700	MDVL	84047	2177	A1
7500	MDVL	84047	2176	E4
7600	SNDY	84047	2176	E4
7800	SNDY	84070	2176	E4
7800	SNDY	84094	2176	E4
8400	SLkC	84094	2176	E7
9100	SNDY	84070	2282	E1
9100	SNDY	84094	2282	E1
9800	SLkC	84094	2282	E1
10200	SLkC	84070	2282	E4
11400	DRPR	84020	2282	E7
SR-71 S 700 E				
400	SLCY	84102	1858	E5
900	SLCY	84105	1858	E5
1600	SLCY	84105	1964	E1
2100	SLCY	84106	1964	E1
2700	SLkC	84106	1964	E1
2800	SSLK	84106	1964	E7
3900	SLkC	84107	1964	E7
3900	SLkC	84124	1964	E7
4000	SLkC	84107	2070	E1
4000	SLkC	84124	2070	E1
4500	MRRY	84107	2070	E1
4600	MRRY	84107	2071	A3
4600	SLkC	84107	2071	A3
7700	SNDY	84047	2176	E4
7800	SNDY	84070	2176	E4
7800	SNDY	84094	2176	E4
8400	SLkC	84094	2176	E5
9100	SNDY	84070	2282	E1
9100	SNDY	84094	2282	E1
9800	SLkC	84094	2282	E1
10200	SLkC	84070	2282	E4
11400	DRPR	84020	2282	E7
12000	DRPR	84020	2388	E1

STREET
Block City ZIP Map# Grid

SR-71 S 900 E
4800 MRRY 84107 2071 A3
4800 SLkC 84117 2071 A3
4900 MRRY 84117 2071 A4
5600 MRRY 84121 2071 A5
6400 MRRY 84047 2177 A1
6400 MRRY 84107 2177 A1
6400 MRRY 84121 2177 A1
6700 MDVL 84047 2177 A1
7500 MDVL 84047 2176 E4
7600 SNDY 84047 2176 E4
SR-71 E 12300 S
10 DRPR 84020 2388 E1
SR-71 W 12300 S
10 DRPR 84020 2388 C1
SR-71 W 12600 S
900 DRPR 84020 2387 E2
900 DRPR 84020 2388 A1
1200 RIVN 84065 2387 E2
2900 RIVN 84065 2386 D2
SR-71 Van Winkle Expwy
- MRRY 84107 2071 A3
- SLkC 84107 2071 A3
SR-73
- EGMN 84043 2601 A7
- UthC 84043 2601 A7
10 LEHI 84043 2603 E6
10 SRSP 84043 2602 B6
8800 LEHI 84043 2602 D6
10800 SRSP 84043 2601 E6
SR-73 W 8570 N
8700 LEHI 84043 2603 A6
8800 LEHI 84043 2602 E6
10800 SRSP 84043 2601 E6
10800 SRSP 84043 2602 A6
SR-73 Cedar Fort Rd
- EGMN 84043 2601 A7
- SRSP 84043 2601 B7
- UthC 84043 2601 A7
SR-73 Main St
10 SRSP 84043 2602 B6
SR-73 E Main St
10 LEHI 84043 2603 C6
SR-73 W Main St
500 LEHI 84043 2603 B6
SR-74
10 ANFK 84003 2711 C1
100 ANFK 84003 2604 C7
400 ALPN 84004 2497 D7
1200 UthC 84003 2604 D4
9600 HILD 84003 2604 D4
10900 HILD 84003 2497 D7
SR-74 N 100 E
10 ANFK 84003 2711 C1
100 ANFK 84003 2604 C7
1200 UthC 84003 2604 D4
SR-74 Alpine Hwy
400 ALPN 84004 2497 D7
SR-74 N Alpine Hwy
9600 HILD 84003 2604 D4
10900 HILD 84003 2497 D7
SR-74 N Main St
10 ALPN 84004 2497 E4
SR-74 S Main St
10 ALPN 84004 2497 E5
SR-75
- UthC 84606 3035 E6
100 SGVL 84663 3036 C6
1200 SGVL 84663 3035 E6
SR-75 W 1400 N
100 SGVL 84663 3036 C6
SR-75 W 1500 N
- UthC 84606 3035 E6
1200 SGVL 84663 3035 E6
1200 SGVL 84663 3036 C6
SR-77
10 SGVL 84663 3143 B3
700 SGVL 84660 3142 B3
700 SGVL 84663 3142 E3
700 SPFK 84660 3142 B3
700 SPFK 84663 3142 B3
700 UthC 84660 3142 B3
800 UthC 84660 3141 D3
SR-77 W 400 S
10 SGVL 84663 3143 B3
700 SGVL 84663 3142 E3
SR-77 W 3900 S
- SGVL 84660 3142 C3
- SGVL 84663 3142 C3
SR-77 W 4000 S
700 SGVL 84660 3142 C3
700 SGVL 84663 3142 C3
700 SPFK 84660 3142 B3
700 SPFK 84663 3142 B3
700 UthC 84660 3142 B3
800 UthC 84660 3141 D3
SR-77 W 4400 S
2700 UthC 84660 3141 A4
SR-77 Palmyra Dr
4000 UthC 84660 3141 A4
SR-79
- OGDN 84401 1114 E6
- OGDN 84405 1114 E6
- ROY 84067 1114 E6
- ROY 84401 1114 E6
- WbrC 84401 1114 E6
- WbrC 84405 1114 E6
100 OGDN 84401 1115 E5
500 OGDN 84403 1115 E5
600 OGDN 84403 1116 A5
1300 OGDN 84405 1115 A6
SR-79 30th St
100 OGDN 84401 1115 E5
500 OGDN 84403 1115 E5
600 OGDN 84403 1116 A5
SR-79 W 30th St
100 OGDN 84401 1115 E5
SR-79 31st St
- OGDN 84401 1115 D5
- OGDN 84405 1115 C5
SR-79 Hinckley Dr
- OGDN 84401 1114 E6
- OGDN 84405 1114 E6
- ROY 84067 1114 E6
- ROY 84401 1114 E6
- WbrC 84401 1114 E6
- WbrC 84405 1114 E6
1300 OGDN 84401 1115 A6
1300 OGDN 84405 1115 A6
SR-79 Washington Blvd
3000 OGDN 84401 1115 E5

STREET
Block City ZIP Map# Grid

SR-82
- BxEC 84312 521 B1
10 GRLD 84312 520 E2
300 GRLD 84312 521 A2
600 TMTN 84337 520 E5
SR-82 300 St E
600 TMTN 84337 520 E5
SR-82 E 600 St N
- TMTN 84337 520 E5
SR-82 E Factory St
- BxEC 84312 521 B2
10 GRLD 84312 520 E2
300 GRLD 84312 521 A2
SR-82 S Main St
10 GRLD 84312 520 E2
800 TMTN 84337 520 E2
SR-82 North St
- TMTN 84337 520 E5
SR-82 N Tremont St
- TMTN 84337 520 E5
SR-83
- BxEC 84307 704 B6
- CRNN 84307 704 B6
SR-90
10 BMCY 84302 766 E6
100 BMCY 84302 767 B6
SR-90 E 200 S
10 BMCY 84302 766 E6
100 BMCY 84302 767 B6
SR-92
- LEHI 84043 2495 D7
- LEHI 84043 2496 D7
- LEHI 84043 2497 A7
- UthC 84004 2498 E7
- UthC 84043 2496 D7
- UthC 84043 2497 A7
3800 CRHL 84003 2498 E7
3800 CRHL 84062 2498 E7
3800 HILD 84003 2498 E7
4800 HILD 84003 2497 E7
SR-92 W 11000 N
- LEHI 84043 2495 D7
- LEHI 84043 2496 D7
- LEHI 84043 2497 A7
- UthC 84043 2496 D7
- UthC 84043 2497 A7
3800 CRHL 84003 2498 E7
3800 CRHL 84062 2498 E7
3800 HILD 84003 2498 E7
4800 HILD 84003 2497 E7
SR-92 Alpine Loop Rd
- HILD 84003 2498 C7
- UthC 84004 2498 E7
SR-92 American Fork Canyon Rd
- UthC 84004 2498 E7
SR-92 Highland Hwy
- HILD 84003 2497 E7
SR-93
- NSLK 84087 1653 C4
- WDCR 84087 1653 C4
400 NSLK 84054 1653 C4
400 WDCR 84010 1653 C4
600 BNFL 84010 1653 C4
600 NSLK 84010 1653 C4
SR-93 W 2600 S
- NSLK 84087 1653 C4
- WDCR 84087 1653 C4
400 NSLK 84054 1653 C4
400 WDCR 84010 1653 C4
600 BNFL 84010 1653 C4
600 NSLK 84010 1653 C4
SR-97
1600 ROY 84067 1171 B5
3400 ROY 84067 1170 E5
4300 HOPR 84315 1170 A4
5200 HOPR 84315 1169 D4
SR-97 W 5500 S
3700 ROY 84067 1170 E5
4300 HOPR 84315 1170 A4
5200 HOPR 84315 1169 D4
SR-97 W 5600 S
1600 ROY 84067 1171 B5
3400 ROY 84067 1170 E5
SR-101
- CchC 84319 650 C1
- CchC 84321 651 D2
- CchC 84339 650 C1
- HYRM 84319 650 C1
- WELV 84319 650 A1
- WELV 84339 650 A1
10 HYRM 84319 651 A2
10 WELV 84339 649 E2
1400 CchC 84319 652 A3
1400 CchC 84321 652 A3
1400 HYRM 84319 652 A3
1400 HYRM 84321 652 A3
SR-101 N 400 W
10 HYRM 84319 651 A2
SR-101 Blacksmith Fork Cyn Rd
1400 CchC 84319 652 B3
1400 CchC 84321 652 C3
1400 HYRM 84319 652 B3
1400 HYRM 84321 652 B3
SR-101 Main St
10 HYRM 84319 651 B2
SR-101 E Main St
10 WELV 84339 649 E2
SR-101 W Main St
10 HYRM 84319 651 B2
SR-102
- BxEC 84309 521 D6
- BxEC 84309 522 A5
- BxEC 84337 520 A6
- DWVL 84309 521 D6
- DWVL 84309 522 A5
10 TMTN 84337 520 E6
600 TMTN 84337 521 A6
1900 BxEC 84337 521 A6
SR-102 11200 Rd N
- BxEC 84337 520 A6
1500 TMTN 84337 520 B6
SR-102 E Main St
10 TMTN 84337 520 E6
600 TMTN 84337 521 A6
1900 BxEC 84337 521 B6
SR-102 W Main St
10 TMTN 84337 520 E6
SR-103
10 CRFD 84015 1227 D3

STREET
Block City ZIP Map# Grid

SR-103 E 650 N
10 CRFD 84015 1227 D3
SR-104
100 OGDN 84401 1115 D2
700 WHVN 84401 1115 B2
1400 WHVN 84401 1114 E2
SR-104 W 20th St
100 OGDN 84401 1115 D2
SR-104 W 21st St
100 OGDN 84401 1115 B2
SR-104 Wilson Ln
700 WHVN 84401 1115 B2
1400 WHVN 84401 1114 E2
SR-105
10 CTRV 84014 1551 D3
SR-105 W Parrish Ln
10 CTRV 84014 1551 D3
SR-106
- WDCR 84010 1653 C2
10 CTRV 84014 1551 E1
10 FMTN 84025 1346 C6
10 FMTN 84025 1448 D1
200 BNFL 84010 1653 D1
400 BNFL 84010 1551 D7
1500 CTRV 84014 1448 D7
SR-106 S 185 E
10 FMTN 84025 1448 D2
SR-106 N 200 W
10 BNFL 84010 1551 D7
SR-106 S 200 E
100 FMTN 84025 1448 D1
SR-106 S 200 W
10 BNFL 84010 1551 D7
200 BNFL 84010 1653 D1
SR-106 S 300 W
1400 BNFL 84010 1653 D2
SR-106 W 600 N
10 FMTN 84025 1346 C7
SR-106 N Main St
10 CTRV 84014 1551 E1
10 FMTN 84025 1448 D1
400 BNFL 84010 1551 D7
600 FMTN 84025 1346 C7
1500 CTRV 84014 1448 D7
SR-106 S Main St
10 CTRV 84014 1551 E3
1000 BNFL 84010 1551 E5
SR-106 Shepard Ln
10 FMTN 84025 1346 C6
SR-106 W Shepard Ln
600 FMTN 84025 1346 B6
SR-106 E State St
10 FMTN 84025 1448 D2
SR-106 E Willey St
10 BNFL 84010 1551 D7
SR-106 W Willey St
10 BNFL 84010 1551 D7
SR-107
10 CRFD 84015 1227 C4
1400 CLTN 84015 1227 A4
1500 WPT 84015 1227 A4
1700 WPT 84015 1226 E4
4000 WPT 84015 1225 E4
SR-107 W 300 N
10 CRFD 84015 1227 D4
SR-107 West Point Rd
500 CRFD 84015 1227 C4
1400 CLTN 84015 1227 A4
1500 WPT 84015 1227 A4
1700 WPT 84015 1226 E4
4000 WPT 84015 1225 E4
SR-108
10 CRFD 84015 1281 E1
10 CRFD 84016 1281 E1
300 WPT 84015 1226 E3
400 LYTN 84041 1282 D1
600 SRCS 84015 1226 E7
600 SRCS 84075 1281 E1
700 CLTN 84015 1226 E3
700 SRCS 84016 1281 A1
800 CRFD 84015 1282 A1
1700 SRCS 84075 1280 E1
1800 CLTN 84015 1170 E6
1900 WbrC 84067 1114 C7
1900 WHVN 84067 1114 C7
1900 WHVN 84401 1114 C7
3600 ROY 84067 1114 C7
3900 ROY 84067 1171 A1
3900 WHVN 84067 1171 A1
4200 WbrC 84067 1171 A1
4500 ROY 84067 1170 E2
4500 WbrC 84067 1170 E2
4500 WHVN 84067 1170 E2
SR-108 W 1700 S
1200 SRCS 84075 1281 A1
1700 SRCS 84075 1280 E1
SR-108 S 2000 W
600 SRCS 84075 1226 E6
SR-108 S 3500 W
4700 ROY 84067 1170 E3
SR-108 E Antelope Dr
10 CRFD 84015 1281 E1
10 CRFD 84016 1281 E1
800 CRFD 84015 1282 A1
SR-108 W Antelope Dr
10 CRFD 84015 1281 D1
10 CRFD 84016 1281 D1
400 LYTN 84041 1282 D1
600 SRCS 84075 1281 C1
700 SRCS 84016 1281 B1
SR-108 Midland Dr
1900 WbrC 84067 1114 C7
1900 WHVN 84067 1114 C7
1900 WHVN 84401 1114 C7
3600 ROY 84067 1114 C7
3900 ROY 84067 1171 A1
3900 WHVN 84067 1171 A1
4200 WbrC 84067 1171 A1
4500 ROY 84067 1170 E2
4500 WbrC 84067 1170 E2
4500 WHVN 84067 1170 E2
SR-108 Two Mile Rd
- SRCS 84075 1226 E7
300 WPT 84015 1226 E3
700 CLTN 84015 1226 E3
1800 CLTN 84015 1170 E7
SR-109
10 LYTN 84041 1282 E5
10 LYTN 84041 1283 A5
1100 LYTN 84040 1283 C4
1500 DvsC 84040 1283 C4
2200 LYTN 84040 1284 A4

STREET
Block City ZIP Map# Grid

SR-109 E Gentile St
10 LYTN 84041 1282 E5
10 LYTN 84041 1283 A5
1100 LYTN 84040 1283 C4
SR-109 Oak Hills Dr
1300 LYTN 84040 1283 C4
1500 DvsC 84040 1283 C4
2200 LYTN 84040 1284 A4
SR-110
10 WPT 84015 1225 E5
700 DvsC 84075 1225 E5
700 WPT 84075 1225 E5
1200 SRCS 84075 1225 E5
SR-110 N 4500 W
10 WPT 84015 1225 E5
SR-110 S 4500 W
10 WPT 84015 1225 E4
700 DvsC 84075 1225 E6
700 WPT 84075 1225 E6
1200 SRCS 84075 1225 E7
SR-111
- SLkC 84084 2066 E6
- WJDN 84084 2173 A2
- WJDN 84088 2173 A5
- WVCY 84006 2066 E6
- WVCY 84006 2066 E6
- WVCY 84084 2067 A7
- WVCY 84084 2173 A2
2600 SLkC 84044 1960 B3
3700 SLkC 84006 1960 B7
3800 SLkC 84006 2066 B1
3800 SLkC 84044 2066 B1
4100 WVCY 84044 2066 B1
SR-111 S 8400 W
2600 SLkC 84044 1960 B3
3700 SLkC 84006 1960 B7
3800 SLkC 84006 2066 B1
3800 SLkC 84044 2066 B1
4100 WVCY 84044 2066 B1
SR-113
- WshC 84032 2504 B1
10 HRCY 84032 2398 C4
10 MIDW 84049 2397 B4
600 WshC 84049 2397 B4
800 WshC 84032 2397 E4
900 WshC 84032 2398 A4
2500 CSTN 84032 2504 B1
SR-113 W 100 S
10 HRCY 84032 2398 C4
SR-113 S Center St
10 MIDW 84049 2397 B3
600 WshC 84049 2397 B5
SR-113 Charleston Rd
- WshC 84032 2397 B7
- WshC 84032 2504 B1
900 WshC 84049 2397 B5
2500 CSTN 84032 2504 B1
SR-113 E Main St
10 MIDW 84049 2397 B4
SR-113 Midway Ln
800 MIDW 84049 2397 D3
800 WshC 84032 2397 E4
800 WshC 84049 2397 E4
900 HRCY 84032 2398 A4
900 WshC 84032 2398 A4
SR-114
10 LNDN 84042 2712 D5
10 OREM 84057 2819 E4
10 OREM 84058 2819 E4
10 PRVO 84601 2927 D6
10 VNYD 84057 2819 E4
400 LNDN 84042 2819 E4
400 VNYD 84058 2819 E7
500 PRVO 84601 2928 B7
500 PTGV 84062 2712 D4
900 OREM 84058 2926 E1
1000 OREM 84058 2927 B3
1200 OREM 84601 2927 B3
1200 UthC 84058 2927 B3
1200 UthC 84601 2927 B3
SR-114 W Center St
500 PRVO 84601 2928 B7
1300 PRVO 84601 2927 E7
SR-114 Geneva Dr
500 PTGV 84062 2712 D4
SR-114 N Geneva Rd
10 LNDN 84042 2712 D6
10 OREM 84057 2819 E4
10 PRVO 84601 2927 D6
10 VNYD 84057 2819 E4
1800 UthC 84601 2927 B3
1900 UthC 84058 2927 B3
SR-114 S Geneva Rd
10 LNDN 84042 2712 D7
10 OREM 84058 2819 E5
10 VNYD 84057 2819 E5
200 OREM 84058 2819 E6
400 LNDN 84042 2819 E1
400 VNYD 84058 2819 E6
900 OREM 84058 2926 E1
1000 OREM 84058 2927 B3
1200 OREM 84601 2927 B3
1200 UthC 84058 2927 B3
1200 UthC 84601 2927 B3
SR-115
10 SPFK 84660 3249 A3
100 PYSN 84651 3354 E4
700 UthC 84660 3249 A3
800 UthC 84651 3354 E4
1200 SPFK 84660 3248 D4
1400 UthC 84660 3248 D4
1600 UthC 84660 3354 E1
SR-115 W 100 S
10 SPFK 84660 3249 A3
SR-115 W 900 S
1600 SPFK 84660 3248 D4
1600 SPFK 84660 3249 A4
SR-115 S 3200 W
9300 UthC 84651 3354 E2
9300 UthC 84660 3354 E2
SR-115 W 6800 S
400 SPFK 84660 3249 C3
700 UthC 84660 3249 B3
SR-115 W 7300 S
1200 SPFK 84660 3248 E4
1400 UthC 84660 3248 E4
SR-115 Benjamin Rd
8500 UthC 84651 3354 E1
8500 UthC 84660 3354 E1
SR-115 N Main St
100 PYSN 84651 3354 E5
800 UthC 84651 3354 E3

STREET
Block City ZIP Map# Grid

SR-126
- BxEC 84340 941 C7
- BxEC 84340 997 C1
- BxEC 84404 997 C1
10 CRFD 84015 1227 E5
10 LYTN 84041 1282 E4
10 LYTN 84041 1283 A5
100 MTSV 84404 1055 D6
700 CRFD 84015 1228 A6
800 FRWT 84404 1055 D2
800 SNST 84015 1227 D3
1200 MTSV 84401 1055 D6
1200 MTSV 84401 1114 D1
1400 WHVN 84401 1114 D1
1500 LYTN 84041 1228 A7
1800 FRWT 84404 997 D7
1800 SNST 84015 1171 D6
2100 LYTN 84015 1228 A7
2500 OGDN 84401 1114 D3
3100 WbrC 84401 1114 D7
3300 WbrC 84067 1114 D7
3300 WHVN 84067 1114 D7
3400 ROY 84067 1114 D7
3400 ROY 84401 1114 D7
3400 WbrC 84405 1114 D7
3600 OGDN 84405 1114 D7
4000 ROY 84067 1171 D1
4100 OGDN 84067 1171 D1
4100 OGDN 84405 1171 D1
4100 ROY 84405 1171 D1
SR-126 N 1900 W
100 MTSV 84404 1055 D5
SR-126 S 1900 W
100 MTSV 84404 1055 D5
1200 MTSV 84401 1055 D7
1200 MTSV 84401 1114 D1
1400 WHVN 84401 1114 D1
2500 OGDN 84401 1114 D3
3100 WbrC 84401 1114 D7
3300 WbrC 84067 1114 D7
3300 WHVN 84067 1114 D7
3400 ROY 84067 1114 D7
3400 ROY 84401 1114 D7
3400 WbrC 84405 1114 D7
3600 OGDN 84405 1114 D7
4000 ROY 84067 1171 D1
4100 OGDN 84067 1171 D1
4100 OGDN 84405 1171 D1
4100 ROY 84405 1171 D1
SR-126 N 2000 W
400 MTSV 84404 1055 D2
800 FRWT 84404 1055 D2
1800 FRWT 84404 997 D7
SR-126 N Main St
10 CRFD 84015 1227 E5
10 LYTN 84041 1282 E4
800 SNST 84015 1227 D3
1800 SNST 84015 1171 D7
2000 LYTN 84041 1228 B7
2100 CRFD 84015 1228 B7
2100 LYTN 84015 1228 B7
SR-126 S Main St
10 CRFD 84015 1227 D4
10 LYTN 84041 1282 E5
10 LYTN 84041 1283 A5
SR-126 State St
10 CRFD 84015 1227 D4
700 CRFD 84015 1228 A6
1500 LYTN 84041 1228 A7
SR-127
2000 SRCS 84075 1280 E1
3000 DvsC 84075 1280 E1
SR-127 W 1700 S
2000 SRCS 84075 1280 E1
3000 DvsC 84075 1280 E1
SR-131
- WBNF 84087 1551 D7
200 BNFL 84010 1551 D7
500 WBNF 84010 1551 D7
SR-131 W Willey St
- WBNF 84087 1551 D7
200 BNFL 84010 1551 D7
500 WBNF 84010 1551 D7
SR-134
10 WbrC 84404 1054 B5
900 WbrC 84401 1054 B7
1100 PTVW 84404 998 A6
1100 PTVW 84414 998 A6
1100 WbrC 84404 998 A6
1200 WbrC 84401 1113 B2
1300 PNCY 84404 1054 B1
1300 PTVW 84404 997 E6
1300 WbrC 84404 997 E6
1700 FRWT 84404 997 E6
1900 PNCY 84404 996 B7
2500 PNCY 84404 997 C6
3300 WHVN 84315 1113 B7
3400 WbrC 84404 996 D6
SR-134 W 2200 N
4200 PNCY 84404 996 C7
SR-134 W 2575 N
4200 PNCY 84404 996 C6
SR-134 W 2600 N
2500 FRWT 84404 997 B6
2500 PNCY 84404 997 A6
2500 WbrC 84404 997 A6
3400 PNCY 84404 996 E6
3400 WbrC 84404 996 E6
SR-134 W 2700 N
1100 PTVW 84404 998 A6
1100 PTVW 84414 998 A6
1100 WbrC 84404 998 A6
1300 PTVW 84404 997 E6
1300 WbrC 84404 997 E6
1700 FRWT 84404 997 E6
SR-134 N 4200 W
2500 PNCY 84404 996 C6
SR-134 N 4275 W
2200 PNCY 84404 996 C6
SR-134 N 4650 W
1900 PNCY 84404 996 B7
SR-134 N 4700 W
10 WbrC 84404 1054 B5
1300 PNCY 84404 1054 B2
SR-134 S 4700 W
100 WbrC 84404 1054 B5
900 WbrC 84401 1054 B7
1200 WbrC 84401 1113 B2
3300 WHVN 84315 1113 B7
SR-140
300 BFDL 84065 2388 B7
300 DRPR 84020 2388 B7

STREET
Block City ZIP Map# Grid

SR-140
900 BFDL 84065 2387 D7
SR-140 W 14400 S
1700 BFDL 84065 2387 D7
SR-140 W 14600 S
300 BFDL 84065 2388 B7
300 DRPR 84020 2388 B7
900 BFDL 84065 2387 E7
SR-140 Highland Dr
- DRPR 84020 2388 B7
SR-140 S Redwood Rd
14300 BFDL 84065 2387 C7
SR-141
- GNLA 84655 3460 A4
5600 UthC 84651 3460 D1
12000 UthC 84655 3460 A4
SR-141 S 5600 W
11300 UthC 84651 3460 D1
SR-141 W 11600 S
5600 UthC 84651 3460 D1
SR-141 S West Mountain Rd
11800 UthC 84651 3460 C2
12000 UthC 84655 3460 B3
SR-145
- ANFK 84003 2711 A1
- UthC 84003 2711 A1
SR-146
- CRHL 84003 2498 C7
- CRHL 84062 2498 C7
- CRHL 84062 2605 C3
- HILD 84003 2498 C7
10 PTGV 84062 2712 D3
1400 PTGV 84062 2605 D7
SR-146 N 100 E
10 PTGV 84062 2712 D3
1400 PTGV 84062 2605 D7
SR-146 S 100 E
10 PTGV 84062 2712 D3
SR-146 Canyon Rd
- CRHL 84003 2498 C7
- CRHL 84062 2498 C7
- CRHL 84062 2605 C3
- HILD 84003 2498 C7
SR-147
- SPFK 84663 3249 E2
10 MPTN 84664 3144 A7
10 MPTN 84664 3250 E2
10 MPTN 84664 3251 A2
10 SPFK 84660 3249 E2
100 PYSN 84651 3354 E5
500 UthC 84660 3249 A2
600 MPTN 84664 3143 E7
900 UthC 84651 3354 E5
1000 UthC 84660 3248 E2
1100 SPFK 84660 3250 A2
1100 SPFK 84663 3250 A2
1100 UthC 84660 3250 A2
1100 UthC 84663 3250 A2
1600 UthC 84664 3250 A2
SR-147 E 400 N
1100 SPFK 84660 3250 A2
1100 SPFK 84663 3250 A2
1600 UthC 84660 3250 A2
SR-147 W 400 N
10 SPFK 84660 3249 C2
600 UthC 84660 3249 B2
SR-147 W 1600 S
10 MPTN 84664 3250 E2
10 MPTN 84664 3251 A2
SR-147 S 4400 W
10200 PYSN 84651 3354 B5
10200 UthC 84651 3354 B5
SR-147 E 6400 S
- MPTN 84664 3250 D2
1100 UthC 84660 3250 B2
1100 UthC 84663 3250 B2
1600 UthC 84664 3250 C2
SR-147 W 6400 S
500 UthC 84660 3249 A2
1000 UthC 84660 3248 E2
SR-147 W 10400 S
1600 PYSN 84651 3354 B5
1600 UthC 84651 3354 B5
SR-147 S Main St
10 MPTN 84664 3144 A7
10 MPTN 84664 3251 A1
SR-147 W Maple St
10 MPTN 84664 3144 A7
600 MPTN 84664 3143 E7
SR-147 S State Rd
- SPFK 84660 3249 C2
- SPFK 84663 3249 E2
SR-147 W Utah Av
100 PYSN 84651 3354 E5
900 UthC 84651 3354 E5
SR-151
- SJDN 84070 2282 B4
- SNDY 84070 2282 B4
- SNDY 84095 2282 B4
200 SJDN 84095 2282 B4
900 SJDN 84095 2281 E4
3000 SJDN 84095 2280 E3
SR-151 W 10600 S
- SJDN 84070 2282 B4
- SJDN 84095 2282 B4
- SNDY 84070 2282 B4
- SNDY 84095 2282 B4
SR-151 W South Jordan Pkwy
200 SJDN 84095 2282 B4
900 SJDN 84095 2281 E4
3000 SJDN 84095 2280 E3
SR-152
- CDHT 84121 2177 D1
- HLDY 84121 2177 D1
- MRRY 84121 2071 C6
- MRRY 84121 2177 D1
- SLkC 84121 2071 C6
5500 MRRY 84117 2071 C6
5500 SLkC 84117 2071 C6
6100 HLDY 84121 2071 D7
SR-152 Highland Dr
- CDHT 84121 2177 D1
- HLDY 84121 2177 D1
- MRRY 84121 2177 D1
6100 HLDY 84121 2071 D7
6100 MRRY 84121 2071 D7
SR-152 Van Winkle Expwy
- MRRY 84121 2071 C6
- SLkC 84121 2071 C6
5500 MRRY 84117 2071 C6

STREET
Block City ZIP Map# Grid

SR-152 Van Winkle Expwy
5500 SLkC 84117 2071 C6
6100 HLDY 84121 2071 D7
SR-154
- BFDL 84065 2387 C5
- BFDL 84065 2388 B5
- DRPR 84020 2388 D5
- RIVN 84065 2280 D7
- RIVN 84065 2386 C1
- RIVN 84065 2387 A5
- SJDN 84095 2280 D5
- SLCY 84104 1856 C5
- SLCY 84104 1962 C1
- SLCY 84120 1962 C1
- TYVL 84084 2068 D7
- TYVL 84084 2174 D3
- TYVL 84118 2068 D5
- WJDN 84084 2068 D7
- WJDN 84084 2174 D5
- WJDN 84088 2174 D5
- WJDN 84088 2280 D1
- WVCY 84120 1962 D3
- WVCY 84120 2068 D1
SR-154 Bangerter Hwy
- BFDL 84065 2387 A5
- BFDL 84065 2388 B5
- DRPR 84020 2388 D5
- RIVN 84065 2280 D7
- RIVN 84065 2386 C1
- RIVN 84065 2387 C5
- SJDN 84095 2280 D1
- SLCY 84104 1856 C5
- SLCY 84104 1962 C1
- SLCY 84120 1962 C1
- TYVL 84084 2068 D7
- TYVL 84084 2174 D3
- TYVL 84118 2068 D5
- WJDN 84084 2068 D7
- WJDN 84084 2174 D5
- WJDN 84088 2174 D5
- WJDN 84088 2280 D1
- WVCY 84120 1962 D3
- WVCY 84120 2068 D5
SR-156
- SPFK 84660 3142 C7
10 SPFK 84660 3249 C2
SR-156 N Main St
- SPFK 84660 3142 C7
10 SPFK 84660 3249 C2
SR-156 S Main St
10 SPFK 84660 3249 C3
SR-158
- WbrC 84317 1059 C6
400 WbrC 84310 1059 E4
700 WbrC 84310 1060 A3
2400 WbrC 84310 1001 E7
SR-158 Powder Mountain Rd
4400 WbrC 84310 1001 E1
SR-158 Wolf Creek Dr
3200 WbrC 84310 1001 E3
SR-164
- SPFK 84660 3249 B5
- UthC 84660 3249 B5
800 SALM 84660 3248 D6
800 SALM 84660 3249 B5
800 SPFK 84660 3248 D6
800 UthC 84660 3248 D6
SR-164 W 8000 S
800 SALM 84660 3248 D6
800 SALM 84660 3249 A6
800 SPFK 84660 3248 D6
800 SPFK 84660 3249 A6
800 UthC 84660 3248 D6
800 UthC 84660 3249 A6
SR-164 Arrowhead Trail Rd
- SPFK 84660 3249 B5
SR-165
- CchC 84319 591 D6
- CchC 84319 651 D6
- CchC 84319 710 D2
- CchC 84321 527 D7
- CchC 84328 651 D6
- CchC 84328 710 D2
- CchC 84332 527 D7
- LOGN 84321 527 D7
- MLVI 84321 591 D2
- PVDN 84321 527 D7
- PVDN 84332 527 D7
10 HYRM 84319 651 D2
200 CchC 84321 651 D2
2400 CchC 84321 591 D2
2400 CchC 84332 591 D2
2400 MLVI 84332 591 D2
2400 NBLY 84321 591 D2
2500 NBLY 84332 591 D2
8600 PARA 84319 710 D2
8600 PARA 84328 710 D2
SR-165 S 200 W
400 HYRM 84319 651 D4
SR-165 200 St W
8600 PARA 84319 710 D4
8600 PARA 84328 710 D4
SR-165 N 800 St E
10 HYRM 84319 651 D2
200 CchC 84321 651 D2
SR-165 S 800 St E
10 HYRM 84319 651 D3
SR-165 S Main St
2400 CchC 84321 591 D2
2400 CchC 84332 591 D2
2400 MLVI 84332 591 D2
2400 NBLY 84321 591 D2
2500 NBLY 84332 591 D2
SR-167
- WbrC 84317 1060 E7
SR-167 Trappers Loop Rd
- WbrC 84317 1060 E7
SR-171
10 SSLK 84115 1964 D5
400 SSLK 84119 1964 A5
500 SSLK 84106 1964 D5
700 SLkC 84106 1964 D5
700 SLkC 84106 1965 A5
900 SSLK 84119 1963 E5
1100 SLCY 84106 1965 A5
1100 WVCY 84119 1963 E5
2000 SLkC 84109 1965 E5
2300 SLkC 84109 1966 A5
3000 WVCY 84119 1962 E6
3600 WVCY 84120 1962 E6

STREET Block City ZIP Map# Grid

SR-171
5000 WVCY 84120 1961 E6
5600 WVCY 84128 1961 E6
7000 WVCY 84128 1960 D6
7200 SLkC 84044 1960 D6
SR-171 E 3300 S
10 SSLK 84115 1964 D5
500 SSLK 84106 1964 E5
700 SLkC 84106 1964 E5
700 SLkC 84106 1965 A5
1100 SLCY 84106 1965 A5
2000 SLkC 84109 1965 E5
2300 SLkC 84109 1966 A5
SR-171 W 3300 S
10 SSLK 84115 1964 D5
400 SSLK 84119 1964 A5
900 SSLK 84119 1963 E5
1100 WVCY 84119 1963 E5
SR-171 W 3500 S
1300 WVCY 84119 1963 A6
3000 WVCY 84119 1962 E6
3600 WVCY 84120 1962 E6
5000 WVCY 84120 1961 E6
5600 WVCY 84128 1961 E6
7000 WVCY 84128 1960 D6
7200 SLkC 84044 1960 D6
SR-172
- SLCY 84116 1855 D3
- SLCY 84120 1961 D1
- SLCY 84128 1961 D1
100 SLCY 84104 1855 D3
1300 SLCY 84104 1961 D1
2100 WVCY 84120 1961 D4
2100 WVCY 84128 1961 D4
4000 WVCY 84120 2067 D1
4000 WVCY 84128 2067 D1
4700 SLkC 84118 2067 D1
4700 WVCY 84118 2067 D1
SR-172 S 5600 W
- SLCY 84116 1855 D3
- SLCY 84120 1961 D1
- SLCY 84128 1961 D1
100 SLCY 84104 1855 D3
1300 SLCY 84104 1961 D1
2100 WVCY 84128 1961 D4
3500 WVCY 84120 1961 D7
4000 WVCY 84120 2067 D1
4000 WVCY 84128 2067 D1
4700 SLkC 84118 2067 D1
4700 WVCY 84118 2067 D1
SR-172 Wolverine Wy
3500 WVCY 84120 1961 D6
3500 WVCY 84128 1961 D6
SR-173
300 MRRY 84107 2070 B5
300 MRRY 84123 2070 B5
800 MRRY 84123 2069 E5
1000 TYVL 84123 2069 E5
1700 TYVL 84118 2069 E5
3000 TYVL 84118 2068 E5
4800 SLkC 84118 2068 B5
5000 SLkC 84118 2067 E5
5600 WVCY 84118 2067 E5
6400 SLkC 84006 2066 D5
6400 WVCY 84006 2066 D5
6400 WVCY 84044 2066 D5
6400 WVCY 84044 2067 A5
6400 WVCY 84084 2066 D5
6400 WVCY 84084 2067 A5
SR-173 W 5300 S
300 MRRY 84107 2070 B5
300 MRRY 84123 2070 B5
SR-173 W 5400 S
800 MRRY 84123 2069 E5
800 MRRY 84123 2070 A5
1000 TYVL 84123 2069 E5
1700 TYVL 84118 2069 E5
3000 TYVL 84118 2068 E5
4800 SLkC 84118 2068 B5
5000 SLkC 84118 2067 E5
5600 WVCY 84118 2067 E5
6400 SLkC 84006 2066 D5
6400 WVCY 84006 2066 D5
6400 WVCY 84044 2066 D5
6400 WVCY 84044 2067 A5
6400 WVCY 84084 2066 D5
6400 WVCY 84084 2067 A5
SR-173 Spartan Wy
- MRRY 84107 2070 C4
SR-180
100 ANFK 84003 2711 D2
400 UthC 84003 2711 D2
SR-180 S 500 E
100 ANFK 84003 2711 D2
400 UthC 84003 2711 D2
SR-181
500 SLCY 84102 1859 B6
900 SLCY 84105 1859 B6
1600 SLCY 84105 1965 B1
2100 SLCY 84106 1965 B1
3000 SLkC 84106 1965 B4
3900 SLkC 84124 1965 B7
4000 SLkC 84124 2071 B1
4500 SLkC 84117 2071 B1
SR-181 S 1300 E
500 SLCY 84102 1859 B6
900 SLCY 84105 1859 B6
1600 SLCY 84105 1965 B1
2100 SLCY 84106 1965 B1
3100 SLkC 84106 1965 B4
3900 SLkC 84124 1965 B7
4000 SLkC 84124 2071 B1
4500 SLkC 84117 2071 B1
SR-181 Richmond St
2900 SLCY 84106 1965 B4
3000 SLkC 84106 1965 B4
SR-184
- SLCY 84116 1754 C7
10 SLCY 84103 1858 D2
500 SLCY 84103 1754 C7
SR-184 E 300 N
10 SLCY 84103 1858 C2
SR-184 Columbus St
300 SLCY 84103 1858 C2
SR-184 N State St
100 SLCY 84103 1858 D2
SR-184 Victory Rd
- SLCY 84116 1754 C7
500 SLCY 84103 1754 C7
500 SLCY 84103 1858 D2
SR-186
- SLkC - 1966 B3

SR-186
10 SLCY 84101 1858 B3
10 SLCY 84103 1858 B3
10 SLCY 84111 1858 D4
500 SLCY 84102 1858 D4
500 SLCY 84108 1859 D4
500 SLCY 84112 1859 D4
500 SLCY 84116 1858 B3
700 SLCY 84102 1859 A4
900 SLCY 84116 1857 D2
1000 SLCY 84104 1857 D2
1500 SLCY 84108 1860 A7
1600 SLCY 84108 1966 A1
2100 SLCY 84109 1966 B3
SR-186 N 300 W
10 SLCY 84103 1858 B3
SR-186 S 300 W
10 SLCY 84101 1858 B3
SR-186 E 400 S
10 SLCY 84101 1858 D4
10 SLCY 84111 1858 D4
500 SLCY 84102 1858 D4
700 SLCY 84102 1859 A4
SR-186 W 400 S
10 SLCY 84101 1858 C4
SR-186 E 500 S
1000 SLCY 84102 1859 D4
1400 SLCY 84108 1859 D4
1400 SLCY 84112 1859 D4
SR-186 S 2100 E
800 SLCY 84108 1859 E5
SR-186 Foothill Blvd
500 SLCY 84108 1859 D4
500 SLCY 84112 1859 D4
SR-186 Foothill Dr
1100 SLCY 84108 1859 E6
1500 SLCY 84108 1860 A7
1600 SLCY 84108 1966 A1
2100 SLCY 84109 1966 B3
SR-186 W North Temple
300 SLCY 84103 1858 B3
400 SLCY 84101 1858 B3
500 SLCY 84116 1858 B3
900 SLCY 84116 1857 D2
1000 SLCY 84104 1857 D2
SR-190
- CDHT 84121 2072 B7
- HLDY 84121 2072 B7
- SLkC 84098 2182 D2
- SLkC 84098 2183 A3
- WshC 84049 2183 C4
3800 CDHT 84121 2178 E2
4000 SLkC 84121 2178 E2
6600 HLDY 84121 2178 C1
SR-190 E 6200 S
- CDHT 84121 2072 B7
- HLDY 84121 2072 B7
- HLDY 84121 2178 C1
SR-190 E Big Cottonwd Cyn Rd
- SLkC 84098 2182 D2
- SLkC 84098 2183 A3
3800 CDHT 84121 2178 D2
4000 SLkC 84121 2178 E2
SR-190 Wasatch Blvd
6600 CDHT 84121 2178 C2
6600 HLDY 84121 2178 C1
SR-193
- CRFD 84015 1227 E6
- CRFD 84015 1228 A6
- DvsC 84040 1229 E5
- DvsC 84041 1229 A6
- DvsC 84056 1229 A6
- LYTN 84040 1230 A5
- LYTN 84041 1229 A6
- LYTN 84056 1228 E6
- LYTN 84056 1229 A6
10 DvsC 84041 1228 E6
10 DvsC 84056 1228 E6
10 LYTN 84041 1228 E6
1300 LYTN 84040 1229 A6
SR-193 E 3000 N
1300 LYTN 84040 1229 C6
SR-193 W 3000 N
10 DvsC 84041 1228 E6
10 DvsC 84056 1228 E6
10 LYTN 84041 1228 E6
SR-193 Bernard Fisher Hwy
- CRFD 84015 1227 E6
- CRFD 84015 1228 A6
SR-195
- HLDY 84124 1965 E7
2700 SLCY 84109 1965 E5
2700 SLkC 84109 1965 E5
4100 HLDY 84124 2071 E2
SR-195 S 2300 E
2700 SLCY 84109 1965 E5
2700 SLkC 84109 1965 E5
4100 HLDY 84124 2071 E2
SR-197
10 LEHI 84043 2603 B5
SR-197 N 500 W
10 LEHI 84043 2603 B5
SR-198
- SNQN 84655 3461 B6
- UthC 84651 3355 D4
10 PYSN 84651 3354 E5
10 SPFK 84660 3249 D3
300 PYSN 84651 3355 A5
400 SALM 84653 3356 B3
500 SALM 84653 3355 D4
900 UthC 84653 3356 C1
1200 SPFK 84660 3250 B4
1200 UthC 84660 3249 D3
1400 PYSN 84651 3461 D2
8600 UthC 84660 3356 C1
11600 UthC 84651 3461 D2
SR-198 E 100 N
10 PYSN 84651 3354 E5
300 PYSN 84651 3355 A5
SR-198 N 100 W
10 PYSN 84651 3354 E5
SR-198 S 100 W
10 PYSN 84651 3354 E5
SR-198 W 100 N
10 PYSN 84651 3354 E5
SR-198 E 300 S
10 SPFK 84660 3249 D3
SR-198 E Canyon Rd
600 SPFK 84660 3249 E3
1200 SPFK 84660 3250 B4

SR-198 S Main St
300 SPFK 84660 3249 C3
1200 UthC 84660 3249 C5
SR-198 State Rd
- PYSN 84651 3354 E5
- PYSN 84651 3355 A5
- SALM 84653 3355 D4
- UthC 84651 3355 D4
SR-198 N State Rd
400 SALM 84653 3356 B2
900 UthC 84653 3356 B1
SR-198 S State Rd
- SALM 84653 3356 B3
500 SALM 84653 3355 E4
1400 PYSN 84651 3461 D2
1800 SPFK 84660 3249 C6
8100 UthC 84660 3249 C7
8600 UthC 84660 3356 C1
11000 PYSN 84651 3354 D7
11600 UthC 84651 3461 D2
SR-198 S State St
13200 UthC 84651 3461 B6
SR-201
- WVCY 84128 1960 E3
- SLCY - 1961 A3
- SLCY - 1962 B2
- SLCY - 1963 A2
- SSLK - 1963 E2
- WVCY - 1961 E2
- WVCY - 1962 D2
- WVCY - 1963 E2
10 SLCY 84115 1964 C2
10 SSLK 84115 1964 C2
600 SLCY 84104 1964 A2
600 SLCY 84119 1964 A2
600 SSLK 84119 1964 A2
7200 SLkC 84044 1960 A3
8600 SLkC 84044 1959 A2
9100 SLkC 84006 1959 D3
SR-201 E 2100 S
10 SLCY 84115 1964 C2
10 SSLK 84115 1964 C2
SR-201 W 2100 S
10 SLCY 84115 1964 C2
10 SSLK 84115 1964 C2
600 SLCY 84104 1964 A2
600 SLCY 84119 1964 A2
600 SSLK 84119 1964 A2
SR-201 2100 S Frwy
- SLCY - 1961 E2
- SLCY - 1962 D2
- SLCY - 1963 A2
- SLCY - 1964 A2
- SSLK - 1963 E2
- SSLK - 1964 A2
- WVCY - 1961 E2
- WVCY - 1962 D2
- WVCY - 1963 E2
SR-201 W 2400 S
- WVCY 84128 1960 E3
- WVCY 84128 1961 A3
7200 SLkC 84044 1960 A3
8600 SLkC 84044 1959 A2
9100 SLkC 84006 1959 D3
SR-203
1200 OGDN 84404 1116 C1
1500 OGDN 84401 1116 C1
2700 OGDN 84403 1116 B6
3900 OGDN 84403 1173 B1
4800 SOGN 84403 1173 B3
5300 WbrC 84403 1173 B3
5900 SOGN 84405 1173 B3
SR-203 Harrison Blvd
1200 OGDN 84404 1116 C1
1500 OGDN 84401 1116 C1
2700 OGDN 84403 1116 B6
3900 OGDN 84403 1173 B1
4800 SOGN 84403 1173 B3
5300 WbrC 84403 1173 B3
5900 SOGN 84405 1173 B3
SR-204
100 OGDN 84404 1056 D4
400 HARR 84404 1056 D4
1200 OGDN 84404 1115 D2
1800 OGDN 84401 1115 D2
3600 OGDN 84405 1115 D6
3600 SOGN 84405 1115 D6
SR-204 Wall Av
100 OGDN 84404 1056 D5
1200 OGDN 84404 1115 D2
1800 OGDN 84401 1115 D2
3600 OGDN 84405 1115 D6
3600 SOGN 84405 1115 D6
SR-204 N Wall Av
100 OGDN 84404 1056 D4
400 HARR 84404 1056 D4
SR-209
- SLkC 84088 2176 A7
- WJDN 84088 2176 A7
10 SNDY 84070 2176 D7
700 SNDY 84094 2176 D7
700 SNDY 84094 2177 A7
800 SNDY 84094 2283 A1
900 WJDN 84088 2175 E7
1300 SLkC 84092 2283 C1
1300 SNDY 84092 2283 A1
1300 SNDY 84093 2283 A1
2400 SNDY 84092 2284 A1
2700 SLkC 84092 2284 A1
3000 WJDN 84088 2174 E7
3100 SNDY 84093 2284 A1
SR-209 E 9000 S
10 SNDY 84070 2176 D7
700 SNDY 84094 2176 D7
700 SNDY 84094 2177 A7
800 SNDY 84094 2283 A1
SR-209 W 9000 S
- SLkC 84088 2176 A7
- WJDN 84088 2176 A7
10 SNDY 84070 2176 C7
900 WJDN 84088 2175 E7
3000 WJDN 84088 2174 E7
SR-209 E 9400 S
1000 SNDY 84094 2283 A1
1300 SLkC 84092 2283 C1
1300 SNDY 84092 2283 A1
1300 SNDY 84093 2283 A1
SR-209 S Little Cottonwood Rd
2400 SNDY 84092 2284 A1
2700 SLkC 84092 2284 A1
3100 SNDY 84093 2284 A1

SR-209 S Little Cottonwood Rd
9400 SNDY 84092 2283 E1
9400 SNDY 84093 2283 E1
SR-210
- ALTA 84049 2181 E6
- ALTA 84049 2182 A6
- SLkC 84049 2181 E6
- SLkC 84049 2287 B1
3800 SLkC 84092 2284 D1
3800 SLkC 84121 2284 D1
7000 CDHT 84121 2178 D3
8900 CDHT 84093 2178 D7
9000 CDHT 84092 2178 D7
9000 SLkC 84092 2178 D7
9000 SLkC 84121 2178 D7
SR-210 N Little Cottonwood Rd
3800 SLkC 84092 2284 D1
3800 SLkC 84121 2284 D1
SR-210 Little Cottonwd Cyn Rd
- ALTA 84049 2181 E6
- ALTA 84049 2182 A6
- SLkC 84049 2181 E6
- SLkC 84049 2287 B1
8900 CDHT 84093 2178 D7
8900 CDHT 84121 2178 D7
9000 CDHT 84092 2178 D7
9000 SLkC 84092 2178 D7
9000 SLkC 84092 2284 D1
9000 SLkC 84121 2178 D7
9000 SLkC 84121 2284 D1
SR-210 Wasatch Blvd
- CDHT 84093 2178 D7
7000 CDHT 84121 2178 D3
SR-218
- CchC 84335 398 A1
- CchC 84335 399 B2
- SHFD 84335 399 B2
2800 AMGA 84335 398 A1
SR-218 W 6200 N
2800 AMGA 84335 398 B1
SR-224
- PKCY 84060 2184 E1
- PKCY 84098 2078 B1
- SmtC 84060 2078 B1
- SmtC 84098 1971 E3
- SmtC 84098 2078 B1
1100 PKCY 84060 2078 B1
SR-224 Deer Valley Dr
1100 PKCY 84060 2078 D4
SR-224 Marsac Av
10 PKCY 84060 2078 E5
SR-224 Park Av
1600 PKCY 84060 2078 B1
SR-225
300 FMTN 84025 1346 B7
SR-225 Park Ln
300 FMTN 84025 1346 B7
SR-227
- FMTN 84025 1448 C2
SR-227 S 200 W
- FMTN 84025 1448 C2
SR-227 W State St
10 FMTN 84025 1448 D2
SR-232
700 LYTN 84041 1282 E2
2000 LYTN 84041 1228 E7
SR-232 N Hill Field Rd
900 LYTN 84041 1282 E2
2000 LYTN 84041 1228 E7
SR-232 W Hill Field Rd
700 LYTN 84041 1282 D3
SR-235
100 NHON 84414 998 E7
100 OGDN 84404 1056 E5
100 PTVW 84414 998 B6
400 HARR 84404 1056 E4
1500 NHON 84404 1056 E2
1500 NHON 84414 1056 E2
1500 WbrC 84404 1056 E2
1700 WbrC 84414 1056 E2
SR-235 E 2550 N
100 NHON 84414 998 D6
SR-235 W 2550 N
100 NHON 84414 998 D6
100 PTVW 84414 998 D6
SR-235 Washington Blvd
100 OGDN 84404 1056 E5
1700 NHON 84404 1056 E2
1700 NHON 84414 1056 E2
1700 WbrC 84404 1056 E2
1700 WbrC 84414 1056 E2
2400 NHON 84414 998 E7
SR-235 N Washington Blvd
100 OGDN 84404 1056 E5
400 HARR 84404 1056 E4
1500 NHON 84404 1056 E2
1500 NHON 84414 1056 E2
1500 WbrC 84404 1056 E1
2300 NHON 84414 998 E6
SR-238
- PVDN 84332 527 E4
- PVDN 84332 591 E2
- RVHT 84321 528 A4
10 LOGN 84321 527 E4
10 MLVI 84332 591 E3
200 NBLY 84321 591 E3
300 RVHT 84321 527 E4
800 CchC 84332 591 E2
SR-238 E 300 S
10 LOGN 84321 527 E4
SR-238 S 400 E
- LOGN 84321 527 E4
300 RVHT 84321 527 E4
SR-238 N Main St
10 MLVI 84332 591 E3
800 CchC 84332 591 E1
SR-238 S Main St
10 MLVI 84332 591 E3
SR-238 E Mill Rd
- MLVI 84332 591 E3
200 NBLY 84321 591 D3
SR-240
2600 HYVL 84314 646 C2
SR-240 W 6900 St N
2600 HYVL 84314 646 C2
SR-241
1600 LNDN 84042 2819 E1
1600 OREM 84057 2819 E1

SR-241 W 1600 N
1600 LNDN 84042 2819 E1
1600 OREM 84057 2819 E1
SR-248
- SmtC 84017 1973 D7
- SmtC 84017 2079 E1
- SmtC 84098 1973 D7
700 PKCY 84060 2078 D3
2400 PKCY 84060 2079 B2
2600 PKCY 84098 2079 B2
2600 SmtC 84098 2079 B2
SR-248 Kearns Blvd
700 PKCY 84060 2078 D3
2400 PKCY 84060 2079 A3
2600 PKCY 84098 2079 C2
2600 SmtC 84098 2079 C2
SR-265
10 OREM 84058 2927 E1
400 OREM 84097 2927 E1
500 OREM 84097 2928 A1
900 OREM 84604 2928 A1
900 PRVO 84097 2928 A1
900 PRVO 84604 2928 C3
SR-265 University Pkwy
400 OREM 84097 2927 E1
500 OREM 84097 2928 A1
900 OREM 84604 2928 A1
900 PRVO 84097 2928 A1
900 PRVO 84604 2928 A1
SR-265 E University Pkwy
10 OREM 84058 2927 D1
SR-265 N University Pkwy
1800 PRVO 84604 2928 C3
SR-265 W University Pkwy
10 OREM 84058 2927 E1
SR-266
10 MRRY 84107 2070 E2
200 SLkC 84107 2070 E2
400 MRRY 84123 2070 A2
600 TYVL 84123 2070 A2
700 SLkC 84107 2071 A2
800 TYVL 84123 2069 E2
900 SLkC 84117 2071 A2
900 SLkC 84124 2071 A2
1700 HLDY 84117 2071 C2
1700 HLDY 84124 2071 C2
1700 TYVL 84118 2069 C3
1700 TYVL 84119 2069 C3
2500 HLDY 84117 2072 A2
2500 HLDY 84124 2072 A2
2700 SLkC 84124 2072 A2
SR-266 E 4430 S
2500 HLDY 84117 2072 A2
2500 HLDY 84124 2072 A2
2700 SLkC 84124 2072 A2
SR-266 E 4500 S
10 MRRY 84107 2070 C2
200 SLkC 84107 2070 D2
700 SLkC 84107 2071 A2
900 SLkC 84117 2071 A2
900 SLkC 84124 2071 A2
1700 HLDY 84117 2071 D2
1700 HLDY 84124 2071 D2
SR-266 W 4500 S
10 MRRY 84107 2070 A2
400 MRRY 84123 2070 A2
600 TYVL 84123 2070 A2
SR-266 W 4700 S
800 TYVL 84123 2069 E2
800 TYVL 84123 2070 A2
1700 TYVL 84118 2069 C3
1700 TYVL 84119 2069 C3
SR-268
300 SLCY 84103 1858 B1
400 SLCY 84116 1858 B1
SR-268 W 600 N
300 SLCY 84103 1858 B1
400 SLCY 84116 1858 B1
SR-269
- SLCY 84104 1858 C4
10 SLCY 84101 1858 C4
10 SLCY 84111 1858 C5
SR-269 W 6th S
200 SLCY 84101 1858 B5
SR-269 E 500 S
10 SLCY 84111 1858 C4
SR-269 W 500 S
10 SLCY 84101 1858 C4
SR-269 E 600 S
10 SLCY 84111 1858 C5
SR-269 W 600 S
10 SLCY 84101 1858 C5
SR-270
400 SLCY 84101 1858 C5
SR-270 S West Temple
400 SLCY 84101 1858 C5
SR-272
1200 FMTN 84025 1346 B5
SR-272 N Main St
1200 FMTN 84025 1346 B5
SR-273
- FMTN 84025 1346 A4
10 KYVL 84037 1345 C1
800 DvsC 84037 1345 E3
900 FTHT 84037 1345 E3
1100 DvsC 84037 1346 A4
1100 FMTN 84037 1346 A4
1100 FTHT 84037 1346 A4
1100 KYVL 84037 1346 A4
SR-273 W 200 N
10 KYVL 84037 1345 C1
SR-273 N Main St
10 KYVL 84037 1345 C1
SR-273 S Main St
- FMTN 84025 1346 A4
10 KYVL 84037 1345 C1
800 DvsC 84037 1345 E3
900 FTHT 84037 1345 E3
1100 DvsC 84037 1346 A4
1100 FMTN 84037 1346 A4
1100 FTHT 84037 1346 A4
1100 KYVL 84037 1346 A4
SR-282
- SLCY 84102 1859 C3
- SLCY 84103 1859 C3
100 SLCY 84112 1859 C3
500 SLCY 84108 1859 D4
1900 SLCY 84113 1859 D4
SR-282 E 400 S
1300 SLCY 84102 1859 B4
SR-282 North Campus Dr
- SLCY 84102 1859 C3

SR-282 North Campus Dr
- SLCY 84103 1859 C3
- SLCY 84112 1859 C3
SR-282 E South Campus Dr
1500 SLCY 84112 1859 D4
1900 SLCY 84113 1859 D4
SR-282 Wasatch Dr
100 SLCY 84112 1859 D3
200 SLCY 84113 1859 D3
500 SLCY 84108 1859 D4
SR-284
- OGDN 84403 1116 B7
- OGDN 84403 1173 B1
SR-284 E 3850 S
- OGDN 84403 1116 B7
SR-284 E 4000 S
- OGDN 84403 1173 B1
SR-284 E 4100 S
1200 OGDN 84403 1173 C1
SR-284 Dixon Dr
- OGDN 84403 1116 B7
- OGDN 84403 1173 B1
SR-284 Edvalson St
1200 OGDN 84403 1116 B7
SR-315
10 WLRD 84340 885 B4
SR-315 W 750 N
10 WLRD 84340 885 B4
US-6
- UthC 84655 3460 D7
- SPFK - 3248 E4
- SPFK 84660 3249 E1
- PYSN - 3354 D4
- UthC - 3248 B7
- UthC - 3355 A2
- UthC - 3461 B3
- SPFK 84660 3250 A2
- UthC - 3249 C1
- GNLA 84655 3460 A6
- SPFK 84660 3142 D7
- SPFK 84660 3251 A7
- UthC - 3354 B7
- UthC - 3461 B3
10 SNQN 84655 3460 D7
400 SNQN 84655 3461 A7
US-6 E Main St
10 SNQN 84655 3460 E7
400 SNQN 84655 3461 A7
US-6 W Main St
10 SNQN 84655 3460 D7
US-6 Veterans Memorial Hwy
- PYSN - 3354 D4
- SNQN - 3461 B3
- SPFK - 3142 D7
- SPFK - 3248 E4
- SPFK - 3249 C1
- UthC - 3248 B7
- UthC - 3249 C1
- UthC - 3354 B7
- UthC - 3355 A2
- UthC - 3461 B3
US-40
- SmtC - 1973 A3
- SmtC - 2079 C1
- HRCY 84032 2505 E1
- SmtC - 1972 E2
- WshC - 2079 C1
- WshC - 2186 A7
- WshC 84032 2398 D7
- WshC 84032 2505 E1
- WshC - 2185 E1
- WshC - 2292 B2
- WshC 84032 2292 D7
10 HRCY 84032 2398 D5
US-40 N Main St
10 HRCY 84032 2398 D5
US-40 S Main St
10 HRCY 84032 2398 D7
US-89
- CchC 84339 648 E6
- LEHI - 2495 C7
- BMCY 84302 767 B7
- BMCY 84302 828 B1
- BxEC 84324 708 B7
- BxEC 84340 997 D1
- CchC 84339 708 A5
- DRPR - 2388 C3
- BxEC 84302 828 B1
- BxEC 84324 768 A2
- BxEC 84340 941 D2
- CchC 84321 527 B7
- CchC 84321 528 E1
- CchC 84321 590 D4
- CchC 84321 591 A1
- CchC 84328 708 B7
- CchC 84339 707 D1
- DvsC 84037 1284 A6
- FMTN 84025 1346 B6
- HARR 84414 1056 C2
- MNTU 84324 768 C4
- PRRY 84302 885 C1
- PTVW 84404 997 E3
- PTVW 84414 998 A5
- SOGN 84405 1173 E7
- UNTH 84403 1230 A1
- WELV 84319 650 A1
- WELV 84339 650 A1
- BNFL - 1551 C5
- DvsC 84040 1230 A6
- UNTH 84403 1173 E7
- CTRV - 1448 C6
- BxEC 84324 767 E7
- DvsC 84405 1230 A4
- WELV 84319 590 B7
- LEHI - 2602 D2
- FTHT 84037 1284 A6
- UNTH 84405 1173 E7
- DRPR - 2495 C7
- HARR 84404 998 B7
- UthC - 2495 C7
- CchC 84339 590 D4
- CchC 84339 649 E2
- CchC 84339 650 A1
- LOGN 84321 591 A1
- LYTN 84040 1230 A4
- LYTN 84040 1284 A1
- NSLK 84054 1754 A2
- PTVW 84404 998 A5
- SLCY 84116 1754 A2
- SOGN 84403 1173 A4
- SPFK 84660 3251 A6

US-89
- WbrC 84405 1173 E7
- BNFL - 1551 C5
- HARR 84414 998 B7
- UNTH 84405 1174 A7
- WbrC 84403 1173 E7
- WBNF - 1551 C5
- KYVL 84037 1284 A6
- CTRV - 1551 C5
- FMTN - 1448 C6
- DvsC 84037 1346 B6
- DvsC 84040 1284 A6
- FTHT 84037 1346 A2
- NBLY 84321 590 D4
- PTVW 84414 997 E3
- SPFK 84660 3250 E6
- SWBR 84405 1230 A4
- UNTH 84405 1174 A7
- UNTH 84405 1230 A1
- UthC 84660 3250 E6
- WbrC 84414 997 D1
- WELV 84321 590 B7
- WELV 84339 649 E2
- CTRV - 1551 C5
10 ANFK 84003 2711 B1
10 LEHI 84043 2603 C5
10 LNDN 84042 2713 B6
10 LOGN 84321 527 E2
10 MPTN 84664 3143 D7
10 OGDN 84404 1056 E4
10 OREM 84057 2820 D5
10 OREM 84058 2820 D5
10 PRVO 84601 2928 B6
10 PRVO 84606 2928 D7
10 PTGV 84062 2712 C3
10 SGVL 84663 3143 C2
10 SLCY 84103 1858 D4
10 SLCY 84111 1858 D4
10 WLRD 84340 885 C7
100 ANFK 84003 2604 A7
100 OREM 84057 2713 B6
100 WBNF 84010 1551 C6
100 WBNF 84010 1653 C1
200 BNFL 84010 1653 C1
300 HARR 84404 1056 E4
400 LNDN 84042 2712 E5
500 PRVO 84606 3035 E1
600 LOGN 84321 528 A2
600 SGVL 84663 3036 C7
600 WDCR 84010 1653 C1
600 WLRD 84340 941 C5
700 ANFK 84003 2712 A2
700 MPTN 84664 3250 D1
700 OREM 84097 2820 E7
700 UthC 84003 2711 E1
700 UthC 84003 2712 A2
800 PRVO 84604 2928 B6
900 UthC 84043 2603 E6
1000 OREM 84058 2927 E1
1000 OREM 84097 2927 E1
1100 BMCY 84302 827 E2
1100 SLCY 84103 1754 B7
1300 OGDN 84404 1115 E1
1300 PRRY 84302 827 E2
1300 SLCY 84115 1858 D7
1400 ANFK 84003 2603 E6
1400 PRVO 84606 3036 B4
1400 UthC 84664 3250 D1
1500 ANFK 84003 2604 A7
1500 PRVO 84663 3036 C7
1500 SGVL 84606 3036 C7
1500 SLCY 84115 1964 D1
1500 UthC 84003 2604 A7
1600 OREM 84058 2928 A3
1600 OREM 84097 2928 A3
1600 UthC 84606 3036 B4
1800 OGDN 84401 1115 E1
1800 SLCY 84103 1753 E4
1800 SLCY 84116 1753 E3
2100 SSLK 84115 1964 D1
2600 NSLK 84010 1653 C3
2600 NSLK 84054 1653 C3
3200 DvsC 84010 1653 B6
3400 DvsC 84054 1653 B6
3500 OGDN 84403 1115 E7
3600 SOGN 84403 1115 E7
3600 SOGN 84405 1115 E7
3900 SLkC 84107 1964 D7
3900 SOGN 84403 1172 E1
3900 SOGN 84405 1172 E1
4000 SLkC 84107 2070 D1
4000 WbrC 84405 1172 E1
4200 MRRY 84107 2070 D1
4300 WSTR 84403 1172 E1
4300 WSTR 84405 1172 E1
6400 MRRY 84107 2176 C1
6500 MRRY 84047 2176 C1
6600 MDVL 84047 2176 C1
6600 MDVL 84107 2176 C1
7800 MDVL 84070 2176 C4
8200 SNDY 84070 2176 C4
9200 SNDY 84070 2282 C1
11400 DRPR 84020 2282 C6
US-89 E 300 S
10 PRVO 84606 2928 C7
US-89 N 300 W
100 SLCY 84103 1858 B1
700 SLCY 84103 1754 B7
US-89 W 300 S
10 PRVO 84601 2928 C7
US-89 S 400 E
1500 SGVL 84663 3143 D5
1700 MPTN 84664 3143 D5
US-89 400 St N
10 LOGN 84321 527 E2
600 LOGN 84321 528 A2
US-89 N 500 W
10 BNFL 84010 1551 C6
10 PRVO 84601 2928 B6
100 WBNF 84010 1551 C6
600 PRVO 84604 2928 B5
US-89 S 500 W
10 BNFL 84010 1551 C7
10 PRVO 84601 2928 B7
100 WBNF 84010 1653 C1
200 BNFL 84010 1653 C1
600 WDCR 84010 1653 C1
US-89 W 1100 S
- BMCY 84302 827 E2
- BMCY 84302 828 A2
- BxEC 84302 828 A2

STREET
Block City ZIP Map# Grid

US-89 N 1200 W
- LEHI 84043 2603 A3
US-89 N 1600 W
10 MPTN 84664 3143 D6
US-89 S 1600 W
10 MPTN 84664 3143 D7
700 MPTN 84664 3250 D1
1400 UthC 84664 3250 D1
US-89 Beck St
- NSLK 84054 1754 A1
1100 SLCY 84103 1754 B7
1100 SLCY 84116 1754 B7
1800 SLCY 84103 1753 E4
1800 SLCY 84116 1753 E3
US-89 N Harrisville Rd
10 OGDN 84404 1056 E4
300 HARR 84404 1056 E4
US-89 E Main St
10 ANFK 84003 2711 C1
US-89 N Main St
10 LOGN 84321 527 D4
10 SGVL 84663 3143 C2
10 WLRD 84340 885 C5
600 SGVL 84663 3036 C7
1500 PRVO 84606 3036 C6
1500 PRVO 84663 3036 C6
1500 SGVL 84606 3036 C6
1600 UthC 84606 3036 C5
US-89 S Main St
10 LOGN 84321 527 D3
10 SGVL 84663 3143 D7
10 WLRD 84340 885 C7
600 WLRD 84340 941 C5
1100 BMCY 84302 827 E3
1300 PRRY 84302 827 E3
2200 BNFL 84010 1653 C3
2200 WDCR 84010 1653 C3
2600 NSLK 84010 1653 C4
2600 NSLK 84054 1653 C4
3200 DvsC 84010 1653 B5
3400 DvsC 84054 1653 B5
US-89 W Main St
10 ANFK 84003 2711 B1
US-89 E North Temple
10 SLCY 84103 1858 C2
US-89 W North Temple
10 SLCY 84103 1858 C2
US-89 E State Rd
200 ANFK 84003 2711 D1
400 LNDN 84042 2712 E5
700 ANFK 84003 2712 A2
700 UthC 84003 2711 E1
700 UthC 84003 2712 A2
1100 PTGV 84062 2712 A2
US-89 State St
6800 MDVL 84047 2176 C1
7800 MDVL 84070 2176 C4
8200 SNDY 84070 2176 C5
9200 SNDY 84070 2282 C1
US-89 E State St
10 LEHI 84043 2603 C5
900 UthC 84043 2603 D6
1400 ANFK 84003 2603 E6
1500 ANFK 84003 2604 A7
1500 ANFK 84043 2604 A7
1500 UthC 84043 2604 A7
US-89 N State St
10 LNDN 84042 2713 B6
10 OREM 84057 2820 D5
10 SLCY 84103 1858 D3
500 LNDN 84042 2712 E5
1200 PRVO 84604 2928 B4
1700 OREM 84057 2713 B6
US-89 S State St
10 LNDN 84042 2713 B6
10 OREM 84058 2820 D5
10 SLCY 84111 1858 D3
100 OREM 84057 2713 B7
300 PRVO 84606 2928 D7
500 PRVO 84606 3035 E1
700 OREM 84097 2820 E7
1000 OREM 84058 2927 E1
1000 OREM 84097 2927 E1
1300 SLCY 84115 1858 D7
1400 PRVO 84606 3036 B4
1500 SLCY 84115 1964 D1
1600 OREM 84058 2928 A3
1600 OREM 84097 2928 A3
1600 UthC 84606 3036 B4
1800 PRVO 84604 2928 A3
2100 SSLK 84115 1964 D1
3900 SLkC 84107 1964 D7
4000 SLkC 84107 2070 D1
4200 MRRY 84107 2070 D1
6400 MRRY 84107 2176 C1
6500 MRRY 84047 2176 C1
6600 MDVL 84047 2176 C1
6600 MDVL 84107 2176 C1
8600 SNDY 84070 2176 C7
11400 DRPR 84020 2282 C6
US-89 W State St
10 ANFK 84003 2711 B1
10 LEHI 84043 2603 C5
100 ANFK 84003 2604 A7
US-89 Veterans Memorial Hwy
- BNFL - 1551 C5
- CTRV - 1448 C6
- CTRV - 1551 C5
- DRPR - 2282 C7
- DRPR - 2388 C3
- DRPR - 2495 C7
- FMTN - 1448 C6
- LEHI - 2495 C7
- LEHI - 2602 D2
- UthC - 2495 C7
- WBNF - 1551 C5
US-89 Washington Blvd
- SOGN 84403 1173 A4
- SOGN 84405 1173 A4
200 OGDN 84404 1056 E5
1300 OGDN 84404 1115 E1
1800 OGDN 84401 1115 E1
3500 OGDN 84403 1115 E7
3600 SOGN 84403 1115 E7
3600 SOGN 84405 1115 E7
3900 SOGN 84403 1172 E1
3900 SOGN 84405 1172 E1
4000 WbrC 84405 1172 E1
4300 WSTR 84403 1172 E1
4300 WSTR 84405 1172 E1
US-91
- BMCY 84302 767 B7
- BMCY 84302 828 B1
- BxEC 84302 827 E2
- BxEC 84302 828 B1
- BxEC 84324 708 B7
- BxEC 84324 767 E7
- BxEC 84324 768 A2
- BxEC 84340 827 E2
- CchC 84318 399 D7
- CchC 84321 527 B7
- CchC 84321 590 D4
- CchC 84321 591 A1
- CchC 84328 708 B7
- CchC 84335 399 D7
- CchC 84339 590 D4
- CchC 84339 648 E6
- CchC 84339 649 E2
- CchC 84339 650 A1
- CchC 84339 707 D1
- CchC 84339 708 A5
- CchC 84341 399 D7
- CchC 84341 463 D1
- HDPK 84318 399 D7
- HDPK 84318 463 D1
- HDPK 84341 399 D7
- HDPK 84341 463 D1
- LOGN 84321 591 A1
- MNTU 84324 768 C4
- NBLY 84321 590 D4
- NHLN 84341 463 D4
- WELV 84319 590 B7
- WELV 84319 650 A1
- WELV 84321 590 B7
- WELV 84339 649 E2
- WELV 84339 650 A1
10 BMCY 84302 827 E2
10 LOGN 84321 527 D4
10 SHFD 84335 399 D1
900 LOGN 84321 463 D7
1000 LOGN 84341 463 D7
US-91 W 1100 S
- BMCY 84302 828 A2
- BxEC 84302 827 E2
- BxEC 84302 828 A2
- BxEC 84340 827 E2
10 BMCY 84302 827 E2
US-91 N Main St
10 LOGN 84321 527 D4
10 SHFD 84335 399 D1
900 LOGN 84321 463 D7
1000 LOGN 84341 463 D7
US-91 S Main St
10 LOGN 84321 527 D3
10 SHFD 84335 399 D3
US-189
- PRVO 84604 2822 A1
- UthC 84604 2822 A1
- WshC 84032 2292 D7
- WshC 84032 2503 E7
10 HRCY 84032 2398 D5
10 PRVO 84601 2928 C7
10 PRVO 84606 2928 C7
10 WshC 84032 2398 B7
800 PRVO 84601 3035 C1
800 PRVO 84604 2928 C5
800 PRVO 84606 3035 C1
1200 HRCY 84032 2505 A1
1200 WshC 84032 2505 A1
1600 WshC 84032 2504 E2
2100 CSTN 84032 2504 E2
2300 OREM 84097 2714 E7
2300 OREM 84604 2714 E7
2300 OREM 84604 2821 D1
2300 PRVO 84604 2714 E7
2300 PRVO 84604 2821 D1
2300 UthC 84604 2714 E7
5000 UthC 84604 2821 C4
US-189 S Charleston Rd
10 HRCY 84032 2398 B7
10 WshC 84032 2398 B7
1200 HRCY 84032 2505 A1
1200 WshC 84032 2505 A1
1600 WshC 84032 2504 E2
2100 CSTN 84032 2504 E2
US-189 N Main St
10 HRCY 84032 2398 D5
US-189 S Main St
10 HRCY 84032 2398 D4
US-189 E Provo Canyon Rd
- PRVO 84604 2822 A1
- UthC 84604 2821 D1
- UthC 84604 2822 A1
2300 OREM 84097 2714 E7
2300 OREM 84604 2714 E7
2300 OREM 84604 2821 D1
2300 PRVO 84604 2714 E7
2300 PRVO 84604 2821 D1
2300 UthC 84604 2714 E7
US-189 N University Av
10 PRVO 84601 2928 C7
10 PRVO 84606 2928 C7
800 PRVO 84604 2928 C5
3300 PRVO 84604 2821 C7
5000 UthC 84604 2821 C4
5600 OREM 84604 2821 C3
US-189 S University Av
10 PRVO 84601 2928 C7
10 PRVO 84606 2928 C7
800 PRVO 84601 3035 C1
800 PRVO 84606 3035 C1

A

A Av
- OGDN 84404 1056 C7
- OGDN 84404 1115 C1
- PTVW 84404 997 E5
2400 OGDN 84401 1115 C4
A Ln
200 DvsC 84056 1228 D4
A St
- BMCY 84302 767 A7
- CRFD 84016 1227 D7
- KYVL 84041 1283 B7
- ROY 84067 1114 B7
- RVDL 84405 1172 A3
10 SGVL 84663 3143 E3
10 SLCY 84103 1858 D2
600 OREM 84057 2820 C3
Aaron Av
10 SGVL 84663 3143 D2
Aaron Wy
4700 SLkC 84118 2068 C3
Abbedale Ln
1700 SNDY 84092 2283 C2
Abbey Cir
- PVDN 84332 528 B7
Abbey Ct
4300 TYVL 84123 2069 D2
Abbey Ln
10 PVDN 84332 528 B7
Abbeyon Dr
2800 WbrC 84310 1001 B5
Abbey Ridge Ln
10100 SNDY 84092 2283 E3
Abbey View Rd
2000 WJDN 84088 2281 B1
Abbotts Ford Ct
600 SNDY 84070 2282 E6
Abbotts Ford Ln
600 SNDY 84070 2282 E7
Abercrombie Ln
7800 WJDN 84088 2174 A4
Aberdeen Cir
1000 FMTN 84025 1346 A6
10000 SJDN 84095 2280 C2
Aberdeen Ln
10400 HILD 84003 2605 A2
Abilene Wy
900 SmtC 84098 1972 A4
Abinadi Rd
4100 SLkC 84124 2072 E2
Abrams Wy
200 FTHT 84037 1346 A1
Absaroka Ct
900 DRPR 84020 2389 A7
Acheron Cir
4300 SJDN 84095 2280 B2
Achilles Dr
4000 SLkC 84124 2072 C1
Acoma Rd
300 MDVL 84047 2176 E1
Acoma St
3500 WVCY 84120 1962 A6
Acord Cir
4400 WVCY 84120 1962 B5
Acord Wy
200 HRCY 84032 2398 D7
3900 WVCY 84120 1962 C7
3900 WVCY 84120 2068 C1
Acorn Cir
1800 OGDN 84403 1173 D1
Acorn Ct
700 SLCY 84111 1858 E5
Acorn Dr
10 NSLK 84054 1653 C7
Acorn Ln
2900 SLkC 84093 2178 B6
Acorn Wy
- HRCY 84032 2398 D7
Adaley Av
400 MRRY 84107 2070 D6
Adams
- ANFK 84003 2604 C6
Adams Av
- LOGN 84321 528 A2
- SOGN 84405 1172 E3
- WSTR 84405 1172 E3
10 PTGV 84062 2712 D3
100 OGDN 84404 1056 E5
1600 OGDN 84404 1115 E1
2000 OGDN 84401 1115 E2
2700 OGDN 84403 1115 E4
3600 OGDN 84403 1115 E7
3900 SOGN 84403 1172 E1
4000 WbrC 84403 1172 E1
N Adams Av
1000 OGDN 84404 1056 D3
Adams Cir
10 CTRV 84014 1551 E2
2900 SSLK 84115 1964 E5
4000 CRFD 84015 1228 B5
Adams Rd
3600 SLkC 84044 1960 D7
Adams St
600 LYTN 84041 1283 B5
900 LYTN 84040 1283 B3
2500 SSLK 84115 1964 E3
7800 MDVL 84047 2176 B4
Adams Av Pkwy
- SOGN 84403 1172 E5
- SOGN 84405 1172 E5
- SWBR 84405 1172 E5
- WbrC 84405 1172 E5
5300 WSTR 84405 1172 E5
Adamson Cir
5500 WJDN 84088 2173 D7
N Adamswood Rd
100 LYTN 84040 1283 B4
S Adamswood Rd
10 LYTN 84040 1283 C4
Addington Cir
900 SNDY 84094 2177 A5
Adelaide Dr
2300 RIVN 84065 2387 B2
Adeline Ct
5600 HRMN 84065 2385 D5
Adirondack Wy
6300 TYVL 84084 2069 A7
Administrative Lp
1100 SNST 84056 1227 D2
Admiral Dr
13600 RIVN 84065 2386 A5
Admiral Byrd Rd
100 SLCY 84116 1855 E2
Adobe Cir
2600 TYVL 84118 2069 A3
Adobe Mill Ln
- OGDN 84404 1056 C4
Adobe School Dr
14100 DRPR 84020 2389 A6
Adonis Cir
4000 SLkC 84124 2072 E1
Adonis Dr
3700 SLkC 84124 2072 D1
Adventure Wy Dr
6600 WJDN 84084 2173 D2
Aerie Cir
300 NSLK 84054 1754 C1
1500 PKCY 84060 2078 E4
Aerie Dr
900 PKCY 84060 2078 E5
Aerie Cove
3700 CDHT 84121 2178 D4
Aerie Heights Cove
2100 SNDY 84092 2283 E5
Aerie Hill Cir
5000 WJDN 84084 2174 A2
Aerie Hill Dr
4800 WJDN 84084 2174 A3
After Glow Ln
- LEHI 84043 2495 C5
Afton Av
300 MRRY 84107 2070 D7
Afton Cir
400 SNDY 84070 2282 E1
1700 LYTN 84041 1282 A1
Aggie Village Dr
10 LOGN 84321 464 B7
10 LOGN 84341 464 B7
Aileen Wy
200 FMTN 84025 1448 C2
Ainsley Cir
6800 HILD 84003 2603 E2
Ainsley Wy
10400 HILD 84003 2603 E2
Aintree Av
- DRPR 84020 2389 C3
Aircraft Av
10 LYTN 84041 1283 A4
Aire Dr
4500 WJDN 84088 2174 B5
Airfield Av
700 DvsC 84056 1172 C7
900 DvsC 84056 1228 C4
Airlane Dr
10 CRFD 84015 1228 A5
Airport Dr
600 LEHI 84043 2603 D3
5000 ROY 84067 1171 D3
Airport Rd
- CchC 84341 463 A3
- LOGN 84341 463 A3
2400 CchC 84341 462 B1
3300 OGDN 84405 1115 A7
3800 OGDN 84405 1172 A1
4000 OGDN 84405 1171 E3
4400 ROY 84067 1171 E3
4800 RVDL 84067 1171 E3
6200 WJDN 84084 2068 B7
6200 WJDN 84084 2174 B2
7800 WJDN 84088 2174 B3
E Airport Rd
- WshC 84032 2398 D7
10 HRCY 84032 2398 D7
N Airport Rd
1400 BMCY 84302 765 E1
1400 BMCY 84302 766 A2
1400 BxEC 84302 765 E1
1400 BxEC 84302 766 A2
S Airport Rd
600 HRCY 84032 2398 B7
1900 WshC 84032 2398 C7
W Airport Rd
10 HRCY 84032 2398 C7
10 WshC 84032 2398 C7
1800 BMCY 84302 765 E2
Akagi Ln
1300 DRPR 84020 2389 C4
Akers Wy
900 SNDY 84094 2177 A5
Alabama Av
3600 WJDN 84084 2174 D2
Alabama Dr
- DvsC 84056 1227 E3
10 MDVL 84047 2176 C3
900 DvsC 84056 1228 B3
Alabaster Cir
12100 HRMN 84065 2386 B1
Alameda Av
400 SLCY 84111 1858 D3
1200 SLCY 84102 1859 B3
Alamo St
2900 WVCY 84120 1961 E4
Alan Av
3400 WVCY 84119 1962 D7
Alan Cir
300 SNDY 84070 2282 D1
Alane St
2900 WVCY 84120 1962 C4
Alan Point Cir
700 DRPR 84020 2282 A7
Alan Point Dr
700 DRPR 84020 2282 A7
Alanwood Dr
1100 LYTN 84040 1283 C4
Alaska Av
2000 PRVO 84606 3036 B3
Alaska Dr
900 DvsC 84056 1228 B3
Alba Lucia Dr
8200 WJDN 84088 2175 A5
Albany Bay
3200 WVCY 84128 1961 B5
Albardado Ct
- SLkC 84044 1960 B7
Alberly Wy
3900 HLDY 84124 1965 E7
Albermarle Av
300 SLCY 84115 1858 B7
Albert Ct
13300 HRMN 84065 2385 D4
Alberta Pl
3100 WJDN 84084 2174 E3
Albertville Pl
6000 SLkC 84121 2071 E6
Albion Cir
9400 SNDY 84092 2283 C1
Albion Dr
1700 SNDY 84092 2283 C1
Albion Alps Rd
- ALTA 84049 2288 C2
Albion Basin Rd
- ALTA 84049 2182 A6
- ALTA 84049 2288 B1
Albion Village Wy
100 SNDY 84070 2282 C1
Albright Dr
4200 HLDY 84124 2071 D1
Albury Rd
1700 SNDY 84092 2283 C2
Alby Wy
3700 WVCY 84119 1963 D7
Alcott Cir
8000 SLkC 84044 1960 C4
Aldan Ct
5600 SmtC 84098 1972 C4
Alden St
2400 SLCY 84106 1965 B3
Alder Rd
1300 TYVL 84123 2069 D1
Alder St
1600 LYTN 84041 1282 D1
Alderbrook Cir
12900 DRPR 84020 2389 B3
Alder Glen Ln
15000 DRPR 84020 2496 D1
Alder Grove Wy
10200 SJDN 84095 2280 C3
Alder Hill Rd
- DRPR 84020 2388 D7
- DRPR 84020 2495 D1
Alderstone Bay
3000 WVCY 84128 1961 B5
Alderwood Cir
800 LYTN 84041 1283 B3
Alderwood Ct
3600 WVCY 84120 1961 E7
Alderwood Dr
- OGDN 84403 1173 E3
Aldo Cir
2000 SLCY 84108 1859 D7
W Aleen Av
8300 SLkC 84044 1960 B5
Alena Cove
3800 RIVN 84065 2386 D1
Alesa St
2000 WVCY 84119 1963 B6
Alex St
5000 SLkC 84118 2068 B4
Alexander Ct
1000 SNDY 84094 2177 A5
Alexander Dr
400 EKMT 84651 3463 A2
Alexander St
1700 WVCY 84119 1963 B3
Alexandria Ln
- HARR 84414 998 D6
Alfalfa Cir
- MIDW 84049 2397 B1
6800 WJDN 84084 2175 B1
Alford Ct
300 NSLK 84054 1652 C6
E Alfred Av
10 KYVL 84041 1283 C5
10 LYTN 84041 1283 C5
N Alfred Av
1100 DvsC 84040 1283 C5
1100 DvsC 84041 1283 C5
1100 KYVL 84040 1283 C5
1100 KYVL 84041 1283 C5
1100 LYTN 84041 1283 C5
W Alfred Av
10 KYVL 84041 1283 C5
10 LYTN 84041 1283 C5
Alfred Cir
1700 LYTN 84041 1282 B1
6500 MRRY 84123 2176 B1
Alfred Wy
500 MRRY 84123 2176 B1
Alice Cir
2900 WVCY 84119 2069 A1
8400 SLkC 84044 1960 B6
Alice Dr
2400 WJDN 84088 2281 A1
Alice Wy
1100 FMTN 84025 1346 C6
2800 WVCY 84119 2069 A2
Alice May Cir
300 FMTN 84025 1448 D3
Alice Susanna Pl
1800 WJDN 84084 2175 C1
Alice Susanna Wy
6600 WJDN 84084 2175 C1
Alicia Cir
300 DRPR 84020 2388 D3
Alicia Park Wy
4700 MRRY 84107 2071 A3
Alida Cir
2500 WJDN 84084 2175 A3
Alida Dr
2600 WJDN 84084 2175 A3
Alida Pl
100 SLCY 84103 1858 C1
Alisa Meadow Dr
11200 SJDN 84095 2281 E6
Alison Cir
2000 HLDY 84124 2071 D1
Alisway Rd
- PTGV 84062 2712 C3
Allanwood Pl
500 LYTN 84040 1283 C4
Alla Panna Wy
1800 SNDY 84093 2283 D1
Allegheny Cir
800 ALPN 84004 2497 E6
Allegheny Dr
1500 TYVL 84123 2069 C7
E Allegheny Wy
10 ALPN 84004 2497 E6
200 ALPN 84004 2498 A6
W Allegheny Wy
10 ALPN 84004 2497 E6
N Allen St
10 MDVL 84047 2176 A3
S Allen St
10 MDVL 84047 2176 B4
500 SNDY 84070 2176 B4
W Allen Cove
600 MDVL 84047 2176 A4
Allendale Dr
5200 MRRY 84123 2070 A4
Allenhurst
10 PTGV 84062 2712 D2
Allen Park Dr
1300 SLCY 84105 1965 B1
Allen Peak Cir
1000 OGDN 84404 1057 B2
Allison Cir
9700 SNDY 84070 2282 D2
Allison Wy
1700 SRCS 84075 1281 A2
Allison Dee Cir
11800 RIVN 84065 2280 E7
Allison Park Ct
12000 DRPR 84020 2388 A1
Allred Cir
2800 TYVL 84118 2069 A5
Allred Park Rd
300 LEHI 84043 2603 A6
Almaden Ct
- BFDL 84065 2387 D5
Almina Rd
4300 WVCY 84120 2068 B1
Almira Ct
3200 CDHT 84121 2178 C2
Almond Ln
1500 WJDN 84088 2175 D6
Almond St
200 SLCY 84103 1858 C2
Almont Cir
6100 WVCY 84128 2067 C1
Aloha Ln
300 SNDY 84070 2282 E3
Aloha Rd
600 SLCY 84103 1754 E7
600 SLCY 84103 1858 E1
600 SLCY 84103 1859 A1
Alondra Wy
11300 SNDY 84094 2283 A6
Alonzo Ln
13300 HRMN 84065 2385 C4
Alpen Cir
8600 CDHT 84121 2178 C6
Alpen Wy
8600 CDHT 84121 2178 D6
Alpen Glow Ct
5100 HRMN 84065 2385 E6
Alpen Glow St
- WbrC 84310 1002 A2
Alphorn Wy
- WshC 84049 2396 D3
Alpine Blvd
10 ALPN 84004 2498 B4
Alpine Cir
1300 LYTN 84040 1283 C3
4900 HILD 84003 2604 E1
S Alpine Cir
200 ALPN 84004 2498 B5
Alpine Ct
10 ANFK 84003 2711 D1
Alpine Dr
10 PTGV 84062 2712 D4
5300 MRRY 84107 2070 D4
E Alpine Dr
10 EKMT 84651 3463 A2
800 ALPN 84004 2498 B5
S Alpine Dr
200 ALPN 84004 2498 B5
Alpine Hwy
400 ALPN 84004 2497 E6
Alpine Hwy SR-74
400 ALPN 84004 2497 E6
N Alpine Hwy
9600 HILD 84003 2604 D3
10900 HILD 84003 2497 E7
N Alpine Hwy SR-74
9600 HILD 84003 2604 D3
10900 HILD 84003 2497 E7
Alpine Lp
1200 PRVO 84606 3036 A2
Alpine Pl
1100 SLCY 84105 1859 B5
Alpine Wy
1200 PRVO 84606 3036 A2
Alpine Air Wy
1100 PRVO 84601 3034 B2
Alpine Brook Cir
5300 SLkC 84118 2067 E6
Alpine Cove Cir
4000 UthC 84004 2498 B1
Alpine Cove Dr
4100 UthC 84004 2498 B1
Alpine Fir Cove
7900 MDVL 84070 2176 D5
Alpine Flower Cir
5300 SLkC 84118 2067 C6
Alpine Loop Rd
- HILD 84003 2498 D7
- UthC 84004 2498 D7
Alpine Loop Rd SR-92
- HILD 84003 2498 D7
- UthC 84004 2498 D7
Alpine Meadows Cir
4300 WVCY 84120 1962 A4
Alpine Meadows Dr
2900 WVCY 84120 1962 B5
Alpine Point Cir
5500 SLkC 84118 2067 D5
Alpine Trail Dr
10 DRPR 84020 2388 D1
Alpine Valley Cir
3900 SLkC 84092 2284 D2
Alpinhof Cir
200 MIDW 84049 2396 E2
Alpinhof Ct
200 MIDW 84049 2396 E2
200 WshC 84049 2396 E2
Alpinhof Ln
300 MIDW 84049 2396 E2
Alps Wy
1700 SLCY 84116 1753 C7
Alsace Wy
1500 WVCY 84119 1963 C5
Alstead Cove
3800 SJDN 84095 2280 D3
Alta Cir
1400 SLCY 84103 1859 C2
Alta St
100 SLCY 84103 1859 C2
Alta Approach Rd
3800 SLkC 84092 2284 D2
Alta Canyon Cir
2400 SNDY 84093 2178 A5
Alta Canyon Dr
2000 SNDY 84093 2177 E6
2400 SNDY 84093 2178 A6
8500 SLkC 84093 2178 A6
Alta Cove Cir
2100 SNDY 84093 2177 E6
Alta Cove Dr
8600 SNDY 84093 2177 E6
Alta Heights Dr
1200 SNDY 84094 2283 B5
Alta Hills Cir
8700 CDHT 84093 2178 B6
Alta Hills Dr
3100 CDHT 84093 2178 B6
Altair Cir
1500 SNDY 84093 2177 C7
1700 SLCY 84116 1857 C2
Altair Dr
8600 SNDY 84093 2177 C6
8700 SLkC 84093 2177 C6
Alta Loma Dr
3700 SLkC 84106 1965 B7
Alta Mesa Cir
11100 SNDY 84094 2283 B5
Altamont Cir
2500 SNDY 84092 2284 A2
Altamont Dr
9600 SNDY 84092 2284 A2
Altamont Lake Ln
700 SNDY 84094 2177 A7
Alta Peak Rd
2900 SJDN 84095 2281 A5
Altara Cir
700 SNDY 84094 2282 E5
Altara Hills Dr
700 SNDY 84094 2282 E5
Alta Ridge Cir
3600 SLkC 84092 2284 D2
Alta View Cir
9700 SNDY 84070 2282 C2
Alta View Ct
9800 SNDY 84070 2282 C2
W Alta View Dr
300 MDVL 84047 2176 B4
Alta View Wy
10 SNDY 84070 2282 C2
Altavilla Dr
10000 SLkC 84092 2284 A3
Alta Vista Cir
1500 OGDN 84404 1057 C6
Alta Vista Dr
200 OREM 84058 2927 C2
Alta Vista St
3500 SLkC 84106 1965 B6
Altawood Dr
- SLkC 84092 2284 B1
10 SNDY 84093 2284 B1
Altawood Ln
10 SNDY 84093 2284 C1
Alton Wy
1000 SLCY 84108 1860 D6
Altonia Cir
4500 WVCY 84120 2067 E2
Altura Cir
400 SNDY 84070 2282 E3
Alturas Cir
200 OREM 84058 2927 C3
Alva Cir
2200 SLkC 84109 1965 E6
Alvera Cir
5200 HLDY 84117 2072 B4
Alvera Dr
2900 HLDY 84117 2072 B4
Alveron Dr
3600 TYVL 84118 2068 D5
S Alvey Dr
600 MPTN 84664 3143 D7
W Alvey Dr
1600 MPTN 84664 3143 D7
Alvey Ln
9100 SNDY 84093 2177 E7
9100 SNDY 84093 2283 E1
Alysum Cir
11800 RIVN 84065 2281 D7
N Ama Fille Cir
300 EKMT 84651 3463 A1
E Ama Fille Ln
10 EKMT 84651 3463 A1
Amalfi Wy
1400 SNDY 84093 2177 C7
Amanda Av
800 SLCY 84105 1859 C5
Amanda Lynn Ln
100 MDVL 84047 2176 B6
Amaryllis St
10100 SLkC 84094 2283 A3
Ambassador Wy
1300 SLCY 84108 1860 A7
Amber Av
100 TMTN 84337 521 A6
400 TMTN 84337 520 E6
Amber Ct
1700 PKCY 84060 2079 B5
Amber Ln
9500 SLkC 84094 2283 A2
Amber Rd
1300 PKCY 84060 2079 A6
Amber Crest Ln
1500 DRPR 84020 2496 C1
Amberfields Dr
300 HYRM 84319 651 D2
Amber Meadow Ct
9400 SJDN 84095 2280 B2
Amber Ridge Ln
5200 WVCY 84120 1961 E6
Amber Rose Ln
5000 HRMN 84065 2386 A6
5100 HRMN 84065 2385 E6
Amber Stone Dr
11700 SJDN 84095 2279 D7
Amberview Cove
5200 WVCY 84120 1961 E7
Amberwick Ln
2700 SNDY 84093 2178 A7
Amberwood Cir
9700 SJDN 84095 2281 E2
Ambiance Ct
8500 SLkC 84044 1960 B7
Amblewood Ln
1500 SLkC 84124 2071 C1
Amby Cir
1100 BNFL 84010 1552 B7
Ambyr Lynn Wy
4300 SJDN 84095 2280 B2
Amelia Earhart Dr
4700 SLCY 84116 1856 A2
5100 SLCY 84116 1855 D2
American Av
300 SLCY 84101 1858 B6
1300 SLCY 84104 1857 D6
W American Av
10 MRRY 84107 2070 C5
American Dr
3600 WVCY 84119 1963 A6

American Wy
10 BMCY 84302 766 D5
500 PYSN 84651 3354 B6
1500 UthC 84651 3354 B6
2800 OGDN 84401 1114 E5
American Beauty Dr
600 SLCY 84116 1857 E1
700 SLCY 84116 1753 E7
American Fork Canyon Rd
- UthC 84004 2498 E7
American Fork Canyon Rd SR-92
- UthC 84004 2498 E7
S American Park Cir
- WVCY 84119 1963 B4
W American Park Cir
1700 WVCY 84119 1963 B4
W American Park Dr
1700 WVCY 84119 1963 C5
American Saddler Dr
2600 PKCY 84060 2078 D1
N Amerigo Ln
300 EKMT 84651 3462 E2
300 EKMT 84651 3463 A1
Amesbury Cir
1300 MRRY 84121 2071 B7
Amethyst Av
700 LYTN 84041 1283 A3
Amethyst Dr
4800 WJDN 84088 2174 A4
5100 WJDN 84088 2173 E5
Amherst Av
2900 WVCY 84119 1963 A5
Amidan Dr
700 OGDN 84404 1056 B5
Amiga Dr
1000 SLCY 84104 1857 E7
N Amiron Wy
1300 OREM 84057 2820 C1
W Amiron Wy
300 OREM 84057 2820 C1
Amundsen Ct
2400 PKCY 84060 2079 B5
Ananyu Ct
9300 CRHL 84062 2605 D4
Anasazi Dr
1800 OGDN 84403 1173 D4
Ancestor Pl
5900 TYVL 84123 2069 D6
Ancora Ct
6400 WVCY 84128 1961 B5
Andalusian Ct
5600 HRMN 84065 2385 D4
Andermatt Cir
2200 SNDY 84093 2177 E6
Anderson Av
300 MRRY 84107 2070 D6
400 MRRY 84123 2070 A6
600 HYRM 84319 651 D2
Anderson Dr
600 BMCY 84302 767 B4
N Anderson Ln
10 LNDN 84042 2712 C6
W Anderson Ln
1200 LNDN 84042 2712 D5
Anderson Wy
6800 WJDN 84084 2175 D1
Anderson Farm Cove
13800 DRPR 84020 2388 D5
Anderwood Ln
14600 BFDL 84065 2387 C7
Andes Dr
800 ALPN 84004 2497 E6
Andes Wy
6300 TYVL 84084 2069 A7
6400 TYVL 84084 2175 A2
Andlor St
4800 HLDY 84117 2072 A3
Andorra Ln
8100 SNDY 84093 2177 C5
Andover Ct
1200 SNDY 84094 2283 B6
Andra Dr
4100 WVCY 84120 2068 D1
Andrea Cir
700 SLCY 84116 1753 C7
W Andrea Cir
700 KYVL 84037 1345 B2
Andrea Dee Cir
3000 RIVN 84065 2386 E1
Andrew Av
300 SLCY 84115 1858 B7
1200 SLCY 84104 1857 D7
2300 SLCY 84104 1856 E7
Andrew Dr
11200 HILD 84003 2497 C7
Andrews Ln
- SRSP 84043 2601 D5
Andrew View Cir
12100 DRPR 84020 2388 A1
Andrus Ln
1700 PRVO 84604 2928 D3
Andy Av
- SSLK 84115 1964 B2
Angel Ct
300 SNDY 84070 2176 D4
Angel St
100 MDVL 84070 2176 D5
8000 SNDY 84070 2176 D5
N Angel St
10 KYVL 84037 1344 D1
200 KYVL 84037 1282 D7
300 DvsC 84037 1282 D7
300 DvsC 84041 1282 D7
300 KYVL 84041 1282 D7
700 LYTN 84041 1282 C3
S Angel St
10 DvsC 84041 1282 C6
10 KYVL 84037 1344 E2
10 LYTN 84041 1282 C6
500 KYVL 84037 1345 A3
Angela Wy
10 NSLK 84054 1653 C7
Angel Creek Cir
3400 RIVN 84065 2280 E7
Angelico Ct
3700 WVCY 84119 1963 E6
Angelina Av
800 SLkC 84106 1965 A5
Angelita Ct
1100 SLCY 84106 1965 B3
E Angelo Av
10 SSLK 84115 1964 C5
W Angelo Av
10 SSLK 84115 1964 C5
Angelous Rd
- SNQN 84655 3461 B7
Angels Wy
1600 KYVL 84037 1344 E2
S Angelsea Cir
7000 WJDN 84084 2174 C2
Angelsea Dr
7000 WJDN 84084 2174 E2
Angelus St
4200 MRRY 84107 2070 C3
Angie Cir
600 MDVL 84047 2176 E1
Angle Ln
5800 TYVL 84118 2069 B6
Angus Ct
1100 SmtC 84098 1972 A4
Angus Dr
3600 SJDN 84095 2280 C1
Anita Av
1400 SLkC 84106 1965 C7
Anita Dr
500 KYVL 84037 1282 D7
Ann Dr
3800 WVCY 84119 1962 E7
Ann St
300 CRFD 84015 1227 C3
1300 SRCS 84075 1227 A7
1800 LYTN 84041 1282 B1
Anna Cir
11000 SJDN 84095 2282 A5
Anna Ln
200 MIDW 84049 2397 C1
Annabelle Ln
1000 SNDY 84094 2283 A4
Anna Bow Cir
4700 HLDY 84117 2072 A3
Annalyn Cir
300 SNDY 84070 2282 D1
Annalyn Dr
300 SNDY 84070 2282 D2
Annapolis Dr
4100 WVCY 84120 2068 B2
Anna Raquel Cir
4700 TYVL 84123 2070 A3
Annas Cir
7700 WJDN 84084 2175 D4
Ann Christine Ct
12600 RIVN 84065 2387 B2
Ann Dell Ln
1700 MRRY 84121 2071 D6
S Anne Cir
1000 OREM 84058 2820 D7
1000 OREM 84058 2927 D1
Anne Marie Dr
2900 CDHT 84121 2178 B1
Annie Lace Cir
13700 DRPR 84020 2389 C5
Annie Lace Wy
1300 DRPR 84020 2389 C5
Annie Oakley Dr
2300 PKCY 84060 2078 E4
2300 PKCY 84060 2079 A3
W Annika Cir
1100 SJDN 84095 2281 E6
E Antelope Dr
10 CRFD 84015 1281 E1
10 CRFD 84016 1281 E1
10 LYTN 84041 1282 A1
100 LYTN 84041 1283 A1
800 CRFD 84015 1282 A1
800 LYTN 84040 1283 D1
2200 LYTN 84040 1229 E7
2600 LYTN 84040 1230 A7
E Antelope Dr SR-108
10 CRFD 84015 1281 E1
10 CRFD 84016 1281 E1
800 CRFD 84015 1282 A1
W Antelope Dr
10 CRFD 84015 1281 C1
10 CRFD 84016 1281 C1
10 LYTN 84041 1282 E1
100 LYTN 84041 1281 C1
600 SRCS 84075 1281 C1
700 SRCS 84016 1281 C1
W Antelope Dr SR-108
10 CRFD 84015 1281 C1
10 CRFD 84016 1281 C1
400 LYTN 84041 1282 A1
600 SRCS 84075 1281 C1
700 SRCS 84016 1281 C1
Antelope Rd
6900 WVCY 84128 1961 A4
7100 WVCY 84128 1960 E4
Antelope Hills Dr
8400 SLkC 84044 1960 B7
Anthem Ct
11700 SJDN 84095 2280 E7
Anthony Cir
1400 SLCY 84104 1857 D7
Antilles Cir
1100 SLCY 84116 1753 C6
Antilles Dr
1100 SLCY 84116 1753 C6
Antimony Cir
9400 SNDY 84094 2283 A1
Antimony Ln
9800 SLkC 84094 2283 A2
Antler Wy
3200 CDHT 84121 2178 C2
Antonio Dr
7400 SLkC 84044 1960 E6
Anvil Blvd
- CchC 84319 652 B3
- HYRM 84319 652 B3
Anvil Dr
1300 DRPR 84020 2389 C2
Apache Cir
2700 SLCY 84108 1860 B7
Apache Ln
2900 PRVO 84604 2928 D1
Apache Tr
2000 SmtC 84098 1971 D7
Apache Wy
1500 OGDN 84403 1173 C3
2900 PRVO 84604 2928 E1
Apaloosa Dr
7000 WVCY 84128 1960 E3
7000 WVCY 84128 1961 A3
Apen Ridge Ln
- PVDN 84332 592 B1
Aplomado Cir
9900 SNDY 84092 2283 D2
Aplomado Dr
9800 SNDY 84092 2283 D2
Apollo Dr
3500 SLkC 84124 2072 C1
Apollo Rd
100 SLCY 84116 1855 D2
Apollo Wy
- HILD 84003 2497 B5
10 SNDY 84070 2176 C5
Appaloosa Rd
400 WBNF 84087 1551 B6
Appian Cir
5500 TYVL 84118 2069 A5
Appian Wy
2800 TYVL 84118 2069 A5
Appian Cove
3000 TYVL 84118 2068 C4
3000 TYVL 84118 2069 A4
Apple Av
100 SRSP 84043 2601 E4
1200 PRVO 84604 2928 E5
1400 PRVO 84604 2929 A4
Apple Ct
2400 SRSP 84043 2601 E4
9500 CRHL 84062 2605 A4
11000 SNDY 84070 2282 E5
Apple Dr
100 HYRM 84319 651 D2
Apple Hl
10 SNDY 84092 2283 E5
Apple Ln
400 PYSN 84651 3355 B7
400 PYSN 84651 3462 A1
Apple Vw
- SNQN 84655 3461 B7
- UthC 84655 3461 B7
Apple Blossom Cir
4600 CRHL 84062 2605 A3
Apple Blossom Ln
500 PTGV 84062 2712 E4
2600 HLDY 84117 2072 A2
E Apple Blossom Wy
10 SALM 84653 3356 B4
W Apple Blossom Wy
10 SALM 84653 3356 A5
Apple Creek Ct
6400 WVCY 84118 2067 B7
6400 WVCY 84118 2173 B1
Apple Farms Cir
3700 WVCY 84119 1963 C7
Apple Farms Rd
1900 WVCY 84119 1963 B7
Applegate Dr
- MRRY 84123 2070 A4
Apple Gate Wy
- LEHI 84043 2495 D6
Apple Grove Ln
300 PTGV 84062 2712 E4
800 PTGV 84062 2713 A4
Applegrove Ln
11300 SJDN 84095 2281 B6
Apple Hollow Cove
2900 SLkC 84092 2284 B3
Apple Honey Ln
7200 MDVL 84047 2176 D2
Apple Mill Cove
- SLkC 84109 1966 C6
Apple Orchard Ct
1600 DRPR 84020 2389 D4
Apple Orchard Ln
- MPTN 84664 3143 D4
13300 DRPR 84020 2389 C4
Apple Park Pl
800 SLkC 84106 1965 A5
Apple Park Wy
800 SLkC 84106 1965 A5
Apple Pear Cir
13200 DRPR 84020 2389 C3
Appleseed Rd
2100 WVCY 84119 1963 B6
Appleton Dr
2800 WVCY 84119 1963 A4
3000 WVCY 84119 1962 E4
Apple Tree Dr
500 SNDY 84070 2282 E5
Appletree Dr
300 ALPN 84004 2498 A3
Applevale Dr
5400 MRRY 84123 2070 A5
Applewood Av
2100 HLDY 84121 2071 E6
Applewood Cir
10300 CRHL 84062 2605 A2
Applewood Dr
100 ALPN 84004 2498 B4
400 CTRV 84014 1551 C2
500 BNFL 84010 1653 C5
5000 TYVL 84118 2068 D4
Appomattox Cir
4200 DvsC 84056 1228 A4
Appomattox Wy
1300 TYVL 84123 2175 D1
Apricot Av
10 SLCY 84103 1858 C2
Apricot Pl
2400 SRSP 84043 2601 E4
April Ann Ct
1600 DRPR 84020 2389 C2
April Meadows Dr
6200 TYVL 84084 2068 C7
6200 WJDN 84084 2068 C7
April Moon Cove
13800 HRMN 84065 2385 C5
Aquarius Cir
4000 SLkC 84118 2068 C6
Aquarius Ct
4000 SLkC 84118 2068 C7
Aquarius Dr
6000 SLkC 84118 2068 C7
Aqua Vista Cove
6600 CDHT 84121 2178 B1
Arabian Cir
2600 WVCY 84128 1960 D3
Arabian Dr
2900 PKCY 84060 2078 C1
Arabian Wy
2500 WVCY 84128 1961 A4
7000 WVCY 84128 1960 E4
Arapaho Cir
1900 OGDN 84403 1173 D4
Arapaho Ct
800 BMCY 84302 828 A1
Arapaho Dr
5200 OGDN 84403 1173 D4
Arapahoe Av
800 SLCY 84104 1858 A5
1100 SLCY 84104 1857 D5
Arapahoe Ln
2700 PRVO 84604 2928 E1
Arapeen Dr
500 SLCY 84108 1859 E4
Arbor Cir
4800 HLDY 84117 2071 E3
Arbor Dr
100 SRSP 84043 2601 E5
Arbor Ln
2000 HLDY 84117 2071 D4
Arbor Wy
900 DvsC 84041 1282 C7
900 LYTN 84041 1282 C7
Arborfield Cir
1800 SNDY 84092 2283 D2
Arbor Hill Ct
2000 RIVN 84065 2387 B1
S Arbor Meadows Ln
8500 WJDN 84088 2175 D5
Arbor Park Dr
3500 SLkC 84044 1960 B6
Arbor Rose Cir
14200 HRMN 84065 2385 D6
Arbor Rose Dr
5700 HRMN 84065 2385 D6
Arbor View Wy
1400 SJDN 84095 2281 D4
Arbutus Cir
5300 WJDN 84084 2173 E1
Arcadia Ln
1900 HLDY 84124 2071 D2
4400 HLDY 84117 2071 D2
Arcadia Green Wy
800 SLkC 84107 2071 A2
Arcadia Heights Cir
2700 SLCY 84109 1966 B2
Arcadia Rose Ln
14300 HRMN 84065 2385 D6
Arcata Rd
3400 SLkC 84124 2072 C2
Archard Av
300 SSLK 84115 1964 A6
Archer Ln
4500 WVCY 84120 1962 B5
Arches Dr
2200 TYVL 84118 2069 B5
Archie Av
100 FTHT 84037 1346 B1
Archmore Ct
2800 WVCY 84128 1961 D4
S Archmore Dr
1300 SGVL 84663 3143 A4
W Archmore Dr
1200 SGVL 84663 3142 E5
1200 SGVL 84663 3143 A5
Archmore Lp
1400 SGVL 84663 3142 E5
1400 SGVL 84663 3143 A5
Archmore St
10 SRSP 84043 2710 A3
Arco Cir
3900 HLDY 84124 1965 D7
Arctic Ct
500 SLCY 84103 1858 C1
Arctic Fox Cir
3700 TYVL 84118 2068 D7
Ardelle Cove
600 DRPR 84020 2388 E2
Arden Ct
4300 TYVL 84123 2069 D2
Ardmore Pl
200 SLCY 84103 1858 B2
Ardonna Wy
10800 SNDY 84070 2282 E5
Argaus Cir
6200 WVCY 84128 2067 C1
Argenta Dr
8200 WJDN 84088 2174 A5
Argo Cir
- HILD 84003 2497 B5
Argonaut Dr
4500 WVCY 84120 2068 A2
Argyle Ct
300 SLCY 84116 1858 A2
Argyll Cir
4300 SJDN 84095 2280 B2
Argyll Ct
400 HRCY 84032 2398 C3
Ariane Wy
400 CTRV 84014 1551 D2
A Richards Hall
100 PRVO 84604 2928 D4
Aries Cir
1700 SLCY 84116 1857 C2
Aries Dr
6000 SLkC 84118 2068 C6
Aristada Av
5400 WJDN 84084 2173 C2
Arizona Av
2000 PRVO 84606 3036 B4
Arizona Dr
100 MDVL 84047 2176 B3
1200 CRFD 84056 1227 D3
1200 SNST 84056 1227 D3
1300 DvsC 84056 1228 B3
Arizona St
3800 CRNN 84307 765 A1
3900 CRNN 84307 704 E7
3900 CRNN 84307 764 E1
Arkansas Dr
- DvsC 84056 1227 E2
- SNST 84056 1227 E2
10 MDVL 84047 2176 C3
Arlen Wy
1800 SNDY 84093 2177 D7
Arlington Av
100 MRRY 84107 2070 D3
Arlington Cir
- BNFL 84010 1654 B3
100 SLCY 84103 1859 C2
Arlington Ct
8200 WJDN 84088 2175 D5
Arlington Dr
500 PRVO 84606 2928 E5
1300 OGDN 84403 1116 C5
1300 SLCY 84103 1859 C2
Arlington Wy
- HARR 84414 998 D6
900 BNFL 84010 1654 A3
Arlington Park Dr
4600 SLkC 84120 2068 A3
4600 WVCY 84120 2068 A3
Arlinridge Dr
5700 HRMN 84065 2385 D3
Arlo Av
300 SLkC 84070 2176 D5
Arminta St
5200 SLkC 84117 2071 B4
Armor Ct
2900 WVCY 84120 1962 B4
Armoridge Cir
8100 SLkC 84044 1960 C7
Armoridge Dr
3700 SLkC 84044 1960 C7
Armoridge Ln
3700 SLkC 84044 1960 C7
Arnecia Pl
800 SLkC 84106 1965 A7
Arnett Dr
2300 SLkC 84109 1965 E7
2400 SLkC 84109 1966 A7
Arnette Cir
3700 SLkC 84109 1966 A7
Arnica Ridge Cir
5500 SLkC 84118 2067 C5
Arno Ct
4700 WJDN 84084 2174 A1
Arno Wy
4700 WJDN 84084 2174 B1
Arnold Ct
500 ALPN 84004 2498 B5
Arnold Dr
- LYTN 84041 1282 E1
200 DvsC 84056 1228 E5
Arnold Pl
300 SLCY 84111 1858 D3
Arnold Wy
2100 WVCY 84119 1963 A2
Arosa Cir
2200 SNDY 84093 2177 E5
Arrow Creek Dr
13800 DRPR 84020 2388 E5
Arrowhead Cir
5000 MRRY 84107 2070 E4
Arrowhead Ln
700 MRRY 84107 2070 E4
700 MRRY 84107 2071 A4
5300 OGDN 84403 1173 D4
Arrowhead Tr
600 PYSN 84651 3355 A4
800 UthC 84651 3355 A4
Arrowhead Trail Rd
- PYSN 84651 3355 B2
- SPFK 84660 3249 C5
- UthC 84651 3355 B2
8900 SALM 84653 3355 B2
8900 UthC 84660 3355 B2
Arrowhead Trail Rd SR-164
- SPFK 84660 3249 C5
Arrow Wood Ct
6700 WJDN 84084 2173 E1
Arroyo Rd
3800 SLkC 84106 1965 C7
Arsenal Rd
- CRFD 84056 1227 E3
800 DvsC 84056 1227 E3
800 DvsC 84056 1228 A4
1000 CLTN 84015 1227 A2
1100 SNST 84056 1227 D2
1800 CLTN 84015 1226 D2
3000 WPT 84015 1226 B2
4000 WPT 84015 1225 D2
Artesian Rd
800 OREM 84058 2819 E7
Artesian Wy
2000 CDHT 84121 2177 D1
Arthur Dr
1300 PRVO 84601 2927 E5
1900 WJDN 84084 2175 C3
Arthur St
- SLkC 84044 1854 C7
Arthurs Ct
3000 WVCY 84120 1962 A3
Artist Wy
400 LYTN 84040 1283 D3
Artistic Cir
1600 BNFL 84010 1653 D2
3500 SJDN 84095 2280 D7
S Artistic Cir
800 SGVL 84663 3143 C3
Artistry Ln
13500 HRMN 84065 2385 D4
Ascot Cir
1400 SNDY 84092 2283 C4
Ascot Dr
1000 NSLK 84054 1652 C5
Ascot Pkwy
1300 SNDY 84092 2283 C4
Ascot Downs Ct
10100 SJDN 84095 2280 C3
Ascot Downs Dr
4000 SJDN 84095 2280 C3
Ash Av
1000 PRVO 84604 2928 E4
Ash Cir
200 WDHL 84653 3356 C7
3300 SLkC 84109 1966 C7
Ash Dr
700 DvsC 84056 1229 A3
1000 LYTN 84040 1283 C2
Ash Briar Ln
3300 WJDN 84084 2174 E4
Ashbrook Cir
200 MDVL 84047 2176 D1
Ashbury Ln
6200 HLDY 84121 2071 E7
Ashby Dr
3400 WVCY 84128 1961 A5
Ashby Ln
9600 HILD 84003 2604 C4
Ashby Pl
1000 OREM 84097 2821 C2
Ashby Wy
6800 WVCY 84128 1961 A6
Ashby Cove
3400 WVCY 84128 1961 A6
Ashdown Ln
- DRPR 84020 2496 E3
Ashe Cir
100 BMCY 84302 767 B5
Ashe Dr
100 BMCY 84302 767 B5
Ashford Dr
1200 KYVL 84037 1283 E5
1500 SLkC 84124 2071 C1
Ashland Cir
3600 WJDN 84084 2174 D1
Ashland Dr
3800 SLkC 84109 1966 B7
Ashland Wy
2800 SLkC 84109 1966 B7
Ashley Av
10 PKCY 84060 2078 D1
8200 SLkC 84093 2178 B5
Ashley Cir
900 BNFL 84010 1654 A4
8200 SLkC 84093 2178 B5
Ashley Downs Ct
7800 CDHT 84093 2177 D4
Ashley Hills Cir
10200 SNDY 84092 2283 E3
Ashley Meadows Cir
10300 SNDY 84092 2283 E3
Ashley Mesa Ln
1800 SNDY 84092 2283 D3
Ashley Park Dr
10200 SNDY 84092 2283 E3
Ashley Ridge Rd
1800 SNDY 84092 2283 D3
Ashridge Cir
1900 SNDY 84093 2177 C6
Ashton Av
700 SLCY 84106 1964 E3
700 SLCY 84106 1965 A3
Ashton Blvd
- LEHI 84043 2495 C7
- LEHI 84043 2602 C1
Ashton Cir
2000 SLCY 84109 1965 D2
Ash Tree Cove
1200 SLkC 84106 1965 B6
Ashwood Cir
1300 MRRY 84121 2071 B7
Ashwood Dr
6300 MRRY 84121 2071 B7
Aspen Av
- ROY 84067 1171 D7
- RVDL 84405 1171 D7
300 SLCY 84101 1858 B6
1100 PRVO 84604 2928 E4
1100 SNST 84056 1227 D1
1700 SNST 84056 1171 D7
2000 BFDL 84065 2387 B7
Aspen Cir
100 SmtC 84098 1864 C6
1100 HRCY 84032 2398 E1
2700 SLCY 84109 1966 A2
Aspen Ct
- TMTN 84337 520 D6
5600 SOGN 84403 1173 C5
Aspen Dr
10 MPTN 84664 3144 C7
10 NHLN 84341 463 E3
10 SmtC 84098 1864 B5
10 SmtC 84098 1971 D7
500 BMCY 84302 767 B4
1100 LOGN 84341 464 D7
4200 UthC 84004 2498 B1
Aspen Grv
- CRFD 84015 1227 D4
Aspen Ln
100 SmtC 84098 1864 B6
200 SmtC 84098 1866 D3
4100 WbrC 84310 1001 E2
S Aspen Ln
4600 TYVL 84123 2069 E3
Aspen Pk
- LOGN 84321 591 A1
Aspen Pl
100 SmtC 84098 1864 C6
Aspen Rd
- SNST 84056 1227 D2
Aspen St
- SGVL 84663 3035 E6
200 LYTN 84041 1282 E4
200 LYTN 84041 1283 A4
Aspen Ter
10 SmtC 84098 1864 B5
Aspen Wy
400 CTRV 84014 1551 E2
700 LYTN 84040 1283 B3
2500 SNDY 84093 2178 A6
8600 SLkC 84093 2178 A6
W Aspen Wy
10 SALM 84653 3356 A5
Aspen Cove
10 WPT 84015 1227 A4
W Aspen Cove
4300 CRHL 84062 2605 B3
Aspen E Dr
600 LYTN 84041 1283 B3
Aspen Glen Cir
12800 RIVN 84065 2387 C3
Aspen Heights Dr
700 MRRY 84123 2070 A5
Aspen Hills Cir
9600 SNDY 84092 2283 E1
Aspen Hills Dr
2100 SNDY 84092 2283 E1
Aspen Hills Pl
2300 SNDY 84092 2283 C4
Aspen Hollow Ln
4400 HLDY 84117 2072 B2
N Aspen Leaf Dr
5600 SmtC 84098 1972 E3
5600 SmtC 84098 1973 A3
Aspen Leaf Pl
1800 DRPR 84020 2496 D1
E Aspen Meadows Ct
400 SLkC 84107 1964 E7
Aspen Park Dr
4800 WJDN 84084 2068 A7
Aspen Ridge Ln
300 UthC 84004 2498 B3
Aspen Ridge Ln
400 ALPN 84004 2498 B3
1100 PRVO 84604 2821 E5
Aspen Ridge Rd
11800 SNDY 84094 2283 B7
12000 SNDY 84094 2389 B1
Aspen Shadow Ct
4900 WJDN 84084 2068 A7
Aspen Springs Dr
2400 PKCY 84060 2078 A2
4800 RIVN 84065 2386 A3
Aspen View Ct
1900 SNDY 84092 2283 D5
2000 DRPR 84020 2496 D1
Aspen View Dr
5200 WJDN 84088 2173 E6
Aspenwood Wy
2100 SNDY 84092 2283 E2
Asplund Cir
2900 WVCY 84119 1962 E5
Associated Av
1700 SLCY 84104 1963 C1
Aster Ct
7800 PKCY 84060 2185 A2
Aster Ln
7800 PKCY 84060 2184 E1
7800 PKCY 84060 2185 A2
9900 SLkC 84094 2283 A2
S Astor Ln
10 EKMT 84651 3463 A2
Astor Park Ct
9400 SJDN 84095 2281 B1
Astro Cir
3600 SLkC 84109 1966 D6
Astro Wy
3600 SLkC 84109 1966 D6
Atala Wy
- RIVN 84065 2386 A4
Athena Dr
2500 SLkC 84044 1960 C4
11800 HILD 84003 2497 B5
Athens Dr
4600 WJDN 84088 2174 B5
Atherton Ct
1100 TYVL 84123 2069 E2
Atherton Dr
900 TYVL 84123 2069 E2
900 TYVL 84123 2070 A2
Atherton Wy
10 LYTN 84041 1228 E6
Athleen Dr
1100 WJDN 84084 2175 D2
Atkin Av
1500 SLCY 84106 1965 C4
2000 SLkC 84109 1965 D4
Atkinson Rd
- WshC 84049 2396 D2
Atlanta Cir
3600 WJDN 84084 2174 D2
Atlantis Dr
600 OREM 84057 2820 D3
Atlas Ln
900 DvsC 84056 1228 A3
Atlas Wy
3500 WVCY 84120 1962 B6
Atmore Rd
3600 WJDN 84084 2068 D7
Atwood Blvd
4500 MRRY 84107 2070 D2
Aubrey Ln
4100 WVCY 84128 2067 C1
Aubrey Dee Cir
3100 RIVN 84065 2280 E7
Aubrey Meadow Cir
11200 SJDN 84095 2281 E5
Auburn Dr
600 MRRY 84123 2070 A5
Auburn Ridge Ln
1700 DRPR 84020 2496 C1
Audrey Ct
6200 WVCY 84128 1961 B4
Audrey St
2900 WVCY 84128 1961 B4
August Ln
6000 WJDN 84084 2173 C1
Augusta Ct
10 PKCY 84060 2078 D1
Augusta Dr
- LEHI 84043 2602 C2
3600 SRCS 84075 1226 A7
Augusta Wy
1000 SLCY 84108 1860 B6
Augustus Wy
5500 HRMN 84065 2385 D2
August View Cir
6000 WJDN 84084 2173 C1
Aura Cir
3300 SLkC 84124 1966 C7
Aura Dr
3900 SLkC 84124 1966 C7
3900 SLkC 84124 2072 C1
Aurora Cir
3600 SLkC 84124 1966 D7
Aurora Wy
2100 SRSP 84043 2601 E5
Austin Av
900 OREM 84097 2821 B7
1000 SLCY 84106 1965 A4
1000 SLkC 84106 1965 A4
Austin Rd
1700 SLCY 84112 1859 D3
Austrian Wy
3300 CDHT 84121 2178 C5
Auto Blvd
10 MRRY 84107 2070 C2
Auto Mall Dr
10600 SNDY 84070 2282 C5
Autumn Av
900 SLCY 84116 1857 E1
Autumn Cir
4400 CRHL 84062 2605 B3
E Autumn Cir
600 EKMT 84651 3463 B2
Autumn Dr
- MPTN 84664 3250 D1
7400 WJDN 84084 2175 A3
Autumn Bluff Dr
1100 MRRY 84123 2069 E7
Autumn Creek Dr
4900 RIVN 84065 2385 E4
Autumn Dusk Cove
5800 HRMN 84065 2385 C5

Salt Lake City Street Index

STREET / Block City ZIP Map# Grid

Autumn Farm Dr
2200 SJDN 84095 2281 B5
Autumn Field Dr
700 SNDY 84094 2176 E6
Autumn Gate Ct
3500 SLkC 84044 1960 B7
Autumn Glen Ct
5400 TYVL 84118 2068 C5
Autumn Gold Cir
8500 WJDN 84088 2174 C5
Autumn Heights Dr
5200 RIVN 84065 2385 D4
Autumn Hill Cir
1200 SNDY 84094 2283 B6
Autumn Hill Dr
11400 SNDY 84094 2283 B6
Autumn Hollow Ct
500 DRPR 84020 2388 E3
Autumn Hue Cir
4800 HRMN 84065 2386 A6
Autumn Leaf Cir
10 WDHL 84653 3463 C2
Autumn Leaf Ln
1100 TYVL 84123 2069 E3
Autumn Meadow Cir
9400 SJDN 84095 2280 B2
Autumn Oak Cir
1300 WJDN 84088 2175 D6
Autumn Park Cir
300 KYVL 84037 1345 C2
Autumn Park Dr
5200 TYVL 84118 2069 B4
Autumn Ridge Dr
2300 SNDY 84092 2283 E7
Autumn Ridge Cove
11700 SNDY 84092 2284 A7
Autumn Rose Dr
13400 RIVN 84065 2385 E4
Autumn Spice Ln
4600 TYVL 84123 2069 E3
Autumn View Ct
11200 SJDN 84095 2281 B5
Autumn Wood Ln
2200 TYVL 84118 2069 B4
Avalon
10500 CRHL 84062 2605 B1
Avalon Dr
1500 LYTN 84041 1282 B1
5300 MRRY 84107 2070 E5
Avalon Hills Dr
800 OGDN 84404 1057 B3
Avant Cir
4800 TYVL 84118 2069 A3
Avanyu Cir
9400 CRHL 84062 2605 C4
Avanyu Dr
3600 CRHL 84062 2605 D4
AVC Ln
400 OGDN 84404 1056 E5
500 OGDN 84404 1057 A5
Averett Av
400 SGVL 84663 3143 D3
N Avery Av
10600 HILD 84003 2604 A1
W Avery Av
6500 HILD 84003 2604 A1
Avery Cir
6800 HILD 84003 2604 A1
Aviary Pl
1100 SLkC 84117 2071 B3
Aviation Dr
500 PRVO 84601 3034 B1
7000 WJDN 84084 2174 D3
Avignon Pl
- WJDN 84088 2175 E7
9200 WJDN 84088 2281 E1
Avila Ct
900 SNDY 84094 2283 A5
Avila Dr
800 SNDY 84094 2283 A5
Avion St
5000 WVCY 84120 1961 E5
Avon Pl
400 SSLK 84115 1964 E4
Avondale Dr
3500 CDHT 84121 2178 C4
10300 CRHL 84062 2605 C2
Avonly Bay
8500 SLkC 84044 1960 B7
Avonmore Cir
11000 HILD 84003 2497 C7
Axel Park Rd
5200 WJDN 84088 2279 E1
Ayrshire Dr
5700 MRRY 84107 2070 E6
Aztec Dr
5000 OGDN 84403 1173 D4
9500 CRHL 84062 2605 C4
Aztec Rd
11800 DRPR 84020 2282 B7
Azul Wy
8300 SNDY 84093 2177 D5
Azure Cir
300 DRPR 84020 2388 D3
Azure Meadow Cir
3800 TYVL 84118 2068 C7
Azure Meadow Dr
5800 TYVL 84118 2068 D7
Azurite Cir
12100 HRMN 84065 2386 A1

B

B Av
- PTVW 84404 997 E5
300 DvsC 84056 1228 D5
2300 OGDN 84401 1115 C3
B St
- BMCY 84302 767 A6
- BMCY 84302 827 E2
- CRFD 84016 1227 D7
- KYVL 84041 1283 B7
- ROY 84067 1114 B7
- RVDL 84405 1172 B4
10 SGVL 84663 3143 E3
10 SLCY 84103 1858 D2
Babbling Brook Ct
900 FMTN 84025 1448 D4
Back Nine Cir
9300 SmtC 84098 1865 A3
Badger Hllw
- SmtC 84098 1864 E7
Badger Ln
4900 RIVN 84065 2386 A2
Baer Canyon Rd
1300 FTHT 84037 1346 B1
Baer Creek Cir
1700 KYVL 84037 1345 C5
Baer Creek Dr
10 KYVL 84037 1345 C5
Bagend St
1700 SLkC 84106 1965 D5
Bagley Park Rd
5300 WJDN 84088 2279 E1
5400 WJDN 84088 2173 D7
Bagpiper Cir
10000 SJDN 84095 2280 C3
Bailey Pl
200 SLCY 84101 1858 C5
Bailiff Dr
5400 SLkC 84118 2067 D4
Bainbridge Cir
7300 CDHT 84121 2177 E3
Bainbridge Rd
1500 SNDY 84092 2283 C2
Baird Av
100 SSLK 84115 1964 D6
Baird Cir
300 SSLK 84115 1964 D6
Baker Dr
700 MDVL 84047 2176 E2
800 MDVL 84047 2177 A2
3300 OGDN 84403 1116 C6
Baker St
5300 MRRY 84107 2070 E4
Balboa Dr
7300 MDVL 84047 2176 D3
Bald Eagle Ct
2100 DRPR 84020 2496 E1
Bald Eagle Dr
7700 PKCY 84049 2185 A2
7700 PKCY 84060 2185 A2
8000 WshC 84049 2185 A2
Bald Mountain Cir
1400 ALPN 84004 2498 C3
N Bald Mountain Dr
10 ALPN 84004 2498 C4
S Bald Mountain Dr
10 ALPN 84004 2498 C4
Baldwin Av
6700 WJDN 84084 2174 E1
Baldwin Pk
5300 MRRY 84123 2070 A5
Baldy Dr
4600 WJDN 84088 2174 A4
Balfour Ln
6600 TYVL 84084 2175 E1
Balham Rd
2200 TYVL 84119 2069 B2
Ballerina Wy
5700 HRMN 84065 2385 D4
Ballif Rd
1700 SLCY 84112 1859 D3
Ballot Rd
11800 DRPR 84020 2282 B7
Balmoral Wy
4400 WVCY 84119 2069 A2
Balsa Av
5300 WJDN 84084 2067 D7
Balsa Cir
6200 WJDN 84084 2067 E7
Balsam Av
4400 TYVL 84123 2069 D2
Balsam Cir
1400 TYVL 84123 2069 D2
Balsam Dr
100 CTRV 84014 1551 E2
1400 LYTN 84040 1283 C2
4700 SmtC 84098 1864 C6
Balsam Fir Ct
1400 SJDN 84095 2281 D4
Balsam Pine Dr
4500 WJDN 84088 2174 B7
Baltic Ct
400 SLCY 84103 1858 C1
Bamberger Ct
- NSLK 84054 1653 A7
Bamberger Dr
700 ANFK 84003 2711 E1
700 UthC 84003 2711 E1
800 UthC 84003 2712 A1
Bamberger Rd
- NSLK 84054 1653 A6
- UthC 84651 3354 E2
- UthC 84651 3355 A3
- UthC 84660 3354 E2
- UthC 84660 3355 A3
Bamberger Wy
- CTRV 84014 1551 D4
Bambrough Pl
1700 SLCY 84108 1965 E1
Bamburgh Wy
3400 WVCY 84128 1961 A6
Bamell Dr
6400 WVCY 84128 1961 B4
Bampton Ln
4100 SLkC 84118 2068 C3
Banburry Dr
- SRCS 84075 1227 A6
Banbury Cir
500 NSLK 84054 1652 D5
7300 CDHT 84121 2178 A3
Banbury Dr
1200 SRCS 84075 1227 A7
1500 SRCS 84075 1281 A1
Banbury Ln
4700 OGDN 84403 1173 D3
Banbury Rd
2700 CDHT 84121 2178 B3
Bancroft Ct
10 PKCY 84060 2078 D2
Baneberry Wy
3600 TYVL 84118 2068 D5
Bangerter Hwy
- BFDL 84065 2387 C5
- BFDL 84065 2388 A5
- DRPR 84020 2388 A5
- RIVN 84065 2280 D7
- RIVN 84065 2386 C2
- RIVN 84065 2387 C5
- SJDN 84095 2280 D7
- SLCY 84104 1856 C3
- SLCY 84104 1962 C3
- SLCY 84120 1962 C3
Bangerter Hwy
- TYVL 84084 2068 D6
- TYVL 84084 2174 D3
- TYVL 84118 2068 D3
- WJDN 84084 2068 D6
- WJDN 84084 2174 D3
- WJDN 84088 2174 D7
- WJDN 84088 2280 D4
- WVCY 84120 1962 C3
- WVCY 84120 2068 D3
Bangerter Hwy SR-154
- BFDL 84065 2387 C5
- BFDL 84065 2388 A5
- DRPR 84020 2388 A5
- RIVN 84065 2280 D7
- RIVN 84065 2386 C2
- RIVN 84065 2387 C5
- SJDN 84095 2280 D7
- SLCY 84104 1856 C7
- SLCY 84104 1962 C3
- SLCY 84120 1962 C3
- TYVL 84084 2068 D6
- TYVL 84084 2174 D3
- TYVL 84118 2068 D3
- WJDN 84084 2068 D6
- WJDN 84084 2174 D3
- WJDN 84088 2174 D7
- WJDN 84088 2280 D4
- WVCY 84120 1962 C3
- WVCY 84120 2068 D3
Bank Av
100 SSLK 84115 1964 D5
Banks Ct
200 SLCY 84102 1859 A3
W Banks Rd
2200 UthC 84660 3141 B5
Banner Dr
2900 SJDN 84095 2281 A3
3100 SJDN 84095 2280 E3
Bannock Cir
5000 WVCY 84120 2068 A1
Bannock Dr
2900 PRVO 84604 2928 D1
4100 WVCY 84120 2068 A1
Bannock St
3600 WVCY 84120 1962 A7
Bannor Hill Cir
10000 SNDY 84092 2283 D2
Bannor Hill Rd
10000 SNDY 84092 2283 D2
Banquet Av
4800 WJDN 84084 2068 A7
5100 WJDN 84084 2067 E7
Barbara Cir
1500 WJDN 84084 2175 C2
Barbara Pl
1000 SLCY 84102 1859 A4
Barbara Wy
3700 SLkC 84124 1966 D7
Barbara Ast
200 LYTN 84041 1282 E3
W Barberry Dr
1000 TYVL 84123 2069 E3
Barbey Dr
2500 SLkC 84109 1966 A4
Barcelona Dr
2400 SLkC 84093 2178 A5
Barcon Rd
1500 SLkC 84117 2071 C5
Bard Ln
8200 WJDN 84088 2175 D5
Bardee Ln
100 KYVL 84037 1345 C5
Bareback Rd
10 FMTN 84025 1447 D2
Baringwood Cir
3500 TYVL 84118 2068 D5
Barium Ln
9800 SLkC 84094 2283 A2
Barium St
9500 SNDY 84094 2283 A1
Barke Cir
4700 TYVL 84123 2069 D3
Barker Pkwy
2300 NHON 84414 999 B6
Barker Rd
2000 WVCY 84119 2069 B1
4100 TYVL 84119 2069 B1
Barletta Ct
4700 WJDN 84084 2174 A1
Barley Cir
2200 WJDN 84084 2175 B2
Barley Wy
2100 SRSP 84043 2601 D5
Barlow St
300 CRFD 84015 1227 B3
Bar M Cir
2800 WVCY 84119 2069 A1
Barnard St
10 CTRV 84014 1551 E1
Barnes Cir
1000 LEHI 84043 2603 B5
Barnes Dr
100 KYVL 84037 1345 A1
W Barnett Ln
3400 UthC 84651 3461 E4
Barney St
3100 WVCY 84119 1963 A5
Barneys Peak Cir
13900 HRMN 84065 2385 E5
Barnfield Wy
3500 WVCY 84119 1962 D7
Barnhill Bay
3100 CDHT 84121 2178 D2
Barnsley Ln
4500 SJDN 84095 2280 B3
Barnstable Dr
8300 WJDN 84088 2173 D6
Barnwood Wy
1000 SNDY 84094 2177 C3
Barnwood Bay
3100 CDHT 84121 2178 D2
Baronay Cir
9100 SNDY 84093 2178 A7
Baroness Pl
1700 SLCY 84116 1753 C5
Baroness St
1400 SLCY 84116 1753 C5
Barrel Ct
13600 HRMN 84065 2385 C5
Barrett Av
10 ANFK 84003 2711 C1
Barrett Cir
200 ANFK 84003 2711 B2
Barrett Park Cir
11100 SNDY 84092 2283 D5
Barrett Park Dr
1700 SNDY 84092 2283 D5
Barrington Cir
9000 WJDN 84088 2174 B7
Barrington Dr
- KYVL 84037 1344 E2
4400 WJDN 84088 2174 B7
Barrington Wy
10 LYTN 84041 1228 E6
Barrows Av
700 SLkC 84106 1964 E5
700 SLkC 84106 1965 A5
Barry Cir
300 NSLK 84054 1653 B7
Bartels Cir
3200 WJDN 84084 2174 E3
Barton Ct
900 BNFL 84010 1654 C2
Barton Creek Cir
1300 BNFL 84010 1654 B1
Barton Creek Ln
1300 BNFL 84010 1654 C1
Barton Creek Wy
900 WBNF 84087 1551 B5
Barton Crest Ct
3800 WVCY 84120 1962 D7
Barton Hollow Dr
1300 WJDN 84084 2175 D3
Barton Park Dr
4800 WJDN 84084 2068 A7
Barton's Ln
3200 BFDL 84065 2386 E7
Basel Dr
1300 WshC 84049 2396 D3
Basils Wy
4000 WVCY 84120 2068 C2
Basin St
9200 SNDY 84070 2176 A7
9200 SNDY 84070 2282 A1
Basswood Cove
3500 WVCY 84120 1961 E6
Bastile Dr
5400 TYVL 84118 2069 A5
Bateman Ln
500 ALPN 84004 2497 E5
Bateman Pl
1200 WJDN 84084 2175 D1
Bateman Dell Wy
6800 WJDN 84084 2175 E1
Bateman Field Dr
6800 WJDN 84084 2175 E1
Bateman Point Dr
1100 WJDN 84084 2175 D1
Bateman Ponds Cir
6800 WJDN 84084 2175 E1
Bateman Ponds Wy
1100 WJDN 84084 2175 D2
Battle Creek Ct
6300 WVCY 84118 2067 C7
Battlefield Cove
7600 WJDN 84084 2175 D4
Baty Dr
2800 WVCY 84119 1963 A4
Baur Av
10 PVDN 84332 592 A1
Bavarian Ct
8200 CDHT 84093 2178 B5
Bawden Av
3600 WVCY 84120 2068 D1
Baxter Dr
800 SJDN 84095 2282 A4
1900 HRCY 84032 2398 D7
Baxter Ln
- CchC 84319 650 D6
Bay Cir
3500 LEHI 84043 2495 A6
E Bay Wy
- SGVL 84663 3035 E6
Bayberry Cir
11500 DRPR 84020 2282 D6
13300 UthC 84004 2498 B1
Bayhill Dr
10200 CRHL 84062 2605 C2
Bay Leaf Dr
1700 SRSP 84043 2601 E6
Bay Meadow Cir
10800 SNDY 84092 2283 B5
Bay Meadow Dr
10600 SNDY 84092 2283 B4
Bayport Wy
700 TYVL 84123 2070 A3
N Bayview Dr
800 FMTN 84025 1346 C7
W Bayview Dr
100 FMTN 84025 1346 C7
Baywood Cir
5300 SLkC 84117 2071 D5
Baywood Dr
1800 SLkC 84117 2071 D5
Beachwood Dr
- FRWT 84404 1055 D3
500 DRPR 84020 2388 E5
Beacon Av
10 LYTN 84041 1283 B4
Beacon Dr
1300 SLCY 84108 1859 E7
2300 SLCY 84108 1860 A7
Beacon Hill Cir
1300 TYVL 84123 2069 D5
Beacon Hill Dr
1300 TYVL 84123 2069 D5
Beagle Dr
2400 SNDY 84092 2284 A1
Bear Canyon Dr
3300 CRHL 84062 2605 D5
11600 DRPR 84020 2283 A6
11600 SNDY 84020 2283 A6
11600 SNDY 84094 2283 A6
Bear Canyon Rd
800 SNDY 84094 2283 A6
Bear Castle Cove
12500 DRPR 84020 2389 D2
Bearcat Dr
300 SSLK 84115 1964 B2
Bear Claw Cir
1800 DRPR 84020 2389 D3
Bear Creek Cir
12400 DRPR 84020 2389 D1
Bear Creek Dr
12400 DRPR 84020 2389 D1
Bear Cub Cir
12400 DRPR 84020 2389 D2
Beardsley Pl
900 SSLK 84119 1963 E3
Beargrass Rd
6600 WJDN 84084 2174 A1
6700 WJDN 84084 2173 E2
Bear Hills Cir
2300 DRPR 84020 2283 E7
2400 DRPR 84020 2284 A7
Bear Hills Ct
2300 DRPR 84020 2389 E1
Bear Hills Dr
2300 DRPR 84020 2284 A7
2300 DRPR 84020 2389 E1
12000 DRPR 84020 2283 E7
Bear Hollow Cir
1100 DRPR 84020 2389 B3
Bear Hollow Dr
1900 SmtC 84098 1971 D5
13200 DRPR 84020 2389 B4
Bear Hollow Cove
1100 DRPR 84020 2389 B4
Bear Mountain Cir
2000 DRPR 84020 2389 D2
Bear Mountain Dr
1800 DRPR 84020 2389 D2
Bear Park Pl
12500 DRPR 84020 2389 D2
Bear Ridge Dr
5100 SmtC 84098 1971 D4
Bear Ridge Cove
2000 DRPR 84020 2389 D2
Bear River Rd
3300 SJDN 84095 2280 E4
Beartooth Cir
900 DRPR 84020 2389 A7
Bear View Dr
4800 SmtC 84098 1971 C5
Beau Cir
4800 SLkC 84118 2068 A5
Beau Meadow Ln
11600 DRPR 84020 2282 D7
Beaumont Cir
1800 SLkC 84121 2071 D6
Beaumont Ct
400 SLCY 84116 1858 B1
Beaumont Dr
- KYVL 84037 1344 D2
5700 SLkC 84121 2071 C6
8000 SLkC 84093 2177 C5
8000 SNDY 84093 2177 C5
Beau View Ct
3700 WVCY 84120 1962 D4
Beaven Cir
2600 WVCY 84128 1961 A4
Beaver Cir
- WVCY 84119 1962 E6
3000 WVCY 84119 1963 A6
Beaver St
3100 WVCY 84119 1963 A5
Beaverbrook Ln
4900 MRRY 84117 2071 A4
Bechers Brook Wy
13300 DRPR 84020 2389 C4
Beck St
- NSLK 84054 1754 A1
1100 SLCY 84103 1754 B6
1100 SLCY 84116 1754 B6
1800 SLCY 84103 1753 E4
1800 SLCY 84116 1753 E4
Beck St US-89
- NSLK 84054 1754 A1
1100 SLCY 84103 1754 B6
1100 SLCY 84116 1754 B6
1800 SLCY 84103 1753 E4
1800 SLCY 84116 1753 E4
Beckford Cir
3400 WJDN 84088 2174 E4
Beckstead Ln
- SJDN 84095 2281 C5
Becky Cir
3700 SLkC 84109 1965 E7
Becky's Cove
800 OREM 84097 2821 A7
Becraft Ln
- OGDN 84404 1056 C6
Bedford Cir
4100 DvsC 84056 1228 A5
Bedford Dr
1000 KYVL 84037 1284 A6
4300 PRVO 84604 2821 E5
Bedford Rd
1000 KYVL 84037 1284 A6
2700 WVCY 84119 2069 A2
3000 WVCY 84119 2068 E2
Bedrock Ln
10200 SNDY 84092 2284 C3
Bee Ct
2300 OGDN 84401 1115 C3
Beecher Av
10 BMCY 84302 767 B5
Beechnut Wy
1300 DvsC 84056 1228 A2
Beechwood Cir
1500 TYVL 84123 2069 C2
E Beechwood Dr
1400 LYTN 84040 1283 C1
Beechwood Rd
4300 TYVL 84123 2069 D3
Beehive Av
1300 WDCR 84010 1653 C2
Beehive Cir
3400 WVCY 84119 1963 A6
Beehive Dr
700 SmtC 84098 1867 A7
800 SmtC 84098 1866 E7
Beehive St
3300 WVCY 84119 1963 A5
Beetdigger Blvd
10 SNDY 84070 2282 C2
Begonia Cir
5200 WJDN 84084 2067 E7
Begonia Dr
6300 WJDN 84084 2067 E7
6400 WJDN 84084 2173 E1
Begonia Pl
5200 WJDN 84084 2173 E1
Begonia Wy
5200 WJDN 84084 2173 E1
Bekkemellom Wy
7400 CDHT 84093 2177 D3
Belaire Dr
2000 SLCY 84108 1966 B2
2000 SLCY 84109 1966 B2
Beldon Pl
300 SLCY 84111 1858 D4
Belfast Dr
3800 SLkC 84044 1960 C7
Belfort Dr
3600 WVCY 84120 2068 D2
Bell Av
1400 SLCY 84104 1857 D6
Bellagio Ct
5400 HRMN 84065 2385 D2
Bellagio Wy
5500 HRMN 84065 2385 E2
Bella Rosa Cove
5800 HRMN 84065 2385 C5
Bella Verde Ct
4500 SLkC 84107 2071 A2
Bella Vie Ct
1400 MRRY 84121 2071 B6
Bella Vista Ct
200 FMTN 84025 1346 C4
Bella Vista Dr
1800 FMTN 84025 1346 C4
6800 CDHT 84121 2177 D2
N Bella Vista Dr
500 OREM 84097 2821 B3
Bellaviti Cir
3300 WJDN 84084 2174 E3
Bell Canyon Cir
10000 SLkC 84092 2284 B3
Bell Canyon Dr
900 SNDY 84094 2283 A4
Bell Canyon Rd
3000 SLkC 84092 2284 B2
10000 SNDY 84092 2284 C3
Bellcastle Cir
1100 SNDY 84094 2283 B5
Belle Ct
- FTHT 84037 1346 B3
Belle Isis Bay
13800 HRMN 84065 2385 D5
Belle Meadows Wy
1000 MRRY 84121 2071 A6
Bellemont Ct
10 PKCY 84060 2184 E1
10 PKCY 84060 2185 A1
Belle Starr Ct
2100 PKCY 84060 2078 E3
Bellevue Ct
10 PKCY 84060 2078 E7
10 PKCY 84060 2079 A7
Bell Flower St
- SLCY 84104 1856 E5
Bello Av
6800 WVCY 84128 1961 A6
7000 WVCY 84128 1960 E6
Bell Oaks Cir
3200 SLkC 84092 2284 C2
Bell Oaks Dr
9700 SLkC 84092 2284 C2
Bell Ridge Dr
11200 SNDY 84094 2283 B6
Bell Tower Ln
1900 SLkC 84109 1965 D5
Bell View Cir
1200 SNDY 84094 2283 B4
Bellwood Ln
900 MRRY 84123 2069 E5
Bel Mar Dr
600 SOGN 84403 1116 A7
800 OGDN 84403 1116 A7
Belmont Av
200 SLCY 84111 1858 D6
700 SLCY 84105 1858 E6
700 SLCY 84105 1859 A6
Belmont Dr
- FMTN 84025 1448 A2
1000 BMCY 84302 767 B4
Belmont Pl
300 PRVO 84606 2928 E6
Belmont Downs Ct
6100 WVCY 84128 1961 C4
Belmont Downs Ln
2700 WVCY 84128 1961 C4
Belmont Hills Pl
11100 SJDN 84095 2281 A5
Belmore Dr
10 KYVL 84037 1345 C2
Belmour Wy
4600 HLDY 84117 2071 E2
Belnap Cir
700 OGDN 84403 1116 A6
8000 WJDN 84088 2174 A5
Belsaw Cir
1100 SNDY 84094 2283 B5
Belton Cir
2800 SNDY 84093 2178 B7
Belton Ln
9200 SNDY 84093 2178 B7
9200 SNDY 84093 2284 B1
Belvedere Wy
- LYTN 84041 1282 E1
Belview Av
300 MRRY 84107 2070 D6
Ben Air Cir
1800 TYVL 84084 2069 C7
Ben Air Dr
1800 TYVL 84084 2069 C7
Ben Armine Cir
4100 SJDN 84095 2280 C2
Benbow St
500 MRRY 84107 2070 E4
Bench Cove
13200 DRPR 84020 2389 A3
Benchland Cir
2500 RIVN 84065 2387 B2
Benchmark Cir
2200 SLCY 84109 1966 B2
Benchmark Dr
2800 SLCY 84109 1966 B2
2900 SLkC 84109 1966 B2
Bench View Dr
1000 OGDN 84404 1057 B3
Benchview Cove
12900 DRPR 84020 2388 E3
Bendamere Cir
2100 SLCY 84109 1965 E4
Ben Davis Pk
5200 MRRY 84123 2070 A5
Bendixon Cir
2600 WVCY 84128 1960 E4
Bendixon Dr
6900 WVCY 84128 1961 A4
7100 WVCY 84128 1960 E4
Bendixon Wy
2600 WVCY 84128 1961 A4
Benecia Dr
6600 CDHT 84121 2178 A1
Bengal Blvd
2000 CDHT 84093 2177 E3
2000 CDHT 84121 2177 E3
2300 CDHT 84093 2178 B4
2300 CDHT 84121 2178 B4
Bengal Bend Cove
2400 CDHT 84093 2178 A3
2400 CDHT 84121 2178 A3
Bengal Hills Cove
2000 CDHT 84121 2177 D3
Benjamin Rd
8500 UthC 84651 3354 E2
8500 UthC 84660 3354 E2
Benjamin Rd SR-115
8500 UthC 84651 3354 E2
8500 UthC 84660 3354 E2
Ben Lomond Av
4800 SOGN 84403 1172 E3
Ben Lomond Dr
500 SOGN 84403 1172 E3
500 SOGN 84403 1173 A4
Ben Lomond Peak Dr
13800 RIVN 84065 2386 A5
Bennett Cir
1300 FMTN 84025 1346 B5
Bennett Rd
1500 SLCY 84104 1857 B7
1500 SLCY 84104 1963 B1
Bennett St
1600 LYTN 84041 1282 D1
Bennion Blvd
1300 TYVL 84123 2069 C7
1700 TYVL 84084 2069 C7
1700 TYVL 84118 2069 C7
2900 TYVL 84084 2068 E7
2900 TYVL 84118 2068 E7
Bennion Cir
3100 TYVL 84118 2068 E6
Bennion Dr
5600 TYVL 84118 2068 E5
Bennion Rd
4100 TYVL 84119 2069 C2
Bennion Heights Cir
2200 TYVL 84084 2069 C6
Bennion Pines Ct
2400 TYVL 84118 2069 A3
Bennion View Ct
6100 TYVL 84118 2069 C7
Benson Wy
10 SNDY 84070 2176 C7
Bentbrook Ln
10 SNDY 84092 2284 A5
Bentham Av
9100 SNDY 84093 2177 D7
Bentley Cir
- KYVL 84037 1344 D2
Bently Cir
9000 SNDY 84093 2178 B7
Bently Ct
- KYVL 84037 1344 D2
Bent Nail Dr
5000 TYVL 84118 2069 B4
Bentoak Dr
3700 WVCY 84120 1962 C4
Bentwood Ln
10 SNDY 84092 2284 B5
Benview Av
3800 WVCY 84120 2068 C2
Benview Dr
4000 WVCY 84120 2068 C2
Be Prepared Wy
900 HRCY 84032 2398 C5
Berault Ct
6700 WJDN 84084 2173 C1
Bergen Cir
12700 RIVN 84065 2386 E2
Berger Ln
100 MRRY 84107 2070 C3
Berghalde Ln
3500 HLDY 84121 2072 C7
Berg Hollow Ln
11200 SJDN 84095 2282 A6
Berkeley Cir
2600 SLCY 84109 1965 E4
Berkeley St
1800 SLCY 84108 1965 E2
2100 SLCY 84109 1965 E3
Berkshire Cir
2800 SLkC 84044 1960 D4
Berkshire Rd
800 WDCR 84087 1653 B3
Bermuda
10600 CRHL 84062 2605 C1
Bermuda Ln
1300 RIVN 84065 2387 D3
Bern Wy
300 WshC 84049 2291 A6
Bernada Cir
4500 SLkC 84124 2072 C2
Bernada Dr
3200 SLkC 84124 2072 C2
Bernadine Dr
2300 SLCY 84109 1965 E2
2300 SLCY 84109 1966 A2
Bernard Fisher Hwy
- CRFD 84015 1227 E6
- CRFD 84015 1228 A6
Bernard Fisher Hwy SR-193
- CRFD 84015 1227 E6
- CRFD 84015 1228 A6
Bernay Cir
900 SNDY 84094 2177 A5
Bernice Wy
100 NSLK 84054 1653 C7
Bernina Dr
2900 TYVL 84118 2069 A6
3000 TYVL 84118 2068 E6
Berridale Cir
4100 SJDN 84095 2280 C2

STREET
Block City ZIP Map# Grid

N Berringer Av
- OGDN 84404 1056 B5
S Berringer Av
- OGDN 84404 1056 B5
Berry Ln
13200 DRPR 84020 2389 C4
Berry Creek Dr
4900 RIVN 84065 2386 A3
Berry Glen Cir
7700 WJDN 84084 2174 B3
Berryknoll Cir
11500 DRPR 84020 2282 D6
Berry Patch Ct
13200 DRPR 84020 2389 C3
Berry Patch Wy
- SRSP 84043 2601 E5
Berrywood Ct
10700 SNDY 84070 2282 E4
Bertha Dr
800 OREM 84057 2820 D3
Berula Cir
6700 WJDN 84084 2173 E1
Berwick Pl
2700 WVCY 84119 2069 A1
Berwick View Ct
13800 HRMN 84065 2385 E5
Beryl Av
100 SSLK 84115 1964 D3
Bessie Ln
- PVDN 84332 592 A1
Best Av
900 SLkC 84106 1965 A6
Beth Cir
3600 TYVL 84118 2068 D5
Bethany Hills Cove
1500 BFDL 84065 2387 C5
Beth Park Cir
3900 WVCY 84120 1962 C7
Beth Park Dr
3700 WVCY 84120 1962 B6
Betsy Ross Cir
7300 SLkC 84044 1960 E5
Bettina Ln
8100 SNDY 84093 2177 C5
Betty Dr
9200 WJDN 84088 2174 C7
9200 WJDN 84088 2280 C1
Betty Gene Dr
6400 MRRY 84107 2176 C1
Betula Dr
1700 RIVN 84065 2387 C1
Beus Dr
1300 SNST 84015 1227 D2
1700 OGDN 84403 1173 D1
Beverlee Ann Dr
100 DRPR 84020 2282 B7
Beverly Av
400 OREM 84057 2820 B4
Beverly Dr
1400 OGDN 84403 1116 C4
Beverly St
2400 SLCY 84106 1965 C3
Beverly Wy
1000 BNFL 84010 1654 A3
Beverly Glen Av
2400 WJDN 84084 2175 A2
Bevwood Cir
4100 SLkC 84124 2072 B1
Beynon Ct
600 MDVL 84047 2176 A4
Biathalon Cir
3400 TYVL 84084 2068 D7
Biathalon Lp
5400 SmtC 84098 1971 D4
Bigarade Ln
3200 TYVL 84118 2068 E4
Big Buck Cove
13800 BFDL 84065 2386 C5
E Big Cottonwood Canyon Rd
- SLkC 84098 2182 D1
- SLkC 84098 2183 A3
3200 CDHT 84121 2178 D2
4000 SLkC 84121 2178 D2
E Big Cottonwd Cyn Rd SR-190
- SLkC 84098 2182 D1
- SLkC 84098 2183 A3
3800 CDHT 84121 2178 D2
4000 SLkC 84121 2178 D2
S Big Cottonwood Canyon Rd
3100 HLDY 84121 2178 B1
6400 CDHT 84121 2178 B1
S Big Hollow Rd
3000 WshC 84032 2505 C2
Big Horn Cir
5300 WJDN 84084 2173 E4
Bighorn Pkwy
5800 WbrC 84310 1002 B4
W Big Leaf Ct
700 PYSN 84651 3461 D1
Bigler Ln
700 MIDW 84049 2397 A2
Big Mountain Dr
700 TYVL 84123 2070 A3
Big Oak Dr
- WVCY 84119 1963 C3
Big Pine Cir
1200 SNDY 84094 2177 B4
Big Pine Dr
1100 SNDY 84094 2177 B4
Big River Ct
900 SSLK 84119 1963 E7
Big River Wy
3800 SSLK 84119 1963 E7
Big Rock Ln
3500 SLkC 84092 2178 C7
Big Sky Dr
400 SNDY 84070 2282 E6
1900 WbrC 84310 1001 B7
E Big Sky Dr
1900 WbrC 84310 1001 B7
Big Snowy Ct
800 DRPR 84020 2389 A7
Big Springs Dr
5300 WJDN 84088 2173 E4
Big Spruce Wy
3200 SmtC 84098 1865 A7
3200 SmtC 84098 1971 B1
Big Var Wy
1500 RIVN 84065 2387 D1
Bilbo Av
7600 WJDN 84084 2175 C3
Bill Bailey Blvd
1100 OGDN 84404 1056 A3
Billinis Rd
500 SSLK 84119 1964 A6
Bills Dr
3800 WVCY 84128 1961 D7
Billy Mitchell Rd
300 SLCY 84116 1855 E2
Biltmore Av
100 MRRY 84107 2070 D1
Binford St
100 OGDN 84401 1115 D4
700 OGDN 84401 1116 A4
W Binford St
800 OGDN 84401 1115 B4
Bing Av
3200 PRRY 84302 827 B7
Bing Cir
400 FMTN 84025 1346 C5
Bing Ct
700 KYVL 84037 1345 E2
Bing St
- SNQN 84655 3461 B7
- UthC 84655 3461 B7
Bingham Creek Dr
3700 WJDN 84088 2174 D7
Bingham Hills Ct
9200 WJDN 84088 2174 E7
Bingham Miner Ct
10000 SJDN 84095 2281 C3
Bingham Park Dr
4400 WJDN 84088 2174 B7
9200 WJDN 84088 2280 B1
Bingham View Cir
4400 WJDN 84088 2174 B6
Bingham View Dr
8400 WJDN 84088 2174 B6
Birch Av
3600 OGDN 84403 1116 C7
Birch Cir
10 CRFD 84015 1228 A5
700 LYTN 84041 1283 B4
1000 ALPN 84004 2498 B2
1100 HRCY 84032 2398 E2
3300 SLkC 84124 1966 C7
W Birch Cir
1400 MPTN 84664 3251 A2
Birch Dr
3700 SLkC 84109 1966 C7
3900 SLkC 84124 1966 C7
S Birch Dr
500 SPFK 84660 3249 E4
Birch Ln
900 PRVO 84604 2928 E4
1300 DvsC 84056 1228 B2
2200 OGDN 84401 1116 A3
Birch St
- SGVL 84663 3035 E6
700 CRFD 84015 1228 A5
7600 MDVL 84047 2176 C3
Birchbrook Cir
1000 CDHT 84121 2177 A1
Birch Canyon Rd
- CchC 84335 400 C1
- SHFD 84335 400 B2
Birchfield Ln
600 MRRY 84107 2176 E1
Birch Hill Ln
10 DRPR 84020 2495 C1
Birch Hollow Cove
2100 DRPR 84020 2389 E1
Birchpoint Dr
1100 MRRY 84117 2071 B5
Birch River Rd
3600 WVCY 84119 1963 E6
Birchtree Ln
10 SNDY 84092 2283 E5
Birchwood Dr
200 OREM 84057 2820 E4
900 MRRY 84121 2071 A6
Birchwood Wy
9600 SNDY 84092 2283 E2
Bird Ct
2100 WJDN 84088 2175 B7
Bird Dr
1300 WshC 84049 2396 D3
Bird Dog Cove
12600 DRPR 84020 2388 E2
Bird Haven Rd
4000 WVCY 84119 2069 B1
Birdie Cir
1000 NSLK 84054 1653 D7
Birdie Ln
600 FTHT 84037 1346 A3
Birdie Wy
4500 SJDN 84095 2280 B2
Bird Refuge Rd
- BxEC 84302 764 E7
- BxEC 84302 765 A6
Birdsong Dr
2200 WVCY 84119 1963 B7
Birmingham Ln
100 NSLK 84054 1652 C5
Birnam Woods Wy
9800 SJDN 84095 2280 C2
Biscayne Dr
7600 CDHT 84121 2178 B4
Bishop Ln
10 KYVL 84037 1345 C1
Bishop Pl
200 SLCY 84103 1858 B1
Bishop St
3600 WVCY 84119 1963 A6
Bishops St
400 KYVL 84037 1345 A2
Bitner Ranch Rd
- SmtC 84098 1866 C7
300 SmtC 84098 1972 A2
1300 SmtC 84098 1971 E1
Bitterbrush Ln
- DRPR 84020 2388 C7
Bitterroot Cir
3200 TYVL 84118 2068 E3
Bitterroot Dr
3300 TYVL 84118 2068 E3
Bitterroot Pl
3200 TYVL 84118 2068 E3
N Black Av
- OGDN 84404 1056 A4
S Black Av
- OGDN 84404 1056 A5
Black Angus Dr
1800 SLCY 84116 1753 B4
Blackberry Cir
13000 DRPR 84020 2388 B3
Blackberry Dr
200 SRSP 84043 2601 E5
Blackburn Cir
2700 HLDY 84117 2072 A3
Black Cherry Cir
3200 PRRY 84302 827 B7
S Black Cherry Wy
11100 SJDN 84095 2281 D5
W Black Cherry Wy
1300 SJDN 84095 2281 D5
Black Currant Ct
8700 SLkC 84044 1960 A5
Black Currant Wy
8700 SLkC 84044 1960 A5
Black Diamond Cove
8700 WJDN 84088 2173 D6
Black Elk Wy
4400 WJDN 84088 2280 B1
E Black Forest Dr
1000 SNDY 84094 2283 A6
S Black Forest Dr
11400 SNDY 84094 2283 A6
Black Fox Ct
1200 DRPR 84020 2389 B2
Blackfriar Cir
7400 WJDN 84084 2174 E3
Black Granite Wy
3200 WVCY 84120 1962 A5
Blackgum Ct
8600 SLkC 84044 1960 B5
Blackhawk Cir
1600 PTGV 84062 2713 C4
Black Hawk Dr
- LOGN 84321 527 C6
Blackhawk Dr
1500 PTGV 84062 2713 C4
3500 WVCY 84120 1962 D6
Blackhawk St
700 PYSN 84651 3355 A3
Blackhawk Tr
- SmtC 84098 1971 E1
- SmtC 84098 1972 A1
Blackhawk Wy
600 SLCY 84108 1859 E5
Black Horn Pl
3700 SLkC 84092 2284 D2
E Black Horse Lp
1100 SPFK 84660 3250 B1
N Black Horse Lp
600 SPFK 84660 3250 A1
Blackjack Rd
- ALTA 84049 2181 D7
Black Mica Av
5800 SLkC 84118 2067 C5
Black Mica Cir
5400 SLkC 84118 2067 C5
Black Mountain Cir
1300 OGDN 84404 1057 B2
Black Mountain Dr
1400 OGDN 84404 1057 B2
Black Oak Dr
6400 WJDN 84088 2173 B5
Black Pine St
8800 WJDN 84088 2174 B7
Black Powder Dr
- HRMN 84065 2386 B1
Blackrock Rd
3200 CchC 84321 462 A2
Blacksmith Ct
- LOGN 84321 527 C7
Blacksmith Ln
1400 DRPR 84020 2389 B2
Blacksmith Rd
3700 SmtC 84098 1864 E6
3700 SmtC 84098 1865 A6
Blacksmith Fork Canyon Rd
1400 CchC 84319 652 D4
1400 CchC 84321 652 D4
1400 HYRM 84319 652 D4
1400 HYRM 84321 652 D4
Blacksmith Fork Cyn Rd SR-101
1400 CchC 84319 652 D4
1400 CchC 84321 652 D4
1400 HYRM 84319 652 D4
1400 HYRM 84321 652 D4
Blackstone Rd
6500 CDHT 84121 2177 D1
Black Swan Dr
4600 SLkC 84117 2071 A3
Blaine Av
300 SLCY 84115 1964 D1
1500 SLCY 84105 1965 C1
1700 SLCY 84108 1965 C1
2300 SLCY 84108 1966 A1
Blaine Cir
2300 SLCY 84108 1965 E1
Blaine Dr
6400 MRRY 84107 2176 C1
Blair Cir
3500 SSLK 84115 1964 D6
Blair St
400 SLCY 84111 1858 D4
1300 SLCY 84115 1858 D7
1600 SLCY 84115 1964 D1
2100 SSLK 84115 1964 D2
Blake Cir
11100 SJDN 84095 2282 A5
Blake Ct
200 LOGN 84321 528 C2
Blake Dr
2400 TYVL 84118 2069 A5
Blanch St
3500 WVCY 84128 1961 D6
Blanck Cir
2400 TYVL 84118 2069 B6
Blayde Dr
13700 HRMN 84065 2385 B5
Blaze Ct
13000 RIVN 84065 2387 D3
Blaze Meadows Rd
- SJDN 84095 2280 E6
3000 SJDN 84095 2281 A6
Blazer Cir
2300 RIVN 84065 2387 B4
Bliss Ct
200 SLCY 84116 1858 B2
Blisswood Ct
100 MDVL 84047 2176 C3
Blisswood Dr
7500 MDVL 84047 2176 C3
Blister Rd
200 MDVL 84047 2176 D1
200 MRRY 84047 2176 D1
Blithfield Cir
1800 SNDY 84092 2283 D2
Bloomfield Pl
1400 SLCY 84116 1753 C5
Bloomsbury Cove
900 MRRY 84123 2069 E6
900 MRRY 84123 2070 A6
Blossom Cir
500 FTHT 84037 1346 B2
Blossom Ct
- SRSP 84043 2601 D4
Blossom Dr
1300 SNDY 84092 2283 B2
Blossom Ln
1400 OGDN 84404 1116 B1
Blossom Glen Wy
4500 ROY 84067 1171 C2
Blossom Tree Ln
10800 SNDY 84070 2282 E5
Blossom Valley Ln
6300 WVCY 84118 2067 C7
Blossomwood Cir
2200 SNDY 84093 2283 D1
Blue Admiral Ct
4800 RIVN 84065 2386 B5
Blue Admiral Dr
13700 RIVN 84065 2386 A5
Bluebell Cir
1400 BNFL 84010 1654 B3
Bluebell Dr
1900 BNFL 84010 1654 B3
2900 SLkC 84124 2072 B1
Blue Bell Dr N
4000 WbrC 84310 1001 B7
Blueberry Hl
1500 SNDY 84093 2177 C5
Blue Beu Dr
3900 WbrC 84310 1001 B7
Bluebird Cir
3800 WVCY 84120 2068 C1
Bluebird Dr
4100 WVCY 84120 2068 D1
Blue Bird Rd
1600 OREM 84097 2713 E7
Bluebird St
1200 WVCY 84119 1963 D7
Bluebonnet Cir
5200 WJDN 84084 2173 E1
Blue Brook Cove
11300 SJDN 84095 2281 D6
Blue Crest Dr
3200 WVCY 84119 2068 E2
Blue Flower Ct
6700 WJDN 84084 2174 A1
Blue Fox Cir
3600 TYVL 84118 2068 D6
Blue Grass Cir
- KYVL 84037 1283 D7
1400 CDHT 84121 2177 B1
Blue Grouse Wy
1500 WVCY 84119 1963 C3
Blue Haven Dr
3200 WVCY 84119 2068 E2
Blue Heron Cir
900 DRPR 84020 2283 D7
Blue Heron Dr
11800 DRPR 84020 2283 A7
Blue Heron Wy
900 DRPR 84020 2283 D7
Blue Holly Ct
5100 WJDN 84088 2173 D7
Blue Iron Wy
5800 SLkC 84118 2067 C6
Blue Jay Cir
8800 CDHT 84121 2178 D6
Blue Jay Ln
3700 CDHT 84121 2178 D6
Blue Jay St
4100 WVCY 84120 2068 A1
Blue Lake Ln
4500 WVCY 84120 1962 B5
Blue Meadow Dr
3900 TYVL 84118 2068 C6
Bluemont Cir
1500 TYVL 84123 2175 C1
Bluemont Dr
1300 TYVL 84123 2069 D7
6400 TYVL 84123 2175 D1
Blue Quail Cir
4700 TYVL 84118 2069 B3
Blue Ribbon Bay Dr
7600 SLkC 84044 1960 D7
Blueridge Cir
4700 TYVL 84118 2068 E3
Blueridge Dr
3200 TYVL 84118 2068 E3
Blue Ridge Ln
700 ALPN 84004 2498 A6
Blue Roan Ln
11300 SNDY 84092 2283 D4
Blue Sage Ln
10 LYTN 84040 1284 A4
Blue Skye Ct
- DRPR 84020 2389 D7
Blue Spruce Cir
5200 HLDY 84117 2072 B5
Blue Spruce Dr
2600 HLDY 84117 2072 A4
Blue Spruce Rd
600 ALPN 84004 2497 C4
Blue Stone Cir
- NHON 84414 998 E7
5900 MRRY 84123 2070 A6
Bluevail Ct
5500 WJDN 84084 2173 D1
Bluewing Wy
13500 RIVN 84065 2386 A4
13600 RIVN 84065 2385 E5
S Bluff Dr
3300 SRCS 84075 1281 B4
Bluff Rd
- SRCS 84075 1226 A5
200 WPT 84015 1226 A5
S Bluff Rd
1200 SRCS 84075 1226 C7
1200 SRCS 84075 1280 D1
2700 SRCS 84075 1281 B4
3200 DvsC 84075 1281 B4
N Bluff St
- PVDN 84332 527 E5
Bluff Pointe Dr
1400 DRPR 84020 2496 C1
Bluff Ridge Dr
- SRCS 84075 1281 C1
Bluffside Cir
1900 SNDY 84092 2283 D2
Bluffside Dr
9600 SNDY 84092 2283 D1
Bluff View Dr
11800 SNDY 84092 2283 B7
11800 SNDY 84092 2389 B1
Boabab Cir
4900 SLkC 84117 2071 C4
Boabab Ct
5000 SLkC 84117 2071 C4
Boabab Dr
1500 SLkC 84117 2071 C4
Boat Harbor Dr
- UthC 84601 2926 E6
- UthC 84601 2927 A6
400 PRVO 84601 2927 C5
Bob Ln
1400 SNDY 84092 2283 C5
Bobolink St
1100 WVCY 84119 1963 E7
Bobsled Blvd
5400 SmtC 84098 1971 D3
Bobsled Cir
3400 TYVL 84084 2174 D1
Bobwhite Ct
4300 OGDN 84403 1173 D2
Bobwhite Wy
3800 WVCY 84120 2068 D1
Bogey Cir
200 NSLK 84054 1653 D6
4400 SJDN 84095 2280 B2
Bogey Dr
1200 FTHT 84037 1346 A3
Boggess Dr
7000 MDVL 84047 2176 E2
Bohm Cir
1000 SNDY 84094 2283 A4
Bohm Pl
10700 SNDY 84094 2283 A5
Boise Cir
9200 SNDY 84070 2176 E7
Boise St
300 SNDY 84070 2176 D7
Bolton Ct
10100 SJDN 84095 2280 B3
Boman Wy
600 SWBR 84405 1229 A1
Bo Mar Dr
2000 CDHT 84121 2177 D1
Bona Ln
100 SGVL 84663 3143 B2
Bona Dea Blvd
6000 WVCY 84128 2067 B1
Bonair St
2200 HLDY 84117 2071 E3
Bonanza Cir
2200 SJDN 84095 2281 B3
Bonanza Ct
10 PKCY 84060 2078 B3
2200 SJDN 84095 2281 B3
Bonanza Dr
1600 PKCY 84060 2078 D4
Bonanza Rd
10 FMTN 84025 1447 E2
Bonanza Wy
2200 SJDN 84095 2281 B2
Bonar Bridge Rd
4000 SJDN 84095 2280 C2
Bona Villa Dr
1700 OGDN 84403 1173 D1
Bona Vista Cir
100 BNFL 84010 1653 D5
Bonham Ln
6600 TYVL 84084 2175 E1
Bonica Ln
5600 HRMN 84065 2385 D5
Bonita Dr
1100 SLkC 84106 1965 B6
Bonito Wy
10 CTRV 84014 1551 E2
Bonne Wy
1600 LYTN 84040 1283 C2
Bonner Cir
4600 SLkC 84117 2071 B3
Bonner Wy
1100 SLkC 84117 2071 B3
Bonnet Dr
9000 SNDY 84093 2177 C7
Bonneview Dr
1500 SLCY 84105 1859 C6
1800 BNFL 84010 1654 A3
Bonneville Av
1000 LOGN 84341 463 E7
E Bonneville Blvd
- SLCY 84103 1858 D1
700 SLCY 84103 1754 D7
W Bonneville Blvd
500 SLCY 84103 1754 D7
500 SLCY 84103 1858 D1
E Bonneville Dr
10 BNFL 84010 1653 E5
N Bonneville Dr
900 SLCY 84103 1755 A7
1000 SLCY 84103 1859 B1
S Bonneville Dr
1000 SLCY 84108 1860 A6
W Bonneville Dr
10 BNFL 84010 1653 D6
Bonneville Terrace Dr
2400 OGDN 84403 1173 E4
2400 WbrC 84403 1173 E4
2500 WbrC 84403 1174 A5
Bonnie Arlene Dr
6800 WVCY 84128 1961 A6
Bonnie Brae Av
2800 SLkC 84124 2072 B1
Bonniebrook Cir
2200 TYVL 84118 2069 B3
Bonniebrook Dr
2200 TYVL 84118 2069 B3
Bonniewood Dr
3800 WVCY 84119 1962 E7
3900 WVCY 84119 2068 C3
Bonnyview Ln
300 MRRY 84107 2070 B3
Bonview Dr
3100 SLkC 84109 1966 C7
Boone Cir
3600 SLkC 84044 1960 E6
Boothill Cir
3900 WVCY 84120 1962 A7
Boot Hill Dr
7600 SmtC 84098 1865 A6
Boothill Dr
3900 WVCY 84120 1962 A7
4000 WVCY 84120 2068 A1
5000 WVCY 84120 1961 D6
Bora Bora Dr
13700 HRMN 84065 2385 A5
Borax Av
5900 SLkC 84118 2067 C6
Borax Cir
5800 SLkC 84118 2067 C6
N Bordeaux Ln
200 ALPN 84004 2497 E4
W Bordeaux Ln
100 ALPN 84004 2497 E4
Bordeaux Wy
4400 WVCY 84120 2068 D2
9000 SNDY 84093 2177 C7
Borg Cir
6200 WbrC 84403 1174 A7
6300 WbrC 84403 1173 E7
Borg Ct
2100 SNDY 84092 2283 E2
Borg Dr
2100 SNDY 84092 2283 E2
Boro St
300 KYVL 84037 1283 B7
Borthwick Wy
1200 TYVL 84084 2175 D1
Bosham Ln
1700 SLkC 84106 1965 D4
1800 SLCY 84106 1965 D4
Boston Cir
7800 CDHT 84093 2177 E4
Boston Dr
- NSLK 84054 1652 C6
Boswell Bay
- SLkC 84044 1960 B7
Bothwell Ct
300 SLCY 84104 1857 E4
Bothwell St
500 SLCY 84104 1857 E4
Bott Av
600 BMCY 84302 767 B5
Botticelli Ct
3600 WVCY 84119 1963 D6
Bouchelle Ln
6400 CDHT 84121 2072 B7
6400 CDHT 84121 2178 A1
Bouchelle Cove
6600 CDHT 84121 2178 A1
Bouck Cir
4000 WVCY 84120 2068 C2
Boughton St
1300 OGDN 84403 1116 C6
Boulder Dr
3000 LYTN 84040 1284 A1
3200 DvsC 84040 1284 A1
6900 CDHT 84121 2177 C2
Boulder Creek Dr
- WJDN 84088 2173 D5
Boulder Creek Rd
8300 WJDN 84088 2173 D5
Boulder Glen Cir
4900 WJDN 84088 2174 A6
Boulder Meadow Dr
4800 HRMN 84065 2386 A6
Boulder Wash Ln
4900 WJDN 84088 2174 A6
Boulevard Gdns
10 SLCY 84115 1964 C1
Boulter St
12700 DRPR 84020 2389 C3
Boulton Wy
10 BNFL 84010 1653 D4
N Bountiful Blvd
- BNFL 84010 1552 C7
S Bountiful Blvd
10 BNFL 84010 1552 C7
300 BNFL 84010 1654 C2
3500 BNFL 84010 1653 D7
4400 BNFL 84054 1653 D7
4400 NSLK 84054 1653 D7
Bountiful Dr
- MPTN 84664 3250 D1
Bountiful Wy
500 SRSP 84043 2601 D5
Bountiful Hills Dr
900 BNFL 84010 1654 A1
Bountiful Ridge Dr
4300 BNFL 84010 1653 D7
Bounty Cove
4000 LEHI 84043 2495 B6
Bourdeaux St
700 MDVL 84047 2176 E1
700 MDVL 84047 2177 A1
Bourne Cir
7400 CDHT 84121 2178 A3
Bouwhuis Dr
3100 WHVN 84401 1114 D5
Bowden Cir
1500 SLkC 84117 2071 C4
Bowden St
10800 SNDY 84070 2282 E5
Bowers Wy
10 SSLK 84115 1964 C2
Bowl Dr
700 OREM 84097 2821 A1
Bowler Cir
8100 SLkC 84044 1960 C7
Bowling Av
1700 TYVL 84119 2069 B2
Box Canyon Rd
8000 WJDN 84088 2173 D4
Box Elder Cir
1300 LOGN 84341 464 B7
1600 ALPN 84004 2498 C2
1600 UthC 84004 2498 C2
Box Elder Dr
1300 ALPN 84004 2498 C1
3700 CRHL 84062 2605 C4
Boxelder Ln
1200 SNST 84056 1227 E3
Box Elder St
4500 MRRY 84107 2070 C2
Box Elder Tr
1500 ALPN 84004 2498 C2
Box Elder Wy
1100 TMTN 84337 520 E3
Boxwood Cir
1300 LOGN 84341 464 B6
Boxwood Rd
6200 HLDY 84121 2071 E7
Boyce Cir
600 LYTN 84041 1283 A6
Boyd Dr
13700 HRMN 84065 2385 A5
Boyes St
2300 HLDY 84117 2071 E3
Boynton Rd
10 DvsC 84040 1283 D5
10 KYVL 84037 1283 C6
10 LYTN 84040 1283 D5
1300 DvsC 84037 1283 D5
Boysenberry Cir
1500 SNDY 84093 2177 C5
Boysenberry Dr
2000 SRSP 84043 2601 E5
8000 SNDY 84093 2177 C5
Braddock Ln
800 ALPN 84004 2497 E6
Bradford Cir
2700 WVCY 84119 2069 A2
Bradford Dr
- NSLK 84054 1652 C5
Bradford Park Dr
3200 WVCY 84119 1962 D3
Bradley Dr
10 CTRV 84014 1551 D4
Bradley Wy
300 SLkC 84070 2176 D5
Bradshaw Cir
2600 SLCY 84109 1966 B2
Brady Cir
7800 CDHT 84093 2177 D4
Brady Ln
- DvsC 84075 1344 D2
- KYVL 84037 1344 D2
- KYVL 84075 1344 D2
Brady Wy
2700 LYTN 84041 1281 E2
Brady Creek Cir
2000 SNDY 84093 2177 D5
Brady Creek Dr
1800 SNDY 84093 2177 D5
Brae Lin Wy
6900 WJDN 84084 2175 D2
Braemar Ct
5600 WVCY 84128 1961 D4
Braenear Cir
9400 SJDN 84095 2280 B1
Braewick Rd
100 SLCY 84103 1754 D7
Braewood Pl
4100 WVCY 84120 2067 E1
Brahma Cir
5500 MRRY 84107 2070 D5
Brahma Dr
200 MRRY 84107 2070 D5
Brahma Rd
- FMTN 84025 1447 E1
Braidhill Dr
300 DRPR 84020 2388 E7
Braintree Ct
1500 SLkC 84124 2071 C2
Bramble Wy
2300 HLDY 84117 2072 A2
Brambleberry Ln
300 DRPR 84020 2282 D6
Bramblewood Ln
5700 SLkC 84118 2068 B6
Brammerton Dr
- TYVL 84123 2070 A2
Brampton Wy
600 SLCY 84104 1857 C4
Bramwell Ct
800 OGDN 84401 1116 A4
Branbury Ct
5400 SLkC 84118 2067 E7
Branch Dr
2800 HLDY 84117 2072 B3
Branden Dr
3100 WVCY 84120 1962 A5
Brandermill Cove
900 MRRY 84123 2069 E6
900 MRRY 84123 2070 A6
Branding Cir
1800 SLCY 84116 1753 C4
Brandon Ct
4000 WVCY 84128 1960 D7
4000 WVCY 84128 2066 E1
Brandon Dr
- SGVL 84663 3144 A2
700 KYVL 84037 1345 B2
Brandon Park Dr
11100 SNDY 84092 2283 D6
Brandon Park Pl
1900 SNDY 84092 2283 D5
Brandon Park Ter
1900 SNDY 84092 2283 D6
Brandon Park Wy
1900 SNDY 84092 2283 D5
Brandonwood Dr
1100 MRRY 84123 2069 D5
Brandt Ct
400 SLkC 84107 1964 E7
Brandy Cir
3500 WJDN 84084 2174 D2
Brandy Buck
3700 TYVL 84118 2068 D6
Brandy Creek Dr
- SNDY 84070 2282 B1
Brandy Spring Ln
9500 SNDY 84070 2282 C1
Brandy Wine
5500 TYVL 84118 2068 D5
Brandy Wood Dr
4500 WVCY 84120 2068 A2
Brass Cir
6000 SLkC 84118 2067 C6

STREET / Block City ZIP Map# Grid

Brass Dr
5800 SLkC 84118 2067 C6
Brass Pl
6000 SLkC 84118 2067 C6
Brava St
1500 SLCY 84104 1857 E7
Braveheart Ct
1300 WVCY 84119 1963 D6
Bravery Ct
3500 WVCY 84119 1963 D6
Braxton Ct
6300 MRRY 84121 2071 D7
Braxton Pl
1500 LOGN 84321 528 C3
Braxton Rd
- DRPR 84020 2388 D7
Brayden Wy
200 DRPR 84020 2388 D7
Breaker Point Cir
12300 RIVN 84065 2387 D1
Breaker Point Wy
1300 RIVN 84065 2387 D1
Breakwater Dr
5400 TYVL 84123 2069 C6
Bree St
5600 TYVL 84118 2068 D6
Breeze Cir
3300 SLkC 84044 1960 C5
Breeze Dr
2700 SLkC 84044 1960 C5
Breeze Wy
- BNFL 84010 1653 D6
1400 WbrC 84404 997 E6
1400 WbrC 84404 998 A6
Breeze Hill Rd
7000 WJDN 84084 2174 A2
Brekenridge Dr
1100 MRRY 84117 2071 B5
Brenda Av
1100 MRRY 84121 2177 A1
Brenda Lee Ln
12700 RIVN 84065 2387 E3
Brent Cir
100 SNDY 84070 2282 D1
Brent Ln
2000 CDHT 84121 2177 E2
Brent St
10 LYTN 84041 1282 E4
Brentmar Cir
8900 SNDY 84070 2176 E7
Brentridge Cir
11400 SJDN 84095 2281 E6
Brentwood Cir
500 BNFL 84010 1653 E1
2200 SLCY 84109 1966 A3
4700 PRVO 84604 2821 E5
Brentwood Dr
2500 HLDY 84121 2072 A6
5800 HLDY 84121 2071 E6
Brentwood Ln
300 BNFL 84010 1654 C1
Brereton Dr
2700 PRVO 84604 2928 D2
E Breton Woods Ln
1000 OREM 84097 2821 A5
Brett Av
3300 WVCY 84119 1962 E7
Brew Rd
400 DRPR 84020 2388 E7
Brewer Av
2000 CDHT 84121 2177 D2
Brewski Bay
1200 TYVL 84084 2175 D1
Brewster Dr
300 DRPR 84020 2388 E7
Brian Head Cir
8600 SNDY 84093 2177 E6
Brian's Wy
4400 WVCY 84119 2068 E2
Briar Av
900 PRVO 84604 2928 E4
Briar Dr
3300 WJDN 84084 2174 E4
Briarcliff Av
900 SLCY 84116 1857 E1
Briarcreek Cir
2400 HLDY 84117 2072 A2
Briarcreek Dr
2300 HLDY 84117 2072 A2
Briar Crest Ct
15100 DRPR 84020 2496 D1
Briarglen Dr
1700 SNDY 84092 2283 C7
Briarglen Ln
1700 SNDY 84092 2283 C7
Briarmeadow Av
700 MRRY 84107 2070 D7
700 MRRY 84107 2071 A7
Briar Rose Pl
1600 SLCY 84104 1963 C1
Briarsprings Cir
500 SNDY 84047 2176 A3
Briarsprings Dr
7600 SNDY 84047 2176 E3
Briar Sweet Cir
400 LYTN 84041 1283 B6
Briarwood Cir
800 CTRV 84014 1551 E2
4400 HLDY 84124 2071 E2
Briarwood Dr
100 CTRV 84014 1551 E2
2300 HLDY 84124 2071 E2
Briar Wood Ln
4300 LEHI 84043 2495 C6
Bricker Dr
200 DRPR 84020 2388 B3
Brickyard Rd
1100 SLCY 84106 1965 B5
N Bridge Cir
4100 DvsC 84056 1228 A4
N Bridge Ct
1900 LYTN 84040 1283 E1
E Bridge Rd
8400 MDVL 84047 2176 C5
Bridge Creek Ln
- DvsC 84041 1282 B7
- LYTN 84041 1282 B7
Bridgecreek Ln
900 LYTN 84041 1282 C7
Bridgecreek Wy
200 DRPR 84020 2388 D2

Bridgecrest Cir
1800 SLCY 84116 1753 B5
Bridgefield Dr
14300 DRPR 84020 2388 D6
Bridge Maple Ln
6500 WJDN 84084 2173 B3
Bridgepark Cir
100 DRPR 84020 2388 D2
Bridge Park Wy
1200 LYTN 84041 1282 C7
Bridgeport Av
2600 CDHT 84093 2178 A4
Bridgeport Wy
1400 WJDN 84084 2175 D2
Bridger Blvd
2500 SLkC 84093 2178 A6
8800 PARA 84328 710 D4
S Bridger Blvd
8900 PARA 84328 710 D5
Bridger Cir
- WDHL 84653 3463 D3
Bridger Dr
200 LOGN 84321 463 C7
200 LOGN 84321 527 C1
2100 SGVL 84663 3143 C6
E Bridger Ln
500 EKMT 84651 3463 A1
Bridger Rd
1800 SLCY 84104 1963 A1
Bridgestone Cir
1500 SLCY 84116 1753 C5
Bridgestone Ln
1800 SLCY 84116 1753 B5
Bridgeview Ct
14000 BFDL 84065 2387 D5
Bridgeview Dr
1200 LYTN 84041 1282 B7
Bridgewater Cir
7500 CDHT 84121 2178 A3
10300 CRHL 84062 2605 A2
Bridgewater Ct
7500 CDHT 84121 2178 A3
Bridgewater Dr
2700 CDHT 84121 2178 B3
Bridgewood Ln
12500 DRPR 84020 2388 D2
Bridgton Cir
3800 SLkC 84044 1960 D7
Bridgton Dr
7600 SLkC 84044 1960 C7
Bridgton Pl
3800 SLkC 84044 1960 D7
Bridle Wy
2200 BFDL 84065 2387 B5
Bridlebrook Cir
1500 SLkC 84117 2071 C5
Bridlechase Ln
5700 MRRY 84107 2070 E6
Bridle Creek Dr
4900 WJDN 84084 2174 A3
5100 WJDN 84084 2173 E3
Bridle Hollow Pl
5200 WJDN 84084 2173 D3
Bridle Mark Wy
7400 WJDN 84084 2173 E3
Bridle Meadow Cir
2300 BFDL 84065 2387 B5
Bridle Oak Dr
2200 SJDN 84095 2281 B2
Bridle Park Cove
13400 DRPR 84020 2388 E4
Bridle Pass Ln
10700 SLkC 84092 2283 E4
Bridle Path Lp
1700 LEHI 84043 2710 B2
Bridle Ridge Cir
7400 WJDN 84084 2173 D3
Bridle Trail Cir
13500 DRPR 84020 2389 B4
Bridle Trail Rd
1200 DRPR 84020 2389 B4
Bridle Vista Cir
5300 WJDN 84084 2173 D3
Bridlewalk Ln
300 MRRY 84107 2070 D6
Bridlewood Dr
300 SLkC 84107 2070 E1
3800 BNFL 84010 1653 D6
Bridle Wood Ln
400 SGVL 84663 3143 B2
Bridlewood Lp
1200 LEHI 84043 2603 A1
Brigadier Cir
1100 SLCY 84116 1753 B6
Brigadoon Ct
1000 SLkC 84117 2071 A3
Brigadoon Park Dr
1400 WJDN 84088 2281 D1
Briggs Blvd
- CRHL 84062 2605 C1
Briggs Dr
10 BNFL 84010 1552 B7
E Brigham Av
400 ANFK 84003 2604 D6
N Brigham Av
300 ANFK 84003 2604 D7
Bright Ct
500 SLCY 84116 1858 A1
Bright Meadow Cir
9500 SJDN 84095 2281 A1
Bright Morning Cir
5100 TYVL 84123 2069 C4
Brighton Cir
3000 CDHT 84121 2178 B4
Brighton Ct
3000 CDHT 84121 2178 B3
Brighton Pl
3000 CDHT 84121 2178 B3
Brighton Wy
7400 CDHT 84121 2178 B3
Brighton Cove Cir
7700 CDHT 84093 2178 A4
Brighton Point Dr
3500 CDHT 84121 2178 C3
Brighton View Dr
9200 SNDY 84070 2176 E7
9200 SNDY 84070 2282 E1
Brimley Wy
4900 TYVL 84118 2068 E4
Brina Ln
3800 SLkC 84044 1960 E7

Bringhurst Cir
400 PVDN 84332 528 B7
400 PVDN 84332 592 B1
Brinker Av
500 OGDN 84404 1057 B6
1300 OGDN 84404 1116 B1
1800 OGDN 84401 1116 B2
2700 OGDN 84403 1116 B4
4000 OGDN 84403 1173 B1
N Brinker Av
600 OGDN 84404 1057 B4
Brinley Ln
- FTHT 84037 1346 B3
Brinton Cir
2800 LYTN 84040 1230 A7
Brinton Wy
2400 LYTN 84040 1230 A7
Brisbane Dr
1200 SNDY 84094 2283 B7
Brister Cir
5400 MRRY 84123 2069 E5
Brister Dr
1100 MRRY 84123 2069 D5
Bristlecone Cir
2300 CDHT 84121 2177 E3
Bristlecone Wy
10200 CRHL 84062 2605 C2
Bristol
10600 CRHL 84062 2605 C1
Bristol Cir
4500 PRVO 84604 2821 E5
Bristol Ct
300 ALPN 84004 2498 A4
Bristol Rd
10 LOGN 84341 464 C6
900 FTHT 84037 1346 A3
Bristol Wy
3400 WVCY 84119 1962 E6
Bristol Ridge Rd
1300 WJDN 84088 2175 D5
Brit Cir
8600 MDVL 84047 2176 C6
Britain Dr
7800 SLkC 84044 1960 C5
Britannia Av
900 SGVL 84663 3142 E4
Britley Bay
10100 SJDN 84095 2280 C3
Brittany Ct
5100 WVCY 84120 1961 E6
Brittany Dr
600 MRRY 84107 2070 E2
Brittany Rd
4600 OGDN 84403 1173 D2
Brittany Park Av
7100 WJDN 84084 2174 A2
Brittany Town Dr
7000 WJDN 84084 2174 A2
Brittney Downs Dr
4300 WVCY 84120 1962 B7
Brixen Ct
600 SLCY 84102 1859 A5
Brixton Rd
3800 TYVL 84118 2068 C4
E Broadhollow Dr
10 WDHL 84653 3463 D3
Broadleaf Cir
200 DRPR 84020 2388 D7
Broadmoor St
1900 SLCY 84108 1966 A2
2100 SLCY 84109 1966 A2
Broadmore Av
300 OGDN 84404 1056 D4
Broadview Wy
2300 SNDY 84092 2283 E6
2300 SNDY 84092 2284 A6
E Broadway
10 SLCY 84111 1858 D4
W Broadway
500 SLCY 84101 1858 B4
Broadway St
3100 SLkC 84044 1960 D5
Brock St
3300 WVCY 84119 1963 A6
Brockbank Dr
3300 SLkC 84124 2072 C2
Brockbank Wy
3900 SLkC 84124 2072 D1
Brockshire Cir
4200 SJDN 84095 2280 C2
Brockway Cir
1200 MRRY 84117 2071 B5
Brockway St
5400 MRRY 84117 2071 B5
Broderick Dr
2300 TYVL 84084 2069 B7
Broderick Wy
6400 TYVL 84084 2069 B7
Broken Fence Ln
800 FTHT 84037 1345 E1
800 FTHT 84037 1346 A1
Broken Hill Dr
2500 SmtC 84098 1865 C3
Broken Ridge Ct
1000 SNDY 84094 2177 A4
Broken Ridge Dr
1000 SNDY 84094 2177 C3
Broken Spoke Wy
2600 PKCY 84060 2078 E1
N Brom Cir
1800 LYTN 84040 1283 E1
Brome Grass Cir
600 KYVL 84037 1283 D6
Bromley Dr
700 ANFK 84003 2711 E4
Bromley Rd
7000 WJDN 84084 2174 E3
Bron Breck Dr
4700 HLDY 84117 2072 B3
Bronco Cir
3600 SLkC 84044 1960 D6
N Bronco Rd
- NHLN 84341 464 C1
Bronson Cir
900 HRCY 84032 2398 C5
Bronze Ln
1100 SLkC 84094 2283 B3
Brook Cir
1000 ALPN 84004 2498 B4
1000 KYVL 84037 1284 B6
Brook Ct
200 SGVL 84663 3143 D2

Brook Ln
2300 SNDY 84092 2283 E7
2300 SNDY 84092 2284 A7
Brook Wy
6600 CDHT 84121 2177 D1
Brookburn Rd
2700 SLkC 84109 1966 A6
Brookbury Wy
4700 TYVL 84123 2069 D3
Brookcrest Cir
800 SJDN 84095 2281 E3
800 SJDN 84095 2282 A3
Brookdale Cir
300 OGDN 84404 1056 D4
Brooke Ln
1100 FMTN 84025 1448 D4
Brooke Ln Cir
100 FMTN 84025 1448 D4
Brookfield Cir
4100 WVCY 84120 2067 D1
Brookfield Ln
200 CTRV 84014 1551 C1
Brookfield Wy
4100 WVCY 84120 2067 D1
Brookglen Dr
2400 SNDY 84092 2284 A7
Brook Haven Dr
900 FTHT 84037 1284 B6
900 KYVL 84037 1284 B6
Brookhaven Dr
3200 TYVL 84118 2068 E4
Brook Haven Cove
12900 DRPR 84020 2388 D3
Brookhill Dr
1800 CDHT 84121 2177 D1
Brook Hollow Ct
3600 WVCY 84128 1961 C6
Brook Hollow Dr
6000 WVCY 84128 1961 C6
Brook Hollow Loop Rd
7300 SmtC 84098 1865 B6
Brookhurst Cir
1300 CTRV 84014 1551 C1
3700 WVCY 84120 1961 E7
Brookings Ct
- DRPR 84020 2496 D3
Brookings Dr
- DRPR 84020 2496 E3
- DRPR 84020 2497 A3
Brooklane Cir
1400 SLkC 84124 1965 C7
Brooklane Dr
3900 SLkC 84124 1965 C7
Brookline Cove
12600 RIVN 84065 2386 B2
Brooklyn Av
200 SLCY 84101 1858 B6
1100 SLCY 84104 1857 E6
Brook Maple Wy
6500 WJDN 84084 2173 B3
Brook Meadow Dr
100 HARR 84404 1056 E3
Brookmill Ln
2400 SNDY 84092 2284 A7
Brook N Lance
11100 SJDN 84095 2282 A5
Brookridge Dr
5500 MRRY 84107 2071 A6
Brook Ridge Ln
1400 TYVL 84123 2069 D3
Brookshire Cir
4600 PRVO 84604 2821 D5
Brookshire Dr
500 RVDL 84405 1115 B7
1300 SLkC 84106 1965 B6
3500 SRCS 84075 1226 B7
4500 PRVO 84604 2821 D5
E Brookshire Dr
700 KYVL 84037 1283 E6
N Brookshire Dr
700 KYVL 84037 1283 E6
Brookshire Hollow Dr
700 KYVL 84037 1283 E7
Brookside Cir
800 OGDN 84404 1056 C7
Brookside Ct
- PYSN 84651 3461 D1
3700 SmtC 84098 1971 E7
3700 SmtC 84098 1972 A7
Brookside Dr
- DRPR 84020 2496 D3
10 SGVL 84663 3143 D3
3200 PRVO 84604 2928 B1
3400 PRVO 84604 2821 B7
Brookside Ln
10 CTRV 84014 1551 D2
N Brookside Ln
3200 PRVO 84604 2928 B2
Brookside Pl
10 LOGN 84321 527 E2
Brookstone Dr
- MRRY 84121 2177 C1
6400 MRRY 84121 2071 C7
Brookview Cir
6500 WVCY 84128 2067 B1
Brook View Ln
3400 SLkC 84106 1965 A6
Brook Water Ct
12900 DRPR 84020 2388 D3
Brookway Dr
2800 WVCY 84119 1962 E4
Brookwillow Cove
4600 SLkC 84117 2071 C2
Brookwood Cir
4600 SLkC 84117 2071 B3
Brookwood Dr
4600 SLkC 84117 2071 B3
8600 SmtC 84098 1866 D4
Brower Cir
2700 WJDN 84084 2175 A1
Brown Av
9200 WJDN 84088 2281 B1
Brown Ln
- OGDN 84404 1056 C5
1400 FMTN 84025 1345 E5
Brown St
4600 MRRY 84107 2070 D3
Brown Bear Pl
13100 DRPR 84020 2389 D3
Brown Farm Ln
300 DRPR 84020 2388 D5

Browning Av
- DvsC 84056 1172 A7
200 SLCY 84115 1858 D7
600 SLCY 84105 1858 E7
800 SLCY 84105 1859 A7
1600 DvsC 84056 1171 E7
1700 SLCY 84108 1859 D7
1700 SNST 84056 1171 E7
2300 WbrC 84404 998 A6
Browning Cir
1500 OGDN 84403 1173 C3
Browning Ct
1800 SmtC 84098 1971 E4
Browning Ln
- FMTN 84025 1345 D7
Browning Pl
- FMTN 84025 1345 D7
Browning St
2300 DvsC 84056 1172 B7
Brown Park Dr
- WJDN 84088 2173 E6
Browns Park Dr
1800 BNFL 84010 1654 B3
Brown's Pond Cove
12800 DRPR 84020 2388 D3
Brown Summit Cir
11300 SJDN 84095 2281 D6
Brown Villa Cove
4800 TYVL 84123 2069 E3
Bruce Cir
300 CRFD 84015 1227 E4
1300 LYTN 84040 1283 C3
Bruce St
300 CRFD 84015 1227 E3
3300 SLkC 84124 2072 C2
Brucemont Dr
2400 TYVL 84118 2069 A5
Brud Dr
5600 WVCY 84128 1961 C5
Bruin Blvd
- TYVL 84119 2069 C2
Brundisi Wy
5300 HRMN 84065 2385 D2
Brunello Dr
1400 BFDL 84065 2387 D5
Brunley Ct
3200 RIVN 84065 2386 E3
Brunswick Ct
4200 TYVL 84123 2069 E1
Brush Creek Bay
5200 WVCY 84120 1961 E6
Brushwood Bay
2900 WVCY 84120 1962 A4
Bryan Av
10 SLCY 84115 1858 C7
600 SLCY 84105 1858 E7
900 SLCY 84105 1859 A7
2000 SLCY 84108 1859 D7
Bryan Cir
2200 SLCY 84108 1859 E7
Bryan Ln
500 CTRV 84014 1551 D4
Bryanston Cove
900 MRRY 84123 2069 E6
900 MRRY 84123 2070 A6
Bryant Dr
2500 SLkC 84044 1960 C4
Bryce Dr
8000 SNDY 84070 2176 D5
8200 SLkC 84070 2176 D5
Bryce Jeffery Dr
1100 RIVN 84065 2387 E2
Brynn Cir
1900 WJDN 84088 2175 C7
Brynwood Pine Bay
3200 WJDN 84088 2174 E6
Bryson Cir
3200 RIVN 84065 2386 E3
Bubbling Brook Ln
100 DRPR 84020 2282 B7
Buccaneer Dr
1000 SLCY 84116 1753 E6
2700 SLkC 84044 1960 B5
Buchanan Av
1900 OGDN 84401 1116 D3
2700 OGDN 84403 1116 D5
Buchnell Dr
1000 SNDY 84094 2177 A5
Buck Cir
3400 CDHT 84121 2178 C2
Buckboard Cir
7600 SmtC 84098 1864 E6
13700 RIVN 84065 2387 C5
Buckboard Dr
3200 SmtC 84098 1865 A7
7200 SmtC 84098 1864 E7
Buckboard Wy
13600 RIVN 84065 2387 C4
Buckeroo Cir
3600 SLkC 84044 1960 C7
Buckeroo Dr
3500 SLkC 84044 1960 D6
Buckeye View Wy
5000 RIVN 84065 2385 E4
5000 RIVN 84065 2386 B4
Buck Hollow Dr
4000 BFDL 84065 2386 C5
Buck Hollow Ln
4000 BFDL 84065 2386 C5
Buck Hollow Cove
13800 BFDL 84065 2386 C5
E Buckhorn Dr
5400 WbrC 84310 1002 A3
Buckingham Ct
8900 SNDY 84093 2177 B7
Buckingham Dr
100 PVDN 84332 528 B7
Buckingham Wy
2000 SNDY 84093 2177 E7
Buckley Av
400 SGVL 84663 3143 D2
Buckley Ln
1700 PRVO 84606 3036 A3
Buckshot Cove
12900 DRPR 84020 2388 D3
Buckskin Ln
1000 WJDN 84088 2175 E6
Buckthorn Cir
6700 WJDN 84084 2173 E1
Buckwheat Cir
1100 RIVN 84065 2281 E7

Buckwheat Wy
11800 RIVN 84065 2281 E7
Bud Cir
2300 TYVL 84084 2069 B7
Budding Cir
1400 SNDY 84092 2283 C2
Budding Dr
1400 SNDY 84092 2283 C2
Buddlea Dr
900 SLkC 84094 2283 A3
Budge Ln
1600 PTVW 84414 997 E3
Buena Verde Ln
3100 SLkC 84044 1960 C5
Buena Vista Dr
3900 PTVW 84414 998 B2
6600 UNTH 84405 1173 D7
6600 UNTH 84405 1229 D1
8600 SNDY 84094 2177 A6
Bueno Av
700 SLCY 84102 1858 E3
700 SLCY 84102 1859 A3
Bueno Vista Dr
2500 WJDN 84088 2175 A5
Buffalo Ct
4900 RIVN 84065 2386 A2
N Buffalo Dr
900 SRSP 84043 2601 D7
W Buffalo Dr
800 SRSP 84043 2601 C7
Buffalo Bill Dr
2200 PKCY 84060 2079 A2
Bufflehead Dr
6700 SmtC 84098 1971 D1
Bugatti Dr
300 SSLK 84115 1964 B2
Bugle Wy
200 PVDN 84332 528 C7
Builders Dr
2400 TYVL 84118 2069 A4
N Buisness Park Loop Rd
6400 SmtC 84098 1973 A2
E Bulldog Blvd
10 PRVO 84604 2928 C4
W Bulldog Blvd
10 PRVO 84604 2928 B4
Bulldog Cir
600 MRRY 84123 2070 A7
Bullen Hall
100 LOGN 84321 528 B1
Bullion St
700 MRRY 84123 2070 A5
900 MRRY 84123 2069 E6
Bull Moose Cir
4500 WJDN 84088 2174 B7
Bullock
- PRVO 84606 3035 E3
- UthC 84606 3035 E3
Bull River Cir
11500 HILD 84003 2497 C6
Bull River Rd
6000 HILD 84003 2497 A6
W Bullriver Rd
400 LEHI 84043 2496 B7
8000 UthC 84043 2496 B7
8800 LEHI 84043 2495 E7
8800 UthC 84043 2495 E7
Bull Run Cir
4200 DvsC 84056 1228 A4
Bullrush Wy
500 SSLK 84106 1964 E5
Bunbury Ln
1600 SLCY 84104 1857 C5
Bunbury Cove
600 SLCY 84104 1857 C5
Bunker Cir
4300 SJDN 84095 2280 B2
Bunker Hill Rd
200 NSLK 84054 1653 C7
200 NSLK 84054 1754 C1
1600 SLkC 84117 2071 C3
Burbank Av
1400 SLCY 84104 1857 D6
N Burbidge Av
- OGDN 84404 1056 B4
Burch Creek Dr
4600 SOGN 84403 1172 E2
4800 SOGN 84403 1173 A3
Burch Creek Hllw
4800 SOGN 84403 1173 A3
Burdock Dr
3000 WVCY 84128 1961 D5
Burgess Rd
3800 TYVL 84118 2068 C5
E Burgi Ln
10 MIDW 84049 2397 C1
10 WshC 84049 2397 C1
W Burgi Ln
10 MIDW 84049 2397 B1
100 WshC 84049 2397 B1
Burgundy St
9200 SNDY 84070 2176 A7
9200 SNDY 84070 2282 A1
Burke Ln
- FMTN 84025 1346 A7
1400 FMTN 84025 1345 E7
Burkman Wy
4100 WVCY 84120 2067 E1
Burkwood Ln
11700 DRPR 84020 2283 A7
Burley Cir
2300 SJDN 84095 2281 B1
Burlingame Dr
2900 WVCY 84120 1962 A3
Burlington Ct
900 FMTN 84025 1346 A4
Burnby Ln
10100 SJDN 84095 2280 C3
Burnell Rd
- UthC 84660 3249 B2
Burnham Dr
700 PTVW 84414 942 C7
Burningham Cir
2000 WVCY 84119 1963 B7
Burningham Dr
3800 WVCY 84119 1963 C7
4000 WVCY 84119 2069 C1
Burning Oak Dr
1600 DRPR 84020 2389 C5
Burns St
10 BNFL 84010 1653 D2

N Burns St
100 OGDN 84404 1056 C4
Burnside Cir
2000 SLkC 84109 1965 D7
Burnt Oak Dr
8500 WJDN 84088 2173 B6
Bur Oak Ln
11700 SNDY 84092 2283 D7
Burr Dr
7400 SLkC 84044 1960 E6
Burrell St
5900 TYVL 84118 2069 A6
Burrey Ct
3400 WVCY 84119 2068 E1
E Burton Av
10 SSLK 84115 1964 D3
W Burton Av
200 SSLK 84115 1964 C3
Burton Ct
1500 OGDN 84403 1173 C4
E Burton Ln
10 KYVL 84037 1345 D3
W Burton Ln
1600 KYVL 84037 1345 B5
Burton Trail Cir
1100 SJDN 84095 2281 E6
Bury Rd
- WJDN 84088 2173 A4
Busby St
- SLkC 84044 1854 C7
Business Park Dr
12100 DRPR 84020 2388 C1
W Business Park Dr
1300 OREM 84058 2927 A2
1400 OREM 84058 2926 E1
Busman Pl
3700 WVCY 84128 1961 C7
Buster Cir
4900 SLkC 84118 2067 D3
Buster St
4900 SLkC 84118 2067 E4
Butch Cassidy Dr
2600 PKCY 84060 2079 A3
Butler Av
1300 SLCY 84102 1859 B3
Butler Cir
5700 MRRY 84107 2070 D6
Butler Hills Dr
7400 CDHT 84121 2177 E3
Butte St
- SLCY 84104 1857 A5
Buttercup Dr
1300 SNDY 84092 2283 C2
Butterfield Cir
4500 TYVL 84123 2069 D2
Butterfield St
4400 TYVL 84123 2069 D2
Butterfield Park Wy
6200 HRMN 84065 2385 C6
Butterfield Peak Cir
5100 RIVN 84065 2385 E5
Butternut Cir
2400 HLDY 84124 2072 A2
Butternut Ln
2400 LEHI 84043 2495 C6
Butternut Rd
4300 HLDY 84124 2071 E1
4300 HLDY 84124 2072 A2
4400 HLDY 84117 2072 A2
Buttonwood Cir
9700 SNDY 84092 2283 C4
Buttonwood Dr
2100 SNDY 84092 2283 E1
Bybee Dr
2600 WbrC 84403 1174 A7
Byde A Wyle
3400 WVCY 84119 1963 E6
Bypass Rd
- ALTA 84049 2181 D7
- ALTA 84049 2287 C1
- SLkC 84049 2181 C7
- SLkC 84049 2287 C1
Byron Cir
2000 WVCY 84119 2069 B1
Byrum Cir
5700 SLkC 84118 2068 A6
Bywater Wy
- BMCY 84302 767 B6

C

C Av
- PTVW 84404 997 E5
10 DvsC 84056 1228 D4
2200 OGDN 84401 1115 C3
C St
- BMCY 84302 767 A6
- BMCY 84302 827 E2
- CRFD 84015 1227 C7
- KYVL 84041 1283 B6
- ROY 84067 1114 B7
- RVDL 84405 1172 A3
10 SGVL 84663 3143 E3
10 SLCY 84103 1858 D2
900 SLCY 84116 1753 A7
Caballero Dr
7600 CDHT 84093 2177 D4
Cabernet Dr
1400 BFDL 84065 2387 D6
Cable Ct
3100 WJDN 84084 2174 E3
Cabot Ln
1100 DRPR 84020 2389 B3
Cabot Cove
12900 DRPR 84020 2389 B3
Cabrito St
1200 SLkC 84117 2071 B4
Cache Cir
3200 SJDN 84095 2280 E4
Cache Dr
7900 PKCY 84060 2185 A1
Cache Creek Cir
4100 WJDN 84088 2174 C7
Cache Point Ln
100 DRPR 84020 2388 D4
Cactus St
300 SLCY 84111 1858 C4
Cactus Berry Dr
12900 RIVN 84065 2386 A3
Cadbury Cir
3800 SRCS 84075 1226 B6

STREET
Block City ZIP Map# Grid

Cadbury Dr
300 SJDN 84095 2282 B5
Cadbury Ln
- SGVL 84663 3142 E4
Caddie Cir
9900 SJDN 84095 2280 B2
Caddis Cir
11800 RIVN 84065 2281 D7
Cadenza Dr
5100 WJDN 84084 2173 E1
Caesar Cir
1300 WVCY 84119 1963 D7
Cahoon Cir
4900 TYVL 84118 2069 A4
Cahoon Dr
700 OGDN 84401 1116 A3
Cahoon St
700 OGDN 84401 1115 B3
700 WbrC 84401 1115 B3
1300 OGDN 84401 1116 C3
W Cahoon St
600 OGDN 84401 1115 B3
800 WbrC 84401 1115 B3
Caithness Cir
9400 SJDN 84095 2280 B1
Caitland Ct
2900 CDHT 84121 2178 B1
Caitlin Cir
1500 SRCS 84075 1281 A3
Cajun Bay
1400 TYVL 84123 2069 D7
Calais Ct
1500 WVCY 84119 1963 D5
Calann Dr
1600 SLkC 84121 2071 C6
Calder Av
1800 BNFL 84010 1653 D3
Calder Ct
500 KYVL 84037 1345 E2
Caleb Dr
100 NSLK 84054 1652 C6
Caledonia Cir
9500 SJDN 84095 2280 A1
Calgary Pl
6000 SLkC 84121 2071 E6
Calico Wy
3900 WVCY 84120 1962 A7
4000 WVCY 84120 2068 A1
Caliente Dr
8700 WJDN 84088 2173 D7
California Av
200 SLCY 84115 1858 A7
800 SLCY 84104 1858 A7
900 SLCY 84104 1857 D7
1700 PRVO 84606 3036 A3
2300 SLCY 84104 1856 D7
California Cir
2000 PRVO 84606 3036 A3
California Dr
200 MDVL 84047 2176 B3
1200 DvsC 84056 1227 D2
1200 SNST 84056 1227 D2
1300 DvsC 84056 1228 B2
Calinas Creek Cir
400 MRRY 84107 2070 E6
Calkary Cir
3200 WVCY 84120 1961 E5
Call Dr
1000 BNFL 84010 1551 C6
Calla Lily Wy
1400 SNDY 84092 2283 C3
Callander Ct
13900 HRMN 84065 2385 E5
Callander Ln
5300 HRMN 84065 2385 D5
Callao Dr
3500 WVCY 84128 1961 A6
Callaway Ct
1300 TYVL 84123 2069 D7
Callaway Dr
1600 HRCY 84032 2398 E1
Callery Ln
6700 WJDN 84084 2173 A4
Callie Dr
- WJDN 84084 2175 D2
Calls Fort Rd
- BxEC 84302 646 B6
- HYVL 84314 646 D6
N Calls Fort Rd
5300 BxEC 84302 646 B6
Calnette Dr
300 SNDY 84070 2282 E3
Calnita Cir
6400 TYVL 84084 2069 A7
6400 TYVL 84084 2175 A1
Cal Pac Av
1300 SPFK 84660 3249 C5
Calumet Cir
2200 PKCY 84060 2078 E3
Calvin Dr
3600 WVCY 84120 1962 C7
W Calvo Dr
1500 WVCY 84119 1963 D7
Calvo View Cir
3700 WVCY 84119 1963 C7
Calypso St
2900 WVCY 84120 1962 A4
Calyx Cir
4800 WJDN 84084 2174 A1
Camaren Dr
300 BMCY 84302 827 D1
Camarilla Cir
600 SLCY 84104 1857 D5
Camas Lilly Cir
- PTVW 84414 998 D2
Camas Meadows Cir
8000 WJDN 84088 2173 E4
Camberley Cir
9700 SNDY 84092 2283 C2
Cambria Cir
7600 CDHT 84121 2178 C4
Cambridge Av
- HARR 84414 998 D6
Cambridge Cir
- LYTN 84040 1229 B6
500 SLCY 84103 1859 B1
2300 PRVO 84604 2928 E2
8800 SNDY 84070 2176 B6
Cambridge Ct
1200 PRVO 84604 2928 E2
4500 BNFL 84010 1653 E7
9800 HILD 84003 2604 D3
Cambridge Dr
3400 WVCY 84119 1962 D6
Cambridge Ln
4000 CRFD 84015 1228 A5
Cambridge Lp
4000 CRFD 84015 1228 A5
Cambridge Pk
- CRFD 84015 1227 A3
Cambridge Rd
900 KYVL 84037 1284 A6
4400 CRHL 84062 2605 A3
Cambridge Wy
500 SLCY 84103 1859 C1
Cambridge Cross Cir
2500 RIVN 84065 2387 A3
Cambridgetown Cove
1200 TYVL 84123 2069 C4
Camden Rd
500 DRPR 84020 2282 E6
Camden Park Ct
400 DRPR 84020 2282 E6
Camden Park Ln
500 DRPR 84020 2282 E6
Camden Pointe Cove
500 DRPR 84020 2282 E6
Camelback Cir
7300 CDHT 84121 2178 A3
Camelback Rd
2400 CDHT 84121 2178 A3
Cameley Cir
1900 SNDY 84093 2177 D6
Camella St
- SLCY 84104 1856 E5
Camelot Dr
- NHLN 84341 464 C6
1200 PRVO 84601 2927 E5
1200 PRVO 84601 2928 A5
W Camelot Dr
1400 LYTN 84041 1282 B1
Camelot Wy
1900 WJDN 84084 2175 C2
Cameo Wy
1700 SNDY 84093 2177 C6
Cameo Park Cir
9300 SJDN 84095 2281 B1
Cameron Ct
900 OGDN 84404 1057 B3
3200 SJDN 84095 2280 E2
Cameron Pl
9800 SNDY 84092 2284 A2
N Cameron St
10 SRSP 84043 2710 A3
S Cameron St
10 SRSP 84043 2710 A3
Cameron Park Ct
3200 SJDN 84095 2280 E2
Cameron Park Dr
9800 SJDN 84095 2280 E2
Cameron Park Ln
3200 SJDN 84095 2280 E2
Camila Av
600 MRRY 84107 2070 E2
Camille Cir
800 CTRV 84014 1551 D2
2600 HLDY 84117 2072 A2
Camille St
4100 HLDY 84124 2072 A1
4400 HLDY 84117 2072 A2
Camino Cir
7300 CDHT 84121 2177 E3
Camino Ct
7300 CDHT 84121 2177 E3
Camino Pl
7300 CDHT 84121 2177 E3
Camino Wy
2000 CDHT 84121 2177 E3
2300 CDHT 84121 2178 A2
Camino Bay
7300 CDHT 84121 2177 E3
Camino Real Dr
4900 SLkC 84117 2071 B4
5100 MRRY 84117 2071 B4
Camlan Ln
- SGVL 84663 3142 E4
Campaign Dr
3100 SJDN 84095 2280 E2
Campbell Dr
4900 SLkC 84118 2067 E4
Campbell St
600 CRFD 84015 1227 E6
600 CRFD 84015 1228 A6
Campden Ct
1700 FMTN 84025 1346 B5
10100 SJDN 84095 2280 B3
Campden Dr
4200 SJDN 84095 2280 B3
Campfire Cir
3800 WVCY 84119 1963 A7
Campground Rd
- ALTA 84049 2288 C1
Campo St
4200 WVCY 84119 2068 D2
Campus Cir
7200 CDHT 84121 2177 E3
Campus Dr
2300 CDHT 84121 2177 E2
2300 CDHT 84121 2178 A2
E Campus Dr
- PRVO 84604 2928 C4
600 OREM 84097 2821 A5
N Campus Dr
- PRVO 84604 2928 D4
S Campus Dr
- PRVO 84604 2928 D5
- PRVO 84606 2928 D5
100 OREM 84097 2820 E6
100 OREM 84097 2821 A6
W Campus Dr
- PRVO 84604 2928 D5
Campus Center Dr
- SLCY 84112 1859 C4
Campus View Dr
7100 WJDN 84084 2174 D2
Camp Williams Rd
- SLkC 84065 2494 D5
- UthC 84043 2494 D5
14400 BFDL 84065 2387 C7
16700 BFDL 84065 2494 C4
Camp Williams Rd SR-68
- SLkC 84065 2494 D5
- UthC 84043 2494 D5
14400 BFDL 84065 2387 C7
Camp Williams Rd SR-68
14800 BFDL 84065 2494 C2
Camron Glen Dr
2700 SLkC 84044 1960 E4
Camstone Dr
5000 WVCY 84120 1962 A7
Cana Cir
700 SLkC 84094 2282 E3
Canabra Ct
500 DRPR 84020 2282 E7
Canal Dr
10 LNDN 84042 2713 D6
3700 WPT 84015 1226 A1
Canal Rd
- CchC 84321 592 A4
- SALM 84653 3356 E4
- UthC 84653 3356 E4
1700 WJDN 84084 2175 B1
Canal St
4800 TYVL 84123 2069 D4
Canal Bank Rd
12000 BxEC 84336 520 A4
12000 TMTN 84337 520 A4
Canal Ridge Rd
1900 TYVL 84118 2069 C6
Canary St
1200 WVCY 84119 1963 D7
Canary Bird Cove
4700 HRMN 84065 2386 A1
Canberra Dr
10 DvsC 84056 1228 C4
1200 LNDN 84042 2713 E7
1200 SNDY 84094 2283 B7
Canbury Cir
13000 DRPR 84020 2389 B3
Cancun Wy
1300 RIVN 84065 2387 D2
Candice Wood Cir
5000 WVCY 84120 1962 A7
Candis Cir
7300 SLkC 84044 1960 E6
Candis Dr
3500 SLkC 84044 1960 E6
Candis Pl
7300 SLkC 84044 1960 E6
Candle Cove
6600 CDHT 84121 2178 A1
Candlelite Ln
600 SNDY 84047 2176 E4
Candle Spruce Cove
2000 SNDY 84092 2283 D1
Candlestick Ln
7800 MDVL 84070 2176 D4
Candle Tree Ln
9400 SNDY 84092 2283 E1
Candle Tree Cove
2000 SNDY 84092 2283 D1
Candlewood Cir
9700 SNDY 84092 2283 C4
Candlewood Ct
2200 SNDY 84092 2283 E2
Candlewood Dr
2100 SNDY 84092 2283 E1
Candlewood Pl
100 PRVO 84604 2928 C1
Candy Crest Cir
2400 TYVL 84118 2069 B5
Candy Pull Dr
14000 DRPR 84020 2389 A5
Candy Tuft St
3100 CDHT 84121 2178 B2
Canfield Dr
400 OGDN 84404 1056 E2
500 OGDN 84404 1057 A2
Cannery St
1200 PRRY 84302 827 B6
Cannes Wy
1600 MRRY 84121 2071 C6
Cannon Av
1000 SLCY 84104 1857 E7
Cannon Cir
10 FMTN 84025 1448 D4
Cannon Dr
1100 FMTN 84025 1448 D5
Cannon Creek Cir
3400 WVCY 84119 1962 D5
Cannon Park Ln
1900 SJDN 84095 2281 B1
Cannonwood Dr
6200 TYVL 84123 2069 C7
Cannonwood Pl
1400 TYVL 84123 2069 D7
Cantel Dr
500 PYSN 84651 3461 D1
Canterbury Cir
- LOGN 84321 528 B3
6800 HILD 84003 2603 E2
6800 HILD 84003 2604 A2
Canterbury Ct
6600 HILD 84003 2604 A1
Canterbury Dr
800 LOGN 84321 528 A3
1300 SLCY 84108 1860 A7
N Canterbury Dr
- HILD 84003 2604 A1
10400 HILD 84003 2603 E2
W Canterbury Dr
6600 HILD 84003 2604 A1
Canterbury Ln
10 LOGN 84321 528 A3
600 ALPN 84004 2498 A4
1300 OREM 84097 2821 B2
2500 CDHT 84121 2178 A3
6600 HILD 84003 2604 A1
Canterbury Pl
10500 HILD 84003 2604 A2
Canterbury Rd
4700 OGDN 84403 1173 D3
Canterbury Wy
6500 HILD 84003 2604 A2
Canterbury Park Cir
9700 HILD 84003 2604 C3
N Canterbury Park Cir
9700 HILD 84003 2604 C4
W Canterbury Park Cir
5800 HILD 84003 2604 C4
Canterwood Cir
1300 SNDY 84093 2177 B4
Canterwood Ct
10800 SJDN 84095 2281 B4
Canterwood Dr
2400 SJDN 84095 2281 A5
Canterwood Ln
7600 SNDY 84093 2177 C4
Canton Ct
11400 SNDY 84092 2284 B6
Canton Ln
2700 SNDY 84092 2284 A6
Cantwell St
3100 WVCY 84119 1963 A5
Canvasback Ln
- WPT 84015 1225 D4
S Canyon Av
10 SGVL 84663 3143 E2
300 SGVL 84663 3144 A2
Canyon Blvd
- LOGN 84321 528 A2
400 LOGN 84321 527 E2
Canyon Cir
1600 FMTN 84025 1346 B5
Canyon Ct
10 PKCY 84060 2078 A2
Canyon Dr
900 SPFK 84660 3249 E3
1300 SWBR 84405 1229 C1
7000 SmtC 84098 1864 E7
7000 SmtC 84098 1970 E1
S Canyon Dr
400 SGVL 84663 3144 A3
Canyon Ln
300 NSLK 84054 1754 B1
Canyon Rd
- CchC 84318 400 C7
- CchC 84321 592 E2
- CchC 84335 400 B1
- CchC 84341 400 D6
- CRHL 84003 2498 C7
- CRHL 84062 2498 C7
- CRHL 84062 2605 C2
- HILD 84003 2498 C7
- OGDN 84401 1116 D1
- SNQN 84655 3567 E3
- UthC 84655 3567 E3
- UthC 84655 3568 A2
- WbrC 84317 1116 D1
10 PVDN 84332 592 B1
10 SHFD 84335 399 E2
100 SLCY 84103 1858 D1
200 LOGN 84321 527 E3
300 MLVI 84332 592 B4
400 OGDN 84404 1115 E1
500 HDPK 84318 400 B7
500 SHFD 84335 400 A2
600 LOGN 84321 528 A2
600 OGDN 84404 1116 A1
600 SLCY 84103 1754 D7
1000 HDPK 84341 400 C7
1100 OGDN 84404 1057 B7
1700 SGVL 84663 3144 D4
Canyon Rd SR-39
- OGDN 84401 1116 D1
- WbrC 84317 1116 D1
Canyon Rd SR-146
- CRHL 84003 2498 C7
- CRHL 84062 2498 C7
- CRHL 84062 2605 C2
- HILD 84003 2498 C7
E Canyon Rd
600 SPFK 84660 3249 E3
1200 SPFK 84660 3250 B4
E Canyon Rd SR-198
600 SPFK 84660 3249 E3
1200 SPFK 84660 3250 B4
N Canyon Rd
2100 PRVO 84604 2928 C2
3300 PRVO 84604 2821 D7
4400 UthC 84604 2821 D7
S Canyon Rd
10 SNQN 84655 3460 E7
100 SNQN 84655 3567 E1
700 PYSN 84651 3354 E6
800 PYSN 84651 3355 A7
900 UthC 84655 3567 E2
1700 SGVL 84663 3144 B4
11300 UthC 84651 3355 A7
Canyon Vw
10 FMTN 84025 1346 D6
Canyon Wy
100 CTRV 84014 1552 A4
3500 SLkC 84106 1965 C6
Canyon Breeze Dr
10 CTRV 84014 1551 E4
Canyon Breeze Ln
700 DRPR 84020 2389 A5
Canyon Cove
- OGDN 84401 1116 C2
10 LOGN 84321 528 A2
10 WPT 84015 1226 E4
Canyon Cove Cir
6200 HLDY 84121 2072 C7
Canyon Cove Ct
6200 HLDY 84121 2072 C7
Canyon Cove Dr
700 PYSN 84651 3355 A7
3400 HLDY 84121 2072 C7
6500 HLDY 84121 2178 D1
Canyon Cove Gln
- OGDN 84401 1116 C2
Canyon Cove Ln
- OGDN 84401 1116 C2
Canyon Cove Pl
6400 HLDY 84121 2072 C7
6400 HLDY 84121 2178 C1
Canyon Cove St
200 LOGN 84321 528 A2
Canyon Cove Crest
- OGDN 84401 1116 C2
Canyon Creek Cir
6900 CDHT 84121 2178 C2
E Canyon Creek Cir
2900 LYTN 84040 1284 A4
N Canyon Creek Cir
300 LYTN 84040 1284 A4
Canyon Creek Dr
900 BNFL 84010 1654 A6
3300 CDHT 84121 2178 C2
Canyon Crest Cir
900 BNFL 84010 1654 B2
Canyon Crest Dr
1100 BNFL 84010 1654 B2
3400 HLDY 84121 2178 C1
6400 HLDY 84121 2072 C7
E Canyon Crest Dr
2500 SPFK 84660 3250 C6
W Canyon Crest Dr
200 ALPN 84004 2497 D5
E Canyon Crest Rd
10 ALPN 84004 2497 E5
100 ALPN 84004 2498 A5
S Canyon Crest Rd
500 ALPN 84004 2498 A6
W Canyon Crest Rd
10 ALPN 84004 2497 E5
Canyon Dr Ct
6800 SmtC 84098 1970 E1
Canyon Estates Cir
400 BNFL 84010 1653 E5
Canyon Estates Dr
400 BNFL 84010 1653 E5
Canyon Gate Cir
9000 SNDY 84093 2178 B7
Canyon Gate Rd
8900 SLkC 84093 2178 B7
8900 SNDY 84093 2178 B7
Canyon Glen Lp
- SPFK 84660 3250 D6
E Canyon Glen Lp
3100 SPFK 84660 3250 D6
Canyon Heights Dr
3500 CRHL 84062 2605 D4
N Canyon Hills Dr
800 OREM 84097 2821 B3
Canyonlands Cir
2200 TYVL 84118 2069 B5
Canyon Meadow Dr
1000 PRVO 84606 3036 A1
6800 SWBR 84405 1173 A7
6800 SWBR 84405 1229 A1
Canyon Oak Cir
3100 SNDY 84092 2284 B3
Canyon Oaks Cir
1600 BNFL 84010 1654 B2
Canyon Oaks Dr
1100 BNFL 84010 1654 B2
Canyon Oaks Wy
200 SLCY 84103 1754 D6
Canyon Park Rd
1200 BNFL 84010 1654 B2
Canyon Pines Cir
6900 CDHT 84121 2178 B2
Canyon Ranch Rd
6400 HLDY 84121 2178 C1
Canyon Ridge Wy
800 MDVL 84047 2177 A3
E Canyon Rim Dr
2200 LYTN 84040 1283 E2
Canyon Rim Ln
3100 SLkC 84109 1966 B4
Canyon River Wy
3800 SSLK 84119 1963 E7
Canyon Rose Cir
5100 HRMN 84065 2385 E6
Canyon Side Ln
100 SLCY 84103 1858 D2
Canyon Side Rd
100 SLCY 84103 1858 D2
Canyon Spring Cir
13300 DRPR 84020 2389 A4
Canyons Resort Dr
1800 SmtC 84098 1971 D7
Canyon View Cir
400 NSLK 84054 1754 B1
500 PTGV 84062 2713 B2
4800 BNFL 84010 1754 E1
S Canyon View Cir
3000 SLkC 84109 1966 B5
Canyon View Ct
1000 FMTN 84025 1346 D6
Canyon View Dr
10 FMTN 84025 1346 C7
300 PTGV 84062 2713 B2
400 OGDN 84404 1056 E3
500 OGDN 84404 1057 A2
700 HYRM 84319 651 D3
2100 LYTN 84040 1229 E6
2700 SLkC 84109 1966 A5
4600 HILD 84003 2605 A1
9100 SmtC 84098 1864 E4
10700 HILD 84003 2498 A7
S Canyon View Dr
300 EKMT 84651 3463 A3
Canyon View Ln
500 PTGV 84062 2713 B2
Canyon View Pl
3900 SLkC 84092 2284 E2
Canyon View Rd
1000 MIDW 84049 2397 B1
1000 WshC 84049 2291 B7
1000 WshC 84049 2397 B1
Canyon Vine Cove
14100 DRPR 84020 2389 C6
Canyon Vista Ln
14000 DRPR 84020 2389 D5
Canyon Vista Rd
1000 PRVO 84606 3036 A1
Canyonwoods Dr
1600 OGDN 84404 1116 B1
Cape Cod Dr
5600 WVCY 84128 2067 D2
Capehart St
5000 SLkC 84118 2068 A4
Capella Wy
1300 SLkC 84093 2177 C6
8800 SNDY 84093 2177 C6
Capernaum Rd
1100 WJDN 84088 2175 D6
Cape Vista Wy
4400 WVCY 84128 2067 D2
Capistrano Dr
1000 SLCY 84116 1753 E7
Capital St
900 OGDN 84401 1116 A3
Capital Reef Dr
2200 TYVL 84118 2069 B5
E Capitol Blvd
600 SLCY 84103 1858 D1
1000 SLCY 84103 1754 D6
Capitol Pl
3000 SJDN 84095 2281 A2
E Capitol St
500 SLCY 84103 1858 D1
W Capitol St
400 SLCY 84103 1858 C1
700 OGDN 84401 1115 B3
Capitol Oaks Ln
300 SLCY 84103 1754 D6
Capitol Park Av
300 SLCY 84103 1858 D1
Caplan St
4600 SLkC 84118 2068 B5
Capri Dr
500 MRRY 84123 2070 B5
Caprice Ln
- FTHT 84037 1346 B3
Capricorn Wy
2400 HLDY 84124 2072 A1
2500 SLkC 84124 2072 A1
Capstone Av
3600 CDHT 84121 2178 D5
Captain Cir
1200 SLCY 84116 1753 B6
Captain Molly Dr
1600 PKCY 84060 2078 C4
Captiva Cove
6800 CDHT 84121 2178 A1
Caracol Cove
6600 CDHT 84121 2178 A1
Cara Vella Ln
- CTRV 84014 1551 D3
Caraway Bay
3200 WJDN 84088 2174 E7
Carbide Ct
11800 HRMN 84065 2280 A7
Carbon Cir
3000 WVCY 84120 1962 C5
Cardiff Cir
3700 BNFL 84010 1653 E6
7600 CDHT 84121 2178 B3
Cardiff Rd
2900 CDHT 84121 2178 B3
Cardiff Wy
3700 BNFL 84010 1653 E6
Cardinal Wy
2300 CDHT 84121 2177 E3
2400 CDHT 84121 2178 A3
Cardington Cir
5800 SLkC 84118 2067 C6
Cardoness Wy
7900 WJDN 84088 2174 E4
Carefree Cir
2000 TYVL 84084 2069 C7
Carefree Dr
2000 TYVL 84084 2069 B7
Cargo Cir
5800 SLkC 84118 2067 C7
Caribbean Wy
5000 MRRY 84107 2070 E4
Caribou Cir
3400 SJDN 84095 2280 D4
Caring Cove
600 SLCY 84103 1858 E1
Carl Cir
2400 TYVL 84084 2069 B7
Carl Dr
6300 TYVL 84084 2069 B7
Carla St
2900 WVCY 84120 1962 C4
Carling Cir
7400 CDHT 84121 2178 A3
Carlington Ct
10100 SJDN 84095 2280 C3
Carlisle Av
200 ALPN 84004 2498 A6
Carlisle St
700 SSLK 84119 1964 A6
Carlisle Park Ln
700 SSLK 84119 1964 A7
900 SSLK 84119 1963 E7
Carlisle Park Pl
3700 SSLK 84119 1963 E7
Carlquist Dr
400 DRPR 84020 2388 D3
Carlson Av
10 MDVL 84047 2176 D2
Carlton Ct
1200 TYVL 84123 2069 E1
Carlton Wy
1300 SRCS 84075 1281 A3
Carmel Dr
500 MDVL 84047 2176 E3
Carmelita Dr
1100 SLkC 84106 1965 B6
S Carmellia Dr
4500 TYVL 84123 2069 E2
W Carmellia Dr
1100 TYVL 84123 2069 D3
Carmen Ct
8300 SNDY 84070 2176 D5
Carnaby Ct
4300 TYVL 84123 2069 E2
Carnation Dr
700 SLkC 84094 2282 E3
700 SLkC 84094 2283 A3
800 SNDY 84094 2283 A3
Carnegie Tech St
4500 WVCY 84120 2068 B3
Carney St
800 SOGN 84403 1116 A7
Carnoustie Ct
13800 HRMN 84065 2385 E5
Carol Wy
100 MDVL 84047 2176 D3
E Carole Cir
300 SSLK 84115 1964 D4
Carole Dr
2700 CDHT 84121 2178 A3
Carolee Hill Cir
5100 WJDN 84084 2173 D2
Caroleen Wy
4200 SLkC 84124 2071 C1
Carolina Dr
3600 WJDN 84084 2174 D1
N Carolina Ln
2000 RVDL 84405 1172 A6
Caroline Day Cove
400 DRPR 84020 2388 D6
Carol Jane Dr
4300 HLDY 84124 2071 E2
Carolyn Pl
1000 BMCY 84302 767 B4
Carolyn St
3500 SLkC 84106 1965 A6
Carolyn Wy
2100 BNFL 84010 1654 A4
Carousel St
1200 SLCY 84116 1753 C6
Carpell Av
5200 WJDN 84084 2173 E1
Carpenter Cove
5200 TYVL 84118 2069 B4
Carranza Dr
2900 TYVL 84118 2069 A6
Carrara Dr
- DRPR 84020 2283 E7
Carriage Av
1800 RIVN 84065 2387 B4
W Carriage Cir
300 OREM 84058 2927 C2
Carriage Ct
- OGDN 84403 1173 D3
Carriage Ln
- NSLK 84054 1653 B4
400 KYVL 84037 1282 E7
2100 HLDY 84117 2071 E2
2800 WbrC 84403 1174 A7
3600 BNFL 84010 1653 C6
4400 CRHL 84062 2605 A2
Carriage Sq
1700 TYVL 84119 2069 C1
Carriage Chase Ln
2000 SNDY 84092 2283 E1
Carriagehouse Ln
9600 SNDY 84092 2284 B2
Carriage Oak Ct
2500 SJDN 84095 2281 A2
Carriage Oak Ln
9900 SJDN 84095 2281 B2
Carriage Park Cir
1700 MRRY 84121 2071 C7
Carrie Dr
1300 FTHT 84037 1346 B1
3900 WVCY 84120 1962 D7
4000 WVCY 84120 2068 D1
Carrie Rim Cir
11300 SJDN 84095 2281 E6
Carrigan Cir
1700 SLCY 84108 1966 C1
Carrigan Canyon Dr
- SLCY 84108 1966 B1
2900 SLkC 84108 1966 B1
Carrington Ct
11600 SNDY 84092 2283 E6
Carrington Ln
10 CTRV 84014 1551 E1
Carrington St
10600 SNDY 84094 2283 A4
Carroll Hall
100 PRVO 84604 2928 E3
Carson Cir
6600 WJDN 84084 2175 B1
Carson Dr
- RVHT 84321 528 A5
Carson Ln
2400 WJDN 84084 2175 B1
N Carston Ct
1700 FMTN 84025 1346 D4
W Carston Ct
1200 FMTN 84025 1346 A5
Carter Cir
4100 HLDY 84124 2071 D1
7000 WJDN 84084 2175 A2
Carter Dr
700 RVDL 84405 1115 B7
E Carter Dr
10 LEHI 84043 2603 C2
N Carter Dr
2200 LEHI 84043 2603 C2
Carterville Rd
1700 PRVO 84604 2928 B3
S Carterville Rd
- PRVO 84604 2928 B2
300 OREM 84097 2821 B6
300 PRVO 84097 2821 B6
1100 OREM 84097 2928 B2
1600 OREM 84604 2928 B2
Cart Path Ct
- TYVL 84123 2069 D7
Casa Blanca Dr
7500 MDVL 84047 2177 A3
Casa Blanco Av
800 MDVL 84047 2177 A3
Casa Blanco Cir
700 MDVL 84047 2177 B3
Casa Bonita Pl
4400 WVCY 84119 2068 D2
Casa Grande Cir
7500 MDVL 84047 2177 A3
Casa Loma Dr
10 CTRV 84014 1551 E1
Casa Morena Cir
7500 MDVL 84047 2177 A3
Casa Negra Av
800 MDVL 84047 2177 A3
Casa Negra Cir
7500 MDVL 84047 2177 A3
Casa Roja St
800 MDVL 84047 2177 A3
Casa Verde Cir
7600 MDVL 84047 2177 A4
Casa Verde St
7500 MDVL 84047 2177 A3
E Cascade Av
10 ALPN 84004 2497 E5
100 ALPN 84004 2498 A5
W Cascade Av
10 ALPN 84004 2497 E6
Cascade Cir
3600 SLkC 84109 1966 D4
Cascade Ct
500 ALPN 84004 2497 E6
Cascade Dr
- OREM 84097 2821 A1
1800 PRVO 84604 2927 D4
Cascade St
400 SNDY 84070 2282 E1
Cascade Wy
2900 SLkC 84109 1966 C5
Cascades Cir
3800 SRCS 84075 1226 A7
Cascade Springs Dr
- WshC 84049 2396 A7
- WshC 84049 2397 A6
- WshC 84049 2503 A1
Cascade Springs Ln
8500 WJDN 84088 2175 A5
Cascade Springs Cove
3500 CRHL 84062 2605 D5
Case Mountain Rd
5100 WJDN 84084 2173 E2

Salt Lake City Street Index

STREET Block City ZIP Map# Grid

Case Mountain Cove
7100 WJDN 84084 2173 E2
Casey Cove
3800 RIVN 84065 2386 D1
Casino Wy
1800 MRRY 84121 2071 D7
Casino Camino St
3400 WVCY 84119 1963 D6
Casper Pl
11600 SNDY 84092 2283 C6
Casper Rd
1500 SNDY 84092 2283 C7
Caspers Park Pl
1800 HLDY 84117 2071 C2
S Casperville Rd
1200 WshC 84032 2397 D7
1900 CSTN 84032 2397 D7
1900 WshC 84032 2504 D1
W Casperville Rd
1200 HRCY 84032 2398 A6
1200 WshC 84032 2398 A6
1300 WshC 84032 2397 E6
Cassatt Cir
5300 SLkC 84118 2067 E7
Cassidy Cir
1200 BNFL 84010 1654 B3
2500 WJDN 84084 2175 B1
Cassidy Ln
6600 WJDN 84084 2175 B1
Cassie Cir
7600 MDVL 84047 2177 A4
Cassie Dr
800 SOGN 84405 1173 A5
Cassowary Cir
2600 SNDY 84092 2284 A6
Cassowary Dr
2600 SNDY 84092 2284 A7
Castle Rd
3900 WVCY 84128 1961 B7
3900 WVCY 84128 2067 B1
Castlecreek Cir
1100 MRRY 84117 2071 A5
Castlecreek Dr
1100 MRRY 84117 2071 B4
Castle Dale Cir
1100 SNDY 84094 2283 B6
Castlefield Ln
6300 MRRY 84107 2070 E7
6400 MRRY 84107 2176 C2
Castleford Dr
6200 WJDN 84084 2068 C7
6400 TYVL 84084 2068 C7
6400 TYVL 84084 2174 C1
Castlegate Dr
5300 MRRY 84117 2071 B5
Castle Hill Av
2000 CDHT 84121 2177 E3
Castle Hill Cir
7400 CDHT 84121 2177 D3
Castle Oaks Cir
2600 TYVL 84118 2069 A3
Castle Park Ct
6500 WVCY 84118 2173 C1
Castle Park Ln
6000 WVCY 84118 2173 C1
Castle Peak Dr
- HRMN 84065 2385 E5
5100 RIVN 84065 2385 E5
Castle Pine Cir
5200 HILD 84003 2604 D1
Castle Pine Dr
10600 HILD 84003 2604 E1
Castle Pine Wy
5200 HILD 84003 2604 D1
Castle Pines Wy
3800 WJDN 84084 2174 C2
Castle Ridge Dr
4700 SLkC 84117 2071 C3
Castle Rock Rd
1000 SNDY 84094 2283 B6
Castle View Dr
3900 WVCY 84128 1961 A7
3900 WVCY 84128 2067 B1
Casto Cir
5000 HLDY 84117 2072 A4
Casto Ln
2500 HLDY 84117 2072 A4
Casto Pines Cove
5000 HLDY 84117 2072 A4
Catalina Dr
2300 CDHT 84121 2177 E2
2300 CDHT 84121 2178 A2
Catalina View Cove
3300 SLkC 84044 1960 C6
Catalpa St
100 MDVL 84047 2176 B3
Catamount Ridge Wy
3700 SLkC 84092 2284 D7
Catania Dr
2100 DRPR 84020 2283 E7
12000 DRPR 84020 2389 E1
Cathay Cir
4600 TYVL 84123 2070 A3
Catherine Cir
600 SLCY 84116 1857 D1
Catherine St
500 SLCY 84116 1857 D1
1700 SLCY 84116 1753 D5
Caton Wy
1200 SLCY 84106 1965 B3
Cattail Cir
12000 DRPR 84020 2389 A1
Cattail Dr
600 OGDN 84404 1057 A4
900 DRPR 84020 2389 A1
Cavalier Cir
7100 CDHT 84121 2178 A2
Cavalier Dr
2300 CDHT 84121 2177 E3
2300 CDHT 84121 2178 A2
N Cavallo Dr
1700 SLCY 84116 1753 C4
1700 SLkC 84116 1753 C4
W Cavallo Dr
1700 SLCY 84116 1753 C5
1700 SLkC 84116 1753 C5
Cave Bay
4300 WVCY 84128 2067 C2
Cave Hollow Cir
10 FMTN 84025 1448 C5
Cave Hollow Ct
10 FMTN 84025 1448 C4
Cave Hollow Ln
1100 FMTN 84025 1448 D5
Cave Hollow Wy
1500 BNFL 84010 1654 C4
Caveman Blvd
- ANFK 84003 2711 E1
300 ANFK 84003 2604 E7
Cavendish Cir
800 SNDY 84094 2283 A4
Cave Peak Dr
4800 RIVN 84065 2386 A6
Cawdor St
3900 SJDN 84095 2280 C2
Cayenne Dr
2700 TYVL 84118 2069 A6
Cayias Dr
500 NSLK 84054 1653 B6
Cayman Cir
12900 RIVN 84065 2387 D3
Cecelia Cir
1800 SLkC 84121 2071 D6
Cecil Dr
2500 HLDY 84124 2072 A1
Cedar Av
- SLCY 84103 1859 B2
900 PRVO 84604 2928 E4
Cedar Cir
1300 PRVO 84604 2928 E4
8100 SWBR 84405 1229 E4
8800 WJDN 84088 2175 D6
Cedar Ct
4600 SmtC 84098 1864 C6
8000 SWBR 84405 1229 D3
Cedar Dr
3300 SmtC 84098 1865 A5
Cedar Ln
- SmtC 84098 1971 D7
1200 CRFD 84056 1227 E2
1200 DvsC 84056 1227 E2
1200 SNST 84056 1227 E2
5800 SOGN 84403 1173 D6
Cedar Pl
2400 SRSP 84043 2601 E4
Cedar St
- SGVL 84663 3035 E6
6100 MRRY 84107 2070 C7
8800 WJDN 84088 2175 D6
Cedar Wy
7700 SmtC 84098 1864 D6
Cedar Bench Dr
1900 SWBR 84405 1229 D3
Cedar Breaks Dr
1900 TYVL 84118 2069 B5
Cedar Brook Pl
10600 SJDN 84095 2280 C4
W Cedar Cove Ct
4300 CRHL 84062 2605 B2
Cedar Creek Cir
4300 CRHL 84062 2605 B3
6500 WVCY 84118 2173 B1
Cedar Crest Dr
1300 SLkC 84092 2283 B1
Cedar Fort Rd
- EGMN 84043 2601 A7
- SRSP 84043 2601 A7
- UthC 84043 2601 A7
Cedar Fort Rd SR-73
- EGMN 84043 2601 A7
- SRSP 84043 2601 A7
- UthC 84043 2601 A7
Cedar Glen Cir
2400 SWBR 84405 1230 A3
Cedar Heights Dr
1100 LOGN 84341 464 D7
Cedar Hill Ct
6600 WJDN 84084 2173 C1
Cedar Hill Dr
- WJDN 84084 2173 B1
Cedar Hill Rd
5800 WJDN 84084 2173 C1
W Cedar Hills Dr
- HILD 84003 2604 E3
- HILD 84003 2605 A3
4000 PTGV 84062 2605 B3
4600 CRHL 84062 2605 A3
Cedar Hills Rd
- WJDN 84084 2173 C1
Cedar Hollow Blvd
1100 LEHI 84043 2603 D4
Cedar Hollow Ct
4800 RIVN 84065 2386 A3
Cedar Hollow Dr
1300 LEHI 84043 2603 E4
Cedar Hollow Rd
600 LEHI 84043 2603 D4
Cedar Loop Dr
1900 SWBR 84405 1229 D3
Cedar Mountain Cir
1200 ALPN 84004 2498 C6
Cedar Park Dr
5500 HRMN 84065 2385 D3
Cedar Pine Ct
800 SLkC 84106 1965 A7
Cedar Point Peak Cir
13900 RIVN 84065 2386 B6
Cedar Point Peak Dr
4800 RIVN 84065 2386 A5
5100 RIVN 84065 2385 E4
Cedar Ridge Cir
11900 SNDY 84094 2283 A7
Cedar Ridge Rd
1000 SNDY 84094 2283 B7
E Cedar Ridge Rd
1100 LEHI 84043 2603 E4
N Cedar Ridge Rd
1300 LEHI 84043 2603 E4
Cedar Run Cir
4600 CRHL 84062 2605 A4
Cedar Springs Ln
10500 SJDN 84095 2280 C4
Cedar Stone Cir
11700 SJDN 84095 2279 D7
Cedar Terrace Cir
900 SNDY 84094 2177 A4
Cedar Terrace Dr
700 SNDY 84094 2176 E4
700 SNDY 84094 2177 A4
Cedar View Cir
11200 SNDY 84094 2283 B5
Cedar View Dr
1100 SNDY 84094 2283 B5
Cedarwood Dr
300 OREM 84057 2820 E4
Cedar Wood Ln
3900 SJDN 84095 2280 C4
Cedro Cir
1400 SNDY 84093 2177 C5
Cee Jay Ct
4600 SJDN 84095 2280 B2
Celebration Dr
3200 WVCY 84128 1961 B6
Celeste Av
10 MDVL 84047 2176 D4
Celeste Cir
3100 SLkC 84109 1966 B6
Celeste Wy
3100 SLkC 84109 1966 B6
Celestial Ct
10500 SJDN 84095 2281 C4
Celia Cir
1900 LYTN 84041 1282 A1
N Celia Wy
1300 LYTN 84041 1282 B2
W Celia Wy
1900 LYTN 84041 1282 A1
Celia Cove
6300 MRRY 84121 2071 B7
Cemetery Rd
- BxEC 84307 764 B1
Centennial
3900 CRHL 84062 2605 C1
Centennial Av
7400 SLkC 84044 1960 E6
Centennial Cir
300 PKCY 84060 2079 A7
1100 SLCY 84116 1753 E7
Centennial Dr
200 NSLK 84054 1653 C7
200 NSLK 84054 1754 C1
300 PKCY 84060 2079 A7
Centennial Pkwy
10000 SNDY 84070 2282 C3
Centennial Rd
3500 SLkC 84044 1960 E6
Centennial Wy
- TYVL 84118 2069 A4
Centennial Cove
100 LEHI 84043 2603 C2
Center Av
400 LOGN 84321 527 B4
1600 OGDN 84404 1115 C2
Center Sq
7600 MDVL 84047 2176 C4
Center St
- BMCY 84302 767 A7
- CRFD 84015 1227 D4
- CRFD 84016 1227 D4
- OGDN 84401 1115 E2
- OGDN 84401 1116 A2
- PRVO 84606 3035 D1
- SLCY 84103 1859 B2
- SNQN 84655 3567 E2
- WELV 84339 589 D7
200 SLCY 84103 1858 C1
700 PRRY 84302 827 C5
4800 MRRY 84107 2070 D3
8500 SNDY 84070 2176 D6
9200 SNDY 84070 2282 D1
E Center St
- MLVI 84332 591 E3
10 ALPN 84004 2497 E4
10 BNFL 84010 1551 E7
10 CRFD 84015 1227 E4
10 CTRV 84014 1551 E3
10 HRCY 84032 2398 E4
10 KYVL 84037 1345 D1
10 LOGN 84321 527 E3
10 MNDN 84325 524 D6
10 MNTU 84324 768 C7
10 NSLK 84054 1653 A7
10 OREM 84057 2820 E5
10 OREM 84058 2820 E5
10 PRVO 84606 2928 D7
10 PTGV 84062 2712 E3
10 SALM 84653 3356 B3
10 SGVL 84663 3143 D2
10 SHFD 84335 399 E2
10 SPFK 84660 3249 D3
10 WLRD 84340 885 C6
100 MLVI 84332 592 A3
100 PVDN 84332 528 A6
200 ALPN 84004 2498 A4
200 HDPK 84318 464 A1
200 LNDN 84042 2713 C6
400 OREM 84097 2820 E5
400 SHFD 84335 400 A3
500 BNFL 84010 1552 A7
500 LOGN 84321 528 A3
500 OREM 84097 2821 A5
600 CTRV 84014 1552 A3
600 PTGV 84062 2713 A3
600 WshC 84032 2398 E4
1000 PRVO 84097 2821 A5
1100 PRVO 84606 2929 A7
1200 SPFK 84660 3250 A3
1300 SGVL 84663 3144 A2
1800 UthC 84606 3144 A2
N Center St
10 ANFK 84003 2711 C1
10 HYRM 84319 651 B2
10 MIDW 84049 2397 B2
10 SNQN 84655 3460 E7
10 WELV 84339 649 D1
10 WLRD 84340 885 C5
1300 ANFK 84003 2604 C4
1500 LEHI 84043 2603 C3
N Center St SR-23
10 WELV 84339 649 D1
S Center St
10 ANFK 84003 2711 C1
10 HYRM 84319 651 B3
10 LEHI 84043 2603 C7
10 MIDW 84049 2397 B4
10 WELV 84339 649 D4
10 WLRD 84340 885 C5
400 UthC 84043 2603 C7
600 WshC 84049 2397 B4
700 LEHI 84043 2710 C1
800 UthC 84043 2710 C1
S Center St SR-23
10 WELV 84339 649 D4
S Center St SR-113
10 MIDW 84049 2397 B4
S Center St SR-113
600 WshC 84049 2397 B4
W Center St
10 ALPN 84004 2497 E4
10 BNFL 84010 1551 D7
10 HDPK 84318 463 E1
10 HRCY 84032 2398 C4
10 KYVL 84037 1345 C1
10 LOGN 84321 527 C3
10 MLVI 84332 591 E3
10 MNDN 84325 524 D6
10 MNTU 84324 768 B7
10 NSLK 84054 1653 A7
10 OREM 84057 2820 A5
10 OREM 84058 2820 A5
10 PTGV 84062 2712 D3
10 PVDN 84332 528 A6
10 SALM 84653 3356 A3
10 SGVL 84663 3143 C2
10 SHFD 84335 399 D2
10 SPFK 84660 3249 C3
100 PVDN 84332 527 E6
100 WLRD 84340 885 C5
200 NSLK 84054 1652 C7
800 CchC 84335 399 D2
800 MDVL 84047 2175 E4
800 MDVL 84047 2176 A4
1000 PRVO 84601 2928 A7
1100 SLkC 84116 1652 C7
1200 LNDN 84042 2712 D6
1300 OREM 84057 2819 E5
1300 OREM 84058 2819 E5
1300 PRVO 84601 2927 D7
2200 SGVL 84663 3142 D2
3100 PRVO 84601 2926 E6
4000 UthC 84601 2926 E6
6000 CchC 84325 524 C3
W Center St SR-114
500 PRVO 84601 2928 A7
1300 PRVO 84601 2927 D7
Centerbrook Dr
2700 WVCY 84119 1962 D4
E Center Creek Rd
1100 HRCY 84032 2505 E1
1100 WshC 84032 2505 E1
Center Fork Cir
900 SNDY 84094 2283 A7
Centerline Dr
1500 WDCR 84087 1652 D3
Center Park Dr
- WJDN 84084 2068 C7
3600 WJDN 84084 2174 C2
Center Point Wy
14500 BFDL 84065 2387 E7
Center View Ct
7500 WJDN 84084 2174 C3
Center View Wy
3600 WJDN 84084 2174 C3
Central Av
- SLCY 84103 1859 A2
- SLkC 84098 2182 C1
E Central Av
10 SLkC 84107 2070 C1
W Central Av
10 SLkC 84107 2070 C1
Central Campus Dr
10 SLCY 84112 1859 C3
Central Park Cir
2500 TYVL 84118 2069 B4
Central Park Dr
5000 TYVL 84118 2069 A4
Central Park Wy
2500 TYVL 84118 2069 A4
Central Valley Rd
700 SSLK 84119 1964 A5
Century Dr
- OGDN 84404 1056 C5
400 MRRY 84123 2070 B2
900 TMTN 84337 520 D7
1000 TMTN 84337 584 D1
S Century Dr
500 OGDN 84404 1056 C6
Century Heights Dr
- HILD 84003 2497 C5
Century Park Wy
10 SSLK 84115 1964 C4
Cephus Cir
12700 DRPR 84020 2388 A2
Cephus Rd
500 DRPR 84020 2388 A2
Ceres Dr
3400 SLkC 84124 2072 C1
Ceri Ln
300 MIDW 84049 2397 A1
Cerromar Dr
1300 SRCS 84075 1226 A7
Cervantes Cir
9700 SLkC 84092 2284 B2
Cessna Cir
8600 SNDY 84093 2177 D6
Cezanne Cir
6100 SLkC 84118 2067 D7
Chablis Cir
9000 SNDY 84093 2177 B7
Chad Cir
700 MDVL 84047 2176 E3
Chad St
7600 MDVL 84047 2176 E3
7600 MDVL 84047 2177 A3
7600 SNDY 84047 2176 E4
7600 SNDY 84047 2177 A4
Chadbourne Dr
3400 CDHT 84121 2178 C4
Chadds Ford Ln
700 MDVL 84047 2177 A3
Chad Heights Ln
300 MDVL 84047 2176 D4
Chadwick Cir
200 ANFK 84003 2711 B2
Chadwick St
2400 SLCY 84106 1965 C3
Chalet Cir
400 BNFL 84010 1653 C5
2500 CDHT 84093 2178 A4
Chalet Dr
3500 SmtC 84098 1971 D7
Chalet Rd
2400 CDHT 84093 2178 A4
Chalice Wy
2900 WVCY 84120 1962 A3
Chalk Creek Wy
11600 SJDN 84095 2281 A7
Chalk Mark Cir
5200 TYVL 84118 2069 A5
Challenger Rd
500 SLCY 84116 1856 A1
Chambers St
700 SOGN 84403 1173 A4
Chambre Dr
5700 SLkC 84118 2067 D5
Champagne Av
1700 TYVL 84118 2069 C4
Champagne Cir
2000 TYVL 84118 2069 B4
Champlain Wy
5900 HRMN 84065 2385 C4
Chancellor Cir
1300 SLCY 84108 1860 B7
Chancellor Pl
2700 SLCY 84108 1860 B7
Chancellor Wy
1300 SLCY 84108 1860 A7
Chancey Dr
2400 SmtC 84098 1865 C4
Chandler Cir
1200 SLCY 84103 1859 B1
Chandler Dr
900 SLCY 84103 1859 B1
Chandler Boy Ct
13000 RIVN 84065 2387 D3
Chandlerpoint Wy
100 DRPR 84020 2388 D7
Chandlery Pl
3500 SLkC 84044 1960 B6
Chandlery Wy
8400 SLkC 84044 1960 B6
Channel Dr
500 MRRY 84107 2070 E6
Channing Dr
9500 SJDN 84095 2280 E2
Chantay Dr
6100 WVCY 84128 1961 C6
Chantilly Cir
5700 SLkC 84118 2067 D5
Chantilly Dr
3400 WVCY 84128 1961 C6
Chantilly Pl
200 PRVO 84604 2928 C3
Chapada Cir
900 SNDY 84094 2283 A5
Chapada Wy
10800 SNDY 84094 2283 A5
Chaparral Dr
700 MRRY 84123 2070 A5
Chaparral Oak Cir
2100 CDHT 84121 2177 E1
Chapel Cir
300 OREM 84058 2927 E2
Chapel Dr
700 BNFL 84010 1551 D6
E Chapel Dr
10 SALM 84653 3356 B5
W Chapel Dr
10 SALM 84653 3356 A5
Chapel Hl
4200 PRVO 84604 2821 E6
Chapel St
10 LYTN 84041 1283 B5
4600 HLDY 84117 2072 A2
N Chapel St
10 MDVL 84047 2176 B3
S Chapel St
10 MDVL 84047 2176 B4
Chapel Hill Cir
7400 MDVL 84047 2177 B3
E Chapel Hill Dr
1000 MDVL 84047 2177 A3
Chapel Oaks Cir
1400 CDHT 84093 2177 C4
Chapel Ridge Cir
11400 SJDN 84095 2281 E6
Chapel Ridge Dr
1200 SJDN 84095 2281 D6
Chapel Ridge Rd
- LEHI 84043 2495 C5
Chapel Rim Cir
2300 SJDN 84095 2281 B6
Chapel Rim Wy
11400 SJDN 84095 2281 B6
Chapel View Cir
1000 SJDN 84095 2281 E6
Chapel View Dr
11300 SJDN 84095 2281 E6
Chapman Pl
400 SLCY 84111 1858 E3
N Chappel Dr
800 SPFK 84660 3249 E1
1200 SPFK 84660 3142 E7
Chappel Valley Lp
800 LEHI 84043 2710 B1
N Chappel Valley Lp
500 LEHI 84043 2710 B1
Chardonnay Wy
14000 BFDL 84065 2387 D5
Charenton Cove Cir
5000 OGDN 84403 1173 E3
Chari Cir
7200 WJDN 84084 2175 D2
Charing Wy
13000 RIVN 84065 2387 B3
Charing Cross Rd
3200 WJDN 84084 2174 D3
Chariot Cir
800 SNDY 84094 2177 A6
Chariot Dr
800 SNDY 84094 2177 A6
Charisma Ln
13900 HRMN 84065 2385 D6
Charismatic Ct
11200 SJDN 84095 2281 B6
Charisse Cir
7200 WJDN 84084 2175 D2
Charity Ln
- SNDY 84070 2176 D6
Charity Cove
300 SLCY 84103 1858 D1
Charlais Dr
1000 FTHT 84037 1284 A7
Charlais Ln
4800 SmtC 84098 1972 A4
Charleen Cir
4900 OGDN 84403 1173 D3
Charlene Dr
700 BNFL 84010 1654 A2
Charlene Ln
5000 WVCY 84120 2068 B2
Charles Dr
800 KYVL 84037 1345 B2
4100 WVCY 84120 2068 B1
Charles Wy
4500 WVCY 84120 2068 B1
Charles Lindbergh Dr
100 SLCY 84116 1856 A2
Charleston Av
- NHON 84414 998 D6
2500 HARR 84414 998 D6
Charleston Cir
800 SNDY 84094 2283 A4
Charleston Dr
9600 CRHL 84062 2605 B4
Charleston Ln
1800 SLkC 84121 2071 D6
3400 CSTN 84032 2504 C3
Charleston Rd
- WshC 84032 2397 B6
- WshC 84032 2504 B2
900 WshC 84049 2397 B6
2500 CSTN 84032 2504 B2
Charleston Rd SR-113
- WshC 84032 2397 B6
- WshC 84032 2504 B2
900 WshC 84049 2397 B6
2500 CSTN 84032 2504 B2
S Charleston Rd
10 HRCY 84032 2398 B7
10 WshC 84032 2398 B7
1200 HRCY 84032 2505 A1
1200 WshC 84032 2505 A1
1600 WshC 84032 2504 C3
2100 CSTN 84032 2504 C3
S Charleston Rd US-189
10 HRCY 84032 2398 B7
10 WshC 84032 2398 B7
1200 HRCY 84032 2505 A1
1200 WshC 84032 2505 A1
1600 WshC 84032 2504 C3
2100 CSTN 84032 2504 C3
Charleston St
700 SNDY 84094 2283 B3
Charlestown Cir
4000 DvsC 84056 1228 A4
Charlestown Lp
4000 DvsC 84056 1228 A5
Charlesworth Cir
3400 WJDN 84088 2174 D4
Charlesworth Ct
500 OGDN 84401 1115 E3
Charlotte Av
5100 SLkC 84118 2068 A4
Charlotte Dr
900 SJDN 84095 2281 E2
Charlton Av
1100 SLCY 84106 1965 B4
Charlton Cir
900 SLCY 84106 1965 A4
Charros Rd
2300 SLkC 84092 2283 E4
2400 SLkC 84092 2284 A4
Charter Wy
6800 WJDN 84084 2173 D2
Charter Oaks Cir
1500 CDHT 84093 2177 C3
Charter Pointe Rd
2300 SJDN 84095 2281 B6
Chartres Av
700 SNDY 84070 2176 A7
800 SNDY 84070 2282 A1
Chartwell Ct
1000 SLCY 84103 1754 D6
Chase Av
800 SLCY 84102 1859 A5
Chase Ln
600 SGVL 84663 3143 D2
E Chase Ln
10 CTRV 84014 1551 E2
600 CTRV 84014 1552 A2
W Chase Ln
10 CTRV 84014 1551 D2
Chase St
200 SLCY 84113 1859 D3
Chase Brook Ln
800 SLkC 84124 1965 A7
Chase Creek Ct
800 SLkC 84124 1965 B7
Chateau Av
1700 TYVL 84118 2069 C4
Chateau Dr
2300 ROY 84067 1171 C5
Chateau Parc Cove
3600 HLDY 84121 2178 C1
Chatelain Rd
900 OGDN 84403 1116 A5
Chatham St
2400 WVCY 84119 1963 D3
Chatsworth Ct
7800 CDHT 84093 2177 C4
Chattel Cir
10000 SJDN 84095 2280 E3
Chatterleigh Av
6200 WVCY 84128 1961 C7
Chatterleigh Rd
3500 WVCY 84128 1961 C7
Chaucer Pl
2900 SLCY 84108 1860 B6
Chaundra Av
3200 SLkC 84124 2072 C2
Chavez Cir
1100 SJDN 84095 2281 E1
Chavez Dr
1000 SJDN 84095 2281 D2
Chaz Ct
400 SLCY 84116 1857 D1
Cheerful Dr
5000 TYVL 84123 2069 D4
Cheerful Vista Rd
3300 WVCY 84120 1961 E6
Cheever Ln
1400 FMTN 84025 1345 E5
Chegwidden Ln
4200 TYVL 84123 2069 D1
Chelemes Wy
10 CRFD 84015 1281 D2
Chelsea Cir
8800 SNDY 84070 2176 C6
Chelsea Dr
400 BNFL 84010 1653 E4
Chelsea Dr
600 BNFL 84010 1654 A4
Chelsie Dr
700 KYVL 84037 1345 B2
Cheltonham Wy
4000 TYVL 84084 2068 C7
4000 WJDN 84084 2068 C7
Chenault Wy
900 DvsC 84056 1228 B4
Chentelle Dr
4700 TYVL 84118 2069 B3
Cherapple Cir
600 OREM 84097 2714 A7
Cherapple Dr
600 OREM 84097 2713 E7
600 OREM 84097 2714 A7
Cherbourg Pl
9000 SNDY 84093 2177 E7
Cherise Cir
3000 SLkC 84106 1965 D5
Cherokee Cir
1500 SLCY 84108 1860 A7
1600 OGDN 84403 1173 C4
1600 WbrC 84403 1173 C4
Cherokee Dr
800 PTGV 84062 2713 C4
Cherokee Ln
2800 PRVO 84604 2928 E1
3200 PRVO 84604 2821 E7
Cherrington Cir
- OREM 84097 2821 B3
Cherry
10 PVDN 84332 528 B6
Cherry Cir
1400 PRVO 84604 2928 E4
1500 FMTN 84025 1346 C5
2300 SRSP 84043 2601 D4
N Cherry Cir
1500 LYTN 84040 1283 C2
Cherry Ct
2800 OGDN 84403 1116 A4
4500 CRHL 84062 2605 A4
Cherry Dr
300 RVDL 84405 1172 C2
500 BMCY 84302 767 A4
600 OREM 84058 2820 B7
2400 PRRY 84302 827 D5
2800 NHON 84414 999 C5
Cherry Ln
- SNQN 84655 3461 B6
- UthC 84655 3461 B6
10 FMTN 84025 1448 D2
1000 PRVO 84604 2928 E4
1400 CTRV 84014 1551 E1
1900 HRCY 84032 2292 E7
10400 HILD 84003 2605 A2
E Cherry Ln
900 LYTN 84040 1283 C2
1600 FTHT 84037 1346 B2
2500 LYTN 84040 1284 A2
N Cherry Ln
1500 LYTN 84040 1284 A1
S Cherry Ln
500 FTHT 84037 1346 B2
Cherry St
400 MRRY 84123 2070 B2
Cherry Blossom Cir
4400 WVCY 84120 2068 A2
Cherry Blossom Dr
1400 FMTN 84025 1346 B5
Cherry Blossom Ln
2800 HLDY 84117 2072 B2
Cherry Canyon Wy
1400 DRPR 84020 2389 C2
Cherry Creek Dr
11400 SNDY 84094 2283 A6
Cherry Creek Ln
1400 DRPR 84020 2389 C3
Cherry Grove Wy
2400 SJDN 84095 2281 A3
Cherry Hill Cir
700 PTGV 84062 2713 A3
Cherry Hill Dr
200 PTGV 84062 2713 A3
11400 SNDY 84094 2283 B6
Cherry Hills Cir
3700 SRCS 84075 1226 B7
Cherry Hollow Cir
4400 WVCY 84120 2068 A2
Cherry Knoll Cir
11500 SNDY 84094 2283 B6
Cherry Knoll Dr
1100 SNDY 84094 2283 B6
Cherry Laurel Ln
4800 WJDN 84088 2174 A7
4900 WJDN 84088 2173 D7
Cherry Meadows Ln
1900 LYTN 84040 1283 D1
Cherry Park Ln
2500 SJDN 84095 2281 A3
Cherry Plum Ct
500 SNDY 84070 2282 E4
Cherry Ridge Dr
1200 PRRY 84302 827 B7
Cherry Springs Ct
6000 WVCY 84118 2067 C7
Cherry Tree Ln
7000 CDHT 84121 2177 D2
Cherry Valley Pl
6200 WVCY 84118 2067 B7
Cherry View Dr
4300 WVCY 84120 2068 A1
5000 WVCY 84120 2067 E1
Cherry Wood Cir
800 DRPR 84020 2283 A6
Cherrywood Cir
700 CTRV 84014 1551 E2
1900 SLkC 84106 1965 D7
Cherrywood Dr
- FRWT 84404 1055 C3
1100 LYTN 84040 1283 D2
Cherrywood Ln
4800 WVCY 84120 2068 A2
5000 WVCY 84120 2067 E2
Cherrywood Rd
500 KYVL 84037 1345 E2
Cherrywoods Ln
10 SNDY 84092 2284 A5
Cheryl Cir
1300 KYVL 84037 1345 E4
S Cheryl St
3800 WVCY 84119 1963 B7

STREET Block City ZIP Map# Grid

Cheryle Wy
2200 LYTN 84040 1230 A7
2300 LYTN 84040 1229 E7
Chesapeake Cir
700 MRRY 84123 2070 A6
3000 SJDN 84095 2281 A2
Chesapeake Dr
9600 SJDN 84095 2281 A2
Cheshire Cir
9000 SNDY 84093 2177 E7
Cheshire Dr
2400 SNDY 84093 2178 A7
8900 SNDY 84093 2177 A7
Chester Ln
700 KYVL 84037 1345 A1
Chester Rd
5200 WVCY 84120 1961 E6
Chester St
100 OGDN 84404 1056 D6
500 OGDN 84404 1057 A7
Chesterbrook Cove
900 MRRY 84123 2069 E6
900 MRRY 84123 2070 A6
Chesterfield Dr
9600 CRHL 84062 2605 A3
Chesterfield St
2400 WVCY 84119 1963 E3
Chester Park Dr
3200 WVCY 84119 1962 E4
Chestnut Cir
7300 CDHT 84121 2178 C3
Chestnut Ln
200 LOGN 84321 527 E1
W Chestnut Ln
10 SHFD 84335 399 D1
Chestnut St
100 OGDN 84404 1056 D5
800 SLCY 84104 1857 B5
Chestnut Glen Dr
4700 MRRY 84107 2070 E3
Chestnut Oak Dr
4200 LEHI 84043 2495 C6
Chestnut Ridge Dr
200 SNDY 84070 2282 D4
Chestnut View Ct
10200 SJDN 84095 2280 C3
Chestnut View Dr
4100 SJDN 84095 2280 C3
Chet's Ct
5300 WVCY 84120 1961 E6
Chevy Chase Cir
1000 MRRY 84117 2071 B5
Chevy Chase Dr
1000 MRRY 84117 2071 A5
Cheyenne Cir
5000 OGDN 84403 1173 C3
Cheyenne St
300 SLCY 84104 1857 D5
Cheyenne Wy
8800 SmtC 84098 1865 C4
Chicago St
200 SLCY 84116 1857 E2
1500 SLCY 84116 1753 E5
Chichory Ln
11400 DRPR 84020 2282 D6
Chickadee Cir
9100 SNDY 84093 2178 A7
Chickadee St
1200 WVCY 84119 1963 D7
Chickasha Dr
4300 MRRY 84107 2070 D2
Child Dr
1200 LYTN 84040 1283 D2
Childs Av
300 OGDN 84404 1056 E5
1400 OGDN 84404 1115 E1
1800 OGDN 84401 1115 E2
3800 SOGN 84405 1115 E7
N Childs Av
100 OGDN 84404 1056 E5
Childs Ln
10 CTRV 84014 1551 C3
1900 WBNF 84087 1551 C4
S Childs Rd
500 SPFK 84660 3250 A1
500 SPFK 84663 3250 A1
S Childs Rd SR-51
500 SPFK 84660 3250 A1
500 SPFK 84663 3250 A1
Chilly Peak Cir
1300 OGDN 84404 1057 B2
Chilly Peak Dr
4800 RIVN 84065 2386 A6
Chimes Cir
10 SOGN 84405 1115 D7
Chimes View Dr
- WbrC 84405 1172 E1
100 SOGN 84405 1115 D7
200 SOGN 84405 1172 E1
Chimney St
3300 WVCY 84119 1962 E6
Chimney Rock Cir
2900 TYVL 84084 2069 A7
Chimney Stone Ct
- DRPR 84020 2496 D3
Chinaberry Cir
9500 SNDY 84092 2283 E1
China Clay Cir
5700 SLkC 84118 2067 C6
China Clay Dr
5400 SLkC 84118 2067 C5
Chinook Cir
5000 MRRY 84107 2070 E4
Chinook Wy
5100 MRRY 84107 2070 E4
Chip Cir
9900 SJDN 84095 2280 B2
Chipeta Wy
200 SLCY 84108 1859 E4
200 SLCY 84113 1859 E4
Chipman
- ANFK 84003 2604 C6
Chipman Av
200 ANFK 84003 2604 E7
Chippewa Pl
5000 WVCY 84120 1961 E6
5000 WVCY 84120 1962 A6
Chippewa Rd
3500 WVCY 84120 1962 A6
Chippewa Wy
2800 PRVO 84604 2928 E1
Chism Ct
3500 TYVL 84118 2068 D7
Chiswick Ct
5900 WJDN 84084 2173 B1
Chloe Wy
100 MDVL 84047 2176 B6
Choctaw Av
4800 WVCY 84120 1962 A6
Choctaw Rdg
1800 OGDN 84403 1173 D4
Chokecherry Cir
400 OREM 84058 2820 C5
1800 BNFL 84010 1654 C4
Choke Cherry Dr
3600 SLkC 84109 1966 D6
Chokecherry Dr
1300 BNFL 84010 1654 B3
Chosen Wy
9800 SJDN 84095 2281 E2
Chris Ln
6900 CDHT 84121 2177 C2
Chris St
400 PTVW 84404 998 A6
Chriskay Dr
- SLkC 84118 2067 E3
- SLkC 84118 2068 A3
Chrisman Dr
- SALM 84653 3356 A4
S Chrisman Dr
300 SALM 84653 3356 A4
Christalee Ct
7200 WJDN 84084 2175 C2
Christan Wy
1500 RIVN 84065 2387 C5
Christensen Av
2700 OGDN 84403 1116 D4
N Christensen Farm Rd
500 SALM 84653 3355 E3
Christine Cir
1000 SLkC 84106 1965 A7
Christine St
3500 SLkC 84106 1965 A6
Christine Wy
200 KYVL 84037 1345 B2
Christmas Box Ln
1100 OGDN 84404 1057 B7
Christoffersen Cir
2700 WbrC 84403 1174 A6
Christopher Cir
700 KYVL 84037 1345 B2
11100 SNDY 84092 2283 C5
Christopher Pl
100 TMTN 84337 521 A6
Christopherson Cir
4400 WVCY 84120 2068 C2
Christopherson Dr
3800 WVCY 84120 2068 C2
Christos Cir
6100 TYVL 84123 2069 D7
Christy Av
3500 WVCY 84119 1962 D5
Christyann Dr
3600 TYVL 84118 2068 D5
Christy Hill Wy
3600 TYVL 84118 2068 D4
Chromalloy Cir
8400 WJDN 84088 2174 C6
Chucker Cir
11800 RIVN 84065 2281 E7
Chugg Ln
400 HARR 84404 1056 C3
Chukar Ln
4700 WbrC 84403 1173 D3
4800 OGDN 84403 1173 D3
Chula Cir
7100 WVCY 84128 1960 E6
Chula Dr
3500 WVCY 84128 1960 E6
7000 WVCY 84128 1961 A6
Chula Vista Cir
3100 CDHT 84121 2178 B2
Church Av
100 LOGN 84321 527 D3
N Church Cir
4000 DvsC 84056 1228 A4
Church St
10 ANFK 84003 2711 C1
10 LYTN 84041 1282 E5
1000 LYTN 84041 1283 A2
N Church St
1700 LYTN 84040 1283 B1
1700 LYTN 84041 1283 B1
2100 LYTN 84040 1229 C6
Churchill Dr
500 CTRV 84014 1448 C6
4200 PRVO 84604 2821 E6
E Churchill Dr
10 SLCY 84103 1754 C7
Churchill Downs Dr
- FMTN 84025 1448 A2
1400 SNDY 84092 2283 C4
Churchwood Dr
3400 TYVL 84118 2068 D4
Chylene Dr
9600 SNDY 84092 2284 B2
9700 SLkC 84092 2284 B2
Cilma Cir
3800 WVCY 84128 1961 C7
Cilma Dr
5700 WVCY 84128 1961 C7
Cilma Pl
3800 WVCY 84128 1961 C7
Cima Dr
1800 SNDY 84093 2177 D6
Cimarron
4000 CRHL 84062 2605 C1
Cimmaron Dr
2100 SGVL 84663 3143 C6
Cimmarron Dr
3600 WVCY 84128 1961 A6
7000 WVCY 84128 1960 E6
Cindy Cir
10900 SNDY 84092 2283 E5
Cindy Ct
9600 SJDN 84095 2280 A1
Cindy Ln
4800 SJDN 84095 2280 A1
12800 DRPR 84020 2389 B3
Cindy Lee Cir
9700 SJDN 84095 2280 A2
Cinnabar Ln
2300 CDHT 84121 2177 E2
2300 CDHT 84121 2178 A2
Cinnamon Cir
- SRSP 84043 2601 D5
2800 TYVL 84118 2069 A6
Cinnamon Dr
300 SRSP 84043 2601 D5
5800 TYVL 84118 2069 A6
Cinnamon Hills Dr
900 PRVO 84606 3036 A1
Cinnamon Ridge Rd
12000 SNDY 84094 2283 B7
12000 SNDY 84094 2389 B1
Cinnamon Tree Cir
4700 WVCY 84120 2068 B2
Cinnamon Wood Ln
4900 SJDN 84095 2280 A1
Circle Dr
1100 SNST 84056 1227 E2
Circle Pl
600 PVDN 84332 592 B1
Circle Wy
1400 SLCY 84103 1859 C2
3000 OGDN 84403 1116 C5
Circle Cove
500 LEHI 84043 2603 B4
Circle Oaks
10 SNDY 84092 2284 A5
Circle View Dr
1100 LOGN 84341 464 D7
Cirrus Cir
6100 SLkC 84118 2068 C7
Cisco Ct
5500 WJDN 84088 2173 D6
Cistena Cir
1100 LYTN 84040 1283 C2
Citadel St
4600 WVCY 84120 2068 B3
Citation Dr
- FMTN 84025 1448 A2
Citori Dr
7800 SNDY 84070 2176 E4
Citrus Cir
3400 SSLK 84106 1964 E6
City Center Ct
- WVCY 84119 1963 B5
City Creek Canyon Rd
- SLCY 84103 1754 E6
- SLCY 84103 1755 D3
City Lights Cir
9900 SJDN 84095 2280 D2
S City Pasture Rd
800 SGVL 84663 3036 B7
Civic Center Dr
100 SNDY 84070 2282 C2
CJ Wy
1200 WVCY 84119 1963 D6
Claim Jumper Cir
7300 CDHT 84121 2178 D3
Claim Jumper Ct
10 PKCY 84060 2078 B3
Claim Staker Wy
4700 HRMN 84065 2280 A7
12000 HRMN 84065 2386 B1
Clairmont Cir
8500 SNDY 84070 2176 E6
Clara Dr
6000 TYVL 84118 2069 B7
6200 TYVL 84084 2069 B7
Clara Pl
200 TMTN 84337 520 E6
Clara St
2000 LYTN 84041 1282 A1
Claremont Dr
1900 BNFL 84010 1654 B4
Claremont Wy
1900 SLCY 84108 1859 E6
Clarenden Pl
5000 HLDY 84117 2072 A4
Claret Cir
7300 CDHT 84121 2178 A3
Claret St
7400 CDHT 84121 2178 A3
Claridge Dr
1500 SLkC 84124 2071 B1
Clark Av
1200 SLCY 84116 1857 D2
N Clark Av
100 OGDN 84404 1056 A5
S Clark Av
- OGDN 84404 1056 A6
Clark Ln
500 WDCR 84010 1653 C2
900 FMTN 84025 1448 A1
1300 FMTN 84025 1447 D1
N Clark Ln
10 EKMT 84651 3463 A2
S Clark Ln
10 EKMT 84651 3463 A2
Clark St
200 MRRY 84107 2070 D3
1700 LYTN 84041 1282 E1
Clarke Ln
4700 WbrC 84310 1001 D6
Clarke St
4800 WbrC 84310 1001 D5
Clarkston Cir
3200 SJDN 84095 2280 E4
Clarmont Dr
900 BNFL 84010 1654 A3
Clarry Cir
3800 SLkC 84044 1960 B5
Classic Dr
1500 WDCR 84087 1652 E4
Classic Cove
14200 BFDL 84065 2387 A6
Claudia St
4000 WVCY 84120 1961 D7
4000 WVCY 84120 2067 D1
Claudia Hill Ln
5100 WJDN 84084 2173 E2
7000 WJDN 84084 2174 A2
Clavinet Cir
3900 WJDN 84088 2174 C6
Clawson Pl
400 SLCY 84111 1858 E3
Clay St
6100 MRRY 84107 2070 C7
Claybourne Av
2100 SLkC 84109 1965 E4
2200 SLCY 84109 1965 E4
E Claybourne Av
10 SSLK 84115 1964 C4
700 SLCY 84106 1965 A4
700 SLkC 84106 1964 E4
700 SLkC 84106 1965 A4
W Claybourne Av
1400 WVCY 84119 1963 C4
Claybourne Cir
2700 SLkC 84109 1965 E4
Clay Creek Wy
- WJDN 84088 2173 D4
Clay Hollow Av
5100 WJDN 84088 2173 D4
Clay Park Dr
10 MRRY 84107 2070 C7
Clayton St
1400 SLCY 84104 1857 D7
1500 SLCY 84104 1963 D1
Clayton Ridge Wy
6800 WJDN 84084 2174 C1
Clear St
6100 MRRY 84107 2070 C7
Clear Berry Cir
300 DRPR 84020 2282 D6
Clearbrook Cir
3400 WVCY 84119 1962 E4
Clearbrook Dr
2800 WVCY 84119 1962 E4
Clear Creek Dr
10 SNDY 84070 2282 C5
Clear Spring Ln
1100 MRRY 84117 2071 B4
Clearview Dr
10200 SNDY 84070 2282 E4
Clearview St
4500 HLDY 84117 2071 E2
4500 HLDY 84117 2072 A2
Clear Vista Cir
5700 SLkC 84118 2067 B6
Clear Vista Dr
5800 SLkC 84118 2067 B6
Clearwater Ct
- LYTN 84041 1283 B6
Clearwater Dr
- KYVL 84041 1283 B6
- LYTN 84041 1283 B6
Clegg Cir
200 ANFK 84003 2711 B2
Cleggs Ln
- SJDN 84095 2281 E2
Clematis Wy
5200 WJDN 84084 2067 E7
6300 WJDN 84084 2173 E1
Clementine Cir
10500 SJDN 84095 2281 A4
Clermont Dr
3600 WVCY 84120 2068 D2
Clernates Cir
6400 WJDN 84084 2067 E7
6400 WJDN 84084 2173 E1
Clernates Dr
5400 SLkC 84118 2067 E6
6200 WJDN 84084 2067 E7
6400 WJDN 84084 2173 E2
Cleveland Av
300 SLCY 84115 1858 E7
500 SLCY 84105 1858 E7
Cleveland Cir
3400 SLkC 84109 1966 A6
Cleveland St
3800 NHON 84414 998 D3
E Cliff Cir
3700 SLkC 84124 2072 D2
Cliff Dr
3800 SLkC 84124 1966 D7
E Cliff Dr
3500 SLkC 84124 2072 D2
Cliffhaven Ln
3900 WVCY 84128 1961 D7
Clifford Cir
11300 SNDY 84092 2283 B6
Cliffs Pl
1800 LYTN 84041 1282 B1
Cliff Side Ct
1000 SNDY 84094 2177 B4
Cliff Side Dr
7900 SNDY 84094 2177 A4
Cliffside Dr
1100 LOGN 84321 528 B3
Cliff Swallow Dr
2300 SNDY 84093 2177 E7
2300 SNDY 84093 2178 A7
Clifton Av
300 ANFK 84003 2604 B6
Clifton Park Ct
4400 RIVN 84065 2386 B1
Clinton Av
2200 SLCY 84116 1857 A1
E Clinton Av
100 SLCY 84103 1858 D1
W Clinton Av
100 SLCY 84103 1858 C1
Clinton Rd
10 SNST 84015 1227 A1
500 CLTN 84015 1227 A1
1700 CLTN 84015 1226 C1
3500 WPT 84015 1226 A1
3700 WPT 84015 1225 E1
Clinton Rd SR-37
10 SNST 84015 1227 A1
500 CLTN 84015 1227 A1
1700 CLTN 84015 1226 C1
3500 WPT 84015 1226 A1
3700 WPT 84015 1225 E1
Clintwood Dr
300 DRPR 84020 2282 B7
Clipper Peak Cir
5400 HRMN 84065 2385 E3
Clipper Ridge Wy
13600 HRMN 84065 2385 C4
Cloud Ln
5800 HRMN 84065 2385 D4
Cloud Peak Ct
3300 WbrC 84310 1002 B4
Cloudywing Wy
- RIVN 84065 2386 A4
5100 RIVN 84065 2385 E4
Clover Cir
10 HRCY 84032 2398 C3
800 OGDN 84404 1056 D7
900 MIDW 84049 2397 B1
6800 WJDN 84084 2175 A1
E Clover Cir
700 RVHT 84321 528 A4
Clover Dr
12500 DRPR 84020 2388 E2
Clover Ln
600 KYVL 84037 1283 D7
4100 HLDY 84124 2071 E1
Clover Blossom Cir
700 MRRY 84123 2070 A4
Clover Creek Ln
5800 WVCY 84118 2067 C7
Clover Crest Dr
600 MRRY 84123 2070 A3
Clover Dale Dr
200 DvsC 84010 1653 B6
200 NSLK 84054 1653 B6
Cloverdale Rd
1600 CDHT 84121 2177 C2
Clover Leaf Ln
1800 DRPR 84020 2496 D1
Clover Meadow Cir
800 MRRY 84123 2070 A4
Clover Meadow Dr
800 MRRY 84123 2070 A4
Clover Meadow Rd
200 KYVL 84037 1283 B6
Clover Ridge Dr
200 SNDY 84070 2282 D4
Clover Spring Ln
8100 CDHT 84121 2178 C5
Clover View Dr
400 MRRY 84123 2070 B4
Cloverwood Cir
400 DRPR 84020 2388 E2
N Cloward Wy
600 EKMT 84651 3462 E1
600 UthC 84651 3462 E1
Club Dr
4000 SmtC 84098 1864 E4
Club Ln
- DvsC 84056 1228 D4
Club House Ct
100 BNFL 84010 1653 D7
100 NSLK 84054 1653 D7
Club House Dr
- LEHI 84043 2495 B7
- LEHI 84043 2602 B1
Clubhouse Dr
- CRHL 84062 2605 B1
1000 TYVL 84123 1963 D7
4000 TYVL 84123 2069 D1
Club Oaks Dr
9000 SNDY 84070 2176 A7
Club View Ln
5800 SOGN 84405 1173 B6
Clyde St
1900 LYTN 84041 1282 A1
Clydesdale Cir
2500 BFDL 84065 2387 A5
Clydesdale Ct
2400 FRWT 84404 997 C7
Clydesdale Dr
2600 WVCY 84128 1960 D3
CO-545
- CchC 84319 650 E4
- CchC 84339 650 E4
- HYRM 84319 650 E4
- HYRM 84319 651 A3
Coachman Cir
7600 CDHT 84093 2178 A3
Coachman Wy
600 RVDL 84405 1172 B2
3900 RVDL 84405 1115 C6
8500 WJDN 84088 2174 D6
Coal Creek Cir
700 SNDY 84094 2282 E5
Coalition View Ct
500 PKCY 84060 2078 E6
500 PKCY 84060 2079 A6
Coalville Wy
400 DRPR 84020 2495 E1
14800 DRPR 84020 2388 E7
Coastal Ct
1400 TYVL 84123 2069 D5
Coates Av
400 LYTN 84041 1283 A4
Coats Dr
3600 TYVL 84118 2068 D3
Coatsville Av
10 SLCY 84115 1964 D1
600 SLCY 84105 1964 E1
800 SLCY 84105 1965 A1
Coba Ct
6600 CDHT 84121 2178 A1
Cobalt Cir
9400 SNDY 84094 2283 A1
Cobalt Ln
1000 SNDY 84094 2283 A2
9800 SLkC 84094 2283 A2
Cobb Cir
4700 SLkC 84118 2068 C3
Cobble Cir
5100 WJDN 84088 2173 D5
Cobble Ter
2300 CchC 84325 588 D2
2300 CchC 84339 588 D2
Cobble Brook Ln
3500 CDHT 84121 2178 E5
Cobble Canyon Cir
8900 SLkC 84093 2178 B7
8900 SNDY 84093 2178 B7
Cobble Canyon Ln
3000 SNDY 84093 2178 B7
3700 SLkC 84093 2178 B7
Cobble Creek Cir
200 FMTN 84025 1448 D2
500 NSLK 84054 1653 A6
Cobble Creek Dr
5100 WJDN 84088 2173 D4
8200 WJDN 84088 2174 A5
Cobble Creek Ln
- WshC 84032 2505 B3
Cobble Creek Rd
10 NSLK 84054 1653 A5
200 FMTN 84025 1448 E2
1300 MRRY 84117 2071 B5
S Cobble Creek Rd
1300 MRRY 84117 2071 B4
1300 SLkC 84117 2071 B4
Cobble Crest Ln
8900 SNDY 84093 2178 B7
Cobblecrest Rd
2200 HLDY 84121 2071 E7
W Cobble Crest Rd
3200 BxEC 84309 522 B3
3200 BxEC 84312 522 B3
W Cobblecrest Rd
3200 BxEC 84309 522 B2
3200 BxEC 84312 522 B2
Cobble Hill Cove
200 LEHI 84043 2603 B3
Cobblemoor Ln
2700 SNDY 84093 2178 A7
Cobble Ridge Dr
3800 WJDN 84084 2174 D2
Cobblerock Ln
6200 HLDY 84121 2072 A7
Cobblestone Dr
500 MDVL 84047 2176 E2
1700 PRVO 84604 2928 A3
Cobblestone Ln
500 MDVL 84047 2176 E2
1400 OGDN 84404 1116 B1
Cobblestone Rd
1700 SGVL 84663 3144 B4
Cobblestone Wy
2400 SNDY 84093 2178 A7
Cobblestone Village Cir
1500 SNDY 84092 2283 C4
Cobble Stream Cir
3000 SNDY 84093 2178 B7
Cobblewood Cove
10 SNDY 84092 2284 B5
Cochise Ct
2800 PKCY 84060 2079 A3
Cochise Dr
3500 WVCY 84120 1962 C6
Cocomo Ct
13200 HRMN 84065 2385 B4
Cody Cir
1100 SJDN 84095 2281 D5
Cody Ln
6600 WJDN 84084 2175 A1
Colander Dr
4500 WJDN 84088 2174 A6
Colby Av
3500 WVCY 84128 1961 A6
Colchester Ct
1700 SNDY 84092 2283 C6
N Colchester Ct
600 LYTN 84040 1283 C3
Colchester Dr
500 LYTN 84040 1283 C3
11500 SNDY 84092 2283 C6
Cold Creek Wy
- LYTN 84041 1282 B4
Cold Springs Cir
4800 RIVN 84065 2386 A2
Cold Stone Ln
5100 WJDN 84088 2173 D4
Cold Water Dr
800 SNDY 84094 2177 A7
E Cold Water Wy
900 OGDN 84404 1057 B2
N Cold Water Wy
1400 OGDN 84404 1057 B2
Colebrook Cove
3100 WVCY 84128 1961 C5
Coleman Rd
800 CchC 84335 399 A1
1200 CchC 84335 398 E1
Colemere Wy
3300 SLkC 84109 1966 A5
Colene Dr
8300 SLkC 84094 2177 B6
8300 SNDY 84094 2177 B6
Coles Camp Cir
11800 HRMN 84065 2280 A7
Coleus Ct
6600 WJDN 84084 2174 A1
Coley Cir
5200 WVCY 84120 1961 E7
W Coleys Cove
10 EKMT 84651 3462 E3
Colfax Av
200 SLCY 84111 1858 D5
Colgate St
4600 WVCY 84120 2068 B3
Colima Cir
11300 SNDY 84094 2283 B6
Colima Dr
1000 SNDY 84094 2283 B6
College Dr
- OREM 84058 2820 A7
- OREM 84058 2927 B1
1500 OGDN 84403 1173 C1
5200 MRRY 84123 2070 B4
College St
- SLkC 84107 2071 A2
1100 SLkC 84117 2071 A2
Colleton Cir
6300 MRRY 84121 2071 C7
Collins Blvd
300 OGDN 84404 1057 B4
Collins Camp Ct
3100 WVCY 84128 1961 C5
Colliseum Ct
5400 TYVL 84118 2069 A5
Colmar Av
900 SLCY 84104 1963 E1
900 SLCY 84104 1964 A1
Colmere St
2600 SNDY 84092 2284 A2
Colonel Rd
1100 SLCY 84116 1753 B6
Colonial
- NSLK 84054 1653 B4
Colonial Av
10 LYTN 84041 1283 B4
Colonial Cir
1300 SLCY 84108 1859 D7
Colonial Dr
- PTVW 84414 998 D6
1300 SLCY 84108 1859 D7
2500 HARR 84414 998 D6
10400 CRHL 84062 2605 C2
Colonial Pl
1200 SLCY 84102 1859 B5
Colony N
800 SLkC 84106 1965 A6
Colony S
800 SLkC 84106 1965 A6
Colony Cir
3000 CRFD 84015 1228 B5
4800 SLkC 84117 2071 C3
Colony Dr
1300 SLkC 84117 2071 C3
Colony Cove
3400 LEHI 84043 2495 B7
Colony Pointe Dr
- LEHI 84043 2602 D4
S Colorado Av
900 PRVO 84606 3035 E2
Colorado Dr
- DvsC 84056 1227 E2
- SNST 84056 1227 E2
200 MDVL 84047 2176 B3
Colorado St
400 SLCY 84116 1857 D1
1000 SLCY 84116 1753 D6
3800 CRNN 84307 705 A7
3900 CRNN 84307 704 E7
Colorow Dr
400 SLCY 84108 1859 E4
400 SLCY 84108 1860 A4
400 SLCY 84113 1859 E4
400 SLCY 84113 1860 A4
Colt Ct
4100 WVCY 84120 2068 B1
Colt Dr
- FMTN 84025 1345 D7
Colter Cir
5000 SLkC 84118 2067 E4
Colter Dr
5300 SLkC 84118 2067 E4
Colter Bay Cir
9100 WJDN 84088 2174 C7
Colt Haven Cir
4000 HLDY 84124 2071 D1
Colt Hollow Ct
5800 HRMN 84065 2385 C4
Colton Mill Ct
4800 WVCY 84120 1962 A5
Columbia Av
10 SLkC 84107 2070 C1
Columbia Cir
600 PRVO 84601 2928 B5
Columbia Dr
10 MDVL 84047 2176 C4
1300 WJDN 84084 2175 D2
Columbia Ln
500 PRVO 84604 2928 A4
S Columbia Ln
1800 OREM 84058 2928 A3
1800 OREM 84097 2928 A3
Columbia St
- SLkC 84044 1854 D7
Columbine Cir
10400 SLkC 84094 2283 B3
Columbine Ct
2500 PKCY 84060 2078 E1
Columbine Wy
10400 SLkC 84094 2283 B4
N Columbus Ln
200 EKMT 84651 3462 E2
Columbus St
300 SLCY 84103 1858 C2
Columbus St SR-184
300 SLCY 84103 1858 C2
Comanche Cir
2600 SLCY 84108 1966 A1
5000 OGDN 84403 1173 D3
Comanche Dr
2600 SLCY 84108 1860 A7
2600 SLCY 84108 1966 A1
Comanche Ln
3000 PRVO 84604 2928 E1
Comanche Tr
2100 SmtC 84098 1971 D7
Comancheria Cir
12100 DRPR 84020 2388 E1
Combe Rd
1600 SOGN 84403 1173 D5
1700 WbrC 84403 1173 D5
2500 WbrC 84403 1174 A6
6000 UNTH 84403 1174 A6
6400 UNTH 84403 1173 D5
Comet Cir
4000 HLDY 84124 2072 A1
Comet Hill Cir
7200 WJDN 84084 2173 E2
Comish Cir
900 KYVL 84037 1344 E3
Commerce Dr
- SRSP 84043 2602 A7
3900 SLkC 84107 1964 B7
4000 MRRY 84107 2070 B1
4000 SLkC 84107 2070 B1
S Commerce Dr
400 OREM 84058 2819 E6
400 OREM 84058 2820 A6
Commerce Lp
300 OREM 84058 2820 A6
Commerce Rd
400 OREM 84058 2820 A6
Commerce Wy
1800 OGDN 84401 1114 D5
1900 WHVN 84401 1114 D5
Commerce Park Dr
600 MDVL 84047 2176 A2
N Commercial St
700 OREM 84057 2820 C3
S Commercial St
900 OREM 84058 2820 E7
Commons Ln
- SLCY 84104 1856 D6
Commonwealth Av
500 SLCY 84106 1964 E2
800 SLCY 84106 1965 A2
2400 SLCY 84109 1966 A2
E Commonwealth Av
100 SSLK 84115 1964 D2
W Commonwealth Av
100 SSLK 84115 1964 C2
Commotion Dr
2100 SNDY 84093 2177 E6
Community Ln
400 DvsC 84056 1228 D5
Como Ln
5700 WJDN 84084 2173 D2
Compass Cir
500 BNFL 84010 1653 C5
Compass Ct
2400 TYVL 84118 2069 A4

Salt Lake City Street Index

STREET
Block City ZIP Map# Grid
Compass Point Ln
1500 WJDN 84084 2175 C2
Compton Ct
500 MRRY 84107 2070 E3
Compton Rd
1100 FMTN 84025 1346 C6
N Compton Rd
1300 FMTN 84025 1346 C5
Comptons Pt
1400 FMTN 84025 1346 C5
Comstock Cir
7300 CDHT 84121 2178 D3
Comstock Dr
2100 PKCY 84060 2078 E3
Concho Wy
100 LEHI 84043 2710 B2
Concord Cir
2100 WJDN 84084 2175 B1
N Concord Cir
1300 HARR 84404 1056 C2
W Concord Dr
200 HARR 84404 1056 D2
Concord Pl
300 SRSP 84043 2601 D5
Concord St
200 SLCY 84104 1857 D4
1500 SLCY 84104 1963 E1
Concord Wy
800 BNFL 84010 1552 A7
3000 CRFD 84015 1228 B5
Concordia Pl
7600 SNDY 84047 2176 A3
Concord Park Dr
14800 BFDL 84065 2388 A7
14800 BFDL 84065 2495 A1
Condie Cir
10 FMTN 84025 1346 D6
Condie Dr
1800 TYVL 84119 2069 C1
Condie Ln
4100 WVCY 84120 2068 B1
Condie Park Cir
4600 WVCY 84120 2068 B1
Condor Cir
11800 RIVN 84065 2281 C7
Coneflower Ct
6800 WJDN 84084 2174 A2
Conestoga Cir
5400 SLkC 84118 2067 E5
Conewood St
5100 WVCY 84120 2067 E2
Confluence Av
500 MRRY 84123 2070 B1
Congress Dr
3800 WVCY 84119 1963 D7
Congress Wy
3100 CRFD 84015 1228 B5
Congressional
10600 CRHL 84062 2605 B1
Congressional Dr
1100 SRCS 84075 1226 A7
Congressional Wy
9800 SJDN 84095 2281 A2
Conifer Pl
10 LOGN 84321 528 A3
Conifer Wy
1500 TYVL 84123 2069 C2
Connecticut Av
1100 HARR 84404 1056 D3
Connecticut Dr
1200 DvsC 84056 1227 D2
1200 SNST 84056 1227 D2
1500 SLCY 84103 1859 D1
Connecticut Ln
300 SLCY 84103 1859 D1
Conner Park Cove
2000 SLkC 84109 1965 E4
Connie Dr
500 MDVL 84047 2176 E3
Connie Wy
1400 TYVL 84123 2069 D7
Connor Ct
5700 HILD 84003 2497 C7
Connor Rd
200 SLCY 84108 1859 E3
200 SLCY 84113 1859 E3
Connor St
800 SLCY 84108 1859 E5
1800 SLCY 84108 1965 E1
2700 SLCY 84109 1965 E4
2700 SLkC 84109 1965 E4
Connor Ridge Cove
900 MDVL 84047 2177 A4
Conrad St
4300 SLkC 84124 2071 C1
Consiline Av
3800 SLkC 84044 1960 D7
Constitution Blvd
2100 WVCY 84119 1963 A2
4000 WVCY 84119 2069 A2
4100 TYVL 84119 2069 A2
Constitution Cir
300 LYTN 84041 1283 A4
Constitution Dr
3000 WVCY 84119 1963 C4
Constitution Wy
200 NSLK 84054 1754 C1
1700 OGDN 84403 1116 C5
3000 CRFD 84015 1228 B5
Contadora Cir
3900 WVCY 84128 1961 C7
Contadora Ct
4000 WVCY 84128 1961 C7
Contadora Dr
6000 WVCY 84128 1961 B7
Contadora Ln
3900 WVCY 84128 1961 C7
Continental Cir
2900 TYVL 84118 2069 A4
Continental Dr
100 FMTN 84025 1448 D3
4000 WVCY 84120 2068 C1
Conway Ct
600 SLCY 84111 1858 D5
Conway Rd
5700 SLkC 84121 2071 C6
Cook Dr
10 LYTN 84041 1282 D4
Cook St
500 OGDN 84404 1056 E5
1200 OGDN 84404 1057 C5
Cooke Dr
1900 PKCY 84060 2078 E3
Cool Breeze Cir
4000 TYVL 84084 2068 C7
Cool Creek Wy
- WJDN 84088 2173 D4
Coolidge St
7700 MDVL 84047 2176 C5
Cool Water Wy
- WJDN 84088 2173 E4
Coon Canyon Wy
8000 SLkC 84044 1960 C5
Cooper Ln
- SmtC 84098 1971 D6
Cooper St
- KYVL 84037 1344 D2
7700 MDVL 84047 2176 A4
Coopers Hawk Bay
4700 SLkC 84117 2071 B3
Coopers Hollow Dr
- LEHI 84043 2603 E6
Copper Ln
- HRMN 84065 2386 B1
9200 WJDN 84088 2280 B1
9300 SJDN 84095 2280 B1
Copper Brook Cir
4600 WJDN 84088 2174 C5
Copper Canyon Wy
4800 WJDN 84088 2174 A5
Copper City Cir
5800 SLkC 84118 2067 C5
Copper City Dr
5400 SLkC 84118 2067 C6
Copper Cove Cir
3100 SLkC 84044 1959 E5
Copper Creek Cir
9100 SNDY 84093 2177 C7
Copper Creek Rd
1300 SNDY 84093 2177 B7
Copper Dale Pl
4600 WJDN 84088 2174 A6
Copperfield Pl
8000 SLkC 84044 1960 C6
Coppergate Cir
2000 WJDN 84084 2175 C3
Copper Glen Ct
4400 WJDN 84088 2174 B6
Copper Hill Dr
6800 WVCY 84128 1961 A7
7000 WVCY 84128 1960 E7
7200 SLkC 84044 1960 E7
Copper Hollow Dr
3600 SLkC 84044 1960 B7
Copper Meadow Ln
4900 WJDN 84088 2174 A5
5100 WJDN 84088 2173 D4
Copper Mine Dr
4600 HRMN 84065 2280 A7
Copper Oaks Dr
4800 HRMN 84065 2386 A6
Copper Park Dr
5500 HRMN 84065 2385 D4
Copper Peak Cir
5500 HRMN 84065 2385 D5
Copper Pit Cir
10000 SJDN 84095 2281 C3
Copper Pot Ln
4400 WJDN 84088 2174 B6
Copper Ridge Dr
3600 SLkC 84044 1960 B7
Copper Springs Ct
4800 RIVN 84065 2386 A2
Copper Stone Dr
5600 SJDN 84095 2279 D6
Copper Valley Ln
4400 WJDN 84088 2174 B6
Copperview Dr
2600 SLkC 84044 1960 E4
Copper Vista Cir
8200 WJDN 84088 2174 A4
Copperwood Dr
5500 WJDN 84088 2173 D7
Copplestone Cir
9700 SNDY 84092 2283 B1
Coquille Av
4800 WVCY 84120 1962 A7
Coquina Ct
2600 CDHT 84121 2178 A1
Cora Wy
5500 TYVL 84118 2069 A5
Cora B Ln
6500 HRMN 84065 2385 B5
Coral Dr
6200 TYVL 84123 2069 D7
Coral St
4100 HLDY 84124 2072 A1
Coral Dawn Ln
14000 HRMN 84065 2385 D6
Coral Dawn Cove
5800 HRMN 84065 2385 D5
Coral Dune Dr
3800 SJDN 84095 2280 C4
Coralroot Cir
6600 WJDN 84084 2174 A1
Coral Rose Pl
5100 WVCY 84120 2067 C3
Corbin Dr
2700 WVCY 84120 1962 D5
Corbin Bay
3700 WVCY 84120 1962 D4
Corby Cir
1400 SNDY 84092 2389 C1
Cordelia Av
10 SSLK 84115 1964 C4
Cordelle Cir
3600 WJDN 84084 2174 D2
Cordon Blue Wy
5000 TYVL 84118 2068 E4
Cordova Cir
1400 SNDY 84093 2177 C7
Cordova Wy
8900 SNDY 84093 2177 B7
Corentine Cir
5700 SLkC 84118 2067 D5
Coriander Ct
4900 SLkC 84118 2068 A6
Coriander Dr
4800 SLkC 84118 2068 A6
Corilyn Cir
5000 WVCY 84120 1962 A7
Corinne Dr
3200 SJDN 84095 2280 E4
Cork Oak Dr
8500 WJDN 84088 2173 B6
Corliss Av
9000 WJDN 84088 2174 B7
Corliss Cir
9000 WJDN 84088 2174 B7
Cormorant Cir
6800 CDHT 84121 2177 C2
Cornell Cir
1700 SLCY 84108 1859 C6
Cornell Dr
8400 SNDY 84094 2177 A6
W Cornell Dr
200 MDVL 84047 2176 B4
Cornell St
100 SLCY 84116 1857 D2
800 SLCY 84116 1753 D7
Corner Bridge Ln
300 DRPR 84020 2388 D4
Corner Canyon Dr
500 DRPR 84020 2388 E4
Corner Creek Cove
900 DRPR 84020 2389 A3
Corner Hills Cove
13900 DRPR 84020 2388 E5
Corner Hollow Ct
13400 DRPR 84020 2388 D4
Corner Ridge Ct
700 DRPR 84020 2388 E5
700 DRPR 84020 2389 A5
Cornerstone Dr
1400 SJDN 84095 2281 D3
Cornerstone Ln
10100 SJDN 84095 2281 D3
Cornerstone Wy
1500 SJDN 84095 2281 C3
Corner Wood Dr
13200 DRPR 84020 2389 A4
Cornflower Cir
5500 WJDN 84084 2067 D7
Cornia Dr
7400 DvsC 84405 1230 B2
7400 SWBR 84405 1230 B2
Cornish Cir
3200 SJDN 84095 2280 E4
Cornwall Ct
1700 SNDY 84092 2283 C6
Cornwall Pl
1700 SLCY 84116 1753 C5
Corona Cir
2800 WJDN 84084 2175 A4
Coronado Wy
1100 MRRY 84123 2069 E7
Coronation Cir
100 BNFL 84010 1653 D6
Coronation Wy
3600 BNFL 84010 1653 D5
Coronet Dr
3100 SLkC 84124 2072 B1
Corral Cir
1000 WJDN 84088 2175 E6
Corral Dr
- DvsC 84037 1284 A5
2900 LYTN 84040 1284 A5
Corral Ln
1800 SLCY 84116 1753 B4
Corridor Ln
3500 WVCY 84119 1963 D6
Corrie Cir
100 SNDY 84070 2282 D1
Corrie Ann Cir
2000 SNDY 84093 2177 D5
N Cortez Dr
200 EKMT 84651 3463 A1
Cortez St
500 SLCY 84103 1858 D1
Cortina Pl
9700 SLkC 84092 2284 D2
Cortina Pt
1200 WbrC 84317 1060 D7
Cortina Crest Dr
12000 DRPR 84020 2283 E7
12000 DRPR 84020 2389 E2
Cortland Cir
6500 TYVL 84084 2175 B1
Cortney Dr
2900 WVCY 84120 1962 B4
Cortney Pl
4200 WVCY 84120 1962 B4
Cory Rd
600 SJDN 84095 2282 A5
Cory Hill Cir
7500 CDHT 84121 2178 B3
Cosmo Cir
5200 WJDN 84084 2067 E7
Cosmo Dr
6200 WJDN 84084 2067 E7
Cosmo Pl
5200 WJDN 84084 2067 E7
Costa Cove
6600 CDHT 84121 2178 A1
Costanza Wy
12700 DRPR 84020 2389 C2
Cotswold Cir
1600 CDHT 84093 2177 C3
Cotswold Ct
6000 MRRY 84121 2071 C6
Cottage Av
10 SNDY 84070 2176 B6
400 SSLK 84111 1858 D5
Cottage Ct
2600 SmtC 84098 1865 B6
Cottage Lp
2600 SmtC 84098 1865 B6
Cottage Wy
1100 MIDW 84049 2291 A7
1100 MIDW 84049 2397 A1
Cottagebrook Cir
4800 WVCY 84120 2068 A1
Cottage Canyon Dr
8800 CRHL 84062 2605 D5
Cottage Cove
8800 CRHL 84062 2605 D6
Cottage Creek Ln
4500 MRRY 84107 2070 D2
Cottagefield Pl
11900 DRPR 84020 2282 D7
Cottagefield Wy
100 DRPR 84020 2282 D7
Cottage Glen Ln
200 MRRY 84107 2070 D2
Cottage Grove Ln
4500 MRRY 84107 2070 D2
Cottage Pines Cove
3400 CDHT 84121 2178 C5
Cottage Rose Cir
5600 HRMN 84065 2385 D5
Cottage Side Wy
11800 DRPR 84020 2282 D7
Cottagestone Ct
11900 DRPR 84020 2282 D7
Cottage View Ln
- DRPR 84020 2282 D7
Cottage Wood Ln
200 MRRY 84107 2070 D2
Cotton Blossom Ln
1900 HLDY 84117 2071 D4
Cotton Ridge Cir
5600 MRRY 84107 2070 D4
Cottontail Dr
6400 WVCY 84128 1961 B5
Cotton Tree Ln
5000 HLDY 84117 2071 E4
Cotton View Ct
7700 CDHT 84121 2178 E4
Cotton Willow Ln
2000 HLDY 84117 2071 D4
Cottonwood Cir
600 BMCY 84302 767 A6
700 BNFL 84010 1654 A2
800 ALPN 84004 2498 B2
2200 HLDY 84117 2071 E5
N Cottonwood Cir
1100 HRCY 84032 2398 E1
S Cottonwood Cir
1100 HRCY 84032 2398 E2
Cotton Wood Ct
1000 TMTN 84337 520 E3
Cottonwood Dr
- FRWT 84404 1055 C2
10 CTRV 84014 1551 E1
100 PTVW 84414 998 D1
600 SWBR 84405 1172 E6
600 SWBR 84405 1173 A6
800 TMTN 84337 520 C5
E Cottonwood Dr
800 HRCY 84032 2398 E2
N Cottonwood Dr
10000 CRHL 84062 2605 B2
Cottonwood Ln
- NHLN 84341 464 C3
- SmtC 84098 1972 A5
- WbrC 84317 1061 B7
1300 DvsC 84056 1228 A2
4800 HLDY 84117 2072 A4
5000 HLDY 84117 2071 E5
5300 HLDY 84121 2071 E5
N Cottonwood Ln
3000 PRVO 84604 2928 B1
3300 PRVO 84604 2821 B7
E Cottonwood Pkwy
2700 CDHT 84121 2072 B7
2700 CDHT 84121 2178 A1
Cottonwood Pl
- FRWT 84404 1055 D3
Cottonwood Rd
100 SHFD 84335 399 E2
Cottonwood St
- MRRY 84107 2070 C4
6400 MRRY 84107 2176 B1
7300 MDVL 84047 2176 B3
Cottonwood Tr
8400 SmtC 84098 1866 D4
Cottonwood Club Cir
1800 SLkC 84117 2071 D4
Cottonwood Club Dr
1800 SLkC 84117 2071 D4
Cottonwood Cove Ln
2000 CDHT 84093 2177 D4
Cottonwood Hills Cir
1000 SNDY 84094 2177 A6
Cottonwood Hills Ct
8100 SNDY 84094 2177 B5
Cottonwood Hills Dr
1100 SNDY 84094 2177 B5
Cougar Dr
800 OREM 84097 2821 A4
Cougar Ln
5400 SLkC 84118 2068 A6
6000 WJDN 84118 2068 A6
6200 WJDN 84084 2068 A6
6500 WJDN 84084 2174 A1
Councilman Cir
1200 WDCR 84087 1653 A1
Countess Wy
2500 SJDN 84095 2281 A2
Count Fleet Ct
2200 SJDN 84095 2281 B5
Country Av
2500 CDHT 84121 2178 A1
Country Cir
1700 CTRV 84014 1448 D7
Country Dr
800 OREM 84097 2821 A5
Country Ln
10 OREM 84097 2821 A5
900 FMTN 84025 1448 A3
1000 DRPR 84020 2389 A4
N Country Ln
10 FTHT 84037 1346 A1
200 FTHT 84037 1284 A7
300 KYVL 84037 1284 A7
S Country Ln
10 FTHT 84037 1346 A1
Country Rd
700 FTHT 84037 1345 E1
800 FTHT 84037 1346 A1
8300 SRSP 84043 2601 C7
Country Wy
10 FTHT 84037 1346 A1
200 FTHT 84037 1284 A7
Country Bend Cir
1700 FMTN 84025 1447 D1
Country Bend Dr
2200 SJDN 84095 2281 B2
Country Bend Ln
- FMTN 84025 1447 E1
Country Bend Rd
10 FMTN 84025 1447 D1
Country Bend Cove
100 FMTN 84025 1447 E1
Country Bluff Rd
3200 SJDN 84095 2280 E6
Country Breeze Cir
600 DRPR 84020 2388 E3
Country Brook Ct
11600 SJDN 84095 2280 C7
Country Cir Dr
10 TMTN 84337 520 C5
Country Classic Dr
2700 BFDL 84065 2387 A6
Country Club Cir
2300 SLCY 84106 1965 D3
2300 SLCY 84109 1965 D3
Country Club Dr
- TMTN 84337 520 C6
100 SOGN 84405 1172 D1
100 WbrC 84405 1172 D1
1700 LOGN 84321 528 D1
1700 LOGN 84341 528 D1
2100 SLCY 84109 1965 E3
2300 SLCY 84109 1966 A3
2700 PRVO 84604 2928 C2
4600 HILD 84003 2498 A7
4600 HILD 84003 2605 A1
4900 HILD 84003 2604 E1
Country Cove Wy
3800 WHVN 84315 1113 B7
Country Creek Dr
500 LYTN 84041 1283 B6
1100 SJDN 84095 2281 D4
Country Creek Cove
10700 SJDN 84095 2281 E4
Country Crossing Ct
4200 SJDN 84095 2280 B7
Country Crossing Rd
11400 SJDN 84095 2280 C7
Country Farm Cir
11500 SJDN 84095 2280 C6
Country Glen Cir
9200 SNDY 84093 2177 C7
Country Hills Dr
700 SOGN 84403 1173 C2
1600 OGDN 84403 1173 C1
5800 TYVL 84118 2068 D7
6000 TYVL 84084 2068 D7
6000 WJDN 84084 2068 D7
Country Hollow Dr
3500 CDHT 84121 2178 C3
Country Knoll Rd
3200 SJDN 84095 2280 E6
Countrylane Rd
1000 SLkC 84117 2071 A2
Country Manor Cir
- ALPN 84004 2498 C6
Country Manor Dr
1300 LOGN 84321 527 C7
N Country Manor Ln
10 ALPN 84004 2498 B4
S Country Manor Ln
10 ALPN 84004 2498 B5
Country Manor Rd
3500 CDHT 84121 2178 C3
Country Meadow Ln
600 ALPN 84004 2498 A5
4100 WVCY 84120 2068 C1
Country Meadow Estates Dr
900 HRCY 84032 2398 B5
900 WshC 84032 2398 B5
Country Mile Dr
1000 RIVN 84065 2281 D7
Country Mill Ct
7600 WJDN 84084 2175 D3
Country Oak Ln
1300 DRPR 84020 2389 B2
Country Oaks Dr
2100 LYTN 84040 1283 E1
2500 LYTN 84040 1284 A1
Country Park Cove
1100 SJDN 84095 2281 E4
Country Pine Cove
2000 HLDY 84117 2071 D3
Country Ridge Dr
1100 SJDN 84095 2281 D6
Country Shire Dr
700 KYVL 84041 1283 B6
700 LYTN 84041 1283 B6
Countryside Cir
10 SmtC 84098 1972 C2
100 OREM 84058 2820 C6
1000 HRCY 84032 2398 B5
Countryside Ct
600 MDVL 84047 2176 A2
Country Side Dr
- LOGN 84321 527 C7
Countryside Dr
100 OREM 84058 2820 C5
E Countryside Dr
1700 SLkC 84106 1965 C6
W Countryside Dr
200 OREM 84058 2820 C5
Countryside Ln
2200 WJDN 84084 2175 B1
Countryside Rd
10 FMTN 84025 1447 D2
E Countryside Wy
400 OGDN 84404 1056 E3
Country Spring Cir
- KYVL 84037 1344 C1
- KYVL 84037 1345 A3
Country Spring Rd
- KYVL 84037 1345 A1
Country Springs Cir
100 BNFL 84010 1551 D5
Country Springs Dr
100 BNFL 84010 1551 D4
Country Springs Ln
1600 BNFL 84010 1551 D5
Country Squire Dr
3700 WJDN 84088 2174 D6
Country Terrace Cir
1600 SNDY 84092 2283 C7
Country View Dr
4500 SOGN 84403 1173 A2
Country View Ln
2100 CDHT 84121 2177 E3
Country Villa Ln
900 TYVL 84123 2069 E3
Country W Dr
3500 SLkC 84044 1960 C6
Countrywood Ct
1700 SNDY 84092 2283 C2
Country Wood Dr
4400 LEHI 84043 2495 C6
Countrywood Dr
9800 SNDY 84092 2283 C3
Countrywood Ln
1300 WJDN 84088 2175 D7
Country Woods Cir
1000 CDHT 84121 2177 A1
County Rd
2800 HLDY 84121 2072 B5
Courage Dr
8900 SNDY 84070 2176 C7
Courchevel Pl
- CDHT 84121 2178 B2
Course View Ln
1900 DRPR 84020 2389 D1
Court Av
100 MRRY 84107 2070 D3
N Courtesy Wy
10 OREM 84057 2820 C4
Courtland Av
6700 CDHT 84121 2177 E1
Courtney Ct
4300 WJDN 84088 2174 B7
Courtney Pl
9000 WJDN 84088 2174 B7
Courtney Down Wy
- WJDN 84084 2174 A3
Courtside Ln
10 SNDY 84092 2284 A5
Courtyard Dr
1300 LEHI 84043 2603 B4
Courtyard Ln
10 CTRV 84014 1551 E5
Cousins Ln
2700 SJDN 84095 2281 A4
Cove Cir
1300 NSLK 84054 1754 E1
3200 LYTN 84040 1284 B4
Cove Dr
- SGVL 84663 3144 C4
N Cove Dr
3800 PRVO 84604 2821 C6
W Cove Dr
10 EKMT 84651 3462 E2
Cove Ln
10 LYTN 84040 1284 B4
2800 BNFL 84010 1654 C4
Cove Canyon Dr
5100 SmtC 84098 1971 D4
Cove Creek Ln
5800 MRRY 84107 2071 A6
Cove Crest Cir
12100 RIVN 84065 2387 D1
Covecrest Dr
4300 SLkC 84124 2072 D2
Cove Hollow Ln
5300 SmtC 84098 1971 D4
Coventry
- LOGN 84341 463 C6
Coventry Cir
- SRCS 84075 1226 B6
300 FTHT 84037 1284 A7
1000 OREM 84097 2821 B7
Coventry Ct
9800 HILD 84003 2604 D3
Coventry Ln
100 NSLK 84054 1653 C7
400 ALPN 84004 2498 B3
1300 PRVO 84604 2821 E7
2700 CDHT 84121 2178 A3
N Coventry Ln
700 ALPN 84004 2498 B3
Coventry Park Dr
3200 WVCY 84119 1962 E4
Coventry View Dr
1800 SLCY 84116 1753 C7
Cove Park Cir
1200 MRRY 84123 2069 D6
Cove Point Dr
3500 SLkC 84124 1966 C7
Cove Point Ln
1900 PRVO 84604 2928 A3
Covewood Pl
1000 WJDN 84088 2175 E6
Covey Ln
12300 RIVN 84065 2387 D1
Covey View Ct
1900 SLCY 84106 1965 D4
Covington Ct
1100 SNDY 84094 2283 B6
Cowan Wy
3900 WVCY 84120 1962 B7
3900 WVCY 84120 2068 B1
Cowdell St
4900 TYVL 84118 2069 B4
Cowley St
600 LYTN 84041 1282 D3
E Cox Ln
10 MDVL 84047 2176 C3
Coybrook Cir
3200 TYVL 84084 2068 E6
Coybrook Ct
3200 TYVL 84084 2174 E1
Coybrook Dr
3200 TYVL 84084 2068 E7
6400 TYVL 84084 2174 E1
Coybrook Pl
3200 TYVL 84084 2068 E7
Coyote Cir
900 NSLK 84054 1653 C7
Coyote Ln
- HRCY 84032 2292 D7
- WshC 84032 2292 D7
Coyote Run
- SRSP 84043 2601 C7
Coyote Cove
9300 WJDN 84088 2281 A1
Coyote Hollow Ct
14100 DRPR 84020 2389 D6
Cozy Dale Dr
4400 OGDN 84405 1172 A2
4400 RVDL 84405 1171 E2
4400 RVDL 84405 1172 A2
CR-2862
- SALM 84653 3248 E7
- SALM 84653 3249 A6
- SALM 84653 3355 D1
- SALM 84660 3248 E7
- SALM 84660 3249 A6
- UthC 84653 3248 E7
- UthC 84660 3249 A6
- UthC 84660 3355 D1
Crab St
- FTHT 84037 1346 A4
Crab Apple Cir
3500 TYVL 84118 2068 D3
Craftsman Ct
1300 LYTN 84041 1282 C7
Craftsman Wy
1600 SLkC 84124 2071 C2
Crag's End
- SLCY 84103 1754 C6
Craig Cir
1200 OGDN 84404 1116 B1
3600 SLkC 84109 1966 A6
Craig Dr
2600 SLkC 84109 1966 A6
Craig Ln
2000 SRCS 84075 1280 E1
Cranberry Cir
8000 SNDY 84093 2177 C4
Cranberry Lp
3600 LEHI 84043 2495 A7
Cranberry Wy
800 SGVL 84663 3144 B4
Cranberry Hill Ct
11400 DRPR 84020 2282 D6
Cranberry Hill Dr
10 DRPR 84020 2282 D6
Crandall Av
900 SLCY 84106 1965 A4
Crandall Cir
1800 SLCY 84106 1965 D4
Crandall Dr
1400 SGVL 84663 3144 A2
Cranston Cove
5800 WVCY 84128 2067 C1
Cranton Pl
1000 BMCY 84302 767 B4
Crape Myrtle Cir
400 DRPR 84020 2282 E6
Cravalan Cir
8200 SLkC 84093 2177 E5
Crawford Av
200 MRRY 84107 2070 D3
Crawford Pl
10 SNDY 84070 2176 C7
Crayon Ct
10 LOGN 84321 527 B5
Creative Pl
2100 SLkC 84093 2177 E5
Cree Dr
3500 WVCY 84120 1962 A6
5100 WVCY 84120 1961 E6
Creek Cir
8100 CDHT 84093 2177 E5
Creek Ct
2700 PKCY 84060 2078 C2
Creek Dr
- SLkC 84098 2182 C1
2400 PKCY 84060 2078 C2
E Creek Dr
10 MRRY 84107 2070 C7
W Creek Dr
10 MRRY 84107 2070 C7
Creek Ln
700 FMTN 84025 1346 A5
4500 MRRY 84107 2070 D2
Creek Pl
10 MIDW 84049 2397 A3
Creek Rd
1100 CDHT 84093 2177 C4
1100 SNDY 84093 2177 C4
1600 SLkC 84093 2177 C4
2400 CDHT 84093 2178 A5
2400 SLkC 84093 2178 A5
2900 CDHT 84121 2178 A5
2900 SmtC 84098 1865 B4
Creek Wy
2100 CDHT 84093 2177 E5
Creek Bed Dr
10 PYSN 84651 3354 E5
W Creekbend Dr
700 SSLK 84119 1964 A7
Creek Bluff Cove
600 SNDY 84070 2282 A1
Creekcove Cir
1100 CDHT 84121 2177 B1
Creekcove Wy
6800 CDHT 84121 2177 B1
Creek Hill Ln
900 MDVL 84047 2177 A3
Creek Hollow Cove
8200 SLkC 84093 2177 E5
8200 SNDY 84093 2177 E5
Creek Park Ct
3400 SLkC 84106 1964 D5
Creek Ridge Cir
11100 SJDN 84095 2281 E5
Creek Ridge Dr
1100 SJDN 84095 2281 D5
Creekside Cir
400 MRRY 84107 2070 E5
500 KYVL 84037 1283 C7
Creekside Ct
900 FMTN 84025 1448 D4
Creekside Dr
700 LYTN 84041 1283 B6
1000 OGDN 84404 1116 B1
Creek Side Ln
1600 SmtC 84098 1971 E4
Creekside Ln
300 KYVL 84037 1283 C7
Creekside Wy
- WbrC 84310 1001 D4
300 KYVL 84037 1283 C7
Creekside Pass
800 ALPN 84004 2497 D6
Creek Stone Ct
5100 SmtC 84098 1971 E4
Creek Trail Ct
11000 SJDN 84095 2281 D5
Creek View Cir
4500 MRRY 84107 2070 E2
Creek View Dr
- LYTN 84041 1283 B6
500 MRRY 84107 2070 D2
1000 FTHT 84037 1346 A3
4600 WbrC 84310 1001 D3
S Creek View Dr
1000 FTHT 84037 1346 A4
Creek View Rd
400 CTRV 84014 1551 C2

STREET
Block City ZIP Map# Grid

Creekview Cove
- CDHT 84093 2177 C3
Creek Vista Dr
13800 HRMN 84065 2385 E5
Creekwood Cir
8200 WJDN 84088 2175 B5
Creekwood Dr
8100 WJDN 84088 2175 B5
Creekwood Ln
700 MRRY 84107 2071 A5
5500 MRRY 84107 2070 D4
Creighton Wy
2500 CDHT 84121 2178 A2
Creponette Dr
9100 SNDY 84093 2177 D7
E Crescent Cir
1100 LYTN 84040 1283 C3
Crescent Dr
- MPTN 84664 3250 D1
400 LOGN 84341 463 E7
3000 SLkC 84106 1965 B5
S Crescent Dr
900 SmtC 84098 1866 E5
900 SmtC 84098 1867 A6
Crescent Dr N
1000 SmtC 84098 1867 A5
Crescent Rd
1300 PKCY 84060 2078 C4
Crescent Wy
- MPTN 84664 3250 D1
Crescent Glen Cir
11200 SNDY 84070 2282 D5
Crescent Park Cir
11200 SNDY 84070 2282 D5
Crescent Park Wy
100 SNDY 84070 2282 D6
Crescentridge Cir
11200 SJDN 84095 2282 A5
Crescent Tram
- PKCY 84060 2078 D6
Crescent View Cir
1600 SNDY 84092 2283 C5
Crescent View Dr
1700 SNDY 84092 2283 C6
Crescent Vista Ln
300 SNDY 84070 2282 D5
Crescentwood Dr
200 SNDY 84070 2282 D6
11300 DRPR 84020 2282 D6
Crespi Ct
3600 WVCY 84119 1963 D6
E Crest
- OGDN 84401 1116 A2
W Crest
- OGDN 84401 1116 A2
Crest Cir
1500 SNDY 84093 2177 C7
Crest Ct
3400 WshC 84049 2079 C7
Crest Dr
700 OREM 84057 2820 B2
Crest St
6600 WVCY 84128 1961 A7
Crestbrook Ln
3300 SLkC 84109 1966 A6
Crested Wheat Cir
500 KYVL 84037 1283 D7
13900 DRPR 84020 2389 B5
Crestfield Dr
3200 WVCY 84119 2068 D2
Crestflower Wy
5500 SLkC 84118 2067 D6
Crest Gate Cir
1100 TYVL 84123 2069 E4
Crest Haven Ct
10400 SJDN 84095 2281 C4
Cresthill Cir
4600 HLDY 84117 2071 D2
Cresthill Dr
1800 HLDY 84117 2071 D2
Crestline Cir
300 SLCY 84103 1859 B2
Crestline Dr
- PRVO 84601 3035 B1
3000 PKCY 84060 2078 C1
Crestmont Wy
- KYVL 84037 1344 E2
W Crestmont Wy
- KYVL 84037 1344 D2
Crestmoor Ct
4600 WJDN 84088 2174 A5
Crestmount Cir
3600 HLDY 84121 2072 D7
Crestmount Dr
6300 HLDY 84121 2072 C7
Crest Oak Cir
4400 SLkC 84124 2072 D2
Crest Oak Dr
4400 SLkC 84124 2072 D2
Crestone Av
200 SSLK 84115 1964 D5
Crest Point Cir
8800 SNDY 84093 2177 E6
Crestridge Cir
12100 SNDY 84094 2389 B1
Crestridge Rd
1200 SNDY 84094 2389 B1
Crest View Av
800 PRVO 84604 2821 D6
W Crestview Av
- BxEC 84312 522 B3
3100 BxEC 84309 522 B3
Crestview Cir
100 SmtC 84098 1864 B6
1000 SLCY 84108 1860 B6
3100 BNFL 84010 1653 C5
Crestview Ct
7400 CDHT 84093 2177 D3
Crestview Dr
200 SLkC 84098 1864 B5
300 BMCY 84302 767 B4
2700 SLCY 84108 1860 A6
3900 HLDY 84124 1965 E7
Crestview Ln
10 SGVL 84663 3036 B7
100 SmtC 84098 1864 B6
Crestview Ter
100 SmtC 84098 1864 B5
Crestwood Cir
600 BNFL 84010 1552 A5
Crestwood Ct
3500 WshC 84049 2185 B1
Crestwood Dr
1200 SOGN 84405 1173 B5
3300 SLkC 84109 1966 D6
Crestwood Ln
- PRVO 84601 3035 B1
Crestwood Rd
10 KYVL 84037 1283 D7
800 KYVL 84037 1284 A6
W Crestwood Rd
10 KYVL 84037 1283 C7
Crestwood St
1700 LYTN 84040 1283 D2
Crichton Cove
- WVCY 84128 1961 A5
Crimson Cir
300 SSLK 84115 1964 D6
Crimson Ct
- HILD 84003 2604 C3
Crimson Ln
800 KYVL 84041 1283 B6
Crimson Wy
4500 ROY 84067 1171 C2
Crimson Glory Ct
13800 HRMN 84065 2385 D5
Crimson Oak Dr
1600 DRPR 84020 2389 C5
Crimson Patch Wy
5000 RIVN 84065 2385 E4
5000 RIVN 84065 2386 B4
Cripple Creek Cir
9100 WJDN 84088 2175 D7
Cristobal St
6600 CDHT 84121 2178 A1
Critchlow St
- OGDN 84404 1056 A6
Critters Cove
12600 RIVN 84065 2386 B2
Crockett Av
10 LOGN 84321 527 C1
100 LOGN 84321 528 A2
Crockett Dr
5000 SLkC 84118 2067 E4
Crocus Cir
800 SLkC 84094 2283 A3
Crocus St
10400 SLkC 84094 2283 A3
Croft Cove
3500 SSLK 84106 1964 E6
Croftwood Cove
6400 WVCY 84128 1961 B4
Croix Cir
12900 RIVN 84065 2387 D3
Cromwell Ct
4300 TYVL 84123 2069 E1
Cromwell Ln
13800 DRPR 84020 2388 E5
Crooked Stick Dr
- LEHI 84043 2602 C2
Cross Ct
5400 TYVL 84123 2069 D5
Cross St
10 LYTN 84041 1282 E4
300 OGDN 84404 1056 E7
700 OGDN 84404 1057 A7
4900 SLkC 84118 2068 A4
Crossbow Cir
5400 TYVL 84123 2069 D5
Cross Country Cir
11500 SJDN 84095 2280 C6
Cross Country Wy
5400 SmtC 84098 1971 D4
Cross Creek Cir
4800 MRRY 84107 2070 D3
Cross Creek Ln
300 MRRY 84107 2070 D3
Crosscut Cir
11800 HRMN 84065 2280 B7
Crosshill Ln
10 SNDY 84092 2284 A5
Crossley Ct
10100 SJDN 84095 2280 B3
Crosspark Dr
1400 TYVL 84123 2069 D5
Crosspointe Cir
5400 TYVL 84123 2069 D5
Crosspointe Ct
5500 TYVL 84123 2069 C6
Crosspointe Wy
1400 TYVL 84123 2069 D5
Crossroad Sq
200 SSLK 84115 1964 B2
Crosswind Dr
800 SPFK 84660 3249 E5
Crosswind Wy
900 DRPR 84020 2389 A4
Crosswood Cir
9400 SNDY 84093 2284 B1
Crosswood Ln
3100 SNDY 84093 2284 B1
Crow Cir
7100 WVCY 84128 1960 E5
W Crowder Cir
3700 WVCY 84120 1962 D7
Crown Av
3800 WVCY 84120 2068 C2
Crown Cir
5500 TYVL 84118 2068 E5
Crown St
3200 TYVL 84118 2068 E5
Crown Pointe Dr
400 MRRY 84107 2070 D5
Crownpointe Dr
4900 WVCY 84120 1962 A4
5100 WVCY 84120 1961 E4
Crown Ridge Cir
400 MRRY 84107 2070 D5
Crown Ridge Rd
400 MRRY 84107 2070 D5
Crown Rose Dr
14000 HRMN 84065 2385 D6
Cruden Bay Ct
13800 HRMN 84065 2385 E5
Cruise Dr
3700 SLkC 84109 1966 B7
Cruise Wy
2900 SLkC 84109 1966 B7
Cruise Bay Ct
2600 CDHT 84121 2178 A1
Crusader Dr
200 MRRY 84107 2070 D1
E Crusader Dr
200 MRRY 84107 2070 C4
Crus Corvi Rd
5000 WJDN 84084 2173 E1
5000 WJDN 84084 2174 A1
Crystal Av
600 LOGN 84321 527 C1
2000 SLCY 84109 1965 D3
E Crystal Av
10 SSLK 84115 1964 C3
600 SLCY 84106 1964 E3
1100 SLCY 84106 1965 B3
W Crystal Av
10 SSLK 84115 1964 C3
1200 WVCY 84119 1963 D3
Crystal Bluffs Dr
1100 MRRY 84123 2069 E7
Crystal Brook Cove
7400 SLkC 84044 1960 E4
Crystal Downs Ln
6800 WJDN 84084 2174 D2
Crystal Lake Wy
2900 WVCY 84120 1962 B4
Crystal Meadow Ln
400 DRPR 84020 2388 E3
Crystal Ridge Dr
1500 WJDN 84084 2175 D2
Crystal River Dr
1100 MRRY 84123 2069 E7
Crystal Rock Av
1700 SLCY 84116 1753 C5
Crystal Springs Dr
400 DRPR 84020 2388 D3
Crystal View Dr
1200 PTGV 84062 2713 B2
Crystal View Wy
1500 SJDN 84095 2281 D5
Crystal Vista Ln
9000 WJDN 84088 2174 B7
Cub Dr
3600 TYVL 84118 2068 D7
Cub Creek Cir
13300 DRPR 84020 2389 B4
Culloden Ct
1200 MRRY 84123 2069 D6
Culmination St
10400 SJDN 84095 2281 C4
Culpepper Cir
1400 TYVL 84123 2175 D1
Culross Ln
300 DRPR 84020 2388 E7
Cumberland Ct
700 ALPN 84004 2497 E6
Cumberland Dr
2100 HLDY 84124 1965 E7
4000 HLDY 84124 2071 D1
Cumberland Rd
4100 HLDY 84124 2071 E1
Cumberland Wy
800 ALPN 84004 2497 E6
Cumbria Cir
3700 WVCY 84119 1963 E6
Cummings Pkwy
- WshC 84049 2289 E7
- WshC 84049 2396 A3
Cummings Rd
3400 SLkC 84109 1966 C6
Cumorah Dr
4100 SLkC 84124 2072 E2
E Cumorah Dr
1000 GNLA 84655 3460 A6
Cumulus Cir
6100 SLkC 84118 2068 C7
Cupecoy Dr
2500 CDHT 84121 2178 A1
Curlew Cir
800 DRPR 84020 2283 A7
Curling Ct
3500 TYVL 84084 2174 D1
Current Creek Cir
11600 SJDN 84095 2281 A7
Current Creek Dr
- SJDN 84095 2280 E7
- SJDN 84095 2281 A7
Currey Ln
400 SGVL 84663 3143 B2
Curry Cir
2800 TYVL 84118 2069 A6
Curry Peak Cir
13900 HRMN 84065 2385 E4
Curtis Dr
1900 CDHT 84093 2177 D3
Cushing Av
100 ANFK 84003 2711 C1
Cushing Wy
100 LYTN 84041 1228 E6
Custer Av
600 OGDN 84404 1057 C6
1500 OGDN 84404 1116 C1
2300 OGDN 84401 1116 C3
3600 OGDN 84403 1116 C7
Custer Rd
2100 SLCY 84104 1963 A1
S Cutbridge Slant Rd
6500 SPFK 84660 3250 A3
6500 UthC 84660 3250 A3
Cutler Av
300 SGVL 84663 3143 D1
Cutler Dr
10 NSLK 84054 1652 D7
Cutler Rd
1100 SLkC 84106 1965 B7
Cutler Cove
13400 DRPR 84020 2389 A4
Cutler Creek Rd
- EKMT 84651 3462 D1
- UthC 84651 3462 D1
Cutter Ln
800 SmtC 84098 1972 A4
1100 SmtC 84098 1971 E4
Cyclamen Cir
6200 WJDN 84084 2067 E7
Cyclamen Ct
5400 WJDN 84084 2173 E1
Cyclamen Dr
6600 WJDN 84084 2173 E1
Cyclamen Pl
5400 WJDN 84084 2173 D1
Cyclamen Sq
6300 WJDN 84084 2067 E7
Cyclamen Wy
5000 WJDN 84084 2067 E7
5000 WJDN 84084 2068 A7
6400 WJDN 84084 2173 C2
Cyclamen Cove
5400 WJDN 84084 2067 E7
Cygnus Hill Cove
5200 WJDN 84084 2173 E2
Cynthia Wy
300 NSLK 84054 1653 B7
400 NSLK 84054 1754 B1
Cynthia Ann Cir
2200 RIVN 84065 2281 B7
Cypress
- CRHL 84062 2605 B1
Cypress Av
- SLCY 84103 1859 B2
Cypress St
7200 MDVL 84047 2176 B3
Cypress Wy
- LEHI 84043 2602 C2
2500 CDHT 84121 2178 A2
Cypress Pine Cove
7900 MDVL 84070 2176 D4
Cypress Point Wy
1500 DRPR 84020 2389 C1
Cyprus Dr
- HILD 84003 2497 B5
Cyprus Grove Cir
2700 SLkC 84044 1960 A4
Cy's Rd
700 SLkC 84094 2176 E6
700 SLkC 84094 2177 A6
700 SNDY 84094 2176 E6
700 SNDY 84094 2177 A6

D

D Av
- PTVW 84404 997 E5
100 DvsC 84056 1228 D5
2200 OGDN 84401 1115 B3
D St
- BMCY 84302 767 A7
- BMCY 84302 827 E2
- CRFD 84016 1227 C7
- KYVL 84041 1283 B6
- RVDL 84405 1172 A3
10 SLCY 84103 1858 E2
Dadola Dr
3400 BNFL 84010 1653 D5
Daffodil Av
5300 WJDN 84084 2173 E1
Daffodil Wy
6400 WJDN 84084 2067 E7
6400 WJDN 84084 2173 E1
Daggerwing Wy
13600 RIVN 84065 2385 E5
13600 RIVN 84065 2386 B4
Dahl Ln
1800 SRCS 84075 1281 A1
Dairy Ln
300 DRPR 84020 2388 D4
Daisy Av
800 SLkC 84094 2283 A4
Daisy Ln
700 MRRY 84123 2070 A4
Daisyfield Dr
100 DRPR 84020 2388 C6
Daisy Meadow Cir
9500 SJDN 84095 2281 A1
Daisy Ridge Dr
10800 SNDY 84070 2282 D4
Dakota Av
2000 PRVO 84606 3036 B3
Dakota Dr
- FMTN 84025 1345 D7
Dakota Ln
1700 PRVO 84606 3036 A3
Dale Av
1400 SLCY 84104 1857 D6
Dale Amour Dr
5500 SLkC 84118 2067 D5
Dale Park Cir
6600 WJDN 84084 2175 C1
Dale Ridge Av
1700 SLCY 84116 1753 C5
Dale Ridge Cir
1700 SLCY 84116 1753 C5
Dalesend Dr
2900 SLkC 84044 1960 C4
Daley Av
400 LYTN 84041 1283 A3
Daley Cir
1200 PYSN 84651 3355 B7
1200 PYSN 84651 3461 E2
Dallas St
1200 SRCS 84075 1227 A7
Dallas Kyle Dr
6600 HRMN 84065 2385 B5
Dallin Cir
1500 SRCS 84075 1281 A3
Dallin St
2100 SLCY 84109 1965 E3
Dalmatian St
3000 WVCY 84128 1960 E5
6900 WVCY 84128 1961 A5
Dalton Av
400 PTGV 84062 2713 B2
800 SLCY 84104 1858 A6
1600 SLCY 84104 1857 C6
Dalton Dr
2300 SGVL 84663 3143 C6
Daly Av
10 PKCY 84060 2078 E7
Damascus Wy
8800 WJDN 84088 2175 E6
Damie Ln
1200 LEHI 84043 2603 E2
Damon Cir
4800 SLkC 84117 2071 C3
Damon Wy
1600 SLkC 84117 2071 C3
Damsel Dr
400 MRRY 84107 2070 E2
Dan Dr
1700 LYTN 84040 1283 D1
7400 WJDN 84084 2175 D3
Dan St
100 OGDN 84404 1056 D4
1100 OGDN 84404 1057 B4
Dana Cir
9600 SNDY 84070 2282 D1
Dana Shelby Ct
3500 WVCY 84119 1963 C6
Danbury Cir
3800 SLkC 84044 1960 C7
Danbury Dr
8000 SLkC 84044 1960 C7
Dandelion Cir
700 FMTN 84025 1346 B5
Daneborg Cir
3300 CDHT 84121 2178 C5
Daneborg Dr
3300 CDHT 84121 2178 C6
Danforth Dr
3000 CDHT 84121 2178 B3
Daniel Ct
500 MRRY 84123 2176 B1
Daniel Dr
- FMTN 84025 1448 C3
200 OREM 84057 2820 C1
800 FTHT 84037 1346 B3
E Daniel Dr
10 KYVL 84041 1283 C6
N Daniel Dr
1100 KYVL 84041 1283 C5
Daniel Wy
500 MRRY 84123 2176 B1
Daniels Dr
- CTRV 84014 1551 D2
S Daniels Rd
1200 HRCY 84032 2398 C7
1200 WshC 84032 2398 C7
2000 WshC 84032 2505 D1
Danish Cir
3200 CDHT 84121 2178 C5
Danish Ct
3200 CDHT 84121 2178 C5
Danish Rd
2900 CDHT 84093 2178 C6
2900 CDHT 84121 2178 C6
Danish Wy
3100 CDHT 84121 2178 B5
Danish Brook Cir
2900 CDHT 84121 2178 B4
Danish Crest Ln
3100 CDHT 84093 2178 B5
Danish Downes Ct
7800 CDHT 84121 2178 B4
Danish Hills Cir
3200 CDHT 84121 2178 C5
Danish Oaks Ct
2800 CDHT 84093 2178 B4
Danish Oaks Dr
7900 CDHT 84093 2178 B4
Danish Point Pl
7800 CDHT 84121 2178 B4
Danish Ridge Wy
2900 CDHT 84121 2178 B4
Danish Springs Cove
3200 CDHT 84093 2178 C6
Danna Cir
4600 TYVL 84119 2069 B3
Dannon Wy
5600 WJDN 84088 2173 C7
Dansere Cir
3900 WJDN 84088 2174 C6
Danshill Cir
5100 TYVL 84118 2068 E4
Dansie Wy
12200 RIVN 84065 2387 C1
Dante Rd
9700 SLkC 84092 2284 C2
Danube Cir
5500 TYVL 84118 2068 E5
Danube Ct
5500 TYVL 84118 2068 E5
Danube Dr
3000 TYVL 84118 2069 A5
3200 TYVL 84118 2068 D5
Danville Dr
2700 SNDY 84092 2284 A6
Dapple Gray Cir
1600 RIVN 84065 2387 D3
Darby Cir
1200 MRRY 84117 2071 B5
Darby Castle Wy
1200 TYVL 84123 2069 D1
Dard Pl
2200 SLkC 84109 1965 E4
Dard Hills Ct
2700 SLkC 84109 1965 E4
Darin Cir
400 SNDY 84070 2282 E2
Darin Dr
9800 SNDY 84070 2282 E2
Darin St
8100 MDVL 84047 2176 B5
Darin Wy
2700 LYTN 84041 1281 E2
Darle Av
5600 WVCY 84128 1961 D6
Darling Cir
600 OGDN 84403 1116 A5
Darling St
400 OGDN 84401 1115 E5
500 OGDN 84403 1115 E5
700 OGDN 84403 1116 A5
Darlington Wy
100 LYTN 84041 1228 E6
Dart Cir
- KYVL 84037 1345 D2
Dart Dr
100 DvsC 84056 1228 D4
Dartmoor Ln
10 SLCY 84103 1754 C7
Dartmoor Pl
10 SLCY 84103 1754 C7
Dartmoor Wy
900 SLCY 84103 1754 C7
Dartmouth Cir
4500 WVCY 84120 2068 B3
Dartmouth Dr
4500 WVCY 84120 2068 B3
4600 SLkC 84120 2068 B3
Dartwhite Ln
- RIVN 84065 2386 B4
Darwin Av
600 LOGN 84321 528 A1
Darwin St
500 SLCY 84103 1858 C1
W Dauntless Av
2100 SLCY 84116 1753 B7
Davencourt Cir
3100 LEHI 84043 2495 B7
N Davencourt Lp
3900 LEHI 84043 2495 B7
W Davencourt Lp
3000 LEHI 84043 2495 B7
Davencrest Ln
2200 TYVL 84119 2069 B1
Davenshire Ln
2200 TYVL 84119 2069 C1
David Cir
300 SNDY 84070 2282 D2
1300 SRCS 84075 1227 A7
David Ct
300 SNDY 84070 2282 D2
E David Dr
300 TMTN 84337 520 E5
500 TMTN 84337 521 A4
David Pl
3800 WVCY 84119 1962 E7
David St
1200 SRCS 84075 1227 A7
9400 SNDY 84070 2282 E1
David Wy
100 NSLK 84054 1653 C7
Davinci Dr
3100 CDHT 84121 2178 B4
Davinci Ln
- CTRV 84014 1551 D4
Davis Av
1300 LOGN 84321 528 B1
Davis Blvd
10 KYVL 84037 1345 C2
300 FTHT 84037 1346 B2
500 DvsC 84037 1346 C2
N Davis Blvd
10 BNFL 84010 1552 B7
S Davis Blvd
10 BNFL 84010 1552 B7
200 BNFL 84010 1654 A2
1800 BNFL 84010 1653 E5
W Davis Blvd
300 BNFL 84010 1653 C6
400 NSLK 84054 1653 C6
Davis Ct
100 PKCY 84060 2078 D2
Davis Dr
1500 LYTN 84041 1282 B2
E Davis Dr
1100 SALM 84653 3356 D5
S Davis Dr
2700 SSLK 84115 1964 B4
2700 SSLK 84119 1964 B4
Davis Ln
100 LEHI 84043 2603 C3
Davis Rd
600 SSLK 84119 1964 A2
Davis St
600 PRRY 84302 827 C4
Davis County Rd
- CTRV 84014 1448 B6
- CTRV 84014 1551 B2
- CTRV 84087 1551 B3
- DvsC 84025 1448 B5
- DvsC 84087 1448 B5
Davis Creek Ln
900 FMTN 84025 1448 D4
Davis View Ln
6100 WVCY 84128 1961 C6
Dawn Dr
500 SNDY 84070 2282 E1
1400 CDHT 84121 2177 C1
Dawn Hill Dr
10 SNDY 84092 2284 A5
Dawn Vista Rd
5600 WJDN 84084 2173 D1
Dawson St
10 LYTN 84041 1282 E5
Dawson Hollow Cir
2300 LYTN 84040 1283 E1
Day Ct
13100 DRPR 84020 2388 D3
Daybreak Cir
9100 SNDY 84093 2177 E7
Daybreak Dr
- SOGN 84403 1173 B4
9000 SNDY 84093 2177 E7
Daybreak Ln
100 SRSP 84043 2601 E5
Daybreaker Dr
2300 SmtC 84098 1865 C4
Daybreak Rim Wy
- SJDN 84095 2280 B6
Day Lodge Rd
- ALTA 84049 2182 A6
Day Meadow Dr
100 DRPR 84020 2388 D3
Day Park Dr
5100 WVCY 84120 1961 E7
Dayspring Ln
2300 HLDY 84124 1965 C6
2300 HLDY 84124 1966 A7
Daystar Cir
2600 PKCY 84060 2079 B5
Dayton St
3100 SLkC 84044 1960 B5
Dayton Crest Cir
2300 SJDN 84095 2281 B2
Dazzling View Cir
7900 CDHT 84093 2178 A4
Dean Cir
1900 KYVL 84037 1282 D7
4400 WVCY 84120 2068 C2
Dean Dr
3800 WVCY 84120 2068 C2
Deann Dr
3500 WVCY 84128 1961 C6
Dearborn St
2400 SLCY 84106 1965 C4
Deauville Av
1500 MRRY 84121 2071 C6
Debbie Cir
9500 SNDY 84070 2282 E1
Debbie St
600 PTVW 84404 998 A7
Debeers Dr
2000 SNDY 84093 2177 E6
Debenham St
1400 WVCY 84119 1963 D7
Debonair Dr
900 SLCY 84116 1753 E7
Deborah Cir
900 BNFL 84010 1654 A3
Deborah Dr
900 BNFL 84010 1654 A3
3800 WJDN 84088 2280 D1
Deborah Ann Ct
8300 SNDY 84070 2176 D5
Debra Cir
6800 MDVL 84047 2176 D2
Debrian Wy
14300 DRPR 84020 2388 D6
Debs Pl
400 SLCY 84111 1858 E5
Decade Dr
- SLCY 84104 1962 E1
- SLCY 84104 1963 A1
Decathlon St
3900 SLkC 84124 1965 B7
4000 SLkC 84124 2071 B1
Decatur Cir
3600 WJDN 84084 2174 D1
Decker Lake Blvd
2300 WVCY 84119 1963 B3
Decker Lake Dr
3000 WVCY 84119 1963 B5
Decker Lake Ln
2500 WVCY 84119 1963 C3
Declaration Pl
2900 SJDN 84095 2281 A2
Decora Wy
4900 WJDN 84084 2174 A2
Dedication Dr
8900 SNDY 84070 2176 A6
Dee Av
500 LOGN 84321 527 D2
Dee Cir
3300 RIVN 84065 2386 E2
Dee Park Dr
2400 TYVL 84118 2069 B6
Deep Creek Cir
8700 WJDN 84088 2173 E6
Deep Creek Dr
5200 WJDN 84088 2173 E7
9800 CRHL 84062 2605 B3
Deep Forest Cir
- WDHL 84653 3463 D3
Deep Woods Dr
1800 DRPR 84020 2389 D7
1800 DRPR 84020 2496 D1
Deer Cr
- CRFD 84015 1227 D4
Deer Brook Cir
9700 SLkC 84092 2284 D2
Deerbrush Cir
5500 WJDN 84084 2173 D1
Deer Creek Cir
3100 CDHT 84121 2178 C4
Deer Creek Rd
7800 CDHT 84121 2178 C4
Deercreek Rd
4600 SLkC 84124 2072 B3
Deer Creek Wy
2200 SGVL 84663 3144 B4
Deer Creek Cove
3200 CDHT 84121 2178 C4
Deer Crest Cir
- FTHT 84037 1346 B4
Deer Crest Dr
- FTHT 84037 1346 B4
Deercrest Dr
5400 WVCY 84120 2067 D2
Deer Crest Estates Dr
- PKCY 84060 2079 B6
3600 WshC 84049 2079 B6
Deere Dr
- MPTN 84664 3250 D1
Deere Valley Dr
1800 LYTN 84040 1229 D6
Deere View Dr
1900 LYTN 84040 1229 D6
Deer Fence Tr
- CchC 84321 592 C3
- CchC 84332 592 C3
- PVDN 84321 592 C3
- PVDN 84332 592 C3
Deerfield Ct
200 ALPN 84004 2497 E4
Deerfield Dr
200 ALPN 84004 2497 E4
1100 CTRV 84014 1551 E1
Deerfield Rd
700 MRRY 84107 2070 E7
700 MRRY 84107 2071 A6
Deer Glen Cir
13500 RIVN 84065 2386 C4
Deer Haven Dr
1000 BMCY 84302 767 B4
Deerhaven Dr
1500 NHLN 84341 464 C5
Deer Haven Cove
14000 BFDL 84065 2386 D6
Deer Hill Wy
3800 BFDL 84065 2386 C5
Deer Hollow Cir
300 CTRV 84014 1551 E3
3300 SLkC 84092 2284 C4
Deerhollow Cir
200 NSLK 84054 1653 C6
Deer Hollow Ct
2600 WshC 84049 2079 D7
Deer Hollow Dr
3000 SLkC 84092 2284 B4
3100 SNDY 84092 2284 C4
Deer Hollow Rd
- WshC 84049 2185 E1
- WshC 84049 2186 A1
2500 WshC 84049 2079 C6
Deer Horn Ct
4000 RIVN 84065 2386 C5
Deer Horn Dr
3900 RIVN 84065 2386 C5
Deer Knoll Cir
13500 RIVN 84065 2386 C4
Deer Lake Dr
2400 PKCY 84060 2079 B5
Deermeadow Cir
5400 WVCY 84120 2067 D2
Deer Meadow Dr
- LEHI 84043 2603 A2
900 NHON 84414 999 B6
Deermeadow Dr
4300 WVCY 84120 2067 E2
Deer Mountain Cir
13500 RIVN 84065 2386 C4

STREET
Block City ZIP Map# Grid

Deer Mountain Dr
3900 RIVN 84065 2386 C4
Deer Orchard Dr
3800 BFDL 84065 2386 D6
Deer Orchard Cove
14000 BFDL 84065 2386 C6
Deer Pointe Dr
2800 WshC 84049 2079 C7
Deer Ridge Dr
- DRPR 84020 2389 D7
- DRPR 84020 2496 B2
Deer Ridge Pl
- SLkC 84092 2284 C4
Deer Ridge Rd
- FTHT 84037 1346 B4
Deer Run Dr
1900 SWBR 84405 1229 D3
2300 SWBR 84405 1230 A3
Deer Run Ln
100 LYTN 84040 1284 B4
Deer Run Pl
9500 SLkC 84092 2284 B1
Deer Run Wy
8100 SWBR 84405 1229 E4
8100 SWBR 84405 1230 A4
Deer Springs Ln
6100 WVCY 84118 2067 C7
E Deer Trail Dr
600 SPFK 84660 3249 E4
Deer Valley Dr
200 PKCY 84060 2078 D4
600 PKCY 84060 2079 A6
3600 WshC 84060 1960 B7
Deer Valley Dr SR-224
1100 PKCY 84060 2078 D4
Deer Valley Dr E
2200 PKCY 84060 2079 B7
Deer Valley Dr N
1200 PKCY 84060 2079 A6
Deer Valley Dr S
1300 PKCY 84060 2079 A6
Deer Valley Lp
- PKCY 84060 2079 A5
400 PKCY 84060 2078 E6
Deer View Cir
700 FTHT 84037 1346 B3
Deer View Pl
13800 BFDL 84065 2386 B5
Deerwalk Ln
1000 OGDN 84404 1057 B7
Deerwalk Rd
900 DRPR 84020 2389 A3
Deer Wood Dr
5000 WVCY 84120 2067 E3
5000 WVCY 84120 2068 A3
Degiorio St
1600 WbrC 84401 1113 D1
Deitrick Cir
6900 WJDN 84084 2173 D2
Del Cir
4200 WVCY 84120 2068 C1
Delaney Ct
3200 WVCY 84128 1961 B5
De Lann Ln
1800 SLkC 84121 2071 D6
Delaware Dr
1200 DvsC 84056 1227 D2
1200 SNST 84056 1227 D2
Delaware Ln
1500 SLkC 84117 2071 C4
Delayne Cir
600 LYTN 84041 1282 D1
Delfina Ct
5300 WVCY 84120 1961 E6
Delia Cir
3700 SLkC 84109 1966 A7
Delia Dr
2300 SLkC 84109 1965 E7
Delicious St
900 FTHT 84037 1346 A4
Dell Rd
7600 CDHT 84121 2178 B4
Dellron Dr
6200 MRRY 84123 2069 E7
Dell Wood Ct
4800 WJDN 84084 2174 A3
Delmar Ct
200 SLCY 84101 1858 C4
Del Mar Dr
3100 SLkC 84109 1966 B7
Delmont Dr
2000 HLDY 84117 2071 D3
S Del Monte Rd
1100 SPFK 84660 3249 B5
Delno Cir
500 SLkC 84107 1964 E7
Delno Dr
500 SLkC 84107 1964 E7
Delong St
500 SLCY 84104 1857 B5
Deloss Ct
6300 WJDN 84084 2173 B2
Delpha Dr
2500 TYVL 84084 2069 A7
Delphinium St
700 SLkC 84094 2282 E3
Del Prado St
4900 SLkC 84117 2071 B4
Del Rio St
1100 SLkC 84117 2071 B4
Delsa Dr
2700 SLkC 84124 1966 A7
3200 SLkC 84124 2072 C1
Delsey Cove
10100 SJDN 84095 2280 C3
Del Sol Ln
3500 SJDN 84095 2280 D5
Delta Dr
- PKCY 84060 2078 B2
Delta Park Cir
4600 WVCY 84120 1962 B5
Del Verde Av
3100 SLkC 84109 1966 C6
Demerest Rd
8000 CDHT 84121 2178 E4
Demeter Dr
- SLkC 84044 1960 C4
Denali Cir
10 LNDN 84042 2714 A6
Denali Dr
10 LNDN 84042 2714 A6
2700 TYVL 84084 2069 A7

Denarles Cir
1600 MRRY 84121 2071 C6
Denby Dale Rd
6800 WJDN 84084 2174 C2
Denise Dr
1900 SLkC 84106 1965 D5
Denman Av
6200 WJDN 84084 2173 C1
Denmark Dr
2900 CDHT 84093 2178 B4
Dennis Cir
3000 WVCY 84120 1962 C5
Dennis Dr
4000 WVCY 84120 1962 C5
S Deno Cr
4200 WVCY 84120 2068 C2
S Deno Dr
4100 WVCY 84120 2068 C1
W Deno Dr
4200 WVCY 84120 2068 C2
Denton Cir
3400 WJDN 84084 2174 E2
Dentwood Dr
1100 BMCY 84302 827 E2
Denver St
- SLCY 84104 1856 E5
400 SLCY 84111 1858 E4
1500 SLCY 84115 1858 E7
1500 SLCY 84115 1964 E1
Depot Dr
300 OGDN 84404 1056 B4
Depot Rd
5700 UthC 84660 3142 B7
5800 UthC 84660 3249 B1
Depot St
200 CRFD 84015 1227 D5
200 CRFD 84016 1227 D5
700 MDVL 84047 2176 A3
Derby Cir
3200 WJDN 84088 2174 E5
Derby Ln
1200 FTHT 84037 1346 A3
Derby St
2300 WVCY 84119 1963 D3
Derby Wy
3200 WJDN 84088 2174 E5
Derbyshire
3000 WVCY 84120 1962 A3
Derbyshire Ct
4200 TYVL 84123 2069 E1
Derek Cir
2300 TYVL 84084 2069 B7
Derek Hollow Cove
7000 MDVL 84047 2177 A2
Dern St
200 SLCY 84113 1859 D4
Desert Creek Cir
14100 HRMN 84065 2385 C6
Desert Dusk Rd
2400 TYVL 84118 2069 B3
Desert Fox Cir
3600 TYVL 84118 2068 D7
Desert Peak Cir
13900 RIVN 84065 2386 A5
Desert Ridge Cove
7900 CDHT 84093 2178 A4
Desert Stone Cir
5600 SJDN 84095 2279 D6
Desert Sun Cir
1400 DRPR 84020 2389 C6
Desert Vista Cir
6200 SLkC 84118 2067 C6
Desoto St
500 SLCY 84103 1858 D1
Despain Wy
9000 CDHT 84093 2178 C7
Detevis Cir
3800 WVCY 84120 1962 C4
Detrobriand St
1900 SLCY 84113 1859 D3
E Detroiter Av
200 MRRY 84107 2070 C4
S Detroiter Cir
100 MRRY 84107 2070 D1
Devan Park Wy
3200 SJDN 84095 2280 E2
Devereaux Wy
2800 SLkC 84109 1966 A4
Deveron Cir
4300 SJDN 84095 2280 B2
Deville Dr
7100 CDHT 84121 2177 D2
Devils Castle Rd
- ALTA 84049 2288 B2
Devin Pl
7700 MDVL 84047 2177 A4
7700 SNDY 84047 2177 A4
Devon Dr
2900 BNFL 84010 1653 E5
2900 BNFL 84010 1654 A4
Devon St
1100 KYVL 84037 1284 A5
Devon Glen Dr
- SGVL 84663 3143 A1
Devonna Rd
5100 WJDN 84084 2173 E2
Devonshire Cir
2900 SLCY 84108 1860 B7
4000 PRVO 84604 2821 E6
Devonshire Dr
1200 PRVO 84604 2821 E6
1300 SLCY 84108 1860 B7
1500 SLCY 84108 1966 B1
4300 BNFL 84010 1653 D7
Dewberry Ln
5200 TYVL 84118 2068 D5
Dew Crest Cir
3900 HLDY 84124 1965 D7
Dewdrops Dr
5900 SLkC 84118 2067 D6
6100 WJDN 84118 2067 E7
6200 WJDN 84084 2067 E7
Dewflower Cir
5200 SLkC 84118 2067 E5
Dexter Cir
- FMTN 84025 1447 E1
Dexter St
500 SLCY 84116 1858 A1
1400 SLCY 84116 1754 A5
Diamond St
700 LYTN 84041 1282 E3

E Diamond St
10 LYTN 84041 1282 E3
10 LYTN 84041 1283 A3
W Diamond St
10 LYTN 84041 1282 E3
Diamond Wy
900 SLkC 84094 2283 A2
1100 SNDY 84094 2283 A2
Diamondback Dr
4900 RIVN 84065 2386 A2
Diamond Dove Dr
8600 WJDN 84088 2175 D6
N Diamond Fork Lp
- SPFK 84663 3250 A2
300 SPFK 84660 3250 A2
Diamond Hills Ln
1900 HLDY 84121 2071 D7
Diamondleaf Wy
4800 WJDN 84084 2174 A2
Diamond Rose Cir
800 SLCY 84116 1858 A1
Diana Wy
4100 SLkC 84124 2072 C1
Diana Hills Wy
800 SNDY 84094 2283 A5
Diane Cir
1300 TYVL 84123 2069 D5
Diane Dr
1300 TYVL 84123 2069 D6
1500 HARR 84404 1056 C1
1500 HARR 84414 1056 C1
1600 NHON 84404 1056 C1
1600 NHON 84414 1056 C1
Dianna St
500 SOGN 84403 1115 E7
Dickens Pl
3000 SLCY 84108 1860 B6
Dickinson Cove
3300 TYVL 84118 2068 E3
Dickson Wy
7400 SLkC 84044 1960 D6
Diestel Rd
800 SLCY 84105 1859 C6
800 SLCY 84108 1859 C6
Dillan Cir
6300 HRMN 84065 2385 C3
Dillon Dr
700 OGDN 84404 1057 B3
Dimond Dr
2700 WJDN 84084 2175 A3
Dimple Dell Cir
3000 SLkC 84092 2284 B3
Dimple Dell Dr
10600 SLkC 84092 2283 E4
Dimple Dell Ln
2900 SLkC 84092 2284 B3
Dimple Dell Rd
2000 SLkC 84092 2283 C4
2000 SNDY 84092 2283 C4
2300 SLkC 84092 2284 B4
2300 SNDY 84092 2284 B4
Dimple View Ln
10200 SLkC 84092 2284 B3
10200 SNDY 84092 2284 B3
Dimrall Dr
3700 TYVL 84118 2068 C5
Dinivan St
700 NSLK 84054 1653 B5
Dipo Pl
4700 SLkC 84117 2071 B3
Dirassy Dr
6500 HRMN 84065 2385 B5
Directors Row
2100 SLCY 84104 1857 A6
2300 SLCY 84104 1856 D6
Director View Ln
14100 DRPR 84020 2389 A6
Discovery Ct
6800 WJDN 84084 2173 C2
Discovery Dr
5600 WJDN 84084 2173 C1
Ditsie Dr
3800 SLkC 84044 1960 D7
Division Ln
100 MRRY 84107 2070 D3
500 SLCY 84106 1964 E3
Division Rd
500 SmtC 84098 1866 D7
Dixie Cir
3600 WJDN 84084 2174 D1
4600 SOGN 84403 1173 A2
Dixie Dr
800 SOGN 84405 1173 A5
5800 WVCY 84128 1961 C7
6200 WJDN 84084 2068 D7
6400 WJDN 84084 2174 D1
Dixie St
600 LYTN 84041 1283 B3
Dixie Ann Dr
4500 WVCY 84119 2068 E2
Dixon Dr
- OGDN 84403 1116 B7
- OGDN 84403 1173 B1
Dixon Dr SR-284
- OGDN 84403 1116 B7
- OGDN 84403 1173 B1
S Dixon Rd
- UthC 84651 3354 D2
8500 UthC 84660 3354 E1
Dixon Pond Rd
- SALM 84653 3355 D3
Dobbin Ln
10100 SJDN 84095 2280 C3
Doc Holiday Dr
2100 PKCY 84060 2078 E3
2200 PKCY 84060 2079 A3
Dogwood Av
1200 DvsC 84056 1227 E3
1200 SNST 84056 1227 E3
Dogwood Ct
8600 SLkC 84044 1960 A6
Dogwood Dr
1200 MPTN 84664 3144 C7
Dogwood Ln
4300 CRHL 84062 2605 B2
Dogwood St
- SGVL 84663 3035 E6
Dokos Ct
1500 SLCY 84104 1857 D7
Dokos Ln
1300 SLCY 84104 1857 C7

Dolley Ct
3900 WVCY 84128 1961 D7
Dolomite Ln
9800 SLkC 84094 2283 A2
9800 SNDY 84094 2283 A2
Dolomite Wy
9400 SNDY 84094 2283 B1
Dolores St
5800 ROY 84067 1171 C5
Dolphin Cir
7700 CDHT 84093 2178 A4
Dolphin Wy
2300 CDHT 84093 2177 E4
2300 CDHT 84093 2178 A4
Domian Ct
3100 WVCY 84128 1961 A5
Dominion Ct
5600 WbrC 84403 1173 E5
Donalbain St
3900 SJDN 84095 2280 C2
Donatello Ct
3700 WVCY 84119 1963 C6
Don Bain St
3900 SJDN 84095 2280 C2
Don Carlos Dr
6000 TYVL 84118 2069 A7
Donegal Cir
2000 SLkC 84109 1965 E5
Donelson Ln
1900 HLDY 84117 2071 D4
Don Felipe Av
3100 TYVL 84118 2068 E6
Don Francisco Dr
3000 TYVL 84118 2068 E6
3000 TYVL 84118 2069 A6
Donibristle Cir
4000 SJDN 84095 2280 C2
Don Jose Cir
5900 TYVL 84118 2068 E6
Don Jose Dr
6000 TYVL 84118 2068 E6
Don Juan Dr
2900 TYVL 84118 2069 A7
Don Leone Dr
6100 TYVL 84118 2069 A7
Donna Cir
300 SNDY 84070 2282 D2
Donna St
200 OGDN 84404 1057 B4
Donna Rae Cir
2200 RIVN 84065 2281 B7
Donnawood Cir
2500 TYVL 84084 2069 C6
Donner Cir
800 SLCY 84108 1860 B5
Donner Wy
800 SLCY 84108 1860 B6
Don Quixote Dr
6000 TYVL 84118 2068 E7
Don Salvador Av
2900 TYVL 84118 2069 A7
3000 TYVL 84118 2068 E7
Donwald St
3900 SJDN 84095 2280 C2
Doodle Bug Pl
2900 WVCY 84128 1961 C5
Dooley Ct
100 SLCY 84102 1859 A3
Doral Dr
1200 SRCS 84075 1226 B7
1500 SRCS 84075 1280 B1
10400 CRHL 84062 2605 C2
Doral Pl
12200 DRPR 84020 2389 C1
Doralma St
300 SLCY 84116 1857 B2
N Dorchester Av
2400 HARR 84414 998 D6
W Dorchester Av
200 HARR 84414 998 C6
Dorchester Dr
9600 CRHL 84062 2605 B3
E Dorchester Dr
10 SLCY 84103 1754 C7
Doreen Cir
4300 SLkC 84107 2070 D1
Doreen Dr
12200 RIVN 84065 2387 C1
Doreen St
300 SLkC 84107 2070 D1
Doren Dr
600 SOGN 84403 1173 A3
Dorie St
3100 SLkC 84106 1965 A5
Dorilee Dr
4500 WJDN 84088 2174 B6
Doris Cir
900 CTRV 84014 1551 E2
Doris Wy
4300 HLDY 84124 2071 D2
Dornoch Dr
13800 HRMN 84065 2385 E5
Dorothea Wy
400 SLCY 84116 1857 C1
700 SLCY 84116 1753 C7
Dorothy Cir
500 SNDY 84070 2282 E1
Dorris St
1000 CTRV 84014 1551 E2
Dorset Cir
7200 CDHT 84121 2177 E2
Dorthea Wy
400 NSLK 84054 1653 C7
400 NSLK 84054 1754 B1
Double Down Ct
9000 SNDY 84093 2177 E7
Double Eagle Dr
- LEHI 84043 2602 C2
Double Jack Cir
10600 SJDN 84095 2281 B4
Double Jack Ct
10 PKCY 84060 2078 B3
Doug Cove
5800 TYVL 84118 2069 B6
S Doughton Av
- OGDN 84404 1056 B7
Douglas Cir
1100 SJDN 84095 2281 E1
Douglas Dr
500 LOGN 84341 463 E7
500 LOGN 84341 464 A7
800 BMCY 84302 827 D1

Douglas Dr
1100 SJDN 84095 2281 E1
1300 SNST 84015 1227 C2
7700 SmtC 84098 1864 C6
Douglas St
100 OGDN 84404 1056 D5
100 SLCY 84102 1859 B3
500 OGDN 84404 1057 A5
1100 SLCY 84105 1859 B6
1900 SLCY 84105 1965 B2
2400 SLCY 84106 1965 B3
Douglas Corrigan Wy
4800 SLCY 84116 1856 A2
5100 SLCY 84116 1855 E2
Douglas Fir Cove
7800 SNDY 84094 2177 C3
Douglass Dr
400 PYSN 84651 3354 E4
Dove St
1200 WVCY 84119 1963 D7
Dove Bend Cir
9800 SJDN 84095 2281 A2
Dove Creek Ln
5100 WJDN 84088 2173 E4
Dove Hollow Cir
1700 TYVL 84118 2069 C7
Dove Meadows Ln
1500 WJDN 84088 2175 C6
Dove Point Rd
2200 WVCY 84119 2069 B1
Dover Cir
600 PVDN 84332 528 B7
9600 CRHL 84062 2605 B4
Dover Dr
900 PRVO 84604 2821 E6
1400 SPFK 84660 3250 A3
Dover Ln
4100 PRVO 84604 2821 E6
Dover Rd
1300 SLCY 84108 1860 A7
Dover St
1100 KYVL 84037 1284 A5
Dover Hills Dr
3500 CDHT 84121 2178 C3
Dove's Landing Dr
11800 RIVN 84065 2280 E7
Dove Tail Dr
3000 WVCY 84128 1961 A5
Downhill Rd
3400 TYVL 84084 2068 E7
Downing Dr
4400 CRHL 84062 2605 A2
Downing St
500 MDVL 84047 2176 E2
Downington Av
100 SLCY 84115 1964 D1
500 SLCY 84105 1964 E1
1500 SLCY 84105 1965 C1
1700 SLCY 84108 1965 C1
2500 SLCY 84108 1966 A1
Downs Cir
200 OGDN 84404 1056 D6
Downs Dr
200 OGDN 84404 1056 D6
Downs Wy
2700 WVCY 84119 1962 D4
Doxey Rd
1500 CLTN 84015 1227 A3
1800 CLTN 84015 1226 E3
1800 WPT 84015 1226 E3
1800 WPT 84015 1227 A3
Doxey St
100 OGDN 84401 1115 D4
1000 CLTN 84015 1227 A3
1000 OGDN 84403 1116 B4
W Doxey St
800 OGDN 84401 1115 B4
Draft Horse Ct
5600 HRMN 84065 2385 D5
Drage Cir
3500 SLkC 84109 1966 B6
Dragon Fly Dr
- LEHI 84043 2710 D2
Drake Ln
1700 WJDN 84084 2175 C3
Draney Ln
10 MDVL 84047 2176 C3
Draper Ln
10 PRVO 84601 2927 E6
Draper Pkwy
900 DRPR 84020 2389 B1
1300 SNDY 84092 2389 B1
Draper St
4300 SLkC 84118 2068 B6
Draper Downs Dr
300 DRPR 84020 2388 D2
Draper Farm Cove
12000 DRPR 84020 2389 E1
Draper Heights Wy
500 DRPR 84020 2388 E7
600 DRPR 84020 2389 A7
Draper Park Ln
100 DRPR 84020 2282 D7
Draper View Rd
600 DRPR 84020 2388 E7
700 DRPR 84020 2389 A7
Draper View Cove
14600 DRPR 84020 2388 E7
Draperville Av
11900 DRPR 84020 2282 C7
Draper Woods Wy
500 DRPR 84020 2388 E7
Draper Woods Cove
14700 DRPR 84020 2388 E7
Drawbridge Wy
2900 WVCY 84120 1962 A3
Dream Cir
9800 SJDN 84095 2281 E2
Dreamfield Dr
14300 DRPR 84020 2388 D6
Driftwood Dr
1700 PRVO 84604 2928 E3
4400 TYVL 84123 2069 D3
Driggs Av
500 SLCY 84106 1964 E3
1200 SLCY 84106 1965 B3
Drone Wy
- DvsC 84056 1228 E2
Dry Bone Cir
5900 SLkC 84118 2067 C5
Dry Canyon Dr
- OREM 84097 2714 A7

Dry Canyon Dr
10 LNDN 84042 2714 A7
Dry Canyon Rd
- CchC 84335 400 B3
- CchC 84341 400 D4
- SHFD 84335 400 B3
- SHFD 84341 400 B3
Dry Creek Cir
6000 HILD 84003 2497 B6
Dry Creek Dr
10 PYSN 84651 3461 D1
2500 RIVN 84065 2387 A2
3700 CRHL 84062 2605 C3
Drycreek Ln
300 ALPN 84004 2498 A4
Dry Creek Rd
10 LEHI 84043 2603 C3
700 SNDY 84094 2282 E6
700 SNDY 84094 2283 A6
6000 HILD 84003 2497 B6
11800 DRPR 84020 2283 A6
Dry Creek Wy
700 SNDY 84094 2282 D5
2000 LEHI 84043 2603 C3
Dry Gulch Cir
900 SNDY 84094 2283 C5
Dry Gulch Rd
900 SNDY 84094 2283 A6
Drystone Av
700 SNDY 84094 2283 A6
11200 SNDY 84094 2282 E5
Drystone Cir
800 SNDY 84094 2283 D4
Dry Sycamore Ln
- WJDN 84088 2173 A4
Dry Willow Ct
800 DRPR 84020 2283 A7
Drywind Dr
6300 TYVL 84084 2068 C7
Dubei Ct
200 SLCY 84111 1858 D3
Dublin Cir
4000 WVCY 84119 2069 A1
Dublin Dr
2400 WVCY 84119 2069 A1
Duchesne Cir
10 DRPR 84020 2495 C1
Duchess St
6000 WJDN 84084 2173 C1
Duck Hook Dr
2500 PKCY 84060 2078 E1
Duck Pond Ln
1400 TYVL 84123 2069 D6
Ducks Horn Dr
- DRPR 84020 2496 E4
Duck Tail Cir
1200 MRRY 84123 2069 E7
Duder St
10 SLCY 84104 1857 C3
Duehl Cir
1300 TYVL 84123 2069 D1
Duffer Cir
1000 NSLK 84054 1653 D7
Duffer Ln
1000 NSLK 84054 1653 D7
Duffys Ln
1500 WJDN 84084 2175 C2
Duke Ln
1200 DvsC 84056 1227 E3
5200 TYVL 84118 2068 C4
Dukewater Cir
3000 WVCY 84120 1962 A4
Dulce Av
- DvsC 84056 1228 C5
Duluth Av
800 SLCY 84116 1754 A5
900 SLCY 84116 1753 E5
Dunbar Cir
9400 SJDN 84095 2281 D1
Dunbar Cove
9400 SJDN 84095 2281 D1
Dunbarton Dr
1000 MRRY 84117 2071 A5
Dundee Cir
1000 SRCS 84075 1226 B6
4500 HILD 84003 2605 A1
Dundee St
3900 SJDN 84095 2280 C2
Dune Buggy Dr
3800 SJDN 84095 2280 C4
Dunes Dr
900 SRCS 84075 1226 B6
Dunford Ct
6000 WVCY 84128 1961 C4
Dunham Ln
3600 WVCY 84119 1963 D7
Dunhammer Dr
12600 RIVN 84065 2387 A2
Dunkeld St
3800 SJDN 84095 2280 C3
Dunlop Ct
100 PKCY 84060 2078 D2
8300 WJDN 84088 2175 A5
Dunlop Dr
2700 WJDN 84088 2175 A5
Dunmore Ct
4200 TYVL 84123 2069 E1
Dunmore Dr
1200 SGVL 84663 3142 E4
1200 SGVL 84663 3143 A4
Dunn Ct
3700 SLkC 84044 1960 C7
Dunning Ct
600 DRPR 84020 2282 A6
Dunraven Dr
2800 WVCY 84119 2069 A2
Dun Roamin Ln
1200 DRPR 84020 2389 B3
Dunrobin Ct
1100 MRRY 84123 2069 E6
Dunsinane Cir
1600 OGDN 84401 1116 C2
Dunsinane Dr
9400 SJDN 84095 2280 D1
Dunsmoore Wy
2900 WVCY 84120 1962 A4
Dunston Av
9100 SNDY 84093 2177 D7
Dupler Rd
800 SNDY 84094 2283 A5
Dupont Av
900 SLCY 84116 1753 D6

Duquesne Av
4600 WVCY 84120 2068 B2
Durango Ct
6000 MRRY 84123 2069 D7
Durban Rd
2600 SNDY 84093 2284 A1
9200 SNDY 84093 2178 B7
Durdham Ln
100 SNDY 84070 2282 C1
Durham Dr
700 NSLK 84054 1652 D5
Durrans Ln
3900 WVCY 84120 1962 B7
3900 WVCY 84120 2068 B1
Durrant St
- ANFK 84003 2604 C6
Duskywing Wy
13600 RIVN 84065 2385 E5
Dusty Cir
6200 TYVL 84084 2068 C7
Dusty Creek Av
700 SNDY 84094 2282 D5
700 SNDY 84094 2283 D4
Dusty Downs Cir
1200 SJDN 84095 2281 D5
Dusty Rock Cir
700 SNDY 84094 2283 A5
Dusty Rock Pl
800 SNDY 84094 2283 A5
Dutch Apple Cove
3500 TYVL 84118 2068 D3
Dutch Canyon Rd
1500 MIDW 84049 2291 D6
1500 WshC 84049 2185 C7
1500 WshC 84049 2291 D3
Dutch Draw Cir
4200 TYVL 84119 2069 A1
Dutch Draw Dr
2400 TYVL 84119 2069 A1
Dutchess Pl
9600 SJDN 84095 2281 B1
Dwayne Dr
500 LEHI 84043 2710 B1
Dwight D Eisenhower Hwy
- SLCY - 1854 B3
- SLCY - 1855 B2
- SLCY - 1856 A3
- SLCY - 1857 D3
- SLCY - 1964 D3
- SLCY - 1965 D3
- SLCY - 1966 B4
- SLkC - 1853 D3
- SLkC - 1854 B3
- SLkC - 1864 A5
- SLkC - 1966 D3
- SmtC - 1865 A4
- SmtC - 1866 E7
- SmtC - 1867 C3
- SmtC - 1971 D1
- SmtC - 1972 C2
- SSLK - 1964 D3
Dwight D Eisenhower Hwy I-80
- SLCY - 1854 B3
- SLCY - 1855 B2
- SLCY - 1856 A3
- SLCY - 1857 D3
- SLCY - 1964 D3
- SLCY - 1965 D3
- SLCY - 1966 B4
- SLkC - 1853 A3
- SLkC - 1854 B3
- SLkC - 1864 A5
- SLkC - 1966 D3
- SmtC - 1865 A4
- SmtC - 1866 E7
- SmtC - 1867 C3
- SmtC - 1971 D1
- SmtC - 1972 C2
- SSLK - 1964 D3
Dyer Ln
4900 TYVL 84118 2068 E4
Dylan Loop Rd
6900 HRMN 84065 2385 A5
Dynamite Cir
11900 HRMN 84065 2280 A7
Dynasty Wy
8200 CDHT 84121 2178 C5
Dynasty Oaks Cir
5600 TYVL 84118 2068 E6

E

E Av
- PTVW 84404 997 E5
10 DvsC 84056 1228 D5
2300 OGDN 84401 1115 B3
E St
- BMCY 84302 767 A6
- BMCY 84302 827 E2
- CRFD 84016 1227 C7
- KYVL 84041 1283 B6
- RVDL 84405 1172 A3
10 SLCY 84103 1858 E2
Eagle Ct
10 PKCY 84060 2079 A7
2100 WJDN 84088 2175 B6
Eagle Dr
- PVDN 84332 528 C7
400 OREM 84097 2820 E2
600 OREM 84097 2821 A2
E Eagle Dr
500 MPTN 84664 3144 C7
600 MPTN 84664 3251 C1
Eagle Wy
- WbrC 84317 1061 D7
200 NSLK 84054 1653 C7
200 NSLK 84054 1754 D1
600 FTHT 84037 1346 A3
1400 PKCY 84060 2078 E4
2600 SLCY 84108 1860 A7
Eagle Bend Cir
11600 SNDY 84094 2283 A7
Eagle Bend Rd
1000 SNDY 84094 2283 A6
Eaglebrook Cir
4600 CRHL 84062 2605 A2
Eaglebrook Dr
200 SNDY 84070 2176 D5
Eagle Chase Dr
2100 DRPR 84020 2496 E1

STREET Block City ZIP Map# Grid

Eagle Crest Cir
3100 SNDY 84092 2284 B5
Eagle Crest Dr
2100 DRPR 84020 2496 E2
Eaglecrest Dr
2300 LEHI 84043 2603 C2
S Eagle Estates Cir
700 BMCY 84302 828 A1
Eagle Glen Wy
3800 WVCY 84120 1962 C7
Eagle Heights Dr
3800 WVCY 84120 1962 C7
Eagle Hill Cir
5000 WJDN 84084 2174 B2
Eagle Landing Ct
10 PKCY 84060 2078 C1
Eagle Nest Dr
- WDHL 84653 3463 C4
1200 MRRY 84123 2069 D6
Eagle Park Ln
4500 WVCY 84120 1962 B4
Eagle Pass
600 NSLK 84054 1754 B2
Eagle Peak Dr
5500 HRMN 84065 2385 D3
Eagle Point Blvd
600 NSLK 84054 1754 C1
Eagle Point Cir
400 NSLK 84054 1754 B1
Eagle Point Dr
3800 SLkC 84124 1966 C7
Eagle Pointe Ct
10 PKCY 84060 2078 C1
Eagle Ray Ct
2100 CDHT 84121 2177 E1
Eagle Ridge Cir
1100 SNDY 84094 2283 B7
Eagle Ridge Dr
- WbrC 84310 1001 D2
400 HYRM 84319 651 A3
400 HYRM 84319 650 E3
700 BNFL 84010 1552 C6
11500 SNDY 84094 2283 B6
E Eagle Ridge Dr
200 NSLK 84054 1653 A7
200 NSLK 84054 1754 B1
S Eagle Ridge Dr
10 NSLK 84054 1653 D7
800 BNFL 84010 1653 D7
Eagle Rock Wy
3100 WVCY 84120 1962 A5
5100 WVCY 84120 1961 E5
Eagles Lndg
- WPT 84015 1225 D4
Eagleslanding Cove
2600 HLDY 84121 2072 A7
Eagles Nest Cir
1000 NSLK 84054 1653 D7
1000 NSLK 84054 1754 C1
Eagles Peak Cove
6000 WVCY 84128 1961 C5
Eagle Stone Wy
14900 DRPR 84020 2496 E1
Eagles View Dr
- LEHI 84043 2495 C4
Eagle View Cir
200 NSLK 84054 1653 D7
3100 SNDY 84092 2284 B5
Eagle View Ct
10 PKCY 84060 2078 D1
Eagle View Dr
600 ALPN 84004 2497 D3
11100 SNDY 84092 2284 B5
Eagle View Cove
11200 SNDY 84092 2284 B6
Eagle Wood Dr
5000 WVCY 84120 2067 E3
5000 WVCY 84120 2068 A3
E Eaglewood Dr
600 DvsC 84054 1653 C6
600 NSLK 84054 1653 C6
N Eaglewood Dr
10 NSLK 84054 1653 C6
S Eaglewood Dr
10 NSLK 84054 1653 C7
Eaglewood Ln
10 SNDY 84092 2284 A5
Eaglewood Lp
800 NSLK 84054 1754 C1
1100 NSLK 84054 1653 E6
Earl Cir
1300 SRCS 84075 1227 A7
Earl Dr
1200 OGDN 84404 1057 B5
1300 SLCY 84104 1857 B7
Earl Pl
5300 HILD 84003 2604 D2
Earl Wy
1100 SNDY 84094 2177 B7
Earl Dally Ln
- HRCY 84032 2398 E2
Earlene Dr
600 SOGN 84403 1172 E2
600 SOGN 84403 1173 A2
Earles Ct Rd
2200 TYVL 84119 2069 B2
Early Dawn Dr
5700 WJDN 84084 2173 D1
Early Duke Dr
5100 WVCY 84120 2067 E2
Early Duke St
4300 WVCY 84120 2067 D1
4300 WVCY 84120 2068 A2
Earnshaw Ln
1600 SLCY 84116 1753 C5
East Ln
300 ANFK 84003 2604 C7
East Pl
900 SLCY 84102 1859 A4
Eastbay Blvd
10 PRVO 84606 3035 C2
Eastborne Ct
500 FMTN 84025 1346 B4
Eastbourne Cir
7400 CDHT 84121 2178 A3
Eastbourne Dr
2400 CDHT 84121 2178 A3
Eastbrook Dr
6300 TYVL 84084 2068 E7
6300 TYVL 84084 2174 E1
Eastcliff Av
4600 PRVO 84604 2821 C5
N Eastcrest Dr
200 LYTN 84040 1283 C4
S Eastcrest Rd
3100 WVCY 84120 1962 C5
Eastdell Dr
9400 SNDY 84092 2283 E2
Eastern Park Ln
4100 WVCY 84119 2069 A1
Eastfork Cir
- FMTN 84025 1447 E1
Eastgate Dr
100 SNDY 84070 2176 B6
900 PRVO 84606 3035 D1
Eastgate Rd
900 MRRY 84117 2071 A4
N East Lisa St
1300 LYTN 84040 1283 C2
Easton St
2400 TYVL 84118 2069 A5
Eastpoint Cir
1400 SLkC 84092 2283 C1
Eastpoint Dr
1300 SLkC 84092 2283 B1
Eastpointe Cir
500 BNFL 84010 1653 B5
Eastpointe Dr
500 BNFL 84010 1653 B5
Eastridge Cir
- LOGN 84321 528 B3
300 ALPN 84004 2498 A3
1200 SNDY 84094 2283 B7
Eastridge Dr
1100 LOGN 84321 528 B3
S Eastridge Dr
600 SGVL 84663 3144 A3
Eastridge Ln
100 LOGN 84321 528 B3
1000 MRRY 84117 2071 B4
4800 SLkC 84117 2071 B4
Eastridge Rd
1000 SNDY 84094 2283 A7
East Side Dr
400 LYTN 84040 1284 A3
Eastview Dr
800 ALPN 84004 2498 A3
5400 SLkC 84118 2067 E5
E Eastview Dr
200 ALPN 84004 2498 A2
Eastview Ln
1000 ALPN 84004 2498 A2
Eastwood Cir
500 PVDN 84332 528 B7
5800 MRRY 84107 2071 A7
Eastwood Dr
10 OREM 84097 2821 A5
1800 SOGN 84403 1173 E6
2000 WbrC 84403 1173 E6
E Eastwood Dr
3500 SLkC 84109 1966 D6
S Eastwood Dr
3300 SLkC 84109 1966 D6
Eastwood Ln
3700 SLkC 84109 1966 A7
3800 HLDY 84109 1966 A7
Eastwood Pl
2400 SNDY 84092 2284 A2
Easy St
800 OGDN 84403 1116 A5
1400 SJDN 84095 2281 D3
Easy Putt Dr
1200 TYVL 84123 2069 D7
Eaton Wy
5900 SLkC 84118 2067 C7
Ebony Av
4300 TYVL 84123 2069 D2
Eccles Av
500 OGDN 84404 1057 B6
1800 OGDN 84401 1116 B2
3000 OGDN 84403 1116 B5
3900 OGDN 84403 1173 B1
N Eccles Av
800 OGDN 84404 1057 B3
S Eccles Av
100 OGDN 84404 1057 B5
N Eccles Dr
200 OGDN 84404 1057 B4
Eccles St
1200 WbrC 84404 997 E6
1200 WbrC 84404 998 A6
1800 FRWT 84404 997 E6
Echo Dr
500 MRRY 84123 2070 B5
Echo Ln
900 SmtC 84098 1866 E7
1000 SmtC 84098 1867 A7
Ecker Hill Dr
3600 SmtC 84098 1865 A6
3700 SmtC 84098 1864 E6
Eclipse Wy
900 SLCY 84116 1753 E7
Eclipse Hill Rd
5100 WJDN 84084 2173 E3
Eddington Ct
5900 SLkC 84118 2067 C7
Eddy Rickenbacker Dr
100 SLCY 84116 1855 D2
Edelweiss Cir
1800 SLkC 84092 2283 C2
Edelweiss Ln
200 MIDW 84049 2291 C6
200 WshC 84049 2291 C6
Eden Dr
11000 SNDY 84094 2283 B5
Edenbrook Dr
1100 SNDY 84094 2283 B5
Edenbrook Wy
9000 WJDN 84088 2175 A7
9200 WJDN 84088 2281 C2
Eden Crest Rd
9800 SJDN 84095 2280 D2
Eden Glen Ct
9800 SJDN 84095 2280 D2
Eden Hills Dr
3300 WbrC 84310 1001 C3
Eden Point Cir
9800 SJDN 84095 2280 D2
Eden Ridge Dr
9800 SJDN 84095 2280 E3
Eden View Ct
9800 SJDN 84095 2280 E2
Eden View Dr
3400 SJDN 84095 2280 D2
Edgeberry Dr
1200 MRRY 84123 2069 D5
Edgecliff Cir
1700 SNDY 84092 2283 D3
Edgecliff Dr
1400 SNDY 84092 2283 C3
Edgecombe Dr
10 SLCY 84103 1754 C7
Edgecrest Dr
100 NSLK 84054 1754 A1
Edgefield Rd
800 SNDY 84094 2177 A5
Edgehill Cir
100 FTHT 84037 1345 E1
100 FTHT 84037 1346 B1
100 LYTN 84040 1284 A4
Edgehill Dr
100 PVDN 84332 592 A1
200 FTHT 84037 1346 A2
500 BNFL 84010 1654 A4
800 BMCY 84302 767 A3
2600 BNFL 84010 1653 E4
4000 OGDN 84403 1173 C1
Edgehill Rd
700 SLCY 84103 1755 A7
Edgemont Dr
200 NSLK 84054 1754 B1
2900 PRVO 84604 2928 D1
Edgemoor Dr
2200 HLDY 84117 2071 E4
Edgemount Dr
10 SLkC 84109 1965 E4
Edgerock Cir
2900 HLDY 84117 2072 B5
Edgeware Ln
2200 TYVL 84119 2069 B2
Edgewater Cir
3800 WVCY 84120 1962 C4
Edgewood Cir
300 PVDN 84332 528 B7
5300 SLkC 84117 2071 C4
Edgewood Dr
300 PVDN 84332 528 B7
600 NSLK 84054 1754 B1
700 SOGN 84403 1173 A3
1000 OGDN 84403 1173 A3
2700 PRVO 84604 2928 C2
4600 SOGN 84403 1172 E2
5000 PRVO 84604 2821 C4
5400 SLkC 84117 2071 C5
Edgewood Pl
300 PVDN 84332 528 B7
N Edgewood Pl
12300 BxEC 84309 522 B3
12300 BxEC 84312 522 B3
Edgewood Rd
4800 PRVO 84604 2821 C5
Edinburgh Ct
1700 ROY 84067 1171 D3
Edinburgh Dr
10300 HILD 84003 2605 B2
Edinburgh Ln
400 HRCY 84032 2398 C2
4700 WJDN 84088 2174 A5
5100 WJDN 84088 2173 E6
Edindrew Cir
400 MRRY 84107 2070 E6
Edindrew Dr
500 MRRY 84107 2070 E6
Edison Av
10 MRRY 84107 2070 C2
Edison St
200 SLCY 84111 1858 D6
1300 SLCY 84115 1858 D7
1800 SLCY 84115 1964 D1
2700 SSLK 84115 1964 D4
Edith Av
200 SLCY 84111 1858 D6
Edith Cir
8700 SLkC 84044 1960 A5
Edith Dr
8600 SLkC 84044 1960 A5
Edith Grove Ln
4000 WVCY 84120 2068 A1
Edman Ln
200 SALM 84653 3355 E3
Ed Mayne St
- SLkC 84118 2068 A6
Edmonds Pl
300 SLCY 84116 1858 A2
Education Cir
2600 WVCY 84128 1961 A4
Edvalson St
1200 OGDN 84403 1116 C7
Edvalson St SR-284
1200 OGDN 84403 1116 C7
Edward Av
1700 SLkC 84106 1965 C5
Edward Cir
3300 SLkC 84124 2072 C1
Edward Dr
4100 SLkC 84124 2072 C1
Edward Wy
3300 SLkC 84124 2072 C1
Edwin Cir
4600 SLkC 84117 2071 B3
Egan St
900 LYTN 84041 1283 B4
Eglantina Ln
13600 HRMN 84065 2385 C5
Egli Ct
600 SLCY 84102 1858 E5
Egret Cove
900 DRPR 84020 2283 A7
Eiger Pt
400 WshC 84049 2291 A6
Eilason Dr
800 FMTN 84025 1346 A6
Eileen Av
1700 TYVL 84084 2069 C7
Eladar Pl
2700 PKCY 84060 2079 B5
Elaine Av
- WVCY 84128 1961 D7
5300 WVCY 84120 1961 D7
Elaine Dr
800 BNFL 84010 1654 B3
3900 WVCY 84120 1962 A7
El Amador Cir
5000 SLkC 84117 2071 B3
El Amador St
1200 SLkC 84117 2071 B4
Elba Av
1000 WVCY 84119 1963 E3
Elbert Av
400 CTRV 84014 1551 E5
600 CTRV 84014 1552 A5
Elbert Cir
600 ALPN 84004 2497 D4
E Elberta Dr
100 NHON 84414 998 E4
W Elberta Dr
100 NHON 84414 998 C4
100 PTVW 84414 998 C4
El Cabrio Dr
3400 WVCY 84119 1962 E4
El Cajon Cir
3400 WVCY 84119 1962 D5
El Cajon Dr
2900 WVCY 84119 1962 E5
El Camino Cir
1800 TYVL 84119 2069 C1
El Camino St
4100 TYVL 84119 2069 C2
El Centro
1000 WVCY 84119 1963 E6
El Cimarron Dr
1100 MRRY 84123 2069 D7
1200 TYVL 84123 2069 D7
Elda Rae Cir
- RIVN 84065 2387 E4
Elderberry Cir
- LOGN 84341 464 C7
Elderberry Wy
2000 SNDY 84092 2283 E7
Eldon Wy
2000 CDHT 84093 2177 D4
El Dorado Dr
1800 HLDY 84124 1965 D7
4000 HLDY 84124 2071 D1
Eldorado Dr
2000 SGVL 84663 3143 C6
El Dorado Pl
10 WJDN 84088 2175 A6
Eldredge St
3100 SSLK 84115 1964 B5
Election Rd
100 DRPR 84020 2282 C6
Electra Ln
1100 SLkC 84094 2283 B2
1100 SNDY 84094 2283 B2
Electra St
9400 SNDY 84094 2283 B1
Elgin Av
700 SLkC 84106 1964 E4
1000 SLCY 84106 1965 A5
1000 SLkC 84106 1965 A5
Elgin Dr
3100 SLkC 84109 1966 B5
El Glen Av
3600 WVCY 84120 1962 D7
Eliason Av
700 BMCY 84302 767 B5
E Eliason Av
1100 BMCY 84302 767 B5
N Eliason Av
10 BMCY 84302 767 B5
Elida St
4500 MRRY 84107 2070 E2
Elise St
300 SNDY 84070 2282 E2
Elizabeth Cir
- KYVL 84037 1344 E3
3300 WJDN 84084 2174 E3
Elizabeth St
10 SLCY 84102 1859 B3
1800 SLCY 84105 1965 B1
2100 SLCY 84106 1965 B2
Elizabeth Day Cove
400 DRPR 84020 2388 E6
Elk Cir
11800 RIVN 84065 2281 E7
Elk Dr
11700 RIVN 84065 2281 E7
Elk Cove Cir
- HILD 84003 2498 B7
Elk Creek Ct
2000 BFDL 84065 2494 C1
Elk Glen Dr
1300 DRPR 84020 2496 B1
Elk Hill Ct
13800 BFDL 84065 2386 C5
Elk Hollow Cir
300 NSLK 84054 1754 D1
Elk Hollow Rd
1100 NSLK 84054 1754 D1
1300 BNFL 84010 1754 D1
1300 DvsC 84010 1754 D1
Elk Horn Cir
8100 CDHT 84093 2178 B5
E Elkhorn Cir
5200 WbrC 84310 1001 E2
5200 WbrC 84310 1002 A3
Elk Horn Dr
700 EKMT 84651 3462 D1
Elkhorn Dr
5800 WbrC 84310 1002 B4
E Elkhorn Dr
- WbrC 84310 1001 E2
5500 WbrC 84310 1002 A3
Elk Horn Ln
2800 CDHT 84093 2178 B5
Elk Horn Peak Dr
5100 RIVN 84065 2385 E6
14000 RIVN 84065 2386 A6
Elkhorn Ranch Rd
2900 NBLY 84321 591 C4
Elk Meadows Dr
4300 WJDN 84088 2280 B1
9100 WJDN 84088 2174 B7
S Elk Meadows Dr
200 EKMT 84651 3462 E2
Elk Mesa Rd
8400 SLkC 84044 1960 B6
Elk Mountain Rd
3600 SLkC 84044 1960 B7
Elk Park Ct
3700 SJDN 84095 2280 D2
W Elk Point Cir
200 WDHL 84653 3463 C2
Elk Point Dr
3600 SLkC 84044 1960 B6
Elk Ridge Cir
3000 WJDN 84084 2175 A3
Elkridge Cir
5400 WbrC 84310 1002 A3
Elk Ridge Dr
3600 SLkC 84044 1960 B7
7600 WJDN 84084 2175 A3
10600 UthC 84651 3355 D7
11100 EKMT 84651 3462 E1
11100 UthC 84651 3462 E1
Elk Ridge Ln
1000 ALPN 84004 2498 A2
1100 UthC 84004 2498 A2
Elkridge Tr
- WbrC 84310 1002 A3
N Elkridge Tr
3400 WbrC 84310 1002 A3
Elk Rim Rd
4200 SJDN 84095 2280 B1
Elk Run Dr
3000 SmtC 84098 1865 B6
Elk Run Ln
4400 WJDN 84088 2280 B1
Elk Valley Ln
3600 SJDN 84095 2280 D1
S Elk View Cir
1900 MPTN 84664 3250 E2
W Elk View Cir
1300 MPTN 84664 3250 E2
Elk View Ct
3700 SJDN 84095 2280 D2
Elk View Dr
9600 SJDN 84095 2280 D2
N Elkview Dr
3500 WbrC 84310 1002 A3
Elk Vista Ln
3600 SJDN 84095 2280 D1
Elkwood Cir
6600 WJDN 84084 2174 A1
Ella St
2800 WJDN 84088 2281 A1
S Ellen Cir
1000 OREM 84058 2820 D7
1000 OREM 84058 2927 D1
Ellen Wy
1700 SNDY 84092 2283 D5
Ellendale Av
1400 LOGN 84321 464 C7
1400 LOGN 84341 464 C7
Ellerbeck Ln
1700 DRPR 84020 2389 D2
Ellerby Av
900 MRRY 84117 2071 A4
Ellerby Ct
5000 SLkC 84117 2071 A3
Ellis Cir
600 WDCR 84087 1653 B2
Ellis Dr
100 OREM 84097 2821 A6
W Ellis St
700 OGDN 84401 1115 B4
Ellison St
10 LYTN 84041 1282 E5
Ellisonwoods Av
2300 CDHT 84121 2071 E7
2300 CDHT 84121 2072 A7
W Elm
10 SHFD 84335 399 D1
Elm Av
- SLCY 84103 1859 B2
500 SLCY 84106 1964 E2
900 SLCY 84106 1965 A2
1000 BMCY 84302 767 B5
1000 PRVO 84604 2928 E4
2400 SLCY 84109 1966 A2
Elm Cir
- LYTN 84041 1283 B5
1400 PRVO 84604 2928 E4
Elm Dr
- LEHI 84043 2602 C2
Elm Ln
1200 DvsC 84056 1227 E2
Elm St
- SGVL 84663 3035 E6
- SHFD 84335 399 D1
200 MRRY 84107 2070 D3
400 ANFK 84003 2711 D1
400 LYTN 84041 1283 A5
7300 MDVL 84047 2176 B3
Elma Cir
3800 WVCY 84120 1962 A7
Elma St
3700 WVCY 84120 1962 A7
5000 WVCY 84120 1961 D6
El Manicero Wy
8200 SNDY 84093 2177 C5
8400 SLkC 84093 2177 C5
Elmcrest Dr
500 MRRY 84107 2176 E1
Elmer St
3100 SLkC 84044 1960 C5
Elm Grove Dr
2400 PRRY 84302 827 D5
Elmhearst Dr
9000 WJDN 84088 2174 D7
Elm Hill Cir
1400 TYVL 84123 2175 D1
Elm Meadows Rd
12400 RIVN 84065 2386 E2
El Monte Dr
1100 SLkC 84117 2071 B4
Elm Ridge Rd
11700 SNDY 84094 2283 B7
W Elm Tree Pl
800 SLCY 84116 1754 B7
Elmwood Dr
300 OREM 84057 2820 D4
3000 RIVN 84065 2387 A1
3100 RIVN 84065 2386 E1
Elmwood St
3600 SLkC 84106 1965 D6
Eloni Cir
7300 WJDN 84084 2175 D3
El Rancho Rd
3300 SLkC 84109 1966 D6
El Rey St
1400 SLCY 84108 1859 D7
Elsbrook Cir
14200 DRPR 84020 2388 E6
El Sendero Cir
1100 SLkC 84117 2071 B4
El Sendero St
1200 SLkC 84117 2071 B4
El Serrito Cir
3400 SLkC 84109 1966 C6
S El Serrito Dr
3300 SLkC 84109 1966 C6
Elsie Cir
6000 TYVL 84123 2069 D7
Elsie Ct
6000 TYVL 84123 2069 D7
Elsie Dr
1400 TYVL 84123 2069 D6
Elswood Av
1100 SNDY 84094 2283 B1
Elusive Wy
3600 SLkC 84044 1960 D6
Elwood Pl
500 SLCY 84102 1858 E5
Elwood Wy
3800 WJDN 84088 2174 C5
Ely Pl
600 SLCY 84102 1858 E5
Embarcadero St
5300 TYVL 84123 2069 C5
Embassy Cir
1300 SLCY 84108 1860 B7
Embassy Wy
1300 SLCY 84108 1860 A7
Emelita St
1200 MRRY 84117 2071 B4
1200 SLkC 84117 2071 B4
Emerald Dr
10 LYTN 84041 1282 E3
10 LYTN 84041 1283 A3
800 SLkC 84094 2283 A1
Emerald St
1000 LYTN 84040 1283 D3
Emerald Green Dr
3900 WVCY 84120 2068 B1
Emerald Hills Ct
2200 CDHT 84121 2177 E2
Emerald Hills Dr
600 BNFL 84010 1654 A3
2200 CDHT 84121 2177 E2
Emerald Isle Ln
10 MRRY 84107 2070 C5
Emerald Lake Cove
9200 CRHL 84062 2605 D5
Emerald Oaks Ct
600 FMTN 84025 1346 B4
Emerald Ridge Cove
6000 HLDY 84121 2071 D7
Emeril Av
800 SLCY 84116 1858 A3
Emerson Av
300 SLCY 84115 1858 D7
500 SLCY 84105 1858 E7
1300 SLCY 84105 1859 C7
2000 SLCY 84108 1859 D7
2400 SLCY 84108 1860 A7
Emerson Cir
8000 SLkC 84044 1960 C3
Emery Av
400 OREM 84057 2820 B4
Emery Cir
1100 SLCY 84104 1857 E4
Emery St
300 SLCY 84104 1857 E5
Emigration Cir
1300 SLCY 84108 1859 D7
Emigration St
1300 SLCY 84108 1859 C7
Emigration Canyon Rd
- SLCY 84108 1860 B5
1500 SLkC 84108 1860 B5
Emilee Kaye Ct
100 SNDY 84070 2282 D4
Emilion Cir
5700 SLkC 84118 2067 D5
Emily Cir
700 SLCY 84116 1753 C7
Emma Cir
4000 SLkC 84124 2071 B1
Emma Jo Av
100 SNST 84015 1227 D2
Emma Mine Dr
4600 HRMN 84065 2280 A7
Emma Sue Cir
5100 WJDN 84084 2173 E2
Emmeline Dr
5300 HRMN 84065 2385 D7
Emmons Dr
4600 WJDN 84088 2174 A4
Emperor Dr
3800 WVCY 84119 1963 D7
Emperor Pl
1300 WVCY 84119 1963 D7
Empire Av
700 SLkC 84106 1964 E6
700 SLkC 84106 1965 A6
800 PKCY 84060 2078 D5
Empire Cir
700 SLkC 84106 1965 A6
Empire Rd
1500 SLCY 84104 1857 C7
1500 SLCY 84104 1963 C1
Empress Ct
5800 WJDN 84088 2173 D1
Empress Ln
6600 WJDN 84088 2173 B1
Emry Ct
- FTHT 84037 1346 A4
Encampment Cir
12100 DRPR 84020 2388 E1
Enchanted Dr
700 MDVL 84047 2176 E1
700 MDVL 84047 2177 A1
Enchanted Hills Dr
3200 CDHT 84121 2178 C3
Enchanted Oak Ln
9000 SNDY 84094 2177 A7
Enchanted View Dr
3300 CDHT 84121 2178 C3
Encino St
5100 SLkC 84117 2071 B4
Endicott Cir
- KYVL 84037 1344 D2
Engine Ln
200 DvsC 84056 1228 E4
Englewood Cir
5000 TYVL 84118 2068 D4
Englewood Dr
200 BMCY 84302 827 E1
3600 TYVL 84118 2068 D4
English Wy
3200 CDHT 84093 2178 C6
English Holly Ct
1400 SJDN 84095 2281 D4
English Oaks Cove
7900 CDHT 84093 2177 C4
7900 SNDY 84093 2177 C4
Engstrom Wy
200 LYTN 84041 1228 E6
Ensign Cir
1600 CDHT 84121 2177 C2
Ensign Ct
1600 CDHT 84121 2177 C3
Ensign Pl
1600 CDHT 84121 2177 C2
Ensign Bay
1700 CDHT 84121 2177 C3
Ensign Park Dr
2800 SLkC 84044 1960 E4
Ensign Peak Cir
14100 RIVN 84065 2385 E6
Ensign Point Ln
13300 DRPR 84020 2388 D4
Ensign Vista Dr
100 SLCY 84103 1754 D7
Enterado Av
3300 WVCY 84119 1962 E7
Enterado Cir
3900 WVCY 84119 1962 E7
Enterprise Pt
300 HDPK 84318 400 C6
Enterprise Wy
- NSLK 84054 1652 C7
- NSLK 84054 1753 C1
- TYVL 84123 2069 E2
- TYVL 84123 2070 A2
Entrada Ln
1500 RIVN 84065 2387 C2
Ephraim Cir
3200 SJDN 84095 2280 E4
Equator Ln
7000 WJDN 84084 2175 D2
Equestrian Ct
2000 PKCY 84060 2078 E2
Equestrian Dr
11400 SJDN 84095 2281 D6
Equestrian Park Cir
9400 SNDY 84092 2283 E1
Equity Dr
- NSLK 84054 1652 C7
Ereckson Ln
5600 MRRY 84107 2070 E6
Erekson View Cir
700 MRRY 84107 2070 E6
Erica Cir
3400 WJDN 84084 2174 E2
Erica Ln
- SWBR 84405 1229 D2
E Erica Wy
1800 SWBR 84405 1229 D2
Erickson Ln
- SWBR 84405 1229 D2
300 MRRY 84107 2070 B3
Erickson Park Dr
1400 WJDN 84084 2175 C3
Erie St
400 SLCY 84116 1858 B1
Erin Cir
1100 TYVL 84123 2069 E3
Erin Ln
4700 TYVL 84123 2069 E3
Erin Loop Rd
13700 HRMN 84065 2385 A5
Erique Wy
7900 CDHT 84093 2177 E4
Erma Av
100 SNST 84015 1227 D2
Erv Cir
4800 SLkC 84118 2067 E3
Escala Ln
- CTRV 84014 1551 D4
Escalade Av
3500 CDHT 84121 2178 D6
Escalade Cir
8600 CDHT 84121 2178 D6
Escalante Dr
100 SPFK 84660 3249 C3
8200 SLkC 84093 2178 A5
8300 SLkC 84093 2177 E5
8400 SNDY 84093 2178 A6
N Escalante Dr
200 EKMT 84651 3463 A2
Escondido St
5000 SLkC 84117 2071 B4
Eskesen Cir
3100 WVCY 84120 1962 A5
Eskesen Dr
3200 WVCY 84120 1962 A5
Espadrille Cir
2100 TYVL 84118 2069 B4
Espadrille Dr
5100 TYVL 84118 2069 C4
Esprit Dr
5600 SLkC 84118 2067 D6
Essex Dr
5200 TYVL 84118 2068 D4
Essex Ct Cir
6900 MDVL 84047 2177 A2
Essex Ct Wy
900 MDVL 84047 2177 A2
Estate Dr
200 ALPN 84004 2497 E4
Estate Wy
100 FTHT 84037 1346 B1
Estates Cir
2800 PKCY 84060 2078 D2
Estates Dr
1100 SOGN 84403 1173 B4
2700 PKCY 84060 2078 D1
Estates Pl
2800 PKCY 84060 2078 D2
Estates Wy
12300 DRPR 84020 2389 B1
Estella Cir
600 CTRV 84014 1552 A4
Esther Cir
4900 SLkC 84117 2071 A3
Esther Ann Cir
13700 DRPR 84020 2389 B5
Estrellita Dr
1300 SNDY 84093 2177 B5

Salt Lake City Street Index

STREET Block City ZIP Map# Grid

Etienne Wy
2700 SLkC 84093 2178 B5
Eton Cir
8800 SNDY 84070 2176 B6
Eton Ct
600 FMTN 84025 1346 B4
600 FTHT 84037 1346 B4
Etruscan Ct
6900 WJDN 84084 2174 A2
Etruscan Wy
6700 WJDN 84084 2174 B1
Ettenmor Cir
3700 TYVL 84118 2068 D5
Etude Dr
8200 WJDN 84088 2174 B5
Eucalyptus Wy
2500 WVCY 84119 1963 A4
Euclid Av
900 SLCY 84104 1857 E3
900 SLCY 84104 1858 B3
Euculpytus Ct
4000 CRHL 84062 2605 C2
Eugene St
100 NSLK 84054 1653 B7
Eugene Hill Wy
3000 TYVL 84118 2069 A4
3100 TYVL 84118 2068 E4
Eugenia Pl
3100 WVCY 84119 1962 E5
Eureka Wy
2000 SJDN 84095 2281 B7
Europa Dr
1300 SLkC 84106 1965 B7
Euston Dr
2100 PKCY 84060 2079 A3
Evalin Cir
1300 SRCS 84075 1227 A7
Evalynn Cir
2200 RIVN 84065 2387 B1
Evan Hill Rd
7300 WJDN 84084 2173 E3
Evans Wy
2000 FMTN 84025 1346 B4
Evelyn Dr
3700 SLkC 84124 2072 D1
Evelyn Rd
3800 SOGN 84403 1116 A7
3900 SOGN 84403 1173 A1
Eveningbreeze
1700 DRPR 84020 2389 C1
Evening Dove Cir
2500 WVCY 84119 1963 A6
Evening Light Cove
3600 SLkC 84044 1960 B6
E Evening Moon Wy
9800 SNDY 84070 2282 C2
W Evening Moon Wy
9800 SNDY 84070 2282 C2
Eveningshade Dr
7600 WJDN 84084 2175 A3
Evening Star Dr
1800 PKCY 84060 2078 E2
2400 HLDY 84124 1966 A7
Evening Star Wy
10 SNDY 84070 2282 C2
Evensen Cir
9700 SJDN 84095 2281 D2
Everest Dr
6300 TYVL 84084 2069 A7
Everett Av
- SLCY 84103 1754 A6
600 SLCY 84116 1754 A6
Everett Cir
5600 TYVL 84118 2069 A6
Everette Av
1300 LYTN 84041 1282 B2
Everettwood Dr
2300 TYVL 84084 2069 A7
Evergreen Av
1900 SLkC 84106 1965 D6
2000 SLkC 84109 1965 D6
2400 SLkC 84109 1966 A6
Evergreen Cir
100 SmtC 84098 1864 B6
5300 HILD 84003 2497 D6
10100 CRHL 84062 2605 A2
E Evergreen Cir
2400 SLkC 84109 1966 A6
Evergreen Dr
700 ANFK 84003 2604 E7
800 ANFK 84003 2605 A7
900 LOGN 84321 528 B1
3700 PTVW 84414 998 A3
Evergreen Ln
1400 SLkC 84106 1965 C6
Evergreen Pl
3300 SLkC 84106 1965 D6
Evergreen Rd
1900 SGVL 84663 3143 C5
1900 UthC 84663 3143 C5
Evergreen Wy
- HILD 84003 2497 D6
10 CRFD 84015 1281 D1
600 OGDN 84404 1056 E4
Evergreen Pine Ln
200 MDVL 84070 2176 D4
Evergreen View Ct
2200 SLkC 84109 1965 E6
Everleigh Cir
1900 SNDY 84093 2177 C6
Evesham Dr
400 MRRY 84107 2070 E6
Ewell Dr
4100 SLkC 84107 2071 A1
Ewe Turn
1300 DvsC 84040 1283 E5
Excaliber Wy
9000 WJDN 84088 2175 C7
Excalibur St
100 NSLK 84054 1653 A5
300 DvsC 84010 1653 B5
Excelsius Cir
7900 CDHT 84121 2178 B4
Exchange Pl
10 SLCY 84111 1858 C4
Exchange Rd
300 OGDN 84401 1115 B3
700 WbrC 84401 1115 B3
Executive Cir
1800 WJDN 84084 2175 C2
Executive Dr
7000 WJDN 84084 2175 C3
Executive Pkwy
2500 LEHI 84043 2602 C1
Executive Park Dr
900 MRRY 84117 2071 A5
Exeter Cir
2300 SNDY 84093 2177 E7
2300 SNDY 84093 2178 B7
Explorer Wy
2300 RIVN 84065 2387 B4
Expressway Ln
700 SPFK 84660 3249 E1
1100 SPFK 84660 3250 A1
Eyrie Dr
1400 OGDN 84404 1057 A2

F

F Av
- PTVW 84404 997 E5
400 DvsC 84056 1228 C5
2300 OGDN 84401 1115 B4
F St
- BMCY 84302 767 A7
- BMCY 84302 827 E2
- CRFD 84016 1227 C6
- KYVL 84041 1283 B6
- RVDL 84405 1172 A3
10 SLCY 84103 1858 E2
Faber Ln
6200 TYVL 84123 2069 D7
Facet Wy
5300 WJDN 84088 2173 E5
Factor St
- DvsC 84056 1228 C5
E Factory St
- BxEC 84312 521 A2
10 GRLD 84312 520 E2
300 GRLD 84312 521 A2
E Factory St SR-82
- BxEC 84312 521 A2
10 GRLD 84312 520 E2
300 GRLD 84312 521 A2
W Factory St
10 GRLD 84312 520 D2
400 BxEC 84336 520 D2
400 GRLD 84337 520 D2
500 BxEC 84337 520 D2
800 GRLD 84336 520 D2
Factory Outlet Dr
11800 DRPR 84020 2282 C7
11800 DRPR 84020 2388 C1
Fahnian Cir
2700 WJDN 84088 2175 A5
Fair Av
800 TMTN 84337 520 C5
Fairbourne Av
4300 MRRY 84107 2070 D2
Fairbrook Ln
4900 HLDY 84117 2071 E4
Fairburn Cir
4000 SJDN 84095 2280 C2
Faircloguh Dr
900 SLkC 84106 1965 A6
Fairfax Cir
200 SLCY 84103 1859 C2
Fairfax Rd
1200 SLCY 84103 1859 B2
Fairfield Cir
4700 SLkC 84124 2072 C3
E Fairfield Dr
200 KYVL 84037 1283 D7
300 DvsC 84037 1283 D7
Fairfield Rd
3200 SLkC 84124 2072 C3
N Fairfield Rd
10 LYTN 84040 1283 B2
10 LYTN 84041 1283 B2
500 KYVL 84037 1283 C6
600 DvsC 84037 1283 C6
700 DvsC 84041 1283 C6
700 KYVL 84041 1283 C6
2000 LYTN 84040 1229 B7
2000 LYTN 84041 1229 B7
2400 DvsC 84040 1229 B7
2400 DvsC 84041 1229 B7
S Fairfield Rd
10 LYTN 84040 1283 C4
10 LYTN 84041 1283 C4
Fairglen Cir
4000 SJDN 84095 2280 C2
Fairgrounds Dr
1000 OGDN 84404 1056 B3
Fair Haven Cir
1000 MRRY 84123 2069 E5
Fair Hill Ct
13400 DRPR 84020 2389 C4
Fair Hope Cir
14300 HRMN 84065 2385 E6
Fair Isle Ln
2700 WVCY 84128 1961 D4
Fairlane Cir
4400 WVCY 84120 2068 C2
Fairlane St
3200 SLkC 84044 1960 D5
Fairmeadows Dr
700 MDVL 84047 2176 E1
700 MDVL 84047 2177 A2
Fairmont Cir
800 SLCY 84106 1965 A3
Fairmont Ln
1200 LYTN 84041 1282 C7
Fairmount Cir
3600 WJDN 84084 2174 D1
Fairoaks Cir
8500 SNDY 84070 2176 E6
Fair Oaks Dr
900 BNFL 84010 1654 A4
Fairoaks Dr
5400 SLkC 84117 2071 C5
Fairoaks Wy
500 SNDY 84070 2176 E5
Fairview Av
900 SLCY 84105 1859 C6
Fairview Cir
100 ALPN 84004 2497 E3
Fairview Dr
700 BMCY 84302 767 A4
4900 HLDY 84117 2071 E4
5400 SmtC 84098 1972 E3
Fairview Rd
400 CTRV 84014 1551 E3
500 CTRV 84014 1552 A3
Fairway Cir
900 FTHT 84037 1345 E4
900 FTHT 84037 1346 A4
1000 FMTN 84025 1346 A6
1100 FMTN 84025 1345 E6
2400 BNFL 84010 1654 A4
3400 SPFK 84660 3250 E6
12100 SNDY 84092 2389 C1
Fairway Ct
- OREM 84058 2819 D7
Fairway Dr
100 SHFD 84335 400 A2
700 BNFL 84010 1654 A4
2200 SPFK 84660 3250 D7
2200 WJDN 84088 2175 B6
E Fairway Dr
900 NSLK 84054 1653 D6
1100 BNFL 84010 1653 D6
N Fairway Dr
10 BNFL 84010 1653 D7
10 NSLK 84054 1653 D7
S Fairway Dr
10 EKMT 84651 3463 A2
10 NSLK 84054 1653 D7
Fairway Ln
- OREM 84058 2819 D7
10 LOGN 84321 527 C5
1300 FMTN 84025 1346 A5
1600 SPFK 84660 3250 D6
Fairway Pl
1000 NSLK 84054 1653 D6
Fairway Hills Ct
3000 PKCY 84060 2079 A1
Fairway Knoll Dr
13900 DRPR 84020 2389 C5
Fairway Ridge Rd
1500 DRPR 84020 2389 C5
Fairways Dr
4900 WbrC 84310 1001 E1
Fairway View Dr
700 SNDY 84070 2282 A1
1000 FTHT 84037 1346 A3
Fairway Village Dr
2400 PKCY 84060 2078 E1
Fairwind Cir
4000 TYVL 84084 2068 B7
Fairwind Dr
6200 TYVL 84084 2068 C7
6200 WJDN 84084 2068 C7
6400 TYVL 84084 2174 C1
Fair Winns Ct
- DRPR 84020 2496 E2
Fair Winns Ln
- DRPR 84020 2496 E3
Fairwood Cir
300 PVDN 84332 528 A7
Fairwood Dr
2000 TYVL 84118 2069 B6
Falcon Cir
1000 MPTN 84664 3251 C1
9100 SNDY 84093 2177 D7
Falcon Ct
7800 PKCY 84060 2185 A1
Falcon St
4100 WVCY 84120 2068 C1
Falcon Wy
800 OREM 84097 2820 E2
1800 SNDY 84093 2177 D7
2300 SNDY 84093 2178 A7
2600 SNDY 84093 2284 A1
Falcon Crest Ct
15200 DRPR 84020 2496 E2
Falconer Wy
1200 WshC 84049 2396 D2
Falcon Hill Cir
1900 SNDY 84092 2283 D2
Falcon Hill Dr
1900 SNDY 84092 2283 E2
Falcon Hurst Cir
1900 SNDY 84092 2283 D1
Falcon Hurst Ct
1900 SNDY 84092 2283 D2
Falcon Hurst Dr
9800 SNDY 84092 2283 D2
Falcon Park Cir
9100 SNDY 84093 2177 D7
Falcon Pointe Ct
15300 DRPR 84020 2496 E2
Falcon Ridge Dr
2100 DRPR 84020 2496 E2
Falcon Ridge Wy
- LEHI 84043 2495 C5
Falconview Dr
1900 SNDY 84092 2283 D2
Falconwood Ln
10 SNDY 84092 2284 A4
Falkirk Rd
- SRCS 84075 1226 B7
Falkridge Ct
- DRPR 84020 2389 B7
Fall St
200 SLCY 84116 1857 D2
Fallbrook Cir
8200 SNDY 84094 2177 A5
Fallbrook Wy
900 SNDY 84094 2177 A5
Fallentine Rd
2800 SLkC 84093 2178 B6
Fall Oak Dr
6300 WJDN 84088 2173 B5
Fall View Dr
1800 SNDY 84093 2177 D6
Fallwood Dr
1900 TYVL 84118 2069 C5
Falstaff Dr
5400 SLkC 84118 2067 E4
Family Cir
600 SNDY 84070 2282 E3
Family Oaks Dr
4700 WbrC 84310 1001 D2
Family Tree Pl
5700 TYVL 84123 2069 C6
Fanfare Ct
6600 WVCY 84128 1961 B5
Fanfare Dr
6600 WVCY 84128 1961 A5
Farah Cir
5300 SLkC 84118 2067 E4
Farah Dr
4800 SLkC 84118 2067 E3
Fardown Av
1900 HLDY 84121 2071 E6
Fardown Ct
5900 HLDY 84121 2071 E6
Fargo Rd
6600 WJDN 84084 2175 B1
Fargo St
2400 WVCY 84119 1963 D3
S Fariway Dr
10 EKMT 84651 3463 A2
Farley Cir
1500 SNDY 84092 2283 C6
Farm Cir
100 FMTN 84025 1447 E1
Farm Ln
700 FMTN 84025 1448 A3
1900 CDHT 84093 2177 D4
Farm Rd
- UthC 84651 3460 D4
- UthC 84655 3460 D4
10 MIDW 84049 2397 B1
1500 FMTN 84025 1447 E1
4000 WJDN 84088 2174 C6
Farm Bridge Cir
4500 SLkC 84117 2071 B2
Farm Brook Wy
2100 CDHT 84093 2177 E5
Farm Cove
100 FMTN 84025 1447 E1
Farm Creek Cir
7900 CDHT 84093 2177 D4
Farmer Cir
4800 WVCY 84120 1962 A4
Farmer Wy
3300 SSLK 84106 1964 E6
3300 SSLK 84115 1964 E6
Farmhaven Dr
2300 SNST 84015 1171 C7
Farm Hill Dr
1300 MRRY 84117 2071 B5
Farm Hollow Ln
13600 DRPR 84020 2388 E4
Farmington Hills Dr
900 FMTN 84025 1346 C7
Farm Ln Cir
1200 OREM 84057 2820 D1
Farm Meadow Cir
1400 SLkC 84117 2071 C3
Farm Meadow Ln
1300 SLkC 84117 2071 C2
Farm Meadow Rd
1500 FMTN 84025 1447 E1
Farm Oak Ct
8200 WJDN 84088 2173 C5
Farm Ridge Rd
1900 TYVL 84118 2069 C6
Farmstead Cir
9700 SJDN 84095 2281 E2
Farmview Ln
10600 SJDN 84095 2281 B4
Farnsworth Ln
11200 SNDY 84070 2282 E5
Farr Av
1000 OGDN 84404 1056 A2
Farr Ct
1100 OGDN 84401 1116 B3
Farr Dr
1500 OGDN 84404 1116 B1
Farrington Ct
3500 WJDN 84084 2174 D3
Farr W Dr
1400 FRWT 84404 1055 E1
1500 FRWT 84404 997 D7
Farthingale Ln
2500 TYVL 84119 2069 A1
Farthington Cir
3800 WJDN 84088 2174 D6
Far Vista Ct
6200 SLkC 84118 2067 C6
Far Vista Dr
5700 SLkC 84118 2067 C6
Fashion Blvd
5600 MRRY 84107 2070 D7
6200 MRRY 84107 2176 C2
Fashion Point Dr
5900 SOGN 84403 1173 C6
Fashionsquare Dr
6000 MRRY 84107 2070 D7
Fassio Cir
4400 WVCY 84120 1962 B5
Fastback Cir
12000 RIVN 84065 2281 E7
Faunsdale Cir
1700 SNDY 84092 2283 C3
Faunsdale Dr
1700 SNDY 84092 2283 C3
Faust Cir
8000 SLkC 84044 1960 C4
Faust Wy
1800 TYVL 84084 2069 C7
Fawn Cir
3400 CDHT 84121 2178 C2
Fawn Dr
3000 SmtC 84098 1865 B6
Fawn Ln
1700 BNFL 84010 1654 C4
Fawn Grove Ln
10 SNDY 84092 2284 A5
Fawn Hill Cir
14200 BFDL 84065 2386 D6
Fawn Hill Ct
3800 BFDL 84065 2386 C6
Fawn Point Ct
1200 DRPR 84020 2496 B1
Fawnwood Cove
3100 SNDY 84092 2284 B4
Faye Cir
600 SNDY 84070 2282 E1
Fayelle Av
10 MRRY 84107 2176 C1
Fayette Av
400 SLCY 84101 1858 B6
800 SLCY 84104 1858 A6
Fayeway Dr
8300 SLkC 84094 2177 B5
8300 SNDY 84094 2177 B5
Feather Gold Ct
2100 DRPR 84020 2496 E1
Feather Hill Ct
2100 DRPR 84020 2496 E1
Featherstone Cir
1700 SLCY 84116 1753 C7
Featherstone Dr
900 SLCY 84116 1753 C7
Featherwood Dr
10400 SJDN 84095 2281 B4
Federal Av
10 LOGN 84321 527 D3
Federal Wy
- SLCY 84112 1859 C3
1300 SLCY 84102 1859 B3
1300 SLCY 84103 1859 B3
Federal Heights Cir
200 SLCY 84103 1859 C2
Federal Heights Dr
1200 SLCY 84103 1859 B2
Federal Pointe Dr
1500 SLCY 84103 1859 C2
Feldspar Wy
5800 WJDN 84084 2173 C2
Felt Hall
10 PRVO 84604 2928 D4
Fenchurch Dr
2100 PKCY 84060 2079 A3
Fenchurch Rd
3400 WJDN 84084 2174 D3
E Fenton Av
300 SSLK 84115 1964 D7
S Fenton Cove
3700 SSLK 84115 1964 D7
Fenway Av
1200 SLCY 84102 1859 B5
Fenwick Cir
4000 SJDN 84095 2280 C2
Feramorz Dr
3900 HLDY 84124 1965 E7
Ferguson Dr
9700 CRHL 84062 2605 A3
Ferguson Wy
4600 CRHL 84062 2605 A4
Fern Av
100 SLCY 84103 1858 B1
Fern Cir
2500 WJDN 84084 2175 A2
8000 MDVL 84047 2176 B4
Fern Dr
10 CRFD 84015 1227 D3
500 MDVL 84047 2176 A4
1600 OGDN 84403 1173 C1
Fernbrook Dr
3200 TYVL 84084 2174 E1
6300 TYVL 84084 2068 E7
Fernbush Cir
7500 SLkC 84044 1960 D5
Fernbush Dr
3000 SLkC 84044 1960 D5
Ferncrest Cir
5200 TYVL 84118 2069 A5
Fernleaf St
1500 SLCY 84116 1753 C5
Fernwood Cir
3200 LYTN 84040 1230 B7
Fernwood Dr
- FRWT 84404 1055 D2
300 HYRM 84319 651 C4
1300 TYVL 84123 2069 D2
3000 DvsC 84040 1284 A1
3000 LYTN 84040 1284 A1
3200 LYTN 84040 1230 B7
Ferron Cir
5700 TYVL 84118 2069 A6
Ferron Dr
2700 TYVL 84118 2069 A5
Fescue Cir
6400 WVCY 84128 1961 B5
Festival Dr
2900 WVCY 84120 1961 E5
5000 WVCY 84120 1962 A5
Festive Wy
8200 WJDN 84088 2174 B5
Fetzer Cir
3000 SLkC 84044 1960 D5
Fetzer Dr
2900 SLkC 84044 1960 D4
Feulner Ct
6600 WVCY 84128 1961 A6
Feulner Dr
3500 WVCY 84128 1961 B6
Feulner Park Cir
5700 WJDN 84088 2279 D1
Feulner Park Rd
9400 WJDN 84088 2279 D1
Fiddlesticks
10600 CRHL 84062 2605 B1
Field Cir
5700 SLkC 84118 2068 B6
E Field Cir
200 ALPN 84004 2498 B4
N Field Cir
2200 PTGV 84062 2605 C6
N Field Dr
900 PTGV 84062 2605 C6
Fieldbury Cir
5300 WVCY 84120 1961 E6
Field Creek Wy
- WJDN 84088 2173 D5
Field Crescent Ln
- RIVN 84065 2385 E3
Fieldcrest Dr
4500 CRHL 84062 2605 A2
Fieldcrest Ln
1400 SLkC 84117 2071 C4
Field Downs Dr
12000 RIVN 84065 2281 B7
12000 RIVN 84065 2387 B1
N Fielding Av
- OGDN 84404 1056 B5
Fielding Hill Ln
- DRPR 84020 2496 E3
Fieldmint Ln
3200 WVCY 84128 1961 D6
Field Point Cir
2600 SNDY 84092 2284 A6
Field Rose Dr
2300 HLDY 84121 2071 E6
6100 HLDY 84121 2072 A7
Fieldstone Cir
3500 CDHT 84121 2178 C3
Fieldstone Ln
- LEHI 84043 2495 D5
7500 CDHT 84121 2178 C3
Fieldview Dr
7100 WVCY 84128 1960 E6
Fiesta Wy
6300 MRRY 84121 2071 D7
Fife Ct
1100 MRRY 84123 2069 E6
W Fig Tree Pl
800 SLCY 84116 1754 A7
Figure Skate Cir
3400 WJDN 84084 2174 D1
Filbert Wy
6000 SLkC 84118 2068 A7
Filbert Park Cir
4800 SLkC 84118 2068 A6
Fillmore Av
1300 OGDN 84404 1057 C7
1300 OGDN 84404 1116 C1
1900 OGDN 84401 1116 C3
2700 OGDN 84403 1116 C4
4400 OGDN 84403 1173 C2
Filly Bay Dr
3700 SLkC 84044 1960 C7
Filmore St
1300 SLCY 84105 1859 C7
2400 SLCY 84106 1965 C3
Finair Dr
4100 WVCY 84120 2068 C1
Finair St
4300 WVCY 84120 2068 C2
Finch Ln
10 SLCY 84102 1859 B3
Fine Dr
500 SSLK 84119 1964 A7
Finlandia Cir
8000 CDHT 84093 2178 A5
Finlandia Ct
3000 CDHT 84093 2178 B5
Finlandia Wy
8000 CDHT 84093 2178 B5
Fiona Cir
3800 WVCY 84120 1962 D4
Fir Av
900 PRVO 84604 2928 E4
1200 DvsC 84056 1227 E3
Fir Cir
1400 PRVO 84604 2928 E4
Fir St
- SGVL 84663 3035 E6
Fire Bud Cir
5400 HRMN 84065 2385 E6
E Fireclay Av
10 MRRY 84107 2070 C1
W Fireclay Av
10 MRRY 84107 2070 C1
Firefox Cir
6900 WJDN 84084 2173 E2
Fire Lily Ln
9200 WJDN 84088 2174 A7
9200 WJDN 84088 2280 A1
Firenze Pl
5900 WJDN 84084 2173 C1
Fireside Cir
1500 SLkC 84093 2177 C5
Firestone Cir
5900 SJDN 84095 2279 C7
Firetip Ct
13500 RIVN 84065 2386 A4
S Fireweed Dr
4500 TYVL 84123 2069 E2
W Fireweed Dr
900 TYVL 84123 2069 E2
First St
6500 HTVL 84317 1060 D5
6500 WbrC 84317 1060 D5
7300 HTVL 84317 1061 A5
7700 WbrC 84317 1061 A5
Firth Cir
4100 SJDN 84095 2280 C2
Firth Farm Rd
6700 SWBR 84405 1172 E7
Fishburn Dr
10 BMCY 84302 827 D1
S Fisher Cir
2900 SLkC 84109 1965 E4
Fisher Ln
2300 SLkC 84109 1965 E4
2300 SLkC 84109 1966 A4
Fisher Wy
3600 WVCY 84119 1963 D7
E Fish Hatchery Rd
10 MNTU 84324 829 C1
Fitz Ln
500 DRPR 84020 2388 E3
Fitzgerald Ct
14000 DRPR 84020 2388 E5
Fitzgerald Ln
900 LEHI 84043 2603 D4
Fitzpatrick Cir
5000 SLkC 84118 2067 E4
Fiver Cir
1500 RIVN 84065 2387 D1
Fjord Cir
5400 TYVL 84118 2069 A5
W Flag Av
1800 WVCY 84119 1963 C5
Flair St
2900 WVCY 84120 1961 E4
Flamingo Dr
2500 HLDY 84117 2072 A4
Flamingo Wy
6800 WJDN 84084 2175 D2
Flanders Rd
10000 SNDY 84092 2283 C3
Flanders Wy
1800 SmtC 84098 1971 D6
Flannery Dr
700 ALPN 84004 2498 B5
Flat Bear Cir
1800 DRPR 84020 2389 D1
Flatbush Cove
12700 RIVN 84065 2386 A3
Flat Creek Cir
4100 WJDN 84088 2174 C7
Flathead Ct
900 DRPR 84020 2389 A7
Flatiron Dr
2200 SNDY 84093 2177 E7
Flax Dr
- SRSP 84043 2601 D5
Fleetwood Dr
3400 SLkC 84109 1966 D6
Fleming Dr
700 ANFK 84003 2604 E7
800 ANFK 84003 2605 A7
800 ANFK 84003 2712 A1
Fletcher Ct
400 SLCY 84102 1859 A4
1400 SmtC 84098 1971 E4
Flight Line Dr
1100 PRVO 84601 3034 B2
Flint Ct
1400 KYVL 84037 1282 E7
Flint Dr
9400 SNDY 84094 2283 B2
9800 SLkC 84094 2283 B2
Flint St
10 LYTN 84041 1282 E5
N Flint St
10 KYVL 84037 1345 A1
200 KYVL 84037 1282 E7
200 KYVL 84037 1283 A7
500 DvsC 84037 1282 E7
600 LYTN 84037 1282 E7
600 LYTN 84041 1282 E7
S Flint St
10 KYVL 84037 1345 A1
Flint Wy
8700 SmtC 84098 1865 C3
Flintbrook Cir
3200 TYVL 84084 2174 D1
Flint Meadow Dr
1000 KYVL 84037 1283 A7
1100 KYVL 84037 1282 E7
Flint Rock Dr
- DRPR 84020 2496 B1
Flonnette Ln
900 SPFK 84660 3249 E3
1100 SPFK 84660 3250 A3
Florabund Cir
3200 SLkC 84044 1960 A5
Florabund Ln
3300 SLkC 84044 1960 A6
Floral St
200 SLCY 84111 1858 D4
Florence Cir
200 FTHT 84037 1346 B2
2800 SLkC 84109 1966 B4
Florence Dr
8600 SLkC 84044 1960 A5
Florence Wy
9800 SJDN 84095 2281 E2
9800 SJDN 84095 2282 A2
Florentine Ct
6900 WJDN 84084 2174 B2
Florentine Ln
- CTRV 84014 1551 D3
Florentine Wy
6700 WJDN 84084 2174 A1
Floret Ln
900 MDVL 84047 2177 A2
Floribunda Dr
400 SRSP 84043 2601 D5
2800 HLDY 84117 2072 B4
Florida St
- DvsC 84056 1227 E2
Florlita Av
3200 WVCY 84119 1962 E7
3300 WVCY 84119 2068 E1
Florlita Cir
4000 WVCY 84119 2068 E1
Flowerfield Cir
14100 DRPR 84020 2388 D6
Flowerfield Dr
100 DRPR 84020 2388 D6
Flowering Plum Ln
11400 HILD 84003 2497 B6
Floyd Dr
400 SNDY 84070 2282 E1
Flyer Wy
1000 SLCY 84116 1753 B7
Flynn Cir
3500 SLkC 84109 1966 B6
Foggio Ct
4700 WJDN 84084 2174 A1
Folker Cir
3600 SLkC 84109 1966 B6
Folklore Pl
5900 TYVL 84123 2069 D6
Folsom Av
900 SLCY 84104 1857 E3
900 SLCY 84104 1858 B3
Fonnesbeck Av
10 LOGN 84321 527 D3
Fontaine Bleu Cir
5800 MRRY 84121 2071 C6
Fontaine Bleu Dr
5800 MRRY 84121 2071 C6
Fools Gold Cir
11800 HRMN 84065 2280 B7
Foothill Blvd
500 SLCY 84108 1859 D4
500 SLCY 84112 1859 D4
Foothill Blvd SR-186
500 SLCY 84108 1859 D4
500 SLCY 84112 1859 D4
Foothill Cir
2300 SLCY 84108 1965 D1
Foothill Dr
800 SLCY 84108 1859 D5
900 PVDN 84332 592 B2
1000 PRVO 84604 2929 A4
1500 SLCY 84108 1860 A7
1600 LOGN 84341 464 C6
1600 SLCY 84108 1966 A2
1700 NHLN 84341 464 C6
2100 SLCY 84109 1966 A2
2600 OGDN 84401 1116 D4
2600 PRVO 84604 2928 E1
2700 OGDN 84403 1116 D4
3400 PRVO 84604 2821 E7
4100 BNFL 84010 1653 D7
6000 HILD 84003 2497 C6
Foothill Dr SR-186
1100 SLCY 84108 1859 E6
1500 SLCY 84108 1860 A7
1600 SLCY 84108 1966 A2
2100 SLCY 84109 1966 A2
Foot Hill Ln
3300 WbrC 84310 1001 C4
Foothill Ln
- CRHL 84062 2605 C2
Foothill Rd
- NHLN 84341 464 D3
Foothill Wy
- BMCY 84302 766 E3
- BMCY 84302 767 A3

STREET Block City ZIP Map# Grid
Forbes Av
300 LYTN 84041 1282 D1
Forbes Ln
- ALPN 84004 2497 E4
Forbes St
1800 LYTN 84040 1283 D2
Forbes Park Wy
1200 SLCY 84116 1753 D5
Forbush Av
10 MDVL 84047 2176 C3
Forbush Dr
1500 SNDY 84093 2177 C4
Forbush Ln
1300 CDHT 84093 2177 B4
1300 SNDY 84093 2177 B4
Ford Av
100 SSLK 84115 1964 D6
Ford Dr
700 CTRV 84014 1551 D4
800 BNFL 84010 1551 D4
Ford Canyon Cross
- CTRV 84014 1448 E7
Ford Canyon Dr
- CTRV 84014 1448 E7
- CTRV 84014 1551 E1
Forefather Pl
5900 TYVL 84123 2069 B6
Forest Cir
4800 TYVL 84118 2068 E3
Forest Ln
- LEHI 84043 2602 B1
E Forest St
10 BMCY 84302 766 E5
100 BMCY 84302 767 A5
W Forest St
- BxEC 84302 766 A6
- BxEC 84340 766 A6
10 BMCY 84302 766 D5
2500 BxEC 84302 765 E6
2500 BxEC 84340 765 E6
Forest Tr
5200 HILD 84003 2604 D3
Forest Bend Dr
1900 CDHT 84093 2177 D4
Forest Brook Cir
800 MRRY 84107 2071 A6
Forest Creek Dr
10100 CRHL 84062 2605 B2
Forest Creek Ln
1800 CDHT 84093 2177 D3
Forest Dale Cir
2500 SLCY 84106 1965 B3
Forest Farm Cir
800 SLCY 84106 1965 A4
Forest Green Dr
1500 OGDN 84403 1173 C2
Forest Hills Dr
1600 SLkC 84106 1965 C7
Forest Lake Cir
8900 CRHL 84062 2605 D5
Forest Meadow Dr
13200 RIVN 84065 2387 A4
Forest Meadow Rd
- SmtC 84098 1867 B1
Forest Oaks Ct
7900 CDHT 84121 2178 B4
Forest Park Ct
800 SLCY 84106 1965 A3
Forest Pointe Cir
9400 SNDY 84093 2284 B1
Forest Ridge Dr
1800 LYTN 84040 1283 D1
Forest Ridge Rd
1200 SNDY 84094 2283 B7
Forest Side Cir
700 MRRY 84107 2071 A6
Forest Side Ln
5800 MRRY 84107 2071 A6
Forest Spring Wy
2700 SLCY 84106 1965 A4
Forest View Av
900 SLCY 84106 1965 A4
Forest Wood Dr
4600 WVCY 84120 2068 A2
Forge Wy
1400 DRPR 84020 2389 C1
Forget Me Not Av
1100 SLkC 84094 2283 B3
Forman Wy
10500 SJDN 84095 2281 B4
Formby Cir
3700 SRCS 84075 1226 A7
Formby Dr
3800 SRCS 84075 1226 A7
Forsythia Dr
3200 WVCY 84119 1962 E5
Fort Cir
400 ALPN 84004 2497 D5
Fort Dr
400 PTGV 84062 2713 B4
Fort Ln
1000 OGDN 84404 1116 B1
1100 PTGV 84062 2713 B3
N Fort Ln
10 LYTN 84041 1283 A4
2000 LYTN 84041 1229 A7
2400 DvsC 84041 1229 A7
S Fort Ln
10 LYTN 84041 1283 A5
E Fort Rd
1500 SmtC 84098 1971 E6
W Fort Rd
1500 SmtC 84098 1971 E6
Fort St
12400 DRPR 84020 2389 A2
13400 DRPR 84020 2388 E5
Fort Canyon Rd
800 ALPN 84004 2497 E1
Fort Creek Dr
100 ALPN 84004 2497 E4
Fort Douglas Blvd
10 SLCY 84113 1859 D3
Fort Douglas Cir
1700 SLCY 84103 1859 C2
Fort Draper Av
11900 DRPR 84020 2282 D7
Fortuna Cir
3600 SLkC 84124 2072 D2
Fortuna Dr
3200 SLkC 84124 2072 C3
Fortuna Wy
4700 SLkC 84124 2072 B3
Fortune Rd
1700 SLCY 84104 1857 C7
Fort Union Blvd
10 MDVL 84047 2176 C2
700 MDVL 84047 2177 C2
1100 CDHT 84121 2177 C2
2300 CDHT 84121 2178 C2
Foss Cir
2800 BNFL 84010 1653 E4
Foss St
200 SLCY 84104 1857 D4
Foster Ln
300 KYVL 84037 1346 A2
Foubert Av
3900 SLkC 84124 2072 D1
Foulger St
1100 SLCY 84111 1858 C6
Foulois Rd
500 DvsC 84056 1229 A6
700 DvsC 84056 1172 C7
700 DvsC 84056 1228 E1
Fountain Cir
500 MRRY 84123 2070 B6
Fountain Crest Wy
- KYVL 84037 1344 E2
Four B Ln
1000 SLkC 84095 2281 E1
1100 SJDN 84095 2281 D1
Four Lakes Dr
2800 PKCY 84060 2078 D1
Four Mile Rd
300 WPT 84015 1226 A3
Four Sox Cove
11300 SNDY 84092 2283 C6
Four Woods Cir
2200 SLkC 84109 1965 E6
Fowler Av
100 OGDN 84404 1057 B5
1600 OGDN 84404 1116 B1
2100 OGDN 84401 1116 B3
2700 OGDN 84403 1116 B4
4000 OGDN 84403 1173 B1
N Fowler Av
1200 OGDN 84404 1057 B2
Fox Cir
9400 SNDY 84092 2284 A1
Fox Ct
400 CTRV 84014 1448 D7
Foxberry Ct
4800 SLkC 84118 2068 A6
Foxboro Dr
100 NSLK 84054 1652 C6
1300 SLkC 84106 1965 C6
Fox Borough Dr
700 LEHI 84043 2603 A4
Foxborough Ln
1800 DRPR 84020 2389 D1
Foxbridge Cir
8400 MDVL 84047 2176 C5
Foxbridge Dr
100 MDVL 84047 2176 B5
Fox Chase Dr
5600 SOGN 84403 1173 B5
Foxcrest Ct
1200 SmtC 84098 1973 A3
E Fox Crest Dr
1000 SmtC 84098 1972 E3
1000 SmtC 84098 1973 A3
Fox Crossing Ln
1200 DRPR 84020 2389 B3
Fox Den Cross
9100 WJDN 84088 2175 C7
9100 WJDN 84088 2281 D2
Fox Den Dr
1100 WJDN 84084 2175 E3
Fox Den Ln
10 MIDW 84049 2397 C4
Fox Farm Pl
400 DRPR 84020 2388 E2
Fox Farm Rd
1000 LOGN 84321 528 B2
Foxfield Ct
13100 DRPR 84020 2389 C4
Foxflower Ct
6900 WJDN 84084 2173 E2
Fox Glen Cir
10 PKCY 84060 2079 B3
Foxglen Dr
3600 ROY 84067 1170 D3
Foxglove Ct
7300 SmtC 84098 1866 B7
S Foxglove Dr
4500 TYVL 84123 2069 D3
W Foxglove Dr
900 TYVL 84123 2069 E2
Foxglove Rd
1200 FMTN 84025 1346 B5
Foxhill Cir
10 NSLK 84054 1653 C7
Fox Hill Dr
800 NSLK 84054 1653 C7
S Fox Hill Dr
700 SPFK 84660 3249 D4
Foxhill Rd
900 NSLK 84054 1653 D6
N Foxhill Rd
10 NSLK 84054 1653 D7
S Foxhill Rd
10 NSLK 84054 1653 C6
Fox Hills Dr
6000 TYVL 84118 2068 D7
Fox Hollow Dr
700 NSLK 84054 1652 C5
Fox Hollow Wy
- LEHI 84043 2495 C4
Fox Hunt Dr
2400 SNDY 84092 2284 A1
2400 SNDY 84093 2284 A1
9300 SNDY 84092 2283 E1
9300 SNDY 84093 2283 E1
Fox Hunters Lp
- LEHI 84043 2495 C4
Fox Meadow Dr
700 DRPR 84020 2388 E3
700 DRPR 84020 2389 A3
Foxmoor Cir
1800 SNDY 84092 2283 D5
Foxmoor Dr
200 OREM 84057 2820 C3
11000 SNDY 84092 2283 D6
Foxmoor Pl
1800 SNDY 84092 2283 D5
Fox Park Dr
1500 WJDN 84088 2175 C7
Fox Point Ln
500 SLkC 84107 2070 E1
Fox Pointe Cir
100 NSLK 84054 1653 D6
N Fox Pointe Cir
5900 SmtC 84098 1971 E3
Fox Pointe Ct
8200 WJDN 84088 2175 D5
Fox Pointe Dr
1200 KYVL 84037 1345 D4
1300 WJDN 84088 2175 D5
Foxridge Dr
200 PVDN 84332 528 B7
Fox Ridge Wy
6800 WJDN 84084 2173 E1
Fox River Ln
5800 WVCY 84118 2067 C7
Fox Run Dr
600 KYVL 84041 1283 C6
600 LYTN 84041 1283 C6
3500 WbrC 84310 1001 E3
Fox Run Wy
12400 DRPR 84020 2388 E2
Fox Shadow Dr
2900 WVCY 84120 1962 A5
Foxstone Cove
400 DRPR 84020 2388 E2
Foxtail Ln
300 KYVL 84037 1283 D7
Fox Tail Tr
3700 PKCY 84060 2079 B3
Fox Tail Bay
7400 WJDN 84084 2175 E3
Foxtail Pine Wy
8800 WJDN 84088 2174 E6
Foxton Cir
3500 WJDN 84084 2174 D2
Foxtrail Cir
4400 LEHI 84043 2495 D6
Foxtrail Dr
2100 LEHI 84043 2495 D6
Fox Trot Cir
1200 WJDN 84084 2175 D3
Foxwood Cir
3000 SLkC 84092 2284 B1
Fox Wood Ct
10 PKCY 84060 2079 A3
Foxwood Ln
9400 SLkC 84092 2284 B1
9400 SNDY 84093 2284 B1
Fragrant Ln
5900 HRMN 84065 2385 C4
Framewood Ln
1000 TYVL 84123 2069 E3
Francis Cir
800 KYVL 84037 1345 A3
Francis St
100 LYTN 84041 1282 E3
Frandsen Cir
11200 SJDN 84095 2281 E5
Frankie Cir
1600 SLCY 84104 1857 C6
Frankin Pkwy
- NSLK 84054 1652 E4
- NSLK 84054 1653 A4
Franklin Cir
10 BNFL 84010 1653 D3
1300 HARR 84404 1056 D2
3200 SLkC 84044 1960 E5
6800 WJDN 84084 2175 C2
Franklin Rd
3600 SLkC 84044 1960 D7
N Franklin Rd
400 LYTN 84040 1283 C3
Franklin St
100 OGDN 84401 1115 D6
800 OGDN 84403 1116 A6
Franklin Wy
3100 CRFD 84015 1228 C5
Franz Cir
10 BNFL 84010 1653 D2
Frederick Pl
3000 WVCY 84119 2068 E2
3000 WVCY 84119 2069 A2
Freedom Av
10 SNDY 84070 2176 C7
N Freedom Blvd
10 PRVO 84601 2928 C6
800 PRVO 84604 2928 C6
S Freedom Blvd
10 PRVO 84601 2928 C7
900 PRVO 84601 3035 C1
Freedom Cir
700 NSLK 84054 1653 B7
3200 CRFD 84015 1228 B5
Freedom Dr
600 NSLK 84054 1653 C7
Freedom Ln
400 HRCY 84032 2398 C5
3200 WJDN 84084 2174 E3
Freedom Hill Wy
6100 HRMN 84065 2385 C1
Free Land Av
500 MDVL 84047 2176 E2
Free Land Pl
6900 MDVL 84047 2176 A2
Freeman Ln
13300 HRMN 84065 2385 D4
Freeman Peak Cir
5200 HRMN 84065 2385 E5
Freeman Peak Dr
13800 HRMN 84065 2385 E5
Freemont Cir
600 CTRV 84014 1448 C7
Freemont Peak Cir
6400 TYVL 84084 2068 E7
Freeport Center Access
- CRFD 84016 1227 D7
- CRFD 84016 1281 B1
S Freeport Industrial Pkwy
700 CRFD 84015 1227 D6
Freestyle Wy
- SmtC 84098 1971 D4
Freeway Park Dr
4900 RVDL 84405 1171 E4
5200 ROY 84067 1171 E4
Fremont Av
100 SLCY 84101 1858 C6
800 SLCY 84104 1858 A6
1100 SLCY 84104 1857 E6
Fremont Dr
1700 SLCY 84104 1963 B1
Fremont Rd
800 BNFL 84010 1654 C2
Fremont Wy
200 LYTN 84041 1228 E6
E Fremont Wy
500 EKMT 84651 3463 A2
S Fremont Wy
10 EKMT 84651 3463 A2
Fremont Crest Av
1900 SRCS 84075 1280 D1
Freshman Cir
1200 SLkC 84117 2071 B2
Friar Wy
1900 WJDN 84084 2175 C3
Friardale St
4500 WVCY 84120 1962 A3
Friborg Wy
1300 WshC 84049 2396 D2
Friendship Dr
13800 HRMN 84065 2385 D5
Friesian Wy
5700 MRRY 84107 2070 E6
Frieze Cir
4900 TYVL 84118 2069 A3
Frisco Dr
- WJDN 84088 2173 D6
Frodo Av
7600 WJDN 84084 2175 B3
Frolic Ct
5600 HRMN 84065 2385 D4
Front Av
400 SSLK 84115 1964 E5
Front St
- LYTN 84041 1283 A5
1400 SLCY 84115 1858 C7
Frontage Rd
- CRFD 84015 1228 A5
- PYSN 84651 3354 E3
- SLCY 84116 1858 A1
- SNQN 84655 3567 D2
- SWBR 84405 1230 A2
- UthC 84651 3354 E3
- UthC 84655 3567 D2
300 FMTN 84025 1448 C3
N Frontage Rd
10 CTRV 84014 1551 C1
400 NSLK 84054 1653 A6
1400 CTRV 84014 1448 C7
10000 LEHI 84043 2495 C7
10000 LEHI 84043 2602 D1
10000 LEHI 84043 2603 A2
11000 UthC 84043 2495 C7
S Frontage Rd
- CTRV 84014 1448 C4
- FMTN 84025 1448 C4
- OREM 84058 2927 C3
- PRVO 84058 2927 C3
300 ANFK 84003 2711 C2
1000 PRVO 84601 3035 B2
1500 DvsC 84037 1345 D5
1500 KYVL 84037 1345 D5
1800 FMTN 84025 1345 D5
W Frontage Rd
100 ANFK 84003 2711 C2
Frontier Cir
1800 FMTN 84025 1447 D1
2400 RIVN 84065 2387 B5
Frontier Dr
200 FMTN 84025 1447 D1
700 ALPN 84004 2497 D5
1800 SLkC 84121 2071 D6
Frontier St
2200 RIVN 84065 2387 B5
Front Nine Wy
1000 FMTN 84025 1346 A5
Frost Ct
14400 BFDL 84065 2387 C6
Frostwood Dr
- SmtC 84098 1971 D7
Fruitland Dr
1600 NHON 84414 1057 B1
1900 NHON 84414 999 B6
S Fruitridge Ln
11200 UthC 84651 3460 D1
Fruitwood Ct
600 SNDY 84070 2282 E5
Fruitwood Ln
500 SNDY 84070 2282 E4
Fuchsia Cir
5000 WJDN 84084 2068 A7
Fuchsia Dr
5100 WJDN 84084 2067 E7
6300 WJDN 84084 2068 A7
Fuchsia Pl
6300 WJDN 84084 2067 E7
Fugal Hall
100 PRVO 84604 2928 E3
Fuhriman Dr
200 PVDN 84332 527 E7
Fulkoner Wy
1300 WshC 84049 2396 D2
Fuller Av
600 SLCY 84102 1858 E4
1000 SLCY 84102 1859 A4
Fuller Dr
1500 SLkC 84124 2071 C1
3300 WbrC 84310 1001 C4
Fullmer Cir
1800 CDHT 84093 2177 D3
Fulton St
500 SLCY 84104 1857 A5
Fur Hollow Cir
9900 SLkC 84092 2284 B2
Fur Hollow Dr
3100 SLkC 84092 2284 B2
Furnace Creek Ct
6300 WVCY 84118 2067 C7

G

G Av
- PTVW 84404 997 E5
800 DvsC 84056 1228 C4
2300 OGDN 84401 1115 B3
G St
- CRFD 84016 1227 C6
- KYVL 84041 1283 B6
- LYTN 84041 1283 B6
- RVDL 84405 1172 B3
10 SLCY 84103 1858 E2
Ga St
7500 WJDN 84084 2175 D3
Gable Ln
700 MDVL 84047 2176 E2
700 MDVL 84047 2177 A2
Gable St
700 MDVL 84047 2176 E2
700 MDVL 84047 2177 A2
Gad Wy
2100 SNDY 84093 2177 E5
Gad Valley Cir
10800 SNDY 84094 2283 A4
E Gadzooks Dr
1000 SNDY 84094 2283 B6
S Gadzooks Dr
11400 SNDY 84094 2283 B6
Gaelic Cir
9300 WJDN 84088 2281 C1
Gainey Ranch Ct
7900 CDHT 84093 2178 A4
Gairlock Cir
9800 SJDN 84095 2280 C2
Gala Wy
6600 WVCY 84128 1961 B5
Galahad St
200 NSLK 84054 1653 B5
Galaxie Dr
1300 SLkC 84093 2177 B6
Galaxy Hill Rd
7100 WJDN 84084 2173 E3
Galaxy Park Pl
3500 WJDN 84088 2174 D6
Galbraith Ln
1500 KYVL 84037 1344 E3
Galbreath Wy
8900 SLkC 84044 1960 A5
9000 SLkC 84044 1959 E5
Gale St
- SLCY 84101 1858 B3
Galena Dr
700 SLkC 84094 2282 E2
700 SLkC 84094 2283 A2
1000 SNDY 84094 2283 A2
Galena Park Blvd
12300 DRPR 84020 2388 B1
Galena Park Dr
12200 DRPR 84020 2388 A1
Galilee Cir
1200 WJDN 84088 2175 E7
Galilee Ct
8900 WJDN 84088 2175 D7
Galilee Wy
8700 WJDN 84088 2175 E7
Galileo Ln
5000 TYVL 84118 2069 C4
Gallagher Pl
500 SLCY 84102 1858 E5
500 SLCY 84111 1858 E5
Gallant Fox Ct
2200 SJDN 84095 2281 B5
Gallantry Wy
6600 CDHT 84121 2177 E1
Gallatin Ln
14500 DRPR 84020 2389 A7
Galleria Dr
4800 MRRY 84123 2070 B3
Gallivan Av
10 SLCY 84111 1858 C4
Gallivan Ct
10 PKCY 84060 1972 D7
Gallivan Lp
2600 PKCY 84060 1972 D7
Galloway Cove
13000 RIVN 84065 2387 E3
Gallup Cir
400 CTRV 84014 1551 D1
Gambel Dr
7900 SmtC 84098 1865 A6
Gambel Oak Cir
11700 SNDY 84092 2283 E7
Gambel Oak Dr
2100 SNDY 84092 2283 E7
Gamblers Cove
4800 RIVN 84065 2386 A2
Gambol Oak Cir
11000 HILD 84003 2497 B7
E Gammon Rd
10 VNYD 84057 2819 D5
10 VNYD 84058 2819 D5
W Gammon Rd
10 VNYD 84058 2819 C5
Gandalf Dr
3700 TYVL 84118 2068 D6
Gander Ln
1800 SLCY 84116 1753 B4
Garden Av
100 SSLK 84115 1964 D4
500 SSLK 84106 1964 E4
700 SLkC 84106 1964 E4
700 SLkC 84106 1965 A4
Garden Cir
300 SSLK 84115 1964 D4
Garden Ct
- OGDN 84403 1173 D3
Garden Dr
- LEHI 84043 2495 A7
- LEHI 84043 2602 C1
900 OREM 84057 2820 D2
900 SLkC 84124 2071 A1
1300 PTGV 84062 2712 B2
E Gardena Av
100 SSLK 84115 1964 D4
Garden Creek Wy
2300 WJDN 84088 2175 B5
Garden Crest Cir
2000 WJDN 84088 2175 C7
Garden Gate Dr
3500 WVCY 84128 1961 C6
Garden Glen Rd
9600 SJDN 84095 2280 D2
Garden Green Cir
5300 WVCY 84120 2067 D1
Garden Grove Ln
3500 SJDN 84095 2280 D2
Gardenia Av
7200 SLkC 84044 1960 D6
Gardenia Cir
7300 SLkC 84044 1960 E5
Gardenia Dr
600 MDVL 84047 2176 A5
E Garden Park Cir
100 SSLK 84115 1964 D4
S Garden Park Cir
2800 SSLK 84115 1964 D4
Garden Park Dr
100 OREM 84057 2820 C4
Garden Rose Ln
14300 HRMN 84065 2385 C6
Garden Spring Ln
4600 SLkC 84117 2071 B3
Garden Stone Cir
5700 SJDN 84095 2279 D6
Garden Tomb Wy
- SLCY 84102 1859 B5
Garden View Dr
10 MDVL 84047 2176 B4
Garden Vista Cove
4700 WVCY 84120 2068 A1
Gardner Ln
1700 WJDN 84088 2175 B6
Gardners Pl
9400 SNDY 84092 2283 D1
Garfield Av
- SLkC 84044 1854 C7
200 SLCY 84115 1964 D1
600 SLCY 84105 1964 E1
700 SLCY 84105 1965 A1
1700 SLCY 84108 1965 C1
E Garland Rd
- BxEC 84312 521 C1
- BxEC 84337 521 C1
Garland Wy
900 DvsC 84056 1228 B3
Garmisch Cove
11400 SLkC 84049 2284 B6
11400 SNDY 84092 2284 B6
Garn Wy
500 SLCY 84104 1857 E4
Garner Ct
5700 SLkC 84118 2068 B6
Garnet Dr
9500 SLkC 84094 2283 A2
Garnet St
800 LYTN 84041 1283 A3
Garnette Cir
1000 SLCY 84116 1753 C6
Garnette St
1000 SLCY 84116 1753 D6
Garrone Av
3800 WJDN 84084 2174 D1
Garrone Ct
6800 WJDN 84084 2174 C2
Garside St
100 SLCY 84116 1857 D2
Garth Cir
6400 TYVL 84084 2069 B7
Gary Av
300 SNDY 84070 2282 D1
Gary Dr
1000 LYTN 84041 1282 C2
Gary Rd
4000 SLkC 84124 1966 D7
4000 SLkC 84124 2072 D1
Gary Wy
10 NSLK 84054 1653 C7
200 NSLK 84054 1754 C1
Gaskill Wy
4800 WJDN 84088 2174 A5
5000 WJDN 84088 2173 E6
Gatehouse Ln
10 SNDY 84092 2283 E4
Gates Av
7000 WVCY 84128 1960 E3
7000 WVCY 84128 1961 A3
Gates Hall
100 PRVO 84604 2928 E3
Gateway Dr
- CchC 84321 527 E5
- LOGN 84341 464 C6
- NHLN 84341 464 C6
- PVDN 84332 527 E5
- RVHT 84321 527 E5
S Gateway Lp
10 SPFK 84660 3250 A3
E Gateway Rd
3500 SLkC 84109 1966 C5
Gateway Park Pl
12300 DRPR 84020 2388 B2
Gatewood Dr
800 SNDY 84094 2177 A7
Gathering Pl
- SJDN 84095 2281 D3
Gause Ln
- SNQN 84655 3460 D7
Gavin Cir
1100 DRPR 84020 2389 B6
Gawaine St
700 NSLK 84054 1653 B5
Gaylar Cir
2600 SLkC 84109 1966 A6
Gaylawood Cir
1500 TYVL 84123 2069 C7
Gaylene Cir
1200 SNDY 84094 2177 B6
Gaynel Autumn Cir
5300 TYVL 84118 2069 B5
Geary St
5300 TYVL 84123 2069 D5
N Geiger Av
- OGDN 84404 1056 B5
S Geiger Av
- OGDN 84404 1056 B5
Geitz St
3500 WVCY 84120 1962 A6
Gelding Ln
1700 SLCY 84116 1753 B5
Gem Cir
1900 SLCY 84116 1753 B5
Gemini Dr
200 SLCY 84116 1857 C2
Gemstone Dr
3000 WJDN 84084 2174 E1
General Dr
1700 SLCY 84116 1753 B5
Gener's Cross
- WVCY 84119 1963 D6
Genesee Av
700 SLCY 84104 1858 A5
900 SLCY 84104 1857 E5
S Genetti Av
- OGDN 84404 1056 B5
Geneva Dr
- MIDW 84049 2396 D2
10 MIDW 84049 2397 D4
500 PTGV 84062 2712 D4
1300 WshC 84049 2396 D2
Geneva Dr SR-114
500 PTGV 84062 2712 D4
N Geneva Rd
10 LNDN 84042 2712 D5
10 OREM 84057 2819 E5
10 VNYD 84057 2819 E5
1700 PRVO 84601 2927 C4
1800 UthC 84601 2927 C4
1900 UthC 84058 2927 C4
N Geneva Rd SR-114
10 LNDN 84042 2712 D5
10 OREM 84057 2819 E5
10 PRVO 84601 2927 C4
10 VNYD 84057 2819 E5
1800 UthC 84601 2927 C4
1900 UthC 84058 2927 C4
S Geneva Rd
10 LNDN 84042 2712 D7
10 OREM 84058 2819 E5
10 VNYD 84058 2819 E5
200 OREM 84057 2819 E5
400 LNDN 84042 2819 E1
400 VNYD 84058 2819 E5
900 OREM 84058 2926 E1
1000 OREM 84058 2927 A2
1200 OREM 84601 2927 A2
1200 UthC 84058 2927 A2
1200 UthC 84601 2927 A2
S Geneva Rd SR-114
10 LNDN 84042 2712 D7
10 OREM 84058 2819 E5
10 VNYD 84058 2819 E5
200 OREM 84057 2819 E5
400 LNDN 84042 2819 E1
400 VNYD 84058 2819 E5
900 OREM 84058 2926 E1
1000 OREM 84058 2927 A2
1200 OREM 84601 2927 A2
1200 UthC 84058 2927 A2
1200 UthC 84601 2927 A2
Genoa Ct
5400 HRMN 84065 2385 E2
Genova Dr
2000 DRPR 84020 2283 D7
Genova Hills Dr
11000 DRPR 84020 2283 D7
Gentile St
- DvsC 84075 1280 D4
- DvsC 84075 1281 A5
500 SRCS 84075 1281 C5
E Gentile St
10 LYTN 84041 1282 E5
10 LYTN 84041 1283 A5
1100 LYTN 84040 1283 B5
2500 LYTN 84040 1284 A3
E Gentile St SR-109
10 LYTN 84041 1282 E5
10 LYTN 84041 1283 A5
1100 LYTN 84040 1283 B5
W Gentile St
10 LYTN 84041 1282 E5
2200 LYTN 84075 1282 A5
2300 DvsC 84041 1281 E5
2300 DvsC 84075 1281 E5
2300 DvsC 84075 1282 A5
2300 LYTN 84041 1281 E5
2300 LYTN 84075 1281 E5
Gentle Creek Cir
3300 RIVN 84065 2280 E7
Gentry Ln
3900 WJDN 84088 2174 C6
Gentry Park Cir
9300 SJDN 84095 2281 B1
Geode Cir
9800 SNDY 84094 2283 B2
Geode Wy
1100 SNDY 84094 2283 B2
George Pl
3100 SLkC 84044 1960 D5
Georges Rd
1300 WJDN 84084 2175 D4
E Georgetown Sq S
2100 SLkC 84109 1965 E5
S Georgetown Sq E
3300 SLkC 84109 1965 E6
S Georgetown Sq W
3300 SLkC 84109 1965 E6
Georgia Av
100 HARR 84404 1056 D2
Georgia Cir
300 SSLK 84115 1964 D7
Georgia Dr
- BMCY 84302 827 D2
6500 WJDN 84084 2174 D1
Georgia St
1100 SNST 84056 1227 E2
1300 DvsC 84056 1228 A2
1500 DvsC 84056 1227 E2
Georgia Wy
2600 SNDY 84092 2284 A1
Geralee Ln
7100 WJDN 84084 2174 A3
Geranium St
700 SLkC 84094 2282 E3
700 SLkC 84094 2283 A3
Germania Av
400 MRRY 84123 2070 A4
Germania Cir
2300 SLkC 84093 2177 E4
3200 CDHT 84093 2178 C6
Germania Pl
5000 MRRY 84123 2070 A4
Geronimo Ct
2500 PKCY 84060 2079 A3
Gertie Av
1700 SLCY 84116 1857 C2
Gertrude Dr
3300 SLkC 84044 1960 E5
Gettysburg Cir
3200 SLkC 84044 1960 E5
4200 DvsC 84056 1228 A4
Gettysburg Dr
7200 SLkC 84044 1960 D5
Ghost Hill Dr
5000 WJDN 84084 2173 D3

Salt Lake City Street Index

STREET
Block City ZIP Map# Grid

Ghost Hill Dr
5000 WJDN 84084 2174 A2
Gibbon St
10 SLCY 84113 1859 D3
S Gibbons Ln
- NBLY 84321 591 B2
Gibbs Cir
10 SOGN 84405 1172 E1
Gibralter Ct
3000 TYVL 84118 2069 A5
Gibson Av
1200 OGDN 84404 1056 D7
1300 OGDN 84404 1115 C1
Gilbert Cir
1200 OREM 84057 2820 D2
Gilbert Dr
2600 RIVN 84065 2387 A2
Gilead Wy
4400 SLkC 84124 2072 E2
Gillen Ln
5900 MRRY 84107 2070 D6
Gillespie Av
1100 SLCY 84104 1857 D4
Gillespie St
- OGDN 84404 1056 B4
Gillman Cir
1200 OREM 84097 2820 E2
N Gillman Ln
200 LNDN 84042 2712 E6
W Gillman Ln
200 LNDN 84042 2712 E5
200 LNDN 84042 2713 A5
Gilly St
10100 SJDN 84095 2280 C3
Gilman Dr
1300 LYTN 84040 1283 E2
Gilmer Dr
1100 SLCY 84102 1859 B6
1100 SLCY 84105 1859 B6
Gilroy Cir
3600 SLkC 84109 1966 D7
Gilroy Rd
3600 SLkC 84109 1966 D6
Gilt Edge Cir
2300 PKCY 84060 2079 B5
Ginger Pl
200 SRSP 84043 2601 E6
Ginger St
5900 TYVL 84118 2069 A6
Ginger Root Ct
11500 DRPR 84020 2282 D6
Gingerwood Ct
5900 SLkC 84118 2068 A6
Ginkgo Ct
- PRVO 84604 2928 E4
Ginny Cir
6000 WVCY 84128 1961 C6
Ginny Dr
3600 WVCY 84128 1961 C6
Girard Av
500 SLCY 84116 1858 B1
1100 SLCY 84116 1857 E1
E Girard Av
10 SLCY 84103 1858 D1
W Girard Av
10 SLCY 84103 1858 C1
Girard Pl
100 SLCY 84103 1858 C1
Girls Home Rd
- BxEC 84324 829 B2
- MNTU 84324 829 B2
Glacier Ln
3300 SLkC 84092 2284 C1
Glacier Park Ln
9600 SLkC 84092 2284 C1
Glacier Point Cir
13000 DRPR 84020 2389 C3
Glacier Ridge Dr
2400 SNDY 84092 2284 A2
Glacier Summit Ct
1800 DRPR 84020 2389 D3
Glacier Summit Dr
12900 DRPR 84020 2389 D3
Glade Hollow Wy
3800 BNFL 84010 1653 E6
Gladiator Wy
800 SNDY 84094 2177 A6
Gladiola St
500 SLCY 84104 1856 E4
Gladstan Dr
10 EKMT 84651 3462 E2
200 PYSN 84651 3462 E2
Gladys Cir
1900 SJDN 84095 2281 C3
Gladys Dr
10400 SJDN 84095 2281 C3
Glasgow Av
1700 OGDN 84404 1115 C2
Glasgow Dr
4200 SJDN 84095 2280 B2
Glasgow Ln
400 HRCY 84032 2398 C2
Glasmann Wy
4500 OGDN 84403 1173 B3
4800 SOGN 84403 1173 B3
Glas Slipper Rd
9500 SNDY 84092 2283 E1
Glen Av
200 FMTN 84025 1448 D2
200 LYTN 84041 1282 E3
1900 RIVN 84065 2387 B1
Glen Cir
300 FTHT 84037 1346 B2
Glen Dr
400 FTHT 84037 1346 B2
Glen Pl
200 LYTN 84041 1282 E3
Glen Arbor St
1500 SLCY 84105 1965 C1
Glenbarr Dr
1200 SGVL 84663 3142 E4
1200 SGVL 84663 3143 A4
Glenbrook Cir
1700 SLkC 84121 2071 D5
Glenbrook St
5700 SLkC 84121 2071 D6
Glen Carter Dr
300 LEHI 84043 2603 B6
Glencoe Ct
6000 MRRY 84123 2069 D6
Glencoe Dr
1200 MRRY 84123 2069 D6
Glencrest Ln
4700 MRRY 84107 2070 E3
Glen Croft Ln
300 SNDY 84070 2282 D5
Glendale Cir
1000 SLCY 84104 1857 D6
Glendale Dr
1000 SLCY 84104 1857 D6
Glendale St
200 SLCY 84104 1857 E4
Glendell Dr
1700 OREM 84058 2927 D2
Glendon Cir
1800 PTGV 84062 2605 C7
Glendon St
5000 MRRY 84123 2070 A4
N Glendon Wy
1900 PTGV 84062 2605 D7
W Glendon Wy
300 PTGV 84062 2605 C6
Glendover Wy
1600 SNDY 84092 2283 C2
Glen Eagle Dr
- WVCY 84128 1961 D4
Gleneagles Dr
1300 SRCS 84075 1226 C7
Glengyle Ct
1200 MRRY 84123 2069 D6
Glen Haven Ln
2100 HLDY 84117 2071 E3
Glen Heather Av
2700 CDHT 84121 2178 A3
Glen Hill Cir
4300 WVCY 84120 1962 B7
Glen Hill Dr
3800 WVCY 84120 1962 C7
Glen Livet Ct
5600 WVCY 84128 1961 D4
Glen Livet Ln
600 HRCY 84032 2398 C3
Glenmare St
1300 SLCY 84105 1859 C7
2400 SLCY 84106 1965 C3
Glen Meadows Cir
1600 TYVL 84123 2069 C7
Glenmoor Hills Dr
4300 SJDN 84095 2280 B2
Glenn St
4800 MRRY 84107 2070 D3
Glenna Dr
2500 HLDY 84124 2072 A1
Glenn Abbey Cir
2700 SNDY 84093 2178 B7
Glenn Abbey Wy
2700 SNDY 84093 2178 A7
9200 SNDY 84093 2284 A1
Glen Oaks Dr
2800 SLCY 84109 1966 B2
Glenoaks Dr
6000 MRRY 84107 2071 A7
Glen Park Ct
5100 WVCY 84120 1961 E5
Glenridge Wy
4700 MRRY 84107 2070 E3
Glenrose Dr
1300 SLCY 84104 1857 D6
Glen Springs Wy
1100 WJDN 84088 2175 E6
Glenview Cir
6500 TYVL 84084 2175 B1
Glenwild Dr
- SmtC 84098 1972 A1
7500 SmtC 84098 1866 A7
Glenwood Av
7600 SLkC 84044 1960 D6
Glenwood Cir
- PRVO 84604 2821 B7
400 PVDN 84332 528 B7
3400 SLkC 84044 1960 D6
Glenwood Dr
- FRWT 84404 1055 C3
400 HYRM 84319 651 C4
400 SGVL 84663 3143 D3
Glenwood Ln
9700 SJDN 84095 2280 A2
Glider Ln
1700 SNDY 84093 2177 C6
Glimmer Bay Dr
3600 SLkC 84044 1960 A6
Gloria Ct
400 SSLK 84115 1964 E4
Gloria St
2900 SLkC 84109 1966 C4
Glorieta Dr
1100 SLkC 84106 1965 B6
Gloucester Ct
4200 TYVL 84123 2069 E1
Glover Av
- OGDN 84404 1056 B3
N Glover Av
- OGDN 84404 1056 B5
S Glover Av
- OGDN 84404 1056 B5
E Glovers Ln
10 FMTN 84025 1448 D4
W Glovers Ln
10 FMTN 84025 1448 C4
1100 DvsC 84025 1448 A4
1100 DvsC 84087 1448 A4
1100 FMTN 84087 1448 A4
1300 DvsC 84025 1447 E4
2000 DvsC 84087 1447 D4
Godatia Cir
10500 SLkC 84094 2283 B4
Godatia Ln
1000 SLkC 84094 2283 B3
Goddard Cir
900 LYTN 84041 1283 B4
9000 WJDN 84088 2174 B7
Goddard St
300 OGDN 84401 1115 E6
800 OGDN 84403 1116 A6
Gold Cir
7400 WJDN 84084 2175 B3
Gold Pl
900 SLCY 84104 1858 B6
Gold Bullion Ct
6100 WJDN 84084 2173 C2
Gold Dust Dr
11400 SJDN 84095 2281 C6
Gold Dust Ln
1800 PKCY 84060 2078 E3
E Golden Av
10 LYTN 84041 1282 D3
10 LYTN 84041 1283 A3
W Golden Av
10 LYTN 84041 1282 E3
Golden Cir
1300 FTHT 84037 1346 B2
4000 SLkC 84124 1965 B7
Golden Dr
5700 MRRY 84123 2070 B6
Golden Wy
1300 PKCY 84060 2078 E4
Golden Arrow Cove
4400 WVCY 84128 2067 D2
Golden Chain St
6300 MRRY 84107 2071 A7
Golden Cir Dr
400 FTHT 84037 1346 B2
Golden Creek Cir
3400 RIVN 84065 2280 D7
Golden Eagle Cir
1400 ALPN 84004 2498 C4
Golden Eagle Dr
- DRPR 84020 2496 E2
200 PKCY 84060 2078 E7
200 PKCY 84060 2079 A6
Golden Eye Dr
2500 SNDY 84093 2178 A7
Golden Field Wy
800 SNDY 84094 2177 A6
8800 SNDY 84094 2176 C7
Golden Fox Cir
4300 RIVN 84065 2280 B7
Golden Gate Cir
5500 WJDN 84084 2173 D1
Golden Grain Cir
3700 WVCY 84120 1962 D7
Golden Harvest Rd
10 DRPR 84020 2388 B3
Golden Hills Av
3500 CDHT 84121 2178 C6
Golden Leaf Ct
14700 DRPR 84020 2389 D7
Golden Leaf Wy
- MPTN 84664 3250 D1
Golden Meadows Dr
2700 RIVN 84065 2387 A3
Golden Oak Ln
5100 HILD 84003 2604 E2
Golden Oaks Dr
3500 CDHT 84121 2178 C6
Golden Pheasant Dr
300 DRPR 84020 2388 D3
700 DRPR 84020 2389 A3
Goldenpointe Wy
2400 WJDN 84088 2175 B4
Goldenrod Av
7500 SLkC 84044 1960 D5
Goldenrod Wy
- SRSP 84043 2601 D6
Golden Stone Cir
11900 RIVN 84065 2280 B7
Golden Valley Dr
1900 RIVN 84065 2387 B4
Golden View Cir
- RIVN 84065 2280 C7
Golden Wheat Cir
11700 SJDN 84095 2280 C7
Golden Wheat Cove
11600 SJDN 84095 2280 C7
Golden Willow Cir
100 SNDY 84070 2282 D3
Golden Willow Dr
10200 SNDY 84070 2282 D3
Goldfinch Cir
7000 WJDN 84084 2174 A2
Goldfinch St
1200 WVCY 84119 1963 D7
Gold Leaf Cir
200 DRPR 84020 2495 D1
Gold Medal Dr
6200 TYVL 84084 2068 D7
6500 TYVL 84084 2174 E1
6500 WJDN 84084 2174 E1
Gold Miners Pl
4700 HRMN 84065 2280 A7
4700 HRMN 84065 2386 A1
Gold Nugget Cir
10100 SJDN 84095 2281 C3
Gold Nugget Dr
1800 SJDN 84095 2281 C3
Gold Ridge Dr
3600 SLkC 84044 1960 B7
Gold River Cir
200 OREM 84057 2713 E7
Gold River Dr
1700 OREM 84057 2713 E7
Gold Rush Cir
1800 WJDN 84084 2175 C2
Goldrush Pl
5900 WVCY 84128 2067 C2
Gold Sands Pl
10100 SJDN 84095 2281 C3
Goldsmith Ct
11800 HRMN 84065 2280 A7
Goldstar Dr
- OGDN 84401 1116 A2
Gold Stone Dr
5600 SJDN 84095 2279 D6
Goldstone Pl
- CRFD 84015 1228 B6
Gold Tip Dr
300 OREM 84058 2819 E6
Gold Valley Ct
6300 WVCY 84118 2067 C7
Golf Cir
4300 SJDN 84095 2280 B2
Golf Course Cir
1200 BNFL 84010 1654 B3
Golf Course Dr
700 DvsC 84056 1229 A3
Golf Course Rd
- PVDN 84332 527 D5
10 LOGN 84321 527 C5
Goltz Av
100 SLCY 84101 1858 C6
Gomex Rd
- SPFK 84660 3250 E6
Gompers Av
7900 SLkC 84044 1960 C5
Gompers Cir
3200 SLkC 84044 1960 C5
Goodnight Dr
2200 MPTN 84664 3143 C6
2200 SGVL 84663 3143 C6
Good Springs Cove
5500 WJDN 84088 2173 D6
Good Trump Ct
2300 PKCY 84060 2079 B6
Goodway Dr
600 MRRY 84123 2070 A5
Goodwin Av
1300 SLCY 84116 1753 D6
Goodwin Cir
1100 SLCY 84116 1753 C6
Goodyear Av
300 OGDN 84404 1056 A2
Gooseberry Ct
3600 TYVL 84118 2068 D5
Goosenest Dr
400 EKMT 84651 3462 C1
400 PYSN 84651 3355 B5
400 UthC 84651 3462 C1
500 UthC 84651 3355 B7
1200 PYSN 84651 3462 C1
W Goosenest Dr
10 EKMT 84651 3462 E1
10 EKMT 84651 3463 A1
E Gordon Av
10 LYTN 84041 1283 A3
10 SLkC 84107 2070 C1
800 LYTN 84040 1283 A3
W Gordon Av
10 SLkC 84107 2070 C1
700 LYTN 84041 1282 D3
2500 LYTN 84041 1281 D3
Gordon Ln
100 SLkC 84107 2070 D1
200 MRRY 84107 2070 D1
Gordon Ln Cir
100 SLkC 84107 2070 D2
Gorgoza Dr
8600 SmtC 84098 1864 D4
Goshawk Ct
300 SmtC 84098 1866 C4
Goshawk Ranch Rd
- SmtC 84098 1866 C4
Goshen St
300 SLCY 84104 1857 E4
Goshen Canyon Rd
- UthC 84655 3567 C3
600 SNQN 84655 3567 C3
S Goshen Canyon Rd
10 SNQN 84655 3460 D7
100 SNQN 84655 3567 D1
Goshute Dr
4500 RIVN 84065 2386 B2
Goslin Ct
7800 WJDN 84088 2174 A4
Governors Cir
1200 WDCR 84087 1652 E1
Governors Wy
1200 WDCR 84087 1652 E1
1200 WDCR 84087 1653 A1
Grace Av
500 OGDN 84404 1056 D6
Grace Cir
12000 DRPR 84020 2388 A1
Grace Ct
900 SLCY 84111 1858 E6
Grace Ln
- LOGN 84341 464 B5
Grace St
2900 SLkC 84109 1966 B5
Graceland Wy
6200 WJDN 84084 2173 B1
Gracey Ln
1700 SNDY 84092 2283 D6
Gracie View Pl
12100 DRPR 84020 2388 A1
S Graff Cir
1100 OREM 84058 2927 E1
Graig Ln S
- SRCS 84075 1280 D1
Grain St
- KYVL 84037 1345 B3
Grainery Cove
1000 RIVN 84065 2387 E1
Grambling Wy
1000 SNDY 84094 2177 B5
Gramercy Av
- OGDN 84401 1116 A1
200 OGDN 84404 1057 A6
1600 OGDN 84401 1116 A1
2700 OGDN 84403 1116 A4
3900 OGDN 84403 1173 A1
3900 SOGN 84403 1173 A1
N Gramercy Av
1200 OGDN 84404 1057 A2
Granada Cir
1300 BNFL 84010 1552 C7
1300 SNDY 84093 2177 B7
Granada Dr
1300 BNFL 84010 1552 B7
1300 SNDY 84093 2177 C7
6200 MRRY 84121 2071 D7
Granada Hills Ct
4700 WJDN 84088 2174 A7
Granada Hills Dr
9000 WJDN 84088 2174 A7
Granary Wy
400 SRSP 84043 2601 D5
Grand Av
- SLCY 84103 1859 A2
900 PRVO 84604 2927 E5
Grand Cir
1000 PRVO 84604 2927 E5
Grand St
600 SLCY 84102 1859 A5
Grand Alpine Ct
800 SLCY 84103 1754 E7
Grand Cayman Dr
700 SLkC 84107 2070 E4
700 SLkC 84107 2071 A1
Grandeur Cir
1800 CDHT 84121 2177 D2
Grandeur Dr
1900 CDHT 84121 2177 D2
Grandeur Peak Cir
800 TYVL 84123 2070 A2
Grand Oak Cir
2600 BNFL 84010 1654 C4
Grand Oak Dr
8600 CDHT 84121 2178 C6
Grand Oaks Cir
600 FTHT 84037 1346 B2
Grand Oaks St
500 FTHT 84037 1346 B2
Grand Pit
- HYVL 84314 646 E3
Grand Point Cir
2500 SNDY 84092 2284 A1
Grandridge Ct
800 SLCY 84103 1754 D7
Grand Ridge Dr
800 SLCY 84103 1754 E7
Grand Teton Dr
4100 WJDN 84088 2280 C1
9200 WJDN 84088 2174 C7
Grand Trotter Wy
13400 HRMN 84065 2385 C4
Grand Valley Pl
6800 WJDN 84084 2173 C1
Grand View Cir
9400 SNDY 84092 2284 A1
Grandview Cir
2700 SLCY 84106 1965 C4
Grand View Ct
200 FMTN 84025 1346 C5
Grand View Dr
300 FMTN 84025 1346 C5
Grandview Dr
700 PVDN 84332 592 B1
900 OGDN 84403 1173 A1
2500 SNDY 84092 2284 A1
2700 SLkC 84092 2284 A1
3800 OGDN 84403 1116 A7
Grandview Ln
1400 PRVO 84604 2928 A4
Grandview Rd
900 BMCY 84302 827 E2
Grand View Wy
9400 SNDY 84092 2284 A1
Grand View Peak Cir
14000 RIVN 84065 2386 A6
Grand View Peak Dr
4800 RIVN 84065 2386 A6
Grand Vista Wy
2600 CDHT 84093 2178 A4
Granger Dr
3600 WVCY 84119 1963 A6
Granite Av
400 SSLK 84115 1964 E5
Granite Cir
11500 HILD 84003 2497 B6
Granite Dr
10700 SNDY 84094 2283 B5
W Granite Dr
1200 LYTN 84041 1282 C7
Granite Pl
2400 SNDY 84092 2284 A2
Granite Brook Ct
1500 DRPR 84020 2496 C1
Granite Canyon Dr
9700 SNDY 84092 2283 D2
Granite Crest Cir
2500 SNDY 84092 2284 A2
Granite Crest Ln
10000 SNDY 84092 2284 A2
Granite Farm Rd
9400 SNDY 84093 2284 B1
9500 SLkC 84092 2284 B1
Granite Flats Rd
11500 HILD 84003 2497 B6
Granite Hills Cir
2400 SNDY 84092 2284 A1
Granite Hills Dr
2300 SNDY 84092 2283 C4
2300 SNDY 84092 2284 A2
Granite Meadow Ln
3000 SLkC 84092 2284 B1
Granite Mesa Cir
10300 SNDY 84092 2283 E3
Granite Mill Ct
1000 SLkC 84106 1965 A5
Granite Peak Dr
800 SNDY 84094 2283 A5
Granite Point Cir
3200 SLkC 84092 2284 C2
Granite Ridge Ln
14700 DRPR 84020 2388 D7
Granite Slope Dr
9800 SLkC 84092 2284 D2
Granite View Ct
400 DRPR 84020 2388 E3
Granite View Dr
9700 SNDY 84092 2284 A2
Granite Woods Cir
9600 SNDY 84092 2284 B2
Granite Woods Ln
3100 SNDY 84092 2284 B2
Grant Av
200 PKCY 84060 2078 D6
300 OGDN 84404 1056 E5
1300 OGDN 84404 1115 E1
1800 OGDN 84401 1115 E1
3800 SOGN 84405 1115 E7
N Grant Av
10 ANFK 84003 2711 D1
100 ANFK 84003 2604 D7
S Grant Av
10 ANFK 84003 2711 D1
Grant Cir
4300 DvsC 84056 1228 A4
Grant Ln
1000 SRCS 84075 1281 B2
Grant St
400 SLCY 84116 1858 A1
1700 SLCY 84104 1964 A1
7600 MDVL 84047 2176 C3
Granville Cir
9100 SNDY 84093 2177 E7
Grape Ivy Wy
900 SLkC 84106 1965 A7
Grasmere Ln
3700 WVCY 84119 1963 E6
Grass Ln
1200 DvsC 84056 1227 E2
Grassland Ct
12200 RIVN 84065 2387 C1
W Grassland Dr
- ANFK 84003 2604 A7
900 ANFK 84003 2603 E6
Grassy Knoll Ct
1800 RIVN 84065 2387 C1
Gravel Rd
1000 SNDY 84094 2177 A6
Gravel Hills Dr
1000 SNDY 84094 2177 B6
Gravenstein Pk
5200 MRRY 84123 2070 A4
Gray Av
10 SLCY 84103 1858 C2
Grayboulder Ct
10200 SLkC 84092 2284 C3
10200 SNDY 84092 2284 C3
Gray Fox Dr
1800 DRPR 84020 2389 D6
Grayhawk Ln
- DRPR 84020 2389 C6
Graymalkin Cir
3800 SJDN 84095 2280 C2
Grayrock Ct
10300 SNDY 84092 2284 B3
Grayson Ct
1200 SNDY 84094 2283 B6
Graystone Ct
12200 DRPR 84020 2389 D1
Graystone Ln
2000 DRPR 84020 2389 D1
Greasewood Dr
1000 RIVN 84065 2281 E7
Great Basin Cir
5000 HRMN 84065 2386 A6
Great Lakes Dr
3600 WVCY 84119 1962 D3
3600 WVCY 84120 1962 D3
Great Pasture Rd
3000 WJDN 84088 2174 E6
3000 WJDN 84088 2175 A5
Greaves Hall
300 LOGN 84321 528 B2
Grecian Dr
6200 WVCY 84128 2067 B1
Green Dr
1400 PRVO 84604 2927 E3
Green St
10 LYTN 84041 1282 E4
10 LYTN 84041 1283 A4
400 SLCY 84102 1858 E4
500 MRRY 84123 2070 B4
1000 FTHT 84037 1346 A2
1400 SLCY 84105 1858 E7
2200 SLCY 84106 1964 E2
3100 SSLK 84106 1964 E5
Green Wy
8600 SNDY 84094 2177 A6
8800 SNDY 84094 2176 E6
Green Acre Dr
3000 WJDN 84088 2174 E5
3000 WJDN 84088 2175 A5
Green Apple St
1400 SJDN 84095 2281 D2
Green Berry Ct
7400 MDVL 84047 2176 E3
Green Blossom Ct
800 SLkC 84107 2071 A2
Greenborough Dr
7000 MDVL 84047 2176 E2
Greenbriar Cir
2000 SLkC 84109 1965 E7
Greenbriar Wy
2100 SLkC 84109 1965 E7
3600 SLkC 84106 1965 E7
Greenbrook Ct
4500 TYVL 84123 2069 D3
Green Canyon Dr
- CchC 84321 464 E5
Green Canyon Rd
1600 PRVO 84606 3036 A1
Green Clover Rd
12900 DRPR 84020 2388 B3
Greendale Rd
6700 CDHT 84121 2177 D1
Greenfield Av
1300 MRRY 84121 2177 B1
Greenfield Cir
100 HRCY 84032 2398 D7
200 FTHT 84037 1346 A2
1200 MRRY 84121 2177 B1
E Greenfield Cir
700 RVHT 84321 528 A4
Greenfield Dr
7200 SmtC 84098 1866 D7
Greenfield Wy
6600 CDHT 84121 2177 D1
Green Flower Ct
800 SLkC 84107 2071 A2
Green Grass Ct
11300 SJDN 84095 2281 D6
Green Haven Dr
400 MDVL 84047 2176 C3
Green Head Ln
- WPT 84015 1225 E4
Green Hedge Wy
1300 WJDN 84084 2175 D3
Green Hills Dr
3400 CDHT 84093 2178 C7
Greenleaf Dr
500 MRRY 84123 2070 B5
Greenmeadow Wy
500 MRRY 84107 2176 C2
Green Mesa Wy
3200 WJDN 84088 2174 E6
Greenmont Cir
3400 WVCY 84120 1962 A6
Greenmont Dr
3300 WVCY 84120 1962 A5
Green Oaks Dr
900 BNFL 84010 1654 A4
Greenoaks Dr
700 MRRY 84123 2070 A6
900 MRRY 84123 2069 E6
Greenpine Dr
- MRRY 84123 2070 B4
S Greenridge Av
800 PYSN 84651 3355 A7
Green Ridge Dr
10800 SNDY 84070 2282 D5
Greens Ln
2200 SPFK 84660 3250 D7
Greenstoke Dr
1000 SLCY 84103 1754 D7
Greenstreak Dr
4900 RIVN 84065 2386 A4
Green Tree Cir
3300 TYVL 84118 2068 E4
Green Tree Wy
4900 TYVL 84118 2068 E4
Green Valley Dr
700 SLkC 84107 2070 E2
700 SLkC 84107 2071 A2
Green Vista Ct
800 SLkC 84107 2071 A2
Greenwich Cir
2000 SNDY 84093 2177 E6
Greenwich Ln
8800 SNDY 84093 2177 D6
Greenwood
- ANFK 84003 2604 C6
Greenwood Av
10 MDVL 84047 2176 C3
300 SNDY 84047 2176 E3
Greenwood Cir
200 MDVL 84047 2176 D3
Greenwood Dr
200 BMCY 84302 827 D1
5900 MRRY 84123 2070 B7
9000 SNDY 84070 2176 E7
9200 SNDY 84070 2282 E1
Greenwood Ter
800 SLCY 84105 1859 C6
Greenwood Village Dr
7400 MDVL 84047 2176 E3
Greer Ln
7400 CDHT 84093 2177 C3
Gregory Av
1900 RIVN 84065 2387 B1
N Gregory Dr
1600 LYTN 84041 1282 B1
W Gregory Dr
1600 LYTN 84041 1282 B1
Gregson Av
800 SLkC 84106 1965 A5
900 SLCY 84106 1965 A5
2100 SLkC 84109 1965 E5
2300 SLkC 84109 1966 A5
E Gregson Av
10 SSLK 84115 1964 C5
W Gregson Av
100 SSLK 84115 1964 B5
Grenoble Dr
700 MDVL 84047 2177 A1
Grenoble St
600 SLCY 84116 1857 E1
Grenwood Cir
4000 SOGN 84405 1172 E1
Grey Goose Rd
- LEHI 84043 2710 D1
Grey Hackle Ln
2500 TYVL 84119 2069 A2
Grey Hawk Dr
- LEHI 84043 2495 C4
Grey Oak Cir
1700 MRRY 84121 2071 E6
Greystone Dr
- FMTN 84025 1448 D4
Griffin Ct
5100 SLkC 84118 2067 E7
Griffin Dr
300 BMCY 84302 767 A3
Griffin Ln
- RVHT 84321 528 A4
Griffiths Pl
7100 CDHT 84121 2178 D2
Grindelwald Ln
900 MIDW 84049 2396 E1
Grippen Ln
- HYVL 84314 647 A6
Grist Mill Pl
1000 MDVL 84047 2177 A3
Grizzly Rd
- WDHL 84653 3463 C4
Grizzly Wy
- WJDN 84088 2174 A4
4300 HOPR 84315 1170 B3
4300 WHVN 84315 1170 B3
7000 WJDN 84084 2173 E2
7300 WJDN 84084 2174 A3
8100 WJDN 84088 2173 E5
Grizzly Gulch St
4100 TYVL 84119 2069 B1
Grizzly Hollow Cove
12200 DRPR 84020 2389 E1
Grossamer Wy
5200 RIVN 84065 2385 E5
Grouse Cir
3800 WVCY 84120 2068 D1
9300 SNDY 84093 2284 A1
Grouse Bend Cir
9800 SJDN 84095 2281 B2
Grouse Creek Cir
2700 SLkC 84092 2284 A3
2700 SNDY 84092 2284 A3
Grouse Pointe Cove
13000 DRPR 84020 2389 A3
Grove Av
10 SLCY 84115 1964 C1
Grove Cir
1000 PTGV 84062 2713 B1
N Grove Cir
100 ALPN 84004 2498 A3
Grove Dr
300 ALPN 84004 2498 A3
1200 UthC 84004 2498 A2
E Grove Dr
800 PTGV 84062 2713 B2
N Grove Dr
900 PTGV 84062 2713 B1
Grove Creek Dr
100 PTGV 84062 2712 E2
600 PTGV 84062 2713 A2
Grove Hideaway
1700 ROY 84067 1171 C2
Grove Hollow Ct
1200 MRRY 84121 2071 B7
Grover Ln
1700 HLDY 84124 2071 D1
Grover St
- LYTN 84041 1282 E4
Grovewood Cir
5200 WVCY 84120 2067 E2
Grubb St
3100 TYVL 84118 2068 E6
Grubstake Cir
2400 SJDN 84095 2281 B3
Guadulahonky Dr
- DRPR 84020 2388 D2

Salt Lake City Street Index

STREET
Block City ZIP Map# Grid

Guard Ct
1800 WJDN 84088 2175 C7
Guardsman Wy
500 SLCY 84102 1859 C5
500 SLCY 84108 1859 C5
700 SLCY 84105 1859 C5
Guardsman Connection Rd
- PKCY 84060 2184 E2
Gudgell Ct
700 SLCY 84111 1858 E5
Guenevere St
100 NSLK 84054 1653 A5
E Guest Av
10 SSLK 84115 1964 C6
W Guest Av
10 SSLK 84115 1964 C6
Guinevere Rd
1400 LYTN 84041 1282 B1
Gum Ln
1200 DvsC 84056 1227 E3
1600 DvsC 84056 1171 E7
Gumwood Av
1500 TYVL 84123 2069 D2
Gun Club Rd
- HLDY 84121 2072 C7
3200 HLDY 84121 2178 C1
Gunderson Ln
1700 HLDY 84124 2071 D1
Gunlock Dr
2400 TYVL 84118 2069 B6
E Gunn Av
1200 SLkC 84106 1965 B5
Gunnell Pl
600 SLCY 84116 1858 A2
Gunn Trail Cir
11200 SJDN 84095 2281 D5
Gunther Dr
1800 CDHT 84121 2177 D2
Gurene Dr
5000 SLkC 84117 2071 C4
Gwen St
100 OGDN 84404 1056 D6
Gynhill Ct
500 FMTN 84025 1448 D3
Gyrfalcon Ct
9900 SNDY 84092 2283 E2
Gyrfalcon Dr
1800 SNDY 84092 2283 D2
Gyrfalcon Ln
2000 SNDY 84092 2283 E2

H

H Av
- PTVW 84404 997 E5
800 DvsC 84056 1228 B4
2800 OGDN 84401 1115 B4
H St
- CRFD 84016 1227 C6
- KYVL 84041 1283 B6
- RVDL 84405 1172 B3
10 SLCY 84103 1858 E2
Hacienda Cir
600 BMCY 84302 766 D7
Hacienda Dr
1100 WVCY 84119 1963 E6
Hackamore Cir
13600 DRPR 84020 2389 B4
Hackamore Dr
1000 DRPR 84020 2389 B4
Hackberry Ln
3300 SLkC 84044 1960 A6
Hackberry Pl
3400 SLkC 84044 1960 A6
Hackney Ct
2800 PKCY 84060 2078 C2
Haddie Cir
200 LOGN 84321 528 C2
Hadley Av
2900 WVCY 84128 1961 C5
Hadley Ct
3000 WVCY 84128 1961 C5
Hadwen Dr
2900 WVCY 84128 1961 B4
Hagan Cir
1500 SNDY 84092 2283 C7
Hagan Rd
11400 SNDY 84092 2283 C6
Hagoth Cir
4400 SLkC 84124 2072 E2
Haight Creek Dr
1100 KYVL 84037 1345 E5
Hail Cir
6300 HILD 84003 2604 B1
Halcyon Dr
800 MRRY 84123 2070 A4
900 MRRY 84123 2069 E4
Hale Av
2200 HLDY 84121 2071 E7
Hale Dr
10 PTGV 84062 2712 D3
3900 SLkC 84124 1966 D7
4000 SLkC 84124 2072 D1
Hale Wy
3000 CRFD 84015 1228 B5
Halelani Dr
7200 MDVL 84047 2176 D3
Haley Cir
8300 SNDY 84094 2177 A5
Haley Ct
400 ALPN 84004 2497 D5
W Haleys Lookout
300 EKMT 84651 3462 E3
Halford Cir
5100 SLkC 84118 2067 E6
Half Penny Cir
3800 WJDN 84088 2174 D6
Halifax Ct
600 FMTN 84025 1346 B4
Halifax Dr
2800 WVCY 84119 1962 E4
Hall Cir
2600 WVCY 84119 1963 A7
S Hall Dr W
7100 WJDN 84084 2175 D2
W Hall Dr S
1100 WJDN 84084 2175 D2
Hallmark Cir
2600 WVCY 84119 1963 A7
Hallmark Dr
2500 WVCY 84119 1963 A7
Halstead Ct
5100 SLkC 84118 2067 E7
Halverson Dr
1200 OGDN 84403 1173 B1
Hamilton Cir
6900 WJDN 84084 2175 C2
Hamilton Dr
1700 RIVN 84065 2387 C4
3200 CRFD 84015 1228 A5
E Hamilton Ln
100 SSLK 84115 1964 D4
Hamlet Cir
5200 SLkC 84118 2067 D4
E Hamlet Cir N
700 MIDW 84049 2397 D3
E Hamlet Cir S
700 MIDW 84049 2397 D4
S Hamlet Cir W
10 MIDW 84049 2397 D3
Hamlin St
5200 MRRY 84123 2070 B4
Hammon Ln
3600 SRCS 84075 1226 A7
Hammond Dr
2100 TYVL 84118 2069 B5
Hammonton Cir
3100 WVCY 84119 1963 C5
Hampshire Cir
3600 WVCY 84119 1963 D7
Hampton Av
300 SLCY 84111 1858 D6
Hampton Cir
2100 OGDN 84403 1173 E5
Hampton Ct
600 ALPN 84004 2498 B3
1700 FMTN 84025 1346 B5
3100 SLkC 84124 2072 B1
5100 HILD 84003 2604 E2
S Hampton Ct
700 FMTN 84025 1346 B5
Hampton Pl
- LOGN 84341 463 C5
Hampton Ct Ln
400 FTHT 84037 1284 A7
Hampton Green Wy
2000 OGDN 84403 1173 D4
Hampton Park Dr
2700 WVCY 84119 1962 E4
Hampton Ridge Cir
2000 OGDN 84403 1173 D5
Hana Ct
1300 DRPR 84020 2389 B4
Hanauer St
4600 MRRY 84107 2070 C3
Hancock Cir
4000 CRFD 84015 1228 B5
6200 MRRY 84121 2071 C7
Hancock Rd
3700 SLkC 84044 1960 E6
Handcart Cir
8400 SNDY 84070 2176 D5
Hand Cart Wy
100 SNDY 84070 2176 D5
Hanks Cir
1400 FMTN 84025 1345 E5
Hanline Cir
- KYVL 84037 1345 A3
Hannibal St
2100 SLCY 84106 1965 D2
Hanover Dr
10 OREM 84058 2820 D7
1500 SLCY 84103 1859 C2
Hanover Park Dr
3200 WVCY 84119 1962 E4
Hansen Av
300 SLCY 84115 1964 B1
Hansen Cir
5700 MRRY 84107 2070 D6
Hansen St
- LOGN 84321 528 A3
7700 MDVL 84047 2176 A4
Hansen Hollow Pl
1300 SLkC 84124 2071 A1
Hansen Meadows Dr
- SRCS 84075 1280 E2
Hansen Ridge Dr
- LEHI 84043 2603 C3
Hansomcab Wy
13600 HRMN 84065 2385 C5
Happiness Cir
6300 TYVL 84084 2069 B7
Happiness Dr
2000 TYVL 84084 2069 B7
Happy Hollow Ln
500 KYVL 84037 1283 E7
Harbonne Ln
6700 WJDN 84084 2174 D1
Harbor Pkwy
600 PRVO 84601 2927 C5
Harbor St
4600 WVCY 84120 1962 B5
Harbor Pointe Dr
1400 TYVL 84123 2069 D5
W Harcliff Cir
100 LNDN 84042 2713 A6
Hard Rock Cir
2400 TYVL 84119 2069 B1
Hard Rock Dr
2400 TYVL 84119 2069 B1
Harker Cir
6100 WVCY 84128 2067 C1
Harker Canyon Dr
3100 SLkC 84044 1960 C5
Harkness Dr
4600 WJDN 84088 2174 A7
Harlech Ln
- WVCY 84128 1961 A6
Harlingen Cir
3100 WVCY 84119 1963 C5
Harman Dr
4600 WVCY 84120 1962 A6
Harmony Cir
3100 SLkC 84109 1966 A5
Harmony Ct
600 SLCY 84102 1858 E5
Harmony Pl
500 BMCY 84302 766 D4
Harmony Bend Wy
- SLkC 84118 2068 A3
Harmony Grove Wy
1900 SNDY 84092 2283 D7
Harmony Rose Cir
900 SJDN 84095 2281 E2
Harms Wy
11200 UthC 84651 3356 A7
Harness Cove
5700 HRMN 84065 2385 D5
Harold St
100 SLCY 84116 1857 C2
Harold Gatty Dr
4800 SLCY 84116 1856 A1
5000 SLCY 84116 1855 D1
Harper St
4800 HLDY 84117 2071 E3
Harper Wy
10 SWBR 84405 1172 D6
Harper Peak Ct
3000 SJDN 84095 2281 A6
Harriger Wy
200 LYTN 84041 1229 A6
Harrington Lp
4000 CRFD 84015 1228 A5
Harris Av
200 SLCY 84115 1858 B7
1300 SLCY 84104 1963 D1
1600 SLCY 84104 1857 C7
E Harris St
100 OGDN 84401 1115 D6
W Harris St
100 OGDN 84401 1115 D6
Harrison Av
10 SLCY 84115 1858 C7
300 ANFK 84003 2711 B1
700 SLCY 84105 1858 E7
700 SLCY 84105 1859 A7
1700 SLCY 84108 1859 C7
Harrison Blvd
100 OGDN 84404 1057 B6
900 OGDN 84404 1116 B2
1500 OGDN 84401 1116 B2
2700 OGDN 84403 1116 B3
3900 OGDN 84403 1173 B2
4800 SOGN 84403 1173 C4
5300 WbrC 84403 1173 C4
5900 SOGN 84405 1173 C4
6100 WbrC 84405 1173 C4
Harrison Blvd SR-203
1200 OGDN 84404 1116 B3
1500 OGDN 84401 1116 B3
2700 OGDN 84403 1116 B3
3900 OGDN 84403 1173 B2
4800 SOGN 84403 1173 C4
5300 WbrC 84403 1173 C4
5900 SOGN 84405 1173 C4
N Harrison Blvd
100 OGDN 84404 1057 B4
Harrison Cir
8200 MDVL 84047 2176 B5
Harrison St
200 MDVL 84047 2176 B5
8800 SNDY 84070 2176 B7
Harrisonwood Cir
4600 WVCY 84119 2068 D3
Harrisonwood Dr
3400 WVCY 84119 2068 D2
N Harrisville Rd
10 OGDN 84404 1056 D4
700 HARR 84404 1056 D3
N Harrisville Rd US-89
10 OGDN 84404 1056 D4
300 HARR 84404 1056 D4
W Harrisville Rd
400 HARR 84404 1056 C2
500 OGDN 84404 1056 C2
1200 FRWT 84404 1056 C2
1300 FRWT 84404 1055 E1
Harrop St
400 OGDN 84404 1056 E6
1400 OGDN 84404 1057 C6
Hartford St
2400 SLCY 84106 1965 C3
Hartwell Av
300 SLCY 84115 1964 B1
Hartwick Ct
8400 SLkC 84044 1960 B6
Harvard Av
10 SLCY 84111 1858 C6
900 SLCY 84105 1859 A6
1700 SLCY 84108 1859 D6
Harvard Cir
300 ANFK 84003 2711 D2
W Harvard Cir
400 MDVL 84047 2176 A5
W Harvard Dr
300 MDVL 84047 2176 B5
Harvard Oaks Cir
2000 SLCY 84108 1859 D6
Harvard Park Dr
8400 SNDY 84094 2177 A6
Harvel Dr
7900 MDVL 84070 2176 D4
Harvest Cir
6800 WJDN 84084 2175 A2
Harvest Ln
- MIDW 84049 2397 B1
2200 WJDN 84084 2175 B3
Harvest Pkwy
- MPTN 84664 3250 D1
Harvest Rd
200 PVDN 84332 527 E6
Harvest St
1500 SLCY 84116 1857 D2
Harvest Berry Ln
11500 DRPR 84020 2282 D6
Harvest Berry Pl
100 DRPR 84020 2282 D6
Harvest Cove
3300 LEHI 84043 2495 B7
Harvest Creek Wy
4300 RIVN 84065 2386 B2
Harvest Crest Wy
11400 SJDN 84095 2280 B6
Harvest Hill Dr
6900 WJDN 84084 2175 E2
Harvest Hills Blvd
200 SRSP 84043 2601 D5
Harvest Hollow Ct
600 DRPR 84020 2388 E3
Harvestland Dr
2200 TYVL 84118 2069 B2
Harvestmill Dr
5300 WJDN 84088 2173 E6
Harvest Moon Ct
11600 SJDN 84095 2280 C7
Harvest Moon Dr
300 SRSP 84043 2601 D4
500 PTGV 84062 2712 E4
500 PTGV 84062 2713 A4
4000 SJDN 84095 2280 B7
Harvest Moon Ln
- MPTN 84664 3250 D1
Harvest Oaks Cir
1800 DRPR 84020 2389 D5
Harvest Rain Av
11400 SJDN 84095 2280 B6
Harvest Ridge Dr
7300 WJDN 84084 2175 B3
Harvest Side Ln
4400 SJDN 84095 2280 B6
Harvest Spring Ln
12500 RIVN 84065 2386 B2
Harvest Sun Ln
- SJDN 84095 2280 B7
Harvest View Wy
1000 WJDN 84084 2175 E2
Harvey Blvd
4100 CRHL 84062 2605 A3
Harvey Cir
9700 CRHL 84062 2605 A3
Harvey Rd
1400 FTHT 84037 1346 B3
Harvey St
3600 WVCY 84119 1962 E7
Harvey Heights Cir
2400 TYVL 84118 2069 B5
Harvey Heights Dr
5400 TYVL 84118 2069 B5
Harwood Ln
800 MRRY 84107 2071 A4
Haslam Cir
1500 SLCY 84116 1753 D7
Hastings Cir
6200 TYVL 84084 2068 E7
Hatch St
500 WDCR 84010 1653 C1
Hathaway Dr
1600 ROY 84067 1171 D2
Hathaway St
6000 TYVL 84123 2069 D7
Hatton Cir
5800 MRRY 84107 2070 C6
Haun Av
2000 HLDY 84121 2071 E7
Haun Dr
2700 WJDN 84088 2175 A6
2900 WJDN 84088 2174 E6
Havanna Rose Cove
14300 HRMN 84065 2385 D6
Havasu Wy
3600 WVCY 84120 1962 A6
Havea Cir
3000 TYVL 84118 2068 E5
E Haven Av
10 SSLK 84115 1964 C2
W Haven Av
100 SSLK 84115 1964 C2
W Haven Cir
500 LOGN 84321 527 C1
Haven Ct
100 KYVL 84037 1284 A7
Haven Dr
2500 SLkC 84109 1966 A7
W Haven Dr
500 LOGN 84321 527 C1
Haven Ln
2300 HLDY 84117 2071 E4
2300 HLDY 84117 2072 A4
4400 CRHL 84062 2605 A2
Haven Wy
3700 SLkC 84109 1966 A7
Haven Brook Cir
1600 MRRY 84121 2071 C7
Haven Chase Ln
1700 MRRY 84121 2071 C7
Haven Cove
3400 LEHI 84043 2495 B6
Haven Crest Rd
300 DRPR 84020 2388 D7
Haven Dale Ct
1700 MRRY 84121 2071 D5
Haven Glen Ln
1600 MRRY 84121 2071 C7
Haven Heights Cir
2000 SJDN 84095 2281 B4
Haven Heights Rd
10500 SJDN 84095 2281 C4
Haven Maple Dr
6500 WJDN 84084 2173 B3
Haven Meadow Ln
13300 RIVN 84065 2387 D4
Haven Moor Cir
6100 MRRY 84121 2071 C7
Haven Oaks Pl
6300 MRRY 84121 2071 C7
Havenstone Ln
1500 SLCY 84116 1753 C5
Haven View Ct
10500 SJDN 84095 2281 C4
Haven View Rd
1700 SJDN 84095 2281 C4
Havenwood Ln
5200 HLDY 84117 2072 A5
Haverford Ct
4300 TYVL 84123 2069 D2
Haverhill Cir
3800 SJDN 84095 2280 D2
Havre Cir
11200 SNDY 84070 2282 E5
Hawarden Cir
4300 WVCY 84119 2068 E2
Hawarden Dr
4400 WVCY 84119 2068 E2
Hawberry Cir
1100 DRPR 84020 2389 B5
Hawberry Rd
1100 DRPR 84020 2389 B5
Hawes Cir
12000 RIVN 84065 2280 D7
Hawk Cir
1900 SNDY 84092 2283 D2
Hawk Ct
7800 PKCY 84060 2185 A2
Hawker Ln
2900 WVCY 84128 1960 E5
Hawker Ln
2900 WVCY 84128 1961 A4
Hawkes Ct
100 SLCY 84102 1858 E3
Hawkeye Cir
3800 WVCY 84120 1962 D6
Hawkeye Dr
3500 WVCY 84120 1962 D6
4000 WVCY 84120 2068 D1
Hawkeye St
3600 WVCY 84120 1962 D7
4300 WVCY 84120 2068 D2
Hawkins Ct
9400 SLkC 84092 2284 B1
Hawk Nest Cir
3600 WVCY 84120 1962 C6
Hawksbill Cir
6500 TYVL 84123 2175 D1
Hawksbill Dr
1300 TYVL 84123 2175 D1
Hawks Nest Dr
700 MPTN 84664 3251 C1
Hawk Stone Cir
- DRPR 84020 2389 E7
- DRPR 84020 2496 E1
Hawkwood Dr
11000 SNDY 84094 2283 A5
Hawley Park Rd
9200 WJDN 84088 2279 D1
Haworth Cir
- NSLK 84054 1652 C5
Haworth Dr
1000 NSLK 84054 1652 C5
Hawthorne Av
500 SLCY 84102 1858 E4
700 SLCY 84102 1859 A4
1300 DvsC 84056 1228 B2
3000 OGDN 84403 1116 B5
W Hawthorne Ct
4300 CRHL 84062 2605 B2
Hawthorne Dr
100 LYTN 84041 1283 A4
300 BMCY 84302 767 B4
300 LYTN 84041 1282 D4
Hawthorne St
2000 SRSP 84043 2710 A3
Hawthorne Glen Cir
7400 WJDN 84084 2174 A3
Hawthorne Hill Ln
10 DRPR 84020 2495 C1
Haxton Pl
10 SLCY 84102 1859 A3
Hayden Ct
800 ALPN 84004 2497 C5
1500 LOGN 84321 528 C3
Hayden Wy
3000 TYVL 84118 2068 E4
3000 TYVL 84118 2069 A5
Hayden Peak Dr
5100 WJDN 84088 2173 D4
5100 WJDN 84088 2174 A4
Hayes Av
1500 SLCY 84104 1857 D6
Hayes Cir
4000 CRHL 84062 2605 B1
Hayes St
8200 MDVL 84047 2176 B5
Hayloft Cove
4800 WVCY 84120 1962 A4
Hays Dr
1600 LYTN 84040 1283 D1
Haystack Ct
5100 SmtC 84098 1972 A5
Haystack Wy
5800 MRRY 84123 2069 D6
Haystack Peak Cir
13900 RIVN 84065 2386 B6
Haywagon Ct
5600 HRMN 84065 2385 D4
E Hazel Dr
10 SALM 84653 3356 A4
S Hazel Dr
400 SALM 84653 3356 B4
Hazel Pl
100 TMTN 84337 521 A6
Hazel Arlene Cir
3400 SLkC 84106 1965 A6
Hazelhurst Dr
2700 TYVL 84118 2069 A6
Hazelnut Cir
2800 TYVL 84118 2069 A6
Hazelnut Dr
2700 TYVL 84118 2069 A6
Hazelwood Wy
2000 CDHT 84121 2177 D2
Hazy Cir
4000 TYVL 84084 2068 C7
Hazy Wy
3800 TYVL 84084 2068 C7
Head Ct
100 PKCY 84060 2078 D2
Healey Blvd
700 ALPN 84004 2498 A6
Healey Ct
800 ALPN 84004 2498 A6
Healey Homestead Cir
800 ALPN 84004 2498 B6
Healy St
300 OGDN 84401 1115 E5
700 OGDN 84403 1116 A5
Hearthstone Cir
9600 SJDN 84095 2280 E2
14200 HRMN 84065 2386 B6
Hearthstone Dr
3200 SJDN 84095 2280 E1
Heartland Cove
5100 HRMN 84065 2385 E6
Heartwood Cir
800 FTHT 84037 1345 E2
Heartwood St
10 FTHT 84037 1345 E1
Heartwood Cove
9700 SNDY 84070 2282 E2
Heath Av
4800 SLkC 84118 2067 E3
5000 SLkC 84118 2068 A4
Heath Cir
5400 SLkC 84118 2067 E3
Heath Ct
4900 SLkC 84118 2068 A5
Heath Ln
1400 DvsC 84056 1228 B1
Heath Blayde Cir
6700 HRMN 84065 2385 A5
Heather Cir
100 HARR 84404 1056 D2
200 OREM 84057 2713 E7
1000 SLkC 84094 2283 A4
1100 FMTN 84025 1346 C6
1500 LYTN 84040 1283 C1
2800 HLDY 84117 2072 B5
2800 HLDY 84121 2072 B5
Heather Dr
1300 LYTN 84040 1283 C2
Heather Ln
500 WBNF 84087 1551 C5
1400 SRCS 84075 1226 B7
5100 SmtC 84098 1971 E4
W Heather Ln
700 PRVO 84601 3035 A1
Heather Rd
100 OREM 84057 2713 E7
400 OREM 84097 2713 E7
600 OREM 84097 2714 A7
Heather St
100 SLCY 84102 1858 E3
E Heather St
600 MDVL 84047 2176 A5
Heather Wy
6800 WJDN 84084 2175 C1
Heatherberry Cir
11500 DRPR 84020 2282 D6
Heather Brae Cir
9400 SJDN 84095 2281 D1
Heather Brae Ct
1300 SJDN 84095 2281 D1
Heather Brook Cir
9400 SJDN 84095 2281 D1
Heather Brook Cove
9400 SJDN 84095 2281 D1
Heathercrest Cir
4400 WVCY 84120 2067 D2
Heather Dale Cir
9400 SJDN 84095 2281 D1
Heather Dee Cir
11900 RIVN 84065 2280 E7
Heather Downs Cir
1500 SJDN 84095 2281 D1
Heather Downs Dr
1300 SJDN 84095 2281 C1
9300 WJDN 84088 2281 C1
Heatherfield Ln
3900 LEHI 84043 2495 D6
Heatherglen Cir
4400 TYVL 84119 2069 B2
Heatherglen Ct
4400 TYVL 84119 2069 B2
Heatherglen Dr
2200 TYVL 84119 2069 B2
Heather Hill Cir
5100 TYVL 84118 2069 A4
Heatheridge Dr
1600 OREM 84097 2713 E7
1600 OREM 84097 2820 D1
Heather Oaks Ct
1800 DRPR 84020 2496 D1
Heather Ridge Cir
300 SNDY 84070 2282 D5
Heather Ridge Dr
10700 SNDY 84070 2282 D4
Heatherstone Cir
15000 DRPR 84020 2496 E1
Heatherton Cir
1300 MRRY 84121 2071 B7
Heatherton Wy
1400 MRRY 84121 2071 E5
Heatherview Ct
4400 WVCY 84120 2067 C2
Heatherwood Cir
1600 SNDY 84092 2283 C7
Heatherwood Ct
1900 LEHI 84043 2495 D6
Heathrow Cir
5500 SLkC 84118 2067 D3
Heavenly Cir
9800 SJDN 84095 2281 E2
Heavens Gate Av
1300 TYVL 84123 2069 D4
Heavy Cloud Cir
5900 HRMN 84065 2385 C6
Hebe Ct
5300 WVCY 84120 1961 E2
Heber Av
100 PKCY 84060 2078 E6
Hector Dr
3200 WVCY 84119 2068 E2
Hedge Hollow Cove
300 DRPR 84020 2388 D2
Hedgelawn Wy
11000 SNDY 84092 2283 C5
Heidelberg Ln
3900 WJDN 84084 2174 C1
S Heights Cir
800 SOGN 84403 1173 A3
Heirloom Pl
5900 TYVL 84123 2069 C6
Heiselts Hollow Dr
9600 CRHL 84062 2605 D4
Helaman Cir
4200 SLkC 84124 2072 E2
Helaman Dr
- PRVO 84604 2928 C4
Helen Cir
8900 SLkC 84044 1960 A5
Helen Dr
1100 LYTN 84041 1282 C2
8600 SLkC 84044 1960 A5
Helena Rose Dr
14400 HRMN 84065 2385 E7
Helenic Ct
8300 WJDN 84088 2174 A5
Helenic Ln
4600 WJDN 84088 2174 A5
Hellas Dr
4800 WVCY 84120 2068 A3
Hellgate Rd
- ALTA 84049 2181 D7
Helm Av
100 SSLK 84115 1964 D6
Helmsdale Cir
4000 SJDN 84095 2280 C2
Helmsdale St
4000 SJDN 84095 2280 D2
Hemingford Ct
4200 TYVL 84123 2069 E1
Hemingway Dr
1100 MRRY 84121 2071 B6
Hemisphere Ct
10400 SJDN 84095 2281 C4
Hemlock Dr
1500 TYVL 84123 2069 C3
Hempstead Rd
10 SLCY 84112 1859 D4
10 SLCY 84113 1859 D4
Hempstead St
2400 WVCY 84119 1963 D3
Henderson Dr
900 OGDN 84404 1057 B7
Henley Dr
5400 SLkC 84118 2067 D4
Henry Ln
- SLCY 84116 1752 E3
Henry St
- SNQN 84655 3461 B7
400 KYVL 84037 1282 D7
Henry Alice Ct
2200 WJDN 84084 2175 B2
Henry Day Ct
400 DRPR 84020 2388 E6
Henry Day Rd
14300 DRPR 84020 2388 D6
Henrys Fork Wy
4800 WJDN 84088 2174 A4
Hensley Cir
4900 TYVL 84118 2069 A4
Herbert Av
10 SLCY 84111 1858 C6
900 SLCY 84105 1859 A6
1700 SLCY 84108 1859 D6
Hercules Dr
4400 WVCY 84120 1962 B7
Herdan Cir
6900 WVCY 84128 1961 A4
Herdon Wy
6600 WVCY 84128 1961 A6
Heredity Pl
5900 TYVL 84123 2069 B6
Heritage Blvd
400 LYTN 84041 1282 D2
Heritage Cir
500 CRFD 84015 1227 C4
Heritage Dr
700 PRVO 84604 2928 D4
1900 FRWT 84404 997 B7
1900 FRWT 84404 1055 C1
3000 WVCY 84119 1963 C4
Heritage Ln
1700 SRCS 84075 1280 E1
Heritage Pkwy
1600 SRCS 84075 1227 A6
1800 SRCS 84075 1226 E6
Heritage Wy
2300 SLCY 84109 1965 E4
2300 SLkC 84109 1965 E4
2400 SLCY 84109 1966 A4
2400 SLkC 84109 1966 A4
Heritage Cove
10 LOGN 84321 527 E1
5100 TYVL 84118 2069 A4
Heritagecrest Wy
14600 BFDL 84065 2388 A7
14800 BFDL 84065 2495 A1
Heritage Hall Dr
- PRVO 84604 2928 D4
Heritage Hill Ct
12500 HRMN 84065 2385 B2
Heritage Hill Dr
6100 HRMN 84065 2385 B2
Heritage Park Blvd
700 LYTN 84041 1282 D1
Heritage Park Rd
2600 TYVL 84118 2069 A4
Heritage Ranch Dr
- FRWT 84404 1055 D2
Heritage School Dr
5600 PRVO 84097 2821 C3
Herman Cir
3000 WVCY 84119 2068 E2
Herman Dr
4300 WVCY 84119 2069 A2
Hermansen Cir
100 SSLK 84115 1964 D7
Hermes Cir
3600 SLkC 84124 2072 D1
Hermes Dr
3400 SLkC 84124 2072 C1
Hermitage Cir
1600 MRRY 84121 2071 D5
Hermosa Wy
2700 SLkC 84124 2072 B2
Heron Wy
1500 WVCY 84119 1963 C3
Heron Ridge Cir
12000 DRPR 84020 2389 A1
Herriman Hwy
- HRMN 84065 2385 D3
Hersey Park Ct
11800 RIVN 84065 2280 B7
Hertford Dr
4400 WVCY 84119 2069 A2
Herzog Av
8200 SLkC 84044 1960 B5
Heughs Cir
3400 HLDY 84121 2178 C1
Heughs Canyon Cir
3500 HLDY 84121 2072 C7
Heughs Canyon Ct
6000 HLDY 84121 2072 C6
Heughs Canyon Dr
6100 HLDY 84121 2072 C7
6200 HLDY 84121 2178 C1
Heughs Canyon Wy
3300 HLDY 84121 2072 C7
Hews Pl
2000 TYVL 84118 2069 C5
Hew Wood Cir
1900 TYVL 84118 2069 C5
Hew Wood Ct
1900 TYVL 84118 2069 C5
Hew Wood Dr
5300 TYVL 84118 2069 C5
Heytesbury Ln
9800 SNDY 84092 2283 C3
Hialeah Rd
2900 WVCY 84119 2068 E1

STREET
Block City ZIP Map# Grid

Hialeah Rd
2900 WVCY 84119 2069 A1
3900 WVCY 84119 1963 A7
Hiawatha Cir
2600 SLCY 84108 1860 A7
Hibiscus Av
700 SLkC 84094 2283 A3
Hicken Ct
800 HRCY 84032 2398 B6
Hicken Ln
- HRCY 84032 2398 B6
Hickenlooper Wy
1100 DRPR 84020 2389 B5
Hickory Ln
1400 MRRY 84121 2177 B1
1600 PRVO 84604 2928 A4
6400 MRRY 84121 2071 C7
Hickory St
- DvsC 84056 1227 E1
900 BMCY 84302 827 E1
6200 DvsC 84056 1171 E7
Hickory Hill Cir
7200 CDHT 84121 2178 C3
Hickory Knolls Ct
12900 DRPR 84020 2389 D3
Hickory Park Cir
12100 RIVN 84065 2386 B1
Hickory Park Rd
- RIVN 84065 2386 B1
Hickory Point Cir
1900 SNDY 84092 2283 D3
Hickory Point Dr
10000 SNDY 84092 2283 D2
Hickory Ridge Ct
1800 DRPR 84020 2389 D2
Hickory Ridge Ln
12700 DRPR 84020 2389 D2
Hickory Valley Cir
1900 SNDY 84092 2283 D6
Hickory Valley Dr
11400 SNDY 84092 2283 D6
Hidden Cir
500 NSLK 84054 1754 B1
11600 SNDY 84092 2283 C6
Hidden Ct
10 PKCY 84060 2079 A4
Hidden Dr
5400 HILD 84003 2604 D3
Hidden Ln
400 NSLK 84054 1754 B1
Hidden Pl
5900 MRRY 84123 2069 D6
Hidden Acres Cir
2200 SLkC 84109 1965 E4
Hidden Bluff Wy
9500 SNDY 84070 2282 A2
Hidden Bluff Cove
600 SNDY 84070 2282 A1
Hidden Brook Blvd
11700 SNDY 84092 2284 A7
Hidden Canyon Ln
2500 SNDY 84092 2284 A7
N Hidden Cove
400 OGDN 84404 1056 E4
Hidden Cove Cir
4800 TYVL 84123 2069 E3
Hidden Cove Dr
4700 TYVL 84123 2069 E3
Hidden Cove Ln
400 LEHI 84043 2603 C5
Hidden Cove Rd
4000 SmtC 84098 1864 D4
Hidden Creek Ct
1300 SLkC 84117 2071 B3
Hidden Creek Dr
100 LEHI 84043 2603 B3
Hidden Crest Wy
10400 SJDN 84095 2281 B3
Hidden Haven Ct
10500 SJDN 84095 2281 C4
Hidden Hollow Cir
- BNFL 84010 1654 A7
Hidden Hollow Dr
1200 LYTN 84040 1229 C7
2000 LYTN 84040 1283 C1
4300 BNFL 84010 1653 E7
4300 BNFL 84010 1654 A7
W Hidden Hollow Dr
200 OREM 84058 2927 C2
Hidden Lake Cir
400 BNFL 84010 1653 E7
Hidden Lake Dr
200 BNFL 84010 1754 E1
200 DvsC 84010 1754 E1
200 NSLK 84054 1754 E1
400 BNFL 84010 1654 A7
4600 BNFL 84010 1653 E7
Hidden Manor Cir
700 LEHI 84043 2603 D4
Hidden Meadow Wy
- FMTN 84025 1346 B6
Hidden Meadows Dr
1700 SLkC 84117 2071 D3
Hidden Oak Dr
3300 CDHT 84121 2178 C6
10100 HILD 84003 2604 E2
Hidden Oaks Cir
8600 CDHT 84121 2178 C6
Hidden Oaks Ln
10 PKCY 84060 2079 B4
Hidden Oaks Cove
100 PKCY 84060 2079 B4
Hidden Park Ln
7900 SNDY 84093 2177 C4
Hidden Point Dr
9400 SNDY 84070 2282 A1
Hidden Pond Dr
10100 HILD 84003 2604 B2
Hidden Quail Cir
4300 HLDY 84124 2071 E1
Hidden Quail Cove
1200 FMTN 84025 1346 C6
Hidden Ridge Ln
10600 SLkC 84092 2284 B4
Hidden Rose Cir
5300 HRMN 84065 2385 E7
Hidden Splendor Ct
10 PKCY 84060 2078 B3
Hidden Springs Pkwy
- FTHT 84037 1346 B4
Hidden Springs Cove
8100 SNDY 84094 2177 B5
Hidden Vale Ln
11200 SNDY 84070 2282 D6
Hidden Valley Blvd
11400 SNDY 84092 2283 E6
Hidden Valley Cir
2300 SNDY 84092 2283 E6
Hidden Valley Dr
900 FTHT 84037 1346 A4
1000 SNDY 84094 2389 A1
1100 SNDY 84094 2283 B7
1300 SNDY 84094 2283 B7
Hidden Valley Rd
1500 SNDY 84092 2283 C7
12000 SNDY 84092 2389 C1
Hidden Valley Club Cir
1600 SNDY 84092 2283 C7
Hidden Valley Club Dr
1600 SNDY 84092 2389 C1
1700 SNDY 84092 2283 C7
Hidden View Dr
11200 SNDY 84070 2282 D5
Hidden Villa Rd
100 SLCY 84115 1964 C1
Hidden Village Dr
11600 SNDY 84092 2283 D6
Hideaway Cove
12700 DRPR 84020 2388 D2
Hideout Cir
2000 RIVN 84065 2387 C5
Higate Av
6200 WVCY 84128 1961 B6
Higbee Cir
3100 WVCY 84119 1963 C5
High Av
200 SLCY 84115 1858 B7
1400 SLCY 84104 1857 D7
High St
2000 PKCY 84060 2078 E4
2000 PKCY 84060 2079 A4
S High Bench Rd
400 ALPN 84004 2498 B5
High Berry Cir
11700 DRPR 84020 2282 E7
High Berry Ln
300 DRPR 84020 2282 D6
High Bluff Dr
6400 WVCY 84118 2067 B7
6400 WVCY 84118 2173 C2
6600 WJDN 84084 2173 C2
High Country Dr
800 OREM 84097 2821 A1
1700 OREM 84097 2714 A7
High Creek Cir
12200 RIVN 84065 2387 E1
High Creek Dr
1000 RIVN 84065 2387 E1
High Crest Cir
- FTHT 84037 1346 B4
High Crest Ln
11200 SJDN 84095 2280 B6
High Danish Cir
3000 CDHT 84093 2178 A5
Highfield Rd
8100 SmtC 84098 1867 A4
Highland
- SNQN 84655 3567 E1
E Highland Blvd
600 BMCY 84302 767 A3
N Highland Blvd
10 BMCY 84302 767 B4
Highland Cir
4800 SLkC 84117 2071 D3
10800 HILD 84003 2605 A1
S Highland Cir
10 EKMT 84651 3463 A2
Highland Ct
3700 BNFL 84010 1653 E6
Highland Dr
- DRPR 84020 2283 E7
- DRPR 84020 2388 C7
- DRPR 84020 2389 B5
- HLDY 84121 2177 D1
- MRRY 84121 2177 D1
- SmtC 84098 1972 B2
- SNQN 84655 3461 A7
- SNQN 84655 3568 A1
300 RVDL 84405 1172 C2
1400 NHLN 84341 464 C6
2100 SLCY 84106 1965 B3
2900 SLkC 84106 1965 C6
3900 HLDY 84124 1965 C6
3900 SLkC 84124 1965 C6
4000 HLDY 84124 2071 C1
4000 SLkC 84124 2071 C1
4500 HLDY 84117 2071 D3
4500 SLkC 84117 2071 D3
5400 HLDY 84121 2071 D3
5600 SLkC 84121 2071 D7
6000 MRRY 84121 2071 D7
6500 CDHT 84121 2177 D1
7400 CDHT 84093 2177 D2
7900 SNDY 84093 2177 D2
8100 SLkC 84093 2177 D2
9200 SNDY 84093 2283 D1
9400 SNDY 84092 2283 D1
Highland Dr SR-140
- DRPR 84020 2388 B7
Highland Dr SR-152
- CDHT 84121 2177 D1
- HLDY 84121 2177 D1
- MRRY 84121 2177 D1
6100 HLDY 84121 2071 D7
6100 MRRY 84121 2071 D7
E Highland Dr
10 SmtC 84098 1972 D1
6100 SmtC 84098 1973 A3
W Highland Dr
100 SmtC 84098 1972 B2
Highland Hwy
- HILD 84003 2497 C7
Highland Hwy SR-92
- HILD 84003 2497 C7
Highland Cove Ln
1400 SLkC 84106 1965 C7
Highland Down Ln
5100 HLDY 84117 2071 D4
Highlander St
3500 WVCY 84128 1961 A6
Highland Hollow Dr
1300 WJDN 84084 2175 D3
Highland Hollow Cove
7500 WJDN 84084 2175 D3
Highland Oaks Cir
11700 SNDY 84092 2284 A7
Highland Oaks Dr
600 BNFL 84010 1653 E6
700 BNFL 84010 1654 A6
Highland Park Cir
5600 SLkC 84121 2071 D5
Highland Rose Ln
1900 HLDY 84117 2071 D4
Highland Springs Cir
1900 SOGN 84403 1173 D6
Highland Springs Rd
1900 SOGN 84403 1173 D6
Highland View Cir
2000 SLCY 84109 1965 D4
Highland View Ct
5500 WbrC 84310 1002 A3
Highline Cir
10500 SJDN 84095 2281 A4
E Highline Dr
10 WDHL 84653 3463 D2
High Line Canal Rd
- UthC 84651 3460 B3
- UthC 84655 3460 B3
S Highline Canal Rd
- PYSN 84651 3355 A7
- PYSN 84651 3462 A1
11800 PYSN 84651 3461 E2
11800 UthC 84651 3461 C4
13100 UthC 84655 3461 B6
High Meadow Dr
9400 SJDN 84095 2280 E1
High Mesa Dr
2000 SNDY 84092 2283 D5
High Mountain Cir
11400 SNDY 84092 2283 E6
High Mountain Dr
2200 SNDY 84092 2283 E6
2300 SNDY 84092 2284 A6
S High Oak Vw
9800 UthC 84653 3356 E4
High Oaks Ln
1600 DRPR 84020 2389 C5
High Pine Cir
1100 RIVN 84065 2387 E1
High Pine Dr
1000 RIVN 84065 2387 E1
High Point Ln
1800 SNDY 84092 2283 D3
Highpoint Pkwy
1200 SNDY 84094 2177 B4
High Pointe Dr
1900 BNFL 84010 1654 C3
High Ridge Cir
600 ALPN 84004 2498 A6
High Ridge Dr
600 ALPN 84004 2498 A6
High Ridge Ln
600 ALPN 84004 2498 A6
2100 SNDY 84092 2283 E4
W High Sierra Dr
10 EKMT 84651 3462 E3
10 EKMT 84651 3463 A3
High Spirit Ct
5600 HRMN 84065 2385 D5
High Summit Cir
8100 WJDN 84088 2174 B5
Hightech Dr
6900 MDVL 84047 2176 C2
Highwood Dr
4900 SLkC 84118 2068 A5
5400 SLkC 84118 2067 D5
N Higley Rd
2900 FRWT 84404 997 D4
Hiland Rd
400 OGDN 84404 1057 C6
Hilda Dr
1400 FTHT 84037 1346 B3
Hilden Ct
7600 CDHT 84093 2177 B4
Hilgard Dr
8000 WJDN 84088 2174 A4
Hill Av
100 SLkC 84107 2070 D1
Hill Blvd
700 LYTN 84041 1283 A3
800 LYTN 84041 1282 E3
Hill Cir
300 RVDL 84405 1172 D2
12200 RIVN 84065 2387 D1
Hill Dr
2700 OGDN 84403 1116 C4
Hill Rd
5400 SOGN 84403 1173 B4
Hill St
1800 KYVL 84037 1282 D7
2000 LYTN 84037 1282 D7
Hill Climb Cir
2600 SNDY 84092 2284 A6
Hillcrest Av
700 LOGN 84321 528 B1
1600 SLCY 84106 1965 D3
Hillcrest Cir
- BxEC 84309 522 C4
- TMTN 84337 520 E4
600 TMTN 84337 521 A5
1800 LYTN 84040 1283 D2
3200 BxEC 84312 522 C4
4000 SOGN 84405 1172 D1
E Hillcrest Cir
10 MRRY 84107 2070 D5
W Hillcrest Cir
10 MRRY 84107 2070 C5
Hillcrest Dr
- BxEC 84309 522 B2
800 SGVL 84663 3143 E2
5300 MRRY 84107 2070 C5
N Hillcrest Dr
12400 BxEC 84309 522 C3
12400 BxEC 84312 522 C3
Hillcrest Ln
- CRHL 84062 2605 C2
Hillcrest High Dr
700 MDVL 84047 2176 E3
700 MDVL 84047 2177 B3
Hilldon Av
100 SLCY 84103 1859 C2
Hillers Dr
8000 WJDN 84088 2174 A4
Hillfield Rd
2600 LYTN 84040 1230 A5
N Hill Field Rd
900 LYTN 84041 1282 E2
2000 LYTN 84041 1228 E7
N Hill Field Rd SR-232
900 LYTN 84041 1282 E2
2000 LYTN 84041 1228 E7
W Hill Field Rd
- LYTN 84041 1281 D4
10 LYTN 84041 1282 D3
W Hill Field Rd SR-232
700 LYTN 84041 1282 D3
Hillgate Wy
300 LYTN 84041 1228 E6
300 LYTN 84041 1229 A6
Hill Haven Dr
100 PRRY 84302 827 E3
Hill Haven Ln
8300 SLkC 84093 2177 C5
8300 SNDY 84093 2177 C5
Hill Mar St
4800 TYVL 84118 2069 C4
Hill Park Cir
500 SLkC 84107 2070 E1
Hillpark Cir
4600 CRHL 84062 2605 A2
Hill Rise Cir
1700 CDHT 84121 2177 C2
E Hills Cir
1400 BNFL 84010 1552 A5
2400 SNDY 84093 2178 A7
E Hills Dr
600 BNFL 84010 1552 A5
8800 SNDY 84093 2178 A6
N Hills Dr
1100 LYTN 84040 1229 C5
1200 DvsC 84040 1229 C5
Hillsboro Cir
3600 WJDN 84084 2174 D1
Hillsboro Dr
1200 LYTN 84040 1283 D1
3300 TYVL 84118 2068 E4
Hillsborough Dr
- PVDN 84332 592 B2
10 PTVW 84414 998 D6
400 MLVI 84332 592 B3
Hillsborough Heights Rd
9500 SNDY 84092 2283 C3
9500 SNDY 84092 2284 A2
Hillsdale Cir
1300 PRVO 84606 2928 E5
Hillsdale Dr
3100 WVCY 84119 1963 A5
Hillsdale Ln
700 PRVO 84604 2928 E5
700 PRVO 84606 2928 E5
14300 HRMN 84065 2385 B6
Hillsden Dr
2500 HLDY 84117 2072 A5
Hillsden Rd
1000 LYTN 84040 1283 C3
Hillside Av
- SLCY 84103 1859 A2
10 PKCY 84060 2078 D6
10 SLCY 84103 1858 C2
Hillside Cir
10 LOGN 84321 528 A1
500 CTRV 84014 1551 E3
500 CTRV 84014 1552 A3
900 PRVO 84604 2821 E5
1700 OGDN 84403 1173 D1
2500 SLkC 84109 1966 A6
N Hillside Cir
400 ALPN 84004 2497 E3
W Hillside Cir
200 ALPN 84004 2497 E3
Hillside Dr
- SRSP 84043 2601 C7
200 SHFD 84335 400 B2
300 MRRY 84107 2070 D5
400 BNFL 84010 1551 E6
400 BNFL 84010 1552 A6
500 ALPN 84004 2497 E3
600 CTRV 84014 1552 A2
900 PRVO 84604 2821 E5
1200 PTGV 84062 2713 B2
9100 CRHL 84062 2605 D5
S Hillside Dr
10 EKMT 84651 3463 A2
Hillside Ln
- DvsC 84010 1653 B6
- NSLK 84010 1653 B6
3400 SLkC 84109 1966 A7
3800 HLDY 84109 1966 A7
E Hillside Garden Dr
10 NSLK 84054 1653 A7
S Hillside Garden Dr
10 NSLK 84054 1653 B7
Hillside Oak Cir
600 NSLK 84054 1653 C7
Hillside Oak Cove
1600 DRPR 84020 2389 C5
Hillside Pines Cir
2600 SLkC 84109 1966 A6
Hillside Village Cir
6800 CDHT 84121 2178 D2
Hillside Village Ct
2500 CDHT 84121 2178 A2
Hill Stone Dr
5600 SJDN 84095 2279 D7
Hilltop Cir
1100 BNFL 84010 1654 B1
Hilltop Ct
4000 SmtC 84098 1864 E4
Hilltop Dr
- OGDN 84401 1115 E2
- OGDN 84401 1116 A2
800 CRFD 84015 1228 A5
Hilltop Ln
1800 NHLN 84341 464 C5
Hilltop Rd
600 SLCY 84103 1754 E7
600 SLCY 84103 1755 A7
600 SLCY 84103 1859 A1
Hilltop Oak Dr
6500 WJDN 84088 2173 B6
Hillview Dr
900 SLkC 84124 2071 A1
Hillview Rd
900 BMCY 84302 827 E1
Hill Villa Dr
600 LYTN 84041 1282 D3
Hill Vista Ct
5100 WJDN 84088 2173 E5
Hillwood Wy
5600 TYVL 84118 2069 B5
Hilmar Cir
1800 TYVL 84118 2069 C3
Hilo St
500 SNDY 84070 2282 E4
Hilton Head Wy
12100 DRPR 84020 2389 C1
Himalaya Ct
10 ALPN 84004 2497 E6
Himalaya Wy
6500 TYVL 84084 2174 E1
Himrod Ct
6000 MRRY 84123 2069 D7
Hinckley Dr
- OGDN 84401 1114 E6
- OGDN 84405 1114 E6
- ROY 84067 1114 E6
- ROY 84401 1114 E6
- WbrC 84401 1114 E6
- WbrC 84405 1114 E6
1300 OGDN 84401 1115 A6
1300 OGDN 84405 1115 A6
Hinckley Dr SR-79
- OGDN 84401 1114 E6
- OGDN 84405 1114 E6
- ROY 84067 1114 E6
- ROY 84401 1114 E6
- WbrC 84401 1114 E6
- WbrC 84405 1114 E6
1300 OGDN 84401 1115 A6
1300 OGDN 84405 1115 A6
Hindenberg Pkwy
2400 PRVO 84606 3036 B4
Hindley Dr
400 ANFK 84003 2604 B7
Hinton Ct
3200 WVCY 84128 1961 B5
Hintze Dr
2300 HLDY 84124 2071 E1
Hislop Dr
800 OGDN 84404 1057 C6
History Dr
11600 SJDN 84095 2280 E7
Hitching Post Ct
5000 HRMN 84065 2385 D4
Hitching Post Dr
7100 SmtC 84098 1864 E7
Hobble Creek Dr
1200 SGVL 84663 3143 E4
1200 SGVL 84663 3144 A4
Hobble Creek Canyon Rd
10 SGVL 84663 3144 E4
10 UthC 84663 3144 E4
Hobbs Dr
2200 SJDN 84095 2281 B1
Hobbs Creek Dr
2100 LYTN 84040 1230 A5
Hobbson Dr
4600 SLkC 84118 2068 A6
Hockey Ln
3400 WJDN 84084 2174 E1
Hod Hill Cir
5100 TYVL 84118 2069 B4
Hods Hollow Dr
500 DvsC 84037 1283 E6
500 KYVL 84037 1283 E6
Hoffman St
4500 SLkC 84118 2068 A5
Hogan St
3300 WVCY 84119 1963 A6
Hog Hollow Rd
400 ALPN 84004 2497 C3
Holbrook Dr
2700 BNFL 84010 1653 D5
E Holdaway Rd
400 OREM 84058 2819 D6
400 VNYD 84058 2819 D6
500 OREM 84057 2819 D6
S Holdaway Rd
10 VNYD 84058 2819 D5
Holden St
7400 MDVL 84047 2176 A3
Holder Dr
4100 WVCY 84120 2067 E1
Holder Knoll Dr
4100 WVCY 84120 2067 E1
Holdershill Ln
2900 TYVL 84118 2068 E4
2900 TYVL 84118 2069 A4
Holiday Dr
300 BMCY 84302 767 B4
3100 NHON 84414 998 E4
Holiday Curve Dr
1500 SmtC 84098 1971 E7
Holiday Park Dr
10600 SNDY 84070 2282 C4
Holiday Ranch Loop Rd
2300 PKCY 84060 2078 C3
Holladay Blvd
1700 HLDY 84124 2071 C1
4400 HLDY 84117 2071 E2
4700 HLDY 84117 2072 A4
5600 HLDY 84121 2072 B6
Holladay Cir
4500 HLDY 84117 2071 D2
S Holladay Oaks Ln
2500 HLDY 84117 2072 A3
Holladay Wood Ln
4600 SLkC 84117 2071 B3
Hollandia Ln
3900 WJDN 84084 2174 C1
Hollie Av
800 FMTN 84025 1448 D4
S Hollow Rd
4100 NBLY 84321 591 E6
4500 CchC 84321 591 E6
4500 CchC 84321 651 E1
4500 NBLY 84321 651 E1
4600 CchC 84321 652 A2
5700 CchC 84319 652 A2
5700 HYRM 84319 652 A2
5700 HYRM 84321 652 A2
Holloway Dr
4100 HLDY 84124 2071 D1
Hollow Creek Rd
400 DRPR 84020 2388 E6
Hollow Dale Cir
6700 CDHT 84121 2177 B1
Hollow Dale Dr
1300 CDHT 84121 2177 B1
Hollow Mill Dr
2600 CDHT 84121 2178 A1
Hollow Moor Cove
7400 WJDN 84084 2175 D3
Hollow Oak Cir
6900 CDHT 84121 2178 B2
Hollow Ridge Dr
500 CchC 84319 650 E3
500 HYRM 84319 650 E3
Hollow Ridge Rd
6900 CDHT 84121 2178 B2
Hollow Springs Cir
5400 MRRY 84123 2069 E5
Hollow Springs Dr
5500 MRRY 84123 2069 E5
Hollow View Wy
6900 WJDN 84084 2175 D2
Holly Av
700 MRRY 84107 2070 E7
700 MRRY 84107 2071 A7
Holly Cir
10 ALPN 84004 2498 C5
700 MRRY 84107 2070 E7
1100 PRVO 84604 2928 E4
9500 SNDY 84070 2282 D1
Holly Dr
10 ALPN 84004 2498 C5
3300 SLkC 84109 1965 D5
Holly Ln
1200 DvsC 84056 1227 E2
4500 HLDY 84117 2071 E2
Holly St
200 PTVW 84404 998 B6
Hollyberry Cir
6000 MRRY 84123 2070 D7
Hollycrest Dr
- PRVO 84601 3035 B1
800 SJDN 84095 2282 A3
900 SJDN 84095 2281 E3
Holly Grove Ct
15100 DRPR 84020 2496 D1
Holly Haven Cir
600 MRRY 84107 2070 E3
Hollyhock Av
800 SLkC 84094 2283 A4
Hollyhock Hl
3100 CDHT 84121 2178 B2
Hollyhock Ln
10 LOGN 84321 527 C5
Hollyhock St
- SmtC 84098 1866 B7
Holly Lily Ln
4900 WJDN 84088 2174 A7
Holly Oak Dr
8300 WJDN 84088 2173 B5
Holly Ridge Rd
1200 SNDY 84094 2283 B7
Hollywood Av
10 SLCY 84115 1964 C2
600 SLCY 84105 1964 E2
900 SLCY 84105 1965 A2
2200 SLCY 84108 1965 E1
Holmberg St
3500 WVCY 84119 1963 A6
E Holmes Creek Dr
100 KYVL 84037 1283 D7
Holmes Creek Ln
- LYTN 84041 1283 C5
Holroyd Dr
700 SOGN 84403 1173 A4
Holstein Wy
300 MRRY 84107 2070 E6
Holt Cir
4900 TYVL 84118 2069 B4
Holyoke Dr
3700 SJDN 84095 2280 D2
Holyoke Pl
3800 SJDN 84095 2280 D2
Homecoming Av
1400 SJDN 84095 2281 D3
Homecrest St
3000 WVCY 84119 1963 C5
Home Front Cir
1200 BFDL 84065 2387 D5
Homer St
2800 WVCY 84119 1963 A6
Home Run Ct
3100 WshC 84049 2079 C7
3100 WshC 84049 2185 C1
Homestake Rd
- ALTA 84049 2288 B2
1800 PKCY 84060 2078 D4
Homestead Cir
600 PTGV 84062 2713 B2
1400 CTRV 84014 1448 E7
1500 FMTN 84025 1447 E1
Homestead Ct
5800 MRRY 84107 2071 A7
Homestead Dr
- LEHI 84043 2495 C5
S Homestead Dr
900 WDHL 84653 3463 D3
Homestead Ln
200 FTHT 84037 1284 A7
1000 FTHT 84037 1346 A1
2200 RIVN 84065 2387 B4
Homestead Rd
200 MIDW 84049 2397 A2
1200 MIDW 84049 2291 A7
1200 WshC 84049 2291 A7
2800 SmtC 84098 1865 B5
Homestead Farms Ln
1700 WVCY 84119 1963 C6
Homewood Cir
2400 SJDN 84095 2281 B4
Homewood Ln
- PTGV 84062 2605 B4
Honda Av
3400 WVCY 84119 1962 D3
Honda Park Dr
700 BFDL 84065 2495 A1
Honey Bee Cir
400 FMTN 84025 1346 C5
Honey Berry Ct
100 DRPR 84020 2282 D6
Honeybrook Pl
1300 SLkC 84106 1965 D6
Honeyclover Ct
5000 MRRY 84123 2070 A4
Honeycomb Cir
7800 CDHT 84121 2178 E4
Honey Comb Rd
3500 CDHT 84121 2178 C4
Honey Crisp Wy
1400 SJDN 84095 2281 D2
Honeycut Cir
1800 SLkC 84106 1965 D6
4500 CRHL 84062 2605 A2
Honeycut Rd
3300 SLkC 84106 1965 D6
Honeyfield Dr
14200 DRPR 84020 2388 D6
Honey Locust Ct
11500 DRPR 84020 2282 E6
Honey Locust Ln
3900 CRHL 84062 2605 C2
Honeysuckle Wy
5500 SLkC 84118 2067 E6
Honeywood Ln
4400 WVCY 84120 2068 A2
Honeywood Cove Dr
7800 CDHT 84121 2178 D4
Honeywood Hill Ln
7800 CDHT 84121 2178 D4
Hook Dr
9900 SJDN 84095 2280 B2
Hoopes Cir
5200 SLkC 84118 2068 A4
Hoopes St
5000 SLkC 84118 2068 A4
5100 SLkC 84118 2067 E4
Hoover Pl
400 SLCY 84111 1858 E5
Hoover St
8200 MDVL 84047 2176 B5
Hope Av
300 SLCY 84115 1858 B7
Hope Cir
600 LYTN 84040 1283 C3
1500 SRCS 84075 1281 A3
Hopi Cir
6300 WJDN 84084 2068 A7
Hopi Dr
4100 WVCY 84119 2068 E1
6200 WJDN 84084 2068 A7
Horizon Av
10 HRCY 84032 2398 D7
Horizon Cir
7000 CDHT 84121 2178 B2
Horizon Dr
- HILD 84003 2497 C5
Horizon Bluff Cir
13800 HRMN 84065 2385 C5
Horizon Downs Cir
3900 TYVL 84118 2068 C6
Horizon Hills Cir
13800 HRMN 84065 2385 C5
Horizon Point Cir
1700 DRPR 84020 2389 C3
Horizon Point Dr
13000 DRPR 84020 2389 C3
Horizon Ridge Ln
6000 HRMN 84065 2385 C5
Horizon View Ct
1700 DRPR 84020 2389 C3
Horman Ct
9400 SJDN 84095 2280 B1
Hornburg Cir
2500 RIVN 84065 2281 B7
Horne Av
1700 SLkC 84106 1965 C5
Horn Silver Cir
5800 SLkC 84118 2067 C5
Horseback Ln
13500 HRMN 84065 2385 D5
N Horseman
1900 LYTN 84040 1283 E1
Horseshoe Cir
2500 SJDN 84095 2281 A2
Horse Spring Ct
5600 HRMN 84065 2385 D4
Horsetail Av
- SmtC 84098 1866 B7
- SmtC 84098 1972 B1
Horsley Cir
900 BNFL 84010 1653 E2
Hospital Dr
- OREM 84057 2820 C4
Hosta Ln
10100 SLkC 84094 2283 B3
Hot Springs Dr
700 MIDW 84049 2397 A2
Hot Springs St
1400 SLCY 84116 1754 A5
Hourglass Cir
500 DRPR 84020 2388 E4
Houtz Av
600 SGVL 84663 3144 A3
Howard Dr
400 SNDY 84070 2282 E1
N Howard St
10 WBNF 84087 1551 A6
S Howard St
10 WBNF 84087 1551 A7
10 WBNF 84087 1653 A1
600 WDCR 84087 1653 A1
Howey Dr
2000 HLDY 84121 2071 D7
Hoyle Cir
6800 WJDN 84084 2173 D2
Hoyt Pl
800 SLCY 84116 1858 A2
Hoyt Peak Cir
13900 RIVN 84065 2386 A5
Hubbard Av
300 SLCY 84111 1858 D6
1500 SLCY 84105 1859 C6
1700 SLCY 84108 1859 D6
Hubbard Cir
600 ALPN 84004 2497 D4
Huckleberry Cir
1500 SNDY 84093 2177 C5
8500 WJDN 84088 2174 E6
Huckleberry Ct
8900 SNDY 84093 2177 A7
Hudson Av
800 SLCY 84106 1965 A4
Hudson Cir
2900 SLCY 84106 1965 B4
E Hudson Dr
10 EKMT 84651 3462 E1

STREET
Block City ZIP Map# Grid
E Hudson Dr
10 EKMT 84651 3463 A2
W Hudson Dr
10 EKMT 84651 3462 E2
Hudson St
1000 OGDN 84404 1057 B6
Huega Ct
4900 SmtC 84098 1971 D5
Hughes St
1000 CTRV 84014 1551 E2
Hugo Av
4600 HLDY 84117 2071 E3
Hugo St
2100 HLDY 84117 2071 E2
Hugoton Cir
2100 TYVL 84118 2069 B5
Hugoton Dr
5400 TYVL 84118 2069 B5
Hulse Av
10 SLkC 84098 2182 C1
Humboldt Ct
8800 WJDN 84088 2173 D7
Humes Ln
100 LEHI 84043 2603 C4
Hummel Cir
4500 SLkC 84118 2068 B6
Hummel Dr
5800 SLkC 84118 2068 B6
Hummelstrasse
4500 HLDY 84117 2071 D2
4500 HLDY 84124 2071 D1
Hummingbird Cir
9000 SNDY 84094 2177 A7
Hummingbird Ln
9000 SNDY 84094 2177 B7
Hummingbird St
1200 WVCY 84119 1963 D7
Hummingbird Wy
3800 WVCY 84120 2068 C1
Hundley Haven Cir
700 SLkC 84106 1964 D7
Hunt Rd
1100 MRRY 84117 2071 B5
Hunter Ct
3200 WVCY 84120 1961 E5
Hunter Dr
5100 WVCY 84120 1961 D5
Hunter Farm Cir
6700 WVCY 84128 1961 A5
Hunter Farm Wy
3100 WVCY 84128 1961 A5
Hunter Glen Dr
4400 WVCY 84128 2067 C2
Hunter Hollow Dr
5600 WVCY 84128 2067 D2
Hunter Hollow Wy
12900 DRPR 84020 2388 E3
Hunter Oak Wy
- WVCY 84128 1961 A5
Hunter Park Cir
5600 WVCY 84128 1961 D6
Hunter Point Cir
3400 WVCY 84128 1961 A6
Hunters Ct
2700 OGDN 84401 1115 E4
Hunters Gln
2000 LYTN 84040 1283 E4
Hunters Hllw
- CRFD 84015 1227 D4
Hunters Meadow Cir
1900 CDHT 84093 2177 D4
Hunters Ridge Cir
3400 SLkC 84124 2072 C2
Hunter View Dr
3100 WVCY 84128 1961 A6
Hunter Vista Cir
6700 WVCY 84128 1961 A5
Hunter Wood Cir
6700 WVCY 84128 1961 A5
Hunting Cir Rd
200 HARR 84404 1056 C1
400 HARR 84414 1056 C1
Huntington Cir
3900 BNFL 84010 1653 E6
5200 TYVL 84118 2068 E4
Huntington Dr
3300 BNFL 84010 1653 E6
Huntington Rd
3200 TYVL 84118 2068 E4
Huntington Rdg
1300 OREM 84097 2821 B2
Huntington St
4600 WVCY 84120 1962 A7
Huntmoor Ct
1100 RIVN 84065 2387 D4
Hunts End Dr
2300 SNDY 84092 2284 A1
N Huntsman Pth
3500 WbrC 84310 1001 E3
Huntsman Wy
500 SLCY 84113 1860 A4
Huron Wy
3100 PRVO 84604 2928 E1
Hurstbourne Cir
6200 TYVL 84084 2068 E7
Hurstbourne Dr
3200 TYVL 84084 2068 E7
Hyacinth Cir
10400 SLkC 84094 2283 B3
Hyannis Av
1800 WVCY 84119 1963 C5
Hyclone Dr
- LOGN 84321 527 B7
Hyclone Rd
1700 LOGN 84321 527 B7
Hyde Park Ct
600 PRVO 84604 2821 D6
Hyde Park Wy
1200 SLCY 84116 1753 C6
Hy Land Acres
5200 HILD 84003 2604 D1
Hyland Hills Rd
2800 SLCY 84108 1966 B2
2800 SLCY 84109 1966 B2
Hyland Lake Dr
900 MRRY 84121 2071 A6
Hyrum Pl
10900 SNDY 84070 2282 D5
Hyrum R Smith Ln
- HRCY 84032 2398 E2

I

I Av
2500 OGDN 84401 1115 B4
I St
- RVDL 84405 1172 B4
10 SLCY 84103 1858 E2
600 SLCY 84103 1754 E7
I-15
- SLCY - 1753 E3
I-15 BUS
- BMCY 84302 765 E2
- BMCY 84302 766 B3
- BxEC 84302 765 E2
- BxEC 84302 766 B3
I-15 BUS W 1100 S
- BxEC 84302 827 C2
- BxEC 84340 827 C2
10 BMCY 84302 827 C2
I-15 BUS N Main St
10 BMCY 84302 766 E5
I-15 BUS S Main St
10 BMCY 84302 766 E6
700 BMCY 84302 827 E1
I-15 Veterans Memorial Hwy
- ANFK - 2603 E7
- ANFK - 2711 A1
- ANFK - 2712 C6
- BMCY - 705 E6
- BMCY - 765 E1
- BMCY - 766 A7
- BNFL - 1551 C6
- BNFL - 1653 C2
- BxEC - 520 C7
- BxEC - 585 E6
- BxEC - 646 C6
- BxEC - 705 D1
- BxEC - 765 E3
- BxEC - 766 A7
- BxEC - 827 A1
- BxEC - 885 A1
- BxEC - 941 B3
- BxEC - 997 D4
- CRFD - 1227 E4
- CRFD - 1228 A4
- CTRV - 1448 C7
- CTRV - 1551 C6
- DRPR - 2282 C6
- DRPR - 2388 B7
- DRPR - 2495 B6
- DvsC - 1227 E4
- DvsC - 1228 B6
- DvsC - 1283 A5
- DvsC - 1345 E6
- ELWD - 584 E2
- ELWD - 585 E6
- FMTN - 1345 E6
- FMTN - 1346 A7
- FMTN - 1448 C7
- FRWT - 997 D4
- FRWT - 1055 D1
- HYVL - 585 E6
- HYVL - 645 E1
- HYVL - 646 C6
- HYVL - 705 D1
- JubC - 3567 B6
- KYVL - 1283 A5
- KYVL - 1345 E6
- LEHI - 2495 B6
- LEHI - 2602 D1
- LEHI - 2603 E7
- LNDN - 2712 A4
- LNDN - 2819 E1
- LYTN - 1228 B6
- LYTN - 1282 E4
- LYTN - 1283 A5
- MDVL - 2176 B1
- MRRY - 2070 B1
- MRRY - 2176 B5
- MTSV - 1055 E6
- MTSV - 1114 E1
- NSLK - 1653 C2
- NSLK - 1754 A2
- OGDN - 1115 A2
- OGDN - 1171 E2
- OGDN - 1172 A2
- OREM - 2819 E1
- OREM - 2820 A2
- OREM - 2927 E6
- PRRY - 827 A1
- PRRY - 885 B6
- PRVO - 2927 B2
- PRVO - 2928 A7
- PRVO - 3035 B1
- PTGV - 2712 C6
- PTVW - 997 D4
- PYSN - 3354 E4
- ROY - 1171 D7
- RVDL - 1115 B7
- RVDL - 1171 E2
- RVDL - 1172 A1
- SGVL - 3035 D7
- SGVL - 3142 D1
- SLCY - 1753 E4
- SLCY - 1754 A2
- SLCY - 1858 A2
- SLCY - 1964 B1
- SLkC - 1964 B7
- SLkC - 2070 B1
- SNDY - 2176 B5
- SNDY - 2282 B1
- SNQN - 3461 A7
- SNQN - 3567 B6
- SNQN - 3568 A1
- SNST - 1171 D7
- SNST - 1227 D1
- SPFK - 3142 D6
- SPFK - 3248 B7
- SPFK - 3249 A3
- SSLK - 1964 B1
- TMTN - 520 C1
- TMTN - 584 E2
- UthC - 2495 B6
- UthC - 2603 E7
- UthC - 2711 E4
- UthC - 2712 A4
- UthC - 3035 D4
- UthC - 3142 D6
- UthC - 3248 E4
- UthC - 3249 C1
I-15 Veterans Memorial Hwy
- UthC - 3354 B7
- UthC - 3355 B1
- UthC - 3461 A7
- UthC - 3567 D2
- WBNF - 1551 C6
- WBNF - 1653 C2
- WbrC - 1115 A2
- WDCR - 1653 C2
- WHVN - 1114 E1
- WHVN - 1115 A2
- WLRD - 885 A1
- WLRD - 941 B3
I-80 Dwight D Eisenhower Hwy
- SLCY - 1854 D3
- SLCY - 1855 E3
- SLCY - 1856 A3
- SLCY - 1857 D3
- SLCY - 1964 D3
- SLCY - 1965 E3
- SLCY - 1966 A4
- SLkC - 1853 B3
- SLkC - 1854 A3
- SLkC - 1864 A5
- SLkC - 1966 A4
- SmtC - 1865 D7
- SmtC - 1866 E7
- SmtC - 1867 C1
- SmtC - 1971 D1
- SmtC - 1972 E1
- SSLK - 1964 D3
I-80 Veterans Memorial Hwy
- SLCY - 1858 A5
- SLCY - 1964 B1
- SSLK - 1964 B1
I-84
- BxEC - 520 A6
- DvsC - 1230 B1
- RVDL - 1172 A2
- SWBR - 1172 D6
- SWBR - 1173 A7
- SWBR - 1229 C1
- TMTN - 520 A6
- TMTN - 584 D1
- UNTH - 1230 B1
- WbrC - 1172 D6
- WbrC - 1229 C1
- WbrC - 1230 B1
I-84 BUS
- BMCY 84302 765 E2
- BMCY 84302 766 B3
- BxEC 84302 765 E2
- BxEC 84302 766 B3
I-84 BUS W 1100 S
- BxEC 84302 827 D2
- BxEC 84340 827 D2
10 BMCY 84302 827 D2
I-84 BUS N Main St
10 BMCY 84302 766 E5
I-84 BUS S Main St
10 BMCY 84302 766 E6
700 BMCY 84302 827 E1
I-84 Veterans Memorial Hwy
- BMCY - 705 E6
- BMCY - 765 E1
- BMCY - 766 A7
- BxEC - 520 C7
- BxEC - 585 E6
- BxEC - 646 C6
- BxEC - 705 D1
- BxEC - 765 E3
- BxEC - 766 A7
- BxEC - 827 A1
- BxEC - 885 A2
- BxEC - 941 B3
- BxEC - 997 D4
- ELWD - 584 E2
- ELWD - 585 C4
- FRWT - 997 D4
- FRWT - 1055 D1
- HYVL - 585 E6
- HYVL - 645 E1
- HYVL - 646 A1
- HYVL - 705 D1
- MTSV - 1055 D1
- MTSV - 1114 E1
- OGDN - 1115 A3
- PRRY - 827 A1
- PRRY - 885 B6
- PTVW - 997 D4
- RVDL - 1115 B7
- RVDL - 1172 A1
- TMTN - 520 C7
- TMTN - 584 E2
- WbrC - 1115 A3
- WHVN - 1114 E1
- WHVN - 1115 A3
- WLRD - 885 A2
- WLRD - 941 B3
I-215
- CDHT - 2071 E7
- CDHT - 2072 A7
- CDHT - 2177 C1
- DvsC - 1753 D1
- HLDY - 2071 E7
- HLDY - 2072 B3
- HLDY - 2177 C1
- MDVL - 2176 E1
- MRRY - 2069 E7
- MRRY - 2070 C7
- MRRY - 2176 E1
- MRRY - 2177 C1
- NSLK - 1753 D1
- SLCY - 1753 D1
- SLCY - 1857 B2
- SLCY - 1963 B1
- SLCY - 1966 B4
- SLkC - 1753 D1
- SLkC - 1966 B4
- SLkC - 2072 B3
- TYVL - 2069 E7
- WVCY - 1963 B3
- WVCY - 2069 B2
Ibis Wy
900 DRPR 84020 2283 A7
N Icabod Ln
1700 LYTN 84040 1283 E1
Ice Skate Cir
3500 WJDN 84084 2174 D1
Ichabod St
4700 HLDY 84117 2072 B3
Ida Cir
400 ANFK 84003 2604 B6
1700 SNDY 84093 2177 D7
2900 SLCY 84106 1965 D4
Ida Ln
8600 SNDY 84093 2177 C6
Idaho Av
400 PRVO 84606 2928 E7
400 PRVO 84606 3035 E1
Idaho St
3900 CRNN 84307 705 A7
4000 CRNN 84307 704 E6
E Ideal Ln
100 SSLK 84115 1964 D4
Idlewild Cir
4700 SLkC 84124 2072 C3
10300 CRHL 84062 2605 A2
Idlewild Rd
4700 SLkC 84124 2072 C3
Illinois Av
1000 SLCY 84104 1857 D6
Impala Cir
2800 WVCY 84128 1961 A4
Imperia Wy
5300 HRMN 84065 2385 E2
Imperial St
1800 SLCY 84105 1965 C2
2400 SLCY 84106 1965 C3
2800 SLkC 84106 1965 C5
Imperial Wy
4000 PRVO 84604 2821 E5
Imperial Oak Dr
6200 WJDN 84088 2173 B5
Imperial Park Ln
1700 SLkC 84106 1965 C5
Imperial Park Sq
1700 SLkC 84106 1965 C5
Impressions Dr
5500 SLkC 84118 2067 E6
Impressions Wy
5200 SLkC 84118 2067 D7
Ina Av
2100 PKCY 84060 2078 E3
Inauguration Rd
200 DRPR 84020 2282 B7
Inca Cir
4600 WVCY 84120 2067 E3
Independance Ln
3100 CRFD 84015 1228 B5
Independence Av
600 PRVO 84601 2927 E5
800 PRVO 84604 2927 D4
Independence Blvd
200 HARR 84404 1056 D2
1700 SLCY 84116 1753 B5
Independence Cir
600 PRRY 84302 827 D5
Independence St
3000 WVCY 84119 1963 C5
Independence Wy
300 NSLK 84054 1754 C1
Indiana Av
1000 SLCY 84104 1857 D5
Indiana Cir
2000 SLCY 84104 1857 B5
Indian Camps Rd
- OGDN 84404 1056 C5
Indian Hills Cir
1400 SLCY 84108 1860 A7
2800 PRVO 84604 2928 E1
Indian Hills Dr
1400 SLCY 84108 1860 A7
2700 PRVO 84604 2928 E1
Indian Hills Ln
2700 LYTN 84040 1229 D6
Indian Hollow Ln
6200 SLkC 84065 2385 B6
Indian Oak Dr
6100 WJDN 84088 2173 C5
Indian Pony Wy
6000 HRMN 84065 2385 C4
Indian Ridge Cir
1300 SLkC 84092 2283 B2
Indian Ridge Dr
9600 SLkC 84092 2283 B2
9700 SNDY 84092 2283 B2
Indian Rock Rd
5400 HLDY 84117 2072 B5
5400 HLDY 84121 2072 B5
Indian Springs Cir
1300 LYTN 84040 1283 C5
Indian Springs Dr
10 LYTN 84040 1283 C5
Indian Springs Rd
400 BNFL 84010 1653 E5
400 BNFL 84010 1654 A5
Indian Summer Dr
1500 SLCY 84116 1857 C2
Indian Tails Rd
- MNTU 84324 768 D5
Indian Trail Cir
1300 BNFL 84010 1654 B1
Indian Trail Rd
500 BNFL 84010 1654 B1
Indian Wells Ln
1500 DRPR 84020 2389 C1
Indigo Ln
1500 DvsC 84056 1227 E2
Indigo Meadow Cir
3900 TYVL 84118 2068 D6
Industrial Cir
1900 SLCY 84104 1963 B1
W Industrial Cir
1300 SGVL 84663 3035 E6
1300 SGVL 84663 3036 A6
Industrial Dr
- PRVO 84606 3036 A3
- UthC 84606 3036 A3
2500 OGDN 84401 1114 E4
2500 OGDN 84401 1115 A4
W Industrial Dr
200 PTGV 84062 2712 D3
1300 OREM 84058 2820 A5
Industrial Ln
500 DvsC 84056 1228 E5
Industrial Pkwy
900 HRCY 84032 2398 C6
900 WshC 84032 2398 C6
S Industrial Pkwy
700 PRVO 84606 3035 E3
Industrial Rd
1300 SLCY 84104 1857 C7
1500 SLCY 84104 1963 C1
Industrial Wy
- BMCY 84302 766 C5
Industrial Park Dr
10 SPFK 84660 3142 C7
800 OREM 84057 2819 E2
800 OREM 84057 2820 A3
Industry Cir
8200 WJDN 84088 2174 B5
Ingersol St
- SLCY 84116 1752 E4
Ingersoll Ln
- SLCY 84116 1752 E3
Ingleby Cir
1600 SLCY 84104 1857 C6
Inglenook Dr
10 MDVL 84047 2176 C2
Inglenook Cove
6900 MDVL 84047 2176 C2
Inglewood Ct
1100 SLCY 84105 1859 A6
Inglewood Dr
100 OREM 84097 2821 A5
Ingot Wy
1800 SJDN 84095 2281 C6
Ingram Dr
9100 WJDN 84088 2174 A7
Innovation Ct
600 PYSN 84651 3354 B6
Innovation Dr
3800 RIVN 84065 2386 C4
Innsbruck Dr
1100 WbrC 84317 1060 D7
Innsbruck Wy
10 SmtC 84098 1864 B6
1800 SLkC 84121 2071 D6
Innsbruck Strasse
10 SmtC 84098 1864 B6
Inspiration Cir
9700 SNDY 84092 2283 C4
Integra Ct
1300 SLkC 84106 1965 B6
Interlaken Cir
2200 SNDY 84093 2177 E4
Interlaken Rd
200 WshC 84049 2291 B6
1000 MIDW 84049 2291 C7
1000 MIDW 84049 2397 C1
Interlaken Wy
- WshC 84049 2396 D3
Interlochen Ln
6600 WJDN 84084 2174 C1
S Intermountain Dr
5200 MRRY 84107 2070 C4
International Wy
100 ALPN 84004 2497 D3
N Interstate Plaza Dr
10 LEHI 84043 2603 E6
S Interstate Plaza Dr
10 LEHI 84043 2603 E7
Intrigue Dr
6000 HRMN 84065 2385 C5
Intrigue Pl
6100 HRMN 84065 2385 C5
Inverary Dr
4300 SLkC 84124 2071 B2
Inverness Cir
7200 WJDN 84084 2175 E3
Inverness Ct
1700 ROY 84067 1171 D3
Inverness Dr
900 SRCS 84075 1226 B7
7100 WJDN 84084 2175 E2
Inverness Ln
400 HRCY 84032 2398 C3
Inwood Dr
2900 TYVL 84118 2069 A5
Iola Av
1100 SLCY 84104 1857 D4
Iowa Av
200 OGDN 84404 1057 B5
2300 OGDN 84401 1116 B3
3000 OGDN 84403 1116 B5
N Iowa Av
100 OGDN 84404 1057 B5
Iowa Ln
- SLCY 84116 1752 D3
Iowa St
200 SLCY 84102 1859 A4
Iowa String Rd
- BxEC 84337 584 C1
- ELWD 84337 584 C1
- TMTN 84337 584 C1
10 TMTN 84337 520 C7
Ira Wy
1500 SRCS 84075 1227 A7
Iraquoi Wy
5000 OGDN 84403 1173 D4
Irene Dr
2700 BNFL 84010 1653 E4
Irie Ln
500 SLCY 84116 1857 C1
Iris Ln
1100 SLkC 84106 1965 B6
Irisfield Cir
14300 DRPR 84020 2388 D6
Irisfield Dr
100 DRPR 84020 2388 D6
Iron Wy
700 SNDY 84070 2176 A7
Iron Boberg Cir
1300 DRPR 84020 2389 B5
Iron Canyon Ct
10 PKCY 84060 2078 A2
Iron Canyon Dr
2400 PKCY 84060 2078 B2
Iron Gate Rd
3200 SJDN 84095 2280 E1
Iron Horse Dr
800 PKCY 84060 2078 D4
Iron Horse Pl
2100 DRPR 84020 2389 D1
Iron Mountain Dr
2400 PKCY 84060 2078 A2
Iron Port Dr
1400 SJDN 84095 2281 D2
Ironside Wy
- FMTN 84025 1447 D1
Ironton Blvd
1900 PRVO 84606 3036 A4
Ironwood Av
1300 MRRY 84121 2177 B1
Ironwood Cir
1100 BNFL 84010 1653 D7
1100 NSLK 84054 1653 D7
Ironwood Dr
10 BNFL 84010 1653 D7
10 NSLK 84054 1653 D7
300 SSLK 84115 1964 B3
3900 CRHL 84062 2605 B2
Ironwood Ln
1600 DvsC 84056 1171 E7
Iroquois Cir
2900 PRVO 84604 2928 E1
Iroquois Dr
2300 PRVO 84604 2928 E2
Iroquois St
1600 DvsC 84056 1171 E7
Irving St
700 SLCY 84116 1753 C7
Irwin Rd
11700 SNDY 84092 2283 C7
Isabella Ct
500 SLCY 84102 1859 B4
Isis Cir
2500 SLkC 84044 1960 D4
Island Cir
3400 WVCY 84120 1962 B6
Island Dr
1200 LOGN 84321 528 B2
Island Wy
3300 WVCY 84120 1962 B5
Island Creek Dr
5400 WJDN 84088 2173 D4
Island Park Dr
5400 WJDN 84088 2173 D5
Island View Cir
400 FMTN 84025 1448 E3
Island View Dr
100 CTRV 84014 1552 A4
900 BNFL 84010 1552 A5
Isom Pl
500 SLCY 84103 1858 E2
Italian Ct
4700 WJDN 84084 2174 B1
Italian St
4600 WJDN 84084 2174 A2
Ithica Dr
- HILD 84003 2497 B5
Ivan Ct
200 SLCY 84102 1859 A4
Ivana St
4000 WVCY 84120 1961 E7
4000 WVCY 84120 2067 E1
Ivanhoe Ct
3000 WVCY 84120 1962 A3
Iverness Cir
9800 SJDN 84095 2280 C2
Iverson St
600 SLCY 84111 1858 D5
Iverson Woods Pl
2100 HLDY 84117 2071 E2
S Ivey Ln
4500 TYVL 84123 2069 E3
Ivory Cir
6500 TYVL 84084 2175 A1
Ivory Wy
2700 TYVL 84084 2175 A1
3100 TYVL 84084 2068 E7
3100 TYVL 84084 2174 E1
Ivy Cir
1600 SLCY 84116 1753 C7
Ivy Dr
8100 MDVL 84047 2176 B5
W Ivy Dr
500 MDVL 84047 2176 B5
Ivy Ln
300 SSLK 84115 1964 D5
4200 PRVO 84604 2821 E6
Ivy Pl
1200 KYVL 84037 1283 E5
3500 SRCS 84075 1226 B7
Ivy Brook Cir
5100 MRRY 84123 2070 B4
Ivy Creek Cove
11100 SJDN 84095 2281 E5
Ivy Gable Dr
8400 WJDN 84088 2173 B5
Ivy Hills Cir
8800 SNDY 84093 2177 E6
Ivy Leaf Pl
8700 WJDN 84088 2174 B6
Ivy Manor Ln
13500 DRPR 84020 2388 E4
13500 DRPR 84020 2389 A4
Ivy Oaks Dr
10 SNDY 84093 2284 C1
Ivy Park Ct
3300 WVCY 84119 1962 E5
Ivy Park Dr
3300 WVCY 84119 1962 E5
Ivy Springs Ln
8400 WJDN 84088 2173 B5
Ivy Woods Ln
300 MDVL 84047 2176 E3

J

J St
- RVDL 84405 1172 B4
10 SLCY 84103 1858 E2
Jack Cir
2300 TYVL 84084 2069 B7
4200 WVCY 84120 2068 C1
Jack D Dr
1200 LYTN 84041 1282 C4
Jackling Wy
5800 WJDN 84084 2173 C2
Jack Rabbit Run
800 SRSP 84043 2601 C7
Jackson Av
500 OGDN 84404 1057 B6
700 SLCY 84116 1858 A2
2000 OGDN 84401 1116 B3
2700 OGDN 84403 1116 B4
3900 OGDN 84403 1173 B1
N Jackson Av
400 OGDN 84404 1057 B4
Jackson Cir
10 ANFK 84003 2711 E1
Jackson Cir
9600 SNDY 84092 2284 A2
Jackson Dr
1700 OGDN 84401 1116 A2
Jackson St
- KYVL 84037 1344 D2
8000 MDVL 84047 2176 B5
Jackson Hole Dr
8400 SNDY 84093 2177 E5
Jacob Rd
1300 SNDY 84092 2389 C1
Jacob Astor Wy
3200 SJDN 84095 2280 E4
Jacob Hill Cir
5300 WJDN 84084 2173 E3
Jacobs Cir
1200 MRRY 84121 2071 B7
Jacobs Wy
- SRSP 84043 2601 D6
Jacob's Mill Rd
- PTVW 84414 997 E4
- PTVW 84414 998 A3
Jacqueline Dr
2500 WbrC 84403 1173 E4
2500 WbrC 84403 1174 A4
Jacquelyn St
3800 WJDN 84088 2280 D1
Jade Cir
900 SLkC 84094 2283 A2
Jade Dr
9700 SLkC 84094 2283 A2
Jade Hill Cove
7300 WJDN 84084 2174 A3
Jade Park Ln
500 DRPR 84020 2388 E6
Jaguar Dr
7800 WJDN 84088 2175 A5
Jake Ln
11900 RIVN 84065 2281 A7
Jake Garn Blvd
500 SLCY 84104 1857 E4
Jamaica Cir
5900 MRRY 84123 2070 B6
Jamaica St
6000 MRRY 84123 2070 B7
Jamboree St
2900 WVCY 84120 1962 A5
James Cir
300 SNDY 84070 2282 D1
James Ct
900 SLCY 84111 1858 E6
James Dr
1500 FTHT 84037 1346 B3
James St
- TMTN 84337 520 D7
500 CRFD 84015 1227 D3
James Brown Dr
- OGDN 84401 1115 C4
James M Mair Ln
- HRCY 84032 2398 D3
Jameson Av
3400 RIVN 84065 2280 E7
Jameson Point Cove
9700 SLkC 84092 2284 C2
James Pointe Dr
600 MRRY 84107 2176 E1
Jamestown Cir
4200 DvsC 84056 1228 A4
6200 MRRY 84121 2071 C7
Jamestown Ct
6200 MRRY 84121 2071 C7
Jamestown Dr
1400 MRRY 84121 2071 C7
Jamiah Dr
5700 MRRY 84123 2070 A6
Jamie Wy
1800 RIVN 84065 2387 C1
Jamileh Cir
200 EKMT 84651 3463 A2
Jana Lee Dr
2800 WJDN 84088 2175 A7
2800 WJDN 84088 2281 A1
Janalynn Dr
11200 SJDN 84095 2281 E6
Jane Cir
1700 SNDY 84092 2283 C5
3600 WVCY 84120 1962 B6
Janella Cir
1700 SNDY 84093 2177 D5
Janella Wy
1700 SNDY 84093 2177 C5
Janene Cir
2100 WBNF 84087 1551 C4
Janet Av
100 SNST 84015 1227 D2
Janet Wy
9200 WJDN 84088 2174 D7
9200 WJDN 84088 2280 D1
Janette Av
4800 WVCY 84120 1962 A7
5300 WVCY 84120 1961 D7
Janice Dr
11800 RIVN 84065 2280 E7
12100 RIVN 84065 2386 E1
Jardim Cir
1900 SNDY 84093 2177 D5
Jardim Wy
8400 SNDY 84093 2177 D5
Jared Cir
13200 RIVN 84065 2387 D4
Jared Wy
2200 WbrC 84403 1173 E5
Jaren Cir
1100 SLCY 84108 1860 B6
Jargon Cir
5900 SLkC 84118 2067 C6
Jargon Wy
5900 SLkC 84118 2067 C6
Jarrad Rd
5000 SLkC 84118 2067 D7
5000 SLkC 84118 2068 A7
Jarrah St
4300 TYVL 84123 2069 D2
Jasmine Av
1300 SNDY 84092 2283 B2
S Jasmine Dr
4600 TYVL 84123 2069 E2
W Jasmine Dr
900 TYVL 84123 2069 E3
Jasmine St
3600 WVCY 84120 2068 D2

STREET
Block City ZIP Map# Grid

Jason Dr
10700 SNDY 84094 2283 B4
Jason Pl
3100 WVCY 84119 1962 E5
Jason K Cir
9000 SNDY 84070 2176 D7
Jasper Cir
900 SLCY 84106 1965 A3
Jasper St
2500 SLCY 84106 1965 A4
Jasper Hill Dr
7200 WJDN 84084 2174 A3
Jay Cir
2600 TYVL 84118 2069 A3
Jay Ln E
200 PYSN 84651 3355 A6
Jay Ln W
200 PYSN 84651 3355 A6
Jay St
400 KYVL 84037 1345 A2
Jayco Dr
- SLkC 84118 2067 E3
- SLkC 84118 2068 A3
Jayden Cove
4400 WVCY 84120 2068 D2
Jay Hill Cir
5100 TYVL 84118 2068 E4
Jazz Ln
5000 MRRY 84117 2071 A4
Jean Cir
- WPT 84015 1225 E4
1300 DRPR 84020 2389 C2
Jean Dr
- WPT 84015 1225 E4
9200 SNDY 84070 2176 E7
9200 SNDY 84070 2282 E1
Jean St
3100 SLkC 84044 1960 C5
Jean Wy
2500 WJDN 84084 2175 A2
Jeanne Av
1100 MRRY 84121 2071 B7
Jeannine Dr
4200 SLkC 84107 2070 D1
Jedediah Dr
5000 SLkC 84118 2067 E4
Jeff St
1200 LYTN 84040 1283 C2
Jefferson Av
100 OGDN 84404 1057 A5
300 ANFK 84003 2711 B1
1300 OGDN 84404 1116 A1
1600 OGDN 84404 1115 E1
2000 OGDN 84401 1116 A3
2700 OGDN 84403 1116 A5
3100 OGDN 84403 1115 E6
3600 SOGN 84403 1115 E7
4000 SOGN 84403 1172 E1
4500 SOGN 84403 1173 A2
N Jefferson Av
1100 OGDN 84404 1057 A2
Jefferson Cir
3600 SLkC 84044 1960 D7
6900 WJDN 84084 2175 C2
Jefferson Ln
9000 SNDY 84070 2176 A7
Jefferson Rd
7200 SLkC 84044 1960 D6
Jefferson St
100 SSLK 84115 1964 C4
800 SLCY 84101 1858 C5
1500 SLCY 84115 1858 C7
1600 SLCY 84115 1964 C1
6400 MRRY 84107 2176 C1
6800 MDVL 84047 2176 C2
Jefferson Cove
600 SNDY 84070 2176 A7
Jeffrey Dr
200 CTRV 84014 1551 D4
Jeffs Cir
4100 WVCY 84128 2067 B1
Jene Dr
500 SNDY 84070 2282 E1
Jenelles Bay
3500 WVCY 84119 1963 B6
Jenks Av
10 ANFK 84003 2711 C1
Jennie Ln
2800 HLDY 84117 2072 B2
Jennies Ct
10 DvsC 84037 1283 C6
Jennifer Dr
1900 WbrC 84403 1173 D5
Jennifer Wy
1700 SLCY 84116 1857 C2
Jennifer Dee Cir
3000 RIVN 84065 2280 E7
E Jennings Ln
10 CTRV 84014 1448 E7
W Jennings Ln
10 CTRV 84014 1448 D7
Jenny Ln
400 PTVW 84414 998 D6
2000 CRFD 84015 1281 C1
Jenny Lake Dr
4000 WJDN 84088 2174 C7
4000 WJDN 84088 2280 C1
Jenny Sue Ct
600 MRRY 84123 2070 A6
Jensen Cir
4100 WVCY 84120 2068 C1
7100 SWBR 84405 1229 C1
Jensen Ln
400 MRRY 84123 2070 B2
Jensen St
300 LYTN 84041 1282 E2
Jensen Meadow Ln
500 SLCY 84116 1857 C1
Jepson Av
700 SLkC 84106 1964 E5
700 SLkC 84106 1965 A5
Jerand Wy
300 SNDY 84070 2282 D6
Jerema Ct
12100 DRPR 84020 2388 A1
Jeremiah Cir
4900 SLkC 84118 2067 D4
Jeremiah Dr
4900 SLkC 84118 2067 D3
Jeremy Cir
1800 MRRY 84121 2071 D7
9000 SmtC 84098 1865 A4
Jeremy Ct
1800 MRRY 84121 2071 D7
Jeremy Dr
1800 MRRY 84121 2071 D7
Jeremy St
10 SLCY 84104 1858 A3
Jeremy Ranch Rd
8700 SmtC 84098 1865 B4
9200 SmtC 84098 1864 E2
Jeremy Woods Dr
4000 SmtC 84098 1864 E4
Jeri Dr
400 BNFL 84010 1653 E3
Jerling Cir
5000 HILD 84003 2604 E1
E Jerling Dr
10600 HILD 84003 2604 E1
N Jerling Dr
10600 HILD 84003 2604 E1
W Jerling Dr
5000 HILD 84003 2604 E1
Jerrie Lee Ln
900 SLkC 84117 2071 A2
Jerry Wy
8300 WJDN 84088 2175 C5
Jersey Cir
10 CTRV 84014 1448 D7
4800 WVCY 84120 1962 A5
Jerusalem Pl
1000 TYVL 84123 2069 E4
Jesse Valley Cir
11900 SNDY 84092 2283 C7
Jessica Ln
2300 SNDY 84092 2284 A3
10000 SNDY 84092 2283 E4
Jessie Ln
13300 RIVN 84065 2387 C4
Jessie Creek Dr
4800 PTVW 84414 942 C7
4800 WbrC 84414 942 C7
4900 PTVW 84324 942 C7
Jessieo Wy
5500 TYVL 84123 2069 D5
Jessi's Meadow Cir
1100 WBNF 84087 1551 A6
Jessi's Meadow Dr
400 WBNF 84087 1551 A6
800 WBNF 84087 1550 E6
Jessi's Meadow Wy
1100 WBNF 84087 1551 A6
Jester Dr
3900 WVCY 84119 1963 D7
Jetway Av
2400 SLCY 84104 1857 A3
Jewell Av
900 SLCY 84104 1963 E1
900 SLCY 84104 1964 A2
W Jewkes Cir
2200 WJDN 84088 2175 B4
Jewkes St
7800 WJDN 84088 2175 B4
Jill's Pl
4400 WVCY 84120 2068 B2
Jim Bridger Dr
500 CTRV 84014 1448 D7
Jimmy Doolittle Rd
100 SLCY 84116 1855 E2
Joan Cir
6400 TYVL 84084 2069 B7
Joan St
1000 SNST 84015 1227 D2
Joann Dr
7700 CDHT 84093 2177 D4
Joanna Cir
9600 SNDY 84070 2282 D1
Joanne St
500 PTVW 84404 998 A6
Joaquin St
4800 SLkC 84118 2067 D3
Jocelyn Wy
4300 WVCY 84128 2067 C1
Jodi Dr
1000 LYTN 84041 1281 E2
Jodie Cir
3600 WVCY 84128 1961 C6
Jodie Ln
3600 WVCY 84128 1961 C7
Jody St
2500 WJDN 84088 2175 A7
Joe Dean Cir
1500 OGDN 84403 1173 C3
Joey Cir
1400 SNDY 84092 2283 C7
Joey Ct
4800 HILD 84003 2498 A7
Joey Park Pl
12000 DRPR 84020 2388 A1
John Ln
- OREM 84057 2820 A4
John St
1800 LYTN 84041 1282 B1
John Wy
4100 WVCY 84120 2067 E1
John Glenn Rd
300 SLCY 84116 1855 C1
John Henry Dr
2300 WVCY 84119 1963 B2
John N Winterose Ln
- HRCY 84032 2398 D2
Johnson Cir
5900 MRRY 84121 2071 B6
Johnson Rd
4100 CchC 84321 591 D6
4100 NBLY 84321 591 D6
Johnson Ridge Cir
7300 WJDN 84084 2175 D3
Johnson Ridge Ln
1100 WJDN 84084 2175 E3
1400 CchC 84321 591 A1
N Johnson's Mill Rd
10 MIDW 84049 2397 D3
10 WshC 84049 2397 D3
S Johnson's Mill Rd
10 MIDW 84049 2397 D3
Johnson Wy Cir
8500 SNDY 84094 2177 A6
Johnson Wy Dr
700 SNDY 84094 2176 E6
700 SNDY 84094 2177 A6
Johnstone Dr
1900 SNDY 84093 2177 D5
Jolley Acres Cir
11400 SLkC 84092 2283 D6
11400 SNDY 84092 2283 D6
Jolly Cir
1600 TYVL 84123 2069 C4
Jolly St
5000 TYVL 84123 2069 C4
Joma St
6400 MRRY 84107 2070 E7
Jonathan Cir
7200 CDHT 84121 2178 D3
Jonathan Dr
3600 CDHT 84121 2178 C2
Jonathan Pl
200 SRSP 84043 2601 D4
Jonathan Rd
4800 HILD 84003 2498 A7
4900 HILD 84003 2497 E7
Jonathan View Ln
12100 DRPR 84020 2388 A1
Jonathon St
- FTHT 84037 1346 A4
N Jones Av
- OGDN 84404 1056 B5
S Jones Av
- OGDN 84404 1056 B5
Jones Ct
4900 MRRY 84107 2070 D4
Jones Dr
200 BMCY 84302 767 A6
2500 WbrC 84310 1001 E5
Jonestead Wy
2200 WJDN 84084 2175 B2
Jonetta Dr
2900 SLkC 84109 1965 E4
Joni Dr
2000 LYTN 84040 1229 E7
2500 LYTN 84040 1230 A7
Jonquil Dr
2900 TYVL 84118 2069 A6
5800 TYVL 84118 2068 E6
Jonquil Ln
1500 DvsC 84056 1227 E2
Jordan Av
1100 PRVO 84604 2928 A4
Jordan Ct
2400 TYVL 84118 2069 B6
Jordan Wy
9600 SJDN 84095 2281 E1
Jordanair Dr
11600 SJDN 84095 2280 D7
Jordan Bend Rd
3200 SJDN 84095 2280 E6
Jordan Bluff Cir
1100 TYVL 84123 2069 E4
Jordan Canal Rd
4900 TYVL 84118 2068 E4
5100 TYVL 84118 2069 A4
S Jordan Canal Rd
5400 TYVL 84118 2069 B6
Jordan Crest Cir
10000 SJDN 84095 2281 A3
Jordan Dale Rd
7400 WJDN 84084 2175 D3
Jordanelle Wy
3000 WshC 84049 2079 C7
Jordanelle View Dr
2900 WshC 84049 2079 C7
Jordan Farms Rd
11400 SJDN 84095 2280 E6
S Jordan Gateway
10200 SJDN 84095 2282 C5
Jordan Haven Ct
2200 SJDN 84095 2281 B2
Jordan Hills Dr
1300 SJDN 84095 2281 D6
Jordan Knoll Cir
3200 SJDN 84095 2280 E6
Jordan Landing Blvd
3600 WJDN 84084 2174 C4
7300 WJDN 84088 2174 C4
Jordan Meadow Ln
11200 SNDY 84070 2282 D5
Jordan Meadows Ln
2200 WJDN 84084 2175 A3
Jordan Meadows Cove
2200 WJDN 84084 2175 B3
Jordan Narrows Rd
1600 BFDL 84065 2494 D6
Jordan Oaks Dr
9000 SNDY 84070 2176 A7
Jordan Park Cir
10000 SJDN 84095 2280 E2
Jordan Point Cir
1600 SNDY 84092 2283 C6
Jordan Point Dr
1500 SNDY 84092 2283 C6
Jordan Ridge Cir
9700 SJDN 84095 2281 E2
Jordan Ridge Ct
1000 SJDN 84095 2281 E2
Jordan Ridge Rd
9700 SJDN 84095 2281 E2
Jordan River Dr
1000 SJDN 84095 2281 E5
Jordan Valley Wy
8700 WJDN 84088 2174 D6
Jordan View Cir
200 SNDY 84070 2282 D6
Jordan View Dr
100 SNDY 84070 2282 D5
Jordan Villa Dr
2000 WJDN 84088 2281 B1
Jordan Village Rd
6800 WJDN 84084 2174 D1
Jordan Vista Rd
- RIVN 84065 2387 E1
N Jorgensen Av
- OGDN 84404 1056 C4
Joseph Dr
8200 SLkC 84044 1960 B4
Joseph View Ln
12100 DRPR 84020 2388 A1
Josh Cir
600 MRRY 84123 2070 A6
Joshua Cir
5500 WJDN 84084 2173 D1
Joshua Dr
300 KYVL 84037 1345 A2
E Jost Rd
1600 FTHT 84037 1346 B2
Joust Ct
1700 SLCY 84116 1753 C6
S Joy Dr
200 FMTN 84025 1448 D2
W Joy Dr
10 FMTN 84025 1448 D2
Joyce Dr
3300 SLkC 84109 1966 C4
Joycelyn Cir
3600 WVCY 84120 1962 A6
Joye St
400 SLkC 84107 2070 E1
Joyes Ln
1100 WJDN 84088 2175 D6
W Joyli Cir
2200 WJDN 84088 2175 B4
Jubilee Ct
6600 WVCY 84128 1961 B6
Jubilee Wy
6600 WVCY 84128 1961 A6
Judd Cir
3700 WJDN 84088 2174 D7
Judd Ln
9000 WJDN 84088 2174 D7
9200 WJDN 84088 2280 D1
Judith St
2900 SLCY 84106 1965 B4
Judy Av
100 SNST 84015 1227 D2
Judy Cir
3400 RIVN 84065 2386 E1
S Judy Dr
8400 MDVL 84047 2176 C5
Julep Cir
400 MRRY 84107 2070 E2
Julep Dr
400 MRRY 84107 2070 E2
Julho St
1600 SNDY 84093 2177 C5
Julia Cir
8800 SLkC 84044 1960 A5
Julia Ln
3100 SLkC 84044 1960 A5
Julie Dr
500 LYTN 84041 1283 B4
Julie Ann Cir
1100 SNDY 84094 2283 B4
Julie Ann Pl
5200 HILD 84003 2604 D2
Julie Ann Wy
2700 WJDN 84088 2281 A1
9000 WJDN 84088 2175 A7
Julie Anna Ct
8200 SNDY 84070 2176 D5
Julie Anna Dr
100 SNDY 84070 2176 D5
Julien Cove
14000 BFDL 84065 2387 D6
Julie's Dr
3100 SmtC 84098 1865 B6
Juliet Wy
2900 CDHT 84121 2178 B1
Junction Cir
15000 DRPR 84020 2495 D1
June Cir
1500 DRPR 84020 2389 C2
Jungfrau Hl
200 WshC 84049 2291 B6
Juniper
10 SHFD 84335 399 D1
Juniper Av
600 PTGV 84062 2713 A4
Juniper Cir
4100 UthC 84004 2498 B1
Juniper Ct
8000 SWBR 84405 1229 D3
Juniper Dr
700 LOGN 84321 528 C1
7900 SmtC 84098 1865 A6
Juniper Ln
- DvsC 84056 1171 E7
1800 RVDL 84405 1172 A6
2100 DvsC 84056 1172 A7
3900 WbrC 84310 1001 E2
W Juniper Rd
4000 CRHL 84062 2605 C2
Juniper St
1600 LYTN 84040 1283 D4
Juniper Wy
2700 HLDY 84117 2072 A4
Juniper Crest Rd
- HRMN 84065 2386 A6
- RIVN 84065 2386 A6
Juniper Hills Dr
4000 SJDN 84095 2280 C4
Juniperpoint Dr
- SLCY 84103 1754 E7
Juno Cir
3600 SLkC 84124 1966 D7
Jupiter Cir
11800 HILD 84003 2497 B5
Jupiter Dr
3500 SLkC 84124 1966 C7
4000 SLkC 84124 2072 D1
Jupiter Hills Cir
800 SRCS 84075 1226 B6
Jupiter Hills Dr
3400 SRCS 84075 1226 B6
Jupiter View Dr
2200 PKCY 84060 2078 C3
Justice St
3000 WVCY 84119 1963 C5
Justin Dr
600 MRRY 84123 2070 A6
Justin Kay Ct
700 SLCY 84104 1858 A6
Justin Park Dr
1900 SNDY 84092 2283 D5

K

K St
- RVDL 84405 1172 B3
10 SLCY 84103 1859 A2
Kadie Ln
1200 KYVL 84037 1345 E4
Kagie Cir
900 CTRV 84014 1551 D2
Kaibab Cir
3600 SLkC 84109 1966 D5
Kaibab Wy
3100 SLkC 84109 1966 D5
Kaitlyn Cir
5700 HILD 84003 2497 C7
12000 DRPR 84020 2388 A1
Kaitlyn Ln
500 ANFK 84003 2605 A6
6600 HILD 84003 2604 A1
Kaitlyn Ann Cir
4700 TYVL 84123 2070 A3
Kalani Dr
4900 HLDY 84117 2072 B4
Kalinda Dr
2200 SNDY 84092 2283 E2
Kallie Cir
3900 WVCY 84120 1962 A7
Kal Ridge Ln
200 HDPK 84318 400 C7
Kamas Cir
5900 TYVL 84118 2069 A6
Kamas Dr
2400 TYVL 84118 2069 B6
Kami Wy
- SLkC 84118 2068 A3
Kanab Ct
15000 DRPR 84020 2495 D1
Kandi Cir
12000 RIVN 84065 2281 C7
Kane Cir
2000 CDHT 84121 2177 D2
Kanesville Meadows Ln
3800 WHVN 84315 1113 C7
Kapalua
3900 CRHL 84062 2605 C1
Kapford Dr
2900 WVCY 84128 1961 B4
Kara Ct
3200 CDHT 84121 2178 C2
Kara Dr
2700 SRCS 84075 1281 A3
Karalee Wy
2100 SNDY 84092 2283 E3
2400 SNDY 84092 2284 A3
Karalynn Ct
5600 HRMN 84065 2385 D3
Karen Dr
10 BNFL 84010 1552 B7
5400 WbrC 84403 1173 E4
Karin Ct
2000 CDHT 84093 2177 E3
Karleen Cir
- BMCY 84302 767 C5
Karleen Dr
1100 BMCY 84302 767 B6
Karl L Nelsen Ln
- HRCY 84032 2398 E2
Karma Av
3900 WVCY 84120 1961 D7
Karon Cir
900 SNDY 84094 2177 A7
Karos Cir
6000 TYVL 84123 2069 D7
Karren St
2400 HLDY 84124 2072 A1
Karsten Ct
5100 SLkC 84118 2067 E6
Kaseys Cir
800 DRPR 84020 2389 A6
Kate Cove
1900 WJDN 84088 2175 C7
Katelyn Park Ct
12000 DRPR 84020 2388 E1
Katey Ct
11400 SNDY 84092 2283 D6
Kathan Wy
- SLkC 84118 2068 A3
Katherine Cir
2800 SLkC 84109 1966 B4
Katherine Dr
3200 SLkC 84044 1960 A5
Kathleen Av
4600 WVCY 84120 1962 A7
5400 WVCY 84120 1961 D7
5400 WVCY 84128 1961 D7
Kathleen Cir
3900 WVCY 84120 1962 B7
Kathrine Ann Ct
6400 WVCY 84118 2173 B1
Kathryn Cir
200 SNDY 84070 2282 D1
Kathy Av
3400 WVCY 84119 2068 D2
Kathy Cir
4500 WVCY 84119 2068 D2
Kathy Dr
2000 SNDY 84092 2283 D6
Katie Cir
1200 LYTN 84041 1281 E2
Katie St
4800 TYVL 84118 2068 E3
Katie Lynn Ln
2300 HLDY 84117 2071 E3
2300 HLDY 84117 2072 A3
Katie's Cross
3000 SmtC 84098 1865 B6
Katie's Wy
1900 CRFD 84015 1281 D1
N Katrina Ct
1800 LYTN 84040 1283 E1
Kavin Spring Cir
700 ALPN 84004 2498 B6
Kawakami Dr
- ANFK 84003 2711 A1
Kay Cir
3800 HLDY 84124 1965 C7
3800 SLkC 84106 1965 C7
E Kay Cir
3000 LYTN 84040 1284 B4
Kay Ln
- SWBR 84405 1229 D2
Kayland Cir
4500 HLDY 84117 2071 E2
Kayland Wy
2000 HLDY 84117 2071 D2
Kaylynne Cir
- BMCY 84302 767 C5
Kays Cr
1700 LYTN 84040 1283 C1
Kays Dr
- KYVL 84037 1345 B3
N Kays Dr
10 KYVL 84037 1345 A1
300 KYVL 84037 1283 A7
S Kays Dr
- KYVL 84037 1345 A1
Kays Creek Dr
1300 LYTN 84040 1283 D1
Kays Creek Pl
1800 LYTN 84040 1283 D1
Kaysville Ct
10 DRPR 84020 2495 C1
Kaywood Cir
2400 SLCY 84109 1966 A3
Kearns Blvd
700 PKCY 84060 2078 D3
2400 PKCY 84060 2079 A2
2600 PKCY 84098 2079 A2
2600 SmtC 84098 2079 A2
Kearns Blvd SR-248
700 PKCY 84060 2078 D3
2400 PKCY 84060 2079 A2
2600 PKCY 84098 2079 A2
2600 SmtC 84098 2079 A2
Keddington Ln
2400 HLDY 84117 2072 A2
Keelcrest Cir
2000 WJDN 84084 2175 B4
Keelcrest Dr
7600 WJDN 84084 2175 B4
Keepsake Ct
1500 SJDN 84095 2281 C2
Keith Dr
1100 SNDY 84094 2177 B7
Keller Ln
- NHLN 84341 464 B5
2000 SLkC 84109 1965 E6
Kelley Dr
8800 WbrC 84317 1061 E4
Kelly Cir
4600 HLDY 84117 2072 A3
Kelly Ln
2700 HLDY 84117 2072 A3
Kelly Brook Dr
9500 SNDY 84092 2284 B2
Kelmscott Ct
1600 SLkC 84124 2071 C2
Kelmscott Ln
4400 SLkC 84124 2071 C2
Kelsch Dr
8500 SLkC 84093 2177 C6
8500 SNDY 84093 2177 C6
Kelsey Av
10 SLCY 84111 1858 C6
Keltic Ct
2800 WVCY 84128 1961 D4
Kelvingrove Cir
4000 SJDN 84095 2280 C2
Kemp Dr
5200 SLkC 84118 2067 E4
Kemper Cir
11600 SJDN 84095 2280 E6
Kempner Rd
2900 SLkC 84109 1966 B6
Kenbridge Ct
4400 SLkC 84108 1860 E4
N Kendell Av
100 OGDN 84404 1056 B5
S Kendell Av
100 OGDN 84404 1056 B5
Kendrick Ct
- LOGN 84321 528 C4
Kenmore Cir
12000 RIVN 84065 2280 E7
Kennedy Dr
2800 SLCY 84108 1860 B6
Kennelly Av
1100 SNDY 84094 2283 B2
Ken Rey St
1400 SLCY 84108 1859 D7
Kensington
- LOGN 84341 463 C5
Kensington Av
10 SLCY 84115 1858 C7
500 SLCY 84105 1858 E7
900 SLCY 84105 1859 A7
1900 SLCY 84108 1859 D7
2400 SLCY 84108 1860 A7
Kensington Cir
5400 HILD 84003 2604 D3
Kensington St
600 FMTN 84025 1346 B5
1900 FTHT 84037 1346 B5
Kensington Park Dr
- WJDN 84088 2175 B7
Kent Cir
1300 LYTN 84041 1282 C2
5400 MRRY 84117 2071 B5
Kent Dr
400 NSLK 84054 1652 C6
Kenton Dr
2700 SLkC 84109 1966 A4
Kentucky Av
2400 HLDY 84117 2071 E3
2400 HLDY 84117 2072 A3
Kentucky Cir
3600 WJDN 84084 2174 D1
Kentucky Dr
3600 WJDN 84084 2174 D1
6300 WJDN 84084 2068 D7
Kentwood Dr
800 BMCY 84302 827 E1
Kenwood Cir
1700 SLCY 84106 1965 C4
Kenwood Dr
5300 MRRY 84107 2070 E5
Kenwood St
2500 SLCY 84106 1965 D3
2800 SLkC 84106 1965 D4
Kenyon Cir
9000 WJDN 84088 2174 B7
Kenyon Park Dr
3700 WVCY 84120 1962 C7
Kenyons Claim Cir
6100 WJDN 84084 2173 C1
Keri Cir
10 NSLK 84054 1653 C7
Keri Lynn Ct
12700 RIVN 84065 2387 B2
Keri Lynn Dr
12800 RIVN 84065 2387 B3
Kerry Cir
5800 MRRY 84107 2070 E6
Kerrybrook Dr
1500 KYVL 84037 1345 C5
Kersh Dr
300 CRFD 84015 1227 C3
Kershaw St
300 OGDN 84401 1115 E4
800 OGDN 84403 1116 A4
W Kershaw St
900 OGDN 84401 1115 A5
Kessler Peak Cir
13900 RIVN 84065 2386 A5
Kessler Peak Dr
4800 RIVN 84065 2386 A5
Kestrel Dr
4000 WVCY 84120 2068 C1
Kestrel Ridge Rd
4500 SJDN 84095 2280 B6
Kestrel Rise Rd
11200 SJDN 84095 2280 B6
Keswick Rd
1500 CDHT 84093 2177 C4
Ketchum Dr
6400 WVCY 84128 1961 B4
Kewanee Cir
3600 WVCY 84120 1962 C4
Kewanee Dr
3600 WVCY 84120 1962 D7
Keyridge Cir
100 OREM 84058 2927 D1
Keys St
2200 WVCY 84119 1963 D3
Keystone Ct
10 PKCY 84060 2078 B3
Keystone Dr
5900 SJDN 84095 2279 C6
Keys View Ct
1700 SLkC 84117 2071 D2
Kidd Cir
1900 SmtC 84098 1971 D5
Kiera Ct
1700 HLDY 84124 2071 C2
Kierstin Pl
1600 SLCY 84105 1965 C1
Kiesel Av
300 OGDN 84404 1056 E6
1500 OGDN 84404 1115 E1
1800 OGDN 84401 1115 E2
3800 SOGN 84405 1115 E7
Kiesta Ct
6800 WJDN 84084 2174 A1
Kikkert Cir
900 SLkC 84124 1965 A7
Kiku Ct
4800 WJDN 84084 2174 A1
Kilberry Wy
- WJDN 84088 2174 C4
Kilbourne Ct
700 SLCY 84102 1858 E5
Kilby Ct
700 SLCY 84101 1858 B5
Kilby Rd
2300 SmtC 84098 1971 D1
2400 SmtC 84098 1865 C6
3800 SmtC 84098 1864 C5
Kilchurn Cir
4000 SJDN 84095 2280 C2
Kildare Cir
4000 WVCY 84119 2069 B1
Kilee Ct
3000 WVCY 84128 1961 C5
Killarney Cir
4000 WVCY 84119 2069 A2
Killarney Dr
700 SRCS 84075 1226 A6
4400 HILD 84003 2605 A2
Kilmuir Cir
9500 SJDN 84095 2280 B1
Kilt St
3800 SJDN 84095 2280 C3
Kilt Rock Cir
2800 WVCY 84128 1961 D4
Kilt Rock Dr
- WVCY 84128 1961 D4
Kim Dr
400 PRRY 84302 827 D5
Kim Wy
6600 CDHT 84121 2177 D1
Kimball Cir
500 MIDW 84049 2397 A1
Kimballfield Ln
100 DRPR 84020 2282 D7
Kimball Hall
200 PRVO 84604 2928 E3
Kimballs Ln
11400 DRPR 84020 2282 E6
Kimbary Cir
3600 SLkC 84109 1966 A6
Kimbary Wy
2500 SLkC 84109 1966 A7
Kimberly Cir
1700 SLCY 84116 1857 C1
Kimberly Dr
1200 LYTN 84040 1283 C2
Kimberly Wy
3800 WVCY 84128 1961 A7
Kimble St
400 LYTN 84041 1283 A6
E Kimbouris Ln
10 FMTN 84025 1448 D5
W Kimbouris Ln
10 FMTN 84025 1448 C5
Kimman Ln
1200 TYVL 84123 2069 D5
Kimman Cove
5300 TYVL 84123 2069 D5
Kimsbrough Ct
10000 SNDY 84092 2283 D2
Kimsbrough Rd
1600 SNDY 84092 2283 C3
Kim Wood Ln
3000 SSLK 84106 1964 E5
King Cir
600 LYTN 84041 1282 D4
King Rd
10 PKCY 84060 2078 E7
King St
10 LYTN 84041 1282 D4
500 ANFK 84003 2711 E1
2100 SLCY 84109 1966 A2
King Arthur Dr
4100 WVCY 84119 2069 A2
King Arthur Wy
500 NSLK 84054 1653 B5

STREET
Block City ZIP Map# Grid

Kingdom Ct
3500 WVCY 84119 1963 D6
Kingdon Ln
10 NSLK 84054 1653 B7
King Hill Dr
3600 NHON 84414 999 A3
Kings Ct
10 LOGN 84321 527 C1
10 PKCY 84060 2078 B4
1100 KYVL 84037 1345 A2
E Kings Ln
600 SSLK 84106 1964 E4
Kings Bridge Dr
7500 WJDN 84084 2175 D3
Kingsbrook Av
3200 TYVL 84084 2068 E7
S Kingsburg Cove
3500 SLkC 84044 1960 C6
Kings Cove Cir
3500 CDHT 84121 2178 C5
Kings Cove Dr
8300 CDHT 84121 2178 C6
Kings Cove Wy
3500 CDHT 84121 2178 C6
Kings Crossing Ct
2900 RIVN 84065 2281 B7
Kings Crossing Dr
800 FMTN 84025 1346 A7
Kings Crossing Wy
- SJDN 84095 2281 A6
11800 RIVN 84065 2281 A7
12000 RIVN 84065 2387 A1
Kings Estate Cir
4000 WVCY 84128 1961 B7
Kings Estate Ct
6600 WVCY 84128 1961 A7
Kings Estate Dr
3900 WVCY 84128 1960 E7
6400 WVCY 84128 1961 A7
Kings Farm Wy
3000 RIVN 84065 2281 A7
Kingsford Av
5600 SmtC 84098 1972 E3
Kings Hill Cir
3500 CDHT 84121 2178 C6
Kings Hill Dr
3400 CDHT 84121 2178 C5
Kings Hill Pl
9000 CDHT 84121 2178 D7
Kingsley Ct
3700 WJDN 84084 2174 D1
Kings Meadow Ct
2900 RIVN 84065 2281 A7
Kings Mountain Ct
2900 RIVN 84065 2281 A7
Kings Peak Dr
10 LNDN 84042 2714 A6
Kings Peak Cove
600 DRPR 84020 2388 E4
Kingspointe Cir
3700 WVCY 84119 1963 E7
Kingspointe Ln
1300 WVCY 84119 1963 D7
Kings Row Cir
4800 SLkC 84117 2071 C3
Kings Row Dr
1300 SLkC 84117 2071 B4
N Kings Row Dr
1500 WVCY 84119 1963 D7
S Kings Row Dr
1500 WVCY 84119 2069 D1
Kingston Av
400 LYTN 84041 1283 A3
Kingston Cir
3500 OGDN 84403 1116 C7
7500 CDHT 84121 2178 C3
Kingston Dr
- SWBR 84405 1172 D6
1300 OGDN 84403 1116 C7
Kingston Pl
600 BMCY 84302 767 A3
Kingston Rd
1800 FMTN 84025 1346 A4
Kingston St
7400 CDHT 84121 2178 C3
Kingston Wy
5800 MRRY 84107 2070 C6
Kingswood Cir
5300 TYVL 84118 2068 C5
Kingswood Dr
5100 TYVL 84118 2068 E4
E Kingswood Rd
800 KYVL 84037 1283 E6
800 KYVL 84037 1284 A6
N Kingswood Rd
900 KYVL 84037 1284 A6
1000 KYVL 84037 1283 E5
King Valley Dr
6200 WVCY 84128 2067 B1
King Valley Ln
4000 WVCY 84128 2067 C1
6100 WVCY 84128 1961 C7
King Valley Rd
6200 WVCY 84128 2067 B1
King Valley St
3900 WVCY 84128 1961 B7
3900 WVCY 84128 2067 B1
King Valley Wy
4000 WVCY 84128 2067 C1
Kinney Cir
11800 RIVN 84065 2281 E7
Kinsmen Cir
5200 SLkC 84118 2067 E4
Kintail Ct
5700 WVCY 84128 1961 D4
Kintail St
10 SRSP 84043 2710 A3
Kiowa Ct
5000 WVCY 84120 1962 A6
Kiowa Wy
5000 WVCY 84120 1962 A6
5100 WVCY 84120 1961 E6
Kipling Cir
7500 CDHT 84121 2178 C3
Kirby Ln
500 SPFK 84660 3142 D7
500 SPFK 84660 3249 D1
Kirk Av
400 LYTN 84041 1283 A3
Kirk Cir
3500 SLkC 84106 1965 D6
Kirk Pl
100 BMCY 84302 827 E2
Kirkcaldy Cir
4100 SJDN 84095 2280 C2
Kirkham Wy
1700 TYVL 84119 2069 C2
Kirkside Dr
3600 SJDN 84095 2280 D1
Kirkwall Cir
4000 SJDN 84095 2280 C2
Kirkwood Cir
8200 SNDY 84094 2177 B5
Kirkwood Pl
8200 SNDY 84094 2177 B5
Kirkwood Wy
1000 SNDY 84094 2177 B5
Kiska Ln
4900 SLkC 84117 2071 B4
Kit Cir
6900 WJDN 84084 2175 D2
Kit Carson Cir
600 CTRV 84014 1448 C7
Kittridge Dr
300 MDVL 84047 2176 E2
Kiwana Dr
4800 SOGN 84403 1172 E3
4800 SOGN 84403 1173 A3
Kiwi Cir
2200 TYVL 84118 2069 B5
Kline Av
2000 HLDY 84117 2071 E2
Klondyke Dr
- WJDN 84088 2173 D7
Klorissa Pl
7000 HRMN 84065 2385 A5
Klosters Cir
2200 SNDY 84093 2177 E6
Knaak Wy
200 PYSN 84651 3354 C5
Knight Cir
400 ALPN 84004 2498 B3
Knights Ct
800 OGDN 84401 1116 A3
Knights Wy
- KYVL 84037 1345 A2
1900 WJDN 84084 2175 C3
Knightsbridge Ln
10 SLCY 84103 1754 C7
Knights Bridge Rd
4500 TYVL 84119 2069 B2
Knob Hl
- SmtC 84098 1972 B1
Knollcrest St
400 MRRY 84107 2070 D5
Knoll Hollow Ln
13900 DRPR 84020 2389 C6
Knolls Ct
700 DRPR 84020 2388 E7
Knollwood Cir
11300 SNDY 84092 2283 C4
Knollwood Dr
1300 SNDY 84092 2283 B6
4800 OGDN 84403 1173 D3
Knowles Ln
300 LOGN 84321 527 A4
Knowley Rd
- WJDN 84088 2173 A4
Knowlton St
300 LYTN 84041 1283 A6
Knox Ct
10100 SJDN 84095 2280 B3
Knox Dr
4300 SJDN 84095 2280 B3
Knudsen Mill Cir
6900 CDHT 84121 2178 B2
Knudsen Ridge Cir
6900 CDHT 84121 2178 A2
Koa Dr
2000 PRVO 84601 2927 D6
Kodiak Ct
2200 DRPR 84020 2389 E1
Kodiak Wy
1300 SJDN 84095 2281 D1
Kodiak Creek Ct
1300 SJDN 84095 2281 D1
Kohala Dr
2900 HLDY 84117 2072 B4
Kohler Ln
700 MIDW 84049 2397 A2
900 MIDW 84049 2396 E2
Kokopelli Ct
6900 WJDN 84084 2173 D2
Kokopelli Dr
5600 WJDN 84084 2173 D2
Kolby Ln
8500 MDVL 84047 2176 B6
Kolob Cir
10 SGVL 84663 3143 D2
Kolton Rd
700 SJDN 84095 2282 A5
Komas Dr
500 SLCY 84108 1859 E5
Koneta Ct
500 SLCY 84102 1859 A4
Koradine Dr
1000 SJDN 84095 2281 E4
Kotter Ln
100 BxEC 84302 766 E2
100 BxEC 84302 767 A2
Kramer Cir
9900 SNDY 84092 2283 D2
Kramer Dr
2000 SNDY 84092 2283 D2
Kress Cir
400 SLCY 84116 1857 D2
Krista Ct
600 MRRY 84123 2176 A1
Kristedell Ct
1100 MRRY 84123 2069 E7
Kristianna Cir
1400 SLCY 84103 1859 C1
Kristian Pine Ln
6300 MRRY 84123 2176 A1
Kristie Ln
1300 SLCY 84108 1859 D7
Kristilyn Ln
7000 WJDN 84084 2174 A2
Kristin Dr
100 SNDY 84070 2282 D2
Kronborg Cir
2900 RIVN 84065 2387 A2
Ksel Cir
2700 SLkC 84092 2284 A1
Ksel Dr
2700 SLkC 84092 2284 A1
2900 SNDY 84093 2284 B1
9500 SNDY 84092 2284 A1
Kudu Ct
1700 DRPR 84020 2389 C3
Kuhni Rd
- SGVL 84663 3035 E6
2300 UthC 84606 3035 E5
Kwanzan Cir
400 OREM 84058 2820 C5
Kyle Dr
4500 SLkC 84118 2068 B6
Kylee Ln
900 OGDN 84404 1116 B1
Kyle Earl Ln
13700 HRMN 84065 2385 A5
Kylie Cove
5300 TYVL 84123 2069 D5

L

L St
- RVDL 84405 1172 B4
10 SLCY 84103 1859 A2
La Barranca Ct
7800 CDHT 84093 2177 E4
La Brea St
4900 SLkC 84118 2067 E4
Labrum Av
700 MRRY 84107 2176 E1
La Casa Cir
800 SNDY 84094 2283 A4
La Casa Dr
900 SNDY 84094 2283 A4
Lacey Wy
500 NSLK 84054 1653 C7
Laconia Ct
700 SLCY 84111 1858 D5
La Contessa Dr
1100 SLkC 84117 2071 B4
La Costa Ct
1500 DRPR 84020 2389 C1
La Cresta Dr
1900 CDHT 84121 2177 D1
Lacroix Dr
8400 SNDY 84070 2176 E5
Lacy Ln
800 MIDW 84049 2397 C1
La Dore Dr
700 SLkC 84107 2070 E2
700 SLkC 84107 2071 A2
Lady Dove Ln
3200 SJDN 84095 2280 E1
Lafayette Ct
11200 SNDY 84092 2283 C5
Lafayette Dr
600 SLCY 84116 1857 E1
700 SLCY 84116 1753 E7
Lafayette St
700 SNDY 84094 2282 E4
700 SNDY 84094 2283 A4
N Lagoon Dr
10 FMTN 84025 1448 C1
100 FMTN 84025 1346 B7
S Lagoon Dr
10 FMTN 84025 1448 C2
Lago Vista Cir
200 BNFL 84010 1654 B1
La Grange Wy
9000 SNDY 84093 2177 D7
Laguna Cir
8000 WJDN 84088 2175 B4
Laguna Dr
2300 WJDN 84088 2175 B4
Laguna Vista Cir
200 OREM 84058 2927 C3
Laguna Vista Dr
1800 OREM 84058 2927 C2
E La Har Dr
1700 SLkC 84106 1965 C5
Lahm Ln
500 DvsC 84056 1228 E5
Laily Ct
4800 SLkC 84117 2071 A3
Laine Av
2000 OGDN 84401 1116 A2
Laird Av
1500 SLCY 84105 1859 C6
1700 SLCY 84108 1859 C6
Laird Cir
1400 SLCY 84105 1859 C6
Laird Dr
1900 SLCY 84108 1859 D6
Laird Wy
2100 SLCY 84108 1859 E6
La Jolla
10700 CRHL 84062 2605 B1
La Joya Dr
2800 SLkC 84124 2072 B1
Lake Cir
700 SLkC 84106 1965 A5
E Lake Dr
4900 MRRY 84107 2071 A3
N Lake Dr
- LEHI 84043 2710 B2
Lake St
800 SLCY 84102 1858 E5
800 SLCY 84102 1859 A5
900 SLCY 84105 1859 A6
1300 OGDN 84401 1116 C4
1700 SLCY 84105 1965 A1
2100 SLCY 84106 1965 A2
2700 SLkC 84106 1965 A4
W Lake St
700 OGDN 84401 1115 B4
Lake Ter
1300 LEHI 84043 2603 E4
Lake Breeze Ln
4500 WVCY 84120 1962 B4
Lakecrest Dr
2500 WVCY 84119 1963 C3
Lakecrest Rd
1000 BNFL 84010 1654 C2
Lake Erie Dr
2600 WVCY 84120 1962 D4
Lake Fork Cir
6200 TYVL 84084 2069 A7
Lake Front Ct
1400 SmtC 84098 1971 E5
Lakeline Cir
2100 SLCY 84109 1966 B2
Lakeline Dr
1800 SLCY 84108 1966 B2
1800 SLkC 84108 1966 B2
2000 SLCY 84109 1966 B2
Lake Mary Dr
2900 CDHT 84121 2178 B3
Lake Meadow Dr
2900 WVCY 84120 1962 B5
Lake Mesa Dr
2000 SRCS 84075 1280 D1
Lake Park Blvd
2500 WVCY 84120 1962 C3
Lake Park Cir
2500 WVCY 84119 1963 C3
Lake Park Dr
1700 WVCY 84119 1963 C3
Lake Pines Dr
4900 MRRY 84107 2071 A3
Lake Placid Pl
6000 SLkC 84121 2071 E6
Lakepoint Dr
700 MRRY 84107 2070 D4
Laker Ct
300 SLCY 84102 1859 A4
E Laker Wy
100 WSTR 84405 1172 D3
W Laker Wy
100 WSTR 84405 1172 C3
500 RVDL 84405 1172 C3
Lake Ridge Dr
- KYVL 84037 1345 C5
Laker View Dr
700 SOGN 84403 1173 A1
Lakeshore Dr
600 PRVO 84601 2927 B5
N Lakeshore Dr
800 PRVO 84601 2927 B5
Lakeside Cir
- PKCY 84060 2079 A6
Lakeside Ct
- PKCY 84060 2079 A6
Lakeside Dr
- WbrC 84317 1060 C6
900 WbrC 84310 1059 E2
5700 MRRY 84121 2071 A6
Lakeside Ln
100 CTRV 84014 1551 D2
Lake Stone Cir
11700 SJDN 84095 2279 D7
Lakeview Cir
1600 OGDN 84403 1173 C1
3100 LYTN 84040 1284 A2
S Lakeview Cir
600 WDHL 84653 3463 D2
Lake View Ct
2300 PKCY 84060 2078 E1
Lakeview Ct
- WbrC 84310 1001 D3
Lake View Dr
300 LEHI 84043 2710 B3
Lakeview Dr
10 CRFD 84015 1227 D4
10 LYTN 84041 1228 E6
200 LYTN 84041 1229 A6
300 ALPN 84004 2497 D3
500 BNFL 84010 1654 B1
600 HRCY 84032 2398 E1
1200 PRVO 84604 2927 D4
2000 PKCY 84060 2078 E2
2100 LEHI 84043 2710 A3
2100 SRSP 84043 2710 A3
2300 SLkC 84109 1965 E4
2700 SLkC 84109 1966 A4
3500 NHON 84414 998 E3
4000 OGDN 84403 1173 D1
4200 CRHL 84062 2605 B3
E Lake View Dr
300 EKMT 84651 3463 A3
E Lakeview Dr
100 CRFD 84015 1227 D4
N Lakeview Dr
10 CRFD 84015 1227 E4
S Lakeview Dr
10 CRFD 84015 1227 D4
Lakeview Hts
200 CRFD 84015 1281 E1
W Lakeview Rd
10 LNDN 84042 2713 A6
400 LNDN 84042 2712 E6
Lakeview St
200 BMCY 84302 827 E1
Lakeview Wy
400 FMTN 84025 1448 E3
1500 OGDN 84403 1173 C3
E Lakeview Wy
10 WDHL 84653 3463 D2
400 FMTN 84025 1448 E3
W Lakeview Wy
10 WDHL 84653 3463 D2
Lakewood Cir
1300 MRRY 84117 2071 A5
Lakewood Dr
100 OREM 84058 2927 C2
300 PRVO 84601 3035 B3
1400 SLkC 84117 2071 C5
La Mancha Wy
3200 TYVL 84118 2068 E4
Lamar Cir
900 ALPN 84004 2498 B3
Lamarne St
600 SLCY 84116 1857 E1
Lamasa Cir
11000 SNDY 84092 2283 B5
Lamayrun St
3100 SLkC 84044 1960 A5
Lambert Av
- SNQN 84655 3461 B7
3200 PRRY 84302 827 B7
Lambert Dr
500 OREM 84097 2820 E6
500 OREM 84097 2821 A6
Lambert Ln
1600 PRVO 84604 2928 D3
Lambert Wy
500 KYVL 84037 1345 E2
Lambeth Cir
5100 TYVL 84118 2069 C4
Lambeth St
5000 TYVL 84118 2069 C4
Lambourne Av
400 SSLK 84115 1964 D5
1800 SLkC 84106 1965 D5
2000 SLkC 84109 1965 D5
2300 SLkC 84109 1966 A5
S Lambourne Cir
3100 SLkC 84109 1966 A5
Lame Dog Wy
- PKCY 84060 2078 C4
S La Mesa Rd
3300 SLkC 84109 1966 C5
La Montagne Ln
10 SLkC 84092 2284 C2
Lamplight Ln
3500 SLkC 84044 1960 A6
Lamplighter Dr
1000 LOGN 84321 528 B3
Lamplighter Wy
3900 RVDL 84405 1115 C6
Lampton Cir
9700 SJDN 84095 2281 E2
Lampton Rd
1000 SJDN 84095 2281 D2
Lampton Cove
11900 RIVN 84065 2281 E7
Lampton View Cir
1000 RIVN 84065 2281 E7
Lampton View Dr
11400 SJDN 84095 2281 E6
11700 RIVN 84065 2281 E6
12100 RIVN 84065 2387 E1
Lamus Cir
6100 WVCY 84128 2067 C1
Lana Ct
400 DRPR 84020 2388 E7
Lanark Rd
4600 SLkC 84124 2072 C3
Lancashire Cir
3600 WVCY 84119 1963 D7
Lancaster Cir
1400 SNDY 84092 2283 C5
Lancaster Dr
2700 SLCY 84108 1860 B7
Lancaster Wy
1300 OREM 84097 2821 B2
Lance Cir
2800 CSTN 84032 2504 D3
Lance St
3900 WVCY 84119 1962 E7
3900 WVCY 84119 1963 A7
8100 MDVL 84047 2176 A5
Lancelot Cir
200 NSLK 84054 1653 B5
Lancelot Dr
500 NSLK 84054 1653 B5
1300 PRVO 84601 2927 E5
1300 WVCY 84119 1963 D6
Land Dr
3500 WVCY 84119 1962 D4
Landau Ln
2400 SJDN 84095 2281 B2
Landen Cir
3800 WVCY 84120 1962 C4
Lander Wy
4300 SLkC 84118 2068 B6
Landmark Cir
4500 CRHL 84062 2605 A3
Landmark Dr
6400 SmtC 84098 1971 D1
Landou Dr
11800 DRPR 84020 2282 C7
Landover Cir
8700 SNDY 84093 2177 E6
Land Rush Dr
500 MDVL 84047 2176 E2
Land Rush Pl
7000 MDVL 84047 2176 E2
Lands End Rd
900 FMTN 84025 1346 A4
Lane Cir
300 SNDY 84070 2282 D2
Lanebrook Cir
1500 SLkC 84124 1965 C7
Lanebrook Ln
1500 SLkC 84124 1965 C7
Laneview Ct
4300 SLkC 84108 1860 E4
Laney Av
2200 HLDY 84117 2071 E3
Laney's Wy
500 DRPR 84020 2388 E7
Langdale Cir
1600 CDHT 84093 2177 C4
Langford Ln
10800 SJDN 84095 2282 B5
Lankshire Dr
10 PTVW 84414 998 D5
Lannae Dr
1200 SNDY 84094 2283 B2
Lantana Dr
8800 WJDN 84088 2174 E6
Lantern Ln
1400 DRPR 84020 2389 C6
Lantern Hill Ct
3200 CDHT 84093 2178 B5
Lapis Dr
14300 DRPR 84020 2388 E6
La Quinta
- CRHL 84062 2605 C1
La Quinta Pl
12100 DRPR 84020 2389 D1
Larabrook Wy
6600 WJDN 84084 2174 E1
Larch Ln
- DvsC 84056 1228 A1
Larch Wy
4400 TYVL 84123 2069 C2
Larchmont Dr
3300 SLkC 84109 1966 C4
Larchmont Wy
1200 LYTN 84041 1282 C7
Larchwood Dr
300 MDVL 84047 2176 E1
Laredo Cir
4900 WVCY 84120 2068 A1
Laredo Wy
4000 WVCY 84120 2068 A1
Laree St
2900 WVCY 84120 1962 C4
Lares Cir
4200 SLkC 84124 2072 E1
Lares Wy
3800 SLkC 84124 2072 D1
Lariat Cir
9000 SmtC 84098 1864 E4
Lariat Dr
4800 WVCY 84120 1962 A7
Lariat Rd
3500 SmtC 84098 1865 A3
3700 SmtC 84098 1864 E4
La Rieta Dr
5700 HRMN 84065 2385 D4
Larissa Ln
2300 RIVN 84065 2387 B2
Lark Cir
1300 OGDN 84403 1116 C7
Lark Ln
- WPT 84015 1225 D4
W Lark Rd
400 SNQN 84655 3460 C7
6000 UthC 84655 3460 B6
6600 GNLA 84655 3460 B6
Lark St
- UthC 84655 3460 C6
Lark Wy
4900 WVCY 84120 2068 A1
Larkin Wy
3200 WVCY 84120 1962 A5
Larkin's Ln
100 KYVL 84037 1345 C2
Lark Meadow Cove
7600 SNDY 84047 2176 E3
Larkspur Cir
10300 SLkC 84094 2283 A3
Larkspur Dr
200 LOGN 84321 527 E4
700 SLkC 84094 2282 E3
700 SLkC 84094 2283 A3
1100 WDCR 84087 1653 A3
2500 PKCY 84060 2078 E1
Larkspur Ln
4900 OGDN 84403 1173 D3
Larkwood St
4300 SLkC 84107 2070 E2
La Rosa Ct
6900 CDHT 84121 2177 C2
Larry Cir
3600 WVCY 84120 2068 D1
Larsen Dr
500 BNFL 84010 1653 E1
500 BNFL 84010 1654 A1
Larsen Ln
100 HARR 84404 1056 D3
Larsen Pkwy
2000 PRVO 84606 3036 A4
Larsen Rd
- UthC 84660 3248 E3
- UthC 84660 3249 A3
Larsen St
- PRRY 84302 827 C5
Larson Ln
200 LYTN 84041 1282 E6
Larson Wy
4300 HLDY 84124 2071 D1
La Rue Ln
2900 SLkC 84106 1965 D4
Lasalle Cir
6000 MRRY 84123 2070 A7
La Salle Dr
500 MRRY 84123 2070 A7
W La Salle Dr
300 MDVL 84047 2176 B5
Las Flores St
3900 WVCY 84119 1962 E7
Lasso Ct
14100 DRPR 84020 2389 C6
Lasso Loop Cir
3600 SLkC 84044 1960 C6
Last Chance Cove
11800 HRMN 84065 2280 B7
La Strada Cir
2800 RIVN 84065 2387 A2
La Strada Wy
2700 RIVN 84065 2387 A2
3000 RIVN 84065 2386 E2
Last Run Dr
3800 SmtC 84098 1971 E7
Last Stand Dr
- SmtC 84098 1972 A5
La Sue Sue St
3500 WVCY 84119 1963 E5
Latigo Cir
3900 WVCY 84128 1961 A7
E Latigo Dr
10 SGVL 84663 3143 C7
Latimer Dr
3900 WVCY 84120 1962 B7
3900 WVCY 84120 2068 B1
Latimer View Ct
1800 SLkC 84106 1965 D4
Latitude Ln
1500 WJDN 84084 2175 C2
La Tour Cir
2000 HLDY 84121 2071 D6
La Tour St
5900 HLDY 84121 2071 D6
Launa St
7300 MDVL 84047 2176 E3
Laura Dr
100 KYVL 84037 1345 D3
4900 MRRY 84107 2071 A3
Laura Anne Wy
9100 SNDY 84094 2177 A7
Lauralin Dr
200 LOGN 84321 528 B2
Laura Ln Dr
2800 SNDY 84092 2284 B2
Laurel Cir
3600 SLkC 84109 1966 A6
Laurel Dr
400 SNDY 84070 2176 D7
Laurel St
10 SLCY 84103 1859 B3
1400 OGDN 84403 1116 C5
Laurel Bluff Cove
15200 DRPR 84020 2496 D2
Laurel Canyon Dr
5800 WVCY 84118 2173 C1
6200 WVCY 84118 2067 C7
Laurel Chase Cir
1500 RIVN 84065 2387 C1
Laurel Chase Dr
12000 RIVN 84065 2281 D7
12000 RIVN 84065 2387 D2
Laurelcrest St
3600 SLkC 84109 1966 C7
S Laurel Green Dr
4100 WVCY 84120 2068 C1
Laurel Hill Cir
5300 WJDN 84084 2173 E3
Laurelhurst Dr
1700 SLCY 84108 1966 A1
Laurel Oak Dr
8400 WJDN 84088 2173 B6
Laurel Oaks Ct
14900 DRPR 84020 2496 D1
Laurel Park Ln
13100 DRPR 84020 2389 D3
Laurel Ridge Cir
9300 WJDN 84088 2280 C1
Laurel Ridge Dr
4000 WJDN 84088 2280 C1
Laurelwood Cir
1800 SLkC 84121 2071 D6
Laurelwood Dr
- FRWT 84404 1055 C3
- PRVO 84601 3035 B2
400 KYVL 84037 1345 E2
1000 FTHT 84037 1346 A2
Laurelwood St
5600 SLkC 84121 2071 D6
Lauri Kay Dr
2200 HLDY 84124 2071 E2
Lauritzen Dr
6200 TYVL 84084 2069 B7
Lavell Ln
3000 SSLK 84106 1964 E5
Laver Ct
2100 SNDY 84092 2283 E2
Laver Dr
3700 SLkC 84109 1966 A7
Laver St
2100 SNDY 84092 2283 E2
La Vera Ln
300 SNDY 84070 2282 D6
La Verde St
700 LYTN 84041 1282 E3
Lavina Dr
500 SOGN 84403 1172 E2
600 SOGN 84403 1173 A2
La Vista Dr
10 WJDN 84088 2175 B5
Lavon Cir
1200 SLkC 84106 1965 B6
Lavon Dr
1200 SLkC 84106 1965 B6
Law Cir
4200 SLkC 84118 2068 C3
Law Ct
10 LOGN 84321 527 D3
Law Dr
800 BMCY 84302 827 D1
Law Creek Cir
3300 RIVN 84065 2280 E7
Lawndale Dr
300 SSLK 84115 1964 B3
Lawrence Cir
1700 SJDN 84095 2281 B1
Laxon Ct
100 SLCY 84116 1857 E2
Layne Dr
100 MDVL 84047 2176 D3
Laytham Wy
2900 WJDN 84088 2175 A7
3000 WJDN 84088 2174 E7
Layton Av
10 SLCY 84115 1964 C1
700 SLCY 84104 1964 A1
Layton Cir
10 LYTN 84041 1282 E4
Laytona Dr
1000 LYTN 84041 1282 C2
Layton Hills Pkwy
1400 LYTN 84041 1282 D1
Layton Ridge Dr
- LYTN 84040 1230 B5
Lazon Cir
9100 SNDY 84094 2177 A7
Lazon Dr
700 SNDY 84094 2176 E7
700 SNDY 84094 2177 A7
Lazy Bar Cir
6700 CDHT 84121 2177 E1
Lazy Creek Cove
13000 SLkC 84065 2385 B3
Lazy River Dr
1100 WJDN 84084 2175 E1
Leadville Av
1300 SLCY 84116 1857 D1
Leaf Wing Ln
- RIVN 84065 2386 A4
Leafwood Ln
700 SNDY 84094 2176 C7
Leah Day Cove
400 DRPR 84020 2388 E6
Learned Av
1000 SLCY 84104 1857 E3
Leatherwood Cir
9700 SJDN 84095 2280 E2
E Le Banke Av
100 SSLK 84115 1964 D5
Lebon Cir
600 PRVO 84601 3035 B1
Le Chateau Wy
5400 SLkC 84118 2067 D5
Le Corbusier Cir
3700 SLkC 84106 1965 D7
Ledgemont Dr
4500 SLkC 84124 2072 C3
Ledgewood Cir
2000 TYVL 84084 2069 B7
Ledgewood Dr
2200 TYVL 84084 2069 B7
2400 TYVL 84084 2175 A1
Lee Ln
10 SNDY 84070 2282 D4
Lee Ann St
3200 WVCY 84119 1962 E5
Leeds Ct
- NSLK 84054 1652 C5
Leeds Cove
3400 WVCY 84128 1961 A6
Lee Maur St
3600 WVCY 84119 1963 A7

Salt Lake City Street Index

STREET Block City ZIP Map# Grid

Lee Wy Cir
2000 SLkC 84109 1965 D4
Legacy Dr
2300 NHON 84414 999 A6
Legacy Cove
10200 SJDN 84095 2282 A3
Legacy Hill Dr
5200 WJDN 84084 2173 E3
Legacy Park Ln
2800 SNDY 84093 2178 B7
Legacy Point Dr
- RIVN 84065 2386 A2
Legacy Ranch Blvd
- HRMN 84065 2386 B1
- RIVN 84065 2386 B1
Legacy Springs Dr
4800 RIVN 84065 2386 A2
Legacy View St
1200 SLCY 84104 1855 D6
Legend Ln
10 SNDY 84092 2283 E5
Legend Hills Dr
1300 CRFD 84015 1228 C7
1400 CRFD 84041 1228 C7
1400 LYTN 84015 1228 C7
1400 LYTN 84041 1228 C7
Legrand
100 LOGN 84321 527 D6
Le Grand St
800 SLCY 84108 1859 D6
S Lehi Dr
3100 WVCY 84119 1963 A5
W Lehi Dr
2800 WVCY 84119 1963 A5
3000 WVCY 84119 1962 E5
Lehman Av
2800 WVCY 84119 1963 A6
3000 WVCY 84119 1962 E6
Lehua Ln
3000 HLDY 84117 2072 B4
Leicester Bay
3800 SJDN 84095 2280 D2
Leichen Av
5900 WJDN 84084 2173 C1
Leichen Ct
5500 WJDN 84084 2173 B1
Leila Ln
4900 HRMN 84065 2386 A6
5100 HRMN 84065 2385 E6
Leilani Cir
600 SNDY 84070 2282 E3
Leilani Dr
10200 SNDY 84070 2282 E4
Leisure Cir
1900 TYVL 84118 2069 C4
2700 WJDN 84084 2175 A3
Leisure Ln
1800 TYVL 84118 2069 C4
Leland Av
500 SSLK 84106 1964 E5
Leland Ct
4400 TYVL 84119 2069 B2
Leland Dr
1500 WJDN 84084 2175 C3
Leland Cove
3000 SSLK 84106 1964 E5
Lemans Dr
4300 SLkC 84124 2071 A2
Lemar Wy
4800 WVCY 84120 1962 A5
5000 WVCY 84120 1961 E4
Lemay Av
2700 WVCY 84119 1963 A6
3000 WVCY 84119 1962 E6
Lemel Cir
2700 SSLK 84115 1964 B4
Lemmon Ln
3800 SLkC 84106 1965 C7
Lemon Ln
- RVDL 84405 1172 A5
1400 DvsC 84056 1172 A7
1400 DvsC 84056 1228 A1
Lemonwood Cir
4600 WVCY 84120 2067 E3
Lemonwood St
5200 WVCY 84120 2067 E2
N Lena Cir
12000 BxEC 84337 521 D3
Lena Dr
8000 WJDN 84088 2174 B4
Lennox Cir
9400 SJDN 84095 2280 B1
Lennox Dr
4300 SJDN 84095 2280 B1
4300 WJDN 84088 2280 B1
Lennox Ln
2100 SRSP 84043 2710 A3
Lennox St
600 MDVL 84047 2176 A4
Lenora Cir
7000 CDHT 84121 2177 D2
Lenora Joe Cove
200 MDVL 84047 2176 C1
200 MDVL 84107 2176 C1
200 MRRY 84107 2176 C1
Leo Wy
4400 HLDY 84117 2072 B2
Leon Av
2900 WVCY 84119 1963 A6
Leona Dr
500 SOGN 84403 1115 E7
Leona Ln
500 SLkC 84107 2070 E1
Leonard Cir
2000 SNDY 84093 2177 D5
Leonard Dr
- WbrC 84310 1001 C4
Leonard Ln
600 FMTN 84025 1346 B5
Leonardo Ln
1500 WVCY 84119 1963 C6
Leonidas Dr
3300 SLkC 84044 1960 A5
Leo Park Rd
5400 WJDN 84088 2279 E1
Le Page St
7700 MDVL 84047 2176 A4
Leprechaun Ln
5100 SLkC 84118 2067 E4
Le Rosier Ct
1100 WJDN 84088 2281 D1
Lerwill Av
700 TYVL 84123 2070 A3
Leslie Av
100 SSLK 84115 1964 D3
Leslie Cir
1600 PTGV 84062 2605 B7
Leslie Dr
8000 WJDN 84088 2174 D5
W Lester Av
10 MDVL 84047 2176 C1
10 MDVL 84107 2176 C1
10 MRRY 84107 2176 C1
Lester Dr
1200 SWBR 84405 1229 B2
3200 WVCY 84119 1963 C5
Lester St
2500 WVCY 84119 1963 D4
Leticia Ct
5300 WJDN 84084 2173 E2
Level Dr
2400 TYVL 84118 2069 A4
Levoy Dr
800 TYVL 84123 2070 A2
900 TYVL 84123 2069 E2
Lewis Dr
1200 OGDN 84404 1057 C5
Lewis St
- SLCY 84113 1859 D3
E Lewis Wy
500 EKMT 84651 3463 A2
Lewis & Clark Cir
600 CTRV 84014 1448 C7
Lewis & Clark Dr
500 CTRV 84014 1448 C7
Lewis Acres Ct
5000 WVCY 84120 2068 A1
Lewis-Clark Cir
5000 SLkC 84118 2067 E4
Lewis Clark Dr
5000 SLkC 84118 2067 E4
Lewis Park Cir
100 BNFL 84010 1653 E4
Lewis Park Dr
200 BNFL 84010 1653 E4
Lewis Peak Dr
1000 OGDN 84404 1057 B2
N Lewis Peak Dr
1200 OGDN 84404 1057 B2
Lewisport Dr
3700 WJDN 84084 2068 D7
Lewiston Cir
3200 SJDN 84095 2280 E4
Lewiston Peak Cir
5200 RIVN 84065 2385 E6
Lewiston Peak Dr
- HRMN 84065 2385 E6
14000 RIVN 84065 2385 E6
Lexann Cir
9200 SNDY 84093 2177 E7
Lexington Av
1100 SLCY 84104 1857 E6
Lexington Cir
2400 HLDY 84124 1966 A7
11000 SNDY 84092 2283 C5
Lexington Dr
1300 SNDY 84092 2283 B5
2000 WJDN 84084 2175 B1
3400 BNFL 84010 1653 E5
Lexington Wy
3100 CRFD 84015 1228 B5
Lexington Hills Cir
11500 SNDY 84092 2283 D6
Lexington Hills Dr
2000 SNDY 84092 2283 D6
Lexington View Dr
3300 WJDN 84088 2174 E4
Lexs Ln
700 PVDN 84332 528 B6
Libby Wy
900 SLCY 84116 1753 C7
Liberty Av
100 LYTN 84041 1282 E5
100 OGDN 84404 1057 A5
700 SLCY 84105 1858 E6
700 SLCY 84105 1859 A6
1300 OGDN 84404 1116 A1
2000 OGDN 84401 1116 A2
2700 OGDN 84403 1116 A5
4100 SOGN 84403 1173 A1
N Liberty Av
1100 OGDN 84404 1057 A2
Liberty Cir
600 PRRY 84302 827 D5
W Liberty Dr
1700 WVCY 84119 1963 C5
Liberty Hts
- SNDY 84094 2177 B5
Liberty Rd
200 NSLK 84054 1653 C7
Liberty St
4200 DvsC 84056 1228 A4
Liberty Wy
3100 CRFD 84015 1228 B5
Liberty Creek Dr
4000 SJDN 84095 2280 C1
Liberty Hill Ct
12500 HRMN 84065 2385 C2
Liberty Oaks Cove
6000 MRRY 84107 2070 C7
Liberty Ridge Cir
9400 SJDN 84095 2280 C1
E Liddle Ct
500 PYSN 84651 3355 A7
Liesel St
7200 WJDN 84084 2175 D3
Lieutenant Rd
1900 SLCY 84116 1753 B6
Lighthouse Rd
5400 TYVL 84123 2069 C5
Lightning Peak Cir
5300 RIVN 84065 2385 E4
Lightning Peak Dr
5300 HRMN 84065 2385 E6
5300 RIVN 84065 2385 E6
Lilac Av
5400 WJDN 84084 2067 D7
N Lilac Av
5300 WJDN 84084 2067 E7
W Lilac Dr
6200 WJDN 84084 2067 E7
Liljay Cir
1600 SLCY 84104 1857 C6
Lillehammer Cir
3400 TYVL 84084 2174 B1
Lillehammer Ln
5400 SmtC 84098 1971 D3
Lillian Cir
100 BNFL 84010 1552 B7
Lillie Cir
1200 MRRY 84121 2071 B6
Lilloet St
3500 WVCY 84120 1962 A6
Lillyvale Pl
5900 WJDN 84084 2173 C1
Lillyview Ln
- WJDN 84084 2173 C1
Lillywood Dr
900 NSLK 84054 1653 C6
Lily Dr
4000 ROY 84067 1171 B1
Lily Garden Ct
9600 SJDN 84095 2280 E2
Lily Garden Ln
3400 SJDN 84095 2280 D1
Lily Langtree Ct
2400 PKCY 84060 2079 A3
Lilypad Bay
900 DRPR 84020 2283 A7
Lime Ln
6700 WJDN 84084 2173 E1
Lime Canyon Rd
- MIDW 84049 2290 D7
- MIDW 84049 2396 D1
- WshC 84049 2290 D7
- WshC 84049 2396 D1
700 MIDW 84049 2397 A1
Lime Canyon Wy
1100 MIDW 84049 2396 E1
1100 WshC 84049 2396 E1
Limestone Cir
9500 SJDN 84095 2280 E1
Limousine Ct
- FMTN 84025 1447 E1
Lincoln Av
10 ANFK 84003 2711 B1
500 OGDN 84404 1056 D6
1300 OGDN 84404 1115 D2
1800 OGDN 84401 1115 D2
3600 SOGN 84405 1115 D7
Lincoln Cir
2000 HLDY 84124 2071 D1
2900 SLCY 84106 1965 A4
4300 DvsC 84056 1228 A4
Lincoln Ct
4000 HLDY 84124 2071 E1
Lincoln Dr
2700 SJDN 84095 2281 A2
Lincoln Ln
1000 SmtC 84098 1972 A2
1700 HLDY 84124 2071 D1
2300 HLDY 84124 2072 A1
2500 SLkC 84124 2072 A1
7600 SWBR 84405 1230 B3
Lincoln Pl
500 MRRY 84107 2070 E3
Lincoln St
100 SLCY 84102 1859 A3
900 SLCY 84105 1859 A6
1800 SLCY 84105 1965 A2
2100 SLCY 84106 1965 A2
3000 SLkC 84106 1965 A5
4800 MRRY 84107 2070 E3
7600 MDVL 84047 2176 B4
Lincoln Cove
2800 SJDN 84095 2281 A2
Lincoln Park Dr
4200 TYVL 84123 2069 C1
S Lincolnshire Wy
- KYVL 84037 1344 E2
Linda Cir
3000 SLkC 84109 1966 A5
Linda Wy
200 BMCY 84302 827 E2
2200 PRRY 84302 827 C4
Linda Loma Dr
200 CTRV 84014 1551 E2
Linda Marie Ln
1400 RIVN 84065 2387 D4
Linda Rosa Av
1300 SLkC 84106 1965 B7
Linda Vista Dr
1000 WVCY 84119 1963 E6
Lindell Av
300 SNDY 84070 2176 D6
Linden Av
700 SLCY 84102 1858 E4
700 SLCY 84102 1859 A4
Linden Cir
1600 BNFL 84010 1551 D5
2000 HLDY 84121 2071 D6
Linden Ln
1300 DvsC 84056 1228 A2
1600 BNFL 84010 1551 D5
Linden St
100 CRFD 84015 1227 E5
3100 BNFL 84010 1653 D5
Linden Wy
5900 HLDY 84121 2071 E6
Linden Hill Ln
10 DRPR 84020 2495 C1
Lindfield Cir
8900 SNDY 84093 2178 A7
Lindi Wy
1200 LYTN 84041 1281 E2
Lindon Dr
700 BMCY 84302 767 A4
Lindon Rd
11000 SNDY 84092 2283 B5
Lindon St
5600 MRRY 84107 2070 D6
Lindon Wy
100 MRRY 84107 2070 D6
Lindon Park Cir
300 LNDN 84042 2712 E7
Lindon Park Dr
400 LNDN 84042 2712 E7
400 LNDN 84042 2819 E1
Lindsay Dr
1900 TYVL 84119 2069 C1
Lindsay St
400 LYTN 84041 1283 A4
Lindsay Grove Ct
1300 DRPR 84020 2389 B4
Lindsay Marie Cir
1500 RIVN 84065 2281 D7
Lindsay Wood Ln
2300 SNDY 84092 2283 E4
Lineage Ln
1500 TYVL 84123 2069 C6
Linger Ln
9200 SmtC 84098 1867 B3
Links Dr
4400 WVCY 84120 1962 C3
Links Wy
1300 FMTN 84025 1346 C5
Linton Cir
3000 WJDN 84088 2175 A4
Linton Dr
3000 WJDN 84088 2174 E4
3000 WJDN 84088 2175 A4
Lion Ln
3100 HLDY 84121 2178 B1
Lionel St
200 NSLK 84054 1653 A4
6100 WJDN 84084 2173 C1
Lionheart Wy
3500 WVCY 84119 1963 D6
Lipman Cir
11400 SNDY 84092 2283 C6
Lipman Dr
1600 SNDY 84092 2283 C6
Lisa Av
9000 WJDN 84088 2175 B7
Lisa Dr
4000 SLkC 84124 1966 C7
4000 SLkC 84124 2072 B1
Lisa St
300 PTVW 84404 998 A6
Lisa Hills Cove
900 MRRY 84123 2069 E6
Lisa Ray Cir
200 MRRY 84107 2176 C1
Lisashire Ln
2400 TYVL 84118 2069 B5
Lishawn Dr
3800 TYVL 84118 2068 C6
Lismore Ln
7900 WJDN 84088 2174 C4
Lisonbee Av
700 SLkC 84106 1964 E5
700 SLkC 84106 1965 A5
Liston Cir
600 KYVL 84037 1283 E7
Litson Cir
700 MRRY 84107 2070 E7
Little Cir
7100 WJDN 84084 2175 B2
Little Ln
1200 WVCY 84119 1963 D7
Little Belle Ct
7100 PKCY 84060 2184 E2
Little Bessie Av
2100 PKCY 84060 2078 E3
Littlecloud Cir
2100 SNDY 84093 2177 E6
Littlecloud Rd
8600 SNDY 84093 2177 E6
Little Cottonwood Ln
3500 SLkC 84092 2284 D2
Little Cottonwood Pl
9700 SLkC 84092 2284 D2
N Little Cottonwood Rd
3600 SLkC 84092 2284 D1
3600 SLkC 84121 2284 D1
N Little Cottonwood Rd SR-210
3800 SLkC 84092 2284 D1
3800 SLkC 84121 2284 D1
S Little Cottonwood Rd
2400 SNDY 84092 2284 A1
2700 SLkC 84092 2284 A1
3100 SNDY 84093 2284 A1
9400 SNDY 84092 2283 E1
9400 SNDY 84093 2283 E1
S Little Cottonwood Rd SR-209
2400 SNDY 84092 2284 A1
2700 SLkC 84092 2284 A1
3100 SNDY 84093 2284 A1
9400 SNDY 84092 2283 E1
9400 SNDY 84093 2283 E1
Little Cottonwood Canyon Rd
- ALTA 84049 2181 C7
- ALTA 84049 2182 A6
- SLkC 84049 2181 C7
- SLkC 84049 2287 A1
- SLkC 84092 2284 E2
- SLkC 84121 2284 E2
8900 CDHT 84093 2178 D7
8900 CDHT 84121 2178 D7
9000 CDHT 84092 2178 D7
9000 SLkC 84092 2178 D7
9000 SLkC 84121 2178 D7
Little Cottonwd Cyn Rd SR-210
- ALTA 84049 2181 C7
- ALTA 84049 2182 A6
- SLkC 84049 2181 C7
- SLkC 84049 2287 A1
- SLkC 84092 2284 E2
- SLkC 84121 2284 E2
8900 CDHT 84093 2178 D7
8900 CDHT 84121 2178 D7
9000 CDHT 84092 2178 D7
9000 SLkC 84092 2178 D7
9000 SLkC 84121 2178 D7
Little Creek Dr
1300 WJDN 84088 2175 D7
Little Farm Ln
3400 SLkC 84109 1966 A6
Little Kate Rd
700 PKCY 84060 2078 D2
Little Kay Cir
200 SNDY 84070 2282 D1
Little Lake Dr
1500 SmtC 84098 1971 E5
Little Matterhorn Dr
700 TYVL 84123 2070 A2
Little Mountain Dr
800 TYVL 84123 2070 A2
Littler Cir
1300 SNDY 84092 2283 B7
Littler Rd
11600 SNDY 84092 2283 B7
Little River Wy
800 SSLK 84119 1964 A7
900 SSLK 84119 1963 E7
Littlerock Ct
3800 PRVO 84604 2821 E6
Little Rock Dr
3500 PRVO 84604 2821 E7
Littlerock Ln
3600 PRVO 84604 2821 E7
Little Rock Ter
3600 PRVO 84604 2821 E7
Little Sweden Rd
10 WshC 84032 2505 D2
Little Valley Rd
800 SLCY 84103 1755 A7
1100 FMTN 84010 1448 E3
1100 FMTN 84025 1448 E3
Little Water Peak Cir
13800 RIVN 84065 2385 E5
Little Water Peak Dr
4900 RIVN 84065 2386 A5
5100 RIVN 84065 2385 E5
5200 HRMN 84065 2385 E5
Little Willow Cir
3400 CDHT 84121 2178 C6
Little Willow Cove
- MPTN 84664 3250 E1
Littlewood Cir
8500 SNDY 84094 2177 A6
Live Oak Cir
2800 HLDY 84117 2072 B2
Livingston Av
1700 SLCY 84116 1753 C7
Liza Ln
- WJDN 84084 2173 B1
Lizette Cir
700 FMTN 84025 1448 D3
Lizzi Cove
2700 SJDN 84095 2281 A6
Lloyd Ln
10 WshC 84032 2398 D1
1000 RIVN 84065 2387 D3
Lloyd Rd
- FMTN 84025 1346 A4
- FMTN 84037 1346 A4
800 FTHT 84037 1346 A4
Lloydene Av
2500 ROY 84067 1171 B5
Loader Dr
200 PTGV 84062 2713 A3
Loafer Dr
- WDHL 84653 3463 C4
E Loafer Dr
10 WDHL 84653 3463 C3
N Loafer Dr
300 EKMT 84651 3463 B2
S Loafer Dr
10 WDHL 84653 3463 C3
W Loafer Dr
10 WDHL 84653 3463 C3
N Loafer Canyon Rd
10 EKMT 84651 3463 B2
S Loafer Canyon Rd
200 EKMT 84651 3463 B3
900 SALM 84653 3356 A6
10700 UthC 84651 3356 B7
11400 UthC 84651 3463 B1
E Loafer View Dr
1200 PYSN 84651 3355 C6
S Loafer View Dr
200 PYSN 84651 3355 B5
Lobelia Dr
6200 WJDN 84084 2068 A7
Loch Awe Dr
9400 SJDN 84095 2280 B1
Loch Hawkins Dr
- MRRY 84123 2069 D6
Loch Lomond Dr
1600 LYTN 84040 1283 D1
2100 SRSP 84043 2710 A3
Loch Lomond Wy
1000 SLkC 84117 2071 C3
Lochmor
10600 CRHL 84062 2605 B1
Loch Ness Av
6900 WVCY 84128 1961 A6
7000 WVCY 84128 1960 E6
Loch Raven Ct
5700 WVCY 84128 1961 D4
Lochshire Cir
4200 SJDN 84095 2280 C1
Lockhart Rd
2500 HLDY 84117 2072 A3
Locksley Cir
1500 SNDY 84092 2283 C3
Locksley Rd
10100 SNDY 84092 2283 C3
Lockwood Dr
400 OGDN 84404 1056 E2
500 OGDN 84404 1057 A2
4900 WVCY 84120 2067 D1
N Locust Av
400 LNDN 84042 2713 A5
S Locust Av
200 PTGV 84062 2712 E3
500 PTGV 84062 2713 A4
Locust Cir
1100 PRVO 84604 2928 E4
Locust Grv
600 LEHI 84043 2603 D6
Locust Ln
- LEHI 84043 2603 D5
1100 PRVO 84604 2928 E4
2100 DvsC 84056 1172 A7
4600 HLDY 84117 2071 E2
Locust St
10 CRFD 84015 1227 E4
300 SNDY 84070 2176 E6
7300 MDVL 84047 2176 B3
Locust Ridge Ct
10200 SJDN 84095 2280 C3
Lodder Dr
700 KYVL 84037 1345 B2
Loder Dr
5900 SLkC 84118 2067 E6
Lodestone Av
5500 SLkC 84118 2067 D6
Lodestone Cir
5600 SLkC 84118 2067 B7
Lodgepole Dr
1100 SNDY 84094 2177 B4
Lofgreen Av
3200 PRVO 84604 2821 D7
3200 PRVO 84604 2928 D1
Lofty Ln
200 NSLK 84054 1754 B1
Logan Av
300 SLCY 84115 1964 D1
700 SLCY 84105 1964 E1
1000 SLCY 84105 1965 A1
1900 SLCY 84108 1965 D1
2200 SLCY 84108 1859 E7
Logan Cir
2300 SLCY 84108 1965 D1
Logan Wy
2300 SLCY 84108 1965 E1
2300 SLCY 84108 1966 A1
Loganberry Ct
11400 DRPR 84020 2282 D6
Logan Canyon Rd
10600 SJDN 84095 2280 E4
Logan Falls Ln
14300 HRMN 84065 2385 E6
Logans Run Cove
11800 HRMN 84065 2280 A7
Lois Cir
700 MDVL 84047 2176 E3
Lois Ln
3600 SLkC 84124 2072 D1
3700 SLkC 84124 1966 D7
Lois Meadows Ct
1600 BFDL 84065 2387 C6
Lola Cir
10 SNDY 84070 2176 C6
3000 SLkC 84109 1966 A5
Lolene Cir
2500 TYVL 84118 2069 B5
Lolene Wy
5500 TYVL 84118 2069 B5
Loma Ln
200 SLCY 84103 1858 C2
Loma Wy
1300 SNDY 84092 2283 B5
Lombardy Cir
1400 MRRY 84121 2071 B7
1400 MRRY 84121 2177 A2
Lombardy Ct
1400 MRRY 84121 2071 B7
Lombardy Dr
1400 MRRY 84121 2071 B7
6500 MRRY 84121 2177 B1
Lombardy Pl
1300 MRRY 84121 2071 B7
Lombardy St
900 BMCY 84302 827 E1
E Lomond View Dr
100 NHON 84414 998 D5
W Lomond View Dr
100 NHON 84414 998 D5
100 PTVW 84414 998 D5
Lona Cir
7300 WJDN 84084 2175 D3
London Ln
3000 SLkC 84044 1960 D5
London Rd
100 CTRV 84014 1551 E2
Londonderry Dr
11000 SNDY 84092 2283 C5
London Plane Rd
1700 HLDY 84124 2071 C1
Lonebrook Ct
100 LOGN 84321 528 A3
Lone Brook Ln
3500 CDHT 84121 2178 C5
Lone Hollow Ln
10 SNDY 84092 2284 A6
Lone Hollow Rd
10 SNDY 84092 2283 E5
10 SNDY 84092 2284 A6
Lone Hollow Cove
10 SNDY 84092 2284 A6
Lone Oak Ct
15100 DRPR 84020 2496 C1
Lone Oak Dr
1600 DRPR 84020 2496 C1
Lone Peak Dr
1500 SLkC 84117 2071 C5
E Lone Peak Dr
10 ALPN 84004 2498 B4
N Lone Peak Dr
10 ALPN 84004 2498 B4
S Lone Peak Dr
10 ALPN 84004 2498 B4
Lone Peak Ln
1000 DRPR 84020 2389 B4
Lone Peak Pkwy
11400 DRPR 84020 2282 C6
11900 DRPR 84020 2388 C1
Lone Pine Ct
8700 SmtC 84098 1864 E4
Lone Point Ln
13400 DRPR 84020 2388 D4
Lone Rock Cir
11500 HILD 84003 2497 B6
Lone Rock Dr
13300 DRPR 84020 2388 E4
Lone Rock Rd
6200 HILD 84003 2497 A6
Lonesome Cir
4600 WJDN 84088 2174 B6
Lone Springs Cove
3300 SLkC 84092 2284 C4
Lone Star Cir
3600 SLkC 84044 1960 D6
Lonestar Dr
- FMTN 84025 1447 D1
Lone Tree Ln
2500 TYVL 84119 2069 A2
Lone View Ct
4600 WJDN 84088 2174 A6
Long Ct
2100 WJDN 84088 2175 B7
Long Dr
100 ALPN 84004 2497 D5
8700 WJDN 84088 2175 B6
Longbranch Ct
1700 DRPR 84020 2496 C2
Longbranch Dr
1700 DRPR 84020 2496 C1
Longdale Cir
1600 SNDY 84092 2283 C5
Longdale Dr
1300 SNDY 84092 2283 C5
Long Dr Ct
400 ALPN 84004 2497 D5
Longfellow Ln
5800 MRRY 84107 2070 D6
Longhorn Dr
- FMTN 84025 1447 E1
- FMTN 84025 1448 A1
Longitude Ln
7000 WJDN 84084 2175 D2
Long Leaf Dr
900 NSLK 84054 1652 C5
4500 WJDN 84088 2174 B6
Longmeadow Cir
6500 TYVL 84084 2175 B1
Longmeadow Dr
2200 TYVL 84084 2175 B1
Longmore Dr
4900 SLkC 84118 2068 A7
5000 SLkC 84118 2067 D7
Long Rifle Rd
7700 SmtC 84098 1866 D6
Long Tail Dr
12700 DRPR 84020 2388 E3
Long Tail Cove
400 DRPR 84020 2388 E2
Long Valley Ct
6000 WVCY 84128 2067 C1
Long Valley Dr
4100 WVCY 84128 2067 C1
Longview Dr
1800 HLDY 84124 2071 D1
6100 MRRY 84107 2070 E7
Longwood Ln
10 SNDY 84092 2284 A5
Lonsdale Dr
2000 CDHT 84121 2177 E3
Look Out Pl
7300 MDVL 84047 2176 C3
Lookout Peak Cir
4800 RIVN 84065 2386 A5
Lookout Peak Dr
13800 RIVN 84065 2386 A5
Loomis Ln
5000 SLkC 84118 2067 D7
5000 SLkC 84118 2068 A7
Lopalena Cir
5500 WJDN 84084 2173 D2
Lora Lee Cir
3600 CDHT 84121 2178 D5
Loran Heights Dr
2700 SLkC 84109 1966 A5
Loredell Dr
2700 HLDY 84117 2072 A4
Loredo Dr
11200 SNDY 84094 2283 A6
Loren Wy
3800 WVCY 84120 1962 D7
Loren Mair Ln
- HRCY 84032 2398 E3
Loren-Von Cir
3400 SLkC 84124 2072 C2
Loren-Von Dr
3400 SLkC 84124 2072 C2
Loretta Dr
3700 SLkC 84106 1965 B7
Lori Cir
1200 SNDY 84094 2177 B6
1300 SRCS 84075 1227 A7
Lori Wy
1000 MRRY 84117 2071 A4
Loridan Ln
10100 SNDY 84092 2284 A3
Lorien Ct
1100 BNFL 84010 1654 C2
2800 SLkC 84109 1966 B4
Lorien Dr
1200 BNFL 84010 1654 C2
Lorient Av
3800 WJDN 84084 2174 C1
Lori Leigh Ln
900 SLkC 84117 2071 A2
Lorin Cir
2200 OGDN 84401 1116 B3
Lorita Wy
2100 CDHT 84093 2177 E4
Lorl Ln Dr
1200 OGDN 84404 1116 C1
W Lorna Cir
4400 WVCY 84120 1962 B7
Lorna Dr
3700 WVCY 84120 1962 B7
Lornadale Cir
5600 SLkC 84121 2071 D5
Lorraine Av
900 SLkC 84106 1965 A6
Lorraine Cir
3300 SLkC 84106 1965 A6
Lorreen Cir
1600 MRRY 84121 2071 C7
Lorreen Ct
1600 MRRY 84121 2071 C7
Lorreen Dr
6200 MRRY 84121 2071 C7
Lorreen Pl
6300 MRRY 84121 2071 C7
Los Altos St
3300 SLkC 84109 1966 C6
Los Angeles St
700 SLCY 84116 1753 E7
700 SLCY 84116 1857 E1
Losee Dr
4300 WVCY 84120 2068 B2
Losser Dr
2900 WVCY 84119 1962 E5
Lost Canyon Cir
7300 CDHT 84121 2178 D3
Lost Creek Ln
10 MRRY 84107 2070 C3
Lost Eden Dr
1100 SNDY 84094 2283 B4
Lost Spring Ln
3500 CDHT 84121 2178 C5
Lost Trail Dr
10900 SNDY 84092 2284 B5
Lostwood Dr
2900 SNDY 84092 2284 B5
Lotus Wy
6300 WJDN 84084 2067 D7
6500 WJDN 84084 2173 D1
Lotus Blossom Dr
4200 WVCY 84120 2067 E2
5000 WVCY 84120 2068 A2

STREET Block City ZIP Map# Grid

Louise Av
2700 SLkC 84109 1966 B4
E Louise Av
10 SSLK 84115 1964 C4
W Louise Av
10 SSLK 84115 1964 C4
Louise Meadow Dr
900 SJDN 84095 2281 E6
Louisville Cir
3600 WJDN 84084 2174 D1
Lou Jean St
2700 TYVL 84118 2069 A5
Lourdes Ln
6800 MDVL 84047 2177 A1
Love Ln
300 DvsC 84041 1229 A6
700 LYTN 84041 1229 A6
Lovebug Cir
2500 TYVL 84084 2069 C6
Loveland Av
700 SLCY 84106 1964 E3
700 SLCY 84106 1965 A3
Lovely Rd
1400 TYVL 84123 2069 C4
Lovers Ln
13200 RIVN 84065 2387 E4
Lowell Av
100 SLCY 84111 1858 D5
500 SLCY 84102 1858 E5
900 PKCY 84060 2078 D5
900 SLCY 84102 1859 A5
Lowell H Cir
- HRMN 84065 2385 B5
Lowe Peak Cir
14100 RIVN 84065 2385 E6
Lowe Peak Dr
5100 RIVN 84065 2385 E6
Lower Evergreen Dr
100 SmtC 84098 1864 C6
Lower Huntly Wy
3200 WJDN 84088 2174 C4
Lower Iron Horse Lp
1600 PKCY 84060 2078 D4
Lower Lando Ln
2400 SmtC 84098 1865 C4
Lower Newark Wy
3200 WJDN 84088 2174 E4
Loxwood Av
- SLCY 84104 1856 E5
2900 SLCY 84104 1857 A5
Loyal Av
10 SNDY 84070 2176 C7
Loyal Dr
500 MRRY 84123 2070 B6
Loyola St
4600 WVCY 84120 2068 B3
Lucas Ln
10000 SJDN 84095 2280 E5
Lucerne Cir
600 HRCY 84032 2398 D3
Lucerne Dr
- WshC 84049 2396 D2
10 HRCY 84032 2398 C2
S Lucerne Dr
400 SALM 84653 3356 A4
Lucerne Ln
6600 WJDN 84084 2174 C1
Lucia Cir
2600 WJDN 84088 2175 A5
Lucida Wy
- SLkC 84044 1960 B7
Luck Dr
500 PTGV 84062 2713 B4
Luck Ln
1300 SLkC 84106 1965 C6
Luckspring Dr
1300 SLkC 84106 1965 B6
Lucky Clover Cir
800 MRRY 84123 2070 A7
Lucky Clover Ln
700 MRRY 84123 2070 A4
Lucky Cove
1100 WJDN 84084 2175 D3
Lucky John Dr
1000 PKCY 84060 2078 D3
Lucky Star Wy
- FMTN 84025 1448 D4
Lucy Av
200 SLCY 84101 1858 B6
800 SLCY 84104 1858 A6
Luella Cir
1500 WJDN 84084 2175 D1
Luetta Dr
900 SLkC 84124 1965 A7
Lugano Cir
- WshC 84049 2396 D3
Lugano Dr
5600 WJDN 84084 2173 D2
Luge Ln
3300 TYVL 84084 2174 E1
3300 WJDN 84084 2174 E1
5400 SmtC 84098 1971 D4
Luke Cir
13000 RIVN 84065 2386 E3
Luke St
1600 LYTN 84041 1282 B1
Luna Cir
2000 CDHT 84121 2177 E1
Luna Wy
6800 CDHT 84121 2177 E2
Lund Ln
- CTRV 84014 1448 D6
- CTRV 84025 1448 D6
- FMTN 84025 1448 D6
E Lund Ln
- CTRV 84014 1448 D5
- CTRV 84025 1448 D5
- FMTN 84014 1448 D5
- FMTN 84025 1448 D5
W Lund Ln
10 FMTN 84025 1448 C6
N Lupe Cir
400 OREM 84057 2820 E4
Lupine Dr
400 ALPN 84004 2497 D3
7000 SmtC 84098 1866 A7
7000 SmtC 84098 1972 A1
Lupine Ln
2400 PKCY 84060 2078 E1
Lupine Wy
700 FMTN 84025 1346 B6
5800 MRRY 84121 2071 B6

Lusanne Wy
- WshC 84049 2396 D2
Lusterpointe Ct
7900 WJDN 84088 2175 B4
Lusterpointe Ln
2400 WJDN 84088 2175 A4
Luxor Pk
3000 WVCY 84120 1962 A3
Luzern Rd
300 WshC 84049 2291 B6
Lyman Ct
1200 SLCY 84105 1859 A6
Lynaria Ct
6900 WJDN 84084 2174 A2
Lyndbrook Wy
11000 SNDY 84092 2283 B5
Lyndhurst Dr
- NSLK 84054 1652 D6
Lyndy Dr
700 MDVL 84047 2176 E3
700 MDVL 84047 2177 A3
Lyndzie Ln
2200 CDHT 84121 2177 E2
Lynford Dr
11000 SNDY 84092 2283 C5
Lynn Cir
100 SNDY 84070 2282 D1
Lynn Ln
8000 WJDN 84088 2174 D5
Lynnbrook Dr
500 SPFK 84660 3249 E1
Lynncrest Dr
5200 TYVL 84118 2069 A5
Lynncrest Cove
3100 TYVL 84118 2069 A5
Lynne Ln
4200 HLDY 84124 2071 E1
Lynne St
10 PTVW 84404 998 B7
Lynne Wy
5900 ROY 84067 1171 B6
N Lynne School Ln
100 OGDN 84404 1056 D5
S Lynne School Ln
100 OGDN 84404 1056 D5
Lynnwood Av
1400 LOGN 84341 464 C7
Lynnwood Dr
10 CRFD 84015 1227 E4
1000 OREM 84097 2928 A1
Lynnwood St
8500 SNDY 84070 2176 E6
Lynwood Dr
- FRWT 84404 1055 D3
2300 SLCY 84109 1965 E2
2300 SLCY 84109 1966 A3
W Lynwood Dr
200 BNFL 84010 1653 C1
Lyoni Ct
6800 WJDN 84084 2174 A1

M

M Av
- DvsC 84056 1227 E3
M St
500 SLCY 84103 1859 A1
Mabey Dr
2100 SLCY 84109 1965 E3
Mabey Ln
1100 SJDN 84095 2281 D3
MacArthur Av
100 SSLK 84115 1964 C1
MacDuff Ln
9300 WJDN 84088 2281 D1
Mace St
100 PRRY 84302 827 E2
MacFarland Dr
900 SLCY 84116 1753 E7
E Mach Schnell Dr
1000 SNDY 84094 2283 A6
S Mach Schnell Dr
11400 SNDY 84094 2283 C5
Macintosh Cir
3400 CDHT 84121 2178 C2
Macintosh Ln
3400 CDHT 84121 2178 C3
Macintosh Wy
- PTVW 84414 998 A4
Mackay Dr
4100 TYVL 84119 2069 B1
Mackay St
4200 TYVL 84123 2069 D1
Mackay Meadows Pl
2900 WVCY 84119 2069 A1
Macks Inn Cir
8100 WJDN 84088 2173 D5
Maclane
500 BMCY 84302 767 A7
Macondray Cir
6000 MRRY 84123 2070 D7
Madeline Ln
13300 HRMN 84065 2385 C3
Madera Cir
3700 RIVN 84065 2280 D7
Madera Hills Dr
1200 BNFL 84010 1654 B2
Madill Cir
3800 WVCY 84119 1963 B7
Madison Av
100 OGDN 84404 1057 A5
1500 OGDN 84404 1116 A1
2000 OGDN 84401 1116 A2
2700 OGDN 84403 1116 A5
3700 SOGN 84403 1116 A7
3800 SOGN 84403 1173 A1
7300 SLkC 84044 1960 E5
N Madison Av
400 OGDN 84404 1057 A4
Madison Cir
3200 SLkC 84044 1960 E5
6800 WJDN 84084 2175 C2
Madison Dr
3200 SLkC 84044 1960 E5
Madison Rd
7200 SLkC 84044 1960 E6
Madison Meadow Ln
700 MDVL 84047 2176 A2
Madison Nan Dr
- WJDN 84088 2173 A4
Madison Ridge Ln
1600 RIVN 84065 2387 C1

Madison View Dr
1600 RIVN 84065 2387 C1
Madrid St
6200 MRRY 84121 2071 D7
Madrid Wy
1300 SNDY 84093 2177 C5
Madrona Ln
1300 DvsC 84056 1228 B2
Madsen Ct
8000 SNDY 84093 2177 B4
Madsen Ln
800 NSLK 84054 1653 B5
1600 SNDY 84093 2177 C4
Maeser Hall
10 PRVO 84604 2928 D5
Magda Ln
1300 SLkC 84124 2071 B1
E Magellan Ln
200 EKMT 84651 3463 A1
W Magellan Ln
10 EKMT 84651 3462 E2
Magic Dr
100 MRRY 84107 2070 C5
Magic Hills Cir
3400 CDHT 84121 2178 C3
Magic Hills Dr
7400 CDHT 84121 2178 C3
Magic Isle Ln
100 MRRY 84107 2070 C5
Magic Morning Ln
5100 TYVL 84123 2069 E4
Magic View Cir
7400 CDHT 84121 2178 D3
Magic View Dr
3300 CDHT 84121 2178 C3
Magic Wand St
1300 DRPR 84020 2389 B5
Magnolia
- DvsC 84056 1229 A4
Magnolia Dr
3100 SLkC 84044 1960 D6
Magnolia Tree Cove
1300 WJDN 84084 2175 D3
Magnum Ct
4700 HRMN 84065 2386 A1
Magpie Cir
900 MIDW 84049 2397 B1
Mahogany Dr
300 ANFK 84003 2711 B1
1600 FTHT 84037 1346 B3
N Mahogany Dr
700 PTGV 84062 2713 A1
3400 CRHL 84062 2605 D4
Mahogany Ln
- PTGV 84062 2713 B1
Mahogany Pl
5800 WJDN 84084 2173 B1
N Mahogany Wy
10 EKMT 84651 3463 A2
S Mahogany Wy
10 EKMT 84651 3463 A2
Mahogany Hill Wy
10 DRPR 84020 2495 C1
Mahogany Valley Rd
- NHLN 84341 464 D2
Mahre Dr
1900 SmtC 84098 1971 D5
Maia Cir
7900 SLkC 84044 1960 C4
Maiden Ct
2900 WVCY 84120 1962 A4
Maidie Ln
3500 WVCY 84119 2068 D2
Main St
- PRVO 84606 3035 D1
- SLCY 84103 1859 A2
10 HYRM 84319 651 A2
10 SNDY 84070 2176 D6
10 SRSP 84043 2602 A6
100 PKCY 84060 2078 E5
7200 MDVL 84047 2176 A4
Main St SR-73
10 SRSP 84043 2602 A6
Main St SR-101
10 HYRM 84319 651 A2
E Main St
10 ANFK 84003 2711 D1
10 LEHI 84043 2603 D6
10 MIDW 84049 2397 C3
10 SNQN 84655 3460 E7
10 TMTN 84337 520 E6
10 WELV 84339 649 D2
400 SNQN 84655 3461 A7
600 TMTN 84337 521 A6
700 WshC 84049 2397 C3
1900 BxEC 84337 521 A6
5600 HRMN 84065 2385 D3
E Main St SR-73
10 LEHI 84043 2603 D6
E Main St SR-101
10 WELV 84339 649 D2
E Main St SR-102
10 TMTN 84337 520 E6
600 TMTN 84337 521 A6
1900 BxEC 84337 521 A6
E Main St SR-113
10 MIDW 84049 2397 C3
E Main St US-6
10 SNQN 84655 3460 E7
400 SNQN 84655 3461 A7
E Main St US-89
10 ANFK 84003 2711 C1
N Main St
- LYTN 84037 1283 B7
- MNDN 84325 524 D5
10 ALPN 84004 2497 E4
10 BMCY 84302 766 E5
10 CRFD 84015 1227 D3
10 CTRV 84014 1551 E3
10 FMTN 84025 1448 D1
10 GRLD 84312 520 E1
10 HDPK 84318 400 A7
10 HDPK 84318 464 A1
10 HRCY 84032 2398 D3
10 KYVL 84037 1345 C1
10 LNDN 84042 2713 B6
10 LOGN 84321 527 D2
10 LYTN 84041 1282 C2
10 MLVI 84332 591 E2
10 MNTU 84324 768 C7
10 MPTN 84664 3144 A6
10 NSLK 84054 1653 A6

N Main St
10 PTGV 84062 2712 D2
10 PVDN 84332 528 A6
10 PYSN 84651 3354 E4
10 SALM 84653 3356 A2
10 SGVL 84663 3143 C1
10 SHFD 84335 399 D2
10 SPFK 84660 3249 C2
10 WLRD 84340 885 C2
100 SLCY 84103 1858 C1
200 KYVL 84037 1283 B7
300 OREM 84057 2820 D3
400 BNFL 84010 1551 E6
600 FMTN 84025 1346 B6
600 KYVL 84041 1283 B7
600 SGVL 84663 3036 B5
800 CchC 84332 591 E2
800 SNST 84015 1227 D3
800 UthC 84651 3354 E4
900 LOGN 84321 463 D7
1000 LOGN 84341 463 D7
1200 SPFK 84660 3142 C6
1300 BxEC 84302 766 E5
1500 CTRV 84014 1448 D6
1500 PRVO 84606 3036 B5
1500 PRVO 84663 3036 B5
1500 SGVL 84606 3036 B5
1600 OREM 84057 2713 D7
1600 UthC 84606 3036 B5
1800 SNST 84015 1171 D7
2000 LYTN 84041 1228 B7
2100 CRFD 84015 1228 B7
2100 LYTN 84015 1228 B7
N Main St I-15 BUS
10 BMCY 84302 766 E5
N Main St I-84 BUS
10 BMCY 84302 766 E5
N Main St SR-13
10 BMCY 84302 766 E5
N Main St SR-30
200 LOGN 84321 527 D2
N Main St SR-38
900 BMCY 84302 766 E3
1300 BxEC 84302 766 E3
N Main St SR-74
10 ALPN 84004 2497 E4
N Main St SR-106
10 CTRV 84014 1551 E3
10 FMTN 84025 1448 D1
400 BNFL 84010 1551 E6
600 FMTN 84025 1346 D7
1500 CTRV 84014 1448 D6
N Main St SR-115
100 PYSN 84651 3354 E4
800 UthC 84651 3354 E4
N Main St SR-126
10 CRFD 84015 1227 D3
10 LYTN 84041 1282 C2
800 SNST 84015 1227 D3
1800 SNST 84015 1171 D7
2000 LYTN 84041 1228 B7
2100 CRFD 84015 1228 B7
2100 LYTN 84015 1228 B7
N Main St SR-156
- SPFK 84660 3142 C7
10 SPFK 84660 3249 C2
N Main St SR-238
10 MLVI 84332 591 E2
800 CchC 84332 591 E2
N Main St SR-272
1200 FMTN 84025 1346 B6
N Main St SR-273
10 KYVL 84037 1345 C1
N Main St US-40
10 HRCY 84032 2398 D3
N Main St US-89
10 LOGN 84321 527 D3
10 SGVL 84663 3143 C1
10 WLRD 84340 885 C2
600 SGVL 84663 3036 B5
1500 PRVO 84606 3036 B5
1500 PRVO 84663 3036 B5
1500 SGVL 84606 3036 B5
1600 UthC 84606 3036 B5
N Main St US-91
10 LOGN 84321 527 D2
10 SHFD 84335 399 D2
900 LOGN 84321 463 D7
1000 LOGN 84341 463 D7
N Main St US-189
10 HRCY 84032 2398 D3
S Main St
- FMTN 84025 1346 A4
10 ALPN 84004 2497 E5
10 BMCY 84302 766 E6
10 CRFD 84015 1227 D5
10 CRFD 84016 1227 D5
10 CTRV 84014 1551 E4
10 FMTN 84025 1448 D2
10 GRLD 84312 520 E3
10 HDPK 84318 464 A1
10 HRCY 84032 2398 D5
10 KYVL 84037 1345 D2
10 LNDN 84042 2713 B6
10 LOGN 84321 527 D4
10 LYTN 84041 1282 E5
10 LYTN 84041 1283 A6
10 MNDN 84325 524 D7
10 MNTU 84324 768 C7
10 MNTU 84324 829 C1
10 MPTN 84664 3144 A7
10 MPTN 84664 3251 A1
10 PVDN 84332 528 A7
10 PYSN 84651 3354 E5
10 SALM 84653 3356 A4
10 SGVL 84663 3143 C2
10 SHFD 84335 399 D3
10 SLCY 84101 1858 C4
10 SLCY 84111 1858 C4
10 SPFK 84660 3249 C4
10 WLRD 84340 885 C6
300 BNFL 84010 1653 D1
300 PTGV 84062 2712 D3
400 OREM 84058 2820 D6
500 PVDN 84332 592 A1
600 WLRD 84340 941 C1
700 BMCY 84302 827 E1
700 LYTN 84037 1283 A6
800 DvsC 84037 1345 D2
800 TMTN 84337 520 E3
900 FTHT 84037 1345 D2
900 KYVL 84041 1283 A6

S Main St
1000 BNFL 84010 1551 E4
1000 OREM 84058 2927 D2
1100 DvsC 84037 1346 A4
1100 FMTN 84037 1346 A4
1100 FTHT 84037 1346 A4
1100 KYVL 84037 1346 A4
1200 PYSN 84651 3461 E1
1200 UthC 84660 3249 C4
1300 PRRY 84302 827 E1
1300 SLCY 84115 1858 C4
1500 SLCY 84115 1964 C1
1700 CRFD 84015 1281 D2
2100 SSLK 84115 1964 C1
2200 WDCR 84010 1653 B5
2400 CchC 84321 591 D2
2400 CchC 84332 591 D2
2400 MLVI 84332 591 D2
2400 NBLY 84321 591 D2
2500 LYTN 84015 1281 D2
2500 NBLY 84332 591 D2
2600 NSLK 84010 1653 B5
2600 NSLK 84054 1653 B5
3200 DvsC 84010 1653 B5
3400 DvsC 84054 1653 B5
3900 SLkC 84107 1964 C7
3900 SLkC 84107 2070 C1
4100 MRRY 84107 2070 C1
7500 MDVL 84047 2176 C3
S Main St I-15 BUS
10 BMCY 84302 766 E6
700 BMCY 84302 827 E1
S Main St I-84 BUS
10 BMCY 84302 766 E6
700 BMCY 84302 827 E1
S Main St SR-13
10 BMCY 84302 766 E6
700 BMCY 84302 827 E1
S Main St SR-51
600 SGVL 84663 3143 C3
S Main St SR-74
10 ALPN 84004 2497 E5
S Main St SR-82
10 GRLD 84312 520 E3
800 TMTN 84337 520 E3
S Main St SR-106
10 CTRV 84014 1551 E4
1000 BNFL 84010 1551 E4
S Main St SR-126
10 CRFD 84015 1227 D4
10 LYTN 84041 1282 E5
10 LYTN 84041 1283 A5
S Main St SR-147
10 MPTN 84664 3144 A7
10 MPTN 84664 3251 A1
S Main St SR-156
10 SPFK 84660 3249 C4
S Main St SR-165
2400 CchC 84321 591 D2
2400 CchC 84332 591 D2
2400 MLVI 84332 591 D2
2400 NBLY 84321 591 D2
2500 NBLY 84332 591 D2
S Main St SR-198
300 SPFK 84660 3249 C3
1200 UthC 84660 3249 C3
S Main St SR-238
10 MLVI 84332 591 E3
S Main St SR-273
- FMTN 84025 1346 A4
10 KYVL 84037 1345 D2
800 DvsC 84037 1345 D2
900 FTHT 84037 1345 D2
1100 DvsC 84037 1346 A4
1100 FMTN 84037 1346 A4
1100 FTHT 84037 1346 A4
1100 KYVL 84037 1346 A4
S Main St US-40
10 HRCY 84032 2398 D5
S Main St US-89
10 LOGN 84321 527 D4
10 SGVL 84663 3143 C2
10 WLRD 84340 885 C6
600 WLRD 84340 941 C1
1100 BMCY 84302 827 E2
1300 PRRY 84302 827 E2
2200 BNFL 84010 1653 B5
2200 WDCR 84010 1653 B5
2600 NSLK 84010 1653 B5
2600 NSLK 84054 1653 B5
3200 DvsC 84010 1653 B5
3400 DvsC 84054 1653 B5
S Main St US-91
10 LOGN 84321 527 D4
10 SHFD 84335 399 D3
S Main St US-189
10 HRCY 84032 2398 D5
W Main St
- HYRM 84319 651 A2
10 MIDW 84049 2397 B3
10 SNQN 84655 3460 D7
10 TMTN 84337 520 D6
10 WELV 84339 649 C2
500 LEHI 84043 2603 A7
700 ANFK 84003 2711 A1
700 UthC 84003 2711 A1
1000 ANFK 84003 2710 E1
1000 UthC 84003 2710 E1
6000 HRMN 84065 2385 B3
6600 SLkC 84065 2385 B3
W Main St SR-73
10 LEHI 84043 2603 A7
W Main St SR-101
10 HYRM 84319 651 C2
W Main St SR-102
10 TMTN 84337 520 D6
W Main St US-6
10 SNQN 84655 3460 D7
W Main St US-89
10 ANFK 84003 2711 B1
Maine St
1700 DvsC 84056 1227 E1
1700 SNST 84056 1227 E1
7700 DvsC 84056 1172 A7
7700 DvsC 84056 1228 A1
Main Point Blvd
5700 SOGN 84405 1173 B6
W Main St Ct
10 ALPN 84004 2497 E5
Mainstay Pl
4400 WVCY 84128 2067 C2

Maio Ct
8000 SNDY 84093 2177 C4
Maio Dr
8000 SNDY 84093 2177 C5
Maison Dr
9200 SNDY 84093 2177 D7
9200 SNDY 84093 2283 D1
Majerus Ct
5500 TYVL 84123 2069 D5
Majestic Cir
4400 PTVW 84414 998 D1
Majestic Dr
700 LOGN 84321 527 B5
3100 SLkC 84124 2072 B1
Majestic St
10 KYVL 84037 1345 C2
Majestic Wy
3700 SLkC 84044 1960 E7
Majestic Canyon Rd
10000 SLkC 84092 2284 B3
Majestic Hill Ct
12500 HRMN 84065 2385 C2
Majestic Meadows Dr
200 PYSN 84651 3354 D5
Majestic Peak Dr
5200 HRMN 84065 2385 E5
Majestic Pine Dr
700 MRRY 84107 2070 E6
Majestic Ridge Cir
2700 CDHT 84093 2178 A4
Majestic Ridge Dr
7800 CDHT 84093 2178 A4
Majestic Village Cir
5300 MRRY 84123 2070 A4
Major St
1000 SLCY 84111 1858 C6
1300 SLCY 84115 1858 C7
1900 SLCY 84115 1964 C1
2100 SSLK 84115 1964 C2
6700 MDVL 84107 2176 C1
6700 MRRY 84107 2176 C1
Makai
10500 CRHL 84062 2605 C1
Makenna Ct
2300 HLDY 84117 2071 E2
W Makiya Cir
1100 SJDN 84095 2281 E6
Mala Dr
1000 LYTN 84041 1282 C3
Malan Av
2800 OGDN 84403 1116 C5
Malan Ct
1800 OGDN 84403 1116 D5
Malanie Place Ln
1300 WJDN 84088 2175 D6
Malibu Dr
500 SLkC 84107 2070 E1
Malissa Ann Cir
13900 HRMN 84065 2385 A5
Malissa Ann Dr
6700 HRMN 84065 2385 A5
Mallard Cir
1500 SmtC 84098 1971 E1
9100 SNDY 84093 2178 A7
Mallard Dr
- WPT 84015 1225 D4
Mallard Ln
8000 WJDN 84088 2174 D5
Mallow Ridge Cir
5500 SLkC 84118 2067 C5
Malstrom Ln
10 MRRY 84107 2176 C1
Malvern Av
900 SLCY 84106 1965 A3
1500 WVCY 84119 1963 C3
E Malvern Av
10 SSLK 84115 1964 C3
W Malvern Av
10 SSLK 84115 1964 C3
Manas Wy
6100 HRMN 84065 2385 C5
Manchester Dr
900 NSLK 84054 1652 C6
Manchester Ln
8900 SNDY 84093 2177 D7
Manchester Rd
800 KYVL 84037 1283 E6
900 KYVL 84037 1284 A6
Manchester St
4300 CRHL 84062 2605 B4
Mandalay Rd
1200 SLCY 84116 1753 C6
Mandan Av
4800 WVCY 84120 1962 A7
Manderley Ln
- OGDN 84403 1173 C3
Mandingo Ln
900 DvsC 84056 1228 C3
Mandy Cir
3000 WJDN 84084 2175 A1
Mandy Lee Cove
4500 RIVN 84065 2386 B2
Manfield Wy
1200 DRPR 84020 2389 B2
Mango Cir
4000 TYVL 84123 2069 D1
Mango Rd
1300 TYVL 84123 2069 D1
Manhattan Ct
3600 WVCY 84120 1962 B6
Manhattan Dr
3700 WVCY 84120 1962 B7
Manila Cir
9800 CRHL 84062 2605 B3
Manila Ct
1300 PTGV 84062 2712 B1
Manila Creek Dr
4100 CRHL 84062 2605 B3
Manilla Cir
10 DRPR 84020 2495 C1
Manilla Dr
10 DRPR 84020 2495 D1
200 DRPR 84020 2388 D7
Manitoban Ln
10 HYRM 84319 651 E2
Mann Wy
3600 WVCY 84120 1962 C6
Man of War Cove
1200 SJDN 84095 2281 D6
Manor Cir
1100 SLkC 84124 2071 B1
11000 HILD 84003 2498 A7

Manor Dr
11000 HILD 84003 2498 A7
E Manor Dr
2600 CDHT 84121 2178 A2
Manor Wy
- PKCY 84060 2078 D5
Manorcrest Ct
2900 CDHT 84121 2178 D1
Manorly Cir
6700 CDHT 84121 2178 B1
Manor Ridge Pl
4400 SLkC 84124 2071 B2
Manorview Ct
2900 CDHT 84121 2178 D1
Mansfield Av
300 SSLK 84115 1964 D5
600 SSLK 84106 1964 E5
1000 SLCY 84106 1965 A5
1000 SLkC 84106 1965 A5
Mansfield Cir
3700 WJDN 84084 2174 D1
Manshire Cir
8100 SNDY 84094 2177 A5
Manti Cir
14800 DRPR 84020 2495 E1
Manti Dr
200 DRPR 84020 2388 D7
Mantle Av
1700 TYVL 84119 2069 C1
Mantle Cir
1700 TYVL 84119 2069 C1
Mantova Wy
7000 WJDN 84084 2173 D2
Mantyla St
4900 TYVL 84123 2069 E4
Manzanita Dr
1500 TYVL 84123 2069 C3
Manzano Dr
7800 SNDY 84093 2177 B4
Maple Av
1400 SLkC 84106 1965 C6
Maple Cir
10 NHLN 84341 463 E3
10 SmtC 84098 1864 A5
Maple Ct
- WDHL 84653 3463 E2
N Maple Ct
10100 CRHL 84062 2605 B2
Maple Dr
- SHFD 84335 399 D1
10 SmtC 84098 1864 B5
100 NSLK 84054 1653 A6
200 ALPN 84004 2498 A5
300 SmtC 84098 1866 D5
400 WbrC 84317 1061 E4
900 SPFK 84660 3249 E4
1000 BMCY 84302 767 B5
1300 LOGN 84321 528 C1
E Maple Dr
10 WDHL 84653 3463 D1
S Maple Dr
200 WDHL 84653 3463 D1
W Maple Dr
100 NSLK 84054 1653 A6
Maple Ln
10 PTGV 84062 2712 D4
1200 PRVO 84604 2928 E4
1300 DvsC 84056 1228 A2
1800 BNFL 84010 1654 C4
2000 DvsC 84056 1172 A6
2000 RVDL 84405 1172 A6
E Maple Ln
500 EKMT 84651 3463 A2
Maple Lp
- LEHI 84043 2495 C7
Maple St
100 MRRY 84107 2070 D3
500 CRFD 84015 1227 E4
600 SOGN 84403 1116 A7
800 OGDN 84403 1116 A7
7600 MDVL 84047 2176 C3
E Maple St
10 MPTN 84664 3144 C7
W Maple St
10 MPTN 84664 3144 A7
600 MPTN 84664 3143 E7
W Maple St SR-147
10 MPTN 84664 3144 A7
600 MPTN 84664 3143 E7
Maple Vw
1800 BNFL 84010 1654 C3
Maple Wy
3100 WVCY 84119 1963 A5
Mapleberry Ct
400 DRPR 84020 2282 E7
Maple Bluff Rd
- DRPR 84020 2497 A3
Maple Cove Dr
2800 BNFL 84010 1654 C4
Maple Creek Ln
2400 SNDY 84092 2284 A7
Maple Crest Ct
800 SLkC 84106 1965 A7
Maple Grove Dr
3800 WJDN 84088 2174 C5
Maple Grove Wy
1900 BNFL 84010 1654 D3
Maple Hill Cir
10600 SLkC 84092 2283 E4
Maple Hills Dr
1400 BNFL 84010 1654 C4
Maple Hollow Cir
13900 DRPR 84020 2389 A5
Maple Hollow Rd
700 PVDN 84332 528 B7
Maplehollow Wy
1900 BNFL 84010 1654 C3
Maple Leaf Cv
- MPTN 84664 3143 D5
Mapleleaf Wy
3700 WJDN 84088 2174 C4
Maple Meadows Dr
4300 WVCY 84120 2068 B2
Maple Mesa Dr
7400 WJDN 84084 2173 B3
Maple Park Ct
- DRPR 84020 2389 B7
S Maple Ravine Cir
900 WDHL 84653 3463 C3
Maple Ridge Cir
11800 SNDY 84094 2283 D7

STREET
Block City ZIP Map# Grid

Mapleridge Dr
1900 BNFL 84010 1654 C3
Maple Ridge Rd
11800 SNDY 84094 2283 B7
Maple Run Cir
14200 HRMN 84065 2385 D6
Mapleton Ct
400 DRPR 84020 2388 D4
W Maple Tree Ct
800 SLCY 84116 1754 A7
Maple View Dr
700 SALM 84653 3356 B5
800 SLkC 84106 1965 A7
1900 BNFL 84010 1654 C3
W Maple View Dr
10 SALM 84653 3356 A5
Maplewood Cir
800 LYTN 84041 1283 B3
1300 MRRY 84121 2071 E5
Maplewood Dr
400 BNFL 84010 1551 E6
900 BNFL 84010 1552 A6
1300 MRRY 84121 2071 B7
5600 SOGN 84405 1173 B5
Marabow Cir
4700 HLDY 84117 2072 A3
Marbella Cir
8800 SNDY 84093 2177 B7
Marbella St
1300 SNDY 84093 2177 B7
Marble St
9900 SNDY 84094 2283 B2
10000 SLkC 84094 2283 B2
Marblewood Dr
1900 RIVN 84065 2387 B4
March St
600 SLCY 84104 1857 A5
Marco Ln
500 OGDN 84404 1057 B6
Marco Rd
5600 MRRY 84121 2071 B6
Marco Polo Ln
1100 SJDN 84095 2281 E6
Marcrest Cir
3000 WVCY 84128 1961 B5
Marcrest Dr
3000 WVCY 84128 1961 C5
Marcus Rd
2700 WVCY 84119 1963 A7
Marcy Brook Pl
8100 SLkC 84044 1960 C5
Mardi Gras Ln
4500 WJDN 84088 2174 B6
Mardonna Wy
3500 SLkC 84109 1966 C6
Maren Pl
5900 WJDN 84084 2173 C1
Margaret Av
900 SLCY 84104 1963 E1
900 SLCY 84104 1964 A1
Margaret Park Dr
1200 RIVN 84065 2387 D1
Margaret Rose Dr
1100 RIVN 84065 2387 D1
Margaret View Cir
1200 RIVN 84065 2387 D1
Margie Av
3100 SLkC 84109 1966 C5
Margie Dr
9300 SNDY 84070 2282 E1
Margray Dr
6200 TYVL 84084 2069 C7
Mariah Cir
12200 DRPR 84020 2389 D1
Marialana Wy
500 NSLK 84054 1653 C7
Mariam Wy
7200 SLkC 84044 1960 D7
Marianna Cir
1800 TYVL 84118 2069 C4
Marianna St
4800 TYVL 84118 2069 C4
Maricopa Cir
3500 WVCY 84120 1962 A6
Marie Av
2100 SLkC 84109 1965 E5
3100 SLkC 84109 1966 C5
Marie Cir
300 KYVL 84037 1345 B1
3000 SLkC 84109 1965 E5
Marie Dr
10 BMCY 84302 767 B5
100 MDVL 84047 2176 D3
Marie St
900 LNDN 84042 2713 D5
Marie Jonsson Cir
6700 HILD 84003 2604 A1
Marigold St
3200 SLkC 84044 1960 D6
Marilyn Dr
200 CRFD 84015 1227 E5
700 CRFD 84016 1227 A6
1100 LYTN 84041 1282 C2
1200 OGDN 84403 1116 C4
1200 SRCS 84075 1227 A7
1600 SRCS 84075 1281 A1
2400 PRRY 84302 827 D5
4900 HLDY 84117 2071 E3
Marin Cove
- WVCY 84128 1961 A5
Marinda Wy
3300 CDHT 84121 2178 C3
Marindale Av
10 LOGN 84321 527 C3
Marinwood Av
1100 TYVL 84123 2069 D3
Marinwood Cir
4800 TYVL 84123 2069 D3
Marion Cir
8100 SNDY 84094 2177 A5
Marion Dr
2400 WJDN 84084 2175 A4
Marion St
300 SLCY 84116 1857 E1
Marion View Cir
8100 SNDY 84094 2177 A5
Marion Village Rd
800 SNDY 84094 2177 A5
Mariott Dr
1000 OREM 84057 2820 B2
Mariposa Av
1300 SLkC 84106 1965 B7
Mariposa Wy
11200 SNDY 84094 2283 A6
Mariwood Cir
1000 NSLK 84054 1754 D2
Mar Jane Av
700 MRRY 84107 2071 A7
Marjorie Ct
3300 WJDN 84088 2174 E5
Mark Av
900 SLCY 84106 1965 A3
3000 WVCY 84119 1962 E5
3000 WVCY 84119 1963 A5
Mark St
1700 LYTN 84041 1282 A1
Markea Av
600 SLCY 84102 1858 E4
1000 SLCY 84102 1859 A4
Market St
300 KYVL 84037 1283 B7
3500 WVCY 84119 1963 A6
4000 WVCY 84119 2069 A1
W Market St
10 SLCY 84101 1858 C4
N Market Place Dr
200 CTRV 84014 1551 D3
Marketview Dr
14000 BFDL 84065 2387 D5
Markham Peak Cir
13800 HRMN 84065 2385 E5
S Mark IV Ct
3500 WVCY 84119 1963 A6
Mark Read St
4100 WVCY 84119 2068 E1
Markridge Cir
11400 SJDN 84095 2281 E6
Marks Wy
12700 RIVN 84065 2387 E2
Marksbury Cir
3100 SNDY 84093 2284 C1
Markwood Ct
5100 WVCY 84120 1961 D6
Marla Wy
100 MDVL 84047 2176 D2
Marlette Dr
300 OGDN 84404 1056 D4
Marlis Cir
3900 TYVL 84118 2068 C7
Marmac Cir
2000 BFDL 84065 2494 B1
W Marquette Dr
300 MDVL 84047 2176 B5
Marquis Wy
4100 SLkC 84124 2072 C1
Marrcrest E
2700 PRVO 84604 2928 B2
Marrcrest N
2800 PRVO 84604 2928 C1
Marrcrest S
2800 PRVO 84604 2928 C1
Marrcrest W
2800 PRVO 84604 2928 C1
Marrcrest North Cir
2800 PRVO 84604 2928 C1
Marrcrest West St
- PRVO 84604 2928 B2
Marrwood Cir
2100 HLDY 84124 1965 C6
Marrwood Dr
2000 HLDY 84124 1965 D7
Mars Wy
10 SNDY 84070 2176 C5
4200 SLkC 84124 2072 C1
Marsac Av
10 PKCY 84060 2078 E7
Marsac Av SR-224
10 PKCY 84060 2078 E7
Marseilles Wy
1500 WVCY 84119 1963 D5
Marsh Cir
1000 TMTN 84337 520 E3
Marsha Dr
3700 WVCY 84128 1961 D7
Marsha Brook Cir
2400 TYVL 84118 2069 A5
Marsha Kaye Cir
10800 SNDY 84070 2282 D4
Marshall Av
1600 SLCY 84104 1857 C7
Marshall Wy
300 LYTN 84041 1282 C3
Marsh Cove
700 DRPR 84020 2282 A7
Marshrock Rd
6600 WJDN 84084 2174 A1
Marshwood Ln
500 MRRY 84107 2070 D4
Martha Ln
800 MIDW 84049 2397 C1
Martha Rd
- ALTA 84049 2181 D7
Martha Dunyon Cir
1300 DRPR 84020 2389 B5
Marthas Cove
3200 CDHT 84093 2178 B6
Martin Ln
300 MRRY 84107 2070 B3
Martin St
- OGDN 84401 1115 E2
- OGDN 84401 1116 A2
Martin Wy
6400 WVCY 84128 1961 B7
Martinet Ln
1600 OGDN 84403 1173 C2
Martinez Wy
2800 RIVN 84065 2387 A2
3100 RIVN 84065 2386 E2
Martingale Cir
2500 SJDN 84095 2281 A4
Martingale Dr
10700 SJDN 84095 2281 B4
Martingale Ln
700 SmtC 84098 1972 A4
10700 SJDN 84095 2281 B5
Martin Luther King Jr Blvd
500 SLCY 84102 1858 E5
Martin Luther King Jr St
100 OGDN 84401 1115 D3
Martin Luther King Jr St SR-53
100 OGDN 84401 1115 D3
W Martin Luther King Jr St
300 OGDN 84401 1115 C3
W Martin L King Jr St SR-53
300 OGDN 84401 1115 C3
Marty Cir
1500 WJDN 84084 2175 C2
Marva St
400 LYIN 84041 1283 A3
Marvel Ln
8000 SWBR 84405 1230 A3
Marvelle Cir
6100 SLkC 84118 2067 D7
Marvelle Ct
6000 SLkC 84118 2067 E7
Mar Vian Dr
1200 SLkC 84124 2071 B1
Marvin Wy
2700 LYTN 84040 1230 A7
Marvin Gardens St
1600 SLkC 84121 2071 C5
Marvinwood Dr
2200 TYVL 84119 2069 B2
Mary Cir
1700 CDHT 84121 2177 C2
Mary Dr
10900 SNDY 84092 2283 D5
Mary Wy
200 TMTN 84337 520 E6
Mary Beth Cir
2300 TYVL 84084 2069 C7
Mary Dott Wy
1800 SLCY 84106 1965 D4
1900 SLkC 84106 1965 D4
Mary Esther Cir
7500 CDHT 84093 2177 C3
Mary-Etta Av
300 SSLK 84115 1964 B6
Maryfield Dr
100 SLkC 84108 1860 E3
Maryland Dr
7800 DvsC 84056 1171 E7
Marylebone Rd
7400 WJDN 84084 2174 E3
Mary Leizan Ln
6700 HRMN 84065 2385 A5
Mary Loraine Cir
13800 HRMN 84065 2385 B5
Mary Loraine Dr
6500 HRMN 84065 2385 B5
Marymore Cir
1500 SNDY 84092 2283 C6
Mary Rose Av
400 SLkC 84107 2070 E1
Mascaro Wy
8300 WJDN 84088 2174 A5
Mason Ln
10 NSLK 84054 1653 B7
Mason Wy
7400 SLkC 84044 1960 E6
Mason Hollow Dr
1300 RIVN 84065 2387 D1
S Masonic Cir
2600 SSLK 84115 1964 E3
Masons Mile Dr
2400 TYVL 84118 2069 B4
Mason Vista Wy
3500 SLkC 84044 1960 E6
Massachusetts Cir
1200 HARR 84404 1056 D2
Masters Cir
5700 WVCY 84128 1961 D7
Masters Ct
5700 WVCY 84128 1961 D7
Masters Dr
3600 WVCY 84128 1961 D6
Matanzas Rd
- DRPR 84020 2496 D3
Mateo Wy
1600 SLkC 84117 2071 C5
Mathew Dr
1700 LYTN 84041 1282 B1
Mathews Wy
4100 SLkC 84124 2072 E2
Matisse Ln
200 ALPN 84004 2497 E4
3100 WVCY 84119 1963 D5
Matlock Cir
1600 CDHT 84093 2177 C4
Matson Cir
3900 HLDY 84124 1965 D7
Matterhorn Cir
10 SmtC 84098 1864 C7
Matterhorn Ct
1000 MIDW 84049 2397 C1
Matterhorn Dr
10 SmtC 84098 1864 C7
2700 TYVL 84084 2069 A7
3000 TYVL 84084 2068 E7
N Matterhorn Dr
10 ALPN 84004 2497 D4
S Matterhorn Dr
10 ALPN 84004 2497 D5
Matterhorn Ter
10 SmtC 84098 1864 C7
Matterhorn Wy
200 WshC 84049 2291 C6
300 SmtC 84098 1864 D7
Matthew Av
1100 MRRY 84121 2071 B7
Matthews Wy
1100 RIVN 84065 2281 D7
Maudine Av
5400 WVCY 84120 1961 D7
Maughan Cir
10700 SJDN 84095 2280 E4
Maule Dr
1500 OGDN 84403 1116 C4
Maul Oak Dr
8500 WJDN 84088 2173 B6
Maurice Dr
2700 SLkC 84124 2072 A2
Maverick Cir
6800 CDHT 84121 2178 A1
Maxfield Dr
900 OGDN 84404 1057 D7
1300 OGDN 84404 1116 D1
Maxine Dr
3000 LYTN 84040 1284 A1
Maxine St
3000 WVCY 84120 1962 C5
Maxwell Ln
300 SSLK 84115 1964 D4
May Cir
100 ALPN 84004 2497 E6
3600 WVCY 84120 1962 B6
Mayapple Wy
1400 WVCY 84119 1963 D5
Maybe St
2700 SRCS 84075 1280 D3
Maybeck Pl
4400 SLkC 84124 2071 C2
Mayberry Ct
11400 DRPR 84020 2282 D6
Mayfair Cir
1600 SLCY 84105 1859 C7
Mayfield Dr
14200 DRPR 84020 2388 D6
Mayflower Av
3300 LEHI 84043 2495 B7
Mayflower St
5300 WJDN 84088 2173 E7
Mayfly Wy
600 SNDY 84070 2176 E6
Maynard Ct
3400 RIVN 84065 2386 D4
Mayors Cir
1200 WDCR 84087 1653 A1
Maytime Cir
3900 SLkC 84044 1960 D7
Maytime Dr
7600 SLkC 84044 1960 C7
Maywood Cir
2400 SLCY 84109 1966 A3
Maywood Dr
2300 SLCY 84109 1965 E3
2500 SLCY 84109 1966 A3
W M Bond Ln
- HRCY 84032 2398 E2
- WshC 84032 2398 E2
McBeth Ct
6000 MRRY 84123 2069 E6
McCall St
3600 SSLK 84115 1964 D7
McClanahan Ln
8300 WJDN 84088 2174 A5
McClelland St
100 SLCY 84102 1859 A3
900 SLCY 84105 1859 A6
1800 SLCY 84105 1965 A1
2100 SLCY 84106 1965 A2
3100 SLkC 84106 1965 A5
McCormick Cir
1300 CDHT 84121 2177 B2
McCormick Wy
700 LYTN 84041 1282 C3
1300 CDHT 84093 2177 B2
1300 CDHT 84121 2177 B2
McCuiston Av
6900 HRMN 84065 2385 A5
7000 SLkC 84065 2385 A5
McCune Ct
8300 WJDN 84088 2174 A5
McDaniel Cir
1100 UthC 84004 2498 B3
McDonald Pl
700 SLCY 84102 1859 A4
McDowell Ct
8300 WJDN 84088 2174 A5
McFarland St
800 SOGN 84403 1116 A7
800 SOGN 84403 1173 B1
McGinnis Ln
4900 WJDN 84088 2174 A5
8400 WJDN 84088 2173 E5
McGregor Ln
8300 WJDN 84088 2175 A5
McHenry St
100 MRRY 84107 2070 D3
300 PKCY 84060 2078 E6
McIntyre Ct
4800 WJDN 84088 2174 A5
McIntyre Wy
8400 WJDN 84088 2174 A6
McKaylee Cir
3200 SJDN 84095 2280 E1
McKell Ct
3200 CDHT 84121 2178 C2
McKenzie Ln
8300 WJDN 84088 2174 A6
McKinley Cir
2700 TYVL 84084 2069 A7
McKinley Dr
10 LNDN 84042 2713 E6
10 LNDN 84042 2714 A6
McKinley Ln
6300 TYVL 84084 2069 A7
McKinney Ct
4600 SmtC 84098 1971 D6
McLain Mountain Cir
3600 CDHT 84121 2178 D4
McMillan Cir
5700 MRRY 84107 2070 D5
McMillan Ln
300 MRRY 84107 2070 D6
McNae Wy
6700 WJDN 84088 2175 D1
McNaughton Cir
10000 SJDN 84095 2280 C3
McNeill Cir
3200 CDHT 84093 2178 C6
McVea Ct
9400 SJDN 84095 2280 A1
Mead Av
100 SLCY 84101 1858 C6
1100 SLCY 84104 1857 E6
Mead Cir
1000 SLCY 84104 1857 E6
Meadow Cir
- LOGN 84321 527 B4
1000 ALPN 84004 2498 B4
Meadow Ct
800 DRPR 84020 2283 D7
9100 SNDY 84093 2177 A7
W Meadow Ct
2600 FRWT 84404 997 B5
Meadow Dr
1800 CDHT 84121 2177 D1
3200 OGDN 84403 1116 B6
N Meadow Dr
9700 CRHL 84062 2605 B3
Meadow Ln
- ANFK 84003 2604 A7
- MPTN 84664 3143 D5
10 MIDW 84049 2397 B2
10 SNDY 84070 2176 C7
200 CTRV 84014 1551 D2
600 SLCY 84106 1964 E3
700 ALPN 84004 2497 D5
5600 SOGN 84403 1173 D5
9800 HILD 84003 2604 E3
Meadow Rd
300 MRRY 84107 2070 D2
N Meadow Rd
10 MNTU 84324 768 C7
S Meadow Rd
10 MNTU 84324 768 C7
10 MNTU 84324 829 C1
Meadow Wy
- SOGN 84403 1173 D5
12900 RIVN 84065 2387 B3
Meadoway St
4700 MRRY 84107 2070 D3
Meadow Birch Ct
- PRVO 84601 3035 A2
Meadow Bluff Ln
1400 DRPR 84020 2496 C1
Meadowbrook Cir
3300 WVCY 84119 2068 E1
Meadow Brook Ct
200 LEHI 84043 2603 A7
200 LYTN 84041 1282 E1
Meadowbrook Ct
1200 FMTN 84025 1346 B6
Meadowbrook Dr
200 OGDN 84404 1056 C6
3200 WVCY 84119 2068 D1
E Meadowbrook Dr
800 ALPN 84004 2498 B4
N Meadowbrook Dr
10 ALPN 84004 2498 B4
Meadowbrook Expwy
700 SLkC 84119 1963 E7
700 SLkC 84119 1964 A7
700 SLkC 84123 1963 E7
700 SLkC 84123 1964 A7
700 SSLK 84119 1963 E7
700 SSLK 84119 1964 A7
700 SSLK 84123 1964 A7
700 TYVL 84123 1963 E7
1000 WVCY 84119 1963 E7
1300 TYVL 84123 2069 D1
1300 WVCY 84119 2069 D1
Meadow Brook Ln
1100 LEHI 84043 2603 A7
1300 LEHI 84043 2602 E7
Meadowbrook Ln
10 SGVL 84663 3036 B6
Meadow Creek Ct
2600 PKCY 84060 2078 C2
Meadow Creek Dr
2500 PKCY 84060 2078 C2
Meadow Creek Ln
1600 OGDN 84403 1173 C2
Meadowcreek Ln
400 MIDW 84049 2397 A1
Meadow Crest Dr
5700 MRRY 84107 2070 D6
Meadowcrest Rd
6200 HLDY 84121 2071 E7
Meadow Crossing Dr
1100 WDCR 84087 1653 A3
Meadow Downs Wy
1700 CDHT 84121 2177 C1
Meadow Fork Rd
1100 PRVO 84606 3036 A2
Meadow Gate Cir
4300 WVCY 84120 2068 D2
Meadow Gate Dr
3800 WVCY 84120 2068 C2
Meadow Glen Wy
1100 WJDN 84088 2175 E6
W Meadow Green Dr
3900 WVCY 84120 2068 C1
Meadow Green St
1500 RIVN 84065 2387 C1
Meadow Green Wy
3000 WJDN 84088 2174 E5
3000 WJDN 84088 2175 A5
Meadow Hill Cir
11200 SNDY 84070 2282 E6
Meadow Hill Dr
400 SNDY 84070 2282 E6
Meadowland Av
1800 WJDN 84084 2175 C2
Meadowland Cir
- WBNF 84087 1551 B5
Meadow Lark Cir
300 KYVL 84037 1283 C6
Meadowlark Cir
8900 SNDY 84093 2177 D7
Meadowlark Dr
100 ALPN 84004 2497 E3
3100 WVCY 84119 1963 A6
Meadow Lark Ln
800 KYVL 84037 1283 C6
Meadowlark Ln
500 BNFL 84010 1654 A4
600 SHFD 84335 400 A2
900 WBNF 84087 1551 B4
8400 WJDN 84088 2174 D6
E Meadow Lark Ln
300 SGVL 84663 3143 E2
Meadowlark Rd
500 OREM 84097 2713 E7
1600 OREM 84097 2820 D1
Meadowlark Wy
2000 SNDY 84093 2177 E7
Meadow Lily Ln
9000 WJDN 84088 2174 A7
Meadow Loop Rd
1400 SmtC 84098 1971 E5
N Meadow Loop Rd
- SmtC 84098 1971 D5
Meadow Loop Bay
3200 WVCY 84128 1961 B5
Meadow Marsh Dr
- LEHI 84043 2710 D2
Meadow Moor Cir
1400 SLkC 84117 2071 B4
Meadow Moor Rd
1400 SLkC 84117 2071 C4
Meadow Oak Ct
14800 DRPR 84020 2389 D7
Meadow Park Cir
12100 RIVN 84065 2387 D1
Meadow Park Ct
3200 WVCY 84119 1962 E7
Meadow Pine Ct
800 SLkC 84106 1965 A7
Meadow Point Ct
3000 WVCY 84128 1961 A4
Meadow Ridge Cir
12000 RIVN 84065 2281 E7
Meadowridge Dr
2500 WJDN 84088 2281 A1
Meadow Ridge Ln
1200 SJDN 84095 2281 D1
Meadow Ridge Rd
1200 SNDY 84094 2389 B1
Meadow River Dr
10700 SNDY 84070 2282 D4
N Meadows Cir
2300 PTGV 84062 2605 C6
Meadows Dr
2500 PKCY 84060 2078 B2
3300 PKCY 84060 1972 D7
E Meadows Dr
4800 SmtC 84098 1971 E4
Meadows Connection
1300 SmtC 84098 1971 E5
Meadow Stream Rd
1100 WVCY 84119 1963 D6
Meadow Valley Dr
- DRPR 84020 2389 B7
Meadow View Cir
1700 FMTN 84025 1447 E1
Meadowview Cir
10 HRCY 84032 2398 C3
4600 MRRY 84107 2070 D4
Meadowview Ct
8200 SmtC 84098 1865 A5
Meadow View Dr
- TYVL 84123 2069 E4
100 OGDN 84404 1056 D6
Meadowview Dr
7900 SmtC 84098 1865 A5
Meadow View Ln
- NBLY 84321 591 C5
Meadowview Ln
1200 ANFK 84003 2605 A6
Meadowview Rd
4600 MRRY 84107 2070 D2
8500 SmtC 84098 1866 E4
8500 SmtC 84098 1867 A5
Meadow Vista Ct
8100 SLkC 84044 1960 C5
Meadow Wood Dr
700 DRPR 84020 2282 E7
800 DRPR 84020 2283 A6
4000 RVDL 84405 1172 B1
Meadow Wood Ln
1200 ANFK 84003 2605 A6
Meadow Wood St
- PRVO 84601 3035 B1
Meadow Wood Wy
3200 TYVL 84118 2068 E3
Meadow Wy Dr
800 KYVL 84041 1283 B6
800 LYTN 84041 1283 B6
Meandor Av
6200 WVCY 84128 1961 B6
Mecham Ln
1000 MDVL 84047 2177 A3
Meckailee Cove
9400 SLkC 84094 2283 A1
9400 SNDY 84094 2283 A1
Medallion Cir
9400 SJDN 84095 2281 E1
Medford Dr
3400 BNFL 84010 1653 E5
Medical Dr
10 SLCY 84112 1859 D2
10 SLCY 84113 1859 D2
400 BNFL 84010 1551 E7
400 BNFL 84010 1552 B7
600 BNFL 84010 1654 A1
900 BMCY 84302 827 D2
N Medical Dr
10 SLCY 84103 1859 D2
10 SLCY 84113 1859 D2
S Medical Dr
- SLCY 84113 1859 D3
Medical Plz
10 SLCY 84113 1859 E3
Medical Tower Dr
5700 MRRY 84107 2070 D6
Medinah
4100 CRHL 84062 2605 B1
Medoland Dr
500 BMCY 84302 767 A3
Medoland Pl
700 BMCY 84302 767 B3
Meeting House Rd
800 FTHT 84037 1346 A1
900 FTHT 84037 1284 A7
Megan Cir
2100 WbrC 84403 1173 D5
4100 SLkC 84107 2071 A1
Meier Cir
2400 TYVL 84084 2069 B7
Meier Ct
2400 TYVL 84084 2069 B7
Meier Dr
6200 TYVL 84084 2069 B7
Melanie Ln
300 PTGV 84062 2713 A3
2600 WbrC 84403 1174 A6
E Melanie Ln
100 SALM 84653 3356 B5
S Melanie Ln
1300 SRCS 84075 1227 A7
W Melanie Ln
1200 SRCS 84075 1227 A7
Melba Ln
1500 RIVN 84065 2281 C7
Melbourne Cir
1000 FMTN 84025 1346 C3
Melbourne Ct
900 FMTN 84025 1346 C3
Melbourne St
2500 SLCY 84106 1965 D3
2800 SLkC 84106 1965 D4
Melbrook Ln
7500 WJDN 84084 2173 E3
Melbury Cir
8900 SNDY 84093 2177 D7
Mel Helen Wy
7200 WJDN 84084 2175 B3
Melinda Ln
2100 SLkC 84109 1965 E7
Melissa Cir
11100 SNDY 84092 2283 C5
Melissa Hill Cir
5100 TYVL 84118 2068 D4
Melissa Kaye Dr
10800 SNDY 84070 2282 D5
Mellow Mountain Rd
600 PKCY 84060 2078 E5
600 PKCY 84060 2079 A5
Melodie Ann Wy
2100 HLDY 84124 2071 E2
Melody Ct
900 SJDN 84095 2281 E3
900 SJDN 84095 2282 A3
Melody Ln
800 OGDN 84404 1057 A6
Melody St
200 LYTN 84041 1282 E5
Melody Creek Cir
3400 RIVN 84065 2280 D7
Melony Dr
2400 HLDY 84124 2072 A1
2600 SLkC 84124 2072 A1
Melrose Cir
6500 TYVL 84084 2175 B1
Melville Cir
1700 WJDN 84088 2175 C6
8000 SLkC 84044 1960 C3
Melville Dr
2500 SLkC 84044 1960 C4
Melvina St
3400 SLkC 84106 1965 B6
N Memmo Dr
800 OREM 84057 2820 D3
Memorial Cir
- OGDN 84401 1116 A2
3000 SJDN 84095 2281 A2
Memorial Dr
9800 SJDN 84095 2280 E2
9800 SJDN 84095 2281 A2
Memory Ln
- HLDY 84117 2071 D3
Memorybook Wy
10000 SJDN 84095 2281 D3
Mendon Ct
800 SLCY 84102 1859 A6
Mendon Rd
1000 LOGN 84321 527 A4
1400 LOGN 84321 526 D4
1600 CchC 84321 526 D4
3400 CchC 84321 525 D4
4700 CchC 84325 525 A5
5400 CchC 84325 524 E5
5600 MNDN 84325 524 E5
Menlo Av
800 SLCY 84102 1859 A4
Menteith St
10100 SJDN 84095 2280 D3
Menzel Ct
5100 SLkC 84118 2067 E7
Merced Cir
3700 RIVN 84065 2280 D7
Mercedes Wy
1000 SLCY 84108 1860 B6
Mercer Ct
- DRPR 84020 2497 A2
Mercer Wy
200 SSLK 84115 1964 B3
Mercer Hollow Rd
11500 HILD 84003 2497 B6
Mercer Point Cir
- DRPR 84020 2497 A2
Merchant St
10 ANFK 84003 2711 C1
Mercury Dr
3900 HLDY 84124 1966 A7
3900 HLDY 84124 2072 A1
Merewood Ct
900 SNDY 84094 2177 A5
Meridian Cir
800 TYVL 84123 2070 A2
Meridian Rd
- CchC 84319 709 C2
- CchC 84328 709 C2
- CchC 84339 709 C2
6600 CchC 84319 650 C6
6600 CchC 84339 650 C6
Meridies Dr
2000 SJDN 84095 2281 B4
Merit Pkwy
1600 SJDN 84095 2281 C2
Merlin Dr
1500 PRVO 84601 2927 E5
Merlin St
200 NSLK 84054 1653 B5
Merlin Wy
1400 LYTN 84041 1282 B1
Merlot Wy
6600 WJDN 84088 2173 B6
Merlyn Cir
1800 SLkC 84117 2071 D5
Merlyn Dr
2400 SLkC 84117 2071 D5
Merribee Wy
1600 SLkC 84121 2071 C6
Merrick Ct
8400 WJDN 84088 2173 E5
Merril Cir
4200 WVCY 84120 2068 B1
Merrill Hall
500 LOGN 84321 528 A2
Merrimac Av
10 SLCY 84115 1858 C7
Merriton Ct
8400 SLkC 84044 1960 B6
Merritt Cir
1300 MRRY 84117 2071 B5
Merry Ln
3300 WVCY 84120 1961 E6
Merton Wy
2800 SLkC 84044 1960 A4
Mesa Av
800 LEHI 84043 2603 D3
Mesa Cir
2100 SNDY 84092 2283 E6

Salt Lake City Street Index

STREET Block City ZIP Map# Grid

Mesa Dr
700 BMCY 84302 766 C7
8300 SLkC 84093 2177 C5
8300 SNDY 84093 2177 C5
Mesquite Cir
8600 SLkC 84044 1960 A6
Messina Ct
3700 WVCY 84119 1963 E6
Meteor Hill Cove
5200 WJDN 84084 2173 E2
Metro Wy
3100 SLkC 84109 1966 B5
Metropolitan Wy
2900 SLkC 84109 1966 B5
Meyers Ln
6400 MRRY 84107 2176 C1
Meyer Vista Cove
7900 CDHT 84093 2177 D4
Miami Cir
1300 SLCY 84116 1753 C6
Miami Rd
1300 SLCY 84116 1753 C5
Mica Ln
1400 LYTN 84041 1344 B1
Micah Cir
1900 SJDN 84095 2281 C4
Michael St
2000 CRFD 84015 1281 E1
Michael Wy
1500 SNDY 84093 2177 C7
Michaela Wy
- WJDN 84084 2174 A2
Michaelangelo Ct
3700 WVCY 84119 1963 D6
Michael Mills Pl
900 SLkC 84106 1965 A6
Michaun Ct
10300 SJDN 84095 2281 E3
Michelle Dr
1100 BMCY 84302 827 E2
1100 BMCY 84302 828 A2
Michelle St
100 PTVW 84404 998 A6
Michelle Wy
7500 CDHT 84093 2177 B3
Michigan Av
1100 SLCY 84105 1859 B6
1700 SLCY 84108 1859 D6
2400 SLCY 84108 1860 A6
Mickelsen Pl
12900 DRPR 84020 2389 C3
Midas Cir
4100 WVCY 84128 2067 C1
Midas Creek Dr
1300 SJDN 84095 2281 D6
Midas Gold Rd
4600 HRMN 84065 2386 A1
Midas Park Rd
4600 HRMN 84065 2280 B7
12000 HRMN 84065 2386 B1
Midas Pond Rd
- SJDN 84095 2282 A5
Midas Quarry Rd
12100 HRMN 84065 2386 A1
Midas Ridge Ln
3400 RIVN 84065 2280 E7
Midas Trail Cir
1100 SJDN 84095 2281 E5
Midas Trail Rd
11100 SJDN 84095 2281 E5
Midas View Cir
11200 SJDN 84095 2281 D6
Midas Vista Rd
12000 HRMN 84065 2280 A7
Middlebrook Dr
6200 TYVL 84084 2068 E6
Middle Fork Ln
4900 MRRY 84117 2071 A3
Middlefork Ln
8000 WbrC 84317 1061 B3
Middlepark Ln
4100 WVCY 84119 2068 E1
Middlesex Rd
1100 TYVL 84123 2069 E1
Middleton Wy
2900 SLkC 84124 2072 B1
Middlewood Av
5700 SLkC 84118 2067 D7
Middlewood Cir
6000 SLkC 84118 2067 D7
Midhurst Wy
5000 SLkC 84117 2071 D4
Midland Av
1700 SLCY 84116 1753 D4
Midland Dr
1800 WbrC 84401 1114 E5
1900 WbrC 84067 1114 E5
1900 WHVN 84067 1114 E5
1900 WHVN 84401 1114 E5
2600 OGDN 84401 1115 A4
2700 WbrC 84401 1115 A4
2800 OGDN 84401 1114 E5
3600 ROY 84067 1114 E5
3900 ROY 84067 1171 A2
3900 WHVN 84067 1171 A2
4200 WbrC 84067 1171 A2
4500 ROY 84067 1170 E2
4500 WbrC 84067 1170 E2
4500 WHVN 84067 1170 E2
Midland Dr SR-108
1900 WbrC 84067 1114 D6
1900 WHVN 84067 1114 D6
1900 WHVN 84401 1114 D6
3600 ROY 84067 1114 D6
3900 ROY 84067 1171 A2
3900 WHVN 84067 1171 A2
4200 WbrC 84067 1171 A2
4500 ROY 84067 1170 E2
4500 WbrC 84067 1170 E2
4500 WHVN 84067 1170 E2
Midvalley Cir
1100 WJDN 84088 2175 E7
Midvalley Ct
1100 WJDN 84088 2175 E7
Midvalley Dr
8700 WJDN 84088 2175 E7
Midway Dr
4100 WVCY 84120 2068 C2
Midway Ln
800 MIDW 84049 2397 E4
800 WshC 84032 2397 E4
800 WshC 84049 2397 E4

Midway Ln
900 HRCY 84032 2398 A4
900 WshC 84032 2398 A4
Midway Ln SR-113
800 MIDW 84049 2397 E4
800 WshC 84032 2397 E4
800 WshC 84049 2397 E4
900 HRCY 84032 2398 A4
900 WshC 84032 2398 A4
Midwest Dr
2400 TYVL 84118 2069 A3
3000 TYVL 84118 2068 E3
Miera Ln
4300 WVCY 84120 1962 B6
Mignon Dr
4100 WVCY 84120 2068 B1
Mike Jense Cir
1100 PRVO 84601 3034 B2
Mike Jense Pkwy
3100 PRVO 84601 3034 B2
Mike Wier Dr
1200 DRPR 84020 2389 B7
Milan Dr
1500 SLCY 84116 1753 C7
Milden Cir
6300 WVCY 84128 1961 B5
Milden Ln
6100 WVCY 84128 1961 C5
Mildred St
4600 SLkC 84118 2068 B5
Mile High Cir
5100 OGDN 84403 1173 E4
Mile High Dr
3300 SLkC 84124 2072 C3
4100 PRVO 84604 2821 E5
Miles Cir
4800 TYVL 84118 2068 E3
Miles Dr
3300 TYVL 84118 2068 E3
Milestone Dr
800 SHFD 84335 400 A2
1700 SLCY 84104 1962 E1
1700 SLCY 84104 1963 A1
Milfoil Cir
6600 WJDN 84084 2174 A1
Milhan Ct
6100 MRRY 84123 2069 E7
Military Dr
900 SLCY 84105 1859 C6
900 SLCY 84108 1859 C6
Military Wy
1300 SLCY 84103 1859 C2
Milky Wy
10 CTRV 84014 1448 D7
1000 SNDY 84094 2177 A4
3900 HLDY 84124 1966 A7
3900 HLDY 84124 2072 A1
Mill Cir
500 LYTN 84041 1283 A5
3600 SLkC 84109 1966 C6
Mill Ln
1700 SLkC 84106 1965 C7
Mill Rd
10 LYTN 84041 1283 A5
E Mill Rd
- MLVI 84332 591 D3
200 NBLY 84321 591 D3
E Mill Rd SR-238
- MLVI 84332 591 D3
200 NBLY 84321 591 D3
N Mill Rd
10 HRCY 84032 2398 E3
300 WshC 84032 2398 E3
500 ANFK 84003 2604 C6
S Mill Rd
10 WshC 84032 2398 E4
900 SPFK 84660 3249 B5
1600 UthC 84660 3249 B5
Mill St
200 BNFL 84010 1653 E1
400 BNFL 84010 1654 A1
Millbert Av
1000 SLkC 84106 1965 A6
Millbert Dr
3400 SLkC 84106 1965 A6
Millbridge Ln
1100 WBNF 84087 1551 A7
1300 WBNF 84087 1550 E7
Millbrook Cir
3500 SLkC 84106 1965 D6
E Millbrook Dr
3500 SLkC 84106 1965 D6
Millbrook Rd
1500 SLkC 84106 1965 C6
Millbrook Ter
3600 SLkC 84106 1965 C6
E Millbrook Wy
800 BNFL 84010 1654 B2
S Millbrook Wy
1000 BNFL 84010 1654 A2
Millbury Wy
1700 SNDY 84092 2283 C3
Mill Canyon Dr
10800 SNDY 84094 2283 A5
Mill Canyon Peak Dr
14000 RIVN 84065 2385 E6
Mill Corner Cir
1900 SLkC 84106 1965 D5
Millcreek Cir
1700 SLkC 84106 1965 C6
W Millcreek Cir
300 PTGV 84062 2605 D5
Millcreek Dr
1300 OGDN 84404 1116 C1
E Mill Creek Dr
1900 SLkC 84106 1965 D6
Millcreek Ln
300 KYVL 84037 1283 D7
E Millcreek Rd
2800 SLkC 84109 1966 C6
N Millcreek Rd
3000 PTGV 84062 2605 C5
S Millcreek Rd
3500 SLkC 84109 1966 D6
W Millcreek Rd
400 PTGV 84062 2605 C5
Mill Creek Wy
1400 SLkC 84106 1965 C6
Millcreek Wy
300 BNFL 84010 1653 E2
400 BNFL 84010 1654 A2
500 SSLK 84106 1964 E6

Millcreek Wy
1800 SLkC 84106 1965 D6
E Millcreek Canyon Rd
3700 SLkC 84109 1966 D7
3700 SLkC 84124 1966 D7
S Millcreek Canyon Rd
3400 SLkC 84109 1966 B6
Mill Creek Cove
9000 CRHL 84062 2605 D5
Millcreek Dell Ln
3000 SLkC 84109 1966 B6
Millcreek Park Cir
700 SLkC 84106 1964 E6
Millcrest Cir
1000 BNFL 84010 1654 A2
Millcrest Rd
3700 SLkC 84109 1966 C7
Millen Cir
6600 WVCY 84128 1961 A6
Millennial Ln
- RIVN 84065 2386 C4
Millennium Wy
- MDVL 84047 2176 B3
Miller Av
10 SSLK 84115 1964 C5
400 LYTN 84041 1283 B3
E Miller Av
1200 SLCY 84106 1965 B5
1200 SLkC 84106 1965 B5
E Miller St
10 MRRY 84107 2070 C2
W Miller St
10 MRRY 84107 2070 C3
Miller Wy
- FMTN 84025 1448 B3
Millerama Av
2900 WVCY 84119 2069 A2
3000 WVCY 84119 2068 E2
Millerberg Cir
3500 WJDN 84084 2174 C2
Millerberg Dr
7800 MDVL 84070 2176 D4
Millerberg Wy
3300 WJDN 84084 2174 E2
Millet Cir
2800 WVCY 84120 1962 D4
Millet Pl
2100 SRSP 84043 2601 D4
Millford Cove
3800 SJDN 84095 2280 D2
Millhaven Cir
3500 SLkC 84109 1965 E6
Millhollow Cir
3400 SLkC 84106 1965 C6
Millicent Dr
2800 SLCY 84108 1860 B6
Millpoint Pl
200 SSLK 84115 1964 D6
Millpond Dr
200 LEHI 84043 2603 D7
N Millpond Dr
1200 SGVL 84663 3036 D6
Mill Pond Rd
7300 LEHI 84043 2710 C1
Millrace Ln
4700 MRRY 84107 2070 E3
Millrace Park Ln
800 TYVL 84123 2070 A3
Mill Ridge Cir
12000 SNDY 84094 2283 B7
Mill Ridge Rd
12000 SNDY 84094 2389 B1
Mill Shadow Dr
700 KYVL 84037 1345 A2
Mill Stone Ct
- KYVL 84037 1345 B3
E Millstream Dr
3500 SLkC 84109 1966 D6
Millstream Ln
1300 SLkC 84106 1965 B6
2000 SLkC 84109 1965 D6
3500 SLkC 84109 1966 C6
Millstream Wy
800 BNFL 84010 1654 A2
Mill Valley Ct
6300 WVCY 84118 2067 C7
Mill Valley Ln
6000 WVCY 84118 2067 C7
Millville St
3200 SJDN 84095 2280 E4
Millwood Dr
11200 SNDY 84092 2283 C6
Milne Ln
1300 CDHT 84093 2177 B2
Milo Wy
2500 HLDY 84117 2072 A3
Milos Dr
4800 WVCY 84120 2068 A3
Milstead Ln
5000 SLkC 84118 2068 A6
5100 SLkC 84118 2067 E6
Milton Av
300 SLCY 84115 1964 D1
600 SLCY 84105 1858 E7
1100 SLCY 84105 1859 B7
Mimosa Cir
- RIVN 84065 2386 A4
Mimosa Ln
1300 DvsC 84056 1228 A2
1400 DvsC 84056 1172 A7
Mimosa St
- RIVN 84065 2386 A4
Mindella Wy
200 LYTN 84041 1228 E6
Minden Dr
1700 SLkC 84121 2071 C6
Mindi Meadows Cir
3200 RIVN 84065 2387 B3
Mindy Cir
3300 WVCY 84120 1962 A6
W Mindy Cir
700 KYVL 84037 1345 B2
Miner Dr
2000 SJDN 84095 2281 B3
Mineral Wy
4800 HRMN 84065 2280 A7
Mineral Mt Dr
6800 WJDN 84084 2173 C2
Miners Mesa Dr
6000 WJDN 84084 2173 C2
Mine Shaft Rd
7300 CDHT 84121 2178 D3

Mineside Dr
2600 SLkC 84044 1960 E4
Mingo Park Dr
400 SNDY 84070 2176 E6
Mingo View Av
500 SNDY 84070 2176 E7
Mink Cir
900 NSLK 84054 1653 C7
Minnesota Dr
- DvsC 84056 1172 A7
Mint Green Cir
500 MRRY 84107 2070 E2
Minuet Av
2800 WVCY 84119 2069 A1
3000 WVCY 84119 2068 E1
Minuet Cir
4000 WVCY 84119 2068 E1
Minuet Ct
4000 WVCY 84119 2069 A1
Minuteman Dr
12300 DRPR 84020 2388 C3
14600 DRPR 84020 2495 A3
Minuteman Wy
3000 CRFD 84015 1228 B5
3000 DvsC 84056 1228 B5
Mirabella Dr
5600 HRMN 84065 2385 C5
Miracle Cove
2900 SLkC 84044 1960 E5
Mira Loma St
3400 WVCY 84119 1963 E6
Miramar Wy
3000 SLkC 84109 1965 E5
Miranda Ln
8100 SNDY 84093 2177 C5
Miriam Cir
3800 SLkC 84044 1960 E7
Mirkwood Ln
5600 TYVL 84118 2068 C6
Mirror Lake Dr
5600 WJDN 84088 2173 D5
Mission Rd
1100 SLCY 84104 1857 D6
Misty Cir
4000 TYVL 84084 2068 C7
Misty Dr
3800 TYVL 84084 2068 C7
3900 WJDN 84084 2068 C7
Misty Wy
5800 SLkC 84118 2068 C6
S Misty Breeze Cir
200 KYVL 84037 1344 E2
W Misty Breeze Cir
1400 KYVL 84037 1344 E2
Misty Fen Wy
1300 WJDN 84088 2281 D1
Misty Hollow Wy
1300 WJDN 84084 2175 D3
Misty Meadows Cir
1700 SNDY 84093 2177 C7
Misty Morning Cir
5100 TYVL 84123 2069 C4
Misty Oaks Cir
9500 SJDN 84095 2281 A1
Misty Oaks Dr
2700 SJDN 84095 2281 A1
Misty Sea Rd
12000 RIVN 84065 2281 E7
Misty View Cir
1300 TYVL 84123 2069 D4
Misty View Wy
5100 TYVL 84123 2069 D4
Mistywood Ln
10 SNDY 84092 2283 E5
Mitchell Dr
300 SPFK 84660 3249 B1
1400 OGDN 84403 1116 C6
Mitchell Ln
400 DvsC 84056 1228 D5
Mitchell Cove
400 SSLK 84115 1964 E7
Mitt Ln
7400 CDHT 84121 2177 E3
Mivu Cir
8500 SNDY 84093 2177 D6
Mix Av
8300 SLkC 84044 1960 B6
Moab Wy
15100 DRPR 84020 2495 D1
Moat Cir
2900 WVCY 84120 1962 A4
Mobina Ct
900 SLkC 84117 2071 A3
Mocha Cir
2700 TYVL 84118 2069 A3
Mocha Dr
4700 TYVL 84118 2069 A3
Mockingbird Cir
2400 WVCY 84119 1963 A5
9100 SNDY 84094 2177 B7
Mockingbird Ln
1100 SNDY 84094 2177 B7
Mockingbird Wy
2500 WVCY 84119 1963 B6
Mockorange Dr
2500 WVCY 84119 1963 A4
Modesto Av
1000 SLCY 84104 1857 E6
Modesto Cir
1100 SLCY 84104 1857 E6
Moen Hall
100 LOGN 84321 528 A2
Moffat Ct
300 SSLK 84111 1858 D4
Moffat Farm Ln
6100 MRRY 84121 2071 B7
Mohave Wy
3500 WVCY 84120 1962 A6
Mohawk Av
600 PTGV 84062 2713 C4
Mohawk Cir
1700 SLCY 84108 1966 A1
3200 PRVO 84604 2928 E1
5300 OGDN 84403 1173 D4
Mohawk Ln
1600 OGDN 84403 1173 D4
3100 PRVO 84604 2928 E1
Mohawk Wy
1600 SLCY 84108 1966 B1
Mohican Cir
1200 PTGV 84062 2713 B4
6000 MRRY 84123 2070 A7

Mohican Ln
600 PTGV 84062 2713 B4
3200 PRVO 84604 2821 E7
3200 PRVO 84604 2928 E2
Mohican Wy
3200 PRVO 84604 2928 E1
Mojave Dr
1700 SLCY 84116 1753 C5
Mojave Ln
2900 PRVO 84604 2928 E1
Moki Cir
6300 WJDN 84084 2068 A7
Molasses Mill Dr
14200 DRPR 84020 2389 A6
Molly Dr
3700 SLkC 84044 1960 D7
Mombo Dr
1700 SNDY 84092 2283 C1
Mona Ln
4700 WJDN 84084 2174 A2
Monaco Av
1500 MRRY 84121 2071 C6
Monaco Cir
1500 MRRY 84121 2071 C6
Monarch Dr
10 BNFL 84010 1653 D6
10 NSLK 84054 1653 D6
2100 PKCY 84060 2078 E3
Monarch Wy
4000 SLkC 84124 2072 B1
Monarch Meadows Pkwy
- BFDL 84065 2386 A4
- RIVN 84065 2386 A4
Mond St
100 OGDN 84404 1056 D6
Monet Ct
6000 SLkC 84118 2067 E7
Monica Cove
6900 CDHT 84121 2178 C2
Monitor Dr
2000 PKCY 84060 2078 D2
8500 SNDY 84093 2177 E6
Monroe Blvd
100 OGDN 84404 1057 A5
1300 OGDN 84404 1116 A1
1600 OGDN 84401 1116 A1
1700 NHON 84414 1057 A1
2400 NHON 84414 999 A6
2700 OGDN 84403 1116 A5
3600 SOGN 84403 1116 A7
4000 SOGN 84403 1173 A2
N Monroe Blvd
100 OGDN 84404 1057 A4
Monroe Cir
2100 WJDN 84084 2175 B2
Monroe St
8000 MDVL 84047 2176 C5
8600 SNDY 84070 2176 C7
Monroe Plaza Wy
9100 SNDY 84070 2176 C7
Monson Cir
10 PTGV 84062 2713 B3
Monson Pl
- PTGV 84062 2605 C4
3900 CRHL 84062 2605 C4
Montague Av
400 SLCY 84101 1858 B6
800 SLCY 84104 1858 A6
900 SLCY 84104 1857 E6
Montaia Dr
4000 WVCY 84119 1963 A7
4000 WVCY 84119 2069 A1
Montana Av
1900 PRVO 84606 3036 B3
Montana Dr
400 SNDY 84070 2282 E6
Montana St
3700 CRNN 84307 705 A7
3900 CRNN 84307 704 E7
Montane Ct
12100 DRPR 84020 2389 E1
Montane Dr
2000 DRPR 84020 2389 E1
Montane Cove
2000 DRPR 84020 2389 D1
Mont Blanc Dr
2200 RIVN 84065 2387 B2
Montcalm Dr
2300 RIVN 84065 2387 B2
Mont Clair Ct
600 NSLK 84054 1754 C1
Mont Clair Dr
600 NSLK 84054 1754 C1
Montclair Dr
900 SLkC 84106 1965 A6
Montclair St
3100 SLkC 84044 1960 D6
3500 SLkC 84106 1965 A6
E Monte Ct
400 SSLK 84115 1964 E7
Monte Azul
700 TYVL 84123 2070 A2
Monte Bella Dr
700 TYVL 84123 2070 A2
Monte Bello Rd
2500 SNDY 84092 2284 A1
Monte Blanco Dr
700 TYVL 84123 2070 A2
Monte Carlo Dr
1700 MRRY 84121 2071 C6
Montecito St
3700 SLkC 84106 1965 B7
Monte Cristo Dr
1900 MRRY 84121 2071 D7
Monte del Oro
700 TYVL 84123 2070 A2
Montego Pl
1300 SLkC 84117 2071 C3
Monte Grande Dr
4500 TYVL 84123 2070 A2
Monte Hermosa St
700 TYVL 84123 2070 A2
Monte Joseph Dr
6500 HRMN 84065 2385 B5
Monte Luca Wy
- CDHT 84093 2178 B5
- CDHT 84121 2178 B5
Monterey Cir
3600 BNFL 84010 1653 E6
7400 CDHT 84093 2177 B3
Monterey Dr
500 OREM 84057 2820 D3

Monterey Dr
1800 MRRY 84121 2071 E5
Monterey Pine Ln
3200 WJDN 84088 2174 E6
Monte Verde Dr
3200 SLkC 84109 1966 D6
Monte Vista Cir
1700 SLCY 84108 1965 D1
Monte Vista Dr
4500 TYVL 84123 2070 A2
Montgomery Dr
300 SNDY 84070 2176 D7
Montgomery St
500 SLCY 84104 1857 D4
N Montgomery St
400 SLCY 84116 1857 C2
E Monticello Dr
10 KYVL 84037 1345 D4
W Monticello Dr
10 KYVL 84037 1345 B4
Monticello Ln
1100 MRRY 84123 2069 E7
Montrone Dr
2900 WVCY 84119 1962 E4
Montrose Av
200 SLCY 84101 1858 B5
Montrose Ln
10 SRSP 84043 2710 A3
Montrose St
5300 MRRY 84107 2070 D5
Mont Sur Dr
2400 RIVN 84065 2387 B2
Monument Cir
11700 SJDN 84095 2280 E7
Monument Park Cir
800 SLCY 84108 1859 E5
800 SLCY 84108 1860 A6
Monza Dr
3500 SLkC 84109 1966 C7
Moon Cir
600 FMTN 84025 1346 B6
Moon Beam Bay
3500 SLkC 84044 1960 B6
Moon Crest Ct
5700 WJDN 84084 2173 D1
Moon Flower Cir
4900 SLkC 84118 2068 A6
Moonglow Wy
9700 SNDY 84070 2282 C2
Moonlight Dr
9700 SNDY 84070 2282 C2
Moonlite Hill Ct
12500 HRMN 84065 2385 C2
Moon Ridge Dr
10 MRRY 84107 2070 C6
Moonriver Dr
1500 PRVO 84604 2928 B3
Moon Shadow Dr
5700 HRMN 84065 2385 C5
Moonshine Cir
3800 WJDN 84088 2174 C6
Moonstone St
1500 SJDN 84095 2281 C5
Moonwalk Cir
12000 RIVN 84065 2281 D7
Moor Ln
1600 OREM 84057 2713 E7
1600 OREM 84057 2820 E1
2200 WJDN 84084 2175 B1
E Moor Rd
5100 SLkC 84117 2071 C4
Moor Dale Cir
5000 SLkC 84117 2071 C4
Moor Dale Ln
1500 SLkC 84117 2071 C4
Moore Crest Ct
1800 CDHT 84121 2177 D3
Moorgate Av
3800 WVCY 84120 2068 C2
Moorgate Cir
4300 WVCY 84120 2068 D1
Moor Mont Cir
4900 SLkC 84117 2071 D4
Moormont Dr
1800 SLkC 84117 2071 D4
Moose Hollow Cir
1700 DRPR 84020 2389 C3
Moose Hollow Dr
- WbrC 84310 1001 E3
12700 DRPR 84020 2389 C2
Moosehollow Rd
4000 SmtC 84098 1864 D3
Moose Horn Ct
4600 WJDN 84088 2174 B7
Moraine Cir
2700 SLkC 84109 1966 A7
Moray Ct
1100 PKCY 84060 2078 D2
Moreland Cir
3700 WJDN 84084 2174 D1
Morena Wy
- HRMN 84065 2385 E2
Morgan Blvd
3700 CRHL 84062 2605 C1
Morgan Dr
2700 SLkC 84124 2072 A1
Morgan St
300 LYTN 84041 1283 A5
Morgan Grove Wy
10000 SNDY 84092 2283 E2
Morganwood Bay
5100 SLkC 84118 2068 C4
Morning Blush Dr
5300 HRMN 84065 2385 E6
Morning Breeze Dr
5400 SLkC 84118 2068 A5
Morning Cloak Wy
- RIVN 84065 2385 E4
4900 RIVN 84065 2386 A5
Morning Crest Dr
1200 TYVL 84123 2069 D4
Morning Dew Cir
5000 MRRY 84123 2070 A4
Morning Dew Dr
700 MRRY 84123 2070 A3
Morning Dove Cir
- LEHI 84043 2495 C5
2500 WVCY 84119 1963 B5
Morning Dove Dr
- WPT 84015 1225 D4
Morning Glory Cir
12800 RIVN 84065 2387 B3

Morning Laurel Ln
4900 WJDN 84088 2174 A7
5000 WJDN 84088 2173 E7
Morning Light Dr
5300 HRMN 84065 2385 D6
Morning Lily Ct
9100 WJDN 84088 2174 A7
Morning Lily Ln
4900 WJDN 84088 2174 A7
5100 WJDN 84088 2173 E7
Morning Mesa Cir
5200 TYVL 84123 2069 C4
Morning Mist Ct
9100 SNDY 84093 2177 E7
Morning Oaks Dr
1200 TYVL 84123 2069 D4
Morning Ridge Cir
400 DRPR 84020 2388 E4
Morning Side Cir
- KYVL 84037 1344 E3
Morningside Cir
3100 SLkC 84124 2072 B1
Morningside Dr
- FMTN 84025 1447 D1
2700 SLkC 84124 2072 A1
2900 SLkC 84124 1966 B7
Morning Side Ln
900 WbrC 84310 1059 E2
900 WbrC 84310 1060 A3
Morning Sky Cir
5200 TYVL 84123 2069 D5
Morning Sky Ct
2500 PKCY 84060 2079 A1
Morning Star Ct
2400 PKCY 84060 2078 B3
Morning Star Dr
10 PKCY 84060 2078 B3
2000 SRSP 84043 2601 E5
2600 HLDY 84124 1966 A7
2600 SLkC 84124 1966 A7
4000 HLDY 84124 2072 A1
Morning Star Wy
9800 SNDY 84070 2282 C2
Morning Sun Dr
1200 TYVL 84123 2069 D4
Morning Tide Ln
11200 SJDN 84095 2280 B5
Morning View Cir
9200 SNDY 84094 2177 B7
Morningview Dr
9100 SNDY 84094 2177 B7
Morning Vista Ct
5200 TYVL 84123 2069 E5
Morning Vista Dr
1200 TYVL 84123 2069 D4
Morris Av
100 SSLK 84115 1964 D3
Morris St
4100 TYVL 84119 2069 C2
Morristown Ln
100 HARR 84414 998 D6
Morro St
6600 CDHT 84121 2178 A1
N Morton Dr
400 SLCY 84116 1857 C1
1300 SLCY 84116 1753 B6
W Morton Dr
1800 SLCY 84116 1753 C6
Morton Rd
1500 SLCY 84116 1753 B5
Morton Hills Cir
1100 SLCY 84116 1753 C6
Morywood Cir
9400 SJDN 84095 2281 D1
Morywood Ct
1400 SJDN 84095 2281 D2
Morywood Ln
9400 SJDN 84095 2281 D1
Moshier Ln
3700 WVCY 84120 1961 E7
Moshier View Cir
5300 WVCY 84120 1961 D5
Moss Cir
1200 MDVL 84047 2177 B4
Moss Ln
1400 FMTN 84025 1345 E5
Moss Creek Cir
4700 MRRY 84107 2070 E3
Moss Creek Dr
400 MRRY 84107 2070 E3
E Moss Hill Dr
1200 BNFL 84010 1552 C7
N Moss Hill Dr
10 BNFL 84010 1552 C7
S Moss Hill Dr
10 BNFL 84010 1552 C7
100 BNFL 84010 1654 B1
Moss Rose Ct
5400 HRMN 84065 2385 D6
Mother Lode Ct
11800 HRMN 84065 2280 A7
Motor Av
1000 SLCY 84116 1857 E2
Motor Park Av
10 SNDY 84070 2282 C4
E Mott Dr
2100 SLkC 84109 1965 E5
S Mott Dr
3200 SLkC 84109 1965 E5
Moulton Ln
200 WshC 84032 2292 C5
Mound Fort Dr
1200 OGDN 84404 1057 A7
1200 OGDN 84404 1116 A1
E Mountain Cir
700 ALPN 84004 2498 B6
E Mountain Dr
1000 ALPN 84004 2498 B6
Mountain Ln
3300 PKCY 84060 2078 C1
4700 SLkC 84124 2072 C3
Mountain Pkwy N
- SGVL 84663 3035 E5
- SGVL 84663 3036 A5
- UthC 84606 3035 E5
- UthC 84606 3036 A5
Mountain Pl
4900 SLkC 84124 2072 B4
Mountain Rd
- CchC 84321 528 C4
- LOGN 84321 528 B3
- TMTN 84337 520 A4

STREET Block	City	ZIP	Map#	Grid
Mountain Rd				
900	OGDN	84404	1057	C7
1300	OGDN	84404	1116	C1
1700	NHON	84414	1057	B1
3300	NHON	84414	999	B3
N Mountain Rd				
10	FTHT	84037	1346	B1
200	FTHT	84037	1284	A7
700	KYVL	84037	1284	A6
900	OGDN	84404	1057	B2
1400	NHON	84414	1057	B2
S Mountain Rd				
10	FTHT	84037	1346	B2
Mountain Ash Cir				
1800	RIVN	84065	2387	C1
Mountain Aura Dr				
5600	WJDN	84084	2173	D1
Mountain Berry Dr				
300	DRPR	84020	2282	D6
Mountain Brook Dr				
5200	WJDN	84088	2173	E6
Mountain Cove				
3200	SLkC	84124	2072	C3
E Mountain Creek Cove				
10	FMTN	84025	1346	D6
W Mountain Creek Cove				
10	FMTN	84025	1346	D6
Mountain Crest Cir				
13000	DRPR	84020	2389	C3
Mountain Crest Dr				
1700	DRPR	84020	2389	C3
Mountain Estates Dr				
7600	CDHT	84121	2178	C4
Mountain Farm Ct				
3000	RIVN	84065	2281	B7
Mountain Goat Wy				
2900	WVCY	84128	1960	E4
Mountain Hill Dr				
4800	WJDN	84084	2174	A2
5000	WJDN	84084	2173	D3
Mountain Iris Wy				
5200	WJDN	84088	2173	E7
9200	WJDN	84088	2279	E1
Mountainlands Dr				
200	OREM	84058	2820	A5
Mountain Laurel Ln				
4800	WJDN	84088	2280	A1
9000	WJDN	84088	2174	A7
Mountain Meadow Dr				
8600	WJDN	84088	2175	E6
Mountain Meadow Ln				
5200	SmtC	84098	1972	C4
Mountain Men Cir				
5300	SLkC	84118	2067	D3
Mountain Men Dr				
5100	SLkC	84118	2067	D4
Mountain Oak Ct				
700	PKCY	84060	2078	C2
N Mountainoak Dr				
3600	WbrC	84310	1001	D3
Mountain Oaks Cir				
1100	ALPN	84004	2498	B4
8000	CDHT	84121	2178	D5
Mountain Oaks Dr				
800	OREM	84097	2714	A7
800	OREM	84097	2821	A1
3600	CDHT	84121	2178	D5
3800	BNFL	84010	1654	A6
Mountain Oaks Cove				
3700	CDHT	84121	2178	D4
Mountain Orchard Dr				
-	PTVW	84414	997	E3
-	PTVW	84414	998	A3
Mountain Park Cir				
4800	WJDN	84084	2174	A2
Mountain Pass Cir				
8700	WJDN	84088	2173	E6
Mountain Pine Dr				
3200	WJDN	84088	2174	E6
Mountain Ranch Dr				
5700	SmtC	84098	1972	C3
Mountain Ridge Cir				
11400	SNDY	84092	2283	E6
Mountain Ridge Ct				
3100	PKCY	84060	2078	C1
Mountain Ridge Ln				
-	HILD	84003	2604	D2
Mountain Ridge Rd				
-	JubC	84645	3567	A6
1000	PRVO	84604	2821	E7
Mountain Shadow Dr				
-	LOGN	84321	528	C3
Mountain Shadow Rd				
12000	SNDY	84092	2389	E2
Mountain Shadows Ln				
11000	HILD	84003	2497	E7
Mountainside Cir				
2200	BFDL	84065	2494	B1
Mountain Side Dr				
800	FMTN	84025	1448	D4
Mountainside Dr				
2200	BFDL	84065	2494	B1
Mountain Spa Ln				
600	MIDW	84049	2397	C2
Mountain Springs Cir				
400	MIDW	84049	2397	A2
Mountain Springs Dr				
500	MIDW	84049	2397	A2
Mountain Springs Pkwy				
1800	SGVL	84606	3036	A4
1800	SGVL	84663	3036	A4
1800	UthC	84606	3036	A4
Mountain Springs Pkwy N				
1500	SGVL	84663	3036	A5
Mountain Springs Pkwy S				
1000	SGVL	84663	3036	A7
Mountaintop Cir				
-	PTGV	84062	2605	C3
Mountain Top Dr				
10	PKCY	84060	1972	C7
10	PKCY	84060	2078	C1
Mountain Top Ln				
3100	PKCY	84060	2078	C1
E Mountain Vale Wy				
10	WDHL	84653	3463	D2
Mountain Valley Ct				
10	HRCY	84032	2398	C7
Mountain Valley Dr				
8700	WbrC	84317	1061	D6
Mountain Valley Wy				
3700	SLkC	84092	2284	D2
Mountain View Cir				
-	PVDN	84332	528	A5
400	SNDY	84070	2282	E3
600	NSLK	84054	1754	C2
700	CTRV	84014	1551	D2
3500	RIVN	84065	2386	D2
4300	CRHL	84062	2605	B3
4800	HILD	84003	2604	E1
4800	HILD	84003	2605	A1
Mountain View Ct				
900	OREM	84057	2820	B4
1900	WJDN	84084	2175	C2
Mountain View Dr				
-	OREM	84058	2820	B5
10	MDVL	84047	2176	C4
100	HDPK	84318	400	B7
100	MRRY	84107	2070	D3
300	BMCY	84302	767	A5
300	SNDY	84070	2176	D7
700	RVHT	84321	528	A4
1200	CchC	84335	400	B1
1700	SLkC	84106	1965	C6
2800	SLkC	84109	1966	B7
3100	NHON	84414	998	E4
6100	SmtC	84098	1972	D2
10000	HILD	84003	2604	B3
10000	SNDY	84070	2282	E3
12300	RIVN	84065	2386	E1
E Mountain View Dr				
500	PYSN	84651	3355	B6
500	UthC	84651	3355	B6
W Mountain View Dr				
100	SALM	84653	3356	A4
Mountain View Ests				
500	SRCS	84075	1281	B2
Mountain View Pkwy				
2200	PRVO	84606	3036	B4
N Mountain View Rd				
700	CTRV	84014	1551	C2
W Mountain View Rd				
400	CTRV	84014	1551	C2
Mountainville Cir				
400	ALPN	84004	2498	A4
Mountainville Dr				
300	ALPN	84004	2498	A3
Mountain Vista Dr				
5200	WJDN	84088	2173	E7
Mountain Vista Ln				
2000	PRVO	84606	3036	A3
Mountain Vistas Rd				
10	KYVL	84037	1344	E1
Mountain Vu Cir				
300	SGVL	84663	3143	D4
Mountain Willow Ln				
900	SmtC	84098	1973	A3
Mountain Wood Ln				
10	SNDY	84092	2284	A5
Mountain Wy Dr				
10	OREM	84058	2820	A5
200	OREM	84058	2819	E6
Mountair Dr				
3000	SLCY	84106	1965	B5
3000	SLkC	84106	1965	B5
Mt Baldy Dr				
800	TYVL	84123	2070	A3
E Mt Crest Dr				
2500	SLkC	84109	1966	A7
Mt Flora Cir				
5500	SLkC	84118	2067	D6
Mt Helmos Cir				
6200	TYVL	84084	2069	A7
Mt Hood Dr				
6300	TYVL	84084	2069	A7
6300	TYVL	84084	2175	A2
Mt Jordan Rd				
2600	SLkC	84092	2284	A2
2600	SNDY	84092	2284	A2
Mt Langley Cir				
6200	TYVL	84084	2069	A7
Mt Lincoln Ct				
6200	TYVL	84084	2069	A7
Mt Loafer Cir				
900	SPFK	84660	3249	E3
Mt Logan Dr				
-	LOGN	84321	528	C4
Mt Logan Lp				
1300	LOGN	84321	528	C4
Mt Logan Wy				
3000	TYVL	84084	2069	A7
3000	TYVL	84084	2175	A1
3100	TYVL	84084	2068	E7
Mt Lomond Dr				
3100	NHON	84414	998	E4
Mt Majestic Rd				
8500	SLkC	84093	2178	A6
E Mt Manor Cir				
1400	CDHT	84121	2177	C2
Mt Montana Dr				
6000	WVCY	84118	2067	C7
6000	WVCY	84118	2173	C1
Mt Nebo Dr				
800	TYVL	84123	2070	A3
Mt Ogden Cir				
1500	OGDN	84403	1116	C6
Mt Ogden Dr				
3600	OGDN	84403	1116	C7
Mt Ogden Peak Dr				
14000	RIVN	84065	2386	A6
14100	HRMN	84065	2386	A6
14400	HRMN	84065	2385	E6
Mt Olympus Wy				
3900	SLkC	84124	1966	D7
3900	SLkC	84124	2072	D1
Mt Olympus Peak Dr				
13700	RIVN	84065	2386	B5
Mt Pisgah Rd				
-	CchC	84319	709	D3
-	CchC	84319	710	B3
-	CchC	84328	708	D5
-	CchC	84328	709	D3
-	CchC	84328	710	B3
-	CchC	84339	708	D5
-	CchC	84339	709	A5
Mt Spencer Cir				
8100	WJDN	84088	2174	B5
Mt Springs Ct				
4600	HLDY	84117	2072	B2
Mt Springs Rd				
2900	HLDY	84117	2072	B2
Mt Sterling Rd				
2400	CchC	84339	650	A6
3300	CchC	84339	649	C6
Mt Sterling Rd				
3300	WELV	84339	649	C6
3300	WELV	84339	650	A6
Mt Tuscarora Dr				
700	TYVL	84123	2070	A2
Mt Vernon Cir				
600	MRRY	84107	2070	E7
Mt Vernon Dr				
5900	MRRY	84107	2070	E7
Mt View Dr				
1400	SPFK	84660	3250	A3
Mt Vista Dr				
1800	TYVL	84084	2069	B7
Mt Whitney Ln				
6400	WVCY	84118	2067	B7
6400	WVCY	84118	2173	C1
Mourning Dove Cir				
200	KYVL	84037	1345	E2
Mourning Dove Wy				
6500	SmtC	84098	1971	E2
Moutain Cir				
1600	FTHT	84037	1346	B2
Moutain Peak Dr				
10	DRPR	84020	2388	D1
Moyle Cir				
900	ALPN	84004	2498	B2
1700	BFDL	84065	2387	C6
Moyle Dr				
1000	ALPN	84004	2498	B2
Moyle Pk				
700	ALPN	84004	2498	A3
Muddy Ln				
100	LYTN	84040	1283	C5
Mueller Park Rd				
1300	BNFL	84010	1654	B3
Muirfield Dr				
300	HRCY	84032	2398	C3
4400	SLkC	84124	2071	B2
Muirkirk Cir				
5000	WJDN	84088	2174	A6
Muirkirk Rd				
4800	WJDN	84088	2174	A6
Muirwood Cir				
5900	HRMN	84065	2385	C7
Muirwood Dr				
5600	HRMN	84065	2385	D6
Mulberry Dr				
9800	CRHL	84062	2605	B3
Mulberry Ln				
1300	DvsC	84056	1228	B2
1400	DvsC	84056	1172	B7
Mulberry Wy				
1400	SNDY	84093	2177	C5
Mule Deer Dr				
1700	DRPR	84020	2389	D5
Mules Ear Dr				
-	SmtC	84098	1866	A7
Muley Ct				
4000	BFDL	84065	2386	C5
Mulholland St				
4200	SLkC	84124	2072	D1
Mullien Dr				
6800	WJDN	84084	2173	E2
Mulligan Dr				
7600	SLkC	84044	1960	D6
Mumford Cir				
9400	SNDY	84094	2283	B1
Mumford Dr				
1200	SNDY	84094	2283	B2
Mums Cir				
1400	SNDY	84092	2283	C2
Munchkin Rd				
1400	PKCY	84060	2078	D4
Murdoch Peak Cir				
4800	RIVN	84065	2386	A6
Murdoch Peak Dr				
14000	RIVN	84065	2386	A6
14200	HRMN	84065	2386	A6
Murdoch Woods Pl				
6100	HLDY	84121	2071	E7
Murdock Dr				
1000	ANFK	84003	2605	A4
E Murdock Dr				
900	PTGV	84062	2713	B2
1700	LNDN	84042	2713	C4
N Murdock Dr				
600	PTGV	84062	2713	A1
1600	PTGV	84062	2605	E7
S Murdock Dr				
400	PTGV	84062	2713	B3
Muriel Wy				
3400	WVCY	84119	1962	D7
Murnin Wy				
4300	SmtC	84098	1971	E6
Murphys Ln				
1300	SLkC	84106	1965	B6
Murray Blvd				
400	MRRY	84123	2070	B3
Murray Bluffs Ct				
1200	MRRY	84123	2069	E7
Murray Bluffs Dr				
6200	MRRY	84123	2069	E7
6500	MRRY	84123	2175	E1
6700	WJDN	84084	2175	E1
Murray-Holladay Rd				
1500	SLkC	84117	2071	C3
1800	HLDY	84117	2071	C3
2300	HLDY	84117	2072	A2
Murray Links Dr				
5300	MRRY	84107	2070	E5
Murray Park Ln				
4900	MRRY	84107	2070	D4
E Murray Park Ln				
-	MRRY	84107	2070	D4
S Murray Park Ln				
5000	MRRY	84107	2070	D4
Murray Parkway Av				
5300	MRRY	84123	2069	E5
6300	MRRY	84123	2175	E1
Murray-Taylorsville Rd				
300	MRRY	84107	2070	A3
300	MRRY	84123	2070	A3
600	TYVL	84123	2070	A3
900	TYVL	84123	2069	D3
Musser Ct				
600	SLCY	84102	1859	A5
Mustang Cir				
800	SRSP	84043	2601	D7
1100	WJDN	84088	2175	E6
Mustang Ln				
1000	SRSP	84043	2601	D7
Mustang Loop Rd				
7900	SmtC	84098	1865	B6
E Mutton Hollow Rd				
10	DvsC	84037	1283	D5
10	DvsC	84040	1283	D5
10	DvsC	84041	1283	D5
10	KYVL	84037	1283	D5
10	KYVL	84041	1283	D5
900	LYTN	84037	1283	D5
900	LYTN	84037	1284	A5
900	LYTN	84040	1283	D5
900	LYTN	84040	1284	A5
W Mutton Hollow Rd				
10	DvsC	84037	1283	B6
10	DvsC	84041	1283	B6
10	KYVL	84041	1283	B6
100	KYVL	84037	1283	B6
Myers Ln				
1700	RIVN	84065	2281	A7
1800	SJDN	84095	2281	A7
2700	RIVN	84095	2281	A7
3000	RIVN	84065	2280	E7
3000	SJDN	84095	2280	E7
3700	SJDN	84065	2280	E7
3800	RIVN	84095	2280	E7
Myrna Cir				
-	KYVL	84037	1345	D3
Myron Av				
8300	SLkC	84044	1960	B5
Myrtle Av				
100	MRRY	84107	2070	D4
Mystic Cir				
10000	HILD	84003	2604	D3
Mystic Dr				
10100	HILD	84003	2604	D2
Mystic Hllw				
10100	HILD	84003	2604	E2
Mystic Wy				
3500	SLkC	84044	1960	B6
N				
N St				
10	SLCY	84103	1859	A2
Nail Driver Ct				
10	PKCY	84060	2078	C3
Nalder Cir				
1300	LYTN	84040	1283	C2
Nalder St				
1000	LYTN	84040	1283	C3
Namba Wy				
4500	SLkC	84107	2071	A2
Nancy Dr				
700	SOGN	84403	1173	A3
4400	WVCY	84120	1962	B6
Nancy Wy				
700	NSLK	84054	1653	C7
Naniloa Cir				
2800	HLDY	84117	2072	B3
Naniloa Dr				
4600	HLDY	84117	2072	B3
Nansen Ct				
2400	PKCY	84060	2079	B5
Nantucket Dr				
2300	CDHT	84093	2177	E4
2300	CDHT	84093	2178	A4
Naomi Dr				
-	NHLN	84341	464	E2
400	SNDY	84070	2282	E4
Napa Av				
1400	BFDL	84065	2387	D6
Napa Dr				
1900	SRSP	84043	2601	E5
Narra Pl				
1300	PTGV	84062	2712	B1
Narrow Canyon Rd				
300	CchC	84339	649	A4
Narrow Leaf Ct				
5700	SmtC	84098	1973	A3
Nashi Ln				
1300	DRPR	84020	2389	B4
E Nashua St				
200	MRRY	84107	2070	D1
Natalie Ct				
5100	WVCY	84120	1961	E6
10800	HILD	84003	2604	A1
Natalie Dr				
12600	RIVN	84065	2387	B2
Nate Ln				
300	DRPR	84020	2282	B7
Nathan Cir				
4600	HLDY	84117	2071	E3
Nathanael Wy				
2300	WJDN	84088	2175	B4
Nathaniel Dr				
1000	PTGV	84062	2713	B4
National Pl				
10100	SJDN	84095	2280	E3
Nations Wy				
1900	SLkC	84121	2071	D5
Natura St				
1500	SLCY	84104	1857	E7
Nautilus Dr				
5300	SLkC	84118	2067	D5
Navajo Cir				
2900	PRVO	84604	2928	E1
Navajo Dr				
1200	PTGV	84062	2713	B4
1400	OGDN	84404	1173	C3
Navajo Ln				
3000	PRVO	84604	2928	E1
3200	PRVO	84604	2821	E7
Navajo St				
10	SLCY	84104	1857	D4
1500	SLCY	84104	1963	D1
Navajo Tr				
3600	SmtC	84098	1971	D7
Navajo Wy				
2000	RVDL	84405	1172	A5
Naylor Ct				
1200	SLCY	84105	1859	A6
Naylor Ln				
4800	MRRY	84107	2070	E3
Nayon St				
1000	LYTN	84040	1283	C2
Nebo Dr				
4600	WJDN	84088	2174	B4
Nebo St				
300	SPFK	84660	3249	E3
Nebula Wy				
1800	SLCY	84116	1857	C2
Nectar Wy				
100	SRSP	84043	2601	D4
Nectarine Cir				
1300	SJDN	84095	2281	D5
Nectarine Dr				
11100	SJDN	84095	2281	D5
Neff Meadows Dr				
11800	RIVN	84065	2281	A7
Neffs Cir				
2500	SLkC	84109	1966	A6
Neffs Ln				
2300	SLkC	84109	1965	E6
2300	SLkC	84109	1966	A6
Neighbor Ln				
5500	SLkC	84117	2071	C5
Neighborhood Cove				
10000	SJDN	84095	2281	D2
Neil Armstrong Rd				
300	SLCY	84116	1856	A2
Nellies St				
6000	WJDN	84084	2173	C1
Nelsen Peak Cir				
5500	HRMN	84065	2385	D5
Nelson Ct				
4600	SmtC	84098	1971	D6
Nelson Ln				
100	SALM	84653	3356	C3
Nemelka Ln				
900	MPTN	84664	3251	C2
Nena Wy				
5700	MRRY	84107	2070	C6
Neptune Dr				
4100	SLkC	84124	2072	D1
Nerual Cir				
900	SLCY	84108	1859	D6
Nestled Cove				
-	DRPR	84020	2496	E3
14600	DRPR	84020	2388	E7
Netties Pl				
2100	HLDY	84124	2071	E2
Neuchatel Cir				
1400	WshC	84049	2396	D2
Nevada Av				
900	PRVO	84606	3035	E2
1700	PRVO	84606	3036	A3
Nevada Cir				
1900	PRVO	84606	3036	B4
Nevada St				
1700	SLCY	84108	1965	E1
Neville Ct				
1400	WVCY	84119	1963	D7
New Bedford Dr				
1500	SLCY	84103	1859	C1
Newberry Rd				
900	SLCY	84108	1859	E6
New Bingham Hwy				
-	WJDN	84088	2279	A1
4300	WJDN	84084	2174	B4
4300	WJDN	84088	2174	B4
5300	WJDN	84088	2173	D6
New Bingham Hwy SR-48				
-	WJDN	84088	2279	A1
4300	WJDN	84084	2174	B4
4300	WJDN	84088	2174	B4
5300	WJDN	84088	2173	D6
Newbold Cir				
800	MDVL	84047	2177	A2
Newbold Ln				
1700	RIVN	84065	2387	C2
New Bonneville Pl				
600	SLCY	84103	1755	B7
600	SLCY	84103	1859	C1
Newburgh Dr				
13800	HRMN	84065	2385	E5
Newbury Dr				
10100	SNDY	84092	2283	D3
Newbury Ln				
-	HARR	84414	998	D6
-	WbrC	84414	998	D6
Newcastle Cir				
9000	SNDY	84093	2178	A7
Newcastle Ct				
8900	SNDY	84093	2177	E7
Newcastle Dr				
1800	SNDY	84093	2177	D6
2300	SNDY	84093	2178	A7
Newcastle Rd				
8600	WJDN	84088	2174	D6
New Century Ln				
200	SSLK	84115	1964	D6
New Dawn Cir				
5400	HRMN	84065	2385	D6
Newell Dr				
3700	WJDN	84088	2174	D6
Newellwood Cir				
3300	WJDN	84088	2174	D5
New England Dr				
700	SNDY	84094	2282	E1
700	SNDY	84094	2283	A1
New Flower Cir				
5400	HRMN	84065	2385	E6
New Hampshire Av				
1700	SLCY	84116	1753	C5
New Hampshire Dr				
-	DvsC	84056	1172	A6
New Hampton Dr				
800	MRRY	84123	2070	A4
New Harvest Ln				
2200	LEHI	84043	2495	D6
Newhaven Dr				
6100	MRRY	84121	2071	C7
New Heritage Cir				
3600	WJDN	84088	2280	D1
New Heritage Dr				
9100	WJDN	84088	2174	D7
9300	WJDN	84088	2280	D1
New Hope Dr				
900	DRPR	84020	2389	A3
New Horizon Dr				
2000	SNDY	84093	2177	E7
Newhouse Dr				
3300	SLkC	84044	1960	A5
New Jersey Av				
1100	HARR	84404	1056	D3
New Jersey Dr				
1900	RVDL	84405	1171	E5
1900	RVDL	84405	1172	A5
Newkirk St				
9400	SJDN	84095	2280	D1
New Land Lp				
4000	LEHI	84043	2495	A7
New London Rd				
1700	WJDN	84084	2174	C2
Newmans Ln				
2800	HLDY	84121	2072	B6
Newmark Dr				
3200	WVCY	84128	1961	C5
New Peak Cir				
14100	RIVN	84065	2385	E6
Newport Cir				
2400	CDHT	84093	2178	A4
3800	BNFL	84010	1653	E6
Newport Ln				
1100	KYVL	84037	1284	A5
Newport Wy				
7600	CDHT	84093	2178	A4
New River Dr				
1700	DRPR	84020	2389	C3
New Saddle Rd				
1000	DRPR	84020	2389	B5
New Snowbell				
7700	WJDN	84084	2173	A4
E Newsome Park Ln				
300	SSLK	84115	1964	D6
New Spring Rd				
4400	SJDN	84095	2280	B6
New Star Dr				
500	SLCY	84116	1857	C1
Newton Ct				
4200	TYVL	84123	2069	E1
Newton Park St				
1500	SLCY	84116	1753	C5
Newtopia Cir				
2500	CDHT	84121	2178	A1
New Village Rd				
3700	WJDN	84084	2174	D1
New Vintage Ct				
4400	SLkC	84124	2071	B2
New World Dr				
3200	WJDN	84084	2174	E2
New York Av				
1100	HARR	84404	1056	D2
New York Dr				
1700	SLCY	84116	1753	C6
Nez Perce Dr				
5400	SLkC	84118	2068	A5
NF-019				
-	SLkC	84098	2181	C2
NF-023				
-	SLkC	84098	2182	E3
-	SLkC	84098	2183	A3
NF-029				
-	SLkC	84098	2183	B2
-	SmtC	84060	2183	B2
NF-216				
-	SLkC	84098	2181	A3
NF-223				
-	SLkC	84098	2182	E2
-	SLkC	84098	2183	A2
NF-231				
-	ALTA	84049	2181	E6
NF-70007				
-	UthC	84049	2288	D5
NF-70011				
-	UthC	84049	2287	E5
-	UthC	84049	2288	A6
NF-70025				
-	MPTN	84664	3144	E7
-	UthC	84664	3144	E7
NF-70027				
-	UthC	84604	2929	E1
NF-70085				
-	UthC	84049	2288	E7
-	UthC	84049	2289	B7
NF-70191				
-	WshC	84049	2289	D2
NF-70195				
-	UthC	84049	2288	D7
NF-70317				
-	WshC	84049	2289	D7
NF-70421				
-	WshC	84049	2289	C2
NF-70422				
-	UthC	84049	2288	E6
Niagara Cir				
4900	SLkC	84118	2068	A5
Niagara Wy				
4800	SLkC	84118	2068	A5
Nibley Cir				
800	SLCY	84106	1965	A4
E Nibley View Ct				
700	SLkC	84106	1964	E4
Niblick Dr				
3200	SmtC	84098	1865	A3
Nichole Cir				
1600	SNDY	84093	2177	C7
Nichole Dr				
9100	SNDY	84093	2177	C7
E Nicholls Rd				
800	DvsC	84037	1345	E3
800	KYVL	84037	1345	E3
900	FTHT	84037	1345	E3
900	FTHT	84037	1346	A2
Nichols Ln				
12800	RIVN	84065	2387	D3
Nichols Cove				
700	SLkC	84106	1964	E6
Nicklaus Cir				
1600	SNDY	84092	2283	C7
Nicklaus Rd				
1500	SNDY	84092	2283	C7
12100	SNDY	84092	2389	C1
Nickle Wy				
5800	SLkC	84118	2067	C6
Nickoles Ln				
-	ANFK	84003	2604	A7
-	ANFK	84003	2711	A1
Nicole Cir				
3100	WJDN	84084	2174	E2
Nicoletti Dr				
10	MDVL	84047	2176	C2
Nielsen Blvd				
-	CRHL	84062	2605	B2
Nielsen Wy				
3200	WVCY	84119	2068	E2
Nighthawk Dr				
800	SNDY	84094	2177	A4
Nike Dr				
4000	WJDN	84088	2174	C5
Nike Ln				
900	DvsC	84056	1228	A3
Nila Wy				
2700	SLkC	84124	2072	B1
Niles Av				
1700	SLCY	84116	1753	C5
Nimbus Wy				
5900	SLkC	84118	2068	B7
Nimue Cir				
100	NSLK	84054	1653	A4
Nina Cir				
7200	WJDN	84084	2174	E2
Nina Marie Cir				
4700	TYVL	84123	2070	A3
Ninetta Cir				
200	OREM	84057	2820	E4
Ninigret Dr				
3500	SLCY	84104	1856	D7
Noah Cir				
200	MRRY	84107	2070	C7
Noal Dr				
1500	SLkC	84124	2071	C1
Nob Hill Av				
800	ANFK	84003	2604	C5
Nob Hill St				
4500	WVCY	84120	2068	C3
Nobility Cir				
1700	SLCY	84116	1753	C6
Noble Pl				
700	SLCY	84102	1859	A5
Noble Fir Cove				
2900	SLkC	84044	1960	D4
Noble Oaks Cir				
5900	MRRY	84123	2070	A6
Nocturne Dr				
1000	SLCY	84116	1753	E6
Nod Hill Rd				
2000	CDHT	84121	2177	E1
Noelle Rd				
1300	SNDY	84092	2283	B7
Nola Dr				
1200	CTRV	84014	1551	E1
S Noma Linda Cir				
3000	SLkC	84109	1965	E5
Nora Cir				
3900	SLkC	84124	1966	B7
Nora Dr				
2700	SLkC	84124	1966	A7
Nordic Cir				
8100	CDHT	84093	2178	A6
Nordic Dr				
3000	CDHT	84093	2178	B5
Nordic Valley Dr				
2700	WbrC	84310	1001	B5
Nordic Valley Hwy				
3500	WbrC	84310	1001	A5
3500	WbrC	84414	1001	A5
Nordic Valley Rd				
3400	WbrC	84310	1001	A5
Nordic Valley Wy				
-	WbrC	84414	1001	A6
2400	WbrC	84310	1001	A6
Nordin Av				
3800	SOGN	84403	1116	A7
3900	SOGN	84403	1173	A1
Norfolk Av				
700	PKCY	84060	2078	D5
Norfolk Cir				
4500	PRVO	84604	2821	E5
Norfolk Bay				
3700	SJDN	84095	2280	D3
Norfolk Pine Wy				
7800	SNDY	84094	2177	C3
Norma Cir				
1800	MRRY	84121	2071	D6
W Norman Dr				
1700	WVCY	84119	1963	C5
Normandie Cir				
1300	SLCY	84105	1859	B6
Normandie Ln				
4100	SLkC	84107	2070	E1
Normandy Cir				
6800	MDVL	84047	2177	A2
E Normandy Dr				
400	PRVO	84604	2928	D2
Normandy Pl				
6800	MDVL	84047	2177	A1
Normandy Wy				
700	MDVL	84047	2176	E1
700	MDVL	84047	2177	A1
Normandy Oaks Cir				
5900	MRRY	84123	2070	A6
Normandywoods Ct				
2000	HLDY	84117	2071	D4
Normawood Dr				
6000	TYVL	84123	2069	D7
Norris Pl				
1000	SLCY	84102	1859	A3
North Dr				
1900	RVDL	84405	1171	E5
1900	RVDL	84405	1172	A5
North St				
-	BMCY	84302	767	A6
-	OGDN	84401	1116	A2
-	TMTN	84337	520	E5
100	HARR	84404	1056	E4
100	OGDN	84404	1056	E4
500	OGDN	84404	1057	A4
North St SR-82				
-	TMTN	84337	520	E5
W North St				
100	HARR	84404	1056	D4
100	OGDN	84404	1056	D4
Northborough Cir				
6200	TYVL	84084	2068	E7
Northborough Dr				
3200	TYVL	84084	2068	E7
North Campus Dr				
-	SLCY	84102	1859	C2
-	SLCY	84103	1859	C2
-	SLCY	84112	1859	C2
-	SLCY	84113	1859	C2
North Campus Dr SR-282				
-	SLCY	84102	1859	C2
-	SLCY	84103	1859	C2
-	SLCY	84112	1859	C2
N North Canyon Cir				
3200	BNFL	84010	1653	E5
E North Canyon Rd				
10	BNFL	84010	1653	E4
Northcliffe Cir				
600	SLCY	84103	1859	A1
Northcliffe Dr				
700	SLCY	84103	1859	A1
Northcove Dr				
8600	SmtC	84098	1864	D4

STREET Block City ZIP Map# Grid

Northcrest Dr
600 SLCY 84103 1858 E1
600 SLCY 84103 1859 A1
700 SLCY 84103 1755 A7
E North Dam Rd
100 MNTU 84324 768 C5
E North Eden Cir
1200 SNDY 84094 2283 C3
Northern Hills Cir
800 BNFL 84010 1552 B6
Northern Hills Dr
1000 BNFL 84010 1552 B6
E North Fork Cir
900 SNDY 84094 2283 D7
North Forty Rd
8800 SNDY 84093 2177 E7
S Northforty Wy
10400 SJDN 84095 2281 B4
W Northforty Wy
2500 SJDN 84095 2281 A4
North Front St
3800 CRNN 84307 705 A7
4000 CRNN 84307 704 E7
Northgate Dr
4500 PRVO 84604 2821 B5
E North Hills Dr
400 SLCY 84103 1754 E7
North Lake Dr
500 LEHI 84043 2710 B2
800 MRRY 84107 2071 A3
Northland Dr
600 SLCY 84103 1859 B1
E North Lisa St
1200 LYTN 84040 1283 C2
Northmont Wy
400 SLCY 84103 1754 E7
E North Ogden Rd
2700 WbrC 84414 1000 C3
North Ogden Canyon Rd
1000 NHON 84414 999 B4
1300 WbrC 84414 999 D5
1400 WbrC 84414 1000 A5
Northpoint Ct
700 SLCY 84103 1754 E7
Northpointe Dr
800 NSLK 84054 1652 D7
800 NSLK 84054 1753 D1
E North Pond Cir
1300 MPTN 84664 3251 C1
Northridge Ct
700 FMTN 84025 1346 B4
North Ridge Dr
600 BNFL 84010 1552 B6
Northridge Ln
10 SNDY 84092 2284 B5
Northridge Rd
700 FMTN 84025 1346 A4
Northridge Wy
10 SNDY 84092 2284 A5
Northridge Cove
10 SNDY 84092 2284 A4
Northshore Ct
1600 SmtC 84098 1971 E4
Northshore St
700 SLCY 84103 1755 A7
North Star
1000 LYTN 84041 1282 C7
Northstar Dr
900 PKCY 84060 2078 D5
W Northstar Dr
1500 SLCY 84116 1857 C2
E North Temple
10 SLCY 84103 1858 C2
E North Temple US-89
10 SLCY 84103 1858 C2
W North Temple
300 SLCY 84103 1858 A2
500 SLCY 84101 1858 A2
500 SLCY 84116 1858 A2
900 SLCY 84116 1857 E2
2000 SLCY 84104 1857 B2
W North Temple SR-186
300 SLCY 84103 1858 A2
400 SLCY 84101 1858 A2
500 SLCY 84116 1858 A2
900 SLCY 84116 1857 E2
1000 SLCY 84104 1857 E2
W North Temple US-89
10 SLCY 84103 1858 C2
E North Union Av
900 MDVL 84047 2177 A2
Northvale Dr
900 SLCY 84103 1755 A7
North View Cir
- WDHL 84653 3463 C3
Northview Cir
700 SLCY 84103 1859 B1
Northview Dr
700 SLCY 84103 1755 A7
Northwest Av
5200 SLkC 84118 2068 B5
Northwood Av
1600 SLCY 84116 1857 C1
Northwood Rd
2800 HLDY 84117 2072 B5
W Northwood Wy
100 PRVO 84604 2821 C4
Norwalk Rd
1200 TYVL 84123 2069 D1
Norway Maple Ct
- PYSN 84651 3461 C1
Norwich Dr
3000 WJDN 84088 2175 A4
3100 WJDN 84088 2174 E4
Norwood Rd
3300 CDHT 84121 2178 C4
Nottingham Cir
1400 SNDY 84093 2177 C4
6600 WJDN 84084 2175 B1
Nottingham Ct
- PRVO 84604 2928 A3
Nottingham Dr
6600 WJDN 84084 2175 B1
Nottingham Ln
- OREM 84057 2820 A4
Nottingham Rd
800 WDCR 84087 1653 B3
Nottingham Wy
2500 SLCY 84108 1860 A7
Nova Dr
5900 MRRY 84107 2070 C7
W Nova Dr
10 ANFK 84003 2604 C5
Novell Pl
1800 PRVO 84606 3035 C3
Novice Cir
2600 WVCY 84128 1960 E4
Nowell Cir
2100 SSLK 84115 1964 D2
Nugget Dr
4300 WVCY 84128 2067 C1
Nunley Cir
1900 SLkC 84121 2071 D6
Nutmeg St
3200 CDHT 84121 2178 C2
Nutree Dr
3200 CDHT 84121 2178 B3
Nuttall Dr
1200 LEHI 84043 2603 C4
Nutwood Cir
8500 SNDY 84094 2177 A6
Nu Vue Cir
200 OREM 84057 2820 E3
Nye Cir
2100 CDHT 84121 2177 E1
Nye Dr
6600 CDHT 84121 2177 E1
Nyman Ln
- NHLN 84341 464 B6

O

O St
10 SLCY 84102 1859 A3
10 SLCY 84103 1859 A3
Oak Brch
- LOGN 84321 527 A4
Oak Cir
300 RVDL 84405 1172 C2
8200 SNDY 84093 2177 D5
10300 HILD 84003 2604 E2
W Oak Cir
100 WDHL 84653 3463 C1
Oak Cr
- LOGN 84321 527 A4
Oak Ct
10 PKCY 84060 2079 A7
10000 CRHL 84062 2605 B2
Oak Dr
200 NSLK 84054 1653 C6
700 BMCY 84302 767 A4
700 SOGN 84403 1173 A3
1600 LEHI 84043 2603 D4
S Oak Dr
100 WDHL 84653 3463 C1
W Oak Dr
10 WDHL 84653 3463 C1
Oak Ln
200 FMTN 84025 1448 D2
200 KYVL 84037 1283 D7
200 KYVL 84037 1345 D1
400 ALPN 84004 2498 B5
1400 PRVO 84604 2928 E3
1600 FTHT 84037 1346 B3
1600 LYTN 84040 1283 E1
2200 DvsC 84056 1172 A6
2500 LYTN 84040 1284 A1
8800 WJDN 84088 2175 D6
E Oak Ln
400 EKMT 84651 3463 A3
600 SALM 84653 3356 A5
W Oak Ln
600 SALM 84653 3356 A5
Oak Pl
- LOGN 84321 527 A4
1100 BMCY 84302 767 B4
N Oak Rd E
10000 CRHL 84062 2605 C3
N Oak Rd W
9800 CRHL 84062 2605 B3
W Oak Rd N
4000 CRHL 84062 2605 B2
Oak St
400 OGDN 84401 1115 E3
600 OGDN 84401 1116 A2
7700 MDVL 84047 2176 B4
W Oak St
100 OGDN 84401 1115 D2
Oak Ter
4700 SLkC 84124 2072 C3
Oak Acorn Ct
8200 WJDN 84088 2173 B5
Oak Bend Dr
1800 DRPR 84020 2496 D1
Oak Bluff Pl
14700 DRPR 84020 2389 D7
Oak Bridge Dr
6400 WJDN 84088 2173 B5
Oakbrook Cir
2800 SLCY 84108 1860 B7
Oak Brush Dr
11200 SNDY 84070 2282 E6
Oakbrush Dr N
5600 SmtC 84098 1973 A4
Oak Canyon Dr
3400 HLDY 84121 2072 C6
Oak Cliff Dr
1400 PRVO 84604 2929 A5
Oakcliff Dr
3100 SLkC 84124 2072 C2
Oak Creek Cir
2500 CDHT 84093 2178 A5
Oak Creek Dr
800 LEHI 84043 2603 D2
2500 CDHT 84093 2178 A5
Oak Creek Ln
10200 HILD 84003 2604 E2
Oak Crest Cir
1400 CTRV 84014 1551 D1
2300 SPFK 84660 3250 D7
Oakcrest Cir
1200 PRVO 84604 2928 E2
1600 OGDN 84403 1173 C2
6200 HLDY 84121 2071 E7
Oakcrest Dr
1500 OGDN 84403 1173 C2
1600 OREM 84097 2714 A7
1600 OREM 84097 2821 A1
Oak Crest Ln
1200 PRVO 84604 2928 E3
1200 PRVO 84604 2929 A2
Oakcrest Ln
2300 HLDY 84121 2071 E7
2400 HLDY 84121 2072 A7
Oakcrest Ter
2000 PRVO 84604 2928 E3
Oakdale Dr
1700 SLkC 84121 2071 C6
Oakeson Cir
3200 TYVL 84118 2068 E4
Oak Farms Dr
6700 WJDN 84088 2173 A5
Oak Forest Dr
2000 LYTN 84040 1229 E7
2000 LYTN 84040 1283 E1
2500 LYTN 84040 1230 A7
Oak Forest Rd
300 SLCY 84103 1754 D6
Oak Gate Dr
6200 WJDN 84088 2173 C5
Oak Glenn Wy
11700 SNDY 84092 2283 E7
Oak Grove Dr
2400 SNDY 84092 2284 A6
Oak Grove Ln
5000 HILD 84003 2604 E2
Oak Haven Cir
2500 SPFK 84660 3250 D7
Oak Haven Dr
2400 SPFK 84660 3250 D7
Oak Haven Pl
2000 SLkC 84093 2177 E5
Oak Hill Cir
1200 PRVO 84604 2929 A4
1500 LYTN 84040 1283 E1
Oakhill Cir
300 ALPN 84004 2498 B5
Oakhill Dr
900 ALPN 84004 2498 B5
2300 HLDY 84121 2071 E6
2300 HLDY 84121 2072 A6
Oak Hills Cir
8000 CDHT 84121 2178 C4
Oak Hills Dr
1300 LYTN 84040 1283 D4
1500 DvsC 84040 1283 D4
2200 LYTN 84040 1284 A4
Oak Hills Dr SR-109
1300 LYTN 84040 1283 D4
1500 DvsC 84040 1283 D4
2200 LYTN 84040 1284 A4
Oak Hills Wy
900 SLCY 84108 1860 A6
Oak Hollow Cir
3300 CDHT 84093 2178 C6
Oakhurst Dr
2800 SLCY 84108 1860 B6
Oak Knoll Dr
6100 MRRY 84121 2071 D7
E Oakland Av
100 SSLK 84115 1964 C3
W Oakland Av
10 SSLK 84115 1964 C3
Oakland Hills Rd
6800 WJDN 84084 2174 D1
Oak Leaf Ct
3300 PKCY 84060 2079 B4
Oakleaf Dr
200 NSLK 84054 1653 C6
Oak Leaf Ln
500 NSLK 84054 1653 B6
Oak Leaf Pl
11700 SNDY 84092 2283 E7
Oak Leaf Wy
2100 SNDY 84092 2283 E7
Oakledge Rd
3300 CDHT 84121 2178 C4
Oakley St
300 SLCY 84116 1857 D1
1000 SLCY 84116 1753 D7
Oak Manor Dr
1900 SNDY 84092 2283 D7
Oak Meadows Dr
4100 TYVL 84123 2069 C1
Oak Mill Dr
8300 WJDN 84088 2173 B5
Oakmont
- CRHL 84062 2605 C1
Oakmont Av
700 MRRY 84107 2070 D7
700 MRRY 84107 2071 A7
Oakmont Dr
400 BNFL 84010 1653 E3
Oakmont Ln
700 FTHT 84037 1284 A6
900 PRVO 84604 2929 A4
Oakmont Rd
900 KYVL 84037 1284 A6
Oak Mountain Cir
3900 SLkC 84108 1860 E3
Oak Park Ln
2900 HLDY 84117 2072 B5
Oak Point Dr
2000 BFDL 84065 2387 B7
Oak Ridge Cir
- PRVO 84604 2929 A4
Oakridge Cir
- SOGN 84403 1173 B2
1000 BNFL 84010 1654 B2
1000 SNDY 84094 2283 A7
2000 LYTN 84040 1283 D2
3500 BNFL 84010 1653 E6
S Oak Ridge Cir
300 WDHL 84653 3463 C1
Oakridge Ct
3700 BNFL 84010 1653 E6
Oak Ridge Dr
2400 SPFK 84660 3250 D7
Oakridge Dr
10 BNFL 84010 1653 D6
100 FMTN 84025 1346 C7
1000 CTRV 84014 1551 E1
1000 LYTN 84040 1283 D2
1400 OGDN 84403 1116 C6
1700 SLkC 84106 1965 C7
13400 UthC 84004 2498 B1
E Oakridge Dr
10 EKMT 84651 3462 E1
10 EKMT 84651 3463 A1
2800 SLkC 84109 1966 B7
W Oakridge Dr
10 EKMT 84651 3462 E1
Oakridge Ln
1000 BNFL 84010 1654 B2
1200 FMTN 84025 1345 E6
1500 FMTN 84037 1345 E6
1600 DvsC 84025 1345 E6
1600 DvsC 84037 1345 E6
1600 KYVL 84037 1345 E6
Oakridge Rd
11800 SNDY 84094 2283 A7
Oakridge Rd N
800 SmtC 84098 1866 E3
800 SmtC 84098 1867 A3
Oakridge Rd S
800 SmtC 84098 1866 E3
800 SmtC 84098 1867 A3
Oakridge Park Dr
1000 FMTN 84025 1346 A5
Oak Rim Ln
3000 PKCY 84060 2078 C1
Oak Rim Wy
3500 SLkC 84124 1966 D7
Oak Run Dr
8300 WJDN 84088 2173 C5
E Oaks Dr
300 FTHT 84037 1346 B2
3400 SLkC 84124 2072 C2
W Oaks Dr
100 OGDN 84404 1056 D6
Oakshade Ct
6700 WJDN 84084 2173 B1
S Oakshade Ln
6600 WJDN 84084 2173 B1
W Oakshade Ln
5900 WJDN 84084 2173 C1
Oakshadow Cir
7700 CDHT 84121 2178 E4
Oakshire Cir
1900 SNDY 84092 2283 D6
Oakshire Ln
1900 SNDY 84092 2283 D6
Oak Side Cir
3000 CDHT 84121 2178 B4
Oak Springs Dr
1700 SLCY 84108 1966 A1
Oak Summit Dr
1800 DRPR 84020 2496 D1
Oak Tree Ct
800 SLCY 84116 1754 A7
Oakvale Ct
3500 WVCY 84120 1962 B6
Oak Valley Cir
2900 SLkC 84093 2178 B6
Oak Valley Dr
8600 SLkC 84093 2178 B6
Oak View Cir
1600 OREM 84097 2714 A7
1600 OREM 84097 2821 A1
Oakview Cir
1800 PRVO 84604 2928 E3
2900 CDHT 84121 2178 B4
4200 UthC 84004 2498 B1
Oak View Ct
500 NSLK 84054 1653 C7
Oakview Dr
- LOGN 84321 528 C4
3400 SLkC 84124 2072 D1
4400 UthC 84004 2498 B1
5800 HILD 84003 2497 C6
Oakview Ln
400 BNFL 84010 1654 B1
S Oak View Ln
1400 SPFK 84660 3250 D5
Oak Vista Dr
6700 WJDN 84088 2173 A5
Oak Wood
- LOGN 84321 527 A4
Oakwood Cir
10 SGVL 84663 3144 A2
300 OREM 84057 2820 E4
800 BNFL 84010 1654 A4
1200 ALPN 84004 2498 B5
2500 SLkC 84109 1966 A5
Oakwood Ct
3600 PKCY 84060 2079 B4
5600 SOGN 84403 1173 D5
Oak Wood Dr
3400 PKCY 84060 2079 B4
Oakwood Dr
- HRCY 84032 2292 E7
10 LYTN 84040 1284 A4
100 LYTN 84040 1283 E4
900 BNFL 84010 1654 A5
5700 SOGN 84405 1173 B5
N Oakwood Dr
10 NSLK 84054 1653 C7
S Oakwood Dr
10 NSLK 84054 1653 C7
Oakwood Ln
9600 SLkC 84092 2284 C1
Oakwood Pl
9000 WJDN 84088 2175 B6
Oakwood St
3500 SLkC 84109 1966 A6
Oakwood Park Cir
8700 SNDY 84094 2177 A6
Oakwood Park Dr
700 SNDY 84094 2176 C7
700 SNDY 84094 2177 A6
W Oberland Ct
10 MIDW 84049 2291 B7
Oberland Dr
1000 MIDW 84049 2396 E1
Oberland Rd
2900 SNDY 84092 2284 B6
Oberlin Rd
3700 WVCY 84120 1962 C7
Obsidian Wy
5000 SLkC 84118 2068 A5
5100 SLkC 84118 2067 E5
E Ocampo Ln
300 EKMT 84651 3463 A2
Ocean Ct
1300 TYVL 84123 2069 D5
October Wy
4400 WVCY 84120 2067 E2
October Cove
11700 SNDY 84092 2283 E7
O'Dell Dr
4800 WVCY 84120 1962 A6
O'Dell Ln
100 NSLK 84010 1653 A6
100 NSLK 84054 1653 A6
200 DvsC 84010 1653 A6
200 DvsC 84054 1653 A6
Odin Ln
4500 WJDN 84088 2174 A5
Officers Cir
10 SLCY 84113 1859 D3
Ogallala Dr
3500 WVCY 84119 2068 D1
Ogden Av
500 OGDN 84404 1056 E6
1700 OGDN 84404 1115 E1
2000 OGDN 84401 1115 E2
3500 OGDN 84403 1115 E7
3600 SOGN 84403 1115 E7
3900 SOGN 84403 1172 E1
N Ogden Av
1200 OGDN 84404 1056 E2
Ogden Canyon
10 WbrC 84317 1117 B1
100 WbrC 84317 1058 B7
Ogden Canyon Rd
- OGDN 84401 1116 E1
- WbrC 84317 1116 E1
- WbrC 84317 1117 A1
500 WbrC 84317 1058 E6
600 WbrC 84310 1058 E6
600 WbrC 84310 1059 B6
600 WbrC 84317 1059 B6
Ogden Canyon Rd SR-39
- OGDN 84401 1116 E1
- WbrC 84317 1116 E1
- WbrC 84317 1117 A1
600 WbrC 84310 1058 E6
600 WbrC 84310 1059 B6
600 WbrC 84317 1058 E6
600 WbrC 84317 1059 B6
Ogden Peak Cir
1400 OGDN 84404 1057 B2
O'Hara Cir
7800 SLkC 84044 1960 D4
O'Henry Rd
11000 SNDY 84070 2282 E5
Okehampton Ct
600 FMTN 84025 1346 B4
Okeson Cir
2400 HLDY 84117 2072 A2
Olani Wy
3800 WVCY 84120 1962 C7
Old Barn Dr
8000 SNDY 84094 2177 A4
Old Bauerhof Rd
700 MIDW 84049 2397 B2
Old Bingham Hwy
- SJDN 84088 2279 A3
- SJDN 84095 2279 D2
- WJDN 84095 2279 D2
3400 WJDN 84088 2174 E5
4700 WJDN 84088 2280 A1
4800 WJDN 84088 2279 D2
Old Church Ct
4700 WJDN 84084 2174 A2
Old Colony Cir
2800 HLDY 84117 2072 B4
Old Coventry Cir
8000 SLkC 84093 2177 D5
Old Creek Rd
5000 WJDN 84088 2174 A6
5100 WJDN 84088 2173 E6
Old Cyprus Ct
1400 SJDN 84095 2281 C4
Old Dairy Rd
1000 SNDY 84094 2177 A4
Old Dobbin Ln
13800 DRPR 84020 2389 B5
Old England Rd
11000 SNDY 84092 2283 C5
Old English Rd
500 DRPR 84020 2388 E4
700 DRPR 84020 2389 A4
Olden Raintree Dr
800 CTRV 84014 1551 E2
Old Factory Dr
8100 WJDN 84088 2175 C5
Old Farm Cir
400 CTRV 84014 1551 D1
Old Farm Ln
3900 SLkC 84107 1964 E7
4000 SLkC 84107 2070 E3
Old Farm Rd
100 FTHT 84037 1345 E1
600 SLkC 84107 2070 E1
800 FTHT 84037 1284 A7
800 FTHT 84037 1346 A1
Old Farm Wy
500 SLkC 84107 2070 E1
Old Fashion Pl
5900 TYVL 84123 2069 B6
Old Fort Cir
- FMTN 84025 1447 D1
12600 RIVN 84065 2387 B2
Old Fort Dr
12600 RIVN 84065 2387 B2
Old Fort Rd
- FMTN 84025 1447 D1
Old Glory Cir
3100 SLkC 84044 1960 E5
Oldham Cir
3600 WVCY 84120 1962 C6
Oldham Dr
900 NSLK 84054 1652 C6
Oldham St
3600 WVCY 84120 1962 C6
Old Hargis Hill Rd
1400 WLRD 84340 885 C1
3700 PRRY 84302 885 C1
Old Haul Rd
10 CTRV 84014 1448 D6
Old Highway 30
2600 UNTH 84403 1230 A1
Old Highway 40 Frontage Rd
4500 SmtC 84098 1973 C6
Old Hollow Wy
1100 WJDN 84084 2175 E2
Old Homestead Ln
8700 WJDN 84088 2174 B6
Old Lake Ln
700 FTHT 84037 1346 B3
Old Lexus Dr
- SGVL 84663 3142 D4
Old Maple Ct
1300 MRRY 84117 2071 B5
Old Mill Cir
3100 HLDY 84121 2178 B1
Old Mill Ln
500 KYVL 84037 1345 B2
Old Miller Ct
4200 SLkC 84118 2068 C3
Old Mission Rd
1300 SNDY 84093 2177 B4
Old Oak Ln
10 SNDY 84092 2284 A5
4900 HILD 84003 2604 E2
Old Orchard Cir
2500 HLDY 84121 2072 A7
Old Orchard Ln
4100 CRHL 84062 2605 B4
6000 HLDY 84121 2072 A7
Old Oxford Rd
4700 SLkC 84118 2068 C3
Old Pond Ct
8100 SLkC 84044 1960 C5
Old Post Rd
4600 OGDN 84403 1173 B3
5300 WbrC 84403 1173 C4
Old Post Office Rd
600 SWBR 84405 1229 A1
Old Ranch Pl
9700 SLkC 84092 2284 D2
E Old Ranch Rd
10 SmtC 84098 1972 C5
N Old Ranch Rd
4500 SmtC 84098 1972 C4
W Old Ranch Rd
10 SmtC 84098 1972 B6
4300 SmtC 84098 1971 E6
Old Rosebud Ln
2200 SJDN 84095 2281 B5
Old Saddle Rd
1100 DRPR 84020 2389 B5
Old Sandy Ct
300 SNDY 84070 2176 D6
Old Shepherd Rd
1400 FMTN 84025 1346 A5
Old Silo Wy
3600 WVCY 84119 1963 D7
Old Springs Rd
- OGDN 84404 1056 C5
Old Station Wy
- NSLK 84054 1653 A7
Old Stone House Wy
1000 SmtC 84098 1972 A2
Old Trenton Wy
5300 MRRY 84123 2070 A7
Old US-40
4700 WshC 84049 2186 B7
4700 WshC 84049 2292 B2
Old Villa Wy
- WJDN 84084 2174 A2
Ole Bish Ln
4700 HILD 84003 2605 A2
Olene Cir
3600 WVCY 84120 1962 C6
Oles Ln
6200 HLDY 84121 2072 A7
Olive Cir
4100 TYVL 84123 2069 D1
Olive Dr
1500 SLkC 84124 2071 C1
Olive Ln
1300 DvsC 84056 1228 B2
1400 DvsC 84056 1172 B7
Olive St
- SLCY 84103 1859 B2
1300 TYVL 84123 2069 D1
Olive Berry Ln
100 DRPR 84020 2282 D6
Olive Brook Cir
2800 SLkC 84044 1960 E4
Olive Brook Dr
7400 SLkC 84044 1960 D4
Olive Dunn Dr
3900 WVCY 84120 1962 C5
Olive Grove Wy
3300 WJDN 84088 2174 E7
Olive Hain Ct
3700 SLkC 84044 1960 B6
Olive Leaf Ct
8900 WJDN 84088 2174 E7
Olive Leaf Ln
3200 WJDN 84088 2174 E7
Oliver Cir
2100 HLDY 84124 2071 E1
Oliver Dr
3900 HLDY 84124 1965 E7
Olivet Dr
6700 CDHT 84121 2177 B1
Olive Tree Cir
3300 WJDN 84088 2174 E7
Olpin Ln
- HRCY 84032 2398 E2
Olsen Ln
500 SALM 84653 3356 C3
Olsen Plz
500 LYTN 84041 1282 D3
Olsen Wy
1800 WBNF 84087 1551 A5
Olympiad Ln
5900 HRMN 84065 2385 C4
Olympic Ln
1400 OGDN 84404 1116 B1
N Olympic Ln
600 EKMT 84651 3462 E1
W Olympic Ln
10 EKMT 84651 3462 E1
Olympic Wy
- MIDW 84049 2396 E2
3900 SLkC 84124 1966 C7
4100 SLkC 84124 2072 C1
Olympus Cir
7700 MDVL 84047 2176 B4
Olympus Dr
2300 HLDY 84124 2071 E1
2500 HLDY 84124 2072 A1
2600 SLkC 84124 2072 A1
Olympus St
7700 MDVL 84047 2176 C4
Olympus Oaks Ln
2900 SLkC 84109 1966 B7
Olympus View Dr
3400 SLkC 84124 2072 C1
Olympus Vista Ct
2300 HLDY 84124 2071 E1
Omega Wy
3900 WVCY 84120 1962 C7
Omni Av
1700 SLCY 84116 1753 C7
Omni Cir
1000 SLCY 84116 1753 C7
Omni Dr
900 SLCY 84116 1753 C7
Oneida Cir
2600 PRVO 84604 2928 E2
Oneida Ln
2600 PRVO 84604 2928 E2
Oneida St
1700 SLCY 84108 1965 E1
2300 SLCY 84109 1965 E2
Onieda St
- DvsC 84056 1172 A6
Onion St
700 NSLK 84054 1653 B4
N Onion St
10 WBNF 84087 1551 B6
S Onion St
10 WBNF 84087 1551 B7
10 WBNF 84087 1653 B1
Ontario Av
100 PKCY 84060 2078 E6
Ontario Dr
1100 SLCY 84104 1857 E6
On the Green Wy
1100 FMTN 84025 1346 C5
Onyx Ln
800 SLkC 84094 2283 A1
Onyx St
700 LYTN 84041 1282 E3
Opal Cir
9900 SLkC 84094 2283 A2
Opal Hill Dr
4800 WJDN 84084 2174 A3
Opal Mist Ct
14000 HRMN 84065 2385 E4
Open Hill Dr
4200 SJDN 84095 2280 B6
Ophelia Ln
5700 HRMN 84065 2385 D4
Oquirlane St
3300 SLkC 84044 1960 C6
Oquirrh Dr
1200 PRVO 84604 2927 E4
2700 SLCY 84108 1860 B6
Oquirrh Hills Dr
8400 SLkC 84044 1960 B6
Oquirrh Meadows Dr
9200 WJDN 84088 2174 E7
9200 WJDN 84088 2280 B1
Oquirrh Point Rd
6200 WJDN 84084 2173 B1
Oquirrh Ridge Ct
6000 WJDN 84084 2173 C2
Oquirrh Ridge Rd
6600 WJDN 84084 2173 C2
Oquirrh View Dr
2400 RIVN 84065 2387 A3
Oram Cir
3800 SOGN 84403 1116 A7
Orange St
10 SLCY 84104 1857 C3
Orangewood Ln
600 SNDY 84070 2282 E5
Orchard Av
100 OGDN 84404 1057 A5
400 ANFK 84003 2711 D2
1300 OGDN 84404 1116 A1
2000 OGDN 84401 1116 A2
2900 OGDN 84403 1116 A5
3600 SOGN 84403 1116 A7
4000 SOGN 84403 1173 A1
N Orchard Av
1100 OGDN 84404 1057 A2
Orchard Cir
1800 SLkC 84106 1965 D7
2900 OGDN 84403 1116 A5
Orchard Ct
700 FTHT 84037 1346 B3
Orchard Dr
100 BNFL 84010 1653 C5
600 OREM 84057 2820 D3
600 PTGV 84062 2713 A4
700 RVHT 84321 528 A4
900 CchC 84321 528 A4
1000 BMCY 84302 767 B4
1500 SLkC 84106 1965 C6
1600 ROY 84067 1171 D2
3200 NSLK 84010 1653 C5
3400 DvsC 84010 1653 C5
3400 NSLK 84054 1653 C5
3500 DvsC 84054 1653 C5
E Orchard Dr
2900 SLkC 84109 1966 B7
N Orchard Dr
10 NSLK 84054 1653 B6
100 DvsC 84010 1653 B6
100 DvsC 84054 1653 B6
100 NSLK 84010 1653 B6
S Orchard Dr
10 NSLK 84054 1653 A7
Orchard Ln
800 ALPN 84004 2498 B3
N Orchard Ln
10 SNQN 84655 3461 A7
200 UthC 84655 3461 A7
Orchard Pl
10 BNFL 84010 1653 E4
200 SLCY 84101 1858 B4
1100 BMCY 84302 767 B4
Orchard St
3100 SLkC 84106 1965 C5
Orchard Wy
2200 SRSP 84043 2601 E4
Orchard Grass Cir
600 KYVL 84037 1283 D6
Orchard Heights Dr
1200 LOGN 84321 528 B4
Orchard Hills Wy
3500 WVCY 84128 1961 A6
Orchard Park Dr
1300 OGDN 84404 1116 C1
Orchard View Cir
1800 SJDN 84095 2281 C2
Orchard View Dr
1700 SJDN 84095 2281 C2
S Orchard View Dr
12500 UthC 84651 3460 B4

STREET
Block City ZIP Map# Grid

S Orchard View Dr
12500 UthC 84655 3460 B4
Orchid Cir
4500 WVCY 84120 2068 C2
E Oregon Av
1900 PRVO 84606 3036 B3
S Oregon Av
1700 PRVO 84606 3036 B3
Oregon St
2900 SLkC 84106 1965 C4
Oregon Trail Wy
4700 HRMN 84065 2386 A1
S Orem Blvd
10 OREM 84058 2820 D6
1000 OREM 84058 2927 E1
Orgil Band Rd
14100 DRPR 84020 2389 A6
Origin Pl
5900 TYVL 84123 2069 B6
Oriole Cir
2500 WVCY 84119 1963 B5
Oriole Wy
2500 WVCY 84119 1963 B5
Oriole Grove Wy
2400 WVCY 84119 1963 C3
Orion Cir
2300 WVCY 84119 1963 B6
Orion Wy
2200 WVCY 84119 1963 B6
Orion Hill Rd
7000 WJDN 84084 2173 E2
Orion Hills Cove
5300 WJDN 84084 2173 E2
Orkney Cir
9900 SJDN 84095 2280 C2
Orlando Pl
800 SSLK 84119 1964 A4
Orlean Dr
1800 OREM 84097 2928 B2
Orleans Wy
4400 WVCY 84120 2068 D2
Oros Av
1200 SLkC 84124 1965 B7
Orpheum Av
10 SLCY 84111 1858 C3
Orson F Dr
2900 LYTN 84040 1284 A2
Orton Cir
2300 WVCY 84119 1963 B3
S Orton Rd
9200 UthC 84653 3356 D3
Osage Orange Av
1700 HLDY 84124 2071 C2
Osborne Cir
100 NSLK 84054 1653 B7
600 DRPR 84020 2388 E5
Osborne Ln
13800 DRPR 84020 2388 E6
Osborne Estate Cir
600 DRPR 84020 2388 E5
Oskaloosa Dr
3600 WJDN 84084 2174 D1
Oslo Bay
6000 SLkC 84121 2071 E6
Osmond Dr
6000 WbrC 84403 1174 A6
Osmond Ln
700 PRVO 84604 2821 D6
1000 PRRY 84302 827 B6
Osprey Av
4000 WVCY 84120 2068 C2
Osteen Cir
3700 SLkC 84044 1960 E7
Ostler Ct
900 ALPN 84004 2498 B6
Ott Dr
3300 TYVL 84118 2068 E4
Ottawa Dr
3400 WVCY 84119 2068 D1
Ouray Av
300 SLCY 84103 1858 B1
800 SLCY 84116 1858 A1
1300 SLCY 84116 1857 D1
Outlook Cove
500 DRPR 84020 2388 E7
Ovation Ct
6600 WVCY 84128 1961 B6
Ovation Dr
3300 WVCY 84128 1961 B5
Over Hill Cir
8000 CDHT 84121 2178 C4
Over Hill Rd
- SmtC 84098 1866 E2
Overland Rd
700 NSLK 84054 1653 B5
900 NSLK 84087 1653 B5
Overland Park Rd
11900 RIVN 84065 2280 B7
11900 RIVN 84065 2386 C1
Overlay North Pl
- LOGN 84341 463 D5
Overleigh Ct
9400 SJDN 84095 2281 A1
Overview Wy
1000 WJDN 84084 2175 E2
Owens St
200 LYTN 84041 1282 E4
Owensboro Dr
3700 WJDN 84084 2174 D1
6400 WJDN 84084 2068 C7
Owenwood Cir
1500 SNDY 84092 2283 C6
Oxbow Cir
1500 TYVL 84123 2069 C3
Ox Cart Ln
14800 DRPR 84020 2388 D7
14800 DRPR 84020 2495 D1
Oxford Cir
8800 SNDY 84070 2176 C6
Oxford Ct
9800 HILD 84003 2604 D3
Oxford Dr
4700 OGDN 84403 1173 B3
E Oxford Dr
700 KYVL 84037 1283 E6
800 KYVL 84037 1284 A6
N Oxford Dr
1200 KYVL 84037 1284 A5
Oxford Rd
100 SNDY 84070 2282 C1
Oxford St
4300 CRHL 84062 2605 B3
Oxford Wy
3600 WVCY 84119 1962 E7
4400 BNFL 84010 1653 E7
Oxford Club Cir
1600 DRPR 84020 2389 C3
Oxford Farms Dr
11800 RIVN 84065 2280 D7
Oxford Hills Dr
- DRPR 84020 2283 E7
Oxford Park Dr
3200 WVCY 84119 1962 D3
Ozone Cir
5700 SLkC 84118 2067 C6

P

P St
10 SLCY 84103 1859 A3
Pace Dr
- SmtC 84098 1972 A5
Pace Pl
7000 SmtC 84098 1866 E7
Pace Rd
1100 SmtC 84098 1867 A5
N Pace Frontage Rd
6300 SmtC 84098 1973 A2
6400 SmtC 84017 1867 A7
6400 SmtC 84098 1866 D7
6400 SmtC 84098 1867 A7
6400 SmtC 84098 1972 E1
Pacific Av
- RVDL 84405 1172 C1
10 CRFD 84015 1227 C4
10 CRFD 84016 1227 D4
10 NSLK 84054 1653 A5
700 SLCY 84103 1858 A4
1100 SLCY 84104 1857 D4
2100 OGDN 84401 1115 D2
3100 OGDN 84405 1115 D6
3800 RVDL 84405 1115 C7
Pacific Dr
- ANFK 84003 2604 A7
100 ANFK 84003 2711 C1
1000 UthC 84003 2712 A2
Pacific St
- SLCY 84104 1856 E5
Pack Cove
2300 PTGV 84062 2605 B6
Packlan Pl
1500 TYVL 84123 2069 D4
Packsaddle Cir
3800 SmtC 84098 1864 E6
Paddington Dr
1900 PKCY 84060 2078 E3
1900 PKCY 84060 2079 A3
Paddington Rd
7000 WJDN 84084 2174 E2
Paddock Ct
1100 OREM 84097 2821 B4
N Paddock Dr
- FMTN 84025 1447 E2
- FMTN 84025 1448 A2
Padley St
800 SLCY 84108 1859 E5
Page Cir
- WBNF 84087 1551 B6
600 LYTN 84041 1283 B6
Pagentry Pl
4600 WVCY 84120 2068 C3
E Pages Ln
10 CTRV 84014 1551 E5
400 CTRV 84014 1552 A5
700 BNFL 84010 1552 A5
W Pages Ln
10 BNFL 84010 1551 D5
10 CTRV 84010 1551 D5
10 CTRV 84014 1551 D5
400 BNFL 84087 1551 D5
400 CTRV 84087 1551 D5
400 WBNF 84087 1551 D5
1100 DvsC 84087 1551 A5
1500 DvsC 84087 1550 E5
Pages Place Dr
1600 BNFL 84010 1551 C5
Pagoda Tree Ln
8800 WJDN 84088 2174 E7
Pagos Av
1200 SLkC 84124 1965 B7
Paige Cir
3300 SLkC 84109 1966 B6
Paige Ln
3600 CRHL 84062 2605 D5
Paine Rd
3700 SLkC 84044 1960 E7
Paintbrush Dr
6400 WJDN 84084 2068 A7
6400 WJDN 84084 2174 A1
Paintbrush Ln
- LOGN 84321 528 C4
Paisley Cir
9600 SJDN 84095 2280 C1
Paisley Wy
7400 WJDN 84084 2175 D3
Paiute Dr
3400 WVCY 84119 2068 D1
Palace Wy
1400 WVCY 84119 1963 D7
Palamino Cir
1600 NHLN 84341 464 C2
Pale Moon Ln
4400 SJDN 84095 2280 B6
Palermo St
12700 HRMN 84065 2385 D2
Pali St
500 SNDY 84070 2282 E4
Palimino Wy
900 WBNF 84087 1551 A6
Palisade Cir
1300 LOGN 84321 528 B4
Palisade Dr
900 OREM 84097 2821 A7
3500 SLkC 84109 1966 D5
N Palisade Dr
- OREM 84097 2821 B4
S Palisade Dr
600 OREM 84097 2821 A7
1000 OREM 84097 2928 A1
Palisade Rim Cir
11100 SJDN 84095 2281 E5
Palisade Rim Dr
11200 SJDN 84095 2281 E6
Palisade View Dr
11200 SJDN 84095 2281 E5
Palladium Dr
7800 WJDN 84088 2174 E4
Palm Dr
500 MRRY 84123 2070 B6
Palma Wy
2700 CDHT 84121 2178 B1
Palmer Ct
4200 WVCY 84120 2068 C1
Palmer Dr
4000 RVDL 84405 1172 D1
4000 SOGN 84405 1172 D1
4400 WVCY 84120 2068 B2
Palmer Park Ln
1300 SJDN 84095 2281 D1
Palmer Vista Dr
800 SJDN 84095 2282 A3
900 SJDN 84095 2281 E3
Palmetto Dr
2300 TYVL 84084 2069 B7
Palm Frond Ct
5800 WJDN 84084 2173 D1
Palmyra Dr
5000 UthC 84660 3141 C6
5500 UthC 84660 3142 A7
5600 UthC 84660 3249 A1
Palmyra Dr SR-77
4000 UthC 84660 3141 A4
Paloma Wy
11300 SNDY 84094 2283 B6
S Paloma Wy
11400 SNDY 84094 2283 D4
Palomino Dr
7000 WVCY 84128 1960 E4
7000 WVCY 84128 1961 A4
Palos Verdes Dr
400 OREM 84058 2927 C1
1000 OREM 84058 2820 C7
S Palos Verdes Dr
900 KYVL 84037 1345 D3
Palo Verde Wy
1500 CDHT 84121 2177 C2
Pamela Cir
1000 LYTN 84041 1282 C2
Pamela Dr
2700 CDHT 84121 2178 A4
Pamela Wy
400 SLCY 84116 1857 C1
S Pamela Wy
8400 MDVL 84047 2176 B5
W Pamela Wy
200 MDVL 84047 2176 C6
Pampas Dr
10800 SNDY 84094 2283 A5
Panama St
2100 SSLK 84115 1964 C2
E Pan American Dr
200 MRRY 84107 2070 C4
S Pan American Dr
4300 MRRY 84107 2070 C4
Panamint Rd
4800 WVCY 84120 1962 A6
Panarama Cir
- WbrC 84310 1001 B6
Pando Wy
7700 WJDN 84084 2175 B4
Panguitch Pl
15000 DRPR 84020 2495 D1
Panorama Cir
2000 WbrC 84310 1001 B6
2200 HLDY 84124 2071 E1
Panorama Dr
700 SOGN 84403 1173 A2
2200 HLDY 84124 2071 E1
N Panorama Dr
10800 HILD 84003 2604 E1
10900 HILD 84003 2498 B7
W Panorama Dr
4700 HILD 84003 2498 A7
4700 HILD 84003 2605 A1
4800 HILD 84003 2604 E1
Panorama Wy
2100 HLDY 84124 2071 E1
Panoramic Dr
200 HYRM 84319 651 D2
Pantera Ln
1300 SLkC 84106 1965 B7
Panther Wy
200 SLCY 84103 1858 B2
Pappadopulos Ln
7400 CDHT 84093 2177 C3
Paprika Cir
5900 TYVL 84118 2069 A6
Paprika Dr
2700 TYVL 84118 2069 A6
Par Cir
2100 WJDN 84088 2175 B6
Par Ct
9200 SmtC 84098 1865 B3
Parachute Dr
3900 WVCY 84120 1962 C5
Paracle Cir
100 FMTN 84025 1448 D2
E Paradise Dr
400 OREM 84097 2820 E4
N Paradise Dr
10 OREM 84097 2820 E5
10 OREM 84097 2821 A5
W Paradise Dr
- CchC 84319 710 A3
- CchC 84328 710 A3
Paradise Ln
100 ALPN 84004 2497 D5
100 ALPN 84004 2498 A5
1400 TYVL 84123 2069 C4
Paradise Rd
100 SmtC 84098 1864 C7
Paradise Cove Ln
- ALPN 84004 2497 E5
Paradise Dry Canyon
- CchC 84328 711 C7
Paradiso Ln
- CTRV 84014 1551 D4
Parakeet Dr
9000 SNDY 84093 2178 B7
Paramount Av
200 SLCY 84115 1858 B7
Parc Cir
400 CRFD 84015 1227 D5
Par Four Lp
2200 WJDN 84088 2175 B6
Paris Ln
900 SLkC 84124 2071 A2
Park Av
10 HYRM 84319 651 D2
100 PKCY 84060 2078 E6
200 LYTN 84041 1282 E5
400 LOGN 84321 527 B4
800 TMTN 84337 520 C5
1700 RIVN 84065 2387 C2
Park Av SR-224
1600 PKCY 84060 2078 B2
Park Blvd
400 OGDN 84401 1115 E2
400 OGDN 84404 1115 E2
1400 OGDN 84401 1116 C1
Park Cir
- HILD 84003 2498 B7
10 LOGN 84321 527 C4
2500 SLkC 84109 1966 A6
N Park Cir
100 EKMT 84651 3463 A2
W Park Cir
1500 PTVW 84404 997 E5
Park Ct
3100 SSLK 84106 1964 E5
Park Dr
- HILD 84003 2498 B7
600 HYRM 84319 651 D2
2200 PRRY 84302 827 C4
E Park Dr
10 EKMT 84651 3463 A2
10 KYVL 84037 1345 D4
N Park Dr
300 EKMT 84651 3462 E1
S Park Dr
800 MNTU 84324 768 B7
1000 BxEC 84324 829 B2
1500 MNTU 84324 829 B1
W Park Dr
10 EKMT 84651 3462 E1
10 EKMT 84651 3463 A3
10 KYVL 84037 1345 C4
Park Ln
- FMTN 84025 1448 A1
200 CTRV 84014 1551 D2
300 FMTN 84025 1346 C7
500 DvsC 84056 1228 D5
5700 SOGN 84403 1173 D5
6000 WVCY 84118 2173 C1
Park Ln SR-225
300 FMTN 84025 1346 B7
Park Ln E
1800 OREM 84058 2927 D2
Park Ln N
10 OREM 84058 2927 D2
Park Ln W
1800 OREM 84058 2927 D3
Park Pl
200 BMCY 84302 827 E1
1500 SmtC 84098 1971 E5
3500 SSLK 84106 1964 E6
Park Pl E
5600 SLkC 84121 2071 C6
Park Pl N
1500 SLkC 84121 2071 C5
Park Pl W
5600 SLkC 84121 2071 C6
Park St
- SLCY 84103 1859 A2
100 MDVL 84047 2176 C3
800 SLCY 84102 1858 E5
1500 SLCY 84105 1858 E7
1700 SLCY 84105 1964 E1
1900 PRVO 84606 3036 B3
2400 SSLK 84106 1964 E3
4200 SLkC 84107 2070 E1
S Park St
- GRLD 84312 521 A2
Park Vw
700 LOGN 84321 527 B5
Park Bend Ct
4500 RIVN 84065 2280 B7
Parkbrook Ct
3500 WVCY 84120 1961 D5
Park Centre Dr
1300 CDHT 84121 2177 B2
Park Commons Wy
3100 WVCY 84120 1962 A4
Park Creeke Ln
300 SSLK 84115 1964 D5
Park Crest Cir
1200 SLkC 84124 2071 B1
Parkcrest Ct
7400 CDHT 84093 2177 D3
Parkcrest Dr
2500 WVCY 84119 1963 C3
Parkcrest Ln
- PRVO 84601 3035 B1
Parker Dr
3400 OGDN 84405 1115 C6
3500 RVDL 84405 1115 C6
4000 RVDL 84405 1172 A1
Parker Ln
500 BMCY 84302 827 D1
700 SLkC 84106 1964 E4
700 SLkC 84106 1965 A4
Parker Rd
- OGDN 84405 1115 C5
Parker St
200 ANFK 84003 2604 E7
Park Glen Ct
7700 WJDN 84088 2174 A4
S Park Green Dr
4100 WVCY 84120 2068 C1
Parkham Wy
5900 SLkC 84118 2067 C6
Park Haven Ln
11800 RIVN 84065 2280 B7
12000 RIVN 84065 2386 B1
Park Hill Dr
4500 SLkC 84124 2072 C2
Park Hill Wy
200 SLkC 84107 1964 D7
Park Hills Dr
- CTRV 84025 1448 D5
- DvsC 84010 1448 D5
- FMTN 84025 1448 D5
2000 CTRV 84014 1448 D5
Park Hollow Ln
4100 RIVN 84065 2280 B7
12000 RIVN 84065 2386 B1
Park Hurst Cir
8300 SNDY 84094 2177 A5
Park Hurst Ln
800 SNDY 84094 2177 A5
Parkinson Dr
400 BMCY 84302 766 D4
Parkland Dr
400 SNDY 84070 2176 B6
Parklane Dr E
1800 OREM 84058 2927 D3
Park Manor Dr
4500 SLkC 84117 2071 C2
Park Maple Dr
7400 WJDN 84084 2173 A3
Park Meadow Cir
200 HDPK 84318 464 A2
Park Meadow Dr
200 HDPK 84318 464 A2
W Park Meadows Dr
1000 MPTN 84664 3250 E2
Park Meadows St
3300 SSLK 84106 1964 E6
Park Mesa Wy
700 SNDY 84094 2282 E6
700 SNDY 84094 2283 A6
Park Oak Pl
400 SLkC 84107 2070 E1
Park Palisade Dr
900 SJDN 84095 2281 E5
900 SJDN 84095 2282 A5
Park Pl Ln
10 CTRV 84014 1551 D3
Park Point Dr
4800 WJDN 84084 2068 A7
Parkridge Cir
7400 CDHT 84093 2177 D3
Park Ridge Dr
6100 SmtC 84098 1972 C2
Parkridge Dr
1500 CDHT 84093 2177 C3
1500 CDHT 84121 2177 C3
Park Round Rd
1000 WDHL 84653 3463 C3
Park Row St
900 SLCY 84105 1859 C5
Park School Rd
700 DRPR 84020 2389 A6
Park Shadows Cir
100 BNFL 84010 1551 D6
Park Shadows Ct
100 BNFL 84010 1551 D6
Park Shadows Ln
700 BNFL 84010 1551 D6
Parkside Cir
100 ANFK 84003 2711 C2
500 CTRV 84014 1551 C1
S Parkside Ct
200 PRVO 84601 2927 E7
Parkside Dr
1500 WDCR 84087 1653 A2
2600 LEHI 84043 2602 C4
5100 MRRY 84107 2070 E4
W Parkside Dr
1400 PRVO 84601 2927 E7
Parkside Ln
10 SNDY 84092 2284 A5
1200 LYTN 84041 1282 C7
S Parkside Pl
200 PRVO 84601 2927 E7
Park Springs Cir
1000 PTVW 84414 998 A5
Park Springs Dr
3100 WVCY 84120 1961 E5
Parkstone Ct
12300 DRPR 84020 2389 B1
Parkstone Dr
1100 DRPR 84020 2389 B1
Park Terrace Dr
4200 SLkC 84124 2072 E1
Park Vale Dr
4800 WJDN 84084 2174 A3
Park View Cir
- BNFL 84010 1653 E4
Parkview Cir
100 SmtC 84098 1864 B6
400 SHFD 84335 400 A2
3800 SLkC 84124 1966 D7
Parkview Dr
100 SmtC 84098 1864 B5
3700 SLkC 84109 1966 D7
3700 SLkC 84124 1966 D7
4300 SLkC 84124 2072 D2
4400 OGDN 84403 1173 C2
E Parkview Dr
1300 PRVO 84604 2929 A2
S Parkview Dr
2000 MPTN 84664 3250 E3
Parkview Pl
100 SmtC 84098 1864 C6
Parkview Ter
100 SmtC 84098 1864 B5
Park Village Dr
4800 WJDN 84084 2174 A3
Park Vista Ct
- WVCY 84120 1961 E6
Park Vista Dr
3300 WVCY 84120 1961 E6
Parkway
100 PRVO 84604 2928 C1
Parkway W
100 ALPN 84004 2497 E5
Parkway Av
2100 SLCY 84109 1965 E3
E Parkway Av
700 SLCY 84106 1965 A3
W Parkway Av
1000 WVCY 84119 1963 D3
Parkway Blvd
1700 WVCY 84119 1963 A4
2700 WVCY 84119 1962 E4
3600 WVCY 84120 1962 E4
5600 WVCY 84128 1961 B4
7000 WVCY 84128 1960 D4
7200 SLkC 84044 1960 D4
Parkway Cir
10 CTRV 84014 1551 D1
200 OREM 84057 2820 D3
Parkway Dr
100 CRFD 84015 1227 E5
500 SmtC 84098 1866 E7
600 NSLK 84054 1754 B1
900 SmtC 84098 1867 A7
1300 CTRV 84014 1551 D1
1400 CTRV 84014 1448 D7
7500 MDVL 84047 2176 B3
Parkway Ln
1100 WVCY 84119 1963 E7
Park West Run
- HILD 84003 2497 C5
Park Wood Ct
4800 WJDN 84084 2174 A4
Park Wood Dr
5900 SLkC 84118 2068 A7
6100 WJDN 84118 2068 A7
Parleys Cir
2300 SLCY 84109 1965 D3
Parleys Rd
300 SmtC 84098 1866 D5
Parleys Ter
2100 SLCY 84109 1965 E3
Parleys Wy
2300 SLCY 84109 1965 E2
2300 SLCY 84109 1966 A2
Parleys Canyon Blvd
1700 SLCY 84106 1965 D2
2000 SLCY 84109 1965 D2
Parliament Av
1300 WVCY 84119 1963 D7
Parowan Wy
400 DRPR 84020 2388 E7
14800 DRPR 84020 2495 D1
Parr Ct
4800 WJDN 84088 2174 A5
Parr Dr
4800 WJDN 84088 2174 A6
5100 WJDN 84088 2173 E6
Parrish Dr
5100 SLkC 84118 2067 D4
E Parrish Ln
10 CTRV 84014 1551 E3
400 CTRV 84014 1552 A3
W Parrish Ln
10 CTRV 84014 1551 D3
W Parrish Ln SR-105
10 CTRV 84014 1551 D3
Parrott St
1100 WVCY 84119 1963 E7
Parry St
300 OGDN 84404 1115 E1
Parsley Ct
1700 SRSP 84043 2601 D5
Parthenon Ct
5400 TYVL 84118 2069 A5
Par Three Cir
900 FTHT 84037 1346 A4
Partridge Cir
9300 SNDY 84093 2284 A1
Partridge Ln
- LYTN 84040 1229 B5
Partridge Wy
2000 OGDN 84403 1173 E3
2500 SNDY 84093 2178 A7
Partridge Run Wy
8000 WJDN 84088 2174 D5
Partridge View Ln
8100 WJDN 84088 2174 D5
Pasadena St
2500 SLCY 84109 1966 B3
Pascall Bay
13700 HRMN 84065 2385 C5
Paschal Cir
1800 SLCY 84108 1966 A1
Paskay Dr
4000 WVCY 84120 2068 C2
S Pasque Dr
4600 TYVL 84123 2069 E3
W Pasque Dr
900 TYVL 84123 2069 E3
Patchwork Cir
11600 SJDN 84095 2280 C6
N Patiosprings Cir
4600 WbrC 84310 1001 D2
N Patiosprings Dr
3700 WbrC 84310 1001 D3
Patricia Cir
2900 SLkC 84044 1960 B4
Patricia Dr
2800 SLkC 84044 1960 B4
Patricia Ln
5900 WbrC 84403 1173 D6
Patricia Wy
1700 SLCY 84116 1857 C2
W Patrick Cir
7300 SLkC 84044 1960 E6
Patrick Dr
3100 SLkC 84044 1960 E5
Patrick Wy
- DvsC 84056 1228 B4
Patriot Cir
7400 SLkC 84044 1960 D6
Patriot Dr
3500 SLkC 84044 1960 D6
Patrol Rd
- CRFD 84016 1227 E6
- CRFD 84016 1281 D1
N Patterson Ln
600 ALPN 84004 2498 A3
Patterson St
100 OGDN 84401 1115 D5
600 OGDN 84403 1116 A5
W Patterson St
200 OGDN 84401 1115 D5
Patti Cir
3700 WVCY 84128 1961 C7
Patti Dr
3700 WVCY 84128 1961 C7
Patty Cir
500 CTRV 84014 1551 D4
Paty Cir
400 SNDY 84070 2176 E4
Paul Av
300 LYTN 84041 1282 D1
Paul Cir
2300 TYVL 84118 2069 B7
Paula Cir
10 SNDY 84070 2176 C6
Paula Dr
10 SNDY 84070 2176 C6
Paula Ann St
3200 TYVL 84118 2068 E4
Paulette Av
5400 WVCY 84120 1961 D7
Paulette Wy
200 FMTN 84025 1448 D3
Pauline Wy
2200 WJDN 84088 2175 B5
Paulista Wy
1500 SNDY 84093 2177 C5
Paul Ream Av
10 PRVO 84604 2928 C4
Paulson Cir
12200 RIVN 84065 2387 D1
Pavant Av
4800 WVCY 84120 1962 A7
5100 WVCY 84120 1961 E6
Pavant Cir
5100 WVCY 84120 1961 D5
Pavant Dr
3700 WVCY 84120 1961 E7
3800 WVCY 84120 1962 A7
Pawnee Cir
4800 WJDN 84084 2068 A7
Pawnee Dr
3400 WVCY 84119 2068 D1
4900 WJDN 84084 2068 A7
Pax Cir
3600 SLkC 84124 2072 D1
Paxton Av
- SLCY 84104 1857 C6
200 SLCY 84101 1858 B6
700 SLCY 84104 1858 A6
Paxton Pl
200 BMCY 84302 827 E1
Payday Dr
10 PKCY 84060 2078 B3
Pay Dirt Cir
11800 HRMN 84065 2280 B7
Paydon Ln
1100 RIVN 84065 2387 E2
Payne Cir
10 LYTN 84041 1282 E4
S Payson Canyon Rd
- EKMT 84651 3462 C3
- UthC 84655 3462 D7
11300 PYSN 84651 3355 A7
11300 UthC 84651 3355 A7
11300 UthC 84651 3462 A1
12000 PYSN 84651 3462 C3
Peacefield Dr
- LYTN 84040 1283 C3
Peaceful Pl
9400 SJDN 84095 2281 C1
Peaceful View Wy
1600 SJDN 84095 2281 C1
Peach Ct
9600 CRHL 84062 2605 A3
Peach Dr
1000 OGDN 84404 1057 C7
Peach Ln
200 BNFL 84010 1653 E1
Peach Pl
300 SRSP 84043 2601 D4
Peach St
- SNQN 84655 3461 B7
2400 PRRY 84302 827 D5
4400 HLDY 84117 2072 B2
Peach Blossom Cir
900 SNDY 84094 2177 A7
Peach Blossom Dr
900 SNDY 84094 2283 A1
9000 SNDY 84094 2177 A7
Peach Creek Ct
1600 WJDN 84088 2175 D5
Peach Flower Ln
3600 WVCY 84128 1961 A6
Peach Grove Cir
9900 SJDN 84095 2281 C2
Peach Orchard Ct
1400 DRPR 84020 2389 B4
Peach Park Cove
9900 SJDN 84095 2281 C3
Peach Tree Cir
400 ALPN 84004 2498 A3
1800 SJDN 84095 2281 C2
Peach Tree Dr
10 CTRV 84014 1551 E1
Peachwood Cir
5300 TYVL 84118 2068 E5
Peachwood Dr
3900 WVCY 84119 1962 E7
4000 WVCY 84119 2068 C2
7800 SWBR 84405 1230 A3
Peachwood Wy
2400 SWBR 84405 1230 A3
Peacock Cir
- LYTN 84040 1229 B5
Peacock Dr
- LYTN 84040 1229 B5
9200 SNDY 84093 2178 A7
9200 SNDY 84093 2284 A1
Peacock Ln
- PVDN 84332 528 A7
Peak Dr
4600 WJDN 84088 2174 A4
Peak Ridge Wy
400 DRPR 84020 2388 E4
Peaks Cir
1000 MRRY 84117 2071 A5
Peak View Cir
700 DRPR 84020 2388 E5
Pear Pl
2400 SRSP 84043 2601 E4
Pear Apple Cir
3700 WVCY 84119 1963 C7
Pearblossom Cir
3600 SLkC 84109 1966 C7
Pearce Dr
3200 WVCY 84119 1963 A5
Pearce St
3100 WVCY 84119 1963 A5
Pearhollow Cir
500 OREM 84058 2820 C7
Pearl Cir
300 MDVL 84047 2176 E2
Pearl Crescent Ln
- RIVN 84065 2385 E4
Pearl Harbor St
700 SLCY 84116 1753 E7
700 SLCY 84116 1857 E1
Pear Orchard Ct
1500 DRPR 84020 2389 D4
Pearson Cir
2600 WVCY 84128 1960 E4

STREET
Block City ZIP Map# Grid

Pear Tree Cir
7800 SNDY 84094 2177 B4
Pear Tree Dr
1100 SNDY 84094 2177 B4
Pearwood Cir
5300 TYVL 84118 2068 E5
Pebble Ln
3700 PRVO 84604 2821 E6
Pebble Beach Cir
1600 SNDY 84092 2283 C7
Pebble Beach Dr
3700 NHON 84414 998 E2
Pebblebrook Wy
200 DRPR 84020 2388 D2
Pebble Creek Cir
8400 SNDY 84093 2177 D6
Pebble Creek Dr
2000 SGVL 84663 3144 B4
S Pebblecreek Dr
1300 LYTN 84041 1282 B7
1300 LYTN 84041 1344 B1
W Pebblecreek Dr
1400 LYTN 84041 1282 C7
1400 LYTN 84041 1344 B1
Pebble Creek Ln
2400 LEHI 84043 2495 C6
Pebblecreek Rd
8600 WJDN 84088 2174 A6
Pebble Crest Wy
8600 WJDN 84088 2174 A6
Pebble Glen Cir
2700 SLkC 84109 1966 A6
9100 SNDY 84094 2176 E7
Pebble Hills Cir
1000 SNDY 84094 2177 B6
Pebble Hills Dr
1000 SNDY 84094 2177 B6
Pebblerock Cir
5000 WJDN 84088 2173 D6
5000 WJDN 84088 2174 C5
Pebble Springs Ct
7500 CDHT 84093 2177 B3
Pebblestone Cir
5000 WJDN 84088 2173 D6
5000 WJDN 84088 2174 C5
Pebblestone Ln
- LEHI 84043 2495 D5
Pebblewood Cir
1600 SNDY 84092 2389 C1
Pebblewood Ln
100 CTRV 84014 1551 D2
Pecan Cir
7200 CDHT 84121 2178 C2
8800 WJDN 84088 2175 D6
Peck Cir
300 BMCY 84302 767 A3
N Peck Ln
100 LEHI 84043 2603 C6
Pecos Dr
700 SNDY 84094 2282 E4
700 SNDY 84094 2283 A4
Peel St
8400 SLkC 84044 1960 B5
Peggy Cir
5300 WVCY 84120 2067 E1
Peggy Ct
5300 WVCY 84120 2067 E1
Peggy Dr
4200 WVCY 84120 2067 E2
Peggy Ln
4200 WVCY 84120 2067 E1
Peggy Wy
4200 WVCY 84120 2067 E1
N Pelican Dr
3100 FRWT 84404 997 D4
S Pelican Pond Rd
2200 CchC 84339 589 E2
Pellinore St
100 NSLK 84054 1653 B5
Pelton Dr
1700 CDHT 84093 2177 C4
Pembroke Cir
1400 OREM 84097 2821 C2
Pembroke Ln
3000 WVCY 84120 1962 A5
Pence Dr
4600 WJDN 84088 2174 A6
N Pendleton Av
- OGDN 84404 1056 C4
S Pendleton Av
- OGDN 84404 1056 C5
Pendleton Wy
2200 SJDN 84095 2281 B1
Penguin Cir
5200 MRRY 84117 2071 B4
Penhurst Pl
10 LOGN 84341 463 C6
Penman Ln
10 BNFL 84010 1653 D4
Penn Av
- SLCY 84116 1752 E3
Penn St
1300 SLCY 84105 1859 C7
Penney Av
300 SSLK 84115 1964 D6
S Penney Cove
3500 SSLK 84115 1964 E6
Pennsylvania Av
2400 OGDN 84401 1115 A5
2600 WbrC 84401 1115 A5
3400 OGDN 84405 1115 A5
Pennsylvania Av SR-53
- WbrC 84401 1115 A4
2400 OGDN 84401 1115 B3
Pennsylvania Dr
100 HARR 84404 1056 D2
Pennsylvania Pl
900 SLCY 84102 1859 A3
Penny Cir
100 LYTN 84041 1282 D4
4400 WJDN 84088 2174 B6
Penny Ln
10 LOGN 84341 463 C6
400 LYTN 84041 1282 D4
Penny Parade Dr
200 SLCY 84103 1858 D1
Penrose Dr
1500 SLCY 84103 1859 C2
Pensacola Cir
3600 WJDN 84084 2068 D7
Penstemmon Ln
6900 WJDN 84084 2174 A2

Peony Wy
10100 SLkC 84094 2282 E3
Pepi Band Rd
14000 DRPR 84020 2389 A5
Pepper Cir
11300 SNDY 84092 2284 B6
Peppercorn Cir
2700 TYVL 84118 2069 B6
Peppercorn Rd
2300 LEHI 84043 2495 D6
Pepperell Cir
800 SNDY 84094 2283 A4
Pepper Grass Ln
14200 HRMN 84065 2385 E6
Pepperidge Cir
7000 MDVL 84047 2176 E2
Pepperidge Ct
7000 MDVL 84047 2176 D2
Pepperidge Dr
300 MDVL 84047 2176 E2
Pepperidge Pl
7000 MDVL 84047 2176 D2
Peppermint Cir
200 SRSP 84043 2601 E5
Peppermint Ct
200 SRSP 84043 2601 E5
Peppermint Pl
1800 SRSP 84043 2601 E5
Pepper Pond Ln
6100 WVCY 84128 1961 C5
Pepper Tree Ct
4700 WVCY 84120 1962 A7
Pepperwood Dr
10 SNDY 84092 2284 B5
2000 SNDY 84092 2283 D4
Pepperwood Pointe
10 SNDY 84092 2284 A4
Percival St
200 NSLK 84054 1653 B5
Peregrine Ln
10 BNFL 84010 1551 D7
900 SNDY 84094 2177 A5
Peregrine Pl
8000 SNDY 84094 2177 A4
Peregrine Cove
400 LYTN 84040 1283 D4
Perennial Dr
7500 SLkC 84044 1960 D4
Perigrine Wy
4100 WVCY 84120 2068 C2
N Perimeter Rd
- DvsC 84056 1172 B6
- DvsC 84056 1228 D1
700 DvsC 84056 1229 B3
1900 RVDL 84405 1171 E4
1900 RVDL 84405 1172 A4
Peron Ln
5800 WVCY 84128 1961 C5
Perrine Dr
300 MDVL 84047 2176 D1
Perry Av
1300 SLCY 84103 1859 B3
Perry St
2300 PRRY 84302 827 C4
3600 PRRY 84302 885 B1
3600 PRRY 84340 885 B1
3600 WLRD 84340 885 B1
Perry's Hollow Dr
1300 SLCY 84103 1859 C1
Perry's Hollow Rd
500 SLCY 84103 1859 B1
1200 SLCY 84103 1755 B7
Perrywill Av
1000 SLkC 84124 2071 A1
Perschon Cir
2400 BFDL 84065 2387 B7
Perserverance Ct
10 PKCY 84060 2185 A1
Persille Dr
3200 TYVL 84118 2068 E4
Persimmon Pl
1300 TYVL 84123 2069 D1
N Perth St
10 LEHI 84043 2710 B3
10 SRSP 84043 2710 B3
S Perth St
10 LEHI 84043 2710 A3
10 SRSP 84043 2710 A3
Peruvian Cir
1700 SNDY 84093 2177 D7
Peruvian Dr
9100 SNDY 84093 2177 D7
9300 SNDY 84093 2283 D1
Peruvian Acre Rd
- ALTA 84049 2181 D7
Pescara Ct
4700 WJDN 84084 2174 A1
Petal Cir
1400 SNDY 84092 2283 C2
W Peter Dr
700 KYVL 84037 1345 B2
Peterborough Rd
1600 MRRY 84121 2071 C7
Petersenbluff Dr
1100 RIVN 84065 2387 E1
Peterson Cir
300 PRVO 84604 2928 C3
Peterson Ln
4000 WVCY 84120 1962 C6
Peterson Pkwy
400 SWBR 84405 1172 E7
600 SWBR 84405 1173 A7
Petunia Wy
1400 SLkC 84092 2283 C2
1400 SNDY 84092 2283 C2
W Pfeifferhorn Ct
900 ALPN 84004 2497 C4
N Pfeifferhorn Dr
10 ALPN 84004 2497 C4
S Pfeifferhorn Dr
10 ALPN 84004 2497 C5
W Pfeifferhorn Dr
900 ALPN 84004 2497 C4
Pharaoh Cir
3900 WVCY 84119 1963 D7
Pharaoh Rd
1300 WVCY 84119 1963 D7
Pheasant Cir
- LYTN 84040 1229 B6
500 BNFL 84010 1654 A4
800 KYVL 84037 1345 E2
1900 HLDY 84121 2071 D5

Pheasant Dr
9700 HILD 84003 2604 D3
Pheasant Ln
2000 HLDY 84121 2071 E6
Pheasant Run
- WPT 84015 1225 E4
Pheasant Wy
- LYTN 84040 1229 B6
400 KYVL 84037 1345 E2
500 BNFL 84010 1654 A4
500 CTRV 84014 1551 E3
1300 SmtC 84098 1971 E1
1900 HLDY 84121 2071 D5
Pheasant Bend Cir
2200 SJDN 84095 2281 B2
Pheasantbrook Cir
700 CTRV 84014 1551 D2
Pheasantbrook Dr
- CTRV 84014 1551 D2
W Pheasantbrook Dr
10 CTRV 84014 1551 D2
Pheasant Brook Rd
1600 SNDY 84092 2283 D7
Pheasant Creek Dr
900 LOGN 84321 527 B5
Pheasant Glen Dr
3700 WVCY 84120 1962 B7
Pheasant Haven Ct
500 DRPR 84020 2388 E3
Pheasant Hill Cir
100 PTVW 84414 998 D2
4100 WVCY 84120 2067 E1
Pheasant Hollow Ln
3600 BFDL 84065 2386 D6
Pheasant Meadow Dr
10 SGVL 84663 3143 B2
Pheasant Moor Dr
12800 DRPR 84020 2388 E2
Pheasant Moor Cove
12900 DRPR 84020 2388 D3
Pheasant Park Dr
4100 WVCY 84120 2067 D1
Pheasant Pointe Dr
- LEHI 84043 2602 E1
- LEHI 84043 2603 A1
Pheasant Ridge Cir
200 BNFL 84010 1552 B7
600 ALPN 84004 2498 A6
Pheasant Ridge Ct
600 ALPN 84004 2498 A6
Pheasant Ridge Dr
200 ALPN 84004 2498 A6
Pheasant Ridge Rd
3800 SLkC 84124 1966 D7
Pheasant Ridge Tr
2000 LEHI 84043 2495 D5
Pheasant Run Cir
8100 WJDN 84088 2174 E5
Pheasant Run Ct
4200 LEHI 84043 2495 D6
Pheasant Run Dr
3400 WJDN 84088 2174 E5
E Pheasant Run Dr
900 SGVL 84663 3144 A4
Pheasant View Cir
- FTHT 84037 1346 A3
Pheasant View Dr
400 DRPR 84020 2388 E3
1000 FTHT 84037 1346 A3
E Pheasant View Dr
1000 LYTN 84041 1283 C6
1100 KYVL 84041 1283 C6
S Pheasant View Dr
600 KYVL 84041 1283 B6
600 LYTN 84041 1283 B6
Pheasant Wood Dr
7700 CDHT 84093 2177 C4
Phebe Ln
1600 SLCY 84105 1965 C2
1600 SLCY 84108 1965 C2
Philadelphian Ct
5400 WJDN 84088 2173 D7
Phillips Ln
1300 TYVL 84123 2069 D2
Phillips St
10 DvsC 84037 1282 E7
10 DvsC 84037 1283 A6
10 KYVL 84037 1283 A6
10 KYVL 84041 1283 A6
10 LYTN 84041 1282 E7
10 LYTN 84041 1283 A6
200 LYTN 84037 1283 A6
W Phillips St
1400 LYTN 84037 1282 D7
1400 LYTN 84041 1282 D7
1900 KYVL 84037 1282 D7
1900 KYVL 84041 1282 D7
Phlox St
10100 SLkC 84094 2283 A3
Phylden Dr
2300 HLDY 84117 2071 E2
Piagentini Wy
4700 WJDN 84084 2174 B1
Picabo St
1900 SmtC 84098 1971 D6
3400 TYVL 84084 2068 E7
Piccadilly Cir
3800 WJDN 84088 2174 C6
Pickett Cir
500 SLCY 84104 1964 B1
Pickett Fence Ln
12800 RIVN 84065 2387 A3
Pico St
500 SNDY 84070 2282 E3
Picture Dr
700 SLCY 84116 1753 E7
700 SLCY 84116 1857 E1
Pieper Blvd
4900 SLkC 84118 2068 A4
Piera Cir
3400 WJDN 84084 2174 D3
Pierce Av
1900 OGDN 84401 1116 D3
2700 OGDN 84403 1116 D4
5100 OGDN 84403 1173 C4
Pierpont Av
300 SLCY 84101 1858 B3
900 SLCY 84104 1857 E4
Pika Dr
2800 WVCY 84128 1961 B5
Pike Cir
5000 SLkC 84118 2067 D4

Pikes Peak Ct
6500 TYVL 84084 2175 A1
Pilgrim Dr
5400 WJDN 84088 2173 E7
Pilgrims Cir
4100 LEHI 84043 2495 B6
Pilgrims Loop Rd
- LEHI 84043 2495 B6
Pilot Peak Cir
6500 TYVL 84084 2175 A1
Pimlico Pl
1400 SNDY 84092 2283 C4
Pine Cir
1100 HRCY 84032 2398 E2
1300 PTVW 84414 998 A3
8800 WJDN 84088 2175 D6
Pine Ct
600 OGDN 84404 1056 E4
N Pine Ct
10000 CRHL 84062 2605 C3
Pine Ln
1600 PRVO 84604 2928 E3
Pine St
1300 DvsC 84056 1228 C2
7300 MDVL 84047 2176 B3
Pinebrook Blvd
1600 SmtC 84098 1865 B6
Pinebrook Dr
9600 SJDN 84095 2281 B2
Pinebrook Rd
7000 SmtC 84098 1864 E7
7200 SmtC 84098 1865 A7
E Pine Brush Dr
1100 SmtC 84098 1973 A4
Pine Canyon Rd
200 MIDW 84049 2397 B2
1100 MIDW 84049 2291 A7
1100 WshC 84049 2291 A7
Pinecastle Dr
- WJDN 84088 2173 D5
Pine Cone Ln
- LEHI 84043 2495 C5
Pine Cone St
7000 CDHT 84121 2178 C2
S Pine Cone Wy
500 OGDN 84404 1056 C6
Pine Cove
7500 SWBR 84405 1229 E2
Pine Cove Ln
300 KYVL 84037 1345 B2
Pinecreek Cir
2200 CDHT 84093 2177 E5
Pinecreek Ln
8000 CDHT 84093 2177 E5
Pine Creek Rd
10 WPT 84015 1226 E4
Pinecrest
7000 SmtC 84098 1864 E7
Pinecrest Ln
2000 SNDY 84092 2283 E6
Pine Crossing Cir
8800 WJDN 84088 2174 A7
Pine Crossing Dr
4500 WJDN 84088 2174 B6
Pinedale Cir
9400 SNDY 84092 2283 E1
Pine Flats Ct
4000 SJDN 84095 2280 C4
Pine Grove Wy
4000 SJDN 84095 2280 C4
Pine Haven Cove
12900 DRPR 84020 2389 B3
Pinehill Dr
4900 MRRY 84107 2071 A3
Pine Hills Ln
- DRPR 84020 2389 C6
Pine Hollow Dr
- CRHL 84062 2605 D5
Pinehollow Ln
14900 BFDL 84065 2494 C1
Pinehurst Cir
1100 FMTN 84025 1346 A5
3800 WVCY 84120 2068 B1
Pinehurst Ct
10 PKCY 84060 2078 D1
Pinehurst Dr
5100 WbrC 84310 1001 E2
9800 SNDY 84092 2283 C3
Pinehurst Ln
1500 FMTN 84025 1346 A5
Pine Knot Dr
6700 CDHT 84121 2177 B1
Pine Landing Wy
3800 WJDN 84084 2174 D1
Pine Laurel Ln
4800 WJDN 84088 2174 A7
9000 WJDN 84088 2173 E7
Pine Meadow Pl
2400 TYVL 84118 2069 B4
Pine Meadow Wy
9700 SJDN 84095 2281 B2
Pine Mesa Dr
13900 DRPR 84020 2389 B6
Pinemont Dr
500 MRRY 84123 2070 B4
Pine Mountain Dr
6800 CDHT 84121 2178 B1
Pine Needle Pl
2400 TYVL 84118 2069 A3
Pinenut Cir
8900 WJDN 84088 2174 B7
Pinenut St
- WJDN 84088 2174 B7
E Pine Ridge Cir
1200 ALPN 84004 2498 C4
Pineridge Rd
1000 SNDY 84094 2283 A7
12000 SNDY 84094 2389 B1
Pine Rock Cir
6800 CDHT 84121 2178 B1
Pine Rock Dr
6800 CDHT 84121 2178 B1
Pine Shadow Rd
10500 SJDN 84095 2280 C4
Pines Point Wy
6600 WJDN 84084 2174 C1
Pine Springs Cove
8200 SLkC 84093 2177 E5
Pinetree Cir
900 WBNF 84087 1551 B6
Pine Tree Dr
3900 SLkC 84124 1966 B7

Pinevale Ct
3500 WVCY 84120 1962 B6
Pine Valley Ln
6100 WVCY 84118 2067 C7
Pine Valley Wy
12100 DRPR 84020 2389 E2
Pine View Cir
- SNQN 84655 3567 E2
- UthC 84655 3567 E2
Pineview Cir
6700 CDHT 84121 2178 B1
Pine View Dr
3000 CDHT 84121 2178 B2
Pineview Dr
10 HDPK 84318 464 A1
200 ALPN 84004 2498 B5
8800 WbrC 84317 1061 D3
S Pineview Dr
900 WDHL 84653 3463 D3
Pinewood Cir
700 SNDY 84094 2176 E4
700 SNDY 84094 2177 C3
1400 LYTN 84040 1283 C2
Pine Wood Dr
10 LOGN 84321 527 E3
Pinewood Dr
- FRWT 84404 1055 D3
700 SNDY 84094 2176 E4
700 SNDY 84094 2177 A4
1100 TYVL 84123 2069 D4
5600 SOGN 84403 1173 C5
Pinewood Ln
2500 LYTN 84040 1283 E5
2600 LYTN 84040 1284 A5
Pine Wy Dr
800 MRRY 84107 2071 A3
Piney Ct
8200 WJDN 84088 2175 C5
Pingree Av
200 OGDN 84404 1056 D5
1700 OGDN 84404 1115 D1
2100 OGDN 84401 1115 D3
N Pingree Av
100 OGDN 84404 1056 D5
Pinion Cir
800 HRCY 84032 2398 E1
N Pinion Dr
10100 CRHL 84062 2605 B2
Pinion Ln
8700 WJDN 84088 2175 D6
Pinion St
200 LYTN 84040 1283 D4
Pink Coral Cir
2100 CDHT 84121 2177 E1
Pinnacle Ct
1200 PKCY 84060 2079 A6
Pinnacle Dr
1000 PKCY 84060 2079 A6
4200 CRHL 84062 2605 B3
Pinnacle Pl
4800 SLkC 84124 2072 C3
Pinnacle Point Wy
13300 DRPR 84020 2388 C4
Pinnacle Terrace Wy
2000 CDHT 84093 2177 E4
Pinnocchio Dr
900 SLCY 84116 1753 E7
Pin Oak Cir
200 KYVL 84037 1283 D7
200 KYVL 84037 1345 D1
Pin Oak Dr
6400 WJDN 84088 2173 B5
Pin Oak Ln
200 KYVL 84037 1345 D1
300 KYVL 84037 1283 D7
Pin Oak St
- SLkC 84124 2072 D1
Pinon Pl
3200 CDHT 84121 2178 C2
Pinon Hill Ln
- DRPR 84020 2389 D6
Pinta Cir
7200 WJDN 84084 2174 E2
Pintail Cir
1600 SmtC 84098 1971 E1
Pintail Ct
4700 SLkC 84117 2071 C3
Pintail Wy
- WPT 84015 1225 D4
Pintain Wy
- WPT 84015 1225 E4
Pinto Wy
12900 RIVN 84065 2387 D3
Pinyon Cir
6100 WVCY 84128 2067 C1
Pinyon Pines Ct
10500 SJDN 84095 2281 D4
Pinyon Pines Wy
1400 SJDN 84095 2281 D4
Pioche Ct
2800 WshC 84049 2079 D7
Pioneer Av
10 SNDY 84070 2176 E6
Pioneer Cir
200 MDVL 84047 2176 B4
600 PRVO 84601 2928 B6
900 SLCY 84104 1857 E5
2400 SLkC 84109 1966 A5
Pioneer Dr
10 ALPN 84004 2497 E3
10 ALPN 84004 2498 A3
Pioneer Pkwy
3300 WVCY 84120 1962 C6
Pioneer Rd
600 DRPR 84020 2388 E1
900 SLCY 84104 1857 A7
1300 DRPR 84020 2389 D1
1500 SLCY 84104 1963 A1
12100 DRPR 84020 2283 E7
12100 DRPR 84092 2283 E7
12100 SNDY 84092 2283 E7
W Pioneer Rd
1900 MTSV 84404 1055 D4
3000 MTSV 84404 1054 D2
4100 PNCY 84404 1054 D2
Pioneer St
100 LOGN 84321 527 D3
3300 SLkC 84109 1966 A6
7700 MDVL 84047 2176 B4
N Pioneer St
12500 HRMN 84065 2385 C2

S Pioneer St
13100 HRMN 84065 2385 C3
Pioneer Park Dr
5500 HRMN 84065 2385 E3
Pioneer Peak Cir
13800 HRMN 84065 2385 D5
Piper Cir
8700 SNDY 84093 2177 D6
Piper Ln
8600 SNDY 84093 2177 D6
Pipkin Cove
1500 RIVN 84065 2387 C1
Pippin Dr
7200 CDHT 84121 2178 C3
Pitchfork Ct
15400 BFDL 84065 2494 C2
Pitchfork Rd
1200 MRRY 84123 2069 D6
Pitford Dr
400 CTRV 84014 1551 D4
Piute Dr
3000 PRVO 84604 2928 E1
3300 PRVO 84604 2821 E7
3300 UthC 84604 2821 E7
Placer Claim Wy
6000 WJDN 84084 2173 C1
N Plain City Rd
2200 FRWT 84404 997 B4
2700 PNCY 84404 997 B4
2800 PNCY 84404 996 D5
Planada Wy
5300 SLkC 84118 2067 D3
Plantation Dr
1200 SNDY 84094 2283 B4
Planter Pl
5200 TYVL 84118 2069 B5
Plata Wy
1300 SNDY 84093 2177 C7
Plateau Dr
2900 SLkC 84109 1966 C4
Platinum Cir
7400 WJDN 84084 2175 C3
Platinum Dr
2000 WJDN 84084 2175 C3
Platinum Wy
900 SLkC 84094 2283 A2
Player Cir
11600 SNDY 84092 2283 C6
Player Rd
11400 SNDY 84092 2283 C6
Plaza Wy
3400 SLkC 84109 1966 C6
Plaza Center Dr
7300 WJDN 84084 2174 D3
Pleasant Cir
500 OREM 84097 2820 E3
Pleasant Ct
400 SLCY 84101 1858 C4
Pleasant Dr
400 PTGV 84062 2713 A3
Pleasant Green Dr
3500 SLkC 84044 1960 C6
S Pleasant Grove Blvd
- LNDN 84042 2712 A5
10 PTGV 84062 2712 B4
Pleasant Hill Dr
10800 SNDY 84092 2283 D5
Pleasant Ridge Dr
5400 SLkC 84118 2067 E6
Pleasant View Dr
300 KYVL 84037 1282 E7
10800 SNDY 84092 2283 D5
E Pleasant View Dr
100 NHON 84414 998 C5
W Pleasant View Dr
100 NHON 84414 998 A3
600 PTVW 84414 998 A3
1500 PTVW 84404 997 D2
1500 PTVW 84414 997 D2
Plum Al
100 SLCY 84111 1858 C3
Plum Pl
300 SRSP 84043 2601 E4
Plum St
4700 MRRY 84123 2070 B3
Plumbago Av
5600 SLkC 84118 2067 D5
Plumb Bob Cir
5100 TYVL 84118 2069 A4
Plum Blossom Cir
8300 WJDN 84088 2175 D5
Plum Creek Cir
8300 WJDN 84088 2175 D5
Plum Creek Dr
1500 WJDN 84088 2175 C5
Plum Creek Ln
7700 CDHT 84093 2177 C3
Plum Tree Dr
1200 LYTN 84040 1283 B2
Plum Tree Ln
3200 BNFL 84010 1653 C5
Plumtree Ln
10 MDVL 84047 2176 C2
Plum Tree Wy
700 MDVL 84047 2176 D2
Pluto Wy
3900 SLkC 84124 1966 D7
Plymouth Av
200 SSLK 84115 1964 B7
Plymouth Rock Cove
3400 LEHI 84043 2495 B6
Plymouth View Dr
4800 TYVL 84123 2069 C4
Poacher Cir
5500 SLkC 84118 2067 D5
Poet's Rest
- LYTN 84040 1283 D4
Poinsettia Dr
800 SLCY 84116 1753 E7
Point Dr
10 DRPR 84020 2388 D4
N Pointe Dr
700 SLCY 84103 1858 E1
900 SLCY 84103 1754 E7
Pointe Rd
8200 SmtC 84098 1865 A5
Pointe Meadow Dr
2100 LEHI 84043 2602 D2
Pointe Meadow Lp
1800 LEHI 84043 2602 D3
Pointer Ln
4100 WVCY 84120 2067 E1

Pointe Ridge Ct
7400 WJDN 84084 2175 E3
Point Hills Cove
14000 DRPR 84020 2389 A5
Point of View Cir
100 FMTN 84025 1346 C5
Point View Ct
13900 DRPR 84020 2388 E5
Poison Creek Ln
- PKCY 84060 2078 E3
Poison Oak Dr
6700 WJDN 84088 2173 A6
Polaris Ct
5300 SLkC 84118 2067 E5
Polaris Wy
1800 SLCY 84116 1857 C2
Pole Patch Dr
4600 PTVW 84414 942 D7
4600 PTVW 84414 998 C1
Polk Av
100 OGDN 84404 1057 C6
2200 OGDN 84401 1116 C3
2700 OGDN 84403 1116 C4
N Polk Av
100 OGDN 84404 1057 C5
Pollock Rd
100 SLCY 84108 1859 D4
100 SLCY 84113 1859 D4
Polo Ln
1300 WJDN 84088 2281 D1
Polo Club Ct
11400 SJDN 84095 2281 C6
W Pommel Dr
10 PYSN 84651 3461 E1
Pommell Dr
10 PYSN 84651 3461 E1
N Pond Cir
1200 MPTN 84664 3251 C1
S Pond Cir
1300 MPTN 84664 3251 C2
Ponderosa Cir
7800 SNDY 84094 2177 A4
Ponderosa Ct
4600 SmtC 84098 1864 C6
Ponderosa Dr
300 ALPN 84004 2498 A5
700 SNDY 84094 2176 E4
700 SNDY 84094 2177 A4
4400 SmtC 84098 1864 C6
7000 CDHT 84121 2177 D2
Ponderosa Ln
1500 WJDN 84088 2175 D6
Ponderosa St
1700 LYTN 84040 1283 D4
Ponderosa Wy
7800 SNDY 84094 2177 A4
Pondoray Cir
1200 SLkC 84117 2071 B3
Pond Ridge Dr
900 DRPR 84020 2283 A7
12000 DRPR 84020 2389 A1
Pond Ridge Bay
900 DRPR 84020 2389 A1
Ponds Lodge Dr
8000 WJDN 84088 2173 D5
Pond View Wy
800 SLkC 84106 1965 A6
Pontiac Cir
5100 MRRY 84107 2070 E4
Pontiac Dr
700 MRRY 84107 2070 E4
700 MRRY 84107 2071 A4
Pony Ln
3600 BFDL 84065 2386 D5
Pony Express Rd
- BFDL 84065 2495 A3
- DRPR 84065 2495 A3
12300 DRPR 84020 2388 C2
14600 BFDL 84065 2388 B7
14600 DRPR 84020 2495 B1
Pony Express Wy
500 CTRV 84014 1551 D1
1400 CTRV 84014 1448 D7
Poplar Cir
800 CTRV 84014 1551 E2
800 LYTN 84041 1283 B3
Poplar Ct
- TMTN 84337 520 E4
200 SLCY 84101 1858 C4
10000 CRHL 84062 2605 B3
Poplar Dr
10 BMCY 84302 767 B5
Poplar Ln
2200 DvsC 84056 1172 A6
Poplar St
4800 MRRY 84107 2070 C3
Poplar Brook Pl
10800 SJDN 84095 2280 C4
Poplar Grove Dr
10800 SJDN 84095 2280 C4
Popperton Park Wy
- SLCY 84103 1859 B2
Poppy Ln
700 SLkC 84094 2282 E2
700 SLkC 84094 2283 A2
9400 SNDY 84094 2283 A2
Porcupine Ridge Dr
5600 WbrC 84310 1002 A3
Portal Wy
1700 SNDY 84093 2177 C5
Porter Av
200 OGDN 84404 1057 A5
600 OGDN 84404 1056 E6
2300 OGDN 84401 1115 E3
2800 OGDN 84403 1115 E4
3600 SOGN 84403 1115 E6
4000 SOGN 84403 1172 E1
4600 SOGN 84403 1173 A3
N Porter Av
1100 OGDN 84404 1056 E2
1100 OGDN 84404 1057 A2
Porter Cir
3300 WJDN 84084 2174 E3
W Porter Ln
700 WBNF 84087 1551 B4
800 CTRV 84014 1551 B4
800 CTRV 84087 1551 B4
800 DvsC 84087 1551 B4
Porterfield Pl
3500 SLkC 84044 1960 B7
E Porters Ln
10 CTRV 84014 1551 E4

STREET
Block City ZIP Map# Grid

E Porters Ln
600 CTRV 84014 1552 A4
W Porters Ln
10 CTRV 84014 1551 D4
500 WBNF 84087 1551 C4
Porto Fino Ct
3200 CDHT 84093 2178 B5
Portrush Ct
13900 HRMN 84065 2385 E5
Portside Wy
1300 TYVL 84123 2069 D5
Portsmouth Av
2500 CDHT 84093 2178 A4
Poseidon Dr
4500 WVCY 84120 2068 A3
Post St
300 SLCY 84104 1857 E4
Postwood Cir
5200 WVCY 84120 2067 E3
Potenza Ct
4700 WJDN 84084 2174 A1
Potomac Cir
900 MRRY 84123 2069 E6
Potomac Dr
700 MRRY 84123 2070 A7
900 MRRY 84123 2069 E6
Pot Rock Rd
700 MIDW 84049 2397 A1
Potter St
10 SLCY 84113 1859 D3
Potters Ln
10 PKCY 84060 2079 A6
W Potters Ln
100 WshC 84032 2292 B6
Potterstone Cir
5900 HRMN 84065 2385 C6
Poultry Dr
11800 DRPR 84020 2282 B7
Powder Cove
11800 HRMN 84065 2280 A7
Powderhorn Ct
8900 SNDY 84093 2177 E7
Powderhorn Dr
8800 SNDY 84093 2177 E7
Powderkeg Dr
2100 SNDY 84093 2177 E6
Powder Mountain Rd
4400 WbrC 84310 1001 E1
Powder Mountain Rd SR-158
4400 WbrC 84310 1001 E1
Powder Ridge Dr
- ALTA 84049 2181 D7
4000 WVCY 84128 2067 C1
Powder Run Rd
- ALTA 84049 2181 D7
Powder View Cir
4000 WVCY 84128 2067 C1
Powderwood Dr
4000 WVCY 84128 2067 C1
6600 SmtC 84098 1971 D1
Powell Av
400 CTRV 84014 1551 E1
8300 SLkC 84044 1960 B5
N Powell Rd
10 EKMT 84651 3463 B2
E Powerhouse Rd
1500 SPFK 84660 3250 D7
1500 UthC 84660 3250 D7
Powers Cir
4000 SLkC 84124 2072 E1
Prairie Cir
2200 RIVN 84065 2387 B4
2600 FRWT 84404 997 B6
Prairie Dawn Ln
5400 HRMN 84065 2385 E6
Prairie Dog Cir
1900 RIVN 84065 2387 B1
W Prairie Dunes Dr
3800 WJDN 84084 2174 D1
Prairie Hill Cir
12900 RIVN 84065 2387 A3
Prairie Lake St
- WJDN 84088 2173 D5
Prairie View Dr
6000 TYVL 84118 2068 E7
Pratts St
900 CRFD 84015 1228 A7
Preamble Rd
11800 DRPR 84020 2282 B7
Premier Ln
5700 HRMN 84065 2385 D4
Prescott Dr
11000 SNDY 84092 2283 C5
Prescott Park Cir
11100 SNDY 84092 2283 C5
Presidential Dr
1100 WDCR 84087 1653 A1
1200 WDCR 84087 1652 E1
9800 SJDN 84095 2281 A2
Presidents Cir
200 SLCY 84112 1859 B3
Presidents Dr
2200 WVCY 84120 1962 D3
Prestbury Pl
10600 SNDY 84094 2283 A4
Preston Av
100 LOGN 84321 528 A3
E Preston Dr
1100 ALPN 84004 2498 C5
S Preston Dr
10 ALPN 84004 2498 C4
Preston St
- KYVL 84037 1344 D1
1400 SLCY 84108 1859 D7
2100 SLCY 84106 1965 D2
2900 SLkC 84106 1965 D4
Prestwick Cir
900 FMTN 84025 1346 A6
3800 SRCS 84075 1226 A7
10000 SJDN 84095 2280 C3
Prestwick Dr
1300 SRCS 84075 1226 A7
Price Av
100 SSLK 84115 1964 C6
Price Ln
3800 PTVW 84414 997 E2
Price St
600 MDVL 84047 2176 A4
Prichard St
2000 WVCY 84119 1963 B7

Primavera Wy
1000 WJDN 84084 2175 E2
Primrose Ct
300 FMTN 84025 1346 C4
Primrose Dr
10500 SLkC 84094 2283 B4
Primrose Pl
- SmtC 84098 1866 A6
Prince Cir
4400 WVCY 84120 2068 C2
Prince Ct
10 PKCY 84060 2078 D2
Prince Dr
4400 WVCY 84120 2068 C2
Princes Cir
1100 SRCS 84075 1226 B7
Princess Cove
9600 SJDN 84095 2281 A1
Princeton Av
700 SLCY 84105 1858 E6
800 SLCY 84105 1859 A6
1700 SLCY 84108 1859 C6
Princeton Cir
300 ANFK 84003 2711 D2
Princeton Ct
8300 MDVL 84047 2176 C5
Princeton Dr
3200 CRFD 84015 1228 B5
W Princeton Dr
10 MDVL 84047 2176 C5
Princeville Dr
3500 SRCS 84075 1226 B7
Pringle Cir
2400 WbrC 84403 1173 E6
2400 WbrC 84403 1174 A6
Printers Row
1700 WVCY 84119 1963 B2
Pristine Dr
14600 DRPR 84020 2388 E7
Pristine View Cove
14600 DRPR 84020 2388 E7
Probst Wy
400 MIDW 84049 2397 B2
Proctor Ln
- LNDN 84042 2712 B6
- PTGV 84042 2712 B6
- PTGV 84062 2712 B5
S Proctor Ln
10 PTGV 84062 2712 B4
Proctor Farm Cir
1800 SLkC 84093 2177 D5
Prodo Vista
1000 WVCY 84119 1963 E6
Professional Wy
10 PYSN 84651 3355 B5
Progress Dr
2400 WVCY 84119 1963 C3
Promenade Cir
2600 CDHT 84121 2178 A2
Promenade Dr
4500 ROY 84067 1171 E2
6800 CDHT 84121 2178 A2
Promontory Dr
2300 SLCY 84109 1966 B3
Promontory Wy
1000 SNDY 84094 2177 B4
Promontory Ranch Rd
- SmtC 84017 1867 D1
Prospect Cir
1600 SLCY 84104 1857 C6
Prospect Ln
1500 ALPN 84004 2498 C1
Prospect St
10 PKCY 84060 2078 E7
700 SLCY 84104 1857 C5
1600 SLCY 84104 1963 C1
Prospector Av
1600 PKCY 84060 2078 E3
Prospector Cir
3700 CDHT 84121 2178 D4
Prospector Dr
10 PKCY 84060 2078 C3
3700 CDHT 84121 2178 D3
Prosperity Dr
900 SLCY 84116 1753 E7
Prosperity Rd
- WJDN 84088 2173 C7
9400 WJDN 84088 2279 C2
Prospero Ct
14000 HRMN 84065 2385 D6
Prospero Ln
5400 HRMN 84065 2385 D5
Provence Ln
3100 LEHI 84043 2602 E1
Providence Cir
2300 SJDN 84095 2281 B1
Providence Dr
- SRSP 84043 2601 D5
Providence Wy
9500 SJDN 84095 2281 B2
Provo Canyon Pkwy
900 OREM 84097 2821 C3
E Provo Canyon Rd
- PRVO 84604 2822 A1
- UthC 84604 2821 D1
- UthC 84604 2822 A1
2300 OREM 84097 2714 E7
2300 OREM 84604 2714 E7
2300 OREM 84604 2821 D1
2300 PRVO 84604 2714 E7
2300 PRVO 84604 2821 D1
2300 UthC 84604 2714 E7
E Provo Canyon Rd US-189
- PRVO 84604 2822 A1
- UthC 84604 2821 D1
- UthC 84604 2822 A1
2300 OREM 84097 2714 E7
2300 OREM 84604 2714 E7
2300 OREM 84604 2821 D1
2300 PRVO 84604 2714 E7
2300 PRVO 84604 2821 D1
2300 UthC 84604 2714 E7
Provost Cir
3200 SJDN 84095 2280 E4
Prows Cir
10 LYTN 84041 1283 A3
Ptarmigan Ct
1300 SmtC 84098 1971 D5
1300 SmtC 84098 1972 A5
Ptarmigan Lp
10 LOGN 84321 528 C3
1300 SmtC 84098 1971 D5

Ptarmigan Cove
10900 SJDN 84095 2281 D5
Ptarmigan Gate Rd
13000 DRPR 84020 2389 A3
Publishers Ln
- LYTN 84040 1283 D4
Pueblo St
100 SLCY 84104 1857 D3
Pugsley St
400 SLCY 84103 1858 B1
Pumpkin Patch Cir
3600 WVCY 84120 1962 B6
Pumpkin Patch Dr
400 SRSP 84043 2601 D4
Pumpkin Ridge Cove
14000 DRPR 84020 2389 D6
Purcell Ct
300 MRRY 84107 2070 D4
Purple Lilac Ln
500 SNDY 84070 2282 E1
Purple Sage Dr
6400 WJDN 84084 2068 A7
6400 WJDN 84084 2174 A1
Putnam Ct
3000 WVCY 84128 1961 C5
Putnam Dr
2900 WVCY 84128 1961 C4
Putters Cir
1000 TYVL 84123 1963 E7
Pyreness Dr
200 ALPN 84004 2498 A6
Pyrite Dr
3400 SLkC 84044 1960 A6

Q

Q St
10 SLCY 84103 1859 B3
Quail Cir
1100 FMTN 84025 1346 C6
5600 TYVL 84118 2069 B5
Quail Dr
600 SPFK 84660 3249 E4
2400 LEHI 84043 2603 C2
Quail Ln
4900 OGDN 84403 1173 D3
Quail Rd
500 OREM 84097 2713 E7
500 OREM 84097 2820 E1
Quail Run
- WPT 84015 1225 D4
Quail Wy
10 LOGN 84321 528 C2
Quailbrook Cir
4700 TYVL 84118 2069 C3
Quailbrook Dr
1900 TYVL 84118 2069 B3
Quail Brook Ln
9800 SJDN 84095 2281 A2
Quail Canyon Dr
1500 LOGN 84321 528 C3
Quail Covey Cir
1300 RIVN 84065 2387 D1
Quail Creek Cir
9100 SNDY 84094 2177 B7
Quail Creek Dr
1200 SNDY 84094 2177 B7
Quail Creek Ln
5800 HILD 84003 2497 C6
Quail Crossing Ln
1900 SNDY 84092 2283 D7
3200 SLkC 84092 2284 C1
Quail Estates Wy
1900 SLCY 84106 1965 D4
1900 SLkC 84106 1965 D4
Quail Flight Rd
200 FMTN 84025 1346 C6
Quail Haven Cir
2800 SLCY 84106 1965 D4
Quail Hollow Cir
800 ALPN 84004 2498 B3
9300 SNDY 84093 2284 A1
Quail Hollow Dr
2400 SNDY 84093 2284 A1
3800 SLkC 84124 1966 D7
8800 SNDY 84093 2178 A7
9300 SNDY 84093 2283 E1
Quail Hollow Ln
400 ALPN 84004 2498 B3
Quail Hollow Rd
100 LOGN 84321 528 C3
Quail Meadow Rd
4600 SmtC 84098 1971 D5
W Quail Meadow Rd
1300 SmtC 84098 1971 E5
Quail Nest Cir
300 FMTN 84025 1346 C6
Quail Park Dr
900 SLkC 84117 2071 A2
Quail Point Rd
4700 SLkC 84124 2072 C3
Quail Rdge
500 FTHT 84037 1284 B7
Quail Ridge Cir
1300 RIVN 84065 2387 D1
Quail Ridge Dr
- LYTN 84040 1229 B5
3900 PRVO 84604 2821 E6
Quail Ridge Rd
1300 RIVN 84065 2387 D2
2800 LYTN 84040 1229 B6
9600 SLkC 84092 2284 C1
Quail Run Ct
- LEHI 84043 2495 C5
Quail Run Dr
1700 OGDN 84403 1173 D2
2300 SNDY 84093 2283 D1
2300 SNDY 84093 2284 A1
3800 PRVO 84604 2821 E6
8800 SNDY 84093 2177 E7
Quail Run Rd
300 FMTN 84025 1346 B6
400 SPFK 84660 3249 B6
400 UthC 84660 3249 B6
Quail Springs Cir
7500 SNDY 84047 2176 A3
Quailstone Cir
4700 TYVL 84118 2069 C3
Quailstone Dr
1900 TYVL 84118 2069 B3
Quail Summit Ln
1000 PRVO 84604 2821 E7

Quail Valley Dr
600 PRVO 84604 2821 D7
Quail Vista Ct
1000 SLkC 84117 2071 A2
Quail Vista Ln
1000 SLkC 84117 2071 A3
Quail Vista Cove
1000 SLkC 84117 2071 A2
Quail Wing Rd
1100 FMTN 84025 1346 C6
Quailwood Cir
1600 SNDY 84092 2389 E2
Quaking Aspen Ct
700 PKCY 84060 2078 C2
Quaking Aspen Dr
700 MRRY 84123 2070 A5
Qual Cir
- LYTN 84040 1229 B6
Qual Ln
- LYTN 84040 1229 B5
Quality Dr
600 ANFK 84003 2711 E3
600 UthC 84003 2711 E3
Quarry Dr
3900 SLkC 84092 2284 E2
Quarry Rd
- SLkC 84092 2284 E2
Quarry Hill Cir
5400 SLkC 84118 2067 C5
Quarry Point Ln
14800 DRPR 84020 2388 D7
14800 DRPR 84020 2495 D1
Quarry Ridge Cove
11800 HRMN 84065 2280 A7
Quarter Cir
10 NBLY 84321 591 D5
Quarter Horse Av
1800 SLCY 84116 1753 C5
Quartz Dr
1500 SJDN 84095 2281 D5
Quartz Hill Dr
7200 WJDN 84084 2173 D3
7200 WJDN 84084 2174 A3
Quartzridge Dr
1900 SNDY 84092 2283 D2
Quartz Valley Cir
4800 RIVN 84065 2386 A3
Quayle Av
10 SLCY 84115 1964 C1
900 SLCY 84104 1963 E1
900 SLCY 84104 1964 A1
Quayle Ln
1000 PRRY 84302 827 B5
Queen Esther Dr
2300 PKCY 84060 2079 B6
Queens Ferry Dr
4200 SJDN 84095 2280 B3
Queensland Ct
200 LNDN 84042 2713 E5
Queenspointe Cir
3700 WVCY 84119 1963 E7
Queenspointe Ln
3600 WVCY 84119 1963 D7
Queenswood Cir
5300 TYVL 84118 2068 C5
Queenswood Dr
3300 TYVL 84118 2068 D4
Quest Cir
2900 WVCY 84120 1962 A3
Quicksilver Dr
7500 CDHT 84121 2178 D4
Quick Water Wy
- WJDN 84088 2173 D4
Quiet Cir
4600 MRRY 84107 2070 E2
Quiet Acres Cove
1100 SJDN 84095 2281 D5
Quiet Meadow Ln
10 MPTN 84664 3144 D5
Quiet Ridge Cir
3600 SLkC 84092 2284 C2
Quiet Spring Cove
5000 SLkC 84117 2071 B4
Quietwood Ln
10 SNDY 84092 2283 E5
Quince Ln
- DvsC 84056 1172 B6
Quince St
200 SLCY 84103 1858 C2
Quincee Ct
13000 RIVN 84065 2386 E3
Quincy Av
100 OGDN 84404 1057 A5
2000 OGDN 84401 1116 A2
2700 OGDN 84403 1116 A5
N Quincy Av
100 OGDN 84404 1057 A5
Quincy Ct
300 ALPN 84004 2498 A3
Quindaro St
9600 SNDY 84070 2282 E2
Quinette Ln
4100 SLkC 84124 2072 B1
Quinn Ct
- OGDN 84404 1057 A6
Quintail Cir
2800 SJDN 84095 2281 A2
Quintail Ln
2800 SJDN 84095 2281 A2
Quirrh Av
- SLCY 84103 1859 A1

R

R St
10 SLCY 84103 1859 B3
R&D Cir
600 OREM 84097 2820 E1
600 OREM 84097 2821 A1
Rabscuttle Ln
1500 RIVN 84065 2387 C1
Rachelle Dr
3100 WJDN 84084 2174 C2
Rachel Marie Wy
8500 MDVL 84047 2176 B6
Racquet Club Cir
- CDHT 84121 2178 D3
Racquet Club Dr
10 PKCY 84060 2078 D2
7200 CDHT 84121 2178 D3
Radcliffe St
4600 WVCY 84120 2068 B3

Raddon Dr
1400 SNDY 84092 2283 B7
N Radford Ln
400 WbrC 84310 1059 E3
Radial Ln
14100 DRPR 84020 2389 A6
Radley Cir
6200 WVCY 84128 1961 C5
Rae St
2900 WVCY 84120 1962 C4
Raelyn Wy
2300 LYTN 84040 1229 E7
Railroad St
1700 LEHI 84043 2603 A3
Rainbow Cir
1300 LYTN 84040 1283 C2
4700 MRRY 84107 2070 D3
Rainbow Dr
100 MRRY 84107 2070 D2
800 LYTN 84041 1283 A3
900 LOGN 84321 527 B5
2500 LYTN 84040 1284 A2
Rainbow Ln
300 MIDW 84049 2397 A2
E Rainbow Wy
10 HRCY 84032 2398 D7
W Rainbow Wy
10 HRCY 84032 2398 C7
Rainbow Oaks Cir
2800 SNDY 84092 2284 B6
Rainbow Point Dr
2000 HLDY 84124 1965 D7
Rain Crest Ct
6300 HLDY 84121 2071 E7
Rainforest Dr
700 MRRY 84107 2070 D4
700 MRRY 84107 2071 A6
Rainier Av
1200 LNDN 84042 2713 E6
3000 SLkC 84109 1966 D5
Rainsborough Cir
6200 MRRY 84121 2071 B7
Rainsborough Rd
1300 MRRY 84121 2071 E5
Raintree Av
800 SNDY 84094 2177 A4
Raintree Cir
800 WBNF 84087 1551 B6
2100 SNDY 84092 2283 E1
Raintree Dr
9400 SNDY 84092 2283 E2
Raintree Pl
9600 SNDY 84092 2283 C4
Rain Tree Wy
4600 WVCY 84120 1962 A6
Rainy Ln
6100 MRRY 84107 2070 C7
Rainy Brook Ct
2100 RIVN 84065 2281 B7
Raleigh Ct
12200 DRPR 84020 2389 D1
Ralph Dr
5500 TYVL 84118 2069 A5
Ralph St
4000 SLkC 84124 1965 B7
4000 SLkC 84124 2071 B1
Ralph H Cir
6400 HRMN 84065 2385 B5
Ralph H Wy
13800 HRMN 84065 2385 B5
Ram Blvd
2100 SLCY 84106 1965 C2
Ramanee Dr
7200 MDVL 84047 2176 D3
Rambler Dr
600 SLCY 84116 1857 E1
Rambling Rd
- DRPR 84020 2389 B5
Rambouillet Dr
900 SJDN 84095 2281 E6
Ramola St
1300 KYVL 84037 1344 E3
1300 KYVL 84037 1345 A3
Ramona Av
300 SLCY 84115 1964 D1
700 SLCY 84105 1964 E1
1300 SLCY 84105 1965 C1
1700 SLCY 84108 1965 D1
Ramsey Cir
3300 WVCY 84120 1962 A5
Ramseyer Ln
- MRRY 84107 2070 B7
Rams Gate Cir
2200 TYVL 84119 2069 B3
Ramsgate Rd
600 FMTN 84025 1346 B4
Ranch Av
100 TMTN 84337 520 C5
Ranch Cir
800 DRPR 84020 2389 A5
S Ranch Cir
500 ALPN 84004 2497 D5
W Ranch Cir
600 ALPN 84004 2497 D6
1100 MIDW 84049 2396 E2
Ranch Dr
300 ALPN 84004 2497 D5
2500 WshC 84032 2505 E1
Ranch Pl
5300 SmtC 84098 1971 E4
Ranch Rd
1500 FMTN 84025 1447 E2
Ranch Wy
500 MIDW 84049 2396 E2
N Ranch Creek Ln
4300 SmtC 84098 1972 D6
Ranchero Dr
1000 DRPR 84020 2389 B4
Ranches Loop Rd
5200 WJDN 84088 2173 E4
Ranches Park Ln
- WJDN 84088 2173 E4
Ranchfield Rd
4500 SLkC 84117 2071 B2
Ranchhand Rd
- WJDN 84088 2173 E4
Ranch Hollow Ln
1200 MRRY 84123 2175 D1
Ranchhouse Rd
- WJDN 84088 2173 E4
Rancho Blvd
900 OGDN 84404 1057 B5

E Rancho Ct
100 MRRY 84107 2070 D4
Rancho Dr
200 PYSN 84651 3461 E1
Rancho Martin Cir
6200 WVCY 84128 1961 C7
Rancho Vista Dr
1000 OGDN 84404 1057 B3
Rancho Vista Ln
3700 WVCY 84120 1961 E7
4000 WVCY 84120 2067 E1
Ranch Park Dr
1000 WJDN 84088 2175 E6
Ranch View Dr
3400 SLkC 84124 2072 C1
Ranchwood Ct
8300 WJDN 84088 2173 D5
Randall Cir
7400 MDVL 84047 2176 D3
Randell Wy
200 CTRV 84014 1551 E4
Randers Ln
1100 DRPR 84020 2389 B4
Randolf Cir
15000 DRPR 84020 2495 D1
Randy Cir
8500 MDVL 84047 2176 B6
Range Cir
4500 SLkC 84117 2071 B2
Range Rd
1000 SLkC 84117 2071 A2
Range St
700 DvsC 84056 1229 A3
Raphael Ct
3700 WVCY 84119 1963 D7
Rappahannock Cir
5900 MRRY 84123 2070 D7
Rappel Ct
8400 WJDN 84088 2173 E5
Raptor Cove
8000 SNDY 84094 2177 A4
Raquel Cir
3300 WVCY 84120 1962 A5
Rasmussen Rd
2000 SmtC 84098 1865 B5
2000 SmtC 84098 1971 D1
4000 SmtC 84098 1864 E5
Raspberry Ct
11400 DRPR 84020 2282 D6
Raspberry Dr
200 SRSP 84043 2601 E5
Raton Ln
1100 MRRY 84123 2069 E7
Rattler Rd
800 SRSP 84043 2601 C7
Raven St
100 MRRY 84107 2070 D4
E Raven St
5200 MRRY 84107 2070 D4
W Raven St
5200 MRRY 84107 2070 D4
Raven Crest Ln
- LEHI 84043 2495 C5
Ravenna Ct
5200 HRMN 84065 2385 E2
Ravenwood Ln
10 SNDY 84092 2284 A5
Rawhide Dr
3800 WVCY 84120 1962 C6
Rawlins Cir
100 DRPR 84020 2388 D2
400 CTRV 84014 1551 D4
Rawlins Ln
100 DRPR 84020 2388 D2
Ray Cir
8500 SNDY 84094 2177 A6
Ray St
100 OGDN 84404 1056 D6
Rayco Cir
1300 TYVL 84123 2069 D7
Rayford Cir
4900 SLkC 84118 2067 E4
Raygene Wy
600 NSLK 84054 1653 C7
Raymond Av
3700 SOGN 84403 1116 A7
3900 SOGN 84403 1173 A1
Raymond Ct
10 LOGN 84321 527 E2
4400 TYVL 84119 2069 B2
Raymond Dr
6300 SWBR 84405 1172 D7
Raymond Rd
800 FTHT 84037 1345 E2
800 FTHT 84037 1346 A1
Raymond Klauck Wy
800 SGVL 84663 3036 A5
Reaper Cir
2300 WJDN 84084 2175 B2
Rebecca Cir
1300 SLkC 84117 2071 B3
Rebecca Ann Cir
2000 TYVL 84084 2175 B1
Recreation Wy
- NSLK 84054 1753 C1
Red Admiral Ct
13700 RIVN 84065 2386 A5
Red Admiral Dr
4800 RIVN 84065 2386 A5
W Red Angus Dr
1800 SLCY 84116 1753 C4
Red Barn Rd
1700 SGVL 84663 3144 A4
Redberry Cir
13000 DRPR 84020 2388 B3
Redberry Rd
10 DRPR 84020 2388 B3
Redberry Fox Cove
5200 WJDN 84088 2173 E4
Redbirch Cove
1900 CDHT 84093 2177 D4
Red Blossom Cir
4400 WVCY 84120 2068 A2
Red Brick Ct
300 SLCY 84103 1858 D1
Redbud Ct
8700 SLkC 84044 1960 A6
Redbud Wy
8600 SLkC 84044 1960 B6
Red Bur Ct
- WVCY 84119 1963 C3

Red Canyon Ct
11300 SJDN 84095 2281 D6
Red Castle Wy
8000 WJDN 84088 2174 A4
Red Cherry Cir
4400 WVCY 84120 2068 A2
Red Cliff Dr
5400 TYVL 84123 2069 D5
Red Cloud Wy
8100 WJDN 84088 2174 A5
Redclover Dr
1900 SLCY 84116 1753 B7
Redden Rd
200 SmtC 84098 1866 D5
Redding Ct
1100 SNDY 84094 2283 B6
Red Elm Cir
6800 WJDN 84084 2174 A1
Red Elm Wy
3000 RIVN 84065 2386 E2
3000 RIVN 84065 2387 A2
Redfeather Dr
- SNDY 84092 2283 C6
Redfield Av
300 SSLK 84115 1964 B5
Red Flower Cir
5100 WVCY 84120 2067 C2
Redford Dr
600 PRVO 84604 2821 D5
Red Fox Cir
6100 TYVL 84118 2068 D7
Red Fox Ct
4900 SmtC 84098 1972 A4
Red Fox Rd
1400 SmtC 84098 1866 A5
Red Fox Trc
1300 LOGN 84321 528 B4
Redhaven Dr
900 SNDY 84094 2283 A1
9300 SLkC 84094 2283 A1
Red Hawk Cir
3700 WbrC 84310 1002 B3
Red Hawk Ct
1700 SmtC 84098 1865 E6
Red Hawk Ln
- SmtC 84098 1866 D1
Redhawk Rd
3800 WVCY 84119 1963 B7
4000 WVCY 84119 2069 B1
Red Hawk Tr
1300 SmtC 84098 1866 A4
1500 SmtC 84098 1865 E6
N Red Hawk Tr
9100 SmtC 84098 1865 E4
9100 SmtC 84098 1866 A4
Red Heather Ln
1300 WJDN 84084 2175 D3
Red Hen Rd
800 SRSP 84043 2601 C7
Red Leaf Dr
200 DRPR 84020 2495 D1
Red Lodge Cir
4800 SLkC 84118 2068 A5
Red Lodge Dr
4800 SLkC 84118 2068 A5
Redmaple Cir
700 SLkC 84106 1965 A6
Red Maple Ct
- PYSN 84651 3461 D1
700 PKCY 84060 2078 D2
Redmaple Rd
700 SLkC 84106 1964 E6
700 SLkC 84106 1965 C6
Red Mountain Cir
4800 RIVN 84065 2386 A3
Red Narrows Dr
5600 WJDN 84088 2173 D5
Red Oaks Dr
700 MRRY 84123 2070 A7
Redondo Av
10 SLCY 84115 1964 C2
500 SLCY 84105 1964 D2
1400 SLCY 84105 1965 C2
1700 SLCY 84108 1965 D2
2300 SLCY 84108 1966 A2
Redondo Pl
2000 SLCY 84108 1965 D2
Red Pine Cir
8800 WJDN 84088 2174 B7
Red Pine Ct
2500 PKCY 84060 2078 C2
W Red Pine Ct
- SmtC 84098 2077 C1
Red Pine Dr
10 ALPN 84004 2497 E5
300 ALPN 84004 2498 A5
Red Pine Rd
2100 SmtC 84098 2077 C1
3500 SmtC 84098 1971 D7
Red River Rd
8300 SNDY 84093 2177 E5
Red Robin Rd
2200 WVCY 84119 1963 B7
Red Rose Ln
1100 MRRY 84123 2069 E7
Red Sage Ct
4500 SLkC 84107 2071 A2
Red Sage Ln
800 SLkC 84107 2071 A2
Red Slide Dr
- CchC 84339 649 C1
- WELV 84339 649 C1
N Red Slide Dr
200 WELV 84339 649 C1
Red Springs Wy
8100 WJDN 84088 2174 A4
Red Spruce Dr
4600 WJDN 84088 2174 B7
Red Stone
1700 SmtC 84098 1971 E2
Redstone Wy
3200 WVCY 84119 1963 D5
Red Tail Ct
7800 PKCY 84060 2185 A2
7800 WshC 84049 2185 A2
7900 PKCY 84049 2185 A2
Red Tail Dr
3900 RIVN 84065 2386 C5
Redtail Hawk Bay
4700 SLkC 84117 2071 B3
Red Top Cir
- KYVL 84037 1283 D7

Salt Lake City Street Index

STREET
Block City ZIP Map# Grid

Red Tree Ct
1600 DRPR 84020 2389 C4
Red Vista Wy
3200 WVCY 84119 1963 D5
Red Willow Cir
8800 SNDY 84093 2177 D7
Redwing St
3800 WVCY 84119 1963 A7
W Redwood Ct
4300 CRHL 84062 2605 B2
N Redwood Dr
10200 CRHL 84062 2605 A2
S Redwood Dr
1100 SLCY 84104 1857 D6
W Redwood Dr
4500 CRHL 84062 2605 B2
Redwood Ln
5600 SOGN 84403 1173 D5
W Redwood Pl
1500 WVCY 84119 1963 C7
Redwood Rd
1400 DvsC 84056 1228 C1
6600 WJDN 84084 2175 C2
7800 WJDN 84088 2175 C2
9100 WJDN 84088 2281 C1
Redwood Rd SR-48
7000 WJDN 84084 2175 C3
Redwood Rd SR-68
6600 WJDN 84084 2175 C2
7800 WJDN 84088 2175 C2
9100 WJDN 84088 2281 C1
N Redwood Rd
10 NSLK 84054 1652 D5
10 SLCY 84104 1857 C1
100 SLCY 84116 1857 C1
500 WDCR 84087 1652 D1
500 DvsC 84087 1652 D5
700 SLCY 84116 1753 C6
1700 SLkC 84116 1753 C3
N Redwood Rd SR-68
10 NSLK 84054 1652 D5
10 SLCY 84104 1857 C1
100 SLCY 84116 1857 C1
500 WDCR 84087 1652 D5
500 DvsC 84087 1652 D5
700 SLCY 84116 1753 C6
1700 SLkC 84116 1753 C3
S Redwood Rd
10 NSLK 84054 1652 D7
10 SLCY 84104 1857 C5
300 NSLK 84054 1753 C2
600 DvsC 84054 1753 C2
600 SLkC 84116 1753 C2
1600 SLCY 84104 1963 C1
2100 WVCY 84119 1963 C1
3900 WVCY 84119 2069 C2
4100 TYVL 84119 2069 C2
4100 TYVL 84123 2069 C2
4700 TYVL 84118 2069 C4
6200 TYVL 84084 2069 C7
6200 WJDN 84084 2069 C7
6400 TYVL 84123 2175 C1
6400 WJDN 84084 2175 C1
9400 SJDN 84095 2281 C2
11600 RIVN 84065 2281 C7
12100 RIVN 84065 2387 C1
13800 BFDL 84065 2387 C6
14800 BFDL 84065 2494 D1
S Redwood Rd SR-68
10 NSLK 84054 1652 D7
10 SLCY 84104 1857 C5
300 NSLK 84054 1753 C2
600 DvsC 84054 1753 C2
600 SLkC 84116 1753 C2
1600 SLCY 84104 1963 C1
2100 WVCY 84119 1963 C1
3900 WVCY 84119 2069 C2
4100 TYVL 84119 2069 C2
4100 TYVL 84123 2069 C2
4700 TYVL 84118 2069 C4
6200 TYVL 84084 2069 C7
6200 WJDN 84084 2069 C7
6400 TYVL 84123 2175 C1
6400 WJDN 84084 2175 C1
9400 SJDN 84095 2281 C2
11600 RIVN 84065 2281 C6
12100 RIVN 84065 2387 C1
13800 BFDL 84065 2387 C4
S Redwood Rd SR-140
14300 BFDL 84065 2387 C6
Red Zinc Dr
5900 SLkC 84118 2067 C6
Reed Av
200 SLCY 84103 1754 B7
Reeder Hall
300 LOGN 84321 528 A2
N Rees Av
400 SPFK 84660 3250 A2
400 SPFK 84663 3250 A2
Reese Dr
1100 PRVO 84601 2927 C4
Reeves Av
1200 OGDN 84404 1056 D7
2100 OGDN 84401 1115 D3
Reeves Ln
11700 SJDN 84095 2281 E7
11800 RIVN 84065 2281 E7
Reeves Ter
300 SLCY 84102 1859 A4
Regal St
10 MRRY 84107 2070 C3
Regal Hill Dr
7300 WJDN 84084 2173 E3
Regalia Rd
3400 CDHT 84121 2178 C5
Regal Stream Cove
1900 CDHT 84093 2177 D4
Regan Ct
3200 CDHT 84121 2178 C1
Regency Dr
2300 WbrC 84403 1173 E5
Regency St
4800 HLDY 84117 2072 A4
Regency Wy
200 NSLK 84054 1653 D6
Regency Park Dr
3200 WVCY 84119 1962 E4
Regene Wy
2800 WVCY 84119 2069 A1
Regent Ct
1100 OREM 84057 2820 C2
Regent St
100 SLCY 84111 1858 C3
2100 SSLK 84115 1964 C2
Regent Hill Cir
200 MDVL 84047 2176 D3
Regent Park Ct
200 MDVL 84047 2176 D3
Regent Park Ln
7500 MDVL 84047 2176 D3
7500 SNDY 84047 2176 D3
Reid Av
1200 LYTN 84041 1282 B2
Reindeer Dr
7100 CDHT 84121 2178 C2
Relation St
12100 DRPR 84020 2389 C2
Reliance Dr
8900 SNDY 84070 2176 C7
Rembrandt Cir
10 SNDY 84070 2282 D4
Rembrandt Ln
10 SNDY 84070 2282 D4
Remembrance Ln
10000 SJDN 84095 2281 D2
Remington Ln
- FMTN 84025 1345 D7
1600 SmtC 84098 1971 E4
Remington Wy
700 SLCY 84104 1858 A6
Remuda Dr
2400 FRWT 84404 997 B2
Rena Av
300 MDVL 84047 2176 D2
Rena Cir
6800 MDVL 84047 2176 E2
Renae St
2700 WJDN 84084 2175 A1
Renaissance Ct
2400 PTGV 84062 2605 B6
Renaissance Dr
9000 CRHL 84062 2605 D5
Renaissance Pl
1300 PTGV 84062 2605 B6
Renaissance Wy
1500 SGVL 84663 3142 E4
Renardo Pl
4400 WVCY 84119 2068 E2
Renault Cir
3900 WVCY 84119 1963 C7
Rendon Ct
200 SLCY 84116 1858 A2
Renedezvous Wy
3000 WVCY 84120 1962 A4
Renegade Rd
2200 SNDY 84093 2177 E7
Renoir Cir
2000 HLDY 84121 2071 D6
Research Rd
1800 SLCY 84112 1859 D4
Research Wy
1200 OREM 84097 2821 A2
1700 WVCY 84119 1963 C4
Research Park Wy
500 LOGN 84341 463 E6
Reservoir Dr
200 MNTU 84324 768 D7
200 MNTU 84324 829 C1
Reuben Cir
6200 WVCY 84128 1961 C5
Reunion Av
1600 SJDN 84095 2281 C2
Reunion Glen Dr
- SJDN 84095 2281 E2
Reunion Glen Wy
9800 SJDN 84095 2281 D2
Reva Cir
6500 TYVL 84123 2175 D1
Reveille Cir
1100 SLCY 84116 1753 C6
Revelle Wy
1300 SLkC 84106 1965 B7
Revere Cir
900 MRRY 84117 2071 A5
2100 WJDN 84084 2175 B1
3100 CRFD 84015 1228 C5
Revere Dr
5300 MRRY 84117 2071 A5
Rexford Pl
3300 CDHT 84121 2178 C4
Reynolds Ct
4700 SLkC 84117 2071 C3
Rhinehurst Cir
1900 WJDN 84084 2175 B4
Rhinestone Cir
3700 SLkC 84044 1960 D7
Rhode Island Cir
1100 HARR 84404 1056 D2
Rhonda Av
1500 WJDN 84084 2175 D1
Rhonda Crest Cir
1100 RIVN 84065 2387 E2
Rialto Wy
5600 WJDN 84084 2173 D2
Ribbon Ln
2000 HLDY 84117 2071 D2
Ribbonwood Dr
1800 OREM 84057 2713 B7
Rice Cir
800 FMTN 84025 1448 D4
E Rice Ln
10 FMTN 84025 1448 D4
W Rice Ln
10 FMTN 84025 1448 C4
Rich Wy
1800 CDHT 84121 2177 D3
Richard Rd
1700 SNDY 84093 2177 C7
Richard Crest Dr
4200 TYVL 84119 2069 B1
Richards St
800 SLCY 84101 1858 C5
1500 SLCY 84115 1858 C7
1500 SSLK 84115 1964 C1
2100 SSLK 84115 1964 C2
Richards Wy
200 FMTN 84025 1346 C6
Richards Hall
500 LOGN 84321 528 B1
E Richards Hall
200 PRVO 84604 2928 E3
Richardson Cir
4100 WVCY 84128 2067 D1
Richardson Ln
6000 WVCY 84128 2067 C1
Riches Av
1000 SLCY 84106 1965 A5
1000 SLkC 84106 1965 A5
Richey Rd
1600 DRPR 84020 2389 C5
Richfield Av
4600 WVCY 84120 1962 A6
Richfield Cir
3600 WVCY 84120 1962 B6
Richfield Ct
3600 WVCY 84120 1962 A6
Richland Cir
1800 WJDN 84084 2175 C2
Richland Dr
600 SLCY 84103 1859 B1
Richmond Cir
4300 DvsC 84056 1228 A4
Richmond Dr
700 SmtC 84098 1972 E3
Richmond Ln
10 SRSP 84043 2710 A3
Richmond St
2900 SLCY 84106 1965 B5
3000 SLkC 84106 1965 B5
Richmond St SR-181
2900 SLCY 84106 1965 B5
3000 SLkC 84106 1965 B5
Rick Cir
11200 SJDN 84095 2282 A6
Rick's Creek Cir
- CTRV 84014 1448 E7
Rick's Creek Wy
10 CTRV 84014 1448 D7
Ricky's Dr
3400 WVCY 84119 2068 D2
Rideout Hall Ln
100 DRPR 84020 2282 D7
Riderwood Wy
600 PRVO 84601 2927 C5
Ridge Av
100 PKCY 84060 2078 E7
N Ridge Ct
1100 SPFK 84663 3250 A1
Ridge Dr
- PRVO 84606 2928 E6
300 HRCY 84032 2398 D1
3500 WVCY 84119 1962 D4
E Ridge Dr
200 ALPN 84004 2498 A5
Ridge Ln
300 ALPN 84004 2498 A5
S Ridge Ln
400 PYSN 84651 3355 B6
Ridge Rd
- LYTN 84040 1283 C4
- SNQN 84655 3461 A7
- SNQN 84655 3568 A1
100 OREM 84057 2713 D7
6000 HILD 84003 2497 B6
N Ridge Rd
- JubC 84645 3567 A6
Ridge Wy
7200 SmtC 84098 1864 D7
N Ridge Wy
1000 SPFK 84663 3250 A1
Ridge Break Ln
11800 RIVN 84065 2281 D7
Ridge Brook Wy
5300 SLkC 84118 2067 E6
Ridge Canyon Rd
4900 PTVW 84414 942 D7
Ridge Creek Cir
5700 MRRY 84107 2070 D6
Ridge Creek Rd
5700 MRRY 84107 2070 E6
Ridge Crest Cir
4400 BNFL 84010 1653 E7
Ridgecrest Cir
- PRVO 84601 3035 C1
3900 TYVL 84118 2068 C4
Ridge Crest Ct
700 ALPN 84004 2498 B5
Ridge Crest Dr
10 SmtC 84098 1972 C2
Ridgecrest Dr
300 HYRM 84319 651 D1
1600 OGDN 84403 1173 C1
3800 TYVL 84118 2068 C3
S Ridgecrest Dr
100 OREM 84058 2820 B5
Ridgedale Cir
1100 SLkC 84106 1965 B5
2100 OGDN 84403 1173 E4
Ridgedale Dr
1900 OGDN 84403 1173 E3
5200 WbrC 84403 1173 E3
Ridgedale Ln
1100 SLkC 84106 1965 B6
E Ridgefield Rd
1500 SPFK 84663 3250 A1
Ridge Flower Wy
5200 SLkC 84118 2067 E6
Ridge Gate Cir
10000 SNDY 84092 2283 D3
Ridgehill Dr
1800 BNFL 84010 1654 D3
Ridge Hill Ln
- MDVL 84047 2177 A3
Ridge Hollow Cir
200 SHFD 84335 400 A3
5800 SLkC 84118 2067 E6
Ridgehollow Dr
1800 BNFL 84010 1654 C3
Ridgehollow Rd
400 SHFD 84335 400 A3
Ridge Hollow Wy
5300 SLkC 84118 2067 E6
Ridgeland Cir
3500 WVCY 84119 1962 D3
Ridgeland Dr
2500 WVCY 84119 1962 E3
Ridgeline Cir
800 CTRV 84014 1552 A5
Ridge Line Dr
1400 RIVN 84065 2281 D7
E Ridgeline Dr
10 WSTR 84405 1172 E4
1400 SOGN 84405 1173 C6
S Ridgeline Dr
4400 RVDL 84405 1172 C2
S Ridgeline Dr
4400 WSTR 84405 1172 C2
W Ridgeline Dr
10 WSTR 84405 1172 D4
Ridgemark Dr
1300 SLkC 84092 2283 C2
1300 SNDY 84092 2283 C2
Ridge Meadow Ln
1200 CDHT 84093 2177 B2
Ridge Place Dr
- OGDN 84404 1056 D3
Ridgepoint
7800 PKCY 84060 2184 E1
Ridge Point Dr
1700 WPT 84015 1227 A4
1800 WPT 84015 1226 E4
E Ridge Point Dr
1600 BNFL 84010 1654 C2
S Ridge Point Dr
1400 BNFL 84010 1654 C2
Ridge Point Rd
8300 SNDY 84093 2177 E5
Ridgeside Ct
1000 SJDN 84095 2281 E5
Ridgeside Dr
10900 SJDN 84095 2281 E5
Ridge Stone Dr
5400 SLkC 84118 2067 D5
Ridge Top Cir
600 NSLK 84054 1754 C1
Ridge Top Ln
500 NSLK 84054 1754 B1
Ridgetop Cove
1000 SJDN 84095 2281 E5
Ridgeview Cir
1500 FMTN 84025 1346 B5
1600 LYTN 84040 1283 D2
Ridgeview Dr
10 BNFL 84010 1552 A7
200 BNFL 84010 1654 A1
700 SOGN 84403 1173 A2
2900 NHLN 84341 464 D3
3000 PKCY 84060 2078 C1
S Ridgeview Dr
100 OREM 84058 2820 A5
Ridgeview Wy
3800 TYVL 84118 2068 C4
Ridge Village Dr
5300 WVCY 84118 2067 D5
Ridgewood Cir
500 FMTN 84025 1346 B5
Ridgewood Ln
1300 BNFL 84010 1654 B3
Ridgewood Pl
9000 WJDN 84088 2175 B7
Ridgewood Wy
- BNFL 84010 1654 B4
Rifle St
4700 MRRY 84107 2070 C3
Rigdon Av
100 SSLK 84115 1964 D7
Riggs Cir
9800 SNDY 84092 2283 E2
Riggs Dr
2000 SNDY 84092 2283 D2
Rildah Cir
- KYVL 84037 1344 E3
Riley Cir
800 SLCY 84104 1858 A7
Riley Dr
1200 PYSN 84651 3355 A7
1200 PYSN 84651 3462 A1
Riley Ln
5300 MRRY 84107 2070 C5
Rimrock Ln
1100 MRRY 84123 2069 E7
Ring Rd
- LYTN 84041 1282 D2
N Ring Rd
600 LYTN 84041 1282 D2
S Ring Rd
- LYTN 84041 1282 D2
Ringneck Cir
400 DRPR 84020 2388 E2
Ringtail Cove
12800 DRPR 84020 2389 B2
Rio Cir
1800 SNDY 84093 2177 D5
Rio Ct
1900 SNDY 84093 2177 D5
Rio Wy
1800 SNDY 84093 2177 D5
Rio Bravo Pl
10 WJDN 84088 2175 B5
Rio Camino
3400 WVCY 84119 1963 E6
Rio Grande Pl
10 WJDN 84088 2175 A6
Rio Grande Rd
1400 SmtC 84098 1971 E6
N Rio Grande St
100 MDVL 84047 2176 B3
S Rio Grande St
10 SLCY 84101 1858 B4
Rio Vista
1100 WVCY 84119 1963 E6
Riparian Dr
800 DRPR 84020 2283 A7
Ripple Dr
4400 WJDN 84088 2174 B7
Ripple Creek Cir
4500 WJDN 84088 2174 B7
Rips Ct
1800 RIVN 84065 2387 C2
Rishel Cir
6100 WVCY 84128 2067 C1
Rising Star Ln
3600 PKCY 84060 2079 B4
3600 SmtC 84098 2079 B4
Ritter Dr
1100 RVDL 84405 1172 A4
1500 RVDL 84405 1171 E4
Rivendell Rd
3700 TYVL 84118 2068 C6
River Dr
- WbrC 84310 1001 B1
400 OGDN 84404 1115 E1
800 OGDN 84401 1116 A1
800 OGDN 84404 1116 A1
N River Dr
3100 WbrC 84310 1001 C4
River Ln
3700 UthC 84660 3141 A3
3700 WVCY 84119 1963 E7
S River Ln
5100 UthC 84660 3141 C6
6000 UthC 84660 3248 C1
River Rd
200 ALPN 84004 2497 E5
N River Rd
10 MIDW 84049 2397 C2
300 WshC 84049 2397 C2
1000 MIDW 84049 2291 E7
1000 WshC 84049 2291 E7
1700 WshC 84049 2292 A5
3300 WshC 84032 2292 A5
8800 BxEC 84337 585 D4
8800 ELWD 84337 585 D4
W River Rd
900 WshC 84032 2292 B4
900 WshC 84049 2292 B4
River Vw
- LEHI 84043 2602 B7
River Wy
200 LEHI 84043 2602 C7
River Bank Rd
1100 WVCY 84119 1963 E6
River Bend Ct
200 LEHI 84043 2602 E7
Riverbend Dr
800 MRRY 84123 2070 A7
River Bend Ln
200 PRVO 84097 2821 B4
1000 OGDN 84404 1116 B1
River Bend Rd
11400 HILD 84003 2497 B6
Riverbend Rd
200 LOGN 84321 527 C5
Riverbirch Cir
600 ANFK 84003 2604 E6
River Birch Ct
700 PKCY 84060 2078 C2
River Birch Dr
500 SHFD 84335 400 A2
River Bluffs Rd
1100 MRRY 84123 2069 E7
Riverboat Rd
4100 TYVL 84123 2070 A1
River Bottom Rd
1700 SGVL 84663 3144 B4
E River Bottom Rd
600 SPFK 84660 3249 E6
700 SPFK 84660 3250 A6
700 UthC 84660 3249 E6
700 UthC 84660 3250 A6
S River Bottom Rd
7000 SPFK 84660 3249 D4
7000 UthC 84660 3249 D4
River Bottoms Rd
- UthC 84660 3250 A6
3000 SPFK 84660 3250 D6
Riverbreeze Dr
1000 OREM 84097 2821 B6
S River Breeze Dr
500 OREM 84097 2821 B7
River Cir Dr
10 LOGN 84321 527 B4
River Creek Cir
1000 RIVN 84065 2387 E1
Rivercrest Cir
1000 SJDN 84095 2281 E5
River Cross Ct
1400 TYVL 84123 2069 D3
Rivercross Rd
400 SPFK 84660 3249 C5
Riverdale Av
400 RVHT 84321 527 E4
Riverdale Dr
10 LOGN 84321 528 A3
Riverdale Rd
1600 ROY 84067 1171 D4
1600 RVDL 84405 1171 D4
3400 OGDN 84401 1115 D7
3500 SOGN 84405 1115 D7
4000 RVDL 84405 1115 D7
4000 RVDL 84405 1172 C1
Riverdale Rd SR-26
1600 ROY 84067 1171 D4
1600 RVDL 84405 1171 D4
3400 OGDN 84401 1115 D7
3500 SOGN 84405 1115 D7
4000 RVDL 84405 1115 D7
4000 RVDL 84405 1172 C1
W Riverdale Rd
- ROY 84067 1171 E3
600 RVDL 84405 1172 A2
1200 RVDL 84405 1171 E3
W Riverdale Rd SR-26
- ROY 84067 1171 E3
600 RVDL 84405 1172 A2
1200 RVDL 84405 1171 E3
Riverdell Rd
1100 MRRY 84123 2069 E7
River Edge Ln
1200 MRRY 84123 2175 E1
River Front Pkwy
10600 SJDN 84095 2282 A4
11300 SJDN 84095 2281 E6
River Glen Cir
6000 MRRY 84123 2070 A7
River Glen Dr
700 MRRY 84123 2070 A7
River Grande Wy
- TYVL 84123 2070 A2
E River Haven Cir
1000 OREM 84097 2821 B7
River Heights Blvd
- RVHT 84321 527 E4
600 RVHT 84321 528 A4
1000 LOGN 84321 528 A4
River Hills Dr
1100 RIVN 84065 2281 D7
River Hollow Rd
700 SLkC 84123 1964 A7
River Horse Rd
1100 WVCY 84119 1963 E6
River House Cir
1200 MRRY 84123 2069 D7
River Meadow Wy
700 TYVL 84123 2070 A3
River Meadows Dr
100 ALPN 84004 2498 A5
Rivermist Ln
4000 LEHI 84043 2495 D7
River Oaks Cir
1400 SNDY 84093 2177 C4
River Oaks Dr
1400 SNDY 84093 2177 C4
River Park Dr
- RVDL 84405 1172 A3
10 LOGN 84321 528 A2
100 PRVO 84097 2821 B4
100 PRVO 84604 2821 B4
5700 MRRY 84123 2069 E6
Riverpark Dr
600 RVDL 84405 1172 B1
W River Park Wy
5000 PRVO 84604 2821 C4
River Pine Cir
1000 RIVN 84065 2387 E1
River Point Cir
900 MRRY 84123 2069 E6
900 MRRY 84123 2070 D7
River Pointe Dr
10 LOGN 84321 528 A3
River Ridge Dr
1300 WJDN 84088 2175 D7
River Ridge Ln
1100 OREM 84097 2821 B6
1100 PRVO 84097 2821 B6
1200 SPFK 84660 3249 C5
River Rock Pl
5800 WVCY 84118 2173 C1
River Rock Rd
- SPFK 84660 3249 C5
River Rose Ln
13400 RIVN 84065 2385 E4
River Run Dr
5200 PRVO 84097 2821 C4
River Run Wy
3800 SSLK 84119 1964 A7
Riverside Av
1700 PRVO 84604 2928 B3
Riverside Cir
1400 SLCY 84116 1857 D1
Riverside Dr
- MRRY 84123 2070 A4
10 LOGN 84321 528 A3
500 SLCY 84116 1857 D1
700 SLCY 84116 1753 C7
700 SNDY 84070 2176 A7
800 SNDY 84070 2282 A1
1400 SLCY 84104 1857 E7
1500 SLCY 84104 1963 E1
9400 SJDN 84070 2282 A1
9400 SJDN 84095 2282 A1
Riverside Ln
- SPFK 84660 3249 C5
1000 OREM 84097 2821 B7
Riverton Dr
1500 RIVN 84065 2387 C1
Riverton Chase Dr
1500 RIVN 84065 2387 C1
Riverton Farms Wy
2900 RIVN 84065 2387 A2
3000 RIVN 84065 2386 E2
Riverton Ranch Rd
1400 RIVN 84065 2387 C3
River Trail Ter
700 SLkC 84123 1964 A7
River Valley Dr
3600 RVDL 84405 1115 B7
Riverview Av
100 LOGN 84321 528 A3
1800 SLCY 84116 1753 D4
River View Dr
200 ALPN 84004 2497 E5
1100 SPFK 84660 3249 C5
1700 BFDL 84065 2494 C3
Riverview Dr
1100 TMTN 84337 520 E4
1200 TMTN 84337 521 A3
River Vista Dr
12000 RIVN 84065 2387 E1
River Vista Cove
1000 RIVN 84065 2387 E1
River Walk Dr
900 RIVN 84065 2281 E7
Riverwalk Dr
500 ANFK 84003 2604 D6
700 LOGN 84321 527 C5
River Willow Dr
1600 BFDL 84065 2387 D7
Riverwood Dr
3700 PRVO 84604 2821 B7
7500 CDHT 84093 2177 C4
River Wy Rd
300 SPFK 84660 3249 B5
Riviera
10500 CRHL 84062 2605 C1
E Riviera Cir
600 SSLK 84106 1964 E6
Riviera Dr
3300 SSLK 84106 1964 E5
Riviera Pass Cir
3000 SJDN 84095 2281 A5
Roamer Ct
7900 PKCY 84060 2185 A1
Roan Cir
3700 SLkC 84044 1960 D7
Roanoke Cir
700 MRRY 84123 2070 A7
Roanoke Ln
2200 SJDN 84095 2281 B6
E Robert Av
10 SSLK 84115 1964 C3
400 SLCY 84115 1964 E3
W Robert Av
10 SSLK 84115 1964 C3
Robert Cir
10 FMTN 84025 1346 C6
7600 WJDN 84084 2175 A3
Roberta St
700 SLCY 84111 1858 D5
1300 SLCY 84115 1858 D7
1800 SLCY 84115 1964 D1
2100 SSLK 84115 1964 D2
Roberts St
500 TMTN 84337 520 D7
Robidoux Rd
2400 SLkC 84093 2178 A5
Robin Rd
400 OREM 84097 2713 E7
2400 WVCY 84119 1963 A5
Robin St
300 SHFD 84335 400 A2
8400 SLkC 84044 1960 B4
Robin Wy
1900 WJDN 84084 2175 B2
Robin Hill Rd
4900 WJDN 84084 2174 A2
Robin Hood Ln
- OREM 84057 2820 A4
Robins Av
700 OGDN 84404 1057 C6
2000 OGDN 84401 1116 C3
Robins Cir
1500 OGDN 84404 1116 C1
Robins Wy
1000 SNDY 84094 2283 B1
Robinson
- ANFK 84003 2604 C6
Robinson Av
200 ANFK 84003 2604 E7
Robinson Cir
11000 SNDY 84092 2283 C5
Robinson Dr
700 NSLK 84054 1652 D6
Robinson Ln
1300 PTGV 84062 2712 B3
Robinson Wy
1300 PTGV 84062 2712 B2
Robinwood Cir
5300 TYVL 84118 2069 A5
Robinwood Dr
2900 TYVL 84118 2069 A4
3000 TYVL 84118 2068 E4
Robison Hall
100 PRVO 84604 2928 D4
Roble Cir
8300 SNDY 84093 2177 C5
Robyn Wy
10 FMTN 84025 1346 C6
Rochelle Cir
3300 WVCY 84120 1962 A6
Rochester Av
11000 SJDN 84095 2282 B5
Rock St
2000 RVDL 84405 1172 A5
Rock Creek Dr
2800 SJDN 84095 2281 A7
Rocket Rd
- TMTN 84337 520 C7
- TMTN 84337 584 C1
Rockface Dr
4700 TYVL 84118 2069 A3
Rockford St
5400 SLkC 84118 2067 E5
Rockhampton Dr
2500 SNDY 84092 2284 A6
Rockhill Cir
800 TYVL 84123 2070 A3
Rockhill Ln
4700 TYVL 84123 2070 A3
Rockhill Pl
800 TYVL 84123 2070 A3
Rockhill Point Cove
800 TYVL 84123 2070 A3
Rock Hollow Rd
1800 BFDL 84065 2494 C1
Rocklin Ct
9700 SNDY 84092 2283 E2
Rocklin Dr
1900 SNDY 84092 2283 D1
Rock Manor Dr
10 CTRV 84014 1448 D6
Rock Mill Ln
700 FMTN 84025 1346 D7
Rock Oak Ct
1400 SJDN 84095 2281 D4
Rockridge Dr
1500 LYTN 84041 1282 B7
Rock Ridge Ln
5000 WJDN 84088 2173 E7
5000 WJDN 84088 2174 A7
Rock River Rd
1200 WVCY 84119 1963 D6
Rock Rose Cir
5500 SLkC 84118 2067 D6
Rock Springs Ln
6100 WVCY 84118 2067 C7
Rockview Cir
10000 SNDY 84092 2284 A3
Rockview Dr
2300 SNDY 84092 2283 E4
2400 SNDY 84092 2284 A3
Rockwell Dr
2500 SNDY 84093 2178 A7
Rockwood Cir
500 PVDN 84332 528 B7
Rockwood Dr
500 NSLK 84054 1754 D1
Rockwood Wy
3700 WVCY 84120 1962 C5
Rocky Rd
1800 TYVL 84118 2069 C4
Rocky Creek Dr
5200 WJDN 84088 2173 E6
E Rocky Dugway Rd
200 MNTU 84324 829 D1
Rocky Knoll Ln
500 DRPR 84020 2388 E7
Rocky Mountain Dr
500 ALPN 84004 2497 E6
Rocky Mountain Wy
1100 HYRM 84319 651 E3
Rocky Mouth Cir
14200 DRPR 84020 2389 A6
Rocky Mouth Ln
600 DRPR 84020 2388 E6
600 DRPR 84020 2389 A6
Rocky Park Ln
100 DRPR 84020 2388 D1
Rocky Point Dr
5400 HRMN 84065 2385 D5
Rocky Ridge Rd
- JubC 84645 3567 A6
Rocky Vista Cir
4900 WJDN 84088 2174 A6
Rodeo Dr
- TMTN 84337 520 D6
100 SGVL 84663 3143 C5
Rodeo Ln
6300 MRRY 84121 2071 C7
6400 MRRY 84121 2177 C1

Salt Lake City Street Index

STREET
Block City ZIP Map# Grid

Rodger St
100 LYTN 84041 1282 E4
Roenewood Cir
1500 TYVL 84123 2069 C7
Roeoaks Ct
6400 MRRY 84121 2071 C7
Roffe Rd
1900 SmtC 84098 1971 D6
Roger Cir
1300 LYTN 84040 1283 C2
Roger Dr
3400 SLkC 84124 2072 C2
Rogers Dr
6500 WVCY 84118 2173 C1
Rogers Hall
10 PRVO 84604 2928 D5
Rogue River Ct
5800 WVCY 84118 2067 C7
Rogue River Ln
5900 WVCY 84118 2067 D7
6400 WVCY 84118 2173 D1
Roland Wy
400 CTRV 84014 1551 E2
Rolling Bluff Dr
- DRPR 84020 2496 E3
- DRPR 84020 2497 A3
Rolling Green Dr
1500 DRPR 84020 2389 C6
Rolling Hills Dr
100 CTRV 84014 1448 E6
Rolling Knolls Dr
2700 PRVO 84604 2928 E1
Rolling Knolls Wy
2000 CDHT 84121 2177 D1
N Rolling Oaks Ln
1900 LYTN 84040 1283 E1
Rolling River Rd
1100 WVCY 84119 1963 E6
Rollingwood Ln
10 SNDY 84092 2283 E5
Romaine Cir
400 SNDY 84070 2176 E5
Romaine Dr
8100 SNDY 84070 2176 E5
8200 SLkC 84070 2176 E5
Roman St
- FTHT 84037 1346 A4
Rome Beauty Pk
5200 MRRY 84123 2070 A4
Rome Cove
3700 WVCY 84119 1963 B7
Romney Park Dr
3900 WJDN 84084 2174 C2
Ron Cir
4200 WVCY 84120 2068 B1
Ronald Av
10 LYTN 84041 1282 D4
Rond Cir
1500 OGDN 84403 1173 C4
Rondelle Cir
1700 SNDY 84093 2177 D5
Ron Hollow St
1100 MRRY 84123 2069 E7
Roosevelt Av
10 ANFK 84003 2711 B1
300 SLCY 84115 1858 D7
600 SLCY 84105 1858 E7
800 SLCY 84105 1859 A7
2100 SLCY 84108 1859 E7
Roosevelt St
7700 MDVL 84047 2176 C5
Rooster Hollow Cir
400 KYVL 84037 1345 E2
Rooster Tail Rd
6900 WVCY 84128 1961 A5
Ropcke Dr
1000 MRRY 84123 2069 E6
Ropner Cir
2800 SLkC 84044 1960 C4
Rory Ln
8500 MDVL 84047 2176 C6
Rosa Cir
1300 SNDY 84092 2283 B2
Rosaleen Cir
5600 HRMN 84065 2385 D6
Rosaleen Ln
13900 HRMN 84065 2385 D6
Rosalie Cir
3000 TYVL 84118 2069 A3
4700 TYVL 84118 2068 E3
Rosalind Cir
7400 CDHT 84121 2177 D3
Rosanna Cir
1600 ALPN 84004 2498 C1
Rosanna Ln
1500 ALPN 84004 2498 C1
Rosa Vista Dr
2900 TYVL 84118 2069 A6
5800 TYVL 84118 2068 E6
Rosberg Dr
12600 RIVN 84065 2386 E2
Rose Cir
10 MRRY 84107 2070 C5
4200 SLkC 84118 2068 C3
Rose Ln
5500 ROY 84067 1171 C5
Rose Rd
- OGDN 84401 1116 A2
Rose St
1000 LOGN 84341 464 C7
Rose Anne Cir
10 PTVW 84414 998 D6
Roseberry Ct
5900 WJDN 84084 2173 B1
Roseberry St
5900 WJDN 84084 2173 C1
Rose Blossom Dr
600 LYTN 84041 1283 B6
Rose Blossom St
4300 WVCY 84120 2068 A2
Roseboro Cir
1800 SNDY 84092 2283 D2
Roseboro Rd
9800 SNDY 84092 2283 D3
Rose Brook Cir
900 DRPR 84020 2389 A4
Rose Bud Ct
600 SRSP 84043 2601 D5
Rosebud Ct
900 DRPR 84020 2389 A7
Rose Canyon Rd
13000 HRMN 84065 2385 B5
W Rose Canyon Rd
6400 HRMN 84065 2385 A6
6400 SLkC 84065 2385 A6
Rosecrest Dr
1400 SLCY 84108 1859 D7
Rosecrest Rd
- HRMN 84065 2386 A6
13100 HRMN 84065 2385 D6
13400 RIVN 84065 2385 D6
Rosefield Ln
800 DRPR 84020 2389 A4
Rose Garden Dr
1800 SRSP 84043 2601 D5
Rose Garden Ln
4300 SLkC 84124 2071 A1
Rosehaven Ct
4400 WVCY 84120 2068 C2
Rose Hill Dr
13500 RIVN 84065 2385 D4
S Rose Hollow Ln
3300 WVCY 84119 1962 E5
W Rose Hollow Ln
3300 WVCY 84119 1962 C4
Roseleaf Dr
5200 MRRY 84123 2070 A7
Roselina Dr
5700 HRMN 84065 2385 D5
Rosella Ct
9600 SJDN 84095 2280 A1
Rosemary Cir
4000 WVCY 84120 2067 E1
Rosemary Dr
1700 SRSP 84043 2601 D5
Rosemary Pl
400 SRSP 84043 2601 D5
Rosemary St
3800 WVCY 84120 1961 E7
Rosemill Cir
13400 RIVN 84065 2385 E4
Rosemill Dr
5300 RIVN 84065 2385 E4
Rosemore Ct
700 SLkC 84107 2071 A2
Rose Park Cir
1500 SLCY 84116 1753 D7
Rose Park Ln
1800 SLCY 84116 1753 B4
1800 SLkC 84116 1753 B4
Rose Petal Wy
4300 WVCY 84120 2068 A2
Rose Summit Dr
14300 HRMN 84065 2385 D6
Rosewater Dr
5100 RIVN 84065 2385 D4
Rosewood Av
200 SLCY 84115 1964 D2
Rosewood Cir
10 CTRV 84014 1448 D7
Rosewood Cir N
5400 UthC 84651 3460 E1
Rosewood Cir S
5300 UthC 84651 3460 E1
Rosewood Ct
9700 SJDN 84095 2280 A2
Rosewood Dr
300 HYRM 84319 651 C4
4800 SJDN 84095 2280 A2
Rosewood Ln
300 NSLK 84054 1754 D1
400 LYTN 84037 1283 A6
400 LYTN 84041 1283 A6
E Rosewood Ln
1200 LYTN 84040 1283 C5
N Rosewood Ln
10 LYTN 84040 1283 C5
Rosewood Wy
- LYTN 84041 1283 A6
Rosewood Park Ln
300 DRPR 84020 2388 D2
Rosie Ln
13700 HRMN 84065 2385 B5
Ross Dr
100 CRFD 84015 1227 E5
100 CRFD 84015 1228 A5
1700 OGDN 84403 1173 D1
Ross St
500 WDCR 84010 1653 C3
Rossbern Cove
6700 CDHT 84121 2178 B1
Rossett Green Ln
8200 SLkC 84093 2177 E5
Rossie Hill Dr
600 PKCY 84060 2078 E6
600 PKCY 84060 2079 A6
Rothchild Cir
3600 WVCY 84119 1963 D7
Rothchild Dr
1300 WVCY 84119 1963 D6
Rothmoor Cir
1500 MRRY 84121 2071 D6
Rothmoor Dr
1400 MRRY 84121 2071 D6
6400 MRRY 84121 2177 C1
Roueche Ln
800 KYVL 84037 1345 A3
Roueche St
800 LYTN 84040 1283 C3
Rough St
- DvsC 84056 1229 A4
Roundelay Bay
13800 HRMN 84065 2385 D5
E Round Mountain Dr
900 ALPN 84004 2498 B6
Round Rock Dr
5800 HRMN 84065 2385 C6
Roundstem Rd
4800 WJDN 84084 2174 A1
Roundtable Cir
4700 WVCY 84120 1962 A3
Roundtable Rd
2900 WVCY 84120 1962 A5
Roundtoft Dr
100 SLCY 84103 1754 D7
Round Tree Ln
15000 DRPR 84020 2496 D1
Roundup Cir
1800 SLCY 84116 1753 C4
1800 SLkC 84116 1753 C4
Round Valley Wy
3100 PKCY 84060 2079 A1
Rowland Dr
4200 HLDY 84124 2072 A1
Rowley Dr
700 SLkC 84107 2070 E1
700 SLkC 84107 2071 A1
Roxborough Ct
4400 WVCY 84119 2069 A2
Roxborough Park St
2800 WVCY 84119 2069 A2
3000 WVCY 84119 2068 E3
Roxbury Cir
2600 SLCY 84108 1860 A7
4000 CRFD 84015 1228 A5
Roxbury Rd
1300 SLCY 84108 1860 A7
Roxey Ct
6000 WVCY 84128 1961 C5
Royal Cir
2000 SLCY 84108 1859 D7
Royal Ct
10 PKCY 84060 2079 A7
Royal Ln
2300 CDHT 84093 2177 E4
2300 CDHT 84093 2178 A4
Royal St
3100 PKCY 84060 2079 A6
5000 PKCY 84060 2078 E7
5000 PKCY 84060 2184 E1
Royal St E
- PKCY 84060 2184 E1
7500 PKCY 84060 2185 A2
Royal St W
7000 PKCY 84060 2184 E1
Royal Ann Cir
100 OREM 84058 2820 C6
4500 WVCY 84120 2068 A2
Royal Ann Ct
700 KYVL 84037 1345 E2
Royal Ann Dr
- PRRY 84302 827 B7
4800 WVCY 84120 2068 A2
Royalanne Av
3200 PRRY 84302 827 B7
Royal Autumn Cir
5300 TYVL 84118 2069 B5
Royal Crest Dr
8600 WJDN 84088 2174 D6
Royal Farm Dr
2000 CDHT 84121 2177 E1
E Royal Garden Ter
200 SSLK 84115 1964 D6
Royal Harvest Wy
2000 CDHT 84121 2177 D1
Royal Heights Dr
2400 SJDN 84095 2281 A1
Royal Oak Cir
1600 SNDY 84092 2283 C2
Royal Oak Ct
800 FMTN 84025 1346 B4
Royal Oaks Dr
200 OGDN 84404 1056 C4
Royal Red Rd
9600 CRHL 84062 2605 B4
Royal Ridge Dr
1600 ROY 84067 1171 D2
Royal River Rd
4300 TYVL 84123 2070 A2
Royal Scott Dr
3500 WVCY 84128 1961 A6
Royal Tee Cove
10400 SJDN 84095 2281 E4
Royalton Dr
5800 MRRY 84107 2070 E6
Royal Troon Dr
300 HRCY 84032 2398 C3
1300 SLkC 84124 2071 B2
Royalty Ln
9600 SJDN 84095 2281 A1
Royalwood Cir
3400 PRVO 84604 2821 C7
3500 TYVL 84118 2068 D4
Royalwood Dr
3200 TYVL 84118 2068 E4
Royal Wulff Ln
3000 WVCY 84120 1962 C5
Roycroft Pl
1600 SLkC 84124 2071 C2
Roy Park Cir
- ROY 84067 1171 B4
Rozanne Cir
1800 TYVL 84084 2069 C7
Rua Branco Cir
1900 SNDY 84093 2177 D5
Rua Branco Dr
1800 SNDY 84093 2177 D5
Ruby Ct
11800 HRMN 84065 2280 A7
Ruby Wy
900 WBNF 84087 1551 B5
1300 SRCS 84075 1227 A7
Ruby Ridge Cove
6000 HLDY 84121 2071 D7
Rue Ann Ct
1100 OGDN 84401 1116 B3
Ruflin Cir
600 WDCR 84087 1653 B2
Ruflin Acres Dr
1100 WDCR 84087 1653 B2
Rugby Ct
4300 TYVL 84123 2069 E1
Ruger Pl
- FMTN 84025 1345 D7
Rulon St
3100 SLkC 84044 1960 B6
Rulon White Blvd
1800 FRWT 84404 1056 A1
1800 HARR 84404 1056 A1
1800 WbrC 84404 1056 A1
1900 WbrC 84404 998 A7
2100 WbrC 84404 997 E6
Rumel Pl
400 SLCY 84111 1858 E4
Ruminant Rd
2500 PKCY 84060 2078 A2
Rundquist Dr
1500 WJDN 84084 2175 C3
Rungsted Cir
3800 SRCS 84075 1226 A7
Running Bear Ln
- DRPR 84020 2389 D3
Running Creek Wy
- UthC 84043 2603 E1
Running Springs Dr
1900 WJDN 84084 2175 C2
Rupp Ct
4200 TYVL 84119 2069 B2
Rushford Ct
4100 WVCY 84128 2067 C1
Rushton Ln
3200 TYVL 84118 2068 E3
Rushton St
100 OGDN 84401 1115 D2
900 OGDN 84401 1116 A2
W Rushton St
100 OGDN 84401 1115 D2
Rushton Acres Ct
5000 WVCY 84120 2068 A1
Rushton Acres Ln
4100 WVCY 84120 2068 A1
Rushton Park Dr
2900 WVCY 84120 1962 C4
Rushton View Dr
- SJDN 84095 2280 C4
Ruskin Cir
9500 SLkC 84092 2284 C1
Ruskin Ct
3200 SLkC 84092 2284 C2
Russell Cir
2400 HLDY 84117 2072 A2
Russell St
4500 HLDY 84117 2071 E2
4500 HLDY 84117 2072 A2
Russell Park Rd
8600 CDHT 84121 2178 C6
Russett Av
10 SSLK 84115 1964 C4
1400 WVCY 84119 1963 C4
Russian Frost Dr
14400 HRMN 84065 2385 E7
Rustic Cir
- KYVL 84037 1345 B3
Rustic Dr
5300 MRRY 84123 2069 E5
Rustic Meadow Cir
2500 SJDN 84095 2281 A4
Rustic Oak Ct
8200 WJDN 84088 2173 B5
Rustic Roads Dr
2200 SJDN 84095 2281 B4
Rustic Spring Ln
3500 CDHT 84121 2178 C5
Rustler Rd
8600 CDHT 84093 2178 B6
Rusty Dr
7200 MDVL 84047 2176 D3
Rutgers Av
4300 WVCY 84120 2068 B3
Ruth Av
100 SNST 84015 1227 D2
Ruth Dr
3700 SLkC 84124 1966 D7
3700 SLkC 84124 2072 D1
4000 SLkC 84118 2068 C3
Rutherford Av
1400 BFDL 84065 2387 D6
Rutherford Ridge Rd
1600 OGDN 84403 1173 C3
Ruth Meadows Cove
4700 SLkC 84117 2071 C3
Rutland Pl
3300 CDHT 84121 2178 C4
RWK Park Dr
300 MRRY 84107 2070 B7
Ryan Cir
2000 WbrC 84403 1173 D5
5600 TYVL 84118 2069 A5
Ryan Dr
2900 TYVL 84118 2069 A5
3000 TYVL 84118 2068 E5
Ryan Hill Cir
5100 TYVL 84118 2068 C4
Ryan Park Av
1800 SNDY 84092 2283 D5
Ryans Ln
100 MIDW 84049 2397 E3
100 WshC 84049 2397 E3
Rye Cir
6800 WJDN 84084 2175 B2
Rye Grass Cir
- KYVL 84037 1283 D7

S

S St
10 SLCY 84102 1859 B3
10 SLCY 84103 1859 B3
Sabal Av
2400 CDHT 84093 2178 A4
Sable Av
2700 TYVL 84118 2069 A3
Sable Cir
900 NSLK 84054 1653 C6
2000 TYVL 84118 2069 A3
Sackett Dr
2300 SmtC 84098 1865 C4
Saddle Ct
6800 SmtC 84098 1970 E1
Saddle Wy
2200 TYVL 84118 2069 B6
Saddle Back Cir
500 SGVL 84663 3143 A2
Saddleback Cir
8600 SmtC 84098 1864 E4
Saddle Back Dr
400 SGVL 84663 3143 B2
Saddleback Dr
5100 SLkC 84117 2071 C4
Saddleback Rd
400 CchC 84335 399 B1
400 SHFD 84335 399 B1
3200 SmtC 84098 1865 A4
3700 SmtC 84098 1864 E4
Saddleback View Cir
2200 BFDL 84065 2387 B6
Saddle Bluff Dr
1100 WJDN 84084 2175 E1
Saddle Brook Cir
8000 CDHT 84093 2177 E4
Saddlebrook Dr
300 PYSN 84651 3461 D1
Saddlebrooke Cir
10800 SJDN 84095 2281 D5
Saddle Creek Cir
5200 WJDN 84084 2173 E3
Saddlecrest Cir
5200 WJDN 84084 2173 E3
Saddle Hill Dr
1600 LOGN 84321 528 C1
1600 LOGN 84341 528 C1
Saddle Hill Rd
600 SLCY 84103 1859 B1
Saddle Hollow Pl
5200 WJDN 84084 2173 E3
Saddle Horn Cir
2300 BFDL 84065 2387 B5
Saddlehorn Cir
- KYVL 84037 1344 E2
- KYVL 84037 1345 A2
1500 FMTN 84025 1447 E2
Saddle Horn Ct
2300 BFDL 84065 2387 B5
Saddle Horn Dr
13900 BFDL 84065 2387 B6
Saddle Leaf Ct
14800 DRPR 84020 2496 D1
Saddle Mount Cir
5300 WJDN 84084 2173 E4
Saddle Oaks Ct
8200 WJDN 84088 2173 C5
Saddle Park Dr
5100 WJDN 84084 2173 E3
Saddler Cir
8500 WJDN 84088 2174 D6
Saddler Dr
3600 WJDN 84088 2174 D6
Saddle Ridge Dr
13400 DRPR 84020 2388 E4
Saddle View Wy
300 PKCY 84060 2078 C3
Saddle Wood Cir
400 CTRV 84014 1448 C7
Saddlewood Ln
10 SNDY 84092 2284 A5
Sage Cir
300 LOGN 84321 528 C4
800 PTGV 84062 2713 A1
900 HRCY 84032 2398 E2
4300 SLkC 84124 2071 A1
S Sage Cir
10 OREM 84097 2820 E5
Sage Dr
- WPT 84015 1225 E4
10 OREM 84097 2820 E5
700 PTGV 84062 2713 A1
Sage Ln
- FTHT 84037 1346 B3
Sage Lp
3000 LEHI 84043 2602 E1
N Sage Rd E
10000 CRHL 84062 2605 C3
N Sage Rd W
10000 CRHL 84062 2605 B3
W Sage Rd N
4000 CRHL 84062 2605 B2
Sage St
700 DvsC 84056 1229 A3
Sage Wy
2500 SLCY 84109 1966 A2
Sage Brook Cir
3700 SLkC 84044 1960 B7
Sagebrook Dr
5700 SmtC 84098 1972 E3
Sagebrush Cir
3100 CDHT 84121 2178 D2
Sagebrush Pl
300 SmtC 84098 1866 D3
Sagebrush Rd
4600 SmtC 84098 1972 A4
Sagebrush Wy
7000 CDHT 84121 2178 B2
Sage Creek Cir
200 SGVL 84663 3143 D4
Sage Creek Rd
10400 SJDN 84095 2280 D4
Sage Crest Cir
9200 SNDY 84093 2177 E7
Sage Crest Dr
14500 BFDL 84065 2387 C7
Sage Flats Wy
3800 SJDN 84095 2280 D4
Sage Hen Rd
1600 OREM 84097 2713 E7
Sage Hill Dr
- SRSP 84043 2601 C7
Sagehill Dr
1000 SLkC 84124 2071 A1
Sage Hollow Dr
1700 DRPR 84020 2389 D5
Sage Hollow Wy
- SJDN 84095 2280 C3
Sage Meadow Dr
3800 SJDN 84095 2280 D4
Sage Mesa Dr
11400 SNDY 84094 2282 E6
Sage Park Ln
900 SLkC 84117 2071 A2
Sage Point Wy
3800 SJDN 84095 2280 C3
Sage Ridge Cir
12000 SNDY 84094 2283 B7
Sage Ridge Rd
1100 SNDY 84094 2283 B7
Sage Rim Cove
3800 SJDN 84095 2280 D3
Sagers Wy
4000 WVCY 84128 1961 B7
4000 WVCY 84128 2067 B1
Sage Springs Cir
10200 SJDN 84095 2280 D3
Sage View Ct
- SJDN 84095 2280 D3
Sage Vista Dr
10300 CRHL 84062 2605 C1
Sage Vista Wy
- SJDN 84095 2280 C3
Sage Willow Dr
3800 SJDN 84095 2280 D4
Sagewood Av
500 PRVO 84604 2928 D3
Sage Wood Dr
6200 SmtC 84098 1971 E2
Sagewood Dr
5700 MRRY 84107 2070 C6
Sagewood Rd
1600 PRVO 84604 2928 D3
Sagramore St
600 NSLK 84054 1653 B5
Saguaro Dr
4800 WJDN 84084 2174 B1
5000 WJDN 84084 2173 E1
Sahalee
10500 CRHL 84062 2605 B1
Sahara Dr
2000 HLDY 84124 2071 D1
St. Andrews Ct
10 PKCY 84060 2078 D1
St. Andrews Dr
700 SRCS 84075 1226 B6
4400 SJDN 84095 2280 A2
N St. Andrews Dr
1600 FMTN 84025 1346 A5
W St. Andrews Dr
1200 FMTN 84025 1346 D4
St. Benedicts Wy
5400 WSTR 84405 1172 E4
St. Charles Pl
1600 SLkC 84121 2071 C5
St. Francis Cir
3900 HLDY 84124 1965 D7
St. George Cir
15000 DRPR 84020 2495 D1
St. Gregory Dr
1700 LYTN 84041 1282 B1
St. Ives Ln
7900 WJDN 84088 2174 E4
St. James Pl
1600 SLkC 84121 2071 C6
St. John St
700 SLCY 84104 1856 B6
St. Marks Ct
1500 SLkC 84124 1965 C7
St. Marys Cir
2900 SLCY 84108 1860 B6
St. Marys Dr
1900 SLCY 84108 1859 D7
2300 SLCY 84108 1860 A7
W St. Marys Dr
100 MDVL 84047 2176 C5
St. Mary's Wy
2600 SLCY 84108 1860 A6
St. Moritz Cir
10 SmtC 84098 1864 C6
2200 SNDY 84093 2177 E6
St. Moritz Rd
200 WshC 84049 2291 C6
St. Moritz Ter
10 SmtC 84098 1864 C7
St. Moritz Wy
10 SmtC 84098 1864 C6
St. Moritz Strasse
100 SmtC 84098 1864 C7
St. Tropez Cove
8200 CDHT 84093 2178 A6
Sako Wy
7800 SNDY 84070 2176 E4
Sakura Ct
4800 WJDN 84084 2174 A1
Salem Av
5800 SLkC 84118 2068 B6
Salem Cir
5900 SLkC 84118 2068 B6
Salem Ct
4500 SLkC 84118 2068 B6
E Salem Canal Rd
10 SALM 84653 3356 B4
800 UthC 84653 3356 B4
S Salem Canal Rd
10 SALM 84653 3356 A5
300 SALM 84653 3355 E6
1400 SALM 84651 3355 E6
1400 UthC 84651 3355 E6
W Salem Canal Rd
1100 PYSN 84651 3355 C6
1100 UthC 84651 3355 C6
E Salem Hills Cir
400 EKMT 84651 3463 A2
E Salem Hills Dr
10 EKMT 84651 3462 E3
10 EKMT 84651 3463 A3
N Salem Hills Dr
10 EKMT 84651 3463 A1
S Salem Hills Dr
10 EKMT 84651 3463 A2
W Salem Hills Dr
10 EKMT 84651 3462 E3
S Salem Lake Dr
300 SALM 84653 3356 A4
W Salem Lake Dr
- SALM 84653 3356 A4
Salerno St
5500 HRMN 84065 2385 D2
Salinas Dr
3600 RIVN 84065 2386 D1
Salisbury Ct
8100 SNDY 84094 2177 A5
Salish Cir
4600 RIVN 84065 2386 A3
Salix Cir
6800 WJDN 84084 2173 E2
Sallie Av
300 SLCY 84103 1858 D1
Sallybrooke Wy
4800 WJDN 84088 2174 A6
Salt Creek Rd
- HYVL 84314 646 B1
N Salt Creek Rd
- HYVL 84314 646 B2
Salt Grass Rd
3700 WVCY 84119 1963 E7
Salt Lick Cir
3700 SLkC 84044 1960 D7
Salvia Pl
1400 WVCY 84119 1963 D5
Salz Wy
12900 DRPR 84020 2389 C3
Sam Giles Rd
- OGDN 84404 1056 C5
Sammy Cir
1100 RIVN 84065 2387 D2
Sam Oliver St
5800 MRRY 84107 2070 C6
Sample Cove
2000 CDHT 84093 2177 E4
Sampson Av
10 PKCY 84060 2078 E7
Sampson Ct
4800 HILD 84003 2498 A6
Sampson Dr
11100 HILD 84003 2498 A7
Sam's Blvd
4000 SLkC 84118 2068 C4
Samson Cir
12100 DRPR 84020 2388 A1
Samuel Cir
5200 TYVL 84118 2069 B4
Samuel Ct
5200 TYVL 84118 2069 B4
Samuel Dr
2200 TYVL 84118 2069 B5
Samuel Colt Ct
2200 PKCY 84060 2078 E3
San Andreas Ct
10 WJDN 84088 2175 B5
San Carlos Dr
3400 WVCY 84119 2068 D2
San Carlos Pl
4400 WVCY 84119 2068 D2
Sanctuary Cir
1800 WJDN 84084 2175 C4
Sandalwood Cir
4700 TYVL 84118 2069 B3
E Sandalwood Dr
1500 SWBR 84405 1229 C2
Sandbar Wy
- SPFK 84660 3249 B5
Sandcrest Cir
11200 SNDY 84094 2283 A5
Sandcrest Dr
900 SNDY 84094 2283 A5
Sand Dollar Dr
700 SNDY 84094 2282 E3
Sand Dune Dr
- SJDN 84095 2280 D4
Sanders Cir
11600 SNDY 84092 2283 B6
Sanders Ln
200 KYVL 84037 1283 D7
200 KYVL 84037 1345 D1
Sanders Rd
1100 SNDY 84094 2283 B6
1300 SNDY 84092 2283 B6
Sanders Hill Cir
1200 SNDY 84094 2283 B6
Sand Hill Cir
3700 SJDN 84095 2280 D3
Sandhill Ct
- LEHI 84043 2710 D2
5200 SmtC 84098 1972 B4
Sandhill Rd
1200 OREM 84058 2927 B2
1800 PRVO 84058 2927 B2
Sandhurst Dr
800 SLCY 84103 1754 C7
Sandi Dr
1200 LYTN 84041 1281 E2
Sandia Hills Dr
800 SNDY 84094 2177 A6
Sandlewood Dr
4000 CRHL 84062 2605 B2
Sandlily Cir
6800 WJDN 84084 2173 E2
Sandpiper Cir
1400 SLkC 84117 2071 C4
Sandpiper Dr
1300 SLkC 84117 2071 B4
Sandpiper Wy
1300 SLkC 84117 2071 C4
Sand Pointe Ln
2200 SJDN 84095 2281 B6
Sandra Cir
1200 MRRY 84121 2071 B6
Sandra Wy
7600 MDVL 84047 2176 D4
7700 MDVL 84070 2176 D4
Sandridge Av
100 PKCY 84060 2078 E6
Sandridge Cir
9000 SNDY 84093 2177 A7
Sandridge Dr
9700 SNDY 84092 2283 C2
N Sandrun Rd
100 SLCY 84103 1754 D7
S Sandrun Rd
100 SLCY 84103 1754 D7
Sands Dr
2000 HLDY 84124 2071 D1
Sandstone Cir
700 SNDY 84094 2282 E5
Sandstone Cove
10 PKCY 84060 2078 C1
Sand Trap Cir
4300 SJDN 84095 2280 B2
Sandtrap Cir
1100 NSLK 84054 1653 D7
Sand Trap Ct
9000 SmtC 84098 1865 B3
Sandtrap Ln
1300 FMTN 84025 1346 A6
Sandusky Cir
5900 MRRY 84123 2070 A6
Sandviken Cir
12700 RIVN 84065 2387 A2
Sandwedge Cir
6200 MRRY 84123 2070 A6
Sandwood Dr
9700 SJDN 84095 2280 A2
Sandy Cir
300 SNDY 84070 2282 D2
Sandy Pkwy
600 SNDY 84070 2176 B5
Sandy Creek Cir
9100 WJDN 84088 2175 D7
Sandy Creek Dr
11000 SNDY 84094 2283 A5
Sandy Dunes Cir
700 SNDY 84094 2282 E5
Sandy Dunes Dr
700 SNDY 84094 2282 D5
700 SNDY 84094 2283 A6
Sandy Gulch Cir
800 SNDY 84094 2283 A6
Sandy Gulch Pl
800 SNDY 84094 2283 A6
Sandy Gulch Rd
11100 SNDY 84094 2283 A5
Sandy Heights Dr
7700 SNDY 84047 2176 E4
Sandy Highland Dr
1000 SNDY 84094 2177 A5
Sandy Hills Dr
1300 SNDY 84093 2283 B1

STREET
Block City ZIP Map# Grid

Sandy Hollow Cir
400 SNDY 84047 2176 E4
Sandy Land Ln
300 SNDY 84047 2176 D3
Sandy Marie Wy
8500 MDVL 84047 2176 C6
Sandy Oaks Dr
300 SNDY 84070 2176 E5
9000 SNDY 84094 2177 A7
Sandy Park Cir
300 SNDY 84047 2176 D3
Sandy Park Dr
400 SNDY 84047 2176 E3
Sandy Point Dr
700 SNDY 84094 2282 E4
Sandy Ridge Cir
11200 SNDY 84094 2283 C4
Sandy Ridge Dr
1200 SNDY 84094 2283 B6
Sandy Stone Cir
5600 SJDN 84095 2279 D6
Sandy Woods Cir
7500 SNDY 84047 2176 C3
Sandy Woods Ln
300 SNDY 84047 2176 E3
San Fernando Dr
1100 SLCY 84116 1753 E7
Sanford Dr
5400 MRRY 84123 2070 B5
Sanibel Cove
2600 CDHT 84121 2178 A2
San Jose St
700 OGDN 84401 1115 A5
San Juan Ct
10 WJDN 84088 2175 B5
San Lucas Ct
4600 SLkC 84117 2071 C2
San Marcos Cir
3400 WVCY 84119 1962 D5
San Miguel St
10 WJDN 84088 2175 A6
E San Rafael Av
3800 SLkC 84109 1966 D6
San Rafael Ct
10 WJDN 84088 2175 A6
San Simeon Wy
700 BNFL 84010 1654 A4
Santa Ana
- SNST 84015 1171 C6
Santa Anita Ct
13500 HRMN 84065 2385 C4
Santa Cruz Dr
6900 CDHT 84121 2177 C2
E Santa Fe Dr
10 SGVL 84663 3143 C7
Santa Maria Cir
7200 WJDN 84084 2174 E2
Santa Rita Pl
10 WJDN 84088 2175 A6
Santa Rosa Av
3200 SLkC 84109 1966 C5
Santa Rosa Dr
3400 SLkC 84109 1966 C6
Santa Rosa Pl
10 WJDN 84088 2175 A6
Santa Ynez Cir
1100 SLCY 84104 1857 E6
Santee Cir
900 MRRY 84123 2070 D7
Santex Cir
2700 TYVL 84118 2069 A3
Santiago Ln
1400 CDHT 84121 2177 C2
Saphire Cir
9600 SNDY 84094 2283 B1
Saphire Dr
1000 SNDY 84094 2283 B1
Sapphire Dr
700 LYTN 84041 1282 E3
Sapporo Cir
3400 TYVL 84084 2174 E1
Sara Ln
1000 OGDN 84404 1116 B1
Sarah Cir
1000 OREM 84058 2820 D7
1000 OREM 84058 2927 D1
6200 WVCY 84128 1961 C7
Sarah St
10 PVDN 84332 528 B6
Sarah Jane Cir
5200 SLkC 84118 2067 E5
Sarah Jane Dr
5400 SLkC 84118 2067 E6
Saralee Dr
8500 WJDN 84088 2174 B6
Saratoga Rd
1300 SLkC 84117 2071 B3
N Saratoga Rd
10 LEHI 84043 2602 D7
Saratoga Wy
3300 CRFD 84015 1228 B5
Sarbo St
4700 SLkC 84118 2068 A5
Saris Cir
2700 WVCY 84120 1962 D4
Sarto Av
2400 CDHT 84093 2178 A4
Satori Cir
1100 SLCY 84116 1753 C6
Satsuma
- PVDN 84332 528 B6
N Satsuma Dr
10 PVDN 84332 528 B6
S Satsuma Dr
10 PVDN 84332 528 B6
Saturn Av
3900 HLDY 84124 1966 A7
Saunders St
300 MRRY 84107 2070 D5
Saunton Cir
3900 SRCS 84075 1226 A7
Savannah Cir
3600 WJDN 84084 2174 D1
Savannah Ct
700 SNDY 84094 2283 A4
Savannah Dr
10600 SNDY 84094 2282 E5
10600 SNDY 84094 2283 A4
Savannah Ln
100 HARR 84414 998 D6
Saw Wy
- WJDN 84088 2173 A4
Sawgrass Cir
1800 DRPR 84020 2389 D1
Sawmill
- CRHL 84062 2605 B1
E Sawmill Rd
4300 SmtC 84098 1971 E6
W Sawmill Rd
4400 SmtC 84098 1971 E6
Saw Mill Cove
13400 DRPR 84020 2388 E4
Sawtell Cir
8000 WJDN 84088 2173 E4
Sawtell Wy
5300 WJDN 84088 2173 E4
Sawtooth Cir
6400 TYVL 84084 2174 E1
Sawtooth Oak Dr
8300 WJDN 84088 2173 B5
Saxby Pl
9100 WJDN 84088 2175 A7
Saxon Cir
1500 SGVL 84663 3142 E4
Saxon Brook Rd
700 OGDN 84404 1116 A1
Saxony Cir
4700 SLkC 84117 2071 B3
Saxony Pl
1300 SLkC 84117 2071 B3
Saybrook Ln
3800 WVCY 84128 1961 D7
Scandia Cir
8100 CDHT 84093 2178 B5
Scandia Ct
8100 CDHT 84093 2178 B5
Scandia Wy
2900 CDHT 84093 2178 B5
Scare Crow Ct
11600 SJDN 84095 2280 B6
Scaret West Ln
- OREM 84057 2820 A4
Scarlet Oak Dr
6400 WJDN 84088 2173 B5
Scarsborough Ln
- WJDN 84084 2174 C1
Scarsdale Ct
2600 TYVL 84118 2069 A4
Scenic Cir
2000 SLCY 84108 1966 B2
2000 SLCY 84109 1966 B2
2000 SLkC 84108 1966 B2
4200 BNFL 84010 1653 D7
Scenic Dr
- PTVW 84404 997 E5
200 ALPN 84004 2498 B5
300 SPFK 84660 3249 E5
1900 SLCY 84108 1966 B2
1900 SLCY 84109 1966 B2
E Scenic Dr
600 PRVO 84604 2821 D6
N Scenic Dr
4000 PRVO 84604 2821 D6
Scenic Hills Cir
10 NSLK 84054 1653 C7
Scenic Hills Dr
500 NSLK 84054 1653 C6
Scenic Oaks Cove
2100 SNDY 84092 2283 D5
Scenic Park Cir
5200 SLkC 84118 2067 E6
Scenic Peak Cove
- DRPR 84020 2388 D4
Scenic Ridge Cir
5300 SLkC 84118 2067 E6
Scenic View Dr
200 HYRM 84319 651 D1
Scenicview Dr
200 PRVO 84097 2821 B3
Scera Ln
500 OREM 84097 2820 E6
Schaub Av
800 LOGN 84321 464 A7
800 LOGN 84321 528 A1
Schick Ln
2700 KYVL 84037 1282 D7
2700 KYVL 84037 1344 D1
2800 DvsC 84037 1344 C1
2800 DvsC 84037 1344 C1
Schiess Ct
200 NBLY 84321 591 C5
Schmidt Cir
9300 WJDN 84088 2281 A1
Schneitter Cir
800 MIDW 84049 2396 E1
Schofield Cir
8900 SNDY 84093 2178 B7
E Schoolhouse Dr
10 WDHL 84653 3463 D2
E School House St
10 LNDN 84042 2713 B6
W School House St
10 LNDN 84042 2713 B6
Schoolhouse Wy
- HRCY 84032 2398 B5
- WshC 84032 2398 B5
School Park Rd
- HILD 84003 2604 D3
Schorr Cir
3300 WJDN 84084 2174 E3
Schorr Dr
3400 WJDN 84084 2174 D3
Schuler Av
7000 WVCY 84128 1960 E3
7000 WVCY 84128 1961 A3
Scirlein Dr
700 SNDY 84094 2177 A7
9000 SNDY 84094 2176 E7
Scobey Cir
11200 SNDY 84070 2282 E5
Scone St
10100 SJDN 84095 2280 C3
Scorpio Dr
4000 SLkC 84118 2068 C7
Scotch Pine Ln
3200 WJDN 84088 2174 E6
Scotia Ln
8600 SLkC 84093 2178 A6
Scots Field Ct
1200 MRRY 84123 2069 D6
Scott Av
300 SSLK 84115 1964 D6
500 SSLK 84106 1964 E6
700 SLkC 84106 1964 E6
Scott Av
700 SLkC 84106 1965 A6
Scott Cir
1400 LYTN 84041 1282 C2
3400 SSLK 84115 1964 D6
Scott Ct
3300 SLkC 84106 1964 E5
Scott Ln
2900 WHVN 84401 1114 D5
Scottish Dr
3200 CDHT 84093 2178 C6
Scottsdale Dr
3100 WVCY 84120 1962 C5
Scranton Dr
3700 WJDN 84084 2174 D1
6400 WJDN 84084 2068 C7
Scrub Oak Dr
6700 WJDN 84088 2173 A5
W Seagull Dr
3800 WVCY 84120 2068 C1
Sean Heights Cir
7300 WJDN 84084 2174 A3
Searle Av
900 MRRY 84117 2071 A4
Searle Cir
5100 MRRY 84117 2071 A4
Seasons St
300 KYVL 84037 1345 C2
Seaton Pl
9100 WJDN 84088 2175 A7
Secluded Cir
1500 OGDN 84403 1173 C2
Secluded Oak Cir
6300 MRRY 84121 2071 E5
Second St
3700 SSLK 84115 1964 D7
Secret Rd
- ALTA 84049 2288 B2
Secret Wy
100 LEHI 84043 2603 B3
Secretariat Dr
13800 DRPR 84020 2389 A5
Secretariat Wy
- FMTN 84025 1447 E2
Sedgemoor Ln
7900 WJDN 84088 2174 C4
Sedonia Ct
6600 WJDN 84084 2173 E1
Seemore Dr
200 KYVL 84037 1282 E7
200 KYVL 84037 1344 E1
Segal Cir
3800 WVCY 84120 1962 C4
Segilla
4100 CRHL 84062 2605 B1
Sego Av
400 SLCY 84111 1858 E5
600 SLCY 84102 1858 E5
800 SLCY 84102 1859 A5
Sego Lily Cir
600 NSLK 84054 1754 D1
Sego Lily Dr
- SRSP 84043 2601 D5
E Sego Lily Dr
100 SNDY 84070 2282 D2
800 SLkC 84094 2283 A2
1100 SNDY 84094 2283 A2
1300 SNDY 84092 2283 E3
2300 SNDY 84092 2284 A3
9800 SLkC 84094 2282 E2
9800 SNDY 84094 2282 E2
W Sego Lily Dr
10 SNDY 84070 2282 C2
300 SJDN 84070 2282 C2
300 SJDN 84095 2282 C2
Sego Lily Ln
400 PVDN 84332 528 B7
600 PVDN 84332 592 B1
Segovia Cir
10900 SNDY 84094 2283 A5
Segura Ct
10 PKCY 84060 2078 D2
Selina Ln
400 DRPR 84020 2388 D6
Seminole
10500 CRHL 84062 2605 B1
Seminole Cir
4600 RIVN 84065 2386 B2
Senate Cir
600 SLCY 84104 1857 E5
Senator Cir
1200 WDCR 84087 1653 A1
Senatorial Pl
10100 SJDN 84095 2280 E3
Senda Cir
8500 SNDY 84093 2177 D6
Seneca Dr
1600 ROY 84067 1171 E2
Seneca Rd
4800 WVCY 84120 1962 A7
Senegal Dove Dr
8600 WJDN 84088 2175 C6
Senior Wy
10 SSLK 84115 1964 C2
Senior Band Rd
900 DRPR 84020 2389 A6
Sennie Dr
3800 SLkC 84044 1960 D7
Senoma Dr
6200 HLDY 84121 2071 D7
September Cove
11800 SNDY 84092 2283 E7
September Morn Cir
1200 TYVL 84123 2069 C4
September Morn Ln
5100 TYVL 84123 2069 D4
Sequioa Dr
1300 SNST 84015 1227 C2
Sequoia Av
2900 SLkC 84109 1966 D5
Sequoia Cir
100 ALPN 84004 2497 D5
Sequoia Tree Ln
7800 SNDY 84094 2177 C3
Seraphine Cove
2600 CDHT 84121 2178 A1
Serena Cir
5300 WVCY 84120 1961 E6
Serengeti Dr
4800 RIVN 84065 2386 A2
Serenity Oak Ln
400 SLkC 84107 2070 A1
Serenity View Dr
3900 WJDN 84084 2174 C1
Sereno Cir
1300 BNFL 84010 1552 A5
Sergeant Dr
1800 SLCY 84116 1753 C6
Serpentine Cir
10300 SLkC 84094 2283 B3
Serpentine Wy
800 SLkC 84094 2283 A2
1100 SNDY 84094 2283 A2
Service Rd
- SSLK 84119 1964 A5
1400 DvsC 84056 1228 A1
Service Wy
1100 DvsC 84056 1227 D2
1100 SNST 84056 1227 D2
Sesame Cir
2800 TYVL 84118 2069 A6
Sesame St
5800 TYVL 84118 2069 A6
Set Ct
1100 FMTN 84025 1345 E6
Set Point Cir
8200 SLkC 84093 2177 E5
Settlement Cir
10 MDVL 84047 2176 C6
Settlement Dr
1300 SmtC 84098 1971 E6
S Settlement Dr
900 WDHL 84653 3463 D3
Settlers Wy
1400 TYVL 84123 2069 D3
Settlers Bend Rd
2500 SJDN 84095 2281 A3
Settlers Point Dr
5900 WVCY 84128 1961 B5
Seven Oaks Ln
1700 DRPR 84020 2496 C1
1700 OGDN 84403 1173 D2
1800 DRPR 84020 2389 D7
N Seven Peaks Blvd
100 PRVO 84606 2928 E6
Seven Springs Cir
10400 SNDY 84092 2284 C3
Seven Springs Dr
3100 SLkC 84092 2284 C4
3100 SNDY 84092 2284 C4
Severn Cir
1900 HLDY 84124 2071 D1
4000 SJDN 84095 2280 C1
Severn Dr
1700 HLDY 84124 2071 D1
Seville Rd
6300 MRRY 84121 2071 E5
Seville Wy
1300 BNFL 84010 1552 B7
Seward Av
600 SLCY 84116 1858 A2
Sextant Ln
7000 WJDN 84084 2175 D2
Seychelles Ct
2600 CDHT 84121 2178 A1
Seymore Dr
600 ANFK 84003 2711 E1
Shad Cir
9100 SNDY 84093 2177 E7
Shad Ln
9100 SNDY 84093 2177 E7
9200 SNDY 84093 2283 E1
Shadberry Cir
5500 WJDN 84084 2173 D1
Shading Ln
700 DRPR 84020 2282 E7
700 DRPR 84020 2283 A7
S Shadow Ln
10 WDHL 84653 3356 C7
Shadow Breeze Rd
- KYVL 84037 1344 E1
- KYVL 84037 1345 A1
Shadowbrook Cir
3100 PRVO 84604 2928 C1
Shadow Brook Ct
9400 SJDN 84095 2281 A1
Shadowbrook Dr
3200 PRVO 84604 2821 D7
3200 PRVO 84604 2928 B2
E Shadowbrook Ln
10 KYVL 84037 1345 D4
Shadow Cove
1600 CDHT 84121 2177 C2
Shadow Gate Cir
1200 SNDY 84094 2283 B7
Shadow Grove Ct
14700 DRPR 84020 2389 D7
Shadowlands Ln
13000 DRPR 84020 2389 C3
Shadow Mountain Cir
900 CTRV 84014 1551 E2
E Shadow Mountain Cir
2100 OGDN 84403 1173 E5
Shadow Mountain Dr
10 LOGN 84321 528 C3
Shadow Mountain Ln
- SmtC 84098 1971 E6
5500 OGDN 84403 1173 E5
5600 WbrC 84403 1173 E5
13500 DRPR 84020 2388 E5
Shadow Oak Ln
1800 SNDY 84092 2283 D7
Shadow Park Dr
2800 WVCY 84119 2069 A2
Shadow Ridge Cir
1700 OGDN 84403 1173 D3
Shadow Ridge Dr
1200 CDHT 84093 2177 B2
Shadowridge Dr
1000 KYVL 84037 1345 D4
Shadow Ridge Rd
10 PKCY 84060 2078 D5
Shadow Valley Dr
1400 OGDN 84403 1173 C4
Shadow Wood Cir
2300 HLDY 84117 2071 E3
2400 HLDY 84117 2072 A3
Shadowwood Dr
700 MRRY 84123 2070 A5
Shadow Wood Ln
10 SNDY 84092 2284 A5
Shady Ct
3300 SLkC 84106 1965 A5
Shady Ln
- WbrC 84310 1001 B6
1000 SOGN 84403 1173 B4
N Shady Ln
10 SALM 84653 3356 C3
S Shady Ln
10 SALM 84653 3356 C3
Shady Acres Ct
11800 RIVN 84065 2281 A7
Shady Bend Ln
- LEHI 84043 2495 C5
Shadybrook Ln
10 SGVL 84663 3036 B6
2700 HLDY 84121 2072 A6
Shady Creek Ln
10 FMTN 84025 1448 D4
Shady Creek Pl
700 SLkC 84106 1965 A6
3300 SLkC 84106 1964 D5
Shady Dell Dr
10800 SNDY 84094 2283 B5
Shady Farm Ln
5600 MRRY 84107 2070 E5
Shady Glen Ln
9800 SJDN 84095 2281 D2
Shady Grove Cir
6300 MRRY 84121 2071 D7
Shadyhollow Ct
- LEHI 84043 2495 C6
Shady Hollow Ln
- LEHI 84043 2495 C5
Shadyhollow Lp
- LEHI 84043 2495 C6
Shady Lake Dr
700 SLkC 84106 1964 D5
700 SLkC 84106 1965 A6
E Shady Ln Wy
1300 FTHT 84037 1346 B3
Shady Maple Cove
1300 MRRY 84117 2071 B5
Shady Meadow Dr
8700 SNDY 84093 2177 D7
Shady Oak Ln
11700 SNDY 84092 2283 E7
Shady Red Ct
- WVCY 84119 1963 D3
Shady Ridge Ct
3500 RIVN 84065 2280 D7
Shady River Wy
700 TYVL 84123 2070 A1
W Shady River Wy
4200 TYVL 84123 2070 A1
Shady Stone Dr
5700 SJDN 84095 2279 D6
Shady Tree Ct
700 SLkC 84106 1964 D5
700 SLkC 84106 1965 A6
Shadyvale Ln
3500 WVCY 84120 1962 B6
Shady View Cir
- LEHI 84043 2495 C6
Shady View Ln
- LEHI 84043 2495 C5
Shady Willow Cir
9000 SNDY 84093 2177 C7
Shadywood Wy
3000 WVCY 84119 1963 D4
Shady Woods Cir
7200 MDVL 84047 2176 E3
Shafer Ln
3500 WVCY 84119 1963 C6
Shaggy Peak Cir
5100 RIVN 84065 2385 E3
Shaggy Peak Dr
- RIVN 84065 2386 A4
5100 RIVN 84065 2385 E5
5300 HRMN 84065 2385 E5
Shakespeare Pl
2900 SLCY 84108 1860 B6
Shakestone Dr
4700 TYVL 84118 2069 A3
Shalee St
5100 SLkC 84118 2067 E4
Shalimar St
3600 WVCY 84128 1961 A6
Shalisan Cir
1500 SNDY 84092 2283 C2
Shalise Cir
3300 WVCY 84120 1962 A6
Shallow Creek Rd
- WJDN 84088 2173 D6
Shamrock Cir
2400 ROY 84067 1171 C3
5200 SLkC 84118 2067 E5
Shamrock Dr
300 MRRY 84107 2070 D2
500 BMCY 84302 767 A3
2600 OGDN 84401 1116 D4
2700 OGDN 84403 1116 D5
Shane Cir
1400 SNDY 84092 2389 C1
Shangri Ln
5800 HLDY 84121 2071 E6
Shangrila Cir
8200 SNDY 84094 2177 B5
Shanna St
4100 SLkC 84124 2072 B1
Shannel Cir
12000 RIVN 84065 2281 B7
12000 RIVN 84065 2387 B1
Shannon Cir
300 BMCY 84302 827 E2
1700 SLCY 84116 1857 C1
Shannon Dr
100 FMTN 84025 1346 C6
Shannon Rd
700 KYVL 84037 1283 E6
Shannon St
1300 SLCY 84105 1859 C7
Sharene Cir
7700 MDVL 84047 2176 D4
Shari Cir
200 BNFL 84010 1552 B7
200 BNFL 84010 1654 B1
Sharlyn Hill Cir
5100 WJDN 84084 2173 D2
Sharolyn Ln
9700 SJDN 84095 2280 A2
Sharon Cir
3300 SLkC 84044 1960 C5
5900 WbrC 84403 1174 A6
Sharon Dr
7700 SLkC 84044 1960 C5
Sharon Ln
300 MIDW 84049 2397 A2
Sharon St
5800 ROY 84067 1171 B5
Sharp Cir
2100 SLCY 84104 1963 D2
Sharp Mountain Dr
1000 OGDN 84404 1057 B2
Sharron Cir
5800 TYVL 84118 2069 A6
Sharron Ct
1000 OGDN 84404 1057 B4
Sharron Dr
2300 TYVL 84118 2069 A6
Shashas Wy
1100 RIVN 84065 2387 E2
Shasta Cir
3700 RIVN 84065 2280 D7
Shatton Ln
8200 WJDN 84088 2175 D5
Shauhna Ln
13300 HRMN 84065 2385 D4
Shawnee Av
5000 OGDN 84403 1173 C3
Shawnee Dr
12800 RIVN 84065 2386 B3
Shay Ln
1800 SWBR 84405 1229 D2
S Shayda Cir
200 EKMT 84651 3463 A2
Shayla Dr
3000 WJDN 84088 2174 E4
Shayn Hill Dr
4800 WJDN 84084 2174 A2
Shea Dr
5400 SLCY 84104 1855 E5
Sheen Rd
10 SALM 84653 3355 E3
Sheffield Cross
- PRVO 84097 2821 B6
Sheffield Dr
400 PRVO 84097 2821 B6
Sheffield Wy
8800 SNDY 84093 2177 E7
Sheila Cir
- KYVL 84037 1345 D3
Shelba Ct
8300 SNDY 84070 2176 D5
Shelbourne Ln
800 TYVL 84123 2070 A3
Shelbrooke Dr
1300 SJDN 84095 2281 D5
Shelbrooke Ln
1300 SJDN 84095 2281 C5
Shelbrooke Cove
1300 SJDN 84095 2281 D5
Shelby Ct
3200 CDHT 84121 2178 D2
Shelley Av
10 SSLK 84115 1964 C4
1400 WVCY 84119 1963 C4
Shelly Av
600 ANFK 84003 2604 E7
Shelly Louise Dr
100 SNDY 84070 2282 D3
Shellywood Cir
9400 SJDN 84095 2281 D1
Shelmerdine Ct
300 SLCY 84111 1858 D4
1700 SLCY 84115 1964 D1
Shelter Cove
4000 LEHI 84043 2495 B7
Shelton Av
10 LEHI 84043 2603 C4
Shelton Dr
- CchC 84328 711 A3
Shelwood Cir
10900 SJDN 84095 2281 D5
Shenandoah Cir
1500 TYVL 84123 2069 C7
4200 DvsC 84056 1228 A4
Shenandoah Park Av
6200 MRRY 84121 2071 C7
Shepard Ln
10 FMTN 84025 1346 A6
1300 FMTN 84025 1345 E6
2900 WVCY 84120 1962 A5
Shepard Ln SR-106
10 FMTN 84025 1346 B6
E Shepard Ln
10 KYVL 84037 1345 D6
400 FMTN 84025 1345 D6
400 FMTN 84037 1345 D6
W Shepard Ln
10 KYVL 84037 1345 C5
600 FMTN 84025 1346 B6
W Shepard Ln SR-106
600 FMTN 84025 1346 B6
Shepard Creek Pkwy
800 FMTN 84025 1346 A6
Shepard Ridge Rd
300 FMTN 84025 1346 B5
Shepherd Wy
300 SmtC 84098 1866 D6
Sheraton Cir
700 SNDY 84094 2282 E4
700 SNDY 84094 2283 A4
Sheri
2800 BNFL 84010 1653 E5
Sheri Cir
1200 BMCY 84302 767 B5
Sheri Wy
3900 WVCY 84120 1962 A7
4000 WVCY 84120 2068 A1
Sheridan
10700 CRHL 84062 2605 B1
Sheridan Cir
400 CTRV 84014 1551 E4
Sheridan Dr
1200 OGDN 84404 1057 B5
Sheridan Rd
1900 SLCY 84108 1859 D7
2300 SLCY 84108 1860 A7
Sheringham Ct
700 FMTN 84025 1346 B5
Sherington Dr
3600 WVCY 84120 1961 E6
Sherleen Cir
1500 SLkC 84124 2071 C1
Sherlene Cir
3600 WVCY 84120 2068 D1
Sherm Cir
4200 WVCY 84120 2068 B1
Sherma Dr
1100 LYTN 84041 1282 B2
Sherman Av
300 SLCY 84115 1858 D7
500 SLCY 84105 1858 E7
800 SLCY 84105 1859 A7
2100 SLCY 84108 1859 E7
Sherwood
4100 CRHL 84062 2605 B1
Sherwood Av
400 PVDN 84332 528 C7
Sherwood Cir
3000 SLCY 84108 1860 B7
7200 WJDN 84084 2175 C3
Sherwood Dr
400 LYTN 84041 1283 A3
700 KYVL 84037 1283 E6
1000 KYVL 84037 1284 A5
1000 OGDN 84404 1057 B5
2500 SLCY 84108 1860 B7
3800 PRVO 84604 2821 E6
Sherwood Ln
- OREM 84057 2820 A4
Shetland Cir
10000 SJDN 84095 2280 C3
Shetland Dr
2600 WVCY 84128 1960 E3
Shetland Ln
900 FMTN 84025 1346 A7
Shettleston Cir
9600 SJDN 84095 2280 C1
Sheva Cir
7900 SLkC 84044 1960 C3
Shields Ln
900 SJDN 84095 2281 E2
Shilling Av
10800 SJDN 84095 2282 B5
Shiloh Wy
600 MRRY 84107 2070 E6
700 MRRY 84107 2071 A7
Shiloh Park Ln
4500 SLkC 84117 2071 C2
Shiloh Rim Dr
- SLkC 84118 2068 A3
Shingle Oak Ct
6100 WJDN 84088 2173 C5
Shinnecock
4000 CRHL 84062 2605 B1
Shire Cir
3700 TYVL 84118 2068 D5
Shirecliff Rd
900 SLCY 84108 1859 E6
Shirl St
6000 TYVL 84123 2069 D7
Shirley Ln
4200 SLkC 84124 2072 A1
Shirley Rae Dr
700 FMTN 84025 1448 A3
700 FMTN 84087 1448 A3
Shooting Star Av
4800 WJDN 84084 2174 A1
S Shore Dr
1500 SmtC 84098 1971 E5
Shoreline Cir
- DvsC 84037 1230 B5
- LYTN 84040 1230 B5
Shoreline Dr
- HILD 84003 2498 C7
2900 WVCY 84120 1962 A5
Short Ct
- DRPR 84020 2389 C2
Short Hills Dr
8000 CDHT 84121 2178 C5
Short Iron Cir
6200 MRRY 84123 2070 A6
Short Leaf Dr
4300 WJDN 84088 2174 B6
Short Line Av
500 SLCY 84116 1858 B2
Short Line Rd
1600 PKCY 84060 2078 D4
Shoshone Av
1300 SLkC 84092 2283 B1
Shoshone Cir
5300 OGDN 84403 1173 D4
9500 SLkC 84092 2283 C1
Shoshone Ct
9500 SLkC 84092 2283 C1
Shoshone Dr
1600 OGDN 84403 1173 D4
Shoshone Lake Dr
4100 WJDN 84088 2174 C7
Shotgun Cir
3600 SLkC 84044 1960 C7
Showcase Ln
7800 SNDY 84094 2177 B4
Shuler Ln
1700 EKMT 84651 3462 D1
1700 PYSN 84651 3462 D1
N Shuler Ln
500 EKMT 84651 3462 D1
Shulsen Ln
8300 WJDN 84088 2175 C6
Shumard Oak Dr
6700 WJDN 84088 2173 A5
Shupe Ln
400 OGDN 84401 1115 E2
Sid Cir
9400 SJDN 84095 2280 B1
Sid Dr
4300 SJDN 84095 2280 B1
Sider Dr
500 NSLK 84054 1653 B6
Sidewinder Cir
4900 RIVN 84065 2386 A2
Sidewinder Dr
1700 PKCY 84060 2078 E3
2500 PKCY 84060 2079 A3
Sidney Av
1900 BNFL 84010 1653 D3
Sidney Cir
7200 SLkC 84044 1960 E5
Sidney Wy
3300 SLkC 84044 1960 E6
Siena Cir
1600 SLCY 84116 1753 C7
Siena Dr
200 PTGV 84062 2605 D7

Salt Lake City Street Index

STREET
Block City ZIP Map# Grid

Sienna Ct
- TYVL 84123 2069 E3
Sienna Ln
- CTRV 84014 1551 D4
Sienna Wy
1100 TYVL 84123 2069 D2
Sienna Dune Dr
10700 SJDN 84095 2280 D4
Sierra Av
200 ALPN 84004 2498 A5
Sierra Cir
600 ALPN 84004 2498 A6
Sierra Dr
2300 WbrC 84310 1002 A6
Sierra Ln
500 PTGV 84062 2712 E4
Sierra Wy
1100 SLkC 84106 1965 B6
Sierra Bonita Ct
- MPTN 84664 3144 B7
Sierra Dawn
1100 WVCY 84119 1963 E6
Sierra Glow Ln
13900 HRMN 84065 2385 E5
Sierra Grande Cir
2900 TYVL 84118 2069 A6
Sierra Grande Ct
2900 TYVL 84118 2069 A6
Sierra Grande Dr
5600 TYVL 84118 2069 A7
Sierra Oaks Dr
6500 WJDN 84088 2173 B5
Sierra Park Cir
2700 SLCY 84106 1965 A4
Sierra Point Pl
2900 SLkC 84109 1965 E4
Sierra Ridge Ct
2000 SLkC 84109 1965 D4
Sierra Rose Dr
5400 HRMN 84065 2385 E7
Sierra View Cir
2000 SLkC 84109 1965 E4
Sierra View Dr
- MPTN 84664 3251 B1
Sierra Vista
1100 WVCY 84119 1963 E6
Siesta Dr
1200 CDHT 84093 2177 B3
Siesta Hills Ct
7500 CDHT 84093 2177 B3
Siggard Dr
1500 SLkC 84106 1965 C6
1900 SLkC 84109 1965 C6
Signal Hl
1500 FTHT 84037 1346 B3
Signal Point Cir
2200 SLCY 84109 1966 B3
Signe Ln
4600 OGDN 84403 1173 C2
Signora Dr
900 SLCY 84116 1857 E1
900 SLCY 84116 1858 A1
Sigsbee Av
1400 SLCY 84103 1859 C3
Silcox Dr
- RIVN 84065 2387 D2
Silent Rain Dr
4400 SJDN 84095 2280 B6
Silica Dr
900 SLkC 84094 2283 A2
Silk Tree Ct
1300 SJDN 84095 2281 D4
Silkwood Ct
15100 DRPR 84020 2496 D1
Sills Ln
10 LYTN 84041 1282 E5
Silo Dr
5300 WJDN 84088 2173 E5
W Silver Av
100 SSLK 84115 1964 C6
Silver Cir
300 ALPN 84004 2498 A5
7400 WJDN 84084 2175 B3
Silver Ln
400 ALPN 84004 2498 A5
Silverado Dr
2000 SGVL 84663 3143 D6
3600 TYVL 84118 2068 D5
5100 WbrC 84310 1001 E2
Silver Bell St
6300 MRRY 84107 2071 A7
Silverbrook Ct
- LEHI 84043 2495 C5
Silver Buckle Wy
11300 SNDY 84092 2283 D4
Silver Charm Ln
11300 SNDY 84092 2283 D4
Silver Cloud Ct
2500 PKCY 84060 2079 A1
Silver Cloud Dr
2400 PKCY 84060 2078 E1
2400 PKCY 84060 2079 A1
Silver Creek Dr
2400 RIVN 84065 2387 A3
6300 SmtC 84098 1973 A2
W Silvercreek Dr
1300 LYTN 84041 1344 C1
Silver Creek Rd
7100 SmtC 84098 1972 D1
8000 SmtC 84098 1867 A4
8800 SmtC 84098 1866 E4
Silvercrest Dr
1300 SNDY 84093 2283 B1
Silver Dollar Dr
- PKCY 84060 2184 E1
Silver Fork Dr
- SLkC 84098 2182 C1
7500 CDHT 84121 2178 B3
Silver Fox Cir
100 PVDN 84332 528 B7
Silver Fox Dr
4700 SLkC 84118 2068 A6
Silverglen Cir
3500 TYVL 84118 2068 D6
Silver Hawk Dr
3000 HLDY 84121 2072 B6
Silver Hills Cir
11200 SNDY 84094 2283 B5
Silver King Cir
7300 CDHT 84121 2178 D3
Silver King Dr
400 PKCY 84060 2078 C4
Silver Lake Dr
3000 CDHT 84121 2178 B4
5700 PKCY 84060 2184 E1
5900 PKCY 84060 2078 E7
5900 PKCY 84060 2079 A7
6400 PKCY 84060 2185 A1
8800 CRHL 84062 2605 D5
Silverleaf Cir
6800 WJDN 84084 2173 E1
Silver Leaf Dr
- MPTN 84664 3250 D1
300 ALPN 84004 2498 A5
Silver Maple Cir
3600 SLkC 84106 1964 E7
Silver Maple Ct
- PYSN 84651 3461 D1
Silver Meadow Wy
2300 WJDN 84088 2175 B4
Silver Meadows Dr
1400 SmtC 84098 1971 E5
Silver Medal Dr
3400 TYVL 84084 2068 E7
6400 TYVL 84084 2174 E1
Silver Mesa Cir
1100 SNDY 84094 2283 B5
Silver Mountain Dr
10400 SLkC 84094 2283 A4
10400 SNDY 84094 2283 A4
Silver Nugget Ct
1800 SJDN 84095 2281 C3
Silver Pine Ct
1800 WJDN 84088 2174 A7
Silverpoint Cir
15300 BFDL 84065 2494 B2
Silverpoint Wy
2200 BFDL 84065 2494 B2
Silver Queen Cir
11100 SNDY 84094 2283 B5
Silver Queen Ct
10 PKCY 84060 2078 B3
Silver Reef Ct
12000 HRMN 84065 2386 B1
Silver Ridge Dr
11100 SNDY 84094 2283 B6
Silver River Cove
1000 RIVN 84065 2281 E7
Silver Rose Cir
5700 HRMN 84065 2385 D6
Silver Saddle Wy
5800 HRMN 84065 2385 C5
Silver Sage Cir
4200 UthC 84004 2498 B1
Silver Sage Dr
700 SmtC 84098 1972 E2
700 SNDY 84094 2282 E4
700 SNDY 84094 2283 A4
Silver Shadow Dr
600 MRRY 84107 2070 E7
700 MRRY 84107 2071 A7
Silver Shine Ct
10100 SJDN 84095 2281 C3
Silversmith Cir
11100 SNDY 84094 2283 D4
Silversmith Dr
1100 SNDY 84094 2283 B5
Silver Spot Ct
5300 RIVN 84065 2385 E5
Silver Spring Cir
9400 SJDN 84095 2281 C1
Silver Springs Dr
1600 SmtC 84098 1971 E4
W Silver Springs Dr
1500 SmtC 84098 1971 E5
Silver Spur Cir
3800 SmtC 84098 1864 E4
3800 SmtC 84098 1865 A4
Silver Spur Ln
11700 DRPR 84020 2282 D7
Silver Spur Rd
8600 SmtC 84098 1865 A4
8700 SmtC 84098 1864 E4
Silver Spur Wy
- FMTN 84025 1447 D1
Silver Star Dr
200 SLCY 84116 1857 C2
Silverstone Cir
2100 SNDY 84093 2177 B7
Silverstone Wy
8800 SNDY 84093 2177 B7
Silver Streak Dr
1900 SJDN 84095 2281 C2
Silver Summit Ct
4300 RIVN 84065 2280 B7
Silver Summit Pkwy
5800 SmtC 84098 1972 E3
5800 SmtC 84098 1973 A3
Silvertip Dr
4800 SLkC 84118 2068 A5
5300 SLkC 84118 2067 E5
Silverton Cir
1800 WJDN 84084 2175 C2
Silver Trace Cir
11800 HRMN 84065 2280 A7
Silver Tree Cir
2100 RIVN 84065 2387 B1
Silver Willow Cir
10200 SNDY 84070 2282 D3
Silver Willow Dr
100 SNDY 84070 2282 D3
Silver Wolf Run
2900 PNCY 84404 997 A7
3300 PNCY 84404 996 D7
Silver Wolf Wy
11800 RIVN 84065 2281 A7
12000 RIVN 84065 2387 A2
Silvery Creek Cove
- RIVN 84065 2280 C7
Simmental Dr
4700 TYVL 84123 2069 D3
Simondi Av
800 SLCY 84116 1858 A2
1100 SLCY 84116 1857 E2
Simoron Dr
400 OGDN 84404 1057 C7
Simplicity Pl
13500 HRMN 84065 2385 C4
Simpson Av
600 SLCY 84106 1964 E2
900 SLCY 84106 1965 A2
2400 SLCY 84109 1966 A2
Singing Wood Ct
1900 WJDN 84084 2175 C1
Single Jack Cir
10600 SJDN 84095 2281 B4
Single Jack Ct
10 PKCY 84060 2078 C3
Singletree Ln
2500 SJDN 84095 2281 A4
Sioux Cir
5000 OGDN 84403 1173 D3
Sir Andrew Wy
1900 SLCY 84116 1753 B7
Sir Anthony Cir E
500 SLCY 84116 1857 C1
Sir Anthony Cir W
500 SLCY 84116 1857 C1
Sir Anthony Dr
600 SLCY 84116 1857 C1
Sir Barton Ln
11000 SJDN 84095 2281 B5
Sir Charles Dr
1800 SLCY 84116 1753 B7
Sir James Cir
1800 SLCY 84116 1857 B3
Sir James Dr
1800 SLCY 84116 1857 B1
Sir James Wy
1700 SLCY 84116 1857 B3
Sir Jeffery Dr
1800 SLCY 84116 1857 C1
Sir Jeffrey Cir
1800 SLCY 84116 1857 B3
Sir Jeffrey Wy
1700 SLCY 84116 1857 B3
Sir Joseph Wy
900 SLCY 84116 1753 B7
Sir Kay Wy
300 NSLK 84054 1653 A4
Sir Michael Dr
500 SLCY 84116 1857 B1
800 SLCY 84116 1753 B7
Sirmingo Wy
1000 RIVN 84065 2281 E7
Sir Patrick Dr
700 SLCY 84116 1753 B7
700 SLCY 84116 1857 B3
Sir Philip Dr
700 SLCY 84116 1857 B3
1200 SLCY 84116 1753 B6
Sir Robert Dr
1900 SLCY 84116 1857 B1
Sir Timothy Av
1800 SLCY 84116 1753 B7
Sitka Dr
2100 SNDY 84093 2177 E6
Sitzmark Dr
1700 SLkC 84092 2283 C1
Six Shooter Cir
8500 SNDY 84093 2177 E6
Skeeswood Cir
5300 TYVL 84118 2068 C5
Skeeswood Dr
5200 TYVL 84118 2068 D4
Skipperling Ct
- RIVN 84065 2386 A4
Skipperling Ln
- RIVN 84065 2386 B4
Skipton
- NSLK 84054 1652 C5
Ski View Dr
1700 SNDY 84092 2283 C1
Skye Dr
3800 SJDN 84095 2280 C2
Skye Park Rd
9500 SJDN 84095 2280 A2
Sky Haven Cir
7000 SLkC 84065 2385 A6
Skyhaven Cove
1000 SWBR 84405 1229 B1
S Skylake Dr
600 WDHL 84653 3463 E3
Skylark Dr
600 SPFK 84660 3249 E5
Skylark Ln
500 SNDY 84047 2176 E3
Skyler Dr
1000 DRPR 84020 2389 A6
Skyline Cir
2400 SLCY 84108 1860 A7
Skyline Dr
- DvsC 84010 1346 E6
- DvsC 84010 1552 C4
- DvsC 84025 1346 D6
- DvsC 84037 1346 E5
- FMTN 84010 1346 D6
- FMTN 84025 1346 D6
- WbrC 84403 1173 E4
10 BMCY 84302 827 E2
10 HRCY 84032 2398 D7
100 BMCY 84302 828 A2
200 BNFL 84010 1552 B7
500 PTVW 84414 998 C2
1500 SOGN 84405 1173 C6
1600 OREM 84097 2714 A7
1600 OREM 84097 2821 A1
1700 NHLN 84341 464 C6
1700 SOGN 84403 1173 C6
1900 LNDN 84042 2714 A7
2400 SLCY 84108 1860 A7
2500 SLCY 84108 1966 A1
3600 OGDN 84403 1116 C7
4600 OGDN 84403 1173 D3
E Skyline Dr
1400 SOGN 84405 1173 C6
1400 WbrC 84405 1173 C6
N Skyline Dr
6200 HLID 84003 2497 B6
S Skyline Dr
6300 HLID 84003 2497 B6
W Skyline Dr
11500 HLID 84003 2497 B6
Skyline Pkwy
3800 OGDN 84403 1116 C7
3800 OGDN 84403 1173 C1
Sky Meadow Dr
- WJDN 84088 2173 D5
Sky Park Dr
2200 WDCR 84087 1652 E4
Sky Pines Ct
2300 HLDY 84117 2071 E2
Skyridge Cir
10 LOGN 84341 463 D7
2800 SLCY 84109 1966 B2
Skyscape Wy
1300 SJDN 84095 2281 D5
Skyview Cir
600 NSLK 84054 1754 C1
3900 SLkC 84124 1965 C7
Sky View Dr
2600 LYTN 84040 1230 A7
Skyview Dr
1300 SLkC 84124 1965 B7
Skyvue Cir
3000 WJDN 84088 2175 A5
3100 WJDN 84088 2174 E5
Slade Pl
400 SLCY 84111 1858 E3
Slalom Wy
3400 TYVL 84084 2174 E1
6600 WJDN 84084 2174 E1
Slant Rd
10 MPTN 84664 3143 D7
10 MPTN 84664 3250 C1
10 UthC 84663 3143 D7
10 UthC 84663 3250 C1
100 MPTN 84663 3250 C1
100 UthC 84664 3250 C1
S Slate Canyon Dr
600 PRVO 84606 2929 A7
600 PRVO 84606 3036 A1
N Slater Av
- OGDN 84404 1056 C5
S Slater Av
- OGDN 84404 1056 C5
Sleepy Hollow Cir
- NHON 84414 998 E7
1900 LYTN 84040 1283 E1
9600 SNDY 84094 2283 B2
Sleepy Hollow Dr
2800 HLDY 84117 2072 B3
Sleepy Hollow Ln
1000 SNDY 84094 2283 B1
Sleepy Hollow Wy
- NHON 84414 998 E7
Sleepy Ridge Dr
- OREM 84058 2819 D7
S Sleepy Ridge Dr
400 OREM 84058 2819 D6
400 VNYD 84058 2819 D6
Slick Rock Cove
4500 HRMN 84065 2280 B7
Smallwood Wy
5700 TYVL 84118 2069 B6
Smart Ln
1000 SNDY 84094 2177 A5
Smeath Av
800 PRVO 84604 2928 E5
Smedley Dr
300 SNST 84015 1227 C2
Smelter St
700 MDVL 84047 2176 A3
Smiley Dr
1500 TYVL 84123 2069 D4
Smith Cir
1100 BMCY 84302 767 B5
Smith Ln
10 PTGV 84062 2712 D3
800 KYVL 84037 1345 A3
Smithfield Cir
3200 SJDN 84095 2280 E4
E Smith Ridge Dr
10 LEHI 84043 2603 C3
N Smith Ridge Dr
1800 LEHI 84043 2603 C3
Smith View Cir
600 ANFK 84003 2604 E7
Smoketree Cir
9400 SNDY 84092 2283 E1
Smokey Cir
6200 TYVL 84084 2068 D7
Smoot Dr
500 FMTN 84025 1448 B2
Smoot Park Wy
1500 CTRV 84014 1448 D7
Snaffle Cir
13700 DRPR 84020 2389 B5
Snake Creek Dr
- MIDW 84049 2290 E7
- MIDW 84049 2291 B7
- WshC 84049 2289 D2
- WshC 84049 2291 B7
1300 WshC 84049 2290 B5
Snapdragon Cove
5500 WJDN 84084 2067 D7
Sneddon Dr
9200 SNDY 84070 2176 E7
9200 SNDY 84070 2282 E1
Snoqualamie Dr
2000 LYTN 84040 1230 B7
Snow Cir
1400 SNDY 84092 2283 C3
Snowball Cir
1300 SNDY 84092 2283 B2
Snow Basin Cir
2200 SNDY 84093 2177 E3
Snow Basin Dr
8300 SNDY 84093 2177 E5
Snow Basin Rd
5700 WbrC 84317 1060 C7
Snow Bell Dr
5100 WJDN 84088 2173 E7
Snow Berry St
- SmtC 84098 1865 E7
- SmtC 84098 1866 A7
- SmtC 84098 1972 A1
Snowbird Cir
8700 SNDY 84093 2178 A6
Snowbird Dr
8500 SNDY 84093 2178 A6
Snowbush Ln
5800 WVCY 84128 1961 C5
Snowcloud Cir
3000 PKCY 84060 2079 B5
N Snowcreek Cir
500 LYTN 84040 1283 B3
Snow Creek Dr
900 LYTN 84040 1283 B3
1100 PKCY 84060 2078 C3
Snowdon Park Dr
2800 WVCY 84119 1962 E4
Snowdrop Pl
5500 WJDN 84084 2173 D1
Snowflake Cir
1000 SJDN 84095 2281 E3
4300 WbrC 84310 1001 E1
Snowflake Dr
4900 WbrC 84310 1001 E1
Snow Flower Ct
4800 RIVN 84065 2386 A2
Snow Forest Ln
10 SNDY 84092 2284 A6
Snow Forest Cove
10 SNDY 84092 2284 B6
Snow Hollow Dr
6400 WVCY 84128 1961 B5
Snow Iris Cir
1400 SNDY 84092 2283 C3
Snow Iris Wy
1400 SNDY 84092 2283 C3
Snowmass Ct
4400 SLkC 84124 2071 C2
Snow Mountain Cir
2700 SLkC 84093 2178 B6
8700 SNDY 84093 2178 A6
Snow Mountain Dr
2300 SNDY 84093 2177 E6
2300 SNDY 84093 2178 A6
2600 SLkC 84093 2178 A6
Snows Ln
100 PKCY 84060 2078 B4
Snowshoe Dr
3000 WVCY 84128 1961 B5
Snow Springs Dr
1700 LEHI 84043 2602 E7
Snowstar Ln
10 SNDY 84092 2283 E5
Snow Top Ct
3400 WshC 84049 2079 B6
Snow Top Rd
11200 PKCY 84060 2079 C5
11200 SmtC 84060 2079 C5
11200 WshC 84049 2079 B6
Snowview Dr
6000 SmtC 84098 1972 D2
Snowville Dr
8400 SNDY 84093 2177 E5
Snyders Wy
4400 SmtC 84098 1971 E6
Soapberry Dr
8700 SLkC 84044 1960 A6
Soapstone Cir
5900 SJDN 84095 2279 C7
Social Hall Av
100 SLCY 84111 1858 D3
Solace Ct
8400 WJDN 84088 2173 E5
Solamere Dr
1900 PKCY 84060 2079 B5
Solano Cir
4600 WVCY 84120 2067 E3
Solar Cir
- HLDY 84124 2072 A1
Solar Dr
2400 HLDY 84124 2072 A1
2500 HLDY 84124 1966 A7
Solar Wy
8400 SNDY 84070 2176 D6
Soldier Hollow Ln
- WshC 84049 2396 E7
- WshC 84049 2397 A7
Soldiers Cir
100 SLCY 84113 1859 D4
Solena Wy
9100 SNDY 84093 2177 E7
9100 SNDY 84093 2283 E1
Solitaire Dr
1300 SLkC 84106 1965 B6
Solitude Cir
10300 CRHL 84062 2605 A2
Solitude Dr
7600 CDHT 84121 2178 B3
Solitude Rdg
4200 TYVL 84119 2069 A1
Solomon Cir
9800 SNDY 84092 2283 D1
Sol Rise Dr
6500 WJDN 84084 2173 D1
Somerdowns Ct
12500 DRPR 84020 2389 B2
Somerlin Ct
1700 DRPR 84020 2389 C2
Somerlin Dr
1700 DRPR 84020 2389 C2
Somerset Ct
1600 FMTN 84025 1346 B5
Somerset Dr
1000 OREM 84097 2821 B2
2000 CDHT 84121 2177 E3
2300 WbrC 84310 1001 A6
6500 WJDN 84084 2174 D1
E Somerset Dr
3000 SPFK 84660 3250 D5
S Somerset Dr
1200 SPFK 84660 3250 D5
Somerset Pl
10 LOGN 84341 463 C5
Somerset St
600 FMTN 84025 1346 B5
Somerset Wy
1000 MRRY 84117 2071 A5
Somerset Hills Ct
13900 DRPR 84020 2389 C5
Somersetridge Dr
1700 DRPR 84020 2389 C2
Somerset Village Wy
2900 SPFK 84660 3250 D5
Somerton Cir
8900 SNDY 84093 2177 D7
Somerville Dr
1800 SNDY 84093 2177 D7
Sommet Dr
2700 HLDY 84117 2072 A3
Sonata St
700 SLCY 84116 1857 D1
1100 SLCY 84116 1753 D6
Sondrio St
5400 HRMN 84065 2385 D2
Sonia Rose Ct
4400 HLDY 84124 2071 D2
Sonnet Dr
2700 SLCY 84106 1965 C4
Sonoma Ct
1300 SLkC 84106 1965 B7
Sonora Wy
14000 BFDL 84065 2387 D5
Sophia Cir
1200 MRRY 84123 2069 D7
Sophomore Cir
1200 SLkC 84117 2071 B2
Sorensen Cir
5600 TYVL 84118 2069 A5
Sorenson Wy
3400 SLkC 84109 1966 B6
Sorrell Ct
5700 HRMN 84065 2385 D4
Sorrento Cir
2200 WDCR 84087 1653 B3
Sorrento Dr
1500 WDCR 84087 1653 C3
Sorrento Wy
5600 WJDN 84084 2173 D2
Sotogrande Wy
1300 SRCS 84075 1226 A7
Soulero Cir
3900 WJDN 84088 2174 C6
South Ln
7400 SPFK 84660 3249 D5
7400 UthC 84660 3249 D5
E South Ln
10 SPFK 84660 3249 C4
10 UthC 84660 3249 C4
South St
- OGDN 84401 1115 E2
- OGDN 84401 1116 A2
Southampton Dr
- NSLK 84054 1652 D6
Southampton Rd
1100 TYVL 84123 2069 E1
Southbluff Cir
14900 BFDL 84065 2494 B1
Southbourne Cir
3000 WVCY 84119 1962 E7
Southbourne Wy
3000 WVCY 84119 1963 A7
South Bridge Wy
1800 SNDY 84093 2177 D7
Southbrook Ln
1000 MRRY 84117 2071 A4
E South Campus Dr
1500 SLCY 84112 1859 C4
1900 SLCY 84113 1859 C4
E South Campus Dr SR-282
1500 SLCY 84112 1859 C4
1900 SLCY 84113 1859 C4
Southcrest Cir
7400 MDVL 84047 2176 A3
7400 MDVL 84047 2177 B3
Southdale Dr
900 TMTN 84337 520 D7
1000 TMTN 84337 584 D1
E South Eden Cir
1200 SNDY 84094 2283 C3
Southern Cross Ct
- HLID 84003 2497 C5
Southfield Rd
10 HRCY 84032 2398 A7
10 WshC 84032 2398 A7
2400 HRCY 84032 2505 B2
2400 WshC 84032 2505 B2
E Southfield Rd
10 SPFK 84660 3249 D7
10 UthC 84660 3249 D7
10 UthC 84660 3356 D1
N Southfield Rd
10 WshC 84032 2398 B4
W Southfield Rd
10 UthC 84660 3249 C7
E South Fork Cir
900 SNDY 84094 2283 A7
Southfork Dr
100 DRPR 84020 2388 D6
700 DRPR 84020 2389 A5
South Front St
3700 CRNN 84307 705 A7
3900 CRNN 84307 704 E7
Southgate Av
10 DvsC 84056 1228 D4
500 HLFD 84041 1228 E5
E Southgate Av
10 SSLK 84115 1964 C4
W Southgate Av
1400 WVCY 84119 1963 C4
W South Jordan Pkwy
200 SJDN 84095 2282 A4
900 SJDN 84095 2281 B3
3000 SJDN 84095 2280 E3
W South Jordan Pkwy SR-151
200 SJDN 84095 2282 A4
900 SJDN 84095 2281 B3
3000 SJDN 84095 2280 E3
Southlake Dr
800 MRRY 84107 2071 A3
E South Lisa St
1200 LYTN 84040 1283 C2
W South Meadow Cir
1200 SJDN 84095 2281 D4
South Moor Cir
5000 SLkC 84117 2071 D4
South Moor Dr
1700 SLkC 84117 2071 C4
South Pointe Dr
- WSTR 84405 1172 E4
Southpointe Rd
2700 SJDN 84095 2281 A1
Southridge Cir
- SNDY 84070 2176 B6
Southridge Ct
4200 SmtC 84098 1864 E5
Southridge Dr
4800 TYVL 84118 2068 C3
8500 SmtC 84098 1864 E5
E South Temple
10 SLCY 84103 1858 E3
10 SLCY 84111 1858 E3
500 SLCY 84102 1858 E3
700 SLCY 84102 1859 B3
700 SLCY 84103 1859 B3
W South Temple
10 SLCY 84101 1858 B3
10 SLCY 84103 1858 B3
600 SLCY 84104 1858 A3
600 SLCY 84116 1858 A3
900 SLCY 84104 1857 E3
900 SLCY 84116 1857 E3
W South Temple St
1300 SLCY 84104 1857 D3
E South Union Av
900 MDVL 84047 2177 A2
Southview
- LOGN 84321 591 A1
E South Weber Dr
10 RVDL 84405 1172 D6
10 SWBR 84405 1172 D6
400 SWBR 84405 1228 E1
400 SWBR 84405 1229 A1
E South Weber Dr SR-60
10 RVDL 84405 1172 D6
10 SWBR 84405 1172 D6
400 SWBR 84405 1228 E1
400 SWBR 84405 1229 A1
Southwell St
1000 OGDN 84404 1057 B5
E Southwell St
100 OGDN 84404 1056 D5
W Southwell St
100 OGDN 84404 1056 D5
Southwest St
500 LOGN 84321 527 B4
Southwillow Dr
12700 DRPR 84020 2389 B2
Southwood Dr
700 MRRY 84107 2070 E7
700 MRRY 84107 2071 A7
9200 SNDY 84070 2282 A1
Sovereign Wy
4100 SLkC 84124 2072 B1
Spacerama Dr
500 MRRY 84123 2070 B6
Spanish Oak Wy
700 MRRY 84123 2070 A7
Spanish Oaks Dr
2300 SPFK 84660 3250 D7
Spanish Ridge Dr
1600 SPFK 84660 3250 C6
Spanish Trails Blvd
100 SPFK 84660 3249 C3
Sparrowtail Rd
6700 WJDN 84084 2173 E1
Spartan Dr
800 SNDY 84094 2177 A6
Spartan Wy
- MRRY 84107 2070 C4
Spartan Wy SR-173
- MRRY 84107 2070 C4
Spaulding Cir
10 PKCY 84060 2078 D2
8300 WJDN 84088 2175 A5
Spaulding Dr
- SWBR 84405 1172 E7
Spaulding Ln
2700 WJDN 84088 2175 A5
Spaulding Rd
3400 WJDN 84088 2174 D4
S Specialty Cir
2900 SSLK 84115 1964 C5
Spectrum Cove
8000 CDHT 84093 2177 E5
Speed Skate Cir
3400 WJDN 84084 2174 E1
Spencer Av
100 SSLK 84115 1964 D5
Spencer Cir
200 FMTN 84025 1448 D3
Spencer Ct
200 SLCY 84103 1858 D2
E Spencer Wy
200 FMTN 84025 1448 D3
S Spencer Wy
300 FMTN 84025 1448 E3
Spencer Crest Dr
2200 BFDL 84065 2387 B7
Spencer Crest Ln
3900 WJDN 84084 2174 C1
Spendlove Ln
- NHLN 84341 464 B6
Spicewood Cir
4700 TYVL 84118 2069 A2
Spicewood Wy
4700 TYVL 84118 2069 A3
Spiers Ln
900 DRPR 84020 2389 A6
Spike Av
5400 WVCY 84120 2067 E2
Spinnaker Row
1400 TYVL 84123 2069 D5
Spinner Ln
2900 WVCY 84120 1962 C5
Spirea Wy
11700 DRPR 84020 2283 A7
Spirit Lake Cir
4800 RIVN 84065 2386 A3
Splendor Cir
3300 SLkC 84124 2072 C1
Splendor Wy
3200 SLkC 84124 1966 C7
3300 SLkC 84124 2072 C1
Splendor View Cir
500 MDVL 84047 2176 E1
Split Rail Ln
- SmtC 84098 1972 A6
N Split Rail Ln
100 SLCY 84116 1753 C5
N Sportsplex Dr
500 KYVL 84037 1282 E7
500 KYVL 84037 1283 A7
W Sportsplex Dr
1100 KYVL 84037 1283 A7
Sprague Ln
13800 DRPR 84020 2388 D5
Spratling Dr
5200 WJDN 84088 2173 E5
Spring Cir
4500 CRHL 84062 2605 A3
Spring Dr
- WshC 84049 2396 D3
3100 WJDN 84084 2174 E3
3100 WJDN 84084 2175 A3
4200 OGDN 84403 1173 D1
E Spring Dr
10 WDHL 84653 3463 D3
W Spring Dr
10 WDHL 84653 3463 D2
Spring Ln
400 LOGN 84341 463 C6
1300 SLkC 84117 2071 C4
Spring St
500 SOGN 84403 1172 E3
1500 SLCY 84116 1857 C2
Spring Azure Wy
13600 RIVN 84065 2386 A5

STREET
Block City ZIP Map# Grid

Springbrook Dr
7500 WJDN 84084 2174 E4
Springbrook Wy
6700 CDHT 84121 2177 C1
Spring Canyon Rd
5800 WbrC 84403 1174 A5
Spring Clover Dr
800 MRRY 84123 2070 A4
Spring Creek Dr
- PVDN 84332 528 A7
- PVDN 84332 592 A1
400 BNFL 84010 1653 E3
1100 LYTN 84041 1228 C7
1600 LEHI 84043 2710 B2
1800 BNFL 84010 1654 A4
Spring Creek Pkwy
100 PVDN 84332 527 E6
Spring Creek Pl
800 SGVL 84663 3036 A6
1200 SGVL 84663 3035 E6
Spring Creek Rd
300 PVDN 84332 528 B7
700 PVDN 84332 592 B1
1600 CchC 84321 592 B1
2600 HLDY 84117 2072 A2
Spring Creek Ranch Rd
- LEHI 84043 2710 D2
Spring Crest Ct
900 MDVL 84047 2177 A3
Springcrest Ln
10100 SJDN 84095 2282 A3
Springdale Wy
1700 DRPR 84020 2389 D3
Spring Day Ln
3200 SJDN 84095 2280 E5
Springdell Cir
1400 UthC 84604 2822 B1
Springdell Dr
1300 UthC 84604 2822 A1
Springer Ln
2900 SJDN 84095 2281 A6
Springfield Cir
9400 SJDN 84095 2281 B1
Springfield Dr
1800 SJDN 84095 2281 C1
Springfield Rd
1700 SLCY 84116 1753 C6
Spring Gate Dr
5200 SLkC 84117 2071 C4
Spring Glen Cir
3200 WVCY 84119 2068 E1
Spring Glen St
4100 WVCY 84119 2068 E1
Spring Harvest Cir
9400 SJDN 84095 2281 C1
Spring Haven Ct
300 KYVL 84037 1345 B2
Spring Haven Dr
2500 SLkC 84109 1966 A7
Springheather Cir
5000 HRMN 84065 2386 A6
Spring Hill Cir
400 NSLK 84054 1653 B7
Spring Hill Dr
600 MRRY 84107 2070 E4
Springhill Dr
100 NSLK 84054 1653 B7
Spring Hollow Dr
2600 SLkC 84109 1966 A7
Spring House Ln
600 MRRY 84107 2070 E4
Spring Lake Rd
12600 UthC 84651 3461 C4
S Spring Lake Rd
12000 UthC 84651 3461 D4
Spring Leaf Dr
1400 SLkC 84117 2071 C4
Spring Meadow Cir
4700 BNFL 84010 1653 E7
4700 BNFL 84010 1754 E1
Spring Meadow Dr
4400 BNFL 84010 1653 E7
Springmeadow Dr
4100 SLkC 84107 2070 E1
Spring Meadow Ln
- KYVL 84037 1345 A1
Spring Meadow Rd
700 MRRY 84107 2070 D4
700 MRRY 84107 2071 A5
Spring Mountain Dr
1400 SGVL 84663 3036 C6
Spring Oak Dr
6700 WJDN 84088 2173 A6
Spring Oaks Dr
1600 SGVL 84663 3144 A2
Spring Park Cir
4400 RIVN 84065 2386 B1
Spring Ridge Cir
12000 SNDY 84094 2389 B1
Springridge Cir
900 NSLK 84054 1653 D6
Spring Ridge Dr
1000 SNDY 84094 2389 B1
Springridge Dr
200 NSLK 84054 1653 C6
Spring Run Dr
1400 SLkC 84117 2071 C4
Springshire Dr
7900 SmtC 84098 1865 A6
Springshire Ln
1200 MRRY 84123 2069 D5
Springside Ct
1300 WVCY 84119 1963 D5
Spring Stone Cir
5700 SJDN 84095 2279 D6
Spring Stone Dr
11400 SJDN 84095 2279 D6
Spring Tree Dr
900 LYTN 84040 1283 B2
Springtree Ln
600 MRRY 84107 2070 E5
Spring Valley Ct
1500 SLkC 84117 2071 C4
Spring View Dr
600 SSLK 84106 1964 E5
700 SLkC 84106 1964 E5
800 SLkC 84106 1965 A5
S Spring Vista Cir
3700 WVCY 84120 1962 D6
W Spring Vista Cir
3600 WVCY 84120 1962 D6
W Spring Vista Dr
3600 WVCY 84120 1962 D6
Springwater Dr
1400 OREM 84058 2819 D7
S Spring Water Dr
3700 WVCY 84120 1962 D7
W Spring Water Dr
3600 WVCY 84120 1962 D7
Spring Wheat Cir
12000 RIVN 84065 2386 C1
Spring Willow Cir
9400 SJDN 84095 2281 C1
Springwood Cir
800 NSLK 84054 1653 C6
Springwood Dr
600 FMTN 84025 1346 B4
800 NSLK 84054 1653 C6
900 BNFL 84010 1653 C6
900 BNFL 84054 1653 C6
Springwood Ln
9200 SNDY 84093 2283 D1
Spruce Av
600 PTGV 84062 2713 A4
Spruce Cir
4300 SLkC 84124 2072 C1
4500 CRHL 84062 2605 B2
S Spruce Cir
1700 MPTN 84664 3251 A2
Spruce Ct
5400 OGDN 84403 1173 E4
Spruce Dr
1300 PTVW 84414 998 A3
3600 SLkC 84124 2072 D1
Spruce Ln
1300 DvsC 84056 1228 C2
Spruce St
7300 MDVL 84047 2176 B3
Spruceberry Cir
11600 DRPR 84020 2282 E7
Spruce Creek Ct
9800 SJDN 84095 2281 C2
W Spruce Creek Ln
2000 SJDN 84095 2281 B2
Spruce Dale Dr
9800 SJDN 84095 2281 B2
Spruce Glen Cir
4700 MRRY 84107 2070 E3
Spruce Glen Rd
400 MRRY 84107 2070 E3
Spruce Grove Wy
9800 SJDN 84095 2281 C2
Spruce Leaf Cir
4200 SJDN 84095 2280 C3
Spruce Leaf Dr
4200 SJDN 84095 2280 C3
Spruce Mesa Wy
700 SNDY 84094 2282 E6
700 SNDY 84094 2283 A6
Spruce Tree Ln
700 SNDY 84094 2177 A4
Spruce View Ct
2200 SLkC 84109 1965 B5
Spruce View Ln
3400 SLkC 84109 1965 E6
Sprucewood Cir
5200 WVCY 84120 2067 E3
Spur Cir
7100 WVCY 84128 1960 D7
Spur Ct
1500 PYSN 84651 3461 E1
Spurlock St
300 LYTN 84041 1282 E4
Spurrier Rd
5400 MRRY 84107 2070 C5
Spyglass
4200 CRHL 84062 2605 B1
Spyglass Cir
1600 SNDY 84092 2283 C7
Spyglass Ct
10 PKCY 84060 2078 D1
Spyglass Hill Dr
1500 DRPR 84020 2389 C6
Squaw Peak Rd
- PRVO 84604 2821 E1
- PRVO 84604 2822 A1
- UthC 84604 2821 E3
- UthC 84604 2822 A1
- UthC 84604 2929 D1
Squire Ct
4400 HLDY 84124 2071 D2
Squire Crest Dr
3800 TYVL 84118 2068 C4
Squirewood Cir
3400 WVCY 84120 1962 A6
Squirewood Dr
3300 WVCY 84120 1962 A6
SR-13
- BMCY 84302 765 B1
- BMCY 84302 766 D3
- BxEC 84302 765 B1
- BxEC 84302 766 D3
- BxEC 84307 704 C5
- BxEC 84307 765 B1
- BxEC 84312 521 B4
- BxEC 84314 645 D5
- BxEC 84337 521 B6
- BxEC 84337 585 C7
- BxEC 84337 645 D5
- CRNN 84307 704 D5
- CRNN 84307 705 A7
- CRNN 84307 765 B1
- ELWD 84337 521 B6
- ELWD 84337 585 C7
- ELWD 84337 645 D5
- GRLD 84312 521 B1
- TMTN 84337 521 B6
SR-13 N 4700 W
- BRCY 84302 704 C4
- BRCY 84307 704 C4
- BRCY 84337 704 C4
5000 BRCY 84302 645 D7
5200 BRCY 84301 645 D7
SR-13 N 4800 W
3300 BxEC 84307 704 C4
4000 BxEC 84337 704 C3
4600 BRCY 84302 704 D1
4600 BRCY 84307 704 D1
4600 BRCY 84337 704 D1
SR-13 N 5200 St W
8000 ELWD 84337 585 B5
10400 BxEC 84337 521 B7
10400 BxEC 84337 585 B2
SR-13 N 5200 St W
10400 ELWD 84337 521 B7
SR-13 N Main St
10 BMCY 84302 766 E4
SR-13 S Main St
10 BMCY 84302 766 E6
700 BMCY 84302 827 E1
SR-23
- CchC 84325 524 D5
- CchC 84325 588 E2
- CchC 84339 588 E2
- CchC 84339 589 A4
- MNDN 84325 524 D5
- MNDN 84325 588 E2
- WELV 84339 589 B6
SR-23 W 500 N
- CchC 84339 589 C7
- WELV 84339 589 C7
SR-23 N 6000 W
100 CchC 84325 524 D2
SR-23 N Center St
10 WELV 84339 649 D2
SR-23 S Center St
10 WELV 84339 649 D1
SR-26 Riverdale Rd
1600 ROY 84067 1171 E4
1600 RVDL 84405 1171 E3
3400 OGDN 84401 1115 D7
3500 SOGN 84405 1115 D7
4000 RVDL 84405 1115 D7
4000 RVDL 84405 1172 C1
SR-26 W Riverdale Rd
- ROY 84067 1171 E3
600 RVDL 84405 1172 C2
1200 RVDL 84405 1171 E3
SR-30
- BxEC - 520 A6
- CchC 84321 525 E1
- CchC 84321 526 A2
- CchC 84325 524 E1
- TMTN - 520 A6
- CchC 84325 525 B1
SR-30 W 200 N
10 LOGN 84321 527 D2
1300 LOGN 84321 526 E2
2100 CchC 84321 526 D2
SR-30 N Main St
200 LOGN 84321 527 D2
SR-30 Veterans Memorial Hwy
- BxEC - 520 B6
- TMTN - 520 C1
SR-32
- WshC 84032 2186 E6
- WshC 84032 2292 C2
- WshC 84049 2186 E6
- WshC 84049 2292 C2
SR-37 W 4000 S
- ROY 84067 1171 A1
2900 WHVN 84067 1170 E1
2900 WHVN 84067 1171 A1
3500 WHVN 84315 1170 E1
5100 HOPR 84315 1170 A1
5300 HOPR 84315 1169 D2
SR-37 N 5000 W
1800 DvsC 84315 1169 D7
1800 DvsC 84315 1225 D1
1800 WPT 84015 1225 D1
2400 HOPR 84315 1169 D6
SR-37 S 5900 W
4100 HOPR 84315 1169 D1
SR-37 Clinton Rd
10 SNST 84015 1227 B1
500 CLTN 84015 1227 B1
1700 CLTN 84015 1226 E1
3500 WPT 84015 1226 A1
3700 WPT 84015 1225 E1
SR-38
- BxEC 84302 647 A6
- BxEC 84302 706 B1
- BxEC 84302 766 E2
- BxEC 84309 522 B4
- BxEC 84309 586 C3
- BxEC 84312 522 B1
- BxEC 84314 647 A6
- DWVL 84309 522 C7
- DWVL 84309 586 C3
- DWVL 84312 522 C7
- HYVL 84302 647 A6
- HYVL 84314 586 C3
- HYVL 84314 646 D3
- HYVL 84314 647 A6
SR-38 N 2600 St W
- HYVL 84314 646 D2
SR-38 N 2800 St W
- HYVL 84314 586 C7
- HYVL 84314 646 D1
SR-38 N Main St
900 BMCY 84302 766 E3
1300 BxEC 84302 766 E2
SR-39
- OGDN 84401 1116 D1
- OGDN 84404 1116 D1
- WbrC 84317 1059 D6
- WbrC 84317 1060 B6
- WbrC 84317 1061 B6
- WbrC 84317 1116 D1
SR-39 12th St
100 OGDN 84404 1056 D7
500 OGDN 84404 1057 A7
SR-39 W 12th St
100 OGDN 84404 1056 C7
700 MTSV 84404 1056 A7
1200 MTSV 84401 1056 A7
1500 MTSV 84401 1055 E7
1500 MTSV 84404 1055 E7
SR-39 E 100 S
7800 WbrC 84317 1061 B5
SR-39 E 900 S
6500 WbrC 84317 1060 E7
7400 WbrC 84317 1061 A7
SR-39 W 1150 S
4400 WbrC 84401 1054 C7
4400 WbrC 84404 1054 C7
SR-39 W 1200 S
2000 MTSV 84401 1055 D7
2000 MTSV 84404 1055 D7
2300 WbrC 84401 1055 D7
2300 WbrC 84404 1055 D7
2800 WbrC 84401 1054 E7
2800 WbrC 84404 1054 E7
SR-39 S 7800 E
500 HTVL 84317 1061 B5
500 WbrC 84317 1061 B5
SR-39 Canyon Rd
- OGDN 84401 1116 D1
- WbrC 84317 1116 E1
SR-39 Ogden Canyon Rd
- OGDN 84401 1116 D1
- WbrC 84317 1116 D1
- WbrC 84317 1117 A1
600 WbrC 84310 1058 E6
600 WbrC 84310 1059 B6
600 WbrC 84317 1058 E6
600 WbrC 84317 1059 B6
SR-48 W 7000 S
1300 WJDN 84084 2175 C2
SR-48 W 7200 S
- MDVL 84047 2175 E2
10 MDVL 84047 2176 C2
SR-48 W 7800 S
1700 WJDN 84084 2175 C4
1700 WJDN 84088 2175 C4
3000 WJDN 84084 2174 E4
3000 WJDN 84088 2174 E4
SR-48 New Bingham Hwy
- WJDN 84088 2279 B1
4300 WJDN 84084 2174 C4
4300 WJDN 84088 2174 C4
5300 WJDN 84088 2173 E6
SR-48 Redwood Rd
7000 WJDN 84084 2175 C3
SR-51
- SGVL 84663 3143 C5
SR-51 S 1100 E
400 SPFK 84660 3249 E2
400 SPFK 84660 3250 A2
400 SPFK 84663 3249 E2
400 SPFK 84663 3250 A2
SR-51 S Childs Rd
500 SPFK 84660 3250 A1
500 SPFK 84663 3250 A1
SR-51 S Main St
600 SGVL 84663 3143 C5
SR-51 State Rd
1800 SGVL 84663 3143 B6
2600 UthC 84663 3143 B7
SR-51 S State Rd
- SGVL 84663 3143 B7
- SPFK 84660 3143 B7
- SPFK 84660 3250 A1
- SPFK 84663 3143 A7
- UthC 84660 3143 B7
- UthC 84663 3143 B7
3400 SPFK 84663 3250 A1
3400 UthC 84660 3250 A1
3400 UthC 84663 3250 A1
SR-52 E 800 N
- OREM 84604 2821 A3
10 OREM 84057 2820 D3
400 OREM 84097 2820 E3
600 OREM 84097 2821 A3
SR-52 W 800 N
10 OREM 84057 2820 D3
1400 OREM 84057 2819 E3
SR-53 Martin Luther King Jr St
100 OGDN 84401 1115 D3
SR-53 W Martin L King Jr St
300 OGDN 84401 1115 D3
SR-53 Pennsylvania Av
- WbrC 84401 1115 A4
2400 OGDN 84401 1115 B3
SR-60
- SWBR 84405 1229 E2
- SWBR 84405 1230 A2
SR-60 S 1050 W
4700 RVDL 84405 1172 A4
SR-60 E South Weber Dr
10 RVDL 84405 1172 C6
10 SWBR 84405 1172 C6
400 SWBR 84405 1228 E1
400 SWBR 84405 1229 A1
SR-60 S Weber Dr
5400 RVDL 84405 1172 A4
5500 SWBR 84405 1172 C6
SR-68
- LEHI 84043 2601 E5
- LEHI 84043 2602 A6
- SRSP 84043 2601 E5
- SRSP 84043 2602 A6
- UthC 84043 2494 D5
- UthC 84043 2601 E1
- WDCR 84087 1652 D1
SR-68 W 500 S
- BNFL 84087 1653 C1
200 BNFL 84010 1653 C1
500 WBNF 84010 1653 C1
600 WBNF 84087 1653 C1
600 WDCR 84010 1653 C1
1300 WDCR 84087 1652 E1
SR-68 Camp Williams Rd
- SLkC 84065 2494 D7
- UthC 84043 2494 D7
14400 BFDL 84065 2387 C6
14900 BFDL 84065 2494 C1
SR-68 Redwood Rd
6600 WJDN 84084 2175 C3
7800 WJDN 84088 2175 C5
9300 WJDN 84088 2281 C1
SR-68 N Redwood Rd
10 NSLK 84054 1652 D7
10 SLCY 84104 1857 C2
100 SLCY 84116 1857 C2
500 WDCR 84087 1652 D2
700 DvsC 84087 1652 D2
700 SLCY 84116 1753 C7
1700 SLkC 84116 1753 C4
SR-68 S Redwood Rd
10 NSLK 84054 1652 D7
10 SLCY 84104 1857 C3
300 NSLK 84054 1753 D1
600 DvsC 84054 1753 C2
600 SLkC 84116 1753 C2
1600 SLCY 84104 1963 C1
2100 WVCY 84119 1963 C3
3900 WVCY 84119 2069 C1
4100 TYVL 84119 2069 C1
4100 TYVL 84123 2069 C1
4700 TYVL 84118 2069 C4
6200 TYVL 84084 2069 C7
6200 WJDN 84084 2069 C7
SR-68 S Redwood Rd
6400 TYVL 84123 2175 C1
6400 WJDN 84084 2175 C1
9400 SJDN 84095 2281 C1
11600 RIVN 84065 2281 C7
12100 RIVN 84065 2387 C2
13800 BFDL 84065 2387 C4
SR-71 S 700 E
400 SLCY 84102 1858 E5
900 SLCY 84105 1858 E5
1600 SLCY 84105 1964 E1
2100 SLCY 84106 1964 E1
2700 SLkC 84106 1964 E1
2800 SSLK 84106 1964 E7
3900 SLkC 84107 1964 E7
3900 SLkC 84124 1964 E7
4000 SLkC 84107 2070 E1
4000 SLkC 84124 2070 E1
4500 MRRY 84107 2070 E1
4600 MRRY 84107 2071 A3
4600 SLkC 84107 2071 A3
7700 SNDY 84047 2176 E4
7800 SNDY 84070 2176 E4
7800 SNDY 84094 2176 E4
8400 SLkC 84094 2176 E5
9100 SNDY 84070 2282 E1
9100 SNDY 84094 2282 E1
9800 SLkC 84094 2282 E1
10200 SLkC 84070 2282 E4
11400 DRPR 84020 2282 E7
12000 DRPR 84020 2388 E1
SR-71 S 900 E
4800 MRRY 84107 2071 A3
4800 SLkC 84117 2071 A3
4900 MRRY 84117 2071 A4
5600 MRRY 84121 2071 A5
6400 MRRY 84047 2177 A1
6400 MRRY 84107 2177 A1
6400 MRRY 84121 2177 A1
6700 MDVL 84047 2177 A1
7500 MDVL 84047 2176 E4
7600 SNDY 84047 2176 E4
SR-71 E 12300 S
10 DRPR 84020 2388 E1
SR-71 W 12300 S
10 DRPR 84020 2388 C1
SR-71 W 12600 S
900 DRPR 84020 2387 E2
900 DRPR 84020 2388 A1
1200 RIVN 84065 2387 E2
2900 RIVN 84065 2386 D2
SR-71 Van Winkle Expwy
- MRRY 84107 2071 A3
- SLkC 84107 2071 A3
SR-73
- LEHI 84043 2603 E6
SR-73 W 8570 N
8700 LEHI 84043 2603 A6
8800 LEHI 84043 2602 E6
10800 SRSP 84043 2601 E6
10800 SRSP 84043 2602 A6
SR-73 Cedar Fort Rd
- EGMN 84043 2601 A7
- SRSP 84043 2601 B7
- UthC 84043 2601 A7
SR-73 Main St
10 SRSP 84043 2602 B6
SR-73 E Main St
10 LEHI 84043 2603 C6
SR-73 W Main St
500 LEHI 84043 2603 B6
SR-74 N 100 E
10 ANFK 84003 2711 C1
100 ANFK 84003 2604 C7
1200 UthC 84003 2604 D4
SR-74 Alpine Hwy
400 ALPN 84004 2497 D7
SR-74 N Alpine Hwy
9600 HILD 84003 2604 D4
10900 HILD 84003 2497 D7
SR-74 N Main St
10 ALPN 84004 2497 E4
SR-74 S Main St
10 ALPN 84004 2497 E5
SR-75 W 1400 N
100 SGVL 84663 3036 C6
SR-75 W 1500 N
- UthC 84606 3035 E6
1200 SGVL 84663 3035 E6
1200 SGVL 84663 3036 C6
SR-77
- UthC 84660 3141 B3
SR-77 W 400 S
10 SGVL 84663 3143 B3
700 SGVL 84663 3142 E3
SR-77 W 3900 S
- SGVL 84660 3142 C3
- SGVL 84663 3142 C3
SR-77 W 4000 S
700 SGVL 84660 3142 C3
700 SGVL 84663 3142 C3
700 SPFK 84660 3142 B3
700 SPFK 84663 3142 B3
700 UthC 84660 3142 B3
800 UthC 84660 3141 D3
SR-77 W 4400 S
2700 UthC 84660 3141 A4
SR-77 Palmyra Dr
4000 UthC 84660 3141 A4
SR-79 30th St
100 OGDN 84401 1115 E5
500 OGDN 84403 1115 E5
600 OGDN 84403 1116 A5
SR-79 W 30th St
100 OGDN 84401 1115 E5
SR-79 31st St
- OGDN 84401 1115 D5
- OGDN 84405 1115 C5
SR-79 Hinckley Dr
- OGDN 84401 1114 E6
- OGDN 84405 1114 E6
- ROY 84067 1114 E6
- ROY 84401 1114 E6
- WbrC 84401 1114 E6
- WbrC 84405 1114 E6
1300 OGDN 84401 1115 A6
1300 OGDN 84405 1115 A6
SR-79 Washington Blvd
3000 OGDN 84401 1115 E5
SR-82
- BxEC 84312 521 B1
SR-82 300 St E
600 TMTN 84337 520 E5
SR-82 E 600 St N
- TMTN 84337 520 E5
SR-82 E Factory St
- BxEC 84312 521 B2
10 GRLD 84312 520 E2
300 GRLD 84312 521 A2
SR-82 S Main St
10 GRLD 84312 520 E2
800 TMTN 84337 520 E2
SR-82 North St
- TMTN 84337 520 E5
SR-82 N Tremont St
- TMTN 84337 520 E5
SR-83
- BxEC 84307 704 B6
- CRNN 84307 704 B6
SR-90
- BMCY 84302 767 B7
SR-90 E 200 S
10 BMCY 84302 766 E6
100 BMCY 84302 767 B6
SR-92
- HILD 84003 2497 B7
SR-92 W 11000 N
- LEHI 84043 2495 D7
- LEHI 84043 2496 D7
- LEHI 84043 2497 A7
- UthC 84043 2496 D7
- UthC 84043 2497 A7
3800 CRHL 84003 2498 E7
3800 CRHL 84062 2498 E7
3800 HILD 84003 2498 E7
4800 HILD 84003 2497 E7
SR-92 Alpine Loop Rd
- HILD 84003 2498 C7
- UthC 84004 2498 E7
SR-92 American Fork Canyon Rd
- UthC 84004 2498 E7
SR-92 Highland Hwy
- HILD 84003 2497 E7
SR-93 W 2600 S
- NSLK 84087 1653 C4
- WDCR 84087 1653 C4
400 NSLK 84054 1653 C4
400 WDCR 84010 1653 C4
600 BNFL 84010 1653 C4
600 NSLK 84010 1653 C4
SR-97 W 5500 S
3700 ROY 84067 1170 E5
4300 HOPR 84315 1170 A4
5200 HOPR 84315 1169 D4
SR-97 W 5600 S
1600 ROY 84067 1171 B5
3400 ROY 84067 1170 E5
SR-101
- CchC 84319 650 C1
- CchC 84319 652 A3
- CchC 84321 651 D2
- CchC 84321 652 A3
- CchC 84339 650 C1
- HYRM 84319 650 C1
- HYRM 84319 651 D2
- HYRM 84319 652 A3
- HYRM 84321 652 A3
- WELV 84319 650 A1
- WELV 84339 649 E2
- WELV 84339 650 A1
SR-101 N 400 W
10 HYRM 84319 651 A2
SR-101 Blacksmith Fork Cyn Rd
1400 CchC 84319 652 B3
1400 CchC 84321 652 C3
1400 HYRM 84319 652 B3
1400 HYRM 84321 652 B3
SR-101 Main St
10 HYRM 84319 651 B2
SR-101 E Main St
10 WELV 84339 649 E2
SR-101 W Main St
10 HYRM 84319 651 B2
SR-102
- BxEC 84309 521 D6
- BxEC 84309 522 A5
- BxEC 84337 521 D6
- DWVL 84309 521 D6
- DWVL 84309 522 A5
SR-102 11200 Rd N
- BxEC 84337 520 A6
1500 TMTN 84337 520 B6
SR-102 E Main St
10 TMTN 84337 520 E6
600 TMTN 84337 521 A6
1900 BxEC 84337 521 B6
SR-102 W Main St
10 TMTN 84337 520 E6
SR-103 E 650 N
10 CRFD 84015 1227 D3
SR-104 W 20th St
100 OGDN 84401 1115 D2
SR-104 W 21st St
100 OGDN 84401 1115 B2
SR-104 Wilson Ln
700 WHVN 84401 1115 B2
1400 WHVN 84401 1114 E2
SR-105 W Parrish Ln
10 CTRV 84014 1551 D3
SR-106
- BNFL 84010 1653 C2
- WDCR 84010 1653 C2
SR-106 S 185 E
10 FMTN 84025 1448 D2
SR-106 N 200 W
10 BNFL 84010 1551 D7
SR-106 S 200 E
100 FMTN 84025 1448 D1
SR-106 S 200 W
10 BNFL 84010 1551 D7
200 BNFL 84010 1653 D1
SR-106 S 300 W
1400 BNFL 84010 1653 D2
SR-106 W 600 N
10 FMTN 84025 1346 C7
SR-106 N Main St
10 CTRV 84014 1551 E1
10 FMTN 84025 1448 D1
400 BNFL 84010 1551 D7
600 FMTN 84025 1346 C7
1500 CTRV 84014 1448 D7
SR-106 S Main St
10 CTRV 84014 1551 E3
1000 BNFL 84010 1551 E5
SR-106 Shepard Ln
10 FMTN 84025 1346 C6
SR-106 W Shepard Ln
600 FMTN 84025 1346 B6
SR-106 E State St
10 FMTN 84025 1448 D2
SR-106 E Willey St
10 BNFL 84010 1551 D7
SR-106 W Willey St
10 BNFL 84010 1551 D7
SR-107 W 300 N
10 CRFD 84015 1227 D4
SR-107 West Point Rd
500 CRFD 84015 1227 C4
1400 CLTN 84015 1227 A4
1500 WPT 84015 1227 A4
1700 WPT 84015 1226 E4
4000 WPT 84015 1225 E4
SR-108 W 1700 S
1200 SRCS 84075 1281 A1
1700 SRCS 84075 1280 E1
SR-108 S 2000 W
600 SRCS 84075 1226 E6
SR-108 S 3500 W
4700 ROY 84067 1170 E3
SR-108 E Antelope Dr
10 CRFD 84015 1281 E1
10 CRFD 84016 1281 E1
800 CRFD 84015 1282 A1
SR-108 W Antelope Dr
10 CRFD 84015 1281 D1
10 CRFD 84016 1281 D1
400 LYTN 84041 1282 D1
600 SRCS 84075 1281 C1
700 SRCS 84016 1281 B1
SR-108 Midland Dr
1900 WbrC 84067 1114 C7
1900 WHVN 84067 1114 C7
1900 WHVN 84401 1114 C7
3600 ROY 84067 1114 C7
3900 ROY 84067 1171 A1
3900 WHVN 84067 1171 A1
4200 WbrC 84067 1171 A1
4500 ROY 84067 1170 E2
4500 WbrC 84067 1170 E2
4500 WHVN 84067 1170 E2
SR-108 Two Mile Rd
- SRCS 84075 1226 E7
300 WPT 84015 1226 E3
700 CLTN 84015 1226 E3
1800 CLTN 84015 1170 E7
SR-109 E Gentile St
10 LYTN 84041 1282 E5
10 LYTN 84041 1283 A5
1100 LYTN 84040 1283 C4
SR-109 Oak Hills Dr
1300 LYTN 84040 1283 C4
1500 DvsC 84040 1283 C4
2200 LYTN 84040 1284 A4
SR-110 N 4500 W
10 WPT 84015 1225 E5
SR-110 S 4500 W
10 WPT 84015 1225 E4
700 DvsC 84075 1225 E6
700 WPT 84075 1225 E6
1200 SRCS 84075 1225 E7
SR-111
- SLkC 84006 2066 D5
- SLkC 84084 2066 E6
- WJDN 84084 2173 A2
- WJDN 84088 2173 A5
- WVCY 84006 2066 D5
- WVCY 84044 2066 C4
- WVCY 84084 2066 D5
- WVCY 84084 2067 A7
- WVCY 84084 2173 A2
SR-111 S 8400 W
2600 SLkC 84044 1960 B3
3700 SLkC 84006 1960 B7
3800 SLkC 84006 2066 B1
3800 SLkC 84044 2066 B1
4100 WVCY 84044 2066 B1
SR-113 W 100 S
10 HRCY 84032 2398 C4
SR-113 S Center St
10 MIDW 84049 2397 B3
600 WshC 84049 2397 B5
SR-113 Charleston Rd
- WshC 84032 2397 B7
- WshC 84032 2504 B1
900 WshC 84049 2397 B5
2500 CSTN 84032 2504 B1
SR-113 E Main St
10 MIDW 84049 2397 B4
SR-113 Midway Ln
800 MIDW 84049 2397 D3
800 WshC 84032 2397 E4
800 WshC 84049 2397 E4
900 HRCY 84032 2398 A4
900 WshC 84032 2398 A4
SR-114
- PTGV 84062 2712 D4
SR-114 W Center St
500 PRVO 84601 2928 B7
1300 PRVO 84601 2927 E7
SR-114 Geneva Dr
500 PTGV 84062 2712 D4
SR-114 N Geneva Rd
10 LNDN 84042 2712 D6
10 OREM 84057 2819 E4
10 PRVO 84601 2927 D6
10 VNYD 84057 2819 E4
1800 UthC 84601 2927 B3
1900 UthC 84058 2927 B3
SR-114 S Geneva Rd
10 LNDN 84042 2712 D7
10 OREM 84058 2819 E5
10 VNYD 84057 2819 E5
200 OREM 84057 2819 E6
400 LNDN 84042 2819 E1
400 VNYD 84058 2819 E6
900 OREM 84058 2926 E1
1000 OREM 84058 2927 B3
1200 OREM 84601 2927 B3
1200 UthC 84058 2927 B3
1200 UthC 84601 2927 B3
SR-115
- SPFK 84660 3249 A3
- UthC 84660 3249 A3

Salt Lake City Street Index

STREET
Block City ZIP Map# Grid

SR-115 W 100 S
10 SPFK 84660 3249 A3
SR-115 W 900 S
1600 SPFK 84660 3248 D4
1600 SPFK 84660 3249 A4
SR-115 S 3200 W
9300 UthC 84651 3354 E2
9300 UthC 84660 3354 E2
SR-115 W 6800 S
400 SPFK 84660 3249 C3
700 UthC 84660 3249 B3
SR-115 W 7300 S
1200 SPFK 84660 3248 E4
1400 UthC 84660 3248 E4
SR-115 Benjamin Rd
8500 UthC 84651 3354 E1
8500 UthC 84660 3354 E1
SR-115 N Main St
100 PYSN 84651 3354 E5
800 UthC 84651 3354 E3
SR-126
- BxEC 84340 941 C7
- BxEC 84340 997 C1
- BxEC 84404 997 C1
SR-126 N 1900 W
100 MTSV 84404 1055 D5
SR-126 S 1900 W
100 MTSV 84404 1055 D5
1200 MTSV 84401 1055 D7
1200 MTSV 84401 1114 D1
1400 WHVN 84401 1114 D1
2500 OGDN 84401 1114 D3
3100 WbrC 84401 1114 D7
3300 WbrC 84067 1114 D7
3300 WHVN 84067 1114 D7
3400 ROY 84067 1114 D7
3400 ROY 84401 1114 D7
3400 WbrC 84405 1114 D7
3600 OGDN 84405 1114 D7
4000 ROY 84067 1171 D1
4100 OGDN 84067 1171 D1
4100 OGDN 84405 1171 D1
4100 ROY 84405 1171 D1
SR-126 N 2000 W
400 MTSV 84404 1055 D2
800 FRWT 84404 1055 D2
1800 FRWT 84404 997 D7
SR-126 N Main St
10 CRFD 84015 1227 E5
10 LYTN 84041 1282 E4
800 SNST 84015 1227 D3
1800 SNST 84015 1171 D7
2000 LYTN 84041 1228 B7
2100 CRFD 84015 1228 B7
2100 LYTN 84015 1228 B7
SR-126 S Main St
10 CRFD 84015 1227 D4
10 LYTN 84041 1282 E5
10 LYTN 84041 1283 A5
SR-126 State St
10 CRFD 84015 1227 D4
700 CRFD 84015 1228 A6
1500 LYTN 84041 1228 A7
SR-127 W 1700 S
2000 SRCS 84075 1280 E1
3000 DvsC 84075 1280 E1
SR-131 W Willey St
- WBNF 84087 1551 D7
200 BNFL 84010 1551 D7
500 WBNF 84010 1551 D7
SR-134 W 2200 N
4200 PNCY 84404 996 C7
SR-134 W 2575 N
4200 PNCY 84404 996 C6
SR-134 W 2600 N
2500 FRWT 84404 997 B6
2500 PNCY 84404 997 A6
2500 WbrC 84404 997 A6
3400 PNCY 84404 996 E6
3400 WbrC 84404 996 E6
SR-134 W 2700 N
1100 PTVW 84404 998 A6
1100 PTVW 84414 998 A6
1100 WbrC 84404 998 A6
1300 PTVW 84404 997 E6
1300 WbrC 84404 997 E6
1700 FRWT 84404 997 E6
SR-134 N 4200 W
2500 PNCY 84404 996 C6
SR-134 N 4275 W
2200 PNCY 84404 996 C6
SR-134 N 4650 W
1900 PNCY 84404 996 B7
SR-134 N 4700 W
10 WbrC 84404 1054 B5
1300 PNCY 84404 1054 B2
SR-134 S 4700 W
100 WbrC 84404 1054 B5
900 WbrC 84401 1054 B7
1200 WbrC 84401 1113 B2
3300 WHVN 84315 1113 B7
SR-140 W 14400 S
1700 BFDL 84065 2387 D7
SR-140 W 14600 S
300 BFDL 84065 2388 B7
300 DRPR 84020 2388 B7
900 BFDL 84065 2387 E7
SR-140 Highland Dr
- DRPR 84020 2388 B7
SR-140 S Redwood Rd
14300 BFDL 84065 2387 C7
SR-141
- GNLA 84655 3460 A4
- UthC 84651 3460 B3
- UthC 84655 3460 B3
SR-141 S 5600 W
11300 UthC 84651 3460 D1
SR-141 W 11600 S
5600 UthC 84651 3460 D1
SR-141 S West Mountain Rd
11800 UthC 84651 3460 C2
12000 UthC 84655 3460 B3
SR-145
- ANFK 84003 2711 A1
- UthC 84003 2711 A1
SR-146
- CRHL 84062 2605 C2
- PTGV 84062 2605 C3
SR-146 N 100 E
10 PTGV 84062 2712 D3
1400 PTGV 84062 2605 D7
SR-146 S 100 E
10 PTGV 84062 2712 D3
SR-146 Canyon Rd
- CRHL 84003 2498 C7
- CRHL 84062 2498 C7
- CRHL 84062 2605 C3
- HILD 84003 2498 C7
SR-147 E 400 N
1100 SPFK 84660 3250 A2
1100 SPFK 84663 3250 A2
1600 UthC 84660 3250 A2
SR-147 W 400 N
10 SPFK 84660 3249 C2
600 UthC 84660 3249 B2
SR-147 W 1600 S
10 MPTN 84664 3250 E2
10 MPTN 84664 3251 A2
SR-147 S 4400 W
10200 PYSN 84651 3354 B5
10200 UthC 84651 3354 B5
SR-147 E 6400 S
- MPTN 84664 3250 D2
1100 UthC 84660 3250 B2
1100 UthC 84663 3250 B2
1600 UthC 84664 3250 C2
SR-147 W 6400 S
500 UthC 84660 3249 A2
1000 UthC 84660 3248 E2
SR-147 W 10400 S
1600 PYSN 84651 3354 B5
1600 UthC 84651 3354 B5
SR-147 S Main St
10 MPTN 84664 3144 A7
10 MPTN 84664 3251 A1
SR-147 W Maple St
10 MPTN 84664 3144 A7
600 MPTN 84664 3143 E7
SR-147 S State Rd
- SPFK 84660 3249 C2
- SPFK 84663 3249 E2
SR-147 W Utah Av
100 PYSN 84651 3354 E5
900 UthC 84651 3354 E5
SR-151 W 10600 S
- SJDN 84070 2282 B4
- SJDN 84095 2282 B4
- SNDY 84070 2282 B4
- SNDY 84095 2282 B4
SR-151 W South Jordan Pkwy
200 SJDN 84095 2282 B4
900 SJDN 84095 2281 E4
3000 SJDN 84095 2280 E3
SR-152 Highland Dr
- CDHT 84121 2177 D1
- HLDY 84121 2177 D1
- MRRY 84121 2177 D1
6100 HLDY 84121 2071 D7
6100 MRRY 84121 2071 D7
SR-152 Van Winkle Expwy
- MRRY 84121 2071 C6
- SLkC 84121 2071 C6
5500 MRRY 84117 2071 C6
5500 SLkC 84117 2071 C6
6100 HLDY 84121 2071 D7
SR-154 Bangerter Hwy
- BFDL 84065 2387 A5
- BFDL 84065 2388 B5
- DRPR 84020 2388 D5
- RIVN 84065 2280 D7
- RIVN 84065 2386 C1
- RIVN 84065 2387 C5
- SJDN 84095 2280 D1
- SLCY 84104 1856 C5
- SLCY 84104 1962 C1
- SLCY 84120 1962 C1
- TYVL 84084 2068 D7
- TYVL 84084 2174 D3
- TYVL 84118 2068 D5
- WJDN 84084 2068 D7
- WJDN 84084 2174 D5
- WJDN 84088 2174 D5
- WJDN 84088 2280 D1
- WVCY 84120 1962 D3
- WVCY 84120 2068 D5
SR-156 N Main St
- SPFK 84660 3142 C7
10 SPFK 84660 3249 C2
SR-156 S Main St
10 SPFK 84660 3249 C3
SR-158
- WbrC 84317 1059 C6
SR-158 Powder Mountain Rd
4400 WbrC 84310 1001 E1
SR-158 Wolf Creek Dr
3200 WbrC 84310 1001 E3
SR-164
- SPFK 84660 3249 C5
- UthC 84660 3249 C5
SR-164 W 8000 S
800 SALM 84660 3248 D6
800 SALM 84660 3249 A6
800 SPFK 84660 3248 D6
800 SPFK 84660 3249 A6
800 UthC 84660 3248 D6
800 UthC 84660 3249 A6
SR-164 Arrowhead Trail Rd
- SPFK 84660 3249 B5
SR-165
- CchC 84319 591 D7
- CchC 84319 651 D4
- CchC 84319 710 D2
- CchC 84321 527 D7
- CchC 84321 591 D6
- CchC 84328 651 D7
- CchC 84328 710 D2
- CchC 84332 527 D7
- HYRM 84319 651 D2
- LOGN 84321 527 D7
- MLVI 84321 591 D1
- MLVI 84332 591 D2
- NBLY 84321 591 D6
- PVDN 84321 527 D7
- PVDN 84332 527 D7
SR-165 S 200 W
400 HYRM 84319 651 D4
SR-165 200 St W
8600 PARA 84319 710 D4
8600 PARA 84328 710 D4
SR-165 N 800 St E
10 HYRM 84319 651 D2
200 CchC 84321 651 D2
SR-165 S 800 St E
10 HYRM 84319 651 D3
SR-165 S Main St
2400 CchC 84321 591 D2
2400 CchC 84332 591 D2
2400 MLVI 84332 591 D2
2400 NBLY 84321 591 D2
2500 NBLY 84332 591 D2
SR-167 Trappers Loop Rd
- WbrC 84317 1060 E7
SR-171 E 3300 S
10 SSLK 84115 1964 C5
500 SSLK 84106 1964 E5
700 SLkC 84106 1964 E5
700 SLkC 84106 1965 A5
1100 SLCY 84106 1965 A5
2000 SLkC 84109 1965 E5
2300 SLkC 84109 1966 A5
SR-171 W 3300 S
10 SSLK 84115 1964 D5
400 SSLK 84119 1964 A5
900 SSLK 84119 1963 E5
1100 WVCY 84119 1963 E5
SR-171 W 3500 S
1300 WVCY 84119 1963 A6
3000 WVCY 84119 1962 E6
3600 WVCY 84120 1962 E6
5000 WVCY 84120 1961 E6
5600 WVCY 84128 1961 E6
7000 WVCY 84128 1960 E6
7200 SLkC 84044 1960 D6
SR-172 S 5600 W
- SLCY 84116 1855 D3
- SLCY 84120 1961 D1
- SLCY 84128 1961 D1
100 SLCY 84104 1855 D3
1300 SLCY 84104 1961 D1
2100 WVCY 84128 1961 D4
3500 WVCY 84120 1961 D7
4000 WVCY 84120 2067 D1
4000 WVCY 84128 2067 D1
4700 SLkC 84118 2067 D1
4700 WVCY 84118 2067 D1
SR-172 Wolverine Wy
3500 WVCY 84120 1961 D6
3500 WVCY 84128 1961 D6
SR-173
- SLkC 84118 2068 A5
SR-173 W 5300 S
300 MRRY 84107 2070 B5
300 MRRY 84123 2070 B5
SR-173 W 5400 S
800 MRRY 84123 2069 E5
800 MRRY 84123 2070 A5
1000 TYVL 84123 2069 E5
1700 TYVL 84118 2069 E5
3000 TYVL 84118 2068 E5
4800 SLkC 84118 2068 B5
5000 SLkC 84118 2067 E5
5600 WVCY 84118 2067 E5
6400 SLkC 84006 2066 D5
6400 WVCY 84006 2066 D5
6400 WVCY 84044 2066 D5
6400 WVCY 84044 2067 A5
6400 WVCY 84084 2066 D5
6400 WVCY 84084 2067 A5
SR-173 Spartan Wy
- MRRY 84107 2070 C4
SR-180 S 500 E
100 ANFK 84003 2711 D2
400 UthC 84003 2711 D2
SR-181 S 1300 E
500 SLCY 84102 1859 B6
900 SLCY 84105 1859 B6
1600 SLCY 84105 1965 B1
2100 SLCY 84106 1965 B1
3100 SLkC 84106 1965 B4
3900 SLkC 84124 1965 B7
4000 SLkC 84124 2071 B1
4500 SLkC 84117 2071 B1
SR-181 Richmond St
2900 SLCY 84106 1965 B4
3000 SLkC 84106 1965 B4
SR-184 E 300 N
10 SLCY 84103 1858 C2
SR-184 Columbus St
300 SLCY 84103 1858 C2
SR-184 N State St
100 SLCY 84103 1858 D2
SR-184 Victory Rd
- SLCY 84116 1754 C7
500 SLCY 84103 1754 C7
500 SLCY 84103 1858 D2
SR-186
- SLCY 84104 1857 A3
- SLCY - 1966 B3
- SLkC - 1966 B3
- SLCY 84116 1857 A3
SR-186 N 300 W
10 SLCY 84103 1858 B3
SR-186 S 300 W
10 SLCY 84101 1858 B3
SR-186 E 400 S
10 SLCY 84101 1858 D4
10 SLCY 84111 1858 D4
500 SLCY 84102 1858 D4
700 SLCY 84102 1859 A4
SR-186 W 400 S
10 SLCY 84101 1858 C4
SR-186 E 500 S
1000 SLCY 84102 1859 D4
1400 SLCY 84108 1859 D4
1400 SLCY 84112 1859 D4
SR-186 S 2100 E
800 SLCY 84108 1859 E5
SR-186 Foothill Blvd
500 SLCY 84108 1859 D4
500 SLCY 84112 1859 D4
SR-186 Foothill Dr
1100 SLCY 84108 1859 E6
1500 SLCY 84108 1860 A7
1600 SLCY 84108 1966 A1
2100 SLCY 84109 1966 B3
SR-186 W North Temple
300 SLCY 84103 1858 B3
400 SLCY 84101 1858 B3
500 SLCY 84116 1858 B3
900 SLCY 84116 1857 D2
1000 SLCY 84104 1857 D2
SR-190
- SLkC 84098 2183 A3
- WshC 84049 2183 C4
SR-190 E 6200 S
- CDHT 84121 2072 B7
- HLDY 84121 2072 B7
- HLDY 84121 2178 C1
SR-190 E Big Cottonwd Cyn Rd
- SLkC 84098 2182 D2
- SLkC 84098 2183 A3
3800 CDHT 84121 2178 D2
4000 SLkC 84121 2178 E2
SR-190 Wasatch Blvd
6600 CDHT 84121 2178 C2
6600 HLDY 84121 2178 C1
SR-193
- CRFD 84015 1228 B6
- DvsC 84040 1229 A6
- DvsC 84041 1229 A6
- DvsC 84056 1228 C6
- DvsC 84056 1229 A6
- LYTN 84040 1229 E5
- LYTN 84040 1230 A5
- LYTN 84041 1228 E6
- LYTN 84041 1229 A6
- LYTN 84056 1228 E6
- LYTN 84056 1229 A6
SR-193 E 3000 N
1300 LYTN 84040 1229 C6
SR-193 W 3000 N
10 DvsC 84041 1228 E6
10 DvsC 84056 1228 E6
10 LYTN 84041 1228 E6
SR-193 Bernard Fisher Hwy
- CRFD 84015 1227 E6
- CRFD 84015 1228 A6
SR-195
- HLDY 84124 1965 E7
- HLDY 84124 2071 E1
SR-195 S 2300 E
2700 SLCY 84109 1965 E5
2700 SLkC 84109 1965 E5
4100 HLDY 84124 2071 E2
SR-197 N 500 W
10 LEHI 84043 2603 B5
SR-198
- SNQN 84655 3461 B6
- UthC 84651 3461 C4
SR-198 E 100 N
10 PYSN 84651 3354 E5
300 PYSN 84651 3355 A5
SR-198 N 100 W
10 PYSN 84651 3354 E5
SR-198 S 100 W
10 PYSN 84651 3354 E5
SR-198 W 100 N
10 PYSN 84651 3354 E5
SR-198 E 300 S
10 SPFK 84660 3249 D3
SR-198 E Canyon Rd
600 SPFK 84660 3249 E3
1200 SPFK 84660 3250 B4
SR-198 S Main St
300 SPFK 84660 3249 C3
1200 UthC 84660 3249 C5
SR-198 State Rd
- PYSN 84651 3354 E5
- PYSN 84651 3355 A5
- SALM 84653 3355 D4
- UthC 84651 3355 D4
SR-198 N State Rd
400 SALM 84653 3356 B2
900 UthC 84653 3356 B1
SR-198 S State Rd
- SALM 84653 3356 B3
500 SALM 84653 3355 E4
1400 PYSN 84651 3461 D2
1800 PYSN 84651 3249 C6
8100 UthC 84660 3249 C7
8600 UthC 84660 3356 C1
11000 PYSN 84651 3354 D7
11600 UthC 84651 3461 D2
SR-198 S State St
13200 UthC 84651 3461 B6
SR-201 E 2100 S
10 SLCY 84115 1964 C2
10 SSLK 84115 1964 C2
SR-201 W 2100 S
10 SLCY 84115 1964 C2
10 SSLK 84115 1964 C2
600 SLCY 84104 1964 A2
600 SLCY 84119 1964 A2
600 SSLK 84119 1964 A2
SR-201 2100 S Frwy
- SLCY - 1961 A3
- SLCY - 1962 D2
- SLCY - 1963 E2
- SLCY - 1964 A2
- SSLK - 1963 E2
- SSLK - 1964 A2
- WVCY - 1961 E2
- WVCY - 1962 D2
- WVCY - 1963 E2
SR-201 W 2400 S
- WVCY 84128 1960 E3
- WVCY 84128 1961 A3
7200 SLkC 84044 1960 A3
8600 SLkC 84044 1959 A2
9100 SLkC 84006 1959 D3
SR-203 Harrison Blvd
1200 OGDN 84404 1116 C1
1500 OGDN 84401 1116 C1
2700 OGDN 84403 1116 B6
3900 OGDN 84403 1173 B1
4800 SOGN 84403 1173 B3
5300 WbrC 84403 1173 B3
5900 SOGN 84405 1173 B3
SR-204 Wall Av
100 OGDN 84404 1056 D5
1200 OGDN 84404 1115 D2
1800 OGDN 84401 1115 D2
3600 OGDN 84405 1115 D6
3600 SOGN 84405 1115 D6
SR-204 N Wall Av
100 OGDN 84404 1056 D4
400 HARR 84404 1056 D4
SR-209 E 9000 S
10 SNDY 84070 2176 D7
700 SNDY 84094 2176 D7
700 SNDY 84094 2177 A7
SR-209 E 9000 S
800 SNDY 84094 2283 A1
SR-209 W 9000 S
- SLkC 84088 2176 A7
- WJDN 84088 2176 A7
10 SNDY 84070 2176 C7
900 WJDN 84088 2175 E7
3000 WJDN 84088 2174 E7
SR-209 E 9400 S
1000 SNDY 84094 2283 A1
1300 SLkC 84092 2283 C1
1300 SNDY 84092 2283 A1
1300 SNDY 84093 2283 A1
SR-209 S Little Cottonwood Rd
2400 SNDY 84092 2284 A1
2700 SLkC 84092 2284 A1
3100 SNDY 84092 2284 A1
9400 SNDY 84092 2283 E1
9400 SNDY 84093 2283 E1
SR-210 N Little Cottonwood Rd
3800 SLkC 84092 2284 D1
3800 SLkC 84121 2284 D1
SR-210 Little Cottonwd Cyn Rd
- ALTA 84049 2181 E6
- ALTA 84049 2182 A6
- SLkC 84049 2181 E6
- SLkC 84049 2287 B1
8900 CDHT 84093 2178 D7
8900 CDHT 84121 2178 D7
9000 CDHT 84092 2178 D7
9000 SLkC 84092 2178 D7
9000 SLkC 84092 2284 D1
9000 SLkC 84121 2178 D7
9000 SLkC 84121 2284 D1
SR-210 Wasatch Blvd
- CDHT 84093 2178 D7
7000 CDHT 84121 2178 D3
SR-218
- AMGA 84335 398 E2
- CchC 84335 398 E2
- CchC 84335 399 B2
- SHFD 84335 399 B2
SR-218 W 6200 N
2800 AMGA 84335 398 B1
SR-224
- PKCY 84060 2078 A1
- PKCY 84060 2184 E1
- PKCY 84098 2078 A1
- SmtC 84060 2078 A1
- SmtC 84098 1971 E3
- SmtC 84098 2078 A1
SR-224 Deer Valley Dr
1100 PKCY 84060 2078 D4
SR-224 Marsac Av
10 PKCY 84060 2078 E5
SR-224 Park Av
1600 PKCY 84060 2078 B1
SR-225 Park Ln
300 FMTN 84025 1346 B7
SR-227 S 200 W
- FMTN 84025 1448 C2
SR-227 W State St
10 FMTN 84025 1448 D2
SR-232 N Hill Field Rd
900 LYTN 84041 1282 E2
2000 LYTN 84041 1228 E7
SR-232 W Hill Field Rd
700 LYTN 84041 1282 D3
SR-235 E 2550 N
100 NHON 84414 998 D6
SR-235 W 2550 N
100 NHON 84414 998 D6
100 PTVW 84414 998 D6
SR-235 Washington Blvd
100 OGDN 84404 1056 E5
1700 NHON 84404 1056 E2
1700 NHON 84414 1056 E2
1700 WbrC 84404 1056 E2
1700 WbrC 84414 1056 E2
2400 NHON 84414 998 E7
SR-235 N Washington Blvd
100 OGDN 84404 1056 E5
400 HARR 84404 1056 E4
1500 NHON 84404 1056 E2
1500 NHON 84414 1056 E2
1500 WbrC 84404 1056 E1
2300 NHON 84414 998 E6
SR-238
- CchC 84332 591 E2
- MLVI 84332 591 E3
- PVDN 84332 527 E7
- PVDN 84332 591 E2
- RVHT 84321 527 E7
- RVHT 84321 528 A4
SR-238 E 300 S
10 LOGN 84321 527 E4
SR-238 S 400 E
- LOGN 84321 527 E4
300 RVHT 84321 527 E4
SR-238 N Main St
10 MLVI 84332 591 E3
800 CchC 84332 591 E1
SR-238 S Main St
10 MLVI 84332 591 E3
SR-238 E Mill Rd
- MLVI 84332 591 E3
200 NBLY 84321 591 D3
SR-240 W 6900 St N
2600 HYVL 84314 646 C2
SR-241 W 1600 N
1600 LNDN 84042 2819 E1
1600 OREM 84057 2819 E1
SR-248
- PKCY 84060 2079 B2
- SmtC 84017 1973 D7
- SmtC 84017 2079 E1
- SmtC 84098 1973 D7
- SmtC 84098 2079 B2
SR-248 Kearns Blvd
700 PKCY 84060 2078 D3
2400 PKCY 84060 2079 A3
2600 PKCY 84098 2079 C2
2600 SmtC 84098 2079 C2
SR-265 University Pkwy
400 OREM 84097 2927 E1
500 OREM 84097 2928 A1
900 OREM 84604 2928 A1
900 PRVO 84097 2928 A1
900 PRVO 84604 2928 A1
SR-265 E University Pkwy
10 OREM 84058 2927 D1
SR-265 N University Pkwy
1800 PRVO 84604 2928 C3
SR-265 W University Pkwy
10 OREM 84058 2927 E1
SR-266
- HLDY 84117 2071 E2
- HLDY 84117 2072 A2
- HLDY 84124 2071 E2
- HLDY 84124 2072 A2
- SLkC 84124 2072 C2
SR-266 E 4430 S
2500 HLDY 84117 2072 A2
2500 HLDY 84124 2072 A2
2700 SLkC 84124 2072 A2
SR-266 E 4500 S
10 MRRY 84107 2070 C2
200 SLkC 84107 2070 D2
700 SLkC 84107 2071 A2
900 SLkC 84117 2071 A2
900 SLkC 84124 2071 A2
1700 HLDY 84117 2071 D2
1700 HLDY 84124 2071 D2
SR-266 W 4500 S
10 MRRY 84107 2070 A2
400 MRRY 84123 2070 A2
600 TYVL 84123 2070 A2
SR-266 W 4700 S
800 TYVL 84123 2069 E2
800 TYVL 84123 2070 A2
1700 TYVL 84118 2069 C3
1700 TYVL 84119 2069 C3
SR-268 W 600 N
300 SLCY 84103 1858 B1
400 SLCY 84116 1858 B1
SR-269
- SLCY 84104 1858 A4
SR-269 W 6th S
200 SLCY 84101 1858 B5
SR-269 E 500 S
10 SLCY 84111 1858 C4
SR-269 W 500 S
10 SLCY 84101 1858 C4
SR-269 E 600 S
10 SLCY 84111 1858 C5
SR-269 W 600 S
10 SLCY 84101 1858 C5
SR-270 S West Temple
400 SLCY 84101 1858 C5
SR-272 N Main St
1200 FMTN 84025 1346 B5
SR-273 W 200 N
10 KYVL 84037 1345 C1
SR-273 N Main St
10 KYVL 84037 1345 C1
SR-273 S Main St
- FMTN 84025 1346 A4
10 KYVL 84037 1345 C1
800 DvsC 84037 1345 E3
900 FTHT 84037 1345 E3
1100 DvsC 84037 1346 A4
1100 FMTN 84037 1346 A4
1100 FTHT 84037 1346 A4
1100 KYVL 84037 1346 A4
SR-282 E 400 S
1300 SLCY 84102 1859 B4
SR-282 North Campus Dr
- SLCY 84102 1859 C3
- SLCY 84103 1859 C3
- SLCY 84112 1859 C3
SR-282 E South Campus Dr
1500 SLCY 84112 1859 D4
1900 SLCY 84113 1859 D4
SR-282 Wasatch Dr
100 SLCY 84112 1859 D3
200 SLCY 84113 1859 D3
500 SLCY 84108 1859 D4
SR-284 E 3850 S
- OGDN 84403 1116 B7
SR-284 E 4000 S
- OGDN 84403 1173 B1
SR-284 E 4100 S
1200 OGDN 84403 1173 C1
SR-284 Dixon Dr
- OGDN 84403 1116 B7
- OGDN 84403 1173 B1
SR-284 Edvalson St
1200 OGDN 84403 1116 B7
SR-315 W 750 N
10 WLRD 84340 885 B4
Stable Bay Dr
3700 SLkC 84044 1960 C7
Stablewood Cir
1500 SLkC 84117 2071 C4
Stacey Cir
800 FMTN 84025 1448 D4
9600 SNDY 84070 2282 D1
Staci Ct
500 OGDN 84404 1056 E6
500 OGDN 84404 1057 A6
Stadium Av
100 PRVO 84604 2928 D3
Stadium Cir
1800 PRVO 84604 2928 D3
E Stadium Dr
1100 LOGN 84341 464 B7
Stadium Ln
2000 PRVO 84604 2928 D3
Stafford Cir
2700 WVCY 84119 2069 A2
Stafford Ct
4300 PRVO 84097 2821 B5
Stafford Pl
2700 WVCY 84119 2069 A2
Stafford Wy
4300 WVCY 84119 2069 A2
Stag Wy
- PKCY 84060 2185 A2
Stagecoach Cir
400 CTRV 84014 1551 D1
1900 RIVN 84065 2387 C5
Stagecoach Dr
7300 SmtC 84098 1864 E6
7300 SmtC 84098 1865 A7
Stagg St
7600 MDVL 84047 2176 A4
Staheli Ln
- UthC 84660 3250 B2
Staker Cir
1600 CDHT 84121 2177 C2
Stalbridge Cir
1900 SNDY 84093 2177 C6
Stallion Ln
1700 SLCY 84116 1753 C5
Stamford Ct
700 ALPN 84004 2498 A3
Stamford Dr
300 NSLK 84054 1652 C6
Stampede Dr
- DRPR 84020 2389 C6
- FMTN 84025 1447 D1
Standard Ct
9000 SLkC 84044 1959 E5
Standard Wy
300 OGDN 84404 1056 C5
Standel Dr
500 SLkC 84108 1860 D4
Standing Oak Dr
1700 DRPR 84020 2389 D5
Stane Av
4200 WVCY 84120 1962 B5
Stanford Ct
10 PKCY 84060 2079 A7
1400 DRPR 84020 2389 C3
Stanford Dr
1400 LYTN 84041 1282 B2
Stanford Ln
2500 HLDY 84117 2072 A4
Stanida Cir
5800 SLkC 84121 2071 D6
Stanley Av
400 SSLK 84115 1964 E5
Stanley Dr
- TMTN 84337 520 D7
1300 SNDY 84093 2177 C7
1400 SNDY 84093 2283 C1
Stanley Glen Ln
1000 TYVL 84123 2069 E4
Stansbury Wy
1000 SLCY 84108 1860 B6
Stanton Av
300 SLCY 84111 1858 D4
Stanton Dr
3100 WVCY 84120 1962 B6
Stanwick Rd
2000 CDHT 84121 2177 D1
E Staples Dr
4700 WbrC 84310 1001 D5
Star Cir
11100 SNDY 84092 2283 C5
N Star Dr
- HILD 84003 2497 C5
Star Ln
500 EKMT 84651 3462 E1
Starboard Ln
5400 TYVL 84123 2069 C5
Starburst Cir
10700 SNDY 84094 2283 B4
Star Crest Dr
300 SLCY 84116 1857 C2
700 SLCY 84116 1753 C7
Starcrest Dr
100 OREM 84058 2927 D1
Stardust Cir
3800 WJDN 84088 2174 C6
Stardust Dr
1700 TYVL 84118 2069 C4
Star Fire Rd
3200 SJDN 84095 2280 E1
Starflower Wy
5400 WJDN 84084 2173 E2
Stargazer Cir
8500 SNDY 84093 2177 E6
Star Lily Cir
9200 WJDN 84088 2174 A7
9200 WJDN 84088 2280 A1
Starling Av
2400 WVCY 84119 1963 A5
Starling Cir
2400 WVCY 84119 1963 B5
Starling Dr
2500 CDHT 84121 2178 A3
Starlite Dr
3200 WJDN 84088 2174 E5
5900 MRRY 84107 2070 C7
Starlite Hill Ln
12500 HRMN 84065 2385 C2
Star Pine Dr
1100 SNDY 84094 2283 B5
Starr Av
500 PRVO 84601 2928 A5
800 PRVO 84604 2928 B5
Star View Cir
4300 WVCY 84128 2067 D2
Starview Dr
10 SmtC 84098 1972 C2
Starwood Cir
1200 SNDY 84094 2283 B5
4000 WVCY 84120 2068 C1
Starwood Dr
1100 SNDY 84094 2283 B5
Starwood St
3800 WVCY 84120 1962 D7
4000 WVCY 84120 2068 B1
State Cir
1000 SLCY 84104 1857 E4
S State Cir
1500 SRCS 84075 1281 A3
State Rd
- PYSN 84651 3354 E5
- PYSN 84651 3355 C4
- SALM 84653 3355 C4
- UthC 84651 3355 C4
1800 SGVL 84663 3143 B6
2600 UthC 84663 3143 B6
State Rd SR-51
1800 SGVL 84663 3143 B6
2600 UthC 84663 3143 B6
State Rd SR-198
- PYSN 84651 3354 E5
- PYSN 84651 3355 C4
- SALM 84653 3355 C4
- UthC 84651 3355 C4
E State Rd
200 ANFK 84003 2711 D1
400 LNDN 84042 2712 E4
700 ANFK 84003 2712 A2
700 UthC 84003 2711 D1
700 UthC 84003 2712 A2
1100 PTGV 84062 2712 A2
E State Rd US-89
200 ANFK 84003 2711 D1

STREET Block City ZIP Map# Grid

E State Rd US-89
400 LNDN 84042 2712 E4
700 ANFK 84003 2712 A2
700 UthC 84003 2711 D1
700 UthC 84003 2712 A2
1100 PTGV 84062 2712 A2
N State Rd
400 SALM 84653 3356 B2
900 UthC 84653 3356 B2
N State Rd SR-198
400 SALM 84653 3356 B2
900 UthC 84653 3356 B2
S State Rd
- SALM 84653 3356 A3
- SGVL 84663 3143 A7
- SPFK 84660 3143 A7
- SPFK 84660 3249 D2
- SPFK 84660 3250 A1
- SPFK 84663 3143 A7
- SPFK 84663 3249 D2
- UthC 84660 3143 A7
- UthC 84663 3143 A7
500 SALM 84653 3355 E4
1400 PYSN 84651 3461 D3
3400 SPFK 84663 3250 A1
3400 UthC 84660 3250 A1
3400 UthC 84663 3250 A1
8100 UthC 84660 3249 C6
8600 UthC 84660 3356 C1
11000 PYSN 84651 3354 D7
11600 UthC 84651 3461 D3
S State Rd SR-51
- SGVL 84663 3143 A7
- SPFK 84660 3143 A7
- SPFK 84660 3250 A1
- SPFK 84663 3143 A7
- UthC 84660 3143 A7
- UthC 84663 3143 A7
3400 SPFK 84663 3250 A1
3400 UthC 84660 3250 A1
3400 UthC 84663 3250 A1
S State Rd SR-147
- SPFK 84660 3249 D2
- SPFK 84663 3249 D2
S State Rd SR-198
- SALM 84653 3356 A3
500 SALM 84653 3355 E4
1400 PYSN 84651 3461 D3
1800 SPFK 84660 3249 C6
8100 UthC 84660 3249 C6
8600 UthC 84660 3356 C1
11000 PYSN 84651 3354 D7
11600 UthC 84651 3461 D3
State St
10 CRFD 84015 1227 E5
700 CRFD 84015 1228 A7
1500 LYTN 84041 1228 A7
6800 MDVL 84047 2176 C2
7800 MDVL 84070 2176 C5
8200 SNDY 84070 2176 C5
9200 SNDY 84070 2282 C2
State St SR-126
10 CRFD 84015 1227 E5
700 CRFD 84015 1228 A7
1500 LYTN 84041 1228 A7
State St US-89
6800 MDVL 84047 2176 C2
7800 MDVL 84070 2176 C5
8200 SNDY 84070 2176 C5
9200 SNDY 84070 2282 C2
E State St
10 FMTN 84025 1448 D2
10 LEHI 84043 2603 C5
900 UthC 84043 2603 C5
1400 ANFK 84003 2603 C5
1500 ANFK 84003 2604 A6
1500 ANFK 84043 2604 A6
1500 UthC 84043 2604 A6
E State St SR-106
10 FMTN 84025 1448 D2
E State St US-89
10 LEHI 84043 2603 C5
900 UthC 84043 2603 C5
1400 ANFK 84003 2603 C5
1500 ANFK 84003 2604 A6
1500 ANFK 84043 2604 A6
1500 UthC 84043 2604 A6
N State St
10 LNDN 84042 2713 A5
10 OREM 84057 2820 C3
10 SLCY 84103 1858 D2
500 LNDN 84042 2712 E4
1200 PRVO 84604 2928 B3
1700 OREM 84057 2713 A5
N State St SR-184
100 SLCY 84103 1858 D2
N State St US-89
10 LNDN 84042 2713 A5
10 OREM 84057 2820 C3
10 SLCY 84103 1858 D3
500 LNDN 84042 2712 E4
1200 PRVO 84604 2928 B3
1700 OREM 84057 2713 A5
S State St
10 LNDN 84042 2713 B7
10 OREM 84058 2820 E7
10 SLCY 84111 1858 D3
100 OREM 84057 2713 B7
300 PRVO 84606 2928 D7
500 PRVO 84606 3035 E2
700 OREM 84097 2820 E7
1000 OREM 84058 2927 E1
1000 OREM 84097 2927 E1
1300 SLCY 84115 1858 D5
1400 PRVO 84606 3036 A3
1500 SLCY 84115 1964 D1
1600 UthC 84606 3036 A3
1700 OREM 84058 2928 A2
1700 OREM 84097 2928 A2
1800 PRVO 84604 2928 A2
2100 SSLK 84115 1964 D6
3900 SLkC 84107 1964 D6
4000 SLkC 84107 2070 D1
4200 MRRY 84107 2070 D1
6400 MRRY 84107 2176 C1
6500 MRRY 84047 2176 C1
6600 MDVL 84107 2176 C1
8600 MDVL 84047 2176 C6
8600 SNDY 84070 2176 C6
11400 DRPR 84020 2282 C6
13200 UthC 84651 3461 B6
S State St SR-198
13200 UthC 84651 3461 B6
S State St US-89
10 LNDN 84042 2713 B7
10 OREM 84058 2820 E7
10 SLCY 84111 1858 D3
100 OREM 84057 2713 B7
300 PRVO 84606 2928 D7
500 PRVO 84606 3035 E2
700 OREM 84097 2820 E7
1000 OREM 84058 2927 E1
1000 OREM 84097 2927 E1
1300 SLCY 84115 1858 D5
1400 PRVO 84606 3036 A3
1500 SLCY 84115 1964 D1
1600 OREM 84058 2928 A2
1600 OREM 84097 2928 A2
1600 UthC 84606 3036 A3
1800 PRVO 84604 2928 A2
2100 SSLK 84115 1964 D6
3900 SLkC 84107 1964 D6
4000 SLkC 84107 2070 D1
4200 MRRY 84107 2070 D1
6400 MRRY 84107 2176 C1
6500 MRRY 84047 2176 C1
6600 MDVL 84107 2176 C1
8600 MDVL 84047 2176 C6
8600 SNDY 84070 2176 C6
11400 DRPR 84020 2282 C6
W State St
10 ANFK 84003 2711 A1
10 FMTN 84025 1448 C2
10 LEHI 84043 2603 A4
100 ANFK 84003 2604 A7
W State St SR-227
10 FMTN 84025 1448 D2
W State St US-89
10 ANFK 84003 2711 A1
10 LEHI 84043 2603 A4
100 ANFK 84003 2604 A7
Statehood Dr
2200 BFDL 84065 2387 B7
Statesman Pl
10100 SJDN 84095 2281 A3
Statice Av
800 SLkC 84094 2283 A3
S Statice Cir
10400 SLkC 84094 2283 A3
Station Creek Wy
7100 CDHT 84093 2177 B2
Station Loop Rd
1000 SmtC 84098 1972 A1
E Stauffer Ln
- MRRY 84107 2070 C6
W Stauffer Ln
10 MRRY 84107 2070 C5
Stauning Cove
2900 CDHT 84093 2178 B4
Stayner Dr
1400 FMTN 84025 1345 E5
Steed Dr
900 CRFD 84015 1227 B3
Steele
- ANFK 84003 2604 C6
Steele St
5000 SLkC 84118 2068 C4
Steeple Chase Ln
6100 MRRY 84121 2071 C7
Steep Mountain Dr
10 DRPR 84020 2495 D1
14700 DRPR 84020 2388 E7
Steffensen Dr
7500 CDHT 84121 2178 A4
W Stegen St
700 OGDN 84404 1056 C7
Stein Wy
7700 PKCY 84060 2184 E2
Stellaria Cir
1300 BNFL 84010 1654 B3
Stephanie Cir
400 SNDY 84070 2282 E1
Stephanie Wy
1400 KYVL 84037 1345 E5
Stephen Ln
2300 RIVN 84065 2387 B2
Stephens Av
1800 OGDN 84401 1115 D2
3500 OGDN 84405 1115 D6
Stephens Cir
4500 SOGN 84403 1173 A2
Stephens Ct
3200 OGDN 84403 1115 E6
Stephens View Cir
12200 DRPR 84020 2388 A1
Stephens View Wy
700 DRPR 84020 2388 A1
Stephie Marie Ln
400 SLCY 84115 1964 D3
400 SSLK 84115 1964 D3
Sterling Cir
100 BNFL 84010 1653 D6
E Sterling Cir
900 SPFK 84660 3249 E4
Sterling Dr
100 BNFL 84010 1653 D6
300 FTHT 84037 1346 B2
900 SLCY 84116 1753 E7
7400 PKCY 84060 2184 E1
7600 PKCY 84060 2185 A1
9100 SNDY 84093 2177 C7
9200 SNDY 84093 2283 C1
E Sterling Dr
900 SPFK 84660 3249 E4
1100 SPFK 84660 3250 A4
Sterling Hills Cove
2000 DRPR 84020 2389 E1
Sterling Park Cir
9800 SJDN 84095 2280 E2
Sterling View Dr
10800 SJDN 84095 2282 B5
Sterling Wood Cove
2000 DRPR 84020 2389 D1
Stern Dr
1300 TYVL 84123 2069 D7
Sternwood Dr
6200 TYVL 84084 2069 B7
Stetson Cir
1400 SLCY 84104 1963 D1
Stetson Dr
100 SGVL 84663 3143 C6
E Stetson Dr
10 SGVL 84663 3143 C6
Stetson Wy
1300 SLCY 84104 1963 D1
Steve Ln
13800 HRMN 84065 2385 A5
Steven Cir
1200 FMTN 84025 1346 C6
Steward Wy
- OGDN 84404 1056 C6
Stewart Cir
1300 SLCY 84104 1857 D7
S Stewart Dr
300 OGDN 84404 1056 C6
Stewart St
500 SLCY 84104 1857 D4
1600 SLCY 84104 1963 D1
Stewart Hill Ct
700 RVHT 84321 528 A4
Stewart Hill Dr
300 RVHT 84321 528 A4
Stewart Hill Dr E
900 LOGN 84321 528 A3
900 RVHT 84321 528 A3
Still Blossom Ln
700 SNDY 84070 2282 A1
Stillman Ln
2100 SLkC 84109 1965 E5
Stillwater Cir
9100 SNDY 84093 2177 C7
Stillwater Pl
3900 WVCY 84120 1962 C4
Stillwater Wy
3900 WVCY 84120 1962 C7
3900 WVCY 84120 2068 C1
Stillwood Cir
4600 SLkC 84117 2071 B3
Stillwood Dr
1300 SLkC 84117 2071 B2
Stimpson Spring Rd
4200 RVDL 84405 1172 D1
Stingtown Rd
900 WbrC 84310 1002 B7
900 WbrC 84310 1060 B2
Stirling
- LOGN 84341 463 C6
Stockbridge Ln
1300 SLkC 84117 2071 B3
Stockton St
5200 SLkC 84118 2067 E4
Stoker Ln
1400 SRCS 84075 1227 A7
Stokes Av
300 DRPR 84020 2388 D4
Stokes Dr
2100 WHVN 84401 1114 C3
Stokewater Dr
6200 TYVL 84084 2068 E7
Stone Cross
4100 PRVO 84604 2821 C6
Stone Rd
2900 CDHT 84121 2178 B3
Stone Bluff Wy
5500 SLkC 84118 2067 D5
Stonebridge Cir
1000 PKCY 84060 2079 A6
12500 DRPR 84020 2388 D2
Stonebridge Dr
100 DRPR 84020 2388 D2
S Stonebridge Dr
1300 LYTN 84041 1282 B7
W Stonebridge Dr
1400 LYTN 84041 1282 B7
Stonebrook Cir
2400 SNDY 84092 2284 A7
Stone Brook Ln
100 PRVO 84604 2821 B6
Stonebury Loop Rd
900 SSLK 84663 3144 C3
2600 UthC 84663 3144 C3
Stone Butte Ln
3100 WVCY 84120 1961 E5
Stonecam Av
3800 WVCY 84120 1961 D5
Stone Canyon Dr
13900 DRPR 84020 2389 B6
Stone Cliff Dr
9700 SNDY 84092 2283 D2
Stone Creek Cir
5300 HILD 84003 2497 D6
Stone Creek Dr
5300 HILD 84003 2497 D7
Stonecreek Dr
1900 WVCY 84119 1963 B6
Stonecreek Hllw
5400 HILD 84003 2497 D7
Stone Creek Ln
1100 LYTN 84041 1282 C7
4200 PRVO 84604 2821 B6
Stone Crest Cir
11600 RIVN 84065 2281 D7
Stone Crest Dr
4800 MRRY 84107 2070 D3
Stone Crest Ln
11700 RIVN 84065 2281 D7
Stonecutter Cir
8000 WJDN 84088 2174 A4
Stonefield Cir
900 SNDY 84094 2177 A5
Stonefield Rd
900 SNDY 84094 2177 A5
Stone Field Wy
- PTVW 84404 997 E3
Stone Flower Wy
5200 SLkC 84118 2067 E5
Stonefly Dr
600 SNDY 84070 2176 E5
Stone Gate Cir
10600 SLkC 84092 2283 E4
10600 SNDY 84092 2283 E4
Stone Gate Ln
10 PRVO 84604 2821 B6
Stonehaven Lp
2200 LEHI 84043 2495 D6
Stonehaven Rd
- LEHI 84043 2495 C6
Stonehaven St
9900 SJDN 84095 2280 C2
Stonehedge
4100 CRHL 84062 2605 B1
Stonehedge Dr
300 SLkC 84107 2070 D1
Stonehedge Rd
700 ALPN 84004 2498 B6
Stonehedge Wy
1800 SGVL 84663 3142 D4
Stonehenge Cir
- PVDN 84332 528 B7
Stonehenge Dr
100 PVDN 84332 528 B7
900 NSLK 84054 1652 C5
Stonehill Ln
3300 CDHT 84121 2178 C5
Stonehollow Cir
6200 TYVL 84084 2068 E7
Stone Hollow Ct
1600 BNFL 84010 1654 D2
11700 RIVN 84065 2281 D7
Stone Hollow Dr
1400 BNFL 84010 1654 C2
Stoneleigh Heights Dr
- DRPR 84020 2389 D7
Stoneleigh Heights Rd
- DRPR 84020 2389 D7
Stone Meadow Dr
1300 WJDN 84088 2175 D7
Stone Mesa Ct
10000 SNDY 84092 2284 C3
Stonemoor Cir
1500 MRRY 84121 2177 C1
Stone Mountain Cir
1400 OGDN 84403 1173 C3
Stone Mountain Ln
3300 SNDY 84092 2284 C2
Stone Mountain Cove
10000 SNDY 84092 2284 C3
Stonepark Cir
100 DRPR 84020 2388 D2
Stone Pine Ln
4800 HLDY 84117 2072 B3
Stone Point Pl
9100 SNDY 84093 2177 A7
Stone Pond Rd
- OGDN 84404 1056 C4
Stone Quarry Cir
5100 WJDN 84088 2173 D6
Stone Ridge Cir
1700 BNFL 84010 1654 C3
9100 SNDY 84093 2177 E7
Stone Ridge Ct
11700 RIVN 84065 2281 C6
E Stone Ridge Dr
1600 BNFL 84010 1654 C2
S Stone Ridge Dr
1400 BNFL 84010 1654 C2
Stone Ridge Ln
1300 RIVN 84065 2281 D7
Stone Spring Cir
8800 WJDN 84088 2174 C6
Stone Valley Wy
1000 SNDY 84094 2283 A7
Stoneview Cir
9100 SNDY 84093 2177 A7
Stone Vista Ln
5000 WJDN 84088 2174 A7
8800 WJDN 84088 2173 D6
Stonewall Ct
10000 SNDY 84092 2284 C3
Stone Wheel Cir
5300 HRMN 84065 2385 E7
Stonewood Cir
2000 SNDY 84093 2177 D5
Stonewood Ct
2000 SNDY 84093 2177 D5
Stonewood Dr
- FRWT 84404 1055 C3
4400 WVCY 84119 2069 A2
8200 SNDY 84093 2177 D5
Stoney Ct
7200 SLkC 84044 1960 E4
Stoney Brook Cir
4300 UthC 84004 2498 B1
Stoneybrook Cir
600 FMTN 84025 1346 D7
Stoneybrook Rd
800 KYVL 84037 1283 E6
Stoney Brook Wy
4500 LEHI 84043 2495 C6
Stoney Creek Cir
3200 WVCY 84128 1961 C5
Stonne Ln
600 KYVL 84037 1283 B6
Stony Brook Cir
5300 SLkC 84118 2067 E6
Stonybrook Ln
10 SGVL 84663 3036 B7
Stony Brook Wy
5600 SLkC 84118 2067 E6
Stony Hill Wy
2600 SPFK 84660 3250 C6
Stony Park Dr
5200 SLkC 84118 2067 E6
Stony Ridge Cir
5400 SLkC 84118 2067 E5
Stony View Dr
1600 SPFK 84660 3250 C6
Stony Vista Dr
5300 SLkC 84118 2067 E6
Storm Mountain Dr
800 TYVL 84123 2070 A3
Stormy Creek Cir
800 SNDY 84094 2283 D4
Stormy Creek Rd
800 SNDY 84094 2283 D4
Stormy Meadow Dr
4800 RIVN 84065 2386 A2
Stornoway Cir
9500 SJDN 84095 2280 A1
Storrs Av
200 ANFK 84003 2711 B2
400 UthC 84003 2711 B2
Stover St
200 SLCY 84113 1859 E3
Stowe Ct
800 FMTN 84025 1346 B4
Stowe Dr
900 OGDN 84404 1057 D7
Strasbourg Cir
9100 SNDY 84093 2177 E7
E Stratford Av
500 SLCY 84106 1964 E3
1300 SLCY 84106 1965 C3
W Stratford Av
10 SSLK 84115 1964 C3
1500 WVCY 84119 1963 C3
Stratford Cir
8800 SNDY 84070 2176 C6
Stratford Dr
2000 SLCY 84109 1965 D3
Stratford Ln
8200 WJDN 84088 2175 D5
Stratler St
5900 MRRY 84107 2070 B7
Strato Dr
1600 SNDY 84093 2177 C5
8400 SLkC 84093 2177 C5
Stratton Dr
4400 HLDY 84117 2072 B2
Stratus St
4100 SLkC 84118 2068 B7
Straw Cir
2200 WJDN 84084 2175 B1
Strawberry Dr
7600 WJDN 84084 2175 A4
Strawberry Lp
7600 WJDN 84084 2175 A4
Strawberry Pl
300 SRSP 84043 2601 D5
Straw Hat Ln
1000 DRPR 84020 2389 A6
Streamside Ct
3600 SLkC 84109 1966 D7
Stream View Dr
2100 CDHT 84093 2177 E5
Streatham Rd
9400 SNDY 84070 2282 C1
Street Ln
100 MIDW 84049 2397 B4
500 WshC 84049 2397 B4
Strickland Pl
5800 WVCY 84128 2067 C1
N Stringer Av
- OGDN 84404 1056 B5
S Stringer Av
- OGDN 84404 1056 B5
Stringfellow Ct
600 SLCY 84111 1858 D5
Stringham Av
- SLCY 84106 1965 B2
500 SLCY 84106 1964 E2
2300 SLCY 84109 1965 E2
2500 SLCY 84109 1966 A2
Stringtown Rd
500 WshC 84049 2397 A5
Strong Ln
10 ALPN 84004 2497 E4
Strongs Ct
300 SLCY 84102 1859 A4
Stryker Av
1900 PKCY 84060 2078 E3
S Stubbs Av
600 PRVO 84601 3035 A1
Stubbs St
700 PTGV 84062 2713 A4
Suada Cir
4000 HLDY 84124 2071 E1
Suada Dr
2100 HLDY 84124 2071 E1
Sublette Cir
8300 SLkC 84093 2177 E5
Sublette Pl
2100 SNDY 84093 2177 E5
2300 SLkC 84093 2177 E5
Suburban Dr
600 BMCY 84302 766 D7
700 BMCY 84302 827 D1
Success Ln
1500 SNDY 84092 2283 C5
Sudbury Av
1300 SNDY 84093 2177 B6
Sue Cir
3400 PRVO 84604 2821 E7
Sue St
3300 SSLK 84115 1964 C5
Suffolk Cir
3700 WVCY 84119 1963 E6
Sugar Ct
700 PYSN 84651 3461 D1
Sugar Pl
2300 WJDN 84088 2175 B5
Sugar St
10 LYTN 84041 1282 C4
Sugar Beet Dr
3800 WVCY 84120 1962 C6
Sugar Berry Rd
11500 DRPR 84020 2282 D6
Sugar Bowl Ln
3000 WVCY 84128 1961 C5
Sugarbush Ct
10700 SJDN 84095 2281 D4
Sugar Creek Wy
1800 WJDN 84088 2175 C4
Sugar Factory Rd
1700 WJDN 84088 2175 A5
Sugarhill Cir
4700 TYVL 84123 2070 A3
Sugarloaf Cir
8600 CDHT 84093 2178 B6
Sugar Loaf Dr
10400 CRHL 84062 2605 C2
Sugarloaf Dr
1700 SNDY 84092 2283 C1
8600 CDHT 84093 2178 B6
Sugarloaf Ln
2300 SLkC 84093 2177 E5
8500 SNDY 84093 2177 E5
8500 SNDY 84093 2178 A6
Sugar Maple Cir
4300 WVCY 84120 2068 B2
Sugarmont Dr
900 SLCY 84106 1965 A2
Sugar Pine Cir
12800 RIVN 84065 2387 C2
Sugarplum Rd
- ALTA 84049 2181 D7
Sulky Cove
13700 HRMN 84065 2385 C5
Sullivan Ln
- PKCY 84060 2078 D4
Sullivan Rd
700 OGDN 84403 1116 A5
1300 PKCY 84060 2078 D4
S Sultan Cir
5900 MRRY 84107 2070 C7
Sultan Downs Dr
3000 WVCY 84120 1962 A4
Sumac Av
400 PRVO 84604 2928 D3
Sumac Cir
- LOGN 84321 528 B2
Sumac Ct
4200 CRHL 84062 2605 B2
Sumac Dr
800 LOGN 84321 528 A3
Sumac Ln
300 PRVO 84604 2928 D3
Sumac Wy
10 BMCY 84302 827 E1
1300 MRRY 84121 2071 B7
6400 MRRY 84121 2177 B1
Summer Cir
4400 CRHL 84062 2605 B3
Summer St
200 SLCY 84116 1857 C2
3100 WJDN 84084 2174 E4
4700 MRRY 84107 2070 C3
Summerborne Cir
1900 SNDY 84093 2177 C5
Summer Chase Cir
300 KYVL 84037 1345 C2
Summer Crest Dr
8800 SNDY 84093 2177 D7
Summercrest Dr
1400 LEHI 84043 2603 D4
Summer Crest Cove
1900 SNDY 84093 2177 A7
Summer Day Dr
10900 SJDN 84095 2280 E5
Summer Estates Cir
3500 CDHT 84121 2178 E4
Summerfield Cir
11500 SNDY 84092 2284 A6
Summerfield Ln
2300 SNDY 84092 2283 E7
2300 SNDY 84092 2284 A6
Summerfield Rd
- SHFD 84335 400 A2
Summer Harvest Dr
1100 DRPR 84020 2389 B3
Summerhill Cir
7600 CDHT 84121 2178 D3
Summer Hill Ct
7600 CDHT 84121 2178 C4
Summer Hill Dr
3300 CDHT 84121 2178 C4
7800 SmtC 84098 1865 A6
Summeridge Dr
1900 TYVL 84118 2069 C6
Summer Leaf Dr
200 DRPR 84020 2495 D1
Summer Meadow Cir
1800 SNDY 84093 2177 D6
Summermeadow Cir
200 BNFL 84010 1653 E7
Summer Meadow Dr
1800 SNDY 84093 2177 A7
Summermeadow Rd
4100 BNFL 84010 1653 E7
Summer Mesa Cir
8900 SNDY 84093 2177 D7
Summer Oak Cir
2300 SNDY 84092 2283 E7
2300 SNDY 84092 2284 A6
Summer Oaks Cir
3500 CDHT 84121 2178 C4
Summer Park Cir
1800 SNDY 84093 2177 A7
Summer Pine Ln
300 SSLK 84115 1964 D6
Summer Place Dr
1600 CRFD 84015 1228 B6
Summerset Cir
13800 DRPR 84020 2388 E5
Summerspring Ln
2300 HLDY 84124 1965 E7
2300 HLDY 84124 1966 A7
Summerstar Cove
2600 WJDN 84088 2175 A5
Summer Stone Dr
5600 SJDN 84095 2279 D6
Summer Trail Dr
3200 WVCY 84120 1961 E4
Summertree Cir
10 OREM 84058 2820 D6
Summer Tree Dr
800 WBNF 84087 1551 B6
Summer Tree Ln
2600 WJDN 84088 2175 A5
Summertree Ln
300 OREM 84058 2820 D6
Summerview Cir
4300 BNFL 84010 1653 E7
Summerview Rd
4400 BNFL 84010 1653 E7
Summer View Wy
5200 TYVL 84123 2069 D5
Summerwild Av
600 RVHT 84321 527 E5
Summer Willow Dr
1800 SNDY 84093 2177 C6
Summer Willow Pl
1900 SNDY 84093 2177 A7
Summer Wind Ct
5300 HRMN 84065 2385 E6
Summer Wind Ln
14200 HRMN 84065 2385 E6
Summerwood Cir
400 BNFL 84010 1653 E7
Summerwood Dr
1800 FMTN 84025 1346 B4
2000 LYTN 84040 1283 E5
2600 LYTN 84040 1284 A4
4400 BNFL 84010 1653 D7
4700 BNFL 84010 1754 D1
4700 DvsC 84010 1754 D1
4700 DvsC 84054 1754 D1
4700 NSLK 84054 1754 D1
S Summerwood Dr
4200 BNFL 84010 1653 E7
Summerwood St
4400 TYVL 84123 2069 E2
Summit Cir
2300 SLCY 84109 1966 B3
Summit Dr
- CchC 84335 400 B2
- PRVO 84606 2928 E6
- PRVO 84606 2929 A6
100 SHFD 84335 400 A2
Summit Dr
300 SmtC 84098 1866 E2
Summit Wy
600 ALPN 84004 2497 D3
Summit Brook Cir
5300 SLkC 84118 2067 E5
Summit Creek Dr
- SHFD 84335 400 A2
Summit Creek Rd
200 SHFD 84335 399 E2
Summit Flower Cir
5300 SLkC 84118 2067 E5
Summit Hollow Cir
1400 RIVN 84065 2387 D1
Summit Point Cir
5500 SLkC 84118 2067 C5
Summit Trail Dr
3100 WVCY 84120 1961 E4
Summit Valley Dr
4600 WJDN 84088 2174 B5
Summit View Dr
9800 WshC 84049 2079 B7
9800 WshC 84049 2185 B1
9900 SNDY 84092 2284 A2
Sumter Dr
3700 WJDN 84084 2068 D7
Sun Cir
7400 SLkC 84044 1960 E5
Sun Dr
4000 SLkC 84118 2068 C6
Sun Arbor Ter
100 SLCY 84116 1857 C2
Sunberry Dr
900 MRRY 84123 2069 E4
900 MRRY 84123 2070 A4
Sunbird Wy
7600 SNDY 84047 2176 E4
Sun Bloom Cir
5200 HRMN 84065 2385 E6
Sun Bloom Ln
14200 HRMN 84065 2385 E7
Sun Blossom Cir
4300 WJDN 84088 2174 B7
Sunbow Ct
5700 SLkC 84118 2067 D6
Sunbow Dr
5600 SLkC 84118 2067 D6
Sunbright Ln
5700 HRMN 84065 2385 D6
Sunbrook Cir
900 ALPN 84004 2498 B3
Sunbrook Pl
2900 WVCY 84119 1962 E4
Sunburn Cir
11600 SNDY 84094 2283 A6
Sunburn Ln
700 DRPR 84020 2282 E6
700 DRPR 84020 2283 A6
700 SNDY 84094 2282 E6
700 SNDY 84094 2283 A6
800 SNDY 84020 2283 A6
Sunburst Cir
7000 CDHT 84121 2178 A2
Sunburst Ct
8900 SNDY 84093 2177 A7
Sunburst Dr
1300 WJDN 84088 2175 D2
Sunburst Ln
700 ALPN 84004 2498 B3
1100 MIDW 84049 2396 E2
Sunburst Wy
- LEHI 84043 2495 C5
Sunbury Pl
5500 SLkC 84118 2067 D6
Sunbury Wy
5400 SLkC 84118 2067 D6
Sun Cliff Ct
5500 SLkC 84118 2067 D6
Suncrest Cir
- KYVL 84037 1344 E3
1300 CTRV 84014 1551 D1
Sun Crest Dr
1000 OGDN 84404 1057 B6
Suncrest Dr
- DRPR 84020 2389 E7
- DRPR 84020 2496 E3
- DRPR 84020 2497 A1
- HILD 84003 2497 A5
- LEHI 84043 2497 A7
- UthC 84020 2497 A5
4500 HLDY 84117 2071 D2
Suncrest Ln
- KYVL 84037 1344 E4
- KYVL 84037 1345 A4
100 SRSP 84043 2601 E5
Sundance Cir
1200 BNFL 84010 1654 B3
1300 LYTN 84040 1283 C2
Sundance Dr
2500 SNDY 84093 2178 A6
Sunderland Cir
10100 SNDY 84092 2284 A3
Sundew Ct
9100 WJDN 84088 2174 A7
Sundew Ln
4800 WJDN 84088 2174 A7
Sundown Av
2300 CDHT 84121 2177 E1
2300 CDHT 84121 2178 A1
Sundown Cir
2100 RIVN 84065 2387 B5
2300 CDHT 84121 2178 A2
Sun Drift Cir
3000 CDHT 84121 2178 B2
Sundrop Cir
4900 SLkC 84118 2068 A5
Sunfalls Ct
5400 SLkC 84118 2067 D7
Sunflare Cove
13800 HRMN 84065 2385 D5
Sunflower Cir
1000 LYTN 84040 1283 C2
1200 NSLK 84054 1754 D1
Sunflower Dr
800 OGDN 84404 1056 D7
11000 HILD 84003 2497 A7
Sunflower Ln
- MPTN 84664 3250 D1
9800 SLkC 84094 2283 A2
9800 SNDY 84094 2283 A2
Sunglow Cir
5200 SLkC 84118 2067 E5

Salt Lake City Street Index

STREET
Block City ZIP Map# Grid

Sunhill Cir
7400 CDHT 84121 2178 A3
Sunhill Rd
7300 CDHT 84121 2178 A3
Sun Hollow Cir
4300 WJDN 84088 2174 B7
Suniland Cir
3500 SLkC 84109 1966 C6
Suniland Dr
3500 SLkC 84109 1966 C6
Sunkist Dr
5600 SLkC 84118 2067 D6
Sun Leaf Dr
8800 WJDN 84088 2174 B6
Sunlight Dr
5700 SLkC 84118 2067 D6
Sunlight Wy
- SRSP 84043 2601 E5
Sunlight Hill Ct
12500 HRMN 84065 2385 C2
Sun Meadow Cir
1900 SLkC 84106 1965 B5
S Sunny Ln
700 OREM 84058 2820 B7
W Sunny Ln
700 OREM 84058 2820 B7
E Sunny Pl
300 SSLK 84115 1964 D7
Sunny Brea Cir
9000 SNDY 84093 2177 C7
Sunnybrook Dr
3200 WVCY 84119 2068 D1
Sunnybrook Wy
2100 HLDY 84124 1965 E7
Sunnydale Dr
3600 SLkC 84109 1966 B7
3900 SLkC 84124 1966 B7
Sunnydale Ln
1400 SLkC 84108 1860 D4
Sunny Glen Cir
1900 SNDY 84093 2177 D7
S Sunny Glen Cir
100 KYVL 84037 1344 E1
Sunnyhill Cir
300 PYSN 84651 3355 B5
Sunnyhill Ln
200 LEHI 84043 2603 C4
Sunny Knoll Ct
2400 PKCY 84060 2078 E1
2400 PKCY 84060 2079 A1
Sunny Meadow Ct
9400 SJDN 84095 2280 B1
W Sunny Meadow Dr
4400 SJDN 84095 2280 B1
Sunnyoak Cir
7900 CDHT 84121 2178 C4
Sunnypark Ln
4100 WVCY 84119 2068 E1
Sunny Peak Cir
5500 SLkC 84118 2067 D5
Sunny River Rd
600 TYVL 84123 2070 A1
Sunnyside Av
1100 SLCY 84102 1859 B5
1400 SLCY 84105 1859 C5
1600 SLCY 84108 1859 C5
2300 SLCY 84108 1860 A5
Sunnyside Dr
600 PKCY 84060 2078 E6
600 PKCY 84060 2079 A6
Sunny Slopes Ct
2900 PKCY 84060 2078 E1
Sunny Slopes Dr
2300 PKCY 84060 2078 E1
2900 PKCY 84060 2079 A1
W Sunny Stone Cir
5800 SJDN 84095 2279 D7
Sunny Stone Dr
11400 SJDN 84095 2279 D6
Sunnyvale Dr
3600 WVCY 84120 1962 C6
Sunny Vista Ln
4800 WJDN 84088 2174 A5
Sunoak Cir
2900 WVCY 84128 1961 B4
Sun Peak Dr
1700 SmtC 84098 1971 E6
Sunridge Cir
1900 SNDY 84093 2177 D6
Sun Ridge Ct
3100 PKCY 84060 2079 A4
5400 SLkC 84118 2067 E6
Sun Ridge Dr
3300 PKCY 84060 2079 B4
Sunridge Dr
1700 PRRY 84302 827 E4
1900 SNDY 84093 2177 D6
3500 SmtC 84098 1864 E6
3500 SmtC 84098 1865 A6
Sun Ridge Cove
10 PKCY 84060 2079 B3
10 SmtC 84098 2079 B3
Sunrise Av
700 HYRM 84319 651 D2
700 SLCY 84103 1754 E7
700 SLCY 84103 1755 A7
Sunrise Cir
700 CTRV 84014 1552 A5
2100 PKCY 84060 2078 E3
3400 WJDN 84084 2174 E2
9000 SNDY 84093 2177 E7
11600 HILD 84003 2497 B6
W Sunrise Cir
10 FMTN 84025 1448 C5
Sunrise Dr
- LYTN 84041 1229 A6
100 LYTN 84041 1228 E6
600 OREM 84097 2714 A7
4000 SmtC 84098 1864 E5
4100 WbrC 84310 1001 D2
6100 HILD 84003 2497 B6
N Sunrise Dr
10 ALPN 84004 2497 D4
S Sunrise Dr
10 ALPN 84004 2497 D4
Sunrise Ln
1100 FMTN 84025 1448 C5
Sunrise Pl
1200 BNFL 84010 1654 B5
1600 WJDN 84084 2175 C3
Sunrise Pl E
7600 WJDN 84084 2175 D4
Sunrise Pl N
1500 WJDN 84084 2175 C3
Sunrise Pl S
1500 WJDN 84084 2175 D3
Sunrise Pl W
7600 WJDN 84084 2175 D4
Sunrise Rd
3500 WVCY 84119 1963 D6
E Sunrise Wy
10 FMTN 84025 1448 C4
S Sunrise Wy
1100 FMTN 84025 1448 D4
W Sunrise Wy
10 FMTN 84025 1448 C4
Sunrise Hills Cir
6900 CDHT 84121 2178 A2
Sunrise Meadow Dr
1500 SNDY 84093 2283 C1
Sunrise Oak Dr
6500 WJDN 84088 2173 B6
Sunrise Park Cir
1700 SNDY 84093 2283 C1
Sunrise Park Dr
1700 SNDY 84093 2283 C1
Sunrise View Dr
700 DRPR 84020 2283 A7
Sunrise Vista Cir
5900 SLkC 84118 2067 B6
Sun River Dr
1100 RIVN 84065 2387 D3
Sunrose Pl
1400 WVCY 84119 1963 D5
E Sunset Av
10 SSLK 84115 1964 C4
W Sunset Av
10 SSLK 84115 1964 C4
1400 WVCY 84119 1963 D4
Sunset Cir
- WbrC 84310 1002 A2
10 ALPN 84004 2497 D6
200 CTRV 84014 1448 D7
700 HYRM 84319 651 D2
2900 SLCY 84108 1860 B7
4400 BNFL 84010 1653 D7
7600 WJDN 84084 2175 A3
Sunset Ct
2100 PKCY 84060 2078 E2
3200 RIVN 84065 2386 E1
Sunset Dr
- SOGN 84405 1173 A4
10 ALPN 84004 2497 E6
10 FMTN 84025 1448 E2
10 LYTN 84041 1228 E6
400 KYVL 84037 1345 B3
600 BMCY 84302 767 A4
900 BNFL 84010 1654 B2
1000 CRFD 84015 1227 B3
1600 LOGN 84321 528 C1
2100 LEHI 84043 2603 A2
4300 CRHL 84062 2605 B3
5100 SOGN 84403 1173 A4
E Sunset Dr
1800 LYTN 84040 1229 E7
2600 LYTN 84040 1230 A7
N Sunset Dr
2000 LYTN 84040 1283 D1
2100 LYTN 84040 1229 D7
W Sunset Dr
1200 SLCY 84116 1753 D6
Sunset Ln
- PVDN 84332 592 B1
600 SOGN 84403 1173 A3
4800 SOGN 84403 1172 E3
Sunset Rd
900 LOGN 84321 528 B3
1800 HRCY 84032 2398 D7
Sunset Wy
- LEHI 84043 2495 C5
- LEHI 84043 2602 C2
4500 BNFL 84010 1653 D7
4500 NSLK 84054 1653 D7
7700 WJDN 84084 2175 A4
Sunset Hills Ct
- HILD 84003 2497 A5
Sunset Hills Dr
- HILD 84003 2497 A6
8400 SLkC 84044 1960 B6
Sunset Hollow Dr
1000 BNFL 84010 1654 A5
Sunset Links Dr
600 MRRY 84123 2070 A7
Sunset Loop Rd
3200 BNFL 84010 1654 B5
Sunset Maple Dr
7400 WJDN 84084 2173 A3
Sunset Oaks Dr
1500 SLCY 84108 1860 B7
1500 SLCY 84108 1966 B1
Sunset Park Cir
4800 WJDN 84088 2174 A4
Sunset Park Ln
4800 WJDN 84088 2174 A5
Sunset Peak Ln
700 TYVL 84123 2070 A3
Sunset Ponds Dr
700 DRPR 84020 2282 E7
700 DRPR 84020 2283 A7
Sunset Ridge Cir
9300 SNDY 84093 2284 B1
Sunset Ridge Dr
2900 SNDY 84093 2284 B1
Sunset View Cir
1400 CTRV 84014 1551 D1
Sunset View Dr
10 CTRV 84014 1551 D1
4100 SLkC 84124 2072 C1
Sunset Vista Dr
5900 SLkC 84118 2067 B6
Sunshade Dr
3300 WVCY 84120 1961 E6
Sunshade Cove
5400 WVCY 84120 1961 D6
Sunshine Ct
700 OREM 84097 2714 A7
Sunshine Dr
5200 WVCY 84120 1961 E6
Sunspot Cir
2100 SNDY 84093 2177 E5
Sunspring Dr
8800 WJDN 84088 2174 B7
Sunsprite Ct
13800 HRMN 84065 2385 D5
Sunstone Rd
4500 TYVL 84123 2070 A3
Suntree Av
5400 WVCY 84120 1961 E5
S Sun Tree Dr
4500 ROY 84067 1171 E2
Sun Valley Dr
8400 SNDY 84093 2177 E6
Sunview Cir
1000 OGDN 84404 1057 C7
Sunview Ct
5700 SLkC 84118 2067 D5
Sunview Dr
1400 OGDN 84404 1057 C7
5600 SLkC 84118 2067 D6
N Sun Village Dr
100 OREM 84057 2820 D5
W Sun Village Dr
100 OREM 84057 2820 D5
Sunwood Ln
10 SNDY 84092 2283 E5
Superior Cir
10600 SNDY 84094 2283 A4
Superior Dr
10700 SNDY 84094 2283 B3
Superior Peak Dr
700 TYVL 84123 2070 A3
Supernal Cir
3500 CDHT 84121 2178 E5
Supernal Wy
3600 CDHT 84121 2178 D5
Supreme Ct
10 PKCY 84060 2079 A7
Supreme Rd
- ALTA 84049 2288 C1
Surf Ct
3300 WJDN 84084 2174 E2
Surrey
- NSLK 84054 1653 B4
Surrey Cir
2000 TYVL 84118 2069 B6
Surrey Ct
6100 MRRY 84121 2071 C7
Surrey Ln
1600 MRRY 84121 2071 C7
Surrey Rd
2200 TYVL 84118 2069 A6
Surrey Meadow Dr
1300 SJDN 84095 2281 D5
Surrey Meadow Cove
10000 SJDN 84095 2281 D4
Surreyrun Rd
400 MRRY 84107 2070 E6
Susan Cir
- KYVL 84037 1345 D3
300 SNDY 84070 2282 D1
8500 WJDN 84088 2174 D6
Susan Dr
1700 SNDY 84092 2283 C5
Susan Wy
2000 CDHT 84121 2177 D2
8200 WJDN 84088 2174 D5
Susan's Cir
7400 SmtC 84098 1865 B6
Susie Cir
3600 WVCY 84120 1962 C6
Susquehanna
700 MRRY 84123 2070 A6
Sussex Ct
3000 WVCY 84119 2069 A2
Sussex Pl
2800 WVCY 84119 2069 A2
Sutter St
5300 TYVL 84123 2069 D5
Sutton Cir
3500 CDHT 84121 2178 C6
Sutton Ct
3500 CDHT 84093 2178 C7
Sutton Wy
8700 CDHT 84121 2178 C6
8900 CDHT 84093 2178 C7
Sutton Commons Cir
1900 SLkC 84121 2071 D6
Suwannee Cir
5900 MRRY 84123 2070 A6
Suzette Cir
1800 SLkC 84106 1965 D5
Swallow St
3800 WVCY 84119 1963 E7
Swallowtail Cir
9500 SJDN 84095 2280 E1
Swallow Wood Ln
10 SNDY 84092 2284 A4
Swan St
1300 OGDN 84401 1116 C3
Swanbridge Dr
5800 SLkC 84118 2067 C6
6100 WVCY 84118 2067 C6
Swaner Pl
2500 OGDN 84401 1116 C4
Swaner Rd
1100 SLCY 84104 1857 B7
1500 SLCY 84104 1963 B1
Swan Hill Dr
7000 WJDN 84084 2174 A3
Swan Hill Cove
4900 WJDN 84084 2174 A2
Swan Lake Cir
3500 SLkC 84044 1960 D6
Swasey Cir
4800 TYVL 84118 2069 B3
Swasey Ct
4800 TYVL 84118 2069 B3
Swasey Dr
2400 TYVL 84118 2069 A3
Swasont Wy
2600 HLDY 84117 2072 A4
Swede Al
100 PKCY 84060 2078 E6
Swede Ln
4000 UthC 84660 3141 A3
Sweet Basil N
2700 TYVL 84118 2069 A6
Sweet Basil S
2700 TYVL 84118 2069 A6
Sweet Basil Cir
2900 TYVL 84118 2069 A6
Sweet Berry Ct
10 DRPR 84020 2282 C6
Sweet Berry Dr
100 DRPR 84020 2282 C6
Sweet Blossom Dr
2800 SJDN 84095 2281 A1
3000 SJDN 84095 2280 E1
Sweetbriar Ln
2000 SNDY 84092 2283 D3
Sweet Caroline Dr
1200 RIVN 84065 2387 D4
Sweet Clover Ln
2900 SJDN 84095 2280 D1
2900 SJDN 84095 2281 A1
Sweet Corn Dr
300 SRSP 84043 2601 D5
Sweetgum Dr
3300 SLkC 84044 1960 A5
Sweet Meadow Ln
700 SNDY 84070 2282 A1
Sweetwater Cir
3800 WVCY 84120 1962 C7
Sweetwater Dr
100 SGVL 84663 3143 C6
300 MPTN 84664 3143 C6
300 SGVL 84664 3143 C6
Sweetwater Ln
1200 FMTN 84025 1346 A5
1300 FMTN 84025 1345 E5
Sweetwood Cir
5400 MRRY 84123 2069 E5
Swensen Cir
12000 RIVN 84065 2386 B1
Swensen Farm Dr
4000 RIVN 84065 2386 B1
11800 RIVN 84065 2280 B7
Swenson Av
400 SGVL 84663 3143 D3
Swenson Ln
- UthC 84660 3249 D6
Swift Creek Dr
- LYTN 84041 1282 B4
Swift Creek Rd
8400 WJDN 84088 2173 D5
Swiftwater Wy
5100 WJDN 84088 2173 E4
Swindon Ct
10100 SJDN 84095 2280 B3
Swinton Ln
1300 FMTN 84025 1345 E5
1700 FMTN 84025 1346 A5
Swiss Alpine Rd
900 MIDW 84049 2396 E2
900 MIDW 84049 2397 A2
900 WshC 84049 2396 E2
Swiss Farm Cir
800 MIDW 84049 2397 B1
Swiss Farm Wy
100 MIDW 84049 2397 B1
Swiss Oaks Dr
900 MIDW 84049 2396 E1
Switzer Dr
1400 WshC 84049 2396 D2
Swordsman Cove
7600 WJDN 84084 2175 D3
Sycamore Av
1000 BMCY 84302 767 B5
Sycamore Cir
10 CRFD 84015 1227 E4
Sycamore Dr
1100 BMCY 84302 767 B5
4500 HLDY 84117 2071 D2
Sycamore Ln
1300 DvsC 84056 1228 C2
1800 HLDY 84117 2071 D3
10200 CRHL 84062 2605 B2
Sycamore Glen Cir
7400 WJDN 84084 2174 B3
Sycamore Hill St
- DRPR 84020 2388 D7
- DRPR 84020 2495 C1
Sycamore Tree Cove
8300 SNDY 84094 2177 B6
Sydette Cir
5200 TYVL 84118 2068 D5
Sylvan Av
1900 SLCY 84108 1965 D2
Sylvia Dr
10 SOGN 84405 1115 D7
Symphony Cir
900 OGDN 84404 1057 A6
4000 WVCY 84119 2069 A1
Syrena Cir
900 SNDY 84094 2177 A7

T

T St
10 SLCY 84103 1859 B3
Tabby Ln
- SLCY 84103 1859 E4
Table Rock Cir
6300 TYVL 84084 2069 A7
Table Rock Dr
2700 TYVL 84084 2069 A7
Taffeta Dr
1000 SLCY 84116 1753 E6
Tafoya Cir
5500 WJDN 84084 2173 D2
Taft St
7800 MDVL 84047 2176 C4
Taft Hill Dr
8800 SNDY 84093 2178 A7
Taft Hills Ct
8800 SNDY 84093 2178 A7
Tafton Rd
3500 WVCY 84120 1961 E6
Taggart Wy
3000 SLkC 84044 1960 C5
Tahnia Bay
5800 MRRY 84121 2071 A6
Tahnia Park Cir
900 MRRY 84121 2071 A6
Tail Trail Ct
3700 SLkC 84044 1960 D7
Taitlynn Cir
1100 SLkC 84106 1965 B5
N Talbot Dr
10 LYTN 84041 1283 B4
S Talbot Dr
10 LYTN 84041 1283 B5
Talisman Cir
1600 SLCY 84116 1753 C7
Talisman Dr
800 SLCY 84116 1753 E7
Tall Oak Ln
6100 MRRY 84121 2071 D7
Tall Oaks Cir
7300 SmtC 84098 1865 A7
Tall Oaks Dr
7000 SmtC 84098 1971 B1
7200 SmtC 84098 1865 A7
Tallowood Cir
1400 CDHT 84093 2177 C3
Tall Pine Ln
8300 CDHT 84121 2178 C5
Tall Pines Wy
1900 SNDY 84092 2283 D5
Tally Ho Dr
900 SLCY 84116 1753 E6
Talon Cir
4800 SLkC 84118 2068 A5
Talon Ct
600 NSLK 84054 1754 C1
Talon Dr
- LOGN 84321 527 C7
1500 PVDN 84332 527 C7
Talon Wy
200 NSLK 84054 1754 C1
Talons Reach Ct
15000 DRPR 84020 2496 E1
Tam Dr
7500 SLkC 84044 1960 D5
Tamara St
1100 SNDY 84094 2283 B2
Tamarack Cir
11200 HILD 84003 2497 B6
Tamarack Dr
10200 CRHL 84062 2605 C2
10700 SNDY 84094 2283 B4
11000 HILD 84003 2497 A7
Tamarack Rd
1100 TYVL 84123 2069 D3
Tameron Cir
9800 SNDY 84092 2283 C2
Tameron Dr
1400 SNDY 84092 2283 C2
Tamra Dr
2400 TYVL 84084 2069 A7
6400 TYVL 84084 2175 A1
Tams Rd
900 WLRD 84340 941 C1
Tanager Ln
200 DRPR 84020 2388 D2
Tangiers Cir
3800 WVCY 84120 1962 D5
Tanglewood Ct
3900 WbrC 84310 1001 D2
Tanglewood Dr
2900 LYTN 84040 1284 A4
4500 HLDY 84117 2071 D2
Tanglewood Lp
500 NSLK 84054 1754 D1
Tanker Dr
600 SLCY 84116 1857 B1
700 SLCY 84116 1753 B7
Tanner Ln
200 MIDW 84049 2396 E2
300 WshC 84049 2396 E2
6400 MRRY 84121 2071 D7
6400 MRRY 84121 2177 D1
Tanner Wy
6400 MRRY 84121 2177 D1
Tannevista Rd
800 BMCY 84302 828 B1
Tanya Av
2400 WJDN 84088 2175 B7
9200 WJDN 84088 2281 B1
9300 SJDN 84095 2281 B1
Taos Cir
8500 SNDY 84093 2177 E6
Taos Dr
8400 SNDY 84093 2177 E5
Tapestry Ln
6000 HRMN 84065 2385 C4
Tappen Park Ln
4400 RIVN 84065 2386 B1
Tara Cir
700 MDVL 84047 2177 A2
Tara Ln
2200 HLDY 84117 2071 E2
Tarali Ct
10400 SJDN 84095 2281 C3
Tarali Wy
1800 SJDN 84095 2281 C3
Tara Woods Ln
11400 SJDN 84095 2281 A6
Tarbert Cir
9500 SJDN 84095 2280 B1
Targhee Dr
9000 WJDN 84088 2174 C7
9200 WJDN 84088 2280 C1
Taroona Dr
5000 SLkC 84117 2071 C4
Tarragon Ct
5900 SLkC 84118 2068 A6
Tartan Av
1500 SLCY 84108 1965 D1
1900 SLCY 84108 1859 D7
Tartan Wy
1400 LYTN 84040 1283 C1
Tartarian Cir
10 BNFL 84010 1552 A7
Taryn's Ln
1300 WJDN 84088 2175 D6
Taryton Ct
4200 TYVL 84123 2069 E1
Tate Ln
10 WshC 84049 2397 B7
Tatteredangel Cove
11600 RIVN 84065 2281 D6
Taunton Ln
400 SJDN 84095 2282 B5
6600 WJDN 84084 2173 B1
Taurus Cir
200 SLCY 84116 1857 C2
Taylor Av
200 OGDN 84404 1057 C5
2300 OGDN 84401 1116 C3
2900 OGDN 84403 1116 C6
4000 OGDN 84403 1173 C1
Taylor Cir
1500 OGDN 84404 1116 C1
Taylor Dr
2700 OGDN 84403 1116 C4
Taylor Rd
2400 FRWT 84404 997 C7
Taylor St
1200 OGDN 84404 1057 C7
1300 OGDN 84404 1116 C1
Taylors Claim Ct
11800 HRMN 84065 2280 A7
Taylors Hill Dr
4700 TYVL 84123 2070 A3
Taylors Hill Cove
700 TYVL 84123 2070 A3
Taylors Meadow Ct
1000 TYVL 84123 2069 E3
Taylors Park Cir
1000 TYVL 84123 2069 E3
Taylors Park Dr
4800 TYVL 84123 2069 E3
Taylorsville Blvd
- TYVL 84118 2069 A5
Tayside Dr
9600 SJDN 84095 2280 B1
Teaberry Dr
3600 TYVL 84118 2068 D5
Teakwood Cir
11200 SNDY 84092 2283 D5
Teakwood Dr
1300 TYVL 84123 2069 C2
1700 SNDY 84092 2283 C6
Teal Cir
9200 SNDY 84093 2178 A7
9200 SNDY 84093 2284 A1
Teal Dr
1700 SmtC 84098 1971 E1
Teal Wy
2600 SNDY 84093 2178 A7
Teal Vista Cir
3300 WVCY 84120 1962 A5
Teancum Rd
500 WshC 84032 2505 D1
Tearose Cir
6500 TYVL 84084 2175 B1
Tea Rose Ct
400 SRSP 84043 2601 D5
Teasel Av
6200 WVCY 84128 1961 B5
Technology Av
500 OREM 84097 2820 E1
500 OREM 84097 2821 A1
Technology Dr
2200 WVCY 84119 1962 D2
N Technology Dr
1800 SGVL 84663 3036 A5
N Technology Wy
1300 OREM 84097 2821 A1
Technology Park Wy
2100 WVCY 84119 1962 D2
Tecumseh St
3700 WVCY 84120 1962 A7
Ted Wy
5200 WVCY 84120 2067 E1
Tee Box Dr
4400 SJDN 84095 2280 B2
Teer Dr
2300 SNST 84015 1171 D6
Tee Shot Cir
9900 SJDN 84095 2280 B2
Tee Time Dr
1000 FMTN 84025 1346 A6
Telegraph Hill Dr
1300 TYVL 84123 2069 D5
Telemark Dr
2400 PKCY 84060 2079 B4
Telford Wy
8000 SLkC 84093 2177 D5
8100 SNDY 84093 2177 D5
Tempest Ridge Cir
14100 HRMN 84065 2385 D6
Temple Av
200 LOGN 84321 527 E2
Temple Ct
1600 BNFL 84010 1654 C3
Temple Dr
6600 TYVL 84084 2175 D2
6600 WJDN 84084 2175 D2
7800 WJDN 84088 2175 D5
11700 RIVN 84065 2281 D7
12000 RIVN 84065 2387 D3
N Temple Dr
700 PRVO 84604 2928 E2
Temple Ln
1500 SJDN 84095 2281 C3
Temple Hill Cir
500 BNFL 84010 1654 C1
Temple Hill Dr
2000 PRVO 84604 2928 E2
Temple Meadows Cir
1200 ANFK 84003 2605 B6
Temple Shadows Dr
4500 CRHL 84062 2605 A4
Temple View Cir
2200 SJDN 84095 2281 B3
Temple View Dr
100 LOGN 84321 528 A4
100 RVHT 84321 528 A4
1900 PRVO 84604 2928 E3
10200 SJDN 84095 2281 B3
Templeview Dr
200 BNFL 84010 1654 C1
Temple View Ln
2200 SJDN 84095 2281 B3
Tempo Rd
7500 SLkC 84044 1960 D1
Tennessee Av
2300 PRVO 84606 3036 B4
Tennyson Cir
7800 MDVL 84070 2176 D4
Ten Sleep Cir
14600 BFDL 84065 2387 A7
Tenway Dr
7100 WVCY 84128 1960 E6
Terah Maria Dr
2400 TYVL 84118 2069 A4
Terendale Ln
11500 SNDY 84092 2283 E6
E Terrace Av
1300 SGVL 84663 3144 A3
Terrace Ct
1900 SNDY 84093 2177 D6
Terrace Dr
- OREM 84097 2928 A3
- PRVO 84604 2928 A3
900 BNFL 84010 1654 B1
900 PRVO 84604 2929 A4
1800 SNDY 84093 2177 D5
E Terrace Dr
1300 FTHT 84037 1346 A1
1400 FTHT 84037 1284 B7
N Terrace Dr
10 CRFD 84015 1227 E4
S Terrace Dr
10 CRFD 84015 1227 E4
Terrace Pl
10 LOGN 84321 528 A2
Terrace Creek Cir
8200 SNDY 84093 2177 D5
Terrace Heights Cir
3600 SLkC 84109 1966 B6
S Terrace Heights Rd
3600 SLkC 84109 1966 B7
Terrace Hills Dr
400 SLCY 84103 1859 A1
700 SLCY 84103 1755 A7
E Terrace View Cir
3100 SLkC 84109 1966 C6
Terrace View Dr
3300 SLkC 84109 1966 C6
Terra Linda Dr
1900 HLDY 84124 2071 D2
Terra Pointe Wy
8600 WJDN 84088 2175 E6
Terra Vista Wy
1900 SNDY 84093 2177 D6
Terrell Cir
7000 MDVL 84047 2176 D2
Terri Lynn Dr
9000 SNDY 84094 2177 A7
Terry Dr
1300 SNST 84015 1227 C2
Tess Av
2800 WVCY 84119 1963 A5
3000 WVCY 84119 1962 E5
Tess Pl
2500 PRRY 84302 827 D5
Teton Dr
1700 PRVO 84604 2927 D4
3000 SLkC 84109 1966 D5
E Teton Dr
1200 LNDN 84042 2713 E6
N Teton Dr
10 LNDN 84042 2713 E6
Teton Estates Dr
4000 WJDN 84088 2174 C7
9200 WJDN 84088 2280 C1
Texas Av
2200 PRVO 84606 3036 B4
Texas St
1700 SLCY 84108 1966 A1
2100 SLCY 84109 1965 E2
Thackeray Pl
2900 SLCY 84108 1860 B6
Thackie Cir
1300 SLCY 84104 1963 D1
Thames Ct
900 FMTN 84025 1346 B4
1200 TYVL 84123 2069 E1
N Thanksgiving Wy
1800 LEHI 84043 2603 A3
2100 LEHI 84043 2602 E2
3100 LEHI 84043 2495 A5
11500 UthC 84043 2495 A5
11700 LEHI 84065 2495 A5
Thatcher Wy
500 MDVL 84047 2176 E2
Thaxton Cir
2000 RIVN 84065 2387 B4
W Thayn Cir
4400 WVCY 84120 1962 B7
Thayn Dr
4400 WVCY 84120 1962 B7
Thaynes Canyon Dr
10 PKCY 84060 2078 B3
Thaynes Canyon Wy
10 PKCY 84060 2078 B3
Theckston Rd
1900 TYVL 84119 2069 B1
Theresa Cove
2000 WVCY 84119 1963 B6
Thimbleleaf Cir
6600 WJDN 84084 2174 A1
Thirty Oaks Dr
2800 SGVL 84663 3144 D4
Thistle Av
1100 SLCY 84102 1859 B3
Thistle St
3000 PKCY 84060 2079 B4
Thistledown Dr
1300 SNDY 84092 2283 C4
Thistle Tree Dr
1900 SGVL 84663 3144 B4
Thistlewood Wy
2100 SNDY 84092 2283 E2
Thomas Cir
7600 WJDN 84084 2175 A3
Thomas Ct
- LOGN 84321 527 A3
Thomas Dr
- KYVL 84037 1344 E4
1200 KYVL 84037 1345 A3
Thomas Brook Ct
8100 SLkC 84044 1960 C5
Thomas Brook Wy
3100 SLkC 84044 1960 C5
Thompson Pl
1800 SRSP 84043 2601 E5
Thor Wy
6200 WVCY 84128 2067 B1
Thoreau Dr
2500 SLkC 84044 1960 C3
Thornberry Ct
11500 DRPR 84020 2282 D6
Thornberry Dr
100 DRPR 84020 2282 D6
W Thornberry Wy
100 PTGV 84062 2712 D3
Thorncrest Wy
4700 SLkC 84118 2068 A6
Thornfield Rd
800 KYVL 84037 1283 E6
1300 DvsC 84037 1283 E5
Thornton Av
1300 SLCY 84105 1859 B6
Thornton Cir
7800 CDHT 84093 2177 D4
Thornwood Av
4400 TYVL 84123 2069 D2

STREET
Block City ZIP Map# Grid

Thornwood Dr
400 ANFK 84003 2604 C7
Thoroughbred Dr
11500 SJDN 84095 2281 D6
Thorpe Creek Rd
3100 WVCY 84128 1961 C5
Thorpe View Cir
3200 WVCY 84128 1961 C5
Thorton Cir
6100 HILD 84003 2604 B3
Thorton Ln
6000 HILD 84003 2604 B3
Thorup Cir
3000 WVCY 84119 1962 E5
Thousand Oaks Cir
3700 SLkC 84124 2072 D2
Thousand Oaks Dr
4500 SLkC 84124 2072 D2
Three Fountains Cir
700 MRRY 84107 2071 A4
5000 MRRY 84107 2070 E3
Three Fountains Dr
10 NHON 84414 998 E6
200 PRVO 84604 2821 C5
600 MRRY 84107 2070 E3
600 MRRY 84107 2071 A3
Three Kings Ct
2000 PKCY 84060 2078 C3
Three Kings Dr
1400 PKCY 84060 2078 C3
Three Mile Rd
300 WPT 84015 1226 C2
800 CLTN 84015 1226 C2
1800 CLTN 84015 1170 C7
Three Mile Canyon Rd
- SmtC 84017 1973 E1
Three Point Av
700 LOGN 84321 527 A4
Three Pointe Av
1000 LOGN 84321 527 A4
Thresher Ct
5300 WJDN 84088 2173 E5
Thrush Rd
1200 WVCY 84119 1963 D7
Thrush Hill Dr
- WJDN 84084 2173 D3
4800 WJDN 84084 2174 A3
Thrushwood Dr
1000 LOGN 84321 528 B3
N Thrushwood Dr
100 LOGN 84321 528 B3
Thunder Rd
3600 RIVN 84065 2386 D1
Thunderbird Dr
1900 WDCR 84087 1652 E3
2600 SLCY 84109 1966 B2
Thunderbird Wy
3600 TYVL 84118 2068 D3
Thunderhead Wy
2200 BFDL 84065 2494 B1
Thyme Cir
10100 SJDN 84095 2280 D3
Tiara St
1200 SLkC 84117 2071 B4
Tibble Fork Cir
3400 CRHL 84062 2605 D5
Tibble Fork Cove
13300 DRPR 84020 2388 E4
Ticaboo Mine Rd
11800 HRMN 84065 2280 B7
Tick Ln
13900 SLkC 84065 2385 B5
Ticklegrass Rd
4800 WJDN 84084 2174 A2
5100 WJDN 84084 2173 D1
Tico Dr
7100 WJDN 84084 2173 E3
Tidwell St
4200 SLkC 84118 2068 B6
Tierney Cir
1200 SNDY 84094 2177 B4
Tierra Dr
5800 SLkC 84118 2068 B6
Tierra Rose Dr
2000 TYVL 84084 2175 B1
Tiffany Town Dr
500 MDVL 84047 2176 B5
Tifftan Cir
8100 SNDY 84094 2177 A5
Tiger Eye Dr
1100 SNDY 84094 2283 B2
Tiger Lily Ct
5500 WJDN 84084 2173 D1
N Timber Dr
700 LEHI 84043 2603 A5
W Timber Dr
1000 LEHI 84043 2603 A5
Timber Wy
1200 SLkC 84117 2071 B4
Timber Brook Dr
- DRPR 84020 2496 D4
E Timbercraft Ln
700 MDVL 84047 2176 E1
W Timbercreek Wy
700 SSLK 84119 1964 A7
Timber Crest Cove
3000 CDHT 84093 2178 B5
Timberline Cir
7600 CDHT 84121 2178 D3
Timberline Dr
3700 CDHT 84121 2178 D4
Timber Oaks Ln
4100 WVCY 84128 2067 D1
Timber Ridge Dr
13900 DRPR 84020 2389 B6
Timber River Dr
12700 RIVN 84065 2386 A3
Timber Run Dr
4800 RIVN 84065 2386 A3
Timberwolf Tr
1500 OREM 84057 2820 D1
Timeless Ct
5600 HRMN 84065 2385 D5
Timeron Dr
3000 WVCY 84128 1961 C5
Timmerman Pl
6300 WVCY 84128 1961 B6
Timoney Rd
1500 DRPR 84020 2389 C5
Timothy Cir
- KYVL 84037 1283 C7
6800 WJDN 84084 2175 B2
Timothy Wy
200 PTGV 84062 2605 D6
2000 BNFL 84010 1654 A3
Timpanogos Blvd
10 OREM 84057 2820 D1
Timpanogos Dr
1300 PRVO 84604 2927 D4
Timpanogos Pkwy
400 OREM 84097 2820 E1
400 OREM 84097 2821 A1
Timpanogos Wy
6200 TYVL 84084 2069 A7
6400 TYVL 84084 2175 A2
Timpie Dr
1000 SNDY 84094 2283 A5
Timp View Dr
12600 RIVN 84065 2387 B3
Timpview Dr
1000 ANFK 84003 2604 C5
2100 PRVO 84604 2928 D3
3300 PRVO 84604 2821 D7
Timp Vista Dr
1100 RIVN 84065 2387 E1
Tina Wy
700 SLkC 84107 2070 E4
4600 SLkC 84107 2071 A2
Tingey Hall
200 PRVO 84604 2928 D4
Tin Snip Cir
2400 TYVL 84118 2069 B4
Tin Stone Cir
5800 SLkC 84118 2067 C5
Tiny Wood Dr
10 SNDY 84070 2176 C7
Tithing Hill Dr
1000 RIVN 84065 2387 E1
Tithing Hill Pl
1000 RIVN 84065 2387 E2
Tithing Point Dr
12400 RIVN 84065 2387 E1
Tithing Ridge Dr
1000 RIVN 84065 2387 E2
Tithing View Ct
1000 RIVN 84065 2387 E2
Titian Wy
7800 CDHT 84121 2178 B4
Tivoli Dr
2000 DRPR 84020 2389 D1
Tivoli Ln
2800 TYVL 84118 2069 A5
TJ Cir
100 SNDY 84070 2282 D1
TJ Dr
200 SNDY 84070 2282 D1
Tobe Dr
200 BNFL 84010 1551 D4
200 CTRV 84010 1551 D4
200 CTRV 84014 1551 D4
Todd Wy
2000 TYVL 84119 2069 B2
Tolcate Ln
5800 HLDY 84121 2072 B6
Tolcate Hills Dr
3100 HLDY 84121 2072 B6
3100 SLkC 84124 2072 B6
Tolcate Woods Ln
5800 HLDY 84121 2072 B6
Tolin Cir
4900 WVCY 84120 1962 A5
Tolin St
3100 WVCY 84120 1962 A5
Tolkin Av
2000 WJDN 84084 2175 B3
Tollgate Rd
900 SmtC 84098 1866 E2
900 SmtC 84098 1867 A2
Tollgate Canyon Rd
- SmtC 84017 1867 B2
- SmtC 84098 1867 B2
Tolman Crest Wy
2900 WVCY 84119 1962 E5
Tomahawk Dr
600 PYSN 84651 3355 A4
1200 SLCY 84103 1859 C1
Tomahawk Ln
5300 OGDN 84403 1173 D4
Tommy Moe Pl
1900 SmtC 84098 1971 D6
N Tommy Thompson Rd
10 SLCY 84116 1856 B2
Tompkins Dr
2200 CDHT 84121 2177 E2
Tom Shoemaker Cir
13700 DRPR 84020 2389 C5
Tom Shoemaker Rd
13700 DRPR 84020 2389 B5
Toms's Ln
1500 WDCR 84087 1652 E3
Tonalea Dr
5400 MRRY 84107 2070 E5
Toni Cir
2600 CDHT 84121 2178 A3
Toni Dr
3200 WVCY 84119 1962 E7
Toni Lee Cir
9100 WJDN 84088 2175 A7
Toni Lee St
2400 WJDN 84088 2175 A7
Tonya Dr
300 SNDY 84070 2282 D2
Tooele Ln
14800 DRPR 84020 2495 D1
Toolson Dr
3500 SLkC 84044 1960 C6
Topaz Dr
1000 SLCY 84116 1753 E7
Top of the World Cir
8500 CDHT 84121 2178 D5
Top of the World Dr
3600 CDHT 84121 2178 D5
Topowa Dr
10 MRRY 84107 2070 C6
Torrey Pines Cir
1600 DRPR 84020 2389 E2
Torrington Ct
5900 SLkC 84118 2067 C6
Torry Cir
400 SNDY 84070 2282 E2
Tortellini Dr
9100 SNDY 84093 2177 D7
9200 SNDY 84093 2283 D1
Tortuga Cove
2600 CDHT 84121 2072 A7
Torwood Ct
1200 MRRY 84123 2069 E6
Toscana Wy
5300 HRMN 84065 2385 D2
Totorica Cir
12600 RIVN 84065 2386 B2
Tottenham Ct Rd
2200 TYVL 84119 2069 B2
Toulouse Cir
4400 WVCY 84120 2068 D2
Toulouse St
3600 WVCY 84120 2068 D2
Towerbell Ln
3000 WVCY 84120 1962 A3
S Towers Dr
400 SALM 84653 3356 A4
Towerview Wy
3500 WVCY 84119 1963 D6
N Town Ln
- NSLK 84054 1653 A7
Town & Country Rd
1200 SGVL 84663 3144 A4
Town Center Blvd
- HILD 84003 2497 D7
- HILD 84003 2604 D1
Town Center Dr
- DRPR 84020 2389 A5
10 TMTN 84337 520 C5
Towncrest Dr
7000 CDHT 84121 2177 E2
Towne Cir
7700 CDHT 84121 2178 A4
Towne Dr
2600 CDHT 84121 2178 A4
Towne Center Dr
1600 SJDN 84095 2281 C4
Towne Centre Blvd
1200 PRVO 84601 3035 C2
Towne Ridge Pkwy
- SNDY 84070 2282 C1
E Townhouse Villa St
200 SSLK 84115 1964 D6
W Townley St
6100 WJDN 84084 2173 C1
Town Meadows Ct
1800 SJDN 84095 2281 C2
Townsend Cir
4700 SLkC 84118 2067 E3
Townsend Wy
4700 SLkC 84118 2067 D3
Township Ct
3900 WVCY 84128 1961 D7
Town View Cir
8400 WJDN 84088 2173 D5
Tracy Cir
8900 SLkC 84093 2178 B7
Tracy Dr
500 KYVL 84037 1345 E4
8500 SLkC 84093 2178 B6
8900 SNDY 84093 2178 B6
Tracy Loop Rd
6900 HRMN 84065 2385 A5
Traditions Ln
5900 TYVL 84123 2069 C6
Trafalga Wy
1700 SLCY 84116 1753 C6
Trail Av
4800 WVCY 84120 1962 A7
Trail Crest Ct
1400 DRPR 84020 2496 C1
Trailorama Av
200 MRRY 84107 2070 D1
Trail Rider Cir
13200 DRPR 84020 2389 A4
Trail Ridge Cir
10600 SLkC 84092 2283 E4
10600 SNDY 84092 2283 E4
Trailsend Ct
600 PTGV 84062 2713 A4
Trailside Dr
5700 SmtC 84098 1972 C3
Trailside Lp
5800 SmtC 84098 1972 D3
Trailside Rd
10 FMTN 84025 1447 E2
Trailwood Cove
11000 SNDY 84092 2284 B5
Tralee Cir
4000 WVCY 84119 2069 B1
Tramway Cir
9500 SNDY 84092 2283 D1
Tramway Dr
1700 SNDY 84092 2283 C1
Tranmere Av
10100 SJDN 84095 2280 B3
Tranquil Ln
8500 SLkC 84044 1960 A6
Transwest Dr
1500 SNDY 84092 2283 C5
Trappers Ct
3400 WbrC 84310 1002 B4
Trappers Wy
- PKCY 84060 2078 E6
Trappers Loop Rd
- WbrC 84317 1060 E7
Trappers Loop Rd SR-167
- WbrC 84317 1060 E7
Traverse Cir
1800 BFDL 84065 2494 C2
Traverse Mountain Blvd
- LEHI 84043 2495 C5
Traverse Pointe Dr
200 DRPR 84020 2388 D7
Traverse Ridge Rd
200 DRPR 84020 2388 D7
600 DRPR 84020 2389 B7
1900 DRPR 84020 2496 D1
Travis Cir
4700 WJDN 84088 2174 A7
Travis Ln
4600 WJDN 84088 2174 B7
Travis Boyd Cir
13800 HRMN 84065 2385 B5
Travis James Ln
200 MRRY 84107 2176 C1
Treasure Cir
9800 SJDN 84095 2281 E2
Treasure Wy
9000 CDHT 84093 2178 C7
Treasure Mountain Cir
2300 SNDY 84093 2177 E6
Treasure Mountain Dr
8400 SLkC 84093 2177 E6
8500 SNDY 84093 2177 E6
Treasure Ridge Cir
7100 CDHT 84121 2177 C2
Tree Ln
4100 TYVL 84119 2069 B1
Treebeard Rd
5500 TYVL 84118 2068 D6
Tree Farm Ln
3300 CDHT 84121 2178 C5
Treeline Dr
400 ALPN 84004 2497 D3
8300 WJDN 84088 2174 E5
Treena Cir
7300 WJDN 84084 2175 D3
Treetop Cir
5000 MRRY 84107 2070 D4
Tree View Dr
1500 SLkC 84124 2071 C1
Trelawney Ln
9100 SmtC 84098 1865 C3
Trellis Cir
400 SRSP 84043 2601 D5
Trellis Pl
1900 SRSP 84043 2601 D5
N Tremont St
800 TMTN 84337 520 E5
N Tremont St SR-82
- TMTN 84337 520 E5
S Tremont St
10 TMTN 84337 520 E7
800 TMTN 84337 584 E1
Tremont Wy
7000 MDVL 84047 2176 D2
Trendland Cove
10 SNDY 84092 2284 A5
Trent Dr
11100 SJDN 84095 2282 A6
Trento Cir
7000 WJDN 84084 2173 D2
Trenton Cir
4000 DvsC 84056 1228 A5
Trenton Dr
10 CRFD 84015 1281 D1
Tresa Dr
6400 TYVL 84084 2069 B7
6400 TYVL 84084 2175 B1
Treseder St
14800 DRPR 84020 2388 D7
14800 DRPR 84020 2495 C1
Tressler Rd
5800 SLkC 84118 2068 B6
Trestle Ct
2400 RIVN 84065 2387 B4
Trestle Ln
13200 RIVN 84065 2387 B4
Treven Pl
500 DRPR 84020 2388 E7
Trevino Rd
1400 SNDY 84092 2283 C7
Trevisto St
- HRMN 84065 2385 D2
Trevor Ln
2300 TYVL 84118 2069 B6
Trident Cir
5300 SLkC 84118 2067 D5
Trident Dr
5400 SLkC 84118 2067 D5
Trifford Pl
3200 TYVL 84084 2068 E6
Trimble Ln
1100 WJDN 84088 2175 E7
Trimble Creek Dr
1000 WJDN 84088 2281 E1
1100 WJDN 84088 2175 E7
Trinity Av
4300 WVCY 84120 2068 B3
Trinnaman Ln
900 LEHI 84043 2603 A4
Triple Crown Ln
6100 HRMN 84065 2385 C5
Tripp Ln
700 MRRY 84123 2070 A6
800 DRPR 84020 2389 A4
Tristram St
700 NSLK 84054 1653 B5
Tritoma Av
900 SLkC 84094 2283 A3
Triton Ct
400 MRRY 84107 2070 E2
Triton Dr
4500 MRRY 84107 2070 E2
Triumph Blvd
- LEHI 84043 2495 D7
Triumph Ln
6700 WJDN 84084 2175 E1
Trojan Dr
4500 WVCY 84120 2068 A3
Troon
3900 CRHL 84062 2605 C1
Troon Cir
1500 SRCS 84075 1226 B7
2600 CDHT 84093 2178 A4
Troon Dr
500 SRCS 84075 1226 B7
Trophy Cir
5400 WVCY 84120 2067 E2
Trotter Ct
13000 RIVN 84065 2387 D3
Trowbridge Wy
5600 SLkC 84118 2067 D6
Troy Wy
200 SLkC 84107 2070 D1
E Truman Av
10 SSLK 84115 1964 D2
W Truman Av
10 SSLK 84115 1964 C2
Truman Cir
4300 DvsC 84056 1228 A4
Trunk Bay Cir
500 MRRY 84107 2070 E5
Truscott Ct
2800 SLkC 84044 1960 E4
Truth Ln
3500 SLkC 84044 1960 C6
Tryall Dr
3000 SRCS 84075 1226 C7
Tuckington Cir
5700 SLkC 84118 2067 D6
Tudor Ct
4600 WVCY 84120 1962 B4
Tuft Ct
6600 WJDN 84084 2173 B1
Tulane Cir
1100 SNDY 84094 2177 B6
Tulare Ct
3700 SJDN 84095 2280 D7
Tule Dr
- HYRM 84319 651 E3
Tulip Dr
9800 SLkC 84094 2282 E2
9800 SLkC 84094 2283 A2
9800 SNDY 84094 2282 E2
Tumbleweed Wy
1400 DRPR 84020 2389 B6
Tumerick Ct
5900 SLkC 84118 2068 A6
Tungsten Ct
5500 WJDN 84088 2173 D6
Tupelo Ln
6700 WJDN 84084 2173 A4
Turf Farm Rd
- UthC 84651 3354 C7
800 PYSN 84651 3354 C7
Turin Dr
800 SLCY 84116 1753 C7
Turley Av
400 PTGV 84062 2712 D4
Turnagain Cove
3100 CDHT 84121 2178 D2
Turnberry Cir
1000 FMTN 84025 1346 A6
Turnberry Ct
- LEHI 84043 2602 B2
Turnberry Ln
- LEHI 84043 2602 B1
Turnberry Pl
4600 TYVL 84123 2069 E3
Turnberry Wy
1000 TYVL 84123 2069 E3
Turner Dr
5600 MRRY 84121 2071 B6
Turnpike Ln
9400 SNDY 84070 2282 C1
Turpin St
6200 MRRY 84107 2070 E7
Turquoise Cir
10000 SNDY 84094 2283 B2
Turquoise Wy
1000 SLkC 84094 2283 B2
1200 SNDY 84094 2283 B2
Turtle Creek Ct
5800 WVCY 84118 2067 C7
Turtle Dove Ln
1500 WJDN 84088 2175 C6
Tuscalee Wy
1700 DRPR 84020 2389 C4
Tuscaloosa Wy
3600 WJDN 84084 2068 D7
Tuscan St
4900 SLkC 84118 2067 E4
Tuscanny Creek Wy
- DRPR 84020 2389 E2
Tuscan Rose Cir
5600 HRMN 84065 2385 D6
Tuscany Cir
1900 PTGV 84062 2605 D7
Tuscany Dr
1800 SRSP 84043 2601 E5
6900 WJDN 84084 2174 A2
Tuscany Wy
1800 PTGV 84062 2605 D7
Tuscany Cove Dr
- FMTN 84025 1448 D5
Tuscany Downs Wy
3100 WVCY 84128 1961 B5
N Tuttle Ct
400 SLCY 84116 1858 B1
Tuxedo Cir
2500 CDHT 84093 2178 A4
Tuxedo Wy
2400 CDHT 84093 2178 A4
Twain Cir
8000 SLkC 84044 1960 C4
Twain Dr
2500 SLkC 84044 1960 C4
Tweed Rd
9700 SJDN 84095 2280 B2
Twelve Pines Cir
1200 SNDY 84094 2177 B4
Twelve Pines Dr
7800 SNDY 84094 2177 B4
Twilight Cir
5900 SLkC 84118 2068 C6
Twilight Ct
2100 PKCY 84060 2078 E2
Twilight Dr
4000 SLkC 84118 2068 B6
Twilight Ln
1800 HRCY 84032 2398 D7
Twin Aspen Cove
6900 CDHT 84121 2178 B2
Twinbrook St
3600 SLkC 84109 1966 B7
Twin Creek Cir
400 KYVL 84037 1283 D7
Twinkenham Dr
1000 SLCY 84103 1754 C6
Twin Lake Cir
7600 CDHT 84121 2178 B3
Twin Oaks Dr
1300 WJDN 84088 2175 D6
Twin Peaks Cir
3300 LYTN 84040 1284 B5
Twin Peaks Dr
100 LYTN 84040 1284 B4
Twin Pines Ct
11700 DRPR 84020 2282 D7
Twin Ridge Dr
100 DRPR 84020 2282 D7
Twin River Lp
200 ALPN 84004 2497 E5
S Twin River Wy
4200 TYVL 84123 2070 A1
W Twin River Wy
700 TYVL 84123 2070 A1
Twin Springs Ct
2900 TYVL 84084 2069 C7
Twin Trees Ln
400 LYTN 84041 1283 A5
Twin View Dr
2000 SLkC 84109 1965 D6
Twin Willows Cir
5800 MRRY 84123 2070 B6
Two Mile Rd
- SRCS 84075 1226 E5
300 WPT 84015 1226 E5
700 CLTN 84015 1226 E2
1800 CLTN 84015 1170 E7
Two Mile Rd SR-108
- SRCS 84075 1226 E5
300 WPT 84015 1226 E5
700 CLTN 84015 1226 E2
1800 CLTN 84015 1170 E7
Tyler Av
100 OGDN 84404 1057 C5
1500 OGDN 84404 1116 C1
2000 OGDN 84401 1116 C3
3000 OGDN 84403 1116 C5
N Tyler Av
100 OGDN 84404 1057 C5
Tyler Cir
800 OGDN 84404 1057 B7
Tyler St
1300 SLCY 84105 1858 E7
Tynedale Ct
7800 CDHT 84093 2177 C4
Tysonbrook Ct
3200 TYVL 84084 2068 E6

U

U St
10 SLCY 84103 1859 B2
Udine Ct
4700 WJDN 84084 2174 A1
Ufizzi Ct
6900 WJDN 84084 2174 A2
Uinta Dr
1200 PRVO 84604 2927 D4
Uintah Av
- SLCY 84103 1859 A1
Uintah Cir
1400 SLCY 84105 1859 C6
Uintah Ct
2700 PKCY 84060 2079 A1
Uintah Wy
1700 SmtC 84098 1971 E2
Uinta Hills Ct
4300 WJDN 84088 2174 B7
Uinta Hills Dr
9000 WJDN 84088 2174 C7
9200 WJDN 84088 2280 C1
Uintah Peak Dr
6300 TYVL 84084 2069 A7
Uinta Pines Cir
3000 SJDN 84095 2280 E6
3000 SJDN 84095 2281 A6
Uinta Point Ln
100 DRPR 84020 2388 C4
Uinta Ridge Ct
3000 TYVL 84084 2068 E7
3000 TYVL 84084 2069 A7
Un Rd
- WELV 84339 649 E2
500 DvsC 84056 1229 A5
Union Av
10 NSLK 84054 1653 A5
2100 OGDN 84401 1115 D2
N Union Av
1100 MDVL 84047 2177 B2
Union St
10 SLCY 84104 1856 E5
Union Creek Wy
7300 MDVL 84047 2177 B2
Union Garden Ct
600 MDVL 84047 2176 E3
Union Mill Ct
7400 MDVL 84047 2176 D3
Union Mill Dr
300 MDVL 84047 2176 C3
Union Park Av
- MRRY 84047 2177 B3
- MRRY 84121 2177 B3
6900 CDHT 84121 2177 B3
6900 MDVL 84047 2177 B3
7000 CDHT 84093 2177 B3
7300 SNDY 84093 2177 B3
7500 SNDY 84047 2177 B3
Union Park Ctr
6900 CDHT 84121 2177 B2
7000 MDVL 84047 2177 B2
Union Pines Ct
600 MDVL 84047 2176 E3
Union Station Cir
11600 SJDN 84095 2280 D6
Union Station Ln
3400 SJDN 84095 2280 D6
Union View Pl
7300 MDVL 84047 2176 C2
Union Village Cir
7300 MDVL 84047 2176 D3
Union Village Ln
300 MDVL 84047 2176 C2
Unionwood Dr
400 SNDY 84047 2176 E4
Universal Cir
400 SNDY 84070 2176 B7
N University Av
10 PRVO 84601 2928 C6
10 PRVO 84606 2928 C6
800 PRVO 84604 2928 C6
4900 PRVO 84604 2821 C5
5000 UthC 84604 2821 C5
5600 OREM 84604 2821 C5
N University Av US-189
10 PRVO 84601 2928 C6
10 PRVO 84606 2928 C6
800 PRVO 84604 2928 C6
3300 PRVO 84604 2821 C5
5000 UthC 84604 2821 C5
5600 OREM 84604 2821 C5
S University Av
10 PRVO 84601 2928 C7
10 PRVO 84606 2928 C7
600 PRVO 84601 3035 C1
600 PRVO 84606 3035 C1
S University Av US-189
10 PRVO 84601 2928 C7
10 PRVO 84606 2928 C7
800 PRVO 84601 3035 C2
800 PRVO 84606 3035 C2
University Pkwy
400 OREM 84097 2927 E1
500 OREM 84097 2928 A1
900 OREM 84604 2928 A1
900 PRVO 84097 2928 A1
900 PRVO 84604 2928 A1
University Pkwy SR-265
400 OREM 84097 2927 E1
500 OREM 84097 2928 A1
900 OREM 84604 2928 A1
900 PRVO 84097 2928 A1
900 PRVO 84604 2928 A1
E University Pkwy
10 OREM 84058 2927 D1
10 PRVO 84604 2928 C4
E University Pkwy SR-265
10 OREM 84058 2927 D1
N University Pkwy
1800 PRVO 84604 2928 B3
N University Pkwy SR-265
1800 PRVO 84604 2928 B3
W University Pkwy
10 OREM 84058 2927 C1
W University Pkwy SR-265
10 OREM 84058 2927 C1
University St
100 SLCY 84112 1859 B4
400 SLCY 84102 1859 B4
University Hill Wy
10 LOGN 84321 528 A1
University Mall
100 OREM 84097 2927 E1
100 OREM 84097 2928 A1
University Park Blvd
2000 LYTN 84041 1228 C7
2000 LYTN 84041 1282 C1
2200 CRFD 84041 1228 C7
Upland Cir
3200 PKCY 84060 2078 C1
Upland Dr
2700 SLkC 84109 1966 B7
Upper Canyon Rd
200 SHFD 84335 399 E2
500 CchC 84335 400 A1
500 SHFD 84335 400 A1
Upper Evergreen Dr
200 SmtC 84098 1864 B6
Upper Huntly Wy
3200 WJDN 84088 2174 C4
Upper Iron Horse Loop Rd
1500 PKCY 84060 2078 D4
Upper Lando Ln
8800 SmtC 84098 1865 C3
Upper Newark Wy
3200 WJDN 84088 2174 C4
Upper Norfolk Av
100 PKCY 84060 2078 E6
Uranium Dr
7400 WJDN 84084 2175 C4
Uri Ln
900 MIDW 84049 2396 E1
Urry Cir
8300 SNDY 84093 2177 C5
US-6
- GNLA 84655 3460 A6
- SNQN 84655 3460 A6
- SPFK 84660 3142 D7
- SPFK 84660 3249 E1
- SPFK 84660 3250 A2
- SPFK 84660 3251 A7
- UthC 84655 3460 D7
US-6 E Main St
10 SNQN 84655 3460 E7
400 SNQN 84655 3461 A7
US-6 W Main St
10 SNQN 84655 3460 D7
US-6 Veterans Memorial Hwy
- PYSN - 3354 D4
- SNQN - 3461 B3
- SPFK - 3142 D7
- SPFK - 3248 E4
- SPFK - 3249 C1
- UthC - 3248 B7
- UthC - 3249 C1
- UthC - 3354 B7
- UthC - 3355 A2
- UthC - 3461 B3
US-40
- WshC - 2079 C1
- WshC - 2185 E1
- HRCY 84032 2398 D6
- SmtC - 1972 E2
- WshC - 2292 B2
- HRCY 84032 2505 E1
- WshC 84032 2292 D7
- SmtC - 1973 A3
- WshC 84032 2505 E1
- SmtC - 2079 C1
- WshC - 2186 A7
- WshC 84032 2398 D7
US-40 N Main St
10 HRCY 84032 2398 D5
US-40 S Main St
10 HRCY 84032 2398 D7
US-89
- ANFK 84003 2604 A7
- ANFK 84043 2604 A6
- BMCY 84302 767 B7
- BMCY 84302 828 B1
- BNFL 84010 1653 C3
- BxEC 84302 828 B1
- BxEC 84324 708 B7
- BxEC 84324 767 E7
- BxEC 84324 768 A2
- BxEC 84340 941 D2
- BxEC 84340 997 D1
- CchC 84321 527 B7
- CchC 84321 528 E1
- CchC 84321 590 D4
- CchC 84321 591 A1
- CchC 84328 708 B7
- CchC 84339 590 D4
- CchC 84339 648 E6
- CchC 84339 649 E2
- CchC 84339 650 A1
- CchC 84339 707 D1
- CchC 84339 708 A5
- DvsC 84037 1284 A6
- DvsC 84037 1346 A2
- DvsC 84040 1230 A6
- DvsC 84040 1284 A6

Block	City	ZIP	Map#	Grid
US-89				
-	DvsC	84405	1230	A4
-	FMTN	84025	1346	B6
-	FTHT	84037	1284	A6
-	FTHT	84037	1346	A2
-	HARR	84404	998	B7
-	HARR	84414	998	B7
-	HARR	84414	1056	C2
-	KYVL	84037	1284	A6
-	LOGN	84321	527	D5
-	LOGN	84321	528	E1
-	LOGN	84321	591	A1
-	LYTN	84040	1230	A4
-	LYTN	84040	1284	A1
-	MNTU	84324	768	C4
-	MPTN	84664	3143	D5
-	NBLY	84321	590	D4
-	NSLK	84010	1653	B6
-	NSLK	84054	1653	A7
-	NSLK	84054	1754	A2
-	PRRY	84302	827	E2
-	PRRY	84302	885	C1
-	PTGV	84062	2712	C2
-	PTVW	84404	997	E3
-	PTVW	84404	998	A5
-	PTVW	84414	997	E3
-	PTVW	84414	998	A5
-	SGVL	84663	3143	D5
-	SLCY	84116	1753	E3
-	SLCY	84116	1754	A2
-	SOGN	84403	1173	B5
-	SOGN	84405	1173	D6
-	SPFK	84660	3250	E6
-	SPFK	84660	3251	A6
-	SWBR	84405	1230	A4
-	UNTH	84403	1173	E7
-	UNTH	84403	1174	A7
-	UNTH	84403	1230	A1
-	UNTH	84405	1173	E7
-	UNTH	84405	1174	A7
-	UNTH	84405	1230	A1
-	UthC	84660	3250	E4
-	WbrC	84403	1173	D7
-	WbrC	84405	1173	D6
-	WbrC	84414	997	D1
-	WDCR	84010	1653	C3
-	WELV	84319	590	B7
-	WELV	84319	650	A1
-	WELV	84321	590	B7
-	WELV	84339	649	E2
-	WELV	84339	650	A1
700	HARR	84404	1056	C2
US-89 E 300 S				
10	PRVO	84606	2928	C7
US-89 N 300 W				
100	SLCY	84103	1858	B1
700	SLCY	84103	1754	B7
US-89 W 300 S				
10	PRVO	84601	2928	C7
US-89 S 400 E				
1500	SGVL	84663	3143	D5
1700	MPTN	84664	3143	D5
US-89 400 St N				
10	LOGN	84321	527	E2
600	LOGN	84321	528	A2
US-89 N 500 W				
10	BNFL	84010	1551	C6
10	PRVO	84601	2928	B6
100	WBNF	84010	1551	C6
800	PRVO	84604	2928	B5
US-89 S 500 W				
10	BNFL	84010	1551	C7
10	PRVO	84601	2928	B7
100	WBNF	84010	1653	C1
200	BNFL	84010	1653	C1
600	WDCR	84010	1653	C1
US-89 W 1100 S				
-	BMCY	84302	827	E2
-	BMCY	84302	828	A2
-	BxEC	84302	828	A2
US-89 N 1200 W				
-	LEHI	84043	2603	A3
US-89 N 1600 W				
10	MPTN	84664	3143	D6
US-89 S 1600 W				
10	MPTN	84664	3143	D7
700	MPTN	84664	3250	D1
1400	UthC	84664	3250	D1
US-89 Beck St				
-	NSLK	84054	1754	A1
1100	SLCY	84103	1754	B7
1100	SLCY	84116	1754	B7
1800	SLCY	84103	1753	E4
1800	SLCY	84116	1753	E3
US-89 N Harrisville Rd				
10	OGDN	84404	1056	E4
300	HARR	84404	1056	E4
US-89 E Main St				
10	ANFK	84003	2711	C1
US-89 N Main St				
10	LOGN	84321	527	D4
10	SGVL	84663	3143	C2
10	WLRD	84340	885	C5
600	SGVL	84663	3036	C7
1500	PRVO	84606	3036	C6
1500	PRVO	84663	3036	C6
1500	SGVL	84606	3036	C6
1600	UthC	84606	3036	C5
US-89 S Main St				
10	LOGN	84321	527	D3
10	SGVL	84663	3143	D7
10	WLRD	84340	885	C7
600	WLRD	84340	941	C5
1100	BMCY	84302	827	E3
1300	PRRY	84302	827	E3
2200	BNFL	84010	1653	C3
2200	WDCR	84010	1653	C3
2600	NSLK	84010	1653	C4
2600	NSLK	84054	1653	C4
3200	DvsC	84010	1653	B5
3400	DvsC	84054	1653	B5
US-89 W Main St				
10	ANFK	84003	2711	B1
US-89 E North Temple				
10	SLCY	84103	1858	C2
US-89 W North Temple				
10	SLCY	84103	1858	C2
US-89 E State Rd				
200	ANFK	84003	2711	D1
400	LNDN	84042	2712	E5
700	ANFK	84003	2712	A2
700	UthC	84003	2711	E1
US-89 E State Rd				
700	UthC	84003	2712	A2
1100	PTGV	84062	2712	A2
US-89 State St				
6800	MDVL	84047	2176	C1
7800	MDVL	84070	2176	C4
8200	SNDY	84070	2176	C5
9200	SNDY	84070	2282	C1
US-89 E State St				
10	LEHI	84043	2603	C5
900	UthC	84043	2603	D6
1400	ANFK	84003	2603	E6
1500	ANFK	84003	2604	A7
1500	ANFK	84043	2604	A7
1500	UthC	84043	2604	A7
US-89 N State St				
10	LNDN	84042	2713	B6
10	OREM	84057	2820	D5
10	SLCY	84103	1858	D3
500	LNDN	84042	2712	E5
1200	PRVO	84604	2928	B4
1700	OREM	84057	2713	B6
US-89 S State St				
10	LNDN	84042	2713	B6
10	OREM	84058	2820	D5
10	SLCY	84111	1858	D3
100	OREM	84057	2713	B7
300	PRVO	84606	2928	D7
500	PRVO	84606	3035	E1
700	OREM	84097	2820	E7
1000	OREM	84058	2927	E1
1000	OREM	84097	2927	E1
1300	SLCY	84115	1858	D7
1400	PRVO	84606	3036	B4
1500	SLCY	84115	1964	D1
1600	OREM	84058	2928	A3
1600	OREM	84097	2928	A3
1600	UthC	84606	3036	B4
1800	PRVO	84604	2928	A3
2100	SSLK	84115	1964	D1
3900	SLkC	84107	1964	D7
4000	SLkC	84107	2070	D1
4200	MRRY	84107	2070	D1
6400	MRRY	84107	2176	C1
6500	MRRY	84047	2176	C1
6600	MDVL	84047	2176	C1
6600	MDVL	84107	2176	C1
8600	SNDY	84070	2176	C7
11400	DRPR	84020	2282	C6
US-89 W State St				
10	ANFK	84003	2711	B1
10	LEHI	84043	2603	C5
100	ANFK	84003	2604	A7
US-89 Veterans Memorial Hwy				
-	BNFL	-	1551	C5
-	CTRV	-	1448	C6
-	CTRV	-	1551	C5
-	DRPR	-	2282	C7
-	DRPR	-	2388	C3
-	DRPR	-	2495	C7
-	FMTN	-	1448	C6
-	LEHI	-	2495	C7
-	LEHI	-	2602	D2
-	UthC	-	2495	C7
-	WBNF	-	1551	C5
US-89 Washington Blvd				
-	SOGN	84403	1173	A4
-	SOGN	84405	1173	A4
200	OGDN	84404	1056	E5
1300	OGDN	84404	1115	E1
1800	OGDN	84401	1115	E1
3500	OGDN	84403	1115	E7
3600	SOGN	84403	1115	E7
3600	SOGN	84405	1115	E7
3900	SOGN	84403	1172	E1
3900	SOGN	84405	1172	E1
4000	WbrC	84405	1172	E1
4300	WSTR	84403	1172	E1
4300	WSTR	84405	1172	E1
US-91				
-	BMCY	84302	767	B7
-	BMCY	84302	828	B1
-	BxEC	84302	828	B1
-	BxEC	84324	708	B7
-	BxEC	84324	767	E7
-	BxEC	84324	768	A2
-	CchC	84318	399	D6
-	CchC	84321	527	B7
-	CchC	84321	590	D4
-	CchC	84321	591	A1
-	CchC	84328	708	B7
-	CchC	84335	399	D6
-	CchC	84339	590	D4
-	CchC	84339	648	E6
-	CchC	84339	649	E2
-	CchC	84339	650	A1
-	CchC	84339	707	D1
-	CchC	84339	708	A5
-	CchC	84341	399	D6
-	CchC	84341	463	D1
-	HDPK	84318	399	D6
-	HDPK	84318	463	D1
-	HDPK	84341	399	D6
-	HDPK	84341	463	D1
-	LOGN	84321	527	D5
-	LOGN	84321	591	A1
-	LOGN	84341	463	D4
-	MNTU	84324	768	C4
-	NBLY	84321	590	D4
-	NHLN	84341	463	D4
-	SHFD	84335	399	D3
-	WELV	84319	590	B7
-	WELV	84319	650	A1
-	WELV	84321	590	B7
-	WELV	84339	649	E2
-	WELV	84339	650	A1
US-91 W 1100 S				
-	BMCY	84302	828	A2
-	BxEC	84302	827	E2
-	BxEC	84302	828	A2
-	BxEC	84340	827	E2
10	BMCY	84302	827	E2
US-91 N Main St				
10	LOGN	84321	527	D4
10	SHFD	84335	399	D1
900	LOGN	84321	463	D7
1000	LOGN	84341	463	D7
US-91 S Main St				
10	LOGN	84321	527	D3
10	SHFD	84335	399	D3
US-189				
-	CSTN	84032	2504	B5
-	WshC	84032	2292	D7
-	WshC	84032	2398	D1
-	WshC	84032	2503	E7
-	WshC	84032	2504	B5
US-189 S Charleston Rd				
10	HRCY	84032	2398	B7
10	WshC	84032	2398	B7
1200	HRCY	84032	2505	A1
1200	WshC	84032	2505	A1
1600	WshC	84032	2504	E2
2100	CSTN	84032	2504	E2
US-189 N Main St				
10	HRCY	84032	2398	D5
US-189 S Main St				
10	HRCY	84032	2398	D4
US-189 E Provo Canyon Rd				
-	PRVO	84604	2822	A1
-	UthC	84604	2821	D1
-	UthC	84604	2822	A1
2300	OREM	84097	2714	E7
2300	OREM	84604	2714	E7
2300	OREM	84604	2821	D1
2300	PRVO	84604	2714	E7
2300	PRVO	84604	2821	D1
2300	UthC	84604	2714	E7
US-189 N University Av				
10	PRVO	84601	2928	C7
10	PRVO	84606	2928	C7
800	PRVO	84604	2928	C5
3300	PRVO	84604	2821	C7
5000	UthC	84604	2821	C4
5600	OREM	84604	2821	C3
US-189 S University Av				
10	PRVO	84601	2928	C7
10	PRVO	84606	2928	C7
800	PRVO	84601	3035	C1
800	PRVO	84606	3035	C1
E UT 193				
1300	LYTN	84040	1229	C6
Utah Av				
300	PRVO	84606	2928	E7
500	PRVO	84606	3035	E1
E Utah Av				
10	PYSN	84651	3354	E5
200	PYSN	84651	3355	A5
W Utah Av				
10	PYSN	84651	3354	E5
900	UthC	84651	3354	D3
W Utah Av SR-147				
100	PYSN	84651	3354	D5
900	UthC	84651	3354	D5
Utah St				
1400	SLCY	84104	1857	C7
Utah Boys Ranch Ln				
5500	WJDN	84088	2173	E7
Utah Highlands Dr				
600	LEHI	84043	2603	D2
Utahna Cir				
1300	SLCY	84104	1857	E7
Utahna Dr				
1300	SLCY	84104	1857	E7
5600	MRRY	84107	2070	C6
E Utah Valley Dr				
600	ANFK	84003	2711	E3
600	ANFK	84003	2712	A3
600	UthC	84003	2711	E3
600	UthC	84003	2712	A3
S Utah Valley Dr				
600	ANFK	84003	2711	E3
600	UthC	84003	2711	E3
Ute Blvd				
1500	SmtC	84098	1971	E2
Ute Cir				
700	MRRY	84107	2071	A4
Ute Dr				
1400	SLCY	84108	1860	A7
Utility Dr				
5100	DvsC	84056	1227	E1
5100	SNST	84056	1227	E1
Utopia Av				
200	SSLK	84115	1964	B2
E Utopia Av				
10	SSLK	84115	1964	C2
W Utopia Av				
10	SSLK	84115	1964	C2
Uyeda Ct				
6300	WJDN	84084	2067	D7
V				
E Vagabond Dr				
200	MRRY	84107	2070	D1
S Vagabond Dr				
4300	MRRY	84107	2070	C4
Vahe St				
700	DRPR	84020	2388	A1
12100	DRPR	84020	2387	E1
Vail Cir				
2400	SNDY	84093	2178	A6
Valais Pkwy				
-	MIDW	84049	2291	C7
-	MIDW	84049	2397	C1
Valais Pkwy W				
-	MIDW	84049	2397	B1
Valcrest Cir				
3300	WVCY	84119	1962	E5
Valcrest Ct				
3300	WVCY	84119	1962	E5
Valcrest Dr				
3200	WVCY	84119	1962	E5
Val de Neige Cir				
2200	SNDY	84093	2177	E5
Valderrama				
4000	CRHL	84062	2605	C1
Valdown Av				
4200	WVCY	84120	1962	B5
Valence Ln				
6700	WJDN	84084	2174	D1
Valencia Cir				
8200	SNDY	84093	2177	B5
Valencia Pl				
8200	SNDY	84093	2177	C5
Valene St				
4900	HLDY	84117	2072	A4
Valentine St				
1200	SLCY	84116	1753	E6
Valeria Dr				
400	LYTN	84041	1283	B3
Valerian Cir				
5300	WJDN	84084	2173	E1
Valerie Ct				
1400	SRCS	84075	1227	A7
Valerie St				
1400	SRCS	84075	1227	A7
Valewood Dr				
1100	MRRY	84123	2069	E5
Valhalla Dr				
1200	CRFD	84015	1228	B6
Valiant				
-	DvsC	84056	1229	A4
Valiant Dr				
8200	CDHT	84121	2178	C5
Vallejo Dr				
4200	SLkC	84124	2072	B1
Valley Cir				
400	SNDY	84070	2176	E5
Valley Dr				
10	MRRY	84107	2070	C7
300	CTRV	84014	1448	D7
300	HRCY	84032	2398	E2
300	SmtC	84098	1866	D7
600	SPFK	84660	3249	C1
1200	OGDN	84401	1116	C2
Valley St				
2900	SLkC	84109	1966	C5
Valley Vw				
-	CRFD	84015	1227	D4
Valley Crest Wy				
2700	BFDL	84065	2387	A6
Valley Field Cir				
2500	SJDN	84095	2281	B4
Valley Forge Rd				
3700	SLkC	84044	1960	D7
Valley Haven Ct				
4000	WVCY	84120	2068	C3
Valley Heights Dr				
3500	TYVL	84118	2068	D4
Valley High Rd				
3600	WVCY	84128	1961	C6
Valley Hills Blvd				
700	HRCY	84032	2398	E1
1500	HRCY	84032	2292	E7
1500	WshC	84032	2292	E7
Valley Hills Dr				
500	HRCY	84032	2398	E2
500	WshC	84032	2398	E2
Valley Home Av				
3200	WVCY	84119	2068	E1
Valley Junction Dr				
2300	WbrC	84310	1001	D6
Valley Maple Dr				
7400	WJDN	84084	2173	A3
Valley Oak Dr				
6500	WJDN	84088	2173	B5
Valley Point Dr				
5800	WVCY	84128	1961	C6
Valley Pointe Ct				
3700	WVCY	84128	1961	C7
Valley Ridge Dr				
1000	HRCY	84032	2398	D1
1300	SNDY	84093	2177	B4
Valley Sage Dr				
900	SGVL	84663	3144	B4
Valley Side Cir				
800	DvsC	84010	1653	B6
Valley Spring Cir				
9400	SJDN	84095	2281	C1
Valley View Av				
2700	HLDY	84117	2072	A3
Valley View Cir				
600	NSLK	84054	1653	C6
1800	OGDN	84403	1173	D1
N Valley View Cir				
700	EKMT	84651	3463	B1
W Valley View Cir				
300	WDHL	84653	3463	C1
Valley View Dr				
-	TMTN	84337	520	A4
-	WbrC	84310	1059	E3
10	NSLK	84054	1653	B7
300	PTGV	84062	2713	A3
400	HYRM	84319	650	E3
400	HYRM	84319	651	A3
800	FTHT	84037	1346	A3
1200	LYTN	84040	1284	A2
2600	DvsC	84040	1230	A6
3000	LYTN	84040	1230	A6
3600	CRHL	84062	2605	C4
4800	WVCY	84120	2068	A1
6000	HILD	84003	2497	B5
E Valley View Wy				
10	WDHL	84653	3463	D2
W Valley View Wy				
10	WDHL	84653	3463	C2
Valley Villa Dr				
4600	WVCY	84120	1962	A6
Valley Vista Dr				
4200	HLDY	84124	2071	E1
Valley W Dr				
3600	WJDN	84088	2174	D6
Valois Cir				
4900	TYVL	84118	2069	B4
Valois Ct				
5000	TYVL	84118	2069	B4
Valois Dr				
4900	TYVL	84118	2069	B3
Vampire				
-	DvsC	84056	1229	A4
Van St				
2400	WJDN	84088	2281	B1
Van Buren Av				
200	OGDN	84404	1057	B5
300	SLCY	84115	1858	B7
1300	SLCY	84104	1857	D7
1800	OGDN	84401	1116	B2
3200	OGDN	84403	1116	B7
4800	OGDN	84403	1173	B3
N Van Buren Av				
400	OGDN	84404	1057	B4
Van Buren Cir				
1500	SLCY	84104	1857	D7
Van Buren St				
8200	MDVL	84047	2176	C5
Vance Ct				
9600	SJDN	84095	2280	A1
Vance View Cir				
10	LEHI	84043	2603	C4
Vance View Ln				
1200	LEHI	84043	2603	C4
Van Cherry Wy				
4800	WVCY	84120	2068	A2
Van Cott Rd				
6200	HLDY	84121	2072	A7
Van Cott Peak Cir				
14000	RIVN	84065	2386	A5
Van Cott Peak Dr				
4800	RIVN	84065	2386	A5
5100	RIVN	84065	2385	E5
Vandyck Ct				
-	WVCY	84119	1963	D6
Van Gogh Cir				
6000	SLkC	84118	2067	E7
Van Ness Pl				
400	SLCY	84111	1858	D5
Van Ross Dr				
2400	SJDN	84095	2281	A5
Vans Wy				
400	PVDN	84332	528	B6
Vantage Cir				
14400	BFDL	84065	2387	A7
Vantage Ct				
10	PKCY	84060	2078	D2
Vantana Ct				
200	MDVL	84047	2176	D1
200	MRRY	84047	2176	D1
Van Winkle Expwy				
-	MRRY	84107	2071	B3
-	MRRY	84121	2071	C6
-	SLkC	84107	2071	B3
-	SLkC	84121	2071	C6
5500	MRRY	84117	2071	C6
5500	SLkC	84117	2071	C6
6100	HLDY	84121	2071	C6
Van Winkle Expwy SR-71				
-	MRRY	84107	2071	A3
-	SLkC	84107	2071	A3
Van Winkle Expwy SR-152				
-	MRRY	84121	2071	C6
-	SLkC	84121	2071	C6
5500	MRRY	84117	2071	C6
5500	SLkC	84117	2071	C6
6100	HLDY	84121	2071	C6
Vaquero Dr				
8600	SNDY	84094	2177	A6
Varden Wy				
1300	TYVL	84123	2069	D2
Varenna St				
12500	HRMN	84065	2385	D1
Vassar Cir				
4200	WVCY	84120	2068	C3
Vassar St				
-	SLkC	84120	2068	C3
4600	WVCY	84120	2068	C3
Vauna St				
5800	ROY	84067	1171	B5
Vauna Lee St				
8600	SNDY	84093	2177	B6
8700	SLkC	84093	2177	B6
Vegas Wy				
4200	HLDY	84124	2071	D1
Venar Cir				
2700	SLkC	84109	1965	E4
Vendee Av				
3800	WJDN	84084	2174	C1
Venenzio Ln				
-	CTRV	84014	1551	D3
Venetia St				
5300	HRMN	84065	2385	D2
Venice Ct				
12700	HRMN	84065	2385	E2
Ventnor Av				
1500	SLkC	84121	2071	C5
Venture Wy				
100	SLCY	84115	1964	C1
Venus Cir				
2500	HLDY	84124	1966	A7
Venus Ct				
1900	PKCY	84060	2078	E2
Vera Cir				
3200	CDHT	84121	2178	C4
Vera Ln				
3000	BFDL	84065	2386	E7
3000	BFDL	84065	2387	A7
Verano Cir				
6600	WJDN	84084	2173	E1
Verbenia Av				
700	SLkC	84094	2283	A3
Verdant Cir				
3200	SLkC	84109	1965	E5
Verde Cir				
1400	SNDY	84093	2177	C5
Verde St				
5100	SLkC	84118	2067	E4
Verdugo Dr				
5000	SLkC	84118	2067	E4
5000	SLkC	84118	2068	A4
Vermer Wy				
10600	SNDY	84070	2282	D4
Vermont Ct				
3900	WVCY	84128	1961	D7
Verna Cir				
3900	WVCY	84120	1962	C7
Vernal Cove				
15000	DRPR	84020	2495	D1
Verne Wy				
400	TMTN	84337	520	E6
Vernon Cir				
3900	SLkC	84124	1965	C7
4000	SLkC	84124	2071	B1
Verona Cir				
2100	PTGV	84062	2605	C7
2500	HLDY	84117	2072	A4
Verona Ln				
2400	PTGV	84062	2605	D6
Verona Wy				
2300	PTGV	84062	2605	C6
Verona Meadows Ct				
700	MRRY	84107	2070	E6
Veronica St				
10100	SLkC	84094	2283	A3
Versailles Av				
-	WJDN	84084	2174	C1
Vespa Dr				
2500	WVCY	84119	1962	D3
Vestry Cir				
1300	DRPR	84020	2389	C4
Vestry Rd				
600	DRPR	84020	2388	E6
600	DRPR	84020	2389	A6
Veterans				
-	ANFK	84003	2604	C6
Veterans Memorial Hwy				
-	ANFK	-	2603	C5
-	ANFK	-	2711	C2
-	ANFK	-	2712	D6
-	BMCY	-	705	E6
-	BMCY	-	765	E1
-	BMCY	-	766	A6
-	BNFL	-	1551	C7
-	BNFL	-	1653	B3
-	BxEC	-	520	B2
-	BxEC	-	585	D5
-	BxEC	-	646	C7
-	BxEC	-	705	D3
-	BxEC	-	765	E3
-	BxEC	-	766	A6
-	BxEC	-	827	A3
-	BxEC	-	885	B5
-	BxEC	-	941	B5
-	BxEC	-	997	C2
-	CRFD	-	1227	E3
-	CRFD	-	1228	A5
-	CTRV	-	1448	C5
-	CTRV	-	1551	C7
-	DRPR	-	2282	C6
-	DRPR	-	2388	C6
-	DRPR	-	2495	A2
-	DvsC	-	1227	E3
-	DvsC	-	1228	B6
-	DvsC	-	1283	A6
-	DvsC	-	1345	C4
-	ELWD	-	584	D1
-	ELWD	-	585	D5
-	FMTN	-	1345	C4
-	FMTN	-	1346	A7
-	FMTN	-	1448	C5
-	FRWT	-	997	D7
-	FRWT	-	1055	D2
-	HYVL	-	585	D5
-	HYVL	-	645	E1
-	HYVL	-	646	B3
-	HYVL	-	705	D3
-	JubC	-	3567	B7
-	KYVL	-	1283	A6
-	KYVL	-	1345	C4
-	LEHI	-	2495	A5
-	LEHI	-	2602	D1
-	LEHI	-	2603	C5
-	LNDN	-	2712	B5
-	LNDN	-	2819	E1
-	LYTN	-	1228	B6
-	LYTN	-	1282	C2
-	LYTN	-	1283	A6
-	MDVL	-	2176	B5
-	MRRY	-	2070	B4
-	MRRY	-	2176	B5
-	MTSV	-	1055	D2
-	MTSV	-	1114	E1
-	NSLK	-	1653	B3
-	NSLK	-	1754	A3
-	OGDN	-	1115	B4
-	OGDN	-	1171	E4
-	OGDN	-	1172	A1
-	OREM	-	2819	E1
-	OREM	-	2820	A4
-	OREM	-	2927	C3
-	PRRY	-	827	A3
-	PRRY	-	885	B5
-	PRVO	-	2927	D6
-	PRVO	-	2928	A7
-	PRVO	-	3035	C4
-	PTGV	-	2712	B5
-	PTVW	-	997	C2
-	PYSN	-	3354	D4
-	ROY	-	1171	E4
-	RVDL	-	1115	B7
-	RVDL	-	1171	E4
-	RVDL	-	1172	A1
-	SGVL	-	3035	C4
-	SGVL	-	3142	D5
-	SLCY	-	1753	E5
-	SLCY	-	1754	A3
-	SLCY	-	1858	A2
-	SLCY	-	1964	B7
-	SLkC	-	1964	B7
-	SLkC	-	2070	B4
-	SNDY	-	2176	B5
-	SNDY	-	2282	B2
-	SNQN	-	3461	B5
-	SNQN	-	3567	D3
-	SNQN	-	3568	A1
-	SNST	-	1171	E4
-	SNST	-	1227	E3
-	SPFK	-	3142	D5
-	SPFK	-	3248	D5
-	SPFK	-	3249	A3
-	SSLK	-	1964	B7
-	TMTN	-	520	B2
-	TMTN	-	584	D1
-	UthC	-	2495	A5
-	UthC	-	2603	C5
-	UthC	-	2711	E3
-	UthC	-	2712	D6
-	UthC	-	3035	C4
-	UthC	-	3142	D5
-	UthC	-	3248	D5
-	UthC	-	3249	A3
-	UthC	-	3354	C6
-	UthC	-	3355	A2
-	UthC	-	3461	B5
-	UthC	-	3567	D3
-	WBNF	-	1551	C7
-	WBNF	-	1653	B3
-	WbrC	-	1115	B4
-	WDCR	-	1653	B3
-	WHVN	-	1114	E1
-	WHVN	-	1115	B7
-	WLRD	-	885	B5
-	WLRD	-	941	B5
Veterans Memorial Hwy I-15				
-	ANFK	-	2603	C5
-	ANFK	-	2711	C2
-	ANFK	-	2712	D6
-	BMCY	-	705	E6
-	BMCY	-	765	E1
-	BMCY	-	766	A6
-	BNFL	-	1551	C7
-	BNFL	-	1653	B3
-	BxEC	-	520	B6
-	BxEC	-	585	D5
-	BxEC	-	646	C7
-	BxEC	-	705	D3
-	BxEC	-	765	E3
Veterans Memorial Hwy I-15				
-	BxEC	-	766	A6
-	BxEC	-	827	A3
-	BxEC	-	885	B5
-	BxEC	-	941	B5
-	BxEC	-	997	C2
-	CRFD	-	1227	E3
-	CRFD	-	1228	A5
-	CTRV	-	1448	C5
-	CTRV	-	1551	C7
-	DRPR	-	2282	C6
-	DRPR	-	2388	C6
-	DRPR	-	2495	A5
-	DvsC	-	1227	E3
-	DvsC	-	1228	B6
-	DvsC	-	1283	A6
-	DvsC	-	1345	C4
-	ELWD	-	584	D1
-	ELWD	-	585	A2
-	FMTN	-	1345	C4
-	FMTN	-	1346	A7
-	FMTN	-	1448	C5
-	FRWT	-	997	C2
-	FRWT	-	1055	D2
-	HYVL	-	585	D5
-	HYVL	-	645	E1
-	HYVL	-	646	B3
-	HYVL	-	705	D3
-	JubC	-	3567	B7
-	KYVL	-	1283	A6
-	KYVL	-	1345	C4
-	LEHI	-	2495	A5
-	LEHI	-	2602	D1
-	LEHI	-	2603	C5
-	LNDN	-	2712	B5
-	LNDN	-	2819	E1
-	LYTN	-	1228	B6
-	LYTN	-	1282	C2
-	LYTN	-	1283	A6
-	MDVL	-	2176	B5
-	MRRY	-	2070	B4
-	MRRY	-	2176	B5
-	MTSV	-	1055	D2
-	MTSV	-	1114	E1
-	NSLK	-	1653	B3
-	NSLK	-	1754	A3
-	OGDN	-	1115	B4
-	OGDN	-	1171	E4
-	OGDN	-	1172	A1
-	OREM	-	2819	E1
-	OREM	-	2820	A4
-	OREM	-	2927	C3
-	PRRY	-	827	A3
-	PRRY	-	885	B5
-	PRVO	-	2927	D6
-	PRVO	-	2928	A7
-	PRVO	-	3035	C4
-	PTGV	-	2712	B5
-	PTVW	-	997	C2
-	PYSN	-	3354	D4
-	ROY	-	1171	E4
-	RVDL	-	1115	B7
-	RVDL	-	1171	E4
-	RVDL	-	1172	A1
-	SGVL	-	3035	C4
-	SGVL	-	3142	D2
-	SLCY	-	1753	E5
-	SLCY	-	1754	A3
-	SLCY	-	1858	A2
-	SLCY	-	1964	B7
-	SLkC	-	1964	B7
-	SLkC	-	2070	B4
-	SNDY	-	2176	B5
-	SNDY	-	2282	B2
-	SNQN	-	3461	B5
-	SNQN	-	3567	D3
-	SNQN	-	3568	A1
-	SNST	-	1171	E4
-	SNST	-	1227	E3
-	SPFK	-	3142	D5
-	SPFK	-	3248	D5
-	SPFK	-	3249	A3
-	SSLK	-	1964	B7
-	TMTN	-	520	C7
-	TMTN	-	584	D1
-	UthC	-	2495	A5
-	UthC	-	2603	C5
-	UthC	-	2711	E3
-	UthC	-	2712	B5
-	UthC	-	3035	C4
-	UthC	-	3142	D5
-	UthC	-	3248	D5
-	UthC	-	3249	A3
-	UthC	-	3354	C6
-	UthC	-	3355	A2
-	UthC	-	3461	B5
-	UthC	-	3567	D3
-	WBNF	-	1551	C7
-	WBNF	-	1653	B3
-	WbrC	-	1115	B4
-	WDCR	-	1653	B3
-	WHVN	-	1114	E1
-	WHVN	-	1115	B7
-	WLRD	-	885	B5
-	WLRD	-	941	B5
Veterans Memorial Hwy I-80				
-	SLCY	-	1858	B7
-	SLCY	-	1964	B7
-	SSLK	-	1964	B7
Veterans Memorial Hwy I-84				
-	BMCY	-	705	E6
-	BMCY	-	765	E1
-	BMCY	-	766	A6
-	BxEC	-	520	C7
-	BxEC	-	585	D5
-	BxEC	-	646	C7
-	BxEC	-	705	D3
-	BxEC	-	765	E3
-	BxEC	-	766	A6
-	BxEC	-	827	A3
-	BxEC	-	885	B5
-	BxEC	-	941	B5
-	BxEC	-	997	D7
-	ELWD	-	584	D1
-	ELWD	-	585	D5
-	FRWT	-	997	D7
-	FRWT	-	1055	D2
-	HYVL	-	585	D5
-	HYVL	-	645	E1

STREET
Block City ZIP Map# Grid

Veterans Memorial Hwy I-84
- HYVL - 646 C7
- HYVL - 705 D3
- MTSV - 1055 D2
- MTSV - 1114 E1
- OGDN - 1115 B4
- PRRY - 827 A3
- PRRY - 885 B5
- PTVW - 997 C2
- RVDL - 1115 B7
- RVDL - 1172 A1
- TMTN - 520 C7
- TMTN - 584 D1
- WbrC - 1115 B4
- WHVN - 1114 E1
- WHVN - 1115 B7
- WLRD - 885 B5
- WLRD - 941 B5
Veterans Memorial Hwy SR-30
- BxEC - 520 B6
- TMTN - 520 B2
Veterans Memorial Hwy US-6
- PYSN - 3354 D4
- SNQN - 3461 B5
- SPFK - 3142 D7
- SPFK - 3248 D5
- SPFK - 3249 C1
- UthC - 3248 D5
- UthC - 3249 B1
- UthC - 3354 C6
- UthC - 3355 A2
- UthC - 3461 B5
Veterans Memorial Hwy US-89
- BNFL - 1551 C7
- CTRV - 1448 C7
- CTRV - 1551 C7
- DRPR - 2282 C7
- DRPR - 2388 C1
- DRPR - 2495 A5
- FMTN - 1448 C1
- LEHI - 2495 A5
- LEHI - 2602 D1
- UthC - 2495 A5
- WBNF - 1551 C7
W Veterans Park Rd
10 PRVO 84604 2821 C5
Via Arboles Ct
11300 SJDN 84095 2280 D6
Via Bello Ct
3500 SJDN 84095 2280 D5
Via Bonito Dr
11200 SJDN 84095 2280 D6
Via Cortina St
6600 WbrC 84317 1060 D7
Via Delepaz Cir
3500 SJDN 84095 2280 D6
Via Encantada Wy
3300 SJDN 84095 2280 E5
Via Esperanza Wy
3500 SJDN 84095 2280 D5
Via Felicidad Wy
3400 SJDN 84095 2280 E5
Via la Costa Cir
- KYVL 84037 1345 D3
Via la Costa Wy
900 KYVL 84037 1345 D3
Via Riviera Wy
8300 CDHT 84093 2178 B5
Via Rossa Wy
1500 WVCY 84119 1963 D5
Via Sudeste Wy
3500 SJDN 84095 2280 D6
Via Terra
3500 SSLK 84115 1964 C6
Viburnum Av
6600 WJDN 84084 2174 A1
Vice Admiral Dr
13700 RIVN 84065 2386 B5
Vickie Cir
1500 WJDN 84084 2175 C1
Vickie Ln
200 CRFD 84015 1227 D3
Victoria Av
1000 SGVL 84663 3142 E4
Victoria Cir
- PKCY 84060 2079 A4
4500 PRVO 84604 2821 E5
Victoria Ln
1700 OGDN 84403 1173 D2
Victoria Pl
400 SLCY 84103 1858 E1
Victoria Wy
1000 SLCY 84116 1753 E6
Victorian Dr
2700 RIVN 84065 2281 A7
Victorian Wy
2400 RIVN 84065 2281 A7
Victoria Park Cir
2400 RIVN 84065 2281 B7
Victoria Park Dr
2700 WVCY 84119 1962 E4
Victors Wy
900 DRPR 84020 2283 A7
Victory Dr
1600 OGDN 84404 1057 D7
Victory Rd
- SLCY 84116 1754 B7
500 SLCY 84103 1754 B7
500 SLCY 84103 1858 C1
Victory Rd SR-184
- SLCY 84116 1754 B7
500 SLCY 84103 1754 B7
500 SLCY 84103 1858 C1
Vidas Av
100 SSLK 84115 1964 D3
View Cir
700 CTRV 84014 1551 C2
S View Cir
2700 BNFL 84010 1653 C4
View Dr
1900 SWBR 84405 1229 D2
2500 SWBR 84405 1230 A3
6100 SmtC 84098 1972 C2
View St
500 LYTN 84040 1283 D4
S View St
1900 SLCY 84105 1965 B2
View Crest Cir
- NHLN 84341 464 D3
Viewcrest Cir
10 BNFL 84010 1552 C7
3600 SLkC 84124 2072 D2
Viewcrest Dr
10 BNFL 84010 1552 C7
3700 SLkC 84124 2072 D2
View Crest Ln
- KYVL 84037 1344 E3
Viewmont Cir
4900 HLDY 84117 2071 E4
Viewmont Dr
10 BNFL 84010 1551 D6
Viewmont St
4700 HLDY 84117 2071 E3
4900 HLDY 84117 2072 A4
View Point Dr
1000 SNDY 84094 2177 B4
View Pointe Dr
- HILD 84003 2498 B7
W View Pointe Dr
3900 SmtC 84098 1864 E4
View Vista Rd
3600 WVCY 84119 1963 E6
Viking Dr
2300 WbrC 84310 1001 A6
2500 WbrC 84414 1001 A6
5000 SOGN 84403 1173 A3
S Viking Rd
3700 SLkC 84109 1966 B7
Viking Wy
10 PTGV 84062 2712 E3
Vilas Dr
10200 SNDY 84092 2283 E3
Villa Cir
100 SPFK 84660 3249 C3
600 BMCY 84302 766 D7
Villa Dr
10 CRFD 84015 1227 D3
3700 HLDY 84109 1966 A7
3700 SLkC 84109 1966 A7
Villa Bluff Dr
600 SNDY 84070 2282 A1
Villa Capri Ct
- MDVL 84047 2176 A4
Village Cir
500 MDVL 84047 2176 B5
700 SNDY 84094 2177 A6
2400 SLCY 84108 1860 A7
5800 SOGN 84403 1173 D5
E Village Cir
10 MIDW 84049 2397 C1
N Village Cir
10 MIDW 84049 2291 B7
W Village Cir
10 MIDW 84049 2397 B1
1100 MIDW 84049 2291 B7
Village Ct
10 ALPN 84004 2498 B4
10 MIDW 84049 2291 B7
7000 MDVL 84047 2176 E2
Village Dr
400 OREM 84058 2820 C5
Village Ln
1600 OREM 84058 2927 E2
S Village Ln
4100 TYVL 84119 2069 B1
W Village Ln
100 PRVO 84604 2821 C4
2600 TYVL 84119 2069 A1
Village Pl
7000 MDVL 84047 2176 E2
Village Rd
800 OGDN 84404 1057 A4
1800 CDHT 84121 2177 D1
Village Wy
- WbrC 84310 1001 D4
700 SNDY 84094 2176 E6
800 ALPN 84004 2498 B5
5600 SOGN 84403 1173 D5
E Village Wy
700 FTHT 84037 1345 E1
N Village Wy
10 FTHT 84037 1345 E1
S Village Wy
10 FTHT 84037 1345 E1
800 FTHT 84037 1346 A1
Village Wy N
700 SNDY 84094 2176 E6
700 SNDY 84094 2177 A6
Village Commons Wy
500 MDVL 84047 2176 A2
Village Crest Dr
2100 DRPR 84020 2496 D1
Village Dell Dr
4800 WJDN 84084 2174 A3
Village Ford Rd
3700 WJDN 84084 2174 D2
Village Gate Wy
- WVCY 84120 1962 A4
Village Glen Cir
4800 WJDN 84084 2174 A3
Village Glen Dr
4800 WJDN 84084 2174 A4
Village Green Cir
2000 DRPR 84020 2389 D7
2000 DRPR 84020 2496 D1
Village Green Rd
1600 CDHT 84121 2177 C1
W Village Hill Av
1800 SLCY 84116 1753 C6
N Village Hill Cir
1200 SLCY 84116 1753 C6
Village Oak Ln
1900 SNDY 84092 2283 D7
Village Park Av
1800 SLCY 84116 1753 B6
Village Point Wy
2000 SNDY 84093 2177 D7
Villager Ln
500 MDVL 84047 2176 E2
Village Rim Rd
3700 SmtC 84098 1971 E7
Village Round Dr
- SmtC 84098 1971 E7
E Village Round Rd
10 WDHL 84653 3463 D3
Village Three Rd
1500 MRRY 84121 2071 C7
Village View St
1200 SLCY 84116 1753 D6
Village Vista Dr
2100 DRPR 84020 2496 D1
2200 DRPR 84020 2389 D7
Village Wood Ct
5100 WVCY 84120 1961 E7
Village Wood Dr
3800 WVCY 84120 1961 E7
Villaire Av
2000 CDHT 84121 2177 D3
Villa Ridge Wy
700 SNDY 84070 2282 A1
Villa Springs Cove
9600 SNDY 84070 2282 A1
Villa View Dr
3500 WVCY 84120 1962 A6
Villosa Cir
6700 WJDN 84084 2174 A1
Vimont Av
2000 SLkC 84109 1965 E4
Vincent Ct
300 SLCY 84102 1858 E4
Vine Cir
10 CRFD 84015 1227 D3
Vine St
900 MRRY 84121 2071 A6
E Vine St
10 MRRY 84107 2070 D4
700 MRRY 84107 2071 A6
N Vine St
200 SLCY 84103 1858 C2
300 CRFD 84015 1227 D3
W Vine St
10 MRRY 84107 2070 B4
300 MRRY 84123 2070 B4
Vine Wy
6100 MRRY 84121 2071 D7
Vine Creek Cir
700 MRRY 84107 2071 A6
Vinecrest Cir
1100 MRRY 84121 2177 B1
Vinecrest Dr
6400 MRRY 84121 2071 B7
6400 MRRY 84121 2177 B1
Vine Field Ln
6100 MRRY 84121 2071 A7
Vine Gate Dr
1200 MRRY 84121 2071 A7
Vine Hill Ln
6100 MRRY 84121 2071 B7
E Vine Meadow Cir
1400 MRRY 84121 2071 C6
Vine Park Dr
6100 MRRY 84121 2071 A7
Vine Ridge Cir
- MRRY 84121 2071 A7
Vine Ridge Wy
1200 MRRY 84121 2071 B7
Vine Side Ln
- MRRY 84121 2071 B7
Vineway Cir
6100 MRRY 84121 2071 C7
Vineyard Cir
1400 BNFL 84010 1552 C7
Vineyard Ct
1400 SLkC 84106 1965 C7
Vineyard Dr
1300 BNFL 84010 1552 B7
Vineyard Pl
1900 SRSP 84043 2601 E5
N Vineyard Rd
100 VNYD 84057 2819 D4
100 VNYD 84058 2819 D4
S Vineyard Rd
- VNYD 84057 2819 E5
- VNYD 84058 2819 E5
100 OREM 84057 2819 E5
100 OREM 84058 2819 E5
W Vineyard Rd
200 VNYD 84057 2819 C4
200 VNYD 84058 2819 C4
Vineyard Wy
- MPTN 84664 3144 C6
100 SRSP 84043 2601 D5
Vinson Cir
3900 WVCY 84120 1962 C7
Vintage Cir
4200 PRVO 84097 2821 B6
Vintage Dr
400 PRVO 84097 2821 B5
Vintage Ln
1200 SLkC 84124 2071 B2
6000 HILD 84003 2604 B3
Vintage Rd
4200 PRVO 84097 2821 B6
Vintage Oak Ln
1700 MRRY 84121 2071 D7
Vintage View Ln
- DRPR 84020 2389 A7
- DRPR 84020 2496 A1
Vintage Woods Ct
1800 SLkC 84117 2071 D4
Vintry Cir
1400 MRRY 84121 2071 C7
Vintry Ln
1300 MRRY 84121 2071 B7
Viola Cir
10 BNFL 84010 1653 D2
Violet Cir
1000 SLkC 84094 2283 A3
Violet Dr
900 SLkC 84094 2283 A3
Violet Peak Dr
- HRMN 84065 2385 C4
Virdann St
400 LYTN 84041 1282 D4
Virden Cir
3900 WVCY 84120 1962 C7
N Virginia Av
1100 HARR 84404 1056 C2
W Virginia Av
200 HARR 84404 1056 D2
Virginia Cir
1000 OREM 84058 2820 D7
1000 OREM 84058 2927 D1
Virginia St
10 SLCY 84103 1859 B2
200 KYVL 84037 1345 D2
500 MRRY 84107 2070 E4
Virginia Wy
2800 OGDN 84403 1116 C5
3400 SLkC 84109 1966 C6
S Virginia Wy
3500 SLkC 84109 1966 C6
Virginia Hills Dr
6700 CDHT 84121 2178 A2
Virginia Pine Ln
3200 WJDN 84088 2174 E6
Vironcia Wy
1400 WVCY 84119 1963 D5
Viscaya Dr
- DRPR 84020 2496 E3
Viscayne Dr
7300 CDHT 84121 2177 D3
Viscounti Cir
8000 SLkC 84093 2177 B4
Viscounti Dr
1700 SLkC 84093 2177 D6
1800 SNDY 84093 2177 D6
Viscounti Cove
1900 SNDY 84093 2177 D6
Vista Cir
10 WDHL 84653 3463 C1
7600 SmtC 84098 1866 E6
Vista Dr
600 FTHT 84037 1346 B3
700 SOGN 84403 1173 A2
4600 HILD 84003 2605 A1
4900 ROY 84067 1170 D4
Vista Wy
11000 SNDY 84070 2282 D5
Vista Bonita Cir
3100 CDHT 84121 2178 B2
Vista Cir Dr
2900 BNFL 84010 1653 D5
Vista Glen Ct
11800 SNDY 84092 2284 A7
Vista Glen Dr
2500 SNDY 84092 2284 A7
Vista Grande Cir
3200 CDHT 84121 2178 B2
Vista Grande Dr
6700 CDHT 84121 2178 B1
Vista Hills Dr
2600 BFDL 84065 2387 A7
Vista Meadows Dr
2500 RIVN 84065 2387 A4
Vista Park Ln
9400 SJDN 84095 2281 B1
Vista Peak Dr
5200 WJDN 84088 2173 E6
Vista Point Dr
5200 SLkC 84118 2067 E6
Vista Ridge Cir
5200 SLkC 84118 2067 E6
Vista Ridge Ct
1800 DRPR 84020 2496 D1
Vista Ridge Wy
5400 SLkC 84118 2067 E5
Vista Royale
200 SALM 84653 3356 A2
Vista Valley Dr
- DRPR 84020 2389 B7
Vista View Dr
- KYVL 84037 1344 E1
900 SLCY 84108 1860 B6
Vista View Ln
500 NSLK 84054 1754 C1
Vista Villa Ln
3500 WVCY 84120 1962 A6
Vista W Dr
3600 WJDN 84088 2174 D7
9200 WJDN 84088 2280 D1
Vitt Dr
900 OGDN 84404 1057 B5
Vivante Wy
1500 WVCY 84119 1963 C5
Vivian St
3100 SLkC 84044 1960 B5
Vixen Wy
3600 TYVL 84118 2068 D6
Voelker Ct
3900 SmtC 84098 1971 E7
Vogue Ct
5800 HRMN 84065 2385 D4
Vollum St
- SLCY 84113 1859 D3
Volney Ct
600 SLCY 84101 1858 C5
Volta Av
3900 WVCY 84120 1962 C7
Volunteer Dr
- SPFK 84660 3249 C4
Von Baron Pl
1500 SLCY 84104 1857 D7
Vons Wy Dr
400 PVDN 84332 528 B6
Voyager Pl
6800 MRRY 84107 2176 C1

W

Wabash Cir
6000 MRRY 84123 2070 A7
Waco Dr
5100 OGDN 84403 1173 C3
Wade Ct
2200 OGDN 84401 1116 A3
Wade Pl
600 BMCY 84302 767 A4
Wade Wy
4200 WVCY 84119 2068 E1
Wadman Dr
2600 OGDN 84401 1115 A4
Wadsworth Park Dr
10 DRPR 84020 2388 C5
Wagner Cir
9000 SNDY 84093 2178 A7
Wagon Trail Dr
- HRMN 84065 2386 A1
Wagon Wheel Cir
10 FMTN 84025 1447 D1
3500 SmtC 84098 1865 A6
Wagonwheel Cir
1500 SLkC 84093 2177 C6
N Wagon Wheel Cir
10 FMTN 84025 1447 E1
Wagon Wheel Wy
3500 SmtC 84098 1864 E6
3500 SmtC 84098 1865 A6
Wagonwheel Wy
2400 LEHI 84043 2603 A2
Wagstaff Dr
1800 HLDY 84117 2071 D2
Wahlquist Ln
5900 MRRY 84123 2070 B6
Wailaki Cir
12700 RIVN 84065 2386 A2
Wailua Wy
2900 HLDY 84117 2072 B3
Waimea Wy
4800 HLDY 84117 2072 B3
Wainwright Rd
2800 SLkC 84109 1966 A4
Wakara Wy
300 SLCY 84113 1859 E4
500 SLCY 84108 1859 D5
Wake Cir
3300 WJDN 84084 2174 E2
S Wakefield Wy
6000 SLkC 84118 2067 D7
6200 WVCY 84118 2067 D7
6600 WJDN 84084 2173 C1
W Wakefield Wy
6000 WJDN 84084 2173 C1
6400 WVCY 84118 2067 C7
6400 WVCY 84118 2173 C1
Wakegan Rd
- BxEC 84307 704 C1
- BxEC 84337 645 A7
- BxEC 84337 704 A1
Wake Point Dr
4800 WVCY 84120 1962 A3
Wakeport Bay
4400 WVCY 84128 2067 D2
Wake Robin Dr
4800 WJDN 84084 2174 A1
5100 WJDN 84084 2173 E1
Walburk Av
1000 LYTN 84040 1283 C3
Walcott St
1300 OGDN 84403 1116 C5
Walden Ln
1100 DRPR 84020 2389 B2
Walden Glen Dr
5400 MRRY 84123 2069 D5
Walden Hills Dr
700 MRRY 84123 2070 A5
900 MRRY 84123 2069 E5
Walden Meadows Cir
5500 MRRY 84123 2069 E4
Walden Meadows Ct
5400 MRRY 84123 2070 A7
Walden Meadows Dr
800 MRRY 84123 2070 A5
900 MRRY 84123 2069 E5
Walden Meadows Pl
5500 MRRY 84123 2070 A5
Walden Park Dr
1000 MRRY 84123 2069 E5
Walden Ridge Dr
900 MRRY 84123 2069 E6
Walden Wood Cir
5400 MRRY 84123 2069 E5
Walden Wood Dr
5500 MRRY 84123 2069 E5
Waldo Dr
2000 HLDY 84117 2071 D2
Walker Ct
10 PKCY 84060 2078 B3
1700 SmtC 84098 1971 E5
Walker Ln
10 FMTN 84025 1448 C1
1400 FMTN 84025 1345 E5
2000 HLDY 84117 2071 E5
2000 HLDY 84121 2071 E5
2100 CTRV 84014 1448 D6
2300 HLDY 84117 2072 A5
2300 HLDY 84121 2072 A5
Walker Estates Cir
5400 HLDY 84117 2071 E5
5400 HLDY 84121 2071 E5
Walker Haven Cir
3900 HLDY 84124 1965 D7
Walker Meadows Cir
1900 HLDY 84117 2071 D4
Walker Mill Ct
3100 CDHT 84121 2178 B1
Walker Mill Dr
3100 CDHT 84121 2178 B1
Walker Oaks Ct
3200 CDHT 84121 2178 C1
Walker Vista Pl
13800 HRMN 84065 2385 C5
Walker Woods Ln
5400 HLDY 84121 2071 E5
Wall Av
100 OGDN 84404 1056 D7
1200 OGDN 84404 1115 D3
1800 OGDN 84401 1115 D3
3600 OGDN 84405 1115 D6
3600 SOGN 84405 1115 D6
Wall Av SR-204
100 OGDN 84404 1056 D7
1200 OGDN 84404 1115 D3
1800 OGDN 84401 1115 D3
3600 OGDN 84405 1115 D6
3600 SOGN 84405 1115 D6
N Wall Av
100 OGDN 84404 1056 D4
400 HARR 84404 1056 D4
N Wall Av SR-204
100 OGDN 84404 1056 D4
400 HARR 84404 1056 D4
Wall St
300 SLCY 84103 1858 C1
700 SLCY 84103 1754 C7
Wallace Dr
1300 SGVL 84663 3142 E5
2800 WbrC 84403 1174 A6
Wallace Ln
4400 HLDY 84117 2072 B2
Wallace Rd
1500 SLCY 84104 1857 B7
1500 SLCY 84104 1963 B1
Waller Ln
6200 WJDN 84084 2067 E7
Wallin St
300 MRRY 84107 2070 B7
Walnut Av
700 PRVO 84604 2928 D2
Walnut Cir
400 SLCY 84116 1857 D2
Walnut Dr
1300 SLCY 84116 1857 D2
Walnut Wy
3100 CDHT 84121 2178 B2
Walnut Brook Dr
500 MRRY 84107 2070 E6
Walnut Canyon Ln
10200 SJDN 84095 2280 B3
Walnut Cove
4200 CRHL 84062 2605 B3
Walnut Creek Ct
5800 WVCY 84118 2067 C7
Walnut Glen St
- SGVL 84663 3143 D3
Walnut Grove Dr
1700 DRPR 84020 2496 C2
Walnut Mill Cove
1900 SLkC 84106 1965 D5
Walnut Ridge Cir
5600 SLkC 84118 2067 B7
Walnut Ridge Dr
6000 SLkC 84118 2067 D7
Walnut Springs Ct
15200 DRPR 84020 2496 D1
Walnut View Cir
5600 SLkC 84118 2067 B7
Walnut View Dr
5600 SLkC 84118 2067 D7
Walnut Wood Dr
5600 SLkC 84118 2067 D7
Walpole Wy
7200 CDHT 84121 2177 E2
Walter Cir
4400 WVCY 84120 2068 B2
Walter Ct
4300 WVCY 84120 2068 C2
Walter Wy
4200 WVCY 84120 2068 B2
Walton Av
100 SSLK 84115 1964 C5
Walton Ln
10 CTRV 84014 1551 D4
Wanda Wy
2600 HLDY 84117 2072 A2
Wandamere Av
600 SSLK 84106 1964 E4
Wander Cir
2700 HLDY 84117 2072 A3
Wander Ln
4200 HLDY 84124 2072 A2
4600 HLDY 84117 2072 A2
Wanderwood Wy
10 SNDY 84092 2283 E5
10 SNDY 84092 2284 A5
Wandsworth Cir
2200 TYVL 84119 2069 B3
Wanlass Wy
2200 BFDL 84065 2387 B7
Wapiti Cir
5400 WbrC 84310 1002 A3
Wapiti Lp
10 HYRM 84319 651 E3
Warbler St
1100 WVCY 84119 1963 E7
N Ward Pkwy
- OGDN 84404 1056 B5
S Ward Pkwy
- OGDN 84404 1056 B5
Ward Rd
700 KYVL 84037 1283 E7
800 KYVL 84037 1284 A7
1100 FTHT 84037 1284 A7
Wardleigh Rd
- DvsC 84056 1171 E7
- RVDL 84067 1171 E5
- SNST 84056 1171 E7
10 DvsC 84056 1228 C4
1100 DvsC 84056 1227 E1
1800 ROY 84067 1171 E5
1800 RVDL 84405 1171 E5
Wardway Dr
2700 SLkC 84124 1965 E7
Warehouse Rd
4700 SLkC 84118 2068 A3
4800 SLkC 84118 2067 E3
Warm Springs Cir
800 KYVL 84037 1345 E3
Warm Springs Dr
500 KYVL 84037 1345 D3
Warm Springs Rd
700 SLCY 84116 1753 E5
700 SLCY 84116 1754 A6
1000 MIDW 84049 2291 B7
1000 MIDW 84049 2397 A1
1200 WshC 84049 2291 B7
Warnick Wy
500 ANFK 84003 2605 B6
Warnock Av
400 SLCY 84115 1964 E3
400 SSLK 84115 1964 E3
500 SLCY 84106 1964 E3
1100 SLCY 84106 1965 B3
W Warnock Av
1500 WVCY 84119 1963 C3
Warnock Dr
10 FMTN 84025 1448 D2
Warr Rd
2900 SLkC 84109 1966 C4
Warr Barton Cir
3800 WVCY 84120 1962 C4
Warren Cir
2900 BFDL 84065 2387 A5
Warren Row
10 OGDN 84401 1115 E2
Warrior Wy
- RVDL 84405 1172 A5
Warwick St
- NSLK 84054 1652 C5
Wasa St
1900 WJDN 84088 2175 C5
Wasatch Av
- SLCY 84103 1859 A1
200 SLCY 84101 1858 B5
900 PRVO 84606 2928 E7
1200 SLCY 84104 1857 D5
Wasatch Blvd
400 SHFD 84335 399 D1
1700 SNDY 84092 2283 D6
2400 SNDY 84092 2284 B6
2900 SLkC 84109 1966 C7
3800 SLkC 84124 1966 C7
4000 SLkC 84124 2072 B4
4800 HLDY 84117 2072 B4
4800 HLDY 84121 2072 C6
Wasatch Blvd
6400 HLDY 84121 2178 C1
6600 CDHT 84121 2178 C1
8900 CDHT 84093 2178 C7
9100 CDHT 84092 2178 C7
9100 SLkC 84092 2178 C7
9100 SLkC 84093 2178 C7
9500 SLkC 84092 2284 C2
Wasatch Blvd SR-190
6600 CDHT 84121 2178 C1
6600 HLDY 84121 2178 C1
Wasatch Blvd SR-210
- CDHT 84093 2178 D3
7000 CDHT 84121 2178 D3
Wasatch Cir
700 TMTN 84337 521 A4
1600 SLCY 84105 1859 C6
Wasatch Ct
4900 OGDN 84403 1173 C3
Wasatch Dr
10 LYTN 84041 1283 A4
100 SLCY 84112 1859 D3
200 SLCY 84113 1859 D3
500 SLCY 84108 1859 D3
900 SLCY 84108 1860 A6
1100 LOGN 84341 463 E7
1200 PRVO 84604 2927 E4
1500 OGDN 84403 1173 C3
1500 SLCY 84108 1966 A1
2100 SLCY 84109 1966 A2
4600 HILD 84003 2498 A7
5600 SOGN 84403 1173 D6
5900 WbrC 84403 1173 D6
Wasatch Dr SR-282
100 SLCY 84112 1859 D3
200 SLCY 84113 1859 D3
500 SLCY 84108 1859 D3
N Wasatch Dr
400 LYTN 84041 1283 A4
800 LYTN 84040 1283 B4
Wasatch Ln
800 SmtC 84098 1866 E6
Wasatch St
700 PYSN 84651 3355 A3
4800 MRRY 84107 2070 D3
W Wasatch St
700 MDVL 84047 2176 A4
Wasatch Wy
200 SmtC 84098 1866 D6
Wasatch Cove Cir
3600 SLkC 84109 1966 B6
Wasatch Downs Cir
9400 SJDN 84095 2281 E1
Wasatch Downs Dr
1100 SJDN 84095 2281 D1
Wasatch Grove Ln
3500 CDHT 84121 2178 E5
Wasatch Hills Ln
3500 CDHT 84121 2178 E5
Wasatch Meadows Ct
4400 WJDN 84088 2174 D7
Wasatch Meadows Dr
4100 WJDN 84088 2174 B7
Wasatch Oaks Cir
3100 SLkC 84124 2072 C2
Wasatch Park Cove
12600 DRPR 84020 2389 A2
Wasatch Pines Ln
3200 SLkC 84092 2284 C2
Wasatch Point Ln
100 DRPR 84020 2388 D4
Wasatch View Cir
9400 SJDN 84095 2281 E1
Wasatch View Dr
- PTVW 84404 997 E5
Wasatch Vista Dr
3600 BFDL 84065 2386 D5
Washakie Cir
1400 OGDN 84403 1173 C4
Washington Av
300 ANFK 84003 2711 B1
1800 PRVO 84606 3036 B3
E Washington Av
10 MRRY 84107 2070 D5
W Washington Av
10 MRRY 84107 2070 C5
Washington Blvd
- SOGN 84403 1173 A4
- SOGN 84405 1173 A4
100 OGDN 84404 1056 E7
1300 OGDN 84404 1115 E2
1700 NHON 84404 1056 E1
1700 NHON 84414 1056 E1
1700 WbrC 84404 1056 E1
1700 WbrC 84414 1056 E1
1800 OGDN 84401 1115 E2
2400 NHON 84414 998 E6
3500 OGDN 84403 1115 E7
3600 OGDN 84405 1115 E7
3600 SOGN 84405 1115 E7
3900 SOGN 84403 1172 E2
3900 SOGN 84405 1172 E2
4000 WbrC 84405 1172 E2
4300 WSTR 84403 1172 E2
4300 WSTR 84405 1172 E2
Washington Blvd SR-79
3000 OGDN 84401 1115 E5
Washington Blvd SR-235
100 OGDN 84404 1056 E7
1700 NHON 84404 1056 E1
1700 NHON 84414 1056 E1
1700 WbrC 84404 1056 E1
1700 WbrC 84414 1056 E1
2400 NHON 84414 998 E7
Washington Blvd US-89
- SOGN 84403 1173 A4
- SOGN 84405 1173 A4
200 OGDN 84404 1056 E6
1300 OGDN 84404 1115 E2
1800 OGDN 84401 1115 E2
3500 OGDN 84403 1115 E7
3600 SOGN 84403 1115 E7
3600 SOGN 84405 1115 E7
3900 SOGN 84403 1172 E2
3900 SOGN 84405 1172 E2
4000 WbrC 84405 1172 E2
4300 WSTR 84403 1172 E2
4300 WSTR 84405 1172 E2
N Washington Blvd
100 OGDN 84404 1056 E2
400 HARR 84404 1056 E2
1500 NHON 84404 1056 E2

STREET
Block City ZIP Map# Grid

N Washington Blvd
1500 NHON 84414 1056 E2
1500 WbrC 84404 1056 E2
2300 NHON 84414 998 E7
N Washington Blvd SR-235
100 OGDN 84404 1056 E2
400 HARR 84404 1056 E2
1500 NHON 84404 1056 E2
1500 NHON 84414 1056 E2
1500 WbrC 84404 1056 E2
2300 NHON 84414 998 E7
Washington Cir
1800 PRVO 84606 3036 B3
4300 DvsC 84056 1228 A4
Washington Dr
3700 SLkC 84044 1960 D7
Washington Lp
3700 SLkC 84044 1960 D6
Washington Rd
7400 SLkC 84044 1960 D6
Washington St
600 SLCY 84101 1858 B5
1300 SLCY 84115 1858 C7
3100 SSLK 84115 1964 C5
3900 CRNN 84307 705 A7
4000 CRNN 84307 704 E7
4300 DvsC 84056 1228 A4
8100 MDVL 84047 2176 B4
Washington Terrace Rd
4100 RVDL 84405 1172 D2
4200 WbrC 84405 1172 D2
4300 WSTR 84405 1172 D2
Washoe Cove
5500 WJDN 84088 2173 D6
Wassail Rd
400 SNDY 84070 2282 E5
Watchwood Dr
5600 TYVL 84118 2069 C5
Water St
100 LOGN 84321 527 D3
Waterbury Cir
10300 CRHL 84062 2605 A2
E Waterbury Cir
5700 MRRY 84121 2071 E5
Waterbury Dr
- MRRY 84121 2071 C6
Waterbury Wy
1500 MRRY 84121 2071 C5
Watercress Ln
1000 MDVL 84047 2177 A2
Waterfall Dr
4900 PTVW 84414 942 D7
Waterfall Dr N
5000 PTVW 84414 942 D7
Waterfall Ln
2900 OGDN 84403 1116 D5
Waterfall Wy
1400 FTHT 84037 1346 B2
Waterford Ct
4200 PRVO 84604 2821 E6
Waterford Dr
900 PRVO 84604 2821 E6
Waterford Wy
400 MDVL 84047 2176 D3
Waterfront Dr
5400 TYVL 84123 2069 C6
Water Leaf Wy
3000 WVCY 84128 1961 D5
Water Lily Dr
500 SSLK 84106 1964 E5
Waterloo Cir
7400 WJDN 84084 2174 E3
Waterloo Ct
10 PKCY 84060 2079 A3
Watermill Cir
7000 CDHT 84121 2178 B2
Water Mill Wy
- KYVL 84037 1345 B3
Watermill Wy
7000 CDHT 84121 2178 C2
Water Oak Dr
8200 WJDN 84088 2173 C5
Water Pointe Dr
1900 WJDN 84088 2175 B5
Waters Cir
9000 SNDY 84093 2177 C7
Waters Ln
1300 SNDY 84093 2177 C7
Watership Down Ln
1500 RIVN 84065 2387 D1
Waterside Cir
2200 SJDN 84095 2281 B6
Waterside Ct
11600 SJDN 84095 2281 B6
Waterside Rd
11400 SJDN 84095 2281 B6
Waterside Cove
1100 CDHT 84093 2177 B2
Waterton Cir
7800 CDHT 84093 2177 E4
Water Tower Wy
- OGDN 84401 1115 A3
2400 WbrC 84401 1115 A3
Water Trough Rd
500 CchC 84321 462 A7
500 CchC 84321 526 A1
1400 CchC 84341 462 A7
Water Trun Dr
- FMTN 84025 1448 D4
Water View Rd
3600 WVCY 84119 1963 E6
Water Vista Wy
2500 CDHT 84093 2178 A5
2500 SLkC 84093 2178 A5
Water Way Rd
- LEHI 84043 2602 B7
Water Wood Dr
4600 WVCY 84120 2067 D3
Watery Ln
- BxEC 84302 766 A3
1000 BMCY 84302 766 A3
Watkins Ln
1000 ALPN 84004 2498 B6
Watkins Wy
3900 WJDN 84084 2174 C1
Watson Rd
1300 SNDY 84092 2283 B7
Watt Ln
6000 WVCY 84128 2067 C1
Wave Ct
3300 WJDN 84084 2174 E2

STREET
Block City ZIP Map# Grid

Waverly Ct
4200 TYVL 84123 2069 D1
Waxwing St
1200 WVCY 84119 1963 D7
Wayfield Dr
100 DRPR 84020 2388 D6
Wayman Ln
5300 HLDY 84117 2072 B5
5400 HLDY 84121 2072 B5
Wayman View Ct
2800 HLDY 84117 2072 A5
Way Mar Cir
7100 CDHT 84121 2177 C2
Waymark Cir
3000 SLkC 84109 1966 B6
Wayne Cir
3700 SLkC 84109 1965 E7
Wayne Ct
200 SLCY 84101 1858 B4
Waynes World Dr
1100 DRPR 84020 2389 B5
Wayside Cir
8200 SNDY 84094 2177 B5
Wayside Dr
1100 SLkC 84094 2177 B5
1200 SNDY 84094 2177 B5
Wayward Cir
4300 WVCY 84128 2067 D2
S Weathervane Dr
5500 MRRY 84117 2071 B6
Weatherwood Ln
4800 HRMN 84065 2386 A6
Weaver Ln
- DvsC 84075 1282 B7
600 DvsC 84041 1282 D6
1200 LYTN 84041 1282 B7
Weaver St
- OGDN 84404 1056 B4
Webb Cir
600 DRPR 84020 2388 A2
Webb Ln
1000 KYVL 84037 1345 A2
1300 KYVL 84037 1344 E2
Webb Rd
600 DRPR 84020 2388 A2
S Weber Dr
5400 RVDL 84405 1172 A4
5500 SWBR 84405 1172 B6
S Weber Dr SR-60
5400 RVDL 84405 1172 A4
5500 SWBR 84405 1172 B6
Weber High Dr
10 NHON 84414 998 C4
100 PTVW 84414 998 C4
Weber River Dr
4300 RVDL 84405 1172 C2
S Weber River Dr
4500 RVDL 84405 1172 B2
Webster Ct
10 PKCY 84060 2078 C3
Webster Dr
900 SNDY 84094 2283 B1
2000 PKCY 84060 2078 B3
W Webster Ln
2400 WshC 84032 2397 D7
Webster St
900 SLkC 84094 2283 A1
Webwood Ct
3400 WVCY 84119 2068 E1
Wedge Cir
2900 SmtC 84098 1865 B3
Wedgecliffe Dr
4700 WVCY 84120 1962 A4
Wedgefield Dr
9100 SNDY 84093 2178 B7
Wedgewood Dr
4400 CRHL 84062 2605 C3
4400 PTGV 84062 2605 C3
4500 ROY 84067 1171 C2
Wedgewood Rd
3600 SLkC 84106 1965 B7
Wedgewood Wy
1200 SOGN 84405 1173 B5
Weechquootee Pl
- SLCY 84111 1858 C4
Weeping Willow Dr
10200 SNDY 84070 2282 C3
S Weight Av
400 SGVL 84663 3143 E3
Weir Dr
3300 SLkC 84044 1959 E5
Welby Av
300 SSLK 84115 1964 D4
1000 SLkC 84106 1965 A5
Welby Farm Rd
8400 WJDN 84088 2174 C6
Welby Hills Dr
4300 WJDN 84088 2174 B7
9200 WJDN 84088 2280 B1
Welby Park Dr
7900 WJDN 84088 2174 B5
Welch Cir
5700 SLkC 84118 2068 A6
Welling Wy
300 FMTN 84025 1346 B5
Wellingford Cir
500 NSLK 84054 1652 D5
Wellington Cir
1800 HLDY 84117 2071 D2
Wellington Ct
9900 HILD 84003 2604 D3
Wellington Dr
- KYVL 84037 1344 D2
S Wellington Dr
- KYVL 84037 1344 D2
Wellington St
2100 SLCY 84106 1965 D2
3500 SLkC 84106 1965 D6
4500 HLDY 84117 2071 D2
Wells Cir
9500 WJDN 84088 2279 D1
Wells Park Rd
5300 WJDN 84088 2279 C1
Well Spring Rd
900 MDVL 84047 2177 A1
Wellsville Cir
3200 SJDN 84095 2280 E4
Well Wood Rd
6900 MDVL 84047 2177 A2
Wenco Cir
1000 SLCY 84104 1857 E7

STREET
Block City ZIP Map# Grid

Wenco Dr
1000 SLCY 84104 1857 E7
Wendell Cir
3500 SSLK 84115 1964 D6
Wendell Dr
400 SSLK 84115 1964 E7
Wendell Ln
1900 HRCY 84032 2398 C7
Wendell Wy
400 SSLK 84115 1964 D6
Wending Ln
6000 WVCY 84128 1961 C7
Wendy Av
3900 WVCY 84120 1962 C4
Wendy Cir
2900 WVCY 84120 1962 C4
Wendy Wy
500 TMTN 84337 521 A6
E Wentworth Av
100 SSLK 84115 1964 D2
W Wentworth Av
100 SSLK 84115 1964 C2
Wesley Rd
1000 MRRY 84117 2071 B4
West Ct
200 SLCY 84102 1859 A4
2300 OGDN 84401 1115 E3
West Ln
100 PRVO 84601 2927 E7
West St
- BMCY 84302 767 A7
Westbench Cir
5800 SLkC 84118 2067 C6
Westbench Dr
5700 SLkC 84118 2067 D6
Westborough Wy
6700 WJDN 84084 2175 D1
Westbridge Dr
1300 PRVO 84601 2927 E7
West Bridge Rd
8400 MDVL 84047 2176 C5
Westbrook Cir
600 KYVL 84037 1283 E6
Westbrook Dr
3200 TYVL 84084 2174 E1
6200 TYVL 84084 2068 E7
Westbrook Rd
700 KYVL 84037 1283 E6
Westbury Ct
1000 NSLK 84054 1652 C5
Westbury Dr
8000 SLkC 84044 1960 C6
Westbury Wy
- LEHI 84043 2602 E1
Westcove Dr
2800 WVCY 84119 2069 A2
3100 WVCY 84119 2068 E2
Westcove Ln
- HILD 84003 2497 C5
S Westcrest Rd
3200 WVCY 84120 1962 C5
West Crimson Ct
- HILD 84003 2604 C3
Westerling Wy
2700 CDHT 84121 2178 A3
Western Dr
8200 SLkC 84044 1960 B4
Western Charm Dr
1700 RIVN 84065 2387 B4
Western Coil Rd
1000 LNDN 84042 2712 D7
S Western Coil Rd
100 LNDN 84042 2712 D7
Western Hills Dr
4700 RIVN 84065 2386 A2
Western Sun Cir
7500 SLkC 84044 1960 D5
Westfall Cir
3800 SLkC 84044 1960 E7
Westfield Cir
300 ALPN 84004 2497 C5
2000 WJDN 84084 2175 B4
Westfield Rd
- UthC 84003 2497 B5
- UthC 84020 2497 B5
300 ALPN 84004 2497 D5
900 ALPN 84003 2497 D5
900 HILD 84003 2497 D5
Westfield Cove Rd
11800 HILD 84003 2497 C5
Westfold Cir
2500 RIVN 84065 2281 B7
Westfold Wy
11800 RIVN 84065 2281 B7
Westgate Cir
3800 SLkC 84044 1960 E7
Westgene Cir
3200 WVCY 84119 1962 D5
N West Geneva Rd
4000 LNDN 84013 2819 B2
4000 VNYD 84013 2819 B2
4000 VNYD 84057 2819 B2
West Glen Dr
- PYSN 84651 3354 B5
Westhaven Dr
3800 WVCY 84120 2068 C1
Westheather Wy
6900 WJDN 84084 2175 B1
Westhill Cir
3800 SLkC 84044 1960 E7
Westlake Av
4000 WVCY 84120 2068 C2
Westlake Cir
3400 WVCY 84119 1962 E5
Westlake Dr
3200 WVCY 84119 1962 D5
4000 ROY 84067 1171 B1
Westlake Rd
3400 WVCY 84119 1962 D5
Westland Dr
400 BMCY 84302 827 D2
3600 WJDN 84088 2280 C1
Westlane Ct
1500 PRVO 84601 2927 E7
Westley Park Cir
9800 SJDN 84095 2280 E2
Westminster Av
100 SLCY 84115 1964 D1
800 SLCY 84105 1965 A1
1800 SLCY 84108 1965 D1
2500 SLCY 84108 1966 A1

STREET
Block City ZIP Map# Grid

West Moor Rd
4900 SLkC 84117 2071 C4
Westmoor Wy
6900 WJDN 84084 2175 B1
Westmoreland Ct
900 FMTN 84025 1346 C3
Westmoreland Dr
- SLCY 84105 1859 C7
S West Mountain Rd
11800 UthC 84651 3460 C3
12000 UthC 84655 3460 C3
S West Mountain Rd SR-141
11800 UthC 84651 3460 C3
12000 UthC 84655 3460 C3
West Oaks Cir
200 OGDN 84404 1056 D6
Weston Av
- LOGN 84321 528 B4
10 SLkC 84107 1964 C7
Weston Dr
- LOGN 84321 528 B4
West Park Av
7200 SLkC 84044 1960 E7
West Park Dr
- SPFK 84660 3249 B4
West Park Rd
5300 HILD 84003 2604 D2
West Point Cir
4900 WVCY 84120 2068 A2
Westpoint Dr
4500 WVCY 84120 2068 A2
West Point Rd
500 CRFD 84015 1227 A4
1400 CLTN 84015 1227 A4
1500 WPT 84015 1227 A4
1700 WPT 84015 1226 D4
4500 WPT 84015 1225 D4
West Point Rd SR-107
500 CRFD 84015 1227 A4
1400 CLTN 84015 1227 A4
1500 WPT 84015 1227 A4
1700 WPT 84015 1226 D4
4000 WPT 84015 1225 E4
West Point Wy
4500 WVCY 84120 2068 A3
Westpointe Cir
800 SLCY 84116 1753 C7
Westridge Blvd
4700 WVCY 84118 2067 C3
5600 SLkC 84118 2067 D4
Westridge St
6400 MRRY 84107 2070 D7
Westshire Cir
2500 WVCY 84119 1963 A7
Westshire Dr
2500 WVCY 84119 2069 A1
3900 WVCY 84119 1963 B7
Westside Cir
5500 SLkC 84118 2067 E5
West Side Dr
1000 LYTN 84041 1282 B7
1000 LYTN 84075 1282 B7
1100 DvsC 84041 1282 B7
1100 DvsC 84075 1282 B7
Westside Dr
5200 SLkC 84118 2067 E5
Westslope Cir
4900 SLkC 84118 2067 D3
Westslope Dr
5200 SLkC 84118 2067 E4
N West Temple
900 SLCY 84103 1858 C3
S West Temple
10 SLCY 84101 1858 C5
1300 SLCY 84115 1858 C5
1500 SLCY 84115 1964 C1
2100 SSLK 84115 1964 C2
3900 SLkC 84107 1964 C7
4000 SLkC 84107 2070 C1
S West Temple SR-270
400 SLCY 84101 1858 C5
West View Cir
100 OREM 84058 2927 D3
Westview Cir
1800 WJDN 84088 2175 C4
3200 SLkC 84124 2072 B3
Westview Dr
10 OREM 84058 2927 D2
4400 SLkC 84124 2072 C2
Westwind Ct
3900 RVDL 84405 1172 B1
Westwind Wy
5000 SLkC 84118 2067 E4
5000 SLkC 84118 2068 A5
Westwood Av
100 SLCY 84115 1964 C2
Westwood Dr
10 OREM 84097 2821 A5
900 PTVW 84414 998 B3
3400 SLkC 84109 1966 D6
Westwood Rd
10 SmtC 84098 1866 C4
1100 BNFL 84010 1653 E2
Weybridge Ln
1700 SNDY 84092 2283 C2
Weymouth Cir
4300 WVCY 84119 2069 A2
Weymouth Pl
4300 WVCY 84119 2069 A2
Weymouth Rd
2900 WVCY 84119 2069 A2
Whatta View Pl
11700 SJDN 84095 2281 E7
Wheatcrest Cir
5100 WJDN 84084 2173 E2
Wheatfield Cir
10 DRPR 84020 2388 C3
Wheatfield Wy
12900 DRPR 84020 2388 C3
Wheat Leigh Ct
9400 SJDN 84095 2281 A1
Wheat Meadow Ct
12000 RIVN 84065 2280 C7
12000 RIVN 84065 2386 C1
Wheatridge Ct
8300 WJDN 84088 2173 D5
Wheatridge Ln
5200 WJDN 84088 2173 E5
Wheatwood Cir
3500 WJDN 84084 2174 C2

STREET
Block City ZIP Map# Grid

Wheeler Ln
1900 HRCY 84032 2398 D7
Wheeler Creek Rd
- WbrC 84317 1059 C6
Wheelock Av
2800 OGDN 84403 1116 C5
Wherry Ln
600 DvsC 84056 1229 A4
Whileaway Rd E
1000 SmtC 84098 1866 E6
1000 SmtC 84098 1867 A6
Whileaway Rd W
7200 SmtC 84098 1866 E7
Whimpy Wy
600 MDVL 84047 2176 A2
Whipoorwhil St
4100 WVCY 84120 2068 A1
Whipple Dr
700 LEHI 84043 2603 D5
Whirlabout Ln
- RIVN 84065 2386 B4
Whirlaway Ln
10600 SNDY 84092 2283 C5
Whisper St
2900 WVCY 84120 1962 A5
Whisper Bend Dr
700 DRPR 84020 2388 E2
700 DRPR 84020 2389 A2
Whisper Brook Bay
12600 DRPR 84020 2388 E2
Whisper Cove Rd
700 SNDY 84094 2177 A7
Whisper Creek Ln
12700 DRPR 84020 2388 E2
Whisper Creek Cove
12600 DRPR 84020 2388 E2
Whisper Grove Cir
12700 DRPR 84020 2389 A2
Whispering Pns
- CRFD 84015 1227 D4
Whispering Breeze Cir
1500 KYVL 84037 1344 C1
W Whispering Meadow Ln
1200 KYVL 84037 1345 A3
1300 KYVL 84037 1344 C2
Whispering Oaks Dr
1600 OGDN 84403 1173 D3
Whispering Pine Cir
5600 MRRY 84107 2071 A5
Whispering Pine Dr
700 MRRY 84107 2070 D4
700 MRRY 84107 2071 A6
Whispering Sands Cir
10300 SJDN 84095 2280 D3
Whispering Sands Dr
3700 SJDN 84095 2280 D3
Whisper Point Ct
12600 DRPR 84020 2388 E1
Whisper Ridge Rd
12700 DRPR 84020 2388 E2
Whisper Rose Cir
14100 HRMN 84065 2385 D6
Whisper Rose Dr
5700 HRMN 84065 2385 D6
Whisper Spring Cove
12600 DRPR 84020 2388 E2
Whisper Wind Pl
12700 DRPR 84020 2388 E2
Whisperwood Cir
1800 SNDY 84092 2283 D1
Whisper Wood Cove
900 KYVL 84037 1345 E3
Whistler Cir
5300 SLkC 84118 2067 E7
Whitaker Dr
2200 TYVL 84118 2069 B4
Whitaker Wy
5000 TYVL 84118 2069 B4
Whitby Ct
4300 TYVL 84123 2069 D2
White Av
1700 SLCY 84106 1965 D4
1700 SLkC 84106 1965 C4
White Cir
2900 SLkC 84109 1965 D4
N White Cir
2000 SLkC 84109 1965 D4
S White Cir
2000 SLkC 84109 1965 D4
White Pl
10 SSLK 84115 1964 C5
White St
- OGDN 84404 1056 B6
900 PRRY 84302 827 B5
White Wy
4200 SLkC 84124 2072 E1
White Aspen Cove
7000 CDHT 84121 2178 B2
White Barn Dr
10 PTVW 84414 998 C5
Whitebird Cir
3800 WVCY 84120 1962 C4
White Blossom Wy
5100 WVCY 84120 2067 E2
5100 WVCY 84120 2068 A2
White Cherry Wy
4500 WVCY 84120 2068 A2
White Cony Cir
2900 WVCY 84128 1961 A4
Whitecrest Wy
7200 MDVL 84047 2176 D2
White Dawn Cir
5300 HRMN 84065 2385 E6
White Diamond Wy
3200 WVCY 84120 1962 A4
White Doe Cir
13500 RIVN 84065 2386 C4
White Flower Cir
5100 WVCY 84120 2067 C2
White Flower Wy
4400 WVCY 84120 2067 E2
Whitehall Ct
700 FMTN 84025 1346 B5
Whitehall Dr
2700 WVCY 84119 1963 A7
3000 WVCY 84119 1962 E7
Whitemaple Wy
700 SLkC 84106 1965 A7
White Oaks Cir
1700 MRRY 84121 2071 D7
White Pine Ct
600 PKCY 84060 2078 C2

STREET
Block City ZIP Map# Grid

White Pine Dr
400 MRRY 84123 2070 B4
White Pine Ln
2300 SmtC 84060 2077 D1
White Pine Wy
7800 SNDY 84094 2177 A4
White Pine Canyon Rd
10 SmtC 84060 2077 A3
1300 SmtC 84098 1971 E7
1300 SmtC 84098 2077 D1
White Rail Ln
3800 WHVN 84315 1113 D7
3900 WHVN 84315 1170 C1
White River Dr
100 SNDY 84070 2282 D4
White Rose Cir
300 DRPR 84020 2388 D2
White's Wy
2900 SLkC 84044 1960 D5
White Sands Dr
10400 SNDY 84070 2282 E4
White Sands Ln
1300 SRCS 84075 1281 A2
Whitesides St
10 LYTN 84041 1283 B5
White Springs Dr
5400 MRRY 84123 2070 A5
White Spruce Cove
100 MDVL 84070 2176 D4
White Tail Cove
13800 BFDL 84065 2386 D5
Whitewater Cir
5800 HLDY 84121 2072 B6
Whitewater Dr
3000 HLDY 84121 2072 B6
White Willow Dr
- KYVL 84037 1345 A2
Whitewood Cir
3600 TYVL 84118 2068 D5
Whitewood Ct
3600 TYVL 84118 2068 D5
Whitewood Dr
5400 TYVL 84118 2068 D6
Whitlock Av
1100 SLCY 84106 1965 B3
E Whitlock Av
100 SSLK 84115 1964 D3
W Whitlock Av
10 SSLK 84115 1964 C3
1400 WVCY 84119 1963 C3
Whitman Dr
- SLkC 84044 1960 C4
Whitmore Wy
2100 CDHT 84121 2177 E1
Whitney Av
300 SLCY 84115 1858 B7
Whitney Hall
200 PRVO 84604 2928 D4
S Whits End
300 KYVL 84037 1345 A2
Whitworth Cir
2800 SLkC 84044 1960 D4
E Wicker Ln
10 BNFL 84010 1653 D3
W Wicker Ln
10 BNFL 84010 1653 D3
Widstoe Building
25100 PRVO 84604 2928 D5
Wigwam Ln
12100 DRPR 84020 2389 C1
Wilcox Camp Rd
- WbrC 84317 1059 C6
Wild Acres Dr
4800 WJDN 84088 2174 A7
9000 WJDN 84088 2173 E7
Wildberry Ct
2500 LEHI 84043 2495 C6
Wildcat Ln
1600 OGDN 84403 1173 C1
Wildcat Wy
- NSLK 84054 1653 C3
1900 WDCR 84010 1653 C3
Wild Cherry Cir
4400 WVCY 84120 2068 A2
Wild Clover Ln
9100 WJDN 84088 2174 A7
9200 WJDN 84088 2280 A1
Wildcreek Rd
4100 SLkC 84092 2284 E2
Wild Duck Ln
1100 SLkC 84117 2071 B3
Wilde Cherry Wy
400 SNDY 84070 2282 E5
Wilderland Ln
5600 TYVL 84118 2068 C6
Wilderness Dr
400 ALPN 84004 2498 A3
Wild Flower Cir
10 ALPN 84004 2498 C5
Wildflower Cir
600 NSLK 84054 1754 D1
9800 CRHL 84062 2605 B3
S Wildflower Cir
800 OGDN 84404 1056 C6
Wildflower Ct
2900 SmtC 84098 1865 B6
Wild Flower Dr
10 ALPN 84004 2498 C5
Wildflower Dr
1900 SLCY 84116 1753 B7
8000 SmtC 84098 1865 B6
Wildflower Ln
- MPTN 84664 3250 D1
300 OGDN 84404 1056 C7
5200 MRRY 84123 2069 E5
Wildflower Rd
1700 SNDY 84092 2283 C2
Wild Flower Wy
1000 SGVL 84663 3144 B4
Wild Hay Cir
13900 DRPR 84020 2389 B5
Wild Hay Ln
1200 DRPR 84020 2389 B5
Wilding Wy
12600 DRPR 84020 2389 D2
Wild Maple Ct
- DRPR 84020 2389 B7
Wild Mare Wy
12900 RIVN 84065 2386 A3
Wild Mustang Ct
5600 HRMN 84065 2385 D4

STREET
Block City ZIP Map# Grid

Wild Oak Dr
5400 WJDN 84088 2173 D6
Wildrose Dr
4300 WVCY 84120 2067 E2
5000 WVCY 84120 2068 A2
S Wild Rose Ln
3600 SLkC 84109 1965 D7
Wildrose Wy
1400 OGDN 84404 1116 C1
Wild Tree Cir
1100 DRPR 84020 2389 B5
Wild West Dr
- DRPR 84020 2389 C6
Wild Willow Cir
8900 SNDY 84093 2177 D7
Wild Willow Ln
1800 SNDY 84093 2177 D7
Wildwood Cir
5700 HLDY 84121 2071 D5
Wildwood Dr
300 BMCY 84302 827 E1
1900 HLDY 84121 2071 D6
Wild Wood Ln
4500 LEHI 84043 2495 C6
Wiley Post Wy
4700 SLCY 84116 1856 A2
5100 SLCY 84116 1855 E2
Wilford Av
300 MRRY 84107 2070 D7
Wilford Dr
1600 KYVL 84037 1345 C5
Wilkie St
200 KYVL 84037 1282 E7
200 KYVL 84037 1344 E1
Wilkins Peak Ct
2900 SJDN 84095 2281 A5
Willard Ct
10 OGDN 84403 1115 E4
Willard Bay Rd
- WLRD 84340 885 A4
N Willard Peak Cir
1200 OGDN 84404 1057 B2
N Willard Peak Dr
900 OGDN 84404 1057 B2
Willard Peak Rd
- BxEC 84310 886 C7
- BxEC 84324 942 C1
- BxEC 84324 886 C7
- BxEC 84414 942 D1
- WbrC 84324 886 E4
200 MNTU 84324 829 C1
500 BxEC 84324 829 C3
Willem Pl
5200 HILD 84003 2604 D2
Willette Cir
3000 WJDN 84084 2175 A1
E Willey St
10 BNFL 84010 1551 E7
E Willey St SR-106
10 BNFL 84010 1551 D7
W Willey St
- WBNF 84087 1551 C7
10 BNFL 84010 1551 C7
500 WBNF 84010 1551 C7
W Willey St SR-106
10 BNFL 84010 1551 D7
W Willey St SR-131
- WBNF 84087 1551 C7
200 BNFL 84010 1551 C7
500 WBNF 84010 1551 C7
William Cir
7600 WJDN 84084 2175 A4
William Wy
700 SLkC 84107 2070 E2
700 SLkC 84107 2071 A2
Williams Av
100 SLCY 84111 1858 D6
1000 SLCY 84105 1859 A6
Williams Ct
800 SLkC 84107 2071 A2
Williams Ln
200 CTRV 84014 1551 D4
Williamsburg Av
2400 HARR 84414 998 D7
Williamsburg Cir
2200 WJDN 84088 2175 B7
6300 WVCY 84128 2067 B1
Williamsburg Ct
9100 WJDN 84088 2175 B7
Williamsburg Dr
4100 WVCY 84128 2067 B1
Williamsburg Park Cir
600 SNDY 84070 2176 E5
Williamson Cir
1500 SNDY 84092 2283 C6
Williamstown Ct
900 SmtC 84098 1972 E3
Willingcott Wy
5900 SLkC 84118 2067 C7
Willmar Cir
12100 RIVN 84065 2387 D1
Willmott Dr
2000 SLkC 84109 1965 D6
Willow
- DvsC 84056 1229 A4
Willow Av
400 SLkC 84107 2070 E2
Willow Cir
500 CTRV 84014 1551 C1
500 HRCY 84032 2398 E2
2700 LEHI 84043 2602 C7
7900 CDHT 84093 2177 D4
N Willow Ct
10000 CRHL 84062 2605 B3
Willow Dr
300 LOGN 84321 527 B4
1500 KYVL 84037 1282 E7
1600 LYTN 84037 1282 E7
2700 LEHI 84043 2602 C7
Willow Ln
- LEHI 84043 2602 B7
- MPTN 84664 3250 D1
10 TMTN 84337 520 E3
1100 PRVO 84604 2928 E4
1100 PRVO 84604 2929 A4
1400 SmtC 84098 1971 E4
5500 MRRY 84107 2070 E5
Willow Lp
1400 SmtC 84098 1971 E5
Willow Rd
- LEHI 84043 2602 C7
1500 PRVO 84604 2928 E3

STREET
Block City ZIP Map# Grid

Willow Rd
4500 HLDY 84117 2071 D2
Willow St
- SLkC 84098 2182 C1
10 LYTN 84041 1283 A4
900 BMCY 84302 827 E1
1400 KYVL 84037 1282 E7
W Willow St
100 OGDN 84401 1115 D2
Willow Wy
- CRFD 84015 1227 D4
- LEHI 84043 2602 C7
- LEHI 84043 2710 D2
300 PTVW 84414 998 C5
700 HRCY 84032 2398 E2
1600 LOGN 84341 464 C6
6800 CDHT 84121 2177 C1
Willow Bank Cir
10200 SNDY 84070 2282 D3
Willow Bend Dr
2600 SNDY 84093 2178 A6
2900 SLkC 84093 2178 A6
Willow Bend Ln
400 LYTN 84041 1228 D7
Willow Bend St
- LEHI 84043 2602 B7
Willow Bend Wy
600 LYTN 84041 1228 D7
Willow Brook Cir
- KYVL 84037 1344 E1
11300 SNDY 84092 2283 E6
Willowbrook Cir
1700 PRVO 84604 2928 A3
Willow Brook Dr
1300 WBNF 84087 1551 B5
Willowbrook Dr
1600 PRVO 84604 2928 A3
Willow Brook Ln
- KYVL 84037 1344 E2
- KYVL 84037 1345 A2
Willowbrook Ln
1100 SGVL 84663 3144 B4
3400 WbrC 84310 1001 D3
Willow Brook Wy
2000 SNDY 84092 2283 E6
E Willowbrooke Cir
4800 WbrC 84310 1001 D4
Willow Canyon Rd
3600 CDHT 84121 2178 D7
Willow Cove Dr
1100 OREM 84057 2820 A3
Willow Creek Dr
800 HARR 84404 1056 B1
2700 SLkC 84093 2178 A5
4300 SmtC 84098 1971 E6
N Willow Creek Ln
3500 WbrC 84310 1001 D3
Willow Creek Lp
4800 WbrC 84310 1001 D4
Willow Creek Rd
300 LYTN 84040 1283 D4
Willow Creek Wy
10 SmtC 84098 1971 D7
Willowcrest Cir
7800 CDHT 84121 2178 B4
Willowcrest Rd
3200 CDHT 84121 2178 E4
Willow Draw
- SmtC 84098 1971 D6
Willow Glen Cir
1800 SNDY 84093 2177 D6
Willow Green Cir
8600 SLkC 84093 2178 B6
Willow Green Ct
8600 SLkC 84093 2178 B6
Willow Green Dr
8600 SLkC 84093 2178 B6
8700 SNDY 84093 2178 B6
Willow Haven Cove
400 DRPR 84020 2388 D3
Willow Hill Dr
11300 SNDY 84092 2283 E6
Willow Hills Ct
8800 SNDY 84093 2178 A6
Willow Hills Dr
2200 SNDY 84093 2177 E6
2300 SNDY 84093 2178 A6
Willow Hollow Rd
3600 WVCY 84119 1963 D5
Willowmere Dr
- KYVL 84037 1345 A1
Willow Moor Cove
400 DRPR 84020 2388 D2
Willow Oak Cir
1700 MRRY 84121 2071 D7
Willowood Av
700 MRRY 84107 2070 D7
700 MRRY 84107 2071 A7
Willow Park Ln
2000 SLkC 84093 2177 E5
Willow Park Rd
- LEHI 84043 2602 C6
Willow Patch
2800 LEHI 84043 2602 C7
Willowpond Wy
6800 WJDN 84084 2173 E2
Willow Reed
- LEHI 84043 2602 B7
Willow Ridge Cir
300 CTRV 84014 1448 D7
Willow Ridge Rd
3200 CDHT 84121 2178 C3
Willow River Rd
3600 WVCY 84119 1963 D5
Willow Run Dr
1200 WJDN 84084 2175 E1
Willow Springs Cir
1200 ALPN 84004 2498 C4
Willow Springs Ln
- DRPR 84020 2389 A2
300 DRPR 84020 2388 D2
Willow Sprout
2800 LEHI 84043 2602 C7
Willowstone Cir
10600 SJDN 84095 2281 B4
Willow Stream Dr
7900 CDHT 84093 2177 E4
Willow Vale Cir
300 CTRV 84014 1448 D7
Willow Valley Cir
300 CTRV 84014 1448 D7
Willow Valley Dr
400 CTRV 84014 1448 D7
1300 CTRV 84014 1551 D1
Willow Valley Rd
3400 SJDN 84095 2280 E4
Willow View Cir
2400 SNDY 84092 2283 E7
2400 SNDY 84092 2284 A6
Willow View Wy
2200 SNDY 84092 2283 E6
Willow Vista Dr
1300 SNDY 84093 2177 B4
Willow Wick Ct
2500 SNDY 84093 2178 A6
Willow Wick Dr
2500 SNDY 84093 2178 A6
Willow Wood Cir
- CTRV 84014 1448 C7
Willow Wood Ct
5600 SOGN 84403 1173 C5
Willow Wood Dr
400 CTRV 84014 1448 C7
800 DRPR 84020 2283 A7
Willow Wood Ln
900 KYVL 84037 1345 E3
1900 SOGN 84403 1173 D6
Willowwood Wy
8800 WJDN 84088 2175 D7
Willson Hollow Ln
1500 LYTN 84040 1283 D1
Wil Mar Pl
1000 CTRV 84014 1551 E2
Wilmington Av
500 SLCY 84106 1964 E2
1900 SLCY 84106 1965 D2
2000 SLCY 84109 1965 D2
2400 SLCY 84109 1966 A2
Wilmington Cir
2100 SLCY 84109 1965 E2
Wilshire Cir
- SLCY 84109 1966 A3
Wilshire Ct
900 FMTN 84025 1346 A4
Wilshire Dr
2400 SLCY 84109 1966 A3
Wilshire Pl
800 SLCY 84102 1859 A5
Wilson Av
10 ANFK 84003 2711 B1
700 SLCY 84105 1964 E1
1600 SLCY 84105 1965 C1
2100 SLCY 84108 1965 E1
2400 SLCY 84108 1966 A1
E Wilson Av
10 MRRY 84107 2070 C5
100 SLCY 84115 1964 D1
W Wilson Av
10 MRRY 84107 2070 C5
Wilson Ct
10 PKCY 84060 2078 D2
Wilson Ln
700 WHVN 84401 1115 A2
1400 WHVN 84401 1114 E2
Wilson Ln SR-104
700 WHVN 84401 1115 A2
1400 WHVN 84401 1114 E2
N Wilson Ln
1800 WHVN 84401 1115 A2
Wilson Rd
100 NSLK 84054 1653 A5
Wilson St
7800 MDVL 84047 2176 C4
S Wilson St
7900 MDVL 84047 2176 C4
Wilson Ln Rd
800 WbrC 84401 1115 A2
800 WHVN 84401 1115 A2
Wilton Dr
700 NSLK 84054 1652 C5
Wilton Wy
1300 SLCY 84108 1860 B7
Wiltshire Wy
2800 WVCY 84119 2069 A2
Wimbledon Ct
7200 WJDN 84084 2175 E3
Wimbledon Dr
4400 PRVO 84604 2821 E5
Wimbledon Ridge Ln
1100 WJDN 84084 2175 D2
Wimbleton Dr
9800 SNDY 84092 2283 E2
Wimbleton Pl
9000 WJDN 84088 2175 B7
Winchester Cir
4200 WVCY 84119 2068 E1
Winchester Ct
4700 SmtC 84098 1971 E4
Winchester Dr
- NSLK 84054 1652 D6
200 SGVL 84663 3143 C6
2700 WVCY 84119 2069 A1
3100 WVCY 84119 2068 E2
9600 CRHL 84062 2605 B4
Winchester Ln
- FMTN 84025 1345 D7
5200 OGDN 84403 1173 C4
E Winchester St
10 MRRY 84107 2070 C7
10 MRRY 84107 2176 C1
700 MRRY 84107 2177 A1
W Winchester St
10 MRRY 84107 2176 A1
300 MRRY 84123 2176 A1
700 MRRY 84123 2175 E1
1200 TYVL 84084 2175 E1
1200 TYVL 84123 2175 E1
1200 WJDN 84084 2175 E1
Wind Bloom Cir
5200 HRMN 84065 2385 E6
Windchime Cir
1000 RIVN 84065 2281 E7
W Windcrest Cir
4400 WVCY 84120 1962 B7
Windcrest Wy
- KYVL 84037 1344 E2
Win-Del Cir
4000 SLkC 84124 2071 C1
Windemere Ln
800 SOGN 84403 1173 A4
Winder Ln
1300 SLkC 84124 2071 C1
Winderbrook Ct
4300 SLkC 84124 2071 C1
Winderbrook Wy
1300 SLkC 84124 2071 B1
Winder Farm Pl
4300 SLkC 84124 2071 C2
Winder Meadow Cir
4200 SLkC 84124 2071 C1
Windermere Ct
9400 SJDN 84095 2281 A1
Windfield Ct
1100 WJDN 84088 2175 E6
Windflower Ln
700 SNDY 84070 2282 A1
Windham Cir
2000 SLkC 84109 1965 D5
Winding Wy
100 LOGN 84321 528 C3
2400 SJDN 84095 2281 A2
Winding Creek Ln
3300 RIVN 84065 2280 E7
Winding Creek Cove
3400 RIVN 84065 2280 D7
Windmill Ct
- KYVL 84037 1345 A1
Windmill Dr
5400 WJDN 84088 2173 E5
Window Ranch Wy
- WJDN 84088 2173 E4
Window Rock Wy
- WJDN 84088 2173 D4
Windrift Ln
400 PKCY 84060 2078 C3
Windrift Bay
4600 WJDN 84088 2174 B5
Wind River Cir
9100 WJDN 84088 2174 C7
Wind River Dr
10 LYTN 84040 1284 A4
4000 WJDN 84088 2174 C7
Windriver Ln
10 LNDN 84042 2713 E6
Wind River Wy
900 KYVL 84037 1345 E3
Windsong Dr
10 SNDY 84092 2284 A5
E Windsong Dr
10 PTGV 84062 2605 D7
W Windsong Dr
10 PTGV 84062 2605 D7
Windsong Ln
- NSLK 84054 1754 C1
Windsor Av
3200 PRRY 84302 827 B7
Windsor Cir
2600 SLCY 84106 1965 A4
4500 CRHL 84062 2605 A3
Windsor Ct
10 BNFL 84010 1653 D7
500 CTRV 84014 1551 D4
500 NSLK 84054 1652 C5
600 ALPN 84004 2498 A3
1300 OREM 84097 2821 B2
Windsor Dr
900 PRVO 84604 2821 E5
1000 LOGN 84321 528 B4
1000 NSLK 84054 1652 C6
1000 RVHT 84321 528 B4
1200 SOGN 84403 1173 B4
4400 CRHL 84062 2605 B3
Windsor Ln
200 CTRV 84014 1551 D4
600 KYVL 84037 1283 E5
800 BNFL 84010 1653 E5
800 BNFL 84010 1654 A5
900 KYVL 84037 1284 A5
5200 HILD 84003 2604 D2
Windsor Pl
9000 WJDN 84088 2175 B6
Windsor St
100 SLCY 84102 1859 A3
900 SLCY 84105 1859 A6
1700 SLCY 84105 1965 A1
2200 SLCY 84106 1965 A3
Windsor Manor Ct
2400 SJDN 84095 2281 B2
Windsor Oak Cove
2000 SNDY 84092 2283 D7
Windsor Park Cir
2000 BNFL 84010 1654 D3
Windsor Park Dr
- HILD 84003 2604 D3
1300 SLkC 84117 2071 C2
Windstone Cir
11500 SJDN 84095 2279 D6
Windstone Dr
11600 SJDN 84095 2279 D7
Windwood Cir
2500 TYVL 84084 2069 A7
7600 CDHT 84121 2178 C4
Windy Hills Dr
10000 SLkC 84092 2284 A2
10000 SNDY 84092 2284 A2
Windy Peak Cir
1100 SNDY 84094 2283 D4
Windy Peak Wy
1000 SNDY 84094 2283 A6
Windy Peak Ridge Dr
11000 SNDY 84094 2283 B5
Winesap Cir
7300 CDHT 84121 2178 D3
Winesap Ct
7200 CDHT 84121 2178 C3
Winesap Rd
3300 CDHT 84121 2178 C2
Winesap St
- FTHT 84037 1346 A4
Winfield Rd
4200 TYVL 84123 2069 E1
Winfield Scott Wy
14100 DRPR 84020 2389 B6
Wing Pl
5300 HILD 84003 2604 D2
Winged Bluff Ln
14900 DRPR 84020 2496 E1
Winged Trace Ct
- DRPR 84020 2496 E2
- DRPR 84020 2497 A2
Wingfield Cir
13700 DRPR 84020 2389 B5
Wingfoot Ct
12200 DRPR 84020 2389 D1
Wing Point Cir
7600 SLkC 84044 1960 D6
Wing Point Dr
3500 SLkC 84044 1960 D6
Wing Stone Wy
- DRPR 84020 2496 E2
Winifred St
10 SLCY 84116 1857 C2
Winners Cir
1500 WJDN 84084 2175 C3
Winslow Av
100 SSLK 84115 1964 D6
Winston Dr
2900 WVCY 84128 1961 C4
E Winston Dr
1100 KYVL 84037 1284 A6
N Winston Dr
1100 KYVL 84037 1284 A5
Winter Cir
4400 CRHL 84062 2605 B3
Winter St
200 SLCY 84116 1857 D2
Winter Berry Dr
9200 WJDN 84088 2174 A7
9200 WJDN 84088 2280 A1
Winterbrook Cir
4800 HRMN 84065 2386 B6
Winter Canyon Wy
800 SNDY 84094 2283 A6
Winterdale Cir
7600 CDHT 84121 2178 C3
Winter Glen Ln
1500 DRPR 84020 2389 C2
Wintergreen Cir
1400 LYTN 84040 1283 C3
5000 MRRY 84123 2070 A4
Wintergreen Ct
1100 ALPN 84004 2498 B3
Winter Hill Ln
4900 WJDN 84088 2174 A2
Winter Hill Cove
7000 WJDN 84084 2174 A2
Winterton Cir
- CSTN 84032 2397 D7
Winterton Rd
- CSTN 84032 2504 C1
2900 CSTN 84032 2397 C7
Winter Wheat Cir
12100 RIVN 84065 2386 C1
Winter Wheat Wy
- SRSP 84043 2601 D4
Winterwood Cir
1400 SLkC 84092 2283 C2
Winterwood Dr
9700 SLkC 84092 2283 C2
9700 SNDY 84092 2283 C2
Winter Wren Dr
9000 SNDY 84093 2178 A7
Winthrope Cir
3600 WJDN 84088 2174 D7
Winthrope Dr
3700 WJDN 84088 2174 D7
Winton St
2400 WVCY 84119 1963 E3
Winward Dr
1500 SLkC 84117 2071 C5
Wirthlin Dr
500 MRRY 84123 2070 A4
Wisteria Wy
- WJDN 84088 2280 A1
5100 WJDN 84088 2279 E1
9000 WJDN 84088 2173 E7
Witfield Ct
8300 WJDN 84088 2175 D5
Withers Ln
1000 RIVN 84065 2387 D2
Witney Cir
900 NSLK 84054 1652 C5
N Wolcott St
10 SLCY 84103 1859 C3
S Wolcott St
10 SLCY 84102 1859 C3
10 SLCY 84103 1859 C3
Wolf Creek Cir
5800 WVCY 84118 2067 C7
Wolf Creek Dr
3200 WbrC 84310 1001 E3
Wolf Creek Dr SR-158
3200 WbrC 84310 1001 E3
N Wolf Creek Dr
3600 WbrC 84310 1001 D3
Wolfe Cir
4200 SmtC 84098 1864 D4
Wolf Hollow Dr
5700 SLkC 84117 2071 B4
S Wolf Hollow Dr
700 SPFK 84660 3249 E4
Wolf Point Cir
11200 SNDY 84070 2282 E5
Wolf Ridge Cir
4000 WbrC 84310 1001 E2
Wollemi Pine Wy
8800 WJDN 84088 2174 E6
Wolverine Wy
3500 WVCY 84120 1961 D6
3500 WVCY 84128 1961 D6
Wolverine Wy SR-172
3500 WVCY 84120 1961 D6
3500 WVCY 84128 1961 D6
Wood Av
10 SLCY 84115 1858 C7
500 SLCY 84105 1858 E7
1000 SLCY 84105 1859 A7
Wood Cir
5700 MRRY 84107 2070 D6
Wood Dr
200 ALPN 84004 2498 A5
Wood Ln
1200 NHLN 84341 464 B6
Wood St
800 OGDN 84404 1116 A1
8000 MDVL 84047 2176 C5
Woodacre Rd
4900 WJDN 84084 2174 A3
Woodash Cir
5200 WVCY 84120 2067 E2
Woodbend Rd
4900 WJDN 84084 2174 A3
Woodbine Cir
9500 SNDY 84092 2283 E1
Woodbine St
700 SLCY 84101 1858 B5
Woodbine Wy
1900 PKCY 84060 2078 D4
Wood Briar Cir
1100 NSLK 84054 1754 D2
Wood Briar Wy
600 NSLK 84054 1754 D1
Woodbridge Dr
1600 SLkC 84117 2071 C3
Woodbrook Ln
2800 SLkC 84044 1960 D4
Woodburne Rd
4900 WJDN 84084 2174 A3
Woodbury Cir
4500 WVCY 84120 1962 B7
Woodchuck Cir
2300 SNDY 84093 2283 D1
Wood Chuck Wy
2200 SNDY 84093 2283 E1
2300 SNDY 84093 2177 A7
2300 SNDY 84093 2178 A7
2300 SNDY 84093 2284 A1
Woodcove Ln
- LEHI 84043 2495 D6
Woodcreek St
4500 WVCY 84119 2068 E3
Woodcrest Dr
1600 SLkC 84117 2071 C4
Woodcrest Ln
1100 NSLK 84054 1754 D1
Woodcutter Ln
4600 WVCY 84120 1962 A4
Wood Duck Ln
4500 SLkC 84117 2071 A3
Wooden Ln
800 SLCY 84116 1753 C7
Woodfield Dr
- WJDN 84084 2174 B3
Woodfield Rd
11000 SJDN 84095 2281 D5
Woodgate Cir
200 MDVL 84047 2176 A4
3800 WVCY 84120 1962 D7
Woodglen Cir
10300 SNDY 84092 2283 C3
Wood Glen Rd
1500 SNDY 84092 2283 C3
Woodgreen Rd
7000 WJDN 84084 2174 E3
Woodgrove Cir
5200 WVCY 84120 2067 E2
Woodgrove Dr
4400 WVCY 84120 2067 E2
Woodhampton Cir
2700 SNDY 84092 2284 B6
Woodhampton Dr
11500 SNDY 84092 2284 A6
Woodhaven Cir
1300 TYVL 84123 2069 D4
Woodhaven Dr
4800 TYVL 84123 2069 D3
Woodhill Cir
1300 SNDY 84092 2283 C4
2500 TYVL 84084 2069 A7
Woodhill Dr
1300 SNDY 84092 2283 C5
Wood Hill Ln
100 NSLK 84054 1653 C6
Wood Hollow Dr
15500 BFDL 84065 2494 C2
Wood Hollow Wy
2100 BNFL 84010 1654 C4
Woodhue Ct
7600 WJDN 84084 2174 B3
Woodlake Dr
300 SLkC 84107 1964 D7
300 SLkC 84107 2070 A1
Woodlake Ln
400 SLkC 84107 2070 D1
Woodlake Cove
300 SLkC 84107 1964 D7
Woodland Av
400 SSLK 84115 1964 E5
E Woodland Av
1300 SLCY 84106 1965 B5
1300 SLkC 84106 1965 B5
Woodland Cir
500 BNFL 84010 1654 A2
5500 OGDN 84403 1173 E4
Woodland Ct
1200 FMTN 84025 1346 C6
Woodland Dr
100 OREM 84097 2821 A6
200 SmtC 84098 1864 B6
500 FMTN 84025 1448 E3
1600 PRVO 84604 2928 A3
2200 OGDN 84403 1173 E5
2300 WbrC 84403 1173 E5
2500 WbrC 84403 1174 A5
5300 ALPN 84004 2497 D6
11200 HILD 84003 2497 D6
Woodland Ln
1100 BNFL 84010 1654 A2
1200 BNFL 84010 1653 E2
Woodland Pl
100 SmtC 84098 1864 C6
Woodland Hills Cir
900 BNFL 84010 1654 A1
Woodland Hills Dr
500 BNFL 84010 1654 A1
S Woodland Hills Dr
300 WDHL 84653 3463 D1
8400 UthC 84660 3249 C7
8400 UthC 84660 3356 C2
8800 SALM 84653 3356 C2
9800 UthC 84653 3356 D4
11000 WDHL 84653 3356 D6
Woodland Park Dr
1500 LYTN 84041 1282 D1
W Woodland Ridge Cir
10 WDHL 84653 3463 C1
Woodland Valley Dr
600 KYVL 84037 1345 E3
Woodland View Dr
7300 PKCY 84060 2184 E1
8100 PKCY 84060 2185 A1
Woodledge Av
5100 WVCY 84120 2067 E2
Woodman Ct
7800 WJDN 84088 2174 B4
Wood Mesa Dr
7500 WJDN 84084 2173 D3
7500 WJDN 84084 2174 A3
Woodmont St
5000 SLkC 84117 2071 D4
Woodmoor Cir
700 BNFL 84010 1654 B2
Woodmoor Dr
900 BNFL 84010 1654 B1
Woodmore Dr
600 OREM 84058 2820 C7
Woodoak Ln
600 MRRY 84107 2070 E5
700 MRRY 84107 2071 A5
900 MRRY 84117 2071 A5
Wood Park Ln
9500 SJDN 84095 2280 A1
Woodpine Cir
500 SNDY 84047 2176 E3
Wood Ranch Ct
9400 SJDN 84095 2280 A1
Wood Ranch Dr
4800 SJDN 84095 2280 A1
5000 SJDN 84095 2279 E2
Wood Ranch Ln
9500 SJDN 84095 2280 A1
Woodridge Cir
1200 MRRY 84121 2071 B7
Woodridge Dr
500 LYTN 84040 1284 A3
4900 SJDN 84095 2280 A2
9700 SJDN 84095 2279 E2
Woodridge Rd
11800 SNDY 84094 2283 B7
12000 SNDY 84094 2389 B1
Woodrose Cir
500 SNDY 84047 2176 A3
Woodrow St
- MRRY 84107 2070 C4
Woodruff Wy
800 SLCY 84108 1860 A5
Woods Cir
600 LEHI 84043 2603 A5
Woods Dr
1300 BNFL 84010 1654 B1
N Woods Dr
400 LEHI 84043 2603 A5
W Woods Dr
1000 LEHI 84043 2603 A5
Woods Ln
7500 SNDY 84047 2176 D3
Woodsborough Cir
5700 SLkC 84118 2067 D6
Woodsborough Wy
6000 SLkC 84118 2067 D7
Woods Cross Dr
500 WDCR 84010 1653 C1
Woods Cross Rd
100 CRFD 84015 1227 D5
Wood Shade Ct
5100 WJDN 84084 2173 E4
Woodshire Av
800 MRRY 84107 2071 A7
Woodshire Cir
700 MRRY 84107 2070 D6
700 MRRY 84107 2071 A7
Woodshire Ct
5600 SOGN 84403 1173 D5
Woodshire Pl
5600 SOGN 84403 1173 D5
Woods Hollow Ln
- HILD 84003 2497 A5
Woodside Av
1300 PKCY 84060 2078 D4
Woodside Dr
10 PRVO 84604 2821 B7
1700 HLDY 84124 2071 B1
1900 HLDY 84124 1965 D7
N Woodside Dr
1700 HLDY 84124 1965 D7
1700 HLDY 84124 2071 C1
S Woodside Dr
1700 HLDY 84124 2071 D1
Woods Park Dr
- HRMN 84065 2385 D3
Woods Peak Cir
5200 HRMN 84065 2385 E5
Wood Spring Dr
4900 WJDN 84084 2174 A3
Wood Springs Dr
10 SGVL 84663 3143 B2
Woodstep Av
5200 WVCY 84120 2067 E2
Woodstock Av
1100 MRRY 84121 2071 B6
Woodstock Cir
900 NSLK 84054 1652 D5
Wood Stone Cir
10800 SJDN 84095 2281 D4
Wood Thrush Cir
9100 SNDY 84093 2178 B7
Wood Thrush Dr
2300 SNDY 84093 2177 E7
2300 SNDY 84093 2178 A7
Woodtree Cir
5200 WVCY 84120 2067 E2
Woodview Cir
700 NSLK 84054 1653 C6
6300 SLkC 84118 2067 B6
Woodview Dr
1800 LEHI 84043 2495 D6
5700 SLkC 84118 2067 B6
Wood Village Ct
5100 WVCY 84120 1961 D5
Wood Vista Cir
9600 SJDN 84095 2280 A1
Woodworth Rd
5100 WJDN 84084 2173 D3
5100 WJDN 84084 2174 B3
Woolley Wy
2800 SLkC 84044 1960 C5
Worchester Dr
2000 CDHT 84121 2177 E2
Wormwood Dr
4300 WVCY 84120 2067 E2
5000 WVCY 84120 2068 A3
Worthington Ct
11600 SNDY 84092 2283 C6
Worthington Dr
4000 SmtC 84098 1971 D6
Worwood Cir
2100 TYVL 84118 2069 B5
Wrangler Cir
13300 DRPR 84020 2389 B4
Wrangler Rd
300 FMTN 84025 1447 E1
Wrangler Wy
3400 SmtC 84098 1865 A4
Wren Cir
4800 HLDY 84117 2072 A3
Wren Rd
2500 HLDY 84117 2072 A3
Wrenhaven Ln
2300 HLDY 84121 2071 E7
2300 HLDY 84121 2072 A7
Wrenhaven Rd
6200 HLDY 84121 2072 A7
Wren Hollow Cir
4800 HLDY 84117 2072 A3
Wrens Grove St
2400 WVCY 84119 1963 D3
Wright Cir
1600 SLCY 84104 1857 C4
Wright Ct
1700 SLCY 84105 1964 E1
Wright Ln
2900 WVCY 84119 1963 A6
3000 WVCY 84119 1962 E6
Wright Wy
500 TMTN 84337 521 A6
1000 SNDY 84094 2283 A1
Wright Brothers Dr
100 SLCY 84116 1856 A2
Wyandotte Av
300 SNDY 84070 2282 E1
Wyatt Earp Wy
2200 PKCY 84060 2079 A3
Wylie Ln
1500 DRPR 84020 2389 C5
Wymount Dr
10 PRVO 84604 2928 E3
Wyndcastle Dr
2500 SNDY 84092 2284 A6
E Wyndom Wy
1000 LYTN 84040 1229 B6
N Wyndom Wy
2800 LYTN 84040 1229 C5
Wyndon Sq
- LYTN 84040 1229 C5
Wynford Cir
3200 CDHT 84121 2178 C3
Wynford St
7500 CDHT 84121 2178 C3
Wyngate Cir
1900 SNDY 84092 2283 D5
Wyngate Ln
11100 SNDY 84092 2283 D5
S Wyngate Park Dr
1500 SJDN 84095 2281 D4
Wynview Ln
1500 SJDN 84095 2281 D5
Wyoming St
1800 SLCY 84108 1966 A1
2200 SLCY 84109 1966 A2

X

Xanadu Cir
4600 TYVL 84123 2070 A3

Y

N Yacht Club Dr
600 WbrC 84310 1059 E3
Yale Av
100 SLCY 84111 1858 D6
700 SLCY 84105 1858 E6
1500 SLCY 84105 1859 C6
2000 SLCY 84108 1859 E6
Yale Cir
300 ANFK 84003 2711 D2
Yale Dr
10 SOGN 84405 1172 D1
Yalecrest Av
1500 SLCY 84105 1859 C6
1700 SLCY 84108 1859 C6
Yamaha Ct
10 PKCY 84060 2078 D2
Yarrow Cir
1800 BNFL 84010 1654 C4
4500 WVCY 84120 2067 E2
11000 HILD 84003 2497 A7
S Yarrow Ln
4500 TYVL 84123 2069 E2
W Yarrow Ln
1000 TYVL 84123 2069 D3
Yeager Rd
5200 SLCY 84116 1855 E2
Yearling Dr
13600 RIVN 84065 2386 C5
Yellow Pine St
8800 WJDN 84088 2174 B7
Yellow Rose Cir
3300 WVCY 84119 1962 C4
Yellow Sage Ct
5000 HRMN 84065 2386 B6
Yellowstone Cir
5800 SJDN 84095 2279 D6
Yellow Wood Ln
- WJDN 84084 2173 A3
Yermo Av
2500 SLCY 84109 1966 A2
Yonex Ct
100 PKCY 84060 2078 D2
York Ct
2100 FMTN 84025 1346 B4
York Dr
900 NSLK 84054 1652 C5
York St
5300 MRRY 84117 2071 B5
York Ridge Rd
12100 SNDY 84094 2389 B1
Yorkshire Cir
4100 SJDN 84095 2280 C1
Yorkshire Ct
9900 HILD 84003 2604 C3
Yorkshire Dr
3800 SJDN 84095 2280 C1
Yorkshire Rd
3600 WVCY 84119 1962 E7
Yorkton Ln
5600 SmtC 84098 1972 E3
Yorktown Cir
1400 SLkC 84117 2071 B3
Yorktown Dr
4700 SLkC 84117 2071 C3

STREET
Block City ZIP Map# Grid

Yorktown Wy
3300 CRFD 84015 1228 B5
Yosemite Dr
3100 SLkC 84109 1966 C5
Young Hall
200 PRVO 84604 2928 D4
Young Haven Cir
3100 SLkC 84109 1966 A5
S Yucca Dr
4600 TYVL 84123 2069 D3
W Yucca Dr
900 TYVL 84123 2069 E3
Yuma Cir
2700 SLkC 84109 1965 D4
Yuma St
1300 SLCY 84108 1859 E7
1700 SLCY 84108 1965 D1
2100 SLCY 84106 1965 D2
2100 SLCY 84109 1965 D2
2700 SLkC 84109 1965 D4
Yuma View Dr
2000 SLCY 84109 1965 D4
2000 SLkC 84109 1965 D4
Y Worry Ln
1300 SJDN 84095 2281 D3

Z

Zachary Dr
1900 SLCY 84116 1753 C7
1900 SLCY 84116 1857 B1
Zacks Cove
3500 SJDN 84095 2280 D5
Zadok Ln
3600 WJDN 84088 2280 D1
Zana Ln
3900 SLkC 84044 1960 E7
E Zane Av
10 SLCY 84103 1858 D1
W Zane Av
10 SLCY 84103 1858 C1
Zarahemla Dr
4200 SLkC 84124 2072 E2
Zenda Wy
1800 MRRY 84121 2177 D1
Zenia Meadows Ct
700 SLkC 84107 2071 A2
Zenith Av
1300 SLCY 84106 1965 C4
1700 SLkC 84106 1965 C4
Zenith Cir
2800 SLCY 84106 1965 A4
Zermat Strasse
100 SmtC 84098 1864 B6
Zermatt Cir
2200 SNDY 84093 2177 E5
Zermatt Dr
700 MIDW 84049 2396 E1
Zermatt St
- WbrC 84310 1002 A2
Zeus Dr
4100 WVCY 84128 2067 C1
Zevex Park Pl
4200 MRRY 84123 2070 A1
Zia Ct
4600 RIVN 84065 2386 B2
Zina Cir
5800 WVCY 84128 1961 C7
Zinnia Ct
6600 WJDN 84084 2173 E1
Zinnia Wy
700 SLkC 84094 2282 E3
700 SNDY 84094 2282 E3
10100 SLkC 84094 2283 A3
Zions Cir
5400 TYVL 84118 2069 B5
Zions Dr
2200 TYVL 84118 2069 B5
Zircon Cir
10 LYTN 84041 1282 E3
Zobell Dr
800 OREM 84097 2821 A5
Zodiac Dr
3900 TYVL 84118 2068 C6
4000 SLkC 84118 2068 C6
Zona Cir
100 SNDY 84070 2176 C6
Zuni Dr
4500 RIVN 84065 2386 B3
Zurich Ln
700 MIDW 84049 2397 D3

#

E 1st N
10 TMTN 84337 520 E6
5800 HRMN 84065 2385 D3
E 1st S
10 TMTN 84337 520 E6
5900 HRMN 84065 2385 C3
N 1st E
10 TMTN 84337 520 E5
12900 HRMN 84065 2385 D3
N 1st W
800 TMTN 84337 520 E4
12900 HRMN 84065 2385 C3
S 1st E
10 TMTN 84337 520 E6
1200 ELWD 84337 584 E1
13100 HRMN 84065 2385 D3
S 1st W
10 TMTN 84337 520 E6
13100 HRMN 84065 2385 C3
W 1st N
10 TMTN 84337 520 E6
6000 HRMN 84065 2385 C3
W 1st S
500 TMTN 84337 520 D6
6100 HRMN 84065 2385 C3
1st Av
- OGDN 84401 1115 E2
100 SLCY 84103 1858 D3
500 MDVL 84047 2176 A3
600 SLCY 84103 1859 A3
1st St
- CRFD 84016 1227 C7
- LYTN 84041 1283 A5
10 DvsC 84056 1228 D3
10 PTVW 84404 998 B6
500 OGDN 84404 1056 E5
500 OGDN 84404 1057 A5
W 1st St
600 OGDN 84404 1056 B5
1st Light Cir
5800 HRMN 84065 2385 D6
E 2nd N
10 TMTN 84337 520 E5
E 2nd S
10 TMTN 84337 520 E6
N 2nd E
10 TMTN 84337 520 E5
100 ANFK 84003 2604 D7
100 ANFK 84003 2711 D1
1400 OREM 84057 2820 D1
12900 HRMN 84065 2385 D3
N 2nd W
10 TMTN 84337 520 D5
S 2nd N
1200 SLCY 84116 1857 D2
S 2nd W
10 TMTN 84337 520 D6
1300 OREM 84058 2927 D1
1700 KYVL 84037 1345 C5
W 2nd N
10 TMTN 84337 520 E5
W 2nd S
500 SPFK 84660 3249 B3
700 TMTN 84337 520 D6
1400 LEHI 84043 2602 E7
2nd Av
- OGDN 84401 1115 E2
100 SLCY 84103 1858 D2
500 MDVL 84047 2176 A3
1200 SLCY 84103 1859 C2
E 2nd Av
10 MRRY 84107 2070 C3
2nd St
- LYTN 84041 1283 A5
10 PTVW 84404 998 A7
100 OGDN 84404 1056 E5
500 OGDN 84404 1057 A5
2200 SLCY 84116 1857 A1
W 2nd St
- OGDN 84404 1056 B5
E 3rd N
10 TMTN 84337 520 E5
1100 SGVL 84663 3143 E1
E 3rd S
10 TMTN 84337 520 E6
800 PYSN 84651 3355 B5
N 3rd E
10 TMTN 84337 520 E5
100 BxEC 84337 520 E5
1400 OREM 84057 2820 E1
N 3rd W
10 TMTN 84337 520 D5
W 3rd N
10 TMTN 84337 520 D5
W 3rd S
10 TMTN 84337 520 E6
900 LEHI 84043 2603 A7
1400 LEHI 84043 2602 E7
3rd Av
- OGDN 84401 1115 E2
100 SLCY 84103 1858 D2
500 MDVL 84047 2176 A3
600 SLCY 84103 1859 A2
3rd St
- CRFD 84016 1281 D1
- LYTN 84041 1283 A5
100 DvsC 84056 1228 D4
100 OGDN 84404 1056 D5
500 OGDN 84404 1057 A5
1600 CRFD 84016 1227 C7
2200 SLCY 84116 1753 A7
E 4th N
1300 PRVO 84606 2928 E6
N 4th E
900 TMTN 84337 520 E4
N 4th W
100 TMTN 84337 520 D5
3600 PRVO 84604 2821 B7
S 4th E
- HRCY 84032 2398 D6
S 4th W
10 SPFK 84660 3249 C3
W 4th S
600 TMTN 84337 520 D6
1400 LEHI 84043 2602 E7
4th Av
- OGDN 84401 1115 E2
100 SLCY 84103 1858 D2
500 MDVL 84047 2176 A3
600 SLCY 84103 1859 A2
E 4th Av
10 MRRY 84107 2070 C3
W 4th Av
10 MRRY 84107 2070 C3
4th St
- PKCY 84060 2078 E6
100 DvsC 84056 1228 D4
100 OGDN 84404 1056 D6
500 OGDN 84404 1057 A6
2200 SLCY 84116 1753 A7
N 5 E
2100 LYTN 84041 1228 E7
E 5th N
- LEHI 84043 2603 E5
10 TMTN 84337 520 E5
S 5th E
1200 PYSN 84651 3355 A7
1200 SGVL 84663 3143 D4
W 5th N
1000 PTGV 84062 2712 C2
3200 WPT 84015 1226 B3
W 5th S
200 TMTN 84337 520 E7
5th Av
- OGDN 84401 1115 E2
200 SLCY 84103 1858 D2
500 MDVL 84047 2176 A3
600 SLCY 84103 1859 A2
E 5th Av
10 MRRY 84107 2070 C3
W 5th Av
100 MRRY 84107 2070 C3
5th St
- CRFD 84016 1227 C6
- PKCY 84060 2078 E6
300 OGDN 84404 1056 E6
500 OGDN 84404 1057 A6
800 DvsC 84056 1228 B4
2200 SLCY 84116 1753 A7
W 5th St
300 OGDN 84404 1056 C6
E 6th S
- DvsC 84037 1345 E2
- KYVL 84037 1345 E2
N 6th E
200 SALM 84653 3356 C3
N 6th W
1800 MPTN 84664 3144 A4
S 6th W
100 TMTN 84337 520 D6
1000 TMTN 84337 584 D1
W 6th N
10 TMTN 84337 520 D5
1600 CLTN 84015 1227 A3
W 6th S
10 TMTN 84337 520 D7
200 SLCY 84101 1858 B5
1200 LEHI 84043 2603 A7
W 6th S SR-269
200 SLCY 84101 1858 B5
6th S
- HDPK 84318 464 A2
- HDPK 84341 464 A2
- NHLN 84341 464 A2
6th Av
- OGDN 84401 1115 E2
- OGDN 84401 1116 A2
200 SLCY 84103 1858 D2
600 SLCY 84103 1859 A2
W 6th Av
500 MDVL 84047 2176 A3
6th St
- DvsC 84015 1228 B5
300 DvsC 84056 1228 D5
400 OGDN 84404 1056 E6
600 DvsC 84056 1229 A5
800 CRFD 84015 1228 B5
1200 DvsC 84056 1227 E3
1400 OGDN 84404 1057 C6
2200 SLCY 84116 1753 B7
E 7th N
10 SGVL 84663 3036 C7
10 SGVL 84663 3143 C1
10 TMTN 84337 520 E4
E 7th S
800 SGVL 84663 3143 E3
1600 SGVL 84663 3144 B3
N 7th E
2900 LEHI 84043 2603 D1
N 7th W
3200 LEHI 84043 2603 B1
S 7th E
1300 PTGV 84062 2713 C4
S 7th W
100 TMTN 84337 520 D6
600 LYTN 84041 1282 D6
8300 MDVL 84047 2176 A6
8300 SNDY 84070 2176 A6
8400 SLkC 84047 2176 A6
8400 SLkC 84070 2176 A6
8400 SLkC 84088 2176 A6
W 7th N
10 TMTN 84337 520 E4
W 7th S
10 LYTN 84041 1282 E6
7th Av
- OGDN 84401 1116 A2
200 SLCY 84103 1858 D2
500 MDVL 84047 2176 A3
600 SLCY 84103 1859 A2
7th St
- CRFD 84016 1227 C6
- PKCY 84060 2078 E6
100 OGDN 84404 1056 E6
300 DvsC 84056 1228 D5
1200 OGDN 84404 1057 A6
2200 SLCY 84116 1753 A7
W 7th St
200 OGDN 84404 1056 D6
E 8th N
10 TMTN 84337 520 E4
E 8th S
800 SGVL 84663 3143 E3
1100 SPFK 84660 3249 E4
1100 SPFK 84660 3250 A4
N 8th E
3000 LEHI 84043 2603 D1
S 8th E
400 KYVL 84037 1345 E2
S 8th W
10 TMTN 84337 520 C6
100 SPFK 84660 3249 B3
W 8th N
10 TMTN 84337 520 E4
1000 LEHI 84043 2603 A5
W 8th S
100 LYTN 84041 1282 E6
400 TMTN 84337 520 D7
8th Av
- OGDN 84401 1116 A2
200 SLCY 84103 1858 D1
500 MDVL 84047 2176 A3
600 SLCY 84103 1859 A2
8th St
- PKCY 84060 2078 D5
500 OGDN 84404 1056 E6
500 OGDN 84404 1057 A6
800 DvsC 84056 1228 C5
E 9th N
800 ANFK 84003 2604 E6
800 ANFK 84003 2605 A5
E 9th S
600 PYSN 84651 3355 A7
N 9th E
400 LNDN 84042 2713 D5
N 9th W
600 TMTN 84337 520 D4
S 9th E
300 SGVL 84663 3143 E2
S 9th W
1500 WDCR 84087 1653 B2
W 9th N
10 TMTN 84337 520 E4
W 9th S
300 LYTN 84041 1282 E7
9th Av
- OGDN 84401 1116 A2
200 SLCY 84103 1858 D1
600 SLCY 84103 1859 A1
E 9th Av
10 MDVL 84047 2176 A3
9th St
- CRFD 84016 1227 C6
- PKCY 84060 2078 D5
100 OGDN 84404 1056 D7
400 DvsC 84056 1228 D5
600 OGDN 84404 1057 A7
W 9th St
100 OGDN 84404 1056 D7
9th S Cir
2300 SLCY 84108 1860 A5
E 10 S
700 UthC 84003 2711 E1
N 10 W
2100 LYTN 84041 1228 E7
S 10 W
400 FMTN 84025 1448 D3
W 10 N
400 OREM 84057 2820 C5
500 LNDN 84042 2712 E6
E 10th S
400 LNDN 84042 2712 E4
400 PTGV 84042 2712 E4
400 PTGV 84062 2712 E4
900 PRVO 84606 3035 E1
N 10th W
3200 LEHI 84043 2603 A1
10th Av
- OGDN 84401 1116 A2
200 SLCY 84103 1858 D1
600 SLCY 84103 1859 A1
10th St
- PKCY 84060 2078 D5
500 OGDN 84404 1056 E7
500 OGDN 84404 1057 A7
E 11 S
- PVDN 84332 592 A2
E 11th N
900 LEHI 84043 2603 D5
N 11th E
700 ANFK 84003 2605 A5
S 11th E
900 SGVL 84663 3143 E4
11th Av
- OGDN 84401 1116 A2
200 SLCY 84103 1858 D1
600 SLCY 84103 1859 A1
11th St
- CRFD 84016 1227 D6
- CRFD 84016 1281 E1
- PKCY 84060 2078 D5
300 OGDN 84404 1056 E7
400 DvsC 84056 1228 D5
1500 OGDN 84404 1057 C7
W 11th St
- OGDN 84404 1056 C7
E 12th N
- SPFK 84660 3249 E1
E 12th S
10 HRCY 84032 2398 E6
400 WshC 84032 2398 E6
N 12th W
1100 PTGV 84062 2712 B1
W 12th N
400 SGVL 84663 3036 B6
W 12th S
- HRCY 84032 2398 B6
12th Av
- OGDN 84401 1116 A2
300 SLCY 84103 1858 E1
600 SLCY 84103 1859 A1
12th St
- CRFD 84015 1228 C5
- DvsC 84056 1228 C5
- PKCY 84060 2078 D5
100 OGDN 84404 1056 E7
500 OGDN 84404 1057 A7
12th St SR-39
100 OGDN 84404 1056 E7
500 OGDN 84404 1057 A7
W 12th St
100 OGDN 84404 1056 A7
700 MTSV 84404 1056 A7
1200 MTSV 84401 1056 A7
1500 MTSV 84401 1055 E7
1500 OGDN 84404 1055 E7
W 12th St SR-39
100 OGDN 84404 1056 A7
700 MTSV 84404 1056 A7
1200 MTSV 84401 1056 A7
1500 MTSV 84401 1055 E7
1500 MTSV 84404 1055 E7
E 13th N
1600 LYTN 84040 1283 D2
N 13th E
- SPFK 84660 3250 A1
1000 LEHI 84043 2603 E4
N 13th W
100 SLCY 84116 1857 D2
3000 LEHI 84043 2603 A1
S 13th W
10 LEHI 84043 2603 A6
100 LEHI 84043 2602 E7
2500 SRCS 84075 1281 A2
W 13th N
400 SGVL 84663 3036 B6
2200 LYTN 84041 1282 A2
13th Av
400 SLCY 84103 1858 E1
600 SLCY 84103 1859 A1
13th St
- CRFD 84016 1227 D6
- CRFD 84016 1281 E1
- PKCY 84060 2078 D5
200 OGDN 84404 1056 D7
900 OGDN 84404 1057 A7
W 13th St
300 OGDN 84404 1056 C7
E 14th S
- PRVO 84606 3036 A2
N 14th E
500 SPFK 84660 3250 A2
2300 LEHI 84043 2603 E2
S 14th E
1300 PRVO 84606 3036 B2
W 14th N
2400 LYTN 84041 1282 A2
2500 LYTN 84041 1281 E2
14th Av
500 SLCY 84103 1858 E1
14th St
- CRFD 84016 1227 E7
- CRFD 84016 1281 E1
- PKCY 84060 2078 D5
200 OGDN 84404 1115 E1
600 OGDN 84404 1116 A1
W 14th St
100 OGDN 84404 1115 D1
S 15 W
- SNQN 84655 3567 E2
E 15th N
200 OREM 84057 2820 E1
S 15th E
1300 PRVO 84606 3036 A2
S 15th W
2900 SRCS 84075 1281 A3
W 15th N
100 LEHI 84043 2603 B4
15th St
- PKCY 84060 2078 D4
100 OGDN 84404 1115 D1
500 OGDN 84404 1116 A1
W 16th N
2300 LEHI 84043 2602 D4
16th Av
400 SLCY 84103 1754 E7
600 SLCY 84103 1755 A7
16th St
- CRFD 84016 1227 D6
400 OGDN 84404 1115 E1
800 OGDN 84404 1116 A1
E 17th N
10 LEHI 84043 2603 C3
E 17th S
1400 SPFK 84660 3250 A6
W 17th N
100 LEHI 84043 2603 B3
200 NHON 84404 1056 D1
300 NHON 84414 1056 D1
17th Av
600 SLCY 84103 1754 E7
600 SLCY 84103 1755 A7
17th St
100 OGDN 84404 1115 D1
600 OGDN 84404 1116 A1
W 17th St
100 OGDN 84404 1115 D1
800 MTSV 84404 1115 B1
S 18 W
8800 SNDY 84070 2176 C6
S 18th E
- SGVL 84663 3144 B4
18th Av
500 SLCY 84103 1754 E7
500 SLCY 84103 1755 A7
18th St
100 OGDN 84404 1115 D1
N 19th W
1500 LEHI 84043 2602 D4
S 19th W
5400 TYVL 84118 2069 C5
W 19th N
10 SPFK 84660 3142 C6
19th St
1000 OGDN 84401 1116 B2
E 20 N
- SHFD 84335 400 B3
E 20 S
- SHFD 84335 400 B3
300 ANFK 84003 2711 D1
1000 LNDN 84042 2713 E6
N 20 E
1400 ANFK 84003 2604 C4
N 20 S
200 SHFD 84335 399 C3
N 20 W
200 PTGV 84062 2712 D2
S 20 E
500 OREM 84058 2820 D6
5800 MRRY 84107 2070 C6
W 20 N
600 OREM 84057 2820 B5
W 20 S
600 LNDN 84042 2712 E6
W 20th N
2000 CLTN 84015 1170 E7
20th St
100 OGDN 84401 1115 D2
500 OGDN 84401 1116 A2
W 20th St
100 OGDN 84401 1115 C2
W 20th St SR-104
100 OGDN 84401 1115 C2
N 21st W
- CLTN 84015 1170 E7
21st St
200 OGDN 84401 1115 E2
500 OGDN 84401 1116 A2
E 21st St
100 OGDN 84401 1115 D2
W 21st St
200 OGDN 84401 1115 C2
W 21st St SR-104
100 OGDN 84401 1115 C2
S 22nd W
13000 RIVN 84065 2387 B3
22nd St
200 OGDN 84401 1115 E3
500 OGDN 84401 1116 A3
E 22nd St
100 OGDN 84401 1115 D3
W 22nd St
100 OGDN 84401 1115 D3
S 23rd E
900 SGVL 84663 3144 B4
23rd St
100 OGDN 84401 1115 D3
500 OGDN 84401 1116 A3
N 24th W
1600 LEHI 84043 2602 D4
24th St
400 OGDN 84401 1115 E3
500 OGDN 84401 1116 A3
W 24th St
900 OGDN 84401 1115 A3
900 WbrC 84401 1115 A3
E 25 S
- DvsC 84037 1284 A5
1000 LNDN 84042 2713 D6
2000 LYTN 84040 1283 E5
2600 LYTN 84040 1284 A5
N 25 E
100 LYTN 84041 1228 E6
1500 LYTN 84041 1282 E1
N 25 W
700 OREM 84057 2820 D3
2900 PRVO 84604 2928 C1
S 25 E
- PRRY 84302 827 E2
400 KYVL 84037 1345 C2
900 LYTN 84041 1282 E6
S 25 W
1000 KYVL 84037 1345 C4
W 25 N
1400 CRFD 84015 1227 A4
1500 WPT 84015 1227 A4
W 25 S
500 WBNF 84010 1551 C7
1000 CRFD 84015 1227 B4
1100 LYTN 84041 1282 C5
25 S
- HYRM 84319 652 A2
E 25th N
1300 LEHI 84043 2603 E2
E 25th S
100 SGVL 84663 3143 C6
S 25th W
2000 SRCS 84075 1280 D1
25th St
100 OGDN 84401 1115 D3
500 OGDN 84401 1116 A3
W 25th St
500 OGDN 84401 1115 B3
N 26th W
1600 LEHI 84043 2602 C4
26th St
100 OGDN 84401 1115 E4
600 OGDN 84401 1116 A4
W 26th St
700 OGDN 84401 1115 B4
N 27th W
500 WPT 84015 1226 D3
S 27th W
11600 SJDN 84095 2281 A7
27th St
100 OGDN 84401 1115 D4
500 OGDN 84401 1116 A4
500 OGDN 84403 1115 E4
500 OGDN 84403 1116 A4
W 27th St
1000 OGDN 84401 1115 A4
N 28th W
2100 CLTN 84015 1170 C7
28th St
100 OGDN 84401 1115 D4
300 OGDN 84403 1115 E4
600 OGDN 84403 1116 A4
W 28th St
1000 OGDN 84401 1115 A4
E 29th N
600 LEHI 84043 2603 D1
29th St
100 OGDN 84401 1115 D5
500 OGDN 84403 1115 E5
600 OGDN 84403 1116 A5
W 29th St
100 OGDN 84401 1115 D5
E 30 N
300 ANFK 84003 2711 D1
700 OREM 84097 2821 A5
800 ANFK 84003 2712 A1
800 UthC 84003 2712 A1
E 30 S
1000 PTGV 84062 2713 B3
1100 HYRM 84319 651 E2
N 30 E
400 KYVL 84037 1283 C7
800 DvsC 84037 1283 C6
N 30 W
300 KYVL 84037 1283 C7
400 ANFK 84003 2604 C6
S 30 E
- SNQN 84655 3567 E2
700 OREM 84058 2820 D7
1500 PYSN 84651 3461 E1
S 30 W
8800 SNDY 84070 2176 B6
W 30 N
400 ANFK 84003 2711 B1
W 30 S
400 SNQN 84655 3460 D7
800 OREM 84058 2820 B5
N 30th W
2300 CLTN 84015 1170 C6
W 30th N
1200 LEHI 84043 2603 A1
1300 LEHI 84043 2602 E1
30th St
100 OGDN 84401 1115 E5
500 OGDN 84403 1115 E5
600 OGDN 84403 1116 A5
30th St SR-79
100 OGDN 84401 1115 E5
500 OGDN 84403 1115 E5
600 OGDN 84403 1116 A5
W 30th St
100 OGDN 84401 1115 D5
W 30th St SR-79
100 OGDN 84401 1115 D5
N 31st W
10 LYTN 84041 1281 D4
31st St
- OGDN 84401 1115 D5
- OGDN 84405 1115 D5
500 OGDN 84403 1115 D5
700 OGDN 84403 1116 A5
31st St SR-79
- OGDN 84401 1115 D5
- OGDN 84405 1115 D5
W 31st St
400 OGDN 84401 1115 C5
400 OGDN 84405 1115 C5
W 32nd N
- LEHI 84043 2602 E1
- LEHI 84043 2603 A1
- UthC 84043 2602 E1
- UthC 84043 2603 A1
32nd St
100 OGDN 84401 1115 D5
500 OGDN 84403 1115 E5
600 OGDN 84403 1116 A5
W 32nd St
100 OGDN 84401 1115 D6
33rd St
100 OGDN 84401 1115 D6
500 OGDN 84403 1115 E6
1400 OGDN 84403 1116 C6
W 33rd St
- OGDN 84405 1115 C6
100 OGDN 84401 1115 D6
E 34 S
400 OREM 84097 2820 E5
S 34th E
1000 SPFK 84660 3250 D5
34th St
100 OGDN 84401 1115 D6
500 OGDN 84403 1115 E6
800 OGDN 84403 1116 A6
S 35 E
1300 FMTN 84025 1448 D5
1600 BNFL 84010 1653 D2
35th St
100 OGDN 84401 1115 D6
400 OGDN 84403 1115 E6
600 OGDN 84403 1116 A6
W 36th S
1800 WVCY 84119 1963 C6
36th St
100 OGDN 84401 1115 D7
100 SOGN 84405 1115 D7
400 OGDN 84403 1115 E7
400 SOGN 84403 1115 E7
500 OGDN 84403 1116 A7
500 SOGN 84403 1116 A7
W 36th St
100 OGDN 84401 1115 D7
100 OGDN 84405 1115 D7
37th St
200 SOGN 84405 1115 D7
400 SOGN 84403 1115 E7
600 SOGN 84403 1116 A7
800 OGDN 84403 1116 A7
S 38th W
- SRCS 84075 1226 B6
38th St
300 SOGN 84405 1115 E7
400 SOGN 84403 1115 E7
700 SOGN 84403 1116 A7
1100 OGDN 84403 1116 B7
N 39th W
10100 CRHL 84062 2605 C2
S 39th W
12200 RIVN 84065 2386 D1
39th St
200 SOGN 84405 1115 E7
400 SOGN 84403 1115 E7
600 SOGN 84403 1116 A7
600 OGDN 84403 1116 B7
E 40 N
400 LNDN 84042 2713 C6
400 OREM 84097 2820 E5
900 SGVL 84663 3143 E2
1100 OREM 84097 2821 B5
N 40 E
1300 OREM 84057 2820 D1
1500 LEHI 84043 2603 C4
1800 OREM 84057 2713 D7
N 40 W
400 LNDN 84042 2713 B5
900 OREM 84057 2820 D2
1400 SNST 84015 1227 D1
1800 PRVO 84604 2928 C3
S 40 E
400 FMTN 84025 1448 D3
600 SALM 84653 3356 B5
1300 PRVO 84606 3035 C2
8500 SNDY 84070 2176 D6
S 40 W
1700 OREM 84058 2927 D2
W 40 N
600 OREM 84057 2820 B5
W 40 S
10 LNDN 84042 2713 A6
400 LNDN 84042 2712 E6
1000 OREM 84058 2820 A5
S 40th W
4100 WHVN 84315 1170 D1
40th St
100 SOGN 84405 1115 D7
100 SOGN 84405 1172 D1
300 WbrC 84405 1172 D1
400 SOGN 84403 1172 D1
400 WbrC 84403 1172 D1
600 SOGN 84403 1173 A1
41st St
500 SOGN 84403 1172 E1
700 SOGN 84403 1173 A1
42nd St
500 SOGN 84403 1172 E1
600 SOGN 84403 1173 A1
W 43rd N
- PTVW 84414 997 E1
- PTVW 84414 998 B2
43rd St
500 SOGN 84403 1172 E2
600 SOGN 84403 1173 A2
S 44th W
- SLCY 84104 1856 B7
N 45 W
1900 OREM 84057 2713 D7
S 45 W
1800 OREM 84058 2927 D3
W 47th S
4000 ROY 84067 1170 D2
N 48 W
300 HDPK 84318 399 E7
N 48th W
9500 ANFK 84003 2605 A2
9500 HILD 84003 2605 A2
9600 ANFK 84062 2605 A2
9800 UthC 84062 2605 A2
10000 CRHL 84062 2605 A2
10900 HILD 84003 2498 A7
W 48th S
6100 HOPR 84315 1169 C3
E 50 N
- ANFK 84062 2712 A1
- TMTN 84337 520 E6
- TMTN 84337 521 A6
100 FMTN 84025 1448 D2
200 SHFD 84335 399 E2
300 HDPK 84318 400 A7
400 NSLK 84054 1653 C7
600 HRCY 84032 2398 E4
600 HYRM 84319 651 D2
700 ANFK 84003 2711 E1
700 LOGN 84321 528 A3

Salt Lake City Street Index

STREET Block	City	ZIP	Map#	Grid
E 50 N				
900	LNDN	84042	2713	D6
1000	SGVL	84663	3143	E2
1100	PTGV	84062	2713	B3
1400	SGVL	84663	3144	A2
E 50 S				
200	NSLK	84054	1653	B7
300	ANFK	84003	2711	E1
700	PRVO	84606	2928	D7
700	UthC	84003	2711	E1
800	PTGV	84062	2713	A3
900	ANFK	84003	2712	A1
900	UthC	84003	2712	A1
1000	LNDN	84042	2713	E6
1000	OREM	84097	2821	B5
1100	LOGN	84321	528	B3
1100	PTGV	84003	2712	A1
2400	DvsC	84040	1283	E5
2400	LYTN	84040	1283	E5
2500	LYTN	84040	1284	A5
N 50 E				
-	SNQN	84655	3460	E6
100	OREM	84057	2820	D4
800	DvsC	84037	1283	C6
800	PRVO	84604	2928	C5
1300	CTRV	84014	1551	E1
1500	SGVL	84663	3036	C6
1700	OREM	84057	2713	D7
1800	CTRV	84014	1448	D7
1900	LYTN	84041	1283	A1
N 50 W				
100	CTRV	84014	1551	D3
100	NSLK	84054	1653	A6
300	PRVO	84601	2928	C6
600	LOGN	84321	527	D1
700	MIDW	84049	2397	B1
800	SNST	84015	1227	D3
900	LOGN	84321	463	D7
1300	PTGV	84062	2712	D1
1400	OREM	84057	2820	D1
1800	LYTN	84041	1282	E1
1800	OREM	84057	2713	D7
2000	LYTN	84041	1228	E7
3300	PRVO	84604	2821	C7
S 50 E				
-	CTRV	84014	1551	E5
300	HDPK	84318	464	A2
400	KYVL	84037	1345	C2
400	SHFD	84335	399	D4
700	NHLN	84341	464	A2
800	FMTN	84025	1448	D3
800	LYTN	84041	1282	E6
900	OREM	84058	2820	D7
1100	OREM	84058	2927	D1
2000	CRFD	84015	1281	D1
3400	BNFL	84010	1653	E5
4500	MRRY	84107	2070	C2
5500	WSTR	84405	1172	D4
S 50 W				
10	KYVL	84037	1345	C3
200	OREM	84058	2820	D6
400	FMTN	84025	1448	D3
600	PTGV	84062	2712	D4
800	SGVL	84663	3143	C4
900	LYTN	84041	1282	E6
1400	PYSN	84651	3461	E1
1500	OREM	84058	2927	D2
2000	BNFL	84010	1653	D3
2000	CRFD	84015	1281	D1
2900	NBLY	84321	591	D3
W 50 N				
-	SLCY	84101	1858	B3
300	ANFK	84003	2711	B1
500	BNFL	84010	1551	C7
500	WBNF	84010	1551	C7
1600	PRVO	84601	2927	E7
3000	LYTN	84041	1281	D5
W 50 S				
10	ANFK	84003	2711	C1
10	CTRV	84014	1551	D3
300	MNTU	84324	768	B7
1200	LEHI	84043	2603	A7
1400	LEHI	84043	2602	E7
1500	WPT	84015	1227	A4
E 55 N				
500	ANFK	84003	2711	E1
S 55 W				
1000	FMTN	84025	1448	D4
E 60 N				
-	LNDN	84042	2713	E6
600	OREM	84097	2821	A5
600	SALM	84653	3356	C3
E 60 S				
-	UthC	84003	2712	A1
300	ANFK	84003	2711	D1
900	SPFK	84660	3249	E3
1200	LNDN	84042	2713	E6
1300	LOGN	84321	528	C3
N 60 E				
700	ANFK	84003	2604	C5
800	OREM	84057	2820	D3
1000	LYTN	84041	1283	A2
1900	OREM	84057	2713	D7
N 60 W				
1300	LYTN	84041	1282	E2
S 60 E				
8500	SNDY	84070	2176	D6
S 60 W				
400	OREM	84058	2820	D6
1400	OREM	84058	2927	D1
W 60 N				
-	LNDN	84042	2713	A6
600	NSLK	84054	1652	D7
700	SPFK	84660	3249	B3
800	LYTN	84041	1282	D5
W 60 S				
900	OREM	84058	2820	B5
E 60 N Cir				
600	OREM	84097	2821	A5
E 65 S				
800	LNDN	84042	2713	D6
S 65 E				
-	ANFK	84003	2711	C2
-	DRPR	84020	2388	C7
7000	MDVL	84047	2176	C2
N 69th W				
10300	HILD	84003	2603	E2
E 70 N				
1000	ANFK	84003	2712	A1
E 70 S				
900	LNDN	84042	2713	D6

STREET Block	City	ZIP	Map#	Grid
N 70 E				
1100	ANFK	84003	2604	C5
1600	PTGV	84062	2605	D7
N 70 W				
-	ANFK	84003	2604	C4
10	CTRV	84014	1551	D3
400	OREM	84057	2820	D4
1400	HILD	84003	2604	C4
S 70 E				
500	OREM	84058	2820	D6
S 70 W				
-	CTRV	84014	1551	D3
100	OREM	84058	2820	D5
1100	FMTN	84025	1448	C4
6600	MRRY	84107	2176	C1
W 70 N				
400	ANFK	84003	2711	B1
1900	PRVO	84601	2927	D6
W 70 S				
200	LNDN	84042	2713	B6
1300	LNDN	84042	2712	C7
1800	PRVO	84601	2927	D7
E 75 N				
700	KYVL	84037	1345	E1
800	BNFL	84010	1552	A7
E 75 S				
1000	BNFL	84010	1552	B7
1800	LYTN	84040	1283	D5
N 75 E				
300	NSLK	84054	1653	A6
1100	CTRV	84014	1551	E1
1400	OREM	84057	2820	D1
1700	LYTN	84041	1283	A1
2100	LYTN	84041	1229	A7
N 75 W				
300	CRFD	84015	1227	D3
400	SGVL	84663	3143	C1
600	LNDN	84042	2713	B5
900	MIDW	84049	2397	B1
1000	LYTN	84041	1282	E2
1300	CTRV	84014	1551	D1
1400	SNST	84015	1227	D1
1500	CTRV	84014	1448	D7
1900	SNST	84015	1171	D7
3900	CchC	84341	399	D7
S 75 E				
600	KYVL	84037	1345	D3
800	OREM	84058	2820	D7
1400	BNFL	84010	1653	E2
2500	CRFD	84015	1281	D3
S 75 W				
300	FMTN	84025	1448	D2
500	PVDN	84332	591	E1
500	PVDN	84332	592	A1
900	LYTN	84041	1282	E6
2500	BNFL	84010	1653	D4
6700	MRRY	84107	2176	C1
W 75 N				
-	BNFL	84010	1551	C7
400	OREM	84057	2820	C5
800	KYVL	84037	1345	B1
1000	CRFD	84015	1227	B4
1200	CTRV	84014	1551	B3
3000	LYTN	84041	1281	E4
W 75 S				
-	CRFD	84015	1227	C4
1100	LYTN	84041	1282	C5
1600	KYVL	84037	1344	E1
1800	WPT	84015	1226	E4
N 76th W				
-	LEHI	84043	2603	D3
E 80 N				
-	SHFD	84335	400	B2
900	OREM	84097	2821	A5
900	SGVL	84663	3143	E2
1100	ANFK	84062	2712	A1
E 80 S				
700	ANFK	84003	2711	E1
900	OREM	84097	2821	A5
1300	LNDN	84042	2713	E6
N 80 E				
1100	ANFK	84003	2604	D5
1700	OREM	84057	2713	D7
1900	PRVO	84604	2928	C3
N 80 W				
400	LNDN	84042	2713	B5
600	LOGN	84321	527	D1
1300	OREM	84057	2820	D1
1700	OREM	84057	2713	D7
1800	PRVO	84604	2928	C3
S 80 E				
100	MNTU	84324	829	C1
700	LOGN	84321	527	D5
S 80 W				
-	NBLY	84321	591	D2
1700	OREM	84058	2927	D2
8800	SNDY	84070	2176	C6
W 80 N				
600	OREM	84057	2820	B5
W 80 S				
1600	PRVO	84601	2927	E7
E 85 S				
400	HDPK	84318	464	B1
N 85 E				
100	OREM	84057	2820	D4
N 85 W				
1900	OREM	84057	2713	D7
S 85 E				
7000	MDVL	84047	2176	D2
10800	SNDY	84070	2282	D5
S 85 W				
6600	MRRY	84107	2176	C1
W 85 S				
1000	OREM	84058	2820	A5
E 90 N				
400	OREM	84097	2820	E5
700	ANFK	84003	2711	E1
E 90 S				
700	ANFK	84003	2711	E1
1100	LNDN	84042	2713	E6
N 90 W				
1900	OREM	84057	2713	D7
S 90 E				
6800	MDVL	84047	2176	D2
8500	SNDY	84070	2176	D6
W 90 N				
200	CRFD	84015	1227	D4
300	ANFK	84003	2711	B1
W 90 S				
300	SALM	84653	3356	A3
400	SALM	84653	3355	E3
2300	PRVO	84601	2927	C7

STREET Block	City	ZIP	Map#	Grid
S 95 E				
7400	MDVL	84047	2176	D3
S 96 W				
8800	SNDY	84070	2176	C6
W 97th N				
5500	HILD	84003	2604	D3
W 98th N				
-	HILD	84003	2604	D3
98th St				
-	HILD	84003	2604	C3
E 100 N				
10	ALPN	84004	2497	E4
10	ANFK	84003	2711	C1
10	BMCY	84302	766	E5
10	BNFL	84010	1551	E7
10	CRFD	84015	1227	D4
10	CTRV	84014	1551	E3
10	FMTN	84025	1448	D1
10	GRLD	84312	520	E1
10	HRCY	84032	2398	D3
10	KYVL	84037	1345	D1
10	LEHI	84043	2603	C6
10	LOGN	84321	527	D3
10	MIDW	84049	2397	C3
10	MNDN	84325	524	D6
10	OREM	84057	2820	D5
10	PRVO	84606	2928	C6
10	PTGV	84062	2712	E2
10	PVDN	84332	528	A6
10	PYSN	84651	3354	E5
10	SALM	84653	3356	B3
10	SGVL	84663	3143	D2
10	SHFD	84335	399	D2
10	SNQN	84655	3460	E7
10	SPFK	84660	3249	D2
10	WELV	84339	649	E1
10	WLRD	84340	885	C5
100	ALPN	84004	2498	A4
100	BMCY	84302	767	A5
200	HDPK	84318	400	A7
300	GRLD	84312	521	A2
300	PYSN	84651	3355	B5
400	CTRV	84014	1552	A3
400	HYRM	84319	651	C2
400	NSLK	84054	1653	B7
500	LNDN	84042	2713	C6
500	LOGN	84321	528	A3
500	SHFD	84335	400	A2
600	BNFL	84010	1552	A7
600	OREM	84097	2821	A5
600	PTGV	84062	2713	A2
1100	SPFK	84660	3250	A3
E 100 N SR-198				
10	PYSN	84651	3354	E5
300	PYSN	84651	3355	B5
E 100 S				
-	LYTN	84041	1283	B5
10	ALPN	84004	2497	E4
10	ALPN	84004	2498	A5
10	ANFK	84003	2711	C1
10	BMCY	84302	766	E6
10	CTRV	84014	1551	E3
10	FMTN	84025	1448	D2
10	GRLD	84312	520	E2
10	HDPK	84318	464	A1
10	HRCY	84032	2398	D4
10	HYRM	84319	651	C3
10	KYVL	84037	1345	D1
10	LEHI	84043	2603	C6
10	LOGN	84321	527	D3
10	MIDW	84049	2397	B3
10	MNDN	84325	524	D7
10	PRVO	84606	2928	C7
10	PTGV	84062	2712	E3
10	PVDN	84332	528	A6
10	PYSN	84651	3354	E5
10	SALM	84653	3356	B3
10	SGVL	84663	3143	C2
10	SHFD	84335	399	E3
10	SLCY	84111	1858	C3
10	SNQN	84655	3460	E7
10	SPFK	84660	3249	D3
10	WELV	84339	649	D2
10	WLRD	84340	885	C6
100	BMCY	84302	767	A6
300	NSLK	84054	1653	B7
300	PYSN	84651	3355	A5
400	BNFL	84010	1551	E7
400	CTRV	84014	1552	A3
400	OREM	84097	2820	E5
400	SNQN	84655	3461	A7
500	BNFL	84010	1552	A7
500	LOGN	84321	528	A3
500	SLCY	84102	1858	E3
600	PTGV	84062	2713	A3
700	RVHT	84321	528	A3
700	SLCY	84102	1859	A3
1000	LNDN	84042	2713	E7
1100	SPFK	84660	3250	A3
1100	UthC	84651	3355	B5
1200	SGVL	84663	3144	A2
1300	SLCY	84112	1859	C3
1800	LYTN	84040	1283	D5
7800	WbrC	84317	1061	D5
E 100 S SR-39				
7800	WbrC	84317	1061	D5
N 100 E				
-	CchC	84325	524	E4
-	SGVL	84663	3036	C6
10	ALPN	84004	2497	E4
10	ANFK	84003	2711	C1
10	BMCY	84302	766	E5
10	FMTN	84025	1448	D1
10	GRLD	84312	520	E1
10	HDPK	84318	464	A1
10	HRCY	84032	2398	D3
10	HYRM	84319	651	B2
10	KYVL	84037	1345	D1
10	LEHI	84043	2603	C6
10	MIDW	84049	2397	C3
10	PRVO	84606	2928	C6
10	PTGV	84062	2712	D1
10	PVDN	84332	528	A6
10	PYSN	84651	3354	E4
10	SALM	84653	3356	B3
10	SGVL	84663	3143	C2
10	SHFD	84335	399	D2
10	SNQN	84655	3460	E6
10	SPFK	84660	3249	D2
10	WELV	84339	649	D1
10	WLRD	84340	885	C5
100	ANFK	84003	2604	C7

STREET Block	City	ZIP	Map#	Grid
N 100 E				
200	KYVL	84037	1283	C7
200	NSLK	84054	1653	A6
200	OREM	84057	2820	D4
300	HDPK	84318	400	A6
400	WELV	84339	589	D7
500	CchC	84318	400	A6
500	FMTN	84025	1346	D7
500	LOGN	84321	527	D1
500	MNDN	84325	524	E4
700	BNFL	84010	1551	E6
900	CTRV	84014	1551	E2
1100	HARR	84404	1056	D2
1100	LYTN	84041	1282	E2
1200	UthC	84003	2604	D4
1400	PTGV	84062	2605	D7
1800	CTRV	84014	1448	D6
1800	LOGN	84341	463	E5
1900	OREM	84057	2713	D7
3000	NHON	84414	998	D4
3300	PRVO	84604	2928	C1
4200	PRVO	84604	2821	C6
N 100 E SR-74				
10	ANFK	84003	2711	C1
100	ANFK	84003	2604	C7
1200	UthC	84003	2604	D4
N 100 E SR-146				
10	PTGV	84062	2712	D1
1400	PTGV	84062	2605	D7
N 100 W				
-	SGVL	84663	3142	C3
-	SGVL	84663	3143	C1
-	SPFK	84660	3142	C3
-	SPFK	84663	3142	C3
-	UthC	84655	3460	D6
10	ALPN	84004	2497	E4
10	ANFK	84003	2711	C1
10	BMCY	84302	766	E4
10	FMTN	84025	1448	C1
10	GRLD	84312	520	E1
10	HDPK	84318	399	E7
10	HDPK	84318	463	E1
10	HRCY	84032	2398	C3
10	HYRM	84319	651	B2
10	KYVL	84037	1345	C1
10	LEHI	84043	2603	C6
10	LOGN	84321	527	D2
10	MIDW	84049	2397	B3
10	PRVO	84601	2928	C6
10	PTGV	84062	2712	D1
10	PVDN	84332	527	E6
10	PYSN	84651	3354	E4
10	SALM	84653	3356	A3
10	SHFD	84335	399	D2
10	SNQN	84655	3460	D6
10	SPFK	84660	3249	C2
10	WELV	84339	649	C1
10	WLRD	84340	885	C5
100	ANFK	84003	2604	C6
200	CTRV	84014	1551	D3
400	CchC	84318	399	E6
400	MNTU	84324	768	C6
400	WELV	84339	589	C7
500	KYVL	84037	1283	C7
500	OREM	84057	2820	D3
600	FMTN	84025	1346	C7
700	CRFD	84015	1227	D3
800	SNST	84015	1227	D3
1100	LYTN	84041	1282	E2
1300	BNFL	84010	1551	D5
2500	SNST	84015	1171	D6
2900	PRVO	84604	2928	C1
3000	NHON	84414	998	D4
4500	PRVO	84604	2821	C5
N 100 W SR-198				
10	PYSN	84651	3354	E5
S 100 E				
-	DvsC	84037	1283	A6
-	FMTN	84025	1345	D6
-	KYVL	84037	1283	A6
-	LYTN	84041	1281	D3
-	MNTU	84324	829	C1
10	ANFK	84003	2711	C1
10	BMCY	84302	766	E7
10	BNFL	84010	1551	E7
10	CTRV	84014	1551	E4
10	FMTN	84025	1448	D2
10	GRLD	84312	520	E2
10	HDPK	84318	464	A1
10	HRCY	84032	2398	D4
10	HYRM	84319	651	B3
10	KYVL	84037	1345	D1
10	LEHI	84043	2603	C7
10	LNDN	84042	2713	B6
10	LOGN	84321	527	D3
10	MIDW	84049	2397	C3
10	MNDN	84325	524	E7
10	PTGV	84062	2712	D3
10	PVDN	84332	528	A7
10	PYSN	84651	3354	E5
10	SALM	84653	3356	B4
10	SGVL	84663	3143	C3
10	SHFD	84335	399	D3
10	SNQN	84655	3460	E7
10	SPFK	84660	3249	D3
10	WELV	84339	649	D2
10	WLRD	84340	885	C6
100	PRVO	84606	2928	C7
100	SNQN	84655	3567	E1
200	BNFL	84010	1653	E1
400	CchC	84325	588	E1
400	MNDN	84325	588	E1
400	PVDN	84332	592	A1
700	PRVO	84606	3035	C1
900	LYTN	84041	1282	E6
900	LYTN	84041	1283	A6
900	OREM	84058	2820	D7
1100	OREM	84058	2927	D1
1300	PYSN	84651	3461	E1
1800	CRFD	84015	1281	D1
5100	WSTR	84405	1172	D3
6700	MDVL	84047	2176	D1
6700	MRRY	84047	2176	D1
8000	MDVL	84070	2176	D5
8200	SlkC	84070	2176	D5
8200	SNDY	84070	2176	D5
11000	SNDY	84070	2282	D5
13700	DRPR	84020	2388	D5
S 100 E SR-146				
10	PTGV	84062	2712	D3
S 100 W				
-	NHLN	84341	463	E2

STREET Block	City	ZIP	Map#	Grid
S 100 W				
-	SNQN	84655	3567	E3
10	ALPN	84004	2497	E5
10	ANFK	84003	2711	C1
10	BMCY	84302	766	E6
10	BNFL	84010	1551	D7
10	FMTN	84025	1448	C2
10	GRLD	84312	520	E2
10	HDPK	84318	463	E1
10	HRCY	84032	2398	C5
10	HYRM	84319	651	B3
10	KYVL	84037	1345	C1
10	LEHI	84043	2603	C7
10	LOGN	84321	527	D4
10	MIDW	84049	2397	B3
10	MNTU	84324	768	C7
10	PRVO	84601	2928	C7
10	PTGV	84062	2712	D3
10	PVDN	84332	527	E6
10	PYSN	84651	3354	E6
10	SGVL	84663	3143	C2
10	SHFD	84335	399	D3
10	SNQN	84655	3460	D7
10	SPFK	84660	3249	C3
10	WELV	84339	649	C3
10	WLRD	84340	885	C6
100	MNTU	84324	829	C1
100	SALM	84653	3356	A4
400	UthC	84003	2711	C2
500	OREM	84058	2820	D6
500	PRVO	84601	3035	C1
600	TMTN	84337	520	E7
700	BMCY	84302	827	E1
700	LEHI	84043	2710	C1
800	BNFL	84010	1653	D1
1400	OREM	84058	2927	D1
1900	CRFD	84015	1281	D1
1900	PRRY	84302	827	E4
3700	NBLY	84321	591	D5
4300	WSTR	84405	1172	D2
5200	MRRY	84107	2070	C4
8800	SNDY	84070	2176	B6
S 100 W SR-198				
10	PYSN	84651	3354	E6
W 100 N				
-	TMTN	84337	520	B6
-	WPT	84015	1226	C4
10	ALPN	84004	2497	E4
10	BMCY	84302	766	E5
10	HDPK	84318	399	E7
10	HDPK	84318	400	A6
10	HRCY	84032	2398	C4
10	HYRM	84319	651	B2
10	LOGN	84321	527	C3
10	MIDW	84049	2397	B3
10	MNDN	84325	524	D6
10	MNTU	84324	768	C7
10	PRVO	84601	2928	C6
10	PTGV	84062	2712	D3
10	PYSN	84651	3354	E5
10	SALM	84653	3356	A3
10	SNQN	84655	3460	D7
10	WELV	84339	649	C1
10	WLRD	84340	885	C5
100	LEHI	84043	2603	B6
200	GRLD	84312	520	E2
200	PVDN	84332	527	E6
200	SGVL	84663	3143	B2
300	ANFK	84003	2711	B1
300	CRFD	84015	1227	C4
400	LYTN	84041	1282	D4
500	BNFL	84010	1551	C7
500	FMTN	84025	1448	B1
500	KYVL	84037	1345	B1
500	WBNF	84010	1551	C7
600	SPFK	84660	3249	B2
700	HYRM	84319	650	E2
700	OREM	84057	2820	B5
800	LNDN	84042	2712	E6
800	NSLK	84054	1652	D6
1500	WPT	84015	1227	A4
2800	PRVO	84601	2927	C6
W 100 N SR-198				
10	PYSN	84651	3354	E5
W 100 S				
-	BxEC	84337	521	B6
-	MNTU	84324	768	B7
10	ANFK	84003	2711	C1
10	BMCY	84302	766	E6
10	GRLD	84312	520	E2
10	HDPK	84318	463	E1
10	HDPK	84318	464	A1
10	HRCY	84032	2398	C4
10	HYRM	84319	651	A3
10	MIDW	84049	2397	B3
10	MNDN	84325	524	D7
10	MNTU	84324	829	B1
10	NSLK	84054	1653	A7
10	PRVO	84601	2928	C7
10	PTGV	84062	2712	D3
10	PVDN	84332	528	A6
10	PYSN	84651	3354	D5
10	SALM	84653	3356	A4
10	SGVL	84663	3143	C2
10	SLCY	84101	1858	C3
10	SNQN	84655	3460	D7
10	SPFK	84660	3249	C3
10	WELV	84339	649	C2
100	PVDN	84332	527	E6
200	WLRD	84340	885	C6
300	BNFL	84010	1551	C7
400	LEHI	84043	2603	B7
400	LNDN	84042	2713	A6
500	KYVL	84037	1345	B1
600	LOGN	84321	527	B3
700	SHFD	84335	399	B3
700	SLCY	84104	1858	A3
800	OREM	84058	2820	B5
900	SLCY	84104	1857	E3
1000	LYTN	84041	1282	C5
1200	LNDN	84042	2712	D6
1500	LEHI	84043	2602	E7
1500	WPT	84015	1227	A4
1800	PRVO	84601	2927	D7
4400	WbrC	84404	1054	C5
W 100 S SR-113				
10	HRCY	84032	2398	C4
W 100 S SR-115				
10	SPFK	84660	3249	C3
N 100 St E				
10	MNDN	84325	524	E6

STREET Block	City	ZIP	Map#	Grid
100 St E				
9000	PARA	84328	710	D5
N 100 E St				
10	MLVI	84332	591	E3
S 100 E St				
10	MLVI	84332	591	E3
W 100 N				
10	PVDN	84332	528	A6
E 100 N St				
10	MLVI	84332	591	E3
100	MLVI	84332	592	A3
W 100 N St				
10	MLVI	84332	591	E3
100 S St				
-	HYRM	84319	652	A3
E 100 S St				
10	MLVI	84332	591	E3
100	MLVI	84332	592	A3
200	HDPK	84318	464	A1
W 100 S St				
10	MLVI	84332	591	E3
300	NBLY	84321	591	E3
300	NBLY	84321	591	E3
300	SNQN	84655	3460	D7
N 100 W St				
10	MLVI	84332	591	E2
700	TMTN	84337	520	E4
900	LOGN	84321	463	D7
900	LOGN	84321	527	D1
S 100 W St				
10	MLVI	84332	591	E3
8800	PARA	84328	710	D5
W 103th N				
6500	HILD	84003	2604	A2
W 105 N				
1000	OREM	84057	2820	A5
E 110 N				
400	LEHI	84043	2603	C6
600	HRCY	84032	2398	E3
E 110 S				
900	LNDN	84042	2713	D7
N 110 E				
1600	LEHI	84043	2603	C3
N 110 W				
1300	OREM	84057	2820	D1
1900	PRVO	84604	2928	C3
S 110 W				
-	NBLY	84321	591	D2
1000	FMTN	84025	1448	C4
1000	OREM	84058	2820	D7
13500	DRPR	84020	2388	C4
W 110 N				
2700	PRVO	84601	2927	C6
W 110 S				
300	LNDN	84042	2713	A7
W 110th S				
1400	SJDN	84095	2281	D5
S 115 E				
8400	SNDY	84070	2176	D5
S 115 W				
5900	MRRY	84107	2070	C7
W 115 N				
10	CTRV	84014	1551	D3
E 120 N				
1000	OREM	84097	2821	B5
1100	ANFK	84062	2605	A7
1100	PTGV	84062	2713	B2
E 120 S				
300	SHFD	84335	399	E3
400	SHFD	84335	400	A3
900	OREM	84097	2821	A5
900	SPFK	84660	3249	E3
N 120 E				
600	OREM	84057	2820	D3
1700	OREM	84057	2713	D7
N 120 W				
400	LNDN	84042	2713	B5
600	LEHI	84043	2603	C5
1200	LOGN	84341	463	D7
1700	OREM	84057	2713	D7
2000	PRVO	84604	2928	C3
S 120 E				
-	SHFD	84335	399	D4
8500	SNDY	84070	2176	D6
S 120 W				
400	OGDN	84404	1056	D6
1900	OREM	84058	2927	D3
5700	MRRY	84107	2070	C6
W 120 N				
-	SPFK	84660	3249	B2
200	ANFK	84003	2711	B1
400	OREM	84057	2820	C5
W 120 S				
10	ALPN	84004	2497	E5
300	LNDN	84042	2713	A7
1500	PRVO	84601	2927	D7
N 120 Cir W				
1100	ANFK	84003	2604	C5
E 125 N				
-	CchC	84321	528	B6
100	OGDN	84404	1056	D5
400	PVDN	84332	528	B6
1200	OGDN	84404	1057	C5
E 125 S				
900	OGDN	84404	1057	B5
N 125 E				
300	NSLK	84054	1653	A6
500	SGVL	84663	3143	C1
1000	LYTN	84041	1283	A2
1100	HARR	84404	1056	D2
N 125 W				
500	SGVL	84663	3143	C1
1400	BNFL	84010	1551	D5
1400	SNST	84015	1227	D1
1500	LYTN	84041	1282	E1
2100	LYTN	84041	1228	E7
2200	SNST	84015	1171	D7
3100	PRVO	84604	2928	B2
4000	PTVW	84414	998	D2
S 125 E				
10	CRFD	84015	1227	D4
700	LYTN	84041	1282	E6
1300	KYVL	84037	1345	D4
1500	OREM	84058	2927	D2
2500	CRFD	84015	1281	D2
4500	WSTR	84405	1172	D2
6900	MDVL	84047	2176	D1
12500	DRPR	84020	2388	D2
S 125 W				
500	LYTN	84041	1282	E6
4500	WSTR	84405	1172	D2
12500	DRPR	84020	2388	C2

STREET Block	City	ZIP	Map#	Grid
W 125 N				
100	OGDN	84404	1056	D5
W 125 S				
-	CTRV	84014	1551	D4
1200	LEHI	84043	2603	A7
1300	LEHI	84043	2602	E7
S 129 W				
5800	MRRY	84107	2070	C6
E 130 N				
200	OREM	84057	2820	E5
400	OREM	84097	2820	E5
1300	SGVL	84663	3144	A2
E 130 S				
-	SNQN	84655	3461	A7
N 130 E				
100	OREM	84057	2820	D4
S 130 E				
10	NSLK	84054	1653	A7
10	SPFK	84660	3249	D3
800	SALM	84653	3356	B5
S 130 W				
400	OREM	84058	2820	D6
6500	MRRY	84107	2176	C1
W 130 N				
800	OREM	84057	2820	B4
W 130 S				
-	PRVO	84601	2927	D7
200	LNDN	84042	2713	A7
1300	OREM	84058	2819	E5
1300	OREM	84058	2820	A5
1800	MPTN	84664	3143	D7
W 131st S				
1200	RIVN	84065	2387	D3
E 135 N				
10	OREM	84057	2820	D5
E 135 S				
10	MNTU	84324	829	C1
1000	LNDN	84042	2713	E7
N 135 W				
100	OGDN	84404	1056	D5
200	LNDN	84042	2713	B5
1800	OREM	84057	2713	D7
S 135 W				
1400	OREM	84058	2927	D1
E 140 N				
200	LNDN	84042	2713	C6
700	ANFK	84003	2604	E7
900	SGVL	84663	3143	E1
1100	OREM	84097	2821	B5
E 140 S				
200	ANFK	84003	2711	D1
1400	PTGV	84062	2713	C3
N 140 E				
1000	OREM	84057	2820	D2
2500	PRVO	84604	2928	C2
N 140 W				
800	ANFK	84003	2604	C5
2500	SNST	84015	1171	D6
3100	PRVO	84604	2928	C1
S 140 E				
-	SHFD	84335	399	E4
800	FMTN	84025	1448	D4
1500	OREM	84058	2927	D2
5400	MRRY	84107	2070	D5
S 140 W				
400	OREM	84058	2820	D6
2000	OREM	84058	2927	D3
W 140 N				
100	OGDN	84404	1056	D5
400	MIDW	84049	2397	A3
1200	SLCY	84116	1857	D2
W 140 S				
1700	OREM	84058	2819	D5
E 145 N				
10	OREM	84057	2820	D5
S 145 E				
1700	OREM	84058	2927	D2
7200	MDVL	84047	2176	D3
N 146 E				
300	SALM	84653	3356	B2
E 150 N				
-	SNQN	84655	3461	A7
10	ANFK	84003	2604	C7
100	OREM	84057	2820	D5
300	HDPK	84318	400	A7
400	BNFL	84010	1551	E7
700	OREM	84097	2821	A4
700	PRVO	84606	2928	D6
700	SGVL	84663	3143	D2
800	LOGN	84321	528	A3
1300	PTGV	84062	2713	C2
E 150 S				
-	CTRV	84014	1551	E4
-	SNQN	84655	3568	A1
500	LNDN	84042	2713	C7
600	BNFL	84010	1552	A7
600	KYVL	84037	1345	E1
600	PTGV	84062	2713	A3
700	PRVO	84606	2928	D7
900	LYTN	84041	1283	B5
900	SGVL	84663	3143	E2
1100	SPFK	84660	3250	A3
1300	SGVL	84663	3144	A2
2500	LYTN	84040	1283	E5
2500	LYTN	84040	1284	A5
N 150 E				
-	SNQN	84655	3460	E6
-	SPFK	84660	3142	D6
300	SGVL	84663	3143	C1
400	KYVL	84037	1283	D7
400	LNDN	84042	2713	B5
400	WELV	84339	589	D7
400	WELV	84339	649	D1
500	FMTN	84025	1346	D7
500	OREM	84057	2820	D3
700	LOGN	84321	527	D1
800	PRVO	84604	2928	C5
1100	LYTN	84041	1283	A2
1200	SGVL	84663	3036	C6
1400	CTRV	84014	1551	E1
1500	PTGV	84062	2605	D7
1800	CTRV	84014	1448	E6
1800	NHON	84404	1056	D1
1900	NHON	84414	1056	D1
1900	OREM	84057	2713	D7
2000	WbrC	84414	998	D2
3000	NHON	84414	998	D4
N 150 W				
-	NHON	84404	1056	D1
-	PVDN	84332	527	E6
-	SNQN	84655	3460	D6
400	PYSN	84651	3354	E4

STREET Block City ZIP Map# Grid

N 150 W
500 CTRV 84014 1551 D2
500 KYVL 84037 1283 C7
600 LOGN 84321 527 D1
700 LYTN 84041 1282 E3
700 SGVL 84663 3036 C7
800 SNST 84015 1227 D3
900 ANFK 84003 2604 C5
900 LOGN 84321 463 D7
1000 OREM 84057 2820 D2
1100 PTGV 84062 2712 D1
1200 HARR 84404 1056 D2
1400 BNFL 84010 1551 D5
1800 OREM 84057 2713 D7
2800 NHON 84414 998 D4
3100 PRVO 84604 2928 C1
4500 PRVO 84604 2821 C5
S 150 E
- SHFD 84335 399 D5
100 KYVL 84037 1345 D1
400 FMTN 84025 1448 D3
700 SGVL 84663 3143 C3
900 OREM 84058 2820 D7
2000 CRFD 84015 1281 D1
2800 BNFL 84010 1653 E4
4700 WSTR 84405 1172 D2
7100 MDVL 84047 2176 D2
11400 DRPR 84020 2282 D6
13100 DRPR 84020 2388 D4
S 150 W
- KYVL 84037 1345 C5
10 CRFD 84015 1227 D4
300 OGDN 84404 1056 D6
500 CTRV 84014 1551 D4
600 OREM 84058 2820 D6
700 TMTN 84337 520 E7
800 BNFL 84010 1653 D1
1100 OREM 84058 2927 D1
1100 PYSN 84651 3354 E7
1400 PYSN 84651 3461 E1
2000 PRRY 84302 827 E4
2200 CRFD 84015 1281 D2
4500 WSTR 84405 1172 D2
4600 MRRY 84107 2070 C3
W 150 N
- PVDN 84332 527 E6
10 NSLK 84054 1653 A6
100 ALPN 84004 2497 E4
300 HDPK 84318 399 E7
400 CRFD 84015 1227 C4
400 OREM 84057 2820 C4
400 SHFD 84335 399 C2
400 LNDN 84042 2712 E6
800 LYTN 84041 1282 D4
1600 PRVO 84601 2927 E6
1600 TMTN 84337 520 B5
1700 WPT 84015 1227 A4
3000 LYTN 84041 1281 D4
3800 WPT 84015 1226 A4
W 150 S
200 OGDN 84404 1056 D5
300 BNFL 84010 1551 D7
900 KYVL 84037 1345 A1
1000 LYTN 84041 1282 C5
1200 CRFD 84015 1227 A5
1500 WPT 84015 1227 A4
5200 SLCY 84104 1855 E3
S 151 W
5300 MRRY 84107 2070 C5
E 155 S
900 LNDN 84042 2713 D7
1400 LNDN 84042 2714 A7
S 157 W
5800 MRRY 84107 2070 C6
E 160 N
200 OREM 84057 2820 D4
300 ANFK 84003 2604 D7
E 160 S
300 SHFD 84335 399 E3
1300 LNDN 84042 2713 E7
N 160 E
200 OGDN 84404 1056 D4
500 MNDN 84325 524 E5
1100 ANFK 84003 2604 D5
1400 MPTN 84664 3144 B5
N 160 W
1200 OREM 84057 2820 D2
1400 LYTN 84041 1282 E1
1700 OREM 84057 2713 C7
1900 PRVO 84604 2928 C3
2500 SNST 84015 1171 D6
3400 PRVO 84604 2821 C7
S 160 E
700 SALM 84653 3356 B5
5400 MRRY 84107 2070 D5
6600 MDVL 84047 2176 D1
6600 MRRY 84047 2176 D1
8400 SNDY 84070 2176 D6
S 160 W
200 CTRV 84014 1551 D4
300 MIDW 84049 2397 B4
4600 MRRY 84107 2070 C2
W 160 N
1200 OREM 84057 2820 A4
2200 SLCY 84116 1857 B2
2800 PRVO 84601 2927 C6
N 165 E
1700 OREM 84057 2713 D7
S 165 E
- KYVL 84037 1345 D4
S 165 W
100 OREM 84058 2820 D5
1600 OREM 84058 2927 D2
W 165 S
10 OREM 84058 2820 D5
E 170 N
100 ANFK 84003 2604 C7
700 HRCY 84032 2398 E3
E 170 S
300 LNDN 84042 2713 C7
500 LOGN 84321 527 E3
500 LOGN 84321 528 A3
N 170 E
800 DvsC 84037 1283 D6
900 BNFL 84010 1551 E6
1200 SGVL 84663 3036 C6
1400 BxEC 84302 767 A2
1400 OREM 84057 2820 D1
N 170 W
200 CTRV 84014 1551 D3
1600 WLRD 84340 885 C1
1800 CTRV 84014 1448 D7
2100 PRVO 84604 2928 C2
S 170 E
- PRVO 84606 3035 C1
8600 SNDY 84070 2176 D6
9400 SNDY 84070 2282 D1
S 170 W
- LOGN 84321 527 C6
400 SGVL 84663 3143 C3
2700 SSLK 84115 1964 C4
W 170 N
100 OREM 84057 2820 C4
600 SPFK 84660 3249 B2
1500 WPT 84015 1227 A4
2700 PRVO 84601 2927 C6
W 170 S
900 OREM 84058 2820 B5
1600 PRVO 84601 2927 E7
E 175 N
500 NSLK 84054 1653 B6
600 LNDN 84042 2713 D6
E 175 S
900 LYTN 84041 1283 B5
N 175 E
- LOGN 84321 527 D2
100 NHON 84414 998 E3
300 NSLK 84054 1653 A6
1100 CTRV 84014 1551 E1
1400 LYTN 84041 1283 A2
2700 PRVO 84604 2928 C1
3200 PRVO 84604 2821 C7
N 175 W
1000 SNST 84015 1227 D2
1400 BNFL 84010 1551 D5
1400 LYTN 84041 1282 E2
2500 SNST 84015 1171 D6
3000 NHON 84414 998 D4
4300 PTVW 84414 998 D1
S 175 E
- FMTN 84025 1345 D6
200 OREM 84058 2820 D5
700 LYTN 84041 1282 E6
1300 KYVL 84037 1345 D4
1400 OREM 84058 2927 E2
2100 CRFD 84015 1281 E2
4300 WSTR 84405 1172 D2
S 175 W
800 BNFL 84010 1653 D1
800 OGDN 84404 1056 D6
4600 WSTR 84405 1172 D3
W 175 N
- CRFD 84015 1227 C4
- LYTN 84041 1281 C4
- NHON 84414 998 D4
- WPT 84015 1226 C4
100 OGDN 84404 1056 D5
300 ANFK 84003 2604 B7
400 OREM 84057 2820 C4
W 175 S
300 KYVL 84037 1345 B2
1100 FMTN 84025 1448 A2
E 180 N
- SNQN 84655 3461 A7
10 OREM 84057 2820 D4
500 SALM 84653 3356 C3
700 UthC 84653 3356 C3
900 LNDN 84042 2713 D6
1100 OREM 84097 2821 B4
1100 SGVL 84663 3143 E1
E 180 S
400 ANFK 84003 2711 D1
400 SHFD 84335 399 E3
400 SHFD 84335 400 A3
900 SPFK 84660 3249 E3
N 180 E
- NHON 84414 998 E4
200 OGDN 84404 1056 D4
500 CTRV 84014 1551 E3
2000 PRVO 84604 2928 C3
2600 LEHI 84043 2603 C2
3500 PRVO 84604 2821 C7
N 180 W
1000 LOGN 84341 463 D7
1200 ANFK 84003 2604 C4
1300 LEHI 84043 2603 B4
1800 OREM 84057 2713 C7
2100 PTGV 84062 2605 D6
S 180 E
- SHFD 84335 399 E4
1100 PRVO 84606 3035 C2
7800 MDVL 84070 2176 D4
S 180 W
10 LNDN 84042 2713 A6
100 OREM 84058 2820 D5
600 SALM 84653 3356 A5
1800 OREM 84058 2927 D3
W 180 N
400 CRFD 84015 1227 C4
700 SPFK 84660 3249 B2
900 OREM 84057 2820 A4
1200 SLCY 84116 1857 E2
W 180 S
- SPFK 84660 3249 B3
700 LEHI 84043 2603 A7
800 OREM 84058 2820 B5
1500 PRVO 84601 2927 E7
1700 OREM 84058 2819 D5
N 185 W
900 OREM 84057 2820 C2
S 185 E
10 FMTN 84025 1448 D2
S 185 E SR-106
10 FMTN 84025 1448 D2
S 185 W
1400 OREM 84058 2927 D2
N 190 E
500 NSLK 84054 1653 B5
1100 LEHI 84043 2603 C4
1900 OREM 84057 2713 D7
N 190 W
4100 PRVO 84604 2821 C6
S 190 E
6800 MDVL 84047 2176 D1
S 190 W
900 OREM 84058 2820 D7
4800 MRRY 84107 2070 C3
W 190 S
900 LEHI 84043 2603 A7
S 198 W
- NBLY 84321 591 D6
E 200 N
- GRLD 84312 520 E1
- GRLD 84312 521 A1
10 ALPN 84004 2497 E4
10 ANFK 84003 2604 D7
10 BMCY 84302 766 E5
10 FMTN 84025 1448 D1
10 HDPK 84318 400 A7
10 HRCY 84032 2398 D3
10 HYRM 84319 651 B2
10 KYVL 84037 1345 D1
10 LEHI 84043 2603 C6
10 MLVI 84332 591 E2
10 MNDN 84325 524 D6
10 NSLK 84054 1653 A6
10 OREM 84057 2820 D4
10 PRVO 84606 2928 C6
10 PTGV 84062 2712 E2
10 PVDN 84332 528 A6
10 PYSN 84651 3354 E5
10 SALM 84653 3356 A3
10 SGVL 84663 3143 D1
10 SHFD 84335 399 E2
10 SLCY 84103 1858 C2
10 SNQN 84655 3460 E7
10 SPFK 84660 3249 E2
10 WELV 84339 649 D1
100 BMCY 84302 767 A5
100 MLVI 84332 592 A2
100 MPTN 84664 3144 B7
200 ALPN 84004 2498 A4
200 LNDN 84042 2713 B6
200 PYSN 84651 3355 A5
400 BNFL 84010 1551 E7
400 BNFL 84010 1552 A7
400 OREM 84097 2820 E4
500 LOGN 84321 527 E2
500 LOGN 84321 528 A2
600 OREM 84097 2821 A4
600 PTGV 84062 2713 A2
700 FTHT 84037 1345 D1
800 ANFK 84003 2605 A7
800 KYVL 84037 1283 E7
900 FTHT 84037 1283 E7
900 GNLA 84655 3460 B4
900 KYVL 84037 1284 A7
900 UthC 84655 3460 B4
1100 FTHT 84037 1284 A7
2400 LYTN 84040 1283 E4
2700 LYTN 84040 1284 A4
5600 HRMN 84065 2385 D2
6600 HTVL 84317 1060 D5
6800 WbrC 84317 1060 D5
7500 HTVL 84317 1061 A5
7500 WbrC 84317 1061 A5
E 200 S
- SNQN 84655 3568 A1
- UthC 84003 2712 A1
- WbrC 84317 1061 D5
10 ANFK 84003 2711 D1
10 BMCY 84302 766 E6
10 BNFL 84010 1551 E7
10 CRFD 84015 1227 D5
10 CTRV 84014 1551 E4
10 FMTN 84025 1448 D2
10 HRCY 84032 2398 D4
10 HYRM 84319 651 C3
10 LEHI 84043 2603 C7
10 LOGN 84321 527 E3
10 MLVI 84332 591 E3
10 MNDN 84325 524 D7
10 PRVO 84606 2928 D7
10 PTGV 84062 2712 E3
10 PVDN 84332 528 A7
10 PYSN 84651 3354 E5
10 SALM 84653 3356 B4
10 SGVL 84663 3143 D2
10 SHFD 84335 399 E3
10 SLCY 84111 1858 C3
10 SNQN 84655 3567 E1
10 SPFK 84660 3249 D3
10 WELV 84339 649 E2
10 WLRD 84340 885 C6
100 BMCY 84302 767 A6
100 KYVL 84037 1345 D2
100 MLVI 84332 592 A3
100 OREM 84058 2820 E5
200 MIDW 84049 2397 C4
200 PYSN 84651 3355 A5
300 HDPK 84318 464 A1
500 CchC 84318 464 A1
500 PTGV 84062 2713 A3
500 SLCY 84102 1858 E3
600 BNFL 84010 1552 A7
600 CTRV 84014 1552 A4
700 CRFD 84015 1228 A5
700 DvsC 84015 1228 A5
700 DvsC 84056 1228 A5
700 SLCY 84102 1859 A3
800 CRFD 84056 1228 A5
800 FTHT 84037 1345 E2
800 HDPK 84341 464 B1
800 NHLN 84341 464 B1
800 OREM 84097 2821 A5
900 FTHT 84037 1346 B1
900 GNLA 84655 3460 A5
1300 SGVL 84663 3144 A2
1900 LYTN 84040 1283 D5
3300 CchC 84339 650 A2
3300 WELV 84339 650 A2
3400 CchC 84339 649 E2
6800 HTVL 84317 1060 E5
7300 HTVL 84317 1061 A5
E 200 S SR-90
10 BMCY 84302 766 E6
100 BMCY 84302 767 A6
N 200 E
- CchC 84339 589 D7
- DvsC 84040 1283 D5
- WbrC 84414 998 E6
10 ALPN 84004 2498 A4
10 ANFK 84003 2711 D1
10 BMCY 84302 767 A5
10 CTRV 84014 1551 E3
10 FMTN 84025 1448 D1
10 GRLD 84312 520 E1
10 HDPK 84318 400 A7
10 HDPK 84318 464 A1
10 HRCY 84032 2398 D3
10 HYRM 84319 651 B2
10 KYVL 84037 1345 D1
10 LNDN 84042 2713 B6
10 LOGN 84321 527 D2
10 MIDW 84049 2397 C3
10 PRVO 84606 2928 C6
10 PTGV 84062 2712 E2
10 PVDN 84332 528 A6
10 PYSN 84651 3354 E4
10 SALM 84653 3356 B3
10 SGVL 84663 3143 C1
10 SHFD 84335 399 E2
10 SNQN 84655 3460 E6
10 SPFK 84660 3249 D2
10 WELV 84339 649 D1
10 WLRD 84340 885 D5
100 MLVI 84332 592 A2
200 ANFK 84003 2604 D7
400 KYVL 84037 1283 D7
400 WELV 84339 589 D7
500 FMTN 84025 1346 D7
700 PTGV 84062 2713 B5
800 LEHI 84043 2603 C5
800 OREM 84057 2820 E2
900 LOGN 84321 463 E7
1000 BNFL 84010 1551 E6
1000 LOGN 84341 463 E7
1000 SPFK 84660 3142 D7
1100 HARR 84404 1056 E2
1100 LYTN 84041 1283 A2
1200 MPTN 84664 3144 B5
1300 SGVL 84663 3036 C6
1300 UthC 84003 2604 D5
1400 HILD 84003 2604 D5
1900 CTRV 84014 1448 E6
2100 PRVO 84604 2928 C3
2400 NHLN 84341 463 E4
2600 NHON 84414 998 D5
4800 PRVO 84604 2821 C5
N 200 W
- NHON 84404 1056 D1
- SGVL 84663 3143 C1
- UthC 84655 3460 D5
10 ANFK 84003 2711 C1
10 BMCY 84302 766 E5
10 BNFL 84010 1551 D7
10 GRLD 84312 520 E2
10 HDPK 84318 399 E7
10 HDPK 84318 463 E1
10 HRCY 84032 2398 C3
10 HYRM 84319 651 A2
10 KYVL 84037 1345 C1
10 LEHI 84043 2603 B6
10 LOGN 84321 527 C3
10 MIDW 84049 2397 B3
10 PYSN 84651 3354 E4
10 SHFD 84335 399 D2
10 SLCY 84103 1858 C3
10 SNQN 84655 3460 D7
10 SPFK 84660 3249 C2
10 WLRD 84340 885 C5
100 OGDN 84404 1056 D5
200 WELV 84339 649 C1
300 CchC 84319 651 A2
300 CRFD 84015 1227 D3
300 FMTN 84025 1448 C1
300 KYVL 84037 1283 C7
300 MNDN 84325 524 D5
400 CchC 84339 649 C1
500 WELV 84339 589 C7
800 PTGV 84062 2712 D1
900 FMTN 84025 1346 C6
900 LOGN 84321 463 C7
1000 LOGN 84341 463 D6
1000 SGVL 84663 3036 C7
1200 ANFK 84003 2604 B4
1300 MPTN 84664 3144 A5
1400 OREM 84057 2820 C1
1400 SNST 84015 1227 D1
1700 CTRV 84014 1551 D5
1700 OREM 84057 2713 C7
1800 SNST 84015 1171 D7
1900 LYTN 84041 1282 E1
2100 NHLN 84341 463 D5
2600 LYTN 84041 1228 E7
2800 NHON 84414 998 D5
3900 PTVW 84414 998 D2
N 200 W SR-106
10 BNFL 84010 1551 D7
S 200 E
- GRLD 84312 520 E2
- LYTN 84041 1281 E2
10 ALPN 84004 2498 A4
10 ANFK 84003 2711 D1
10 BMCY 84302 767 A7
10 BNFL 84010 1551 E7
10 CTRV 84014 1551 E4
10 HDPK 84318 464 A1
10 HRCY 84032 2398 D4
10 HYRM 84319 651 B3
10 KYVL 84037 1345 D1
10 LEHI 84043 2603 C6
10 LNDN 84042 2713 B7
10 LOGN 84321 527 D3
10 MIDW 84049 2397 C3
10 OREM 84058 2820 D5
10 PRVO 84606 2928 C7
10 PTGV 84062 2712 E3
10 PVDN 84332 528 A7
10 PYSN 84651 3354 E5
10 SALM 84653 3356 B4
10 SGVL 84663 3143 C3
10 SHFD 84335 399 E3
10 SLCY 84111 1858 D3
10 SNQN 84655 3460 E7
10 SPFK 84660 3249 D3
10 WELV 84339 649 D2
10 WLRD 84340 885 D6
100 FMTN 84025 1448 D2
100 MLVI 84332 592 A3
100 SNQN 84655 3567 E1
200 BNFL 84010 1653 E1
500 PRVO 84606 3035 C1
700 BMCY 84302 828 A1
700 LYTN 84041 1282 E6
800 LYTN 84041 1283 A6
900 KYVL 84041 1283 A6
1000 OREM 84058 2927 E1
1300 SLCY 84115 1858 D7
1800 SLCY 84115 1964 D1
2100 SSLK 84115 1964 D1
2400 CRFD 84015 1281 E2
3900 SLkC 84107 1964 D7
4000 SLkC 84107 2070 D1
4500 MRRY 84107 2070 D2
4600 WSTR 84405 1172 D2
6200 CchC 84339 649 D5
6700 MDVL 84047 2176 D1
8600 PARA 84328 710 E4
13800 DRPR 84020 2388 D5
S 200 E SR-106
100 FMTN 84025 1448 D2
S 200 W
- FMTN 84025 1448 C2
- NBLY 84321 591 D5
- SNQN 84655 3567 D1
- WDHL 84653 3463 C1
10 ANFK 84003 2711 C1
10 BMCY 84302 766 E7
10 BNFL 84010 1551 D7
10 CchC 84339 649 C2
10 GRLD 84312 520 E2
10 HDPK 84318 463 E1
10 HRCY 84032 2398 C4
10 HYRM 84319 651 A3
10 KYVL 84037 1345 C1
10 LEHI 84043 2603 B7
10 LOGN 84321 527 C3
10 MIDW 84049 2397 B3
10 MNDN 84325 524 D7
10 MNTU 84324 768 B7
10 MNTU 84324 829 B1
10 PYSN 84651 3354 E5
10 SALM 84653 3356 A3
10 SGVL 84663 3143 C2
10 SHFD 84335 399 D3
10 SLCY 84101 1858 C3
10 SPFK 84660 3249 C3
10 WELV 84339 649 C2
10 WLRD 84340 885 C6
100 MLVI 84332 591 E3
100 OREM 84058 2820 D5
200 BNFL 84010 1653 D1
300 CchC 84319 651 A3
700 BMCY 84302 827 E1
800 OGDN 84404 1056 D6
1200 OREM 84058 2927 D1
1300 SLCY 84115 1858 C7
1300 SLCY 84115 1964 C1
1800 CRFD 84015 1281 D1
4200 CchC 84335 399 D6
4300 WSTR 84405 1172 D2
4500 MRRY 84107 2070 C2
9100 PARA 84328 710 D5
9300 CchC 84328 710 D6
11000 WDHL 84653 3356 C7
13400 DRPR 84020 2388 C4
S 200 W SR-106
10 BNFL 84010 1551 D7
200 BNFL 84010 1653 D1
S 200 W SR-165
400 HYRM 84319 651 D4
S 200 W SR-227
- FMTN 84025 1448 C2
W 200 N
- LYTN 84041 1281 D4
- PRVO 84601 2927 B6
- PVDN 84332 527 E6
- WPT 84015 1226 D4
10 ALPN 84004 2497 E4
10 BMCY 84302 766 E5
10 BNFL 84010 1551 D7
10 CTRV 84014 1551 D3
10 GRLD 84312 520 E1
10 HDPK 84318 399 E7
10 HDPK 84318 400 A6
10 HRCY 84032 2398 C3
10 HYRM 84319 651 A2
10 KYVL 84037 1345 A1
10 LEHI 84043 2603 B6
10 LOGN 84321 527 B2
10 MLVI 84332 591 E2
10 MNDN 84325 524 D6
10 MNTU 84324 768 C7
10 NSLK 84054 1653 A6
10 PRVO 84601 2928 C6
10 PTGV 84062 2712 D2
10 PVDN 84332 528 A6
10 SHFD 84335 399 D2
10 SNQN 84655 3460 D7
10 SPFK 84660 3249 C2
10 WELV 84339 649 C1
100 LNDN 84042 2713 A6
100 MIDW 84049 2397 B3
200 WLRD 84340 885 B5
300 SGVL 84663 3143 B1
400 ANFK 84003 2604 B7
400 NSLK 84054 1652 E6
400 PYSN 84651 3354 D5
400 SLCY 84103 1858 B2
500 HYRM 84319 650 E2
700 SLCY 84116 1858 A2
800 OGDN 84404 1056 B5
800 OREM 84057 2820 B4
1000 WBNF 84087 1551 A7
1200 CRFD 84015 1227 A4
1300 LOGN 84321 526 E2
1300 SLCY 84116 1857 D2
1400 KYVL 84037 1344 D1
1700 LNDN 84042 2712 B6
2100 CchC 84321 526 E2
6000 HRMN 84065 2385 C3
W 200 N SR-30
10 LOGN 84321 527 B2
1300 LOGN 84321 526 E2
2100 CchC 84321 526 E2
W 200 N SR-273
10 KYVL 84037 1345 C1
W 200 S
- BxEC 84337 521 B6
- SLCY 84104 1857 D3
10 ANFK 84003 2711 A1
10 BMCY 84302 766 E6
10 FMTN 84025 1448 C2
10 GRLD 84312 520 E2
10 HDPK 84318 464 A2
10 HRCY 84032 2398 C4
10 HYRM 84319 651 A3
10 LEHI 84043 2603 B7
10 MNDN 84325 524 D7
10 PRVO 84601 2928 C7
10 PTGV 84062 2712 D3
10 PVDN 84332 528 A7
10 SHFD 84335 399 D3
10 SLCY 84101 1858 B3
10 SNQN 84655 3567 D1
10 WELV 84339 649 C2
10 WLRD 84340 885 C6
100 ALPN 84004 2497 E5
100 PVDN 84332 527 E7
200 HDPK 84318 463 E1
200 LNDN 84042 2713 A7
200 LNDN 84057 2713 A7
200 SALM 84653 3356 A4
300 BNFL 84010 1551 C7
300 CRFD 84015 1227 C5
300 CRFD 84016 1227 C5
300 SPFK 84660 3249 C3
400 HYRM 84319 650 E3
400 SGVL 84663 3143 B2
500 UthC 84003 2711 A1
600 LOGN 84321 527 B3
600 SLCY 84104 1858 A3
700 LNDN 84042 2712 E7
800 PYSN 84651 3354 D5
1000 SRCS 84015 1227 B5
1000 SRCS 84016 1227 B5
1200 MTSV 84044 1056 A5
1400 LOGN 84321 526 E3
1500 SRCS 84075 1227 B5
1500 WPT 84015 1227 B5
1800 SRCS 84075 1226 E5
1800 WPT 84015 1226 E5
1900 CchC 84321 526 D3
2000 LNDN 84013 2712 C7
2000 VNYD 84013 2712 C7
2100 MTSV 84404 1055 D5
2400 PRVO 84601 2927 C7
3800 CchC 84321 525 D3
4500 WPT 84015 1225 E5
200 W
10 CchC 84339 649 C2
10 WELV 84339 649 C2
200 St S
10 HDPK 84318 464 A1
200 St W
8600 PARA 84319 710 D5
8600 PARA 84328 710 D5
200 St W SR-165
8600 PARA 84319 710 D4
8600 PARA 84328 710 D4
E 205 N
- SLCY 84103 1859 A2
N 205 W
1900 OREM 84057 2713 C7
W 205 N
100 OREM 84057 2820 C4
E 210 S
400 SHFD 84335 399 E3
400 SHFD 84335 400 A3
1700 SGVL 84663 3144 A2
N 210 E
10 MPTN 84664 3144 B6
1300 PTGV 84062 2712 D1
1500 PTGV 84062 2605 D7
1600 OREM 84057 2713 D7
1600 OREM 84057 2820 D1
N 210 W
- CTRV 84014 1551 D3
100 OREM 84057 2820 C4
1100 ANFK 84003 2604 B5
3500 PRVO 84604 2821 C7
S 210 E
- CTRV 84014 1551 E4
7800 MDVL 84070 2176 D4
7800 SLkC 84070 2176 D4
S 210 W
- CTRV 84014 1551 D3
- MDVL 84047 2176 C2
800 OREM 84058 2820 D7
3900 SLkC 84107 1964 C7
3900 SLkC 84107 2070 C1
W 210 N
700 OREM 84057 2820 B4
W 210 S
700 OREM 84058 2820 B5
800 SPFK 84660 3249 B3
E 215 N
600 LNDN 84042 2713 D6
E 220 N
- SLCY 84103 1858 D2
- SLCY 84103 1859 A2
600 ANFK 84003 2604 E7
700 HRCY 84032 2398 E3
900 ANFK 84003 2605 A7
E 220 S
- UthC 84003 2712 A2
800 OREM 84058 2820 E7
N 220 E
500 CTRV 84014 1551 E3
1300 LEHI 84043 2603 C4
2800 PRVO 84604 2928 C1
N 220 W
- PVDN 84332 527 E5
300 SALM 84653 3356 A3
1000 OREM 84057 2820 C2
1300 LOGN 84341 463 C6
S 220 E
600 SHFD 84335 399 E4
2000 OREM 84058 2927 E3
7600 MDVL 84047 2176 D3
8700 SNDY 84070 2176 D6
9400 SNDY 84070 2282 D1
S 220 W
10 OREM 84058 2820 C5
1100 OREM 84058 2927 C1
2600 SSLK 84115 1964 C3
W 220 N
700 WBNF 84087 1551 B7
1100 PRVO 84601 2928 A6
2600 PRVO 84601 2927 C6
W 220 S
200 OREM 84058 2820 C5
400 PTGV 84062 2712 C3
1600 PRVO 84601 2927 E7
E 225 N
800 LYTN 84041 1283 B4
1100 SGVL 84663 3143 E1
1100 SGVL 84663 3144 A1
N 225 E
- NHLN 84341 463 E4
- WbrC 84414 998 E7
300 HDPK 84318 400 A7
700 BNFL 84010 1551 E6
1100 LOGN 84341 463 E5
1400 LYTN 84041 1283 A2
1900 CTRV 84014 1448 E6
3500 NHON 84414 998 E3
N 225 W
800 BNFL 84010 1551 D6
1100 CTRV 84014 1551 D1
1500 HARR 84404 1056 D1
1600 NHON 84404 1056 D1
1700 LYTN 84041 1282 E1
2600 SNST 84015 1171 D6
3300 NHON 84414 998 D3
S 225 E
300 KYVL 84037 1345 D2
400 CTRV 84014 1551 E4
500 PVDN 84332 592 A1
800 SALM 84653 3356 B5
900 LYTN 84041 1283 A6
2100 CRFD 84015 1281 E2
4300 WSTR 84405 1172 D2
S 225 W
800 LYTN 84041 1282 E6
1700 PRRY 84302 827 E3
W 225 N
- PVDN 84332 527 E6
10 LYTN 84041 1282 D4
300 NSLK 84054 1652 E6
400 CRFD 84015 1227 C4
W 225 S
- PVDN 84332 527 E7
600 SHFD 84335 399 B3
800 OREM 84058 2820 B5
800 TMTN 84337 520 C6
900 CchC 84335 399 B3
900 LYTN 84041 1282 C5
E 228 S
- CRFD 84015 1227 E5
E 230 N
- SNQN 84655 3461 B7
600 ANFK 84003 2604 E7
600 LNDN 84042 2713 D6
E 230 S
- SLCY 84112 1859 D4
- SNQN 84655 3568 A1
300 OREM 84058 2820 E6
1000 OREM 84097 2821 B5
1000 PRVO 84606 2928 E7
1100 PYSN 84651 3355 B5
1400 SPFK 84660 3250 A3
N 230 E
400 SHFD 84335 399 E1
1500 LOGN 84341 463 E6
1800 OREM 84057 2713 D7
2500 NHLN 84341 463 E3
3500 PRVO 84604 2821 C7
N 230 W
- LOGN 84341 463 C5
300 PYSN 84651 3354 E4
1200 ANFK 84003 2604 B4
1400 OREM 84057 2820 C1
S 230 E
200 OREM 84058 2820 D5
6600 MDVL 84047 2176 D1
6600 MRRY 84047 2176 D1
8100 MDVL 84070 2176 D5
11000 SNDY 84070 2282 D5
13200 DRPR 84020 2388 D4
S 230 N
2800 PRVO 84601 2927 C6
S 230 W
300 OREM 84058 2820 C6
400 KYVL 84037 1345 C2
W 230 N
400 OREM 84057 2820 C4
W 230 S
400 ANFK 84003 2711 B2
700 SPFK 84660 3249 B3
1100 OREM 84058 2820 A5
2300 PRVO 84601 2927 C7
N 235 E
400 SGVL 84663 3143 D1
700 OREM 84057 2820 E3
N 235 W
900 OREM 84057 2820 C2
S 235 E
5400 MRRY 84107 2070 D5
S 235 W
1400 OREM 84058 2927 C2
W 235 N
- WELV 84339 649 C1
E 240 N
- OREM 84057 2820 E4
- SLCY 84103 1859 A2
E 240 S
700 OREM 84097 2821 A5
800 SALM 84653 3356 C4
N 240 E
- LOGN 84341 463 E7
600 KYVL 84037 1283 D7
800 DvsC 84037 1283 D6
900 ANFK 84003 2604 D5
1100 HARR 84404 1056 E2
1100 OREM 84057 2820 E2
N 240 W
- SNQN 84655 3460 D6
- UthC 84655 3460 D6
1300 LOGN 84341 463 C6
1600 OREM 84057 2713 C7
1600 OREM 84057 2820 C1
S 240 E
100 OREM 84058 2820 E5
500 SALM 84653 3356 B5
800 SGVL 84663 3143 C3
1400 OREM 84058 2927 E2
5000 WSTR 84405 1172 E3
7300 MDVL 84047 2176 D3
8500 SNDY 84070 2176 D6
S 240 W
100 OREM 84058 2820 C5
200 LNDN 84042 2713 A7
200 LNDN 84057 2713 A7
9800 SNDY 84070 2282 C2
W 240 N
- PRVO 84601 2927 B6
300 OREM 84057 2820 C4
400 LOGN 84321 527 C2
900 LNDN 84042 2712 D6
1200 SLCY 84116 1857 D2
W 240 S
600 LEHI 84043 2603 A7
700 OREM 84058 2820 B5
E 245 N
- SLCY 84103 1859 B2

Salt Lake City Street Index

STREET Block City ZIP Map# Grid

E 245 S
400 SGVL 84663 3143 D2
S 245 E
7200 MDVL 84047 2176 D2
S 245 W
13100 DRPR 84020 2388 C3
E 248 S
- CRFD 84015 1227 E4
E 250 N
- SLCY 84103 1859 B2
10 MIDW 84049 2397 C2
10 NSLK 84054 1653 A6
300 KYVL 84037 1345 D1
400 BNFL 84010 1551 E7
400 SGVL 84663 3143 D1
600 BNFL 84010 1552 A7
600 HRCY 84032 2398 E3
1200 PTGV 84062 2713 B2
2000 LYTN 84040 1283 E4
E 250 S
- SNQN 84655 3568 A1
10 ANFK 84003 2711 C2
400 HDPK 84318 464 B1
500 CRFD 84015 1227 E5
500 MIDW 84049 2397 D4
600 KYVL 84037 1345 E2
700 CRFD 84015 1228 A5
700 RVHT 84321 528 A4
800 BNFL 84010 1654 A1
900 BNFL 84010 1552 A7
900 LYTN 84041 1283 B5
900 OREM 84097 2821 A6
1700 SGVL 84663 3144 A2
N 250 E
- LYTN 84041 1229 A7
100 SHFD 84335 399 E2
300 MLVI 84332 592 A2
400 KYVL 84037 1283 D7
900 HARR 84404 1056 E3
1000 CTRV 84014 1551 E2
1300 BNFL 84010 1551 E5
1400 OREM 84057 2820 E1
1500 LOGN 84341 463 E6
1500 LYTN 84041 1283 A1
2900 NHON 84414 998 E4
2900 PRVO 84604 2928 C1
4000 SmtC 84098 1972 D6
4300 PRVO 84604 2821 C6
N 250 W
- CTRV 84014 1551 D2
- HARR 84414 998 D7
10 ANFK 84003 2711 B1
300 SHFD 84335 399 D2
400 SGVL 84663 3143 C1
500 HRCY 84032 2398 C3
700 BMCY 84302 766 E3
700 CRFD 84015 1227 D3
700 SGVL 84663 3036 C7
800 BNFL 84010 1551 D6
800 LOGN 84321 527 C1
800 PRVO 84604 2928 C5
800 SNST 84015 1227 D2
1000 LOGN 84341 463 C7
1400 ANFK 84003 2604 B4
1500 HARR 84404 1056 D1
1600 LYTN 84041 1282 E1
1900 SNST 84015 1171 D7
2600 LYTN 84041 1228 E6
2800 LEHI 84043 2603 B1
3000 NHON 84414 998 D3
3500 PRVO 84604 2821 C7
4300 PTVW 84414 998 D1
S 250 E
- CchC 84318 399 E5
- CchC 84321 591 E5
- CchC 84335 399 E4
- NBLY 84321 591 E5
- OREM 84058 2927 E2
10 HDPK 84318 464 A2
300 OREM 84058 2820 E6
400 SHFD 84335 399 E4
500 KYVL 84037 1345 D2
900 LYTN 84041 1283 A6
900 PRVO 84606 3035 C1
2200 BNFL 84010 1653 E4
2900 NHLN 84341 464 A2
4300 WSTR 84405 1172 D1
8600 SNDY 84070 2176 D6
9400 SNDY 84070 2282 D1
S 250 W
- PVDN 84332 527 E7
10 WLRD 84340 885 B6
200 BNFL 84010 1653 D3
300 LYTN 84041 1282 E5
400 KYVL 84037 1345 C2
400 PTGV 84062 2712 D4
500 ANFK 84003 2711 B2
500 UthC 84003 2711 B2
800 OREM 84058 2820 C7
900 PRVO 84601 3035 C1
1800 CRFD 84015 1281 D1
3200 NBLY 84321 591 D4
3700 NSLK 84054 1653 D6
4600 WSTR 84405 1172 D2
W 250 N
- LYTN 84041 1282 B4
10 CRFD 84015 1227 D4
10 MIDW 84049 2397 B3
300 BNFL 84010 1551 D7
600 LNDN 84042 2712 E6
700 HYRM 84319 650 E2
700 SPFK 84660 3249 B2
1600 WPT 84015 1227 A4
1900 MTSV 84404 1055 D4
3800 WPT 84015 1226 A4
W 250 S
- TMTN 84337 520 C6
10 KYVL 84037 1345 C2
200 LNDN 84042 2713 A7
300 BNFL 84010 1653 D1
400 FMTN 84025 1448 B2
500 SPFK 84660 3249 B3
600 MPTN 84664 3143 E7
600 MPTN 84664 3144 A7
900 LEHI 84043 2603 A7
1000 OREM 84058 2820 A5
4400 WbrC 84404 1054 C5
250 E
- CchC 84318 399 E6
- HDPK 84318 399 E6
S 250 E
900 FMTN 84025 1448 D4

E 255 S
1000 LYTN 84041 1283 C5
N 255 E
- LOGN 84321 527 E1
S 255 W
9000 SNDY 84070 2176 C7
9200 SNDY 84070 2282 B2
W 255 N
700 OREM 84057 2820 B4
W 255 S
10 OREM 84058 2820 C5
E 260 N
- PVDN 84332 528 A6
400 SHFD 84335 400 A2
800 HDPK 84318 400 C7
900 OREM 84097 2821 A4
1100 SPFK 84660 3249 E2
1300 LOGN 84321 528 C2
E 260 S
- SHFD 84335 400 A3
200 OREM 84058 2820 E6
1000 LYTN 84041 1283 C5
1000 OREM 84097 2821 B5
1000 PYSN 84651 3355 B5
N 260 E
- LEHI 84043 2603 C2
100 OREM 84057 2820 E4
200 PTGV 84062 2605 E7
1200 LOGN 84341 463 E7
1400 PTGV 84062 2712 E1
N 260 W
1200 OREM 84057 2820 C2
1300 LOGN 84341 463 C6
S 260 E
200 OREM 84058 2820 E5
500 ANFK 84003 2711 D2
7000 MDVL 84047 2176 D2
9100 SNDY 84070 2176 D7
S 260 W
200 OREM 84058 2820 C5
1200 PYSN 84651 3354 E7
1400 PYSN 84651 3461 E1
3800 NBLY 84321 591 D5
W 260 N
600 SPFK 84660 3249 B2
W 260 S
800 OREM 84058 2820 B5
E 265 N
10 OREM 84057 2820 D4
N 265 E
4600 PRVO 84604 2821 C5
N 265 W
2100 LEHI 84043 2603 B3
S 265 W
12300 DRPR 84020 2388 B2
W 265 N
1500 WPT 84015 1227 A4
W 265 S
900 OREM 84058 2820 A6
E 268 S
- CRFD 84015 1227 E5
E 270 N
- SALM 84653 3356 A3
500 LNDN 84042 2713 C6
700 HRCY 84032 2398 E3
E 270 S
- SNQN 84655 3568 B1
10 KYVL 84037 1345 C2
N 270 E
500 ANFK 84003 2604 D6
1800 OREM 84057 2713 E7
2500 NHLN 84341 463 E3
4000 PRVO 84604 2821 C6
N 270 W
300 TMTN 84337 520 D5
1600 PTGV 84062 2605 D7
S 270 E
900 SALM 84653 3356 B5
4400 MRRY 84107 2070 D2
7400 MDVL 84047 2176 D3
8100 MDVL 84070 2176 D5
S 270 W
10 OREM 84058 2820 C5
1600 OREM 84058 2927 C2
W 270 N
200 OREM 84057 2820 C4
W 270 S
10 KYVL 84037 1345 C2
10 OREM 84058 2820 D6
1700 PRVO 84601 2927 E7
E 275 N
200 LOGN 84321 528 A2
500 HDPK 84318 400 B7
1000 OREM 84097 2821 B4
1300 LYTN 84040 1283 C4
N 275 E
400 BNFL 84010 1551 E7
800 OREM 84057 2820 E3
1100 HARR 84404 1056 E3
3500 NHON 84414 998 E3
N 275 W
- HARR 84414 998 D7
- PTVW 84414 998 D4
800 BNFL 84010 1551 D6
800 LOGN 84321 527 C1
1100 CTRV 84014 1551 D1
1500 LYTN 84041 1282 E1
1500 OREM 84057 2820 C1
1700 NHON 84404 1056 D1
2500 SNST 84015 1171 D6
S 275 E
400 FMTN 84025 1448 D3
400 KYVL 84037 1345 D2
1800 CRFD 84015 1281 E1
4700 WSTR 84405 1172 E3
S 275 W
- CRFD 84015 1281 D2
700 LYTN 84041 1282 E6
2000 PRRY 84302 827 E4
4600 WSTR 84405 1172 D2
5900 MRRY 84107 2070 C6
W 275 N
100 CTRV 84014 1551 D3
400 CRFD 84015 1227 C4
W 275 S
600 TMTN 84337 520 D6
900 LYTN 84041 1282 C5
E 280 N
- SLCY 84103 1859 A2
800 OREM 84097 2821 A4
E 280 S
300 ALPN 84004 2498 A5

E 280 S
800 OREM 84097 2821 A6
800 PYSN 84651 3355 B5
N 280 W
- PVDN 84332 527 E5
- SNQN 84655 3460 D6
1100 PTGV 84062 2712 D1
1200 ANFK 84003 2604 B4
1400 OREM 84057 2820 C1
1600 OREM 84057 2713 C7
S 280 E
10 OREM 84058 2820 E5
1400 OREM 84058 2927 E2
7800 MDVL 84070 2176 D4
8600 SNDY 84070 2176 D6
S 280 W
- LEHI 84043 2710 B2
- UthC 84043 2710 B2
200 OREM 84058 2820 C6
300 LNDN 84042 2713 A7
400 LNDN 84057 2713 A7
1500 PYSN 84651 3461 E1
3900 NBLY 84321 591 D6
10000 SNDY 84070 2282 B2
W 280 N
- PVDN 84332 527 E5
800 OREM 84057 2820 B4
1200 SLCY 84116 1857 D2
W 280 S
- CTRV 84014 1551 D4
2300 PRVO 84601 2927 C7
N 285 E
1400 LYTN 84041 1283 A2
1800 OREM 84057 2713 E7
N 285 W
1700 LYTN 84041 1282 E1
S 285 E
9500 SNDY 84070 2282 D2
S 285 W
300 BNFL 84010 1653 D1
W 285 N
- WELV 84339 649 C1
W 285 S
1000 OREM 84058 2820 A6
E 288 S
- CRFD 84015 1227 E5
E 290 N
300 OREM 84057 2820 E4
900 PTGV 84062 2713 B2
1300 LOGN 84321 528 C2
N 290 E
- OREM 84057 2820 E2
- PRVO 84604 2821 C7
800 ANFK 84003 2604 D5
N 290 W
1300 LOGN 84341 463 C6
S 290 E
1700 OREM 84058 2927 E2
S 290 W
1000 PRVO 84601 3035 B2
W 290 N
100 OREM 84057 2820 D4
600 LNDN 84042 2712 E5
W 290 S
500 SPFK 84660 3249 B3
900 OREM 84058 2820 B6
E 300 N
10 ANFK 84003 2604 D7
10 BMCY 84302 766 E5
10 BNFL 84010 1551 E7
10 CRFD 84015 1227 E4
10 FMTN 84025 1448 D1
10 HDPK 84318 400 A7
10 HRCY 84032 2398 D3
10 HYRM 84319 651 C2
10 LEHI 84043 2603 C6
10 LOGN 84321 527 E2
10 MLVI 84332 591 E2
10 MNDN 84325 524 E5
10 PRVO 84606 2928 C6
10 PYSN 84651 3354 E4
10 SHFD 84335 399 E2
10 SLCY 84103 1858 C2
10 SNQN 84655 3460 E7
10 SPFK 84660 3249 D2
10 WELV 84339 649 D1
100 BMCY 84302 767 A5
100 CchC 84325 524 E5
100 MLVI 84332 592 A2
100 OREM 84057 2820 D4
100 PVDN 84332 528 A5
200 ALPN 84004 2498 A4
200 CTRV 84014 1551 E3
200 MIDW 84049 2397 C2
200 PTGV 84062 2712 E2
200 PYSN 84651 3355 A4
200 SALM 84653 3356 B3
200 KYVL 84037 1283 E7
600 LNDN 84042 2713 C5
600 MPTN 84664 3144 B6
600 PTGV 84062 2713 A2
700 NSLK 84054 1653 C6
700 OREM 84097 2821 A4
800 ANFK 84003 2605 A7
800 LYTN 84041 1283 B4
900 SGVL 84663 3143 E1
900 UthC 84003 2605 A7
1000 BNFL 84010 1552 B7
1000 KYVL 84037 1284 A7
1100 ANFK 84062 2605 B7
1100 LOGN 84321 528 B2
1100 LYTN 84040 1283 C4
1100 UthC 84062 2605 B7
1400 PRVO 84606 2929 A6
1400 PTGV 84062 2605 B7
6800 WbrC 84317 1060 D4
8600 WbrC 84317 1061 D4
E 300 N SR-184
10 SLCY 84103 1858 C2
E 300 S
- FMTN 84025 1448 D2
- MIDW 84049 2397 D4
- MNTU 84324 829 C1
- PVDN 84332 528 A7
- WshC 84049 2397 D4
10 BMCY 84302 766 E6
10 BNFL 84010 1653 E1
10 CTRV 84014 1551 E4
10 GRLD 84312 520 E2
10 HRCY 84032 2398 D4
10 HYRM 84319 651 C3
10 KYVL 84037 1345 C2

E 300 S
10 LEHI 84043 2603 C7
10 LOGN 84321 527 D4
10 MLVI 84332 591 E4
10 MNDN 84325 524 D7
10 PRVO 84606 2928 D7
10 PYSN 84651 3354 E5
10 SALM 84653 3356 B4
10 SGVL 84663 3143 C2
10 SHFD 84335 399 E3
10 SPFK 84660 3249 D3
10 WLRD 84340 885 C6
100 BMCY 84302 767 A6
100 MLVI 84332 592 A4
200 HDPK 84318 464 A1
200 WELV 84339 649 D3
300 PYSN 84651 3355 A5
400 OREM 84097 2820 E6
400 RVHT 84321 527 D4
400 SNQN 84655 3567 E1
400 SNQN 84655 3568 A1
500 ANFK 84003 2711 E2
500 CRFD 84015 1227 E5
500 SHFD 84335 400 A3
500 SLCY 84102 1858 E4
600 CTRV 84014 1552 A4
600 OREM 84097 2821 A6
700 CRFD 84015 1228 A5
700 SLCY 84102 1859 A4
900 KYVL 84037 1346 B1
1000 BNFL 84010 1654 A1
1100 PTGV 84062 2713 B3
1300 PRVO 84606 2929 A7
1400 SGVL 84663 3144 A2
1400 SPFK 84660 3250 A3
7100 HTVL 84317 1060 E5
7300 HTVL 84317 1061 A5
E 300 S SR-198
10 SPFK 84660 3249 D3
E 300 S SR-238
10 LOGN 84321 527 D4
E 300 S US-89
10 PRVO 84606 2928 D7
N 300 E
- MLVI 84332 592 A2
- WELV 84339 649 D4
10 ALPN 84004 2498 A4
10 ANFK 84003 2711 D1
10 BMCY 84302 767 A4
10 CRFD 84015 1227 E4
10 GRLD 84312 520 E1
10 HDPK 84318 400 A7
10 HDPK 84318 464 A1
10 HRCY 84032 2398 D3
10 HYRM 84319 651 C2
10 KYVL 84037 1345 D1
10 MIDW 84049 2397 C3
10 MPTN 84664 3144 B7
10 PRVO 84606 2928 D6
10 PYSN 84651 3355 A4
10 SALM 84653 3356 B3
10 SGVL 84663 3143 D1
10 SNQN 84655 3460 E7
100 ANFK 84003 2604 D7
100 FMTN 84025 1448 D1
100 LOGN 84321 527 E2
200 SHFD 84335 399 E2
300 KYVL 84037 1283 D7
300 PVDN 84332 528 B5
500 BNFL 84010 1551 E6
800 OREM 84057 2820 E2
800 SPFK 84660 3249 D1
900 LOGN 84321 463 E7
1000 CTRV 84014 1551 E2
1000 LEHI 84043 2603 C4
1300 PTGV 84062 2712 E1
1500 LOGN 84341 463 E6
1500 LYTN 84041 1283 A1
1500 PTGV 84062 2605 E7
1800 CTRV 84014 1448 E6
1800 NHON 84404 1056 E1
2200 PRVO 84604 2928 D2
2300 NHLN 84341 463 E3
2800 NHON 84414 998 E4
3700 PRVO 84604 2821 C7
N 300 W
- MNDN 84325 524 C5
- PVDN 84332 527 E6
10 ANFK 84003 2711 B1
10 BMCY 84302 766 E4
10 CRFD 84015 1227 D4
10 GRLD 84312 520 E2
10 HRCY 84032 2398 C3
10 KYVL 84037 1345 C1
10 LEHI 84043 2603 B5
10 LOGN 84321 527 C3
10 MIDW 84049 2397 B3
10 MPTN 84664 3144 A6
10 SLCY 84103 1858 B2
10 SNQN 84655 3460 D7
10 SPFK 84660 3249 C2
200 HYRM 84319 651 A1
200 SGVL 84663 3143 B1
300 KYVL 84037 1283 C7
400 SHFD 84335 399 C1
500 ANFK 84003 2604 B6
600 PRVO 84601 2928 B5
600 SGVL 84663 3036 B7
700 SLCY 84103 1754 B7
800 PRVO 84604 2928 B5
800 PTGV 84062 2712 D1
900 LOGN 84321 463 C7
1000 LYTN 84041 1282 E2
1000 OREM 84057 2820 C3
1200 SPFK 84660 3142 C7
1200 UthC 84660 3142 C7
1300 BNFL 84010 1551 D5
1400 LOGN 84341 463 C6
1400 SNST 84015 1227 D1
1700 CTRV 84014 1448 D7
1700 NHON 84404 1056 D1
1800 SNST 84015 1171 D7
2600 LYTN 84041 1228 E6
3300 PTVW 84414 998 D4
3700 PRVO 84604 2821 B6
4600 PRVO 84097 2821 B4
4600 SmtC 84098 1972 C5
N 300 W SR-186
10 SLCY 84103 1858 B3
N 300 W US-89
100 SLCY 84103 1858 B2
700 SLCY 84103 1754 B7

S 300 E
- CchC 84328 710 E5
- GRLD 84312 520 E2
- GRLD 84312 521 A2
10 ALPN 84004 2498 A4
10 ANFK 84003 2711 D1
10 BMCY 84302 767 A6
10 BNFL 84010 1551 E7
10 CTRV 84014 1551 E4
10 HRCY 84032 2398 D4
10 HYRM 84319 651 C3
10 KYVL 84037 1345 D1
10 LNDN 84042 2713 C7
10 LOGN 84321 527 E3
10 OREM 84058 2820 E5
10 PRVO 84606 2928 C7
10 PTGV 84062 2712 E3
10 PVDN 84332 528 A7
10 PYSN 84651 3355 A5
10 SALM 84653 3356 B4
10 SGVL 84663 3143 D2
10 SLCY 84111 1858 D3
10 SNQN 84655 3460 E7
10 SPFK 84660 3249 D3
10 WELV 84339 649 E2
100 MNTU 84324 768 D7
100 MNTU 84324 829 D1
100 SHFD 84335 399 E3
100 WLRD 84340 885 D6
200 LEHI 84043 2603 C7
200 MLVI 84332 592 A3
300 SNQN 84655 3567 E1
400 UthC 84043 2603 C7
500 PRVO 84606 3035 C1
600 PVDN 84332 592 A1
700 LYTN 84041 1283 A5
800 FMTN 84025 1448 D4
1300 SLCY 84111 1858 D6
1600 SLCY 84115 1964 D1
2100 SSLK 84115 1964 D2
2200 BNFL 84010 1653 E4
3900 SLkC 84107 1964 D6
4000 SLkC 84107 2070 D1
4300 WSTR 84405 1172 E2
6200 MRRY 84107 2070 D7
6400 MRRY 84107 2176 D1
6600 MDVL 84047 2176 D2
7400 UthC 84660 3249 D5
7500 SNDY 84047 2176 D3
8000 MDVL 84070 2176 D4
8000 SNDY 84070 2176 D4
8200 SLkC 84070 2176 D5
9000 PARA 84328 710 E5
9200 SNDY 84070 2282 D1
11900 DRPR 84020 2282 D7
12200 DRPR 84020 2388 D1
S 300 W
- CchC 84319 591 D7
- DRPR 84020 2282 B6
- SJDN 84095 2282 B4
- SNDY 84095 2282 B4
- TMTN 84337 520 D6
10 ANFK 84003 2711 B1
10 BMCY 84302 766 E6
10 BNFL 84010 1551 D7
10 CRFD 84015 1227 C4
10 FMTN 84025 1448 C2
10 GRLD 84312 520 E2
10 HRCY 84032 2398 C5
10 KYVL 84037 1345 C1
10 LNDN 84042 2713 A6
10 LOGN 84321 527 C4
10 MIDW 84049 2397 B3
10 MNTU 84324 768 B7
10 PRVO 84601 2928 B7
10 PYSN 84651 3354 E6
10 SALM 84653 3356 A3
10 SGVL 84663 3143 B2
10 SHFD 84335 399 C3
10 SLCY 84101 1858 B6
10 SNQN 84655 3460 D7
10 SPFK 84660 3249 C3
100 SNQN 84655 3567 D1
200 HYRM 84319 651 A3
300 CchC 84319 651 A3
300 WELV 84339 649 C2
500 LEHI 84043 2603 B7
600 BNFL 84010 1653 D1
600 LEHI 84043 2710 B1
600 PRVO 84601 3035 B1
600 UthC 84043 2710 B1
700 BMCY 84302 827 E1
800 OREM 84058 2820 C7
900 OGDN 84404 1056 D7
1000 OREM 84058 2927 C1
1300 SLCY 84115 1858 B6
1400 PYSN 84651 3461 E1
1600 SLCY 84115 1964 B1
1700 CRFD 84015 1281 D1
2100 SSLK 84115 1964 B4
3600 NBLY 84321 591 C5
4000 RVDL 84405 1172 C1
4400 WSTR 84405 1172 D3
5500 MRRY 84107 2070 C5
6300 MRRY 84107 2176 A1
6800 MDVL 84047 2176 B2
8600 CchC 84319 710 C4
8600 PARA 84319 710 C4
8700 PARA 84328 710 C4
8900 SNDY 84070 2176 B7
9000 SNDY 84070 2282 B2
10000 SJDN 84070 2282 B2
S 300 W SR-106
1400 BNFL 84010 1653 D2
S 300 W SR-186
10 SLCY 84101 1858 B3
W 300 N
10 ANFK 84003 2604 C7
10 BNFL 84010 1551 D7
10 FMTN 84025 1448 C1
10 HDPK 84318 399 E7
10 HDPK 84318 400 A6
10 HRCY 84032 2398 C3
10 HYRM 84319 651 A2
10 LOGN 84321 527 C2
10 MLVI 84332 591 E2
10 MNDN 84325 524 D5
10 OREM 84057 2820 D4
10 SGVL 84663 3143 C1
10 SNQN 84655 3460 D7
10 WELV 84339 649 C1
100 CRFD 84015 1227 D4

W 300 N
400 SHFD 84335 399 C2
400 SLCY 84103 1858 B2
500 LEHI 84043 2603 A6
500 SLCY 84116 1858 A2
600 BMCY 84302 766 D5
600 PTGV 84062 2712 C2
600 PYSN 84651 3354 D4
600 SPFK 84660 3249 B2
800 KYVL 84037 1283 A7
800 PRVO 84601 2928 A6
900 SLCY 84116 1857 E2
1000 UthC 84043 2603 A6
1100 LYTN 84041 1282 C4
2200 PRVO 84601 2927 D6
7100 CchC 84325 523 E2
7100 CchC 84325 524 A2
W 300 N SR-107
10 CRFD 84015 1227 D4
W 300 S
- BxEC 84337 521 B6
- MIDW 84049 2397 B4
10 BMCY 84302 766 E6
10 BNFL 84010 1653 D1
10 GRLD 84312 520 D2
10 HRCY 84032 2398 C4
10 HYRM 84319 651 B3
10 KYVL 84037 1345 C2
10 LOGN 84321 527 C4
10 MLVI 84332 591 E4
10 OREM 84058 2820 D6
10 PRVO 84601 2928 B7
10 PTGV 84062 2712 D3
10 PVDN 84332 528 A7
10 PYSN 84651 3354 E5
10 SGVL 84663 3143 C2
10 SHFD 84335 399 D3
10 SNQN 84655 3567 D1
10 WELV 84339 649 C3
100 ANFK 84003 2711 B2
100 PVDN 84332 527 E7
100 SALM 84653 3356 A4
400 LYTN 84041 1282 D5
400 SALM 84653 3355 E4
600 LEHI 84043 2603 A7
700 SLCY 84104 1858 A4
700 SPFK 84660 3249 B3
900 SLCY 84104 1857 D4
1200 LNDN 84042 2712 D7
1800 PRVO 84601 2927 D7
2500 DvsC 84087 1652 D1
2500 WDCR 84087 1652 D1
5200 SLCY 84104 1855 E4
W 300 S US-89
10 PRVO 84601 2928 B7
300 St E
600 TMTN 84337 520 E4
300 St E SR-82
600 TMTN 84337 520 E4
S 300 E
300 RVHT 84321 527 E4
E 300 S Cir
100 ANFK 84003 2711 D2
W 301 N
- LYTN 84041 1282 E4
E 310 N
- LEHI 84043 2603 E6
- SLCY 84103 1859 B2
E 310 S
900 OREM 84097 2821 A6
N 310 W
1300 LOGN 84341 463 C6
S 310 W
- SJDN 84095 2282 B5
900 PRVO 84601 3035 B1
2300 PRRY 84302 827 E4
W 310 N
200 OREM 84057 2820 C4
1300 MIDW 84049 2396 D2
E 315 S
500 LYTN 84041 1283 A5
800 OREM 84097 2821 A6
N 315 W
600 LOGN 84321 527 C1
W 315 S
10 OREM 84058 2820 D6
E 320 N
- KYVL 84037 1283 C7
- PRVO 84606 2928 C4
100 SALM 84653 3356 B3
300 OREM 84057 2820 E4
500 OREM 84097 2820 E4
600 HRCY 84032 2398 E3
900 LOGN 84321 528 A2
E 320 S
600 SALM 84653 3356 C4
1000 LYTN 84041 1283 C5
N 320 E
400 SALM 84653 3356 B2
500 KYVL 84037 1283 D7
N 320 W
200 OREM 84057 2820 C4
300 HDPK 84318 399 E7
1100 ANFK 84003 2604 B5
1100 LOGN 84341 463 C7
1700 OREM 84057 2713 C7
S 320 E
100 OREM 84058 2820 E5
800 SALM 84653 3356 B5
1400 OREM 84058 2927 E2
6200 MRRY 84107 2070 D7
S 320 W
10 OREM 84058 2820 C5
100 TMTN 84337 520 D6
300 LNDN 84042 2713 A7
300 SHFD 84335 399 E1
600 PRVO 84601 3035 B1
1700 OREM 84058 2927 C2
1900 OREM 84057 2713 C7
W 320 N
700 LNDN 84042 2712 E5
W 320 S
1100 OREM 84058 2820 A6
E 325 N
- SLCY 84103 1859 B2
E 325 S
900 KYVL 84037 1346 A2
900 LYTN 84041 1283 B5
N 325 E
400 OREM 84057 2820 E4
700 BMCY 84302 767 A3
1000 HARR 84404 1056 E3
1200 BNFL 84010 1551 E5

N 325 E
1200 CTRV 84014 1551 E1
1300 LYTN 84041 1283 A2
1900 OREM 84057 2713 E7
N 325 W
700 BNFL 84010 1551 C6
800 KYVL 84037 1283 C6
900 HARR 84404 1056 D3
1400 OREM 84057 2820 C1
2500 SNST 84015 1171 C6
3000 PTVW 84414 998 D4
4600 PRVO 84097 2821 B5
S 325 E
1200 BNFL 84010 1653 E2
4700 WSTR 84405 1172 E2
S 325 W
- SNQN 84655 3567 D1
100 OREM 84058 2820 C5
1500 OREM 84058 2927 C2
2300 CRFD 84015 1281 D2
3300 BNFL 84010 1653 D5
W 325 N
- BMCY 84302 766 D4
- LYTN 84041 1281 E4
400 CRFD 84015 1227 C3
800 LNDN 84042 2712 D5
1000 HYRM 84319 650 D1
W 325 S
400 LYTN 84041 1282 E6
2000 MPTN 84664 3143 D7
E 330 N
- PRVO 84606 2929 A6
- SLCY 84103 1859 B2
400 LNDN 84042 2713 C5
400 OREM 84097 2820 E4
1100 PYSN 84651 3355 B4
1300 PTGV 84062 2713 C2
1400 LEHI 84043 2603 E6
E 330 S
500 ANFK 84003 2711 E2
1300 PRVO 84606 2928 E7
1400 PRVO 84606 2929 A7
N 330 E
10 ANFK 84003 2711 D1
10 SHFD 84335 399 E2
200 OREM 84057 2820 E4
2500 NHLN 84341 463 E3
N 330 W
- SNQN 84655 3460 D6
1400 PTGV 84062 2605 D7
S 330 E
400 ANFK 84003 2711 D2
500 UthC 84003 2711 D2
S 330 W
500 OREM 84058 2820 C6
1200 PYSN 84651 3354 E7
1200 PYSN 84651 3461 E1
13100 DRPR 84020 2388 B3
W 330 N
- MIDW 84049 2396 E2
W 330 S
600 ANFK 84003 2711 A2
600 UthC 84003 2711 A2
800 LOGN 84321 527 B4
800 OREM 84058 2820 B6
E 335 N
- SLCY 84103 1859 D1
S 335 E
3400 SSLK 84115 1964 D6
S 335 W
200 OREM 84058 2820 C6
E 340 N
- SLCY 84103 1859 B2
600 LNDN 84042 2713 C5
700 ANFK 84003 2604 E7
E 340 S
200 OREM 84058 2820 E6
400 SHFD 84335 400 A3
700 ANFK 84003 2711 E2
700 ANFK 84003 2712 A2
900 SALM 84653 3356 C4
N 340 E
600 LNDN 84042 2713 C5
600 OREM 84057 2820 E3
800 ANFK 84003 2604 D5
1500 PTGV 84062 2605 E7
1500 PTGV 84062 2712 E1
N 340 W
100 PYSN 84651 3354 E5
600 OREM 84057 2820 C3
1300 LOGN 84341 463 C6
1700 LEHI 84043 2603 B3
S 340 E
6200 MRRY 84107 2070 D7
W 340 N
2200 SLCY 84116 1857 B2
S 345 E
4600 MRRY 84107 2070 D2
6700 MDVL 84047 2176 D1
W 345 N
10 HDPK 84318 399 E7
10 HDPK 84318 400 A7
W 345 S
1100 LYTN 84041 1282 C5
E 350 N
- LYTN 84040 1283 E4
- PVDN 84332 592 A2
- SLCY 84103 1859 A2
10 NSLK 84054 1653 A6
10 OREM 84057 2820 D4
100 NSLK 84054 1653 A6
200 ALPN 84004 2498 A4
200 MLVI 84332 592 A2
300 SALM 84653 3356 B3
300 SHFD 84335 399 E1
400 BNFL 84010 1551 E7
500 SHFD 84335 400 A1
600 BNFL 84010 1552 A7
700 KYVL 84037 1283 E7
700 PTGV 84062 2713 A2
700 PYSN 84651 3355 B4
800 ANFK 84003 2605 A7
800 LYTN 84041 1283 B4
800 PRVO 84606 2928 D6
1100 OREM 84097 2821 B4
E 350 S
- PRVO 84606 2928 C7
10 CRFD 84015 1227 D5
10 CRFD 84016 1227 D5
100 LOGN 84321 527 D4
300 HYRM 84319 651 C3
300 LEHI 84043 2603 D7

Salt Lake City Street Index

STREET Block	City	ZIP	Map#	Grid
E 350 S				
400	ANFK	84003	2711	D2
400	OREM	84097	2820	E6
400	SNQN	84655	3568	A1
600	BMCY	84302	767	B6
700	CRFD	84015	1228	A5
700	RVHT	84321	528	A4
700	SHFD	84335	400	A3
800	KYVL	84037	1345	E2
900	OREM	84097	2821	B6
1500	SGVL	84663	3144	A2
N 350 E				
-	TMTN	84337	521	A3
300	SHFD	84335	399	E1
400	HDPK	84318	400	A6
400	KYVL	84037	1283	D7
500	SGVL	84663	3143	D1
700	ANFK	84003	2604	D6
800	TMTN	84337	520	E4
900	LOGN	84321	463	E7
900	LOGN	84321	527	E1
1000	FMTN	84025	1345	D6
1400	OREM	84057	2820	E1
1500	LYTN	84041	1283	A1
1800	CTRV	84014	1448	E6
2100	PRVO	84604	2928	D3
3200	PRVO	84604	2821	C7
3400	NHON	84414	998	E3
N 350 W				
-	SNQN	84655	3460	D6
-	UthC	84655	3460	D6
10	ANFK	84003	2711	B1
10	SHFD	84335	399	C2
600	KYVL	84037	1283	C7
600	SGVL	84663	3036	B7
600	SGVL	84663	3143	B1
1100	CTRV	84014	1551	D1
1200	ANFK	84003	2604	B4
1400	BNFL	84010	1551	C5
1400	SNST	84015	1227	C1
1600	OREM	84057	2820	C1
1600	PTGV	84062	2605	D7
1700	LYTN	84041	1282	E1
1700	NHON	84404	1056	C1
1800	OREM	84057	2713	C7
1800	SNST	84015	1171	C7
2300	HARR	84414	998	C6
2600	LYTN	84041	1228	E6
3900	PTVW	84414	998	D3
S 350 E				
-	SPFK	84660	3142	D4
10	CRFD	84015	1227	E4
10	FMTN	84025	1448	D2
10	LOGN	84321	527	E3
10	NSLK	84054	1653	B7
10	OREM	84058	2820	E5
10	PTGV	84062	2712	E3
300	SHFD	84335	399	E3
400	SNQN	84655	3567	E1
500	KYVL	84037	1345	D2
900	PRVO	84606	3035	D2
1000	PYSN	84651	3355	A7
1600	SGVL	84663	3143	D5
1700	OREM	84058	2927	E2
1800	BNFL	84010	1653	E3
1900	CRFD	84015	1281	E1
5100	WSTR	84405	1172	E3
7100	MDVL	84047	2176	D2
S 350 W				
-	OGDN	84404	1056	C6
-	UthC	84043	2710	B2
10	CRFD	84015	1227	D4
100	BNFL	84010	1551	D7
600	LYTN	84041	1282	E6
600	OREM	84058	2820	C7
700	LNDN	84042	2713	A4
700	LOGN	84321	527	C5
800	SALM	84653	3356	A5
900	GRLD	84312	520	E3
1000	OREM	84058	2927	C1
1300	BNFL	84010	1653	C2
1400	PYSN	84651	3461	E1
1600	PRRY	84302	827	D3
2300	CRFD	84015	1281	C2
5900	MRRY	84107	2070	B6
W 350 N				
-	WbrC	84404	1054	B4
10	CRFD	84015	1227	D4
300	HDPK	84318	399	E7
300	OREM	84057	2820	C4
600	TMTN	84337	520	D5
600	UthC	84660	3249	B2
800	KYVL	84037	1283	A7
1200	PRVO	84601	2928	A6
1600	WPT	84015	1227	A4
1700	WPT	84015	1226	E4
1800	PRVO	84601	2927	D6
3000	LYTN	84041	1281	D4
W 350 S				
10	KYVL	84037	1345	C2
10	MIDW	84049	2397	B4
400	ANFK	84003	2711	B2
500	SPFK	84660	3249	C3
600	LEHI	84043	2603	B7
600	OREM	84058	2820	B6
900	LYTN	84041	1282	C5
1100	LOGN	84321	527	A4
1400	LEHI	84043	2602	E7
1800	PRVO	84601	2927	D7
3500	LNDN	84042	2712	D7
E 355 N				
-	SLCY	84103	1859	B2
N 355 W				
500	OREM	84057	2820	C3
W 355 S				
10	OREM	84058	2820	D6
E 360 N				
900	PTGV	84062	2713	B2
E 360 S				
200	LEHI	84043	2603	C7
700	OREM	84097	2821	A6
900	PRVO	84606	2928	E7
N 360 E				
200	OREM	84057	2820	E4
400	SALM	84653	3356	B2
500	ANFK	84003	2604	D6
1500	LOGN	84341	463	E6
1800	PTGV	84062	2605	E7
1900	PRVO	84604	2928	D3
N 360 W				
10	CRFD	84015	1227	C4
600	OREM	84057	2820	C3
S 360 E				
10	ANFK	84003	2711	D1
600	SALM	84653	3356	B5
2600	SSLK	84115	1964	D4
8800	SNDY	84070	2176	D6
10100	SNDY	84070	2282	D3
S 360 W				
10	CRFD	84015	1227	C4
10	OREM	84058	2820	C5
1200	PYSN	84651	3354	E7
1200	PYSN	84651	3461	E1
1400	OREM	84058	2927	C2
W 360 N				
100	SHFD	84335	399	D1
2300	PRVO	84601	2927	C6
W 360 S				
500	SPFK	84660	3249	B3
1000	OREM	84058	2820	A6
2100	PRVO	84601	2927	D7
S 365 W				
11400	WDHL	84653	3356	B7
11400	WDHL	84653	3463	B1
W 365 N				
1300	MIDW	84049	2396	D2
E 370 N				
1000	UthC	84003	2605	A7
1300	PTGV	84062	2713	B2
E 370 S				
-	SNQN	84655	3568	B1
100	KYVL	84037	1345	D2
800	OREM	84097	2821	A6
1000	LYTN	84041	1283	C5
1100	PYSN	84651	3355	B5
N 370 E				
10	ANFK	84003	2711	D1
800	ANFK	84003	2604	D5
1500	PTGV	84062	2605	E7
2500	NHLN	84341	463	E3
N 370 W				
300	OREM	84057	2820	C4
600	SPFK	84660	3249	C2
3800	PRVO	84604	2821	B6
S 370 E				
200	SHFD	84335	399	E3
300	LEHI	84043	2603	C7
6200	MRRY	84107	2070	E7
6300	MRRY	84107	2176	E1
S 370 W				
300	SNDY	84070	2282	B1
2000	PRRY	84302	827	D4
W 370 N				
200	PYSN	84651	3354	E4
900	OREM	84057	2820	B4
1000	HYRM	84319	650	D1
2400	PRVO	84601	2927	C6
W 370 S				
300	ANFK	84003	2711	B2
800	LOGN	84321	527	B4
E 375 N				
800	OREM	84097	2821	A4
8600	WbrC	84317	1061	D4
E 375 S				
1000	LYTN	84041	1283	C5
N 375 E				
900	HARR	84404	1056	E3
1500	OREM	84057	2820	E1
3300	NHON	84414	998	E3
N 375 W				
1000	LOGN	84341	463	C7
1400	OREM	84057	2820	C1
2300	HARR	84414	998	C6
2500	SNST	84015	1171	C6
4200	PTVW	84414	998	C2
S 375 E				
-	OGDN	84401	1115	E4
200	CRFD	84015	1227	E5
1400	KYVL	84037	1345	D4
1700	SGVL	84663	3143	D5
1800	OREM	84058	2927	E3
4700	WSTR	84405	1172	E2
5000	SOGN	84405	1172	E3
7600	MDVL	84047	2176	D3
S 375 W				
500	OGDN	84404	1056	C6
1900	LEHI	84043	2710	B3
4800	WSTR	84405	1172	C3
W 375 N				
-	BNFL	84010	1551	D7
200	HDPK	84318	399	E7
400	CRFD	84015	1227	C3
W 375 S				
100	OGDN	84404	1056	D5
700	TMTN	84337	520	D6
N 376 E				
10	SHFD	84335	399	E2
E 380 N				
-	UthC	84003	2605	A7
400	ANFK	84003	2604	D7
600	HYRM	84319	651	D1
700	HRCY	84032	2398	E3
1000	LNDN	84042	2713	D5
1000	PRVO	84606	2928	E6
E 380 S				
400	SHFD	84335	400	A4
N 380 E				
1100	PTGV	84062	2712	E1
N 380 W				
-	SNQN	84655	3460	D6
10	OREM	84057	2820	C5
700	PRVO	84601	2928	B5
1200	PRVO	84604	2928	B4
2300	LEHI	84043	2603	B5
4000	PRVO	84604	2821	B6
S 380 E				
100	SHFD	84335	399	E3
400	ANFK	84003	2711	D2
4000	SLkC	84107	2070	D1
S 380 W				
6100	MRRY	84107	2070	B7
6500	MRRY	84107	2176	B1
W 380 N				
-	OGDN	84404	1056	C4
200	WLRD	84340	885	C5
W 380 S				
400	ANFK	84003	2711	B2
1600	PRVO	84601	2927	E7
E 380 N Cir				
1000	UthC	84003	2605	A7
E 385 N				
-	SLCY	84103	1859	D1
N 385 W				
-	BNFL	84010	1551	C7
400	SHFD	84335	399	C1
S 385 E				
10300	SNDY	84070	2282	D3
S 385 W				
2200	PRRY	84302	827	D4
W 385 N				
10	HDPK	84318	399	E7
10	HDPK	84318	400	A7
E 390 N				
900	LNDN	84042	2713	D5
1000	UthC	84003	2605	A7
N 390 E				
-	PTGV	84062	2712	E1
900	ANFK	84003	2604	D5
1500	PTGV	84062	2605	E7
2200	PRVO	84604	2928	D2
N 390 W				
900	SNST	84015	1227	C2
1000	ANFK	84003	2604	B5
1500	PTGV	84062	2605	D7
S 390 E				
-	RVHT	84321	527	E5
4300	SLkC	84107	2070	D1
10600	SNDY	84070	2282	E4
W 390 N				
2100	PRVO	84601	2927	D6
E 400 N				
-	PTGV	84062	2713	B2
-	UthC	84003	2605	A7
-	UthC	84655	3460	A3
10	ANFK	84003	2604	D7
10	BMCY	84302	766	E4
10	FMTN	84025	1448	D1
10	HRCY	84032	2398	D3
10	LNDN	84042	2713	B5
10	MIDW	84049	2397	B2
10	MNDN	84325	524	D5
10	MPTN	84664	3144	B6
10	OREM	84057	2820	E4
10	PRVO	84606	2928	D6
10	PTGV	84062	2712	D2
10	PYSN	84651	3354	E4
10	SALM	84653	3356	B2
10	SGVL	84663	3143	D1
10	SHFD	84335	399	E1
10	SNQN	84655	3460	E6
10	WELV	84339	649	E1
100	BMCY	84302	767	A4
200	BNFL	84010	1551	E7
200	CchC	84319	651	C1
200	PYSN	84651	3355	A4
200	TMTN	84337	520	E5
400	HYRM	84319	651	C1
400	OREM	84097	2820	E4
400	SNQN	84655	3461	A6
500	BNFL	84010	1552	B7
600	OREM	84097	2821	A4
600	WELV	84339	650	A1
800	GNLA	84655	3460	A3
800	KYVL	84037	1283	E7
800	WELV	84339	650	A1
1100	FTHT	84037	1284	A7
1100	KYVL	84037	1284	A7
1100	SPFK	84660	3250	A2
1100	SPFK	84663	3250	A2
1400	LEHI	84043	2603	E6
1600	UthC	84660	3250	A2
6800	HTVL	84317	1060	D4
6800	WbrC	84317	1060	D4
E 400 N SR-147				
1100	SPFK	84660	3250	A2
1100	SPFK	84663	3250	A2
1600	UthC	84660	3250	A2
E 400 S				
-	PRVO	84606	3035	D1
-	PTGV	84062	2713	B3
-	WELV	84339	649	D3
10	ANFK	84003	2711	D2
10	BMCY	84302	766	E6
10	BNFL	84010	1653	E1
10	HRCY	84032	2398	D4
10	HYRM	84319	651	B4
10	LOGN	84321	527	D4
10	MNDN	84325	524	E7
10	OREM	84058	2820	D6
10	PRVO	84606	2928	D7
10	PVDN	84332	528	A7
10	SGVL	84663	3143	E3
10	SHFD	84335	399	E4
10	SLCY	84101	1858	E4
10	SLCY	84111	1858	E4
10	SNQN	84655	3567	E1
100	BMCY	84302	767	A7
100	PYSN	84651	3354	E6
300	PYSN	84651	3355	A6
300	SPFK	84660	3249	D3
400	BNFL	84010	1654	A2
400	OREM	84097	2820	E6
400	RVHT	84321	527	E4
400	SNQN	84655	3568	A1
500	CRFD	84015	1227	E5
500	LEHI	84043	2603	D7
500	OREM	84097	2821	A6
500	SLCY	84102	1858	E4
600	RVHT	84321	528	A4
700	CRFD	84015	1228	A5
700	KYVL	84037	1345	E2
700	SHFD	84335	400	A4
700	SLCY	84102	1859	A4
900	FTHT	84037	1346	A2
900	KYVL	84037	1346	A2
900	LYTN	84041	1283	B6
1100	SGVL	84663	3144	A3
1400	LOGN	84321	528	C4
1700	UthC	84606	3144	A3
7400	HTVL	84317	1061	A5
E 400 S SR-186				
10	SLCY	84101	1858	E4
10	SLCY	84111	1858	E4
500	SLCY	84102	1858	E4
700	SLCY	84102	1859	A4
E 400 S SR-282				
1300	SLCY	84102	1859	B4
N 400 E				
-	MLVI	84332	592	A2
10	ANFK	84003	2711	D1
10	BMCY	84302	767	A4
10	BNFL	84010	1551	E6
10	CTRV	84014	1551	E2
10	GRLD	84312	521	A1
10	HDPK	84318	400	B7
10	HDPK	84318	464	B1
10	HRCY	84032	2398	D3
10	HYRM	84319	651	C2
10	KYVL	84037	1345	D1
10	LNDN	84042	2713	C5
10	OREM	84057	2820	E4
10	OREM	84097	2820	E4
10	PRVO	84606	2928	D6
10	PTGV	84062	2712	E2
10	PVDN	84332	528	B6
10	PYSN	84651	3355	A4
10	SALM	84653	3356	B3
10	SGVL	84663	3143	D1
10	SNQN	84655	3460	E7
10	SPFK	84660	3249	D2
100	LOGN	84321	527	E2
300	CchC	84321	528	B6
300	LOGN	84321	527	C3
300	PVDN	84321	528	B6
400	KYVL	84037	1283	D7
500	CchC	84318	400	B7
600	LEHI	84043	2603	C5
700	SGVL	84663	3036	D7
900	ANFK	84003	2604	D5
900	LOGN	84321	463	E7
1000	LOGN	84341	463	E7
1300	MPTN	84664	3144	B5
1700	OREM	84057	2713	E7
1700	OREM	84097	2713	E7
2200	NHLN	84341	463	E4
3300	NHON	84414	998	E3
4400	CchC	84335	400	B7
N 400 W				
-	PRVO	84604	2928	B3
-	PRVO	84606	3035	D1
-	PVDN	84332	527	E6
-	SNQN	84655	3460	D6
10	BMCY	84302	766	E4
10	CRFD	84015	1227	C4
10	CTRV	84014	1551	D3
10	HRCY	84032	2398	C3
10	HYRM	84319	651	A2
10	KYVL	84037	1345	C1
10	LEHI	84043	2603	B6
10	LOGN	84321	527	C3
10	MIDW	84049	2397	A3
10	NSLK	84054	1652	E6
10	PRVO	84601	2928	B6
10	PYSN	84651	3354	E4
10	SGVL	84663	3143	B1
10	SLCY	84101	1858	B2
10	SLCY	84103	1858	B2
200	ALPN	84004	2497	D4
300	KYVL	84037	1283	B7
500	SHFD	84335	399	C1
600	LNDN	84042	2713	A4
600	SGVL	84663	3036	B7
700	OREM	84057	2820	C3
700	SLCY	84103	1754	B7
700	SLCY	84116	1754	B7
800	LYTN	84041	1282	E3
800	PTGV	84062	2712	D1
900	LOGN	84321	463	C7
1300	ANFK	84003	2604	B4
1400	BNFL	84010	1551	C5
1400	CTRV	84014	1448	D7
1400	SNST	84015	1227	C1
1600	MPTN	84664	3144	A5
1700	OREM	84057	2713	C7
2300	HARR	84414	998	C6
2300	SNST	84015	1171	C6
2400	LOGN	84341	463	C4
3000	SPFK	84660	3142	C4
3100	PTVW	84414	998	C4
4600	SmtC	84098	1972	B5
6200	CchC	84335	399	C1
14000	CchC	84325	523	E1
14000	CchC	84325	524	A1
N 400 W SR-101				
10	HYRM	84319	651	A2
S 400 E				
-	GRLD	84312	521	A2
-	MLVI	84332	592	B2
-	PTGV	84062	2712	E3
-	RVHT	84321	527	E4
10	ANFK	84003	2711	D2
10	BMCY	84302	767	A6
10	BNFL	84010	1551	E7
10	CRFD	84015	1227	E4
10	CTRV	84014	1551	E4
10	HRCY	84032	2398	D4
10	HYRM	84319	651	C3
10	KYVL	84037	1345	D1
10	LEHI	84043	2603	C6
10	LNDN	84042	2713	C7
10	LOGN	84321	527	E3
10	MIDW	84049	2397	C3
10	OREM	84058	2820	E6
10	OREM	84097	2820	E6
10	PRVO	84606	2928	D7
10	PYSN	84651	3355	A5
10	SALM	84653	3356	B4
10	SGVL	84663	3143	D4
10	SLCY	84111	1858	D3
10	SNQN	84655	3460	E7
10	SPFK	84660	3249	D3
100	ALPN	84004	2498	A4
200	HDPK	84318	464	B1
300	SNQN	84655	3567	E1
400	SNQN	84655	3568	A1
500	PRVO	84606	3035	D1
700	FMTN	84025	1448	E3
900	BMCY	84302	828	A1
900	PVDN	84332	592	B2
1000	CchC	84321	528	B5
1000	PVDN	84332	528	B5
1200	MPTN	84664	3251	B1
1300	SLCY	84115	1858	D6
1400	OREM	84058	2927	E2
1600	SLCY	84115	1964	E1
1700	MPTN	84664	3143	D4
1800	BNFL	84010	1653	E3
2100	MPTN	84663	3143	D4
2100	SGVL	84664	3143	D4
3300	SSLK	84115	1964	D5
3900	SLkC	84107	1964	D7
6200	MRRY	84107	2070	E7
8700	SNDY	84070	2176	D6
8800	UthC	84653	3356	E2
8800	UthC	84660	3356	E2
10200	SNDY	84070	2282	D3
S 400 E SR-238				
-	LOGN	84321	527	E4
300	RVHT	84321	527	E4
S 400 E US-89				
1500	SGVL	84663	3143	D5
1700	MPTN	84664	3143	D5
S 400 W				
-	PRVO	84606	3035	D1
-	SNQN	84655	3460	D7
-	SNQN	84655	3567	D1
-	TMTN	84337	520	D6
10	BMCY	84302	766	E7
10	CTRV	84014	1551	D4
10	HRCY	84032	2398	C4
10	HYRM	84319	651	A3
10	KYVL	84037	1345	B1
10	LNDN	84042	2713	A7
10	LOGN	84321	527	C3
10	OREM	84058	2820	C7
10	PRVO	84601	2928	B7
10	SGVL	84663	3143	B2
10	SHFD	84335	399	C3
10	SLCY	84101	1858	B3
200	SALM	84653	3356	A4
300	ANFK	84003	2711	B2
400	LNDN	84042	2820	A1
500	LEHI	84043	2603	B7
600	PRVO	84601	3035	B1
700	BMCY	84302	827	E1
800	BNFL	84010	1653	C2
800	CchC	84335	399	C6
1200	OREM	84058	2927	C1
1200	PYSN	84651	3354	D7
1300	SLCY	84115	1858	B7
1400	PYSN	84651	3461	E1
1500	SLCY	84115	1964	B1
2100	SSLK	84115	1964	B2
2300	CRFD	84015	1281	C2
4500	WSTR	84405	1172	C2
6500	MRRY	84107	2176	B2
6700	MDVL	84047	2176	B2
7900	CchC	84319	710	C3
8200	CchC	84319	651	C7
8500	UthC	84660	3249	B7
8500	UthC	84660	3356	B1
W 400 N				
-	LYTN	84041	1282	B4
-	SALM	84653	3355	E2
-	UthC	84043	2603	A6
-	WLRD	84340	883	C4
10	ANFK	84003	2604	B7
10	BMCY	84302	766	E4
10	CRFD	84015	1227	D3
10	FMTN	84025	1448	D1
10	HRCY	84032	2398	C3
10	KYVL	84037	1283	C7
10	LEHI	84043	2603	C6
10	LNDN	84042	2713	A5
10	MLVI	84332	591	E2
10	MNDN	84325	524	D5
10	OREM	84057	2820	D4
10	PRVO	84601	2928	C6
10	PTGV	84062	2712	D2
10	PYSN	84651	3354	E4
10	SALM	84653	3356	A2
10	SGVL	84663	3143	C1
10	SHFD	84335	399	D1
10	SNQN	84655	3460	D6
10	SPFK	84660	3249	C2
10	WELV	84339	649	C1
100	SLCY	84103	1858	B2
200	CchC	84319	651	A1
200	HYRM	84319	651	A1
400	TMTN	84337	520	D5
500	HYRM	84319	650	E1
500	OGDN	84404	1056	B4
600	UthC	84660	3249	C2
600	WBNF	84087	1551	B7
700	SLCY	84116	1858	A2
900	LOGN	84321	527	B2
900	UthC	84651	3354	D4
1200	MTSV	84404	1056	A4
1200	OREM	84057	2819	E4
1300	MTSV	84404	1055	E4
1300	WBNF	84087	1550	E7
1700	SLCY	84116	1857	C2
1800	WPT	84015	1226	E3
1800	WPT	84015	1227	A3
4300	LNDN	84042	2712	B5
4300	UthC	84003	2712	B5
W 400 N SR-147				
10	SPFK	84660	3249	C2
600	UthC	84660	3249	C2
W 400 S				
-	BxEC	84337	521	B6
-	CchC	84339	649	C3
-	GRLD	84312	520	E2
-	LEHI	84043	2602	C7
-	PRVO	84606	3035	D1
-	SNQN	84655	3567	C1
10	BNFL	84010	1653	D1
10	HRCY	84032	2398	C4
10	HYRM	84319	651	B4
10	KYVL	84037	1345	C2
10	LOGN	84321	527	C4
10	NSLK	84054	1754	A1
10	OREM	84058	2820	C6
10	PRVO	84601	2928	B7
10	PVDN	84332	528	A7
10	PYSN	84651	3354	E6
10	SHFD	84335	399	D4
10	SLCY	84101	1858	B4
100	ANFK	84003	2711	C2
100	CchC	84319	651	B4
100	PVDN	84332	527	E7
100	WELV	84339	649	C3
200	LNDN	84042	2713	A7
200	LNDN	84057	2713	A7
300	LEHI	84043	2603	B7
300	SALM	84653	3356	A4
400	SGVL	84663	3143	A3
500	LNDN	84042	2712	E7
600	BMCY	84302	766	D7
700	SGVL	84663	3142	D3
700	SLCY	84104	1858	B4
900	LYTN	84041	1282	D5
900	SLCY	84104	1857	D4
1300	OREM	84058	2819	E6
3700	WbrC	84404	1054	D5
3800	CchC	84321	525	D4
5300	CchC	84325	524	E4
5300	CchC	84325	525	A4
W 400 S SR-77				
10	SGVL	84663	3143	A3
700	SGVL	84663	3142	D3
W 400 S SR-186				
10	SLCY	84101	1858	C4
400 E				
-	TMTN	84337	521	A4
400 St N				
10	LOGN	84321	527	D2
500	LOGN	84321	528	A2
400 St N US-89				
10	LOGN	84321	527	D2
500	LOGN	84321	528	A2
400 St S				
-	LOGN	84321	527	B4
E 400 S Cir				
1600	BNFL	84010	1654	C1
E 400N				
-	MLVI	84332	592	A2
E 405 N				
-	SLCY	84103	1859	A1
E 405 S				
400	LYTN	84041	1283	A5
E 410 N				
400	HDPK	84318	400	B7
E 410 S				
-	WELV	84339	649	D3
1100	SPFK	84660	3249	E4
1100	SPFK	84660	3250	A3
S 410 E				
700	SALM	84653	3356	B5
7400	MDVL	84047	2176	E3
S 410 W				
700	OGDN	84404	1056	C6
W 410 N				
600	ANFK	84003	2604	A7
800	LNDN	84042	2712	D5
W 410 S				
1900	PRVO	84601	2927	D7
E 415 N				
-	SLCY	84103	1859	D1
S 415 E				
7600	MDVL	84047	2176	E4
10000	SNDY	84070	2282	D3
E 420 N				
600	PRVO	84606	2928	D6
700	ANFK	84003	2604	E7
E 420 S				
400	PTGV	84062	2712	E3
400	SHFD	84335	400	A4
1100	PYSN	84651	3355	B6
1300	PRVO	84606	2928	E7
N 420 E				
10	OREM	84097	2820	E5
2500	PRVO	84604	2928	D2
N 420 W				
600	LEHI	84043	2603	B5
1000	ANFK	84003	2604	B5
4700	PRVO	84097	2821	B5
S 420 E				
100	SHFD	84335	399	E3
300	PTGV	84062	2712	E3
500	SALM	84653	3356	B5
8000	SNDY	84070	2176	E4
8600	UthC	84660	3356	E1
10300	SNDY	84070	2282	E3
S 420 W				
200	ANFK	84003	2711	B2
900	SALM	84653	3356	A6
4000	MRRY	84123	2070	B1
7500	BxEC	84340	941	D3
W 420 N				
1000	OREM	84057	2820	A4
W 420 S				
2300	PRVO	84601	2927	C7
S 424 E				
1800	OREM	84058	2927	E3
E 425 N				
-	LYTN	84040	1283	E4
300	HDPK	84318	400	A6
800	ANFK	84003	2604	E7
800	ANFK	84003	2605	A7
1000	OGDN	84404	1057	B4
E 425 S				
200	KYVL	84037	1345	D2
500	LYTN	84041	1283	A6
600	OGDN	84404	1057	A6
N 425 E				
10	SHFD	84335	399	E2
300	ALPN	84004	2498	A4
500	TMTN	84337	520	E5
900	OGDN	84404	1056	E3
1700	NHON	84414	1056	E1
3400	NHON	84414	998	E3
N 425 W				
800	OREM	84057	2820	C3
1000	CTRV	84014	1551	D2
1900	HARR	84414	998	C7
2600	SNST	84015	1171	C6
2900	LEHI	84043	2603	B1
3400	LEHI	84043	2496	B7
4100	PTVW	84414	998	C2
S 425 E				
-	OGDN	84401	1115	E3
200	HDPK	84318	464	B1
500	CRFD	84015	1227	E5
700	BMCY	84302	828	A1
7600	SNDY	84047	2176	E3
S 425 W				
-	PVDN	84332	527	E7
10	BNFL	84010	1551	C7
200	BNFL	84010	1653	C1
400	PRRY	84302	827	D3
1800	CRFD	84015	1281	C1
4900	WSTR	84405	1172	C3
7400	BxEC	84340	941	D3
W 425 N				
-	SGVL	84663	3143	A1
500	LNDN	84042	2712	E5
W 425 S				
100	OGDN	84404	1056	D6
200	CTRV	84014	1551	D4
300	LYTN	84041	1282	D6
E 426 N				
200	ALPN	84004	2498	A4
E 430 N				
500	ANFK	84003	2604	E7
900	PTGV	84062	2713	B2
1200	OREM	84097	2821	B4
E 430 S				
-	PTGV	84062	2713	C3
-	SNQN	84655	3567	D1
-	SNQN	84655	3568	B1
N 430 E				
1100	OGDN	84404	1056	E2
1300	OREM	84097	2820	E1
4100	PRVO	84604	2821	D6
N 430 W				
1700	OREM	84057	2713	C7
2200	LEHI	84043	2603	B3
S 430 E				
-	PTGV	84062	2712	E4
10	OREM	84097	2820	E5
4100	SLkC	84107	2070	E1
6900	MDVL	84047	2176	E2
S 430 W				
-	PRVO	84601	2928	B7
500	OGDN	84404	1056	C6
800	HRCY	84032	2398	C5
800	SALM	84653	3356	A5
1400	OREM	84058	2927	C1
W 430 N				
2400	PRVO	84601	2927	C6
W 430 S				
-	LOGN	84321	527	B4
1100	OREM	84058	2820	A6
1200	PRVO	84601	2928	A7
1800	PRVO	84601	2927	D7
E 435 N				
1100	OREM	84097	2821	B4
N 435 E				
800	OREM	84097	2820	E3
W 435 S				
-	SRCS	84075	1226	C5
E 440 N				
-	PRVO	84606	2929	A6
700	OREM	84097	2821	A4
900	PTGV	84062	2713	B2
900	SGVL	84663	3143	E1
1100	SPFK	84663	3250	A2
1300	PRVO	84606	2928	E6
E 440 S				
600	HYRM	84319	651	D4
N 440 E				
-	PRVO	84604	2928	D3
N 440 W				
-	OGDN	84404	1056	C4
-	SNQN	84655	3460	D7
10	ANFK	84003	2711	B1
700	PRVO	84601	2928	B5
000	PRVO	84604	2928	B6
1000	OREM	84057	2820	C2
1400	MPTN	84664	3144	A5
1800	LYTN	84041	1282	E1
3500	PRVO	84604	2821	B7
S 440 E				
2200	SSLK	84115	1964	E2
6200	MRRY	84107	2070	E7
6300	MRRY	84107	2176	E1
8500	SNDY	84070	2176	E6
10100	SNDY	84070	2282	E3
S 440 W				
500	OREM	84058	2820	C6
700	OGDN	84404	1056	C6
1700	WDCR	84010	1653	C2
W 440 N				
-	SNQN	84655	3460	D6
200	PYSN	84651	3354	E4
500	ANFK	84003	2604	B7
500	OREM	84057	2820	C4
W 440 S				
10	SALM	84653	3356	B4
500	OREM	84058	2820	C6
E 442 N				
100	LOGN	84321	527	E2
E 442 S				
-	CRFD	84015	1227	D5
E 445 N				
-	SLCY	84103	1859	A1
E 445 S				
500	OREM	84097	2821	A6
S 445 E				
-	ANFK	84003	2711	D2
S 445 W				
11200	SJDN	84095	2282	B6
W 445 S				
900	OREM	84058	2820	B6
E 450 N				
-	LEHI	84043	2603	E6
-	MLVI	84332	591	E2
-	MLVI	84332	592	A2
10	OREM	84057	2820	D4
200	LNDN	84042	2713	C5
300	SGVL	84663	3143	D1
500	OGDN	84404	1056	E4
600	PYSN	84651	3355	A4
700	OGDN	84404	1057	A4
700	WshC	84032	2398	E3
800	ANFK	84003	2604	E7
800	ANFK	84003	2605	A7
900	PRVO	84606	2928	E6
1000	BNFL	84010	1552	B6
E 450 S				
-	ANFK	84003	2711	D2
10	FMTN	84025	1448	D3
10	MIDW	84049	2397	C4
10	SHFD	84335	399	D4
300	CRFD	84015	1227	E5
300	HDPK	84318	464	A2
400	OREM	84097	2820	E6
400	SNQN	84655	3568	A1
500	BNFL	84010	1654	A1
600	CRFD	84015	1228	A5
800	SHFD	84335	400	B4
900	PTGV	84062	2713	B3
1400	SGVL	84663	3144	A3
N 450 E				
-	PTGV	84062	2605	E7
-	PTGV	84062	2712	E1
-	SGVL	84663	3143	D1
10	WELV	84339	649	E1
200	ANFK	84003	2604	D7
600	LNDN	84042	2713	C5
700	TMTN	84337	520	E4
900	OGDN	84404	1056	E3
1300	BNFL	84010	1551	E5
1300	OREM	84097	2820	E1
1400	PRVO	84604	2928	D4
1700	NHON	84414	1056	E1
2900	NHON	84414	998	E4
N 450 W				
-	PTGV	84062	2605	C5
-	SNQN	84655	3460	D6

Block	City	ZIP	Map#	Grid
N 450 W				
100	LYTN	84041	1282	E4
300	CRFD	84015	1227	C3
400	OREM	84057	2820	C3
600	LOGN	84321	527	C1
700	SGVL	84663	3036	B6
800	KYVL	84041	1283	B6
800	PTGV	84062	2712	D1
800	SNST	84015	1227	C2
1000	BMCY	84302	766	E3
1100	ANFK	84003	2604	B5
1100	CTRV	84014	1551	D1
1700	PRVO	84604	2928	B3
1900	CTRV	84014	1448	D6
2300	HARR	84414	998	C6
2500	PTVW	84414	998	C6
2500	SNST	84015	1171	C6
3100	SGVL	84663	3143	B1
3800	PRVO	84604	2821	B6
4600	PRVO	84097	2821	B5
S 450 E				
10	CRFD	84015	1227	E4
10	OREM	84097	2820	E5
100	WELV	84339	649	E2
200	HDPK	84318	464	B2
300	SALM	84653	3356	B4
400	PRVO	84606	2928	D7
900	BMCY	84302	828	A1
1000	OREM	84097	2927	E1
1100	KYVL	84037	1345	D4
1700	OREM	84058	2927	E2
2800	BNFL	84010	1653	E4
6000	MRRY	84107	2070	E7
7800	SNDY	84070	2176	E4
12300	DRPR	84020	2388	E1
S 450 W				
-	BMCY	84302	767	A6
-	NBLY	84321	591	C3
10	LNDN	84042	2713	A6
100	OREM	84058	2820	C5
200	LYTN	84041	1282	E5
300	ANFK	84003	2711	B2
300	LOGN	84321	527	C4
700	BNFL	84010	1653	C1
1500	PRVO	84601	3035	B3
1600	LEHI	84043	2710	B2
1700	SLCY	84115	1964	B1
2200	PRRY	84302	827	D4
2300	CRFD	84015	1281	C2
3000	MPTN	84664	3251	A4
4500	WSTR	84405	1172	C2
W 450 N				
-	CRFD	84015	1227	B3
-	LYTN	84041	1281	D4
-	SGVL	84663	3143	C1
-	SNQN	84655	3460	D6
10	LNDN	84042	2713	B5
10	OREM	84057	2820	D4
100	HDPK	84318	399	E6
400	TMTN	84337	520	D5
700	ANFK	84003	2604	A7
800	KYVL	84037	1283	A7
1000	PRVO	84601	2928	A6
1800	PRVO	84601	2927	D6
3000	WPT	84015	1226	C3
W 450 S				
10	FMTN	84025	1448	D3
700	OREM	84058	2820	B6
800	PYSN	84651	3354	D6
900	LYTN	84041	1282	D5
2300	SGVL	84663	3142	C3
E 450 N Cir				
1000	UthC	84003	2605	A7
S 455 E				
10	SHFD	84335	399	E3
300	SHFD	84335	400	A4
3500	SSLK	84115	1964	E6
6800	MDVL	84047	2176	E2
10700	SNDY	84070	2282	E4
S 455 W				
9200	SNDY	84070	2176	B7
9200	SNDY	84070	2282	B1
E 460 N				
-	SLCY	84103	1859	A1
400	MPTN	84664	3144	B6
E 460 S				
300	LEHI	84043	2603	C7
800	OREM	84097	2821	A6
900	PRVO	84606	2928	E7
N 460 E				
1600	MPTN	84664	3144	B5
2500	PRVO	84604	2928	D2
N 460 W				
10	OREM	84057	2820	C5
10	SALM	84653	3355	E3
800	LEHI	84043	2603	B5
800	SALM	84653	3248	E7
800	UthC	84660	3248	E7
1400	PTGV	84062	2605	C7
S 460 E				
100	LOGN	84321	527	E3
200	ANFK	84003	2711	D2
2200	SSLK	84115	1964	E2
10200	SNDY	84070	2282	E3
S 460 W				
10	SALM	84653	3355	E3
10	SALM	84653	3356	A3
600	TMTN	84337	520	D7
1300	OREM	84058	2927	C1
1400	PYSN	84651	3461	D1
1900	LEHI	84043	2710	B3
W 460 N				
500	OREM	84057	2820	C4
600	ANFK	84003	2604	A7
2300	PRVO	84601	2927	C6
W 460 S				
200	OREM	84058	2820	C6
1900	PRVO	84601	2927	D7
S 465 E				
10400	SNDY	84070	2282	E4
S 465 W				
1300	OREM	84058	2927	C1
W 465 N				
1000	OREM	84057	2820	A4
W 465 S				
400	SPFK	84660	3249	B4
1300	OREM	84058	2819	E6
1300	OREM	84058	2820	A6
E 470 N				
-	LEHI	84043	2603	D6
10	BNFL	84010	1551	E6
1100	OREM	84097	2821	B4
E 470 S				
1000	PYSN	84651	3355	B6
1100	PTGV	84062	2713	B3
N 470 E				
10	SHFD	84335	400	A2
800	OREM	84097	2820	E3
800	PTGV	84062	2712	E1
1800	OREM	84097	2713	E7
2200	PRVO	84604	2928	D2
N 470 W				
10	ANFK	84003	2711	B1
400	LEHI	84043	2603	B6
1000	OREM	84057	2820	C2
S 470 E				
10	OREM	84097	2820	E5
100	ANFK	84003	2711	D1
500	SGVL	84663	3143	D3
700	RVHT	84321	527	E5
S 470 W				
200	SGVL	84663	3143	B2
400	SPFK	84660	3249	B4
W 470 N				
-	LEHI	84043	2603	B6
100	SHFD	84335	399	D1
300	SPFK	84660	3249	C2
600	LOGN	84321	527	B2
2000	WPT	84015	1226	E3
2200	SLCY	84116	1857	B1
2700	PRVO	84601	2927	C6
W 470 S				
-	PRVO	84601	2928	B7
200	ANFK	84003	2711	B2
200	LNDN	84042	2713	A7
600	OREM	84058	2820	B6
1600	PRVO	84601	2927	D7
E 475 N				
10	NSLK	84054	1653	B6
300	ANFK	84003	2604	D7
400	OGDN	84404	1056	E4
700	OREM	84097	2821	A4
800	ANFK	84003	2605	A7
E 475 S				
10	KYVL	84037	1345	D2
N 475 E				
700	SGVL	84663	3036	D7
900	OREM	84097	2820	E2
1100	OGDN	84404	1056	E2
1700	NHON	84414	1057	A1
3500	NHON	84414	998	E3
3700	NHON	84414	999	A3
N 475 W				
300	CRFD	84015	1227	C3
400	HRCY	84032	2398	C3
1400	SNST	84015	1227	C1
2300	SNST	84015	1171	C6
S 475 E				
-	ANFK	84003	2711	D2
-	SGVL	84663	3143	D3
300	OREM	84097	2820	E6
600	CTRV	84014	1551	E4
6500	SWBR	84405	1172	E7
6800	SWBR	84405	1228	E1
9800	SNDY	84070	2282	E2
S 475 W				
-	SPFK	84660	3249	C3
1000	FMTN	84025	1448	B4
1900	WDCR	84010	1653	C3
3200	BNFL	84010	1653	C5
4500	WSTR	84405	1172	C2
7400	BxEC	84340	941	D3
W 475 N				
400	CTRV	84014	1551	E3
500	CRFD	84015	1227	C3
1600	WPT	84015	1227	A3
W 475 S				
-	FMTN	84025	1447	E3
-	FMTN	84025	1448	A3
100	OGDN	84404	1056	D6
E 480 N				
-	SPFK	84663	3249	E2
-	SPFK	84663	3250	A2
200	SHFD	84335	399	E1
E 480 S				
900	ALPN	84004	2498	B5
1500	PTGV	84062	2713	C4
N 480 E				
3900	PRVO	84604	2821	D6
N 480 W				
10	HYRM	84319	651	A2
300	ANFK	84003	2604	B7
700	OREM	84057	2820	C3
S 480 E				
2200	SSLK	84115	1964	E2
S 480 W				
-	TMTN	84337	520	D6
900	SALM	84653	3355	E6
7500	BxEC	84340	941	D4
9200	SNDY	84070	2176	B7
9200	SNDY	84070	2282	B1
W 480 N				
10	LNDN	84042	2713	B5
500	ANFK	84003	2604	A7
500	SPFK	84660	3249	B2
2100	PRVO	84601	2927	D6
W 480 S				
900	LOGN	84321	527	B4
E 485 S				
500	OREM	84097	2821	A6
S 485 W				
-	PVDN	84332	527	D7
E 490 N				
-	OGDN	84404	1057	A4
10	ANFK	84003	2604	C7
10	SHFD	84335	399	D1
800	LNDN	84042	2713	D5
1000	PTGV	84062	2713	B2
N 490 E				
10	SHFD	84335	400	A2
4200	PRVO	84604	2821	D6
N 490 W				
10	ANFK	84003	2711	B1
100	LYTN	84041	1228	E6
1800	OREM	84057	2713	C7
2200	LEHI	84043	2603	B2
S 490 E				
-	CRFD	84015	1227	E6
-	SHFD	84335	400	A3
4100	SLkC	84107	2070	E1
S 490 W				
500	OREM	84058	2820	C6
1200	OREM	84058	2927	C1
W 490 N				
1000	OREM	84057	2820	A4
2400	PRVO	84601	2927	C6
W 490 S				
500	OREM	84058	2820	B6
1100	PRVO	84601	2928	A7
N 490 W Cir				
500	ANFK	84003	2604	B6
E 500 N				
-	HYRM	84319	651	C1
-	SNQN	84655	3460	E6
-	WbrC	84317	1060	E4
-	WbrC	84317	1061	A4
10	BMCY	84302	766	E4
10	FMTN	84025	1346	D7
10	HRCY	84032	2398	D3
10	KYVL	84037	1283	D7
10	LEHI	84043	2603	C6
10	LOGN	84321	527	E2
10	MLVI	84332	591	E2
10	MLVI	84332	592	A2
10	OREM	84057	2820	D4
10	PRVO	84606	2928	D6
10	PYSN	84651	3354	E4
10	SLCY	84103	1858	D1
10	SPFK	84660	3249	D2
100	ANFK	84003	2604	D6
100	BMCY	84302	767	A4
100	CTRV	84014	1551	E3
100	WELV	84339	589	D7
200	CchC	84339	589	D7
300	SGVL	84663	3143	D1
400	LNDN	84042	2713	C5
500	CchC	84319	651	C1
500	OREM	84097	2820	E4
500	PYSN	84651	3355	A4
600	LOGN	84321	528	A2
600	OGDN	84404	1057	A4
600	OREM	84097	2821	A4
600	WshC	84032	2398	D3
800	ANFK	84003	2605	A6
1000	LYTN	84040	1283	C4
1300	BNFL	84010	1552	B6
E 500 S				
-	SHFD	84335	400	B4
10	ANFK	84003	2711	D2
10	BMCY	84302	766	E7
10	BNFL	84010	1653	E1
10	FMTN	84025	1448	D3
10	GRLD	84312	520	E2
10	HRCY	84032	2398	D5
10	HYRM	84319	651	B4
10	MIDW	84049	2397	C4
10	PRVO	84606	2928	D7
10	PVDN	84332	592	A1
10	PYSN	84651	3354	E6
10	SGVL	84663	3143	C3
10	SHFD	84335	399	D4
10	SLCY	84111	1858	E4
10	WELV	84339	649	D3
100	BMCY	84302	767	A7
100	LOGN	84321	527	D4
100	PTGV	84062	2712	E3
100	PYSN	84651	3355	A6
100	RVHT	84321	527	D4
300	CRFD	84015	1227	E5
400	OREM	84097	2820	E6
400	UthC	84003	2711	D2
500	BNFL	84010	1654	A1
500	SGVL	84663	3144	A3
500	SLCY	84102	1858	E4
600	RVHT	84321	528	A4
800	OREM	84097	2821	A6
1000	PTGV	84062	2713	B3
1000	SLCY	84102	1859	B4
1100	SPFK	84660	3249	E4
1100	SPFK	84660	3250	A3
1400	SLCY	84108	1859	B4
1400	SLCY	84112	1859	B4
7400	HTVL	84317	1061	C6
7800	WbrC	84317	1061	C6
E 500 S SR-186				
1000	SLCY	84102	1859	B4
1400	SLCY	84108	1859	B4
1400	SLCY	84112	1859	B4
E 500 S SR-269				
10	SLCY	84111	1858	C4
N 500 E				
-	LOGN	84341	463	E5
10	ANFK	84003	2711	D1
10	CRFD	84015	1227	E4
10	GRLD	84312	521	A1
10	HDPK	84318	400	B7
10	HDPK	84318	464	B1
10	HRCY	84032	2398	D3
10	HYRM	84319	651	C2
10	KYVL	84037	1345	E1
10	LEHI	84043	2603	D6
10	PRVO	84606	2928	D6
10	PTGV	84062	2712	E2
10	PYSN	84651	3355	A5
10	SALM	84653	3356	B3
100	ANFK	84003	2604	D7
100	OREM	84097	2820	E4
200	BMCY	84302	767	A4
200	CTRV	84014	1551	E3
200	LOGN	84321	527	E2
200	SGVL	84663	3143	D1
300	KYVL	84037	1283	E7
400	SPFK	84660	3249	D1
500	LNDN	84042	2713	C5
600	BNFL	84010	1551	E6
800	SGVL	84663	3036	D7
800	UthC	84651	3355	A4
900	LOGN	84321	463	E7
1000	NSLK	84054	1653	B4
1000	OGDN	84404	1056	E3
1300	MPTN	84664	3144	B5
1400	PTGV	84062	2605	E7
1800	NHON	84414	1057	A1
1900	OREM	84097	2713	E7
2700	NHON	84414	999	A5
3100	NHON	84414	998	E4
3100	PRVO	84604	2928	D1
3600	PRVO	84604	2821	D7
4300	CchC	84318	400	B6
N 500 W				
-	BxEC	84302	766	E2
-	SNQN	84655	3460	C6
-	UthC	84655	3460	C6
10	BMCY	84302	766	D5
10	BNFL	84010	1551	C7
10	CRFD	84015	1227	C4
10	HRCY	84032	2398	C3
10	NSLK	84054	1652	E7
10	PRVO	84601	2928	B5
100	WBNF	84010	1551	C7
200	HYRM	84319	650	E2
400	PYSN	84651	3354	D4
400	SPFK	84660	3249	C2
500	SLCY	84103	1858	B1
500	SLCY	84116	1858	B1
600	LOGN	84321	527	C1
600	SLCY	84103	1754	B7
600	SLCY	84116	1754	B7
800	CTRV	84014	1551	D2
800	PRVO	84604	2928	B5
800	PTGV	84062	2712	C1
1100	ANFK	84003	2604	B4
1400	OREM	84057	2820	C1
1800	MPTN	84664	3144	A4
1900	CTRV	84014	1448	D6
2000	HARR	84414	998	C7
2200	LYTN	84041	1228	D7
3000	PTVW	84414	998	C4
3200	LEHI	84043	2603	B1
3400	LEHI	84043	2496	B7
N 500 W SR-197				
10	LEHI	84043	2603	B5
N 500 W US-89				
10	BNFL	84010	1551	C7
10	PRVO	84601	2928	B5
100	WBNF	84010	1551	C7
800	PRVO	84604	2928	B5
S 500 E				
-	CchC	84321	591	E4
-	PVDN	84332	592	B1
-	SHFD	84335	400	A4
10	ANFK	84003	2711	D2
10	BMCY	84302	767	A6
10	BNFL	84010	1551	E7
10	CRFD	84015	1227	E5
10	HDPK	84318	464	B1
10	HRCY	84032	2398	D4
10	HYRM	84319	651	C3
10	KYVL	84037	1345	D2
10	LNDN	84042	2713	C6
10	LOGN	84321	527	E3
10	PRVO	84606	2928	D7
10	PTGV	84062	2712	E3
10	PYSN	84651	3355	A6
10	SLCY	84102	1858	E3
10	SLCY	84111	1858	E3
10	SPFK	84660	3249	D3
200	BNFL	84010	1654	A1
200	SGVL	84663	3143	D2
200	SNQN	84655	3568	A1
300	RVHT	84321	527	E4
400	LEHI	84043	2603	D7
400	SALM	84653	3356	B4
400	UthC	84003	2711	D2
500	OREM	84097	2820	E7
500	PRVO	84606	3035	D1
800	BMCY	84302	828	A1
800	PVDN	84332	527	E5
900	SLCY	84105	1858	E6
1000	OREM	84097	2927	E1
1200	UthC	84651	3356	B6
1300	SLCY	84115	1858	E7
1500	SLCY	84105	1964	E1
1500	SLCY	84115	1964	E1
1700	BNFL	84010	1653	E3
1700	OREM	84058	2927	E2
1800	CRFD	84015	1281	E1
2100	SLCY	84106	1964	E2
2800	SSLK	84106	1964	E4
3500	SSLK	84115	1964	E7
3900	SLkC	84107	1964	E7
4000	SLkC	84107	2070	E1
6700	MDVL	84047	2176	E1
8700	SNDY	84070	2176	E6
10000	MLVI	84332	592	B3
13500	DRPR	84020	2388	E4
S 500 E SR-180				
100	ANFK	84003	2711	D2
400	UthC	84003	2711	D2
S 500 W				
-	CchC	84321	527	C7
-	TMTN	84337	520	D6
10	BMCY	84302	766	D7
10	BNFL	84010	1551	C7
10	CRFD	84015	1227	C4
10	HRCY	84032	2398	C4
10	LEHI	84043	2603	B7
10	LOGN	84321	527	C3
10	PRVO	84601	2928	B7
10	PYSN	84651	3354	D6
10	SLCY	84101	1858	B3
100	HYRM	84319	650	E3
100	OREM	84058	2820	C5
100	WBNF	84010	1653	C4
200	ANFK	84003	2711	B2
200	SALM	84653	3355	E4
200	SHFD	84335	399	C3
200	SPFK	84660	3249	C3
200	UthC	84003	2711	B2
300	LYTN	84041	1282	D5
500	LNDN	84042	2713	A7
500	LNDN	84042	2820	A1
500	PRVO	84601	3035	B1
500	SNQN	84655	3567	C2
500	UthC	84655	3567	C2
600	WDCR	84010	1653	C4
700	BMCY	84302	827	D1
700	UthC	84043	2710	B1
1000	OREM	84058	2927	C1
1300	SLCY	84104	1858	B7
1300	SLCY	84104	1964	B1
1300	SLCY	84115	1858	B7
1300	SLCY	84115	1964	B1
1400	PYSN	84651	3461	D1
1900	LEHI	84043	2710	B3
1900	SPFK	84660	3142	B6
1900	UthC	84660	3142	B6
2200	CRFD	84015	1281	C2
2800	BNFL	84010	1653	C4
3300	SSLK	84115	1964	B7
3300	SSLK	84119	1964	B7
3900	SLkC	84115	1964	B7
3900	SLkC	84123	2070	B1
4100	MRRY	84123	2070	B1
9000	SNDY	84070	2176	B7
9300	SNDY	84070	2282	B1
S 500 W US-89				
10	BNFL	84010	1551	C7
10	PRVO	84601	2928	B7
100	WBNF	84010	1653	C1
200	BNFL	84010	1653	C1
600	WDCR	84010	1653	C1
W 500 N				
-	BxEC	84324	768	A5
-	MNTU	84324	768	A5
-	SGVL	84663	3142	D1
-	SGVL	84663	3143	C1
-	SLCY	84116	1857	C1
-	SNQN	84655	3460	D6
10	ANFK	84003	2604	B6
10	HRCY	84032	2398	C3
10	KYVL	84037	1283	C7
10	LEHI	84043	2603	B6
10	LOGN	84321	527	C2
10	PRVO	84601	2928	C6
10	PYSN	84651	3354	E4
10	SLCY	84103	1858	C1
10	SPFK	84660	3249	C2
100	NSLK	84054	1652	E5
100	NSLK	84054	1653	A5
100	WELV	84339	589	C7
300	LNDN	84042	2713	A5
300	OREM	84057	2820	C4
400	TMTN	84337	520	D5
500	BMCY	84302	766	D4
500	SLCY	84116	1858	A1
700	PTGV	84062	2712	C2
800	LNDN	84042	2712	D5
1000	CTRV	84014	1551	C3
1200	CRFD	84015	1227	B3
1300	PRVO	84601	2927	E6
1700	WPT	84015	1227	A3
2300	WPT	84015	1226	D3
4300	CchC	84339	589	C7
4500	CchC	84339	648	E1
4500	CchC	84339	649	A1
W 500 N SR-23				
-	CchC	84339	589	C7
-	WELV	84339	589	C7
W 500 S				
-	BNFL	84087	1653	C1
-	HDPK	84318	464	A2
-	SLCY	84104	1858	A4
-	WbrC	84404	1054	B6
10	BMCY	84302	766	D7
10	BNFL	84010	1653	C1
10	GRLD	84312	520	E2
10	HRCY	84032	2398	C5
10	LOGN	84321	527	D4
10	PRVO	84601	2928	C7
10	PVDN	84332	592	A1
10	SLCY	84101	1858	C4
10	SPFK	84660	3249	C4
10	WELV	84339	649	C3
100	HDPK	84318	463	E2
100	PVDN	84332	591	E1
100	SNQN	84655	3567	D1
200	CchC	84332	527	E7
200	MIDW	84049	2397	A4
200	OREM	84058	2820	C6
200	PVDN	84332	527	E7
200	WshC	84049	2397	A4
500	WBNF	84010	1653	C1
600	LEHI	84043	2603	A7
600	PYSN	84651	3354	D6
600	WBNF	84087	1653	C1
600	WDCR	84087	1653	C1
900	LYTN	84041	1282	C6
900	SLCY	84104	1857	D4
1000	PTGV	84062	2712	A2
1200	WDCR	84087	1652	E1
1800	SGVL	84663	3142	E3
2000	MTSV	84044	1055	D6
3000	SLCY	84104	1856	E4
W 500 S SR-68				
-	BNFL	84087	1653	C1
200	BNFL	84010	1653	C1
500	WBNF	84010	1653	C1
600	WBNF	84087	1653	C1
600	WDCR	84087	1653	C1
1200	WDCR	84087	1652	E1
W 500 S SR-269				
10	SLCY	84101	1858	C4
500 E				
-	SNQN	84655	3568	A2
500 S				
-	SNQN	84655	3568	A1
E 510 N				
900	PTGV	84062	2713	A2
E 510 S				
10	ANFK	84003	2711	C2
N 510 E				
800	OREM	84097	2820	E2
N 510 W				
1000	LOGN	84341	463	C7
S 510 E				
600	KYVL	84037	1345	E3
4000	SLkC	84107	2070	A1
9000	SNDY	84070	2176	E7
W 510 N				
-	LOGN	84341	463	C7
2200	PRVO	84601	2927	D6
W 510 S				
10	ANFK	84003	2711	C2
100	UthC	84003	2711	C2
1200	PRVO	84601	2928	A7
N 515 E				
2100	NHON	84414	998	E7
S 515 W				
-	NBLY	84321	591	C3
E 520 N				
-	SHFD	84335	399	D1
300	ANFK	84003	2604	D6
400	LNDN	84042	2713	C5
E 520 S				
100	SHFD	84335	399	E4
400	SHFD	84335	400	A4
1100	PRVO	84606	3035	E1
1400	PRVO	84606	3036	A1
N 520 E				
200	SHFD	84335	400	A2
1000	OREM	84097	2820	E2
2600	LEHI	84043	2603	D2
N 520 W				
300	ANFK	84003	2604	B7
900	OREM	84057	2820	C3
1400	MPTN	84664	3144	A5
1900	OREM	84057	2713	C7
2000	WBNF	84087	1551	C4
S 520 E				
400	OREM	84097	2820	E6
1900	OREM	84058	2927	E3
5900	MRRY	84107	2070	E7
7500	MDVL	84047	2176	E3
7500	SNDY	84047	2176	E3
8400	SNDY	84070	2176	E6
9400	SNDY	84070	2282	E1
12400	DRPR	84020	2388	E1
S 520 W				
300	LNDN	84042	2713	A7
500	OREM	84058	2820	C6
1200	PYSN	84651	3354	D7
6400	MRRY	84123	2176	B1
7500	BxEC	84340	941	D3
W 520 N				
200	OREM	84057	2820	C4
600	SPFK	84660	3249	B2
700	LNDN	84042	2712	E5
900	TMTN	84337	520	C5
2400	PRVO	84601	2927	C6
W 520 S				
900	OREM	84058	2820	B6
1600	PRVO	84601	3034	D1
E 525 N				
-	SNQN	84655	3460	E6
10	LYTN	84041	1282	D3
10	LYTN	84041	1283	A4
1400	LYTN	84040	1283	D3
E 525 S				
300	CRFD	84015	1227	E5
N 525 E				
10	LOGN	84321	527	E3
1100	OGDN	84404	1056	E2
3100	NHON	84414	999	A4
N 525 W				
-	CRFD	84015	1227	C2
10	LYTN	84041	1228	D6
900	CLTN	84015	1227	C2
1600	CTRV	84014	1448	D7
S 525 E				
-	PVDN	84332	592	B1
6300	MRRY	84107	2070	E7
6300	MRRY	84107	2176	E1
7200	MDVL	84047	2176	E2
S 525 W				
-	BxEC	84340	941	D4
10	SGVL	84663	3143	B2
100	CRFD	84015	1227	C4
1800	WDCR	84010	1653	C3
2200	PRRY	84302	827	D4
3200	BNFL	84010	1653	C5
4800	RVDL	84405	1172	C3
5000	WSTR	84405	1172	C3
W 525 N				
10	KYVL	84037	1283	C7
10	LYTN	84041	1282	E4
1000	CRFD	84015	1227	B3
1600	WPT	84015	1227	A3
3000	WPT	84015	1226	C3
W 525 S				
1100	LEHI	84043	2603	A7
1300	LEHI	84043	2602	E7
1500	OREM	84058	2819	E6
E 530 N				
-	SNQN	84655	3460	E6
10	SGVL	84663	3143	C1
700	WshC	84032	2398	E3
800	ANFK	84003	2605	A6
1200	OREM	84097	2821	B4
E 530 S				
10	OREM	84058	2820	D6
200	ANFK	84003	2711	D2
700	SHFD	84335	400	A4
N 530 E				
200	ANFK	84003	2604	E7
700	OREM	84097	2820	E3
2500	PRVO	84604	2928	D2
N 530 W				
100	LYTN	84041	1228	D6
1100	ANFK	84003	2604	B5
1100	PTGV	84062	2712	C1
1400	PTGV	84062	2605	C7
S 530 E				
-	PVDN	84332	592	B1
100	SHFD	84335	400	A3
300	OREM	84097	2820	E6
700	SPFK	84660	3249	D4
4100	SLkC	84107	2070	E1
6200	MRRY	84107	2070	E7
9000	SNDY	84070	2176	E7
S 530 W				
100	OGDN	84404	1056	C5
1000	PYSN	84651	3354	D7
3700	SSLK	84119	1964	B7
7400	BxEC	84340	941	D3
W 530 N				
800	OREM	84057	2820	B3
900	PTGV	84062	2712	C2
2600	PRVO	84601	2927	C6
W 530 S				
800	LOGN	84321	527	B4
1100	OREM	84058	2820	A6
S 534 W				
600	TMTN	84337	520	D7
E 535 S				
400	SGVL	84663	3143	D3
N 535 E				
600	ANFK	84003	2604	E6
700	PTGV	84062	2712	E1
S 535 E				
8200	SNDY	84070	2176	E5
10200	SNDY	84070	2282	E3
S 535 W				
500	LOGN	84321	527	B4
5400	RVDL	84405	1172	C4
E 540 N				
-	SPFK	84660	3250	A2
300	SALM	84653	3356	B2
400	CTRV	84014	1551	E3
500	CTRV	84014	1552	A3
800	MPTN	84664	3144	C6
1100	SPFK	84663	3250	A2
N 540 E				
600	MPTN	84664	3144	B6
1800	OREM	84097	2713	E7
N 540 W				
600	ANFK	84003	2604	B6
1200	OREM	84057	2820	C2
S 540 E				
100	LOGN	84321	527	E4
200	LEHI	84043	2603	D7
3200	SSLK	84106	1964	E5
7100	MDVL	84047	2176	E2
8800	SNDY	84070	2176	E6
9800	SNDY	84070	2282	E2
12000	DRPR	84020	2388	E1
S 540 W				
100	OREM	84058	2820	C5
200	SPFK	84660	3249	B3
500	DRPR	84020	2282	B6
500	SJDN	84095	2282	B6
700	TMTN	84337	520	D7
1000	LEHI	84043	2710	B1
3700	SSLK	84119	1964	B7
W 540 N				
200	OREM	84057	2820	C3
1300	PTGV	84062	2712	B2
2300	PRVO	84601	2927	D6
W 540 S				
100	PVDN	84332	591	E1
1200	OREM	84058	2820	A6
1900	PRVO	84601	3034	D1
E 540 Cir N				
-	ANFK	84003	2604	D6
S 543 E				
1800	OREM	84058	2927	E2
S 545 E				
1000	OREM	84097	2820	E7
1000	OREM	84097	2927	E1
3600	SSLK	84106	1964	E7
E 550 N				
-	MLVI	84332	591	E2
-	SPFK	84663	3250	A2
10	BNFL	84010	1551	E6
100	FMTN	84025	1346	D7
100	SGVL	84663	3143	C1
500	ANFK	84003	2604	E6
500	HRCY	84032	2398	E3
600	LNDN	84042	2713	D5
600	OGDN	84404	1057	A4
700	BNFL	84010	1552	A6
700	WshC	84032	2398	E3
900	LOGN	84321	528	B2
900	SPFK	84660	3249	E2
1300	OREM	84097	2821	B3
E 550 S				
10	CRFD	84015	1227	D5
10	KYVL	84037	1345	D2
400	BNFL	84010	1653	E1
400	CTRV	84014	1551	E4
500	HRCY	84032	2398	E5
500	OREM	84097	2820	E6
700	OGDN	84404	1057	A6
700	SNQN	84655	3568	A1
800	OREM	84097	2821	A6
1000	PTGV	84062	2713	B4
1100	SPFK	84660	3249	E4
1100	SPFK	84660	3250	A4
1300	FTHT	84037	1346	B2
1600	SGVL	84663	3144	A3
N 550 E				
100	NSLK	84054	1653	B6
200	OREM	84097	2820	E4
400	HRCY	84032	2398	E3
400	LNDN	84042	2713	C5
400	SGVL	84663	3143	D1
600	BNFL	84010	1552	A6
600	LOGN	84321	527	E1
700	ANFK	84003	2604	E5
700	WshC	84032	2398	E2
1000	OGDN	84404	1057	A3
1400	BNFL	84010	1551	E5
2700	PRVO	84604	2928	D2
3000	NHON	84414	999	A4
3600	PRVO	84604	2821	D7
N 550 W				
-	BMCY	84302	766	D2
10	LYTN	84041	1228	D6
800	NSLK	84054	1652	E5
1000	WBNF	84087	1551	C5
1300	CLTN	84015	1227	C1
1300	LOGN	84341	463	C7
1300	PTGV	84062	2712	C1
1400	OREM	84057	2820	B1
1800	CLTN	84015	1171	C7
2000	HARR	84414	998	C7
3900	PTVW	84414	998	C2
S 550 E				
200	MIDW	84049	2397	D4
300	RVHT	84321	528	E4
600	KYVL	84037	1345	E3
600	PRVO	84606	3035	D1
700	SGVL	84663	3143	D3
800	CRFD	84015	1227	E6
800	OREM	84097	2820	E7
1400	OREM	84097	2927	E1
2400	BNFL	84010	1653	E4
2400	BNFL	84010	1654	A4
5300	MRRY	84107	2070	E5
5300	WSTR	84405	1172	E4
8600	SNDY	84070	2176	E6
S 550 W				
300	LYTN	84041	1282	D5
300	SALM	84653	3355	E4
400	UthC	84651	3355	E5
400	UthC	84653	3355	E5
1100	TMTN	84337	520	D7
1100	TMTN	84337	584	D1
1500	WDCR	84010	1653	C2
1800	LEHI	84043	2710	B2
2300	SRCS	84075	1281	C2
3300	BNFL	84010	1653	C5
3300	NSLK	84010	1653	C5
3400	NSLK	84054	1653	C5
4200	RVDL	84405	1172	C1
5000	WSTR	84405	1172	C3
W 550 N				
-	SNQN	84655	3460	D6
10	BNFL	84010	1551	D6
10	CTRV	84014	1551	D2
10	MLVI	84332	591	E2
300	LOGN	84321	527	C1
300	OREM	84057	2820	C3
300	SGVL	84663	3143	B1
400	LNDN	84042	2712	E5
400	LNDN	84042	2713	A5
500	ANFK	84003	2604	B6
500	SPFK	84660	3249	B2
500	WBNF	84010	1551	C6
600	PTGV	84062	2712	C2

Salt Lake City Street Index

STREET Block	City	ZIP	Map#	Grid
W 550 N				
800	WBNF	84087	1551	B6
1200	CRFD	84015	1227	B3
1700	WPT	84015	1227	A3
1800	KYVL	84037	1282	D7
1800	WPT	84015	1226	E3
2100	KYVL	84041	1282	D7
4500	WPT	84015	1225	E3
W 550 S				
-	PRVO	84601	2927	A7
-	SNQN	84655	3567	D1
10	CTRV	84014	1551	D4
200	LOGN	84321	527	C4
300	OGDN	84404	1056	D6
300	OREM	84058	2820	C6
500	TMTN	84337	520	D7
900	LYTN	84041	1282	D6
1000	PYSN	84651	3354	C6
1100	PRVO	84601	3035	A1
1400	LEHI	84043	2602	E7
3100	PRVO	84601	3034	B1
550 E				
-	LOGN	84341	464	A5
N 555 W				
100	OREM	84057	2820	C4
S 555 W				
5400	MRRY	84123	2070	B5
W 555 N				
-	CTRV	84014	1551	D2
E 560 N				
700	PRVO	84606	2928	D6
1000	OREM	84097	2821	B3
E 560 S				
-	SHFD	84335	399	D4
400	SHFD	84335	400	A4
N 560 E				
900	OREM	84097	2820	E2
1000	SPFK	84660	3249	D1
2500	PRVO	84604	2928	D2
4100	PRVO	84604	2821	D6
N 560 W				
100	LYTN	84041	1228	D6
400	SPFK	84660	3249	B2
1000	LOGN	84341	463	C7
1100	ANFK	84003	2604	B5
1300	OREM	84057	2820	B1
1600	WBNF	84087	1551	C5
2600	PTGV	84062	2605	C5
3200	LEHI	84043	2603	B1
3300	LEHI	84043	2496	B7
S 560 E				
100	LOGN	84321	527	E3
400	OREM	84097	2820	E7
500	HRCY	84032	2398	E5
5300	MRRY	84107	2070	E5
6800	MDVL	84047	2176	E1
8200	SLkC	84070	2176	E5
8400	SNDY	84070	2176	E5
S 560 W				
500	OREM	84058	2820	C6
700	LEHI	84043	2710	B1
800	TMTN	84337	520	D7
1100	PRVO	84601	3035	B2
2200	PRRY	84302	827	D4
9400	SNDY	84070	2282	B1
W 560 N				
-	SNQN	84655	3460	D6
W 560 S				
10	OREM	84058	2820	D6
600	PRVO	84601	3035	B1
1100	LEHI	84043	2603	A7
2300	PRVO	84601	3034	C1
560 S				
-	SNQN	84655	3568	A1
S 565 E				
3900	SLkC	84107	1964	E7
6700	MDVL	84047	2176	E1
S 565 W				
3700	SSLK	84119	1964	B7
E 570 N				
200	CchC	84318	400	A6
300	HDPK	84318	400	A6
300	SHFD	84335	399	E1
400	OREM	84097	2820	E3
1200	OREM	84097	2821	B3
1200	SPFK	84660	3250	A2
1200	SPFK	84663	3250	A2
E 570 S				
200	ANFK	84003	2711	D2
N 570 E				
-	ANFK	84003	2604	E7
-	ANFK	84003	2711	E1
N 570 W				
400	ANFK	84003	2604	B7
S 570 E				
4000	SLkC	84107	2070	E1
5300	MRRY	84107	2070	E4
9000	SNDY	84070	2176	E7
9800	SNDY	84070	2282	E2
S 570 W				
200	ANFK	84003	2711	B2
200	UthC	84003	2711	B2
1400	PRVO	84601	3035	B2
7500	BxEC	84340	941	D4
W 570 N				
100	OREM	84057	2820	C3
200	LNDN	84042	2713	A5
1200	CLTN	84015	1227	A3
2300	PRVO	84601	2927	D5
E 575 N				
-	FTHT	84037	1284	A7
500	OGDN	84404	1056	E4
800	ANFK	84003	2604	E6
800	ANFK	84003	2605	A6
800	LYTN	84040	1283	B3
E 575 S				
700	LYTN	84041	1283	B6
700	OREM	84097	2821	A6
N 575 E				
100	NSLK	84054	1653	C6
200	HDPK	84318	400	B7
2300	NHON	84414	999	A6
N 575 W				
10	LYTN	84041	1228	D6
400	LNDN	84042	2712	E5
900	CLTN	84015	1227	C2
1100	CTRV	84014	1551	D1
1900	HARR	84414	998	C7
3500	PTVW	84414	998	C3
S 575 E				
1800	CRFD	84015	1281	E1
5600	MRRY	84107	2070	D4
9900	SNDY	84070	2282	E2
S 575 W				
500	LOGN	84321	527	B4
1800	LEHI	84043	2710	B3
2000	WDCR	84010	1653	C3
2900	BNFL	84010	1653	C5
3100	SRCS	84075	1281	C4
3400	NSLK	84054	1653	C5
3500	RVDL	84405	1115	C7
3700	SSLK	84119	1964	B7
4700	RVDL	84405	1172	C3
5100	WSTR	84405	1172	C4
7600	BxEC	84340	941	D4
W 575 N				
10	KYVL	84037	1283	C7
W 575 S				
600	LEHI	84043	2603	A7
1400	OREM	84058	2819	E6
575 E				
-	SNQN	84655	3568	A1
E 580 N				
-	PRVO	84606	2928	E6
-	SNQN	84655	3460	E6
400	ANFK	84003	2604	D6
E 580 S				
1100	PRVO	84606	3035	E1
1300	PRVO	84606	3036	A1
N 580 E				
10	OREM	84097	2820	E5
500	ANFK	84003	2604	E6
600	LOGN	84321	528	A1
800	PRVO	84604	2928	D5
1800	OREM	84097	2713	E7
N 580 W				
100	LYTN	84041	1228	D6
500	ANFK	84003	2604	A6
1400	OREM	84057	2820	B1
S 580 E				
-	SNQN	84655	3568	A1
-	UthC	84003	2711	E5
10	MIDW	84049	2397	D3
3600	SSLK	84106	1964	E7
7200	MDVL	84047	2176	E2
8800	SNDY	84070	2176	E6
10600	SNDY	84070	2282	E4
S 580 W				
600	ALPN	84004	2497	D6
1000	PYSN	84651	3354	D7
1200	OREM	84058	2927	C1
1500	WDCR	84010	1653	C2
W 580 N				
500	ANFK	84003	2604	A6
1200	PRVO	84601	2928	A5
W 580 S				
-	LEHI	84043	2602	B7
10	FMTN	84025	1448	D3
100	PVDN	84332	591	E1
1300	OREM	84058	2820	A6
E 580 N Cir				
1100	UthC	84003	2605	A6
N 585 W				
10	LYTN	84041	1228	D6
W 585 S				
1200	LEHI	84043	2603	A7
1300	LEHI	84043	2602	E7
N 590 W				
-	LOGN	84341	463	C7
500	ANFK	84003	2604	A6
1800	LYTN	84041	1282	D1
S 590 E				
900	OREM	84097	2821	A7
1000	OREM	84097	2928	A1
4100	SLkC	84107	2070	E1
5300	MRRY	84107	2070	E4
7100	MDVL	84047	2176	E2
S 590 W				
200	SPFK	84660	3249	B3
4200	MRRY	84123	2070	B1
W 590 N				
100	LYTN	84041	1282	E3
1000	PRVO	84601	2928	A5
E 600 N				
-	PRVO	84606	3035	D1
-	SGVL	84663	3143	D1
-	WELV	84339	589	D7
10	ANFK	84003	2604	C6
10	BMCY	84302	766	E4
10	FMTN	84025	1346	D7
10	KYVL	84037	1283	C7
10	LEHI	84043	2603	C5
10	LOGN	84321	527	E1
10	MIDW	84049	2397	C2
10	MPTN	84664	3144	B6
10	OREM	84057	2820	D3
10	PRVO	84606	2928	D5
10	PYSN	84651	3354	E4
10	SPFK	84660	3249	D2
100	BMCY	84302	767	A4
100	MNDN	84325	524	E5
200	LNDN	84042	2713	B5
400	OREM	84097	2820	E3
500	PTGV	84062	2712	E2
500	PYSN	84651	3355	A4
600	LOGN	84321	528	A1
600	OREM	84097	2821	A3
700	LYTN	84041	1283	B3
700	WshC	84032	2398	E3
900	ANFK	84003	2605	A6
900	UthC	84003	2605	A6
1300	BNFL	84010	1552	B6
1400	FTHT	84037	1284	B7
1400	KYVL	84037	1284	B7
E 600 S				
-	WbrC	84317	1061	B6
10	BMCY	84302	766	E7
10	HRCY	84032	2398	D5
10	KYVL	84037	1345	D3
10	OREM	84058	2820	D6
10	PRVO	84606	3035	D1
10	PYSN	84651	3354	E6
10	SHFD	84335	399	E4
10	SLCY	84111	1858	D5
10	WELV	84339	649	D3
10	WLRD	84340	885	C7
100	BMCY	84302	767	A7
100	UthC	84003	2711	D3
200	BNFL	84010	1653	E1
200	CchC	84319	651	C4
200	CchC	84335	399	E4
200	CchC	84335	400	A4
200	HYRM	84319	651	C4
200	SHFD	84335	400	A4
300	CTRV	84014	1551	E4
300	PYSN	84651	3355	A6
300	RVHT	84321	527	E4
300	SGVL	84663	3143	D3
400	OREM	84097	2820	E6
500	OREM	84097	2821	A6
500	SALM	84653	3356	C5
600	RVHT	84321	528	A4
700	CTRV	84014	1552	A4
700	SLCY	84102	1858	E5
700	SLCY	84102	1859	A5
800	CchC	84321	528	A4
800	CRFD	84015	1228	A5
800	WshC	84032	2398	D5
1000	PTGV	84062	2713	B4
1200	SPFK	84660	3250	A4
1300	FTHT	84037	1346	B2
1700	SGVL	84663	3144	A3
7500	HTVL	84317	1061	A6
E 600 S SR-269				
10	SLCY	84111	1858	C5
N 600 E				
-	GRLD	84312	521	A1
10	ALPN	84004	2498	A4
10	BMCY	84302	767	A4
10	CTRV	84014	1552	A3
10	HRCY	84032	2398	E3
10	HYRM	84319	651	D2
10	KYVL	84037	1345	E1
10	OREM	84097	2820	E3
10	PYSN	84651	3355	A5
300	HDPK	84318	400	B7
300	LOGN	84321	528	A2
400	CchC	84319	651	D1
400	LNDN	84042	2713	C5
400	SGVL	84663	3143	D1
400	SPFK	84660	3249	D1
600	BNFL	84010	1552	A6
600	CchC	84319	591	D7
600	CchC	84321	591	D7
600	HYRM	84319	591	D7
600	PRVO	84606	2928	D5
600	SGVL	84663	3036	D7
700	PTGV	84062	2713	A1
800	LEHI	84043	2603	D5
900	LOGN	84321	464	A7
1000	LOGN	84341	464	A7
1200	MPTN	84664	3144	B5
1300	PTGV	84062	2712	E1
1700	NHON	84414	1057	A1
1900	OREM	84097	2713	E7
2200	NHLN	84341	464	A4
2600	NHON	84414	999	A5
2900	PRVO	84604	2928	D1
3600	PRVO	84604	2821	D7
N 600 W				
-	LYTN	84041	1228	D7
10	BMCY	84302	766	D5
10	HRCY	84032	2398	C3
10	KYVL	84037	1345	B1
10	LNDN	84042	2712	E6
10	LOGN	84321	527	B3
10	LYTN	84041	1282	D4
10	PRVO	84601	2928	B6
10	PTGV	84062	2712	C2
10	PYSN	84651	3354	D4
10	SLCY	84101	1858	A3
10	SLCY	84116	1858	A3
200	OGDN	84404	1056	C4
700	KYVL	84041	1283	B6
700	WshC	84032	2398	C2
800	PRVO	84604	2928	B6
900	ANFK	84003	2604	A5
900	LOGN	84321	463	B7
1000	CLTN	84015	1227	C2
1000	LOGN	84341	463	B6
1000	WBNF	84087	1551	C5
1200	OREM	84057	2820	B1
1400	CTRV	84014	1448	D7
1500	LEHI	84043	2603	B3
1500	PTGV	84062	2605	C7
1800	WshC	84032	2292	C7
2000	HARR	84414	998	C5
3700	PTVW	84414	998	C5
S 600 E				
-	CchC	84321	592	A6
-	GRLD	84312	521	A2
-	MPTN	84664	3251	B2
-	SNQN	84655	3568	A2
10	ALPN	84004	2498	A5
10	BMCY	84302	767	A6
10	BNFL	84010	1552	A7
10	HYRM	84319	651	D3
10	KYVL	84037	1345	E1
10	LEHI	84043	2603	D7
10	LOGN	84321	528	A3
10	PRVO	84606	2928	D7
10	PTGV	84062	2713	A3
10	PYSN	84651	3355	A6
10	SGVL	84663	3143	D2
10	SLCY	84102	1858	E3
10	SLCY	84103	1858	E3
10	SPFK	84660	3249	D3
200	ANFK	84003	2711	E2
200	CRFD	84015	1227	E5
200	CTRV	84014	1552	A4
300	RVHT	84321	528	A4
300	SHFD	84335	400	A4
500	LEHI	84043	2710	D1
500	PRVO	84606	3035	D1
500	UthC	84043	2603	D7
500	UthC	84003	2710	D1
600	LYTN	84041	1283	B6
800	OREM	84097	2821	A7
800	SLCY	84105	1858	E5
1400	BNFL	84010	1654	A2
1600	SLCY	84105	1964	E1
2100	SLCY	84106	1964	E2
2900	SSLK	84106	1964	E4
3000	WshC	84032	2505	E2
4500	MRRY	84107	2070	E2
5300	WSTR	84405	1172	E4
10000	UthC	84653	3356	E5
10300	SALM	84653	3356	E5
12300	DRPR	84020	2388	E1
S 600 W				
-	MRRY	84123	2070	A4
10	BMCY	84302	766	D6
10	HRCY	84032	2398	C4
10	KYVL	84037	1345	B1
10	LNDN	84042	2712	E6
10	LOGN	84321	527	B3
10	PRVO	84601	2928	B7
10	PYSN	84651	3354	D6
10	SLCY	84101	1858	B4
10	SLCY	84104	1858	B4
100	HYRM	84319	650	E3
100	OGDN	84404	1056	C5
100	OREM	84058	2820	B6
200	LYTN	84041	1282	D5
200	SHFD	84335	399	B4
400	CTRV	84014	1551	D4
400	SNQN	84655	3567	C1
500	CchC	84335	399	B4
700	BMCY	84302	827	D1
700	PRVO	84601	3035	B1
700	TMTN	84337	520	D7
1300	WshC	84032	2398	C5
1400	PYSN	84651	3461	D1
2200	SSLK	84115	1964	B3
2200	SSLK	84119	1964	B3
2300	PRRY	84302	827	D4
2600	NBLY	84321	591	C3
3000	BNFL	84010	1653	C5
3700	RVDL	84405	1115	C7
3700	SRCS	84075	1281	C5
4000	RVDL	84405	1172	B1
5000	WSTR	84405	1172	C3
6100	CchC	84319	651	C5
6100	HYRM	84319	651	C5
7100	MDVL	84047	2176	B2
7400	BxEC	84340	941	D3
9400	SNDY	84070	2282	A1
W 600 N				
-	CchC	84321	526	E1
-	CRFD	84015	1227	B3
-	DvsC	84041	1282	C7
-	KYVL	84041	1282	C7
-	PRVO	84606	3035	D1
-	SNQN	84655	3460	D6
10	BMCY	84302	766	E4
10	FMTN	84025	1346	C7
10	KYVL	84037	1283	C7
10	LEHI	84043	2603	B5
10	LOGN	84321	527	C1
10	MPTN	84664	3144	A6
10	SGVL	84663	3143	C1
10	SPFK	84660	3249	C2
100	BNFL	84010	1551	D6
100	MNTU	84324	768	B6
100	SLCY	84103	1858	B1
300	LNDN	84042	2713	A5
400	LNDN	84042	2712	E5
400	OREM	84057	2820	C3
400	SLCY	84116	1858	B1
500	PRVO	84601	2928	B5
600	ANFK	84003	2604	A6
600	NSLK	84054	1652	D5
800	WBNF	84087	1551	A6
900	OGDN	84404	1056	B3
1100	LOGN	84321	526	E1
1300	PTGV	84062	2712	B2
1700	SLCY	84116	1857	D1
2400	PRVO	84601	2927	C5
2400	WPT	84015	1226	D3
6000	CchC	84325	524	C1
7100	CchC	84325	523	E1
W 600 N SR-106				
10	FMTN	84025	1346	C7
W 600 N SR-268				
300	SLCY	84103	1858	B1
400	SLCY	84116	1858	B1
W 600 S				
-	LNDN	84013	2819	B1
-	SNQN	84655	3567	D2
-	WLRD	84340	885	C7
10	BMCY	84302	766	E7
10	HRCY	84032	2398	C5
10	PYSN	84651	3354	E6
10	SHFD	84335	399	D4
10	SLCY	84101	1858	C5
100	LOGN	84321	527	D5
300	OGDN	84404	1056	C6
500	BNFL	84010	1653	C1
500	WDCR	84010	1653	C1
600	CchC	84335	399	B4
600	SLCY	84104	1858	A5
700	PRVO	84601	3035	A1
800	OREM	84058	2820	B6
900	LYTN	84041	1282	D6
1100	SLCY	84104	1857	D5
1300	PRVO	84601	3034	E1
4000	SLCY	84104	1856	C4
4200	VNYD	84058	2819	B1
4200	VNYD	84057	2819	B1
W 600 S SR-269				
10	SLCY	84101	1858	C5
600 E				
-	SNQN	84655	3568	A2
600 S				
-	SNQN	84655	3568	A2
-	UthC	84655	3568	A2
600 W				
-	ELWD	84337	584	E7
S 600 Blvd W				
200	BMCY	84302	766	D6
E 600 St N				
-	TMTN	84337	520	E5
E 600 St N SR-82				
-	TMTN	84337	520	E5
600 St S				
700	LOGN	84321	527	B4
600 St W				
-	LOGN	84321	527	B4
S 600 E St				
-	CchC	84321	592	A6
E 600 S St				
-	PVDN	84332	592	A1
S 605 E				
1400	OREM	84097	2928	A2
S 605 W				
1300	OREM	84058	2927	B1
E 610 N				
-	SNQN	84655	3460	E6
1200	PRVO	84606	2928	E6
E 610 S				
-	SNQN	84655	3567	E2
N 610 E				
500	ALPN	84004	2498	A3
700	ANFK	84003	2604	E6
800	CTRV	84014	1551	E2
N 610 W				
-	SHFD	84335	399	B2
S 610 E				
300	OREM	84097	2821	A6
3600	SSLK	84106	1964	E7
9800	SNDY	84070	2282	E2
S 610 W				
3700	SSLK	84119	1964	A7
5900	MRRY	84123	2070	B6
W 610 N				
2300	PRVO	84601	2927	D5
W 610 S				
400	OREM	84058	2820	C6
1400	OREM	84058	2819	E6
610 S				
-	SNQN	84655	3568	A2
S 615 E				
4200	SLkC	84107	2070	E1
6700	MDVL	84047	2176	E1
8000	SNDY	84070	2176	E4
10300	SNDY	84070	2282	E3
E 620 N				
400	ANFK	84003	2604	D6
700	PRVO	84606	2928	D5
1200	OREM	84097	2821	B3
E 620 S				
-	SHFD	84335	399	E4
300	SALM	84653	3356	B5
300	UthC	84003	2711	D3
600	ANFK	84003	2711	D3
800	OREM	84097	2821	A6
1300	SGVL	84663	3144	A3
N 620 E				
400	MPTN	84664	3144	B6
900	TMTN	84337	521	A4
3200	LEHI	84043	2603	D1
N 620 W				
10	OREM	84057	2820	B5
3300	LEHI	84043	2496	B7
3300	LEHI	84043	2603	B1
S 620 E				
-	SHFD	84335	400	A4
500	HRCY	84032	2398	E5
1600	OREM	84097	2928	A2
4100	SLkC	84107	2070	E1
5900	MRRY	84107	2070	E6
8600	SNDY	84070	2176	E6
S 620 W				
1200	OREM	84058	2927	B1
1900	LEHI	84043	2710	B3
7600	BxEC	84340	941	D4
W 620 N				
300	OREM	84057	2820	C3
W 620 S				
-	LOGN	84321	526	E5
10	FMTN	84025	1448	C3
10	OREM	84058	2820	D6
E 625 N				
1000	OGDN	84404	1057	B4
1200	LYTN	84040	1283	C3
E 625 S				
-	OGDN	84404	1057	A6
800	LYTN	84041	1283	B6
N 625 E				
600	LEHI	84043	2603	D5
700	KYVL	84037	1283	E6
1700	NHON	84414	1057	A1
N 625 W				
10	LYTN	84041	1282	D4
10	WBNF	84010	1551	C7
400	CRFD	84015	1227	C3
1200	OREM	84057	2820	B2
S 625 E				
1300	SGVL	84663	3143	D4
1600	KYVL	84037	1345	E5
5600	MRRY	84107	2070	E5
S 625 W				
-	WBNF	84010	1551	C7
-	WBNF	84010	1653	C1
1600	WDCR	84010	1653	C3
2600	BNFL	84010	1653	C4
3700	RVDL	84405	1115	B7
7300	BxEC	84340	941	D3
W 625 N				
10	CTRV	84014	1551	D2
10	SLCY	84116	1857	C1
300	LNDN	84042	2713	A5
1700	WPT	84015	1227	A3
2600	WPT	84015	1226	D3
W 625 W				
800	BMCY	84302	766	D3
E 630 N				
100	OREM	84057	2820	D3
400	LNDN	84042	2713	C5
500	ANFK	84003	2604	E6
600	PTGV	84062	2713	A2
E 630 S				
600	HRCY	84032	2398	E5
N 630 E				
-	TMTN	84337	521	A4
300	ANFK	84003	2604	E7
400	OGDN	84404	1057	A4
1100	LOGN	84341	464	A7
1900	OREM	84097	2713	E7
1900	OREM	84097	2714	A7
N 630 W				
10	SPFK	84660	3249	B2
300	UthC	84660	3249	B2
400	LOGN	84321	527	B2
1300	CLTN	84015	1227	C1
1800	CLTN	84015	1171	C7
S 630 E				
-	ANFK	84003	2711	E4
10	LNDN	84042	2713	C6
500	OREM	84097	2821	A6
1500	OREM	84097	2928	A2
5300	MRRY	84107	2070	E5
8800	SNDY	84070	2176	E6
S 630 W				
-	OGDN	84404	1056	C7
10	SPFK	84660	3249	B3
500	OREM	84058	2820	B6
800	ALPN	84004	2497	D6
800	PYSN	84651	3354	D7
6500	MRRY	84123	2176	B1
W 630 N				
-	SNQN	84655	3460	D6
500	ANFK	84003	2604	B6
1000	OREM	84057	2820	A3
W 630 S				
600	OREM	84058	2820	B6
900	PTGV	84062	2712	C4
S 634 W				
600	TMTN	84337	520	D7
N 635 W				
1600	WBNF	84087	1551	C4
S 635 E				
4100	SLkC	84107	2070	E1
S 635 W				
-	SRCS	84075	1281	C1
800	OREM	84058	2820	B7
3600	RVDL	84405	1115	B7
W 635 S				
1200	OREM	84058	2820	A7
E 640 N				
500	ANFK	84003	2604	E6
600	LNDN	84042	2713	D5
600	OREM	84097	2820	E3
600	OREM	84097	2821	A3
E 640 S				
1000	PRVO	84606	3035	E1
1200	PYSN	84651	3355	B6
1300	PRVO	84606	3036	A1
1700	SPFK	84660	3250	B4
N 640 E				
10	ANFK	84003	2711	E1
600	ANFK	84003	2604	E6
2100	LOGN	84341	464	A5
N 640 W				
10	NSLK	84054	1652	E6
500	OREM	84057	2820	B3
900	ANFK	84003	2604	A5
900	UthC	84003	2604	A5
1000	WBNF	84087	1551	C5
2100	LEHI	84043	2603	B3
S 640 E				
300	SHFD	84335	400	A3
900	PYSN	84651	3355	A7
1400	OREM	84097	2928	A1
S 640 W				
100	LNDN	84042	2712	E6
300	LEHI	84043	2603	B7
3600	NBLY	84321	591	C5
5400	MRRY	84123	2070	A5
W 640 N				
100	ANFK	84003	2604	C6
400	LOGN	84321	527	C1
1100	OREM	84057	2820	A3
N 645 E				
400	LNDN	84042	2713	C5
600	LOGN	84321	528	A1
N 645 W				
1600	OREM	84057	2820	B1
1700	OREM	84057	2713	B7
S 645 E				
3600	SSLK	84106	1964	E7
4300	SLkC	84107	2070	E2
E 650 N				
-	CRFD	84056	1227	E3
-	DvsC	84056	1227	E3
10	CRFD	84015	1227	E3
10	MLVI	84332	591	E1
200	LEHI	84043	2603	C5
300	OREM	84057	2820	E3
400	OGDN	84404	1056	E4
500	BNFL	84010	1551	E6
500	BNFL	84010	1552	A6
500	CTRV	84014	1551	E2
500	CTRV	84014	1552	A2
500	OGDN	84404	1057	A4
600	ANFK	84003	2604	E6
900	LOGN	84321	528	B1
1000	OREM	84097	2821	B3
1300	FTHT	84037	1284	A7
E 650 N SR-103				
10	CRFD	84015	1227	D3
E 650 S				
100	FMTN	84025	1448	D3
300	KYVL	84037	1345	D3
500	RVHT	84321	527	E4
600	BMCY	84302	767	A7
600	LYTN	84041	1283	B6
700	CTRV	84014	1552	A4
700	OGDN	84404	1057	A6
1300	FTHT	84037	1346	B3
N 650 E				
100	BNFL	84010	1552	A7
100	KYVL	84037	1345	E1
200	KYVL	84037	1283	E7
200	OREM	84097	2821	A4
400	WshC	84032	2398	E3
600	ANFK	84003	2604	E6
600	LNDN	84042	2713	C4
600	SGVL	84663	3036	D7
600	SGVL	84663	3143	D1
800	LOGN	84321	528	A1
1500	CTRV	84014	1552	A5
1600	PRVO	84604	2928	D3
1700	NHON	84414	1057	A1
2500	NHON	84414	999	A5
3000	DvsC	84056	1229	B6
3000	LYTN	84040	1229	B6
N 650 W				
-	SHFD	84335	399	B2
10	FMTN	84025	1448	B1
100	LNDN	84042	2712	E5
200	KYVL	84037	1283	B7
200	KYVL	84037	1345	B1
300	LNDN	84042	2712	E5
400	ANFK	84003	2604	A6
600	CRFD	84015	1227	C3
1400	OREM	84057	2820	B1
1600	CTRV	84014	1448	D7
1700	PRVO	84604	2928	B3
2000	LYTN	84041	1228	D7
2000	LYTN	84041	1282	D1
2100	HARR	84414	998	B7
2100	LEHI	84043	2603	B3
3700	PTVW	84414	998	C3
S 650 E				
-	OGDN	84404	1057	A6
10	BNFL	84010	1552	A7
300	HYRM	84319	651	D4
300	OREM	84097	2821	A6
400	CRFD	84015	1227	E5
600	HRCY	84032	2398	E5
700	BNFL	84010	1654	A1
700	CTRV	84014	1552	A4
1100	KYVL	84037	1345	E4
2100	CRFD	84015	1281	E1
4100	SLkC	84107	2070	E4
6800	MDVL	84047	2176	E2
S 650 W				
-	CTRV	84014	1448	C6
-	DvsC	84025	1448	C6
-	HRCY	84032	2398	B6
10	FMTN	84025	1448	B3
200	PYSN	84651	3354	D5
800	SALM	84653	3355	E5
1300	OREM	84058	2927	B1
1300	PYSN	84651	3461	D1
2500	PRRY	84302	827	D5
3300	BNFL	84010	1653	C5
3600	RVDL	84405	1115	B7
4300	RVDL	84405	1172	B1
5600	UthC	84660	3142	B7
5600	UthC	84660	3249	B1
7000	CchC	84319	651	C7
W 650 N				
-	LYTN	84041	1281	E3
-	LYTN	84041	1282	A3
-	SNQN	84655	3460	D6
200	BNFL	84010	1551	D6
200	HRCY	84032	2398	C2
200	SGVL	84663	3143	B1
300	LNDN	84042	2713	A4
300	OREM	84057	2820	C3
500	ANFK	84003	2604	B6
600	BMCY	84302	766	D4
600	CRFD	84015	1227	C3
1000	CTRV	84014	1551	C2
1000	PRVO	84601	2928	A5
1000	PTGV	84062	2712	C2
2700	WPT	84015	1226	C3
4500	WPT	84015	1225	E3
W 650 S				
200	BNFL	84010	1653	D1
300	OGDN	84404	1056	D6
600	OREM	84058	2820	B7
700	HRCY	84032	2398	B5
700	WshC	84032	2398	A5
900	LYTN	84041	1282	C6
1100	LEHI	84043	2603	A7
1200	WshC	84032	2397	E5
1400	LEHI	84043	2602	E7
1400	OREM	84058	2819	E6
W 655 N				
900	TMTN	84337	520	C5
E 660 N				
-	SNQN	84655	3460	E6
500	LOGN	84321	527	E1
600	LOGN	84321	528	A1
600	OREM	84097	2820	E3
600	OREM	84097	2821	A3
1000	SPFK	84660	3249	E1
1100	SPFK	84660	3250	B1
1300	PRVO	84606	2928	E6
N 660 E				
400	OGDN	84404	1057	A4
700	OREM	84097	2821	A3
3300	LEHI	84043	2496	D7
3300	LEHI	84043	2603	D1
N 660 W				
-	SRSP	84043	2601	D5
400	WBNF	84087	1551	C6
1100	OREM	84057	2820	B2
1800	CLTN	84015	1171	C7
S 660 E				
4100	SLkC	84107	2070	E1
9600	SNDY	84070	2282	E1
S 660 W				
200	LEHI	84043	2603	B7
500	OREM	84058	2820	B6
800	TMTN	84337	520	D7
2500	NBLY	84321	591	C2
W 660 S				
-	LOGN	84321	526	E5
400	TMTN	84337	520	D7
S 665 W				
800	WDCR	84087	1653	C1
5700	MRRY	84123	2070	A6
W 665 N				
400	OREM	84057	2820	C3
W 665 S				
10	TMTN	84337	520	E7
E 670 N				
500	ANFK	84003	2604	E6
800	OGDN	84404	1057	A4
1200	PRVO	84606	2928	E5
N 670 E				
10	ANFK	84003	2711	E1
10	HRCY	84032	2398	E4
100	ANFK	84003	2604	E7
N 670 W				
400	LOGN	84321	527	B2
1500	CLTN	84015	1227	C1
2400	LEHI	84043	2603	B2
S 670 E				
100	PTGV	84062	2713	A3
500	OREM	84097	2821	A6
6800	MDVL	84047	2176	E2
S 670 W				
5400	MRRY	84123	2070	A5
6500	MRRY	84123	2176	A1
9300	SNDY	84070	2282	A1
W 670 N				
2200	WPT	84015	1226	E3
W 670 S				
900	PTGV	84062	2712	C4
E 675 N				
600	ANFK	84003	2604	E6
600	OGDN	84404	1057	A4
1000	WshC	84032	2398	E2
E 675 S				
700	BMCY	84302	767	A7
800	LEHI	84043	2603	D7
N 675 E				
300	NSLK	84054	1653	C6
400	LNDN	84042	2713	D5
2300	NHON	84414	999	A6
2600	LEHI	84043	2603	D1
3000	LYTN	84040	1229	B5
N 675 W				
-	NSLK	84054	1652	E4
600	BMCY	84302	766	D4
600	CRFD	84015	1227	C3
1000	WBNF	84087	1551	C5
2200	LYTN	84041	1228	D7
S 675 E				
300	HYRM	84319	651	D4
1900	BNFL	84010	1654	B3
4200	SOGN	84403	1173	A1
5600	MRRY	84107	2070	E5
S 675 W				
-	SRCS	84075	1281	C2
400	CTRV	84014	1551	D4

STREET Block City ZIP Map# Grid

S 675 W
1200 WDCR 84087 1653 C2
1900 LEHI 84043 2710 B3
3200 BNFL 84010 1653 C5
11200 SJDN 84095 2282 A6
W 675 N
800 OREM 84057 2820 A3
800 TMTN 84337 520 C5
1600 CLTN 84015 1227 A3
W 675 S
300 LOGN 84321 527 C5
E 680 N
- OREM 84097 2821 A3
200 LNDN 84042 2713 C4
1400 SPFK 84663 3250 A1
E 680 S
10 OREM 84058 2820 D7
10 PRVO 84606 3035 C1
600 HRCY 84032 2398 E5
600 WshC 84032 2398 E5
700 SGVL 84663 3143 D3
N 680 E
600 ANFK 84003 2604 E6
2100 LOGN 84341 464 A5
N 680 W
100 SPFK 84660 3249 B2
400 ANFK 84003 2604 A7
400 OREM 84057 2820 B3
1200 PTGV 84062 2712 C1
1700 OREM 84057 2713 B7
2300 WBNF 84087 1551 B4
S 680 E
600 HRCY 84032 2398 E5
600 PYSN 84651 3355 A6
600 WshC 84032 2398 E5
1400 OREM 84097 2928 A1
S 680 W
10 MPTN 84664 3144 A7
100 LNDN 84042 2712 E7
800 PYSN 84651 3354 D7
1000 PRVO 84601 3035 B2
1400 PYSN 84651 3461 D1
W 680 N
- SNQN 84655 3460 D6
- UthC 84655 3460 D6
10 OREM 84057 2820 D3
400 LOGN 84321 527 C1
500 ANFK 84003 2604 A6
1500 PTGV 84062 2712 A2
2700 PRVO 84601 2927 C5
W 680 S
900 OREM 84058 2820 A7
N 685 W
1200 OREM 84057 2820 B2
1800 WBNF 84087 1551 C4
S 685 E
4000 SLkC 84107 2070 E1
N 690 E
1800 OREM 84097 2714 A7
N 690 W
500 ANFK 84003 2604 A6
700 UthC 84003 2604 A6
2300 CLTN 84015 1171 C6
S 690 E
400 SNQN 84655 3568 A1
700 SPFK 84660 3249 E4
S 690 W
700 LEHI 84043 2710 B1
W 690 N
- SNQN 84655 3460 D6
200 ANFK 84003 2604 B6
W 690 S
900 PRVO 84601 3035 A1
1300 OREM 84058 2819 E7
S 690E
600 SNQN 84655 3568 A2
E 700 N
- LOGN 84321 528 C1
- OREM 84097 2821 A3
10 BMCY 84302 766 E3
10 LOGN 84321 527 E1
10 MLVI 84332 591 E1
10 OREM 84057 2820 D3
10 PRVO 84606 2928 C5
10 PVDN 84332 591 E1
10 SPFK 84660 3249 D1
100 BMCY 84302 767 A3
100 HARR 84404 1056 E4
100 SLCY 84103 1858 D1
200 ANFK 84003 2604 E6
300 BNFL 84010 1653 C5
300 PTGV 84062 2712 E2
300 TMTN 84337 520 E4
400 OGDN 84404 1056 E4
400 PYSN 84651 3355 A4
500 CTRV 84014 1551 E2
500 CTRV 84014 1552 A2
500 NSLK 84010 1653 C5
500 OGDN 84404 1057 A4
500 TMTN 84337 521 A4
600 KYVL 84037 1283 E6
600 OREM 84097 2820 C3
600 SGVL 84663 3036 D7
700 PTGV 84062 2713 A2
800 ANFK 84003 2605 A6
800 MPTN 84664 3144 C6
900 BNFL 84010 1552 A6
900 LEHI 84043 2603 D5
1200 UthC 84003 2605 A6
E 700 S
- DvsC 84056 1229 C3
- HDPK 84318 464 A2
10 BMCY 84302 766 E7
10 CRFD 84015 1227 E6
10 FMTN 84025 1448 D3
10 GRLD 84312 520 E3
10 KYVL 84037 1345 C3
10 LOGN 84321 527 E5
10 OREM 84058 2820 D7
10 PTGV 84062 2712 D4
10 PYSN 84651 3354 E6
10 SGVL 84663 3143 D3
10 SLCY 84111 1858 C5
10 TMTN 84337 520 E3
10 WELV 84339 649 D4
100 BMCY 84302 767 A7
100 PYSN 84651 3355 A6
100 SALM 84653 3356 B5
200 RVHT 84321 527 E5
300 CTRV 84014 1551 E4
400 OREM 84097 2820 E7
500 BNFL 84010 1654 A1
E 700 S
500 SLCY 84102 1858 E5
600 BMCY 84302 828 A1
700 CTRV 84014 1552 A4
700 KYVL 84041 1283 B6
700 LYTN 84041 1283 B6
700 SLCY 84102 1859 A5
900 OREM 84097 2821 A7
1000 CdhC 84321 528 B5
1100 PRVO 84606 3035 E1
1300 PRVO 84606 3036 A1
1300 SGVL 84663 3144 A3
1600 MPTN 84664 3251 C1
7800 LEHI 84043 2603 C7
N 700 E
10 ANFK 84003 2711 E1
10 BMCY 84302 767 A5
10 CTRV 84014 1552 A3
10 PRVO 84606 2928 D6
10 PTGV 84062 2713 A2
10 PVDN 84332 528 C6
10 PYSN 84651 3355 A5
10 SGVL 84663 3143 D1
100 ANFK 84003 2604 E7
200 HDPK 84318 400 B7
200 KYVL 84037 1345 E1
200 NSLK 84054 1653 C6
200 OREM 84097 2821 A4
300 KYVL 84037 1283 E7
300 LOGN 84321 528 A2
400 MPTN 84664 3144 B6
400 SPFK 84660 3249 E1
500 LEHI 84043 2603 D5
900 LOGN 84321 464 A7
900 SGVL 84663 3036 D7
1400 BNFL 84010 1552 A5
2100 LOGN 84341 464 A4
2500 NHON 84414 999 A5
2700 PRVO 84604 2928 D1
3600 PRVO 84604 2821 D7
N 700 W
- ANFK 84003 2604 A7
- OGDN 84404 1056 B4
- TMTN 84337 520 D6
- WBNF 84087 1551 B4
10 KYVL 84037 1345 B1
10 LNDN 84042 2712 E6
10 NSLK 84054 1652 D6
10 PRVO 84601 2928 B6
100 LYTN 84041 1282 D4
100 SPFK 84660 3249 B2
300 CRFD 84015 1227 C3
700 SLCY 84116 1754 A7
700 SLCY 84116 1858 A1
800 PTGV 84062 2712 C2
900 CLTN 84015 1227 C2
1000 OREM 84057 2820 B2
1100 CTRV 84014 1551 D2
1100 FMTN 84025 1346 B6
1200 MPTN 84664 3144 A5
1900 PRVO 84604 2928 B3
2000 CLTN 84015 1171 C7
2000 SGVL 84663 3143 E3
2000 SGVL 84663 3144 A4
2100 HARR 84414 998 B7
2200 LEHI 84043 2603 B2
3000 PTVW 84414 998 B4
S 700 E
- GRLD 84312 521 A2
- OREM 84097 2928 A2
- PTGV 84062 2712 E4
10 ANFK 84003 2711 E1
10 BMCY 84302 828 A1
10 BNFL 84010 1552 A7
10 CTRV 84014 1552 A3
10 HYRM 84319 651 D3
10 MIDW 84049 2397 D3
10 PRVO 84606 2928 D7
10 PTGV 84062 2713 A3
10 PYSN 84651 3355 A5
10 SGVL 84663 3143 D2
10 SLCY 84102 1858 E3
10 SPFK 84660 3249 E3
100 ALPN 84004 2498 B5
100 KYVL 84037 1345 E1
100 UthC 84003 2711 E1
200 CRFD 84015 1228 A5
300 RVHT 84321 528 A4
300 SHFD 84335 400 A4
500 OREM 84097 2821 A6
600 BMCY 84302 767 A7
900 PRVO 84606 3035 D1
900 SLCY 84105 1858 E7
1600 SLCY 84105 1964 E1
1900 BNFL 84010 1654 A3
2100 SLCY 84106 1964 E1
2700 SLkC 84106 1964 E5
2800 SSLK 84106 1964 E5
3900 SGVL 84663 3142 E3
3900 SLkC 84107 1964 E5
3900 SLkC 84124 1964 E5
4000 SLkC 84107 2070 E1
4000 SLkC 84124 2070 E1
4500 MRRY 84107 2070 E1
4600 MRRY 84107 2071 A3
4600 SLkC 84107 2071 A3
5300 SOGN 84405 1173 A4
6700 MDVL 84047 2176 E1
6700 MRRY 84047 2176 E1
7500 SNDY 84047 2176 E3
7800 SNDY 84070 2176 E4
7800 SNDY 84094 2176 E4
8400 SLkC 84094 2176 E6
9100 SNDY 84070 2282 E2
9100 SNDY 84094 2282 E2
9800 SLkC 84094 2282 E2
10200 SLkC 84070 2282 E2
11400 DRPR 84020 2282 E6
12000 DRPR 84020 2388 E1
S 700 E SR-71
400 SLCY 84102 1858 E7
900 SLCY 84105 1858 E7
1600 SLCY 84105 1964 E1
2100 SLCY 84106 1964 E1
2700 SLkC 84106 1964 E5
2800 SSLK 84106 1964 E5
3900 SLkC 84107 1964 E5
3900 SLkC 84124 1964 E5
4000 SLkC 84107 2070 E1
4000 SLkC 84124 2070 E1
4500 MRRY 84107 2070 E1
4600 MRRY 84107 2071 A3
S 700 E SR-71
4600 SLkC 84107 2071 A3
7700 SNDY 84047 2176 E4
7800 SNDY 84070 2176 E4
7800 SNDY 84094 2176 E4
8400 SLkC 84094 2176 E6
9100 SNDY 84070 2282 E2
9100 SNDY 84094 2282 E2
9800 SLkC 84094 2282 E2
10200 SLkC 84070 2282 E2
11400 DRPR 84020 2282 E6
12000 DRPR 84020 2388 E1
S 700 W
- HRCY 84032 2398 B6
- HYRM 84319 651 B1
- LEHI 84043 2710 B2
- SRCS 84075 1281 C1
10 PRVO 84601 2928 B7
10 PYSN 84651 3354 D6
10 SLCY 84104 1858 A3
100 LNDN 84042 2713 A7
100 LOGN 84321 527 B3
200 SPFK 84660 3249 B3
400 BMCY 84302 766 D7
400 LEHI 84043 2603 B7
500 PRVO 84601 3035 B1
600 OREM 84058 2820 B6
800 BMCY 84302 827 D1
800 TMTN 84337 520 D7
800 WDCR 84087 1653 B1
900 SLCY 84101 1858 A6
1400 PYSN 84651 3461 D1
1500 SLCY 84104 1964 A1
2500 PRRY 84302 827 C5
3100 BNFL 84010 1653 C5
3100 NBLY 84321 591 C4
3300 SSLK 84119 1964 A6
3500 CdhC 84321 591 C5
3900 RVDL 84405 1115 B7
3900 RVDL 84405 1172 B1
3900 SLkC 84123 1964 A6
3900 SLkC 84123 2070 A1
4100 MRRY 84123 2070 A1
4400 CdhC 84319 591 C7
4400 CdhC 84319 651 B1
6300 MRRY 84123 2176 A1
6800 MDVL 84047 2176 A1
6800 MDVL 84123 2176 A1
11400 DRPR 84020 2282 A7
11900 DRPR 84020 2388 A1
W 700 N
- NSLK 84054 1652 E5
- SNQN 84655 3460 D6
- WBNF 84087 1551 B6
10 CRFD 84015 1227 D3
10 SPFK 84660 3249 C1
100 ANFK 84003 2604 A6
100 LOGN 84321 527 C1
200 BNFL 84010 1551 D6
300 OREM 84057 2820 B3
300 SLCY 84103 1858 B1
400 SGVL 84663 3036 A7
400 SGVL 84663 3143 B1
600 BMCY 84302 766 D3
600 UthC 84003 2604 A6
700 PRVO 84601 2928 A5
700 SLCY 84116 1858 A1
1500 SLCY 84116 1857 C1
4000 WPT 84015 1226 A3
4300 WbrC 84404 1054 C4
W 700 S
10 BMCY 84302 766 D7
10 CTRV 84014 1551 D4
10 GRLD 84312 520 E3
10 LEHI 84043 2603 B7
10 PTGV 84062 2712 B4
10 PYSN 84651 3354 E6
10 SGVL 84663 3143 C3
10 SLCY 84101 1858 C5
10 WELV 84339 649 C4
100 HRCY 84032 2398 C5
100 SHFD 84335 399 D4
300 LOGN 84321 527 C5
300 PRVO 84601 3035 B1
300 UthC 84043 2603 B7
600 OREM 84058 2820 B7
600 TMTN 84337 520 D7
700 SLCY 84104 1858 A5
700 WDCR 84087 1653 B1
900 SLCY 84104 1857 E5
1000 CRFD 84016 1227 B6
1200 MTSV 84404 1056 A6
1300 LEHI 84043 2602 E7
1300 SRCS 84015 1227 B6
1300 UthC 84043 2602 E7
1400 DvsC 84016 1227 B6
1500 SRCS 84075 1227 B6
1600 MTSV 84404 1055 E6
1700 SRCS 84075 1226 E6
3500 SRCS 84015 1226 B6
3500 WPT 84015 1226 B6
3700 SLCY 84104 1856 A5
4000 DvsC 84075 1225 E6
4000 DvsC 84075 1226 B6
4000 WPT 84015 1225 E6
5300 SLCY 84104 1855 E5
700 E
- CchC 84328 711 A3
700 S
- WELV 84339 649 C4
N 705 W
10 OREM 84057 2820 B5
S 705 E
- OREM 84097 2928 A2
E 710 N
400 LNDN 84042 2713 C4
E 710 S
100 OREM 84058 2820 D7
N 710 E
700 OREM 84097 2821 A3
1700 OREM 84097 2714 A7
N 710 W
10 SPFK 84660 3249 B3
400 LOGN 84321 527 B2
1200 OREM 84057 2820 B2
S 710 E
- LEHI 84043 2710 D2
W 710 N
100 OREM 84057 2820 D3
2200 PRVO 84601 2927 C5
S 715 E
3300 SLkC 84106 1964 E6
E 720 N
300 OREM 84057 2820 E3
500 OREM 84097 2820 E3
700 LEHI 84043 2603 D5
900 OREM 84097 2821 B3
1200 PRVO 84606 2928 E5
E 720 S
10 OREM 84058 2820 D7
300 OREM 84097 2820 E7
300 SPFK 84660 3249 D4
1500 PTGV 84062 2713 C4
N 720 E
300 LEHI 84043 2603 D6
500 PRVO 84606 2928 D5
900 KYVL 84037 1283 E6
N 720 W
1700 OREM 84057 2713 B7
2300 CLTN 84015 1171 C6
S 720 E
200 SALM 84653 3356 C4
1400 OREM 84097 2928 A1
S 720 W
100 LEHI 84043 2603 B7
600 PRVO 84601 3035 B1
1500 WDCR 84087 1653 B2
3400 NBLY 84321 591 C4
W 720 N
- SNQN 84655 3460 C6
- TMTN 84337 520 D4
- UthC 84655 3460 C6
900 ANFK 84043 2604 A6
1000 OREM 84057 2820 A3
W 720 S
10 OREM 84058 2820 D7
800 TMTN 84337 520 D7
900 LOGN 84321 527 A5
E 725 N
- WbrC 84317 1060 E3
- WbrC 84317 1061 A3
800 OGDN 84404 1057 A4
E 725 S
800 CTRV 84014 1552 A4
1900 SGVL 84663 3144 B3
N 725 E
300 HDPK 84318 400 B7
300 NSLK 84054 1653 C6
1500 BNFL 84010 1552 A5
1500 NHON 84414 1057 A1
N 725 W
400 CRFD 84015 1227 C3
600 BMCY 84302 766 D4
1100 CTRV 84014 1551 C1
1200 OREM 84057 2820 B1
1500 CLTN 84015 1227 C1
2000 CTRV 84014 1448 C6
2000 WBNF 84087 1551 B4
2700 LYTN 84041 1228 D6
S 725 E
10 LNDN 84042 2713 D6
300 LYTN 84041 1283 A6
1800 CRFD 84015 1282 A1
5900 MRRY 84107 2070 E7
6400 MRRY 84107 2176 E1
6800 MDVL 84047 2176 E1
S 725 W
800 OREM 84058 2820 B7
2600 PRRY 84302 827 C5
3100 NBLY 84321 591 B4
3200 BNFL 84010 1653 B5
3800 NSLK 84010 1653 B6
3800 NSLK 84054 1653 B6
W 725 N
10 LNDN 84042 2713 A4
200 LOGN 84321 527 C1
1000 CRFD 84015 1227 B3
1000 CTRV 84014 1551 C2
1200 CLTN 84015 1227 B3
2400 WPT 84015 1226 D3
W 725 S
900 BMCY 84302 827 D1
E 730 N
- SNQN 84655 3460 E6
E 730 S
300 RVHT 84321 527 E5
1100 PTGV 84062 2713 B4
N 730 E
700 ANFK 84003 2604 E6
700 OREM 84097 2821 A3
1000 PTGV 84062 2713 A1
1100 LOGN 84341 464 A7
N 730 W
500 ANFK 84003 2604 A6
1700 LOGN 84341 463 B5
2200 CLTN 84015 1171 C7
2400 LEHI 84043 2603 B2
S 730 E
- SNQN 84655 3568 A1
500 OREM 84097 2821 A6
4200 SLkC 84107 2070 E1
9800 SLkC 84094 2282 E2
S 730 W
800 PYSN 84651 3354 D7
1000 LEHI 84043 2710 B1
1300 PYSN 84651 3461 D1
2200 SRCS 84075 1281 C2
W 730 N
- SNQN 84655 3460 D6
100 LOGN 84321 527 D1
2900 PRVO 84601 2927 B5
W 730 S
300 OREM 84058 2820 C7
400 PRVO 84601 3035 B1
600 HRCY 84032 2398 B5
800 BMCY 84302 827 D1
1400 OREM 84058 2819 E7
W 730 N Cir
600 ANFK 84003 2604 A6
E 735 S
- CTRV 84014 1551 E4
W 735 N
1400 CLTN 84015 1227 A3
W 736 N
200 WBNF 84087 1551 B7
E 740 N
10 ANFK 84003 2604 C6
200 LNDN 84042 2713 B4
200 OREM 84057 2820 E3
E 740 S
10 OREM 84058 2820 D7
900 SPFK 84660 3249 E4
1100 PTGV 84062 2713 B4
N 740 E
600 LEHI 84043 2603 D5
1600 MPTN 84664 3144 B5
N 740 W
1500 OREM 84057 2820 B1
1500 PRVO 84604 2928 A4
S 740 E
- LEHI 84043 2710 D2
10 ANFK 84003 2711 E1
200 MIDW 84049 2397 D4
200 RVHT 84321 528 A3
200 WshC 84049 2397 D4
1300 OREM 84097 2928 A1
3700 SLkC 84106 1964 A6
8000 SNDY 84094 2176 E5
8200 SLkC 84094 2176 E5
S 740 W
100 LNDN 84042 2712 E6
700 LEHI 84043 2710 A1
700 WDCR 84087 1653 B1
1500 PYSN 84651 3461 D1
W 740 N
200 ANFK 84003 2604 B6
800 OREM 84057 2820 B3
W 740 S
300 BNFL 84010 1653 C1
N 745 E
300 PTGV 84062 2713 A2
S 745 E
6900 MDVL 84047 2176 E1
8200 SLkC 84094 2176 E5
8200 SNDY 84094 2176 E5
E 750 N
10 BNFL 84010 1551 E6
10 MNTU 84324 768 C5
100 OREM 84057 2820 D3
100 SGVL 84663 3036 C7
200 LNDN 84042 2713 C4
300 ANFK 84003 2604 E6
500 OGDN 84404 1056 E3
600 OGDN 84404 1057 A3
700 BNFL 84010 1552 A6
700 LYTN 84041 1283 B3
700 OREM 84097 2821 A3
700 PRVO 84606 2928 D5
700 PTGV 84062 2713 A2
1200 LOGN 84321 528 B1
E 750 S
- UthC 84660 3250 C4
10 BMCY 84302 828 A1
10 LEHI 84043 2710 C1
100 SALM 84653 3356 B5
300 FMTN 84025 1448 D3
600 OREM 84097 2821 A7
700 SGVL 84663 3143 E3
1400 SPFK 84660 3250 B4
1500 CRFD 84015 1228 B6
1600 SGVL 84663 3144 A3
N 750 E
- PTGV 84062 2713 A1
10 ANFK 84003 2711 E1
10 HRCY 84032 2398 E3
10 KYVL 84037 1345 E1
10 LOGN 84321 528 A3
10 PRVO 84606 2928 D6
100 SGVL 84663 3143 E2
300 KYVL 84037 1283 E7
300 LNDN 84042 2713 D5
300 WshC 84032 2398 E3
400 BNFL 84010 1552 A6
400 PYSN 84651 3355 A4
600 OREM 84097 2821 A3
700 LOGN 84341 464 A5
800 ANFK 84003 2604 E5
2300 PRVO 84604 2928 D2
2600 LEHI 84043 2603 D2
3000 LYTN 84040 1229 B5
3200 NHON 84414 999 A4
3900 PRVO 84604 2821 D6
N 750 W
- PRVO 84604 2928 B2
- SGVL 84663 3143 B1
- WBNF 84087 1551 B4
10 LYTN 84041 1282 D4
100 HYRM 84319 650 E2
300 LNDN 84042 2712 E5
400 LOGN 84321 527 B2
600 OREM 84057 2820 B3
700 CRFD 84015 1227 C3
800 CLTN 84015 1227 C2
1200 PTGV 84062 2712 C1
1200 SGVL 84663 3036 B6
1300 OGDN 84404 1056 B2
1400 HARR 84404 998 B7
1400 HARR 84404 1056 B1
1400 HARR 84414 998 B7
1800 CLTN 84015 1171 C7
1800 FMTN 84025 1346 B5
1900 CTRV 84014 1448 C6
2100 PTVW 84404 998 B7
2200 LEHI 84043 2603 A2
3000 PTVW 84414 998 B4
S 750 E
10 ANFK 84003 2711 E1
10 PRVO 84606 2928 D7
200 BNFL 84010 1552 A7
200 CRFD 84015 1228 A5
300 LYTN 84041 1283 B5
400 OREM 84097 2821 A6
500 BNFL 84010 1654 A1
800 SALM 84653 3356 C6
1000 KYVL 84037 1345 E3
1000 OREM 84097 2928 A1
1000 SGVL 84663 3143 D4
2800 SGVL 84663 3035 E7
2800 SGVL 84663 3142 E2
3700 SLkC 84106 1965 A7
5300 SOGN 84405 1173 A4
S 750 W
10 OREM 84058 2820 B5
100 LNDN 84042 2712 E7
200 SPFK 84660 3249 B3
700 OGDN 84404 1056 B7
1700 SRCS 84075 1281 C1
2000 WDCR 84087 1653 B3
2100 PRRY 84302 827 C4
3900 RVDL 84405 1172 B1
3900 SLkC 84123 1964 A7
3900 SLkC 84123 2070 A1
7200 BxEC 84340 941 C3
W 750 N
- SNQN 84655 3460 D6
W 750 N
10 CRFD 84015 1227 D3
10 WLRD 84340 885 A4
100 SGVL 84663 3036 C7
200 BMCY 84302 766 E3
300 OREM 84057 2820 C3
400 LEHI 84043 2603 B5
400 LOGN 84321 527 C1
500 ANFK 84003 2604 A6
1100 CTRV 84014 1551 C2
2700 PRVO 84601 2927 B5
4000 WPT 84015 1226 A3
W 750 N SR-315
10 WLRD 84340 885 B4
W 750 S
100 LYTN 84041 1282 E6
100 WELV 84339 649 C4
200 BNFL 84010 1653 D1
200 LOGN 84321 527 C5
400 OREM 84058 2820 C7
600 PRVO 84601 3035 B1
700 TMTN 84337 520 D7
800 WDCR 84087 1653 B1
1200 CRFD 84016 1227 A6
2000 SRCS 84075 1226 E6
W 750 N Cir
200 ANFK 84003 2604 C6
S 754 W
500 OREM 84058 2820 B6
757 E
800 OGDN 84404 1057 A3
E 760 N
10 ANFK 84003 2604 C6
300 OREM 84057 2820 E3
400 LNDN 84042 2713 C4
600 LEHI 84043 2603 D5
800 OGDN 84404 1057 A3
1000 OREM 84097 2821 B3
E 760 S
10 OREM 84058 2820 D7
200 WELV 84339 649 D4
1000 OREM 84097 2821 B7
N 760 E
300 ANFK 84003 2604 E7
2700 PRVO 84604 2928 D1
3600 PRVO 84604 2821 D7
N 760 W
1200 FMTN 84025 1346 B6
1200 OREM 84057 2820 B2
1700 OREM 84057 2713 B7
S 760 E
10 FTHT 84037 1345 E1
10 KYVL 84037 1345 E1
10 PTGV 84062 2713 A3
500 SHFD 84335 400 A4
1400 OREM 84097 2928 A1
4200 SLkC 84107 2071 A1
9600 SNDY 84094 2282 E1
S 760 W
- TMTN 84337 520 D6
200 OREM 84058 2820 B6
1300 PRVO 84601 3035 A2
2100 WDCR 84087 1653 B3
W 760 N
1300 OREM 84057 2819 E3
1300 OREM 84057 2820 A3
W 760 S
100 SALM 84653 3356 A5
E 765 N
300 BMCY 84302 767 A3
S 765 W
400 SLCY 84104 1858 A4
W 765 S
200 OREM 84058 2820 C7
E 770 N
300 LOGN 84321 527 E1
400 OREM 84097 2820 E3
500 ALPN 84004 2498 A3
600 ANFK 84003 2605 A6
E 770 S
600 PYSN 84651 3355 A6
N 770 W
1300 OREM 84057 2820 B1
2300 CLTN 84015 1171 C6
S 770 E
200 SALM 84653 3356 C4
700 SPFK 84660 3249 E4
S 770 W
700 WDCR 84087 1653 B1
1000 PRVO 84601 3035 B2
W 770 N
- SNQN 84655 3460 D5
200 KYVL 84037 1283 B6
2900 PRVO 84601 2927 B5
W 770 S
600 WDCR 84087 1653 B1
900 PRVO 84601 3035 A1
1600 SRCS 84075 1227 A6
E 775 N
400 ANFK 84003 2604 D6
400 BNFL 84010 1551 E6
500 BNFL 84010 1552 A6
2800 LYTN 84040 1284 A3
E 775 S
10 LYTN 84041 1282 E6
1500 OGDN 84404 1057 C6
1900 SGVL 84663 3144 B3
N 775 E
10 ANFK 84003 2711 E1
100 ANFK 84003 2604 E7
1800 NHON 84414 1057 A1
1900 NHON 84414 999 A7
N 775 W
700 CRFD 84015 1227 C3
1500 CLTN 84015 1227 C1
1700 WBNF 84087 1551 B4
S 775 E
300 LYTN 84041 1283 B5
500 OGDN 84404 1057 A6
1900 BNFL 84010 1654 A3
3800 SLkC 84106 1965 A7
6800 MDVL 84047 2177 A2
10400 SALM 84653 3356 E5
S 775 W
- CRFD 84016 1227 C5
10 CRFD 84015 1227 C5
1100 BMCY 84302 827 D2
1300 PRRY 84302 827 D2
2000 WDCR 84087 1653 B3
2400 SRCS 84075 1281 C1
3800 DvsC 84010 1653 B6
S 775 W
3800 NSLK 84010 1653 B6
4000 NSLK 84054 1653 B6
4300 RVDL 84405 1172 B2
W 775 N
- LYTN 84041 1282 A3
200 LOGN 84321 527 C1
300 CTRV 84014 1551 D2
800 CRFD 84015 1227 B3
3600 LYTN 84041 1281 C3
W 775 S
10 LYTN 84041 1282 E6
3900 SRCS 84075 1226 A6
S 776 W
600 MIDW 84049 2397 A2
E 780 N
400 OREM 84097 2820 E3
500 PTGV 84062 2712 E2
600 PTGV 84062 2713 A2
900 LYTN 84040 1283 B3
E 780 S
- SNQN 84655 3567 E2
10 PRVO 84606 3035 C1
800 SPFK 84660 3249 E4
N 780 E
700 LEHI 84043 2603 D5
N 780 W
400 LOGN 84321 527 B2
500 ANFK 84003 2604 A6
900 CLTN 84015 1227 C2
1300 LEHI 84043 2603 A4
S 780 E
- UthC 84660 3249 E6
S 780 W
10 LEHI 84043 2603 A7
1100 PYSN 84651 3354 D7
1500 PYSN 84651 3461 D1
5800 MRRY 84123 2070 A6
W 780 N
1100 OREM 84057 2820 A3
W 780 S
- SNQN 84655 3567 E2
- SRCS 84075 1226 D6
10 CTRV 84014 1551 D4
200 LOGN 84321 527 C5
N 785 W
500 LNDN 84042 2712 E5
S 785 E
4300 SLkC 84107 2071 A1
5000 SOGN 84405 1173 A3
5100 MRRY 84107 2071 A4
E 790 S
300 PTGV 84062 2712 E4
N 790 E
500 PRVO 84606 2928 D6
900 LEHI 84043 2603 D5
N 790 W
300 LNDN 84042 2712 E5
2200 LEHI 84043 2603 A2
S 790 W
800 LEHI 84043 2710 A1
1500 PYSN 84651 3461 D2
6400 MRRY 84123 2176 A1
W 790 N
100 ANFK 84003 2604 C6
W 790 S
- CRFD 84016 1227 A6
300 LOGN 84321 527 C5
E 800 N
- MPTN 84664 3144 B6
- OREM 84604 2821 B3
- SPFK 84663 3250 A1
10 LOGN 84321 527 D1
10 OREM 84057 2820 E3
10 PRVO 84604 2928 C5
10 PRVO 84606 2928 C5
10 SPFK 84660 3249 D1
100 BNFL 84010 1551 E6
300 ANFK 84003 2604 D6
400 OGDN 84404 1056 E3
400 OREM 84097 2820 E3
500 BNFL 84010 1653 C5
500 OGDN 84404 1057 A3
600 OREM 84097 2821 A3
700 PTGV 84062 2713 A1
700 SGVL 84663 3036 D7
800 GNLA 84655 3460 A2
1000 BNFL 84010 1552 A6
1000 UthC 84655 3460 A2
1100 LEHI 84043 2603 E5
1100 LYTN 84040 1283 C3
1200 SPFK 84660 3250 A1
1400 LOGN 84321 528 C1
E 800 N SR-52
- OREM 84604 2821 B3
10 OREM 84057 2820 E3
400 OREM 84097 2820 E3
600 OREM 84097 2821 A3
E 800 S
- CRFD 84015 1227 E6
- OGDN 84404 1057 B6
- PVDN 84332 527 E5
- PYSN 84651 3354 E6
- RVHT 84321 527 E5
- WbrC 84404 1061 C6
10 BMCY 84302 827 E1
10 BMCY 84302 828 A1
10 HRCY 84032 2398 D5
10 OREM 84058 2820 E7
10 SGVL 84663 3143 D3
10 SLCY 84111 1858 E5
10 WELV 84339 649 D4
100 PYSN 84651 3355 A6
100 SALM 84653 3356 B5
100 SHFD 84335 399 D5
200 CTRV 84014 1551 E4
200 LYTN 84041 1283 A6
300 OREM 84097 2820 E7
500 OREM 84097 2821 A7
500 SLCY 84102 1858 E5
500 SPFK 84660 3249 E4
700 CTRV 84014 1552 A5
700 SLCY 84102 1859 B5
900 BNFL 84010 1654 A1
900 PRVO 84606 3035 E1
1300 PRVO 84606 3036 A1
1500 CRFD 84015 1228 B6
N 800 E
- ANFK 84003 2605 A6
10 ANFK 84003 2711 E1
10 OREM 84097 2821 A4
10 PRVO 84606 2928 D6

STREET Block City ZIP Map# Grid

N 800 E
10 PYSN 84651 3355 B5
10 SPFK 84660 3249 E2
100 ANFK 84003 2604 E7
100 BMCY 84302 767 B5
200 KYVL 84037 1345 E1
200 PTGV 84062 2713 A2
200 SGVL 84663 3143 E1
300 KYVL 84037 1283 E7
400 LNDN 84042 2713 D5
500 LOGN 84321 528 A1
600 BNFL 84010 1552 A6
800 SGVL 84663 3036 D7
900 LOGN 84321 464 A7
1000 LOGN 84341 464 A7
1300 MPTN 84664 3144 B5
1600 LEHI 84043 2603 D3
1700 NHON 84414 1057 A1
2100 NHLN 84341 464 A3
2200 PRVO 84604 2928 D2
3100 NHON 84414 999 A3
N 800 W
- ANFK 84003 2604 A6
- HYRM 84319 650 E2
- OGDN 84404 1056 B4
- SGVL 84663 3143 A1
10 CchC 84335 399 B2
10 OREM 84057 2820 B4
10 SHFD 84335 399 B2
10 SLCY 84116 1858 A2
100 MIDW 84049 2397 A1
200 SPFK 84660 3249 B2
200 UthC 84660 3249 B2
300 TMTN 84337 520 D5
400 LNDN 84042 2712 E5
400 LOGN 84321 527 B2
500 PRVO 84601 2928 A5
600 BMCY 84302 766 D3
600 CRFD 84015 1227 C3
1000 BxEC 84302 766 C2
1200 MPTN 84664 3143 E5
1300 WBNF 84087 1551 B5
1400 HARR 84404 1056 B1
1400 SLCY 84116 1754 A6
1700 OREM 84057 2713 B7
2100 LYTN 84041 1228 D7
2100 PRVO 84604 2928 A2
2400 LEHI 84043 2603 A2
3400 PTVW 84414 998 B3
S 800 E
- HYRM 84319 652 A3
- HYRM 84321 652 A3
- SHFD 84335 400 B4
- SNQN 84655 3568 A1
10 ALPN 84004 2498 B5
10 BNFL 84010 1552 A7
10 LNDN 84042 2713 D6
10 OREM 84097 2821 A7
10 PTGV 84062 2713 A3
10 PYSN 84651 3355 B5
10 SLCY 84102 1859 A3
10 SPFK 84660 3249 E3
10 UthC 84003 2711 E1
100 HDPK 84318 464 C1
300 MLVI 84332 592 A4
400 CRFD 84015 1228 A5
500 RVHT 84321 528 A4
600 BNFL 84010 1654 A1
600 SGVL 84663 3143 D3
700 CTRV 84014 1552 A4
800 MPTN 84664 3251 B1
900 SLCY 84105 1859 A6
1000 OREM 84097 2928 A1
1100 KYVL 84037 1345 E4
1500 SLCY 84105 1965 A1
2000 CRFD 84015 1282 A1
2100 SLCY 84106 1965 A2
2700 SLkC 84106 1965 A4
3200 CchC 84321 592 A4
4000 SLkC 84124 2071 A1
4900 SOGN 84403 1173 A3
5300 SOGN 84405 1173 A4
6600 CchC 84319 652 A6
6800 MDVL 84047 2177 A2
8800 UthC 84660 3356 E2
11800 DRPR 84020 2282 E7
12000 DRPR 84020 2283 A7
12000 DRPR 84020 2389 A1
S 800 W
- LEHI 84043 2710 A2
10 BMCY 84302 766 D6
10 CchC 84335 399 B3
10 CTRV 84014 1551 C4
10 LNDN 84042 2712 E7
10 MPTN 84664 3143 E7
10 OREM 84058 2820 B5
10 PRVO 84601 2928 A7
10 SHFD 84335 399 B3
10 SLCY 84104 1858 A3
10 TMTN 84337 520 D6
100 PYSN 84651 3354 D6
200 MPTN 84664 3250 E1
300 LNDN 84042 2819 E1
400 CTRV 84087 1551 C4
500 LEHI 84043 2603 A7
500 PRVO 84601 3035 A1
500 WBNF 84087 1653 B3
600 WDCR 84087 1653 B1
700 BMCY 84302 827 D1
700 WBNF 84087 1551 C4
1200 OREM 84058 2927 B1
1800 CchC 84321 527 B7
1800 CchC 84321 591 B1
1800 LOGN 84321 527 B7
1800 LOGN 84321 591 B1
2200 NBLY 84321 591 B1
2200 NSLK 84087 1653 B3
2400 SSLK 84119 1964 A3
2700 SRCS 84075 1281 C3
2800 PRRY 84302 827 C6
2900 UthC 84660 3250 E4
3200 BNFL 84010 1653 B6
3200 DvsC 84010 1653 B6
3200 NSLK 84054 1653 B6
3800 RVDL 84405 1115 B7
4000 SPFK 84660 3142 A4
4000 UthC 84660 3142 A4
4100 CchC 84341 399 B6
4100 RVDL 84405 1172 B1
5600 MRRY 84123 2070 A6
7200 BxEC 84340 941 C3

W 800 N
- BMCY 84302 766 D3
- BxEC 84302 765 C4
- LNDN 84042 2712 E4
- PTGV 84062 3035 D7
10 BNFL 84010 1551 D6
10 CRFD 84015 1227 C3
10 PRVO 84601 2928 B5
10 PRVO 84604 2928 B5
10 SNST 84015 1227 C3
10 SPFK 84660 3249 C1
200 ANFK 84003 2604 B6
200 LEHI 84043 2603 B5
300 LNDN 84042 2713 A4
300 MPTN 84664 3143 E6
300 MPTN 84664 3144 A6
300 PTGV 84062 2713 A4
300 SLCY 84103 1754 B7
500 WBNF 84087 1551 C6
600 CLTN 84015 1227 C3
800 OREM 84057 2820 B3
900 LOGN 84321 527 B1
900 SLCY 84116 1754 A7
1400 OREM 84057 2819 E3
1400 PTGV 84062 2712 B2
1700 SLCY 84116 1753 C7
2200 PRVO 84601 2927 C5
3500 WPT 84015 1226 A3
4300 WPT 84015 1225 E3
5200 CchC 84325 524 E1
5200 CchC 84325 525 A1
W 800 N SR-52
10 OREM 84057 2820 C3
1400 OREM 84057 2819 E3
W 800 S
- CRFD 84016 1227 A6
- GRLD 84312 520 E3
10 MPTN 84664 3250 E1
10 MPTN 84664 3251 A1
10 OREM 84058 2820 D7
10 PYSN 84651 3354 D6
10 SALM 84653 3356 A5
10 SLCY 84101 1858 A5
10 WELV 84339 649 C4
100 SGVL 84663 3143 C3
300 ALPN 84004 2497 D6
300 BNFL 84010 1653 C1
300 CchC 84335 399 C5
300 LOGN 84321 527 C5
300 SHFD 84335 399 C5
400 SALM 84653 3355 E5
500 WDCR 84010 1653 C1
600 SLCY 84104 1858 A5
600 UthC 84651 3355 E5
600 UthC 84653 3355 E5
1200 SLCY 84104 1857 D5
1300 OREM 84058 2819 E7
3600 SLCY 84104 1856 D5
3600 SRCS 84075 1226 B6
E 800 St S
10 SHFD 84335 399 D5
N 800 St E
10 HYRM 84319 651 D2
200 CchC 84321 651 D2
N 800 St E SR-165
10 HYRM 84319 651 D2
200 CchC 84321 651 D2
S 800 St E
10 HYRM 84319 651 D3
S 800 St E SR-165
10 HYRM 84319 651 D3
W 800 N Cir
500 ANFK 84003 2604 B6
S 805 E
3500 SLkC 84106 1965 A6
3900 SLkC 84124 1965 A7
8100 SNDY 84094 2177 A5
E 810 S
700 SPFK 84660 3249 E4
1200 ALPN 84004 2498 C6
N 810 E
200 SHFD 84335 400 A2
N 810 W
500 PTGV 84062 2712 C2
1500 CLTN 84015 1227 C1
1800 CLTN 84015 1171 C7
S 810 E
200 SALM 84653 3356 C4
900 PRVO 84606 3035 D1
3700 SLkC 84106 1965 A7
S 810 W
1400 PRVO 84601 3035 A2
W 810 N
- WBNF 84087 1551 C6
600 PTGV 84062 2712 C2
W 810 S
500 LEHI 84043 2710 B1
W 815 S
200 LOGN 84321 527 C5
E 820 N
700 PRVO 84604 2928 D5
700 PRVO 84606 2928 D5
1400 OREM 84097 2821 C3
1500 PRVO 84604 2929 A5
E 820 S
- CTRV 84014 1551 E5
10 LEHI 84043 2710 C1
100 SALM 84653 3356 B5
200 OREM 84058 2820 E7
400 PTGV 84062 2712 E4
600 PTGV 84062 2713 A4
700 SPFK 84660 3249 E4
1400 SPFK 84660 3250 A4
N 820 E
900 ANFK 84003 2604 E5
2300 PRVO 84604 2928 D2
3600 PRVO 84604 2821 D7
N 820 W
800 OREM 84057 2820 B3
1300 CLTN 84015 1227 C1
1700 OREM 84057 2713 B7
1800 PTGV 84062 2605 C7
2100 FMTN 84025 1346 B4
S 820 E
400 SPFK 84660 3249 E4
1200 ANFK 84003 2711 E4
5100 MRRY 84107 2071 A4
S 820 W
1200 PRVO 84601 3035 A2
W 820 N
400 LEHI 84043 2603 B5
800 PRVO 84601 2928 A5

W 820 N
800 PRVO 84604 2928 A5
1300 PRVO 84601 2927 E5
1300 PRVO 84604 2927 E5
E 825 N
10 LYTN 84041 1282 E3
500 OGDN 84404 1056 E3
500 OGDN 84404 1057 A3
600 LEHI 84043 2603 D5
N 825 E
10 ANFK 84003 2712 A1
100 ANFK 84003 2605 A7
300 ANFK 84003 2604 E7
1900 LEHI 84043 2603 D3
3400 NHON 84414 999 B3
N 825 W
200 HYRM 84319 650 E2
600 CRFD 84015 1227 C3
S 825 E
600 LYTN 84041 1283 B6
2000 CRFD 84015 1282 A1
3300 SLkC 84106 1965 A5
5300 SOGN 84405 1173 A4
6800 MDVL 84047 2177 A2
S 825 W
- SRCS 84075 1281 C2
1700 LEHI 84043 2710 A2
4100 DvsC 84010 1653 B6
4100 RVDL 84405 1172 B1
W 825 N
100 BMCY 84302 766 E3
200 SNST 84015 1227 C3
1100 LYTN 84041 1282 C3
E 830 N
600 ANFK 84003 2604 E5
E 830 S
- CRFD 84015 1227 E6
- SHFD 84335 399 E5
200 FMTN 84025 1448 D3
900 PTGV 84062 2713 A4
N 830 E
- SHFD 84335 400 B2
1000 LEHI 84043 2603 D5
N 830 W
900 OREM 84057 2820 B2
S 830 E
300 SHFD 84335 400 B4
800 OREM 84097 2821 A7
7900 SNDY 84094 2177 A4
8400 SLkC 84094 2177 A5
S 830 W
- SRCS 84075 1281 B1
- TMTN 84337 520 C6
1100 PYSN 84651 3354 D7
1200 PYSN 84651 3461 D1
W 830 N
800 OREM 84057 2820 B3
W 830 S
100 OGDN 84404 1056 D6
E 835 N
400 OREM 84097 2820 E3
N 835 E
100 LNDN 84042 2713 D5
N 835 W
600 OREM 84057 2820 B3
S 835 E
9500 SNDY 84094 2283 A1
S 835 W
10 GRLD 84337 520 D2
1800 WDCR 84087 1653 B3
E 840 N
300 ANFK 84003 2604 D6
400 LEHI 84043 2603 C5
1400 OREM 84097 2821 C3
E 840 S
100 OREM 84058 2820 E7
N 840 E
- ANFK 84003 2604 E5
10 PTGV 84062 2713 A3
500 OGDN 84404 1057 A4
900 OREM 84097 2821 A2
2700 PRVO 84604 2928 D1
N 840 W
1300 OREM 84057 2820 B1
1300 WBNF 84087 1551 B5
1800 PRVO 84604 2928 A3
2300 CLTN 84015 1171 B6
2400 LEHI 84043 2603 A2
S 840 E
3900 SLkC 84124 1965 A7
7000 MDVL 84047 2177 A2
S 840 W
900 LEHI 84043 2710 A1
1200 WDCR 84087 1653 B2
1500 PYSN 84651 3461 D1
5900 MRRY 84123 2070 A6
6400 MRRY 84123 2176 A1
W 840 N
200 BNFL 84010 1551 D6
W 840 S
300 OREM 84058 2820 C7
S 845 E
4200 SLkC 84107 2071 A1
W 845 N
- WBNF 84087 1551 B6
E 850 N
10 ANFK 84003 2604 C6
300 HARR 84404 1056 E3
400 NSLK 84054 1653 B5
400 SGVL 84663 3036 D7
600 LYTN 84041 1283 B3
600 OGDN 84404 1057 A3
1000 OREM 84097 2821 B3
1200 LOGN 84321 528 B1
1300 LYTN 84040 1283 C3
E 850 S
- OGDN 84404 1057 B7
10 LYTN 84041 1282 E6
10 OREM 84058 2820 D7
10 SALM 84653 3356 B5
10 WshC 84049 2397 C5
200 BMCY 84302 828 A1
400 CTRV 84014 1551 E5
400 OREM 84097 2820 E7
600 PYSN 84651 3355 A7
900 SPFK 84660 3249 E4
1300 PRVO 84606 3035 E1
1300 PRVO 84606 3036 A1
1500 SPFK 84660 3250 A4
1600 SGVL 84663 3144 A3
N 850 E
- PTGV 84062 2713 A1

N 850 E
10 LNDN 84042 2713 D6
100 LYTN 84041 1283 B4
200 OREM 84097 2821 A4
400 SGVL 84663 3143 E1
600 ANFK 84003 2604 E6
600 ANFK 84003 2605 A6
1000 BNFL 84010 1552 A6
1700 NHON 84414 1057 B1
2200 LEHI 84043 2603 D2
2300 PRVO 84604 2928 D2
2600 NHON 84414 999 B5
3900 PRVO 84604 2821 D6
N 850 W
- SGVL 84663 3143 A1
10 KYVL 84037 1345 B1
200 HYRM 84319 650 E2
200 LOGN 84321 527 B2
200 OREM 84057 2820 B4
500 PRVO 84601 2928 A5
700 CRFD 84015 1227 B3
1700 OREM 84057 2713 B7
1900 CLTN 84015 1171 C7
2100 PRVO 84604 2928 A2
3300 PTVW 84414 998 B4
S 850 E
- SHFD 84335 400 B4
10 LEHI 84043 2603 D7
10 PRVO 84606 2928 D7
10 PTGV 84062 2713 A3
10 UthC 84003 2712 A1
400 OREM 84097 2821 A6
500 LYTN 84041 1283 B6
600 BMCY 84302 767 B7
700 BNFL 84010 1654 A1
1000 SGVL 84663 3143 E4
1100 SPFK 84660 3249 E5
1500 OREM 84097 2928 A2
4100 SOGN 84403 1173 A1
4200 SLkC 84107 2071 A1
5300 SOGN 84405 1173 A5
7300 SWBR 84405 1229 A1
12000 DRPR 84020 2283 A7
S 850 W
- TMTN 84337 520 C6
100 OREM 84058 2820 B5
600 BMCY 84302 766 D7
1500 WDCR 84087 1653 B2
2700 SRCS 84075 1281 B3
3800 DvsC 84010 1653 B6
3800 NSLK 84010 1653 B6
3800 RVDL 84405 1115 B7
3900 RVDL 84405 1172 B1
14600 BFDL 84065 2388 A7
W 850 N
- LYTN 84041 1282 A3
100 SGVL 84663 3036 B7
200 ANFK 84003 2604 B6
200 BMCY 84302 766 E3
500 PTGV 84062 2712 C1
1000 WBNF 84087 1551 A6
1100 CTRV 84014 1551 C2
2200 PRVO 84601 2927 D5
3600 LYTN 84041 1281 C3
W 850 S
10 CTRV 84014 1551 D5
10 TMTN 84337 520 E7
100 HRCY 84032 2398 C5
400 BNFL 84010 1653 C2
600 LYTN 84041 1282 D6
600 OREM 84058 2820 B7
600 WDCR 84087 1653 B1
700 DvsC 84041 1282 D6
900 PRVO 84601 3035 A1
2000 SRCS 84075 1226 E6
4100 SLCY 84104 1856 B5
S 855 E
- SLkC 84124 1965 A7
6800 MDVL 84047 2177 A2
S 855 W
14600 BFDL 84065 2388 A7
W 855 N
1000 FMTN 84025 1346 A7
E 860 S
- SNQN 84655 3567 E2
700 SPFK 84660 3249 E4
1400 PTGV 84062 2713 C4
N 860 E
800 ALPN 84004 2498 B3
2400 PRVO 84604 2928 D2
N 860 W
10 SPFK 84660 3249 B2
600 OREM 84057 2820 B3
1100 PTGV 84062 2712 C1
1700 OREM 84057 2713 B7
2300 PTGV 84062 2605 C6
S 860 E
10 SGVL 84663 3143 E2
200 OREM 84097 2821 A5
200 SALM 84653 3356 C4
800 SPFK 84660 3249 E4
3500 SLkC 84106 1965 A6
5100 MRRY 84107 2071 A4
6700 MDVL 84047 2177 A1
7800 SNDY 84094 2177 A4
S 860 W
1000 PRVO 84601 3035 A2
W 860 N
500 ANFK 84003 2604 B6
1000 PRVO 84604 2928 A5
1000 PTGV 84062 2712 C1
W 860 S
- SNQN 84655 3567 E2
100 OREM 84058 2820 D7
300 SALM 84653 3356 A5
300 TMTN 84337 520 D7
1400 OREM 84058 2819 E7
E 865 N
100 OREM 84057 2820 D3
N 865 W
1500 CLTN 84015 1227 B1
S 865 E
1000 OGDN 84404 1057 A7
7900 SNDY 84094 2177 A5
8300 SLkC 84094 2177 A5
10600 SNDY 84094 2283 A4
S 865 W
2000 WDCR 84087 1653 B3
3200 SRCS 84075 1281 B4
E 870 N
200 LOGN 84321 527 E1
300 ANFK 84003 2604 D5

E 870 N
500 PRVO 84604 2928 D5
E 870 S
500 PTGV 84062 2712 E4
800 OREM 84097 2821 A7
N 870 E
10 ANFK 84003 2712 A1
400 OREM 84097 2821 A4
1000 ANFK 84003 2604 E5
3600 PRVO 84604 2821 D7
N 870 W
- OGDN 84404 1056 B3
500 WBNF 84087 1551 B6
1300 CLTN 84015 1227 B1
S 870 E
900 OREM 84097 2821 A7
900 SGVL 84663 3143 E4
S 870 W
- LEHI 84043 2710 A2
300 SLCY 84104 1858 A4
1400 PRVO 84601 3035 A2
W 870 N
10 SNST 84015 1227 D2
100 OREM 84057 2820 D3
200 LOGN 84321 527 D1
1700 PTGV 84062 2712 A1
W 870 S
400 OREM 84058 2820 C7
E 875 N
400 OGDN 84404 1056 E3
500 OREM 84097 2820 E3
600 ANFK 84003 2604 E5
600 OGDN 84404 1057 A3
700 OREM 84097 2821 A3
E 875 S
800 BNFL 84010 1654 A1
N 875 E
100 LOGN 84321 528 A3
300 OREM 84097 2821 A4
1700 NHON 84414 1057 B1
2800 NHON 84414 999 B5
N 875 W
10 LYTN 84041 1282 D4
2300 LYTN 84041 1228 D7
S 875 E
500 LYTN 84041 1283 B6
1800 CRFD 84015 1282 A1
3900 OGDN 84403 1173 A1
5000 MRRY 84107 2071 A4
5100 SOGN 84403 1173 A4
5500 SOGN 84405 1173 A4
S 875 W
- BxEC 84340 941 C5
10 OREM 84058 2820 B5
500 WBNF 84087 1653 B1
600 WDCR 84087 1653 B1
3300 SRCS 84075 1281 B4
W 875 N
100 BMCY 84302 766 E3
W 875 S
- LEHI 84043 2710 A1
2400 SRCS 84075 1226 D6
875 E
- CchC 84328 711 A2
E 880 N
900 OREM 84097 2821 A3
E 880 S
700 PTGV 84062 2713 A4
N 880 E
- ANFK 84003 2605 A5
- SHFD 84335 400 B2
400 SGVL 84663 3143 E1
500 SPFK 84660 3249 E2
600 SGVL 84663 3036 D7
2600 PRVO 84604 2928 E2
3000 LEHI 84043 2603 D1
N 880 W
- CTRV 84014 1551 B4
300 LNDN 84042 2712 E5
600 PTGV 84062 2712 C2
S 880 E
100 SGVL 84663 3143 E2
6900 MDVL 84047 2177 A2
8400 SNDY 84094 2177 A5
S 880 W
200 SPFK 84660 3249 B3
400 OREM 84058 2820 B6
1100 PYSN 84651 3354 D7
1200 PYSN 84651 3461 D1
W 880 N
200 ANFK 84003 2604 B6
200 PRVO 84604 2928 B5
300 LOGN 84321 527 C1
800 OREM 84057 2820 B3
2700 PRVO 84601 2927 B5
W 880 S
100 PRVO 84601 3035 C1
N 885 E
900 OREM 84097 2821 A2
S 885 E
1000 OGDN 84404 1057 B7
S 885 W
3100 SRCS 84075 1281 B3
W 885 S
500 BMCY 84302 827 D1
N 890 E
- ANFK 84003 2604 E5
- ANFK 84003 2605 A5
200 OREM 84097 2821 A4
N 890 W
800 OREM 84057 2820 B3
2300 CLTN 84015 1171 B6
S 890 E
800 OREM 84097 2821 A7
1000 OREM 84097 2928 A1
S 890 W
900 PRVO 84601 3035 A1
6400 MRRY 84123 2176 A1
W 890 N
600 PRVO 84604 2928 B5
S 895 E
3900 OGDN 84403 1173 A1
10700 SNDY 84094 2283 A4
895 E
- OGDN 84403 1173 A1
E 900 N
10 ANFK 84003 2604 C5
10 BMCY 84302 766 E3
10 BNFL 84010 1551 E6
10 LEHI 84043 2603 D5
10 PRVO 84604 2928 C5
10 SPFK 84660 3249 D1

E 900 N
100 BMCY 84302 767 A3
200 LOGN 84321 527 E1
300 OREM 84057 2820 E3
300 PTGV 84062 2712 E1
300 TMTN 84337 520 E4
300 TMTN 84337 521 A4
400 NSLK 84054 1653 B4
400 OGDN 84404 1056 E3
400 OREM 84097 2820 E3
400 SGVL 84663 3036 D7
500 LOGN 84321 528 A1
500 OGDN 84404 1057 A3
600 CTRV 84014 1551 E2
600 CTRV 84014 1552 A2
600 KYVL 84037 1283 E6
600 PYSN 84651 3355 A3
700 MPTN 84664 3144 C6
700 PRVO 84606 2928 D5
900 BNFL 84010 1552 A6
1000 OREM 84097 2821 B3
E 900 S
- PTGV 84062 2713 C4
- PVDN 84332 592 B2
- TMTN 84337 520 E3
10 HDPK 84318 464 A3
10 KYVL 84037 1345 C3
10 LYTN 84041 1282 E6
10 MPTN 84664 3251 B1
10 OREM 84058 2820 D7
10 SLCY 84111 1858 E5
10 WELV 84339 649 D4
100 LYTN 84041 1283 A6
100 SALM 84653 3356 B5
200 BMCY 84302 828 A1
200 PYSN 84651 3355 A7
300 OREM 84097 2820 E7
500 SLCY 84102 1858 E5
500 SLCY 84105 1858 E5
600 PRVO 84606 3035 E1
700 OREM 84097 2821 A7
700 SLCY 84102 1859 B5
700 SLCY 84105 1859 B5
800 SGVL 84663 3143 D3
800 SPFK 84660 3249 E4
1100 SPFK 84660 3250 A4
1200 SGVL 84663 3144 A4
1500 CRFD 84015 1228 B6
1500 PRVO 84606 3036 A1
1700 SLCY 84108 1859 E5
6500 WbrC 84317 1060 D6
7400 WbrC 84317 1061 A7
E 900 S SR-39
6500 WbrC 84317 1060 D6
7400 WbrC 84317 1061 A7
N 900 E
- UthC 84043 2603 D6
- WELV 84319 650 A1
- WELV 84339 650 A1
10 ANFK 84003 2712 A1
10 BMCY 84302 767 B5
10 LNDN 84042 2713 D6
10 PRVO 84606 2928 E5
10 PYSN 84651 3355 B5
10 SGVL 84663 3143 E1
100 ANFK 84003 2605 A4
200 HDPK 84318 400 C7
200 KYVL 84037 1283 E7
200 UthC 84003 2605 A5
300 OREM 84097 2821 A4
400 BNFL 84010 1552 A6
500 MPTN 84664 3144 C6
500 PTGV 84062 2713 A1
600 SPFK 84660 3249 E2
700 LOGN 84321 528 A1
800 PRVO 84604 2928 E5
900 LOGN 84321 464 A7
1000 LYTN 84040 1283 B2
1700 LEHI 84043 2603 D3
1700 NHON 84414 1057 B1
3200 NHON 84414 999 B4
3400 LYTN 84040 1229 B5
N 900 W
- MIDW 84049 2396 E2
- PRVO 84606 3035 D1
10 PRVO 84601 2928 A6
10 SLCY 84116 1858 A2
300 HYRM 84319 650 D2
500 ANFK 84003 2604 A6
500 ANFK 84043 2604 A6
500 PTGV 84062 2712 C2
500 UthC 84003 2604 A6
500 UthC 84043 2604 A6
700 SLCY 84116 1754 A7
900 CLTN 84015 1227 B2
1200 OREM 84057 2820 B2
1300 MPTN 84664 3143 E5
1300 OGDN 84404 1056 B2
1500 LEHI 84043 2603 A3
1600 WBNF 84087 1551 B4
1700 OREM 84057 2713 B7
1800 PRVO 84604 2928 A3
1800 PTGV 84062 2605 C7
2100 LYTN 84041 1228 D7
2500 LOGN 84341 463 B3
2600 CLTN 84015 1171 B6
3500 PTVW 84414 998 B3
S 900 E
- SNQN 84655 3568 A1
- UthC 84003 2712 A1
10 ANFK 84003 2712 A1
10 LNDN 84042 2713 D6
10 OREM 84097 2821 A5
10 PRVO 84606 2928 E7
10 PYSN 84651 3355 B5
10 SLCY 84102 1859 A3
10 SPFK 84660 3249 E3
100 SGVL 84663 3143 E2
200 KYVL 84037 1345 E2
300 SHFD 84335 400 B4
500 LYTN 84041 1283 B6
600 BMCY 84302 767 B7
900 PRVO 84606 3035 E1
900 SLCY 84105 1859 A6
1600 SLCY 84105 1965 A2
1800 BNFL 84010 1654 A1
2100 SLCY 84106 1965 A2
3000 SLkC 84106 1965 A6
3900 SLkC 84124 1965 A6
4000 SLkC 84124 2071 A1
4000 SOGN 84403 1173 A1
4100 SLkC 84107 2071 A1

S 900 E
4500 SLkC 84117 2071 A5
4600 MRRY 84107 2071 A5
4600 MRRY 84117 2071 A1
5600 MRRY 84121 2071 A5
5700 SOGN 84405 1173 A5
6400 MRRY 84047 2177 A1
6400 MRRY 84107 2177 A1
6400 MRRY 84121 2177 A1
6700 MDVL 84047 2177 A1
7300 SWBR 84405 1229 A1
7500 MDVL 84047 2176 E3
7600 SNDY 84047 2176 E3
12200 DRPR 84020 2389 A1
S 900 E SR-71
4800 MRRY 84107 2071 A5
4800 SLkC 84117 2071 A5
4900 MRRY 84117 2071 A5
5600 MRRY 84121 2071 A5
6400 MRRY 84047 2177 A1
6400 MRRY 84107 2177 A1
6400 MRRY 84121 2177 A1
6700 MDVL 84047 2177 A1
7500 MDVL 84047 2176 E3
7600 SNDY 84047 2176 E3
S 900 W
- CRFD 84016 1227 B7
- LEHI 84043 2710 A2
- PRVO 84606 3035 D1
- TMTN 84337 520 C6
10 OREM 84058 2820 B5
10 PRVO 84601 2928 A7
10 SLCY 84104 1858 A5
200 PYSN 84651 3354 D6
400 BMCY 84302 766 D7
500 PRVO 84601 3035 A1
500 WBNF 84087 1653 B1
600 WDCR 84087 1653 B1
1500 SLCY 84104 1964 A1
2100 SLCY 84119 1964 A1
2100 SSLK 84119 1964 A4
2300 SRCS 84075 1281 B2
3200 CchC 84321 591 B5
3200 NBLY 84321 591 B5
3700 RVDL 84405 1115 B7
3900 DvsC 84010 1653 B6
3900 NSLK 84010 1653 B6
3900 RVDL 84405 1172 B1
W 900 N
- BMCY 84302 766 D3
- LYTN 84041 1281 C3
- LYTN 84041 1282 A3
- TMTN 84337 520 A4
10 BNFL 84010 1551 D6
10 LOGN 84321 527 D1
10 OREM 84057 2820 D3
10 SGVL 84663 3036 C7
10 SPFK 84660 3249 C1
100 LEHI 84043 2603 B5
300 ANFK 84003 2604 B5
300 NSLK 84054 1652 E4
300 SLCY 84103 1754 B7
600 WBNF 84087 1551 C6
700 PTGV 84062 2712 C1
800 PRVO 84604 2928 A5
900 SLCY 84116 1754 A7
1000 FMTN 84025 1346 B7
1000 UthC 84043 2603 B5
1300 PRVO 84604 2927 E5
1700 SLCY 84116 1753 C7
1900 FMTN 84025 1346 D6
2000 FRWT 84404 1055 D3
W 900 S
- SNQN 84655 3567 E2
- SRCS 84075 1227 A6
10 BNFL 84010 1653 D2
10 GRLD 84312 520 E3
10 LYTN 84041 1282 E6
10 OREM 84058 2820 D7
10 SLCY 84101 1858 C5
100 WELV 84339 649 C4
600 PYSN 84651 3354 D7
600 SLCY 84104 1858 A5
900 SPFK 84660 3249 A4
900 WDCR 84087 1653 B1
1100 PRVO 84601 3034 E1
1100 PRVO 84601 3035 A1
1100 SLCY 84104 1857 D5
1500 OREM 84058 2819 E7
1600 SPFK 84660 3248 E4
2400 SLCY 84104 1856 E5
3500 WbrC 84404 1054 D6
W 900 S SR-115
1600 SPFK 84660 3248 E4
1600 SPFK 84660 3249 A4
900 E
- CchC 84328 711 A2
- SNQN 84655 3568 A2
W 905 N
100 OREM 84057 2820 D3
E 910 N
- ANFK 84003 2605 A5
100 OREM 84057 2820 D3
500 OREM 84097 2820 E2
700 OREM 84097 2821 A2
E 910 S
1400 SPFK 84660 3250 A4
N 910 E
200 LNDN 84042 2713 D5
700 OGDN 84404 1057 A3
800 OREM 84097 2821 A2
1300 ANFK 84003 2605 A4
N 910 W
1300 OREM 84057 2820 B1
2400 LEHI 84043 2603 A2
S 910 E
8600 SNDY 84094 2177 A6
S 910 W
500 PTGV 84062 2712 C4
1400 PYSN 84651 3461 D1
W 910 N
- WBNF 84087 1551 C6
300 LOGN 84321 527 C1
700 CLTN 84015 1227 B2
1000 PTGV 84062 2712 C1
1400 OREM 84057 2819 E3
W 910 S
100 HRCY 84032 2398 C5
900 PRVO 84601 3035 A1
E 915 S
200 FMTN 84025 1448 D4

Salt Lake City Street Index

STREET Block	City	ZIP	Map#	Grid
E 920 N				
-	ANFK	84003	2605	A5
10	ANFK	84003	2604	C5
10	PYSN	84651	3354	E3
10	UthC	84651	3354	E3
300	PYSN	84651	3355	A3
300	UthC	84651	3355	A3
600	OREM	84097	2820	E2
600	OREM	84097	2821	A2
E 920 S				
-	SPFK	84660	3250	B4
700	SPFK	84660	3249	E4
1400	PRVO	84606	3036	A1
N 920 E				
-	SHFD	84335	400	B2
-	SLCY	84103	1859	A1
500	SPFK	84660	3249	E2
2800	NHLN	84341	464	B3
3600	PRVO	84604	2821	E7
N 920 W				
10	SPFK	84660	3249	B2
100	OREM	84057	2820	B4
100	UthC	84660	3249	B2
1900	OREM	84057	2713	B7
2300	PRVO	84604	2928	A2
S 920 E				
-	OGDN	84404	1057	B7
-	UthC	84003	2712	A1
300	SALM	84653	3356	C4
5600	MRRY	84121	2071	A6
8500	SNDY	84094	2177	A6
W 920 N				
800	OREM	84057	2820	B2
1700	PTGV	84062	2712	A1
W 920 S				
200	PRVO	84601	3035	B1
E 925 N				
10	OREM	84057	2820	D2
200	ANFK	84003	2604	D5
600	OGDN	84404	1057	A3
E 925 S				
200	LYTN	84041	1283	A6
N 925 E				
1300	OGDN	84404	1057	A2
1500	NHON	84414	1057	B1
3300	LYTN	84040	1229	B5
N 925 W				
1200	OGDN	84404	1056	B2
1700	CLTN	84015	1227	B1
1800	CLTN	84015	1171	B7
S 925 E				
300	LYTN	84041	1283	B6
400	KYVL	84037	1345	E2
400	KYVL	84037	1346	A2
4900	MRRY	84117	2071	A4
5400	SOGN	84405	1173	A4
7300	SWBR	84405	1229	A1
S 925 W				
-	BxEC	84340	941	C4
-	LEHI	84043	2710	A1
400	OREM	84058	2820	B6
500	LYTN	84041	1282	D6
900	WDCR	84087	1653	B2
2800	OGDN	84401	1115	B5
4100	RVDL	84405	1172	B1
W 925 N				
200	BNFL	84010	1551	D6
400	LOGN	84321	527	C1
500	CTRV	84014	1551	C2
3000	WPT	84015	1226	C2
3600	LYTN	84041	1281	C3
W 925 S				
-	CRFD	84016	1227	A6
-	DvsC	84016	1227	A6
-	SRCS	84075	1227	A6
100	GRLD	84312	520	E3
500	OREM	84058	2820	B7
600	WDCR	84087	1653	B1
800	BMCY	84302	827	D1
925 E				
-	OGDN	84403	1173	B1
E 930 N				
700	PTGV	84062	2713	A1
900	OREM	84097	2821	A2
1100	PRVO	84604	2928	E5
E 930 S				
200	OREM	84058	2820	E7
500	PTGV	84062	2712	E4
500	PTGV	84062	2713	A4
1000	PRVO	84606	3035	E1
N 930 E				
-	SLCY	84103	1859	D1
300	LNDN	84042	2713	D5
2300	PRVO	84604	2928	E2
N 930 W				
10	OREM	84057	2820	B5
S 930 E				
-	UthC	84003	2712	A1
7800	SNDY	84094	2177	A4
10700	SNDY	84094	2283	A4
S 930 W				
-	PYSN	84651	3354	C7
10	OREM	84058	2820	B5
100	OGDN	84404	1056	B5
1400	PYSN	84651	3461	C1
3200	SRCS	84075	1281	B4
W 930 N				
100	OREM	84057	2820	D2
200	SNST	84015	1227	C2
1100	FMTN	84025	1346	A7
1900	PTGV	84062	2712	A1
S 930 Cir E				
-	UthC	84003	2712	A1
E 935 S				
-	WbrC	84317	1061	C7
200	LYTN	84041	1283	A6
N 935 W				
10	LYTN	84041	1282	D4
S 935 E				
5100	MRRY	84117	2071	A4
8400	SNDY	84094	2177	A5
S 938 E				
900	MRRY	84117	2071	A4
E 940 N				
400	OGDN	84404	1056	E3
N 940 E				
-	SLCY	84103	1859	A1
1700	ANFK	84062	2605	A3
2200	LEHI	84043	2603	D2
N 940 W				
400	OREM	84057	2820	B3
1700	OREM	84057	2713	B7
2000	PRVO	84604	2928	A3
S 940 E				
10	OREM	84097	2821	A5
S 940 W				
400	OREM	84058	2820	B6
900	WDCR	84087	1653	B2
1200	PRVO	84601	3035	A2
6400	MRRY	84123	2176	A1
10100	SJDN	84095	2281	E3
W 940 N				
-	TMTN	84337	520	A4
10	OREM	84057	2820	D2
200	PRVO	84604	2928	B5
400	ANFK	84003	2604	B5
E 940 Cir N				
-	ANFK	84003	2605	A5
E 943 S				
1200	FTHT	84037	1346	A3
N 945 W				
600	OREM	84057	2820	B3
S 945 E				
3100	SLkC	84106	1965	A5
E 950 N				
100	DvsC	84037	1283	D6
200	LEHI	84043	2603	C5
400	NSLK	84054	1653	B4
400	SGVL	84663	3036	D7
500	OGDN	84404	1056	E3
600	OGDN	84404	1057	A3
8900	WbrC	84317	1061	E3
E 950 S				
-	BMCY	84302	828	A1
-	PYSN	84651	3355	A7
-	WbrC	84317	1061	B7
10	KYVL	84037	1345	C3
10	LYTN	84041	1282	E6
100	LYTN	84041	1283	A6
200	OREM	84058	2820	E7
600	CRFD	84015	1227	E6
600	PTGV	84062	2713	A4
700	CTRV	84014	1552	A5
700	PRVO	84606	3035	D1
800	OREM	84097	2821	A7
1100	SGVL	84663	3143	E4
1300	SGVL	84663	3144	A4
1400	PRVO	84606	3036	A1
1500	SPFK	84660	3250	A4
6600	WbrC	84317	1060	D7
N 950 E				
100	LNDN	84042	2713	D6
200	LEHI	84043	2603	D6
200	UthC	84043	2603	D6
300	BMCY	84302	767	B5
300	KYVL	84037	1283	E7
600	OGDN	84404	1057	B4
700	BNFL	84010	1552	A6
900	OREM	84097	2821	A2
1100	PTGV	84062	2713	A1
1900	LOGN	84321	464	A5
2100	NHLN	84341	464	A5
2600	NHON	84414	999	B5
N 950 W				
-	CTRV	84014	1551	C2
-	LOGN	84321	527	B2
400	ANFK	84003	2603	E6
1100	OREM	84057	2820	B1
1300	CLTN	84015	1227	B1
1300	OGDN	84404	1056	B2
1400	LEHI	84043	2603	A4
1500	HARR	84404	1056	B1
1700	PRVO	84604	2928	A3
2400	LYTN	84041	1228	D7
2500	CLTN	84015	1171	B6
3300	LEHI	84043	2496	A7
4100	PTVW	84414	998	B2
S 950 E				
-	LOGN	84321	528	B3
-	OGDN	84404	1116	B1
-	RVHT	84321	528	B3
10	OREM	84097	2821	A5
100	PTGV	84062	2713	A3
200	LYTN	84041	1283	B5
700	SPFK	84660	3249	E4
1000	PRVO	84606	3035	E2
1100	SGVL	84663	3143	E4
1200	OGDN	84404	1057	B7
1400	OREM	84097	2928	A2
2800	SGVL	84663	3036	A7
3000	BNFL	84010	1654	A5
4200	SOGN	84403	1173	A1
4500	SLkC	84117	2071	A2
5800	SOGN	84405	1173	A5
S 950 W				
-	BxEC	84340	941	C5
-	CRFD	84016	1227	B6
10	BMCY	84302	766	D6
100	LYTN	84041	1282	D5
300	OREM	84058	2820	B6
500	FMTN	84025	1448	A3
500	WBNF	84087	1653	B1
600	PYSN	84651	3354	C6
700	WDCR	84087	1653	B1
800	BMCY	84302	827	D1
800	PRVO	84601	3035	A1
2300	SRCS	84075	1281	B2
4500	RVDL	84405	1172	A2
W 950 N				
-	CTRV	84014	1551	C2
300	ANFK	84003	2604	B5
400	LOGN	84321	463	C7
900	OREM	84057	2820	A2
1000	CLTN	84015	1227	B2
1100	PTGV	84062	2712	C1
1300	PRVO	84604	2927	E5
2600	PRVO	84601	2927	C5
4400	WbrC	84404	1054	C3
W 950 S				
10	KYVL	84037	1345	C3
10	LYTN	84041	1282	E6
200	OGDN	84404	1056	D7
1400	OREM	84058	2819	E7
S 954 E				
-	OGDN	84404	1116	B1
W 955 N				
1300	CLTN	84015	1227	A2
E 960 N				
400	OGDN	84404	1056	E3
800	ANFK	84003	2605	A5
900	PTGV	84062	2713	B1
E 960 S				
-	BMCY	84302	828	A1
-	SALM	84653	3356	B5
1100	PRVO	84606	3035	E1
1200	FTHT	84037	1346	A3
N 960 E				
-	SLCY	84103	1859	A2
10	ANFK	84003	2712	A1
200	PTGV	84062	2713	B2
600	OREM	84097	2821	A3
N 960 W				
600	PTGV	84062	2712	C2
1000	OREM	84057	2820	B2
S 960 E				
200	OREM	84097	2821	A5
1000	SGVL	84663	3143	E4
1200	PRVO	84606	3035	E2
5300	MRRY	84117	2071	A5
5600	SOGN	84405	1173	B5
10700	SNDY	84094	2283	A4
W 960 N				
-	WPT	84015	1226	A2
10	PRVO	84604	2928	C5
400	ANFK	84003	2604	B5
600	OREM	84057	2820	B2
800	CLTN	84015	1227	B2
1500	OREM	84057	2819	E2
2200	PRVO	84601	2927	C5
2700	CLTN	84015	1226	D2
W 960 S				
200	PRVO	84601	3035	B1
400	OREM	84058	2820	C7
600	TMTN	84337	520	D7
E 965 N				
1000	OREM	84097	2821	B2
S 965 E				
7800	SNDY	84094	2177	A4
W 965 N				
400	OREM	84057	2820	C2
E 970 N				
200	LOGN	84321	463	E7
800	OREM	84097	2821	A2
E 970 S				
-	SPFK	84660	3250	B4
1600	SGVL	84663	3144	A4
N 970 E				
300	LOGN	84321	528	B2
400	SGVL	84663	3143	E1
500	SPFK	84660	3249	E2
700	SGVL	84663	3036	E7
3700	PRVO	84604	2821	E7
N 970 W				
10	OREM	84057	2820	B5
500	PRVO	84601	2928	A5
2300	CLTN	84015	1171	B6
S 970 E				
10	SPFK	84660	3249	E3
12300	DRPR	84020	2389	A1
S 970 W				
900	WDCR	84087	1653	B2
1700	LEHI	84043	2710	A2
W 970 N				
800	OREM	84057	2820	B2
W 970 S				
10	WshC	84049	2397	B5
500	PRVO	84601	3035	B1
E 975 N				
1400	LYTN	84040	1283	C3
E 975 S				
10	LYTN	84041	1283	A6
2300	SGVL	84663	3144	C4
N 975 E				
-	LOGN	84321	528	B1
700	OGDN	84404	1057	B3
1500	NHON	84414	1057	B1
3000	NHON	84414	999	B4
3400	LYTN	84040	1229	B5
N 975 W				
-	TMTN	84337	520	C5
10	CRFD	84015	1227	B4
10	LYTN	84041	1282	C4
900	KYVL	84037	1345	A1
S 975 E				
-	OGDN	84404	1057	B7
100	LYTN	84041	1283	C5
3100	BNFL	84010	1654	A5
4900	MRRY	84117	2071	A4
4900	SLkC	84117	2071	A4
5500	SOGN	84405	1173	A5
S 975 W				
-	LEHI	84043	2710	A1
10	CRFD	84015	1227	B4
10	KYVL	84037	1345	A1
100	LEHI	84043	2603	A7
100	MPTN	84664	3143	E7
W 975 N				
100	OREM	84057	2820	D2
100	SNST	84015	1227	D2
W 975 S				
-	LYTN	84041	1282	B7
500	LEHI	84043	2710	A1
1100	CRFD	84016	1227	B6
3900	SRCS	84075	1226	A6
E 980 N				
-	ANFK	84003	2604	D5
10	OREM	84057	2820	D2
400	OGDN	84404	1056	E3
500	OGDN	84404	1057	A3
N 980 E				
-	SLCY	84103	1859	B1
100	LNDN	84042	2713	D5
1700	ANFK	84062	2605	A3
1700	CRHL	84062	2605	A3
N 980 W				
1400	OREM	84057	2820	A1
1700	OREM	84057	2713	A7
S 980 E				
700	PTGV	84062	2713	B4
1100	SGVL	84663	3143	E4
1200	SPFK	84660	3249	E5
3500	SLkC	84106	1965	A6
S 980 W				
10	OREM	84058	2820	B5
500	PTGV	84062	2712	C4
700	LOGN	84321	527	B5
1100	PRVO	84601	3035	A2
W 980 N				
600	PRVO	84604	2928	B5
W 980 S				
400	SALM	84653	3355	E5
1500	OREM	84058	2819	E7
980 E				
-	CchC	84328	711	B3
981 E				
-	CchC	84328	711	B3
N 985 W				
1300	OREM	84057	2820	A1
W 985 N				
300	SNST	84015	1227	D2
E 990 N				
400	OGDN	84404	1056	D3
500	PTGV	84062	2712	E1
E 990 S				
600	LNDN	84042	2713	A4
600	PTGV	84062	2713	A4
2400	SPFK	84660	3250	C4
N 990 E				
10	ANFK	84003	2712	A1
400	PTGV	84062	2713	B2
N 990 W				
400	ANFK	84003	2603	E6
1200	PTGV	84062	2712	C1
1500	PTGV	84062	2605	C7
S 990 E				
10	ANFK	84003	2712	A1
S 990 W				
200	OREM	84058	2820	B6
1400	PRVO	84601	3035	A2
6400	MRRY	84123	2176	A1
W 990 N				
-	OREM	84057	2820	C2
200	ANFK	84003	2604	B5
1000	PRVO	84604	2928	A5
W 990 S				
10	OREM	84058	2820	D7
400	BMCY	84302	827	D1
E 991 S				
1200	FTHT	84037	1346	A3
E 1000 N				
10	SPFK	84660	3249	D1
100	LOGN	84321	463	E7
100	LOGN	84341	463	E7
200	HARR	84404	1056	E3
200	OREM	84057	2820	E2
300	LEHI	84043	2603	C5
300	PTGV	84062	2712	E1
400	BNFL	84010	1551	E6
400	BNFL	84010	1552	A6
400	MPTN	84664	3144	B6
400	NSLK	84054	1653	B4
400	SGVL	84663	3036	D7
500	LOGN	84321	464	A7
500	LOGN	84341	464	A7
500	SALM	84653	3356	C1
600	OGDN	84404	1057	A3
700	PTGV	84062	2713	A1
800	ANFK	84003	2604	E5
7100	WbrC	84317	1060	E3
7100	WbrC	84317	1061	A3
E 1000 S				
10	BMCY	84302	827	E1
10	BNFL	84010	1653	E2
10	OREM	84058	2820	E7
10	PTGV	84062	2712	E4
200	BMCY	84302	828	A1
400	SGVL	84663	3143	D4
500	ANFK	84003	2711	E4
500	CchC	84321	528	C5
500	OREM	84097	2820	E7
700	KYVL	84037	1345	E4
700	OREM	84097	2821	A7
800	SPFK	84660	3249	E4
1100	PTGV	84062	2713	C4
1400	PRVO	84606	3036	A1
1500	BNFL	84010	1654	C1
1600	SPFK	84660	3250	A4
N 1000 E				
-	LOGN	84321	528	B4
-	RVHT	84321	528	B4
-	SLCY	84103	1859	B2
10	BMCY	84302	767	B5
10	OREM	84097	2821	A4
10	PYSN	84651	3355	B5
200	HDPK	84318	400	C6
200	SPFK	84660	3249	E2
300	BNFL	84010	1552	A6
300	KYVL	84037	1284	A7
700	PRVO	84606	2928	E5
1000	LYTN	84040	1283	B2
1100	MPTN	84664	3144	C5
1100	PTGV	84062	2713	B1
1200	OGDN	84404	1057	B2
1300	ANFK	84003	2605	A4
1900	LOGN	84341	464	B5
2000	LEHI	84043	2603	D3
2300	PRVO	84604	2928	E2
2800	NHLN	84341	464	B3
3200	LYTN	84040	1229	B5
3300	NHON	84414	999	B3
N 1000 W				
10	CRFD	84015	1227	B3
10	KYVL	84037	1345	A1
10	LOGN	84321	527	A1
10	PRVO	84601	2928	A6
10	SLCY	84104	1857	E2
10	SLCY	84116	1857	E2
10	TMTN	84337	520	C5
100	WBNF	84087	1551	B7
400	CTRV	84014	1551	C2
700	CLTN	84015	1227	B3
700	OREM	84057	2820	A3
800	LOGN	84321	463	A7
1100	LOGN	84341	463	A7
1200	MPTN	84664	3143	E5
1800	CchC	84341	463	B4
2100	PRVO	84604	2928	A3
2400	LYTN	84041	1228	D7
2500	CLTN	84015	1171	B7
2500	PTVW	84404	998	B4
3800	PTVW	84414	998	B3
S 1000 E				
-	MPTN	84664	3144	C7
-	SNQN	84655	3568	B1
10	BNFL	84010	1552	A7
10	HYRM	84319	651	E3
10	LYTN	84041	1283	B5
10	OREM	84097	2821	B5
10	PRVO	84606	2928	E7
10	PYSN	84651	3355	B5
10	SLCY	84102	1859	A3
200	BNFL	84010	1654	A1
200	CRFD	84015	1228	A6
200	DvsC	84015	1228	A6
200	GNLA	84655	3460	A5
300	LOGN	84321	528	B4
300	RVHT	84321	528	B4
300	SGVL	84663	3143	E2
500	CchC	84321	528	B4
700	MPTN	84664	3251	C2
900	SLCY	84105	1859	A6
1000	PRVO	84606	3035	E2
1200	OREM	84097	2928	A1
1200	SPFK	84660	3249	E5
1500	LYTN	84041	1228	A6
1500	SLCY	84105	1965	A1
1600	CRFD	84015	1282	A1
1600	LYTN	84041	1282	A1
2100	SLCY	84106	1965	A2
2900	SLkC	84106	1965	A5
3900	SLkC	84124	1965	A7
4500	OGDN	84403	1173	B2
4600	CchC	84318	400	A5
4600	CchC	84335	400	A5
4600	SHFD	84335	400	A5
4800	SOGN	84403	1173	B3
5000	MRRY	84117	2071	A4
5400	SOGN	84405	1173	B4
7300	MDVL	84047	2177	A3
7800	SNDY	84094	2177	A5
8400	SLkC	84094	2177	A5
10000	SLkC	84094	2283	A3
10600	SNDY	84094	2283	A4
11800	DRPR	84020	2283	A7
12100	DRPR	84020	2389	A1
12100	SNDY	84094	2389	A1
S 1000 W				
-	BMCY	84302	827	C1
-	BxEC	84340	941	C5
10	BMCY	84302	766	C6
10	CRFD	84015	1227	B6
10	LOGN	84321	527	A5
10	OREM	84057	2820	A5
10	OREM	84058	2820	A5
10	PRVO	84601	2928	A7
10	SLCY	84104	1857	E3
100	OGDN	84404	1056	B5
200	CRFD	84016	1227	B6
200	SRCS	84015	1227	B6
200	SRCS	84016	1227	B6
300	PYSN	84651	3354	C6
400	LYTN	84041	1282	D6
700	CchC	84321	527	A5
800	PRVO	84601	3035	A1
1100	SRCS	84075	1227	B6
1400	WDCR	84087	1653	A2
1600	SLCY	84104	1963	E1
1700	SRCS	84075	1281	B1
1800	LOGN	84321	591	A1
2700	PRRY	84302	827	C6
3200	DvsC	84075	1281	B4
3300	SSLK	84119	1963	E6
4500	RVDL	84405	1172	A2
8700	WJDN	84088	2175	E7
9800	SJDN	84095	2281	E3
14700	BFDL	84065	2387	E7
W 1000 N				
-	SALM	84653	3356	B1
-	UthC	84660	3356	B1
10	SPFK	84660	3249	C1
200	BNFL	84010	1551	C6
200	FMTN	84025	1346	C6
400	OREM	84057	2820	B2
400	PTGV	84062	2712	C1
400	SGVL	84663	3036	B7
400	SLCY	84103	1754	B7
500	WBNF	84087	1551	B6
600	LOGN	84321	463	B7
600	LOGN	84341	463	B7
800	MPTN	84664	3143	E6
900	SLCY	84116	1753	D7
900	SLCY	84116	1754	B7
1000	CLTN	84015	1227	B2
1200	CchC	84321	463	A7
1200	CchC	84341	463	A7
1300	CchC	84321	462	D7
1300	CchC	84341	462	D7
1400	PRVO	84604	2927	E5
2100	FRWT	84404	1055	C3
2100	TMTN	84337	520	A4
W 1000 S				
10	BNFL	84010	1653	D2
10	CchC	84335	399	D5
10	GRLD	84312	520	E3
10	HRCY	84032	2398	C5
10	KYVL	84037	1345	C3
10	SHFD	84335	399	D5
200	OGDN	84404	1056	D7
400	OREM	84058	2820	C7
500	LOGN	84321	527	A5
900	WDCR	84087	1653	B2
1100	CchC	84321	526	E5
1100	CchC	84321	527	A5
1200	PYSN	84651	3354	C7
1400	OREM	84058	2819	E7
1800	LYTN	84041	1282	A7
1800	LYTN	84075	1282	A7
6400	CchC	84325	524	B5
6400	MNDN	84325	524	B5
6900	CchC	84325	523	E5
W 1000 St N				
10	LOGN	84321	463	C7
10	LOGN	84341	463	C7
S 1000 E St				
-	CchC	84321	592	B7
-	CchC	84321	652	B1
N 1000 W St				
6200	CchC	84335	399	A1
N 1005 W				
1000	OREM	84057	2820	A2
W 1005 N				
10	ANFK	84003	2604	C5
E 1010 N				
10	ANFK	84003	2604	C5
1000	OREM	84097	2821	B2
1000	PTGV	84062	2713	B1
1100	SPFK	84660	3249	E1
1100	SPFK	84660	3250	A1
E 1010 S				
300	OREM	84097	2820	E7
1200	FTHT	84037	1346	A3
N 1010 W				
500	PTGV	84062	2712	C2
W 1010 N				
400	OREM	84057	2820	C2
1500	PTGV	84062	2712	B1
1700	PRVO	84604	2927	D5
2700	CLTN	84015	1226	C2
2700	PRVO	84601	2927	B5
W 1010 S				
3300	PRVO	84601	3034	B1
E 1015 S				
800	OGDN	84404	1057	B7
1200	FTHT	84037	1346	A4
N 1015 W				
1700	OREM	84057	2713	A7
1700	OREM	84057	2820	A1
S 1015 W				
200	OREM	84058	2820	A6
W 1015 N				
100	OREM	84057	2820	D2
E 1020 N				
100	OREM	84057	2820	D2
N 1020 E				
10	ANFK	84003	2712	A1
300	PRVO	84606	2928	E6
600	PTGV	84062	2713	B1
1200	ANFK	84003	2605	A4
1200	UthC	84003	2605	A4
3700	PRVO	84604	2821	E7
N 1020 W				
-	PTGV	84062	2605	C5
-	PTVW	84414	998	A4
10	ANFK	84003	2710	E1
10	OREM	84057	2820	A5
10	UthC	84003	2710	E1
400	PRVO	84601	2928	A6
500	PTGV	84062	2712	C2
S 1020 E				
7200	MDVL	84047	2177	A3
13000	DRPR	84020	2389	A3
S 1020 W				
500	OREM	84058	2820	A6
900	WDCR	84087	1653	A2
1300	UthC	84058	2927	A2
W 1020 N				
700	PRVO	84604	2928	A5
1400	CLTN	84015	1227	A2
W 1020 S				
-	OREM	84058	2820	A7
200	PRVO	84601	3035	C1
S 1021 E				
4900	MRRY	84117	2071	A4
E 1025 S				
800	OGDN	84404	1057	A7
1100	SPFK	84660	3249	E4
1100	SPFK	84660	3250	A5
N 1025 E				
10	LNDN	84042	2713	D6
400	BNFL	84010	1552	B6
600	LYTN	84040	1283	B3
900	OGDN	84404	1057	B3
3000	NHON	84414	999	B4
N 1025 W				
300	CchC	84319	650	D1
300	HYRM	84319	650	D1
500	OREM	84057	2820	A3
500	PRVO	84601	2928	A6
S 1025 E				
10	LNDN	84042	2713	D7
4400	SLkC	84124	2071	A2
4500	SLkC	84117	2071	A2
4600	OGDN	84403	1173	B2
5200	SOGN	84403	1173	B4
5400	SOGN	84405	1173	B5
7300	SWBR	84405	1229	B2
S 1025 W				
100	KYVL	84037	1345	A1
500	FMTN	84025	1448	A3
900	WDCR	84087	1653	A2
1300	SRCS	84075	1227	B7
1700	LEHI	84043	2710	A2
4400	RVDL	84405	1172	A2
W 1025 N				
600	OREM	84057	2820	B2
800	CLTN	84015	1227	B2
2000	FRWT	84404	1055	D3
2500	LYTN	84041	1281	E3
3500	LYTN	84015	1281	C3
W 1025 S				
200	GRLD	84312	520	E3
400	FMTN	84025	1448	C4
2400	SRCS	84075	1226	D6
E 1030 N				
500	PTGV	84062	2712	E1
600	PTGV	84062	2713	A1
800	OREM	84097	2821	A2
1600	LOGN	84341	464	C7
N 1030 E				
-	LEHI	84043	2603	D6
400	PTGV	84062	2713	B2
N 1030 W				
-	PTVW	84414	998	A4
100	OREM	84057	2820	A4
400	LNDN	84042	2712	D5
1600	LNDN	84042	2820	A1
1600	LNDN	84057	2820	A1
1600	OREM	84042	2820	A1
1700	OREM	84042	2713	A7
1700	OREM	84057	2713	A7
S 1030 E				
-	SNQN	84655	3568	B1
10	HYRM	84319	651	E3
700	OREM	84097	2821	B7
1600	OREM	84097	2928	B2
3800	SLkC	84106	1965	A7
S 1030 W				
-	PYSN	84651	3461	C1
600	OREM	84058	2820	A6
900	LEHI	84043	2710	A1
2600	SSLK	84119	1963	E3
8800	WJDN	84088	2175	E6
W 1030 N				
100	OREM	84057	2820	C2
200	ANFK	84003	2604	B5
W 1030 S				
3900	SRCS	84075	1226	A6
S 1034 E				
5000	MRRY	84117	2071	A3
E 1035 S				
2300	SPFK	84660	3250	C4
N 1035 W				
1000	OREM	84057	2820	A2
S 1035 E				
6100	MRRY	84121	2071	A7
7200	MDVL	84047	2177	A2
E 1040 N				
300	OREM	84057	2820	E2
1100	OREM	84097	2821	B2
E 1040 S				
800	PRVO	84606	3035	D1
900	SGVL	84663	3143	E4
N 1040 E				
-	SLCY	84103	1859	B2
100	OREM	84097	2821	B4
200	SGVL	84663	3143	E1
900	LEHI	84043	2603	E5
N 1040 W				
800	MPTN	84664	3143	E6
1400	OREM	84057	2820	A1
S 1040 E				
500	PTGV	84062	2712	A2
600	SPFK	84660	3249	E4
1000	SGVL	84663	3143	E4
1200	OREM	84097	2928	B1
1300	OGDN	84404	1057	B7
1300	OGDN	84404	1116	B1
3900	SLkC	84124	1965	A7
7600	MDVL	84047	2177	A4
9500	SNDY	84094	2283	A1
S 1040 W				
600	OREM	84058	2820	A7
700	PYSN	84651	3354	C6
6400	MRRY	84123	2175	E1
10200	SJDN	84095	2281	E3
W 1040 N				
500	ANFK	84003	2604	A5
700	OREM	84057	2820	B2
W 1040 S				
10	OREM	84058	2820	D7
E 1045 N				
1100	OREM	84097	2821	B2
S 1045 E				
4100	SLkC	84124	2071	A1
5000	MRRY	84117	2071	A4
S 1045 W				
500	OREM	84058	2820	A6
1700	SLCY	84104	1963	E1
W 1045 S				
1000	CRFD	84016	1227	B6
E 1050 N				
10	BNFL	84010	1551	E6
10	DvsC	84037	1283	D6
300	HARR	84404	1056	E3
400	OGDN	84404	1056	E3
400	OREM	84097	2820	E2
400	SGVL	84663	3036	D7
500	OGDN	84404	1057	A3
900	OREM	84097	2821	A2
1100	HRCY	84032	2398	E2
1100	WshC	84032	2398	E2
E 1050 S				
300	PYSN	84651	3355	A7
400	SGVL	84663	3143	D4
700	SPFK	84660	3249	E4
1000	CRFD	84015	1228	A6
1100	SPFK	84660	3250	A5
2200	SGVL	84663	3144	B4
N 1050 E				
-	ANFK	84003	2605	A5
10	BNFL	84010	1552	B7
10	PTGV	84062	2713	B2
10	SGVL	84663	3143	E2
200	KYVL	84037	1284	A7
300	UthC	84003	2605	A7
700	PRVO	84606	2928	E5
1000	OREM	84097	2821	B2
1400	LYTN	84040	1283	B2
1800	LOGN	84341	464	B5
2600	NHON	84414	999	B5
3200	LYTN	84040	1229	B5
N 1050 W				
-	PTVW	84414	998	A4
10	KYVL	84037	1345	A1
500	CRFD	84015	1227	B3
500	PRVO	84601	2928	A5
1300	CLTN	84015	1227	B1
1400	OREM	84057	2820	A1
1600	HARR	84404	1056	A1
1700	PRVO	84604	2928	A3
2300	CLTN	84015	1171	B6
2400	LYTN	84041	1228	C7
S 1050 E				
-	SPFK	84660	3249	E1
10	PTGV	84062	2713	B3
200	LYTN	84041	1283	C5
1200	CRFD	84015	1228	A7
4600	OGDN	84403	1173	B2
5000	SOGN	84403	1173	B3
5400	SOGN	84405	1173	B5
6100	MRRY	84121	2071	A7
8300	SNDY	84094	2177	A5
S 1050 W				
-	PRRY	84302	827	C5
10	CRFD	84015	1227	B4
10	OREM	84058	2820	A5
100	PRVO	84601	2928	A7
400	PYSN	84651	3354	C6
900	WDCR	84087	1653	A2
1200	OREM	84058	2927	A2
1400	UthC	84058	2927	A1
4200	RVDL	84405	1172	A1
5900	UthC	84660	3249	A2
8900	WJDN	84088	2175	E7
S 1050 W SR-60				
4700	RVDL	84405	1172	A3
W 1050 N				
-	LYTN	84015	1281	C2
10	WLRD	84340	885	C3
100	LYTN	84041	1282	E3
200	BNFL	84010	1551	C6
200	LOGN	84341	463	C7
300	LEHI	84043	2603	B5
500	PTGV	84062	2712	C1
800	OREM	84057	2820	B2
900	MPTN	84664	3143	E5
1000	PRVO	84604	2928	A5
1200	PRVO	84604	2927	E5
3000	WPT	84015	1226	C2
W 1050 S				
-	OREM	84058	2819	E7
-	OREM	84058	2926	E1
-	SRCS	84075	1227	A6
200	BNFL	84010	1653	D2
400	SALM	84653	3355	E6
400	SALM	84653	3356	A5
1000	WDCR	84087	1653	A2
1200	PYSN	84651	3354	C7
S 1055 E				
5900	SOGN	84405	1173	A6

Salt Lake City Street Index

STREET Block City ZIP Map# Grid

S 1055 W
10500 SJDN 84095 2281 E4
W 1055 N
300 SNST 84015 1227 C2
E 1060 E
- SNQN 84655 3568 B1
E 1060 N
10 PRVO 84604 2928 C5
100 OREM 84057 2820 D2
1100 SPFK 84660 3249 E1
1100 SPFK 84660 3250 A1
E 1060 S
700 SGVL 84663 3143 D4
900 PRVO 84606 3035 E1
1000 OREM 84097 2821 B7
N 1060 E
300 UthC 84003 2605 A7
2200 LEHI 84043 2603 D2
2200 NHLN 84341 464 B4
2300 PRVO 84604 2928 E2
N 1060 W
300 PRVO 84601 2928 A6
400 OREM 84057 2820 A3
1000 CLTN 84015 1227 B2
1800 PTGV 84062 2605 C7
2000 PRVO 84604 2928 A2
S 1060 E
- SNQN 84655 3568 B1
- UthC 84003 2712 A1
200 SPFK 84660 3249 E3
900 SGVL 84663 3143 E4
1100 PRVO 84606 3035 E2
4200 SLkC 84124 2071 B1
5500 SOGN 84405 1173 B5
8100 SNDY 84094 2177 A5
S 1060 W
- LOGN 84321 527 A4
200 LNDN 84042 2712 D7
W 1060 N
200 ANFK 84003 2604 B5
500 CLTN 84015 1227 C2
500 LOGN 84341 463 C7
1000 FMTN 84025 1346 A6
1000 PRVO 84604 2928 A5
1600 PTGV 84062 2712 B1
1700 PRVO 84604 2927 D5
2600 PRVO 84601 2927 C5
W 1060 S
200 OREM 84058 2820 C7
S 1065 E
- OGDN 84404 1057 B7
- OGDN 84404 1116 B1
4900 MRRY 84117 2071 A3
4900 SLkC 84117 2071 A3
S 1065 W
- SRCS 84075 1281 B3
200 OREM 84058 2820 A6
W 1065 S
1500 SGVL 84663 3142 E4
W 1065 W
- SGVL 84663 3142 E4
E 1070 N
- ANFK 84003 2605 A5
E 1070 S
300 OREM 84097 2927 E1
N 1070 E
200 SPFK 84660 3249 E2
N 1070 W
- PTGV 84062 2605 C6
200 OGDN 84404 1056 A4
1300 PTGV 84062 2712 C1
S 1070 E
10 HYRM 84319 651 E3
4800 SLkC 84117 2071 A3
7700 MDVL 84047 2177 B4
8300 SNDY 84094 2177 B5
S 1070 W
100 OGDN 84404 1056 A5
2300 WVCY 84119 1963 E3
8800 WJDN 84088 2175 E6
W 1070 N
10 OREM 84057 2820 D2
900 WBNF 84087 1551 A6
2100 LYTN 84041 1282 A2
E 1075 N
100 SGVL 84663 3036 D7
7700 WbrC 84317 1061 A3
N 1075 E
1100 OGDN 84404 1057 B3
3100 NHON 84414 999 B4
3300 LYTN 84040 1229 B5
N 1075 W
- FMTN 84037 1346 A5
1400 CLTN 84015 1227 B1
1400 FMTN 84025 1346 A5
1400 OGDN 84404 1056 A2
4000 PTVW 04414 998 B2
S 1075 E
1000 CRFD 84015 1228 A6
4600 OGDN 84403 1173 B2
5000 SOGN 84403 1173 B3
5700 SOGN 84405 1173 B5
S 1075 W
- SRCS 84075 1281 B4
8900 WJDN 84088 2175 E7
W 1075 N
700 OREM 84057 2820 B2
1000 CLTN 84015 1227 B2
1300 LYTN 84041 1282 C3
2600 LYTN 84041 1281 E3
W 1075 S
900 BMCY 84302 827 D2
E 1080 N
10 ANFK 84003 2604 C5
800 OREM 84097 2821 A2
1600 LOGN 84341 464 C7
E 1080 S
1100 PRVO 84606 3035 E1
1600 PRVO 84606 3036 A2
N 1080 E
100 PRVO 84606 2928 E6
400 OREM 84097 2821 B3
N 1080 W
- HYRM 84319 650 D1
500 PRVO 84601 2928 A6
1100 OREM 84057 2820 A2
S 1080 E
200 PRVO 84606 2928 E7
600 OREM 84097 2821 B7
1000 SGVL 84663 3143 E4
6100 MRRY 84121 2071 A7

W 1080 N
200 OREM 84057 2820 C2
400 ANFK 84003 2604 B5
1100 PTGV 84062 2712 B1
2100 CLTN 84015 1226 E2
E 1085 N
10 OREM 84057 2820 D2
N 1085 E
300 LNDN 84042 2713 D5
N 1085 W
2200 LYTN 84041 1228 C7
S 1085 E
6100 MRRY 84121 2071 B7
W 1085 N
500 OREM 84057 2820 C2
W 1085 S
3900 SRCS 84075 1226 A6
E 1090 N
200 OREM 84057 2820 E2
400 OREM 84097 2820 E2
1100 OREM 84097 2821 B2
E 1090 S
800 PRVO 84606 3035 E1
N 1090 E
200 LNDN 84042 2713 D5
N 1090 W
1400 OREM 84057 2820 A1
S 1090 E
10600 SNDY 84094 2283 B4
S 1090 W
2900 SRCS 84075 1281 B3
5600 MRRY 84123 2069 E5
6400 MRRY 84123 2175 E1
W 1090 N
100 OREM 84057 2820 D2
700 CLTN 84015 1227 C2
W 1090 S
- HRCY 84032 2398 B6
S 1095 E
7600 MDVL 84047 2177 B3
S 1095 W
8700 WJDN 84088 2175 E6
E 1100 N
- ANFK 84003 2604 E5
10 BNFL 84010 1551 E6
10 CTRV 84014 1551 E2
10 OREM 84057 2820 D2
10 PTGV 84062 2712 D1
100 HARR 84404 1056 E3
200 LEHI 84043 2603 C4
300 LYTN 84041 1283 A2
400 OGDN 84404 1056 E3
400 SGVL 84663 3036 D7
500 LOGN 84341 463 E7
500 LOGN 84341 464 A7
500 OGDN 84404 1057 A3
500 PTGV 84062 2713 A1
900 ANFK 84003 2605 A5
900 OREM 84097 2821 A2
1100 LYTN 84040 1283 C2
7600 WbrC 84317 1061 B2
E 1100 S
10 KYVL 84037 1345 C4
10 MPTN 84664 3251 B1
10 OREM 84058 2927 D1
100 BNFL 84010 1653 E2
300 TMTN 84337 520 D3
400 PYSN 84651 3355 A7
500 OREM 84097 2927 E1
500 SGVL 84663 3143 D4
800 OREM 84097 2928 A1
800 SPFK 84660 3249 E5
1000 CRFD 84015 1228 A6
1500 SPFK 84660 3250 A5
1600 SGVL 84663 3144 A4
6500 WbrC 84317 1060 D7
N 1100 E
- SLCY 84103 1859 B2
10 ANFK 84003 2712 A1
10 ANFK 84062 2712 A1
10 SPFK 84660 3249 E3
10 UthC 84003 2712 A1
10 UthC 84062 2712 A1
100 ANFK 84062 2605 A7
200 SGVL 84663 3143 E1
200 UthC 84003 2605 A7
200 UthC 84062 2605 A7
400 BNFL 84010 1552 B6
400 PRVO 84606 2928 E5
500 LOGN 84321 528 B1
800 OREM 84097 2821 B2
800 PRVO 84604 2928 E5
900 PTGV 84062 2713 B1
1000 SPFK 84660 3142 E7
1200 ANFK 84003 2605 A4
1400 LYTN 84040 1283 C1
1900 LOGN 84341 464 B5
2500 LYTN 84040 1229 C6
2800 LEHI 84043 2603 E1
2900 NHON 84414 999 B5
2900 WbrC 84414 999 B5
N 1100 N
- LYTN 84041 1282 C2
N 1100 W
- BMCY 84302 766 C3
- BxEC 84302 766 C3
- LYTN 84041 1282 C2
10 NSLK 84054 1652 C7
300 CTRV 84014 1551 C3
300 SLCY 84116 1857 E1
500 CRFD 84015 1227 B3
500 UthC 84043 2603 A5
600 PRVO 84601 2928 A5
900 CLTN 84015 1227 B2
1000 PRVO 84604 2928 A4
1200 FMTN 84025 1346 A6
1500 OREM 84057 2820 A1
1600 DvsC 84087 1551 A4
1600 MPTN 84664 3143 E5
1600 WBNF 84087 1551 A4
1800 CLTN 84015 1171 B7
1800 LEHI 84043 2603 A3
2300 SLCY 84116 1753 E3
2900 LYTN 84041 1228 C6
3600 PTVW 84414 998 B3
4500 BxEC 84302 706 B1
S 1100 E
10 HYRM 84319 651 E3
10 SLCY 84102 1859 B5
100 OREM 84097 2821 B5
100 PYSN 84651 3355 B5
300 BNFL 84010 1654 B1

S 1100 E
300 PTGV 84062 2713 B4
300 SGVL 84663 3143 E3
400 SPFK 84660 3249 E2
400 SPFK 84663 3249 E2
400 SPFK 84663 3250 A2
900 SLCY 84105 1859 B6
1200 OREM 84097 2928 B1
1600 SLCY 84105 1965 B1
1700 SPFK 84660 3250 A6
2200 SLCY 84106 1965 B2
2900 SLkC 84106 1965 B4
3900 SLkC 84124 1965 B6
4000 SLkC 84124 2071 B1
4600 OGDN 84403 1173 B2
5000 SOGN 84403 1173 B3
5700 SOGN 84405 1173 B5
7700 MDVL 84047 2177 B4
8200 UthC 84660 3250 A7
8300 SNDY 84094 2177 B5
13400 DRPR 84020 2389 B4
S 1100 E SR-51
400 SPFK 84660 3249 E2
400 SPFK 84660 3250 A2
400 SPFK 84663 3249 E2
400 SPFK 84663 3250 A2
S 1100 W
- CchC 84321 591 B4
100 FMTN 84025 1448 A2
100 SLCY 84104 1857 E3
300 PRVO 84601 2928 A7
400 OREM 84058 2820 A6
600 PRVO 84601 3035 A2
1200 SRCS 84075 1227 B7
1300 OREM 84058 2820 A7
1300 UthC 84058 2927 A1
2100 LOGN 84321 591 A1
2200 NBLY 84321 591 A1
2200 WHVN 84401 1115 A3
2700 SRCS 84075 1281 B3
3000 SSLK 84119 1963 E5
4200 RVDL 84405 1172 A1
4300 TYVL 84123 2069 E2
7700 BxEC 84340 941 B4
12700 RIVN 84065 2387 E2
W 1100 N
10 FMTN 84025 1346 C6
10 LYTN 84041 1282 E2
10 PTGV 84062 2712 C1
100 HARR 84404 1056 D3
200 LOGN 84341 463 C7
600 WBNF 84087 1551 B6
900 OREM 84057 2820 A2
1000 PRVO 84604 2928 A4
1200 FRWT 84404 1055 E3
1200 FRWT 84404 1056 A3
1400 PRVO 84604 2927 E4
1700 SLCY 84116 1753 C6
2800 LYTN 84041 1281 E2
2800 PRVO 84601 2927 B5
3000 WPT 84015 1226 C2
W 1100 S
- BMCY 84302 828 A2
- BxEC 84302 827 B2
- BxEC 84302 828 A2
- BxEC 84340 827 B2
- GRLD 84312 520 E3
- LOGN 84321 527 D6
10 BMCY 84302 827 E2
10 BNFL 84010 1653 D2
10 FMTN 84025 1448 C4
10 KYVL 84037 1345 C4
500 LEHI 84043 2710 B1
600 PYSN 84651 3354 D7
900 WDCR 84087 1653 B2
1000 CchC 84321 527 A6
1300 OREM 84058 2927 A1
1800 MTSV 84404 1055 D7
2000 SRCS 84075 1226 E6
3200 CchC 84321 525 E6
3200 CchC 84321 526 A6
W 1100 S I-15 BUS
- BxEC 84302 827 B2
- BxEC 84340 827 B2
10 BMCY 84302 827 E2
W 1100 S I-84 BUS
- BxEC 84302 827 B2
- BxEC 84340 827 B2
10 BMCY 84302 827 E2
W 1100 S US-89
- BMCY 84302 827 E2
- BMCY 84302 828 A2
- BxEC 84302 828 A2
W 1100 S US-91
- BMCY 84302 828 A2
- BxEC 84302 827 B2
- BxEC 84302 828 A2
- BxEC 84340 827 B2
10 BMCY 84302 827 E2
S 1105 E
7200 MDVL 84047 2177 B3
E 1110 N
1400 OREM 84097 2821 C2
N 1110 E
100 LNDN 84042 2713 E6
1000 SPFK 84660 3249 E1
1200 OREM 84097 2821 B2
N 1110 W
800 PTGV 84062 2712 C2
2300 CLTN 84015 1171 B7
S 1110 E
4800 SLkC 84117 2071 B3
S 1110 W
1300 UthC 84058 2927 A1
10200 SJDN 84095 2281 E3
S 1115 E
4800 SLkC 84117 2071 B3
S 1115 W
- SRCS 84075 1281 B4
600 OREM 84058 2820 A7
7000 WJDN 84084 2175 E2
E 1120 N
10 ANFK 84003 2604 C5
100 LOGN 84341 463 D7
E 1120 S
- PRVO 84606 3036 A2
800 OGDN 84404 1057 A7
900 OREM 84097 2928 A1
1100 PRVO 84606 3035 E2
2300 SPFK 84660 3250 C5
N 1120 E
100 SGVL 84663 3143 E1

N 1120 E
200 LOGN 84321 528 B2
200 OREM 84097 2821 B4
500 SPFK 84660 3249 E1
2200 LEHI 84043 2603 E2
N 1120 W
300 PRVO 84601 2928 A6
400 OREM 84057 2820 A4
1000 CLTN 84015 1227 B2
1800 PRVO 84604 2928 A3
2400 CLTN 84015 1171 B6
S 1120 E
10600 SNDY 84094 2283 B4
S 1120 W
200 OREM 84058 2820 A5
W 1120 N
10 ANFK 84003 2604 C5
400 OREM 84057 2820 C2
800 PRVO 84604 2928 A5
2700 PRVO 84601 2927 C5
W 1120 S
- SRCS 84075 1227 A6
1500 SGVL 84663 3142 E4
W 1124 N
10 LOGN 84341 463 D7
E 1125 N
800 SGVL 84663 3036 D7
N 1125 E
700 OREM 84097 2821 B3
1400 LEHI 84043 2603 E4
3100 LYTN 84040 1229 C5
3100 NHON 84414 999 C4
N 1125 W
800 LYTN 84041 1282 C3
1100 OREM 84057 2820 A2
1600 LEHI 84043 2603 A4
S 1125 E
- CRFD 84015 1228 A6
2000 BNFL 84010 1654 B3
S 1125 W
300 LYTN 84041 1282 C5
1200 OREM 84058 2927 A1
W 1125 N
200 CTRV 84014 1551 D2
2500 LYTN 84041 1281 E2
2500 LYTN 84041 1282 A2
3300 LYTN 84015 1281 D2
W 1125 S
2200 SRCS 84075 1226 D6
E 1130 N
100 OREM 84057 2820 D2
600 OREM 84097 2820 E2
600 OREM 84097 2821 A2
1100 SPFK 84660 3249 E1
1100 SPFK 84660 3250 A1
E 1130 S
- SPFK 84660 3250 B5
300 PRVO 84606 3035 D2
N 1130 E
300 LNDN 84042 2713 E5
400 PRVO 84606 2928 E5
N 1130 W
- PTGV 84062 2605 B5
200 PRVO 84601 2928 A6
800 PRVO 84604 2928 A5
1200 WshC 84032 2398 B1
1300 OREM 84057 2820 A1
1800 WshC 84032 2292 B7
S 1130 E
700 ALPN 84004 2498 B6
7600 MDVL 84047 2177 B4
S 1130 W
- SRCS 84075 1281 B3
500 LEHI 84043 2603 A7
800 PYSN 84651 3354 C7
1900 WDCR 84087 1653 A3
4800 TYVL 84123 2069 E4
7300 WJDN 84084 2175 E3
13000 RIVN 84065 2387 E3
W 1130 N
300 SNST 84015 1227 C2
500 CLTN 84015 1227 C2
1000 OREM 84057 2820 A2
1100 FMTN 84025 1346 A6
2800 PRVO 84601 2927 B5
W 1130 S
900 PYSN 84651 3354 C7
1200 OREM 84058 2927 A1
S 1135 E
4000 SLkC 84124 2071 B1
E 1140 N
200 OREM 84057 2820 E2
300 LOGN 84341 463 E7
1600 LOGN 84341 464 C7
E 1140 S
900 OGDN 84404 1057 A7
900 PRVO 84606 3035 E2
N 1140 E
200 PYSN 84651 3355 B4
N 1140 W
10 OREM 84057 2820 A5
200 OGDN 84404 1056 A4
400 LOGN 84341 463 C7
800 MPTN 84664 3143 E6
1000 PTGV 84062 2712 C1
1700 PRVO 84604 2928 A3
S 1140 E
100 LNDN 84042 2713 E7
1100 OREM 84097 2928 B1
1100 PRVO 84097 2928 B1
4000 SLkC 84124 1965 B7
4200 SLkC 84124 2071 B1
4800 SLkC 84117 2071 B3
S 1140 W
- DvsC 84041 1282 B6
- LYTN 84041 1282 B6
- WJDN 84088 2175 E4
100 OGDN 84404 1056 A5
2700 SRCS 84075 1281 B3
6400 MRRY 84123 2175 E1
W 1140 N
200 LOGN 84341 463 C7
1000 OREM 84057 2820 A2
1100 PRVO 84604 2928 A4
E 1145 N
400 OREM 84097 2820 E2
1100 OREM 84097 2821 B2
E 1145 S
300 OREM 84097 2928 B1
S 1145 E
5700 MRRY 84121 2071 B6

S 1145 W
1200 OREM 84058 2927 A1
4300 TYVL 84123 2069 E2
W 1145 N
800 CLTN 84015 1227 B2
2100 CLTN 84015 1226 E2
E 1150 N
10 LYTN 84041 1282 D2
10 SGVL 84663 3036 C7
100 HARR 84404 1056 E3
100 LYTN 84041 1283 A2
200 LEHI 84043 2603 C4
400 LOGN 84341 463 E7
600 LOGN 84341 464 A7
600 OGDN 84404 1057 A2
700 PTGV 84062 2713 A1
900 BNFL 84010 1552 A6
900 OREM 84097 2821 A2
1700 LYTN 84040 1283 D2
E 1150 S
10 FMTN 84025 1448 D4
10 PYSN 84651 3354 E7
300 SGVL 84663 3143 D4
400 OREM 84097 2927 E1
500 KYVL 84037 1345 E4
800 OGDN 84404 1057 A7
1000 CRFD 84015 1228 A7
1200 SPFK 84660 3250 A5
N 1150 E
- SLCY 84103 1859 B2
100 LNDN 84042 2713 E6
300 KYVL 84037 1284 A7
400 BNFL 84010 1552 B6
700 LYTN 84040 1283 C3
700 PRVO 84606 2928 E5
1100 ANFK 84003 2605 A4
1100 PTGV 84062 2713 B2
1600 LOGN 84341 464 B6
1900 LEHI 84043 2603 E3
2500 PRVO 84604 2928 E2
3000 NHON 84414 999 C4
3300 LYTN 84040 1229 C5
N 1150 W
100 OREM 84057 2820 A4
600 PRVO 84601 2928 A5
1400 CLTN 84015 1227 B1
1600 LEHI 84043 2603 A4
2500 LYTN 84041 1228 C6
3600 PTGV 84062 2605 B4
S 1150 E
10 BNFL 84010 1552 B7
10 LNDN 84042 2713 E7
10 SPFK 84660 3249 E3
200 PYSN 84651 3355 B5
400 BNFL 84010 1654 B1
600 PRVO 84606 3035 E1
700 PTGV 84062 2713 B4
2900 SGVL 84663 3036 A7
3100 SGVL 84663 3143 A2
4800 OGDN 84403 1173 B3
5000 SOGN 84403 1173 B3
5600 SOGN 84405 1173 B5
10100 SLkC 84094 2283 B3
10100 SNDY 84094 2283 B3
S 1150 W
- DvsC 84056 1172 B5
- SWBR 84405 1172 B5
100 FMTN 84025 1448 A2
500 LYTN 84041 1282 C6
500 OREM 84058 2820 A6
900 CRFD 84016 1227 B6
1300 UthC 84058 2927 A1
2400 SRCS 84075 1281 B2
4400 RVDL 84405 1172 A2
4600 UthC 84660 3141 E5
4600 UthC 84660 3142 A5
9000 WJDN 84088 2175 E7
W 1150 N
10 LOGN 84341 463 D7
100 SGVL 84663 3036 C7
200 SNST 84015 1227 D2
500 LEHI 84043 2603 B5
500 WBNF 84087 1551 C6
700 OREM 84057 2820 B2
1200 LYTN 84041 1282 C2
1200 PRVO 84604 2927 E4
1200 PRVO 84604 2928 A4
3000 WPT 84015 1226 C2
W 1150 S
- OREM 84058 2927 A1
10 FMTN 84025 1448 C4
400 BNFL 84010 1653 C2
700 PRVO 84601 3035 A2
700 PYSN 84651 3354 D7
1200 PRVO 84601 3034 E2
2000 SRCS 84075 1226 E6
4400 WbrC 84401 1054 A7
4400 WbrC 84404 1054 A7
W 1150 S SR-39
4400 WbrC 84401 1054 C7
4400 WbrC 84404 1054 C7
E 1150 N Cir
10 ANFK 84003 2604 C5
N 1155 W
1500 CLTN 84015 1227 B1
S 1155 W
7100 WJDN 84084 2175 E2
10500 SJDN 84095 2281 E4
E 1160 N
600 OREM 84097 2821 A2
1200 LEHI 84043 2603 E5
E 1160 S
- SGVL 84663 3144 A4
1000 PRVO 84606 3035 E2
N 1160 E
400 SPFK 84663 3250 B2
500 OREM 84097 2821 B3
N 1160 W
1400 OREM 84057 2820 A1
1800 PRVO 84604 2928 A3
2300 CLTN 84015 1171 B7
S 1160 E
10 LNDN 84042 2713 E6
S 1160 W
10 OREM 84058 2820 A5
4300 TYVL 84123 2069 E1
7000 WJDN 84084 2175 E2
W 1160 N
500 OREM 84057 2820 C2
600 PTGV 84062 2712 C1
800 PRVO 84604 2928 A4

S 1162 E
13200 DRPR 84020 2389 B3
E 1165 N
200 OREM 84057 2820 E2
N 1165 E
100 LNDN 84042 2713 E6
N 1165 W
1100 OREM 84057 2820 A2
S 1165 E
1400 OGDN 84404 1116 B1
S 1165 W
300 OREM 84058 2820 A6
E 1170 N
600 PTGV 84062 2713 A1
800 OREM 84097 2821 A2
E 1170 S
700 SPFK 84660 3249 E5
2300 SPFK 84660 3250 C5
N 1170 E
10 SGVL 84663 3143 E2
200 LOGN 84321 528 B2
1000 OREM 84097 2821 B2
1500 MPTN 84664 3144 C5
N 1170 W
300 PRVO 84601 2928 A6
1100 CLTN 84015 1227 B2
2400 CLTN 84015 1171 B6
S 1170 E
- SLCY 84106 1965 B4
100 LNDN 84042 2713 E6
100 LOGN 84321 528 B3
900 SPFK 84660 3250 A4
S 1170 W
- FMTN 84025 1448 A3
1200 OREM 84058 2927 A1
7100 WJDN 84084 2175 E2
W 1170 N
100 PTGV 84062 2712 D1
1300 OREM 84057 2820 A2
1400 PRVO 84604 2927 E4
2800 PRVO 84601 2927 B4
E 1175 N
100 HARR 84404 1056 D2
700 OGDN 84404 1057 A3
N 1175 E
3100 LYTN 84040 1229 C5
N 1175 W
- BMCY 84302 766 B4
- BxEC 84302 766 B3
900 CLTN 84015 1227 B2
1600 LEHI 84043 2603 A4
2300 LYTN 84041 1228 C7
S 1175 E
- CRFD 84015 1228 A6
- OGDN 84404 1116 B1
2000 BNFL 84010 1654 B3
4000 OGDN 84403 1173 B1
4000 SLkC 84124 2071 B1
5700 SOGN 84405 1173 B5
S 1175 W
- FMTN 84025 1448 A3
2600 SRCS 84075 1281 B3
4300 TYVL 84123 2069 E2
4500 RVDL 84405 1172 A2
W 1175 N
400 CTRV 84014 1551 C1
600 FMTN 84025 1346 B6
700 WBNF 84087 1551 B6
1000 CLTN 84015 1227 B2
W 1175 S
- LYTN 84041 1282 B7
800 WDCR 84087 1653 B2
2000 SRCS 84075 1226 D7
E 1180 N
600 LEHI 84043 2603 D4
800 PTGV 84062 2713 A1
1000 ANFK 84003 2605 A4
E 1180 S
900 PRVO 84606 3035 E2
1500 SPFK 84660 3250 A5
N 1180 E
200 PTGV 84062 2713 B2
600 OREM 84097 2821 B3
N 1180 W
- OREM 84057 2820 A1
10 OREM 84057 2820 A2
1500 PTGV 84062 2605 B7
S 1180 E
900 SGVL 84663 3143 E4
1100 SPFK 84660 3250 A5
5600 MRRY 84121 2071 B5
S 1180 W
200 OREM 84058 2820 A6
1100 OREM 84058 2927 A1
W 1180 N
2700 PRVO 84601 2927 C4
W 1180 S
1700 WDCR 84087 1652 D2
E 1185 N
1600 LOGN 84341 464 C7
N 1185 E
10 PTGV 84062 2713 B3
N 1185 W
1200 CLTN 84015 1227 B2
S 1185 E
- OGDN 84404 1116 B1
10 PTGV 84062 2713 B3
5800 MRRY 84121 2071 B6
8600 SNDY 84094 2177 B6
8700 SLkC 84094 2177 B6
12900 DRPR 84020 2389 B3
S 1185 W
- SRCS 84075 1281 B2
11600 SJDN 84095 2281 E6
W 1185 N
300 OREM 84057 2820 C2
1100 FMTN 84025 1346 A6
E 1190 N
800 PTGV 84062 2713 A1
E 1190 S
100 FMTN 84025 1448 D4
1400 PRVO 84606 3036 A2
N 1190 E
1100 ANFK 84003 2605 A4
S 1190 E
- SLCY 84106 1965 B4
1100 SGVL 84663 3143 E4
S 1190 W
1300 UthC 84058 2927 A1
6400 MRRY 84123 2175 E1
7100 WJDN 84084 2175 E2
11000 SJDN 84095 2281 E5

W 1190 N
100 LOGN 84341 463 D7
2800 PRVO 84601 2927 C4
S 1195 E
- OGDN 84404 1116 B1
9200 SNDY 84094 2177 B7
S 1195 W
4300 TYVL 84123 2069 E1
E 1200 N
- LYTN 84041 1283 A2
10 MPTN 84664 3144 C5
10 OREM 84057 2820 E2
10 PTGV 84062 2712 D1
200 LOGN 84341 463 E7
400 BNFL 84010 1551 E5
400 BNFL 84010 1552 A5
400 OREM 84097 2820 E2
600 OREM 84097 2821 A2
600 PTGV 84062 2713 A1
700 LOGN 84341 464 A7
900 OGDN 84404 1057 A2
2200 LYTN 84040 1283 E2
2900 LYTN 84040 1284 A2
E 1200 S
- CRFD 84015 1228 B7
- SPFK 84660 3250 B5
10 BNFL 84010 1653 E2
10 LOGN 84321 527 D6
10 OREM 84058 2927 D1
10 PVDN 84332 527 D6
400 KYVL 84037 1345 E4
700 OREM 84097 2928 A1
1200 SGVL 84663 3143 E3
1200 SGVL 84663 3144 A4
1300 BNFL 84010 1654 B2
1400 PRVO 84606 3035 E2
1400 PRVO 84606 3036 B2
N 1200 E
- SLCY 84103 1859 B2
10 LNDN 84042 2713 E6
10 MPTN 84664 3144 C6
200 OREM 84097 2821 B4
300 PTGV 84062 2713 B2
400 BNFL 84010 1552 B6
400 LEHI 84043 2603 E5
500 PRVO 84606 2928 E5
500 UthC 84043 2603 E5
600 LOGN 84321 528 B1
800 PRVO 84604 2928 E5
900 LOGN 84321 464 B7
900 LOGN 84341 464 B7
1200 LYTN 84040 1283 C2
2600 NHLN 84341 464 B3
2700 HILD 84043 2603 E2
2700 NHLN 84318 464 B3
3100 CchC 84318 464 B3
3100 NHON 84414 999 C4
N 1200 W
- BMCY 84302 766 B5
10 OREM 84057 2820 A4
10 MTSV 84404 1056 A4
100 OGDN 84404 1056 A4
200 PRVO 84601 2928 A6
300 LNDN 84042 2712 D5
300 SLCY 84116 1857 E1
400 CRFD 84015 1227 B3
700 SLCY 84116 1753 E6
1000 CchC 84341 463 A7
1000 FRWT 84404 1056 A4
1000 LOGN 84341 463 A7
1200 MPTN 84664 3143 E5
1400 HARR 84404 1056 A1
1600 LEHI 84043 2602 E4
1600 LYTN 84041 1282 C1
1600 PTGV 84062 2605 B7
1800 CLTN 84015 1171 B7
1800 CLTN 84015 1227 A1
2200 LEHI 84043 2603 A2
5200 CchC 84335 399 A3
N 1200 W US-89
- LEHI 84043 2603 A3
S 1200 E
10 LNDN 84042 2713 E6
10 MPTN 84664 3144 C7
10 SLCY 84102 1859 B3
10 SLCY 84103 1859 B3
100 SGVL 84663 3143 E2
200 PRVO 84606 2928 E7
300 BNFL 84010 1654 B1
300 PYSN 84651 3355 B6
400 MPTN 84664 3251 C1
900 SLCY 84105 1859 B6
1200 CRFD 84015 1228 B7
1400 OGDN 84404 1116 B1
1800 SLCY 84105 1965 B1
2800 SLCY 84106 1965 B4
3400 SLkC 84106 1965 B6
4500 SLkC 84117 2071 B2
5000 SOGN 84403 1173 B3
6000 SOGN 84405 1173 B6
6200 MRRY 84121 2071 B7
7200 SWBR 84405 1229 B1
7600 MDVL 84047 2177 B4
13000 DRPR 84020 2389 B3
S 1200 W
- BMCY 84302 766 B7
- BMCY 84302 827 B1
- BxEC 84302 766 B7
- BxEC 84302 827 B1
- CRFD 84016 1227 B6
- LOGN 84321 527 A4
- OREM 84058 2927 A1
10 CRFD 84015 1227 B4
10 LNDN 84042 2712 D6
10 OREM 84058 2820 A5
100 MTSV 84404 1056 A6
100 OGDN 84404 1056 A6
100 PRVO 84601 2928 A7
200 SLCY 84104 1857 E4
500 LEHI 84043 2603 A7
500 WDCR 84087 1653 A1
1200 MTSV 84401 1056 A6
1200 MTSV 84401 1115 A1
1200 MTSV 84404 1115 A1
1800 MPTN 84664 3250 E2
2200 WHVN 84401 1115 A3
2400 SRCS 84075 1281 B2
3100 NBLY 84321 591 A3
3200 CchC 84321 591 A4
3300 WVCY 84119 1963 E6
4300 TYVL 84123 2069 E2
4400 CchC 84319 591 A7

STREET Block City ZIP Map# Grid

S 1200 W
4600 CchC 84319 651 A1
5100 RVDL 84405 1172 A4
5100 UthC 84660 3141 E6
6400 MRRY 84123 2175 E1
7300 SPFK 84660 3248 E5
7700 UthC 84660 3248 E7
8000 SALM 84660 3248 E7
8300 SALM 84653 3248 E7
W 1200 N
- LOGN 84341 463 B7
- SRSP 84043 2601 C7
10 MPTN 84664 3144 A5
10 OREM 84057 2820 C2
10 PTGV 84062 2712 D1
10 WshC 84032 2398 C2
200 BNFL 84010 1551 C6
200 CTRV 84014 1551 D1
200 LEHI 84043 2603 B4
500 ANFK 84003 2604 B5
500 CLTN 84015 1227 C2
700 MPTN 84664 3143 E5
700 PRVO 84604 2928 A4
900 SLCY 84116 1753 E6
1100 WBNF 84087 1551 A6
1200 DvsC 84087 1550 E6
1200 FRWT 84404 1056 A2
1200 LYTN 84041 1282 C2
1200 WBNF 84087 1550 E6
1300 OREM 84057 2819 E2
1300 PRVO 84604 2927 E4
1400 FRWT 84404 1055 E2
2300 PRVO 84601 2927 C4
2600 LYTN 84041 1281 E2
3000 WPT 84015 1226 C2
3800 SLCY 84116 1752 C6
W 1200 S
- GRLD 84312 520 E3
- SRCS 84075 1226 A7
- WPT 84075 1225 E7
- WPT 84075 1226 A7
10 BNFL 84010 1653 D2
10 ELWD 84337 584 D1
10 KYVL 84037 1345 C4
10 LOGN 84321 527 D6
10 PYSN 84651 3354 E7
10 TMTN 84337 584 D1
100 CchC 84325 524 E6
100 MNDN 84325 524 E6
400 OREM 84058 2927 C1
400 SALM 84653 3355 E6
400 SALM 84653 3356 A6
800 PRVO 84601 3035 A2
1100 DvsC 84075 1225 E7
1100 SRCS 84075 1225 E7
1100 WDCR 84087 1653 A2
1300 WDCR 84087 1652 E2
1800 CchC 84321 526 D6
2000 MTSV 84401 1055 C7
2000 MTSV 84404 1055 C7
2300 WbrC 84401 1055 C7
2300 WbrC 84404 1055 C7
2800 WbrC 84401 1054 C7
2800 WbrC 84404 1054 E7
3600 CchC 84321 525 D6
4300 CchC 84325 525 B6
W 1200 S SR-39
2000 MTSV 84401 1055 C7
2000 MTSV 84404 1055 C7
2300 WbrC 84401 1055 C7
2300 WbrC 84404 1055 C7
2800 WbrC 84401 1054 C7
2800 WbrC 84404 1054 C7
1200 S
100 MNDN 84325 524 E6
S 1200 E St
- CchC 84328 711 B3
E 1200 N Cir
10 ANFK 84003 2604 C4
N 1205 W
1300 CLTN 84015 1227 B1
S 1205 E
8800 SNDY 84094 2177 B6
S 1205 W
2900 SRCS 84075 1281 B3
7000 WJDN 84084 2175 E2
E 1210 N
1600 LOGN 84341 464 C7
N 1210 E
400 SPFK 84663 3250 B2
N 1210 W
1900 PTGV 84062 2605 B7
S 1210 E
200 PTGV 84062 2713 B3
9400 SNDY 84094 2283 B2
S 1210 W
13000 RIVN 84065 2387 E3
W 1210 N
2500 PRVO 84601 2927 C4
W 1210 S
700 PYSN 84651 3354 D7
S 1213 E
900 FTHT 84037 1346 A3
S 1215 E
3700 SLkC 84106 1965 B7
W 1215 S
2000 SRCS 84075 1226 E7
E 1220 N
300 PTGV 84062 2712 E1
1100 OREM 84097 2821 B2
1600 LOGN 84341 464 C7
N 1220 E
10 LOGN 84321 528 B3
2000 PRVO 84604 2928 E3
N 1220 W
800 PRVO 84601 2928 A5
1000 PRVO 84604 2928 A4
1600 CLTN 84015 1227 B1
2300 CLTN 84015 1171 B6
S 1220 E
10 LOGN 84321 528 B3
4100 SLkC 84124 2071 B1
5800 MRRY 84121 2071 B6
S 1220 W
400 PRVO 84601 2928 A7
400 PRVO 84601 3035 A1
1200 OREM 84058 2927 A2
1300 UthC 84058 2927 A2
8600 WJDN 84088 2175 E6
11700 SJDN 84095 2281 E7
12400 RIVN 84065 2387 E2
W 1220 N
100 ANFK 84003 2604 B4
700 LEHI 84043 2603 A4
700 PTGV 84062 2712 C1
800 CLTN 84015 1227 B2
1300 LEHI 84043 2602 E4
W 1220 S
500 PRVO 84601 3035 B2
E 1225 N
300 LOGN 84341 463 E7
600 OGDN 84404 1057 A2
1700 LYTN 84040 1283 D2
6800 WbrC 84317 1060 E2
E 1225 S
900 OGDN 84404 1057 A7
1000 CRFD 84015 1228 A7
N 1225 E
300 BNFL 84010 1552 B7
1400 LYTN 84040 1283 C2
2900 NHON 84414 999 C4
N 1225 W
1500 CLTN 84015 1227 B1
1800 CLTN 84015 1171 B7
S 1225 E
10 BNFL 84010 1552 B7
100 BNFL 84010 1654 B1
4500 SLkC 84117 2071 B2
8200 SNDY 84094 2177 B5
8700 SLkC 84094 2177 B6
10600 SLkC 84092 2283 B4
10700 SNDY 84094 2283 B4
S 1225 W
100 FMTN 84025 1448 A2
1900 WDCR 84087 1653 A3
2500 SRCS 84075 1281 B2
5000 RVDL 84405 1172 A3
W 1225 N
100 LYTN 84041 1282 E2
500 CLTN 84015 1227 C2
500 WBNF 84087 1551 C5
800 PRVO 84604 2928 A4
2900 LYTN 84041 1281 E2
E 1230 N
100 SGVL 84663 3036 C7
E 1230 S
500 SGVL 84663 3143 D4
900 PRVO 84606 3035 E2
1400 PRVO 84606 3036 A2
N 1230 E
10 SGVL 84663 3143 E2
500 OREM 84097 2821 B4
N 1230 W
- PTGV 84062 2605 B5
1100 CLTN 84015 1227 B2
1300 OREM 84057 2820 A1
2800 LEHI 84043 2603 A1
S 1230 E
300 SPFK 84660 3250 A3
700 ALPN 84004 2498 B6
S 1230 W
- OREM 84058 2820 A6
10100 SJDN 84095 2281 E3
W 1230 N
100 ANFK 84003 2604 C4
900 OREM 84057 2820 A2
2100 CLTN 84015 1226 E2
W 1230 S
1000 OREM 84058 2927 A1
E 1235 S
100 FMTN 84025 1448 D4
N 1235 W
900 CLTN 84015 1227 B2
W 1235 N
1100 CLTN 84015 1227 B2
W 1235 S
- SRCS 84075 1226 A7
700 PYSN 84651 3354 D7
E 1240 N
200 LOGN 84341 463 E7
E 1240 S
700 SPFK 84660 3249 E5
1100 SPFK 84660 3250 A5
N 1240 E
10 PTGV 84062 2713 B2
900 OREM 84097 2821 B2
S 1240 E
400 PYSN 84651 3355 C6
700 SPFK 84660 3250 A4
8600 SNDY 84094 2177 B6
8700 SLkC 84094 2177 B6
S 1240 W
- OREM 84058 2927 A1
7700 TYVL 84084 2175 D1
8800 WJDN 84088 2175 D7
W 1240 N
500 OREM 84057 2820 C2
700 CLTN 84015 1227 B2
W 1240 S
300 PYSN 84651 3354 D7
1100 SRCS 84075 1227 B7
S 1245 W
7000 WJDN 84084 2175 D2
W 1245 N
2500 LYTN 84041 1281 E2
W 1245 S
2000 SRCS 84075 1226 E7
E 1250 N
10 LYTN 84041 1283 A2
100 ANFK 84003 2604 D4
100 CTRV 84014 1551 E1
100 SGVL 84663 3036 C6
200 BNFL 84010 1551 E5
200 LOGN 84341 463 D7
800 PTGV 84062 2713 A1
900 OREM 84097 2821 A2
1400 LYTN 84040 1283 C2
1700 LOGN 84341 464 D7
3100 LYTN 84040 1284 B2
E 1250 S
- BxEC 84312 521 A3
- TMTN 84337 521 A3
100 TMTN 84337 520 E3
300 PYSN 84651 3355 A7
400 KYVL 84037 1345 E4
500 SGVL 84663 3143 D4
1200 CRFD 84015 1228 B7
1400 OGDN 84404 1057 C7
1400 PRVO 84606 3036 A2
2600 SPFK 84660 3250 C5
N 1250 E
10 LOGN 84321 528 B3
400 BNFL 84010 1552 B6
600 OREM 84097 2821 B3
700 PRVO 84606 2928 E5
1000 LEHI 84043 2603 E4
1400 MPTN 84664 3144 C5
1900 LYTN 84040 1283 C1
2400 NHLN 84341 464 B3
2900 NHON 84414 999 C4
3000 LYTN 84040 1229 C5
N 1250 W
- PTVW 84414 997 E4
- PTVW 84414 998 A3
300 CRFD 84015 1227 B3
800 PRVO 84601 2928 A5
900 PTGV 84062 2712 B1
1000 LYTN 84041 1282 C2
1400 CLTN 84015 1227 B1
1400 OREM 84057 2820 A1
1400 PRVO 84604 2928 A4
1800 LEHI 84043 2603 A3
2000 CLTN 84015 1171 B7
S 1250 E
10 FTHT 84037 1346 A2
100 LOGN 84321 528 B3
200 PTGV 84062 2713 C4
300 LYTN 84041 1283 C6
800 MPTN 84664 3251 C1
1100 SPFK 84660 3250 A5
1200 CRFD 84015 1228 B7
3800 SLkC 84106 1965 B7
5600 MRRY 84121 2071 B5
6000 SOGN 84405 1173 B6
7300 SWBR 84405 1229 B2
S 1250 W
- CRFD 84016 1227 B6
- FMTN 84025 1448 A3
- OREM 84058 2927 A1
10 CRFD 84015 1227 B4
200 LNDN 84042 2712 D7
500 LEHI 84043 2603 A7
1200 SRCS 84075 1227 B7
1500 WDCR 84087 1653 A2
1900 LOGN 84321 591 A1
2800 OGDN 84401 1115 A4
2800 WbrC 84401 1115 A4
3100 SRCS 84075 1281 B3
4500 RVDL 84405 1172 A2
4800 TYVL 84123 2069 D4
6100 MRRY 84123 2069 D7
W 1250 N
- ANFK 84003 2604 B4
10 HARR 84404 1056 D2
10 OREM 84057 2820 D2
100 CTRV 84014 1551 D1
500 CLTN 84015 1227 C2
1500 PRVO 84604 2927 E4
1600 ANFK 84062 2712 B1
1600 PTGV 84062 2712 B1
2000 LYTN 84041 1282 A2
2100 WPT 84015 1226 C2
W 1250 S
- LOGN 84321 527 C6
10 PVDN 84332 527 D6
10 PYSN 84651 3354 E7
400 BNFL 84010 1653 C2
400 OREM 84058 2927 C1
500 HRCY 84032 2398 B6
1250 E
- HYRM 84319 652 A3
E 1250 N Cir
10 ANFK 84003 2604 C4
S 1255 W
10700 SJDN 84095 2281 E4
12400 RIVN 84065 2387 D1
E 1260 N
200 LOGN 84341 463 E7
600 LOGN 84341 464 A7
E 1260 S
10 PYSN 84651 3354 E7
10 PYSN 84651 3461 E1
N 1260 E
- PTGV 84062 2713 B2
N 1260 W
500 CLTN 84015 1227 B3
500 PRVO 84601 2928 A6
S 1260 E
600 PYSN 84651 3355 B6
800 PTGV 84062 2713 B4
3600 SLkC 84106 1965 B6
4400 SLkC 84124 2071 B2
8700 SLkC 84094 2177 B6
S 1260 W
100 LOGN 84321 527 C6
1300 OREM 84058 2927 A1
2900 SRCS 84075 1281 B3
10600 SJDN 84095 2281 D4
W 1260 N
200 SNST 84015 1227 D2
500 LEHI 84043 2603 B4
600 PTGV 84062 2712 C1
900 OREM 84057 2820 A2
S 1265 E
4100 SLkC 84124 2071 B1
E 1270 N
100 SGVL 84663 3036 C6
200 LOGN 84341 463 E7
E 1270 S
1000 PRVO 84606 3035 E2
1400 PRVO 84606 3036 B2
N 1270 E
- LEHI 84043 2603 E6
1000 SPFK 84660 3250 A1
1100 ANFK 84003 2605 B4
N 1270 W
1100 PRVO 84604 2927 E4
3300 PTGV 84062 2605 B5
S 1270 E
1300 SPFK 84660 3250 A5
8700 SLkC 84094 2177 B6
S 1270 W
700 PYSN 84651 3354 C6
W 1270 S
10 PYSN 84651 3461 E1
E 1275 N
400 OGDN 84404 1056 E2
800 OGDN 84404 1057 A2
900 KYVL 84037 1283 E5
900 KYVL 84037 1284 A5
7000 WbrC 84317 1060 E2
E 1275 S
700 KYVL 84037 1345 E4
N 1275 E
1400 LYTN 84040 1283 C2
2700 NHON 84414 999 C5
N 1275 W
500 CRFD 84015 1227 B3
S 1275 E
1900 OGDN 84401 1116 C2
6000 SOGN 84405 1173 B6
8200 SNDY 84094 2177 B5
8300 SLkC 84094 2177 B5
S 1275 W
- FMTN 84025 1448 A2
3100 SRCS 84075 1281 B4
5000 RVDL 84405 1171 E3
8500 WJDN 84088 2175 D6
W 1275 N
10 LYTN 84041 1282 E2
500 LEHI 84043 2603 B4
600 FMTN 84025 1346 B6
2500 LYTN 84041 1281 E2
W 1275 S
- DvsC 84075 1282 B7
- DvsC 84075 1344 B1
- LOGN 84321 527 C7
1100 OREM 84058 2927 A2
2000 SRCS 84075 1226 E7
E 1280 N
400 OREM 84097 2820 E2
600 LOGN 84341 464 A7
1100 ANFK 84003 2605 A4
E 1280 S
- CRFD 84015 1228 B7
900 SALM 84653 3356 C6
1700 PRVO 84606 3036 A2
N 1280 E
500 SPFK 84663 3250 B2
600 OREM 84097 2821 B3
N 1280 W
100 SLCY 84116 1857 D2
200 PRVO 84601 2927 E6
200 PRVO 84601 2928 A6
S 1280 E
300 PRVO 84606 2928 E7
1200 SLkC 84094 2283 B3
6200 MRRY 84121 2071 B7
8200 SNDY 84094 2177 B5
11000 SNDY 84094 2283 B5
S 1280 W
- SJDN 84095 2280 C6
700 CRFD 84016 1227 B6
6100 MRRY 84123 2069 D7
W 1280 N
300 ANFK 84003 2604 B4
800 PRVO 84604 2928 A4
1700 FRWT 84404 1055 E2
W 1280 S
500 PRVO 84601 3035 B2
700 PYSN 84651 3354 D7
N 1285 W
1000 CLTN 84015 1227 B2
1400 OREM 84057 2820 A1
S 1285 W
1100 WDCR 84087 1653 A2
W 1285 N
600 OREM 84057 2820 B2
W 1285 S
10 LOGN 84321 527 D6
10 PVDN 84332 527 D6
E 1290 S
- OREM 84097 2928 B1
300 PYSN 84651 3462 A1
N 1290 E
1000 SPFK 84660 3250 A1
N 1290 W
1000 PRVO 84604 2927 E5
1800 PRVO 84604 2928 B2
S 1290 E
1100 SPFK 84660 3250 A5
W 1290 N
100 ANFK 84003 2604 B4
600 LEHI 84043 2603 B4
1500 FMTN 84025 1345 E6
W 1290 S
100 LOGN 84321 527 D6
1000 OREM 84058 2927 A1
1000 SRCS 84075 1227 B7
W 1295 S
1200 OREM 84058 2927 A1
E 1300 N
10 MPTN 84664 3144 B5
10 OREM 84057 2820 D2
100 LEHI 84043 2603 C4
100 SGVL 84663 3036 C6
200 BNFL 84010 1551 E5
500 LYTN 84041 1283 A2
600 LOGN 84341 464 A7
700 PTGV 84062 2713 A1
900 ANFK 84003 2605 A4
900 OGDN 84404 1057 A2
1100 LYTN 84040 1283 C2
3100 DvsC 84040 1284 B2
3100 LYTN 84040 1284 B2
7800 WbrC 84317 1061 B2
E 1300 S
- ANFK 84003 2711 E4
- ANFK 84003 2712 A4
- CRFD 84015 1228 B7
10 BNFL 84010 1653 D2
10 SLCY 84111 1858 D7
10 SLCY 84115 1858 D7
10 TMTN 84337 520 E3
500 SLCY 84105 1858 D7
700 SLCY 84105 1859 A7
1400 PRVO 84606 3036 A2
1700 SLCY 84108 1859 D7
2300 SLCY 84108 1860 A6
2900 SPFK 84660 3250 D5
8800 WbrC 84317 1061 E7
N 1300 E
- LOGN 84321 528 B3
10 BNFL 84010 1552 B7
10 PTGV 84062 2713 B2
10 SGVL 84663 3144 A2
400 FTHT 84037 1284 A7
700 LYTN 84040 1283 C3
1300 LEHI 84043 2603 E4
3000 NHON 84414 999 C4
3100 LYTN 84040 1229 C5
N 1300 W
10 CRFD 84015 1227 A4
300 SLCY 84116 1857 D1
400 PTGV 84062 2712 B2
500 PRVO 84601 2927 E6
1000 LYTN 84041 1282 C2
1000 SLCY 84116 1753 D6
1300 OREM 84057 2820 A1
1500 CLTN 84015 1227 B1
1500 PTGV 84062 2605 B7
2000 CLTN 84015 1171 B7
S 1300 E
10 BNFL 84010 1552 B7
10 LOGN 84321 528 B3
10 PTGV 84062 2713 B3
10 SGVL 84663 3144 A2
10 SLCY 84102 1859 B4
100 SPFK 84660 3250 A3
300 LYTN 84041 1283 C6
400 KYVL 84037 1283 C6
400 PRVO 84606 2928 E7
900 PRVO 84606 3035 E1
900 SLCY 84105 1859 B7
1100 DvsC 84037 1346 A4
1100 FMTN 84025 1346 A4
1100 FTHT 84037 1346 A4
1600 SLCY 84105 1965 B3
1700 BNFL 84010 1654 B3
1900 OGDN 84401 1116 C2
2100 SLCY 84106 1965 B3
3100 SLkC 84106 1965 B6
3900 SLkC 84124 1965 B6
4000 SLkC 84124 2071 B1
4500 SLkC 84117 2071 B1
5100 MRRY 84117 2071 B5
5100 SOGN 84403 1173 B4
5600 MRRY 84121 2071 B5
6400 MRRY 84121 2177 B1
6600 CDHT 84121 2177 B1
7100 CDHT 84093 2177 B1
7100 MDVL 84047 2177 B1
7400 SWBR 84405 1229 B2
7700 SNDY 84093 2177 B4
7700 SNDY 84094 2177 B4
8100 SLkC 84093 2177 B4
8300 SLkC 84094 2177 B4
9200 SNDY 84093 2283 B1
9200 SNDY 84094 2283 B1
9400 SLkC 84092 2283 B2
9400 SNDY 84092 2283 B1
10200 SLkC 84094 2283 B2
11800 SNDY 84092 2389 B2
11800 SNDY 84094 2389 B2
12200 DRPR 84020 2389 B2
S 1300 E SR-181
500 SLCY 84102 1859 B7
900 SLCY 84105 1859 B7
1600 SLCY 84105 1965 B3
2100 SLCY 84106 1965 B3
3100 SLkC 84106 1965 B6
3900 SLkC 84124 1965 B6
4000 SLkC 84124 2071 B1
4500 SLkC 84117 2071 B1
S 1300 W
- BxEC 84337 520 C6
- TMTN 84337 520 C6
10 CRFD 84015 1227 B5
200 SLCY 84104 1857 D4
300 PRVO 84601 2927 E7
500 WDCR 84087 1652 E1
1200 WDCR 84087 1653 A2
1500 SLCY 84104 1963 D1
2200 WVCY 84119 1963 D2
4000 TYVL 84123 2069 D2
4600 RVDL 84405 1171 E2
4600 RVDL 84405 1172 A3
5400 MRRY 84123 2069 D5
6500 TYVL 84123 2175 D1
9000 WJDN 84088 2175 D7
9200 WJDN 84088 2281 D2
9300 SJDN 84095 2281 D2
11600 RIVN 84065 2281 D6
13200 RIVN 84065 2387 D4
14200 BFDL 84065 2387 C6
14600 BFDL 84065 2494 D1
W 1300 N
10 PTGV 84062 2712 D1
10 SNST 84015 1227 C2
200 BNFL 84010 1551 C5
300 ANFK 84003 2604 B4
500 CLTN 84015 1227 C2
600 FMTN 84025 1346 B6
700 WBNF 84087 1551 B5
900 OREM 84057 2820 A2
1100 PRVO 84604 2928 A4
1200 FRWT 84404 1056 A2
1200 LEHI 84043 2603 A4
1500 FRWT 84404 1055 E2
1700 SLCY 84116 1753 C6
W 1300 S
- GRLD 84312 520 E3
- SLkC 84044 1854 D7
10 BNFL 84010 1653 D2
10 SLCY 84101 1858 A7
10 SLCY 84115 1858 A7
400 PRVO 84601 3035 B2
800 SLCY 84104 1858 A7
1100 WDCR 84087 1653 A2
1300 SLCY 84104 1857 D7
1300 WDCR 84087 1652 E2
1700 SGVL 84663 3142 D4
2400 SRCS 84075 1226 D7
4800 SLCY 84104 1855 E7
4800 SLCY 84104 1856 A7
6000 SLCY 84104 1854 D7
1300 E
- HYRM 84319 652 A3
- HYRM 84321 652 A3
W 1300 St
- SLkC 84044 1854 D7
E 1300 N Cir
10 ANFK 84003 2604 C4
S 1305 W
- CRFD 84016 1227 B6
W 1305 S
- LOGN 84321 527 C6
W 1309 S
100 LOGN 84321 527 D6
E 1310 N
400 OGDN 84404 1056 E2
E 1310 S
200 KYVL 84037 1345 D4
1700 SPFK 84660 3250 B5
N 1310 W
2900 LEHI 84043 2602 E1
W 1310 N
200 OREM 84057 2820 C1
600 LEHI 84043 2603 A4
600 PTGV 84062 2712 C1
2400 PRVO 84601 2927 C4
W 1310 S
- LOGN 84321 527 C6
W 1315 S
- SRCS 84075 1226 A7
10 LOGN 84321 527 D6
10 PVDN 84332 527 D6
1100 OREM 84058 2927 A2
E 1320 N
400 OREM 84097 2820 E1
E 1320 S
10 PYSN 84651 3461 E1
1300 PRVO 84606 3035 E2
1400 PRVO 84606 3036 A2
2700 SPFK 84660 3250 C5
N 1320 E
- LEHI 84043 2603 E6
N 1320 W
- WBNF 84087 1551 A7
100 SLCY 84116 1857 D2
1400 CLTN 84015 1227 B1
S 1320 E
100 LNDN 84042 2713 E7
900 PTGV 84062 2713 B4
1700 SPFK 84660 3250 A6
5900 MRRY 84121 2071 B6
11400 SNDY 84092 2283 B6
S 1320 W
2900 SRCS 84075 1281 A3
W 1320 N
1000 PTGV 84062 2712 B1
1200 PRVO 84604 2927 E4
1600 MPTN 84664 3143 D5
W 1320 S
10 PYSN 84651 3461 E1
100 LOGN 84321 527 C6
400 SALM 84653 3355 E6
400 SALM 84653 3356 A6
E 1325 N
10 LYTN 84041 1283 A2
400 OREM 84097 2820 E2
800 OGDN 84404 1057 A2
1400 LYTN 84040 1283 C2
1500 LOGN 84341 464 C7
6900 WbrC 84317 1060 E2
E 1325 S
- BxEC 84312 521 A4
- TMTN 84337 521 A4
100 PRVO 84606 3035 D2
N 1325 E
2300 LEHI 84043 2603 E2
2600 NHON 84414 999 C5
3100 LYTN 84040 1229 C5
N 1325 W
2600 CLTN 84015 1171 B6
S 1325 E
100 LNDN 84042 2713 E7
4200 OGDN 84403 1173 B1
6000 SOGN 84405 1173 B6
S 1325 W
400 OREM 84058 2820 A6
900 DvsC 84025 1448 A4
900 DvsC 84087 1448 A4
3300 OGDN 84401 1115 A6
3300 WbrC 84401 1115 A6
W 1325 N
- BMCY 84302 766 D2
600 OREM 84057 2820 B1
700 LEHI 84043 2603 A4
1200 PRVO 84604 2928 A4
2400 LYTN 84041 1281 E2
2400 LYTN 84041 1282 A2
W 1325 S
10 LOGN 84321 527 D6
10 PVDN 84332 527 D6
S 1325 West Cir
- SRCS 84075 1281 A1
E 1330 S
- PYSN 84651 3461 E2
200 PYSN 84651 3462 A1
700 SPFK 84660 3249 E5
2300 SPFK 84660 3250 C5
N 1330 E
- LEHI 84043 2603 E6
N 1330 W
10 OREM 84057 2820 A5
100 SLCY 84116 1857 D2
S 1330 E
1600 PRVO 84606 3035 E3
8000 SNDY 84093 2177 B4
8100 SLkC 84093 2177 B5
11000 SNDY 84092 2283 B5
S 1330 W
300 PRVO 84601 2927 E7
400 LEHI 84043 2602 E7
400 PRVO 84601 3034 E1
1500 LOGN 84321 527 A7
8400 WJDN 84088 2175 D5
W 1330 N
200 LOGN 84341 463 C7
700 OREM 84057 2820 B2
1500 FMTN 84025 1345 E6
W 1330 S
1000 OREM 84058 2927 A1
1000 UthC 84058 2927 A1
N 1335 W
1400 OREM 84057 2820 A1
S 1335 E
9400 SLkC 84092 2283 B1
9400 SNDY 84092 2283 B1
S 1335 W
7300 WJDN 84084 2175 D3
W 1335 S
1100 UthC 84058 2927 A2
E 1340 N
10 ANFK 84003 2604 C4
10 OREM 84057 2820 D1
900 ANFK 84003 2605 A4
E 1340 S
10 FMTN 84025 1448 D5
N 1340 E
- PRVO 84606 2928 E6
600 FTHT 84037 1284 A7
N 1340 W
100 SLCY 84116 1857 D2
700 OREM 84057 2820 A3
S 1340 E
1100 SPFK 84660 3250 A5
5300 MRRY 84117 2071 B5
W 1340 N
10 ANFK 84003 2604 C4
800 PRVO 84604 2928 A4
900 OREM 84057 2820 A2
1300 PTGV 84062 2712 B1
3300 CLTN 84015 1226 B2
W 1340 S
10 FMTN 84025 1448 C5
500 PRVO 84601 3035 B2
600 PYSN 84651 3461 D1
N 1345 E
800 LYTN 84040 1283 C3
S 1345 W
5300 RVDL 84405 1171 E4
5300 RVDL 84405 1172 A4
12200 RIVN 84065 2387 D1
W 1345 N
2100 LYTN 84041 1282 A2
E 1350 N
300 PTGV 84062 2712 E1
400 BNFL 84010 1551 E5
500 BNFL 84010 1552 A5
600 OGDN 84404 1057 A2
1000 ANFK 84003 2605 A4
1100 LYTN 84040 1283 C2
1600 LOGN 84341 464 C7
E 1350 S
700 OREM 84097 2928 A1
1100 CRFD 84015 1228 A7
1500 OGDN 84404 1116 D1
1500 PRVO 84606 3036 B2
2300 SPFK 84660 3250 B5
N 1350 E
- PTGV 84062 2713 B2
100 SGVL 84663 3144 A2
3000 NHON 84414 999 C4
N 1350 W
- CRFD 84015 1227 A4
- PTVW 84414 997 E3
- PTVW 84414 998 A3
200 SLCY 84116 1857 D2
500 PRVO 84601 2927 E6
1100 LYTN 84041 1282 C2
1200 FRWT 84404 1056 A2
1300 PRVO 84604 2927 E4
1600 CLTN 84015 1227 A1
2000 CLTN 84015 1171 A7
2900 LEHI 84043 2602 E1
2900 PTGV 84062 2605 B5
S 1350 E
- PTGV 84062 2713 C4
10 LEHI 84043 2603 E7
100 LOGN 84321 528 C3
300 BNFL 84010 1654 B1
300 PRVO 84606 2928 E7
500 FTHT 84037 1346 B2
500 PRVO 84606 3035 E1
600 SGVL 84663 3144 A3
1300 OGDN 84403 1173 C1
1400 CRFD 84015 1228 B7
4200 SLkC 84124 2071 B1
5200 SOGN 84403 1173 B4
6000 SOGN 84405 1173 C6
8700 SLkC 84093 2177 B6
8800 SNDY 84093 2177 B6
9400 SLkC 84092 2283 B1
9400 SNDY 84092 2283 B1
S 1350 W
- FMTN 84025 1448 A3
- OREM 84058 2820 A7
- SRCS 84075 1281 A1
10 LEHI 84043 2602 E6
1100 OREM 84058 2927 A1
1700 WHVN 84401 1115 A2
1900 WDCR 84087 1652 E3
2400 PRRY 84302 827 B4
12000 RIVN 84065 2281 D7
W 1350 N
- LOGN 84341 463 C6
10 ANFK 84003 2604 C4
10 CTRV 84014 1551 D1
100 LYTN 84041 1282 E2
200 BNFL 84010 1551 D5
700 CLTN 84015 1227 B2
800 MPTN 84664 3143 E5
800 OREM 84057 2820 B1
2400 PRVO 84601 2927 C4
W 1350 S
400 OREM 84058 2927 C1
500 WDCR 84010 1653 C2
800 PYSN 84651 3461 D1
1100 SRCS 84075 1227 B7
1700 MTSV 84401 1055 E7
1800 MTSV 84401 1114 D1
2600 SRCS 84075 1226 D7
4500 WbrC 84401 1054 C7
E 1355 S
400 SGVL 84663 3143 D4
S 1355 W
4200 TYVL 84123 2069 D1
W 1355 S
700 SLCY 84104 1858 A7
E 1360 N
1200 LEHI 84043 2603 E4
1300 HILD 84043 2603 E4
1300 UthC 84043 2603 E4
E 1360 S
1200 SPFK 84660 3250 A5
N 1360 E
10 SGVL 84663 3144 A2
N 1360 W
500 CLTN 84015 1227 A3
S 1360 E
300 SPFK 84660 3250 A3
W 1360 N
- CLTN 84015 1226 D1
10 PTGV 84062 2712 D1
200 ANFK 84003 2604 B4
600 OREM 84057 2820 B1
1300 CLTN 84015 1227 A2
W 1360 S
1000 UthC 84058 2927 A1
S 1365 E
1300 SNDY 84093 2177 B4
S 1365 W
3500 WVCY 84119 1963 D6
8600 WJDN 84088 2175 D6
E 1370 N
- CLTN 84015 1226 E1
300 LOGN 84341 463 E6

Salt Lake City Street Index

STREET Block City ZIP Map# Grid
E 1370 N
900 ANFK 84003 2605 A4
E 1370 S
200 PYSN 84651 3462 A1
1300 PRVO 84606 3035 E2
1400 PRVO 84606 3036 B2
2300 SPFK 84660 3250 C5
N 1370 W
400 PTGV 84062 2712 B2
700 OREM 84057 2819 E3
S 1370 E
100 LNDN 84042 2713 E7
1300 PRVO 84606 3035 E2
8300 SNDY 84093 2177 B5
11200 SNDY 84092 2283 B5
S 1370 W
500 LEHI 84043 2602 E7
700 OREM 84058 2819 E7
700 OREM 84058 2820 A7
7100 WJDN 84084 2175 D2
W 1370 N
- CLTN 84015 1226 E1
10 ANFK 84003 2604 C4
1400 PRVO 84604 2927 E4
E 1370 S Pl
10 LOGN 84321 527 C7
E 1370 S St
10 LOGN 84321 527 C7
E 1375 N
100 LYTN 84041 1283 A2
300 CTRV 84014 1551 E1
800 OGDN 84404 1057 A2
E 1375 S
200 KYVL 84037 1345 D4
1500 OGDN 84404 1116 C1
N 1375 E
10 BNFL 84010 1552 B7
2700 WbrC 84414 999 C5
2900 NHON 84414 999 C4
N 1375 W
800 PRVO 84604 2927 E5
1400 CLTN 84015 1227 A1
2600 CLTN 84015 1171 A6
2600 ROY 84015 1171 A6
2600 ROY 84067 1171 A6
S 1375 E
- SOGN 84405 1173 C6
10 FTHT 84037 1346 B1
200 BNFL 84010 1552 B7
200 BNFL 84010 1654 B1
900 SGVL 84663 3144 A4
7200 SWBR 84405 1229 C1
S 1375 W
2900 SRCS 84075 1281 A3
W 1375 N
200 CTRV 84014 1551 D1
700 LEHI 84043 2603 B4
900 OGDN 84404 1056 B2
900 OREM 84057 2820 A1
1600 LYTN 84041 1282 B2
W 1375 S
1500 SRCS 84075 1227 A7
E 1380 N
10 ANFK 84003 2604 C4
1300 LEHI 84043 2603 E4
E 1380 S
900 SPFK 84660 3249 E5
N 1380 E
400 PTGV 84062 2713 C2
1900 NHLN 84341 464 C5
N 1380 W
1200 MPTN 84664 3143 E5
S 1380 E
3900 SLkC 84124 1965 B7
8400 SLkC 84093 2177 B6
9100 SNDY 84093 2177 B7
9400 SLkC 84092 2283 B1
11400 SNDY 84092 2283 C6
S 1380 W
1200 OREM 84058 2927 A1
1500 LOGN 84321 526 E7
7100 WJDN 84084 2175 D2
8400 WJDN 84088 2175 D6
11900 RIVN 84065 2281 D7
W 1380 N
500 LOGN 84341 463 C6
1100 OREM 84057 2820 A1
1100 PRVO 84604 2928 B5
1800 PRVO 84604 2927 E4
W 1380 S
200 PYSN 84651 3461 E1
E 1385 N
1500 LOGN 84341 464 C7
E 1385 S
1000 OREM 84097 2920 D1
N 1385 W
900 CLTN 84015 1227 A2
S 1385 E
7100 CDHT 84121 2177 C2
S 1385 W
- CRFD 84016 1227 A6
W 1385 N
- BMCY 84302 766 D2
1000 CLTN 84015 1227 B1
S 1386 E
- SLCY 84112 1859 C3
E 1390 S
1100 OGDN 84404 1116 B1
N 1390 W
2900 LEHI 84043 2602 E1
S 1390 E
- SWBR 84405 1229 C2
8200 SNDY 84093 2177 C5
S 1390 W
400 PRVO 84601 2927 E7
12000 RIVN 84065 2281 D7
W 1390 N
2400 PRVO 84601 2927 B4
W 1390 S
700 SLCY 84104 1858 A7
1100 UthC 84058 2927 A1
1500 SRCS 84075 1227 A7
1700 SRCS 84075 1226 E7
S 1395 E
4800 SLkC 84117 2071 B3
8500 SLkC 84093 2177 C6
W 1395 N
1000 CLTN 84015 1227 B1
W 1395 S
200 LOGN 84321 527 C7
200 PVDN 84332 527 C7
E 1400 N
10 ANFK 84003 2604 C4
10 BNFL 84014 1551 E5
10 CTRV 84010 1551 E5
10 CTRV 84014 1551 E5
10 LOGN 84341 463 E6
10 MPTN 84664 3144 A5
100 HARR 84404 1056 D2
100 SGVL 84663 3036 C6
200 LEHI 84043 2603 C4
400 BNFL 84010 1551 E5
400 PTGV 84062 2712 E1
500 LOGN 84341 464 A6
600 BNFL 84010 1552 A5
600 PTGV 84062 2713 A1
800 OGDN 84404 1057 A2
1400 LYTN 84040 1283 C2
2500 LYTN 84040 1284 A2
E 1400 S
10 OREM 84058 2927 D1
100 KYVL 84037 1345 D4
400 BNFL 84010 1653 E2
400 MPTN 84664 3251 B2
500 BNFL 84010 1654 A2
500 OREM 84097 2927 E1
500 OREM 84097 2928 A1
1100 SPFK 84660 3249 E5
1100 SPFK 84660 3250 A5
1200 CRFD 84015 1228 B7
N 1400 E
- WbrC 84414 999 C5
10 PTGV 84062 2713 C2
500 LYTN 84040 1283 C3
800 LOGN 84321 528 C1
1100 LOGN 84341 464 C7
1500 LEHI 84043 2603 E4
1700 PRVO 84604 2929 A3
2100 NHLN 84341 464 C4
2300 LYTN 84040 1229 C7
N 1400 W
10 CRFD 84015 1227 A4
10 CTRV 84014 1551 B3
10 LNDN 84042 2712 C6
100 MIDW 84049 2396 D2
300 SLCY 84116 1857 D1
700 SLCY 84116 1753 D7
1100 PRVO 84604 2927 E4
1600 CLTN 84015 1227 A1
1700 LEHI 84043 2602 E3
1900 CLTN 84015 1171 A7
S 1400 E
- PTGV 84062 2712 B3
- SLCY 84112 1859 C4
- SWBR 84405 1229 C2
10 LOGN 84321 528 C3
100 SPFK 84660 3250 A3
300 FTHT 84037 1346 B2
300 PTGV 84062 2713 C3
400 PRVO 84606 2929 A7
400 PRVO 84606 3036 A1
800 SLCY 84102 1859 B5
800 SLCY 84105 1859 B5
900 SGVL 84663 3144 A4
1700 UthC 84660 3250 A6
1800 SLCY 84105 1965 B2
2000 PTGV 84062 2605 B7
2800 SLCY 84106 1965 C4
3900 SLkC 84124 1965 C7
4000 SLkC 84124 2071 B1
5300 SOGN 84403 1173 C4
5800 SOGN 84405 1173 C5
6600 UNTH 84405 1173 C7
8000 SNDY 84093 2177 C4
9400 SLkC 84092 2283 C1
9400 SNDY 84092 2283 C1
13400 DRPR 84020 2389 C4
S 1400 W
- LOGN 84321 527 A4
- UthC 84660 3248 E1
10 LEHI 84043 2602 E7
10 PRVO 84601 2927 E6
10 PRVO 84601 2928 A6
100 SLCY 84104 1857 D3
2400 WDCR 84087 1652 E4
2900 OGDN 84401 1114 E5
2900 WbrC 84401 1114 E5
3400 WVCY 84119 1963 D6
7300 SPFK 84660 3248 E5
12600 RIVN 84065 2387 D2
16500 BFDL 84065 2494 D5
W 1400 N
- SPFK 84660 3142 C7
100 ANFK 84003 2604 B4
100 BNFL 84010 1551 D5
100 HILD 84003 2604 B4
100 LOGN 84341 463 C6
100 SGVL 84663 3036 B6
200 FMTN 84025 1346 B5
300 CTRV 84014 1551 D1
500 CLTN 84015 1227 C1
600 MPTN 84664 3144 A5
700 MPTN 84664 3143 E5
800 OREM 84057 2820 B1
900 OGDN 84404 1056 B2
1100 WBNF 84087 1551 A5
1200 CchC 84341 462 E6
1200 CchC 84341 463 A6
1200 DvsC 84087 1550 E5
1200 DvsC 84087 1551 A5
1200 LEHI 84043 2603 A4
1200 PRVO 84604 2928 A4
1300 FRWT 84404 1056 A2
1500 PRVO 84604 2927 E4
2100 LYTN 84041 1282 A2
2300 LEHI 84043 2602 D4
2600 CLTN 84015 1226 C1
2800 CchC 84321 462 B6
4200 PNCY 84404 1054 C2
5200 WbrC 84404 1054 A2
W 1400 N SR-75
100 SGVL 84663 3036 B6
W 1400 S
10 BNFL 84010 1653 D2
10 OREM 84058 2927 D1
100 GRLD 84312 520 E4
100 TMTN 84337 520 E4
200 SLCY 84115 1858 B7
300 PYSN 84651 3461 D1
500 WDCR 84010 1653 C2
700 PRVO 84601 3035 A2
900 SLCY 84104 1858 A7
900 WDCR 84087 1653 A2
W 1400 S
1100 SLCY 84104 1857 D7
1600 CRFD 84015 1228 B7
2200 CchC 84321 526 D6
2900 WbrC 84401 1113 E1
2900 WbrC 84401 1114 A1
3200 CchC 84321 525 E6
1400 St W
10 BxEC 84337 520 C3
10 GRLD 84337 520 C3
10 TMTN 84337 520 C3
S 1405 E
6700 CDHT 84121 2177 B1
S 1405 W
8700 WJDN 84088 2175 D6
E 1410 S
1500 SPFK 84660 3250 A5
N 1410 E
300 LEHI 84043 2603 E6
N 1410 W
900 PRVO 84604 2927 E5
2900 LEHI 84043 2602 E1
S 1410 E
100 LNDN 84042 2713 E7
300 PRVO 84606 2928 E7
1100 PRVO 84606 3035 E2
1200 PRVO 84606 3036 B2
4900 OGDN 84403 1173 C3
5300 MRRY 84117 2071 B5
S 1410 W
10 LNDN 84042 2712 C7
500 PRVO 84601 3034 E1
7800 WJDN 84088 2175 D4
W 1410 N
1500 FMTN 84025 1345 E5
W 1410 S
300 OREM 84058 2927 C1
600 PYSN 84651 3461 D1
900 UthC 84058 2927 A1
N 1415 W
1000 CLTN 84015 1227 A2
S 1415 W
- SRCS 84075 1281 A3
W 1415 N
100 OREM 84057 2820 C1
E 1420 N
900 ANFK 84003 2605 A4
E 1420 S
- OREM 84058 2927 E1
200 FMTN 84025 1448 D5
900 SPFK 84660 3249 E5
1100 OGDN 84404 1116 B1
N 1420 E
- PRVO 84606 2929 A6
400 LOGN 84321 528 C2
800 OREM 84097 2821 C3
N 1420 W
500 CLTN 84015 1227 A3
800 PTGV 84062 2712 B1
1800 PRVO 84604 2927 E3
2100 PTGV 84062 2605 B6
3100 LEHI 84043 2602 E1
S 1420 E
100 SGVL 84663 3144 A2
1300 PRVO 84606 3036 A2
1400 SPFK 84660 3250 A5
5800 SOGN 84405 1173 C5
7300 CDHT 84093 2177 C3
7300 CDHT 84121 2177 C3
S 1420 W
700 OREM 84058 2819 E7
1200 WDCR 84087 1652 E2
1400 RIVN 84065 2281 D7
4000 TYVL 84123 2069 D1
12000 RIVN 84065 2387 D1
W 1420 N
200 PTGV 84062 2712 D1
300 PTGV 84062 2605 D7
700 CLTN 84015 1227 C1
900 OREM 84057 2820 A1
3300 CLTN 84015 1226 B1
W 1420 S
10 FMTN 84025 1448 D5
200 PYSN 84651 3461 E1
E 1425 N
700 OGDN 84404 1057 A2
1000 LYTN 84040 1283 B2
1400 LOGN 84341 464 C6
N 1425 E
500 LYTN 84040 1283 C3
2200 LYTN 84040 1229 C7
S 1425 E
8600 SNDY 84093 2177 C6
S 1425 W
- CRFD 84016 1227 A6
1800 WDCR 84087 1652 E3
6700 WJDN 84084 2175 D1
W 1425 N
10 SNST 84015 1227 D1
300 LYTN 84041 1282 D2
900 LEHI 84043 2603 A4
1200 CLTN 84015 1227 A1
2700 LYTN 84041 1281 E2
W 1425 S
- UthC 84043 2710 B2
10 PRRY 84302 827 E2
2200 SRCS 84075 1226 D7
W 1428 S
400 OREM 84058 2927 C1
E 1430 N
- PRVO 84604 2928 C4
E 1430 S
2400 SPFK 84660 3250 C5
N 1430 E
300 LOGN 84321 528 C2
1200 PRVO 84604 2929 A2
N 1430 W
800 OREM 84057 2819 E2
1200 PTGV 84062 2712 B1
S 1430 E
800 SPFK 84660 3250 A4
1200 PRVO 84606 3036 A2
5900 MRRY 84121 2071 B6
8400 SLkC 84093 2177 C5
S 1430 W
400 LEHI 84043 2602 E7
8700 WJDN 84088 2175 D6
10600 SJDN 84095 2281 D4
W 1430 S
400 OREM 84058 2927 C2
800 PRVO 84601 3035 A2
N 1435 W
1300 CLTN 84015 1227 A1
S 1435 W
10200 SJDN 84095 2281 D3
W 1435 N
- FMTN 84025 1346 A5
W 1435 S
10 OREM 84058 2927 D1
E 1440 N
400 MPTN 84664 3144 B5
E 1440 S
1200 SPFK 84660 3250 A5
1400 PRVO 84606 3035 E2
1400 PRVO 84606 3036 A2
N 1440 E
10 SGVL 84663 3144 A2
N 1440 W
400 PTGV 84062 2712 B2
S 1440 E
300 SPFK 84660 3250 A3
1000 PRVO 84606 3036 A1
7200 CDHT 84121 2177 C2
S 1440 W
400 PRVO 84601 2927 E7
400 PRVO 84601 3034 E1
2300 WVCY 84119 1963 D3
8700 WJDN 84088 2175 D6
10400 SJDN 84095 2281 D3
W 1440 N
10 OREM 84057 2820 D1
1300 PTGV 84062 2712 B1
1600 FMTN 84025 1345 E5
2500 PRVO 84601 2927 C4
W 1440 S
300 PYSN 84651 3461 E1
600 PRVO 84601 3035 B2
N 1445 W
900 CLTN 84015 1227 A2
W 1445 N
2200 CLTN 84015 1226 D1
E 1450 N
10 OREM 84057 2820 D1
100 LYTN 84041 1283 A2
200 BNFL 84010 1551 E5
400 OREM 84097 2820 E1
500 BNFL 84010 1552 A5
900 OGDN 84404 1057 A2
1000 LYTN 84040 1283 B2
1200 LEHI 84043 2603 E4
7100 WbrC 84317 1060 E2
7200 WbrC 84317 1061 A2
E 1450 S
10 OREM 84058 2927 D1
10 PYSN 84651 3461 E1
200 KYVL 84037 1345 D4
200 OREM 84097 2928 A1
1100 CRFD 84015 1228 B7
1600 OGDN 84404 1116 D1
2200 SPFK 84660 3250 B5
N 1450 E
800 LOGN 84321 528 C1
1200 LYTN 84040 1283 C2
2200 NHLN 84341 464 C4
2300 LEHI 84043 2603 E2
2500 LYTN 84040 1229 C6
N 1450 W
10 CRFD 84015 1227 A4
100 DvsC 84087 1550 E7
100 WBNF 84087 1550 E7
800 PTGV 84062 2712 B1
1100 PRVO 84604 2927 E4
1600 CLTN 84015 1227 A1
1600 LYTN 84041 1282 C1
1800 LEHI 84043 2602 E3
1900 CLTN 84015 1171 A7
2100 PTGV 84062 2605 B7
S 1450 E
- SWBR 84405 1229 C2
300 PRVO 84606 2929 A7
300 PRVO 84606 3036 A1
500 SPFK 84660 3250 A4
700 PTGV 84062 2713 C4
4000 SLkC 84124 1965 C7
5000 OGDN 84403 1173 C3
S 1450 W
- WDCR 84087 1652 E2
10 CRFD 84015 1227 A5
100 LEHI 84043 2602 E6
4600 UthC 84660 3141 E5
5600 UthC 84660 3248 E1
12300 RIVN 84065 2387 D1
W 1450 N
- BMCY 84302 766 D2
200 ANFK 84003 2604 B4
300 BNFL 84010 1551 C5
600 OREM 84057 2820 B1
600 WBNF 84087 1551 B5
1700 CLTN 84015 1227 A1
2100 CLTN 84015 1226 E1
2100 LYTN 84041 1282 A2
W 1450 S
300 OREM 84058 2927 C1
500 PRVO 84601 3035 B2
500 PYSN 84651 3461 D1
S 1452 E
100 SLCY 84112 1859 C3
E 1455 N
1500 LOGN 84341 464 C6
S 1455 E
- SLCY 84112 1859 C3
W 1455 N
900 OREM 84057 2820 A1
W 1455 S
200 OREM 84058 2927 C1
W 1458 S
300 PVDN 84332 527 C7
E 1460 N
800 OREM 84057 2820 D1
1600 LOGN 84341 464 C6
N 1460 E
1500 NHLN 84341 464 C5
S 1460 E
100 SLCY 84112 1859 C3
1200 PRVO 84606 3036 B2
1500 SPFK 84660 3250 A6
4100 SLkC 84124 2071 C1
S 1460 W
- SJDN 84095 2281 E2
3900 WVCY 84119 1963 D7
6400 TYVL 84123 2069 D7
6400 TYVL 84123 2175 D1
6600 WJDN 84084 2175 D1
8000 WJDN 84088 2175 D5
W 1460 N
1000 CLTN 84015 1227 B1
1000 PRVO 84604 2928 A4
1300 PRVO 84604 2927 E4
W 1460 S
600 PYSN 84651 3461 D1
N 1465 W
400 SLCY 84116 1857 D1
W 1465 N
200 CTRV 84014 1551 D1
500 OREM 84057 2820 C1
E 1470 S
10 PYSN 84651 3461 E1
1600 OGDN 84404 1116 C1
2600 SPFK 84660 3250 C5
S 1470 E
100 SGVL 84663 3144 A2
1000 PRVO 84606 3036 A2
S 1470 W
100 PRVO 84601 2927 E7
500 OREM 84058 2819 E6
1500 WDCR 84087 1652 E2
7200 WJDN 84084 2175 D2
W 1470 N
- LOGN 84341 463 C6
700 CLTN 84015 1227 B1
E 1475 N
100 HARR 84404 1056 D2
700 LEHI 84043 2603 D4
E 1475 S
200 KYVL 84037 1345 D4
1100 OGDN 84404 1116 B1
N 1475 E
700 LYTN 84040 1283 C3
1800 LEHI 84043 2603 E3
N 1475 W
1700 LYTN 84041 1282 C1
S 1475 E
- SWBR 84405 1229 C2
5600 SOGN 84403 1173 C5
8000 SNDY 84093 2177 C5
8300 SLkC 84093 2177 C5
S 1475 W
- SRCS 84075 1281 A1
10 LEHI 84043 2602 E7
2900 OGDN 84401 1114 E5
2900 WbrC 84401 1114 E5
5900 TYVL 84123 2069 D6
W 1475 N
100 LYTN 84041 1282 E2
500 OREM 84057 2820 B1
600 CTRV 84014 1448 C7
2500 LYTN 84041 1281 E2
W 1475 S
1300 SRCS 84075 1227 A7
2600 SRCS 84075 1226 D7
E 1480 N
900 ANFK 84003 2605 A4
E 1480 S
2900 SPFK 84660 3250 D5
N 1480 E
- PRVO 84604 2929 A6
- PRVO 84606 2929 A6
10 SGVL 84663 3144 A2
200 LOGN 84321 528 C2
300 LEHI 84043 2603 E6
1800 LYTN 84040 1283 C1
S 1480 E
200 SPFK 84660 3250 A3
6000 MRRY 84121 2071 C7
9100 SNDY 84093 2177 C7
S 1480 W
- WJDN 84084 2175 D2
900 CRFD 84016 1227 A6
900 DvsC 84016 1227 A6
1100 OREM 84058 2926 E1
2300 WVCY 84119 1963 D3
6300 TYVL 84123 2069 D7
8200 WJDN 84088 2175 D5
10300 SJDN 84095 2281 D3
12300 RIVN 84065 2387 D1
W 1480 N
300 LYTN 84041 1282 E2
300 OREM 84057 2820 C1
W 1480 S
10 PYSN 84651 3461 E1
100 OREM 84058 2927 C2
S 1485 E
7800 SNDY 84093 2177 C4
S 1485 W
- SRCS 84075 1281 A1
W 1485 N
100 OREM 84057 2820 D1
S 1490 E
5800 MRRY 84121 2071 C6
S 1490 W
600 OREM 84058 2819 E7
12200 RIVN 84065 2387 D1
E 1490 S Pl
10 LOGN 84321 527 C7
S 1495 E
6600 CDHT 84121 2177 C1
E 1500 N
- LOGN 84341 464 B6
10 LEHI 84043 2603 C4
10 OREM 84057 2820 D1
100 PTGV 84062 2605 D7
100 PTGV 84062 2712 D1
400 OREM 84097 2820 E1
700 BNFL 84010 1552 A5
900 OGDN 84404 1057 A2
1000 LYTN 84040 1283 B2
1200 NHLN 84341 464 B6
1300 PRVO 84604 2928 E4
1300 UthC 84043 2603 E4
1400 PRVO 84604 2929 A4
E 1500 S
- PRVO 84097 2928 B2
10 BNFL 84010 1653 E2
10 OREM 84058 2927 D2
200 KYVL 84037 1345 D5
400 SGVL 84663 3143 D5
500 BNFL 84010 1654 A2
500 OREM 84097 2927 E2
600 OREM 84097 2928 A2
2000 SPFK 84660 3250 B5
N 1500 E
600 LOGN 84321 528 C1
800 LYTN 84040 1283 C3
1200 LOGN 84341 464 C6
1600 PRVO 84604 2929 A3
N 1500 W
- PTVW 84404 997 E3
- PTVW 84414 997 E3
- WDCR 84087 1652 E4
100 MTSV 84404 1055 E5
300 CLTN 84015 1227 A3
300 WPT 84015 1227 A3
500 SLCY 84116 1857 D1
900 OREM 84057 2819 E2
1000 SLCY 84116 1753 D6
1100 LYTN 84041 1282 B2
1300 FRWT 84404 1055 E2
1700 PRVO 84604 2927 E3
1800 CLTN 84015 1171 A7
S 1500 E
- PTGV 84062 2712 B3
- SWBR 84405 1229 C2
200 PTGV 84062 2713 C4
200 SLCY 84112 1859 C4
300 PRVO 84606 2929 A7
500 PRVO 84606 3036 A1
700 CRFD 84015 1228 B6
900 SLCY 84105 1859 C6
900 SPFK 84660 3250 A4
1100 BNFL 84010 1654 C2
1300 LYTN 84041 1228 B7
1600 SLCY 84105 1965 C1
2400 SLCY 84106 1965 C3
3000 SLkC 84106 1965 C5
3900 SLkC 84124 1965 C7
4000 SLkC 84124 2071 C1
4600 SLkC 84117 2071 C2
4700 OGDN 84403 1173 C3
6400 UNTH 84405 1173 C7
S 1500 W
- CchC 84319 651 A6
- CchC 84319 709 E3
- CchC 84328 709 E3
- WDCR 84087 1652 E3
10 LOGN 84321 526 E3
10 OREM 84058 2819 E5
100 MTSV 84404 1055 E5
200 SLCY 84104 1857 D4
300 LEHI 84043 2602 E7
600 CchC 84321 526 E5
3200 CchC 84321 590 E4
3200 NBLY 84321 590 E4
3300 OGDN 84401 1114 E6
3900 WVCY 84119 1963 D7
4000 WVCY 84119 2069 E1
4400 CchC 84319 590 E7
4600 CchC 84319 650 E1
4600 HYRM 84319 650 E1
4800 RVDL 84405 1171 E3
5400 TYVL 84123 2069 D5
8000 WJDN 84088 2175 D5
8700 BxEC 84340 941 B6
12600 RIVN 84065 2387 D2
W 1500 N
- FMTN 84025 1346 A5
- UthC 84606 3035 D6
10 CTRV 84014 1448 D7
100 BMCY 84302 766 D2
100 BxEC 84302 766 D2
200 BNFL 84010 1551 D5
200 HARR 84404 1056 D2
200 PTGV 84062 2605 D7
300 PRVO 84604 2928 B4
400 OREM 84057 2820 C1
600 WBNF 84087 1551 C5
700 LEHI 84043 2603 A4
700 SLCY 84116 1754 A6
1200 MPTN 84664 3143 E5
1200 SGVL 84663 3035 E6
1200 SGVL 84663 3036 A6
1300 FRWT 84404 1055 E2
1300 FRWT 84404 1056 A2
1400 PRVO 84604 2927 E4
1500 FMTN 84025 1345 E5
1500 FMTN 84037 1345 E5
3200 CLTN 84015 1226 B1
4100 MTSV 84404 1054 C2
4100 PNCY 84404 1054 C2
5100 WbrC 84404 1054 A2
W 1500 N SR-75
- UthC 84606 3035 E6
1200 SGVL 84663 3035 E6
1200 SGVL 84663 3036 A6
W 1500 S
- PRRY 84302 827 E2
- PRRY 84302 828 A2
10 BNFL 84010 1653 C2
300 SLCY 84115 1858 B7
300 WDCR 84010 1653 C2
600 WDCR 84087 1653 C2
800 PYSN 84651 3461 D1
900 PRVO 84601 3035 A2
1200 WDCR 84087 1652 E2
1500 SRCS 84075 1227 A7
2100 SLCY 84104 1857 B7
2100 SRCS 84075 1226 D7
3400 SLCY 84104 1856 D7
S 1500 E St
- CchC 84328 711 C7
E 1500 S Pl
10 LOGN 84321 527 C7
S 1505 W
3500 WVCY 84119 1963 D6
E 1510 N
900 NHON 84414 1057 B2
900 OGDN 84404 1057 B2
E 1510 S
1400 SPFK 84660 3250 A5
N 1510 E
1000 OREM 84097 2821 C2
S 1510 E
1200 PRVO 84606 3036 A2
S 1510 W
1000 SGVL 84663 3142 E4
1700 WDCR 84087 1652 E3
9000 WJDN 84088 2175 D7
12300 RIVN 84065 2387 D1
W 1510 N
600 OREM 84057 2820 B1
N 1515 E
1500 LOGN 84341 464 C6
1600 NHLN 84341 464 C6
S 1515 E
- MRRY 84121 2071 B6
S 1515 W
3900 WVCY 84119 1963 D7
3900 WVCY 84119 2069 E1
S 1515 W
14500 BFDL 84065 2387 D7
E 1520 N
100 OREM 84057 2820 D1
900 ANFK 84003 2605 A4
E 1520 S
1100 SPFK 84660 3250 A5
N 1520 E
- LEHI 84043 2603 E5
900 OREM 84097 2821 C2
1100 LOGN 84341 464 C7
N 1520 W
1100 PTGV 84062 2712 B1
1400 PTGV 84062 2605 B7
S 1520 E
800 SPFK 84660 3250 A4
8400 SLkC 84093 2177 C6
9200 SNDY 84093 2177 C7
9200 SNDY 84093 2283 C1
S 1520 W
900 OREM 84058 2819 E7
2200 SRCS 84075 1281 A2
6700 WJDN 84084 2175 D2
8300 WJDN 84088 2175 D5
W 1520 N
300 OREM 84057 2820 C1
500 CLTN 84015 1227 C1
2000 CLTN 84015 1226 E1
2500 PRVO 84601 2927 C4
W 1520 S
100 OREM 84058 2927 D2
5400 SLCY 84104 1855 E7
E 1525 N
200 LYTN 84041 1283 A2
800 NHON 84414 1057 B1
1000 LYTN 84040 1283 C2
2500 LYTN 84040 1284 A2
E 1525 S
100 OREM 84058 2927 D2
1100 CRFD 84015 1228 A7
N 1525 E
1400 LOGN 84341 464 C6
2500 LYTN 84040 1229 C6
N 1525 W
- WPT 84015 1227 A4
10 FMTN 84025 1447 E1
500 FMTN 84025 1345 E7
1700 LYTN 84041 1282 C1
S 1525 E
4700 OGDN 84403 1173 C3
6000 MRRY 84121 2071 C6
S 1525 W
- SRCS 84075 1227 A6
10 FMTN 84025 1447 E3
10 WPT 84015 1227 A4
200 DvsC 84025 1447 E3
6700 WJDN 84084 2175 D1
W 1525 N
10 LYTN 84041 1282 E2
10 OREM 84057 2820 D1
W 1525 S
4600 SLCY 84104 1856 A7
E 1530 S
- LEHI 84043 2710 D2
2900 SPFK 84660 3250 D5
N 1530 E
800 OREM 84097 2821 C3
N 1530 W
10 PRVO 84601 2927 E7
S 1530 E
200 SPFK 84660 3250 A3
300 SLCY 84112 1859 C4
3100 SLkC 84106 1965 C5
5600 MRRY 84121 2071 B6
6600 CDHT 84121 2177 C1
S 1530 W
- LOGN 84321 526 E5
7800 WJDN 84088 2175 D4
W 1530 N
- SLCY 84116 1753 C5
1000 OREM 84057 2820 A1
W 1530 S
10 OREM 84058 2927 D2
E 1530 N St
200 LOGN 84341 463 E6
E 1535 N
10 OREM 84057 2820 D1
N 1535 W
1300 CLTN 84015 1227 A2
S 1535 E
- MRRY 84121 2071 B6
S 1535 W
4000 WVCY 84119 2069 D1
E 1540 N
1500 LOGN 84341 464 C6
E 1540 S
1400 SPFK 84660 3250 A5
N 1540 E
10 SGVL 84663 3144 A2
N 1540 W
900 OREM 84057 2819 E2
S 1540 E
800 PRVO 84606 3036 A1
800 SGVL 84663 3144 A3
5600 MRRY 84121 2071 E5
6600 UNTH 84405 1173 C7
7200 CDHT 84121 2177 C2
7300 CDHT 84093 2177 C2
8700 SLkC 84093 2177 C6
S 1540 W
500 OREM 84058 2819 E6
3200 WVCY 84119 1963 D5
4000 TYVL 84123 2069 D1
10200 SJDN 84095 2281 D3
W 1540 N
700 OREM 84057 2820 B1
2300 LEHI 84043 2602 D4
W 1540 S
1400 WDCR 84087 1652 E2
E 1550 N
- PRVO 84604 2928 D4
200 PTGV 84062 2605 D7
400 OREM 84097 2820 E1
1600 LOGN 84341 464 C6
E 1550 S
- CRFD 84015 1228 A7
300 OREM 84058 2927 E2
500 KYVL 84037 1345 E5
800 OREM 84097 2928 A2
1500 SPFK 84660 3250 A5
N 1550 E
700 OREM 84097 2821 C3

STREET Block City ZIP Map# Grid

N 1550 E
900 LYTN 84040 1283 D3
1400 PRVO 84604 2929 A3
1800 LEHI 84043 2603 E3
2000 NHLN 84341 464 C5
2500 NHON 84414 999 D6
N 1550 W
900 PRVO 84604 2927 E5
2700 PTGV 84062 2605 B6
S 1550 E
- ELWD 84337 521 B7
10 TMTN 84337 521 B7
200 BNFL 84010 1552 C7
200 BNFL 84010 1654 C1
400 PTGV 84062 2713 C3
500 SPFK 84660 3250 A4
1100 OGDN 84404 1057 C7
1300 PRVO 84606 3036 A2
4700 OGDN 84403 1173 C3
5600 MRRY 84121 2071 B6
6000 SOGN 84405 1173 C6
7200 SWBR 84405 1229 C1
S 1550 W
- CchC 84319 650 E6
- CchC 84319 651 A6
10 LNDN 84042 2712 C7
100 WPT 84015 1227 A5
1900 WDCR 84087 1652 E3
4800 RVDL 84405 1171 E3
7300 WJDN 84084 2175 D3
W 1550 N
10 OREM 84057 2820 D1
10 SNST 84015 1227 D1
100 BNFL 84010 1551 D5
200 LYTN 84041 1282 E2
700 WBNF 84087 1551 B5
1000 CLTN 84015 1227 B1
1800 PRVO 84604 2927 D4
2500 CLTN 84015 1226 D1
W 1550 S
700 PYSN 84651 3461 D1
1300 LOGN 84321 527 A7
1300 SRCS 84075 1227 A7
1500 WDCR 84087 1652 E2
4200 DvsC 84075 1225 E7
4200 DvsC 84075 1226 A7
W 1550 Rd S
- PYSN 84651 3461 C1
- UthC 84651 3461 C1
S 1555 E
8500 SLkC 84093 2177 C6
S 1555 W
900 OREM 84058 2819 E7
3900 WVCY 84119 1963 D7
7500 WJDN 84084 2175 D3
E 1560 N
300 PTGV 84062 2605 E7
N 1560 E
900 OREM 84097 2821 C2
1300 LOGN 84341 464 C7
1600 NHLN 84341 464 C6
N 1560 W
2100 PTGV 84062 2605 B6
S 1560 E
- SLCY 84112 1859 D2
- SPFK 84660 3250 A3
500 MPTN 84664 3144 C7
500 MPTN 84664 3251 C1
5600 MRRY 84121 2071 B6
6600 CDHT 84121 2177 C1
S 1560 W
8100 WJDN 84088 2175 D5
W 1560 N
200 OREM 84057 2820 C1
300 LEHI 84043 2603 B4
W 1560 S
10 OREM 84058 2927 D2
500 PRVO 84601 3035 A2
N 1565 W
1000 OREM 84057 2819 E2
S 1565 W
1100 SGVL 84663 3142 E4
3200 WVCY 84119 1963 D5
W 1565 N
10 OREM 84057 2820 D1
E 1570 N
100 OREM 84057 2820 D1
E 1570 S
1100 SPFK 84660 3250 A5
N 1570 E
- LOGN 84321 528 C2
N 1570 W
500 PTGV 84062 2712 B2
S 1570 E
- FTHT 84037 1346 B2
3300 SLkC 84106 1965 C5
4000 SLkC 84124 2071 C1
6500 MRRY 84121 2177 C1
S 1570 W
6600 WJDN 84084 2175 D1
W 1570 N
800 CLTN 84015 1227 B1
2000 CLTN 84015 1226 E1
W 1570 S
300 PRVO 84601 3035 B2
700 PYSN 84651 3461 D1
E 1575 N
10 OREM 84057 2820 D1
1400 PRVO 84604 2929 A4
E 1575 S
100 OREM 84058 2927 D2
N 1575 E
2400 LYTN 84040 1229 C6
N 1575 W
1100 PRVO 84604 2927 E5
S 1575 E
3100 SLkC 84106 1965 C5
4600 OGDN 84403 1173 C2
6200 WbrC 84405 1173 C6
8400 SLkC 84093 2177 C6
S 1575 W
3300 OGDN 84401 1114 E6
3300 WbrC 84401 1114 E6
4800 TYVL 84123 2069 D4
W 1575 N
200 PRVO 84604 2928 B4
2700 PNCY 84404 1055 B1
W 1575 S
1000 SRCS 84075 1227 B7
E 1580 N
1500 LOGN 84341 464 C6
E 1580 S
2300 SPFK 84660 3250 C5
N 1580 E
300 LEHI 84043 2603 E6
N 1580 W
900 OREM 84057 2819 E2
1200 FMTN 84025 1345 E5
S 1580 E
- SLkC 84121 2071 C5
300 SPFK 84660 3250 A3
5700 MRRY 84121 2071 B6
6500 MRRY 84121 2177 C1
S 1580 W
600 OREM 84058 2819 E7
700 LEHI 84043 2602 E7
1100 OREM 84058 2926 E1
2200 WVCY 84119 1963 D2
W 1580 N
100 LEHI 84043 2603 B4
1000 CLTN 84015 1227 B1
3400 CLTN 84015 1226 B1
W 1580 S
- PYSN 84651 3461 C1
S 1585 E
5700 MRRY 84121 2071 C6
E 1590 N
300 PTGV 84062 2605 E7
E 1590 S
- LEHI 84043 2710 D2
2000 SPFK 84660 3250 B5
N 1590 W
1300 CLTN 84015 1227 A2
1600 PRVO 84604 2927 E3
S 1590 E
1300 PRVO 84606 3036 A2
1700 SPFK 84660 3250 A6
4600 SLkC 84117 2071 C3
S 1590 W
900 OREM 84058 2819 E7
8100 WJDN 84088 2175 C5
W 1590 N
1500 CLTN 84015 1227 A1
W 1590 S
700 PYSN 84651 3461 D1
S 1595 E
8700 SLkC 84093 2177 C6
E 1600 N
10 MPTN 84664 3144 C5
10 OREM 84057 2820 D1
10 SGVL 84663 3036 C6
10 SPFK 84660 3142 D7
100 LOGN 84341 463 D6
300 PTGV 84062 2605 E7
400 OREM 84097 2820 D1
600 OREM 84097 2821 A1
1600 LOGN 84341 464 C6
2600 LYTN 84040 1284 A2
E 1600 S
10 MPTN 84664 3251 B2
10 OREM 84058 2927 E2
10 PYSN 84651 3461 E2
100 BNFL 84010 1653 E2
100 PRVO 84606 3035 C2
300 SGVL 84663 3143 C5
500 BNFL 84010 1654 A2
500 OREM 84097 2928 A2
2100 SPFK 84660 3250 B6
N 1600 E
700 LEHI 84043 2603 D4
900 LOGN 84321 528 C1
900 LOGN 84341 528 C1
1000 LOGN 84341 464 C7
1600 MPTN 84664 3144 C5
1600 NHLN 84341 464 C5
2000 LYTN 84040 1229 C7
2500 NHON 84414 999 D6
3100 CchC 84318 464 C2
3100 CchC 84341 464 C2
N 1600 W
10 MPTN 84664 3143 D6
10 PRVO 84601 2927 E6
200 MTSV 84404 1055 E4
300 WPT 84015 1227 A3
800 PTGV 84062 2712 B1
1200 FRWT 84404 1055 E2
1500 CLTN 84015 1227 A1
1600 SGVL 84663 3143 D5
1700 LYTN 84041 1282 B1
2700 PTVW 84404 997 E5
6300 CchC 84335 398 E1
N 1600 W US-89
10 MPTN 84664 3143 D6
S 1600 E
- CRFD 84015 1228 B6
- PTGV 84062 2712 B3
500 SPFK 84660 3250 A4
600 PTGV 84062 2713 C4
900 SGVL 84663 3144 A4
1000 BNFL 84010 1654 C2
1300 SLCY 84105 1859 C7
1500 SLCY 84105 1965 C1
4900 OGDN 84403 1173 C3
6700 UNTH 84405 1173 C7
6800 UNTH 84405 1229 C1
7100 CDHT 84121 2177 C2
7100 SWBR 84405 1229 C1
S 1600 W
- CchC 84319 650 E5
- UthC 84660 3250 E4
10 MPTN 84664 3143 D7
10 PRVO 84601 2927 E7
10 WPT 84015 1227 A4
500 PRVO 84601 3034 E1
700 MPTN 84664 3250 D1
1200 OREM 84058 2926 E1
1200 OREM 84601 2926 E1
1200 SRCS 84075 1227 A7
1200 UthC 84058 2926 E1
1200 UthC 84601 2926 E1
1400 UthC 84664 3250 D2
1500 CchC 84321 526 E7
1500 WDCR 84087 1652 E3
1800 CchC 84321 590 E1
1800 LOGN 84321 526 E7
1800 LOGN 84321 590 E1
3900 WVCY 84119 1963 C7
3900 WVCY 84119 2069 C1
6700 WJDN 84084 2175 D1
7300 SPFK 84660 3248 D5
7300 UthC 84660 3248 D4
8200 WJDN 84088 2175 D5
9600 SJDN 84095 2281 D2
S 1600 W US-89
10 MPTN 84664 3143 D7
700 MPTN 84664 3250 D1
1400 UthC 84664 3250 D2
W 1600 N
10 LOGN 84341 463 D6
10 MPTN 84664 3144 A5
10 OREM 84057 2820 B1
10 SPFK 84660 3142 C7
10 UthC 84660 3142 C7
200 HARR 84404 1056 D1
200 SNST 84015 1227 C1
800 MPTN 84664 3143 E5
800 SLCY 84116 1754 A5
900 LEHI 84043 2603 A4
900 LYTN 84041 1282 D1
1000 LNDN 84042 2820 B1
1000 LNDN 84057 2820 B1
1200 LEHI 84043 2602 E4
1200 PRVO 84604 2928 A4
1300 LNDN 84042 2819 E1
1300 OREM 84057 2819 E1
1600 SGVL 84663 3143 E5
1600 VNYD 84057 2819 D1
1900 PRVO 84604 2927 D4
3200 CLTN 84015 1226 C1
4500 PNCY 84404 1054 B1
W 1600 N SR-241
1600 LNDN 84042 2819 E1
1600 OREM 84057 2819 E1
W 1600 S
- UthC 84651 3461 C1
10 BNFL 84010 1653 D2
10 MPTN 84664 3250 E2
10 MPTN 84664 3251 A2
10 PYSN 84651 3461 E1
300 OREM 84058 2927 C2
300 SLCY 84115 1964 B1
400 SGVL 84663 3142 E5
400 UthC 84660 3142 E5
500 SPFK 84660 3142 E5
500 WDCR 84087 1653 C2
800 LOGN 84321 527 B7
800 SGVL 84663 3143 A5
900 CRFD 84016 1227 B7
1100 WDCR 84087 1653 A2
2600 SRCS 84075 1226 D7
5100 WbrC 84401 1113 A1
5400 CchC 84325 524 E7
5400 CchC 84325 525 A7
5400 MNDN 84325 524 E7
5400 MNDN 84325 525 A7
W 1600 S SR-147
10 MPTN 84664 3250 E2
10 MPTN 84664 3251 A2
S 1600 E St
- CchC 84321 528 C5
- CchC 84321 592 C1
- LOGN 84321 528 C5
- PVDN 84332 592 C1
W 1600 N
5600 BxEC 84307 764 A2
E 1610 N
700 OREM 84097 2821 A1
E 1610 S
2300 SPFK 84660 3250 C6
N 1610 W
900 OREM 84057 2819 E3
S 1610 E
4100 SLkC 84124 2071 C1
6400 MRRY 84121 2071 C7
S 1610 W
300 LEHI 84043 2602 E7
4400 ROY 84067 1171 E2
W 1610 N
2200 LEHI 84043 2602 D4
W 1610 S
300 PRVO 84601 3035 B3
N 1615 W
- CLTN 84015 1171 A7
S 1615 E
1400 OGDN 84404 1116 D1
4100 SLkC 84124 2071 C1
5600 MRRY 84121 2071 E5
6500 MRRY 84121 2177 A3
E 1620 N
10 LEHI 84043 2603 C4
200 OREM 84057 2820 E1
E 1620 S
2600 SPFK 84660 3250 C6
N 1620 W
1400 FMTN 84025 1345 E5
S 1620 E
- SGVL 84663 3144 A4
3300 SLkC 84106 1965 C5
5600 MRRY 84121 2071 E5
6600 CDHT 84121 2177 C1
9000 SNDY 84093 2177 C7
S 1620 W
2400 OGDN 84401 1114 E4
4400 ROY 84067 1171 E2
8100 WJDN 84088 2175 E5
W 1620 N
1300 PTGV 84062 2605 B7
1500 CLTN 84015 1227 A1
1800 LYTN 84041 1282 B1
W 1620 S
700 PYSN 84651 3461 D2
E 1625 N
300 LYTN 84041 1283 A1
1100 LOGN 84341 464 B6
E 1625 S
500 KYVL 84037 1345 E5
N 1625 E
500 LYTN 84040 1283 D3
S 1625 E
800 CRFD 84015 1228 C6
S 1625 W
4400 ROY 84067 1171 E2
W 1625 N
200 PRVO 84604 2928 B3
1200 CLTN 84015 1227 B1
2700 PNCY 84404 1055 B1
W 1625 S
- LEHI 84043 2710 A2
700 SLCY 84104 1858 A7
1100 SRCS 84075 1227 B7
1300 LOGN 84321 527 A7
E 1630 N
1500 NHLN 84341 464 C6
E 1630 S
1000 OREM 84097 2928 B2
1100 SPFK 84660 3249 E6
1400 SPFK 84660 3250 A6
S 1630 W
4400 ROY 84067 1171 E2
9600 SJDN 84095 2281 D1
12600 RIVN 84065 2387 C2
14600 BFDL 84065 2387 C7
W 1630 N
800 OREM 84057 2820 B1
1500 CLTN 84015 1226 D1
S 1635 E
1300 OGDN 84404 1116 D1
S 1635 W
800 OREM 84058 2819 E7
W 1635 N
500 CLTN 84015 1227 C1
E 1640 N
100 PTGV 84062 2605 E7
400 OREM 84057 2820 E1
400 OREM 84097 2820 E1
E 1640 S
1200 PRVO 84606 3035 E3
1300 PRVO 84606 3036 A3
N 1640 E
1400 LOGN 84341 464 C6
N 1640 W
1800 PRVO 84604 2927 E3
S 1640 E
3000 SLkC 84106 1965 C5
S 1640 W
800 OREM 84058 2819 E7
8300 WJDN 84088 2175 C5
W 1640 N
10 OREM 84057 2820 D1
100 LEHI 84043 2603 B4
1000 CLTN 84015 1227 B1
W 1640 S
300 OREM 84058 2927 C2
1400 WDCR 84087 1652 E2
S 1645 E
4900 SLkC 84117 2071 C4
6500 MRRY 84121 2177 A3
8600 SLkC 84093 2177 C6
S 1645 W
6700 WJDN 84084 2175 C1
W 1645 N
200 OREM 84057 2820 C1
E 1650 N
- LOGN 84341 463 E6
- LOGN 84341 464 A6
300 LEHI 84043 2603 C4
600 OREM 84097 2821 A1
1400 PRVO 84604 2929 A3
2600 LYTN 84040 1284 A1
E 1650 S
100 BNFL 84010 1653 E2
200 KYVL 84037 1345 D5
200 OREM 84058 2927 E2
400 SGVL 84663 3143 C5
500 BNFL 84010 1654 A2
600 OREM 84097 2928 A2
2300 SPFK 84660 3250 C6
N 1650 E
- NHLN 84341 464 D5
2000 LYTN 84040 1283 C1
2500 LYTN 84040 1229 D6
N 1650 W
- TMTN 84337 520 B6
300 SGVL 84663 3035 E7
300 SGVL 84663 3142 E1
1100 PRVO 84604 2927 E4
1600 SGVL 84663 3143 D5
S 1650 E
300 SGVL 84663 3144 A3
400 SPFK 84660 3250 A4
1000 BNFL 84010 1654 C2
1000 CRFD 84015 1228 B6
1200 PRVO 84606 3036 A2
1400 OGDN 84404 1116 D1
4200 SLkC 84124 2071 C1
6600 UNTH 84405 1173 C7
6700 UNTH 84405 1229 C1
7600 SWBR 84405 1229 C2
S 1650 W
1200 SRCS 84075 1227 A7
4400 ROY 84067 1171 E2
8000 WJDN 84088 2175 C5
9700 SJDN 84095 2281 C2
11900 RIVN 84065 2281 C7
12900 RIVN 84065 2387 C3
W 1650 N
- WPT 84015 1225 E1
200 HARR 84404 1056 D1
200 NHON 84404 1056 D1
200 PTGV 84062 2605 D7
500 CTRV 84014 1448 D7
700 OREM 84057 2820 B1
1200 SGVL 84663 3035 E6
1200 SGVL 84663 3036 A6
1400 LYTN 84041 1282 C1
2500 LEHI 84043 2602 C4
2700 PNCY 84404 1055 B1
3400 CLTN 84015 1226 B1
4500 PNCY 84404 1054 B1
W 1650 S
1500 WDCR 84087 1652 E2
E 1655 S
300 OREM 84058 2927 E2
S 1655 E
6400 MRRY 84121 2071 C7
6600 CDHT 84121 2177 C1
S 1655 W
7500 WJDN 84084 2175 C3
E 1660 N
200 OREM 84057 2820 E1
E 1660 S
2900 SPFK 84660 3250 D6
N 1660 W
10 WPT 84015 1227 A4
S 1660 E
400 PTGV 84062 2713 C3
800 SPFK 84660 3250 A6
6500 MRRY 84121 2071 C7
6500 MRRY 84121 2177 C1
9000 SNDY 84093 2177 C7
S 1660 W
10 WPT 84015 1227 A4
2400 SRCS 84075 1281 A2
W 1665 N
1000 OREM 84057 2820 A1
E 1670 S
1500 SPFK 84660 3250 A6
N 1670 W
1300 FMTN 84025 1345 E5
1600 PRVO 84604 2927 E3
S 1670 E
4800 SLkC 84117 2071 C3
6500 MRRY 84121 2177 C1
S 1670 W
4200 TYVL 84123 2069 C1
8400 WJDN 84088 2175 C6
9600 SJDN 84095 2281 C1
W 1670 N
900 OREM 84057 2820 B1
1100 PTGV 84062 2605 B7
W 1670 S
10 OREM 84058 2927 D2
300 PRVO 84601 3035 B3
E 1675 N
700 NHON 84414 1057 A1
N 1675 E
1300 LYTN 84040 1283 D2
S 1675 E
300 SGVL 84663 3144 A2
S 1675 W
- OREM 84058 2926 E1
10 LEHI 84043 2602 E7
800 OREM 84058 2819 E7
1800 SRCS 84075 1281 A1
4500 ROY 84067 1171 E2
W 1675 N
10 LYTN 84041 1282 E1
10 SNST 84015 1227 D1
2500 CLTN 84015 1226 D1
4000 SLCY 84116 1752 C5
W 1675 S
- LEHI 84043 2710 A2
E 1680 N
800 LEHI 84043 2603 D4
S 1680 E
400 SGVL 84663 3144 A3
700 PTGV 84062 2713 C4
6400 MRRY 84121 2071 C7
6600 CDHT 84121 2177 C1
S 1680 W
- OREM 84058 2819 E7
- OREM 84058 2926 E1
10 PRVO 84601 2927 E7
500 PRVO 84601 3034 E1
W 1680 N
500 CLTN 84015 1227 C1
2100 CLTN 84015 1226 E1
2500 PRVO 84601 2927 C4
W 1680 S
400 OREM 84058 2927 C2
S 1685 E
1400 OGDN 84404 1116 D1
N 1690 W
1700 LYTN 84041 1282 B1
S 1690 E
4800 SLkC 84117 2071 C3
W 1690 S
1300 LOGN 84321 527 A7
E 1700 N
10 MPTN 84664 3144 B5
10 OREM 84057 2713 D7
100 LEHI 84043 2603 C3
200 LOGN 84341 463 E6
400 NHON 84414 1056 E1
400 NHON 84414 1057 B1
1200 NHLN 84341 464 B6
1600 LOGN 84341 464 C6
2600 LYTN 84040 1284 A1
E 1700 S
- CchC 84321 527 D7
- PVDN 84332 527 D7
- UthC 84003 2711 E5
10 BNFL 84010 1653 E3
10 OREM 84058 2927 D2
10 PRVO 84606 3035 C3
10 SLCY 84115 1964 D1
300 KYVL 84037 1345 D5
500 BNFL 84010 1654 A3
500 OREM 84097 2928 A2
500 SLCY 84105 1964 D1
700 SLCY 84105 1965 A1
1700 SLCY 84108 1965 E1
2300 SLCY 84108 1966 A1
2300 SPFK 84660 3250 C6
N 1700 E
1000 LOGN 84341 464 C7
1100 MPTN 84664 3144 D5
1700 LYTN 84040 1283 D1
1700 NHLN 84341 464 C5
2600 LYTN 84040 1229 D6
N 1700 W
- CLTN 84015 1227 A1
- WDCR 84087 1652 D1
10 WPT 84015 1227 A4
800 LEHI 84043 2602 E4
800 PTGV 84062 2712 B1
1200 FMTN 84025 1345 E6
1900 FRWT 84404 1055 E1
1900 LYTN 84041 1282 B1
2000 LYTN 84041 1228 B7
2100 CRFD 84015 1228 B7
5800 CchC 84335 398 E3
S 1700 E
- CRFD 84015 1228 C6
- SGVL 84664 3144 A4
- SLCY 84112 1859 C4
800 SGVL 84663 3144 A4
800 SPFK 84660 3250 A5
900 SLCY 84105 1859 C6
900 SLCY 84108 1859 C6
1600 SLCY 84105 1965 C1
1600 SLCY 84108 1965 C1
2200 SLkC 84106 1965 C3
6900 CDHT 84121 2177 C2
7200 SWBR 84405 1229 D1
8000 SLkC 84093 2177 C4
8600 SNDY 84093 2177 C6
9400 SNDY 84092 2283 C1
10600 SLkC 84092 2283 C4
11800 SNDY 84092 2389 C1
12300 DRPR 84020 2389 C2
S 1700 W
10 KYVL 84037 1344 E1
10 WPT 84015 1227 A4
1100 MTSV 84401 1055 E7
1100 MTSV 84404 1055 E7
1200 SRCS 84075 1227 A7
1300 SGVL 84663 3142 E5
2500 OGDN 84401 1114 E4
3200 WbrC 84401 1114 E6
4400 ROY 84067 1171 E2
4800 RVDL 84405 1171 E3
10000 UthC 84651 3355 D5
W 1700 N
10 OREM 84057 2820 D1
300 LEHI 84043 2603 B4
800 MPTN 84664 3143 E5
800 WBNF 84087 1551 B5
900 PRVO 84604 2928 A3
1100 CLTN 84015 1227 A1
1300 PRVO 84604 2927 E3
1700 SLCY 84116 1753 B5
1700 SLkC 84116 1753 B5
1900 LYTN 84041 1282 A1
2600 CLTN 84015 1226 D1
3300 PNCY 84404 1055 A1
4100 PNCY 84404 1054 C1
W 1700 S
10 OREM 84058 2927 C2
10 PVDN 84332 527 C7
10 SLCY 84115 1964 A1
100 CchC 84321 527 C7
100 CchC 84332 527 C7
100 PVDN 84321 527 C7
200 BNFL 84010 1653 D3
300 PRRY 84302 827 E3
500 LOGN 84321 527 C7
500 SLCY 84104 1964 A1
900 SLCY 84104 1963 D1
1100 WDCR 84087 1653 A2
1200 SRCS 84075 1281 A1
1900 SRCS 84075 1280 C1
3000 DvsC 84075 1280 C1
3900 WbrC 84401 1113 D1
W 1700 S SR-108
1200 SRCS 84075 1281 A1
1900 SRCS 84075 1280 E1
W 1700 S SR-127
2000 SRCS 84075 1280 C1
3000 DvsC 84075 1280 C1
E 1710 S
1100 SPFK 84660 3250 A6
S 1710 E
1400 PRVO 84606 3036 A2
4800 SLkC 84117 2071 C3
6500 MRRY 84121 2177 C1
7200 CDHT 84121 2177 C2
W 1710 S
- WDCR 84087 1652 E2
S 1715 E
3600 SLkC 84106 1965 C7
8000 SLkC 84093 2177 C5
8100 SNDY 84093 2177 C5
E 1720 N
10 LYTN 84041 1283 A1
E 1720 S
700 OREM 84097 2928 A2
2700 SPFK 84660 3250 C6
N 1720 E
1300 LOGN 84341 464 C7
N 1720 W
1900 CLTN 84015 1171 A7
S 1720 E
4900 SLkC 84117 2071 C3
S 1720 W
4400 ROY 84067 1171 C2
6600 UthC 84660 3248 D3
W 1720 N
100 OREM 84057 2713 D7
500 PRVO 84604 2928 B3
800 OREM 84057 2820 B1
W 1720 S
500 PRVO 84601 3035 B3
S 1722 W
- WVCY 84119 1963 C7
E 1725 N
400 NHON 84414 1057 A1
600 LEHI 84043 2603 D3
600 OREM 84097 2714 A7
E 1725 S
1200 BNFL 84010 1654 B3
N 1725 E
1100 LYTN 84040 1283 D2
N 1725 W
500 CLTN 84015 1227 A3
1200 LYTN 84041 1282 B2
1800 FRWT 84404 1055 E1
S 1725 E
6400 UNTH 84405 1173 D7
6600 WbrC 84405 1173 D7
S 1725 W
3100 WVCY 84119 1963 C5
4500 ROY 84067 1171 E2
W 1725 N
500 OREM 84057 2713 B7
2400 CLTN 84015 1226 D1
W 1725 S
1400 WDCR 84087 1652 E2
E 1730 N
400 OREM 84097 2713 E7
1700 NHLN 84341 464 D6
E 1730 S
300 OREM 84058 2927 E2
N 1730 E
1000 LOGN 84341 464 D7
N 1730 W
1100 PTGV 84062 2712 B1
S 1730 E
3000 SLkC 84106 1965 C5
S 1730 W
800 OREM 84058 2819 E7
1800 SRCS 84075 1281 A1
W 1730 N
800 CLTN 84015 1227 B1
1700 PRVO 84604 2927 D3
W 1730 S
300 LEHI 84043 2710 B2
4800 SLCY 84104 1962 A1
5000 SLCY 84104 1961 E1
N 1735 W
1300 CLTN 84015 1227 A2
E 1740 S
700 OREM 84097 2928 A2
1600 SPFK 84660 3250 A6
N 1740 W
1700 PRVO 84604 2927 E3
S 1740 E
- SPFK 84660 3250 B5
4800 SLkC 84117 2071 C3
S 1740 W
400 PRVO 84601 2927 E7
12200 RIVN 84065 2387 C1
W 1740 N
10 OREM 84057 2713 D7
700 CLTN 84015 1227 C1
1000 OREM 84042 2713 A7
E 1750 N
10 OREM 84057 2713 D7
400 NHON 84414 1056 E1
400 NHON 84414 1057 A1
900 ANFK 84062 2605 A3
1700 LYTN 84040 1283 D1
E 1750 S
500 OREM 84058 2927 E2
1100 SPFK 84660 3250 A6
N 1750 E
1400 LOGN 84341 464 D6
1700 LYTN 84040 1283 D1
1800 NHLN 84341 464 D5
2600 LYTN 84040 1229 D6
N 1750 W
- LEHI 84043 2602 E5
10 WshC 84032 2398 A3
300 WPT 84015 1227 A3
900 PRVO 84604 2927 E4
900 PTGV 84062 2712 B1
1400 CLTN 84015 1227 A1
1400 SGVL 84663 3035 E6
S 1750 E
100 SGVL 84663 3144 A2
500 SPFK 84660 3250 B4
7700 SWBR 84405 1229 D3
S 1750 W
10 WshC 84032 2398 A3
1000 SGVL 84663 3142 E4
4000 UthC 84660 3141 D4
8200 WJDN 84088 2175 C5
W 1750 N
- FRWT 84404 1056 A1
- NHON 84404 1056 D1
10 CTRV 84014 1448 D7
300 LEHI 84043 2603 B3
800 OREM 84057 2713 B7
1400 CLTN 84015 1227 A1
2200 LEHI 84043 2602 D3
2700 PNCY 84404 1055 B1
2800 CLTN 84015 1226 C1
W 1750 S
100 PRRY 84302 827 E3
300 KYVL 84037 1345 C5
500 PYSN 84651 3461 D2
1000 LEHI 84043 2710 A2
1100 WDCR 84087 1653 A3
1300 LOGN 84321 527 A7
2300 SRCS 84075 1280 D1
S 1755 W
3100 WVCY 84119 1963 C5
E 1760 S
2000 SPFK 84660 3250 B6
N 1760 W
800 PRVO 84604 2927 D5
S 1760 W
900 SRCS 84075 1227 A6
2400 OGDN 84401 1114 E3
4700 TYVL 84118 2069 C3
S 1765 W
13000 RIVN 84065 2387 C3
S 1768 E
300 SLCY 84112 1859 C4
E 1770 N
10 LYTN 84041 1283 A1
N 1770 E
1500 LOGN 84341 464 D6
1600 MPTN 84664 3144 D5
S 1770 W
12900 RIVN 84065 2387 C3
W 1770 N
900 OREM 84042 2713 A7
900 OREM 84057 2713 A7
W 1770 S
500 PRVO 84601 3035 B3
2500 SRCS 84075 1280 D1
E 1775 N
10 OREM 84057 2713 D7
600 LEHI 84043 2603 D3
800 NHON 84414 1057 B1
E 1775 S
- OREM 84097 2928 A2
N 1775 W
500 WPT 84015 1227 A3
1800 FRWT 84404 1055 D1
S 1775 E
6600 UNTH 84405 1173 D7
6600 UNTH 84405 1229 D1
S 1775 W
- ROY 84067 1171 E3
1200 MTSV 84401 1055 E7
13400 RIVN 84065 2387 C4
W 1775 N
200 LYTN 84041 1282 E1
200 NHON 84404 1056 D1
1100 LEHI 84043 2603 A3
2300 LEHI 84043 2602 C3
3300 PNCY 84404 1054 E1
3300 PNCY 84404 1055 A1
S 1778 E
- SLCY 84112 1859 D4
E 1780 N
1600 NHLN 84341 464 D6
E 1780 S
300 OREM 84058 2927 E2
N 1780 E
1700 NHLN 84341 464 D6
N 1780 W
1600 LYTN 84041 1282 B1
S 1780 E
- SPFK 84660 3250 B6
500 SGVL 84663 3144 A3
S 1780 W
800 OREM 84058 2819 E7
4600 TYVL 84119 2069 C3
12100 RIVN 84065 2387 C1
W 1780 N
400 OREM 84057 2713 C7
W 1780 S
2100 SRCS 84075 1280 E1
S 1785 E
9900 SNDY 84092 2283 D2

Salt Lake City Street Index

STREET Block City ZIP Map# Grid

E 1790 N
300 PTGV 84062 2605 E7
E 1790 S
1500 SPFK 84660 3250 A6
S 1790 W
10500 SJDN 84095 2281 C4
W 1790 S
300 LEHI 84043 2710 B2
E 1800 N
10 LOGN 84341 463 E5
10 OREM 84057 2713 D7
10 PTGV 84062 2605 D7
400 NHON 84414 1056 E1
500 LOGN 84341 464 A5
500 NHON 84414 1057 A1
6100 WbrC 84310 1060 C1
E 1800 S
10 BNFL 84010 1653 E3
200 OREM 84058 2927 E2
300 KYVL 84037 1345 D5
300 SGVL 84663 3143 D5
500 BNFL 84010 1654 B3
500 CRFD 84015 1281 E1
500 OREM 84058 2928 B2
700 CRFD 84015 1282 A1
3500 SPFK 84660 3250 E6
N 1800 E
- NHLN 84341 464 D5
10 DvsC 84040 1283 D4
10 LYTN 84040 1283 D4
10 MPTN 84664 3144 D7
1400 LOGN 84341 464 D6
N 1800 W
- LEHI 84043 2602 E5
100 WPT 84015 1227 A4
200 LNDN 84042 2712 B6
600 PTGV 84062 2712 B2
800 SLCY 84116 1753 C7
1300 CLTN 84015 1227 A2
1400 CchC 84341 462 D6
S 1800 E
500 SPFK 84660 3250 B4
700 SGVL 84663 3144 A3
1000 SLCY 84108 1859 D6
1800 SLCY 84108 1965 D1
2100 SLCY 84106 1965 D2
3000 SLkC 84106 1965 D5
6400 UthC 84660 3250 C3
6600 UNTH 84405 1173 D7
6600 UNTH 84405 1229 D1
7700 SWBR 84405 1229 D3
7800 CDHT 84093 2177 D4
S 1800 W
100 FMTN 84025 1447 E2
200 PRVO 84601 2927 E7
1200 SRCS 84075 1227 A7
1900 SRCS 84075 1281 A1
3200 WVCY 84119 1963 C5
4700 ROY 84067 1171 D2
7300 UthC 84660 3248 D5
12200 RIVN 84065 2387 C1
14800 BFDL 84065 2494 C1
W 1800 N
- MPTN 84664 3143 E5
- MPTN 84664 3144 A5
10 LOGN 84341 463 C5
10 PTGV 84062 2605 C7
200 CTRV 84014 1448 D7
400 LYTN 84041 1282 D1
500 PRVO 84604 2928 B3
500 WshC 84032 2398 A1
600 OREM 84057 2713 B7
700 WBNF 84087 1551 B4
900 SLCY 84116 1753 E5
1000 LEHI 84043 2603 A3
1200 DvsC 84025 1345 E5
1200 DvsC 84025 1346 D4
1200 DvsC 84037 1345 E5
1200 DvsC 84037 1346 D4
1200 FMTN 84025 1345 E5
1200 FMTN 84025 1346 D4
1200 FMTN 84037 1345 E5
1200 LEHI 84043 2602 E3
1400 KYVL 84037 1345 E5
1800 CchC 84341 462 D5
2500 FRWT 84404 1055 B1
2800 PNCY 84404 1055 B1
W 1800 S
10 BNFL 84010 1653 D3
10 OREM 84058 2927 C2
200 CRFD 84015 1281 C1
300 OGDN 84404 1115 C2
800 LOGN 84321 527 A7
1300 LOGN 84321 526 E7
1400 CchC 84321 526 E7
1900 WHVN 84401 1114 C2
2400 CchC 84339 526 B7
2700 WbrC 84401 1114 C2
3200 WbrC 84401 1113 E2
3400 CchC 84321 525 E7
5900 CchC 84325 524 D7
6000 MNDN 84325 524 D7
S 1800 St W
6400 CchC 84319 650 E5
6400 CchC 84339 650 E5
S 1806 W
1200 WshC 84032 2397 E7
E 1810 N
900 OREM 84097 2714 A7
N 1810 W
10 PRVO 84601 2927 E6
S 1810 E
3000 SLkC 84106 1965 D5
S 1810 W
400 PRVO 84601 2927 E7
900 SRCS 84075 1226 E6
W 1810 N
500 WBNF 84087 1551 C4
W 1810 S
800 SLCY 84104 1964 A1
E 1815 N
- NHLN 84341 464 D5
S 1815 W
4700 TYVL 84118 2069 C3
W 1815 N
600 WBNF 84087 1551 C5
E 1820 S
10 OREM 84058 2927 D2
N 1820 W
1600 PRVO 84604 2927 E3
S 1820 E
- SLCY 84112 1859 D4
S 1820 W
6000 TYVL 84118 2069 C6
W 1820 N
100 OREM 84057 2713 D7
W 1820 S
500 PRVO 84601 3035 B3
1400 WDCR 84087 1652 E3
4100 SLCY 84104 1962 C1
E 1825 N
10 CTRV 84014 1448 E7
2400 LYTN 84040 1283 E1
2400 LYTN 84040 1284 A1
E 1825 S
- SLCY 84108 1966 A1
100 OREM 84058 2927 D2
700 BNFL 84010 1654 A3
N 1825 E
2700 LYTN 84040 1229 D6
N 1825 W
500 WPT 84015 1226 E3
1400 CLTN 84015 1226 E1
1500 LEHI 84043 2602 E4
S 1825 E
2500 OGDN 84401 1116 D4
S 1825 W
4600 TYVL 84119 2069 C3
5000 ROY 84067 1171 D3
7800 WJDN 84088 2175 C4
W 1825 N
- NHON 84404 1056 D1
200 NHON 84414 1056 D1
500 CTRV 84014 1448 C7
1300 PRVO 84604 2927 E3
W 1825 S
800 LEHI 84043 2710 A2
1500 WDCR 84087 1652 E3
1700 SRCS 84075 1281 A1
2200 SRCS 84075 1280 D1
E 1830 S
300 OREM 84058 2927 E2
N 1830 W
1400 PRVO 84604 2927 E4
S 1830 E
- SPFK 84660 3250 B4
6000 MRRY 84121 2071 D6
7700 CDHT 84093 2177 D4
S 1830 W
12600 RIVN 84065 2387 C2
W 1830 N
500 OREM 84057 2713 B7
W 1830 S
300 SLCY 84115 1964 B1
1600 SRCS 84075 1281 A1
E 1834 S
400 OREM 84058 2927 E2
S 1835 E
5800 SLkC 84121 2071 D6
11100 SNDY 84092 2283 D5
S 1835 W
13400 RIVN 84065 2387 C4
13800 BFDL 84065 2387 C5
W 1835 N
- CLTN 84015 1226 D1
1200 LEHI 84043 2603 A3
1800 LEHI 84043 2602 D3
E 1838 S
200 OREM 84058 2927 E3
E 1840 N
300 PTGV 84062 2605 E7
400 OREM 84097 2713 E7
900 LEHI 84043 2603 D3
S 1840 E
600 SGVL 84663 3144 A3
7300 CDHT 84121 2177 D3
12100 DRPR 84020 2389 D1
S 1840 W
800 OREM 84058 2819 D7
1200 OREM 84058 2926 D1
1900 SRCS 84075 1280 E1
12000 RIVN 84065 2281 C7
12000 RIVN 84065 2387 C1
W 1840 S
400 OREM 84058 2927 C3
S 1845 W
- ROY 84067 1171 D2
3800 WVCY 84119 1963 C7
E 1850 N
10 LOGN 84341 463 D5
10 LYTN 84041 1282 E1
10 OREM 84057 2713 D7
400 NHON 84414 1056 E1
400 NHON 84414 1057 A1
600 LOGN 84341 464 A5
1300 PRVO 84604 2929 A3
1400 LYTN 84040 1283 C1
1700 NHLN 84341 464 C5
3000 LYTN 84040 1284 A1
E 1850 S
- SPFK 84660 3250 B6
200 BNFL 84010 1653 E3
700 BNFL 84010 1654 A3
N 1850 E
1700 NHLN 84341 464 D6
1800 LYTN 84040 1283 D1
2700 LYTN 84040 1229 D6
N 1850 W
- LEHI 84043 2602 E5
100 WPT 84015 1226 E4
1300 LYTN 84041 1282 B2
1300 PRVO 84604 2927 E4
2500 FRWT 84404 997 D6
S 1850 E
200 SGVL 84663 3144 B2
200 SLCY 84112 1859 D4
500 SPFK 84660 3250 B4
1900 OGDN 84401 1116 D2
4600 UNTH 84405 1173 D7
7000 CDHT 84121 2177 D2
7800 SWBR 84405 1229 D3
S 1850 W
100 OREM 84058 2819 D5
300 LEHI 84043 2602 E7
300 PRVO 84601 2927 D7
1200 MTSV 84401 1055 D7
1200 SGVL 84663 3142 D4
3100 WVCY 84119 1963 C5
4600 UthC 84660 3141 D5
5000 ROY 84067 1171 D3
5600 UthC 84660 3248 D1
8200 WJDN 84088 2175 C5
14000 BFDL 84065 2387 C6
W 1850 N
- LEHI 84043 2602 D3
10 CTRV 84014 1448 D7
10 SNST 84015 1227 D1
300 LEHI 84043 2603 B3
700 OREM 84057 2713 B7
700 PRVO 84604 2928 A3
900 WBNF 84087 1551 B4
1200 CLTN 84015 1171 B7
1200 CLTN 84015 1227 B1
1400 LYTN 84041 1282 C1
2100 FRWT 84404 1055 C1
2300 CLTN 84015 1170 D7
4700 PNCY 84404 1054 B1
W 1850 S
- SRCS 84075 1281 C1
200 CRFD 84015 1281 C1
400 PRRY 84302 827 D3
1100 WDCR 84087 1653 A3
2500 SRCS 84075 1280 D1
S 1855 W
3100 WVCY 84119 1963 C5
E 1860 N
1400 LEHI 84043 2603 E3
E 1860 S
10 PRVO 84606 3035 E3
800 UthC 84606 3035 E3
900 UthC 84606 3036 A3
S 1860 E
- SPFK 84660 3250 B6
3700 SLkC 84106 1965 D7
S 1860 W
10 PRVO 84601 2927 D7
9400 SJDN 84095 2281 C1
12200 RIVN 84065 2387 C1
W 1860 N
600 CLTN 84015 1171 C7
W 1860 S
300 LEHI 84043 2710 B2
E 1864 S
10 OREM 84058 2927 D3
500 OREM 84058 2928 A3
S 1865 E
4100 HLDY 84124 2071 D1
6400 MRRY 84121 2071 D7
6400 MRRY 84121 2177 D1
S 1865 W
10700 SJDN 84095 2281 C4
E 1870 N
600 OREM 84097 2714 A7
S 1870 E
5100 SLkC 84117 2071 D4
W 1870 N
600 OREM 84057 2713 B7
900 CLTN 84015 1171 A7
1000 LEHI 84043 2603 A3
1100 PRVO 84604 2928 A3
1200 LEHI 84043 2602 E3
1200 PRVO 84604 2927 E3
E 1875 N
10 LYTN 84041 1282 D1
200 CTRV 84014 1448 E6
3200 DvsC 84040 1284 B1
E 1875 S
300 SGVL 84663 3143 D5
600 BNFL 84010 1654 A3
N 1875 W
300 WPT 84015 1226 E3
600 FMTN 84025 1345 D7
S 1875 W
10 WPT 84015 1226 E5
800 SRCS 84075 1226 E6
2400 SRCS 84075 1280 E2
W 1875 N
100 HARR 84414 1056 D1
100 NHON 84404 1056 D1
100 NHON 84414 1056 D1
400 CTRV 84014 1448 C7
400 LYTN 84041 1282 D1
1000 CLTN 84015 1171 B7
1200 DvsC 84025 1346 A4
1200 DvsC 84037 1346 A4
1200 FMTN 84025 1346 A4
1200 FMTN 84037 1346 A4
W 1875 S
- SRCS 84075 1281 A1
400 WDCR 84010 1653 C3
500 LEHI 84043 2710 B2
N 1880 W
1400 PRVO 84604 2927 E4
S 1880 E
1200 SPFK 84660 3250 B5
W 1880 N
10 OREM 84057 2713 D7
W 1880 S
500 WDCR 84010 1653 C3
S 1885 E
3100 SLkC 84106 1965 D5
W 1885 N
400 OREM 84057 2713 C7
E 1890 N
200 OREM 84057 2713 E7
N 1890 W
600 PRVO 84601 2927 E5
600 PRVO 84604 2927 E5
S 1890 W
8200 WJDN 84088 2175 C5
W 1890 N
300 OREM 84057 2713 C7
500 WBNF 84087 1551 C4
2500 CLTN 84015 1170 D7
W 1890 S
1600 SRCS 84075 1281 A1
E 1900 N
10 CTRV 84014 1448 E6
100 NHON 84404 1056 E1
100 NHON 84414 1056 E1
100 WbrC 84404 1056 E1
100 WbrC 84414 1056 E1
300 NHON 84404 998 E7
300 NHON 84414 998 E7
400 NHON 84414 1057 A1
600 LOGN 84341 464 A5
700 NHON 84414 999 A7
800 LEHI 84043 2603 D3
1300 NHLN 84341 464 B5
1800 LYTN 84040 1283 D1
5400 WbrC 84310 1002 C7
E 1900 S
100 BNFL 84010 1653 E3
600 BNFL 84010 1654 A3
600 CRFD 84015 1281 E1
700 CRFD 84015 1282 A1
N 1900 E
- MPTN 84664 3144 D5
N 1900 W
- CchC 84321 462 D7
- MTSV 84404 1055 D3
10 CchC 84321 526 D3
100 WPT 84015 1226 E4
400 LOGN 84321 526 D1
1300 PRVO 84604 2927 D4
1400 CLTN 84015 1226 E1
1800 FRWT 84404 1055 D1
2700 FRWT 84404 997 D5
N 1900 W SR-126
100 MTSV 84404 1055 D4
S 1900 E
800 SGVL 84663 3144 B3
800 SLCY 84108 1859 D5
1600 SLCY 84108 1965 D1
2100 SLCY 84106 1965 D2
3600 SLkC 84106 1965 D7
4700 OGDN 84403 1173 D3
4700 WbrC 84403 1173 D3
5800 SLkC 84121 2071 D6
7400 SWBR 84405 1229 D3
10200 SNDY 84092 2283 D3
S 1900 W
10 CchC 84321 526 D4
10 LNDN 84042 2712 B7
10 LOGN 84321 526 D4
100 MTSV 84404 1055 D6
1200 MTSV 84401 1055 D6
1200 MTSV 84401 1114 D5
1400 WHVN 84401 1114 D1
1900 SRCS 84075 1280 E2
2500 OGDN 84401 1114 D5
3100 WbrC 84401 1114 D5
3300 WbrC 84067 1114 D5
3300 WHVN 84067 1114 D5
3400 ROY 84067 1114 D5
3400 ROY 84401 1114 D5
3400 WbrC 84405 1114 D5
3600 OGDN 84405 1114 D5
3800 WVCY 84119 1963 C7
3900 CchC 84321 590 D7
4000 ROY 84067 1171 D1
4100 OGDN 84067 1171 D1
4100 OGDN 84405 1171 D1
4100 ROY 84405 1171 D1
4400 CchC 84319 590 D7
4600 CchC 84319 650 D1
4900 HYRM 84319 650 D1
8700 WJDN 84088 2175 C6
10000 UthC 84651 3355 D5
12000 RIVN 84065 2281 C7
12000 RIVN 84065 2387 C1
S 1900 W SR-126
100 MTSV 84404 1055 D6
1200 MTSV 84401 1055 D6
1200 MTSV 84401 1114 D5
1400 WHVN 84401 1114 D1
2500 OGDN 84401 1114 D5
3100 WbrC 84401 1114 D5
3300 WbrC 84067 1114 D5
3300 WHVN 84067 1114 D5
3400 ROY 84067 1114 D5
3400 ROY 84401 1114 D5
3400 WbrC 84405 1114 D5
3600 OGDN 84405 1114 D5
4000 ROY 84067 1171 D1
4100 OGDN 84067 1171 D1
4100 OGDN 84405 1171 D1
4100 ROY 84405 1171 D1
W 1900 N
- FRWT 84404 997 D7
10 SNST 84015 1171 D7
100 LYTN 84041 1282 E1
500 CTRV 84014 1448 C6
500 SPFK 84660 3142 B6
600 CLTN 84015 1171 C7
900 MPTN 84664 3143 E4
1100 LEHI 84043 2603 A3
1600 SLCY 84116 1753 C4
2300 FRWT 84404 1055 B1
2700 PNCY 84404 1055 B1
2900 PNCY 84404 997 A7
4400 PNCY 84404 1054 C1
W 1900 S
- SRCS 84075 1281 C1
10 BNFL 84010 1653 D3
10 CRFD 84015 1281 D1
600 MPTN 84664 3251 A2
1200 WDCR 84087 1653 A3
1300 WDCR 84087 1652 E3
1600 MPTN 84664 3250 D2
2300 SRCS 84075 1280 D1
3200 CchC 84321 525 E7
3200 CchC 84321 589 E1
3200 CchC 84321 590 A1
4700 WbrC 84401 1113 A2
S 1905 E
3500 SLkC 84106 1965 D6
E 1910 S
100 OREM 84058 2927 E3
S 1915 E
3700 SLkC 84106 1965 D7
6100 MRRY 84121 2071 D7
S 1915 W
400 LEHI 84043 2602 D7
3900 ROY 84067 1114 D7
5200 TYVL 84118 2069 C4
W 1915 N
2300 CLTN 84015 1170 D7
W 1915 S
1700 SRCS 84075 1281 A1
1800 SRCS 84075 1280 E1
S 1920 W
100 PRVO 84601 2927 D7
400 PRVO 84601 3034 D1
7700 WJDN 84084 2175 C4
8700 WJDN 84088 2175 C6
W 1920 N
700 PTGV 84062 2605 C7
E 1925 N
700 NHON 84414 999 A7
1100 NHON 84414 1057 C1
E 1925 S
200 CRFD 84015 1281 E1
N 1925 E
1200 LYTN 84040 1283 D2
S 1925 E
3900 HLDY 84124 1965 D7
4000 HLDY 84124 2071 D1
7900 SWBR 84405 1229 D3
8300 SNDY 84093 2177 D5
S 1925 W
1200 SRCS 84075 1226 E7
3800 ROY 84067 1114 D7
12200 RIVN 84065 2387 C1
W 1925 N
200 OREM 84057 2713 C7
400 HARR 84414 998 C7
400 LYTN 84041 1282 D1
500 PRVO 84604 2928 B3
600 CTRV 84014 1448 C6
3000 CLTN 84015 1170 C7
5000 DvsC 84315 1169 C7
E 1930 N
10 LYTN 84041 1282 D1
10 LYTN 84041 1283 A1
400 OREM 84097 2713 E7
2500 LYTN 84040 1283 E1
2500 LYTN 84040 1284 A1
N 1930 W
1400 PRVO 84604 2927 D4
2000 CLTN 84015 1170 E7
S 1930 W
9400 SJDN 84095 2281 C1
13400 RIVN 84065 2387 C4
W 1930 N
400 OREM 84057 2713 C7
900 PTGV 84062 2605 C7
1400 CLTN 84015 1171 A7
N 1935 W
1800 LEHI 84043 2602 D3
S 1935 E
3000 SLkC 84106 1965 D4
7000 CDHT 84121 2177 D2
W 1935 S
800 WDCR 84087 1653 B3
E 1940 N
1400 LEHI 84043 2603 E3
N 1940 W
300 WPT 84015 1226 E3
S 1940 E
3100 SLkC 84106 1965 D5
6400 MRRY 84121 2071 D7
S 1940 W
3300 WVCY 84119 1963 C6
W 1940 N
- PRVO 84604 2928 B3
1300 PRVO 84604 2927 E3
W 1940 S
- WDCR 84087 1652 D3
S 1945 E
7300 CDHT 84121 2177 D3
E 1950 N
200 OREM 84057 2713 E7
400 NHON 84414 998 E7
400 NHON 84414 999 A7
500 OREM 84097 2713 E7
600 OREM 84097 2714 A7
700 SPFK 84660 3142 E6
1000 LOGN 84341 464 B5
1300 PRVO 84604 2928 E3
1300 WshC 84032 2398 E1
1500 PRVO 84604 2929 A3
2400 LYTN 84040 1283 E1
3700 WbrC 84310 1001 B7
E 1950 S
10 CRFD 84015 1281 D1
100 OREM 84058 2927 D3
200 BNFL 84010 1653 E3
700 BNFL 84010 1654 A3
700 CRFD 84015 1282 A1
1800 OGDN 84401 1116 D2
N 1950 E
2000 LYTN 84040 1283 D1
2100 LYTN 84040 1229 D7
N 1950 W
100 SLCY 84116 1857 B2
1600 PRVO 84604 2927 D3
S 1950 E
100 LYTN 84040 1283 D5
3700 SLkC 84106 1965 D7
7200 CDHT 84121 2177 D3
7200 SWBR 84405 1229 D1
12100 DRPR 84020 2389 D1
S 1950 W
600 SGVL 84663 3142 D3
2500 SRCS 84075 1280 E2
3500 WVCY 84119 1963 C6
3800 ROY 84067 1114 D7
3900 WVCY 84119 2069 C1
4200 ROY 84067 1171 D1
4700 TYVL 84118 2069 C3
8200 WJDN 84088 2175 C5
10700 SJDN 84095 2281 C4
12700 RIVN 84065 2387 C2
13800 BFDL 84065 2387 C5
W 1950 N
200 OREM 84057 2713 C7
300 SNST 84015 1171 C7
500 CTRV 84014 1448 C6
700 WBNF 84087 1551 B4
1200 PRVO 84604 2928 A3
1400 CLTN 84015 1171 A7
2900 CLTN 84015 1170 C7
W 1950 S
10 BNFL 84010 1653 D3
500 LEHI 84043 2710 B3
700 WDCR 84087 1653 B3
1500 SRCS 84075 1281 A1
1800 WHVN 84401 1114 D2
3200 SRCS 84075 1280 C1
S 1955 E
4000 HLDY 84124 2071 D1
E 1960 N
10 OREM 84057 2713 D7
900 LEHI 84043 2603 D3
E 1960 S
400 OREM 84058 2927 E3
1300 OGDN 84401 1116 C2
N 1960 W
1400 CLTN 84015 1226 E1
2200 LEHI 84043 2602 D3
S 1960 E
4500 HLDY 84117 2071 D2
7800 SWBR 84405 1229 D3
S 1960 W
7600 WJDN 84084 2175 C4
W 1960 N
100 OREM 84057 2713 D7
600 CLTN 84015 1171 C7
1400 LYTN 84041 1282 C1
W 1960 S
1100 LOGN 84321 591 A1
N 1965 E
2100 LYTN 84040 1229 D7
S 1970 W
- SJDN 84095 2281 C1
W 1970 N
1400 PRVO 84604 2927 E3
E 1975 N
- NHON 84414 999 A7
10 CTRV 84014 1448 D6
2100 LYTN 84040 1283 E1
2700 LYTN 84040 1284 A1
E 1975 S
200 CRFD 84015 1281 E1
1500 BNFL 84010 1654 C3
N 1975 E
2000 LYTN 84040 1283 D1
2100 LYTN 84040 1229 D7
N 1975 W
1300 LEHI 84043 2602 D4
S 1975 W
3900 ROY 84067 1114 D7
3900 ROY 84067 1171 D1
7100 WJDN 84084 2175 C3
12100 RIVN 84065 2387 C1
W 1975 N
200 HARR 84414 998 D7
400 PRVO 84604 2928 B3
W 1975 S
1200 WDCR 84087 1653 A3
1300 WDCR 84087 1652 E3
1700 SRCS 84075 1281 A1
1800 SRCS 84075 1280 E1
E 1980 N
200 PRVO 84604 2928 D3
500 LOGN 84341 463 E5
500 LOGN 84341 464 A5
1200 NHLN 84341 464 B5
2400 LYTN 84040 1283 E1
2400 LYTN 84040 1284 A1
N 1980 W
1500 PRVO 84604 2927 D4
S 1980 E
7400 SWBR 84405 1229 D2
10300 SNDY 84092 2283 D3
S 1980 W
10 PRVO 84601 2927 D7
4600 TYVL 84119 2069 C3
9400 SJDN 84095 2281 C1
12800 RIVN 84065 2387 C3
W 1980 N
1200 PRVO 84604 2928 A3
1300 PRVO 84604 2927 E3
W 1980 S
10 CRFD 84015 1281 D1
4100 SLCY 84104 1962 B1
E 1985 S
- HRCY 84032 2398 D7
W 1985 N
200 SNST 84015 1171 C7
W 1987 S
3200 SLCY 84104 1962 D1
E 1990 N
10 PRVO 84604 2928 C3
E 1990 S
1300 OGDN 84401 1116 C2
S 1990 W
100 OREM 84058 2819 D5
10600 SJDN 84095 2281 C4
W 1990 N
10 PRVO 84604 2928 C3
E 2000 N
- LOGN 84341 463 E5
- LOGN 84341 464 A5
10 LNDN 84042 2713 E7
10 LNDN 84057 2713 E7
10 OREM 84057 2713 E7
100 WbrC 84414 998 D7
200 NHON 84414 998 D7
200 OREM 84042 2713 E7
400 OREM 84097 2713 E7
600 LNDN 84042 2714 A7
600 OREM 84097 2714 A7
800 LEHI 84043 2603 D3
1100 PRVO 84604 2928 E3
1500 NHLN 84341 464 C5
E 2000 S
- SLCY 84105 1965 A2
10 OREM 84058 2927 D3
300 PRVO 84058 2927 D3
300 PRVO 84604 2927 D3
400 OREM 84604 2927 D3
500 CRFD 84015 1281 E1
500 OREM 84058 2928 A3
500 PRVO 84604 2928 A3
600 BNFL 84010 1654 A3
700 CRFD 84015 1282 A1
N 2000 E
- SGVL 84663 3144 D4
1600 MPTN 84664 3144 D4
1600 SGVL 84664 3144 D4
2800 NHLN 84341 464 D3
2900 LYTN 84040 1229 D6
N 2000 W
- TMTN 84337 520 B5
10 SGVL 84663 3035 D6
10 SGVL 84663 3142 D1
400 MTSV 84404 1055 D1
800 FRWT 84404 1055 D1
1600 PRVO 84604 2927 D3
1800 FRWT 84404 997 D4
1800 LEHI 84043 2602 D3
4000 CchC 84341 398 D6
5200 CchC 84335 398 D4
N 2000 W SR-126
400 MTSV 84404 1055 D1
800 FRWT 84404 1055 D1
1800 FRWT 84404 997 D4
S 2000 E
10 SLCY 84113 1859 D3
100 LYTN 84040 1283 D5
700 LYTN 84041 1228 C6
700 SGVL 84663 3144 B3
800 SLCY 84108 1859 D5
1500 SPFK 84660 3250 B6
1600 SLCY 84108 1965 D1
S 2000 E
2000 BNFL 84010 1654 D3
2100 SLCY 84106 1965 D3
2600 SLCY 84109 1965 D3
2700 SLkC 84109 1965 D3
2800 SLkC 84106 1965 D5
3900 HLDY 84124 1965 D6
4000 HLDY 84124 2071 D1
6000 WbrC 84403 1173 D6
6400 UNTH 84405 1173 D7
7600 SWBR 84405 1229 D2
10600 SLkC 84092 2283 D4
10600 SNDY 84092 2283 D4
12000 DRPR 84020 2389 D1
S 2000 W
- DvsC 84025 1447 D3
- DvsC 84087 1447 D3
- FMTN 84025 1447 D3
- FMTN 84087 1447 D3
10 SGVL 84663 3142 D2
600 CchC 84321 526 D5
600 SRCS 84075 1226 E6
700 MTSV 84404 1055 D7
1200 SPFK 84660 3142 D5
1700 SRCS 84075 1280 E1
1800 CchC 84321 590 D1
1900 MPTN 84664 3250 D2
2200 WVCY 84119 1963 C2
2500 CchC 84339 590 D3
2700 DvsC 84075 1280 E4
3600 UthC 84660 3141 C3
3700 ROY 84067 1114 D7
4300 ROY 84067 1171 D1
5000 CchC 84319 650 D2
5200 VNYD 84013 2712 B6
5200 VNYD 84013 2819 B1
5200 VNYD 84057 2712 B6
5200 VNYD 84057 2819 B1
5400 LNDN 84042 2712 B6
5600 LNDN 84013 2712 B6
7300 UthC 84660 3248 C5
9300 BxEC 84340 996 E1
S 2000 W SR-108
600 SRCS 84075 1226 E6
W 2000 N
- CLTN 84015 1171 B7
- WBNF 84087 1551 B4
10 LNDN 84042 2713 C7
10 MPTN 84663 3144 A4
10 MPTN 84664 3144 A4
10 OREM 84057 2713 C7
10 SGVL 84663 3144 A4
10 SGVL 84664 3144 A4
10 SNST 84015 1171 D7
100 HARR 84414 998 D7
100 WbrC 84414 998 D7
600 HARR 84404 998 C7
600 PTGV 84062 2605 C7
700 MPTN 84664 3143 E4
700 PRVO 84604 2928 A3
700 SGVL 84663 3143 E4
700 SGVL 84664 3143 E4
2300 CLTN 84015 1170 D7
3500 WPT 84015 1170 B7
4400 CRNN 84307 764 C1
W 2000 S
- MPTN 84664 3250 E3
- MPTN 84664 3251 A2
- PRVO 84606 3035 D1
10 OREM 84058 2927 B3
10 PRRY 84302 827 D4
200 CRFD 84015 1281 D1
400 PRVO 84058 2927 B3
400 PRVO 84601 2927 B3
500 WDCR 84010 1653 C3
700 UthC 84058 2927 B3
700 UthC 84601 2927 B3
700 WDCR 84087 1653 B3
900 WHVN 84401 1115 A2
1100 LOGN 84321 591 A1
1600 SRCS 84075 1281 A1
3200 CchC 84321 590 A1
4800 CchC 84325 589 A1
5400 CchC 84339 588 E1
5400 CchC 84339 589 A1
6200 CchC 84325 588 C1
W 2005 N
700 CLTN 84015 1171 B7
S 2010 W
8300 WJDN 84088 2175 C5
11900 RIVN 84065 2281 C7
12000 RIVN 84065 2387 C1
W 2010 N
1300 PTGV 84062 2605 B7
W 2010 S
- SRCS 84075 1281 B1
S 2020 E
- UthC 84660 3250 D4
7500 SWBR 84405 1229 D2
9000 SNDY 84093 2177 D7
10000 SNDY 84092 2283 D3
W 2020 N
900 PTGV 84062 2605 C7
E 2025 N
500 NHON 84414 999 A7
E 2025 S
200 CRFD 84015 1281 E1
500 BNFL 84010 1654 A3
1300 OGDN 84401 1116 C2
N 2025 W
300 PRVO 84601 2927 D6
1000 LYTN 84041 1282 B2
S 2025 E
6100 WbrC 84403 1173 D6
S 2025 W
3900 ROY 84067 1114 D7
4500 TYVL 84119 2069 C2
4600 ROY 84067 1171 D2
12400 RIVN 84065 2387 C1
W 2025 N
10 CTRV 84014 1448 D6
2800 CLTN 84015 1170 C7
W 2025 S
800 WDCR 84087 1653 B3
2700 SRCS 84075 1280 C1
N 2030 W
1500 CLTN 84015 1226 E1
S 2030 W
4600 TYVL 84119 2069 C3
5200 TYVL 84118 2069 C4
W 2030 S
100 OREM 84058 2927 D3

STREET
Block City ZIP Map# Grid

S 2035 E
3700 SLkC 84109 1965 D7
E 2040 N
900 LEHI 84043 2603 D3
N 2040 W
1400 PRVO 84604 2927 D4
S 2040 W
3100 WVCY 84119 1963 C5
5300 TYVL 84118 2069 C5
9000 WJDN 84088 2175 C7
13400 RIVN 84065 2387 C4
W 2040 N
100 LEHI 84043 2603 B3
W 2040 S
100 OREM 84058 2927 D3
S 2045 E
3100 SLkC 84109 1965 D5
S 2045 W
3500 WVCY 84119 1963 C6
E 2050 N
- LOGN 84341 464 A5
- NHON 84414 999 A7
10 CTRV 84014 1448 D6
10 PRVO 84604 2928 C3
100 NHON 84414 998 D7
1200 NHLN 84341 464 B5
1400 PRVO 84604 2929 A3
2100 LYTN 84040 1283 E1
2500 LYTN 84040 1229 E6
2500 LYTN 84040 1230 A7
3800 WbrC 84310 1001 B7
E 2050 S
400 BNFL 84010 1653 E3
500 BNFL 84010 1654 A3
500 CRFD 84015 1281 E1
700 CRFD 84015 1282 A1
N 2050 E
10 LYTN 84040 1283 D4
2200 LYTN 84040 1229 D7
N 2050 W
500 WPT 84015 1226 E3
1600 PRVO 84604 2927 D3
S 2050 E
10 LYTN 84040 1283 D5
1500 SPFK 84660 3250 B5
5000 HLDY 84117 2071 D4
6200 WbrC 84403 1173 D6
7700 SWBR 84405 1229 E3
10100 SNDY 84092 2283 D3
S 2050 W
10 PRVO 84601 2927 D7
400 PRVO 84601 3034 D1
500 MTSV 84404 1055 D6
1600 WHVN 84401 1114 D1
2000 WJDN 84088 2281 C1
2100 SRCS 84075 1280 E2
3100 WVCY 84119 1963 C5
3700 ROY 84067 1114 D7
4400 ROY 84067 1171 D2
13000 RIVN 84065 2387 C3
W 2050 N
10 SPFK 84660 3142 C6
10 SNST 84015 1171 D7
500 HARR 84414 998 C7
500 WBNF 84087 1551 C4
600 PRVO 84604 2928 B3
1000 CLTN 84015 1171 A7
3000 CLTN 84015 1170 E7
4400 PNCY 84404 996 C7
W 2050 S
10 BNFL 84010 1653 D3
100 CRFD 84015 1281 D1
100 PRRY 84302 827 E4
1100 WHVN 84401 1115 A2
1200 WDCR 84087 1653 A3
1300 WDCR 84087 1652 E3
3300 SRCS 84075 1280 B1
S 2055 W
13900 BFDL 84065 2387 C5
W 2055 S
1600 SRCS 84075 1281 A1
E 2060 N
500 PRVO 84604 2928 D3
1400 NHLN 84341 464 C5
N 2060 W
1800 LEHI 84043 2602 D3
S 2060 E
2100 SLCY 84109 1965 D2
W 2060 N
10 PRVO 84604 2928 C3
200 SNST 84015 1171 D7
W 2060 S
- WDCR 84087 1652 E3
2000 SRCS 84075 1280 E1
S 2065 E
7200 CDHT 84121 2177 D2
E 2070 N
800 LEHI 84043 2603 D3
N 2070 W
2100 CLTN 84015 1170 E7
S 2070 E
3300 SLkC 84109 1965 E6
S 2070 W
8700 WJDN 84088 2175 C6
10700 SJDN 84095 2281 C4
12000 RIVN 84065 2387 C1
W 2070 S
- OREM 84058 2927 D3
E 2075 S
10 OREM 84058 2927 D3
700 BNFL 84010 1654 A3
N 2075 E
1500 LYTN 84040 1283 E2
N 2075 W
900 FRWT 84404 1055 D3
2500 FRWT 84404 997 D6
S 2075 E
3000 SLkC 84109 1965 E5
5800 HLDY 84121 2071 E6
6700 CDHT 84121 2177 E1
S 2075 W
3900 ROY 84067 1114 D7
4200 ROY 84067 1171 D1
7100 WJDN 84084 2175 C2
12400 RIVN 84065 2387 C1
W 2075 N
400 HARR 84414 998 C7
900 CLTN 84015 1171 B7
2100 CLTN 84015 1170 E7
W 2075 S
- SRCS 84075 1281 B1
700 WDCR 84087 1653 B3
2800 SRCS 84075 1280 C1
W 2075 N Cir
500 CTRV 84014 1448 C6
E 2080 N
1100 PRVO 84604 2928 E3
N 2080 W
2200 LEHI 84043 2602 D2
S 2080 E
700 SGVL 84663 3144 B3
S 2080 W
4600 TYVL 84119 2069 B3
13500 RIVN 84065 2387 C4
W 2080 N
500 CLTN 84015 1171 C7
600 WBNF 84087 1551 C4
W 2085 N
600 CLTN 84015 1171 C7
E 2090 N
100 PRVO 84604 2928 C3
N 2090 E
- SRSP 84043 2710 A3
N 2090 W
1400 CLTN 84015 1226 E1
2000 CLTN 84015 1170 E7
S 2090 E
2700 SLCY 84109 1965 E4
2700 SLkC 84109 1965 E4
S 2090 W
12200 RIVN 84065 2387 C1
W 2090 N
- WBNF 84087 1551 B4
N 2095 W
1900 CLTN 84015 1170 E7
W 2095 N
- WBNF 84087 1551 B4
E 2100 N
- LYTN 84040 1230 A7
100 CTRV 84014 1448 E6
100 NHON 84414 998 D7
100 PRVO 84604 2928 C3
400 NHON 84414 999 A7
800 LOGN 84341 464 B5
800 NHLN 84341 464 B5
2000 LYTN 84040 1229 D7
5500 WbrC 84310 1002 A7
E 2100 S
- MLVI 84321 591 D1
10 CRFD 84015 1281 D1
10 SLCY 84115 1964 D2
10 SSLK 84115 1964 D2
200 BNFL 84010 1653 E3
300 CchC 84332 591 E1
500 SLCY 84105 1964 D2
500 SLCY 84106 1964 D2
1000 SLCY 84105 1965 A2
1000 SLCY 84106 1965 A2
1300 SLCY 84106 1965 D2
1700 SLCY 84108 1965 D2
2000 SLCY 84109 1965 D2
2300 SLCY 84108 1966 A2
2300 SLCY 84109 1966 A2
E 2100 S SR-201
10 SLCY 84115 1964 C2
10 SSLK 84115 1964 C2
N 2100 E
2000 LYTN 84040 1229 D7
2000 LYTN 84040 1283 E1
N 2100 W
- CchC 84319 650 D1
- HYRM 84319 650 D1
100 SLCY 84116 1857 B2
500 WPT 84015 1226 E3
1000 LYTN 84041 1282 A2
1400 PRVO 84604 2927 D4
1700 OREM 84058 2927 D4
S 2100 E
500 SGVL 84663 3144 B3
500 UthC 84606 3144 B3
800 SLCY 84108 1859 E7
1600 SLCY 84108 1965 E2
2100 SLCY 84109 1965 E2
3200 SLkC 84109 1965 E5
5000 HLDY 84117 2071 E4
5800 HLDY 84121 2071 E6
7500 SWBR 84405 1229 E3
9000 SNDY 84093 2177 E7
S 2100 E SR-186
800 SLCY 84108 1859 E6
S 2100 W
- LEHI 84043 2602 D7
200 MTSV 84404 1055 D6
1100 SRCS 84075 1226 E7
1600 MPTN 84664 3250 D2
3700 ROY 84067 1114 D7
4400 ROY 84067 1171 D2
9400 SJDN 84095 2281 B1
10000 UthC 84651 3355 C5
W 2100 N
- LYTN 84041 1228 C7
10 LEHI 84043 2603 A3
10 SNST 84015 1171 D7
500 HARR 84414 998 C7
600 PTGV 84062 2605 B7
700 PRVO 84604 2928 A3
1100 CLTN 84015 1171 B7
2000 SLCY 84116 1753 A4
2000 SLkC 84116 1753 B4
2600 CLTN 84015 1170 D7
2700 SLCY 84116 1752 D4
2700 SLkC 84116 1752 D4
3400 PNCY 84404 997 A7
4300 PNCY 84404 996 C7
W 2100 S
- OREM 84058 2927 D3
10 CRFD 84015 1281 D1
10 PRRY 84302 827 D4
10 SLCY 84115 1964 B2
10 SSLK 84115 1964 B2
600 SLCY 84104 1964 B2
600 SLCY 84119 1964 B2
600 SSLK 84119 1964 B2
800 WDCR 84087 1653 B3
900 SLCY 84104 1963 D2
900 SSLK 84119 1963 D2
1000 SLCY 84119 1963 D2
1000 SSLK 84104 1963 D2
1300 WDCR 84087 1652 E3
2100 SRCS 84075 1280 D1
2300 WVCY 84119 1963 A2
3000 SLCY 84104 1962 E2
3100 WVCY 84119 1962 E2
3300 WbrC 84401 1114 A2
3600 WVCY 84120 1962 C2
4000 WbrC 84401 1113 D2
4000 WVCY 84120 1961 E2
5000 SLCY 84104 1961 D2
5600 WVCY 84128 1961 C2
7200 SLCY 84044 1960 E2
7200 SLCY 84104 1960 E2
7200 SLCY 84128 1960 E2
7200 SLkC 84044 1960 E2
W 2100 S SR-201
10 SLCY 84115 1964 B2
10 SSLK 84115 1964 B2
600 SLCY 84104 1964 B2
600 SLCY 84119 1964 B2
600 SSLK 84119 1964 B2
2100 S Frwy
- SLCY - 1961 E2
- SLCY - 1962 B2
- SLCY - 1963 C2
- SLCY - 1964 A2
- SSLK - 1963 C2
- SSLK - 1964 A2
- WVCY - 1961 B2
- WVCY - 1962 D2
- WVCY - 1963 C2
2100 S Frwy SR-201
- SLCY - 1961 E2
- SLCY - 1962 D2
- SLCY - 1963 C2
- SLCY - 1964 A2
- SSLK - 1963 C2
- SSLK - 1964 A2
- WVCY - 1961 B2
- WVCY - 1962 B2
- WVCY - 1963 C2
E 2110 S
200 HRCY 84032 2398 D7
S 2110 E
3500 SLkC 84109 1965 E6
5200 HLDY 84117 2071 E5
S 2110 W
9000 WJDN 84088 2175 B7
12000 RIVN 84065 2281 C7
13000 RIVN 84065 2387 B3
W 2115 S
1600 SRCS 84075 1281 A1
E 2120 N
10 PRVO 84604 2928 C3
600 LOGN 84341 464 A5
S 2120 E
1400 SPFK 84660 3250 B5
4800 HLDY 84117 2071 E3
S 2120 W
10 PRVO 84601 2927 D7
13200 RIVN 84065 2387 C3
W 2120 N
- LEHI 84043 2602 D3
1300 CLTN 84015 1171 A7
2200 CLTN 84015 1170 D7
S 2124 E
4700 HLDY 84117 2071 E3
S 2124 W
7000 UthC 84660 3248 C4
E 2125 N
600 LOGN 84341 464 A5
800 LEHI 84043 2603 D3
1000 LYTN 84040 1229 C7
N 2125 E
2700 LYTN 84040 1229 D6
N 2125 W
900 FRWT 84404 1055 D3
1900 CLTN 84015 1170 E7
2400 FRWT 84404 997 D6
S 2125 E
3200 SLkC 84109 1965 E5
6600 UNTH 84405 1173 E7
8100 SWBR 84405 1229 E4
S 2125 W
700 SRCS 84075 1226 E6
2100 SRCS 84075 1280 E1
5000 ROY 84067 1171 D3
W 2125 N
400 HARR 84414 998 C7
400 SNST 84015 1171 C7
500 LYTN 84041 1228 D7
500 WBNF 84087 1551 C4
4400 PNCY 84404 996 C7
W 2125 S
700 WDCR 84087 1653 B3
1400 SRCS 84075 1281 A1
2700 SRCS 84075 1280 C1
S 2130 E
3300 SLkC 84109 1965 E6
10000 SNDY 84092 2283 E3
S 2130 W
- PRVO 84601 2927 D7
- PRVO 84601 3034 D1
S 2135 E
7400 CDHT 84121 2177 E3
N 2140 E
- NHLN 84341 464 E2
N 2140 W
1600 CLTN 84015 1226 E1
S 2140 E
3600 SLkC 84109 1965 E7
S 2140 W
13500 RIVN 84065 2387 B4
W 2140 N
600 CLTN 84015 1171 C7
700 LEHI 84043 2603 A3
N 2145 W
1800 LEHI 84043 2602 D3
S 2145 E
3500 SLkC 84109 1965 E6
S 2145 W
12400 RIVN 84065 2387 B1
E 2150 N
10 LYTN 84041 1228 E7
10 LYTN 84041 1229 A7
2200 LYTN 84040 1229 E7
E 2150 S
400 BNFL 84010 1653 E3
500 BNFL 84010 1654 A3
800 CRFD 84015 1282 A2
N 2150 E
- NHLN 84341 464 E3
1900 LYTN 84040 1283 E1
3100 DvsC 84040 1229 E5
3100 LYTN 84040 1229 E5
N 2150 W
300 PRVO 84601 2927 D6
500 WPT 84015 1226 E3
1000 LYTN 84041 1282 A2
1400 CLTN 84015 1226 E1
2200 LEHI 84043 2602 D2
6100 AMGA 84335 398 D1
6500 HYVL 84314 646 E3
S 2150 W
300 MTSV 84404 1055 D5
4300 ROY 84067 1171 D2
5200 TYVL 84118 2069 B5
W 2150 N
- LEHI 84043 2602 D3
10 CTRV 84014 1448 D6
10 LYTN 84041 1228 E7
300 LEHI 84043 2603 B3
500 HARR 84414 998 C7
700 PRVO 84604 2928 A3
800 CLTN 84015 1171 B7
1100 WbrC 84404 998 A7
4700 PNCY 84404 996 A7
W 2150 S
- SRCS 84075 1281 C2
100 CRFD 84015 1281 D2
800 WDCR 84087 1653 B3
2100 SRCS 84075 1280 D1
3600 WVCY 84120 1962 D2
S 2155 E
7000 CDHT 84121 2177 E2
E 2160 N
100 SPFK 84660 3142 D6
600 LOGN 84341 464 A5
S 2160 E
- SWBR 84405 1229 E2
7400 CDHT 84121 2177 E3
S 2160 W
6800 WJDN 84084 2175 B2
12000 RIVN 84065 2281 B7
12000 RIVN 84065 2387 B1
W 2160 N
1900 CLTN 84015 1170 E7
N 2165 W
1900 CLTN 84015 1170 E7
S 2165 E
10000 SNDY 84092 2283 E3
E 2170 N
600 LOGN 84341 464 A4
S 2170 W
10800 UthC 84651 3355 C7
W 2170 N
10 PRVO 84604 2928 C3
W 2170 S
- OREM 84058 2927 D3
S 2172 W
7300 WJDN 84084 2175 B3
E 2175 N
- NHON 84414 999 A7
400 NHON 84414 998 E7
N 2175 E
3200 LYTN 84040 1229 E5
3400 DvsC 84040 1229 E5
N 2175 W
1800 FRWT 84404 1055 D1
S 2175 E
3500 SLkC 84109 1965 E6
3900 HLDY 84124 1965 E7
6100 WbrC 84405 1173 E6
6400 UNTH 84405 1173 E7
7800 SWBR 84405 1229 E3
S 2175 W
4000 ROY 84067 1171 D1
W 2175 N
500 LYTN 84041 1228 D7
1100 CLTN 84015 1171 B7
1800 LEHI 84043 2602 D3
2600 CLTN 84015 1170 D7
W 2175 S
100 SGVL 84663 3143 C6
700 WDCR 84087 1653 B3
1100 SRCS 84075 1281 A2
1300 WDCR 84087 1652 E3
2600 SRCS 84075 1280 D2
2700 WHVN 84401 1114 B3
E 2180 N
800 LEHI 84043 2603 D3
1100 NHLN 84341 464 B4
S 2180 E
1500 SPFK 84660 3250 B6
6000 HLDY 84121 2071 E6
S 2180 W
7100 WJDN 84084 2175 B2
W 2180 N
600 LEHI 84043 2603 A3
1000 SLCY 84116 1753 E4
1400 PTGV 84062 2605 B6
E 2190 N
100 PRVO 84604 2928 C3
S 2190 E
1400 SPFK 84660 3250 B5
2100 SLkC 84109 1965 E6
N 2195 W
- CLTN 84015 1226 E2
1900 CLTN 84015 1170 E7
E 2200 N
10 LEHI 84043 2603 C3
10 LOGN 84341 463 E4
10 LYTN 84041 1228 E7
10 NHLN 84341 463 E4
200 PRVO 84604 2928 D2
400 LOGN 84341 464 A4
400 NHLN 84341 464 A4
500 NHON 84414 998 E7
500 NHON 84414 999 A7
1400 LYTN 84040 1229 C7
2900 LYTN 84040 1230 A7
5200 WbrC 84310 1001 E7
5200 WbrC 84310 1002 A7
E 2200 S
- FMTN 84025 1345 D6
- KYVL 84037 1345 D6
10 BNFL 84010 1653 E3
500 CRFD 84015 1281 E2
600 CRFD 84015 1282 A2
1000 BNFL 84010 1654 B4
2200 SPFK 84660 3250 B6
N 2200 E
- NHLN 84341 464 E3
1200 LYTN 84040 1283 E2
3000 LYTN 84040 1229 E5
N 2200 W
10 LYTN 84041 1282 A3
10 LYTN 84075 1282 A3
10 SLCY 84104 1857 B2
100 SLCY 84116 1857 B2
400 WPT 84015 1226 E3
600 PRVO 84601 2927 D5
700 SLCY 84116 1753 B7
1500 CRFD 84015 1282 A3
1500 CRFD 84041 1282 A3
1700 LYTN 84015 1282 A3
1900 SLkC 84116 1753 B3
2400 FRWT 84404 997 D6
3100 SLkC 84116 1652 A7
7000 HYVL 84314 646 E2
S 2200 E
- SGVL 84663 3144 B4
800 SLCY 84108 1859 E5
1600 SLCY 84108 1965 E1
2100 SLCY 84109 1965 E2
6300 HLDY 84121 2071 E7
6500 CDHT 84121 2177 E1
6600 UNTH 84405 1173 E7
S 2200 W
10 LYTN 84041 1282 A6
10 LYTN 84075 1282 A6
1000 SRCS 84075 1226 E7
2100 SRCS 84075 1280 E2
3500 WVCY 84119 1963 B7
4000 WVCY 84119 2069 B1
4100 TYVL 84119 2069 B2
4700 TYVL 84118 2069 B4
5000 ROY 84067 1171 C3
6200 TYVL 84084 2069 B7
6500 TYVL 84084 2175 B2
6500 WJDN 84084 2175 B2
7300 UthC 84660 3248 C5
7800 WJDN 84088 2175 B6
8400 UthC 84660 3355 C1
9200 WJDN 84088 2281 B1
9400 SJDN 84095 2281 B1
12300 RIVN 84065 2387 B2
13800 BFDL 84065 2387 B6
14800 BFDL 84065 2494 B1
W 2200 N
- CchC 84341 463 A4
10 LYTN 84041 1228 E7
10 NHLN 84341 463 D4
100 LEHI 84043 2603 B3
300 SNST 84015 1171 C7
500 HARR 84414 998 C7
600 LOGN 84341 463 B4
700 CLTN 84015 1171 C7
900 PTGV 84062 2605 C6
2900 PNCY 84404 997 A7
2900 WbrC 84404 997 A7
3400 PNCY 84404 996 D7
4100 CRNN 84307 704 E7
4100 CRNN 84307 764 E1
W 2200 N SR-134
4200 PNCY 84404 996 C7
W 2200 S
10 BNFL 84010 1653 D3
10 CRFD 84015 1281 D2
800 CchC 84321 591 A1
800 NBLY 84321 591 A1
1000 LOGN 84321 591 A1
1300 CchC 84321 590 E1
1300 WDCR 84087 1652 E3
1900 WHVN 84401 1114 C3
2000 CchC 84339 590 D1
2100 OREM 84058 2927 D3
2100 PRVO 84604 2927 D3
2700 WVCY 84119 1963 A2
3200 CchC 84321 589 E1
3200 CchC 84339 589 E1
3500 WbrC 84401 1113 D3
4200 DvsC 84075 1280 A2
4200 SRCS 84075 1280 A2
N 2210 W
400 PRVO 84601 2927 D6
S 2210 E
3500 SLkC 84109 1965 E6
S 2210 W
300 PRVO 84601 2927 D7
1700 SRCS 84075 1280 E1
W 2210 S
3100 WVCY 84119 1962 E2
3100 WVCY 84119 1963 A2
S 2215 E
3800 SLkC 84109 1965 E7
N 2220 W
300 PRVO 84601 2927 D6
1000 CLTN 84015 1226 E2
S 2220 E
7100 CDHT 84121 2177 E2
W 2220 N
700 LEHI 84043 2603 A3
2300 CLTN 84015 1170 E7
E 2225 N
500 NHON 84414 999 A7
E 2225 S
10 CRFD 84015 1281 D2
N 2225 E
1900 LYTN 84040 1283 E1
3500 LYTN 84040 1229 E4
N 2225 W
1300 LYTN 84041 1282 A2
1400 CLTN 84015 1226 E1
1800 CLTN 84015 1170 E7
S 2225 E
3000 SLkC 84109 1965 E5
4600 HLDY 84117 2071 E3
6100 WbrC 84403 1173 E6
7700 SWBR 84405 1229 E3
S 2225 W
3800 ROY 84067 1114 D7
6000 ROY 84067 1171 C6
6000 SNST 84015 1171 C6
W 2225 N
100 LEHI 84043 2603 B3
200 SNST 84015 1171 D7
900 CLTN 84015 1171 B7
W 2225 S
300 CRFD 84015 1281 C2
500 SRCS 84075 1281 C2
800 WDCR 84087 1653 B3
2800 SRCS 84075 1280 C2
E 2230 N
10 PRVO 84604 2928 C2
N 2230 E
- SRSP 84043 2710 A3
N 2230 W
- LEHI 84043 2602 D3
S 2230 E
1000 SPFK 84660 3250 B5
6000 HLDY 84121 2071 E6
10300 SNDY 84092 2283 E3
S 2230 W
4100 TYVL 84119 2069 B1
7500 WJDN 84084 2175 B3
W 2230 N
10 PRVO 84604 2928 B2
S 2235 E
3700 SLkC 84109 1965 E7
W 2235 S
- PRRY 84302 827 D4
N 2240 E
1500 LYTN 84040 1283 E2
S 2240 E
6700 CDHT 84121 2177 E1
9800 SNDY 84092 2283 E2
S 2240 W
8700 WJDN 84088 2175 B6
11800 RIVN 84065 2281 B7
12000 RIVN 84065 2387 B1
W 2240 N
600 CLTN 84015 1171 C7
600 PTGV 84062 2605 C6
W 2240 S
1100 WVCY 84119 1963 E2
S 2245 E
3500 SLkC 84109 1965 E6
S 2245 W
8100 WJDN 84088 2175 B5
E 2250 N
10 LEHI 84043 2603 C2
10 LYTN 84041 1228 E7
1200 NHON 84414 999 C7
1400 LYTN 84040 1229 C7
1400 NHLN 84341 464 C4
2500 LYTN 84040 1230 A7
E 2250 S
10 BNFL 84010 1653 E3
10 CRFD 84015 1281 D2
400 SSLK 84115 1964 E2
N 2250 E
200 LYTN 84040 1283 E4
3000 LYTN 84040 1229 E5
N 2250 W
- SGVL 84663 3035 D7
- SGVL 84663 3142 D1
100 MTSV 84404 1055 C4
600 PRVO 84601 2927 D5
900 FRWT 84404 1055 C3
2300 FRWT 84404 997 C6
S 2250 E
1500 SPFK 84660 3250 B5
3900 HLDY 84124 1965 E7
7100 CDHT 84121 2177 E2
7800 SWBR 84405 1229 E3
S 2250 W
- SGVL 84663 3142 D2
100 MTSV 84404 1055 C5
4200 TYVL 84119 2069 B1
4400 ROY 84067 1171 C2
7600 WJDN 84084 2175 B4
W 2250 N
10 LYTN 84041 1228 E7
300 SNST 84015 1171 C7
500 HARR 84414 998 C7
600 WBNF 84087 1551 B4
1100 CLTN 84015 1171 B7
1800 LEHI 84043 2602 D3
2800 CLTN 84015 1170 C7
W 2250 S
700 WDCR 84087 1653 B3
1300 WDCR 84087 1652 E3
1300 WVCY 84119 1963 D2
1800 SRCS 84075 1280 E2
1800 SRCS 84075 1281 A2
E 2260 N
400 PRVO 84604 2928 D2
E 2260 S
800 PRVO 84606 3035 E4
N 2260 W
400 PRVO 84601 2927 D6
1500 LEHI 84043 2602 D4
S 2260 E
7000 CDHT 84121 2177 E2
10300 SNDY 84092 2283 E3
S 2260 W
4100 TYVL 84119 2069 B1
11600 SJDN 84095 2281 B7
13500 RIVN 84065 2387 B5
W 2260 N
700 LEHI 84043 2603 A2
W 2260 S
100 SSLK 84115 1964 C2
S 2265 W
1800 SRCS 84075 1280 E1
W 2265 N
2100 CLTN 84015 1170 E7
E 2270 N
600 PRVO 84604 2928 D2
N 2270 W
- LEHI 84043 2602 D3
200 PRVO 84601 2927 D6
S 2270 E
7200 CDHT 84121 2177 E2
9800 SNDY 84092 2283 E2
S 2270 W
11300 SJDN 84095 2281 B6
W 2270 S
3600 WVCY 84120 1962 D2
E 2275 N
300 NHON 84414 998 E7
5100 WbrC 84310 1001 E6
E 2275 S
10 CRFD 84015 1281 D2
N 2275 E
2000 LYTN 84040 1229 D7
N 2275 W
1300 LYTN 84041 1282 A2
1400 CLTN 84015 1226 E1
2300 CLTN 84015 1170 E6
S 2275 E
6200 HLDY 84121 2071 E7
6200 WbrC 84403 1173 E6
6600 UNTH 84405 1173 E7
6700 UNTH 84405 1229 E1
6700 WbrC 84405 1229 E1
8100 SWBR 84405 1229 E4
S 2275 W
3700 ROY 84067 1114 C7
4000 ROY 84067 1171 C1
10400 SJDN 84095 2281 B4
W 2275 N
900 LYTN 84041 1228 D7
4200 PNCY 84404 996 C7
W 2275 S
1100 SRCS 84075 1281 B2
N 2280 W
100 SLCY 84116 1857 B2
S 2280 E
3900 HLDY 84124 1965 E7
S 2280 W
4600 UthC 84660 3141 C5
8500 WJDN 84088 2175 B6
W 2280 N
100 PRVO 84604 2928 B2
300 LEHI 84043 2603 B2
W 2280 S
- SRCS 84075 1280 B2
1300 WVCY 84119 1963 D2
S 2285 W
1800 SRCS 84075 1280 E1
E 2290 S
- SLCY 84106 1965 B2
N 2290 W
2000 CLTN 84015 1170 E7
S 2290 W
7500 WJDN 84084 2175 B3
W 2290 N
10 LEHI 84043 2603 C2
W 2290 S
- WDCR 84087 1652 E3
E 2300 N
10 LEHI 84043 2603 C2
10 LYTN 84041 1228 E7
100 NHON 84414 998 E6
500 NHON 84414 999 A6
1100 LYTN 84040 1229 C7
1200 NHLN 84341 464 C4
1200 PRVO 84604 2928 E2
1400 PRVO 84604 2929 A2
5500 WbrC 84310 1002 A6
E 2300 S
10 CchC 84332 591 E2
10 MLVI 84321 591 E2
10 MLVI 84332 591 E2
200 BNFL 84010 1653 E4
N 2300 E
- NHLN 84341 464 E2
100 LYTN 84040 1283 E4
3600 LYTN 84040 1229 E4
N 2300 W
- LEHI 84043 2602 D2
- LOGN 84341 526 C2
200 PRVO 84601 2927 D6
300 WPT 84015 1226 D3
400 SLCY 84116 1857 A1
700 TMTN 84337 520 A5
1500 PRVO 84604 2927 D4
1700 FRWT 84404 1055 C1
S 2300 E
800 SGVL 84663 3144 B4
800 SLCY 84108 1859 E5
1000 SPFK 84660 3250 B6
1600 SLCY 84108 1965 E1
2100 SLCY 84109 1965 E1
2700 SLkC 84109 1965 E4
4100 HLDY 84124 2071 E1
4500 HLDY 84117 2071 E1
5900 HLDY 84121 2071 E7
6100 WbrC 84403 1173 E6
6300 CDHT 84121 2071 E7
6500 CDHT 84121 2177 E1
8000 SWBR 84405 1229 E3
S 2300 E SR-195
2700 SLCY 84109 1965 E5
2700 SLkC 84109 1965 E5
4100 HLDY 84124 2071 E1
S 2300 W
- SRCS 84075 1226 E6
900 LEHI 84043 2602 D4
2200 WHVN 84401 1114 C3
4200 ROY 84067 1171 C1
10300 PYSN 84651 3355 C5
10300 UthC 84651 3355 C5
W 2300 N
- PTGV 84062 2605 C6
10 SNST 84015 1171 B7
300 HARR 84414 998 C7
300 WbrC 84414 998 C7
500 CLTN 84015 1171 B7
600 WBNF 84087 1551 B4
700 PRVO 84604 2928 A2
1000 SLCY 84116 1753 D3
1100 LYTN 84041 1228 C7
1500 CLTN 84015 1170 E7
W 2300 S
- WJDN 84088 2175 B5
10 CRFD 84015 1281 D2
200 BNFL 84010 1653 D4
300 PRRY 84302 827 D4
900 SSLK 84119 1963 E2
1300 WDCR 84087 1652 E3
2900 SRCS 84075 1280 C2
5600 WVCY 84128 1961 D3
2300 S
- CchC 84325 588 D2
- CchC 84339 588 D2
S 2305 W
4100 TYVL 84119 2069 B1
N 2310 W
500 PRVO 84601 2927 D5
S 2310 E
7800 SWBR 84405 1229 E3
S 2310 W
5000 TYVL 84118 2069 B4
7000 WJDN 84084 2175 B2
W 2310 N
- CTRV 84014 1551 B4
700 PTGV 84062 2605 C6
S 2315 W
8400 WJDN 84088 2175 B6
E 2320 N
200 PRVO 84604 2928 D2
S 2320 E
1300 SPFK 84660 3250 C5
S 2320 W
6900 WJDN 84084 2175 B2
12300 RIVN 84065 2387 B1
W 2320 S
1000 WVCY 84119 1963 D2

STREET Block City ZIP Map# Grid

E 2325 N
1300 NHON 84414 999 C7
2900 LYTN 84040 1230 A7
E 2325 S
10 CRFD 84015 1281 D2
N 2325 E
2000 LYTN 84040 1229 D7
N 2325 W
- LYTN 84041 1282 A2
700 SLCY 84116 1753 A7
700 SLCY 84116 1857 A1
1500 CRFD 84015 1282 A2
1500 CRFD 84041 1282 A2
S 2325 E
7600 CDHT 84093 2177 E4
7900 SWBR 84405 1229 E3
S 2325 W
2100 SRCS 84075 1280 E2
4200 ROY 84067 1171 C1
W 2325 N
300 LEHI 84043 2603 B2
1000 LYTN 84041 1228 C7
W 2325 S
1300 SRCS 84075 1281 A2
2500 WHVN 84401 1114 B3
E 2330 N
600 NHLN 84341 464 A4
900 LEHI 84043 2603 D2
N 2330 W
300 PRVO 84601 2927 D6
S 2330 E
1500 SPFK 84660 3250 C5
S 2330 W
10400 SJDN 84095 2281 B4
W 2330 S
2800 SRCS 84075 1280 C2
N 2340 W
- PRVO 84601 2927 D5
1500 CLTN 84015 1226 E1
1500 LEHI 84043 2602 D4
S 2340 E
1400 SPFK 84660 3250 C5
7100 CDHT 84121 2177 E2
S 2340 W
4100 ROY 84067 1171 C1
8100 WJDN 84088 2175 B5
9700 SJDN 84095 2281 B2
W 2340 S
3600 WVCY 84120 1962 D3
S 2345 E
6700 CDHT 84121 2177 E1
S 2345 W
7300 WJDN 84084 2175 B3
E 2350 N
10 LEHI 84043 2603 C2
10 LYTN 84041 1228 E7
10 LYTN 84041 1229 A7
200 NHON 84414 998 E6
500 NHON 84414 999 A6
1400 LYTN 84040 1229 C7
E 2350 S
10 BNFL 84010 1653 D4
N 2350 E
200 LYTN 84040 1283 E4
3600 LYTN 84040 1229 E4
N 2350 W
- LEHI 84043 2602 D3
500 WPT 84015 1226 D3
800 PRVO 84601 2927 D5
2300 CLTN 84015 1170 D6
7100 HYVL 84314 646 D2
S 2350 E
- SGVL 84663 3144 C4
8000 SWBR 84405 1229 E3
8000 SWBR 84405 1230 A4
S 2350 W
1500 WHVN 84401 1114 C1
1700 SRCS 84075 1280 D1
4200 ROY 84067 1171 C2
7500 WJDN 84084 2175 B3
W 2350 N
- PNCY 84404 997 A7
300 HARR 84414 998 C7
400 SNST 84015 1171 C7
500 LYTN 84041 1228 D7
600 LEHI 84043 2603 A2
600 WBNF 84087 1551 B4
800 CLTN 84015 1171 B6
1200 WbrC 84404 998 A6
1500 WbrC 84404 997 E7
4200 PNCY 84404 996 C6
W 2350 S
200 BNFL 84010 1653 D4
500 PRRY 84302 827 D5
1300 WDCR 84087 1652 E4
1400 SRCS 84075 1281 A2
1800 SRCS 84075 1280 E2
N 2360 W
400 SLCY 84116 1857 A1
700 SLCY 84116 1753 A7
7000 CLTN 84015 1170 D7
S 2360 W
8100 WJDN 84088 2175 B5
12600 RIVN 84065 2387 B2
S 2365 E
6400 CDHT 84121 2071 E7
6400 CDHT 84121 2177 E1
S 2365 W
5000 TYVL 84118 2069 B4
W 2365 S
2500 WVCY 84119 1963 A3
N 2370 W
200 PRVO 84601 2927 C6
200 SLCY 84116 1857 A2
S 2370 E
1300 SPFK 84660 3250 C5
3900 HLDY 84124 1966 A7
S 2370 W
10 PRVO 84601 2927 D7
7000 WJDN 84084 2175 B2
8200 WJDN 84088 2175 B5
W 2370 N
800 PRVO 84604 2928 A2
E 2375 N
1200 LEHI 84043 2603 E2
1400 LYTN 84040 1229 C7
5400 WbrC 84310 1002 A6
N 2375 E
1200 LYTN 84040 1283 E2
3100 LYTN 84040 1229 E4
N 2375 W
1200 LYTN 84041 1282 A2

S 2375 E
6100 WbrC 84403 1173 E6
7600 CDHT 84093 2177 E4
10200 SNDY 84092 2283 E3
S 2375 W
1100 SRCS 84075 1226 D7
5100 ROY 84067 1171 C4
W 2375 N
300 LEHI 84043 2603 B2
2200 CLTN 84015 1170 D6
W 2375 S
- SRCS 84075 1280 E2
1300 SRCS 84075 1281 A2
N 2380 W
300 PRVO 84601 2927 C6
S 2380 E
1100 SPFK 84660 3250 C5
7400 CDHT 84121 2177 E3
W 2380 S
- CRFD 84015 1281 C2
- SRCS 84075 1281 C2
S 2385 W
8400 WJDN 84088 2175 B5
E 2390 N
800 PRVO 84604 2928 E2
S 2390 W
200 PRVO 84601 2927 D7
W 2390 S
900 PRRY 84302 827 C5
S 2395 W
14400 BFDL 84065 2387 B6
E 2400 N
300 NHLN 84341 463 E4
600 NHON 84414 999 A6
2200 LYTN 84040 1229 E7
E 2400 S
10 CRFD 84015 1281 D2
10 SSLK 84115 1964 D3
N 2400 E
200 LYTN 84040 1283 E4
3000 LYTN 84040 1229 E5
N 2400 W
10 SLCY 84104 1857 A2
100 SLCY 84116 1857 A2
400 WPT 84015 1226 D3
800 PRVO 84601 2927 C5
1400 LEHI 84043 2602 D4
1500 CLTN 84015 1226 D1
1600 CchC 84341 462 C5
2000 BxEC 84302 705 D6
2000 BxEC 84302 765 D1
2000 CLTN 84015 1170 D7
3600 FRWT 84404 997 C2
4500 CchC 84335 398 C5
S 2400 E
800 SGVL 84663 3144 C4
1000 SPFK 84660 3250 C4
1400 SLCY 84108 1860 A7
3500 SLkC 84109 1966 A6
6100 WbrC 84403 1173 E6
6300 UNTH 84405 1173 E7
7200 UthC 84660 3250 D4
S 2400 W
- SRCS 84075 1280 D3
10 SLCY 84104 1857 A3
400 SGVL 84663 3142 D3
1400 CchC 84321 526 C7
1800 CchC 84321 590 C2
1800 CchC 84339 526 C7
1800 CchC 84339 590 C2
3900 WVCY 84119 1963 B7
3900 WVCY 84119 2069 B1
4200 ROY 84067 1171 C1
5000 CchC 84319 650 C2
5000 CchC 84339 650 C2
6000 UthC 84660 3248 B3
7000 WJDN 84084 2175 B2
13700 RIVN 84065 2387 B5
14500 BFDL 84065 2387 B7
W 2400 N
- CTRV 84014 1551 B4
- CTRV 84087 1551 B4
- WshC 84032 2292 B7
10 LOGN 84341 463 D4
10 NHLN 84341 463 D4
200 SNST 84015 1171 C6
300 LYTN 84041 1228 D7
600 LEHI 84043 2603 A2
1000 CLTN 84015 1171 B6
4400 CRNN 84307 704 D7
5200 BxEC 84307 704 B7
W 2400 S
- CchC 84321 591 D2
- CRFD 84015 1281 D2
- WVCY 84128 1960 E3
- WVCY 84128 1961 A3
10 SSLK 84115 1964 C3
200 BNFL 84010 1653 C4
200 PRRY 84302 827 D5
700 SSLK 84119 1964 A3
900 MPTN 84664 3250 E3
1200 HRCY 84032 2505 A1
1200 WshC 84032 2504 E1
1200 WshC 84032 2505 A1
1300 WDCR 84087 1652 E4
1300 WVCY 84119 1963 D3
1700 SRCS 84075 1280 E2
1700 SRCS 84075 1281 A2
2500 CSTN 84032 2504 E1
2500 WHVN 84401 1114 B3
3200 WVCY 84119 1962 E3
3800 WVCY 84120 1962 C3
4500 WbrC 84401 1113 B3
4800 CchC 84325 589 A2
4800 CchC 84339 589 A2
5100 WVCY 84120 1961 E3
5400 CchC 84339 588 E2
7200 SLkC 84044 1960 E3
9000 SLkC 84044 1959 E3
9100 SLkC 84006 1959 E3
W 2400 S SR-201
- WVCY 84128 1960 E3
- WVCY 84128 1961 A3
7200 SLkC 84044 1960 E3
9000 SLkC 84044 1959 E3
9100 SLkC 84006 1959 E3
N 2400 St W
3400 CchC 84341 398 C7
3400 CchC 84341 462 C1
4600 CchC 84335 398 C7
5600 AMGA 84335 398 C1

N 2405 W
1900 CLTN 84015 1170 D7
S 2405 W
7400 WJDN 84084 2175 B3
14900 BFDL 84065 2494 B1
S 2410 E
1600 SPFK 84660 3250 C6
3300 SLkC 84109 1966 A6
W 2410 N
700 PTGV 84062 2605 C6
4100 PNCY 84404 996 C6
S 2415 E
10100 SNDY 84092 2284 A3
W 2415 N
2800 CLTN 84015 1170 C6
E 2420 N
200 NHLN 84341 463 E4
N 2420 W
200 PRVO 84601 2927 C6
S 2420 E
1100 SPFK 84660 3250 C5
10300 SNDY 84092 2284 A3
S 2420 W
7000 WJDN 84084 2175 B2
8100 WJDN 84088 2175 B5
10600 SJDN 84095 2281 B4
12900 RIVN 84065 2387 B3
E 2425 N
1200 LEHI 84043 2603 E2
2200 LYTN 84040 1229 E7
N 2425 W
1200 LYTN 84041 1282 A2
S 2425 E
6400 CDHT 84121 2178 A1
8100 SWBR 84405 1230 A4
S 2425 W
5200 ROY 84067 1171 C4
W 2425 N
300 HARR 84414 998 C6
3400 PNCY 84404 996 E6
4000 CLTN 84015 1170 A6
4000 DvsC 84015 1170 A6
4000 DvsC 84315 1169 E6
4000 DvsC 84315 1170 A6
4400 WbrC 84404 996 C6
W 2425 S
1100 WDCR 84087 1653 A4
1300 SRCS 84075 1281 A2
1800 WDCR 84087 1652 C4
N 2430 W
- TMTN 84337 520 A4
1200 PRVO 84601 2927 C4
1800 CLTN 84015 1226 D1
S 2430 W
300 PRVO 84601 2927 C7
1100 SRCS 84075 1226 D7
W 2430 N
10 PTGV 84062 2605 D6
W 2435 S
2800 SRCS 84075 1280 C2
E 2440 N
300 NHLN 84341 463 E4
N 2440 W
- TMTN 84337 520 A4
S 2440 E
- SPFK 84660 3250 C5
3000 SLkC 84109 1966 A5
S 2440 W
4200 TYVL 84119 2069 B1
8200 WJDN 84088 2175 B5
11800 RIVN 84065 2281 B7
N 2445 W
2600 CLTN 84015 1170 D6
S 2445 E
3500 SLkC 84109 1966 A6
6600 CDHT 84121 2178 A1
E 2450 N
- PRVO 84604 2928 D2
10 LYTN 84041 1228 E7
10 LYTN 84041 1229 A7
600 NHON 84414 999 A6
1000 LYTN 84040 1229 C7
1100 LEHI 84043 2603 E2
E 2450 S
10 CRFD 84015 1281 D2
100 BNFL 84010 1653 E4
N 2450 E
1900 LYTN 84040 1283 E1
2500 LYTN 84040 1229 E6
N 2450 W
- HYVL 84314 646 D2
- TMTN 84337 520 A5
500 WPT 84015 1226 D3
S 2450 E
1600 SPFK 84660 3250 C6
7800 SWBR 84405 1230 A3
S 2450 W
- SGVL 84663 3142 C2
800 SRCS 84075 1226 D6
4200 ROY 84067 1171 C1
7300 UthC 84660 3248 B5
7600 WJDN 84084 2175 B3
W 2450 N
100 LOGN 84341 463 D4
300 HARR 84414 998 C6
400 SNST 84015 1171 C6
600 LEHI 84043 2603 A2
800 PRVO 84604 2928 A2
900 LYTN 84041 1228 C7
1000 CLTN 84015 1171 B6
2300 CLTN 84015 1170 D6
W 2450 S
1400 WDCR 84087 1652 E4
1600 OGDN 84401 1114 E3
S 2455 E
3600 SLkC 84109 1966 A7
W 2455 S
5300 WVCY 84120 1961 E3
N 2460 W
- CLTN 84015 1226 D2
300 PRVO 84601 2927 C6
S 2460 E
10200 SNDY 84092 2284 A3
S 2465 E
9800 SNDY 84092 2284 A2
S 2465 W
1800 SRCS 84075 1280 D1
N 2470 W
1200 PRVO 84601 2927 C4
S 2470 W
200 PRVO 84601 2927 C7
400 PRVO 84601 3034 C1

S 2470 W
7000 WJDN 84084 2175 B2
7800 WJDN 84088 2175 B4
E 2475 N
- NHLN 84341 463 E4
600 NHON 84414 999 A6
1500 LYTN 84040 1229 D7
5400 WbrC 84310 1002 A6
E 2475 S
200 SGVL 84663 3143 C6
1700 BNFL 84010 1654 C4
N 2475 E
2600 LYTN 84040 1229 E6
N 2475 W
200 PRVO 84601 2927 C6
400 MTSV 84404 1055 C4
1400 LYTN 84041 1282 A2
1500 CLTN 84015 1226 D1
1800 CLTN 84015 1170 D7
S 2475 E
2700 SLkC 84109 1966 A4
6400 CDHT 84121 2178 A1
8000 SWBR 84405 1230 A3
S 2475 W
1100 SLCY 84104 1857 B6
3800 WVCY 84119 1963 B7
4600 ROY 84067 1171 C2
4800 TYVL 84118 2069 B4
15000 BFDL 84065 2494 B1
W 2475 N
- CLTN 84015 1170 E6
400 LYTN 84041 1228 D7
2100 FRWT 84404 997 C6
W 2475 S
700 NBLY 84321 591 B2
1600 SRCS 84075 1281 A2
1800 SRCS 84075 1280 E2
2000 WHVN 84401 1114 D3
4100 WbrC 84401 1113 C3
N 2480 W
900 PRVO 84601 2927 C5
S 2480 E
900 SPFK 84660 3250 C5
S 2480 W
7500 WJDN 84084 2175 B3
7800 WJDN 84088 2175 B4
11100 SJDN 84095 2281 B5
13200 RIVN 84065 2387 B4
S 2485 E
6700 CDHT 84121 2178 A1
S 2490 E
1400 SPFK 84660 3250 C5
4300 HLDY 84124 2072 A2
S 2490 W
9100 WJDN 84088 2175 B7
14800 BFDL 84065 2494 B1
S 2495 W
12200 RIVN 84065 2387 B1
W 2495 S
2800 SRCS 84075 1280 C2
E 2500 N
- LYTN 84040 1230 A7
- NHLN 84341 463 D4
100 LYTN 84041 1229 A7
500 NHON 84414 999 A6
700 NHLN 84341 464 A4
1000 PRVO 84604 2928 E2
1100 LYTN 84040 1229 C7
5600 WbrC 84310 1002 B6
E 2500 S
10 CRFD 84015 1281 D2
100 BNFL 84010 1653 E4
N 2500 W
1800 FRWT 84404 1055 C1
2300 CLTN 84015 1170 D6
2700 FRWT 84404 997 C5
6900 HYVL 84314 646 D2
S 2500 E
- SGVL 84663 3144 C3
10 LYTN 84040 1283 E5
1700 SLCY 84108 1966 A1
2300 SLCY 84109 1966 A3
3500 SLkC 84109 1966 A6
5900 WbrC 84403 1174 A6
8000 SWBR 84405 1230 A3
S 2500 W
700 SRCS 84075 1226 D7
1500 SRCS 84075 1280 D1
2200 WHVN 84401 1114 C3
2600 WVCY 84119 1963 B4
4400 ROY 84067 1171 C2
4500 WELV 84319 590 C7
4500 WELV 84319 650 C1
4700 CchC 84319 650 C1
7600 WJDN 84084 2175 B3
9400 SJDN 84095 2281 B1
W 2500 N
10 LOGN 84341 463 C4
10 LYTN 84041 1228 D7
800 LEHI 84043 2603 A2
1100 CLTN 84015 1171 B6
2000 FRWT 84404 997 D6
3000 CLTN 84015 1170 C6
4200 PNCY 84404 996 C6
W 2500 S
- NBLY 84321 591 B2
300 PRRY 84302 827 D5
400 CRFD 84015 1281 C2
500 BNFL 84010 1653 C4
500 WDCR 84010 1653 C4
800 SSLK 84119 1964 A3
1000 SRCS 84075 1281 B2
1400 WDCR 84087 1652 E4
2500 W
- HYVL 84314 646 D1
S 2505 E
10100 SNDY 84092 2284 A3
S 2510 E
1300 SPFK 84660 3250 C5
S 2510 W
11400 SJDN 84095 2281 B6
S 2515 W
2900 WVCY 84119 1963 B5
11200 SJDN 84095 2281 B5
E 2520 N
300 NHLN 84341 463 E3
N 2520 W
200 PRVO 84601 2927 C6
1600 LEHI 84043 2602 D3
S 2520 E
1500 SPFK 84660 3250 C5
2700 SLkC 84109 1966 A4

S 2520 E
6400 CDHT 84121 2072 C7
6400 CDHT 84121 2178 A1
S 2520 W
3800 WVCY 84119 1963 B7
W 2520 S
- BNFL 84010 1653 C4
900 PRRY 84302 827 C5
E 2525 N
1000 LYTN 84040 1229 C7
1400 NHON 84414 999 D6
E 2525 S
200 CRFD 84015 1281 E2
200 SGVL 84663 3143 C6
N 2525 E
1700 LYTN 84040 1283 E1
3700 SWBR 84405 1230 A4
N 2525 W
700 WPT 84015 1226 D3
1000 LYTN 84041 1281 E2
1400 CRFD 84015 1281 E2
2000 CLTN 84015 1170 D7
S 2525 E
8000 SWBR 84405 1230 A3
S 2525 W
- WHVN 84067 1114 B7
3900 ROY 84067 1114 C7
4400 ROY 84067 1171 C2
6200 TYVL 84084 2069 B7
W 2525 N
400 SNST 84015 1171 C6
900 LYTN 84041 1228 C7
W 2525 S
1600 SRCS 84075 1281 A2
N 2530 W
400 PRVO 84601 2927 C6
1400 CLTN 84015 1226 D1
1800 CLTN 84015 1170 D7
S 2530 W
10 PRVO 84601 2927 C7
7000 WJDN 84084 2175 B2
W 2530 N
700 LEHI 84043 2603 A2
N 2540 W
- LEHI 84043 2602 D4
1300 PRVO 84601 2927 C4
S 2540 E
2800 SLkC 84109 1966 A4
S 2540 W
2700 WVCY 84119 1963 B4
4100 TYVL 84119 2069 B2
7400 WJDN 84084 2175 B3
W 2540 N
300 LEHI 84043 2603 B2
E 2550 N
10 LEHI 84043 2603 C2
100 NHON 84414 998 E6
100 NHON 84414 999 A6
700 PRVO 84604 2928 D2
1100 LYTN 84040 1229 C6
2400 LYTN 84040 1230 A6
E 2550 N SR-235
100 NHON 84414 998 E6
E 2550 S
10 CRFD 84015 1281 D2
N 2550 E
1800 LYTN 84040 1284 A1
1900 LYTN 84040 1283 E1
3200 LYTN 84040 1229 E5
3200 LYTN 84040 1230 A4
3700 SWBR 84405 1230 A4
N 2550 W
- FRWT 84404 997 C3
100 MTSV 84404 1055 C5
300 WPT 84015 1226 D3
600 PRVO 84601 2927 C5
2600 CLTN 84015 1170 D6
6900 HYVL 84314 646 D2
S 2550 E
- SPFK 84660 3250 C5
10 LYTN 84040 1284 A5
900 SGVL 84663 3144 C3
5800 WbrC 84403 1174 A5
8000 SWBR 84405 1230 A3
S 2550 W
100 MTSV 84404 1055 C5
5600 ROY 84067 1171 C5
7600 WJDN 84084 2175 B3
13200 RIVN 84065 2387 B4
W 2550 N
100 NHON 84414 998 C6
100 PTVW 84414 998 C6
600 CLTN 84015 1171 B6
900 LEHI 84043 2603 A2
4100 PNCY 84404 996 D6
4900 WbrC 84310 1001 E6
W 2550 N SR-235
100 NHON 84414 998 C6
100 PTVW 84414 998 C6
W 2550 S
10 BNFL 84010 1653 D4
600 PRRY 84302 827 D5
1100 OGDN 84401 1115 A4
1100 WbrC 84401 1115 A4
1400 OGDN 84401 1114 E4
1400 WDCR 84087 1652 E4
1800 WHVN 84401 1114 E4
3100 WbrC 84401 1113 E4
3100 WbrC 84401 1114 A4
S 2555 E
4700 HLDY 84117 2072 A3
S 2555 W
9300 WJDN 84088 2281 B1
9400 SJDN 84095 2281 B1
W 2555 S
3200 WVCY 84119 1962 E3
N 2560 W
10 PRVO 84601 2927 C6
1600 LEHI 84043 2602 C3
S 2560 E
8200 SWBR 84405 1230 A4
S 2560 W
13100 RIVN 84065 2387 B3
S 2565 W
12600 RIVN 84065 2387 B2
W 2565 N
3400 PNCY 84404 996 E6
W 2567 N
10 LYTN 84041 1228 D7
E 2570 N
1000 PRVO 84604 2928 E2

N 2570 W
1100 LYTN 84041 1281 E2
S 2570 W
2300 WVCY 84119 1963 B3
6800 WJDN 84084 2175 B1
11400 SJDN 84095 2281 B6
E 2575 N
- WbrC 84310 1002 A6
N 2575 E
1200 LYTN 84040 1284 A2
1500 LYTN 84040 1283 E1
N 2575 W
500 WPT 84015 1226 D3
1200 LYTN 84041 1281 E2
2200 CLTN 84015 1170 D7
2900 FRWT 84404 997 B4
S 2575 E
8000 SWBR 84405 1230 A3
S 2575 W
4600 ROY 84067 1171 B2
W 2575 N
100 SNST 84015 1171 D6
600 CLTN 84015 1171 C6
4200 PNCY 84404 996 C6
W 2575 N SR-134
4200 PNCY 84404 996 C6
W 2575 S
1600 SRCS 84075 1281 A2
1800 SRCS 84075 1280 E2
N 2580 W
400 PRVO 84601 2927 C6
S 2580 W
2700 WVCY 84119 1963 B4
11200 SJDN 84095 2281 B5
W 2580 N
2200 CLTN 84015 1170 D6
S 2585 W
14400 BFDL 84065 2387 A6
W 2585 N
- CLTN 84015 1226 D2
S 2590 W
1700 SRCS 84075 1280 D1
13200 RIVN 84065 2387 A4
W 2590 S
2500 WVCY 84119 1963 A3
N 2595 N
2000 CLTN 84015 1170 D7
N 2595 W
- CLTN 84015 1170 D7
S 2595 W
5100 TYVL 84118 2069 A4
7200 WJDN 84084 2175 B3
E 2600 N
- PTVW 84414 998 D6
10 LEHI 84043 2603 C2
10 NHLN 84341 463 E3
300 NHON 84414 998 D6
300 PRVO 84604 2928 D2
500 NHON 84414 999 A6
1400 LYTN 84040 1229 C6
E 2600 S
10 CRFD 84015 1281 D2
400 BNFL 84010 1653 E4
N 2600 E
1800 LYTN 84040 1284 A1
2500 LYTN 84040 1230 A6
N 2600 W
- LOGN 84321 526 C2
100 BxEC 84302 765 D5
100 BxEC 84340 765 D5
100 CchC 84321 526 B2
800 CLTN 84015 1226 D2
800 PRVO 84601 2927 C5
4700 WbrC 84310 1001 D6
S 2600 E
1000 SGVL 84663 3144 C4
1000 SPFK 84660 3250 C5
1700 SLCY 84108 1966 A1
3000 SLkC 84109 1966 A5
6400 CDHT 84121 2072 C7
6400 CDHT 84121 2178 A1
7600 SWBR 84405 1230 A3
S 2600 W
- SGVL 84663 3142 C2
1200 SRCS 84075 1226 D7
2700 WVCY 84119 1963 A4
3900 ROY 84067 1114 C7
4400 ROY 84067 1171 B2
5100 CchC 84339 650 C2
13200 RIVN 84065 2387 B3
14600 BFDL 84065 2387 B7
W 2600 N
- CRHL 84062 2605 D6
- PTGV 84062 2605 D6
- WbrC 84404 996 A6
800 CLTN 84015 1171 B6
900 LYTN 84041 1228 C6
1100 LEHI 84043 2603 A2
2500 FRWT 84404 997 A6
2500 PNCY 84404 997 A6
2500 WbrC 84404 997 A6
2700 BxEC 84302 705 C6
3200 CchC 84321 462 A3
3400 PNCY 84404 996 D6
W 2600 N SR-134
2500 FRWT 84404 997 A6
2500 PNCY 84404 997 A6
2500 WbrC 84404 997 A6
3400 PNCY 84404 996 D6
3400 WbrC 84404 996 D6
W 2600 S
10 NBLY 84321 591 D2
200 BNFL 84010 1653 A4
400 NSLK 84054 1653 A4
400 WDCR 84010 1653 A4
500 PRRY 84302 827 D5
600 NSLK 84010 1653 A4
800 NSLK 84087 1653 A4
800 SSLK 84119 1964 A3
900 WDCR 84087 1653 A4
1100 WDCR 84054 1653 A4
1200 CchC 84321 591 A2
1200 MPTN 84664 3250 E3
1200 NSLK 84054 1652 E4
1200 WDCR 84087 1652 E4
1600 CchC 84321 590 E2
1700 WDCR 84054 1652 E4
2400 CchC 84339 590 C2
3300 WVCY 84119 1962 E4
5500 CchC 84339 588 E2
5500 CchC 84339 589 A2
8800 SLkC 84044 1960 A3

W 2600 S
9000 SLkC 84044 1959 E4
W 2600 S SR-93
- NSLK 84087 1653 B4
- WDCR 84087 1653 B4
400 NSLK 84054 1653 B4
400 WDCR 84010 1653 B4
600 BNFL 84010 1653 B4
600 NSLK 84010 1653 B4
N 2600 St W
- HYVL 84314 646 D2
N 2600 St W SR-38
- HYVL 84314 646 D2
W 2610 S
- PRRY 84302 827 C5
900 SSLK 84119 1963 E3
N 2615 W
1500 CLTN 84015 1226 D1
S 2615 W
13100 RIVN 84065 2387 A3
W 2615 S
1000 SRCS 84075 1281 B2
W 2615 S Cir
1900 SRCS 84075 1280 E2
E 2620 N
600 PRVO 84604 2928 E2
N 2620 W
500 PRVO 84601 2927 C6
S 2620 W
- TYVL 84119 2069 A1
2700 WVCY 84119 1963 A4
8100 WJDN 84088 2175 A5
W 2620 S
800 MPTN 84664 3250 E3
E 2625 N
- WbrC 84310 1002 A6
200 NHON 84414 998 E6
1100 LYTN 84040 1229 C6
1100 NHON 84414 999 B6
N 2625 E
1700 LYTN 84040 1284 A1
N 2625 W
500 WPT 84015 1226 D3
S 2625 E
10 LYTN 84040 1284 A5
6000 WbrC 84403 1174 A6
7900 SWBR 84405 1230 A3
S 2625 W
1600 SRCS 84075 1226 D7
1600 SRCS 84075 1280 D1
3900 ROY 84067 1114 C7
4700 ROY 84067 1171 B2
7300 WJDN 84084 2175 A3
9400 SJDN 84095 2281 A1
W 2625 N
200 LYTN 84041 1228 E6
W 2625 S
500 NBLY 84321 591 C2
N 2630 W
1400 PRVO 84601 2927 C4
S 2630 W
- UthC 84660 3248 B2
S 2635 W
- SRCS 84075 1280 D2
N 2640 W
1500 LEHI 84043 2602 C4
2100 CLTN 84015 1170 D7
S 2640 E
1200 SPFK 84660 3250 C5
W 2640 S
1600 SRCS 84075 1281 A3
3400 WVCY 84119 1962 E4
N 2645 W
- CLTN 84015 1170 D7
1000 LYTN 84041 1281 E3
S 2645 W
7200 WJDN 84084 2175 A3
E 2650 N
- WbrC 84310 1001 B6
400 NHON 84414 998 E6
1100 NHON 84414 999 C5
N 2650 E
200 LYTN 84040 1283 E4
3300 LYTN 84040 1230 A5
N 2650 W
10 PRVO 84601 2927 C6
1600 CLTN 84015 1226 D1
6900 HYVL 84314 646 C2
S 2650 W
300 SLCY 84104 1857 A4
1400 SRCS 84075 1226 D7
3600 CchC 84339 590 C5
5600 ROY 84067 1171 B5
7000 UthC 84660 3248 B4
13200 RIVN 84065 2387 A4
W 2650 N
- LEHI 84043 2603 A2
200 LYTN 84041 1228 E6
300 SNST 84015 1171 C6
1200 CLTN 84015 1171 B6
2200 CLTN 84015 1170 D6
4200 PNCY 84404 996 C6
W 2650 S
- WHVN 84401 1114 A4
500 PRRY 84302 827 D5
1500 OGDN 84401 1114 E4
N 2660 W
- CLTN 84015 1226 D2
900 PRVO 84601 2927 C5
S 2660 E
8100 SLkC 84093 2178 A5
W 2660 N
300 LEHI 84043 2603 B2
W 2660 S
- WHVN 84401 1114 A4
S 2665 W
3900 WVCY 84119 1963 A7
3900 WVCY 84119 2069 B2
5600 TYVL 84118 2069 A6
13000 RIVN 84065 2387 A3
N 2670 W
2100 CLTN 84015 1170 D7
S 2670 W
2600 WVCY 84119 1963 A4
W 2670 N
2000 SLCY 84116 1753 B2
W 2670 S
3500 WVCY 84119 1962 E4
E 2675 N
700 NHON 84414 999 A6
1100 LYTN 84040 1229 C6

Salt Lake City Street Index

STREET
Block City ZIP Map# Grid

E 2675 S
10 CRFD 84015 1281 D3
100 LYTN 84041 1281 D3
N 2675 E
1700 LYTN 84040 1284 A1
3700 SWBR 84405 1230 A4
N 2675 W
1000 LYTN 84041 1281 E2
2600 FRWT 84404 997 B5
S 2675 W
1200 SRCS 84075 1226 D7
3900 ROY 84067 1114 B7
4000 ROY 84067 1171 B1
8000 UthC 84660 3248 B6
W 2675 N
- LYTN 84041 1228 E6
E 2680 N
900 PRVO 84604 2928 E2
S 2680 E
6700 CDHT 84121 2178 A1
W 2680 S
700 NBLY 84321 591 B3
2500 WVCY 84119 1963 A4
S 2685 W
- SRCS 84075 1280 D2
N 2690 W
1500 PRVO 84601 2927 C4
S 2690 W
5200 ROY 84067 1171 B4
E 2700 N
100 LEHI 84043 2603 C2
200 SPFK 84660 3142 D5
300 NHLN 84341 463 E3
300 SGVL 84663 3142 D5
300 UthC 84660 3142 D5
400 NHON 84414 998 E5
700 NHON 84414 999 A5
1400 LYTN 84040 1229 C6
1400 NHLN 84341 464 C3
2500 LYTN 84040 1230 A6
5500 WbrC 84310 1002 A5
E 2700 S
10 SSLK 84115 1964 E4
500 SLCY 84106 1964 E4
700 SLCY 84106 1965 C4
700 SLkC 84106 1965 C4
2000 SLCY 84109 1965 C4
N 2700 E
100 LYTN 84040 1284 A4
2500 LYTN 84040 1230 A6
N 2700 W
- CLTN 84015 1170 D7
- CLTN 84015 1226 D1
600 WPT 84015 1226 D3
900 PRVO 84601 2927 C5
3100 FRWT 84404 997 B4
S 2700 E
10 LYTN 84040 1284 A5
1200 SPFK 84660 3250 C5
2700 SLkC 84109 1966 A5
3900 SLkC 84124 1966 A7
4000 SLkC 84124 2072 A1
4200 HLDY 84124 2072 A1
4400 HLDY 84117 2072 A2
7000 CDHT 84121 2178 A3
7700 CDHT 84093 2178 A3
7900 SWBR 84405 1230 A3
9800 SLkC 84092 2284 A2
9900 SNDY 84092 2284 A2
S 2700 W
- RIVN 84065 2387 A6
200 MTSV 84404 1055 B6
700 WbrC 84404 1055 B6
1800 WHVN 84401 1114 B4
3300 WHVN 84067 1114 B6
3700 ROY 84067 1114 B6
4200 ROY 84067 1171 B1
4700 CchC 84319 650 B1
4700 TYVL 84118 2069 A4
6200 TYVL 84084 2069 A7
6500 TYVL 84084 2175 A1
6500 WJDN 84084 2175 A1
8600 WJDN 84088 2175 A7
9200 WJDN 84088 2281 A2
9300 SJDN 84095 2281 A6
13800 BFDL 84065 2387 A6
14800 BFDL 84065 2494 A1
W 2700 N
1000 PTVW 84404 998 B6
1000 PTVW 84414 998 B6
1100 WbrC 84404 998 B6
1300 PTVW 84404 997 E6
1300 WbrC 84404 997 E6
1700 FRWT 84404 997 E6
W 2700 N SR-134
1100 PTVW 84404 998 A6
1100 PTVW 84414 998 A6
1100 WbrC 84404 998 A6
1300 PTVW 84404 997 E6
1300 WbrC 84404 997 E6
1700 FRWT 84404 997 E6
W 2700 S
10 SSLK 84115 1964 C4
400 BNFL 84010 1653 C4
400 PRRY 84302 827 D5
500 NBLY 84321 591 C3
500 SRCS 84075 1281 A3
1500 WVCY 84119 1963 C4
2000 SRCS 84075 1280 E3
3000 DvsC 84075 1280 B3
3800 WVCY 84120 1962 D4
8300 SLkC 84044 1960 B4
9100 SLkC 84006 1959 E4
9100 SLkC 84044 1959 E4
N 2710 W
1200 PRVO 84601 2927 C4
2300 CLTN 84015 1170 D6
S 2720 E
9600 SNDY 84092 2284 A2
W 2720 S
2500 WVCY 84119 1963 A4
E 2725 N
4800 WbrC 84310 1001 E5
N 2725 W
- CRFD 84015 1281 E2
- LYTN 84015 1281 E2
1000 LYTN 84041 1281 E2
S 2725 W
2800 SRCS 84075 1280 D3
4000 ROY 84067 1171 B1
W 2725 N
2500 FRWT 84404 997 C5
W 2725 N
4200 PNCY 84404 996 C6
W 2725 S
300 BNFL 84010 1653 C4
E 2730 N
700 PRVO 84604 2928 D2
S 2730 W
7400 WJDN 84084 2175 A3
13000 RIVN 84065 2387 A3
W 2730 N
300 LEHI 84043 2603 B2
1400 PTGV 84062 2605 B6
W 2730 S
2700 WVCY 84119 1963 A4
E 2735 S
- OGDN 84403 1116 A4
S 2735 W
4100 WVCY 84119 2069 A1
12100 RIVN 84065 2387 A1
N 2740 W
500 PRVO 84601 2927 C5
2200 CLTN 84015 1170 D7
S 2740 E
3700 SLkC 84109 1966 A7
7000 CDHT 84121 2178 A2
S 2740 W
9600 SJDN 84095 2281 A1
11900 RIVN 84065 2281 A7
W 2740 N
10 LEHI 84043 2603 C2
W 2745 S
2500 WVCY 84119 1963 B4
3500 WVCY 84119 1962 D4
E 2750 N
400 NHON 84414 998 E5
500 NHON 84414 999 A5
1000 WbrC 84414 999 C5
2300 LYTN 84040 1229 E6
2400 LYTN 84040 1230 A6
2800 NHLN 84341 464 D3
E 2750 S
10 BNFL 84010 1653 D4
N 2750 E
1800 LYTN 84040 1284 A1
N 2750 W
- CLTN 84015 1170 D7
- CLTN 84015 1226 D1
500 WPT 84015 1226 D3
800 PRVO 84601 2927 C5
1500 PNCY 84404 1055 B1
3800 FRWT 84404 997 B2
7000 HYVL 84314 646 C2
S 2750 E
1600 SPFK 84660 3250 C6
2800 SLkC 84109 1966 A4
8000 SWBR 84405 1230 B3
S 2750 W
4400 ROY 84067 1171 B2
W 2750 N
100 LYTN 84041 1228 D6
5100 WbrC 84404 996 A5
W 2750 S
10 BNFL 84010 1653 D4
400 PRRY 84302 827 D5
1500 OGDN 84401 1114 E4
4300 WbrC 84401 1113 C4
E 2760 N
400 LEHI 84043 2603 D2
N 2760 W
400 PRVO 84601 2927 C6
S 2760 E
4500 HLDY 84117 2072 A2
9600 SNDY 84092 2284 A2
S 2760 W
2000 SLCY 84104 1963 A2
7900 WJDN 84088 2175 A4
12600 RIVN 84065 2387 A2
W 2760 N
- PTGV 84062 2605 C6
W 2760 S
9100 SLkC 84044 1959 E4
N 2770 W
600 PRVO 84601 2927 C5
S 2770 E
1300 SPFK 84660 3250 C5
4500 HLDY 84117 2072 A2
S 2770 W
7400 WJDN 84084 2175 A3
13000 RIVN 84065 2387 A3
W 2770 S
2000 WVCY 84119 1963 B4
W 2771 S
2600 WVCY 84119 1963 A4
N 2775 E
3600 LYTN 84040 1230 A4
N 2775 W
- WPT 84015 1226 D4
1100 LYTN 84041 1281 E2
1300 CLTN 84015 1226 D1
2300 CLTN 84015 1170 D6
S 2775 E
10 LYTN 84040 1284 A5
S 2775 W
5200 ROY 84067 1171 B4
10400 SJDN 84095 2281 A4
12000 RIVN 84065 2281 A7
12000 RIVN 84065 2387 A1
W 2775 N
- LEHI 84043 2603 A2
4200 PNCY 84404 996 C5
W 2775 S
500 NBLY 84321 591 C3
3000 WHVN 84401 1114 A4
E 2780 N
400 PRVO 84604 2928 D1
N 2780 W
1100 PRVO 84601 2927 C4
S 2780 E
3700 SLkC 84109 1966 A7
7000 CDHT 84121 2178 A2
S 2780 W
13600 RIVN 84065 2387 A5
W 2780 S
900 SSLK 84119 1963 E4
900 SSLK 84119 1964 A4
2500 WVCY 84119 1963 B4
S 2785 W
4100 WVCY 84119 2069 A1
S 2790 E
2900 SLkC 84109 1966 A4
S 2790 W
12600 RIVN 84065 2387 A2
S 2795 W
6100 TYVL 84118 2069 A7
6600 WJDN 84084 2175 A1
12100 RIVN 84065 2387 A1
W 2795 N
- WbrC 84404 996 A5
W 2795 S
2800 WVCY 84119 1963 A4
E 2800 N
400 NHON 84414 998 E5
500 NHON 84414 999 A5
800 PRVO 84604 2928 D1
1400 LYTN 84040 1229 C6
E 2800 S
500 SGVL 84663 3035 E7
700 SGVL 84663 3036 A7
N 2800 E
100 LYTN 84040 1284 A4
3600 LYTN 84040 1230 A4
3700 SWBR 84405 1230 A4
N 2800 W
100 MTSV 84404 1055 B4
600 WPT 84015 1226 C3
1600 CLTN 84015 1226 C1
1700 PRVO 84601 2927 C3
1900 BxEC 84302 705 C7
1900 BxEC 84302 765 C1
3200 PNCY 84404 997 B4
3600 FRWT 84404 997 B2
4600 BxEC 84302 646 C7
5800 AMGA 84335 398 B2
S 2800 E
- WbrC 84403 1174 A7
2800 SLkC 84109 1966 B4
7600 SWBR 84405 1230 B3
S 2800 W
- BFDL 84065 2387 A5
- BxEC 84340 996 C1
100 MTSV 84404 1055 B5
400 CchC 84321 526 B4
700 WbrC 84401 1055 B7
700 WbrC 84404 1055 B7
1800 CchC 84339 526 B7
2000 CchC 84339 590 B1
3500 CSTN 84032 2504 D3
4200 ROY 84067 1171 B1
6000 UthC 84660 3248 A2
7000 WJDN 84084 2175 A2
7800 WJDN 84088 2175 A4
11900 RIVN 84065 2281 A7
W 2800 N
10 LYTN 84041 1228 D6
300 LEHI 84043 2603 B2
800 PTGV 84062 2605 C5
3800 PNCY 84404 996 E5
W 2800 S
- SRCS 84075 1281 A3
400 PRRY 84302 827 D6
500 BNFL 84010 1653 C4
1700 OGDN 84401 1114 D4
2500 WVCY 84119 1963 A4
3200 WVCY 84119 1962 D3
4400 WbrC 84401 1113 B4
8900 SLkC 84044 1960 A4
9000 SLkC 84044 1959 E4
N 2800 St W
- HYVL 84314 586 C7
- HYVL 84314 646 C1
N 2800 St W SR-38
- HYVL 84314 586 C7
- HYVL 84314 646 C1
N 2800 W St
7200 HYVL 84314 646 C1
S 2805 W
2700 WVCY 84119 1963 A4
9400 SJDN 84095 2281 A1
12800 RIVN 84065 2387 A3
W 2805 S
3100 WVCY 84119 1962 E4
N 2810 W
700 PRVO 84601 2927 C5
S 2810 W
9600 SJDN 84095 2281 A1
W 2810 S
8700 SLkC 84044 1960 A4
E 2815 S
2300 SLkC 84109 1965 E4
2300 SLkC 84109 1966 A4
N 2820 W
900 PRVO 84601 2927 C5
S 2820 E
3900 SLkC 84124 1966 B7
S 2820 W
4000 WVCY 84119 2069 A1
W 2820 S
700 PRRY 84302 827 C6
8800 SLkC 84044 1960 A4
9100 SLkC 84044 1959 E4
E 2825 N
400 PRVO 84604 2928 D1
900 NHON 84414 999 B5
1000 LYTN 84040 1229 C6
E 2825 S
700 SLkC 84106 1965 A4
N 2825 E
3600 LYTN 84040 1230 A4
N 2825 W
1000 LYTN 84041 1281 E3
3400 FRWT 84404 997 B3
S 2825 E
10 LYTN 84040 1284 A5
7000 CDHT 84121 2178 B2
S 2825 W
- WJDN 84088 2175 A5
5000 ROY 84067 1171 B3
N 2830 W
1100 PRVO 84601 2927 C4
S 2830 W
1900 SRCS 84075 1280 C1
13000 RIVN 84065 2387 A3
W 2830 S
- PRRY 84302 827 C6
N 2835 W
1300 CLTN 84015 1226 C2
S 2835 E
3900 SLkC 84124 1966 B7
4000 SLkC 84124 2072 B1
S 2835 W
4100 WVCY 84119 2069 A1
W 2835 N
700 LYTN 84041 1228 D6
W 2835 S
- SRCS 84075 1281 C3
S 2840 W
7000 WJDN 84084 2175 A2
7900 WJDN 84088 2175 A4
10200 SJDN 84095 2281 A3
S 2845 W
12100 RIVN 84065 2387 A1
N 2845 W
2300 CLTN 84015 1170 C6
E 2850 N
- NHLN 84341 464 D3
400 LEHI 84043 2603 C1
400 NHON 84414 998 E5
500 NHON 84414 999 A5
E 2850 S
2700 SLkC 84109 1966 A4
N 2850 E
3000 LYTN 84040 1230 A5
N 2850 W
1100 PRVO 84601 2927 C4
1500 CLTN 84015 1226 C1
1600 PNCY 84404 1055 B1
S 2850 E
1200 SPFK 84660 3250 C5
3000 SLkC 84109 1966 B5
6000 WbrC 84403 1174 A6
S 2850 W
2900 WHVN 84401 1114 B5
3600 WHVN 84067 1114 B7
4200 ROY 84067 1171 B1
4500 WVCY 84119 2069 A3
6700 WJDN 84084 2175 A1
W 2850 N
- PTGV 84062 2605 B5
10 LYTN 84041 1228 D6
W 2850 S
- SRCS 84075 1281 A3
400 NBLY 84321 591 C3
700 PRRY 84302 827 C6
2500 SRCS 84075 1280 D3
S 2855 E
6100 WbrC 84403 1174 A6
S 2855 W
2700 WVCY 84119 1963 A4
W 2855 S
200 SSLK 84115 1964 B4
E 2860 S
2400 SLkC 84109 1966 A4
S 2860 W
13600 RIVN 84065 2387 A5
W 2860 S
800 SRCS 84075 1281 B3
N 2865 W
1400 CLTN 84015 1226 C1
S 2865 W
11000 SJDN 84095 2281 A5
W 2865 S
3100 WVCY 84119 1962 E4
N 2870 W
400 PRVO 84601 2927 C6
S 2870 E
2800 SLkC 84109 1966 B4
5000 HLDY 84117 2072 B4
7000 CDHT 84121 2178 B2
S 2870 W
3500 WVCY 84119 1963 A6
7100 WJDN 84084 2175 A2
7800 WJDN 84088 2175 A4
W 2870 S
7700 SLkC 84044 1960 D4
E 2875 N
400 PRVO 84604 2928 D1
4800 WbrC 84310 1001 D5
N 2875 W
- WPT 84015 1226 C4
1000 LYTN 84041 1281 E2
S 2875 W
4300 ROY 84067 1171 B1
W 2875 N
200 LEHI 84043 2603 B1
4100 PNCY 84404 996 D5
E 2880 S
2700 SLkC 84109 1966 A4
N 2880 W
- PRVO 84601 2927 B5
S 2880 E
3300 SLkC 84109 1966 B5
S 2880 W
7600 WJDN 84084 2175 A3
8400 WJDN 84088 2175 A6
W 2880 S
300 SSLK 84115 1964 B4
9100 SLkC 84044 1959 E4
S 2885 W
2200 SRCS 84075 1280 C2
N 2890 W
1300 CLTN 84015 1226 C1
S 2890 E
3300 SLkC 84109 1966 C6
S 2890 W
4600 WVCY 84119 2069 A3
W 2890 S
500 SSLK 84115 1964 B4
500 SSLK 84119 1964 B4
1500 SRCS 84075 1281 A3
2700 WVCY 84119 1963 A4
N 2895 W
1800 CLTN 84015 1170 C7
S 2895 W
4500 WVCY 84119 2069 B2
E 2900 N
200 NHON 84414 998 E4
600 NHON 84414 999 A5
800 NHLN 84341 464 A3
2000 LYTN 84040 1229 E6
E 2900 S
10 NBLY 84321 591 D3
600 MLVI 84332 592 B3
900 SGVL 84663 3036 A7
2300 SLkC 84109 1966 A4
N 2900 E
1900 LYTN 84040 1284 A1
3300 WbrC 84310 1000 E3
3300 WbrC 84414 1000 E3
3500 LYTN 84040 1230 A5
N 2900 W
1600 CLTN 84015 1226 C1
S 2900 E
1200 SPFK 84660 3250 D5
2800 SLkC 84109 1966 B5
3900 SLkC 84124 1966 B7
S 2900 E
4200 SLkC 84124 2072 B1
5400 HLDY 84117 2072 B5
6000 WbrC 84403 1174 A6
9800 SNDY 84092 2284 B2
S 2900 W
- WHVN 84067 1114 B7
1200 WbrC 84401 1055 B7
1200 WbrC 84401 1114 B1
1200 WbrC 84404 1055 B7
3000 CSTN 84032 2504 D2
4100 ROY 84067 1171 B2
4500 WELV 84319 590 B7
4500 WELV 84319 650 B1
8100 WJDN 84088 2175 A5
13000 RIVN 84065 2387 A3
W 2900 N
- WbrC 84404 996 A5
10 LYTN 84041 1228 D6
300 PTGV 84062 2605 C5
W 2900 S
10 NBLY 84321 591 D3
500 BNFL 84010 1653 C4
700 PRRY 84302 827 C6
700 SSLK 84119 1964 A4
900 SSLK 84119 1963 E4
1700 OGDN 84401 1114 D5
2700 WHVN 84401 1114 A5
3200 WbrC 84401 1114 A5
3800 WbrC 84401 1113 D5
4700 CchC 84339 589 B3
6100 WVCY 84128 1961 C4
8500 SLkC 84044 1960 A4
E 2910 S
700 SLkC 84106 1964 E4
700 SLkC 84106 1965 A4
S 2910 E
3300 SLkC 84109 1966 B6
S 2910 W
2800 WVCY 84119 1963 A5
W 2910 N
1300 LEHI 84043 2602 E1
W 2910 S
8300 SLkC 84044 1960 B4
N 2920 W
1100 PRVO 84601 2927 B4
S 2920 W
- LEHI 84043 2602 C7
7400 WJDN 84084 2175 A3
8300 WJDN 84088 2175 A5
12100 RIVN 84065 2387 A1
W 2920 S
800 SRCS 84075 1281 B3
2900 WVCY 84119 1963 A4
3000 WVCY 84119 1962 E4
4800 WVCY 84120 1962 A4
6400 WVCY 84128 1961 B4
E 2925 N
1000 NHON 84414 999 C5
N 2925 W
- WPT 84015 1226 C4
1000 LYTN 84041 1281 E2
1400 CRFD 84015 1281 E2
1400 CRFD 84041 1281 E2
1400 LYTN 84015 1281 E2
S 2925 W
300 SRCS 84075 1226 C5
5000 ROY 84067 1171 B3
W 2925 N
300 LEHI 84043 2603 B1
W 2925 S
500 MPTN 84664 3250 E3
500 MPTN 84664 3251 A3
3700 WVCY 84120 1962 D4
S 2930 E
7000 CDHT 84121 2178 B2
S 2930 W
4500 WVCY 84119 2069 A2
N 2930 W
2300 CLTN 84015 1170 C6
W 2935 S
2700 WVCY 84119 1963 A4
E 2940 S
2500 SLkC 84109 1966 A4
S 2940 E
1600 SPFK 84660 3250 D6
3300 SLkC 84109 1966 B6
S 2940 W
2200 SRCS 84075 1280 C2
7800 WJDN 84088 2175 A4
W 2940 S
7600 SLkC 84044 1960 D4
E 2950 N
100 PRVO 84604 2928 D1
300 LEHI 84043 2603 C1
900 NHON 84414 999 B4
1100 LYTN 84040 1229 C6
1700 NHLN 84341 464 D2
N 2950 E
1900 LYTN 84040 1284 A1
2000 LYTN 84040 1230 A7
N 2950 W
- DvsC 84075 1344 B1
1300 CLTN 84015 1226 C2
1900 PNCY 84404 997 B7
1900 PNCY 84404 1055 B1
3600 FRWT 84404 997 B3
3600 WbrC 84404 997 B3
S 2950 E
1300 SPFK 84660 3250 D5
4300 SLkC 84124 2072 B2
S 2950 W
4600 ROY 84067 1171 B2
7200 WJDN 84084 2175 A2
9600 SJDN 84095 2281 A2
13000 RIVN 84065 2387 A3
W 2950 N
10 PRVO 84604 2928 C1
W 2950 S
100 SSLK 84115 1964 C4
500 BNFL 84010 1653 C5
600 PRRY 84302 827 C6
900 SSLK 84119 1963 E4
900 SSLK 84119 1964 A4
S 2955 E
7000 CDHT 84121 2178 B2
S 2955 W
2800 WVCY 84119 1963 A4
S 2956 W
4600 WVCY 84119 2069 A3
E 2960 S
2700 SLkC 84109 1966 B4
N 2960 W
1100 PRVO 84601 2927 B4
S 2960 E
1500 SPFK 84660 3250 D6
S 2960 W
2900 WVCY 84119 1963 A4
6600 WJDN 84084 2175 A1
8300 WJDN 84088 2175 A5
W 2960 N
- LEHI 84043 2603 A1
W 2960 S
2800 WVCY 84119 1963 A4
E 2965 S
2900 SLkC 84109 1966 B4
W 2965 S
- NBLY 84321 591 C3
N 2970 W
10 PRVO 84601 2927 B6
S 2970 E
1100 SPFK 84660 3250 D5
S 2970 W
- LEHI 84043 2602 C7
4600 WVCY 84119 2069 A3
W 2970 S
3700 WVCY 84120 1962 D4
N 2975 E
10 LYTN 84040 1284 A4
2200 LYTN 84040 1230 A7
N 2975 W
- WPT 84015 1226 C4
300 LYTN 84041 1281 D4
3900 WbrC 84404 997 B2
S 2975 W
- WHVN 84401 1114 B4
4200 ROY 84067 1171 A1
W 2975 S
400 BNFL 84010 1653 C5
1300 SRCS 84075 1281 A3
2500 WVCY 84119 1963 B4
E 2980 S
2500 SLkC 84109 1966 A4
S 2980 E
7200 CDHT 84121 2178 B3
9600 SNDY 84092 2284 B1
S 2980 W
4700 TYVL 84118 2069 A3
7000 WJDN 84084 2175 A2
7900 WJDN 84088 2175 A4
13100 RIVN 84065 2387 A3
S 2985 E
7000 CDHT 84121 2178 B2
W 2985 S
800 SRCS 84075 1281 B3
7800 SLkC 84044 1960 D4
E 2990 S
1800 SLkC 84106 1965 D4
S 2990 E
1300 SPFK 84660 3250 D5
4300 SLkC 84124 2072 B2
S 2990 W
13200 RIVN 84065 2387 A3
S 2995 E
4500 HLDY 84117 2072 B2
W 2995 S
2900 WVCY 84119 1963 A5
3000 WVCY 84119 1962 E4
E 3000 N
400 NHON 84414 998 E4
400 NHON 84414 999 A5
2000 LYTN 84040 1229 E6
E 3000 N SR-193
1300 LYTN 84040 1229 C6
E 3000 S
10 BNFL 84010 1653 E5
10 WshC 84032 2505 D2
1300 SLCY 84106 1965 C4
1300 SLkC 84106 1965 C4
2000 SLkC 84109 1965 D5
2300 SLkC 84109 1966 A4
N 3000 E
1100 LYTN 84040 1284 A2
N 3000 W
- BxEC 84302 765 B1
- PRVO 84601 2927 B6
10 WPT 84015 1226 C4
1000 MTSV 84404 1055 A4
2800 CchC 84341 462 B2
3400 FRWT 84404 997 A3
11000 DWVL 84312 522 C6
S 3000 E
6300 CDHT 84121 2072 B7
6300 HLDY 84121 2072 B7
6500 CDHT 84121 2178 B1
S 3000 W
10 WPT 84015 1226 C5
200 SRCS 84075 1226 C5
1700 DvsC 84075 1280 C1
1700 SRCS 84075 1280 C1
2200 CchC 84339 590 B2
2400 CSTN 84032 2504 C1
2700 WHVN 84401 1114 A4
2700 WVCY 84119 1963 A4
3500 CchC 84319 590 B4
3800 WELV 84319 590 B4
3800 WELV 84339 590 B4
4300 ROY 84067 1171 A2
6400 UthC 84660 3248 A2
6800 CchC 84339 650 B6
7800 WJDN 84088 2175 A4
W 3000 N
- PTVW 84414 998 A5
10 DvsC 84041 1228 E6
10 DvsC 84056 1228 E6
10 LYTN 84041 1228 E6
100 SPFK 84660 3142 C4
2300 BxEC 84302 705 D5
W 3000 N SR-193
10 DvsC 84041 1228 E6
10 DvsC 84056 1228 E6
10 LYTN 84041 1228 E6
W 3000 S
- CchC 84321 590 C3
10 WshC 84032 2505 A2
500 BNFL 84010 1653 C5
600 PRRY 84302 827 C6
1200 WshC 84032 2504 D2
2100 CchC 84339 590 C3
2700 CSTN 84032 2504 C2
2900 SSLK 84115 1964 B4
4700 WbrC 84401 1113 B5
4800 WVCY 84120 1962 A5
5100 WVCY 84120 1961 E5
W 3000 S
8600 SLkC 84044 1960 A5
9100 SLkC 84044 1959 E4
E 3010 S
1300 SLCY 84106 1965 C5
1300 SLkC 84106 1965 C5
S 3010 E
3300 SLkC 84109 1966 B5
S 3010 W
10400 SJDN 84095 2281 A4
W 3010 S
8500 SLkC 84044 1960 B5
E 3015 S
1800 SLkC 84106 1965 D5
W 3015 S
3700 WVCY 84120 1962 D5
E 3020 S
3400 SLkC 84109 1966 C5
N 3020 W
1100 PRVO 84601 2927 B4
S 3020 W
8800 WJDN 84088 2175 A7
W 3020 S
4400 WVCY 84120 1962 B5
E 3025 N
900 NHON 84414 999 B4
2200 LYTN 84040 1229 E5
2700 LYTN 84040 1230 A6
S 3025 W
3700 WVCY 84119 1963 A7
4600 ROY 84067 1171 A2
W 3025 S
10 BNFL 84010 1653 D5
S 3030 E
1500 SPFK 84660 3250 D5
3900 SLkC 84124 1966 B7
7300 CDHT 84121 2178 B3
9400 SNDY 84093 2284 B1
S 3030 W
14800 BFDL 84065 2494 A1
W 3030 S
100 SSLK 84115 1964 C5
E 3035 S
2000 SLkC 84109 1965 D5
S 3035 E
4300 SLkC 84124 2072 B2
W 3035 S
4800 WVCY 84120 1962 A5
S 3040 E
3300 SLkC 84109 1966 B5
S 3040 W
- LEHI 84043 2602 C7
4700 TYVL 84118 2069 A3
6600 WJDN 84084 2175 A1
9200 WJDN 84088 2175 A7
13100 RIVN 84065 2387 A3
W 3040 N
1200 PTGV 84062 2605 B5
W 3040 S
2900 WVCY 84119 1963 A5
4400 WVCY 84120 1962 B5
E 3045 S
300 SSLK 84115 1964 D5
1400 SLkC 84106 1965 C5
S 3045 W
13800 BFDL 84065 2387 A5
E 3050 N
- WbrC 84310 1001 E5
400 NHON 84414 998 E4
400 NHON 84414 999 A4
400 PRVO 84604 2928 D1
700 LEHI 84043 2603 D1
3000 DvsC 84040 1230 A5
N 3050 E
1100 LYTN 84040 1284 B2
N 3050 W
- LYTN 84041 1281 D4
1100 WPT 84015 1226 C2
3400 FRWT 84404 997 A3
S 3050 E
1600 SPFK 84660 3250 D6
7000 CDHT 84121 2178 B2
S 3050 W
2700 WVCY 84119 1963 A4
4600 ROY 84067 1171 A2
6000 CLTN 84015 1171 A6
6000 ROY 84015 1171 A6
W 3050 S
300 SSLK 84115 1964 B5
500 MPTN 84664 3250 E4
500 MPTN 84664 3251 A4
800 SRCS 84075 1281 B3
1100 OGDN 84401 1115 A5
E 3060 N
100 PRVO 84604 2928 C1
E 3060 S
1800 SLkC 84106 1965 D5
N 3060 W
1900 CLTN 84015 1170 C7
S 3060 W
3800 WVCY 84119 1963 A7
13600 RIVN 84065 2387 A4
W 3060 N
1200 LEHI 84043 2603 A1
W 3060 S
4400 WVCY 84120 1962 B5
7700 SLkC 84044 1960 D5
E 3065 S
500 SSLK 84106 1964 E5
2000 SLkC 84109 1965 D5
S 3065 W
9600 SJDN 84095 2280 E1
9700 SJDN 84095 2281 A2
E 3070 S
2000 SLkC 84109 1965 E5
E 3075 N
400 NHON 84414 998 E4
1100 LYTN 84040 1229 C6
1200 NHON 84414 999 C4
S 3075 E
3100 SLkC 84109 1966 B5
3900 SLkC 84124 1966 B7
S 3075 W
- WHVN 84401 1114 A4
5500 ROY 84067 1171 A4
7000 WJDN 84084 2174 E2
7000 WJDN 84084 2175 A2
E 3080 S
1900 SLkC 84106 1965 D5
N 3080 W
1000 PRVO 84601 2927 B5

Salt Lake City Street Index

STREET Block City ZIP Map# Grid

S 3080 E
4200 SLkC 84124 2072 B1
7100 CDHT 84121 2178 B2
S 3080 W
2900 WVCY 84119 1962 E5
4000 WVCY 84119 2068 E1
W 3080 N
10 PRVO 84604 2928 C1
W 3080 S
4400 WVCY 84120 1962 B5
E 3085 S
500 SSLK 84106 1964 E5
S 3085 E
7300 CDHT 84121 2178 B3
S 3085 W
3100 WVCY 84119 1962 E5
11800 RIVN 84065 2281 A7
E 3090 N
1200 NHON 84414 999 C4
S 3090 W
9200 WJDN 84088 2175 B7
W 3090 S
- SRCS 84075 1281 B3
S 3095 W
2700 WVCY 84119 1962 E4
4800 TYVL 84118 2068 E3
E 3100 N
10 NHON 84414 998 E4
400 LEHI 84043 2603 D1
400 UthC 84043 2603 D1
500 NHON 84414 999 A4
600 PRVO 84604 2928 D1
1100 DvsC 84040 1229 E5
1200 NHLN 84341 464 C2
2000 LYTN 84040 1229 E5
E 3100 S
10 BNFL 84010 1653 E5
2700 SLkC 84109 1966 A5
N 3100 E
1100 LYTN 84040 1284 B2
N 3100 W
400 WPT 84015 1226 C3
1100 PRVO 84601 2927 B4
2600 BxEC 84302 705 B6
5400 AMGA 84335 398 A3
13000 BxEC 84312 522 B1
S 3100 E
3600 SLkC 84109 1966 B7
4100 SLkC 84124 2072 B1
9500 SLkC 84092 2284 B2
9600 SNDY 84092 2284 B2
S 3100 W
2900 CchC 84339 590 A4
4300 ROY 84067 1171 A2
4300 WbrC 84067 1171 A2
4300 WELV 84339 590 A7
4300 WHVN 84067 1171 A2
7200 WJDN 84084 2174 E3
13000 RIVN 84065 2386 E3
13100 RIVN 84065 2387 A3
W 3100 N
- PTVW 84414 997 E3
- PTVW 84414 998 D5
10 CchC 84341 463 C2
10 LOGN 84341 463 C2
100 PRVO 84604 2928 C1
2500 FRWT 84404 997 B4
W 3100 S
- WVCY 84128 1960 E5
10 BNFL 84010 1653 D5
1400 WVCY 84119 1963 A5
2700 WHVN 84401 1114 B5
3000 WVCY 84119 1962 E5
3600 WVCY 84120 1962 E5
5000 WVCY 84120 1961 E5
6200 WVCY 84128 1961 A5
7200 SLkC 84044 1960 E5
9100 SLkC 84044 1959 E5
E 3110 S
2000 SLkC 84109 1965 D5
N 3110 W
1500 PRVO 84601 2927 B4
1500 UthC 84601 2927 B4
S 3110 W
10 PRVO 84601 2927 B7
10 PRVO 84601 3034 B1
9300 WJDN 84088 2281 A1
E 3115 S
1400 SLkC 84106 1965 C5
S 3115 W
3500 WVCY 84119 1962 E6
12600 RIVN 84065 2386 E2
E 3120 S
2600 SLkC 84109 1966 A5
S 3120 E
1500 SPFK 84660 3250 D5
3900 SLkC 84124 1966 B7
E 3125 N
400 PRVO 84604 2928 D1
600 NHON 84414 999 A4
2400 LYTN 84040 1229 E5
N 3125 E
1200 LYTN 84040 1284 B2
N 3125 W
2300 CLTN 84015 1170 C6
S 3125 E
3400 SLkC 84109 1966 B6
W 3125 S
100 OGDN 84401 1115 D5
4200 WVCY 84120 1962 B4
S 3130 E
3300 SLkC 84109 1966 B5
W 3130 N
2200 SLCY 84116 1753 B1
W 3130 S
- WVCY 84128 1961 A5
E 3135 S
2900 SLkC 84109 1966 B5
E 3140 N
100 PRVO 84604 2928 C1
S 3140 W
2100 WVCY 84119 1962 E2
3900 WVCY 84119 2068 E1
9100 WJDN 84088 2174 E7
9200 WJDN 84088 2280 E1
W 3140 N
10 PRVO 84604 2928 C1
1200 LEHI 84043 2603 A1
W 3140 S
1800 WVCY 84119 1963 C5
4000 WVCY 84120 1962 C5
5800 WVCY 84128 1961 D5
S 3145 E
3700 SLkC 84109 1966 B7
S 3145 W
2700 WVCY 84119 1962 E4
4700 TYVL 84118 2068 E3
W 3145 S
4800 WVCY 84120 1962 A5
E 3150 N
500 NHON 84414 999 A4
700 LEHI 84043 2603 D1
1100 LYTN 84040 1229 C5
E 3150 S
700 SGVL 84663 3142 E1
700 SGVL 84663 3143 A1
1400 SLkC 84106 1965 C5
N 3150 E
1100 LYTN 84040 1284 B2
4300 WbrC 84310 1000 E1
N 3150 W
900 WPT 84015 1226 C2
2600 BxEC 84302 705 B6
S 3150 W
- WHVN 84401 1114 A4
4200 WVCY 84119 2068 E1
4500 ROY 84067 1171 A2
8400 WJDN 84088 2174 E6
12100 RIVN 84065 2386 E1
W 3150 S
700 SRCS 84075 1281 B3
2700 WVCY 84119 1963 A5
3400 CSTN 84032 2504 C2
4200 WVCY 84120 1962 C5
8500 SLkC 84044 1960 A5
E 3155 S
700 SLkC 84106 1964 E5
700 SLkC 84106 1965 A5
S 3155 W
8400 WJDN 84088 2174 E5
S 3160 W
13000 RIVN 84065 2386 E3
W 3160 S
100 SSLK 84115 1964 D5
900 SSLK 84119 1963 E5
900 SSLK 84119 1964 A5
3800 WVCY 84120 1962 D5
S 3165 E
3900 SLkC 84124 1966 B7
E 3170 S
1700 SLkC 84106 1965 D5
S 3170 E
3400 SLkC 84109 1966 B6
S 3170 W
13100 RIVN 84065 2386 E3
W 3170 S
4500 WVCY 84120 1962 B5
E 3175 N
600 NHON 84414 999 A4
E 3175 S
2900 SLkC 84109 1966 B5
N 3175 E
10 LYTN 84040 1284 B4
4300 WbrC 84310 1000 E1
N 3175 W
- WbrC 84404 997 A2
S 3175 E
3300 SLkC 84109 1966 C6
S 3175 W
5100 ROY 84067 1171 A4
W 3175 N
1200 LEHI 84043 2603 A1
1300 LEHI 84043 2602 E1
W 3175 S
100 OGDN 84401 1115 D5
4200 WVCY 84120 1962 C5
E 3180 N
600 PRVO 84604 2928 D1
W 3180 N
- LEHI 84043 2602 E1
W 3180 S
3000 WVCY 84119 1962 E5
3000 WVCY 84119 1963 A5
6100 WVCY 84128 1961 C5
8500 SLkC 84044 1960 B5
E 3185 S
100 SSLK 84115 1964 D5
2000 SLkC 84109 1965 D5
2700 SLkC 84109 1966 B5
W 3185 S
4800 WVCY 84120 1962 A5
S 3190 W
7600 WJDN 84084 2174 E4
W 3190 S
1700 WVCY 84119 1963 C5
E 3195 S
500 SSLK 84106 1964 E5
E 3200 N
100 PRVO 84604 2928 C1
500 NHON 84414 999 A4
E 3200 S
1100 BNFL 84010 1654 A5
N 3200 W
10 LYTN 84041 1281 D4
800 WPT 84015 1226 C2
1000 SLCY 84116 1752 E5
2100 SLkC 84116 1752 E3
3700 CchC 84335 398 A7
4600 BxEC 84302 705 B1
4800 BxEC 84302 646 B7
5100 AMGA 84335 398 A4
S 3200 W
10 LYTN 84075 1281 D5
300 CchC 84321 526 A4
300 DvsC 84075 1281 D6
900 SLCY 84104 1856 E6
1400 CchC 84339 526 A7
1800 CchC 84321 590 A2
1800 CchC 84339 590 A2
1800 SLCY 84104 1962 E3
2100 WVCY 84119 1962 E3
4000 WVCY 84119 2068 E1
4600 ROY 84067 1171 A2
4700 TYVL 84118 2068 E6
5600 CchC 84339 650 A3
6200 TYVL 84084 2068 E6
6500 TYVL 84084 2174 E2
6600 WJDN 84084 2174 E2
7800 WJDN 84088 2174 E6
8500 CchC 84339 709 A4
9300 UthC 84651 3354 E2
9300 UthC 84660 3354 E2
9300 WJDN 84088 2280 E2
9400 SJDN 84095 2280 E2
S 3200 W
11800 RIVN 84065 2280 E7
12000 RIVN 84065 2386 E1
14400 BFDL 84065 2386 E7
14800 BFDL 84065 2493 E1
S 3200 W SR-115
9300 UthC 84651 3354 E2
9300 UthC 84660 3354 E2
W 3200 N
- CchC 84341 463 D2
- LEHI 84043 2602 E1
- PTVW 84414 998 A4
100 HDPK 84318 463 D2
100 HDPK 84341 463 D2
100 PRVO 84604 2928 B1
100 SPFK 84660 3142 C4
2800 BxEC 84302 705 C5
W 3200 S
100 NBLY 84321 591 A4
600 BNFL 84010 1653 B5
700 NSLK 84054 1653 B5
1100 CchC 84321 591 A4
1500 CchC 84321 590 E4
1500 NBLY 84321 590 E4
2000 CchC 84339 590 E4
4200 WVCY 84120 1962 C5
4700 CchC 84339 589 B4
8900 SLkC 84044 1960 A5
9100 SLkC 84044 1959 E5
9200 SLkC 84006 1959 E5
N 3200 St W
3000 CchC 84341 462 A2
3300 CchC 84335 398 A7
3700 CchC 84341 398 A7
E 3205 S
1300 SLkC 84106 1965 B5
2000 SLkC 84109 1965 E5
W 3205 S
4500 WVCY 84120 1962 B5
E 3210 S
1700 SLkC 84106 1965 D5
2500 SLkC 84109 1966 A5
S 3210 E
3900 SLkC 84124 1966 C7
S 3210 W
10500 SJDN 84095 2280 E4
W 3210 S
6400 WVCY 84128 1961 B5
7600 SLkC 84044 1960 D5
E 3215 S
2900 SLkC 84109 1966 B5
E 3220 S
2000 SLkC 84109 1965 D5
2700 SLkC 84109 1966 A5
S 3220 W
8500 WJDN 84088 2174 E5
E 3225 N
500 NHON 84414 999 A4
2100 LYTN 84040 1229 E5
E 3225 S
2300 SLkC 84109 1965 E5
2300 SLkC 84109 1966 A5
N 3225 W
400 WPT 84015 1226 C3
S 3225 W
5700 TYVL 84118 2068 E6
W 3225 S
4200 WVCY 84120 1962 C5
E 3230 N
400 PRVO 84604 2928 D1
600 LEHI 84043 2603 D1
S 3230 W
- WVCY 84119 1962 E1
1700 SLCY 84104 1962 E1
5800 TYVL 84118 2068 E6
S 3235 W
6800 WJDN 84084 2174 E1
12100 RIVN 84065 2386 E1
W 3235 S
4800 WVCY 84120 1962 A5
S 3240 W
12000 RIVN 84065 2280 E7
12300 RIVN 84065 2386 E1
W 3240 N
- PTVW 84414 998 A4
W 3240 S
3700 WVCY 84120 1962 D5
S 3245 W
4500 WVCY 84119 2068 E2
W 3245 S
4500 WVCY 84120 1962 B5
E 3250 N
100 NHON 84414 998 E4
100 PRVO 84604 2928 C1
900 NHON 84414 999 B4
1200 NHLN 84341 464 B2
2100 LYTN 84040 1229 E5
N 3250 E
1700 LYTN 84040 1284 B1
N 3250 W
1800 CLTN 84015 1170 C7
1800 CLTN 84015 1226 C1
S 3250 E
3800 SLkC 84109 1966 C7
S 3250 W
3900 WVCY 84119 1962 E7
7500 WJDN 84084 2174 E3
11800 RIVN 84065 2280 E7
W 3250 N
100 PRVO 84604 2928 C1
2800 PNCY 84404 997 B4
W 3250 S
4200 WVCY 84120 1962 C5
W 3255 S
1800 WVCY 84119 1963 C5
S 3260 W
5700 ROY 84067 1171 A5
7900 WJDN 84088 2174 E4
S 3265 W
9800 SJDN 84095 2280 E2
W 3265 S
900 SSLK 84119 1963 E5
900 SSLK 84119 1964 A5
S 3270 W
3500 WVCY 84119 1962 E6
6800 WJDN 84084 2174 E1
W 3270 S
6400 WVCY 84128 1961 B5
E 3275 N
10 NHON 84414 998 D4
N 3275 W
300 WPT 84015 1226 C3
S 3275 E
3800 SLkC 84109 1966 C7
S 3275 W
5400 ROY 84067 1171 A4
5500 TYVL 84118 2068 E6
W 3275 N
- NHON 84414 998 D4
200 PTVW 84414 998 D4
500 LEHI 84043 2603 B1
W 3275 S
4000 WVCY 84120 1962 C5
E 3280 N
600 LEHI 84043 2603 D1
600 PRVO 84604 2928 D1
S 3280 W
8300 WJDN 84088 2174 E5
12000 RIVN 84065 2280 E7
W 3280 N
900 LEHI 84043 2603 A1
W 3280 S
1500 WVCY 84119 1963 D5
4600 WVCY 84120 1962 A5
5900 WVCY 84128 1961 C5
W 3285 S
4900 WVCY 84120 1962 A5
5000 WVCY 84120 1961 E5
S 3290 W
4200 WVCY 84119 2068 E1
S 3295 W
5500 TYVL 84118 2068 E5
E 3300 N
400 NHON 84414 998 E4
400 PRVO 84604 2928 D1
500 NHON 84414 999 B4
3200 WbrC 84310 1000 E4
3200 WbrC 84310 1001 A4
3200 WbrC 84414 1000 E4
3200 WbrC 84414 1001 A4
E 3300 S
10 BNFL 84010 1653 E5
10 SSLK 84115 1964 E5
500 SSLK 84106 1964 E5
700 SLkC 84106 1964 E5
700 SLkC 84106 1965 A5
1100 SLCY 84106 1965 A5
2000 SLkC 84109 1965 D5
2300 SLkC 84109 1966 B5
E 3300 S SR-171
10 SSLK 84115 1964 E5
500 SSLK 84106 1964 E5
700 SLkC 84106 1964 E5
700 SLkC 84106 1965 A5
1100 SLCY 84106 1965 A5
2000 SLkC 84109 1965 D5
2300 SLkC 84109 1966 B5
N 3300 E
- WbrC 84310 1000 E1
1600 LYTN 84040 1284 B1
1700 DvsC 84040 1284 B1
3900 WbrC 84310 1001 A1
N 3300 W
3600 BxEC 84302 705 B3
S 3300 E
3300 SLkC 84109 1966 C5
S 3300 W
1700 SRCS 84075 1280 C1
2200 CSTN 84032 2504 C1
4700 ROY 84067 1171 A3
5600 CchC 84339 650 A2
5600 WELV 84339 650 A2
6600 WJDN 84084 2174 E1
13100 RIVN 84065 2386 E3
W 3300 N
- PRVO 84604 2821 C7
- PTVW 84414 998 A3
100 PRVO 84604 2928 C1
400 PTGV 84062 2605 C5
2100 FRWT 84404 997 D4
2200 SLkC 84116 1652 A7
2300 SLCY 84116 1652 A7
3400 CRHL 84062 2605 C6
4300 BxEC 84307 704 E4
4400 UthC 84003 2605 B5
W 3300 S
10 SSLK 84115 1964 A5
300 BNFL 84010 1653 C5
400 SSLK 84119 1964 A5
500 NSLK 84010 1653 C5
700 SRCS 84075 1281 B4
900 SSLK 84119 1963 E5
1000 OGDN 84401 1115 A6
1200 WbrC 84401 1115 A6
1300 OGDN 84401 1114 C6
1300 WVCY 84119 1963 C5
1900 WHVN 84067 1114 C6
1900 WHVN 84401 1114 C6
3300 WbrC 84067 1113 E6
3300 WbrC 84067 1114 A6
3300 WbrC 84401 1113 E6
3300 WbrC 84401 1114 A6
3400 CSTN 84032 2504 C2
4200 WVCY 84120 1962 C5
4400 WHVN 84315 1113 B6
4700 WbrC 84315 1113 B6
5800 CchC 84339 588 D4
W 3300 S SR-171
10 SSLK 84115 1964 A5
400 SSLK 84119 1964 A5
900 SSLK 84119 1963 E5
1100 WVCY 84119 1963 E5
S 3305 E
4000 SLkC 84124 2072 C1
S 3310 W
3500 WVCY 84119 1962 E6
8500 WJDN 84088 2174 E5
S 3315 W
5500 TYVL 84118 2068 E5
W 3315 S
5800 WVCY 84128 1961 D5
S 3320 E
4100 SLkC 84124 2072 C1
S 3320 W
4100 WVCY 84119 2068 E1
5400 TYVL 84118 2068 E5
8300 WJDN 84088 2174 E5
W 3320 S
7800 SLkC 84044 1960 C5
E 3325 N
200 NHON 84414 998 E4
2100 LYTN 84040 1229 E5
S 3325 W
3600 WVCY 84119 1962 E6
S 3325 W
4800 ROY 84067 1171 A3
5300 TYVL 84118 2068 E5
W 3325 N
100 NHON 84414 998 D4
W 3325 S
4400 WVCY 84120 1962 B5
E 3330 N
600 PRVO 84604 2821 D7
N 3330 W
1400 CLTN 84015 1226 B1
W 3330 N
500 LEHI 84043 2603 B1
E 3335 S
10 SSLK 84115 1964 C5
2000 SLkC 84109 1965 D5
N 3335 W
300 WPT 84015 1226 C3
S 3335 W
6800 WJDN 84084 2174 E1
W 3335 S
4200 WVCY 84120 1962 B5
S 3340 E
3000 SLkC 84109 1966 C5
4000 SLkC 84124 2072 C1
S 3340 W
- SRCS 84075 1280 C2
3500 WVCY 84119 1962 E6
5800 TYVL 84118 2068 E6
E 3345 S
100 SSLK 84115 1964 D5
1300 SLkC 84106 1966 B6
3000 SLkC 84109 1966 B5
S 3345 W
10000 SJDN 84095 2280 E3
E 3350 N
300 NHON 84414 998 E3
500 NHON 84414 999 A3
2200 LYTN 84040 1229 E5
2900 WbrC 84310 1000 E4
2900 WbrC 84414 1000 E4
E 3350 S
100 SSLK 84115 1964 D5
1400 SLkC 84106 1965 C6
S 3350 W
4700 ROY 84067 1170 E3
4700 TYVL 84118 2068 E3
W 3350 N
200 PTVW 84414 998 D4
900 LEHI 84043 2603 A1
W 3350 S
- SSLK 84115 1964 C5
200 BNFL 84010 1653 D5
1300 OGDN 84401 1115 A6
1700 WVCY 84119 1963 C5
1900 WbrC 84067 1114 D6
4200 WVCY 84120 1962 C5
6700 WVCY 84128 1961 A5
E 3355 S
600 SSLK 84106 1964 E6
1800 SLkC 84106 1965 D6
E 3360 S
300 SSLK 84115 1964 D5
S 3360 E
3100 SLkC 84109 1966 C5
W 3360 S
2500 WVCY 84119 1963 B5
6000 WVCY 84128 1961 C5
E 3365 S
2700 SLkC 84109 1966 B6
E 3370 S
900 SLkC 84106 1965 A6
2200 SLkC 84109 1965 E6
2800 SLkC 84109 1966 B6
S 3370 W
5600 TYVL 84118 2068 E6
6700 WJDN 84084 2174 E1
W 3370 S
8400 SLkC 84044 1960 B5
E 3375 N
400 NHON 84414 999 A3
1600 NHLN 84341 464 C2
E 3375 S
800 SLkC 84106 1965 A6
N 3375 W
1700 PNCY 84404 997 A7
1700 PNCY 84404 1054 E1
1700 PNCY 84404 1055 A1
S 3375 E
8200 CDHT 84121 2178 C5
S 3375 W
- WHVN 84067 1170 E1
4800 ROY 84067 1170 E3
5300 ROY 84067 1171 A4
W 3375 N
400 LEHI 84043 2603 B1
W 3375 S
200 SSLK 84115 1964 D6
1500 OGDN 84401 1114 E6
4100 WVCY 84120 1962 B4
E 3380 S
2100 SLkC 84109 1965 E6
S 3380 E
3000 SLkC 84109 1966 C5
S 3380 W
4500 WVCY 84119 2068 E2
5500 TYVL 84118 2068 E5
6500 TYVL 84084 2174 E1
6600 WJDN 84084 2174 E1
8400 WJDN 84088 2174 E5
W 3380 S
6200 WVCY 84128 1961 B5
8000 SLkC 84044 1960 C5
E 3385 S
900 SLkC 84106 1965 A6
E 3390 S
600 SSLK 84106 1964 E6
E 3395 S
2300 SLkC 84109 1965 E6
2300 SLkC 84109 1966 A6
S 3395 E
7500 CDHT 84121 2178 C3
W 3395 S
1900 WVCY 84119 1963 C6
E 3400 N
400 PRVO 84604 2821 D7
1100 NHON 84414 999 C3
1300 CchC 84341 464 D1
1300 HDPK 84341 464 D1
2300 LYTN 84040 1229 E5
E 3400 S
400 BNFL 84010 1653 E5
E 3400 S
400 SSLK 84115 1964 E6
2700 SLkC 84109 1966 B6
N 3400 W
- PNCY 84404 997 A6
1000 LYTN 84015 1281 D3
11200 DWVL 84309 522 B5
11200 DWVL 84312 522 B5
11400 BxEC 84309 522 B5
11600 BxEC 84312 522 B1
S 3400 E
1000 SGVL 84663 3144 E4
1000 SGVL 84664 3144 E4
S 3400 W
1700 CchC 84321 526 A7
1800 SRCS 84075 1280 B1
2400 WVCY 84119 1962 E3
3000 CchC 84339 589 E4
3000 CchC 84339 590 A4
3000 CSTN 84032 2504 C2
4700 TYVL 84118 2068 E3
4800 WELV 84339 650 A1
5200 ROY 84067 1170 E4
5400 CchC 84339 650 A3
9000 WJDN 84088 2174 E7
9000 WJDN 84088 2280 E1
9400 SJDN 84095 2280 E1
13100 RIVN 84065 2386 E4
14400 BFDL 84065 2386 E7
W 3400 N
1300 CchC 84341 462 E1
1300 CchC 84341 463 A1
3300 PRVO 84604 2821 B7
W 3400 S
10 SSLK 84115 1964 C6
100 NBLY 84321 591 D4
300 BNFL 84010 1653 C5
500 NSLK 84010 1653 C5
500 NSLK 84054 1653 C5
600 DvsC 84010 1653 B5
700 SRCS 84075 1281 C4
1800 CchC 84321 590 D4
3200 CSTN 84032 2504 C2
4200 WVCY 84120 1962 C5
4800 CchC 84339 589 A4
5400 WVCY 84120 1961 E6
5500 CchC 84339 588 E4
6200 WVCY 84128 1961 B6
S 3410 W
8000 WJDN 84088 2174 E4
W 3410 S
500 SSLK 84119 1964 A6
E 3420 N
600 LEHI 84043 2496 D7
N 3420 W
1500 CLTN 84015 1226 B1
S 3420 W
4000 WVCY 84119 2068 E1
6700 WJDN 84084 2174 E1
10900 SJDN 84095 2280 E5
W 3420 N
1100 PTGV 84062 2605 B5
W 3420 S
2000 WVCY 84119 1963 C6
E 3425 N
400 NHON 84414 998 E3
400 NHON 84414 999 A3
N 3425 W
- LYTN 84041 1281 D4
300 WPT 84015 1226 B3
2400 PNCY 84404 996 E6
S 3425 W
- WHVN 84067 1170 E1
2500 WVCY 84119 1962 E3
4100 WVCY 84119 2068 E1
5000 ROY 84067 1170 E3
W 3425 N
2300 FRWT 84404 997 C3
W 3425 S
1500 OGDN 84401 1114 E6
4200 WVCY 84120 1962 C6
S 3430 W
7600 WJDN 84084 2174 E3
W 3430 N
3300 PRVO 84604 2821 B7
W 3430 S
- NBLY 84321 591 B4
W 3435 S
6300 WVCY 84128 1961 B6
S 3440 W
3600 WVCY 84119 1962 E6
W 3440 S
400 SSLK 84115 1964 B6
3400 WVCY 84119 1962 E6
5000 WVCY 84120 1962 A6
E 3450 N
200 PRVO 84604 2821 D7
400 NHON 84414 999 A3
2000 LYTN 84040 1229 E5
2600 LYTN 84040 1230 A5
4300 WbrC 84310 1001 C3
E 3450 S
100 NBLY 84321 591 D5
N 3450 W
1000 LYTN 84015 1281 D2
1000 LYTN 84041 1281 D2
1600 PNCY 84404 1054 E1
1700 PNCY 84404 996 E7
S 3450 W
- WHVN 84067 1170 E2
3100 WVCY 84119 1962 E5
4800 ROY 84067 1170 E3
8200 WJDN 84088 2174 E5
14000 BFDL 84065 2386 E6
W 3450 N
100 SPFK 84660 3142 C4
200 NHON 84414 998 D3
400 PTVW 84414 998 C4
2600 FRWT 84404 997 B3
3300 PRVO 84604 2821 B7
W 3450 S
10 BNFL 84010 1653 D5
10 SSLK 84115 1964 C6
700 SRCS 84075 1281 B4
900 PRRY 84302 827 C7
4200 WVCY 84120 1962 C6
4700 WHVN 84315 1113 B6
8400 SLkC 84044 1960 B6
N 3455 W
1300 CLTN 84015 1226 B1
E 3460 N
400 NHON 84414 998 E3
E 3460 N
400 PRVO 84604 2821 D7
S 3460 W
2500 WVCY 84119 1962 E3
W 3460 S
- WVCY 84119 1963 A6
S 3465 W
5400 TYVL 84118 2068 E5
W 3470 S
3300 WVCY 84119 1962 E6
W 3471 S
2800 CSTN 84032 2504 D3
E 3475 N
300 NHON 84414 998 E3
400 NHON 84414 999 A3
N 3475 W
- LYTN 84041 1281 D4
2000 PNCY 84404 997 A7
S 3475 W
- WHVN 84067 1170 E1
4700 TYVL 84118 2068 E3
W 3475 S
4200 WVCY 84120 1962 C6
8200 SLkC 84044 1960 C6
S 3480 W
1800 SLCY 84104 1962 E1
W 3480 S
- NBLY 84321 591 B4
S 3490 W
8100 WJDN 84088 2174 D5
10000 SJDN 84095 2280 E3
E 3500 N
400 NHON 84414 999 A3
2200 LYTN 84040 1229 E5
E 3500 S
10 BNFL 84010 1653 D6
N 3500 E
2900 WbrC 84310 1001 A4
2900 WbrC 84414 1001 A4
N 3500 W
- LYTN 84041 1281 D3
300 WPT 84015 1226 B3
1000 LYTN 84015 1281 D2
2100 PNCY 84404 996 E7
S 3500 E
7400 CDHT 84121 2178 C4
S 3500 W
800 WbrC 84404 1054 E7
1200 WbrC 84401 1054 E7
1400 WbrC 84401 1113 E1
3000 CSTN 84032 2504 C2
3300 WbrC 84067 1113 E7
3500 WHVN 84067 1113 E7
3500 WHVN 84315 1113 E7
4000 WHVN 84067 1170 E2
4000 WHVN 84315 1170 E2
4600 ROY 84067 1170 E5
4600 ROY 84315 1170 E2
5400 TYVL 84118 2068 E5
6100 CchC 84339 649 E4
10900 SJDN 84095 2280 E5
S 3500 W SR-108
4700 ROY 84067 1170 E5
W 3500 N
700 PTVW 84414 998 B4
2500 FRWT 84404 997 B3
W 3500 S
300 BNFL 84010 1653 C5
500 OGDN 84405 1115 B7
500 RVDL 84405 1115 B7
500 SRCS 84075 1281 C4
600 DvsC 84010 1653 B5
1300 WVCY 84119 1963 C6
1500 CchC 84321 590 E5
3000 CchC 84339 590 A5
3000 WVCY 84119 1962 D6
3200 CSTN 84032 2504 C3
3500 CchC 84339 589 E5
3600 WVCY 84120 1962 D6
5000 WVCY 84120 1961 D6
5600 WVCY 84128 1961 D6
7000 WVCY 84128 1960 E6
7200 SLkC 84044 1960 E6
8900 SLkC 84006 1959 E5
8900 SLkC 84006 1960 A6
8900 SLkC 84044 1959 E5
W 3500 S SR-171
1300 WVCY 84119 1963 C6
3000 WVCY 84119 1962 D6
3600 WVCY 84120 1962 D6
5000 WVCY 84120 1961 D6
5600 WVCY 84128 1961 D6
7000 WVCY 84128 1960 E6
7200 SLkC 84044 1960 E6
E 3510 S
2300 SLkC 84109 1965 E6
2300 SLkC 84109 1966 A6
S 3515 W
3900 WVCY 84119 1962 D7
3900 WVCY 84119 2068 E1
S 3520 W
3800 WVCY 84119 1962 D7
E 3525 N
400 NHON 84414 998 E3
600 NHON 84414 999 A3
2600 LYTN 84040 1230 A5
N 3525 W
2900 PNCY 84404 996 E5
S 3525 W
- SRCS 84075 1226 B6
5600 TYVL 84118 2068 E6
13300 RIVN 84065 2386 D4
S 3530 E
3400 SLkC 84109 1966 C6
S 3530 W
7500 WJDN 84084 2174 D3
7900 WJDN 84088 2174 D4
12200 UthC 84651 3461 E3
W 3530 S
6400 WVCY 84128 1961 B6
S 3535 W
4800 TYVL 84118 2068 D4
6800 WJDN 84084 2174 D2
S 3540 W
8300 WJDN 84088 2174 D5
W 3540 N
10 PRVO 84604 2821 B7
1100 PTGV 84062 2605 B4
W 3540 S
2000 WVCY 84119 1963 C6
3200 WVCY 84119 1962 E6

STREET Block City ZIP Map# Grid

E 3545 S
1200 SLkC 84106 1965 B6
S 3545 E
7700 CDHT 84121 2178 C4
E 3550 N
200 PRVO 84604 2821 C7
300 NHON 84414 998 E3
400 NHON 84414 999 A3
E 3550 S
500 BNFL 84010 1653 E5
500 BNFL 84010 1654 A6
800 SLkC 84106 1965 A6
N 3550 W
- LYTN 84041 1281 C3
2400 PNCY 84404 996 E6
S 3550 W
3600 WHVN 84315 1113 E7
3900 WVCY 84119 1962 D7
3900 WVCY 84119 2068 D1
5000 ROY 84067 1170 E3
9000 UthC 84651 3354 E2
9800 PYSN 84651 3354 E3
W 3550 N
900 PTVW 84414 998 B3
W 3550 S
- PRRY 84302 885 A1
500 RVDL 84405 1115 B7
1200 PRRY 84302 827 B7
3500 WHVN 84315 1113 E6
4200 WVCY 84120 1962 C6
E 3560 N
400 NHON 84414 998 E3
S 3560 W
2500 WVCY 84119 1962 D3
6000 TYVL 84118 2068 D6
W 3560 S
100 SSLK 84115 1964 C6
6400 WVCY 84128 1961 B6
7600 SLkC 84044 1960 D6
W 3565 S
3500 SLkC 84044 1960 C6
S 3570 E
3400 SLkC 84109 1966 D6
S 3570 W
5400 TYVL 84118 2068 D5
W 3570 S
2200 WVCY 84119 1963 B6
3100 WVCY 84119 1962 E6
6200 WVCY 84128 1961 B6
8100 SLkC 84044 1960 C6
E 3575 N
200 NHON 84414 998 E3
500 NHON 84414 999 A3
2600 LYTN 84040 1230 A5
N 3575 W
1000 LYTN 84015 1281 C2
1000 LYTN 84041 1281 C2
S 3575 W
4800 ROY 84067 1170 E3
W 3575 S
- NBLY 84321 591 C5
500 SRCS 84075 1281 C4
5600 WVCY 84128 1961 D6
E 3580 S
800 SLkC 84106 1965 A6
S 3580 W
8200 WJDN 84088 2174 D5
E 3585 S
600 SSLK 84106 1964 E6
W 3595 S
3200 WVCY 84119 1962 E6
E 3600 N
400 NHON 84414 998 E3
500 NHON 84414 999 A3
2100 DvsC 84040 1229 E4
2100 LYTN 84040 1229 E4
2700 LYTN 84040 1230 A5
3600 WbrC 84310 1001 A3
E 3600 S
10 BNFL 84010 1653 D6
1800 SLkC 84106 1965 D6
2700 SLkC 84109 1966 A6
N 3600 W
10 LEHI 84043 2602 B6
10 SRSP 84043 2602 B6
100 WbrC 84404 1054 E4
200 UthC 84043 2602 B6
1900 PNCY 84404 996 E7
4800 BxEC 84302 646 A7
5900 HYVL 84302 646 A6
7300 HYVL 84314 586 A7
7300 HYVL 84314 646 A1
S 3600 W
100 WbrC 84404 1054 E5
200 CchC 84321 525 E5
800 SLCY 84104 1856 D6
1800 CchC 84321 589 E1
1800 SLCY 84104 1962 D3
2100 WVCY 84119 1962 D3
2100 WVCY 84120 1962 D3
3600 WHVN 84315 1113 E7
4000 WHVN 84315 1170 E1
4000 WVCY 84119 2068 D3
4000 WVCY 84120 2068 D3
4300 CchC 84339 589 E7
4500 ROY 84067 1170 E2
4500 ROY 84315 1170 E2
4600 WELV 84339 649 E1
4700 TYVL 84118 2068 D3
6800 CchC 84339 649 E7
7400 CchC 84339 708 E1
11400 SJDN 84095 2280 D6
11800 RIVN 84065 2280 D6
12000 RIVN 84065 2386 D1
13800 BFDL 84065 2386 D4
W 3600 N
- CchC 84341 463 B1
- HDPK 84341 463 C1
700 PTVW 84414 998 B3
2800 FRWT 84404 997 B3
3500 BxEC 84307 704 E4
3500 BxEC 84307 705 A4
3900 WbrC 84404 996 D3
W 3600 S
300 BNFL 84010 1653 C6
400 SSLK 84115 1964 B6
500 RVDL 84405 1115 B7
800 DvsC 84010 1653 B6
800 DvsC 84054 1653 B6
900 PRRY 84302 885 C1
1900 CchC 84321 590 D5
2500 WHVN 84067 1114 B7
W 3600 S
2900 CSTN 84032 2504 C3
3400 WHVN 84067 1113 E7
3500 SLkC 84044 1960 C6
S 3605 E
9000 CDHT 84093 2178 D7
W 3605 S
1900 WVCY 84119 1963 C6
7500 SLkC 84044 1960 D6
S 3608 S
600 SSLK 84106 1964 E6
E 3610 S
500 SSLK 84106 1964 E6
S 3610 E
3400 SLkC 84109 1966 D6
W 3610 N
400 PRVO 84604 2821 B7
S 3615 W
5200 TYVL 84118 2068 D4
W 3615 S
500 SSLK 84119 1964 B6
3300 WVCY 84119 1962 E6
E 3620 N
100 PRVO 84604 2821 C7
S 3620 W
7800 WJDN 84088 2174 D4
12600 UthC 84651 3461 D4
W 3620 S
200 SSLK 84115 1964 C6
6400 WVCY 84128 1961 B6
E 3625 N
300 NHON 84414 998 E3
E 3625 S
900 SLkC 84106 1965 A6
N 3625 W
700 LYTN 84041 1281 C3
W 3625 S
500 SRCS 84075 1281 C4
3700 WHVN 84315 1113 D7
W 3630 S
1300 WVCY 84119 1963 D6
3600 SLkC 84044 1960 C6
E 3635 S
500 SSLK 84106 1964 E6
W 3635 S
6400 WVCY 84128 1961 B6
S 3640 W
4700 TYVL 84118 2068 D3
W 3640 S
5600 WVCY 84128 1961 D6
S 3645 W
8700 WJDN 84088 2174 D6
E 3650 N
400 NHON 84414 998 E3
400 NHON 84414 999 A3
400 PRVO 84604 2821 D7
2500 LYTN 84040 1230 A4
4800 WbrC 84310 1001 D3
E 3650 S
2400 SLkC 84109 1966 A6
N 3650 W
200 WPT 84015 1226 B3
1000 MTSV 84404 1054 E2
2800 PNCY 84404 996 E5
2800 WbrC 84404 996 E5
S 3650 E
3400 SLkC 84109 1966 D6
S 3650 W
3600 WHVN 84315 1113 E7
4500 ROY 84067 1170 E2
4500 ROY 84315 1170 E2
5500 TYVL 84118 2068 D5
W 3650 N
900 PTVW 84414 998 B3
W 3650 S
10 NBLY 84321 591 D5
500 RVDL 84405 1115 B7
2700 WVCY 84119 1963 A6
3000 WVCY 84119 1962 E6
3600 WHVN 84315 1113 E7
4400 WVCY 84120 1962 B6
S 3660 W
3800 WVCY 84120 1962 D7
5100 TYVL 84118 2068 C4
E 3665 S
500 SSLK 84106 1964 E6
900 SLkC 84106 1965 A6
E 3670 S
1000 SLkC 84106 1965 A6
S 3670 W
4000 WVCY 84120 2068 D1
W 3670 S
4000 WVCY 84120 1962 C6
6200 WVCY 84128 1961 C6
E 3675 N
400 NHON 84414 998 E3
600 NHON 84414 999 A3
N 3675 W
- LYTN 84015 1281 C2
- LYTN 84041 1281 C2
1800 WPT 84015 1170 B7
1800 WPT 84015 1226 B1
S 3675 W
3500 WHVN 84315 1113 E7
4500 ROY 84067 1170 E2
W 3675 N
- WbrC 84404 996 D2
W 3675 S
600 RVDL 84405 1115 B7
2800 WHVN 84067 1114 B7
4100 WVCY 84120 1962 C6
E 3680 S
700 SLkC 84106 1964 E7
800 SLkC 84106 1965 A7
S 3680 W
4200 WVCY 84120 2068 D1
8400 WJDN 84088 2174 D5
W 3680 S
200 SSLK 84115 1964 B6
8300 SLkC 84044 1960 B6
E 3685 S
800 SLkC 84106 1965 A7
S 3685 W
4700 TYVL 84118 2068 D3
7900 WJDN 84088 2174 D4
E 3690 S
700 SLkC 84106 1964 A6
700 SLkC 84106 1965 C6
S 3690 W
3100 WVCY 84120 1962 D5
E 3700 N
10 PRVO 84604 2821 C7
200 NHON 84414 998 E3
2400 LYTN 84040 1229 E4
2400 LYTN 84040 1230 A4
E 3700 S
10 NBLY 84321 591 D5
300 CchC 84321 591 E5
400 SSLK 84115 1964 E7
500 CchC 84321 592 A5
700 SLkC 84106 1964 A6
2300 SLkC 84109 1965 E7
2300 SLkC 84109 1966 A7
N 3700 W
- CRFD 84015 1281 C3
- LYTN 84015 1281 C3
- SRCS 84075 1281 C3
100 SLCY 84104 1856 D2
100 SLCY 84116 1856 D2
700 LYTN 84041 1281 C3
1900 PNCY 84404 996 E7
S 3700 W
3800 WVCY 84120 1962 D7
4200 WHVN 84315 1170 E1
4500 ROY 84067 1170 E2
4500 ROY 84315 1170 E2
11800 RIVN 84065 2280 D7
W 3700 N
- HDPK 84341 399 D7
10 PRVO 84604 2821 B7
W 3700 S
100 SSLK 84115 1964 C7
500 RVDL 84405 1115 B7
3500 WHVN 84315 1113 E7
W 3705 S
6200 WVCY 84128 1961 C6
E 3710 S
700 SLkC 84106 1964 A6
S 3710 W
4000 WVCY 84120 2068 D1
5100 TYVL 84118 2068 D4
E 3715 S
2000 SLkC 84109 1965 E7
S 3715 W
8700 WJDN 84088 2174 D6
E 3720 S
700 SLkC 84106 1964 A6
2400 SLkC 84109 1966 A7
S 3720 W
4100 WVCY 84120 2068 D1
8600 WJDN 84088 2174 D6
W 3720 S
4700 WVCY 84120 1962 A7
E 3725 N
100 NHON 84414 998 E3
2700 SWBR 84405 1230 A4
S 3725 W
7800 WJDN 84088 2174 D4
W 3725 S
- ROY 84067 1114 C7
6000 WVCY 84128 1961 C7
E 3730 S
700 SLkC 84106 1964 E7
1300 SLkC 84106 1965 B7
S 3730 W
1800 SLCY 84104 1962 D1
4700 TYVL 84118 2068 D3
E 3735 S
2000 SLkC 84109 1965 E7
W 3735 S
8200 SLkC 84044 1960 C7
E 3740 S
1000 SLkC 84106 1965 A7
S 3740 W
- RIVN 84065 2386 D3
3200 WVCY 84120 1962 D5
4600 WVCY 84120 2068 D3
11700 SJDN 84095 2280 D7
12500 UthC 84651 3461 D4
W 3740 S
500 SSLK 84119 1964 B7
6200 WVCY 84128 1961 C7
E 3745 S
500 SSLK 84106 1964 E7
900 SLkC 84106 1965 A7
2000 SLkC 84109 1965 D7
E 3750 N
400 PRVO 84604 2821 D7
2400 LYTN 84040 1229 E4
2400 SWBR 84405 1229 E4
2500 LYTN 84040 1230 A4
2500 SWBR 84405 1230 A4
E 3750 S
10 SSLK 84115 1964 C7
2300 SLkC 84109 1966 A7
N 3750 E
2300 WbrC 84310 1001 B6
N 3750 W
11200 DWVL 84309 521 E6
S 3750 W
3600 WHVN 84315 1113 E7
4100 WHVN 84315 1170 E1
4700 ROY 84067 1170 E2
W 3750 N
1300 PTVW 84414 998 A3
W 3750 S
- ROY 84067 1114 C7
500 SRCS 84075 1281 C5
600 RVDL 84405 1115 B7
4200 WVCY 84120 1962 C7
S 3760 W
800 SLCY 84104 1856 D5
3600 WVCY 84120 1962 D7
4100 WVCY 84120 2068 D1
4900 TYVL 84118 2068 D4
8800 WJDN 84088 2174 D6
W 3760 S
3000 WVCY 84119 1963 A7
3500 WVCY 84119 1962 D7
W 3765 N
1300 PTVW 84414 998 A3
W 3765 S
500 SSLK 84119 1964 A7
E 3770 S
1200 SLkC 84106 1965 B7
S 3770 W
9400 SJDN 84095 2280 D1
11800 RIVN 84065 2280 D7
12200 RIVN 84065 2386 D1
N 3775 E
1900 WbrC 84310 1001 B7
N 3775 W
1300 WPT 84015 1226 B1
S 3775 E
9700 SLkC 84092 2284 D2
S 3775 W
2400 WbrC 84401 1113 E3
4700 ROY 84067 1170 D3
W 3775 N
1300 PTVW 84414 998 A3
W 3775 S
- NBLY 84321 591 D5
- ROY 84067 1114 C7
2700 WHVN 84067 1114 B7
5700 WVCY 84128 1961 D7
E 3780 S
1800 SLkC 84106 1965 D7
2000 SLkC 84109 1965 E7
S 3780 W
3100 WVCY 84120 1962 D5
8600 WJDN 84088 2174 C6
W 3780 S
3100 WVCY 84119 1962 E7
4300 WVCY 84120 1962 B7
W 3785 S
2700 WVCY 84119 1963 A7
4200 WVCY 84120 1962 C7
5200 WVCY 84120 1961 E7
6300 WVCY 84128 1961 B7
E 3790 S
500 SSLK 84106 1964 E7
W 3790 S
8300 SLkC 84044 1960 B7
S 3795 W
6500 WJDN 84084 2174 D1
E 3800 N
100 PRVO 84604 2821 C7
E 3800 S
500 CchC 84321 591 E5
500 CchC 84321 592 A5
1200 SLkC 84106 1965 B7
3500 SLkC 84109 1966 C7
3500 SLkC 84124 1966 C7
N 3800 E
4100 WbrC 84310 1001 B1
N 3800 W
- BxEC 84307 764 E1
- BxEC 84307 765 A1
- CRNN 84307 764 E1
- PNCY 84404 996 D5
2200 CRNN 84307 765 A1
2300 CRNN 84307 705 A7
S 3800 W
200 CchC 84321 525 D4
900 SLCY 84104 1856 D6
2200 CchC 84321 589 E2
2200 CchC 84339 589 E2
4300 WHVN 84315 1170 D2
4600 ROY 84067 1170 D2
7800 WJDN 84088 2174 D4
11400 SJDN 84095 2280 D6
W 3800 N
300 PRVO 84604 2821 B7
1300 PTVW 84414 998 A2
3100 CchC 84335 398 A7
W 3800 S
- OGDN 84405 1115 A7
600 DvsC 84010 1653 B6
600 DvsC 84054 1653 B6
700 NSLK 84010 1653 B6
700 RVDL 84405 1115 B7
800 NSLK 84054 1653 B6
1500 CchC 84321 590 E6
3000 WVCY 84119 1963 A7
3200 WVCY 84119 1962 E7
3400 CchC 84339 590 A5
3800 WVCY 84120 1962 C7
4400 CchC 84339 589 C5
6600 WVCY 84128 1961 A7
7000 WVCY 84128 1960 E7
W 3800 St N
3400 CchC 84335 398 A7
E 3805 S
700 SLkC 84106 1965 A7
W 3815 S
1300 WVCY 84119 1963 D7
6200 WVCY 84128 1961 C7
E 3820 S
3600 SLkC 84124 1966 D7
S 3820 W
3100 WVCY 84120 1962 D5
8900 WJDN 84088 2174 D7
W 3820 S
500 SSLK 84119 1964 B7
6400 WVCY 84128 1961 B7
E 3825 S
1800 HLDY 84124 1965 D7
1800 SLkC 84106 1965 D7
S 3825 W
2900 WVCY 84120 1962 D5
9200 WJDN 84088 2174 D7
9300 WJDN 84088 2280 D1
9400 SJDN 84095 2280 D1
12300 RIVN 84065 2386 D1
W 3825 S
1900 ROY 84067 1114 D7
4600 WVCY 84120 1962 B7
N 3830 W
9400 CRHL 84062 2605 C4
S 3830 W
8500 WJDN 84088 2174 D6
W 3830 S
4000 WVCY 84120 1962 C7
5200 WVCY 84120 1961 E7
6800 WVCY 84128 1961 A7
E 3835 S
2700 SLkC 84109 1966 A7
W 3835 S
2700 WVCY 84119 1963 A7
3000 WVCY 84119 1962 E7
S 3840 W
9300 SJDN 84095 2280 D1
9300 WJDN 84088 2280 D1
W 3840 S
2400 WVCY 84119 1963 B7
E 3850 N
100 PRVO 84604 2821 C7
E 3850 S
10 NBLY 84321 591 D5
1100 OGDN 84403 1116 B7
E 3850 S SR-284
- OGDN 84403 1116 B7
N 3850 E
1900 WbrC 84310 1001 B7
N 3850 W
1300 WPT 84015 1226 A2
2200 CRNN 84307 765 A1
2300 CRNN 84307 705 A7
S 3850 W
1800 SLCY 84104 1962 D1
2400 WbrC 84401 1113 D3
2400 WVCY 84120 1962 D3
3600 WHVN 84315 1113 D7
4200 WHVN 84315 1170 D1
4500 ROY 84067 1170 D2
4500 ROY 84315 1170 D2
7800 WJDN 84088 2174 D4
W 3850 N
600 PTVW 84414 998 C3
W 3850 S
500 RVDL 84405 1115 B7
4200 WHVN 84315 1113 C7
4800 WVCY 84120 1962 A7
6500 WVCY 84128 1961 B7
E 3850 N N
3800 WbrC 84310 1002 A2
E 3860 N
200 PRVO 84604 2821 C7
S 3860 W
2700 WVCY 84120 1962 D4
4600 WVCY 84120 2068 D3
8900 WJDN 84088 2174 D7
W 3860 S
2000 WVCY 84119 1963 B7
4400 WVCY 84120 1962 B7
6400 WVCY 84128 1961 B7
W 3870 S
1700 WVCY 84119 1963 C7
4300 WVCY 84120 1962 B7
S 3875 W
4300 WHVN 84315 1170 D2
W 3875 S
800 RVDL 84405 1115 B7
1900 ROY 84067 1114 C7
2800 WVCY 84119 1963 A7
3000 WVCY 84119 1962 E7
S 3880 W
10200 SJDN 84095 2280 D3
W 3880 S
6500 WVCY 84128 1961 B7
W 3888 S
- NBLY 84321 591 D5
S 3890 W
11900 RIVN 84065 2280 D7
W 3890 S
3200 WVCY 84119 1962 E7
W 3895 S
4200 WVCY 84120 1962 C7
E 3900 N
10 PRVO 84604 2821 C6
100 NHON 84414 998 E2
3700 WbrC 84310 1001 B3
E 3900 S
10 SLkC 84107 1964 E7
10 SSLK 84115 1964 E7
200 SSLK 84107 1964 E7
500 SLkC 84106 1964 E7
500 SSLK 84106 1964 E7
700 SLkC 84106 1965 B7
700 SLkC 84124 1964 E7
700 SLkC 84124 1965 B7
1600 HLDY 84124 1965 E7
2000 SLkC 84109 1965 E7
2300 HLDY 84109 1965 E7
2300 HLDY 84109 1966 A7
2300 HLDY 84124 1966 A7
2300 SLkC 84109 1966 A7
2500 SLkC 84124 1966 A7
N 3900 W
1900 PNCY 84404 996 D7
2200 CRNN 84307 704 E7
2200 CRNN 84307 764 E1
2300 CRNN 84307 705 A7
3000 WbrC 84404 996 D3
S 3900 W
700 SRCS 84075 1226 A6
3100 WVCY 84120 1962 C5
4000 WHVN 84315 1170 D1
4600 ROY 84067 1170 D2
8800 WJDN 84088 2174 D7
12300 RIVN 84065 2386 D1
W 3900 N
300 PRVO 84604 2821 B6
500 PTVW 84414 998 C3
W 3900 S
- RVDL 84405 1115 B7
- SGVL 84660 3142 C3
- SGVL 84663 3142 C3
10 SLkC 84107 1964 C7
100 OGDN 84405 1115 A7
200 SLkC 84115 1964 B7
400 SLkC 84123 1964 B7
400 SSLK 84115 1964 B7
500 SSLK 84119 1964 B7
800 DvsC 84010 1653 B6
1800 WVCY 84119 1963 C7
1900 CchC 84321 590 D6
2000 ROY 84067 1114 D7
2700 CchC 84319 590 B6
2700 CchC 84339 590 B6
2700 WELV 84319 590 B6
3600 WVCY 84120 1962 D7
3900 WHVN 84315 1113 D7
5200 WVCY 84120 1961 E7
W 3900 S SR-77
- SGVL 84660 3142 C3
- SGVL 84663 3142 C3
W 3910 S
6500 WVCY 84128 1961 B7
S 3920 W
4100 WVCY 84120 2068 C1
6100 TYVL 84118 2068 D7
8600 WJDN 84088 2174 C6
W 3920 S
1900 ROY 84067 1114 C7
E 3925 S
3200 SLkC 84124 1966 C7
S 3925 W
900 SRCS 84075 1226 A6
2700 WbrC 84401 1113 D4
5000 ROY 84067 1170 D3
10300 SJDN 84095 2280 C3
W 3925 N
900 PTVW 84414 998 B2
W 3925 S
2000 ROY 84067 1114 C7
4200 WHVN 84315 1113 C7
E 3930 S
1300 SLkC 84124 1965 B7
S 3930 W
7800 WJDN 84088 2174 C4
W 3930 S
4200 WVCY 84120 1962 B7
E 3935 S
3100 SLkC 84124 1966 B7
W 3935 S
2400 WVCY 84119 1963 B7
6000 WVCY 84128 1961 C7
N 3940 W
9400 CRHL 84062 2605 C4
W 3940 N
400 PRVO 84604 2821 B6
W 3940 S
- NBLY 84321 591 D6
700 SLkC 84123 1964 A7
6500 WVCY 84128 1961 B7
E 3945 S
500 SLkC 84107 1964 E7
E 3950 N
- WbrC 84310 1001 D2
300 PRVO 84604 2821 D6
E 3950 S
10 BNFL 84010 1653 D6
600 SLkC 84107 1964 E7
1000 SLkC 84124 1965 A7
N 3950 W
2200 CRNN 84307 704 E1
2200 CRNN 84307 764 E1
2400 CRNN 84307 705 A7
S 3950 W
700 SRCS 84075 1226 A6
1700 WbrC 84401 1113 D1
3800 WHVN 84315 1113 D7
4600 ROY 84067 1170 D2
9200 UthC 84651 3354 D3
W 3950 N
300 PRVO 84604 2821 B6
800 PTVW 84414 998 C2
W 3950 S
500 RVDL 84405 1115 C7
700 RVDL 84405 1172 B1
1800 WVCY 84119 1963 C7
2600 ROY 84067 1114 B7
3600 WHVN 84315 1113 E7
E 3955 S
500 SLkC 84107 1964 E7
E 3960 S
2900 SLkC 84124 1966 B7
S 3960 W
4200 WVCY 84120 2068 C1
4800 TYVL 84118 2068 C3
7900 WJDN 84088 2174 C4
W 3960 N
10 PRVO 84604 2821 C6
W 3960 S
1900 ROY 84067 1114 C7
1900 ROY 84067 1171 D1
7200 SLkC 84044 1960 E7
S 3965 W
8600 WJDN 84088 2174 C6
W 3965 S
- WHVN 84067 1114 B7
2300 WVCY 84119 1963 B7
3400 WVCY 84119 1962 E7
3600 WVCY 84120 1962 D7
E 3970 S
500 SLkC 84107 1964 E7
1500 SLkC 84124 1965 C7
2100 HLDY 84124 1965 E7
S 3970 W
10300 SJDN 84095 2280 C3
11200 PYSN 84651 3354 C7
W 3970 S
1900 WVCY 84119 1963 C7
E 3975 S
800 SLkC 84124 1965 A7
N 3975 W
2500 PNCY 84404 996 D6
S 3975 W
4800 ROY 84067 1170 D3
6200 TYVL 84084 2068 C7
W 3975 N
300 PTVW 84414 998 C2
2700 FRWT 84404 997 B2
W 3975 S
- WHVN 84067 1114 A7
2800 WHVN 84067 1171 B1
E 3980 S
2200 HLDY 84124 1965 E7
W 3980 S
4400 WVCY 84120 1962 B7
6900 WVCY 84128 1961 A7
7100 WVCY 84128 1960 E7
W 3985 S
1900 ROY 84067 1171 E1
E 3990 S
500 SLkC 84107 1964 E7
1400 SLkC 84124 1965 C7
1600 HLDY 84124 1965 C7
W 3990 S
4500 WVCY 84120 1962 B7
5200 WVCY 84120 1961 E7
W 3995 S
1900 ROY 84067 1171 E1
2400 WVCY 84119 1963 B7
7100 WVCY 84128 1960 E7
7200 SLkC 84044 1960 E7
E 4000 N
200 PRVO 84604 2821 C6
E 4000 S
800 OGDN 84403 1173 A1
1300 SLkC 84124 1965 B7
2200 HLDY 84124 1965 E7
E 4000 S SR-284
- OGDN 84403 1173 B1
N 4000 W
- SLCY 84116 1856 C1
100 WPT 84015 1226 A4
800 CchC 84321 525 D1
1000 SLCY 84116 1752 C5
2200 CRNN 84307 704 E7
2200 CRNN 84307 764 E1
2500 CRNN 84307 705 A6
3700 BxEC 84307 704 E4
8800 PTGV 84062 2605 C5
9400 CRHL 84062 2605 C4
12800 BxEC 84312 521 E1
S 4000 W
10 CchC 84321 525 D3
700 DvsC 84075 1226 A6
700 SRCS 84075 1226 A6
1100 WPT 84075 1226 A6
1700 SRCS 84075 1280 A1
2100 WVCY 84120 1962 C2
2200 DvsC 84075 1280 A1
3800 CchC 84339 589 D6
3800 WELV 84339 589 D6
3900 WHVN 84315 1113 D7
4000 WHVN 84315 1170 D1
4000 WVCY 84120 2068 C2
4600 ROY 84067 1170 D2
4700 SLkC 84118 2068 C2
5800 TYVL 84118 2068 C6
6200 TYVL 84084 2068 C7
6800 CchC 84339 649 D7
7800 WJDN 84088 2174 C6
9300 WJDN 84088 2280 C1
11400 SJDN 84095 2280 C7
11800 RIVN 84065 2280 C7
12600 UthC 84651 3461 D4
13400 RIVN 84065 2386 C4
13800 BFDL 84065 2386 C4
W 4000 N
- NHON 84414 998 D2
1100 PTVW 84414 998 A2
1700 BxEC 84340 997 D2
1700 PTVW 84404 997 D2
1700 PTVW 84414 997 D2
2400 FRWT 84404 997 D2
2800 BxEC 84302 705 C3
2800 WbrC 84404 997 A2
3100 CchC 84335 398 A7
3100 WbrC 84340 996 E2
3100 WbrC 84404 996 E2
3500 PTGV 84062 2605 C4
3900 CRHL 84062 2605 C4
4800 BxEC 84307 704 C3
4800 BxEC 84337 704 C3
W 4000 S
10 NBLY 84321 591 C6
400 CchC 84321 591 C6
700 OGDN 84405 1172 A1
700 SGVL 84660 3142 A3
700 SGVL 84663 3142 A3
700 SPFK 84660 3142 A3
700 SPFK 84663 3142 A3
700 UthC 84660 3142 A3
800 DvsC 84010 1653 B6
800 RVDL 84405 1172 B1
800 UthC 84660 3141 C3
900 NSLK 84010 1653 B6
1800 OGDN 84405 1171 C1
1800 ROY 84067 1171 C1
2200 WbrC 84067 1171 C1
2900 WHVN 84067 1170 B1
2900 WHVN 84067 1171 C1
3500 WHVN 84315 1170 B1
4000 WVCY 84120 1962 C7
5100 HOPR 84315 1170 B1
5300 HOPR 84315 1169 E1
W 4000 S SR-37
- ROY 84067 1171 B1
2900 WHVN 84067 1170 B1
2900 WHVN 84067 1171 B1
3500 WHVN 84315 1170 B1
5100 HOPR 84315 1170 B1
5300 HOPR 84315 1169 E1
W 4000 S SR-77
700 SGVL 84660 3142 A3
700 SGVL 84663 3142 A3
700 SPFK 84660 3142 A3
700 SPFK 84663 3142 A3
700 UthC 84660 3142 A3
800 UthC 84660 3141 C3
E 4010 S
500 SLkC 84107 1964 E7
S 4015 W
4700 SLkC 84118 2068 C4
4700 TYVL 84118 2068 C4
6400 TYVL 84084 2068 C7
6400 TYVL 84084 2174 C1
W 4015 S
6800 WVCY 84128 1961 A7
E 4020 N
400 PRVO 84604 2821 D6
E 4020 S
300 SLkC 84107 1964 D7
1100 SLkC 84124 1965 B7
W 4020 N
200 PRVO 84604 2821 B6
W 4020 S
1400 WVCY 84119 1963 D7
1900 WVCY 84119 2069 C1
4400 WVCY 84120 2068 B1
E 4025 S
600 SLkC 84107 1964 E7
1000 SLkC 84124 1965 A7
S 4025 W
3800 WHVN 84315 1113 D7
5400 ROY 84067 1170 D4
W 4025 S
- WHVN 84067 1171 E1
4500 WVCY 84120 2068 B1
5200 WVCY 84120 2067 E1
6800 WVCY 84128 1961 A7
E 4030 S
500 SLkC 84107 1964 E7
S 4030 W
9400 SJDN 84095 2280 C1
W 4030 S
2400 WVCY 84119 2069 B1
W 4035 S
6800 WVCY 84128 2067 A1
E 4040 S
- SLkC 84124 1965 A7
W 4040 S
3400 WVCY 84119 2068 E1
3600 WVCY 84120 2068 D1
E 4045 S
1300 SLkC 84124 2071 C1
S 4045 W
4300 WVCY 84120 2068 D2
E 4050 S
10 BNFL 84010 1653 D6
500 SLkC 84107 2070 A1
900 OGDN 84403 1173 A1
N 4050 W
2200 CRNN 84307 704 E7

STREET Block City ZIP Map# Grid

S 4050 W
- SRCS 84075 1226 A7
600 SLCY 84104 1856 C5
2500 WbrC 84401 1113 D4
3900 WVCY 84120 1962 C7
3900 WVCY 84120 2068 C1
4800 ROY 84067 1170 D3
W 4050 N
500 PTVW 84414 998 C2
W 4050 S
- WHVN 84067 1170 E1
700 DvsC 84010 1653 B6
800 RVDL 84405 1172 B1
2500 ROY 84067 1171 B1
3500 WVCY 84119 2068 D1
4500 WHVN 84315 1170 B1
4700 WVCY 84120 2068 A1
E 4055 S
500 SLkC 84107 2070 E1
S 4055 W
4700 SLkC 84118 2068 C3
W 4055 S
1900 WVCY 84119 2069 C1
S 4060 W
3100 WVCY 84120 1962 C5
5600 SLkC 84118 2068 C6
W 4060 S
700 SLkC 84123 1964 A7
700 SLkC 84123 2070 A1
3200 WVCY 84119 2068 E1
5300 WVCY 84120 2067 E1
6700 WVCY 84128 2067 A1
E 4065 S
600 SLkC 84107 2070 E3
1300 SLkC 84124 2071 B1
W 4065 S
4500 WVCY 84120 2068 B1
5200 WVCY 84120 2067 E1
6800 WVCY 84128 2067 A1
E 4070 S
700 SLkC 84124 2070 E3
700 SLkC 84124 2071 A1
W 4070 S
- SLkC 84123 2070 B1
400 MRRY 84123 2070 B1
3400 WVCY 84119 2068 E1
E 4075 N
200 PRVO 84604 2821 C6
E 4075 S
500 SLkC 84107 2070 E1
S 4075 W
1600 WbrC 84401 1113 D1
4600 ROY 84067 1170 D2
W 4075 N
300 PTVW 84414 998 D2
W 4075 S
- WHVN 84067 1170 E1
700 RVDL 84405 1172 B1
6900 WVCY 84128 2067 A1
E 4080 S
500 SLkC 84107 2070 E1
1400 SLkC 84124 2071 B1
S 4080 W
4100 WVCY 84120 2068 C1
11700 SJDN 84095 2280 C7
E 4085 S
1100 SLkC 84124 2071 B1
W 4085 S
6800 WVCY 84128 2067 A1
E 4090 S
300 SLkC 84107 2070 D1
3300 SLkC 84124 2072 C1
S 4090 W
5800 SLkC 84118 2068 C6
E 4095 S
1500 SLkC 84124 2071 C1
S 4095 W
4800 SLkC 84118 2068 C3
E 4100 N
- CchC 84341 399 D7
- HDPK 84341 399 D7
10 CchC 84318 399 E7
10 HDPK 84318 399 E7
3000 WbrC 84310 1000 E2
3500 WbrC 84310 1001 A2
E 4100 S
400 SLkC 84107 2070 E1
900 SOGN 84403 1173 C1
1200 OGDN 84403 1173 C1
E 4100 S SR-284
1200 OGDN 84403 1173 C1
N 4100 W
500 WPT 84015 1226 A3
2100 CRNN 84307 764 E1
2200 PNCY 84404 996 D6
2500 CRNN 84307 704 E6
9700 CRHL 84062 2605 C3
S 4100 W
- ROY 84067 1170 D2
400 WbrC 84404 1054 D6
3100 WVCY 84120 1962 C5
4000 WVCY 84120 2068 C1
4100 WHVN 84315 1170 D2
4500 WHVN 84067 1170 D2
13600 RIVN 84065 2386 C5
W 4100 N
10 SmtC 84098 1972 C7
200 PRVO 84604 2821 B6
900 PTVW 84414 998 B2
W 4100 S
- SLkC 84006 2066 B1
700 RVDL 84405 1172 B1
800 DvsC 84010 1653 B6
1600 TYVL 84123 2069 C1
1600 WVCY 84119 2069 C1
1700 TYVL 84119 2069 A1
2600 ROY 84067 1171 B1
3000 WVCY 84119 2068 E1
3600 WVCY 84120 2068 C1
4500 WHVN 84315 1170 B1
5100 WVCY 84120 2067 D1
5600 WVCY 84128 2067 A1
6800 WVCY 84044 2066 E1
6800 WVCY 84044 2067 A1
6800 WVCY 84128 2067 A1
7200 SLkC 84044 2066 E1
E 4100 S St
- CchC 84321 592 A6
S 4105 W
- RIVN 84065 2386 C2
S 4110 W
4300 WVCY 84120 2068 C1

E 4115 S
300 SLkC 84107 2070 D1
E 4119 S
600 SLkC 84107 2070 E1
E 4120 S
400 SLkC 84107 2070 A1
S 4120 W
5400 SLkC 84118 2068 C5
W 4120 S
4500 WVCY 84120 2068 B1
6500 WVCY 84128 2067 B1
E 4125 S
700 SLkC 84107 2070 E3
700 SLkC 84107 2071 A1
700 SLkC 84124 2070 E3
700 SLkC 84124 2071 A1
S 4125 W
4700 ROY 84067 1170 D2
6400 TYVL 84084 2068 C7
W 4125 N
900 PTVW 84414 998 B2
W 4125 S
- ROY 84067 1171 D1
4500 WHVN 84315 1170 B1
E 4129 S
600 SLkC 84107 2070 E3
E 4130 S
1200 SLkC 84124 2071 B1
S 4130 W
1700 SLCY 84104 1962 C1
12000 RIVN 84065 2280 C7
12000 RIVN 84065 2386 C1
W 4130 S
2300 TYVL 84119 2069 B1
4600 WVCY 84120 2068 C3
E 4135 S
2700 SLkC 84124 2072 A1
S 4135 W
4800 SLkC 84118 2068 C3
W 4135 S
2700 WVCY 84119 2069 A1
4100 WVCY 84120 2068 C1
E 4140 S
300 SLkC 84107 2070 D1
S 4140 W
3100 WVCY 84120 1962 C5
4700 SLkC 84118 2068 C3
6500 TYVL 84084 2174 C1
W 4140 N
100 PRVO 84604 2821 B6
E 4145 S
1200 SLkC 84124 2071 B1
W 4145 S
6500 WVCY 84128 2067 A1
E 4149 S
600 SLkC 84107 2070 E1
E 4150 S
- SLkC 84107 2070 D1
800 SOGN 84403 1173 A1
N 4150 E
4300 WbrC 84310 1001 C1
N 4150 W
1500 PNCY 84404 1054 D1
2800 PNCY 84404 996 D5
4000 WbrC 84340 996 C2
4000 WbrC 84404 996 C2
S 4150 W
600 SLCY 84104 1856 C5
2400 WbrC 84401 1113 D4
4000 WVCY 84120 2068 C1
4800 ROY 84067 1170 C3
W 4150 N
300 PRVO 84604 2821 B6
W 4150 S
- WHVN 84067 1170 E1
1000 RVDL 84405 1172 A1
2100 ROY 84067 1171 C1
2300 TYVL 84119 2069 B1
3600 WHVN 84315 1170 E1
3900 WVCY 84120 2068 C1
E 4160 S
1500 SLkC 84124 2071 C1
N 4160 W
9900 CRHL 84062 2605 B3
S 4160 W
6400 TYVL 84084 2068 C7
E 4165 S
1400 SLkC 84124 2071 C1
S 4165 W
4500 WVCY 84120 2068 C2
6500 TYVL 84084 2174 C1
E 4170 N
200 PRVO 84604 2821 C6
E 4170 S
800 SLkC 84107 2071 A1
1300 SLkC 84124 2071 B1
S 4170 W
4400 WVCY 84120 2068 C2
5500 SLkC 84118 2068 C5
13600 RIVN 84065 2386 C5
W 4170 S
600 MRRY 84123 2070 A1
5100 WVCY 84120 2067 E1
6400 WVCY 84128 2067 B1
N 4175 W
2400 PNCY 84404 996 D6
S 4175 W
- WbrC 84401 1113 C3
5500 ROY 84067 1170 C4
W 4175 N
10 PTVW 84414 998 D2
W 4175 S
1000 RVDL 84405 1172 A1
2300 TYVL 84119 2069 C1
2600 ROY 84067 1171 B1
4700 WVCY 84120 2068 A1
5100 HOPR 84315 1170 A1
S 4180 W
3100 WVCY 84120 1962 C5
5000 SLkC 84118 2068 C4
W 4180 S
1400 TYVL 84123 2069 D1
6300 WVCY 84128 2067 B1
E 4181 S
600 SLkC 84107 2070 E4
W 4185 S
2200 TYVL 84119 2069 B1
E 4190 N
400 PRVO 84604 2821 D6
E 4190 S
1600 SLkC 84124 2071 C1

S 4190 W
9500 SJDN 84095 2280 C1
W 4190 S
3600 WVCY 84120 2068 D1
W 4195 S
2300 TYVL 84119 2069 B1
E 4200 S
700 SLkC 84107 2070 E1
700 SLkC 84107 2071 A1
1300 SLkC 84124 2071 C1
1500 OGDN 84403 1173 C1
N 4200 W
100 PRVO 84601 2926 E6
100 UthC 84601 2926 E6
2500 PNCY 84404 996 C6
3000 WbrC 84404 996 D4
N 4200 W SR-134
2500 PNCY 84404 996 C6
S 4200 W
- UthC 84651 3461 C3
- WbrC 84401 1113 C2
1900 CchC 84321 589 D1
3500 WVCY 84120 1962 C6
5000 ROY 84067 1170 C4
7900 CchC 84339 649 D7
7900 CchC 84339 708 D1
W 4200 N
10 CchC 84335 399 D6
10 CchC 84341 399 D6
10 PRVO 84604 2821 C6
300 PTVW 84414 998 C2
1200 CchC 84335 398 E6
1200 CchC 84341 398 E6
W 4200 S
600 CchC 84321 591 B6
1000 RVDL 84405 1172 A1
1300 TYVL 84123 2069 D1
1800 CchC 84321 590 E6
2600 ROY 84067 1171 B1
4400 CchC 84339 589 C6
4500 WHVN 84315 1170 B1
5000 WVCY 84120 2068 A1
5100 WVCY 84120 2067 E1
5500 HOPR 84315 1169 E1
6400 WVCY 84128 2067 B1
S 4205 W
4100 WVCY 84120 2068 C1
E 4215 S
2700 SLkC 84124 2072 A1
W 4215 S
6300 WVCY 84128 2067 B1
E 4220 N
300 PRVO 84604 2821 D6
S 4220 W
3800 WVCY 84120 1962 C7
5300 SLkC 84118 2068 C5
W 4220 S
2200 TYVL 84119 2069 B1
E 4225 S
1200 OGDN 84403 1173 B1
S 4225 W
5500 ROY 84067 1170 C4
W 4225 S
600 RVDL 84405 1172 C1
1900 ROY 84067 1171 D1
3700 WHVN 84315 1170 D1
E 4230 S
1400 SLkC 84124 2071 C1
S 4235 W
3100 WVCY 84120 1962 B4
W 4235 S
1400 TYVL 84123 2069 D1
5000 WVCY 84120 2068 A1
S 4240 W
3500 WVCY 84120 1962 C6
5100 SLkC 84118 2068 C4
9400 SJDN 84095 2280 C1
W 4240 S
2200 TYVL 84119 2069 C1
E 4250 S
600 SOGN 84403 1173 A1
N 4250 W
1400 PNCY 84404 1054 C2
S 4250 W
1700 SLCY 84104 1962 C1
5400 ROY 84067 1170 C4
W 4250 S
1100 RVDL 84405 1172 A1
2100 ROY 84067 1171 C1
4800 WHVN 84315 1170 B1
4800 WVCY 84120 2068 A1
5100 HOPR 84315 1170 A1
E 4255 S
700 SLkC 84107 2070 E1
700 SLkC 84107 2071 A1
S 4260 W
6000 SLkC 84118 2068 C6
12000 UthC 84651 3461 C3
W 4260 S
2200 TYVL 84119 2069 B1
5400 WVCY 84120 2067 D1
S 4265 W
3600 WVCY 84120 1962 C6
E 4270 S
1100 SLkC 84124 2071 B1
S 4270 W
5400 SLkC 84118 2068 C5
W 4270 S
1500 TYVL 84123 2069 C1
E 4275 S
900 SOGN 84403 1173 B1
N 4275 W
2200 PNCY 84404 996 C6
N 4275 W SR-134
2200 PNCY 84404 996 C6
S 4275 W
3900 WVCY 84120 1962 C7
3900 WVCY 84120 2068 C1
5000 ROY 84067 1170 C3
W 4275 S
600 RVDL 84405 1172 C1
2700 ROY 84067 1171 B1
4500 WHVN 84315 1170 B1
5700 HOPR 84315 1169 D1
E 4280 S
600 SLkC 84107 2070 E1
700 SLkC 84107 2071 A1
S 4280 W
4400 WVCY 84120 2068 C2
11300 UthC 84651 3354 C7
11300 UthC 84651 3461 C1

E 4285 S
600 SLkC 84107 2070 E1
W 4290 S
4600 WVCY 84120 2068 A1
E 4300 N
300 PRVO 84604 2821 D6
E 4300 S
- NBLY 84321 591 E7
- SPFK 84660 3142 D4
10 WSTR 84405 1172 E1
300 SGVL 84663 3142 D4
800 SOGN 84403 1173 A2
900 SGVL 84663 3143 A4
N 4300 W
10 WbrC 84404 1054 C4
1400 PNCY 84404 1054 C2
8800 PTGV 84062 2605 B5
S 4300 W
900 WbrC 84401 1054 C7
900 WbrC 84404 1054 C7
1200 CchC 84321 525 D6
1400 WbrC 84401 1113 C2
3100 WVCY 84120 1962 B5
3900 WHVN 84315 1113 C7
3900 WHVN 84315 1170 C1
4500 WHVN 84067 1170 C1
4600 ROY 84067 1170 C5
4700 SLkC 84118 2068 B3
4800 HOPR 84315 1170 C5
5800 ROY 84315 1170 C5
8200 WJDN 84088 2174 C5
W 4300 N
- BxEC 84307 704 D2
100 PTVW 84414 998 D2
1800 BxEC 84340 997 C2
1800 BxEC 84404 997 C2
1800 PTVW 84404 997 C2
W 4300 S
10 WSTR 84405 1172 D2
1100 RVDL 84405 1172 A1
1500 TYVL 84123 2069 C1
2000 ROY 84067 1171 D1
2500 CchC 84319 590 B7
2500 WELV 84319 590 B7
3500 WHVN 84315 1170 D1
4000 WVCY 84120 2068 C1
5500 WVCY 84120 2067 D1
5600 WVCY 84128 2067 D1
W 4305 S
3400 WVCY 84119 2068 D2
S 4310 W
3600 WVCY 84120 1962 B6
5800 SLkC 84118 2068 C6
W 4310 S
3700 WVCY 84120 2068 D1
E 4315 S
700 SLkC 84107 2071 A1
E 4320 N
100 PRVO 84604 2821 C6
S 4320 W
4300 WVCY 84120 2068 B2
5200 SLkC 84118 2068 B5
12100 RIVN 84065 2386 B1
E 4325 N
4000 WbrC 84310 1001 C1
E 4325 S
1300 SLkC 84124 2071 B1
S 4325 W
- HOPR 84315 1170 C5
W 4325 S
2900 ROY 84067 1171 A1
5300 HOPR 84315 1169 E2
5300 HOPR 84315 1170 A2
N 4330 W
1400 PNCY 84404 1054 C2
W 4330 S
500 MRRY 84123 2070 A2
4000 WVCY 84120 2068 C1
5500 WVCY 84120 2067 D2
6100 WVCY 84128 2067 C2
W 4335 S
1900 ROY 84067 1171 D1
E 4340 S
2400 HLDY 84124 2072 A1
S 4340 W
3800 WVCY 84120 1962 B7
4700 SLkC 84118 2068 B3
11400 SJDN 84095 2280 B6
W 4340 S
3200 WVCY 84119 2068 E2
E 4345 S
2900 SLkC 84124 2072 B1
E 4350 N
3600 WbrC 84310 1001 B1
E 4350 S
200 WSTR 84405 1172 E1
600 SLkC 84107 2070 E2
900 SOGN 84403 1173 A2
N 4350 W
- BRCY 84301 645 E5
- BxEC 84301 645 E5
- BxEC 84302 645 E5
2200 PNCY 84404 996 C6
S 4350 W
9200 UthC 84651 3354 B3
W 4350 N
100 PTVW 84414 998 D2
W 4350 S
700 RVDL 84405 1172 B1
2100 ROY 84067 1171 C2
2300 TYVL 84119 2069 B2
4400 WHVN 84315 1170 B1
5500 HOPR 84315 1169 E2
S 4355 W
3100 WVCY 84120 1962 B5
W 4355 S
1100 TYVL 84123 2069 E1
W 4360 S
5400 WVCY 84120 2067 D2
5600 WVCY 84128 2067 D2
E 4365 S
2000 HLDY 84124 2071 D2
W 4365 S
1100 TYVL 84123 2069 E2
4600 WVCY 84120 2068 B2
E 4370 S
100 MRRY 84107 2070 D2
S 4370 W
1600 SLCY 84104 1962 B1
W 4370 S
1100 TYVL 84123 2069 E2
5400 WVCY 84120 2067 E2

S 4375 W
2700 WbrC 84401 1113 C4
4200 WHVN 84315 1170 C1
W 4375 S
700 RVDL 84405 1172 B2
2700 ROY 84067 1171 B1
3600 WHVN 84315 1170 E2
E 4380 N
100 PRVO 84604 2821 C6
E 4380 S
1100 SLkC 84124 2071 B2
S 4380 W
4700 SLkC 84118 2068 B3
11400 SJDN 84095 2280 B6
12400 UthC 84651 3461 C4
S 4385 W
4500 WVCY 84120 2068 B2
5500 SLkC 84118 2068 B5
W 4385 S
5900 WVCY 84128 2067 C2
E 4390 S
2400 HLDY 84124 2072 A2
S 4390 W
6000 SLkC 84118 2068 B7
W 4390 S
2900 ROY 84067 1171 A2
5400 WVCY 84120 2067 D2
E 4400 N
- HDPK 84318 400 D6
10 CchC 84318 399 E6
400 CchC 84318 400 A6
1000 CchC 84341 400 B6
3100 WbrC 84310 1000 E1
E 4400 S
- OGDN 84403 1173 B2
10 WSTR 84405 1172 D2
400 SOGN 84403 1172 E2
400 WbrC 84403 1172 E2
900 SOGN 84403 1173 A2
N 4400 W
- CRNN 84307 704 D6
700 WbrC 84404 1054 C3
1500 PNCY 84404 1054 C2
2100 CRNN 84307 764 D1
4200 BxEC 84307 704 D2
5900 BRCY 84301 645 E5
8500 BxEC 84337 585 E5
9400 ELWD 84337 585 D3
10400 ELWD 84337 521 D7
10800 BxEC 84337 521 D7
S 4400 W
- HOPR 84315 1170 C5
- UthC 84651 3461 C4
3100 WVCY 84120 1962 B5
4000 WVCY 84120 2068 B1
10000 SJDN 84095 2280 B3
10200 PYSN 84651 3354 B5
11300 UthC 84651 3354 B7
12600 RIVN 84065 2386 B2
S 4400 W SR-147
10200 PYSN 84651 3354 B5
10200 UthC 84651 3354 B5
W 4400 N
2400 CchC 84335 398 C6
2400 CchC 84341 398 C6
W 4400 S
- OGDN 84405 1172 A2
10 CchC 84319 591 D7
10 CchC 84321 591 D7
10 WSTR 84405 1172 D2
600 RVDL 84405 1172 A2
1500 CchC 84319 590 D7
1500 CchC 84321 590 D7
1600 OGDN 84067 1171 E2
1600 OGDN 84405 1171 E2
1600 ROY 84405 1171 E2
2700 ROY 84067 1171 B2
2700 UthC 84660 3141 A4
3200 WVCY 84119 2068 D2
3600 WVCY 84120 2068 D2
4700 WHVN 84315 1170 B2
W 4400 S SR-77
2700 UthC 84660 3141 A4
N 4400 W St
- BxEC 84314 645 D3
W 4410 S
4500 WVCY 84120 2068 B2
W 4415 S
4400 WVCY 84120 2068 B2
E 4420 S
1100 SLkC 84124 2071 B2
S 4420 W
4700 SLkC 84118 2068 B4
8800 WJDN 84088 2174 B7
12900 RIVN 84065 2386 B3
W 4420 S
5600 WVCY 84128 2067 D2
E 4425 N
3800 WbrC 84310 1000 E1
E 4425 S
300 WSTR 84405 1172 E2
2000 HLDY 84124 2071 E2
N 4425 W
1900 PNCY 84404 996 C7
1900 PNCY 84404 1054 C1
S 4425 W
- HOPR 84315 1170 C4
4000 WVCY 84120 2068 B1
W 4425 S
2700 ROY 84067 1171 B2
4300 WHVN 84315 1170 C2
6300 HOPR 84315 1169 C2
E 4430 S
2500 HLDY 84117 2072 B2
2500 HLDY 84124 2072 B2
2700 SLkC 84124 2072 B2
E 4430 S SR-266
2500 HLDY 84117 2072 B2
2500 HLDY 84124 2072 B2
2700 SLkC 84124 2072 B2
S 4430 W
5500 SLkC 84118 2068 B5
W 4430 N
3400 PTGV 84062 2605 C3
S 4440 W
3100 WVCY 84120 1962 B5
10000 PYSN 84651 3354 B5
10000 UthC 84651 3354 B5
W 4440 N
- PRVO 84604 2821 C5
S 4445 W
3600 WVCY 84120 1962 B6

E 4450 N
200 UthC 84604 2821 C5
300 PRVO 84604 2821 D5
E 4450 S
200 WSTR 84405 1172 E2
N 4450 W
- PTVW 84414 998 D1
S 4450 W
400 WbrC 84404 1054 C6
2700 WbrC 84401 1113 C4
3800 WHVN 84315 1113 C7
3900 WHVN 84315 1170 C1
12200 UthC 84651 3461 B3
W 4450 S
- WHVN 84067 1170 E2
500 MRRY 84123 2070 B2
700 RVDL 84405 1172 B2
2300 ROY 84067 1171 C2
4600 WHVN 84315 1170 B2
E 4460 S
200 MRRY 84107 2070 D2
S 4460 W
4800 SLkC 84118 2068 B4
9200 WJDN 84088 2174 B7
9200 WJDN 84088 2280 B1
10000 SJDN 84095 2280 B3
W 4460 S
3200 WVCY 84119 2068 E2
E 4470 S
2400 HLDY 84124 2072 A2
W 4470 S
1500 TYVL 84123 2069 D2
E 4475 N
4000 WbrC 84310 1001 B1
E 4475 S
100 WSTR 84405 1172 D2
S 4475 W
4400 WVCY 84120 2068 B2
5500 SLkC 84118 2068 B5
W 4475 S
10 WSTR 84405 1172 D2
2300 ROY 84067 1171 C2
3600 WHVN 84315 1170 E2
S 4480 W
6000 SLkC 84118 2068 B7
W 4480 S
4400 ROY 84067 1171 C2
5600 WVCY 84128 2067 C2
E 4490 S
4100 SLkC 84124 2072 E2
S 4490 W
1600 SLCY 84104 1856 B7
1600 SLCY 84104 1962 B1
W 4490 S
4000 WVCY 84120 2068 C2
W 4495 S
4100 WVCY 84120 2068 C2
E 4500 N
- WbrC 84310 1001 B1
E 4500 S
10 MRRY 84107 2070 D2
200 SLkC 84107 2070 D2
700 SLkC 84107 2071 D2
900 SLkC 84117 2071 D2
900 SLkC 84124 2071 D2
1700 HLDY 84117 2071 D2
1700 HLDY 84124 2071 D2
E 4500 S SR-266
10 MRRY 84107 2070 D2
200 SLkC 84107 2070 D2
700 SLkC 84107 2071 D2
900 SLkC 84117 2071 D2
900 SLkC 84124 2071 D2
1700 HLDY 84117 2071 D2
1700 HLDY 84124 2071 D2
N 4500 W
- HILD 84003 2605 A1
10 WPT 84015 1225 E4
1800 WPT 84015 1169 E7
1900 PNCY 84404 996 C7
1900 PNCY 84404 1054 C1
2000 DvsC 84315 1169 E7
2400 HOPR 84315 1169 E7
5800 BRCY 84301 645 D5
9500 CRHL 84062 2605 A4
N 4500 W SR-110
10 WPT 84015 1225 E4
S 4500 W
10 WPT 84015 1225 E7
700 DvsC 84075 1225 E7
700 WPT 84075 1225 E7
1200 SRCS 84075 1225 E7
3100 WVCY 84120 1962 B5
3500 CchC 84339 589 C5
4200 WHVN 84315 1170 C1
5100 HOPR 84315 1170 C3
5600 SLkC 84118 2068 B6
8400 UthC 84651 3354 B1
S 4500 W SR-110
10 WPT 84015 1225 E7
700 DvsC 84075 1225 E7
700 WPT 84075 1225 E7
1200 SRCS 84075 1225 E7
W 4500 N
10 PRVO 84604 2821 C5
100 PTVW 84414 998 D1
W 4500 S
- WHVN 84067 1170 E2
10 MRRY 84107 2070 C2
100 WSTR 84405 1172 D2
400 MRRY 84123 2070 C2
600 TYVL 84123 2070 C2
1100 RVDL 84405 1172 A2
1700 TYVL 84119 2069 C2
2400 ROY 84067 1171 C2
4500 WHVN 84315 1170 B2
W 4500 S SR-266
10 MRRY 84107 2070 C2
400 MRRY 84123 2070 C2
600 TYVL 84123 2070 C2
E 4505 S
2900 HLDY 84117 2072 B2
W 4505 S
1100 TYVL 84123 2069 D2
E 4510 S
2500 HLDY 84117 2072 B2
W 4510 S
5600 WVCY 84128 2067 D2
N 4512 E
- WbrC 84310 1001 D4
S 4515 W
4300 WVCY 84120 2068 B2

S 4520 W
3900 WVCY 84120 1962 B7
4000 WVCY 84120 2068 B1
6000 SLkC 84118 2068 B7
E 4525 N
300 PRVO 84604 2821 D5
E 4525 S
200 WSTR 84405 1172 E2
900 OGDN 84403 1173 B2
S 4525 W
- HOPR 84315 1170 C5
3600 WVCY 84120 1962 B6
W 4525 S
- WHVN 84067 1170 E2
300 WSTR 84405 1172 C2
2200 ROY 84067 1171 C2
3600 WHVN 84315 1170 D2
5100 HOPR 84315 1170 A2
E 4530 S
900 SLkC 84117 2071 A2
2500 HLDY 84117 2072 A2
S 4540 W
5600 SLkC 84118 2068 B6
E 4550 S
1400 OGDN 84403 1173 C2
3000 HLDY 84117 2072 B2
N 4550 W
500 WPT 84015 1225 E3
1400 PNCY 84404 1054 C2
S 4550 W
- HOPR 84315 1170 C4
2600 WbrC 84401 1113 C4
4000 WHVN 84315 1170 C1
W 4550 S
200 MRRY 84107 2070 C2
1000 RVDL 84405 1172 A2
2200 ROY 84067 1171 C2
3600 ROY 84067 1170 E2
3600 ROY 84315 1170 E2
3900 WHVN 84067 1170 C2
3900 WHVN 84315 1170 C2
E 4555 S
400 MRRY 84107 2070 E2
900 SLkC 84117 2071 A2
E 4560 S
1200 SLkC 84117 2071 B2
N 4560 W
9900 CRHL 84062 2605 A3
S 4560 W
4400 WVCY 84120 2068 B2
W 4560 S
3700 WVCY 84120 2068 D2
E 4565 S
700 SLkC 84107 2070 E2
S 4565 W
3600 WVCY 84120 1962 B7
W 4565 S
5400 WVCY 84120 2067 E2
S 4570 W
- RIVN 84065 2386 B2
W 4570 S
2800 WVCY 84119 2069 A2
4100 WVCY 84120 2068 C2
E 4575 S
200 WSTR 84405 1172 E2
N 4575 W
1600 PNCY 84404 1054 C1
2100 PNCY 84404 996 B7
S 4575 W
4400 WHVN 84315 1170 C2
W 4575 N
500 PTVW 84414 998 C1
1200 BxEC 84302 706 B1
W 4575 S
300 WSTR 84405 1172 C2
1100 RVDL 84405 1172 A2
1600 ROY 84067 1171 E2
E 4580 S
1300 SLkC 84117 2071 B2
S 4580 W
4100 WVCY 84120 2068 B1
4700 SLkC 84118 2068 B3
W 4585 S
4800 WHVN 84315 1170 B2
S 4590 W
6000 SLkC 84118 2068 B7
8200 WJDN 84088 2174 B5
W 4595 S
5000 WVCY 84120 2068 A2
E 4600 N
- CchC 84335 400 B5
E 4600 S
10 WSTR 84405 1172 D2
100 MRRY 84107 2070 D2
500 SOGN 84403 1172 E2
900 OGDN 84403 1173 C2
900 SOGN 84403 1173 B2
1300 SLkC 84117 2071 B2
1800 WbrC 84403 1173 C2
N 4600 W
100 WbrC 84404 1054 B5
1900 PNCY 84404 996 B7
5300 BRCY 84301 645 D6
6900 BxEC 84314 585 D7
6900 BxEC 84314 645 D1
7600 BxEC 84337 585 D7
7600 ELWD 84314 585 D7
7600 ELWD 84337 585 D7
9600 CRHL 84062 2605 A3
S 4600 W
- HOPR 84315 1170 B5
100 WbrC 84404 1054 C5
1300 WbrC 84401 1054 B7
1300 WbrC 84401 1113 B1
3800 CchC 84339 589 C6
4400 WHVN 84315 1170 B2
10400 PYSN 84651 3354 B6
10400 UthC 84651 3354 B6
11200 UthC 84651 3461 B1
W 4600 N
10 PRVO 84604 2821 C5
100 PTVW 84414 998 D1
400 CchC 84335 399 B5
1200 CchC 84335 398 E5
2800 BxEC 84302 705 C1
W 4600 S
- TYVL 84123 2070 A2
- WHVN 84067 1170 E2
200 WSTR 84405 1172 D2
700 CchC 84319 651 B1
1100 RVDL 84405 1172 A2
1200 CchC 84319 591 A7

STREET Block City ZIP Map# Grid

W 4600 S
1400 UthC 84660 3141 D4
1500 CchC 84319 590 D7
2900 ROY 84067 1171 A2
2900 WVCY 84119 2069 A2
3900 ROY 84067 1170 D2
4600 WHVN 84315 1170 B2
5100 HOPR 84315 1170 A2
5300 HOPR 84315 1169 E2
4600 W
- BxEC 84314 645 D3
- BxEC 84337 645 D3
W 4605 S
5400 WVCY 84120 2067 E2
S 4610 W
9100 WJDN 84088 2174 B7
W 4610 S
2800 WVCY 84119 2069 A2
E 4620 N
100 PRVO 84604 2821 C5
E 4620 S
1600 SLkC 84117 2071 C2
S 4620 W
3800 WVCY 84120 1962 B7
4700 SLkC 84118 2068 B4
W 4620 N
300 PRVO 84097 2821 B5
E 4625 S
600 SOGN 84403 1173 A2
N 4625 W
- WPT 84015 1225 E1
S 4625 W
4200 WVCY 84120 2068 B2
6000 SLkC 84118 2068 B6
W 4625 S
100 WSTR 84405 1172 D2
3100 ROY 84067 1171 A2
3600 ROY 84067 1170 E2
E 4630 S
600 MRRY 84107 2070 E2
W 4630 N
300 PRVO 84097 2821 B5
W 4630 S
3200 WVCY 84119 2068 E3
E 4635 N
100 PRVO 84604 2821 C5
E 4640 N
200 PRVO 84604 2821 C5
W 4640 S
100 MRRY 84107 2070 C2
W 4645 S
4000 WVCY 84120 2068 C3
E 4650 N
3000 WbrC 84310 1000 E1
E 4650 S
200 WSTR 84405 1172 E2
N 4650 W
1600 PNCY 84404 1054 B1
1900 PNCY 84404 996 B7
6800 PTGV 84062 2712 A2
7500 PTGV 84003 2712 A1
7500 UthC 84003 2712 A1
N 4650 W SR-134
1900 PNCY 84404 996 B7
S 4650 W
1500 SLCY 84104 1856 B7
1500 SLCY 84104 1962 B1
4000 WVCY 84120 2068 B1
4500 WHVN 84315 1170 B2
5600 HOPR 84315 1170 B5
W 4650 N
300 PRVO 84097 2821 B5
W 4650 S
100 MRRY 84107 2070 C2
300 WSTR 84405 1172 C2
1300 RVDL 84405 1171 E2
1300 RVDL 84405 1172 A2
2800 WVCY 84119 2069 A3
2900 ROY 84067 1171 A2
3400 WVCY 84119 2068 D3
3600 WVCY 84120 2068 D3
4100 ROY 84067 1170 C2
4500 WHVN 84315 1170 C2
W 4655 S
1800 TYVL 84119 2069 C3
E 4660 S
700 SLkC 84107 2070 E3
S 4660 W
5000 SLkC 84118 2068 B4
W 4660 S
2900 WVCY 84119 2069 A3
S 4665 W
3200 WVCY 84120 1962 B5
3900 WVCY 84120 2068 B1
S 4670 W
8400 WJDN 84088 2174 B6
E 4675 S
200 WSTR 84405 1172 E2
1800 HLDY 84117 2071 D3
S 4675 W
3900 WVCY 84120 1962 B7
W 4675 S
300 WSTR 84405 1172 C2
1300 RVDL 84405 1171 E2
3100 ROY 84067 1171 A2
E 4680 N
10 PRVO 84604 2821 C5
E 4680 S
800 SLkC 84107 2071 A3
N 4680 W
9800 CRHL 84062 2605 A3
S 4680 W
4700 SLkC 84118 2068 B3
8700 WJDN 84088 2174 B6
W 4680 S
2000 TYVL 84119 2069 C3
E 4690 S
600 MRRY 84107 2070 C3
E 4695 N
200 PRVO 84604 2821 C5
W 4695 S
4100 SLkC 84118 2068 C3
4100 SLkC 84120 2068 B3
4100 WVCY 84120 2068 B3
E 4700 N
200 PRVO 84604 2821 C5
E 4700 S
10 WSTR 84405 1172 E2
1500 OGDN 84403 1173 C2
N 4700 W
- BRCY 84302 704 D1
- BRCY 84307 704 D1
- BRCY 84337 704 D1
10 WbrC 84404 1054 B4
1300 PNCY 84404 1054 B1
5000 BRCY 84302 645 D7
5200 BRCY 84301 645 D7
N 4700 W SR-13
- BRCY 84302 704 D1
- BRCY 84307 704 D1
- BRCY 84337 704 D1
5000 BRCY 84302 645 D7
5200 BRCY 84301 645 D7
N 4700 W SR-134
10 WbrC 84404 1054 B4
1300 PNCY 84404 1054 B1
S 4700 W
100 WbrC 84404 1054 B7
900 WbrC 84401 1054 B7
1200 WbrC 84401 1113 B3
1300 SLCY 84104 1856 A7
3300 WHVN 84315 1113 B7
3400 WHVN 84315 1170 B1
4800 HOPR 84315 1170 B3
S 4700 W SR-134
100 WbrC 84404 1054 B7
900 WbrC 84401 1054 B7
1200 WbrC 84401 1113 B3
3300 WHVN 84315 1113 B7
3400 WHVN 84315 1170 B1
W 4700 N
3100 CchC 84335 398 A5
W 4700 S
- SLkC 84118 2068 D3
10 WSTR 84405 1172 D2
800 TYVL 84123 2069 B3
800 TYVL 84123 2070 A2
1100 RVDL 84405 1172 A2
1700 TYVL 84118 2069 B3
1700 TYVL 84119 2069 B3
2400 CchC 84319 650 B1
2400 WELV 84319 650 B1
2700 WVCY 84119 2069 B3
2800 WVCY 84118 2069 B3
3000 ROY 84067 1171 A2
3000 TYVL 84118 2068 D3
3000 WELV 84339 650 B1
3000 WVCY 84119 2068 D3
3400 TYVL 84119 2068 D3
3600 WVCY 84120 2068 D3
4100 ROY 84067 1170 C2
4800 WVCY 84118 2068 A3
5100 SLkC 84118 2067 E3
5100 WVCY 84120 2067 E3
5200 SLkC 84120 2067 E3
5600 WVCY 84118 2067 C3
5600 WVCY 84128 2067 C3
6700 HOPR 84315 1169 B2
W 4700 S SR-266
800 TYVL 84123 2069 B3
800 TYVL 84123 2070 A2
1700 TYVL 84118 2069 B3
1700 TYVL 84119 2069 B3
S 4710 W
3900 WVCY 84120 1962 B7
4000 WVCY 84120 2068 A1
W 4715 S
4000 SLkC 84118 2068 C3
4100 SLkC 84120 2068 C3
4700 WVCY 84120 2068 B3
N 4720 W
10400 HILD 84003 2605 A2
S 4720 W
4700 SLkC 84118 2068 A3
W 4720 S
3700 TYVL 84118 2068 D3
E 4725 S
900 OGDN 84403 1173 B2
W 4725 S
300 WSTR 84405 1172 D2
3300 ROY 84067 1171 A2
6400 HOPR 84315 1169 C2
N 4730 W
- HILD 84003 2605 A1
E 4735 N
200 PRVO 84604 2821 C5
S 4745 W
3700 WVCY 84120 1962 A7
W 4745 S
2900 TYVL 84118 2069 A3
3000 TYVL 84118 2068 E3
4700 SLkC 84118 2068 A3
E 4750 N
200 PRVO 84604 2821 D5
E 4750 S
600 SOGN 84403 1173 A3
1000 OGDN 84403 1173 B2
W 4750 N
10 PRVO 84604 2821 C5
W 4750 S
2900 ROY 84067 1171 A3
4000 ROY 84067 1170 D2
S 4755 W
3800 WVCY 84120 1962 A7
4300 WVCY 84120 2068 A2
S 4760 W
2900 WVCY 84120 1962 A4
S 4770 W
8200 WJDN 84088 2174 A5
W 4770 N
400 PRVO 84097 2821 B5
E 4775 S
10 WSTR 84405 1172 D3
W 4775 S
300 WSTR 84405 1172 C3
4700 SLkC 84118 2068 A3
E 4780 S
3300 SLkC 84124 2072 C3
S 4780 W
2900 WVCY 84120 1962 A3
5200 SLkC 84118 2068 A4
W 4780 S
1800 UthC 84660 3141 C5
W 4785 S
3600 TYVL 84118 2068 D3
E 4800 N
200 CchC 84318 399 E5
200 CchC 84318 400 A5
200 CchC 84335 399 E5
200 CchC 84335 400 A5
E 4800 S
10 MRRY 84107 2070 D3
700 MRRY 84107 2071 A3
800 SOGN 84403 1173 A3
1200 OGDN 84403 1173 B3
N 4800 E
3900 WbrC 84310 1001 D2
N 4800 W
1300 WbrC 84404 1054 B2
1400 PNCY 84404 1054 B2
2400 CRNN 84307 704 C5
3200 BxEC 84307 704 C5
4000 BxEC 84337 704 C3
4600 BRCY 84302 704 C3
4600 BRCY 84307 704 C3
4600 BRCY 84337 704 C3
5500 BRCY 84301 645 C5
9600 ELWD 84337 585 C2
10800 BxEC 84337 521 C6
11200 TMTN 84337 521 C6
N 4800 W SR-13
3300 BxEC 84307 704 C3
4000 BxEC 84337 704 C3
4600 BRCY 84302 704 C3
4600 BRCY 84307 704 C3
4600 BRCY 84337 704 C3
S 4800 W
- SNQN 84655 3461 A7
- UthC 84655 3568 B2
700 SLCY 84104 1856 A6
1500 SLCY 84104 1962 A1
2900 WVCY 84120 1962 A7
3300 CchC 84339 589 B4
4000 WVCY 84120 2068 A1
4200 WHVN 84315 1170 B1
4600 SLkC 84120 2068 A3
4700 SLkC 84118 2068 A3
7000 WJDN 84084 2174 A3
8200 WJDN 84088 2174 A7
9200 WJDN 84088 2280 A1
9300 SJDN 84095 2280 A2
11200 UthC 84651 3354 A7
11200 UthC 84651 3461 A1
12900 UthC 84655 3461 A4
W 4800 N
- BxEC 84302 646 C7
- BxEC 84302 705 C1
- BxEC 84337 704 B1
10 PRVO 84604 2821 C5
200 PRVO 84097 2821 C5
400 OREM 84097 2821 C5
3200 CchC 84335 398 A5
W 4800 S
- RVDL 84405 1171 E3
10 MRRY 84107 2070 C3
700 CchC 84319 651 B1
700 SPFK 84660 3142 B5
700 UthC 84660 3142 B5
1600 CchC 84319 650 E1
1700 ROY 84067 1171 B3
1700 RVDL 84067 1171 E3
1900 HYRM 84319 650 E1
2700 UthC 84660 3141 A5
3300 ROY 84067 1170 D3
6300 HOPR 84315 1169 C3
W 4805 S
2800 TYVL 84118 2069 A3
4000 SLkC 84118 2068 C3
S 4820 W
4800 SLkC 84118 2068 A4
W 4820 S
5100 SLkC 84118 2067 E3
E 4825 S
700 SOGN 84403 1173 A3
N 4825 E
3900 WbrC 84310 1001 D2
W 4825 S
500 RVDL 84405 1172 C3
3300 ROY 84067 1170 E3
3300 ROY 84067 1171 A3
4900 HOPR 84315 1170 A3
S 4830 W
8600 WJDN 84088 2174 A6
W 4835 S
4000 SLkC 84118 2068 C3
E 4840 N
200 PRVO 84604 2821 C5
S 4840 W
3200 WVCY 84120 1962 A5
6000 SLkC 84118 2068 A6
W 4840 S
1800 TYVL 84118 2069 C3
E 4850 S
300 WSTR 84405 1172 E3
2100 HLDY 84117 2071 E3
N 4850 W
1700 PNCY 84404 1054 B1
6200 LNDN 84042 2712 A3
6800 ANFK 84003 2712 A3
6800 UthC 84003 2712 A3
S 4850 W
3800 WVCY 84120 1962 A7
4100 WVCY 84120 2068 A1
W 4850 S
100 WSTR 84405 1172 D3
2100 ROY 84067 1171 C3
3300 TYVL 84118 2068 D3
4100 ROY 84067 1170 C3
4900 SLkC 84118 2067 E3
S 4860 W
4700 SLkC 84118 2068 A3
W 4860 S
100 MRRY 84107 2070 C3
W 4865 S
4000 SLkC 84118 2068 C3
4000 TYVL 84118 2068 C3
S 4870 W
8600 WJDN 84088 2174 A6
E 4875 S
800 SOGN 84403 1173 A3
1000 OGDN 84403 1173 B3
S 4875 W
4500 WHVN 84315 1170 B2
W 4875 S
2800 ROY 84067 1171 B3
4100 ROY 84067 1170 C3
S 4880 W
3000 WVCY 84120 1962 A5
6000 SLkC 84118 2068 A7
7400 WJDN 84084 2174 A3
W 4890 S
1400 TYVL 84123 2069 D3
E 4895 S
900 SLkC 84117 2071 A3
S 4895 W
11900 HRMN 84065 2280 A7
W 4895 S
4700 SLkC 84118 2068 A3
E 4900 S
100 WSTR 84405 1172 D3
800 MRRY 84107 2071 A3
1100 OGDN 84403 1173 B3
S 4900 W
2000 WbrC 84401 1113 B2
4100 WVCY 84120 2068 A1
4200 WHVN 84315 1170 B1
4800 SLkC 84118 2068 A4
6800 WJDN 84084 2174 A2
W 4900 S
100 WSTR 84405 1172 C3
500 RVDL 84405 1172 C3
2000 ROY 84067 1171 C3
3000 TYVL 84118 2069 A3
4000 ROY 84067 1170 D3
4900 HOPR 84315 1170 A3
5100 SLkC 84118 2067 E3
S 4910 W
8800 WJDN 84088 2174 A7
W 4915 S
1600 TYVL 84123 2069 C3
S 4920 W
4500 WVCY 84120 2068 A2
W 4920 S
1400 TYVL 84123 2069 D3
E 4925 S
1000 OGDN 84403 1173 B3
S 4925 W
4800 HOPR 84315 1170 B3
W 4925 S
500 RVDL 84405 1172 C3
2800 ROY 84067 1171 B3
3600 ROY 84067 1170 E3
4700 SLkC 84118 2068 A4
W 4935 S
5200 SLkC 84118 2067 E4
S 4940 W
4800 SLkC 84118 2068 A4
8900 WJDN 84088 2174 A7
N 4950 E
2700 WbrC 84310 1001 E5
S 4950 W
5100 HOPR 84315 1170 A4
7400 WJDN 84084 2174 A3
8600 WJDN 84088 2174 A6
W 4950 S
400 WSTR 84405 1172 C3
1400 TYVL 84123 2069 D4
2100 ROY 84067 1171 C3
3400 ROY 84067 1170 E3
5200 HOPR 84315 1170 A3
W 4955 S
3800 TYVL 84118 2068 D4
4700 SLkC 84118 2068 A4
E 4960 N
200 PRVO 84604 2821 C4
S 4960 W
3000 WVCY 84120 1962 A4
W 4960 S
1800 TYVL 84118 2069 C4
3200 TYVL 84118 2068 E4
4000 SLkC 84118 2068 C4
E 4975 S
1000 OGDN 84403 1173 B3
S 4975 W
4200 WHVN 84315 1170 B1
W 4975 S
2000 ROY 84067 1171 C3
3600 ROY 84067 1170 D3
S 4980 W
4800 SLkC 84118 2068 A4
7600 WJDN 84084 2174 A3
W 4980 S
1400 TYVL 84123 2069 D4
S 4985 W
3200 WVCY 84120 1962 A5
W 4985 S
2400 TYVL 84118 2069 B4
4700 SLkC 84118 2068 A4
5000 SLkC 84118 2067 E4
S 4990 W
6400 WJDN 84084 2068 A7
W 4990 S
3800 TYVL 84118 2068 C4
4000 SLkC 84118 2068 C4
E 5000 S
100 WSTR 84405 1172 E3
700 SOGN 84403 1173 A3
1000 MRRY 84117 2071 A4
N 5000 W
300 WPT 84015 1225 D2
1800 DvsC 84315 1169 D7
2400 HOPR 84315 1169 D7
N 5000 W SR-37
1800 DvsC 84315 1169 D7
1800 WPT 84015 1225 D1
2400 HOPR 84315 1169 D7
S 5000 W
3000 WVCY 84120 1962 A5
4200 WHVN 84315 1170 A1
5800 HOPR 84315 1170 A5
W 5000 N
1400 CchC 84335 398 E4
1400 CchC 84335 399 A4
3200 BxEC 84302 646 B7
W 5000 S
100 WSTR 84405 1172 D3
800 UthC 84660 3142 A5
1200 TYVL 84123 2069 D4
1200 UthC 84660 3141 E5
1700 ROY 84067 1171 D3
1700 TYVL 84118 2069 C4
3900 ROY 84067 1170 D3
5300 HOPR 84315 1169 E3
5300 HOPR 84315 1170 A3
5000 W
- BxEC 84337 645 C3
W 5010 S
4000 SLkC 84118 2068 C4
E 5014 S
900 MRRY 84117 2071 A4
E 5015 S
1400 OGDN 84403 1173 C3
W 5015 S
4200 SLkC 84118 2068 B4
S 5020 W
3300 WVCY 84120 1962 A6
4800 SLkC 84118 2068 A4
E 5025 S
1400 OGDN 84403 1173 C3
W 5025 S
500 WSTR 84405 1172 C3
2300 ROY 84067 1171 C3
E 5030 S
1000 MRRY 84117 2071 B4
1100 SLkC 84117 2071 B4
S 5030 W
5300 SLkC 84118 2068 A5
W 5035 S
4900 SLkC 84118 2068 A4
S 5040 W
4500 WVCY 84120 2068 B2
7400 WJDN 84084 2174 A3
W 5040 S
3700 TYVL 84118 2068 D4
E 5050 S
100 WSTR 84405 1172 D3
700 SOGN 84403 1173 A3
1300 OGDN 84403 1173 C3
S 5050 W
4800 HOPR 84315 1170 A3
W 5050 N
300 PRVO 84097 2821 B4
W 5050 S
300 WSTR 84405 1172 C3
1100 RVDL 84405 1172 A3
3300 ROY 84067 1171 A3
3800 ROY 84067 1170 D3
4000 SLkC 84118 2068 C4
5900 HOPR 84315 1169 D3
S 5055 W
6500 WJDN 84084 2174 A1
W 5055 S
4600 SLkC 84118 2068 A4
S 5060 W
8200 WJDN 84088 2174 A5
W 5060 S
4000 ROY 84067 1170 D3
S 5070 W
1700 SLCY 84104 1962 A1
6200 WJDN 84084 2068 A7
S 5075 W
- SLkC 84118 2068 A3
W 5075 S
2300 ROY 84067 1171 C3
3900 ROY 84067 1170 D3
S 5080 W
7600 WJDN 84084 2174 A4
8900 WJDN 84088 2174 A7
W 5085 S
4000 SLkC 84118 2068 C4
S 5090 W
8700 WJDN 84088 2174 A6
S 5095 W
6400 WJDN 84084 2068 A7
6400 WJDN 84084 2174 A1
E 5100 S
100 WSTR 84405 1172 D3
900 SOGN 84403 1173 B4
N 5100 W
1500 PNCY 84404 1054 A1
1500 WbrC 84404 996 A6
1500 WbrC 84404 1054 A1
2000 PNCY 84404 996 A7
11000 HILD 84003 2497 E7
S 5100 E
500 WbrC 84310 1059 E4
S 5100 W
- SLkC 84118 2068 A3
1100 WbrC 84401 1054 A7
2500 HOPR 84401 1113 A4
2500 WbrC 84401 1113 A4
3000 HOPR 84315 1113 A6
3000 WbrC 84315 1113 A6
3300 HOPR 84315 1170 A1
3300 WHVN 84315 1113 A7
3300 WHVN 84315 1170 A1
W 5100 S
- WSTR 84405 1172 C3
1100 RVDL 84405 1172 A3
1200 RVDL 84405 1171 E3
2600 ROY 84067 1171 B3
3600 TYVL 84118 2068 D4
3800 ROY 84067 1170 D4
4600 SLkC 84118 2068 A4
4700 HOPR 84315 1170 A3
5300 HOPR 84315 1169 D3
5600 WVCY 84118 2067 D4
W 5115 S
4000 SLkC 84118 2068 C4
S 5120 W
5200 SLkC 84118 2067 E4
W 5125 S
500 WSTR 84405 1172 C3
2100 ROY 84067 1171 D3
3300 ROY 84067 1170 E3
4300 HOPR 84315 1170 C3
S 5130 W
10 SLkC 84118 2068 A4
6200 WJDN 84084 2067 E7
8700 WJDN 84088 2173 E6
S 5135 W
6400 WJDN 84084 2067 E7
6500 WJDN 84084 2173 E1
W 5135 S
4200 SLkC 84118 2068 B4
E 5140 S
2700 HLDY 84117 2072 A4
S 5140 W
- WJDN 84088 2173 E4
W 5140 S
3600 TYVL 84118 2068 D4
E 5150 S
100 WSTR 84405 1172 D3
1300 SOGN 84403 1173 B4
1800 SLkC 84117 2071 D4
N 5150 W
2600 WbrC 84404 996 A5
S 5150 W
8200 WJDN 84088 2173 E5
W 5150 S
500 WSTR 84405 1172 C3
1000 RVDL 84405 1172 A4
2200 ROY 84067 1171 C4
5200 SLkC 84118 2067 E4
S 5160 W
5100 SLkC 84118 2067 E4
S 5170 W
8800 WJDN 84088 2173 E6
E 5175 S
5100 WSTR 84405 1172 E4
W 5175 S
500 WSTR 84405 1172 C4
1100 RVDL 84405 1172 A4
1200 RVDL 84405 1171 E4
2800 ROY 84067 1171 B4
3500 ROY 84067 1170 E4
4100 SLkC 84118 2068 C4
S 5180 W
5400 SLkC 84118 2067 E5
6300 WJDN 84084 2067 E7
6400 WJDN 84084 2173 E1
W 5180 S
3600 TYVL 84118 2068 D4
S 5185 W
5000 SLkC 84118 2067 E4
E 5190 S
1000 MRRY 84117 2071 A4
W 5195 S
4900 SLkC 84118 2068 A4
E 5200 S
100 WSTR 84405 1172 D4
1300 SOGN 84403 1173 B4
N 5200 W
- CRNN 84307 704 B7
900 WbrC 84404 1054 A3
1800 BxEC 84307 764 B1
1800 CRNN 84307 764 B1
S 5200 W
- SNQN 84655 3460 E5
- UthC 84655 3460 E4
200 SLCY 84104 1855 E4
500 SNQN 84655 3568 A2
1100 WbrC 84401 1054 A7
1700 SLCY 84104 1961 E1
3100 UthC 84655 3568 A2
3500 WVCY 84120 1961 E7
3900 WVCY 84120 2067 E1
4800 SLkC 84118 2067 E3
5200 SJDN 84095 2279 E2
5200 WJDN 84088 2279 E2
7500 WJDN 84088 2173 E3
11900 UthC 84651 3460 E3
W 5200 N
10 SmtC 84098 1972 B4
W 5200 S
- HOPR 84315 1169 C4
- TYVL 84118 2069 A4
100 WSTR 84405 1172 D4
1700 ROY 84067 1171 D4
3400 ROY 84067 1170 E4
5200 SLkC 84118 2067 E4
N 5200 St W
8000 ELWD 84337 585 B6
10400 BxEC 84337 521 B7
10400 BxEC 84337 585 B2
10400 ELWD 84337 521 B7
N 5200 St W SR-13
8000 ELWD 84337 585 B6
10400 BxEC 84337 521 B7
10400 BxEC 84337 585 B2
10400 ELWD 84337 521 B7
5200 W Rd
- BxEC 84337 585 B7
- BxEC 84337 645 B6
- ELWD 84337 585 B7
E 5205 S
900 MRRY 84117 2071 A4
W 5215 S
3600 TYVL 84118 2068 D4
4200 SLkC 84118 2068 B4
N 5220 W
- BxEC 84337 585 B7
- ELWD 84337 585 B2
S 5220 W
8200 WJDN 84088 2173 E5
S 5225 W
4400 HOPR 84315 1170 A2
W 5225 S
500 RVDL 84405 1172 C4
2500 ROY 84067 1171 B4
3500 ROY 84067 1170 E4
N 5230 W
2700 WbrC 84404 996 A5
E 5235 S
1000 MRRY 84117 2071 A4
S 5240 W
5200 SLkC 84118 2067 E4
7600 WJDN 84084 2173 E4
W 5240 S
5200 SLkC 84118 2067 E4
E 5245 S
900 MRRY 84117 2071 A4
W 5245 S
2800 TYVL 84118 2069 A4
E 5250 S
100 WSTR 84405 1172 D4
1300 SOGN 84403 1173 B4
N 5250 W
10700 HILD 84003 2604 E1
10800 HILD 84003 2497 E7
S 5250 W
1100 WbrC 84401 1054 A7
5300 HOPR 84315 1170 A4
10900 UthC 84651 3460 E1
W 5250 S
100 MRRY 84107 2070 C4
100 WSTR 84405 1172 D4
2600 ROY 84067 1171 B4
3900 ROY 84067 1170 D4
W 5255 S
4300 SLkC 84118 2068 B4
S 5260 W
8200 WJDN 84088 2173 E5
E 5275 S
1200 SOGN 84403 1173 B4
S 5275 W
5100 HOPR 84315 1170 A3
W 5275 S
100 MRRY 84107 2070 C4
500 RVDL 84405 1172 C4
500 WSTR 84405 1172 C4
3700 ROY 84067 1170 E4
S 5280 W
- WJDN 84088 2173 E4
7600 WJDN 84084 2173 E4
W 5280 S
2600 TYVL 84118 2069 A4
2700 ROY 84067 1171 B4
E 5285 S
1000 SOGN 84403 1173 B4
E 5290 S
900 MRRY 84117 2071 A4
1100 SLkC 84117 2071 A4
1900 HLDY 84117 2071 D5
W 5295 S
4300 SLkC 84118 2068 B5
E 5300 S
100 MRRY 84107 2070 D4
100 WSTR 84405 1172 D4
500 SOGN 84405 1172 E4
600 SOGN 84403 1173 A4
N 5300 E
- WbrC 84310 1002 A3
N 5300 W
6800 ANFK 84003 2711 D4
6800 UthC 84003 2711 D4
10500 HILD 84003 2604 D1
11000 HILD 84003 2497 D7
S 5300 W
700 SLCY 84104 1856 A5
4800 HOPR 84315 1170 A3
W 5300 N
1900 CchC 84335 398 D4
4700 BRCY 84301 645 D7
W 5300 S
- HOPR 84315 1169 D4
10 MRRY 84107 2070 B5
100 WSTR 84405 1172 D4
300 MRRY 84123 2070 B5
500 RVDL 84405 1172 C4
3300 ROY 84067 1171 A4
4200 ROY 84067 1170 C4
4600 HOPR 84315 1170 B4
W 5300 S SR-173
300 MRRY 84107 2070 B5
300 MRRY 84123 2070 B5
S 5310 W
8200 WJDN 84088 2173 E5
W 5310 S
2000 TYVL 84118 2069 B5
E 5315 S
1700 SLkC 84117 2071 C5
W 5315 S
1900 TYVL 84118 2069 C5
N 5320 W
9900 HILD 84003 2604 D3
S 5320 W
4500 WVCY 84120 2067 E2
7600 WJDN 84084 2173 E4
W 5320 S
500 MRRY 84123 2070 B4
2200 TYVL 84118 2069 B5
4900 SLkC 84118 2068 A5
5100 SLkC 84118 2067 E5
S 5325 W
3800 WVCY 84120 1961 E7
4700 SLkC 84118 2067 E3
W 5325 S
- HOPR 84315 1170 C4
100 MRRY 84107 2070 C5
2700 ROY 84067 1171 B4
4200 ROY 84067 1170 C4
W 5335 S
4300 SLkC 84118 2068 B5
E 5340 S
2100 HLDY 84117 2071 E4
N 5340 W
- WbrC 84404 996 A5
W 5345 S
4000 SLkC 84118 2068 C5
E 5350 S
100 WSTR 84405 1172 D4
S 5350 W
1400 SLCY 84104 1855 E7
1400 SLCY 84104 1961 E1
4000 HOPR 84315 1170 A1
5900 HOPR 84315 1169 E5
8200 WJDN 84088 2173 E5
11500 UthC 84651 3460 E2
12800 UthC 84655 3460 E5
12900 SNQN 84655 3460 E5
W 5350 S
100 WSTR 84405 1172 D4
500 RVDL 84405 1172 C4
2000 TYVL 84118 2069 B5
2600 ROY 84067 1171 B4
3500 ROY 84067 1170 E4
5350 N
- HYVL 84314 647 A6
E 5360 S
1300 MRRY 84117 2071 B5
S 5360 W
7500 WJDN 84084 2173 E3
W 5360 S
4800 SLkC 84118 2068 A5
5000 SLkC 84118 2067 E5
N 5370 W
10500 HILD 84003 2604 D1
S 5370 W
2100 WVCY 84120 1961 E2
E 5375 S
1200 SOGN 84403 1173 B4
S 5375 W
3900 WVCY 84120 1961 E7
4000 WVCY 84120 2067 E1
4600 HOPR 84315 1169 E2
W 5375 S
- HOPR 84315 1170 C4
1300 RVDL 84405 1172 A4
3700 ROY 84067 1170 D4
4400 SLkC 84118 2068 B5
S 5385 W
3300 WVCY 84120 1961 E5
S 5390 W
8200 WJDN 84088 2173 E5
E 5400 S
500 MRRY 84107 2070 E5
500 WSTR 84405 1172 E4
700 SOGN 84405 1173 A4
1200 SOGN 84403 1173 B4
1600 SGVL 84663 3143 B6
1600 UthC 84663 3143 B6
N 5400 W
10800 TMTN 84337 521 B6
S 5400 W
500 CchC 84325 525 A5
1400 MNDN 84325 525 A7
2000 CchC 84325 589 A1
2000 CchC 84339 589 A1
4100 WVCY 84120 2067 E2

Salt Lake City Street Index

STREET Block City ZIP Map# Grid

S 5400 W
4800 HOPR 84315 1169 E3
4800 HOPR 84315 1170 A3
W 5400 N
800 CchC 84335 399 A3
1200 CchC 84335 398 E3
3000 AMGA 84335 398 A3
4500 BRCY 84301 645 D6
W 5400 S
200 MRRY 84107 2070 B5
500 RVDL 84405 1172 C4
500 WSTR 84405 1172 C4
800 MRRY 84123 2069 E5
800 MRRY 84123 2070 A5
1000 TYVL 84123 2069 E5
1700 TYVL 84118 2069 E5
2100 ROY 84067 1171 C4
3000 TYVL 84118 2068 E5
3200 WELV 84339 649 B2
3300 CchC 84339 649 B2
3700 ROY 84067 1170 D4
4800 SLkC 84118 2068 A5
5000 SLkC 84118 2067 D5
5600 WVCY 84118 2067 D5
6400 SLkC 84006 2066 E5
6400 WVCY 84006 2066 E5
6400 WVCY 84044 2066 E5
6400 WVCY 84044 2067 A5
6400 WVCY 84084 2066 E5
6400 WVCY 84084 2067 A5
W 5400 S SR-173
800 MRRY 84123 2069 E5
800 MRRY 84123 2070 A5
1000 TYVL 84123 2069 E5
1700 TYVL 84118 2069 E5
3000 TYVL 84118 2068 E5
4800 SLkC 84118 2068 A5
5000 SLkC 84118 2067 D5
5600 WVCY 84118 2067 D5
6400 SLkC 84006 2066 E5
6400 WVCY 84006 2066 E5
6400 WVCY 84044 2066 E5
6400 WVCY 84044 2067 A5
6400 WVCY 84084 2066 E5
6400 WVCY 84084 2067 A5
S 5415 W
4800 SLkC 84118 2067 E4
S 5420 W
5100 SLkC 84118 2067 E5
6600 WJDN 84084 2173 E1
S 5425 W
5400 SLkC 84118 2067 E5
W 5425 S
1300 RVDL 84405 1172 A4
4200 ROY 84067 1170 C4
E 5440 S
1300 MRRY 84117 2071 B5
S 5440 W
4500 WVCY 84120 2067 E3
W 5440 S
5400 SLkC 84118 2067 E5
W 5442 S
1800 UthC 84660 3141 C7
E 5450 S
100 WSTR 84405 1172 D4
700 SOGN 84405 1173 A4
S 5450 W
3200 WVCY 84120 1961 E5
5000 SLkC 84118 2067 E4
W 5450 S
10 WSTR 84405 1172 D4
1300 RVDL 84405 1172 A4
2700 ROY 84067 1171 B4
3700 ROY 84067 1170 D4
E 5460 S
100 MRRY 84107 2070 D5
W 5460 S
- ROY 84067 1171 B4
4300 SLkC 84118 2068 B5
W 5465 S
500 MRRY 84123 2070 B5
E 5470 S
100 MRRY 84107 2070 D5
N 5470 W
10400 HILD 84003 2604 D1
W 5470 S
3400 TYVL 84118 2068 E5
E 5475 S
800 SOGN 84405 1173 A4
S 5475 W
3300 WVCY 84120 1961 E5
4500 WVCY 84120 2067 E2
5400 SLkC 84118 2067 E5
W 5475 S
1100 RVDL 84405 1172 A4
2100 ROY 84067 1171 D4
4200 ROY 84067 1170 C4
N 5480 W
10000 HILD 84003 2604 D2
W 5485 S
5400 SLkC 84118 2067 E5
E 5490 S
100 MRRY 84107 2070 D5
S 5490 W
7000 WJDN 84084 2173 E3
E 5495 S
2800 HLDY 84117 2072 B5
S 5495 W
5300 SLkC 84118 2067 E5
E 5500 S
100 MRRY 84107 2070 D5
500 WSTR 84405 1172 E4
800 SOGN 84405 1173 A4
N 5500 E
1800 WbrC 84310 1002 A7
1800 WbrC 84310 1060 A1
N 5500 W
1900 DvsC 84315 1169 C7
2400 HOPR 84315 1169 C7
11000 HILD 84003 2497 D7
S 5500 W
10 CchC 84325 524 E3
200 SLCY 84104 1855 E4
1400 SLCY 84104 1961 E1
4000 HOPR 84315 1169 E1
6600 WJDN 84084 2173 E1
W 5500 N
4600 BRCY 84301 645 D6
W 5500 S
400 WSTR 84405 1172 C4
1100 RVDL 84405 1172 A4
2300 CchC 84339 650 C3
2900 ROY 84067 1171 A4
3700 ROY 84067 1170 D4
4000 SLkC 84118 2068 B5
4300 HOPR 84315 1170 D4
5200 HOPR 84315 1169 E4
W 5500 S SR-97
3700 ROY 84067 1170 D4
4300 HOPR 84315 1170 D4
5200 HOPR 84315 1169 E4
S 5505 W
4500 WVCY 84120 2067 D2
W 5505 S
5500 SLkC 84118 2067 D5
S 5510 W
2300 WVCY 84120 1961 D2
W 5510 S
500 MRRY 84123 2070 B5
N 5520 W
9700 HILD 84003 2604 D3
W 5520 S
3900 TYVL 84118 2068 C5
S 5525 W
4200 WVCY 84120 2067 D1
W 5525 S
1100 RVDL 84405 1172 A4
3000 ROY 84067 1171 A4
3900 ROY 84067 1170 D4
E 5530 S
10 MRRY 84107 2070 C5
100 WSTR 84405 1172 E4
S 5530 W
3300 WVCY 84120 1961 D5
E 5540 S
100 WSTR 84405 1172 E4
W 5540 S
1900 TYVL 84118 2069 C5
4400 SLkC 84118 2068 B5
5300 SLkC 84118 2067 E5
E 5550 S
100 WSTR 84405 1172 D4
900 SOGN 84405 1173 A4
1700 SLkC 84117 2071 C5
N 5550 W
10600 HILD 84003 2604 D1
11000 HILD 84003 2497 D7
S 5550 W
- SNQN 84655 3460 E6
- UthC 84655 3460 E6
W 5550 S
200 WSTR 84405 1172 D4
1300 TYVL 84123 2069 D5
2900 ROY 84067 1171 A4
4200 ROY 84067 1170 C4
E 5560 S
200 MRRY 84107 2070 D5
S 5565 W
3200 WVCY 84120 1961 D5
W 5566 S
500 MRRY 84123 2070 B5
S 5570 W
4300 WVCY 84120 2067 D2
W 5570 S
4200 SLkC 84118 2068 B5
E 5575 S
100 WSTR 84405 1172 D5
800 SOGN 84405 1173 A5
S 5575 W
5500 SLkC 84118 2067 D5
W 5575 S
1000 RVDL 84405 1172 A5
3700 ROY 84067 1170 D5
N 5580 W
9700 HILD 84003 2604 D4
W 5580 S
4000 SLkC 84118 2068 C5
W 5585 S
3400 TYVL 84118 2068 D5
E 5600 S
10 WSTR 84405 1172 D5
100 MRRY 84107 2070 D5
700 MRRY 84107 2071 A5
700 SOGN 84405 1173 A5
900 MRRY 84117 2071 A5
900 MRRY 84121 2071 A5
1100 SOGN 84403 1173 B4
1500 SLkC 84117 2071 A5
1500 SLkC 84121 2071 A5
N 5600 E
2200 WbrC 84310 1002 A6
N 5600 W
- BxEC 84312 521 A4
- BxEC 84337 521 A4
- BxEC 84337 645 A6
- BxEC 84337 704 A1
800 CchC 84325 524 E1
1200 BxEC 84307 764 A7
1900 DvsC 84315 1169 C7
2000 BxEC 84307 704 A7
7000 BxEC 84337 585 A7
10400 ELWD 84337 521 A7
10400 ELWD 84337 585 A1
10400 HILD 84003 2604 D1
10600 TMTN 84337 521 A7
10900 HILD 84003 2497 D7
S 5600 W
- SLCY 84116 1855 D4
- SLCY 84120 1961 D1
- SLCY 84128 1961 D1
- WJDN 84088 2173 D5
100 SLCY 84104 1855 D4
1300 SLCY 84104 1961 D1
2100 WVCY 84120 1961 D1
3500 WVCY 84128 1961 D7
4000 WVCY 84120 2067 D4
4000 WVCY 84128 2067 D4
4700 SLkC 84118 2067 D4
4700 WVCY 84118 2067 D4
5000 HOPR 84315 1169 E3
5600 TYVL 84118 2069 C5
6200 WJDN 84084 2067 D6
6400 WJDN 84084 2173 D1
6400 WVCY 84118 2173 D1
11300 UthC 84651 3460 D1
12000 UthC 84655 3460 D3
S 5600 W SR-141
11300 UthC 84651 3460 D1
S 5600 W SR-172
- SLCY 84116 1855 D4
- SLCY 84120 1961 D1
- SLCY 84128 1961 D1
100 SLCY 84104 1855 D4
1300 SLCY 84104 1961 D1
2100 WVCY 84120 1961 D1
3500 WVCY 84128 1961 D7
4000 WVCY 84120 2067 D4
4000 WVCY 84128 2067 D4
4700 SLkC 84118 2067 D4
4700 WVCY 84118 2067 D4
W 5600 N
- BRCY 84301 645 C6
10 PRVO 84604 2821 C3
3500 BxEC 84302 646 A6
3700 BxEC 84302 645 E5
W 5600 S
- CchC 84339 649 B3
300 WSTR 84405 1172 C4
1100 RVDL 84405 1172 A5
1500 TYVL 84123 2069 D5
1600 ROY 84067 1171 D5
1800 UthC 84660 3141 C7
3200 CchC 84339 650 A3
3400 ROY 84067 1170 E5
4600 HOPR 84315 1170 B5
5900 HOPR 84315 1169 C5
W 5600 S SR-97
1600 ROY 84067 1171 D5
3400 ROY 84067 1170 E5
5600 W
- BxEC 84337 645 A4
5600 N Rd
- BxEC 84337 645 B6
W 5615 S
4000 SLkC 84118 2068 B5
W 5620 S
1900 TYVL 84118 2069 B5
3200 TYVL 84118 2068 E5
E 5625 S
900 SOGN 84405 1173 B5
1700 SOGN 84403 1173 C5
S 5625 W
5900 SLkC 84118 2067 D6
W 5625 N
1600 HYVL 84314 646 E5
1600 HYVL 84314 647 A5
W 5625 S
3700 ROY 84067 1170 D5
E 5630 S
1200 SOGN 84403 1173 C5
N 5630 W
11300 HILD 84003 2497 D6
S 5630 W
4400 WVCY 84128 2067 D2
E 5640 S
500 MRRY 84107 2070 E5
1200 SOGN 84403 1173 C5
E 5645 S
1000 MRRY 84121 2071 B5
W 5645 S
2500 TYVL 84118 2069 A5
E 5650 S
800 SOGN 84405 1173 A5
900 MRRY 84121 2071 A5
1700 SOGN 84403 1173 C5
N 5650 W
11000 HILD 84003 2497 D7
S 5650 W
3500 WVCY 84128 1961 D6
W 5650 S
300 WSTR 84405 1172 C4
3000 ROY 84067 1171 A5
3500 TYVL 84118 2068 D5
3900 ROY 84067 1170 D5
W 5655 S
4000 SLkC 84118 2068 B5
E 5660 S
1400 MRRY 84121 2071 B6
N 5660 W
10600 HILD 84003 2604 D1
S 5660 W
5600 TYVL 84118 2068 E5
W 5660 S
3300 TYVL 84118 2068 E5
S 5665 W
4400 WVCY 84128 2067 D2
5900 SLkC 84118 2067 D6
E 5675 S
900 SOGN 84405 1173 B5
1400 SOGN 84403 1173 C5
N 5675 E
3500 WbrC 84310 1002 A3
S 5675 W
- WVCY 84128 1961 D7
W 5675 S
3700 ROY 84067 1170 D5
4600 HOPR 84315 1170 B5
W 5685 S
2900 TYVL 84118 2068 E6
2900 TYVL 84118 2069 A5
E 5690 S
1000 MRRY 84121 2071 B5
W 5695 S
3600 TYVL 84118 2068 D6
E 5700 S
- WbrC 84405 1172 E5
- WSTR 84405 1172 E5
900 MRRY 84121 2071 A5
1100 SOGN 84405 1173 B5
1600 SOGN 84403 1173 C5
2500 WbrC 84403 1174 A5
N 5700 E
1900 WbrC 84310 1002 B7
S 5700 W
3500 WVCY 84128 1961 D6
4300 HOPR 84315 1169 E2
5100 WVCY 84118 2067 D4
13100 HRMN 84065 2385 D3
W 5700 N
4700 BRCY 84301 645 D5
W 5700 S
2200 ROY 84067 1171 C5
2500 CchC 84339 650 B3
2800 TYVL 84118 2069 A6
3200 ROY 84067 1170 E5
3200 TYVL 84118 2068 E6
4000 SLkC 84118 2068 B6
6700 HOPR 84315 1169 B5
E 5710 S
- MRRY 84121 2071 C6
N 5710 W
11200 HILD 84003 2497 C7
S 5710 W
3900 WVCY 84128 1961 D7
3900 WVCY 84128 2067 D1
E 5720 S
600 MRRY 84107 2070 E6
N 5720 W
10600 HILD 84003 2604 C1
S 5720 W
4500 WVCY 84128 2067 D2
W 5720 S
3200 TYVL 84118 2068 E6
E 5725 S
1700 SOGN 84403 1173 C5
S 5725 W
3600 WVCY 84128 1961 D6
5100 HOPR 84315 1169 D3
W 5725 S
2700 ROY 84067 1171 B5
5100 HOPR 84315 1170 A5
E 5730 S
1400 MRRY 84121 2071 B6
N 5730 W
10900 HILD 84003 2497 C7
W 5735 S
500 MRRY 84123 2070 B6
3600 TYVL 84118 2068 D6
E 5740 S
1400 MRRY 84121 2071 C6
N 5740 W
9700 HILD 84003 2604 C3
S 5740 W
4300 WVCY 84128 2067 D1
W 5740 S
4000 SLkC 84118 2068 B6
E 5750 S
800 SOGN 84405 1173 A5
900 MRRY 84121 2071 A6
1700 SOGN 84403 1173 D5
N 5750 W
6400 UthC 84003 2711 C4
7200 ANFK 84003 2711 C3
9600 HILD 84003 2604 C4
10900 HILD 84003 2497 C7
S 5750 W
3500 WVCY 84128 1961 D6
W 5750 S
- HOPR 84315 1170 B5
10 MRRY 84107 2070 C6
500 MRRY 84123 2070 B6
2500 ROY 84067 1171 B5
3700 ROY 84067 1170 D5
E 5760 S
- MRRY 84121 2071 C6
E 5770 S
100 MRRY 84107 2070 D6
W 5770 S
1400 MRRY 84123 2069 D6
1400 TYVL 84123 2069 D6
5700 SLkC 84118 2067 D6
E 5775 S
900 SOGN 84405 1173 B5
1800 SOGN 84403 1173 D5
N 5775 E
3400 WbrC 84310 1002 B3
W 5775 S
2700 ROY 84067 1171 B5
3200 TYVL 84118 2068 E6
S 5780 W
4300 WVCY 84128 2067 D2
W 5780 S
2400 TYVL 84118 2069 B6
4000 SLkC 84118 2068 B6
4000 TYVL 84118 2068 C6
S 5785 W
6800 WJDN 84084 2173 D2
W 5785 S
10 MRRY 84107 2070 C6
E 5800 S
- WSTR 84405 1172 E5
1000 SOGN 84405 1173 B5
1900 SOGN 84403 1173 D5
N 5800 W
- HILD 84003 2604 C3
10900 HILD 84003 2497 C7
S 5800 W
3000 CchC 84339 588 E4
4200 HOPR 84315 1169 D1
13100 HRMN 84065 2385 D3
W 5800 N
2000 CchC 84335 398 D2
2200 AMGA 84335 398 D2
4600 BRCY 84301 645 D5
W 5800 S
- HOPR 84315 1170 B5
2000 CchC 84339 650 D3
2000 ROY 84067 1171 D5
3700 ROY 84067 1170 D5
5900 HOPR 84315 1169 D5
5800 W
- BxEC 84337 645 A3
W 5805 S
3200 TYVL 84118 2068 E6
W 5818 S
100 MRRY 84107 2070 C6
S 5820 W
6800 WJDN 84084 2173 D2
W 5820 S
3800 TYVL 84118 2068 C6
4000 SLkC 84118 2068 C6
E 5825 S
1000 SOGN 84405 1173 B5
1700 SOGN 84403 1173 C5
S 5825 W
11300 UthC 84651 3460 D1
W 5825 S
2700 ROY 84067 1171 A5
3300 ROY 84067 1170 E5
S 5835 W
12700 HRMN 84065 2385 D2
E 5840 S
1100 MRRY 84121 2071 B6
W 5845 S
700 MRRY 84123 2070 A6
E 5850 S
1200 SOGN 84405 1173 B5
1900 SOGN 84403 1173 D5
W 5850 S
600 MRRY 84123 2070 B6
3300 ROY 84067 1171 A5
4100 ROY 84067 1170 C5
4900 HOPR 84315 1170 A5
W 5855 S
4000 SLkC 84118 2068 C6
W 5860 S
3200 TYVL 84118 2068 E6
W 5865 S
4600 SLkC 84118 2068 A6
N 5870 W
10800 HILD 84003 2604 C1
10900 HILD 84003 2497 C7
E 5875 S
800 SOGN 84405 1173 A5
1900 SOGN 84403 1173 D5
W 5875 S
3100 ROY 84067 1171 A5
E 5878 S
10 MRRY 84107 2070 C6
W 5878 S
10 MRRY 84107 2070 C6
W 5885 S
10 MRRY 84107 2070 C6
N 5890 W
10100 HILD 84003 2604 C2
E 5900 S
- WSTR 84405 1172 E5
10 MRRY 84107 2070 E6
700 MRRY 84107 2071 A6
1000 SOGN 84405 1173 B5
1900 SOGN 84403 1173 D5
2400 WbrC 84403 1173 E5
N 5900 W
10500 HILD 84003 2604 C1
10900 HILD 84003 2497 C7
S 5900 W
1800 CchC 84325 588 D1
1800 CchC 84339 588 D1
3700 HOPR 84315 1169 D1
S 5900 W SR-37
4100 HOPR 84315 1169 D1
W 5900 N
2400 AMGA 84335 398 B2
4300 BRCY 84301 645 E5
W 5900 S
10 MRRY 84107 2070 B6
400 MRRY 84123 2070 B6
2000 ROY 84067 1171 D5
3000 UthC 84660 3248 A1
3200 TYVL 84118 2068 E6
4000 SLkC 84118 2068 C6
4100 ROY 84067 1170 C5
5100 HOPR 84315 1170 A5
5300 HOPR 84315 1169 E5
5900 S
900 SOGN 84405 1173 A5
W 5905 S
4600 SLkC 84118 2068 A6
W 5910 S
1400 TYVL 84123 2069 D6
N 5920 W
10700 HILD 84003 2604 C1
W 5920 S
5600 SLkC 84118 2067 D6
W 5925 S
400 MRRY 84123 2070 B6
3100 ROY 84067 1171 A5
E 5930 S
1500 MRRY 84121 2071 C6
W 5930 S
5600 SLkC 84118 2067 D6
E 5935 S
1300 MRRY 84121 2071 B6
E 5950 S
1000 SOGN 84405 1173 A6
2000 WbrC 84403 1173 D6
2500 WbrC 84403 1174 A6
N 5950 W
10100 HILD 84003 2604 C2
S 5950 W
- HOPR 84315 1169 D4
- SNQN 84655 3460 D5
- UthC 84655 3460 D5
W 5950 S
600 UthC 84660 3249 A1
1100 UthC 84660 3248 E1
2500 ROY 84067 1171 C5
4100 ROY 84067 1170 C5
6100 HOPR 84315 1169 C5
W 5960 S
300 MRRY 84107 2070 B6
5600 SLkC 84118 2067 D6
W 5965 S
100 MRRY 84107 2070 C6
E 5975 S
- MRRY 84107 2070 C6
1500 MRRY 84121 2071 C6
W 5975 S
2700 ROY 84067 1171 B6
E 5980 S
400 MRRY 84107 2070 E6
E 5985 S
1300 MRRY 84121 2071 B6
W 5987 S
500 MRRY 84123 2070 A6
S 5990 W
2900 WVCY 84128 1961 C4
E 6000 S
1100 SOGN 84405 1173 B6
2700 WbrC 84403 1174 A6
N 6000 W
100 CchC 84325 524 D2
2400 DvsC 84315 1169 B6
6000 UthC 84003 2711 C5
7400 ELWD 84337 584 E2
8200 BxEC 84337 584 E5
9700 HILD 84003 2604 C2
10900 HILD 84003 2497 C7
11500 ALPN 84004 2497 C7
N 6000 W SR-23
100 CchC 84325 524 D2
S 6000 W
- SNQN 84655 3460 C6
- UthC 84655 3460 C5
3500 WVCY 84128 1961 C7
4000 WVCY 84128 2067 C1
5500 HOPR 84315 1169 D5
11800 HRMN 84065 2279 C7
11800 HRMN 84065 2385 C1
W 6000 N
4300 BRCY 84301 645 D5
W 6000 S
10 MRRY 84107 2070 C7
1900 ROY 84067 1171 B6
2200 UthC 84660 3248 B1
3000 CchC 84339 650 A4
3200 ROY 84067 1170 E6
4000 HOPR 84067 1170 D6
4200 HOPR 84315 1170 D6
E 6015 S
1400 MRRY 84121 2071 C6
W 6015 S
4500 SLkC 84118 2068 B6
N 6020 W
9800 HILD 84003 2604 C3
W 6020 S
10 MRRY 84107 2070 C7
1600 TYVL 84123 2069 C6
2800 TYVL 84118 2069 A6
E 6025 S
2000 WbrC 84403 1173 D6
2600 WbrC 84403 1174 A6
W 6025 S
10 MRRY 84107 2070 C7
E 6030 S
1400 MRRY 84121 2071 C6
S 6035 W
3800 WVCY 84128 1961 C7
N 6040 W
9800 HILD 84003 2604 C3
S 6045 W
9800 WJDN 84088 2279 C2
E 6050 S
1400 MRRY 84121 2071 B6
N 6050 W
9500 HILD 84003 2604 C4
S 6050 W
- HOPR 84315 1169 D3
W 6050 S
2100 ROY 84067 1171 C6
3500 ROY 84067 1170 D6
S 6055 W
- WVCY 84044 2067 C4
5100 WVCY 84118 2067 C4
W 6055 S
5000 SLkC 84118 2068 A6
5100 SLkC 84118 2067 D7
E 6060 S
1900 HLDY 84121 2071 D6
S 6060 W
3100 WVCY 84128 1961 C5
W 6060 S
3500 TYVL 84118 2068 D6
4200 SLkC 84118 2068 B6
E 6070 S
2100 HLDY 84121 2071 E6
S 6070 W
3900 WVCY 84128 1961 C7
6000 SLkC 84118 2067 C7
E 6075 S
1900 WbrC 84403 1173 D6
W 6075 S
2000 ROY 84067 1171 D6
2700 CLTN 84015 1171 B6
2900 ROY 84015 1171 B6
N 6080 W
9800 HILD 84003 2604 C3
W 6090 S
4500 SLkC 84118 2068 B6
W 6095 S
4300 SLkC 84118 2068 B7
E 6100 S
10 MRRY 84107 2070 D7
1200 SOGN 84405 1173 B6
2100 WbrC 84403 1173 E6
N 6100 W
9600 HILD 84003 2604 C4
S 6100 W
5500 HOPR 84315 1169 D5
W 6100 N
4400 BRCY 84301 645 D4
W 6100 S
10 MRRY 84107 2070 C7
3400 CchC 84339 650 A4
3500 CchC 84339 649 E4
3500 TYVL 84118 2068 D7
S 6105 W
6000 SLkC 84118 2067 C7
6000 WVCY 84118 2067 C7
N 6110 W
9800 HILD 84003 2604 C3
W 6110 S
4800 SLkC 84118 2068 A7
S 6115 W
4100 WVCY 84128 2067 C1
6800 WJDN 84084 2173 C2
N 6120 W
10700 HILD 84003 2604 B1
W 6120 S
4600 SLkC 84118 2068 B7
E 6125 S
1200 SOGN 84405 1173 C6
N 6130 W
9800 HILD 84003 2604 B3
W 6130 S
2400 TYVL 84118 2069 B7
4500 SLkC 84118 2068 B7
E 6135 S
1000 MRRY 84121 2071 A7
W 6135 S
3800 TYVL 84118 2068 C7
W 6140 S
800 MRRY 84123 2070 A7
E 6150 S
10 MRRY 84107 2070 C7
2200 WbrC 84403 1173 E6
N 6150 W
- HILD 84003 2497 B5
10500 HILD 84003 2604 B1
S 6150 W
5900 HOPR 84315 1169 C6
9800 WJDN 84088 2279 C2
W 6150 S
1000 UthC 84660 3248 E1
1000 UthC 84660 3249 A1
E 6160 S
1000 MRRY 84121 2071 A7
W 6160 S
300 MRRY 84107 2070 B7
1600 TYVL 84123 2069 C7
6160 W Rd
- ELWD 84337 584 E1
E 6165 S
1000 MRRY 84121 2071 A7
S 6165 W
3900 WVCY 84128 1961 C7
W 6165 S
4300 SLkC 84118 2068 B7
E 6170 S
500 MRRY 84107 2070 E7
W 6170 S
2400 TYVL 84118 2069 B7
E 6175 S
1200 SOGN 84405 1173 B6
2000 WbrC 84403 1173 D6
N 6180 W
9800 HILD 84003 2604 B3
S 6180 W
3300 WVCY 84128 1961 C6
4100 WVCY 84128 2067 C1
E 6185 S
1000 MRRY 84121 2071 A7
N 6190 W
11800 HILD 84003 2497 B5
W 6190 S
1200 MRRY 84123 2069 D7
E 6200 S
- CchC 84319 651 E4
- CchC 84319 652 B4
- CDHT 84121 2072 B7
- HLDY 84121 2178 C1
- HYRM 84319 651 E4
- HYRM 84319 652 B4
1100 MRRY 84121 2071 B7
1500 SOGN 84405 1173 D6
1500 WbrC 84405 1173 D6
1800 SOGN 84403 1173 D6
1800 WbrC 84403 1173 D6
1900 HLDY 84121 2071 E7
2400 HLDY 84121 2072 B7
2700 WbrC 84403 1174 A6
E 6200 S SR-190
- CDHT 84121 2072 B7
- HLDY 84121 2072 B7
- HLDY 84121 2178 C1
N 6200 W
10700 HILD 84003 2604 B1
S 6200 W
- SNQN 84655 3460 C6
- UthC 84655 3460 C6
1800 CchC 84325 524 D7
1800 CchC 84325 588 D1
4700 WVCY 84118 2067 C3
5500 HOPR 84315 1169 C5
13100 HRMN 84065 2385 C3
W 6200 N
2800 AMGA 84335 398 B1
4500 BRCY 84301 645 D4
W 6200 N SR-218
2800 AMGA 84335 398 B1
W 6200 S
3600 TYVL 84084 2068 B7
3600 TYVL 84118 2068 B7
3600 WJDN 84084 2068 B7
4000 SLkC 84118 2068 B7
4700 WJDN 84118 2068 B7
4800 SLkC 84084 2068 B7
5000 SLkC 84118 2067 E7
5000 WJDN 84084 2067 E7
5200 WJDN 84118 2067 E7
5600 WVCY 84118 2067 C7
E 6210 S
1000 MRRY 84121 2071 A7
E 6215 S
300 MRRY 84107 2070 D7
1000 MRRY 84121 2071 B7
E 6220 S
300 MRRY 84107 2070 D7
N 6220 W
9600 HILD 84003 2604 B4
S 6220 W
4200 WVCY 84128 2067 C1
E 6225 S
1200 SOGN 84405 1173 B6
1900 WbrC 84403 1173 D6
N 6225 E
1800 WbrC 84310 1002 C7
1800 WbrC 84310 1060 C1
S 6225 W
3300 WVCY 84128 1961 C5
13000 HRMN 84065 2385 C3
W 6225 S
5000 WJDN 84084 2067 E7
5000 WJDN 84084 2068 A7
E 6230 S
300 MRRY 84107 2070 D7
E 6240 S
300 MRRY 84107 2070 D7
S 6240 W
8200 WJDN 84088 2173 C5
W 6245 S
2000 TYVL 84084 2069 C7
E 6250 S
1500 WbrC 84405 1173 C6
N 6250 E
1700 WbrC 84310 1060 C1
N 6250 W
10500 HILD 84003 2604 B1
S 6250 W
- WVCY 84118 2067 C7
3100 WVCY 84128 1961 C5
8200 WJDN 84088 2173 C5
W 6250 N
3600 HYVL 84314 645 E4
3600 HYVL 84314 646 A4
W 6250 S
3000 TYVL 84084 2068 E7
3000 TYVL 84084 2069 A7
W 6255 S
2400 TYVL 84084 2069 B7
N 6260 W
11800 HILD 84003 2497 B5
S 6265 W
3600 WVCY 84128 1961 C6
E 6270 S
300 MRRY 84107 2070 E7
E 6275 S
2200 WbrC 84403 1173 E6
S 6275 W
14200 HRMN 84065 2385 C6
W 6275 S
5000 WJDN 84084 2068 A7
5100 WJDN 84084 2067 E7
E 6280 S
200 MRRY 84107 2070 D7
S 6285 W
3800 WVCY 84128 1961 C7
E 6290 S
1100 MRRY 84121 2071 B7

STREET Block City ZIP Map# Grid

S 6290 W
3100 WVCY 84128 1961 C5
8200 WJDN 84088 2173 C5
W 6290 S
3800 TYVL 84084 2068 D7
3800 WJDN 84084 2068 D7
E 6295 S
400 MRRY 84107 2070 E7
N 6300 W
10400 HILD 84003 2604 B2
S 6300 W
3700 WVCY 84128 1961 B7
4100 HOPR 84315 1169 C1
W 6300 N
3000 HYVL 84314 646 C4
W 6300 S
300 CchC 84319 651 C5
500 MRRY 84123 2070 A7
2500 TYVL 84084 2069 B7
4100 WJDN 84084 2068 C7
W 6305 S
3900 TYVL 84084 2068 C7
E 6310 S
300 MRRY 84107 2070 D7
S 6310 W
3600 WVCY 84128 1961 C6
S 6315 W
13400 HRMN 84065 2385 B4
E 6320 S
2000 HLDY 84121 2071 E7
N 6320 W
9800 HILD 84003 2604 B3
S 6320 W
3200 WVCY 84128 1961 B5
E 6325 S
400 MRRY 84107 2070 E7
S 6325 W
3800 WVCY 84128 1961 B7
N 6330 W
10900 HILD 84003 2497 B7
10900 HILD 84003 2604 B1
S 6335 W
8200 WJDN 84088 2173 B5
E 6340 S
300 MRRY 84107 2070 D7
300 MRRY 84107 2176 D1
S 6340 W
4200 WVCY 84128 2067 B1
S 6350 W
3700 WVCY 84128 1961 B7
S 6355 W
3600 WVCY 84128 1961 B6
E 6360 S
400 MRRY 84107 2176 E1
S 6360 W
3100 WVCY 84128 1961 B5
E 6380 S
2100 HLDY 84121 2071 E7
E 6400 S
- CchC 84319 651 E5
- MPTN 84664 3250 B2
1100 UthC 84660 3250 B2
1100 UthC 84663 3250 B2
1300 MRRY 84121 2071 D7
1500 UNTH 84405 1173 C7
1500 WbrC 84405 1173 C7
1600 UthC 84664 3250 B2
1700 MRRY 84121 2177 C1
E 6400 S SR-147
- MPTN 84664 3250 B2
1100 UthC 84660 3250 B2
1100 UthC 84663 3250 B2
1600 UthC 84664 3250 B2
N 6400 W
600 CchC 84325 524 C1
7300 UthC 84003 2711 B2
8000 ELWD 84337 584 D6
9100 BxEC 84337 584 D4
10000 TMTN 84337 584 D2
10300 HILD 84003 2604 B1
10900 HILD 84003 2497 B7
S 6400 W
- WJDN 84084 2173 B3
- WJDN 84088 2173 B5
- WVCY 84084 2067 B5
- WVCY 84118 2067 B4
600 CchC 84325 524 C4
2000 CchC 84325 588 C2
2700 WVCY 84128 1961 B5
3900 WVCY 84128 2067 B1
4200 WVCY 84044 2067 B2
4400 HOPR 84315 1169 C2
13800 HRMN 84065 2385 B5
13800 SLkC 84065 2385 B5
W 6400 N
- BxEC 84337 645 C4
4600 BRCY 84301 645 C4
4600 BxEC 84314 645 C4
4800 ANFK 84003 2711 E5
4800 ANFK 84003 2712 A5
4800 UthC 84003 2711 E5
4800 UthC 84003 2712 A5
W 6400 S
500 UthC 84660 3249 A2
1000 UthC 84660 3248 D2
1600 CchC 84319 650 E5
4800 WJDN 84084 2068 A7
W 6400 S SR-147
500 UthC 84660 3249 A2
1000 UthC 84660 3248 D2
6400 Rd N
- BxEC 84337 645 A4
W 6400 N St
- BRCY 84301 645 D4
- BxEC 84314 645 D4
E 6410 S
700 MRRY 84107 2070 E7
W 6410 N
2100 HYVL 84314 646 C4
W 6415 S
1400 TYVL 84123 2069 D7
E 6425 S
2000 HLDY 84121 2071 D7
2600 UNTH 84403 1174 A7
2600 WbrC 84403 1174 A7
E 6430 S
1500 MRRY 84121 2071 C7
S 6430 W
8200 WJDN 84088 2173 B5
W 6435 S
4900 WJDN 84084 2067 E7
4900 WJDN 84084 2068 A7
S 6440 W
4100 WVCY 84128 2067 B1
W 6440 S
- MRRY 84123 2176 A1
4800 WJDN 84084 2068 A7
W 6445 S
4000 TYVL 84084 2068 C7
E 6450 S
1600 MRRY 84121 2071 C7
1700 UNTH 84405 1173 D7
2100 CDHT 84121 2071 E7
S 6450 W
4700 HOPR 84315 1169 C3
S 6460 W
3800 WVCY 84128 1961 B7
W 6460 S
- MRRY 84123 2176 A1
1100 MRRY 84123 2175 E1
S 6465 W
8300 WJDN 84088 2173 B6
E 6470 S
1500 MRRY 84121 2071 C7
S 6470 W
3500 WVCY 84128 1961 B6
E 6480 S
1600 MRRY 84121 2177 A2
W 6480 S
10 MRRY 84107 2176 C1
4000 TYVL 84084 2068 C7
E 6485 S
1600 MRRY 84121 2177 C1
2500 CDHT 84121 2072 A7
S 6485 W
4200 WVCY 84128 2067 B1
E 6500 S
2400 UNTH 84403 1174 A7
2500 WbrC 84403 1174 A7
N 6500 W
- ANFK 84003 2711 A2
2400 DvsC 84315 1169 A6
6700 UthC 84003 2711 A4
S 6500 W
3200 WVCY 84128 1961 B5
5700 HOPR 84315 1169 C5
W 6500 S
- CchC 84319 650 E5
- CchC 84319 651 A5
300 MRRY 84107 2176 B1
900 MRRY 84123 2175 E1
900 MRRY 84123 2176 A1
E 6505 S
1500 MRRY 84121 2177 A2
S 6505 W
3500 WVCY 84128 1961 B6
N 6510 W
10700 HILD 84003 2604 A1
S 6515 W
3800 WVCY 84128 1961 B7
W 6515 S
4000 TYVL 84084 2174 C1
4900 WJDN 84084 2174 A1
5100 WJDN 84084 2173 E1
E 6520 S
1600 MRRY 84121 2177 A3
W 6520 S
4100 TYVL 84084 2174 C1
E 6525 S
1600 UNTH 84405 1173 C7
2100 CDHT 84121 2177 E1
S 6525 E
900 WbrC 84317 1060 D7
N 6530 W
10300 HILD 84003 2604 A2
S 6530 W
4200 WVCY 84128 2067 B1
E 6535 S
1600 MRRY 84121 2177 A3
S 6535 W
3200 WVCY 84128 1961 B5
S 6540 W
7800 WJDN 84088 2173 B4
S 6545 W
3500 WVCY 84128 1961 B6
E 6550 S
- UNTH 84405 1174 A7
1600 MRRY 84121 2177 A3
1800 UNTH 84405 1173 D7
2400 UNTH 84403 1174 A7
W 6550 S
3900 TYVL 84084 2174 C1
S 6555 W
3500 WVCY 84128 1961 B6
8200 WJDN 84088 2173 B5
W 6560 S
4900 WJDN 84084 2174 A1
S 6570 W
13100 UthC 84655 3460 B5
W 6570 S
10 MRRY 84107 2176 C1
500 MRRY 84123 2176 B1
N 6580 W
10000 HILD 84003 2604 A2
S 6580 W
3200 WVCY 84128 1961 B5
4100 WVCY 84128 2067 B1
W 6585 S
4000 TYVL 84084 2174 C1
E 6595 S
2100 CDHT 84121 2177 E1
E 6600 S
10 CchC 84319 651 E5
10 CchC 84319 652 A5
800 UNTH 84405 1173 C7
900 MRRY 84047 2177 A1
900 MRRY 84121 2177 A1
2200 UNTH 84403 1174 A7
2200 UNTH 84405 1174 A7
2300 CDHT 84121 2177 E1
2400 CDHT 84121 2178 A1
S 6600 E
900 WbrC 84317 1060 D7
S 6600 W
13700 HRMN 84065 2385 B5
14200 SLkC 84065 2385 B7
W 6600 S
- CchC 84319 650 E5
- MRRY 84047 2176 D1
10 CchC 84319 651 C5
600 MRRY 84123 2176 A1
4800 WJDN 84084 2174 A1
5100 WJDN 84084 2173 E1
W 6600 St S
1800 CchC 84319 650 D5
1800 CchC 84339 650 D5
N 6610 W
- HILD 84003 2604 A3
W 6610 S
3200 TYVL 84084 2174 E1
3200 WJDN 84084 2174 E1
N 6620 W
9500 HILD 84003 2604 A4
S 6620 W
3800 WVCY 84128 1961 B7
4100 WVCY 84128 2067 B1
W 6620 S
2800 TYVL 84084 2175 A1
2800 WJDN 84084 2175 A1
3000 TYVL 84084 2174 E1
3000 WJDN 84084 2174 E1
E 6630 S
2100 CDHT 84121 2177 E1
N 6630 W
10200 HILD 84003 2604 A2
W 6635 S
5700 WJDN 84084 2173 D1
S 6640 W
3900 WVCY 84128 1961 B7
4000 WVCY 84128 2067 B1
W 6640 S
500 MRRY 84123 2176 B1
W 6645 S
600 MRRY 84123 2176 A1
E 6650 S
100 SWBR 84405 1172 E7
400 SWBR 84405 1173 A7
1400 UNTH 84405 1173 C7
N 6650 W
- UthC 84003 2711 A3
S 6655 W
3600 WVCY 84128 1961 B6
W 6655 S
5600 WJDN 84084 2173 D1
E 6660 S
2300 CDHT 84121 2177 E1
2300 CDHT 84121 2178 A1
S 6660 W
3700 WVCY 84128 1961 B7
4100 WVCY 84128 2067 B1
E 6670 S
1400 CDHT 84121 2177 C1
N 6670 W
9600 HILD 84003 2604 A4
S 6670 W
7400 WJDN 84084 2173 B3
E 6675 S
1600 UNTH 84405 1173 C7
2100 CDHT 84121 2177 E1
W 6675 S
1400 WJDN 84084 2175 D1
6600 MRRY 84123 2176 A1
N 6680 W
10200 HILD 84003 2604 A2
W 6680 S
2700 WJDN 84084 2175 A1
W 6685 S
2900 WJDN 84084 2175 A1
N 6690 W
10000 HILD 84003 2604 A3
W 6690 S
1300 TYVL 84123 2175 D1
1300 WJDN 84084 2175 D1
W 6695 S
3200 WJDN 84084 2174 E1
E 6700 S
1500 UNTH 84405 1173 D7
1700 WbrC 84405 1173 D7
S 6700 W
- WJDN 84088 2173 B4
4400 HOPR 84315 1169 B2
5900 WbrC 84315 1169 B5
W 6700 S
5400 WJDN 84084 2173 C2
E 6710 S
2300 CDHT 84121 2177 E1
2300 CDHT 84121 2178 A1
E 6715 S
100 MDVL 84047 2176 D1
100 MRRY 84047 2176 D1
S 6715 W
8300 WJDN 84088 2173 B5
E 6720 S
2200 CDHT 84121 2177 E1
N 6720 W
7100 UthC 84003 2711 A3
W 6720 S
1400 WJDN 84084 2175 D1
E 6725 S
2100 CDHT 84121 2177 E1
W 6735 S
3200 WJDN 84084 2174 E1
E 6740 S
100 MDVL 84047 2176 D1
900 MDVL 84047 2177 A1
900 MRRY 84047 2177 A1
S 6740 W
3900 WVCY 84128 1961 A7
3900 WVCY 84128 2067 A1
N 6750 W
10400 HILD 84003 2604 A2
S 6750 W
2600 WVCY 84128 1961 A4
W 6750 S
5700 WJDN 84084 2173 D1
E 6765 S
1600 CDHT 84121 2177 C1
E 6775 S
1700 UNTH 84405 1229 D1
W 6775 S
3200 WJDN 84084 2174 E1
E 6780 S
2300 CDHT 84121 2177 E1
2300 CDHT 84121 2178 A1
S 6780 W
3900 WVCY 84128 1961 A7
3900 WVCY 84128 2067 A1
W 6785 S
1300 WJDN 84084 2175 D1
E 6790 S
10 MDVL 84047 2176 D1
10 MRRY 84047 2176 D1
N 6790 W
10400 HILD 84003 2604 A2
E 6800 S
1000 SPFK 84660 3250 B3
1000 UthC 84660 3250 B3
1500 UNTH 84405 1229 C1
1800 MPTN 84664 3250 D3
N 6800 E
100 HTVL 84317 1060 D5
200 WbrC 84317 1060 D5
N 6800 W
8800 UthC 84003 2604 A5
8800 UthC 84043 2604 A5
9400 HILD 84003 2604 A5
9400 HILD 84043 2604 A5
S 6800 E
100 HTVL 84317 1060 D5
900 WbrC 84317 1060 D7
S 6800 W
- BxEC 84307 764 B7
3500 WVCY 84128 1961 A6
5600 HOPR 84315 1169 B5
W 6800 N
- PTGV 84062 2712 A4
4800 ANFK 84003 2711 E4
4800 ANFK 84003 2712 A4
4800 UthC 84003 2711 E4
4800 UthC 84003 2712 A4
5100 BxEC 84337 645 B3
W 6800 S
- CchC 84319 651 C6
400 SPFK 84660 3249 B3
700 UthC 84660 3249 B3
1200 UthC 84660 3248 E3
W 6800 S SR-115
400 SPFK 84660 3249 B3
700 UthC 84660 3249 B3
E 6815 S
300 MDVL 84047 2176 D1
S 6820 W
3900 WVCY 84128 1961 A7
4000 WVCY 84128 2067 A1
W 6825 S
500 MDVL 84047 2176 A1
3400 WJDN 84084 2174 D1
S 6830 W
3500 WVCY 84128 1961 A6
W 6830 S
10 MDVL 84107 2176 C1
300 MDVL 84047 2176 B1
300 MRRY 84107 2176 B1
2300 WJDN 84084 2175 B1
S 6840 W
3800 WVCY 84128 1961 A7
E 6850 S
10 MDVL 84047 2176 D1
1500 UNTH 84405 1229 C1
1500 WbrC 84405 1229 C1
2000 CDHT 84121 2177 D1
W 6850 S
1200 WJDN 84084 2175 D1
E 6856 S
- MDVL 84047 2176 E1
E 6865 S
300 MDVL 84047 2176 D1
S 6865 W
3900 WVCY 84128 1961 A7
4000 WVCY 84128 2067 A1
W 6865 S
2500 WJDN 84084 2175 A1
E 6870 S
500 MDVL 84047 2176 E2
W 6870 S
2700 WJDN 84084 2175 A2
W 6875 S
3400 WJDN 84084 2174 E1
E 6880 S
500 MDVL 84047 2176 E1
S 6880 W
4000 WVCY 84128 1961 B6
W 6880 S
3200 WJDN 84084 2174 E1
E 6890 S
10 MDVL 84047 2176 D1
N 6890 W
10100 HILD 84003 2603 E2
E 6895 S
700 MDVL 84047 2176 E2
800 MDVL 84047 2177 A2
2300 CDHT 84121 2177 E2
2300 CDHT 84121 2178 A2
E 6900 S
1800 UNTH 84405 1229 D1
N 6900 E
100 HTVL 84317 1060 E5
1200 WbrC 84317 1060 E2
S 6900 E
100 HTVL 84317 1060 E5
S 6900 W
3900 WVCY 84128 1961 A7
4000 WVCY 84128 2067 A1
W 6900 N
2300 HYVL 84314 646 D2
4100 BxEC 84314 645 E2
4100 HYVL 84314 645 E2
W 6900 S
1400 WJDN 84084 2175 D1
2900 CchC 84339 650 B6
W 6900 St N
2600 HYVL 84314 646 B2
3700 HYVL 84314 645 E2
W 6900 St N SR-240
2600 HYVL 84314 646 D2
E 6910 S
500 MDVL 84047 2176 A2
W 6915 S
1300 WJDN 84084 2175 D1
W 6920 S
3800 WJDN 84084 2174 D2
W 6925 S
3400 WJDN 84084 2174 E2
W 6930 S
1100 UthC 84660 3248 E3
E 6940 S
100 MDVL 84047 2176 D2
S 6950 W
- HOPR 84315 1169 A5
W 6950 N
- HYVL 84314 646 D2
S 6955 W
3900 WVCY 84128 1961 A7
N 6960 W
10100 HILD 84003 2603 E2
W 6960 S
500 MDVL 84047 2176 A2
2000 WJDN 84084 2175 C2
3200 WJDN 84084 2174 E2
W 6970 S
2600 UthC 84660 3248 B3
W 6975 S
3400 WJDN 84084 2174 E2
E 6980 S
100 MDVL 84047 2176 D2
W 6980 N
2500 HYVL 84314 646 C2
E 6990 S
300 MDVL 84047 2176 E2
S 6990 W
3900 WVCY 84128 1961 A7
N 7000 E
1200 WbrC 84317 1060 E2
S 7000 E
100 HTVL 84317 1060 E5
S 7000 W
3800 WVCY 84128 1961 A7
W 7000 N
2500 HYVL 84314 646 D2
W 7000 S
500 CchC 84319 651 C6
1300 WJDN 84084 2175 D2
4700 WJDN 84084 2174 A2
5100 WJDN 84084 2173 E2
W 7000 S SR-48
1300 WJDN 84084 2175 D2
7000 N
- BxEC 84337 645 C2
E 7000 S St
- CchC 84319 651 D6
N 7015 W
13900 SLkC 84065 2385 A6
E 7020 S
1700 CDHT 84121 2177 C2
S 7025 W
- WJDN 84088 2173 A5
E 7030 S
1800 CDHT 84121 2177 D2
S 7030 W
3900 WVCY 84128 1961 A7
E 7040 S
1900 CDHT 84121 2177 D2
S 7040 W
3800 WVCY 84128 1961 A7
W 7040 S
2800 WJDN 84084 2175 A2
E 7050 S
1600 CDHT 84121 2177 C2
W 7050 S
2900 WJDN 84084 2175 A2
W 7055 S
1000 WJDN 84084 2175 E2
E 7060 S
10 MDVL 84047 2176 D2
S 7060 W
- WJDN 84088 2173 A5
W 7065 S
10 MDVL 84047 2176 C2
E 7070 S
2900 CDHT 84121 2178 B2
E 7075 S
2100 CDHT 84121 2177 E2
E 7080 S
1600 CDHT 84121 2177 C2
S 7080 W
3800 WVCY 84128 1961 A7
W 7085 S
2800 WJDN 84084 2175 A2
E 7090 S
1800 CDHT 84121 2177 D2
W 7095 S
2300 WJDN 84084 2175 B2
E 7100 S
10 MDVL 84047 2176 D2
N 7100 E
- WbrC 84310 1060 E3
- WbrC 84317 1060 E3
N 7100 W
10 CchC 84325 524 A2
S 7100 E
100 HTVL 84317 1060 E5
S 7100 W
5000 HOPR 84315 1169 A4
5900 WbrC 84315 1169 A5
W 7100 N
2500 HYVL 84314 646 D2
E 7105 S
1800 CDHT 84121 2177 D2
S 7105 W
3900 WVCY 84128 1960 E7
W 7105 S
2900 WJDN 84084 2175 A2
E 7110 S
2100 CDHT 84121 2177 E2
2900 CDHT 84121 2178 B2
E 7115 S
1700 CDHT 84121 2177 C2
2700 CDHT 84121 2178 A2
E 7120 S
2200 CDHT 84121 2177 E2
S 7120 W
3400 WVCY 84128 1960 E6
W 7125 S
1100 WJDN 84084 2175 E2
E 7130 S
1800 CDHT 84121 2177 D2
W 7130 S
300 MDVL 84047 2176 B2
2500 WJDN 84084 2175 A2
W 7140 S
2800 WJDN 84084 2175 A2
E 7145 S
2900 CDHT 84121 2178 B2
E 7150 S
600 SWBR 84405 1228 E1
600 SWBR 84405 1229 A1
2200 CDHT 84121 2177 E2
E 7160 S
200 MDVL 84047 2176 D2
1800 CDHT 84121 2177 D2
S 7160 W
3800 WVCY 84128 1960 E7
E 7175 S
2700 CDHT 84121 2178 B2
E 7180 S
- CDHT 84093 2177 B2
2100 CDHT 84121 2177 E2
E 7180 S
2900 CDHT 84121 2178 B2
W 7180 S
2700 WJDN 84084 2175 A2
W 7195 S
2300 WJDN 84084 2175 B2
E 7200 S
1300 CDHT 84093 2177 C2
1300 CDHT 84121 2177 C2
1500 SPFK 84660 3250 C4
2000 UthC 84660 3250 D4
N 7200 E
10 HTVL 84317 1060 E5
N 7200 W
- BxEC 84336 520 B2
7300 BxEC 84337 584 B7
10700 HILD 84043 2603 E1
10700 LEHI 84043 2603 E1
10800 UthC 84043 2603 E1
10900 LEHI 84043 2496 E7
10900 UthC 84043 2496 E7
S 7200 E
100 HTVL 84317 1060 E5
S 7200 W
- SLCY 84044 1854 E3
- SLCY 84104 1854 E6
- SLCY 84116 1854 E3
- SLkC 84044 1854 E6
- SLkC 84104 1854 E5
- WVCY 84044 1960 E3
2100 SLkC 84044 1960 E3
2100 WVCY 84128 1960 E3
3900 SLkC 84044 2066 E1
3900 WVCY 84128 2066 E1
W 7200 N
- UthC 84003 2711 A3
3700 HYVL 84314 646 A2
W 7200 S
- MDVL 84047 2175 E2
10 MDVL 84047 2176 B2
1300 WJDN 84084 2175 D2
W 7200 S SR-48
- MDVL 84047 2175 E2
10 MDVL 84047 2176 B2
E 7205 S
2000 CDHT 84121 2177 D2
W 7225 S
1800 WJDN 84084 2175 C2
E 7230 S
2800 CDHT 84121 2178 B2
N 7230 W
7300 LEHI 84043 2710 E2
7300 UthC 84003 2710 E2
E 7240 S
800 SWBR 84405 1229 A1
1400 CDHT 84121 2177 B2
S 7259 W
- SLkC 84044 1960 E4
E 7260 S
2700 CDHT 84121 2178 A2
W 7260 S
3400 WJDN 84084 2174 E2
W 7265 S
1800 WJDN 84084 2175 C2
W 7268 S
2700 WJDN 84084 2175 A2
S 7270 W
2900 SLkC 84044 1960 E5
N 7275 E
1300 WbrC 84317 1060 E2
1300 WbrC 84317 1061 A2
W 7290 S
1300 WJDN 84084 2175 D2
N 7300 E
900 WbrC 84317 1061 A3
S 7300 E
100 HTVL 84317 1061 A5
W 7300 N
6500 UthC 84003 2711 A3
W 7300 S
1200 SPFK 84660 3248 D4
1400 UthC 84660 3248 D4
W 7300 S SR-115
1200 SPFK 84660 3248 D4
1400 UthC 84660 3248 D4
W 7305 S
1100 WJDN 84084 2175 D3
E 7320 S
2800 CDHT 84121 2178 B3
E 7325 S
1600 SWBR 84405 1229 C2
1800 CDHT 84121 2177 D3
W 7325 S
700 BxEC 84340 941 C3
3100 WJDN 84084 2174 E3
N 7330 W
- LEHI 84043 2603 D7
- LEHI 84043 2710 D1
- UthC 84003 2710 D1
- UthC 84003 2603 D7
- UthC 84043 2710 D1
E 7335 S
1400 CDHT 84121 2177 C3
3000 CDHT 84121 2178 B3
W 7340 S
3400 WJDN 84084 2174 E3
E 7350 S
200 MDVL 84047 2176 D3
2700 CDHT 84121 2178 A3
N 7350 W
7700 LEHI 84003 2710 D1
7700 LEHI 84043 2710 D1
7700 UthC 84003 2710 D1
W 7350 N
8000 LEHI 84043 2710 B3
8500 SRSP 84043 2710 A2
8700 UthC 84043 2710 A2
W 7370 S
2300 WJDN 84084 2175 B3
E 7375 S
900 SWBR 84405 1229 A2
2800 CDHT 84121 2178 B3
E 7380 S
1400 CDHT 84093 2177 C3
1400 CDHT 84121 2177 C3
W 7380 S
2400 WJDN 84084 2175 B3
3400 WJDN 84084 2174 E3
E 7390 S
200 MDVL 84047 2176 D3
E 7400 S
- CchC 84319 651 E7
E 7400 S
- CchC 84319 652 A7
- CchC 84328 651 E7
- CchC 84328 652 A7
- CchC 84328 711 D1
1500 SWBR 84405 1229 C2
2200 SWBR 84405 1230 A2
N 7400 W
7500 LEHI 84003 2710 D2
7500 LEHI 84043 2710 D2
8100 LEHI 84043 2603 D7
S 7400 E
100 HTVL 84317 1061 A5
S 7400 W
2100 SLkC 84044 1960 E2
W 7400 S
- CchC 84319 651 D7
- CchC 84328 651 D7
- WJDN 84084 2173 B3
2900 CchC 84339 649 E7
2900 CchC 84339 650 A7
4800 WJDN 84084 2174 A3
W 7400 S S
300 CchC 84319 651 D7
W 7410 S
2300 WJDN 84084 2175 B3
E 7415 S
400 MDVL 84047 2176 C3
E 7420 S
10 MDVL 84047 2176 D3
W 7420 S
2700 WJDN 84084 2175 A3
5100 WJDN 84084 2173 E3
E 7425 S
- SWBR 84405 1229 C2
N 7425 E
- WbrC 84317 1061 A1
W 7425 S
- BxEC 84324 941 D3
500 BxEC 84340 941 D3
E 7440 S
200 MDVL 84047 2176 D3
E 7450 S
- SWBR 84405 1229 C2
1100 CDHT 84093 2177 B3
S 7450 E
900 WbrC 84317 1061 A7
W 7455 S
1900 WJDN 84084 2175 C3
E 7460 S
100 MDVL 84047 2176 D3
W 7460 S
2700 WJDN 84084 2175 A3
E 7470 S
1900 SWBR 84405 1229 D2
W 7470 S
1400 WJDN 84084 2175 D3
E 7480 S
2300 CDHT 84121 2177 E3
E 7495 S
2100 CDHT 84121 2177 E3
W 7495 S
- WJDN 84084 2175 D3
E 7500 S
- SWBR 84405 1229 C2
N 7500 E
- HTVL 84317 1061 A5
S 7500 E
100 HTVL 84317 1061 A5
S 7500 W
2000 SLCY 84044 1960 D2
2000 SLkC 84044 1960 D2
W 7500 S
2700 WJDN 84084 2175 A3
S 7515 W
3500 SLkC 84044 1960 D6
W 7520 S
3400 WJDN 84084 2174 E3
W 7525 S
2700 WJDN 84084 2175 A3
3300 WJDN 84084 2174 E3
W 7530 S
2300 WJDN 84084 2175 B3
5200 WJDN 84084 2173 E3
W 7545 S
3200 WJDN 84084 2174 E3
E 7550 S
1900 SWBR 84405 1229 D2
S 7550 W
3500 SLkC 84044 1960 D6
W 7550 N
7300 LEHI 84043 2710 D2
W 7550 S
400 BxEC 84340 941 D4
2700 WJDN 84084 2175 A3
4900 WJDN 84084 2174 A3
W 7560 S
2000 WJDN 84084 2175 C3
E 7570 S
500 MDVL 84047 2176 E3
W 7570 S
400 BxEC 84340 941 D4
W 7575 S
2300 WJDN 84084 2175 B3
S 7580 W
3200 SLkC 84044 1960 D6
W 7580 S
3400 WJDN 84084 2174 E3
S 7585 W
3500 SLkC 84044 1960 D6
E 7590 S
3400 CDHT 84121 2178 C3
W 7590 S
2500 WJDN 84084 2175 B3
E 7600 S
1400 SWBR 84405 1229 D2
N 7600 W
8800 BxEC 84337 584 A4
10400 LEHI 84043 2603 D1
11100 BxEC 84337 520 A6
11100 TMTN 84337 520 A6
S 7600 E
100 HTVL 84317 1061 A5
S 7600 W
2100 SLkC 84044 1960 D2
W 7600 S
1700 WJDN 84084 2175 C3
7600 S St
- CchC 84319 710 C1
E 7615 S
10 MDVL 84047 2176 D3

STREET Block	City	ZIP	Map#	Grid
S 7615 W				
3200	SLkC	84044	1960	D5
W 7615 S				
500	BxEC	84340	941	D4
W 7620 N				
7800	LEHI	84043	2710	C2
7800	UthC	84043	2710	C2
E 7625 S				
1000	MDVL	84047	2177	B3
W 7625 S				
2300	WJDN	84084	2175	B3
3300	WJDN	84084	2174	E3
E 7635 S				
300	MDVL	84047	2176	D3
300	SNDY	84047	2176	D3
3200	CDHT	84121	2178	C3
S 7635 W				
2800	SLkC	84044	1960	D4
E 7640 S				
-	SWBR	84405	1229	C2
W 7640 S				
5100	WJDN	84084	2173	D3
E 7645 S				
2300	CDHT	84093	2177	E3
E 7650 S				
100	UthC	84660	3249	D5
300	SPFK	84660	3249	D5
1600	SWBR	84405	1229	C2
3600	CDHT	84121	2178	D3
E 7660 S				
10	MDVL	84047	2176	D3
W 7660 S				
5200	WJDN	84084	2173	E3
E 7670 S				
300	MDVL	84047	2176	E3
400	SNDY	84047	2176	E3
W 7670 S				
3000	WJDN	84084	2175	A3
4900	WJDN	84084	2174	A4
W 7675 S				
3200	WJDN	84084	2174	E4
W 7680 S				
2200	WJDN	84084	2175	B3
5100	WJDN	84084	2173	E4
W 7690 S				
2800	WJDN	84084	2175	A4
E 7700 S				
1000	MDVL	84047	2177	B4
1800	SWBR	84405	1229	D2
S 7700 E				
100	HTVL	84317	1061	B5
W 7700 S				
1500	WJDN	84084	2175	C4
W 7705 S				
1900	WJDN	84084	2175	C4
E 7710 S				
1200	MDVL	84047	2177	B4
E 7720 S				
10	MDVL	84047	2176	D4
W 7720 S				
3000	WJDN	84084	2175	A4
3400	WJDN	84084	2174	D4
E 7725 S				
900	MDVL	84047	2177	A4
W 7725 S				
-	WJDN	84084	2173	B4
W 7730 S				
2800	WJDN	84084	2175	A4
4900	WJDN	84084	2174	A4
5100	WJDN	84084	2173	E4
S 7740 W				
2800	SLkC	84044	1960	D4
W 7740 S				
-	WJDN	84084	2175	A4
E 7745 S				
2400	CDHT	84093	2177	E4
2400	CDHT	84093	2178	A4
S 7750 W				
2800	SLkC	84044	1960	D5
W 7750 N				
6500	ANFK	84003	2711	A1
6500	UthC	84003	2710	E1
6500	UthC	84003	2711	A1
7200	LEHI	84003	2710	E1
7200	LEHI	84043	2710	E1
7200	UthC	84043	2710	E1
E 7755 S				
1200	SNDY	84047	2177	B4
1200	SNDY	84094	2177	B4
W 7770 S				
4900	WJDN	84084	2174	A4
5200	WJDN	84084	2173	E4
E 7775 S				
1700	SWBR	84405	1229	D3
S 7780 W				
3100	SLkC	84044	1960	D5
S 7785 W				
2800	SLkC	84044	1960	D5
E 7800 S				
10	MDVL	84047	2176	D4
10	MDVL	84070	2176	D4
100	SLkC	84070	2176	D4
400	SNDY	84047	2176	E4
400	SNDY	84070	2176	D4
700	SNDY	84047	2177	A4
700	SNDY	84094	2176	E4
700	SNDY	84094	2177	A4
800	MDVL	84047	2177	A4
1900	SWBR	84405	1229	E3
2200	CDHT	84093	2177	E4
2600	SWBR	84405	1230	A3
N 7800 E				
500	WbrC	84317	1061	B3
N 7800 W				
7500	LEHI	84043	2710	C2
7500	UthC	84043	2710	C2
S 7800 E				
500	HTVL	84317	1061	B5
500	WbrC	84317	1061	B5
S 7800 E SR-39				
500	HTVL	84317	1061	B5
500	WbrC	84317	1061	B5
W 7800 S				
800	BxEC	84340	941	C4
1000	WJDN	84084	2175	D4
1000	WJDN	84088	2175	D4
3000	WJDN	84084	2174	D4
3000	WJDN	84088	2174	D4
3100	UthC	84660	3248	A5
5200	WJDN	84084	2173	C4
5200	WJDN	84088	2173	C4
W 7800 S SR-48				
1700	WJDN	84084	2175	B4
1700	WJDN	84088	2175	B4
3000	WJDN	84084	2174	D4
3000	WJDN	84088	2174	D4
7800 S St				
-	CchC	84319	710	C1
W 7800 S St				
-	CchC	84319	710	C1
E 7810 S				
1800	CDHT	84093	2177	D4
W 7820 N				
-	HYVL	84314	586	C7
E 7825 S				
2700	SWBR	84405	1230	B3
N 7825 W				
12000	BxEC	84336	520	A3
12000	TMTN	84337	520	A3
W 7825 S				
3600	WJDN	84088	2174	D4
E 7840 S				
1800	CDHT	84093	2177	D4
1800	SWBR	84405	1229	D3
E 7845 S				
100	MDVL	84070	2176	D4
E 7850 S				
900	SNDY	84094	2177	A4
S 7850 W				
3600	SLkC	84044	1960	D6
E 7855 S				
-	SNDY	84070	2176	E4
S 7860 W				
3300	SLkC	84044	1960	D6
E 7865 S				
800	SNDY	84094	2177	A4
W 7865 S				
3600	WJDN	84088	2174	D4
E 7870 S				
2500	SWBR	84405	1230	A3
W 7870 S				
-	WJDN	84088	2173	E4
E 7875 S				
2100	SWBR	84405	1229	E3
2300	SWBR	84405	1230	A3
W 7875 S				
3800	WJDN	84088	2174	C4
E 7880 S				
1800	SWBR	84405	1229	D3
W 7888 S				
1700	WJDN	84088	2175	C4
E 7890 S				
100	MDVL	84070	2176	D4
S 7895 W				
3300	SLkC	84044	1960	C6
W 7895 S				
-	WJDN	84088	2173	A4
N 7900 E				
1100	WbrC	84310	1061	B1
1100	WbrC	84317	1061	B1
S 7900 E				
600	WbrC	84317	1061	B6
S 7900 W				
3100	SLkC	84044	1960	D5
W 7900 N				
4400	PTGV	84062	2712	B1
4400	UthC	84062	2712	B1
W 7900 S				
700	BxEC	84340	941	C4
1300	WJDN	84088	2175	D4
3000	UthC	84660	3248	A6
W 7900 S St				
-	CchC	84319	710	C2
E 7905 S				
800	SNDY	84094	2177	A4
W 7910 S				
3600	WJDN	84088	2174	D4
E 7925 S				
2200	SWBR	84405	1229	E3
2300	SWBR	84405	1230	A3
W 7925 S				
3800	WJDN	84088	2174	D4
E 7930 S				
100	MDVL	84070	2176	D4
S 7930 W				
2900	SLkC	84044	1960	C4
W 7935 S				
-	WJDN	84088	2173	A4
E 7945 S				
800	SNDY	84094	2177	B4
W 7950 S				
-	BxEC	84340	941	C4
-	WJDN	84088	2173	A4
2700	WJDN	84088	2175	A4
3600	WJDN	84088	2174	D4
W 7965 S				
3800	WJDN	84088	2174	D4
W 7970 S				
3200	WJDN	84088	2174	E4
E 7975 S				
2300	SWBR	84405	1229	E3
2300	SWBR	84405	1230	A3
W 7980 S				
3500	WJDN	84088	2174	D4
E 7985 S				
1000	SNDY	84094	2177	B4
W 7990 S				
3600	WJDN	84088	2174	D4
E 8000 S				
10	MDVL	84070	2176	C4
300	SLkC	84070	2176	D4
300	SNDY	84070	2176	D4
N 8000 W				
7300	LEHI	84043	2710	C2
7300	UthC	84043	2710	C2
10400	LEHI	84043	2603	C1
10800	UthC	84043	2496	C7
10800	UthC	84043	2603	C1
10900	LEHI	84043	2496	C7
S 8000 E				
-	WbrC	84317	1061	B6
S 8000 W				
-	SLkC	84044	1854	C7
2200	SLkC	84044	1960	C2
3900	SLkC	84044	2066	C1
W 8000 N				
3500	HYVL	84314	586	A7
4600	ELWD	84337	585	C6
5700	ELWD	84337	584	D7
6600	BxEC	84337	584	C7
W 8000 S				
-	BxEC	84340	941	A5
800	SALM	84660	3248	D6
W 8000 S				
800	SALM	84660	3249	A6
800	SPFK	84660	3248	D6
800	SPFK	84660	3249	A6
800	UthC	84660	3248	D6
800	UthC	84660	3249	A6
W 8000 S SR-164				
800	SALM	84660	3248	D6
800	SALM	84660	3249	A6
800	SPFK	84660	3248	D6
800	SPFK	84660	3249	A6
800	UthC	84660	3248	D6
800	UthC	84660	3249	A6
8000 N Rd				
-	BxEC	84337	645	B2
W 8010 S				
3800	WJDN	84088	2174	C4
E 8020 S				
1300	SNDY	84093	2177	C4
W 8020 N				
7100	LEHI	84043	2710	E1
7100	UthC	84003	2710	E1
7100	UthC	84043	2710	E1
W 8020 S				
1500	WJDN	84088	2175	D4
W 8025 S				
2900	WJDN	84088	2175	A4
W 8030 S				
-	WJDN	84088	2174	A4
S 8035 W				
3700	SLkC	84044	1960	C7
W 8040 S				
1300	WJDN	84088	2175	D4
E 8045 S				
500	SNDY	84070	2176	E4
W 8045 S				
1500	WJDN	84088	2175	D4
W 8050 S				
-	WJDN	84088	2173	A4
3200	WJDN	84088	2174	E4
S 8070 W				
3200	SLkC	84044	1960	C5
W 8070 S				
3600	WJDN	84088	2174	D4
E 8075 S				
8100	SWBR	84405	1230	B3
E 8080 S				
700	SNDY	84094	2176	E4
700	SNDY	84094	2177	A4
1700	SLkC	84093	2177	C4
E 8085 S				
1300	SNDY	84093	2177	C5
W 8085 S				
1500	WJDN	84088	2175	D5
W 8090 S				
-	WJDN	84088	2173	A5
1500	WJDN	84088	2175	C5
4900	WJDN	84088	2174	A4
E 8100 S				
600	SNDY	84070	2176	E5
2100	SWBR	84405	1229	E3
2300	SWBR	84405	1230	A3
W 8100 S				
-	BxEC	84340	941	C5
8100 S				
-	CchC	84328	711	A2
W 8100 S St				
400	CchC	84319	710	C2
W 8110 S				
3600	WJDN	84088	2174	D5
E 8120 S				
400	SNDY	84070	2176	E5
W 8120 S				
2200	WJDN	84088	2175	B5
E 8125 S				
700	SNDY	84094	2176	E5
700	SNDY	84094	2177	A5
1300	SLkC	84093	2177	B5
2400	SWBR	84405	1230	A3
W 8125 S				
1500	WJDN	84088	2175	D5
W 8130 S				
-	WJDN	84088	2173	A5
E 8135 S				
200	MDVL	84070	2176	D5
S 8140 W				
3800	SLkC	84044	1960	C7
W 8140 S				
4900	WJDN	84088	2174	A5
E 8150 S				
2500	SWBR	84405	1230	A4
S 8150 W				
3500	SLkC	84044	1960	C6
W 8155 S				
1600	WJDN	84088	2175	E5
W 8170 N				
8900	LEHI	84043	2602	E7
E 8175 S				
1000	SNDY	84094	2177	B5
1300	SLkC	84093	2177	C5
1500	SNDY	84093	2177	C5
E 8180 S				
400	SNDY	84070	2176	E5
1700	SNDY	84093	2177	D5
W 8180 S				
4900	WJDN	84088	2174	A5
5200	WJDN	84088	2173	E5
W 8195 S				
1500	WJDN	84088	2175	D5
E 8200 S				
-	SWBR	84405	1230	A4
N 8200 W				
10500	LEHI	84043	2603	B1
S 8200 W				
2700	SLkC	84044	1960	C4
W 8200 N				
3600	HYVL	84314	586	A6
W 8200 S				
-	WJDN	84088	2173	A5
1500	WJDN	84088	2175	C5
2400	UthC	84660	3248	B6
3400	WJDN	84088	2174	E5
3600	CchC	84339	708	E3
8200 S St				
-	CchC	84328	710	D2
E 8220 S				
300	SNDY	84070	2176	E5
1100	SNDY	84094	2177	B5
S 8220 E				
-	WbrC	84317	1061	C7
W 8220 S				
2200	WJDN	84088	2175	B5
E 8230 S				
700	SNDY	84094	2176	E5
700	SNDY	84094	2177	A5
W 8230 S				
1300	WJDN	84088	2175	D5
4500	WJDN	84088	2174	A5
5200	WJDN	84088	2173	E5
S 8235 W				
3600	SLkC	84044	1960	C7
W 8235 S				
6100	WJDN	84088	2173	C5
E 8240 S				
500	SNDY	84070	2176	E5
2400	SWBR	84405	1230	A4
W 8245 S				
3400	WJDN	84088	2174	E5
W 8250 S				
1800	WJDN	84088	2175	C5
3800	WJDN	84088	2174	C5
E 8260 S				
300	SLkC	84070	2176	E5
W 8260 S				
6100	WJDN	84088	2173	C5
E 8270 S				
700	SLkC	84094	2177	A5
700	SNDY	84094	2176	E5
W 8270 S				
1900	WJDN	84088	2175	C5
5100	WJDN	84088	2173	E5
5100	WJDN	84088	2174	A4
E 8280 S				
800	SLkC	84094	2177	A5
800	SNDY	84094	2177	A5
S 8280 W				
3300	SLkC	84044	1960	B6
W 8280 S				
3400	WJDN	84088	2174	D5
E 8285 S				
500	SLkC	84070	2176	E5
500	SNDY	84070	2176	E5
W 8295 S				
1500	WJDN	84088	2175	D5
E 8300 S				
500	SLkC	84070	2176	E5
500	SNDY	84070	2176	E5
2400	SWBR	84405	1230	A4
S 8300 W				
3500	SLkC	84044	1960	B6
W 8300 S				
400	CchC	84319	710	D3
1900	WJDN	84088	2175	C5
W 8305 S				
6700	WJDN	84088	2173	A5
W 8310 S				
5200	WJDN	84088	2173	E5
W 8315 S				
3400	WJDN	84088	2174	D5
E 8320 S				
1000	SNDY	84094	2177	B5
W 8320 S				
5100	WJDN	84088	2173	E5
E 8325 S				
700	SNDY	84094	2176	E5
700	SNDY	84094	2177	A5
1800	SNDY	84093	2177	D5
W 8340 S				
1700	WJDN	84088	2175	C5
E 8350 S				
3300	CDHT	84121	2178	C5
N 8350 W				
7300	LEHI	84043	2710	B2
7400	UthC	84043	2710	B1
W 8350 N				
10800	SRSP	84043	2601	E7
10800	SRSP	84043	2602	A7
W 8350 S				
1900	WJDN	84088	2175	C5
3400	WJDN	84088	2174	D5
E 8355 S				
200	SLkC	84070	2176	D5
W 8360 S				
400	MDVL	84047	2176	B5
400	SNDY	84070	2176	B5
S 8370 W				
3600	SLkC	84044	1960	B7
W 8370 S				
4000	WJDN	84088	2174	C5
E 8375 S				
100	SLkC	84070	2176	D5
700	SNDY	84094	2176	E5
700	SNDY	84094	2177	A5
W 8375 S				
6400	WJDN	84088	2173	B5
E 8380 S				
1000	SNDY	84094	2177	B5
W 8380 S				
2900	WJDN	84088	2175	A5
4000	WJDN	84088	2174	C5
W 8390 S				
2000	WJDN	84088	2175	C5
W 8395 S				
3200	WJDN	84088	2174	E5
E 8400 S				
300	SLkC	84070	2176	E5
300	SNDY	84070	2176	E5
S 8400 W				
2600	SLkC	84044	1960	B4
3700	SLkC	84006	1960	B7
3800	SLkC	84006	2066	B2
3800	SLkC	84044	2066	B2
4100	WVCY	84044	2066	B2
S 8400 W SR-111				
2600	SLkC	84044	1960	B4
3700	SLkC	84006	1960	B7
3800	SLkC	84006	2066	B2
3800	SLkC	84044	2066	B2
4100	WVCY	84044	2066	B2
W 8400 S				
1300	SALM	84653	3248	E7
1800	WJDN	84088	2175	C5
2300	UthC	84660	3248	B7
4600	WJDN	84088	2174	B5
W 8410 S				
3200	WJDN	84088	2174	E5
W 8420 S				
3600	WJDN	84088	2174	D5
E 8425 S				
700	SLkC	84094	2176	E5
700	SLkC	84094	2177	A5
700	SNDY	84094	2176	E5
1300	SLkC	84093	2177	C5
1500	SNDY	84093	2177	C5
W 8430 S				
1500	WJDN	84088	2175	C5
S 8450 E				
-	WbrC	84317	1061	C6
W 8450 S				
1000	WJDN	84088	2175	E5
4500	WJDN	84088	2174	B5
S 8460 W				
4100	SLkC	84006	2066	B1
4100	WVCY	84044	2066	B1
W 8470 S				
1600	WJDN	84088	2175	C6
E 8475 S				
700	SLkC	84094	2176	E6
700	SLkC	84094	2177	A5
700	SNDY	84094	2176	E6
800	SNDY	84094	2177	A5
W 8475 S				
3200	WJDN	84088	2174	E5
S 8480 W				
3300	SLkC	84044	1960	B6
W 8480 S				
100	MDVL	84047	2176	C5
4200	WJDN	84088	2174	B5
E 8490 S				
400	SNDY	84070	2176	E5
S 8490 W				
2600	SLkC	84044	1960	B4
W 8490 S				
-	WJDN	84088	2174	B5
S 8500 W				
2700	SLkC	84044	1960	B4
W 8500 S				
-	UthC	84660	3249	C7
3200	CchC	84339	708	E3
3200	CchC	84339	709	A3
3400	WJDN	84088	2174	E5
E 8505 S				
3400	CDHT	84121	2178	C6
W 8510 S				
1500	WJDN	84088	2175	D6
3200	WJDN	84088	2174	E5
S 8520 W				
3100	SLkC	84044	1960	B5
S 8525 W				
3300	SLkC	84044	1960	B6
W 8525 S				
2900	WJDN	84088	2174	E5
2900	WJDN	84088	2175	A5
E 8545 S				
1400	SLkC	84093	2177	C6
S 8550 W				
2600	SLkC	84044	1960	B4
W 8550 S				
1200	WJDN	84088	2175	D6
E 8555 S				
1300	SLkC	84093	2177	B6
E 8560 S				
900	SNDY	84094	2177	A6
1500	SLkC	84093	2177	C6
S 8560 W				
2700	SLkC	84044	1960	B4
8560 S				
-	CchC	84328	711	B3
W 8565 S				
2900	WJDN	84088	2174	E6
2900	WJDN	84088	2175	A5
W 8570 N				
8700	LEHI	84043	2603	A6
8800	LEHI	84043	2602	E6
10800	SRSP	84043	2601	E6
10800	SRSP	84043	2602	A6
W 8570 N SR-73				
8700	LEHI	84043	2603	A6
8800	LEHI	84043	2602	E6
10800	SRSP	84043	2601	E6
10800	SRSP	84043	2602	A6
E 8575 S				
400	SNDY	84070	2176	E6
W 8575 S				
6400	WJDN	84088	2173	B6
W 8580 S				
2700	WJDN	84088	2175	A6
4600	WJDN	84088	2174	B6
S 8590 W				
2600	SLkC	84044	1960	B4
E 8600 S				
200	CchC	84328	710	E3
200	PARA	84328	710	E3
400	CchC	84328	711	A4
500	SNDY	84070	2176	E6
700	SLkC	84094	2177	A6
700	SNDY	84094	2176	E6
700	SNDY	84094	2177	A6
1300	SLkC	84093	2177	A6
1300	SNDY	84093	2177	A6
S 8600 E				
100	WbrC	84317	1061	D5
W 8600 S				
10	MDVL	84047	2176	C6
100	UthC	84660	3249	C7
100	UthC	84660	3356	C1
1400	WJDN	84088	2175	D6
3200	WJDN	84088	2174	E6
E 8600 S St				
700	CchC	84328	711	C3
W 8605 S				
-	WJDN	84088	2175	C6
S 8620 W				
3100	SLkC	84044	1960	B5
W 8620 S				
1300	WJDN	84088	2175	D6
3600	WJDN	84088	2174	D6
5000	WJDN	84088	2173	E6
S 8630 W				
-	SLkC	84044	1960	B5
E 8640 S				
200	SNDY	84070	2176	D6
1500	SNDY	84093	2177	C6
N 8650 E				
300	WbrC	84317	1061	D4
S 8650 W				
2700	SLkC	84044	1960	B4
W 8650 N				
-	HYVL	84314	586	C5
W 8660 S				
1300	WJDN	84088	2175	D6
3900	WJDN	84088	2174	C6
E 8680 S				
10	SNDY	84070	2176	D6
600	SNDY	84094	2176	E6
W 8680 S				
1100	WJDN	84088	2175	D6
E 8685 S				
1300	SNDY	84093	2177	C6
1600	SLkC	84093	2177	C6
W 8690 S				
3900	WJDN	84088	2174	C6
S 8700 E				
800	WbrC	84317	1061	D7
S 8700 W				
2700	SLkC	84044	1960	A4
W 8700 S				
100	PARA	84319	710	C4
100	PARA	84328	710	C4
800	BxEC	84340	941	B6
1300	WJDN	84088	2175	D6
3800	WJDN	84088	2174	C6
W 8710 S				
-	WJDN	84088	2173	E6
10	SNDY	84070	2176	C6
E 8725 S				
1100	SLkC	84094	2177	B6
E 8730 S				
1300	SLkC	84093	2177	C6
N 8730 W				
10	LEHI	84043	2603	A6
7300	LEHI	84043	2710	A1
7300	SRSP	84043	2710	A1
7300	UthC	84043	2710	A1
W 8730 S				
3900	WJDN	84088	2174	C6
E 8740 S				
3400	CDHT	84121	2178	C6
W 8740 S				
1500	WJDN	84088	2175	C6
4800	WJDN	84088	2174	A6
S 8750 E				
100	WbrC	84317	1061	D5
W 8750 S				
2700	WJDN	84088	2175	A6
2900	WJDN	84088	2174	E6
E 8760 S				
-	SLkC	84094	2177	B6
200	SNDY	84070	2176	D6
W 8760 S				
1700	WJDN	84088	2175	C6
W 8770 S				
2100	WJDN	84088	2175	B6
3900	WJDN	84088	2174	C6
W 8780 S				
2000	WJDN	84088	2175	C6
4800	WJDN	84088	2174	A6
W 8790 S				
4400	WJDN	84088	2174	B6
E 8800 S				
-	CchC	84328	711	C3
10	PARA	84328	710	E4
10	SNDY	84070	2176	D6
10	UthC	84653	3356	E1
10	UthC	84660	3356	E1
N 8800 W				
10300	LEHI	84043	2603	A2
10800	UthC	84043	2496	A7
10800	UthC	84043	2603	A2
S 8800 E				
900	WbrC	84317	1061	D7
S 8800 W				
2600	SLkC	84044	1960	A4
W 8800 N				
4000	ELWD	84337	585	D5
5800	BxEC	84337	584	D5
5800	BxEC	84337	585	A5
5800	ELWD	84337	584	D5
8800	LEHI	84043	2602	E6
8800	LEHI	84043	2603	A6
8800	UthC	84043	2602	E6
8800	UthC	84043	2603	A6
W 8800 S				
10	PARA	84328	710	D4
10	UthC	84653	3356	C1
10	UthC	84660	3356	C1
200	SALM	84653	3356	C1
1800	WJDN	84088	2175	C6
3100	CchC	84339	709	A4
4500	UthC	84651	3354	A1
W 8820 S				
2000	WJDN	84088	2175	C6
4800	WJDN	84088	2174	A6
5000	WJDN	84088	2173	E6
W 8830 S				
10	SNDY	84070	2176	C6
1100	WJDN	84088	2175	E6
W 8835 S				
100	SNDY	84070	2176	B6
E 8840 S				
200	SNDY	84070	2176	D6
E 8850 S				
1300	SLkC	84093	2177	C6
S 8850 W				
2600	SLkC	84044	1960	A4
W 8850 S				
10	SNDY	84070	2176	C6
1800	WJDN	84088	2175	C6
3600	WJDN	84088	2174	D6
E 8860 S				
1200	SLkC	84094	2177	B6
1200	SNDY	84094	2177	B6
W 8860 S				
5000	WJDN	84088	2173	E6
5000	WJDN	84088	2174	A6
W 8865 S				
300	SNDY	84070	2176	C6
W 8870 S				
2000	WJDN	84088	2175	C6
W 8875 S				
-	WJDN	84088	2175	A6
E 8880 S				
200	SNDY	84070	2176	D6
W 8890 S				
3700	WJDN	84088	2174	D6
E 8900 S				
10	PARA	84328	710	E4
S 8900 E				
1300	WbrC	84317	1061	D7
S 8900 W				
2600	SLkC	84044	1960	A4
W 8900 S				
-	WJDN	84088	2173	E7
10	PARA	84328	710	D4
3000	WJDN	84088	2175	A7
W 8910 S				
2100	WJDN	84088	2175	B7
E 8920 S				
200	SNDY	84070	2176	D7
S 8920 W				
3200	SLkC	84044	1960	A5
W 8920 S				
3700	WJDN	84088	2174	D7
W 8925 S				
1000	WJDN	84088	2175	E7
S 8950 E				
-	WbrC	84317	1061	E5
S 8950 W				
2600	SLkC	84044	1960	A4
E 8960 S				
200	SNDY	84070	2176	D7
W 8970 S				
1900	WJDN	84088	2175	C7
4300	WJDN	84088	2174	B7
S 8990 W				
2600	SLkC	84044	1960	A4
E 9000 S				
10	PARA	84328	710	E4
10	SNDY	84070	2176	E7
400	CchC	84328	710	E4
400	CchC	84328	711	A4
700	SNDY	84094	2176	E7
700	SNDY	84094	2177	A7
800	SNDY	84094	2283	A1
E 9000 S SR-209				
10	SNDY	84070	2176	E7
700	SNDY	84094	2176	E7
700	SNDY	84094	2177	A7
800	SNDY	84094	2283	A1
N 9000 E				
100	WbrC	84317	1061	E4
S 9000 E				
-	WbrC	84317	1061	E5
S 9000 W				
2700	SLkC	84044	1960	A4
W 9000 S				
-	SLkC	84088	2176	A7
-	WJDN	84088	2176	A7
10	PARA	84328	710	C4
10	SNDY	84070	2176	A7
300	CchC	84328	710	C4
900	WJDN	84088	2175	E7
4800	WJDN	84088	2173	E7
4800	WJDN	84088	2174	C7
W 9000 S SR-209				
-	SLkC	84088	2176	A7
-	WJDN	84088	2176	A7
10	SNDY	84070	2176	A7
900	WJDN	84088	2175	E7
3000	WJDN	84088	2174	E7
S 9040 W				
2600	SLkC	84044	1960	A4
E 9045 S				
900	SNDY	84094	2177	A7
E 9050 S				
500	SNDY	84070	2176	E7
3500	CDHT	84093	2178	D7
S 9050 W				
2700	SLkC	84044	1960	A4
W 9050 S				
2900	WJDN	84088	2175	A7
3000	WJDN	84088	2174	E7
E 9055 S				
3400	CDHT	84093	2178	C7
E 9060 S				
2000	SNDY	84093	2177	D7
W 9060 S				
2000	WJDN	84088	2175	C7
W 9070 S				
4700	WJDN	84088	2174	A7
S 9080 W				
2600	SLkC	84044	1960	A4
E 9085 S				
700	SNDY	84094	2176	E7
700	SNDY	84094	2177	A7
E 9090 S				
1300	SNDY	84093	2177	C7
E 9100 S				
100	PARA	84328	710	E5
100	SNDY	84070	2176	D7
2000	SNDY	84093	2177	D7
S 9100 W				
2700	SLkC	84044	1959	E5
W 9100 S				
200	PARA	84328	710	C5
2700	WJDN	84088	2175	A7
E 9100 St S				
10	PARA	84328	710	D5
W 9100 St S				
10	PARA	84328	710	D5
W 9110 S				
4700	WJDN	84088	2174	A7
E 9120 S				
300	SNDY	84070	2176	E7
W 9120 S				
300	SNDY	84070	2176	B7
E 9125 S				
200	SNDY	84070	2176	D7
S 9130 W				
2600	SLkC	84044	1959	E4
E 9140 S				
300	SNDY	84070	2176	D7
W 9140 S				
2100	WJDN	84088	2175	B7
E 9150 S				
300	SNDY	84070	2176	E7
N 9150 W				
8100	LEHI	84043	2602	E7
8800	UthC	84043	2602	E6
S 9150 W				
2700	SLkC	84044	1959	E4
W 9150 S				
2800	WJDN	84088	2175	A7
3100	WJDN	84088	2174	E7
E 9165 S				
200	SNDY	84070	2176	D7
E 9180 S				
300	SNDY	84070	2176	D7
S 9180 W				
2400	SLkC	84006	1959	E3
2400	SLkC	84044	1959	E3
W 9190 S				
3100	WJDN	84088	2174	E7
E 9200 S				
10	PARA	84328	710	E5
10	UthC	84653	3356	D2
100	SNDY	84070	2176	D7
1300	SNDY	84093	2177	C7

STREET Block City ZIP Map# Grid

S 9200 E
200 WbrC 84317 1061 E5
S 9200 W
2700 SLkC 84006 1959 E4
2700 SLkC 84044 1959 E4
W 9200 N
4400 ANFK 84003 2605 A5
4400 UthC 84003 2605 A5
6800 BxEC 84337 584 B4
6800 UthC 84043 2603 E5
6800 UthC 84043 2604 A5
8600 LEHI 84043 2603 A5
8700 LEHI 84043 2602 E5
8700 UthC 84043 2602 E5
W 9200 S
100 PARA 84328 710 C5
300 CchC 84328 710 C5
3500 UthC 84651 3354 E2
W 9210 S
100 SNDY 84070 2176 C7
W 9220 N
3600 CRHL 84062 2605 D5
E 9230 S
10 SNDY 84070 2176 D7
W 9230 S
3100 WJDN 84088 2174 E7
W 9240 S
100 SNDY 84070 2176 C7
2900 WJDN 84088 2175 A7
W 9260 S
400 SNDY 84070 2176 B7
3100 WJDN 84088 2174 E7
E 9270 S
10 SNDY 84070 2176 D7
E 9275 S
900 SNDY 84094 2177 A7
S 9275 E
900 WbrC 84317 1061 E7
E 9300 S
10 PARA 84328 710 D5
W 9300 S
10 PARA 84328 710 D5
3100 WJDN 84088 2280 E1
W 9320 S
500 SNDY 84070 2282 B1
W 9330 S
3000 WJDN 84088 2281 A1
W 9340 S
3100 WJDN 84088 2280 E1
W 9365 S
400 SNDY 84070 2282 B1
W 9380 S
4200 WJDN 84088 2280 B1
W 9390 S
3100 WJDN 84088 2280 E1
E 9400 S
- UthC 84653 3356 D2
10 SNDY 84070 2282 D1
700 SNDY 84094 2282 E1
700 SNDY 84094 2283 A1
900 SLkC 84094 2283 A1
1300 SLkC 84092 2283 C1
1300 SNDY 84092 2283 C1
1300 SNDY 84093 2283 C1
E 9400 S SR-209
1000 SNDY 84094 2283 C1
1300 SLkC 84092 2283 C1
1300 SNDY 84092 2283 C1
1300 SNDY 84093 2283 C1
W 9400 S
10 UthC 84653 3356 C3
300 SNDY 84070 2282 B1
1700 SJDN 84095 2281 C1
1700 WJDN 84088 2281 C1
E 9425 S
3200 SNDY 84093 2284 C1
E 9430 S
200 SNDY 84070 2282 D1
1000 SNDY 84094 2283 B1
W 9435 S
2300 SJDN 84095 2281 A1
3000 SJDN 84095 2280 E1
E 9460 S
3100 SNDY 84093 2284 C1
W 9460 S
500 SNDY 84070 2282 B1
W 9470 S
4000 SJDN 84095 2280 C1
S 9490 W
- SJDN 84095 2281 E1
W 9490 S
3700 SJDN 84095 2280 D1
E 9500 S
- SNDY 84092 2283 D1
W 9500 N
6600 HILD 84003 2604 A4
6700 HILD 84043 2604 A4
9500 S
- CchC 84328 710 E6
- CchC 84328 711 A6
E 9503 S
10 SNDY 84070 2282 C1
E 9510 S
2000 SNDY 84092 2283 E1
W 9510 S
4100 SJDN 84095 2280 C1
E 9520 S
1100 SNDY 84094 2283 B1
W 9520 S
- SJDN 84095 2281 B1
W 9525 S
1800 SJDN 84095 2281 C1
E 9530 S
2200 SNDY 84092 2283 E1
E 9545 S
200 SNDY 84070 2282 D1
W 9545 S
2500 SJDN 84095 2281 A1
E 9550 S
10 UthC 84653 3356 C3
N 9550 W
8800 LEHI 84043 2602 D5
W 9560 N
- CRHL 84062 2605 B4
W 9560 S
500 SNDY 84070 2282 B1
W 9580 S
4000 SJDN 84095 2280 C1
E 9585 S
200 SNDY 84070 2282 D1
E 9590 S
700 SNDY 84094 2282 E1
700 SNDY 84094 2283 A1
E 9600 S
600 UthC 84653 3356 E3
600 UthC 84660 3356 E3
W 9600 N
4000 BxEC 84337 586 A3
4000 ELWD 84337 585 E3
4000 ELWD 84337 586 A3
5600 ANFK 84003 2604 C4
5600 HILD 84003 2604 C4
6500 UthC 84003 2604 A4
6800 HILD 84003 2603 E4
6800 HILD 84043 2604 A4
6800 UthC 84043 2603 E4
6800 UthC 84043 2604 A4
8600 LEHI 84043 2603 A4
8700 LEHI 84043 2602 E4
9800 UthC 84043 2602 B4
W 9600 S
3300 UthC 84651 3354 E3
9600 Rd N
- BxEC 84337 584 E3
- BxEC 84337 585 A3
- ELWD 84337 584 E3
- ELWD 84337 585 A3
W 9610 S
3100 SJDN 84095 2280 E1
E 9620 S
1700 SNDY 84092 2283 C1
W 9620 N
5500 HILD 84003 2604 D4
5500 UthC 84003 2604 D4
W 9620 S
1500 SJDN 84095 2281 C1
E 9630 S
700 SNDY 84094 2282 E1
700 SNDY 84094 2283 A1
W 9640 S
1700 SJDN 84095 2281 C1
E 9650 S
400 UthC 84653 3356 E3
400 UthC 84660 3356 E3
9655 S
2100 SNDY 84092 2283 E1
E 9670 S
100 SNDY 84070 2282 D1
W 9680 N
6600 HILD 84003 2604 A4
W 9685 S
1600 SJDN 84095 2281 C1
E 9690 S
2900 SNDY 84092 2284 B2
3000 SLkC 84092 2284 B2
E 9700 N
5700 HILD 84003 2604 D3
E 9710 S
- SLkC 84092 2284 C2
E 9715 S
- SLkC 84092 2283 D2
W 9715 S
3100 SJDN 84095 2280 E2
W 9720 N
6600 HILD 84003 2604 A4
E 9725 S
2700 SNDY 84092 2284 B2
W 9740 N
6000 HILD 84003 2604 B3
W 9755 S
2800 SJDN 84095 2281 A2
E 9760 S
- SLkC 84092 2283 D2
W 9760 S
2700 SJDN 84095 2281 A2
E 9765 S
500 SNDY 84070 2282 E2
W 9765 S
3000 SJDN 84095 2280 E2
W 9770 N
6600 HILD 84003 2604 A3
W 9775 S
1500 SJDN 84095 2281 D2
W 9790 S
6000 WJDN 84088 2279 C2
E 9800 S
10 UthC 84653 3356 D4
1500 SNDY 84092 2283 C2
1600 SLkC 84092 2283 C2
2700 SLkC 84092 2284 A2
2700 SNDY 84092 2284 A2
W 9800 N
4100 CRHL 84062 2605 B3
6000 HILD 84003 2604 B3
W 9800 S
300 SNDY 84070 2282 B2
2000 SJDN 84095 2281 B2
3100 SJDN 84095 2280 E2
E 9800 S St
- CchC 84328 710 E7
- CchC 84328 711 A7
W 9810 N
4500 CRHL 84062 2605 A3
6500 HILD 84003 2604 A3
W 9820 N
4000 CRHL 84062 2605 C3
E 9840 S
2200 SNDY 84092 2283 E2
E 9845 S
1700 SNDY 84092 2283 D2
E 9850 S
600 SNDY 84070 2282 E2
W 9850 N
4600 CRHL 84062 2605 A3
6600 HILD 84003 2604 A3
W 9860 N
4100 CRHL 84062 2605 B3
6200 HILD 84003 2604 B3
W 9860 S
- WJDN 84088 2279 C2
E 9880 S
1700 SNDY 84092 2283 D2
W 9880 N
4000 CRHL 84062 2605 C3
W 9890 N
6300 HILD 84003 2604 B3
E 9898 S
2500 SLkC 84092 2284 A2
E 9900 S
400 SNDY 84070 2282 E2
W 9900 N
4500 CRHL 84062 2605 A3
4700 ANFK 84062 2605 A3
4700 UthC 84062 2605 A3
W 9916 S
1700 SJDN 84095 2281 C2
W 9930 S
- WJDN 84088 2279 C2
E 9940 S
500 SNDY 84070 2282 E2
E 9950 S
600 SNDY 84070 2282 E2
W 9950 N
4100 CRHL 84062 2605 B3
W 9950 S
1300 SJDN 84095 2281 D2
W 9960 N
6300 HILD 84003 2604 B3
W 9970 N
5600 HILD 84003 2604 C3
W 9970 S
1100 SJDN 84095 2281 E2
4800 UthC 84651 3354 A4
W 9980 N
4400 CRHL 84062 2605 A3
E 10000 S
10 SALM 84653 3356 D4
10 UthC 84653 3356 D4
2100 SNDY 84092 2283 E2
2300 SNDY 84092 2284 A2
3100 SLkC 84092 2284 C2
W 10000 N
- LEHI 84043 2602 D3
- UthC 84043 2601 E3
- UthC 84043 2602 A3
4400 ELWD 84337 585 C2
6400 BxEC 84337 584 D2
6400 ELWD 84337 584 D2
W 10000 S
400 SJDN 84095 2282 A2
2700 SJDN 84095 2281 A2
3100 SJDN 84095 2280 E2
4200 UthC 84651 3354 C4
W 10025 S
3400 SJDN 84095 2280 E2
W 10030 N
5400 HILD 84003 2604 D3
W 10040 N
5700 HILD 84003 2604 C3
W 10050 N
6600 HILD 84003 2604 A3
E 10065 S
400 SNDY 84070 2282 E2
W 10080 N
5400 HILD 84003 2604 D3
E 10095 S
2000 SNDY 84092 2283 E3
W 10100 N
5700 HILD 84003 2604 C3
E 10105 S
300 SNDY 84070 2282 D3
E 10120 S
400 SNDY 84070 2282 E3
W 10120 N
6600 HILD 84003 2604 A2
W 10120 S
- WJDN 84088 2279 C3
W 10125 N
6700 HILD 84003 2604 A3
W 10125 S
1000 SJDN 84095 2281 E3
W 10130 N
5400 HILD 84003 2604 D2
E 10140 S
2200 SNDY 84092 2283 E3
E 10145 S
300 SNDY 84070 2282 D3
W 10150 N
6800 HILD 84003 2604 A2
6900 HILD 84003 2603 E2
E 10180 S
1900 SNDY 84092 2283 E3
W 10180 N
5400 HILD 84003 2604 D2
E 10185 S
300 SNDY 84070 2282 D3
E 10195 S
300 SNDY 84070 2282 D3
E 10200 S
10 SNDY 84070 2282 D3
W 10200 N
3000 DWVL 84309 586 B1
6500 HILD 84003 2604 A2
W 10200 S
100 SNDY 84070 2282 C3
200 SALM 84653 3356 C5
300 SJDN 84095 2282 B3
3000 SJDN 84095 2281 A3
3600 SJDN 84095 2280 D3
W 10205 N
6700 HILD 84003 2604 A2
6800 HILD 84003 2603 E2
W 10210 S
1000 SJDN 84095 2281 E3
W 10220 N
3900 CRHL 84062 2605 C2
6200 HILD 84003 2604 B2
E 10225 S
1800 SNDY 84092 2283 D3
2300 SNDY 84092 2284 A3
E 10230 S
400 SNDY 84070 2282 D3
W 10250 N
6400 HILD 84003 2604 A2
W 10250 S
1000 SJDN 84095 2281 E3
E 10260 S
2100 SNDY 84092 2283 E3
W 10260 N
3900 CRHL 84062 2605 C2
W 10260 S
1100 SJDN 84095 2281 E3
E 10265 S
2300 SNDY 84092 2283 E4
2300 SNDY 84092 2284 A3
E 10275 S
- SNDY 84092 2284 C3
E 10285 S
2200 SNDY 84092 2283 E3
W 10290 S
1000 SJDN 84095 2281 E3
E 10300 S
300 SNDY 84070 2282 D3
1800 SNDY 84092 2283 D3
W 10300 N
3900 CRHL 84062 2605 C2
4600 HILD 84003 2605 A2
6800 HILD 84003 2603 E2
6800 HILD 84003 2604 A2
W 10300 S
1300 UthC 84651 3355 E5
E 10305 S
2400 SNDY 84092 2283 E4
2400 SNDY 84092 2284 A3
E 10315 S
500 SNDY 84070 2282 E3
E 10330 S
- SNDY 84092 2284 B3
W 10330 S
1400 SJDN 84095 2281 D3
E 10345 S
500 SNDY 84070 2282 E3
W 10370 N
4700 HILD 84003 2605 A2
E 10375 S
300 SNDY 84070 2282 E3
W 10375 S
800 SJDN 84095 2282 A3
900 SJDN 84095 2281 E3
W 10380 N
6500 HILD 84003 2604 A2
W 10385 S
3800 SJDN 84095 2280 C3
N 10400 W
9300 LEHI 84043 2602 B4
9300 UthC 84043 2602 B4
W 10400 N
- TMTN 84337 584 E1
- UthC 84043 2601 E2
3900 CRHL 84062 2605 C2
4400 BxEC 84337 585 C1
4400 ELWD 84337 585 D1
5000 HILD 84003 2604 E2
5600 ELWD 84337 584 E1
6800 HILD 84003 2603 E2
6900 LEHI 84043 2603 E2
7200 BxEC 84337 584 B1
10400 UthC 84043 2602 A2
W 10400 S
900 SJDN 84095 2281 E3
900 SJDN 84095 2282 A3
1600 PYSN 84651 3354 B5
1600 UthC 84651 3354 B5
W 10400 S SR-147
1600 PYSN 84651 3354 B5
1600 UthC 84651 3354 B5
W 10430 N
6700 HILD 84003 2604 A2
W 10430 S
200 SNDY 84070 2282 D3
E 10450 S
300 SNDY 84070 2282 E3
W 10450 S
2200 SJDN 84095 2281 B3
W 10460 S
2700 SJDN 84095 2281 A3
W 10480 N
5200 HILD 84003 2604 D2
E 10500 S
400 SNDY 84070 2282 E4
W 10500 N
6300 HILD 84003 2604 B2
6800 BxEC 84337 520 C7
6800 TMTN 84337 520 C7
6800 TMTN 84337 584 C1
W 10540 S
3200 SJDN 84095 2280 E4
W 10545 S
2800 SJDN 84095 2281 A4
W 10550 N
5900 HILD 84003 2604 C1
W 10550 S
900 SJDN 84095 2281 E4
900 SJDN 84095 2282 A4
E 10560 S
300 SNDY 84070 2282 D4
W 10570 N
6200 HILD 84003 2604 B1
W 10575 S
2200 SJDN 84095 2281 B4
E 10600 S
10 SNDY 84070 2282 D4
700 SLkC 84094 2283 B4
700 SNDY 84094 2282 E4
700 SNDY 84094 2283 B4
1300 SNDY 84092 2283 B4
W 10600 N
4400 HILD 84003 2605 A1
5300 HILD 84003 2604 D1
W 10600 S
- PYSN 84651 3354 C6
- SJDN 84070 2282 C4
- SJDN 84095 2282 C4
- SNDY 84095 2282 C4
10 SNDY 84070 2282 C4
W 10600 S SR-151
- SJDN 84070 2282 B4
- SJDN 84095 2282 B4
- SNDY 84070 2282 B4
- SNDY 84095 2282 B4
W 10610 S
1100 SJDN 84095 2281 E4
W 10620 N
5600 HILD 84003 2604 C1
E 10655 S
1000 SNDY 84094 2283 B4
W 10675 S
- SJDN 84095 2280 E4
W 10680 N
5600 HILD 84003 2604 D1
W 10690 S
1300 SJDN 84095 2281 D4
E 10695 S
400 SNDY 84070 2282 E4
W 10695 S
1800 SJDN 84095 2281 C4
W 10700 N
5200 HILD 84003 2604 D1
W 10700 S
300 SNDY 84070 2282 D4
E 10710 S
1100 SNDY 84094 2283 B4
E 10715 S
800 SNDY 84094 2283 A4
E 10735 S
400 SNDY 84070 2282 E4
W 10740 N
5200 HILD 84003 2604 E1
W 10740 S
1700 SJDN 84095 2281 C4
W 10750 S
1300 SJDN 84095 2281 D4
W 10755 S
2700 SJDN 84095 2281 A4
3200 SJDN 84095 2280 E4
E 10760 S
1000 SNDY 84094 2283 B4
W 10760 N
6400 HILD 84003 2604 A1
E 10765 S
2000 SLkC 84092 2283 D4
2000 SNDY 84092 2283 D4
W 10770 N
5600 HILD 84003 2604 C1
W 10775 S
1300 SJDN 84095 2281 D4
W 10790 S
- SJDN 84095 2281 C4
W 10800 N
4500 BxEC 84337 521 C7
5200 ELWD 84337 521 B7
5200 HILD 84003 2604 E1
5200 TMTN 84337 521 B7
6700 HILD 84003 2497 A7
6700 HILD 84003 2603 E1
6700 HILD 84043 2497 A7
6700 HILD 84043 2603 E1
6700 HILD 84043 2604 A1
6700 UthC 84003 2497 A7
6700 UthC 84003 2603 E1
6700 UthC 84043 2497 A7
6700 UthC 84043 2604 A1
7200 LEHI 84043 2603 E1
7700 UthC 84043 2603 C1
W 10800 S
- SALM 84653 3356 B6
W 10830 N
6100 HILD 84003 2604 B1
W 10850 N
5200 HILD 84003 2604 D1
W 10875 S
1100 SJDN 84095 2281 E4
W 10880 N
5800 HILD 84003 2604 C1
W 10890 N
6200 HILD 84003 2604 B1
W 10890 S
2700 SJDN 84095 2281 A5
W 10900 N
5700 HILD 84003 2604 C1
6400 HILD 84003 2497 A7
W 10900 S
5000 UthC 84651 3354 A6
W 10920 S
- SJDN 84070 2282 C5
- SJDN 84095 2282 C5
- SNDY 84070 2282 C5
W 10925 N
5800 HILD 84003 2497 C7
E 10930 S
200 SNDY 84070 2282 D5
W 10930 N
5600 HILD 84003 2497 D7
W 10950 N
6200 HILD 84003 2497 B7
W 10950 S
2200 SJDN 84095 2281 B5
E 10980 S
1700 SNDY 84092 2283 D5
E 11000 S
10 SNDY 84070 2282 D5
700 SNDY 84094 2282 E5
700 SNDY 84094 2283 A5
W 11000 N
- LEHI 84043 2495 D7
- LEHI 84043 2496 A7
- LEHI 84043 2497 A7
- UthC 84043 2496 E7
- UthC 84043 2497 A7
3800 CRHL 84003 2498 C7
3800 CRHL 84062 2498 C7
3800 HILD 84003 2498 C7
4800 HILD 84003 2497 E7
W 11000 N SR-92
- LEHI 84043 2495 D7
- LEHI 84043 2496 A7
- LEHI 84043 2497 A7
- UthC 84043 2496 E7
- UthC 84043 2497 A7
3800 CRHL 84003 2498 C7
3800 CRHL 84062 2498 C7
3800 HILD 84003 2498 C7
4800 HILD 84003 2497 E7
W 11000 S
10 SNDY 84070 2282 C5
200 SJDN 84095 2282 B5
W 11010 S
- SJDN 84095 2281 C5
W 11030 N
5600 HILD 84003 2497 D7
W 11030 S
1300 SJDN 84095 2281 D5
W 11060 N
5400 HILD 84003 2497 D7
W 11100 N
5100 HILD 84003 2497 E7
W 11115 S
2400 SJDN 84095 2281 B5
E 11125 S
400 SNDY 84070 2282 E5
W 11140 N
5800 HILD 84003 2497 C7
E 11150 S
800 SNDY 84094 2283 A5
W 11150 S
1300 SJDN 84095 2281 D5
W 11170 S
2400 SJDN 84095 2281 B5
E 11190 S
800 SNDY 84094 2283 A5
W 11200 N
4400 HILD 84003 2498 A7
4800 HILD 84003 2497 E7
W 11200 S
10 WDHL 84653 3356 A7
1200 UthC 84651 3355 E7
1200 UthC 84651 3356 A7
2300 SJDN 84095 2281 B5
4200 PYSN 84651 3354 B7
4200 UthC 84651 3354 B7
11200 Rd N
- BxEC 84337 520 A6
1500 TMTN 84337 520 A6
11200 Rd N SR-102
- BxEC 84337 520 A6
1500 TMTN 84337 520 A6
E 11205 S
1300 SNDY 84092 2283 B5
E 11225 S
800 SNDY 84094 2283 A5
W 11250 S
4200 UthC 84651 3354 C7
E 11265 S
1500 SNDY 84092 2283 C5
E 11270 S
1900 SNDY 84092 2283 D5
W 11270 N
5600 HILD 84003 2497 D7
W 11275 S
2400 SJDN 84095 2281 A6
W 11320 S
2400 SJDN 84095 2281 B6
E 11325 S
900 SNDY 84094 2283 A6
E 11340 S
1900 SNDY 84092 2283 D6
W 11345 S
400 WDHL 84653 3356 C7
W 11350 N
5500 HILD 84003 2497 C6
W 11370 S
2400 SJDN 84095 2281 B6
E 11400 S
10 DRPR 84020 2282 D6
10 SNDY 84020 2282 D6
10 SNDY 84070 2282 D6
700 SNDY 84094 2282 D6
700 SNDY 84094 2283 A6
1300 SNDY 84092 2283 A6
1500 SLkC 84092 2283 A6
W 11400 N
3900 BxEC 84337 521 E5
W 11400 S
10 DRPR 84020 2282 C6
10 SNDY 84070 2282 C6
100 SJDN 84070 2282 C6
100 SJDN 84095 2282 C6
1300 SJDN 84095 2281 D6
3100 SJDN 84095 2280 D6
W 11430 S
4100 SJDN 84095 2280 C6
E 11450 S
1700 SNDY 84092 2283 C6
W 11450 S
5600 UthC 84651 3460 D1
E 11460 S
1300 SNDY 84092 2283 B6
W 11475 S
4200 SJDN 84095 2280 C6
E 11500 S
1900 SNDY 84092 2283 D6
W 11500 S
- DRPR 84020 2282 B6
W 11520 S
3200 SJDN 84095 2280 E6
W 11530 S
- SJDN 84095 2280 B6
W 11560 S
700 DRPR 84020 2282 A6
E 11570 S
1300 SNDY 84092 2283 B6
E 11580 S
2200 SNDY 84092 2283 E6
W 11580 S
3400 SJDN 84095 2280 E6
W 11595 S
4200 SJDN 84095 2280 B6
N 11600 W
8300 SRSP 84043 2601 D7
W 11600 N
4200 BxEC 84337 521 C5
5000 TMTN 84337 521 C5
W 11600 S
2100 PYSN 84651 3462 C1
2100 UthC 84651 3462 C1
4800 UthC 84651 3461 A1
5600 UthC 84651 3460 D1
W 11600 S SR-141
5600 UthC 84651 3460 D1
E 11620 S
2100 SNDY 84092 2283 E6
W 11625 S
2200 SJDN 84095 2281 B6
E 11660 S
2200 SNDY 84092 2283 E6
W 11700 S
1800 SJDN 84095 2281 C7
3500 SJDN 84095 2280 D7
E 11705 S
900 SNDY 84094 2283 A7
W 11715 S
1100 SJDN 84095 2281 E7
W 11745 S
1200 RIVN 84065 2281 D7
1200 SJDN 84095 2281 D7
W 11760 S
2800 SJDN 84095 2281 A7
W 11770 S
4200 SJDN 84095 2280 B7
W 11775 S
1300 RIVN 84065 2281 D7
E 11780 S
1000 SNDY 84094 2283 A7
E 11800 S
- DRPR 84020 2282 E7
W 11800 S
- SJDN 84065 2279 B7
- SLkC 84065 2279 B7
- SLkC 84095 2279 B7
100 DRPR 84020 2282 C7
4500 RIVN 84065 2280 A7
4500 SJDN 84095 2280 A7
4900 HRMN 84065 2280 A7
5000 SJDN 84065 2280 A7
5200 HRMN 84065 2279 E7
5200 SJDN 84095 2279 E7
11800 S
- SNDY 84092 2283 D7
W 11830 N
6000 HILD 84003 2497 C5
W 11830 S
3200 RIVN 84065 2280 E7
W 11860 N
6000 HILD 84003 2497 C5
W 11860 S
1800 RIVN 84065 2281 C7
W 11880 S
3200 RIVN 84065 2280 E7
W 11890 S
3800 RIVN 84065 2280 D7
E 11900 S
500 DRPR 84020 2282 E7
700 DRPR 84020 2283 A7
W 11900 S
- RIVN 84065 2281 E7
W 11925 S
2900 RIVN 84065 2281 A7
3100 RIVN 84065 2280 E7
W 11940 S
1300 RIVN 84065 2281 D7
E 11950 S
- DRPR 84020 2282 D7
W 11950 S
4600 UthC 84651 3461 A2
W 11970 S
1900 RIVN 84065 2281 B7
3700 RIVN 84065 2280 D7
W 11975 S
3200 RIVN 84065 2280 E7
W 11980 S
2700 RIVN 84065 2281 A7
E 12000 S
300 DRPR 84020 2282 E7
700 DRPR 84020 2283 A7
W 12000 N
10 TMTN 84337 520 E4
200 TMTN 84337 521 A4
400 BxEC 84312 521 A4
500 BxEC 84337 521 A4
W 12000 S
3800 UthC 84651 3461 C2
5100 UthC 84651 3460 E2
5300 UthC 84655 3460 E2
W 12015 S
1800 RIVN 84065 2281 C7
W 12020 S
3200 RIVN 84065 2280 E7
W 12040 S
1300 RIVN 84065 2281 D7
3100 RIVN 84065 2280 E7
W 12050 S
1700 RIVN 84065 2281 C7
4000 RIVN 84065 2280 C7
W 12060 N
- HILD 84003 2497 C5
W 12060 S
2000 RIVN 84065 2281 C7
W 12075 S
2700 RIVN 84065 2281 A7
3200 RIVN 84065 2386 E1
E 12100 S
- DRPR 84020 2388 D1
700 DRPR 84020 2389 A1
W 12110 S
1900 RIVN 84065 2281 C7
1900 RIVN 84065 2387 C2
W 12120 S
1700 RIVN 84065 2387 C1
W 12130 S
2700 RIVN 84065 2387 A1
3100 RIVN 84065 2386 E1
W 12140 S
- RIVN 84065 2387 D1
W 12145 S
2100 RIVN 84065 2387 B1
E 12150 S
10 DRPR 84020 2388 D1
W 12165 S
2500 RIVN 84065 2387 A1
W 12175 S
2200 RIVN 84065 2387 B1
W 12180 S
- RIVN 84065 2387 D1
3300 RIVN 84065 2386 E1
W 12190 S
1900 RIVN 84065 2387 C1
W 12195 S
2400 RIVN 84065 2387 B1
E 12200 S
- DRPR 84020 2388 D1
700 DRPR 84020 2389 A1
W 12200 S
100 DRPR 84020 2388 C1
4200 UthC 84651 3461 C3
W 12210 S
1700 RIVN 84065 2387 C1
W 12220 S
1900 RIVN 84065 2387 C1
E 12225 S
1400 DRPR 84020 2389 C1
W 12230 S
1300 RIVN 84065 2387 D1
W 12240 S
3500 UthC 84651 3461 D3
W 12250 S
2200 RIVN 84065 2387 B1
W 12270 S
2500 RIVN 84065 2387 A1
W 12280 S
3600 RIVN 84065 2386 D1
W 12290 S
1300 RIVN 84065 2387 D1
E 12300 S
10 DRPR 84020 2388 D1
700 DRPR 84020 2389 A1
E 12300 S SR-71
10 DRPR 84020 2388 D1
W 12300 S
10 DRPR 84020 2388 B1
3400 UthC 84651 3461 E3
W 12300 S SR-71
10 DRPR 84020 2388 B1
W 12310 S
2300 RIVN 84065 2387 B1
W 12320 S
2700 RIVN 84065 2387 A1
W 12330 S
1400 RIVN 84065 2387 D1
W 12340 S
2300 RIVN 84065 2387 B1

Salt Lake City Street Index

Block	City	ZIP	Map#	Grid
W 12340 S				
3500	RIVN	84065	2386	D1
W 12350 S				
-	UthC	84651	3461	C3
1200	RIVN	84065	2387	D1
3400	RIVN	84065	2386	E1
E 12375 S				
1400	DRPR	84020	2389	C1
W 12380 S				
3800	RIVN	84065	2386	D1
W 12385 S				
1700	RIVN	84065	2387	C1
W 12400 S				
1000	RIVN	84065	2387	D1
3800	UthC	84651	3461	D3
4900	UthC	84651	3460	E3
W 12420 S				
2300	RIVN	84065	2387	B1
W 12440 S				
1200	RIVN	84065	2387	D1
E 12450 S				
10	DRPR	84020	2388	D1
E 12490 S				
1400	DRPR	84020	2389	C2
E 12500 S				
600	DRPR	84020	2388	E2
1500	DRPR	84020	2389	C2
W 12500 S				
1200	RIVN	84065	2387	D2
W 12510 S				
1800	RIVN	84065	2387	C2
W 12525 S				
1400	RIVN	84065	2387	D2
W 12550 S				
1300	RIVN	84065	2387	D2
E 12600 S				
300	DRPR	84020	2388	E2
900	DRPR	84020	2389	A2
W 12600 S				
900	DRPR	84020	2387	D2
900	DRPR	84020	2388	A1
1200	RIVN	84065	2387	D2
2900	RIVN	84065	2386	E2
3700	UthC	84651	3461	D4
5100	HRMN	84065	2385	E2
5100	HRMN	84065	2386	A2
W 12600 S SR-71				
900	DRPR	84020	2387	D2
900	DRPR	84020	2388	A1
1200	RIVN	84065	2387	D2
2900	RIVN	84065	2386	E2
W 12640 S				
2500	RIVN	84065	2387	B2
E 12650 S				
900	DRPR	84020	2389	A2
W 12650 S				
100	DRPR	84020	2388	C2
1300	RIVN	84065	2387	D2
E 12660 S				
1000	DRPR	84020	2389	B2
W 12660 S				
1500	RIVN	84065	2387	D2
E 12675 S				
10	DRPR	84020	2388	C2
W 12680 S				
3500	UthC	84651	3461	D4
W 12696 S				
-	DRPR	84020	2388	C2
E 12700 S				
1500	DRPR	84020	2389	C2
E 12715 S				
1300	DRPR	84020	2389	C2
W 12730 S				
1500	RIVN	84065	2387	D2
W 12800 N				
3400	BxEC	84309	522	A1
3400	BxEC	84312	522	A1
3600	BxEC	84312	521	E2
4800	BxEC	84337	521	C2
6800	BxEC	84336	520	C2
6800	BxEC	84337	520	C2
6800	TMTN	84337	520	C2
W 12800 S				
1400	RIVN	84065	2387	D2
4000	UthC	84651	3461	C4
4500	UthC	84655	3461	A4
4800	UthC	84651	3460	E4
4800	UthC	84655	3460	E4
12800 Rd N				
-	BxEC	84312	521	B2
-	BxEC	84337	521	B2
-	GRLD	84312	521	B2
W 12815 S				
5700	HRMN	84065	2385	D2
W 12820 S				
2500	RIVN	84065	2387	A2
W 12825 S				
2800	RIVN	84065	2387	A2
2900	RIVN	84065	2386	E2
E 12860 S				
600	DRPR	84020	2388	E2
W 12875 S				
2400	RIVN	84065	2387	A2
E 12900 S				
1300	DRPR	84020	2389	B2
W 12900 S				
-	HRMN	84065	2385	E3
1800	RIVN	84065	2387	C3
W 12910 S				
1600	RIVN	84065	2387	C3
W 12920 S				
1900	RIVN	84065	2387	B3
W 12925 S				
2900	RIVN	84065	2387	A3
E 12930 S				
1100	DRPR	84020	2389	B3
W 12950 S				
1500	RIVN	84065	2387	D3
W 12960 S				
2300	RIVN	84065	2387	B3
W 12974 S				
1900	RIVN	84065	2387	C3
W 12975 S				
2200	RIVN	84065	2387	B3
W 12980 S				
1700	RIVN	84065	2387	C3
W 13010 S				
2700	RIVN	84065	2387	A3
3100	RIVN	84065	2386	E3
E 13015 S				
1100	DRPR	84020	2389	B3
W 13035 S				
1700	RIVN	84065	2387	C3
W 13040 S				
1100	RIVN	84065	2387	E3
W 13055 S				
2300	RIVN	84065	2387	B3
W 13070 S				
2200	RIVN	84065	2387	B3
W 13090 S				
6800	SLkC	84065	2385	A3
W 13095 S				
2500	RIVN	84065	2387	A3
W 13100 S				
2300	RIVN	84065	2387	B3
W 13105 S				
2400	RIVN	84065	2387	B3
E 13110 S				
1000	DRPR	84020	2389	A3
W 13120 S				
900	RIVN	84065	2387	E3
3200	RIVN	84065	2386	E3
W 13130 S				
10	DRPR	84020	2388	B3
W 13145 S				
2300	RIVN	84065	2387	B3
W 13150 S				
1700	RIVN	84065	2387	C3
W 13165 S				
10	DRPR	84020	2388	B3
W 13175 S				
3300	RIVN	84065	2386	E3
W 13180 S				
2000	RIVN	84065	2387	B3
W 13190 S				
2300	RIVN	84065	2387	B3
E 13200 S				
10	DRPR	84020	2388	D3
900	DRPR	84020	2389	C3
W 13200 S				
2800	RIVN	84065	2387	A3
3100	RIVN	84065	2386	E3
W 13220 S				
2400	RIVN	84065	2387	B3
W 13235 S				
2300	RIVN	84065	2387	B4
W 13240 S				
200	DRPR	84020	2388	B3
W 13245 S				
2900	RIVN	84065	2387	A3
W 13250 N				
-	BxEC	84312	521	A1
W 13250 S				
-	RIVN	84065	2387	B4
W 13260 S				
3300	RIVN	84065	2386	E4
E 13275 S				
200	DRPR	84020	2388	D3
W 13310 S				
2800	RIVN	84065	2387	A4
W 13330 S				
1800	RIVN	84065	2387	C4
E 13340 S				
200	DRPR	84020	2388	D4
W 13360 S				
2400	RIVN	84065	2387	B4
6000	HRMN	84065	2385	C4
W 13370 S				
3300	RIVN	84065	2386	E4
E 13400 S				
100	DRPR	84020	2388	D4
800	DRPR	84020	2389	A4
W 13400 S				
1300	RIVN	84065	2387	D4
3000	RIVN	84065	2386	E4
4800	HRMN	84065	2386	A4
5000	HRMN	84065	2385	E4
5000	RIVN	84065	2385	E4
E 13430 S				
1300	DRPR	84020	2389	B4
E 13450 S				
900	DRPR	84020	2389	A4
W 13475 S				
6200	HRMN	84065	2385	B4
W 13490 S				
10	DRPR	84020	2388	C4
W 13520 S				
2000	RIVN	84065	2387	B4
W 13550 S				
2200	RIVN	84065	2387	B4
E 13560 S				
100	DRPR	84020	2388	D4
E 13590 S				
1000	DRPR	84020	2389	A4
W 13600 S				
-	SNQN	84655	3461	A6
-	UthC	84655	3461	A6
7100	HRMN	84065	2385	A5
7100	SLkC	84065	2385	A5
E 13630 S				
500	DRPR	84020	2388	E4
W 13640 S				
2700	RIVN	84065	2387	A4
3000	RIVN	84065	2386	E4
W 13680 S				
2900	RIVN	84065	2386	E5
2900	RIVN	84065	2387	A5
5400	HRMN	84065	2385	E4
E 13710 S				
500	DRPR	84020	2388	E4
W 13730 S				
1900	RIVN	84065	2387	C5
W 13750 S				
2300	RIVN	84065	2387	B5
W 13760 S				
2500	RIVN	84065	2387	A5
2700	RIVN	84065	2386	E5
6200	HRMN	84065	2385	C5
E 13800 S				
10	DRPR	84020	2388	D5
700	DRPR	84020	2389	A5
W 13800 S				
10	DRPR	84020	2388	C5
2800	BFDL	84065	2387	A5
2800	RIVN	84065	2387	A5
2900	BFDL	84065	2386	E5
2900	RIVN	84065	2386	E5
W 13900 S				
6000	HRMN	84065	2385	C5
W 13920 S				
-	BFDL	84065	2387	D5
W 13930 S				
1800	BFDL	84065	2387	C5
W 13970 S				
1700	BFDL	84065	2387	C5
W 14000 S				
-	BFDL	84065	2387	A5
-	SNQN	84655	3460	C7
-	UthC	84655	3460	C7
W 14050 S				
2000	BFDL	84065	2387	B5
W 14095 S				
2200	BFDL	84065	2387	B6
W 14165 S				
1600	BFDL	84065	2387	C6
W 14200 S				
1900	BFDL	84065	2387	C6
6200	HRMN	84065	2385	C6
6400	SLkC	84065	2385	B6
W 14270 S				
2100	BFDL	84065	2387	B6
3600	BFDL	84065	2386	D6
W 14300 S				
6000	HRMN	84065	2385	B6
W 14400 S				
1700	BFDL	84065	2387	B6
3000	BFDL	84065	2386	E6
5900	SNQN	84655	3567	B1
5900	UthC	84655	3567	B1
6500	HRMN	84065	2385	B6
6500	SLkC	84065	2385	B6
W 14400 S SR-140				
1700	BFDL	84065	2387	C6
W 14410 S				
6400	HRMN	84065	2385	B6
W 14550 S				
1300	BFDL	84065	2387	D7
W 14600 S				
300	BFDL	84065	2388	A7
300	DRPR	84020	2388	A7
900	BFDL	84065	2387	D7
3000	BFDL	84065	2386	E7
6600	SLkC	84065	2385	B7
W 14600 S SR-140				
300	BFDL	84065	2388	A7
300	DRPR	84020	2388	A7
900	BFDL	84065	2387	D7
W 14730 S				
900	BFDL	84065	2387	E7
900	BFDL	84065	2388	A7
W 14750 S				
2900	BFDL	84065	2386	E7
2900	BFDL	84065	2387	A7
W 14800 S				
6600	HRMN	84065	2385	B7
6600	SLkC	84065	2385	B7
W 14805 S				
1700	BFDL	84065	2387	C7
W 14850 S				
2200	BFDL	84065	2387	B7
W 14865 S				
2500	BFDL	84065	2387	A7
3000	BFDL	84065	2386	E7
W 15000 S				
2200	BFDL	84065	2494	B1
3000	BFDL	84065	2493	E1
W 15090 S				
2600	BFDL	84065	2494	A1
W 17000 S				
1000	BFDL	84065	2494	E6

Salt Lake City Points of Interest Index

Airports

FEATURE NAME Address City ZIP Code	MAP#	GRID
Brigham City, BMCY	765	E1
Heber City Municipal, HRCY	2398	B7
Logan-Cache, LOGN	463	B2
Ogden-Hinckley, OGDN	1172	A1
Provo Municipal, PRVO	3034	A2
Salt Lake City International, SLCY	1752	D7
Salt Lake City Municipal No 2, WJDN	2174	B2
Skypark, DvsC	1652	D3
Spanish Fork-Springville, SPFK	3142	B5
Tremonton Municipal, TMTN	520	C6

Beaches, Harbors & Water Rec

FEATURE NAME Address City ZIP Code	MAP#	GRID
Timp Marina Club, SNDY	2389	B1
Utah Lake State Park Marina, PRVO	2926	E6
Willard Bay State Park-North Marina, WLRD	885	A5

Buildings - Governmental

FEATURE NAME Address City ZIP Code	MAP#	GRID
2nd District Court 805 S Main St, BNFL, 84010	1653	D1
2nd District Court 425 N Wasatch Dr, LYTN, 84041	1283	A4
4th District Court 98 N Center St, ANFK, 84003	2711	C1
4th District Court 40 S Main St, SPFK, 84660	3249	C3
Alpine City Hall 20 N Main St, ALPN, 84004	2497	E4
Alta Town Hall Little Cottonwood Canyon Rd, ALTA, 84049	2181	E7
American Fork City Hall 31 Church St, ANFK, 84003	2711	C1
Bluffdale City Hall 14175 S Redwood Rd, BFDL, 84065	2387	C6
Bluffdale Justice Court 14175 S Redwood Rd, BFDL, 84065	2387	C6
Bountiful City Hall 790 S 100 E, BNFL, 84010	1653	E1
Box Elder 1st District Court 1 S Main St, BMCY, 84302	766	E6
Brigham City Hall 20 N Main St, BMCY, 84302	766	E5
Cache County 1st District Court 140 N 100 W, LOGN, 84321	527	D3
Camp Williams 160 E Broadway, SLCY, 84111	1858	D4
Cedar Hills Town Hall 4393 W Cedar Hills Dr, CRHL, 84062	2605	B3
Centerville City Hall 250 N Main St, CTRV, 84014	1551	E3
Centerville Justice Court 250 N Main St, CTRV, 84014	1551	E3
Charleston Town Hall 3454 W 3400 S, CSTN, 84032	2504	C2
City of Taylorsville Court 5486 S 19th W, TYVL, 84118	2069	C5
Clearfield City Hall 55 State St, CRFD, 84015	1227	D4
Clearfield Justice Court 55 State St, CRFD, 84015	1227	D4
Clinton City Hall 1906 Clinton Rd, CLTN, 84015	1226	E1
Clinton Justice Court 1906 Clinton Rd, CLTN, 84015	1226	E1
Corinne City Hall 2450 N 4000 W, CRNN, 84307	704	E7
Davis County District Court 745 S Main St, BNFL, 84010	1653	D1
Davis County Justice Complex 800 W State St, FMTN, 84025	1448	B1
Davis County Memorial Court 28 E State St, FMTN, 84025	1448	D2
District Court 125 N 100 W, PRVO, 84601	2928	C6
Draper City Hall 12441 S 900 E, DRPR, 84020	2389	A2
Draper Justice Court 12441 S 900 E, DRPR, 84020	2389	A1
Elk Ridge Town Hall 80 E Park Dr, EKMT, 84651	3463	A2
Elmwood Town Hall 5235 W 8800 N, ELWD, 84337	585	B5
Farmington City Hall 130 N Main St, FMTN, 84025	1448	D1
Farr West City Hall 2090 N 2000 W, FRWT, 84404	997	D7
Farr West Justice Court 2090 N 2000 W, FRWT, 84404	997	D7
First District Court 140 N 100 W, LOGN, 84321	527	D3
First Judicial District Court 43 N Main St, BMCY, 84302	766	E5
Fourth District Court HRCY, 84032	2398	D6
Fruit Heights City Hall 910 S Mountain Rd, FTHT, 84037	1346	B3
Fruit Heights Justice Court 910 S Mountain Rd, FTHT, 84037	1346	B3
Garland City Hall 72 N Main St, GRLD, 84312	520	E2
Harrisville City Hall 363 Independence Blvd, HARR, 84404	1056	C2
Harrisville Justice Court 363 Independence Blvd, HARR, 84404	1056	D2
Heber City City Hall 75 N Main St, HRCY, 84032	2398	D4
Heber City Justice Court 75 N Main St, HRCY, 84032	2398	D4
Herriman City Hall 13011 N Pioneer St, HRMN, 84065	2385	C3
Highland City Hall 5378 W 10400 N, HILD, 84003	2604	D2
Highland Justice Court 5378 W 10400 N, HILD, 84003	2604	D2
Holladay City Hall 4707 Holladay Blvd, HLDY, 84117	2071	E3
Holladay Justice Court 4707 Holladay Blvd, HLDY, 84117	2071	E3
Honeyville City Hall 2635 W 6980 N, HYVL, 84314	646	C2
Hooper City Hall 4455 S 5500 W, HOPR, 84315	1169	E2
Huntsville Justice Court 7309 E 200 S, HTVL, 84317	1061	A5
Huntsville Town Hall 7309 E 200 S, HTVL, 84317	1061	A5
Hyde Park City Hall 113 E Center St, HDPK, 84318	464	A1
Hyrum City Hall 83 W Main St, HYRM, 84319	651	B2
Judiciary Courts State of Utah 140 N 100 W, LOGN, 84321	527	D3
Kaysville City Hall 23 E Center St, KYVL, 84037	1345	C1
Layton City Hall 437 N Wasatch Dr, LYTN, 84041	1283	A4
Lehi City Hall 153 N 100 E, LEHI, 84043	2603	C6
Lindon City Hall 100 N State St, LNDN, 84042	2713	B6
Logan City Hall 255 N Main St, LOGN, 84321	527	D2
Mantua City Hall 409 N Main St, MNTU, 84324	768	C6
Mantua Justice Court 409 N Main St, MNTU, 84324	768	C6
Mapleton City Hall 35 E Maple St, MPTN, 84664	3144	A7
Marriott-Slaterville City Hall 1595 W 400 N, MTSV, 84404	1055	E4
Midvale City Hall 644 W Center St, MDVL, 84047	2176	A4
Midvale Justice Court 635 W Center St, MDVL, 84047	2176	A4
Midway City Hall 140 W Main St, MIDW, 84049	2397	B3
Millville City Hall 490 E 300 S, MLVI, 84332	592	B4
Murray City Hall 5025 S State St, MRRY, 84107	2070	D4
Murray Municipal Justice Court 688 E Vine St, MRRY, 84107	2070	E5
Nibley City Hall 625 W 3200 S, NBLY, 84321	591	C4
North Logan City Hall 2185 N 1400 E, NHLN, 84341	464	C4
North Ogden City Hall 505 E 2600 N, NHON, 84414	999	A6
North Ogden Justice Court 505 E 2600 N, NHON, 84414	999	A6
North Salt Lake City Hall NSLK, 84054	1653	A7
Ogden City Hall 2549 Washington Blvd, OGDN, 84401	1115	E3
Ogden District Court House 2525 Grant Av, OGDN, 84401	1115	E4
Orem City Hall 56 N State St, OREM, 84057	2820	D5
Paradise Town Hall 9035 S 100 W St, PARA, 84328	710	D5
Park City City Hall 445 Marsac Av, PKCY, 84060	2078	E6
Payson City Hall 439 W Utah Av, PYSN, 84651	3354	E5
Payson Justice Court 439 W Utah Av, PYSN, 84651	3354	D5
Perry City Hall 3005 Perry St, PRRY, 84302	827	B6
Plain City City Hall 4160 W 2200 N, PNCY, 84404	996	D7
Plain City Justice Court 4160 W 2200 N, PNCY, 84404	996	C7
Pleasant Grove City Hall 70 S 100 E, PTGV, 84062	2712	D3
Pleasant Grove Justice Court 70 S 100 E, PTGV, 84062	2712	D3
Pleasant View City Hall 520 W Elberta Dr, PTVW, 84414	998	C4
Pleasant View Justice Court 520 W Elberta Dr, PTVW, 84414	998	C4
Providence City Hall 15 N Main St, PVDN, 84332	528	A6
Provo City Hall 351 W Center St, PRVO, 84601	2928	B7
Riverdale City Hall 4600 S Weber River Dr, RVDL, 84405	1172	C2
Riverdale Justice Court 4600 S Weber River Dr, RVDL, 84405	1172	C2
River Heights City Hall 520 S 500 E, RVHT, 84321	527	E4
Riverton City Hall 12765 S 1400 W, RIVN, 84065	2387	D2
Riverton Justice Court 12765 S 1400 W, RIVN, 84065	2387	D2
Roy City Hall 5051 S 1900 W, ROY, 84067	1171	D3
Roy City Justice Court House 5551 S 1900 W, ROY, 84067	1171	D4
Salem City Hall 30 W 100 S, SALM, 84653	3356	A3
Salem Justice Court 30 W 100 S, SALM, 84653	3356	A3
Salt Lake City 3rd District Court 451 S 200 E, SLCY, 84111	1858	D4
Salt Lake City City Hall 451 S State St, SLCY, 84111	1858	D4
Salt Lake County 3rd District Court 240 E 400 S, SLCY, 84111	1858	D4
Salt Lake County 3rd District Court 3636 Constitution Blvd, WVCY, 84119	1963	A6
Salt Lake County District Court 210 W Sego Lily Dr, SNDY, 84070	2282	C2
Salt Lake County District Court 2470 S Redwood Rd, WVCY, 84119	1963	C3
Salt Lake County Justice Court 2001 S State St, SLCY, 84115	1964	D1
Sandy City Hall 10000 Centennial Pkwy, SNDY, 84070	2282	C2
Santaquin City Hall 45 W 100 S, SNQN, 84655	3460	D7
Smithfield City Hall 69 N Main St, SHFD, 84335	399	D2
Southeastern District Court 450 S State St, SLCY, 84111	1858	D4
South First District Court 43 N Main St, BMCY, 84302	766	E5
South Jordan City Hall 1600 Towne Center Dr, SJDN, 84095	2281	C4
South Jordan Justice Court 11175 S Redwood Rd, SJDN, 84095	2281	C5
South Ogden City Hall 560 39th St, SOGN, 84403	1115	E7
South Ogden Justice Court 560 39th St, SOGN, 84403	1115	E7
South Salt Lake City Hall 220 Morris Av, SSLK, 84115	1964	D3
South Salt Lake Justice Court 220 Morris Av, SSLK, 84115	1964	D3
South Weber City Hall 1600 E South Weber Dr, SWBR, 84405	1229	C2
South Weber Justice Court 1600 E South Weber Dr, SWBR, 84405	1229	C2
Spanish Fork City Hall 40 S Main St, SPFK, 84660	3249	C3
Springville City Hall 50 S Main St, SGVL, 84663	3143	C2
Springville Justice Court 50 S Main St, SGVL, 84663	3143	C2
Summit County District Court 6300 Silver Creek Dr, SmtC, 84098	1973	A2
Sunset City Hall 85 Clinton Rd, SNST, 84015	1227	D1
Sunset Justice Court 85 Clinton Rd, SNST, 84015	1227	D1
Syracuse City Hall 1787 S 2000 W, SRCS, 84075	1280	E1
Syracuse Justice Court 1787 S 2000 W, SRCS, 84075	1280	E1
Taylorsville City Hall 2600 Taylorsville Blvd, TYVL, 84118	2069	B5
Third District Court 450 S State St, SLCY, 84111	1858	D4
Tremonton City Hall 102 S Tremont St, TMTN, 84337	520	E6
Tremonton Justice Court 102 S Tremont St, TMTN, 84337	520	E6
Uintah Justice Court 2105 E 6550 S, UNTH, 84405	1173	E7
Uintah Town Hall 2105 E 6550 S, UNTH, 84405	1173	E7
Utah County 4th District Court 97 E Center St, OREM, 84057	2820	D5
Utah County 4th District Court 125 N 100 W, PRVO, 84601	2928	C6
Utah County Courthouse 51 S University Av, PRVO, 84606	2928	C7
Utah County Justice Court 51 S University Av, PRVO, 84606	2928	C7
Utah State 2nd District Court 2549 Washington Blvd, OGDN, 84401	1115	E4
Utah Supreme Court 450 N State St, SLCY, 84103	1858	D2
Vineyard Town Hall 240 E Gammon Rd, VNYD, 84058	2819	D5
Wasatch County District Court HRCY, 84032	2398	D6
Wasatch County Justice Court HRCY, 84032	2398	D6
Washington Terrace City Hall 275 E 4425 S, WSTR, 84405	1172	E2
Washington Terrace Justice Court 275 E 4425 S, WSTR, 84405	1172	E2
Weber County 2nd District Court 2549 Washington Blvd, OGDN, 84401	1115	E4
Weber County Justice Court 2380 Washington Blvd, OGDN, 84401	1115	E3
Wellsville City Hall 75 E Main St, WELV, 84339	649	D2
West Bountiful City Hall 550 N Onion St, WBNF, 84087	1551	B6
West Bountiful Justice Court 550 N Onion St, WBNF, 84087	1551	B6
West Haven City Hall 4150 S 3900 W, WHVN, 84315	1170	D1
West Jordan City Hall 8000 Redwood Rd, WJDN, 84088	2175	C4
West Jordan Justice Court 8000 Redwood Rd, WJDN, 84088	2175	C4
West Point City Hall 3016 West Point Rd, WPT, 84015	1226	C4
West Valley City Hall 3600 Constitution Blvd, WVCY, 84119	1963	A6
Willard City Hall 80 S Center St, WLRD, 84340	885	C5
Willard City Justice Court 80 S Center St, WLRD, 84340	885	C5
Woodland Hills City Hall 200 S Woodland Hills Dr, WDHL, 84653	3463	D1
Woods Cross City Hall 1555 S 800 W, WDCR, 84087	1653	B2
Woods Cross Justice Court 1555 S 800 W, WDCR, 84087	1653	B2

Cemeteries

FEATURE NAME Address City ZIP Code	MAP#	GRID
Alpine Cem, ALPN	2498	A3
Alysian Burial Gardens, SLkC	2071	B2
American Fork Cem, ANFK	2604	C6
Aultbrest Memorial Park, OGDN	1116	A6
Ben Lomond Cem, NHON	999	A5
Bountiful Memorial Park Cem, BNFL	1653	D3
Brigham City Cem, BMCY	767	A7
City Cem, SLCY	1859	B2
Evergreen Cem, SGVL	3143	D5
Evergreen Memorial Park, OGDN	1057	A4
Heber City Cem, HRCY	2398	E3
Hyrum City Cem, HYRM	651	C2
Kaysville & Layton Memorial Cem, KYVL	1283	D7
Lake Hill Cem, SNDY	2282	C3
Larkin Sunset Gardens, SNDY	2283	D4
Logan Cem, LOGN	528	B1
Memorial Estates Cem, CDHT	2178	B3
Memorial Gardens of the Wasatch, WbrC	1173	D4
Midway City Cem, WshC	2397	A4
Mount Calvary Cem, SLCY	1859	B2
Mount Olivet Cem, SLCY	1859	C5
Murray City Cem, MRRY	2070	E5
Ogden City Cem, OGDN	1116	A2
Orem Cem, OREM	2821	A1
Payson City Cem, PYSN	3355	A4
Pioneer Memorial Cem, LEHI	2603	C4
Provo City Pioneer Cem, PRVO	3035	E1
Redwood Memorial Estates, WJDN	2175	C1
Riverton Cem, RIVN	2387	D3
Smithfield City Cem, SHFD	399	E3
Valley View Memorial Park, WVCY	2068	B1
Wasatch Lawn Memorial Park, SLkC	1965	C6
Washington Heights Memorial Park, SOGN	1172	E2
Willard Cem, WLRD	885	C4

Colleges & Universities

FEATURE NAME Address City ZIP Code	MAP#	GRID
Brigham Young University 1230 N Canyon Rd, PRVO, 84604	2928	C4
Columbia College 2790 Decker Lake Dr, WVCY, 84119	1963	C4
Eagle Gate College 5588 Green St, MRRY, 84123	2070	B5
ITT Technical Institute 920 Levoy Dr, TYVL, 84123	2070	A2
Kirksville College 69 W University Pkwy, OREM, 84058	2927	D1
LDS Business College 411 E South Temple, SLCY, 84103	1858	E3
Mountain West College 3280 W 3500 S, WVCY, 84119	1962	E6
Ogden Weber Applied Tech College 200 N Washington Blvd, OGDN, 84404	1056	E5
Salt Lake Community College 4600 S Redwood Rd, TYVL, 84119	2069	C2
Salt Lake Community College-Draper Campus 12441 S 900 E, DRPR, 84020	2389	A2
Salt Lake Community College-Jordan Campus 3491 W 9000 S, WJDN, 84088	2174	D7
Salt Lake Comm Coll-Larry H Miller Campus 9750 S 300 W, SNDY, 84070	2282	B2
Salt Lake Community College-Main St Campus 115 S Main St, SLCY, 84111	1858	C3
Salt Lake Community Coll-Meadowbrook Campus 250 W 3900 S, SSLK, 84115	1964	B7
Salt Lake Community College-Sandy Campus 830 E 9400 S, SNDY, 84094	2283	A1
Salt Lake Community Coll-South City Campus 1575 S State St, SLCY, 84115	1858	D7
Stevens Henager College-Murray Campus 635 W 5300 S, MRRY, 84123	2070	A5

Salt Lake City Points of Interest Index

FEATURE NAME Address City ZIP Code	MAP#	GRID
Stevens Henager College-Provo Orem Campus 25 E 1700 S, PRVO, 84606	3035	C2
University of Phoenix-Ogden Campus 2484 Washington Blvd, OGDN, 84401	1115	E3
University of Phoenix-Salt Lake City 5251 Green St, MRRY, 84123	2070	B4
University of Utah 201 S 1460 E, SLCY, 84112	1859	C3
University of Utah-Bountiful 75 E 200 S, BNFL, 84010	1551	E7
University of Utah College of Pharmacy 30 S 2000 E, SLCY, 84113	1859	D3
University of Utah Health Sciences Center 1492 W Antelope Dr, LYTN, 84041	1282	C1
Utah State University E 700 N, LOGN, 84321	528	A1
Utah Valley State College 800 W University Pkwy, OREM, 84058	2927	B1
Washington School of Law 1124 W South Jordan Pkwy, SJDN, 84095	2281	E3
Weber State University 3750 Harrison Blvd, OGDN, 84403	1116	B7
Webster University 2790 Decker Lake Dr, WVCY, 84119	1963	C4
Westminster College 1840 S 1300 E, SLCY, 84105	1965	B1

Entertainment & Sports

FEATURE NAME Address City ZIP Code	MAP#	GRID
Abravanel Concert Hall 123 W South Temple, SLCY, 84101	1858	C3
Alta Ski Resort Day Lodge Rd, ALTA, 84049	2182	A6
Ballet West 50 W 200 S, SLCY, 84101	1858	C3
Beaver Mountain Ski Area 1351 E 700 N, LOGN, 84321	528	B1
Bountiful Performing Arts Center 745 S Main St, BNFL, 84010	1653	D1
Brighton Ski Resort E Big Cottonwood Canyon Rd, SLkC, 84098	2183	A5
Canyons Amphitheater 4000 Canyons Resort Dr, SmtC, 84098	1971	D7
Canyons Ski Resort 4000 Canyons Resort Dr, SmtC, 84098	1971	C7
Capitol Theatre 50 W 200 S, SLCY, 84101	1858	C3
Chateau Apres Lodge 1299 Norfolk Av, PKCY, 84060	2078	C5
Clearfield Community Theater 121 S 350 W, CRFD, 84015	1227	D5
Community College Grand Theatre 1575 S State St, SLCY, 84115	1858	D7
Convention Services & Tech 240 Morris Av, SSLK, 84115	1964	D3
Davis Art Council 445 N Wasatch Dr, LYTN, 84041	1283	A4
Davis County Fairpark Legacy Center 151 S 1100 W, FMTN, 84025	1448	A2
Dee Events Center 4400 Harrison Blvd, OGDN, 84403	1173	B2
Dee Glen Smith Spectrum 850 E 900 N, LOGN, 84321	528	A1
Deer Valley Resort 2250 Deer Valley Dr S, PKCY, 84060	2079	A7
Delta Center 301 W South Temple, SLCY, 84101	1858	B3
Desert Star Playhouse 4861 S State St, MRRY, 84107	2070	D3
Draper Theatre 12366 S 900 E, DRPR, 84020	2389	A1
Eccles Center 1750 Kearns Blvd, PKCY, 84060	2078	E3
E Center of West Valley City 3200 Decker Lake Dr, WVCY, 84119	1963	B5
Egyptian Theatre Company 328 Main St, PKCY, 84060	2078	E6
Ellen Eccles Theatre Box Office 43 S Main St, LOGN, 84321	527	D3
Equestrian Park 10900 S Redwood Rd, SJDN, 84095	2281	C4
Franklin Covey Field 77 W 1300 S, SLCY, 84115	1858	C7
Golden Spike Arena Events Center 1000 N 1200 W, OGDN, 84404	1056	A3
Hale Center Theater 225 W 400 N, OREM, 84057	2820	C4
Hale Centre Theatre 3333 Decker Lake Dr, WVCY, 84119	1963	B5
Heritage Theater PRRY, 84302	827	C5
Hispanic Center for the Arts 7677 Main St, MDVL, 84047	2176	A3
Hogle Zoo 2600 Sunnyside Av, SLCY, 84108	1860	A5
Hughes Center of Performing Arts 3701 Washington Blvd, SOGN, 84405	1115	E7
Jackson Street Junction 2280 Jackson Av, OGDN, 84401	1116	B3
Jon M Huntsman Center 1825 E South Campus Dr, SLCY, 84112	1859	D4
Kimball Art Center 638 Park Av, PKCY, 84060	2078	E6
Kingsbury Hall 1395 Presidents Cir, SLCY, 84112	1859	B3
Lagoon 375 N Lagoon Dr, FMTN, 84025	1346	B7
LaVell Edwards Stadium Stadium Av, PRVO, 84604	2928	C3
Layton City Sports Complex W Hill Field Rd, LYTN, 84041	1282	A3
Lindquist Field 2330 Lincoln Av, OGDN, 84401	1115	E3
Living Planet Aquarium 522 S 400 W, SLCY, 84101	1858	B4
Lumin Technologies 13990 Minuteman Dr, DRPR, 84020	2388	C5
Lyric Theatre 28 W Center St, LOGN, 84321	527	D3
Marriott Center E 1430 N, PRVO, 84604	2928	D4
McKay Events Center 800 W University Pkwy, OREM, 84058	2820	B7
Nordic Valley Ski Area 3567 Nordic Valley Hwy, WbrC, 84414	1001	A5
Off Broadway Theatre 272 S Main St, SLCY, 84101	1858	C4
Ogden Egyptian Center 2415 Washington Blvd, OGDN, 84401	1115	D3
Park City Mountain Resort 1310 Lowell Av, PKCY, 84060	2078	C5
Peery's Egyptian Theatre 2415 Washington Blvd, OGDN, 84401	1115	E3
Prospector Square Conference Center 2200 Sidewinder Dr, PKCY, 84060	2078	E3
Provo Theatre Co 105 E 100 N, PRVO, 84606	2928	C6
Raging Waters 1200 W 1700 S, SLCY, 84104	1963	E1
Rice-Eccles Stadium E 500 S, SLCY, 84112	1859	C4
Rocky Mountain Raceway 6555 W 2100 S, WVCY, 84128	1961	B2
Rodgers Memorial Theatre 292 E Pages Ln, CTRV, 84014	1551	E5
Romney Stadium N 800 E, LOGN, 84341	464	A7
Rose Wagner Performing Arts Center 138 W Broadway, SLCY, 84101	1858	C4
Salt Lake Acting Company 168 W 500 N, SLCY, 84103	1858	C1
Salt Lake Repertory Theater 638 S State St, SLCY, 84111	1858	D5
Salt Lake Visitors Guide 90 S West Temple, SLCY, 84101	1858	C3
Salt Palace Convention Center 100 S West Temple, SLCY, 84101	1858	C3
Scera Summer Shell Outdoor Theatre 699 S State St, OREM, 84058	2820	E7
Snowbird Handicapped Ski 95 Continental Dr, FMTN, 84025	1448	C3
Snowbird Resort Little Cottonwood Canyon Rd, SLkC, 84049	2287	C1
Soldier Hollow Soldier Hollow Ln, WshC, 84049	2396	E7
Solitude Ski Resort E Big Cottonwood Canyon Rd, SLkC, 84098	2182	E2
South Towne Exposition Center 9575 State St, SNDY, 84070	2282	C1
Stageright Theatre Company 5001 Highland Dr, HLDY, 84117	2071	D4
Stewart Stadium Taylor Av, OGDN, 84403	1116	C7
Suntana Raceway 400 W 1600 S, UthC, 84660	3142	E5
Terrace Plaza Playhouse 99 E 4700 S, WSTR, 84405	1172	D2
Usana Amphitheater S 6055 W, WVCY, 84118	2067	C4
Utah Cultural Celebration Center W 3100 S, WVCY, 84119	1963	D5
Utah Escapes 10322 S 2165 E, SNDY, 84092	2283	E3
Utah Musical Theatre 3750 Harrison Blvd, OGDN, 84403	1116	B7
Utah Olympic Oval 5624 Cougar Ln, SLkC, 84118	2068	A5
Utah Olympic Park 3000 Bear Hollow Dr, SmtC, 84098	1971	C4
Utah Opera Company 50 W 200 S, SLCY, 84101	1858	C3
Utah State Fairpark 155 N 1000 W, SLCY, 84116	1857	E2
Utah Symphony 123 W South Temple, SLCY, 84101	1858	C3
Utah Valley State College Theatre 800 W University Pkwy, OREM, 84058	2927	B1
VA Browning Center for Performing Arts E 4100 S, OGDN, 84403	1173	C1
Valley Center Playhouse 780 N 200 E, LNDN, 84042	2713	B4
Villa Playhouse Theatre 239 S Main St, SGVL, 84663	3143	C2
Walker Lane Reception Center 5160 Highland Dr, SLkC, 84117	2071	D4
Waterfall Amphitheater Garden Dr, LEHI, 84043	2495	B7
Weber County Fairgrounds 1000 N 1200 W, OGDN, 84404	1056	A3
Willow Park Zoo 419 W 700 S, LOGN, 84321	527	C5

Golf Courses

FEATURE NAME	MAP#	GRID
Alpine CC, HILD	2604	E1
Ben Lomond GC, HARR	1056	C1
Bonneville GC, SLCY	1860	A6
Bountiful Ridge GC, BNFL	1654	B4
Brigham Willows GC, BMCY	766	E3
Cascade Fairways, OREM	2821	B2
Copper GC, SLkC	1960	A3
Cottonwood CC, SLkC	2071	C5
Davis Park GC, FTHT	1346	A2
Eagle Mountain GC, BMCY	828	B1
Eaglewood GC, NSLK	1754	C1
East Bay GC, PRVO	3035	D3
El Monte GC, OGDN	1116	C1
Fore Lakes GC, TYVL	2069	D3
Forest Dale GC, SLCY	1965	A3
Gladstan GC, PYSN	3462	D2
Glendale GC, SLCY	1963	D1
Glen Eagle GC, SRCS	1226	C7
Glenmoor GC, SJDN	2280	A2
Glenwild GC, SmtC	1866	A6
Golf City, SOGN	1173	C4
Hidden Valley CC, SNDY	2283	E7
Homestead Resort GC, MIDW	2397	A1
Hubbard GC, DvsC	1229	C3
Jeremy Golf & CC, SmtC	1865	B4
Jordan River GC, SLCY	1753	C6
Lakeside GC, WBNF	1551	A5
Logan CC, LOGN	528	D1
Logan River GC, LOGN	527	C6
Meadowbrook GC, TYVL	2069	D1
Mick Riley GC, MRRY	2070	E4
Mountain View GC, WJDN	2175	B6
Mount Ogden GC, OGDN	1116	C5
Mulligan's GC, MTSV	1055	E4
Mulligan's South GC, SJDN	2282	A3
Murray Parkway GC, MRRY	2070	A7
Nibley Park GC, SLkC	1964	E4
Oakridge CC, FMTN	1346	A6
Ogden Golf & CC, WbrC	1172	D1
Old Mill GC, HLDY	2072	B7
Park City GC, PKCY	2078	C4
Park Meadows GC, PKCY	2078	E1
Remuda GC, FRWT	997	B3
Riverbend GC, DRPR	2388	A3
Riverbend GC, RIVN	2387	E2
River Oaks GC, SNDY	2176	A7
Riverside CC, OREM	2928	B1
Rose Park GC, SLCY	1753	C6
Royal Greens GC, ROY	1171	A4
Salt Lake CC & GC, SLCY	1965	D3
Schneiter's Bluff GC, SRCS	1226	B4
Schneiter's Pebblebrook GC, SNDY	2177	B7
Schneiter's Riverside GC, RVDL	1172	A4
Seven Peaks GC, PRVO	2928	E6
Sherwood Hills GC, CchC	707	D2
Skyway GC, TMTN	520	C5
South Mountain GC, DRPR	2389	B6
Spanish Oaks GC, SPFK	3250	D6
Stonebridge GC, WVCY	1962	B3
Summit Park GC, SHFD	400	A2
Sun Hills GC, LYTN	1229	C5
Swan Lakes GC, LYTN	1282	A3
Thanksgiving Point GC, LEHI	2602	B1
The Barn GC, PTVW	998	D5
Tri City GC, ANFK	2604	D4
University GC, SLCY	1859	C3
Valley View GC, LYTN	1283	E3
Wasatch Mountain State Park GC, WshC	2290	E6
West Ridge GC, WVCY	2067	C4
Willow Creek CC, SLkC	2178	A5
Wingpointe GC, SLCY	1856	D2
Wolf Creek GC, WbrC	1001	E2

Historic Sites

FEATURE NAME Address City ZIP Code	MAP#	GRID
Beehive House 67 E South Temple, SLCY, 84103	1858	C3
Brigham City Depot 833 W Forest St, BMCY, 84302	766	D6
Brigham Young Monument S 6660 W, WVCY, 84128	1961	A7
Cathedral Church of St. Mark 231 E 100 S, BMCY, 84302	767	A6
Cathedral of the Madeleine 331 E South Temple, SLCY, 84103	1858	D2
Gardner Historic Village 1100 W 7800 S, WJDN, 84084	2175	E4
Governor's Mansion 603 E South Temple, SLCY, 84103	1858	E3
Heber Valley Historic RR 450 S 600 W, HRCY, 84032	2398	B4
Nightmare Mansion 505 N 100 W, PTGV, 84062	2712	C2
Rocky Point Haunted House 227 Spencer Ct, SLCY, 84103	1858	D2
This Is the Place Monument 2601 Sunnyside Av, SLCY, 84108	1860	A5

Hospitals

FEATURE NAME Address City ZIP Code	MAP#	GRID
Alta View Hosp 9660 S 1300 E, SNDY, 84094	2283	B1
American Fork Hosp 170 N 1100 E, ANFK, 84062	2605	A7
Bear River Valley Hosp 440 W 6th N, TMTN, 84337	520	D5
Brigham City Community Hosp 950 Medical Dr, BMCY, 84302	827	D1
Cache Valley Specialty Hosp 2380 N 400 E, NHLN, 84341	463	E4
Cottonwood Hosp Med Ctr 5770 Fashion Blvd, MRRY, 84107	2070	D6
Davis Hosp & Med Ctr 1600 W Antelope Dr, LYTN, 84041	1282	B1
IHC Health Center 2075 University Park Blvd, LYTN, 84041	1228	C7
IHC Health Center 2400 N Washington Blvd, NHON, 84414	998	E6
IHC Health Center 975 Chambers St, SOGN, 84403	1173	B4
Jordan Valley Hosp 3580 W 9000 S, WJDN, 84088	2174	D7
Lakeview Hosp 630 Medical Dr, BNFL, 84010	1654	A1
LDS Hosp C St, SLCY, 84103	1858	D1
Logan Regional Hosp 1400 N 500 E, LOGN, 84341	463	E6
McKay-Dee Hosp Center 4401 Harrison Blvd, OGDN, 84403	1173	B2
Mountain View Hosp 1000 E 100 N, PYSN, 84651	3355	B5
Ogden Regional Med Ctr 5475 Adams Av Pkwy, WSTR, 84405	1172	E4
Orem Community Hosp 331 N 400 W, OREM, 84057	2820	C4
Park City Health Center 1665 Bonanza Dr, PKCY, 84060	2078	D3
Pioneer Valley Hosp 3460 Pioneer Pkwy, WVCY, 84120	1962	C6
Primary Children's Med Ctr 100 N Medical Dr, SLCY, 84113	1859	D2
St. Marks Hosp 1200 E 3900 S, SLkC, 84124	1965	B7
Salt Lake Regional Med Ctr 1050 E South Temple, SLCY, 84102	1859	A3
Timpanogos Regional Hosp 750 W 800 N, OREM, 84057	2820	B3
University Hosp 50 N Medical Dr, SLCY, 84113	1859	D2
Utah Valley Regional Med Ctr 1034 N 500 W, PRVO, 84604	2928	B5
Veterans Affairs Med Ctr 500 Foothill Blvd, SLCY, 84108	1859	D4

Law Enforcement

FEATURE NAME Address City ZIP Code	MAP#	GRID
Alpine Police Dept 20 N Main St, ALPN, 84004	2497	E4
American Fork Police Dept 98 N Center St, ANFK, 84003	2711	C1
Bountiful Police Dept 805 S Main St, BNFL, 84010	1653	D1
Box Elder County Sheriff 52 S 1000 W, BMCY, 84302	766	C6
Brigham City Police 20 N Main St, BMCY, 84302	766	E5
Centerville Police Dept 250 N Main St, CTRV, 84014	1551	E3
City of Farmington Police 82 N 100 E, FMTN, 84025	1448	D1
Clearfield Police Dept 55 State St, CRFD, 84015	1227	D4
Clinton Police Dept 1906 Clinton Rd, CLTN, 84015	1226	E1
Davis County Sheriff's Dept 800 W State St, FMTN, 84025	1448	B1
Harrisville Police Dept 363 Independence Blvd, HARR, 84404	1056	C2
Heber City Police Dept 75 N Main St, HRCY, 84032	2398	D4
Kaysville Police Dept 58 E 100 N, KYVL, 84037	1345	C1
Layton Police Dept 429 N Wasatch Dr, LYTN, 84041	1283	A4
Lehi Police Dept 152 N Center St, LEHI, 84043	2603	C6
Mapleton Police Dept 305 N Main St, MPTN, 84664	3144	A6
Midvale Police Dept 7912 Main St, MDVL, 84047	2176	A4
Murray Police Dept 5025 S State St, MRRY, 84107	2070	D3
North Ogden Police Dept 505 E 2600 N, NHON, 84414	999	A6
North Salt Lake Police Dept 17 S Main St, NSLK, 84054	1653	A7
Ogden Police Dept 2186 Lincoln Av, OGDN, 84401	1115	D3
Orem Police Dept 56 N State St, OREM, 84057	2820	D5
Park City Police Dept 445 Marsac Av, PKCY, 84060	2078	E6
Payson Police Dept 388 E 100 N, PYSN, 84651	3355	A5

Salt Lake City Points of Interest Index

FEATURE NAME Address City ZIP Code	MAP#	GRID
Pleasant Grove Police Dept 87 E 100 S, PTGV, 84062	2712	D3
Pleasant View Police Dept 520 W Elberta Dr, PTVW, 84414	998	C4
Provo Police Dept 48 S 300 W, PRVO, 84601	2928	B7
Riverdale Police Dept 4580 S Weber River Dr, RDVL, 84405	1172	C2
Roy Police Dept 5051 S 1900 W, ROY, 84067	1171	D3
Salem Police Dept 30 W 100 S, SALM, 84653	3356	A3
Salt Lake City Police Dept 315 E 200 S, SLCY, 84111	1858	D3
Salt Lake City Police Dept 220 Morris Av, SSLK, 84115	1964	D3
Salt Lake County Sheriff 12441 S 900 E, DRPR, 84020	2389	A2
Salt Lake County Sheriff's Dept 2001 S State St, SLCY, 84115	1964	D1
Sandy Police Dept 10000 Centennial Pkwy, SNDY, 84070	2282	C2
South Jordan Police Dept 11725 S Redwood Rd, RIVN, 84065	2281	C7
South Ogden Police Dept 560 39th St, SOGN, 84403	1115	E7
Spanish Fork Police Dept 45 S Main St, SPFK, 84660	3249	C3
Springville Police Dept 45 S Main St, SGVL, 84663	3143	C2
Sunset Police Dept 85 Clinton Rd, SNST, 84015	1227	D1
Syracuse Police Dept 1751 S 2000 W, SRCS, 84075	1280	E1
Utah County Sheriff's Dept 3075 N Main St, SPFK, 84660	3142	C4
Wasatch County Sheriff's Dept HRCY, 84032	2398	D6
Washington Terrace Police Dept 275 E 4425 S, WSTR, 84405	1172	E2
Weber County Sheriff's Dept 457 26th St, OGDN, 84401	1115	E4
West Bountiful Police Dept 550 N Onion St, WBNF, 84087	1551	B6
West Jordan Police Dept 8000 Redwood Rd, WJDN, 84088	2175	C4
West Valley City Police Dept 3600 Constitution Blvd, WVCY, 84119	1963	A6
Willard Police 80 S Center St, WLRD, 84340	885	C6
Woods Cross Police Dept 1555 S 800 W, WDCR, 84087	1653	B2

Libraries

FEATURE NAME Address City ZIP Code	MAP#	GRID
Alta Branch 2197 Fort Union Blvd, CDHT, 84121	2177	E2
Cache County-Providence 15 N Main St, PVDN, 84332	528	A6
Columbus 2530 S 500 E, SLCY, 84115	1964	E3
Davis County-Central 155 Wasatch Dr, LYTN, 84041	1283	A4
Davis County-Headquarters 38 S 100 E, FMTN, 84025	1448	D2
Davis County-North 562 S 1000 E, CRFD, 84015	1228	A5
East Millcreek 2266 Evergreen Av, SLkC, 84109	1965	E6
Family History 35 N West Temple, SLCY, 84103	1858	C3
Holladay 2150 Murray-Holladay Rd, HLDY, 84117	2071	E3
Hyrum City 83 W Main St, HYRM, 84319	651	B2
Kaysville City 44 N Main St, KYVL, 84037	1345	C1
Kearns 5350 S 4220 W, SLkC, 84118	2068	C5
Lehi 120 N Center St, LEHI, 84043	2603	C6
Logan 255 N Main St, LOGN, 84321	527	D2
Mantua 409 N Main St, MNTU, 84324	768	C6
Murray 166 E 5300 S, MRRY, 84107	2070	D4
Ogden Valley Branch Weber County 131 S 7400 E, HTVL, 84317	1061	A5
Orem Public 58 N State St, OREM, 84057	2820	D5
Park City 1255 Park Av, PKCY, 84060	2078	D5
Payson City 66 S Main St, PYSN, 84651	3354	E5
Pleasant Grove Public 30 E Center St, PTGV, 84062	2712	D3
Provo City 550 N University Av, PRVO, 84606	2928	C6
Riverton 12860 S Redwood Rd, RIVN, 84065	2387	C2
Salt Lake City-Anderson/Foothill 1135 S 2100 E, SLCY, 84108	1859	E6
Salt Lake City-Chapman 577 S 900 W, SLCY, 84104	1858	A4
Salt Lake City-Day-Riverside 1575 W 1000 N, SLCY, 84116	1753	D7
Salt Lake City-Sprague 2131 Highland Dr, SLCY, 84106	1965	B2
Salt Lake County Little Cottonwood Canyon Rd, ALTA, 84049	2181	E6
Salt Lake County 455 F St, SLCY, 84103	1858	E1
Salt Lake County 8339 W 3500 S, SLkC, 84044	1960	B6
Salt Lake County 4870 S 2700 W, TYVL, 84118	2069	A3
Salt Lake County 1970 W 7800 S, WJDN, 84084	2175	C4
Salt Lake County-Bingham Creek 4834 W 9000 S, WJDN, 84088	2174	A7
Salt Lake County-Calvin Smith 810 E 3300 S, SLkC, 84106	1965	A5
Salt Lake County-Draper 12400 S 900 E, DRPR, 84020	2389	A1
Salt Lake County-Hunter 4740 W 4100 S, WVCY, 84120	2068	A1
Salt Lake County-West Jordan 2880 W 3650 S, WVCY, 84119	1963	A6
Salt Lake County-Whitmore 2197 Fort Union Blvd, CDHT, 84121	2177	E2
Sandy 10100 Petunia Wy, SNDY, 84092	2283	C3
Santaquin City 20 W 100 S, SNQN, 84655	3460	E7
Smithfield Public 25 N Main St, SHFD, 84335	399	D2
South Branch 725 S Main St, BNFL, 84010	1653	D1
South Jordan 10300 Beckstead Ln, SJDN, 84095	2281	D3
Spanish Fork Public 49 S Main St, SPFK, 84660	3249	C3
Springville Public 50 S Main St, SGVL, 84663	3143	C2
Utah State 450 S State St, SLCY, 84111	1858	D4
Wasatch County 465 E 12th S, HRCY, 84032	2398	E6
Weber County 475 E 2600 N, NHON, 84414	998	E6
Weber County 2464 Jefferson Av, OGDN, 84401	1116	A3
Weber County-SW Branch 1950 W 4800 S, ROY, 84067	1171	D3

Military Installations

FEATURE NAME Address City ZIP Code	MAP#	GRID
Camp Williams State Military Reservation SLkC, 84043	2494	E7
Camp Williams State Military Reservation UthC, 84043	2493	C5
Fort Carson Army Reserve Center OGDN, 84404	1056	B2
Fort Douglas SLCY, 84108	1859	E4
Hill Air Force Base DvsC, 84015	1228	C3

Museums

FEATURE NAME Address City ZIP Code	MAP#	GRID
Alf Engen Ski Mus 2990 Bear Hollow Dr, SmtC, 84098	1971	C5
Bountiful/Davis Art Center 745 S Main St, BNFL, 84010	1653	D1
Brigham City Mus 24 N 300 W, BMCY, 84302	766	E5
Cache Mus N Main St, LOGN, 84321	527	D3
Chase Home Mus of Utah Folk Arts E 1300 S, SLCY, 84105	1858	E6
Children's Mus of Utah 840 N 300 W, SLCY, 84103	1754	B7
Clark Planetarium 110 S 400 W, SLCY, 84101	1858	B3
Crandall Historical Printing Mus 275 E Center St, PRVO, 84606	2928	C7
Daughters of Utah Pioneers Mus 2148 Grant Av, OGDN, 84401	1115	E2
Daughters of Utah Pioneers Mus 175 S Main St, SGVL, 84663	3143	C2
Daughters of Utah Pioneers Mus 300 N Main St, SLCY, 84103	1858	C2
Earth Sciences Mus 1683 N Canyon Rd, PRVO, 84604	2928	C3
Eccles Community Arts Center 2580 Jefferson Av, OGDN, 84401	1116	A4
E Street Gallery 82 E St, SLCY, 84103	1858	E2
Fort Douglas Military Mus 32 Potter St, SLCY, 84113	1859	D4
Hellenic Cultural Mus 279 S 300 W, SLCY, 84101	1858	B4
Heritage Mus of Layton 403 N Wasatch Dr, LYTN, 84041	1283	A4
Hill Aerospace Mus 7961 Wardleigh Rd, RVDL, 84405	1171	E5
John Hutchings Mus of Natual History 55 N Center St, LEHI, 84043	2603	C6
Midvale City Mus 7697 Main St, MDVL, 84047	2176	A4
Millstream Antique Car Mus 1450 Washington Blvd, OGDN, 84404	1115	E1
Monte L Bean Life Science Mus 645 E 1430 N, PRVO, 84604	2928	D4
Museum of Art N Campus Dr, PRVO, 84604	2928	D4
Museum of Church History & Art 45 N West Temple, SLCY, 84103	1858	C3
Museum of Natural History-Weber State Edvalson St, OGDN, 84403	1116	C7
Museum of Natural Science Weber State Edvalson St, OGDN, 84403	1116	C7
Museum of Peoples & Cultures 100 E 700 N, PRVO, 84606	2928	C5
National Award Vehicles Hall of Fame 407 W 100 S, PRVO, 84601	2928	B7
Nora Eccles Harrison Mus of Art 650 N 1100 E, LOGN, 84321	528	B1
North Park Mus 500 W 600 N, PRVO, 84601	2928	B5
Olson Galleries 101 W Main St, MIDW, 84049	2397	B3
Park City Mus & Territorial Jail 528 Main St, PKCY, 84060	2078	E6
Peteetneet Academy & Mus 10 S 600 E, PYSN, 84651	3355	A5
Pioneer Memorial Mus 300 N Main St, SLCY, 84103	1858	C2
Riverton Art Mus 1640 W 13200 S, RIVN, 84065	2387	D3
Robert Duncan Studio 380 E Main St, MIDW, 84049	2397	C3
Roy Historical Mus 5550 Freeway Park Dr, RVDL, 84405	1171	E4
S&S Shortline Train Park & Mus 575 N 1525 W, FMTN, 84025	1345	E7
Salt Lake Art Center 20 S West Temple, SLCY, 84101	1858	C3
Sandy Historical Mus 8744 Center St, SNDY, 84070	2176	D6
Social Hall Heritage Mus 36 S State St, SLCY, 84111	1858	D3
Springville Mus of Art 126 E 400 S, SGVL, 84663	3143	C3
Syracuse Mus 1726 Heritage Ln, SRCS, 84075	1280	E1
Tivoli Gallery 255 S State St, SLCY, 84111	1858	D3
Treehouse Children's Mus 455 23rd St, OGDN, 84401	1115	E3
Union Station Muss 2501 Wall Av, OGDN, 84401	1115	D4
Utah Mus of Fine Arts 410 Campus Center Dr, SLCY, 84112	1859	D4
Utah Mus of Natural History 1390 Presidents Cir, SLCY, 84112	1859	B3
Whitaker Home Mus 168 S Main St, CTRV, 84014	1551	D4

Open Space

FEATURE NAME Address City ZIP Code	MAP#	GRID
Paul Ream Wilderness Pk, PRVO	2927	D6

Other

FEATURE NAME Address City ZIP Code	MAP#	GRID
American West Heritage Center WELV, 84319	590	B6
Assembly Hall W South Temple, SLCY, 84103	1858	C3
Brigham Young's Grave 140 1st Av, SLCY, 84103	1858	D2
Conference Center W North Temple, SLCY, 84103	1858	C2
Mormon Tabernacle W South Temple, SLCY, 84103	1858	C3
Mormon Temple W North Temple, SLCY, 84103	1858	C2
Olympic Cauldron Park 451 S 1400 E, SLCY, 84112	1859	C4
Temple Square SLCY, 84103	1858	C3
Utah State Capitol 350 N State St, SLCY, 84103	1858	C2

Park & Ride

FEATURE NAME Address City ZIP Code	MAP#	GRID
Park & Ride, BNFL	1551	E5
Park & Ride, CRFD	1228	A6
Park & Ride, CTRV	1551	E3
Park & Ride, FMTN	1346	B6
Park & Ride, KYVL	1345	B1
Park & Ride, LYTN	1230	A7
Park & Ride, LYTN	1282	E2
Park & Ride, NHON	998	E5
Park & Ride, NSLK	1653	B7
Park & Ride, PTVW	998	B4
Park & Ride, RVDL	1171	E4
Park & Ride, WDCR	1653	B2
Park & Ride-600 W, KYVL	1345	B1
Park & Ride-900 W, SLCY	1754	A7
Park & Ride-1200 W, OREM	2820	A3
Park & Ride-1600 N, OREM	2819	E1
Park & Ride-1875 N, FMTN	1346	A4
Park & Ride-3500 E, CDHT	2178	C4
Park & Ride-8000 W, SLkC	1960	C3
Park & Ride-Ballpark, SLCY	1858	C7
Park & Ride-Big Cottonwood, CDHT	2178	D2
Park & Ride-Catalpa St, MDVL	2176	B2
Park & Ride-Central Pointe, SSLK	1964	C2
Park & Ride-Cottonwood, MRRY	2177	A1
Park & Ride-E Center, WVCY	1963	B5
Park & Ride-Factory Outlet Dr, DRPR	2388	C1
Park & Ride-Farr West, FRWT	997	D6
Park & Ride-Fashion Place, MRRY	2176	C1
Park & Ride-Fort Union, MDVL	2176	C2
Park & Ride-Frontage Rd, UthC	2495	A5
Park & Ride-Harrison St, SNDY	2176	B7
Park & Ride-Historic Sandy, SNDY	2176	D7
Park & Ride-Hwy 89, PTVW	997	E2
Park & Ride-Hwy 193, LYTN	1282	D3
Park & Ride-I-84, SWBR	1230	B2
Park & Ride-Main St, ANFK	2711	A1
Park & Ride-Main St, PYSN	3354	E3
Park & Ride-Meadowbrook, SSLK	1964	C7
Park & Ride-Millcreek, SSLK	1964	C5
Park & Ride-Murray Central, MRRY	2070	C4
Park & Ride-Murray North, MRRY	2070	C1
Park & Ride-North Ogden, NHON	999	A4
Park & Ride-Ogden, OGDN	1115	D3
Park & Ride-Ogden, WHVN	1114	E2
Park & Ride-Sandy, SNDY	2176	D6
Park & Ride-Sandy Civic Center, SNDY	2282	D2
Park & Ride-The Peaks Ice Arena, PRVO	2928	C3
Park & Ride-UT-13, BMCY	766	E3

Parks & Recreation

FEATURE NAME Address City ZIP Code	MAP#	GRID
9th South Pk, SLCY	1857	E5
11th Avenue Pk, SLCY	1859	A1
1800 South Pk, BNFL	1654	A3
Affleck Pk, OGDN	1115	D6
Akagi Neighborhood Pk, DRPR	2389	C4
Alta Canyon Pk, SNDY	2283	D1
Anderson Pk, PTGV	2713	A3
Andy Adams Pk, LYTN	1283	D2
Andy Ballard Equestrian Pk, DRPR	2389	C4
Art Dye Ball Complex, LEHI	2603	D4
Aspen Meadows Pk, SNDY	2283	D2
Ball Pk, LEHI	2603	A6
Band Wagon Pk, LEHI	2603	C5
Barnes Memorial Pk, KYVL	1283	A7
Bear River City Pk, BRCY	645	D5
Becks Hill Pk, ALPN	2497	E6
Bell Canyon Pk, SNDY	2283	C6
Benjamin Franklin Pk, SLkC	1965	A6
Bernard Fisher Memorial Pk, CRFD	1228	A6
Bicentennial Pk, ANFK	2711	C2
Bicentennial Pk, CRFD	1228	A5
Bicentennial Pk, SNDY	2176	E6
Big Bear Pk, SLkC	2283	A1
Big Cottonwood Pk, SLkC	2071	C2
Big D Sports Pk, OGDN	1116	C1
Bird Pk, SGVL	3143	E3
Bonneville Pk, OGDN	1057	B5
Bonneville Pk, OREM	2820	B1
Bountiful City Pk, BNFL	1551	D6
Brigadoon Pk, WJDN	2175	D7
Brigham Young Pk, BMCY	766	E5
Browns Meadow, WJDN	2175	B7
Bues Pond Pk, OGDN	1173	C2
Burgess Pk, ALPN	2497	E5
Butler Pk, CDHT	2178	A3
Buttercup Pk, SNDY	2283	C2
Bywater Pk, CDHT	2178	B3
Camelot Pk, WJDN	2175	C2
Canterbury Pk, SRCS	1226	D7
Canyon Rim Pk, SLkC	1966	B5
Canyon View Pk, SPFK	3250	D6
Carterville Pk, PRVO	2928	A2
Cascade Pk, OREM	2821	A4
Caveman Pk, ANFK	2604	E7
Centennial Pk, DRPR	2495	D1
Centennial Pk, RIVN	2387	A3
Centennial Pk, SRCS	1280	E1
Centennial Pk, WVCY	1961	E5
Centerville Community Pk, CTRV	1551	C1
Central East Pk, SWBR	1229	C2
Central Pk, CRFD	1227	E4
Central Pk, SWBR	1229	B2
Central Pk, WSTR	1172	D2
Chapel Pk, LYTN	1283	B5
Charles E Steed Memorial Pk, CRFD	1227	B3
Charleston City Pk, CSTN	2504	C3
Cheese Pk, BNFL	1552	A5
Cherry Farms Pk, SWBR	1229	E3
Cherryhill Pk, OREM	2927	E2
Chipman Pk, ANFK	2604	C4
City Center Pk, OREM	2820	D5
City Pk, SJDN	2281	C5
Clinton City Pk, CLTN	1170	E7
Clubhouse Pk, SOGN	1172	D1
Community Pk, OREM	2820	B5
Community Pk, SSLK	1964	E5
Conover Pk, SGVL	3143	D4
Constitution Pk, BMCY	828	A1
Constitution Pk, SLCY	1857	D2
Constitution Pk, WJDN	2174	E2

Salt Lake City Points of Interest Index

Parks & Recreation

FEATURE NAME Address City ZIP Code	MAP#	GRID
Copperview Pk, MDVL	2176	B5
Corinne Ballpark, CRNN	704	E7
Corinne City Pk, CRNN	705	A7
Cougar Pk, WJDN	2174	A1
Creekside Pk, LNDN	2712	E7
Creekside Pk, SLkC	2071	C3
Crescent Pk, SNDY	2282	D5
Crestwood Pk, CDHT	2177	D3
Dale Young Nature Pk, PRRY	827	C4
DATC Pk, KYVL	1345	D2
David Gourley Pk, SLkC	2068	C4
Dee Memorial Pk, OGDN	1116	B3
Deer Creek State Pk, WshC	2504	B2
Dewey Bluth Pk, SNDY	2282	D2
Dilworth Pk, SLCY	1965	E1
Dimple Dell Pk, SNDY	2283	B3
Dixie Valley Pk, WJDN	2068	D7
Donner Trail Pk, SLCY	1860	B5
Dora Lee Pk, WJDN	2174	A6
Draper City Pk, DRPR	2389	B2
Draper Historical Pk, DRPR	2389	A2
East Pk, HYRM	651	D2
East Ridge Pk, SNDY	2389	A1
Eccles Dinosaur Pk, OGDN	1116	C1
Eden Town Pk, WbrC	1002	A7
Ensign Peak, SLCY	1754	D7
Evergreen Pk, ANFK	2604	E7
Evergreen Pk, SLkC	1965	E6
Exchange Pk, PRVO	2928	B5
Fairmont Pk, SLCY	1965	A2
Falcon Pk, SNDY	2177	C7
Farmington Pond Pk, FMTN	1346	D7
Farr West City Pk, FRWT	997	D7
Faultline Gardens, SLCY	1859	A4
Filly & Pony League, ANFK	2604	C6
Flat Iron Mesa Pk, SNDY	2177	C5
Footprinter's Pk, PRVO	3035	A1
Fort Buenaventura State Pk, OGDN	1115	C4
Fort Utah Pk, PRVO	2927	D6
Founders Pk, CTRV	1551	E3
Founders Pk, SRCS	1226	E7
Fourth Street Softball Pk, OGDN	1056	D6
Foxglen Pk, ROY	1170	D2
Francis Pk, OGDN	1057	A4
Fremont Pk, SRCS	1280	C1
Friendship Pk, SOGN	1173	A4
Gailey Pk, KYVL	1345	C2
George Wahlen North Pk, ROY	1171	D1
Germania Pk, MRRY	2069	E4
Glasmann Way Pk, SOGN	1173	B4
Glenn Weaver Memorial Pk, WVCY	1963	B6
Golden Spike Pk, RVDL	1172	A3
Grandview Pk, OGDN	1116	B7
Grandview Pk, PRVO	2928	A4
Granger Pk, WVCY	1962	D6
Granite Pk, SLkC	2284	A4
Grant Pk, MRRY	2070	C7
Greenwood Pk, UthC	2711	D2
Harmon Pk, PRVO	2928	E7
Harmony Pk, SSLK	1964	C7
Harrisville City Millenium Pk, HARR	998	C7
Harrisville City Pk, HARR	1056	D2
Harvey Pk, KYVL	1284	A6
Heber City Pk, HRCY	2398	C4
Heritage Pk, CRHL	2605	B3
Heritage Pk, HILD	2604	D2
Heritage Pk, SGVL	3036	C7
Herman Frank's Pk, SLCY	1859	A7
Hidden Valley Pk, SNDY	2284	A7
Hidden Village Pk, MRRY	2070	B5
High Point Pk, SNDY	2177	A4
Hillman Pk, PYSN	3354	D6
Hillsdale Pk, WVCY	1962	E5
Hindley Pk, ANFK	2604	E7
Hods Hollow Pk, DvsC	1283	D6
Hogan Pk, WDCR	1653	B2
Hogan's Pk, CRFD	1227	C3
Hunter Pk, WVCY	1961	C6
Huntsville Town Pk, HTVL	1061	A5
Hyrum State Pk, CchC	651	B5
Island View Pk, CRFD	1281	D1
Island View Pk, CTRV	1552	A4
Jaycee Pk, OGDN	1116	C3
JC Ball Pk, ANFK	2604	B7
JC Pk, BNFL	1551	D7
Jefferson Pk, OGDN	1115	E6
Jefferson Pk, SLCY	1858	C6
John Adams Pk, BMCY	767	A5
John G White Memorial Pk, SNST	1171	D6
Jordanelle State Pk, WshC	2186	E3
Jordan Meadows, WJDN	2175	B3
Jordan Pk, SLCY	1857	E6
Jordan River Pkway, WJDN	2175	E3
Jordan River State Pkway, SLCY	1857	E4
Jordan River State Pkway, SLkC	1753	C2
Junior High Pk, BNFL	1654	B3
Kaysville City Pk, KYVL	1283	C7
Kimberly Pk, ANFK	2604	B5
Kiwanis Pk, CLTN	1227	B1
Kiwanis Pk, PRVO	2928	E5
Kiwanis Pk, PTGV	2713	A3
Knoll Pk, SALM	3356	B3
Kolob Pk, SGVL	3143	D3
Lambert Pk, ALPN	2498	C2
Layton Commons Pk, LYTN	1283	A3
Lee Olsen Pk, PNCY	996	C7
Legacy Pk, SRCS	1281	B2
Lester Pk, OGDN	1116	A3
Lewis Pk, BNFL	1653	C1
Liberty Community Pk, WbrC	1001	A2
Liberty Pk, OGDN	1116	A2
Liberty Pk, SLCY	1858	E6
Lincoln Pk, LYTN	1282	D1
Linda Vista Pk, SRCS	1280	E3
Lindon Pk, LNDN	2713	B6
Lindsay Pk, BMCY	827	E1
Lindsey Pk, SLCY	1859	A1
Lions Pk, OGDN	1116	D1
Lions Pk, PNCY	996	C6
Lions Pk, WSTR	1172	E3
Lion's Pk, ANFK	2711	B1
Lion's Pk, PRVO	2928	A4
Lomond View, NHON	998	E4
Lorin Farr Pk, OGDN	1116	A1
Lynn Ballard Pk, DRPR	2389	C4
Lyons Club Pk, OGDN	1116	B3
Mack Pk, SHFD	399	E2
Madison Avenue Pk, SOGN	1173	A1
Magna-Copper Pk, SLkC	1960	A3
Main City Pk, FMTN	1448	C2
Main Pk, RIVN	2387	D2
Main Pk, WJDN	2175	C4
Manila Pk, PTGV	2605	D7
Mantua City Pk, MNTU	768	C7
Mapleton City Pk, MPTN	3144	B7
Marriott Pk, MTSV	1056	A7
Marshall White Pk, OGDN	1115	D4
Martin Pk, ANFK	2604	B6
McGriff Pk, NHON	999	B4
Meadows Pk, CLTN	1171	B7
Memorial Pk, BMCY	767	A7
Memorial Pk, PRVO	2928	D6
Memorial Pk, PYSN	3354	E5
Memorial Pk, SGVL	3143	D2
Memory Grove Pk, SLCY	1858	D1
Midvale City Pk, MDVL	2176	B3
Midway City Pk, MIDW	2397	B3
Miguel Field, MPTN	3144	C5
Miles Goodyear Pk, OGDN	1115	C3
Miller Pk, SLCY	1859	C6
Mills Pk, WDCR	1653	A3
Monroe Pk, OGDN	1116	A5
Moon Pk, FMTN	1346	B5
Mountain Meadows Pk, ANFK	2711	B2
Mountain View Pk, FMTN	1448	D3
Mountain View Pk, FRWT	1055	E2
Mountain View Pk, NHON	999	B4
Mountain View Pk, PRRY	827	D5
Mount Eyrie Pk, OGDN	1056	E2
Mount Ogden Pk, OGDN	1116	C5
MTC Learning Pk, OGDN	1116	B1
Mueller Pk, DvsC	1654	E5
Municipal Pk, ROY	1171	C5
Murray Pk, MRRY	2070	D4
Nicholls Pk, FTHT	1346	A2
Ninth Street Pk, OGDN	1057	A7
Nob Hill Pk, ANFK	2604	C5
North Canyon Pk, BNFL	1653	E6
North Ogden Pk, NHON	999	A5
North Pk, PRVO	2928	B6
North Salt Lake Main Pk, NSLK	1653	A7
Oak Forest Pk, LYTN	1229	E7
Oak Lawn Pk, NHON	999	C6
Old Mill Pk, HLDY	2178	B1
Olympus Hills Pk, SLkC	2072	B1
Oquirrh Pk, SLkC	2068	A6
Orchard Pk, OGDN	1116	A6
Orton Greenacres Pk, NHON	999	A7
Parkway Pk, WVCY	1962	E4
Parleys Way, SLkC	1966	B4
Peachwood Pk, WVCY	1962	D7
Peggy Green Pk, RIVN	2387	C1
Perry Pk, PRRY	827	C5
Petersen Pk, ALPN	2498	A5
Pioneer Pk, ANFK	2604	C7
Pioneer Pk, BMCY	766	D5
Pioneer Pk, LNDN	2713	C7
Pioneer Pk, LYTN	1284	A4
Pioneer Pk, PRVO	2928	B7
Pioneer Pk, SLCY	1858	B4
Pleasant Green Pk, SLkC	1960	B5
Pleasant View Pk, PTVW	998	B4
Plum Creek Pk, WJDN	2175	D5
Ponds Pk South, KYVL	1345	C3
Popperton Pk, SLCY	1859	B1
Popular Grove Pk, SLCY	1857	E5
Powerline Pk, PRVO	3035	B2
Provo Rotary Bicentennial Pk, PRVO	3036	A2
Provo Rotary Pk, PRVO	2927	E4
Provost Pk, PRVO	3035	E1
Pueblo del Montana Pk, RIVN	2387	C3
Reservoir Pk, SLCY	1859	B3
Rhomer Pk, WbrC	1172	C4
Riverdale Pk, RVDL	1172	A1
River Front Pk, SJDN	2282	A5
Riverside Pk, PRVO	2928	A5
Riverside Pk, SLCY	1857	D1
Riverview Pk, MRRY	2070	A6
Riverview Pk, PRVO	2821	B5
Robinson Pk, ANFK	2711	C1
Rocket Pk, BNFL	1552	B7
Rolling Hills Pk, OGDN	1057	C7
Romell Pk, OGDN	1056	D6
Ron Claire Pk, OGDN	1057	B3
Ron W. Last Pk, PRVO	2821	C3
Rosewood Pk, SLCY	1753	E6
Rotary Pk, ANFK	2711	D2
Roy Pk, ROY	1171	B4
Russell Swensen Memorial Pk, SPFK	3249	C3
Salt Lake County Hang Gliding Pk, DRPR	2495	C1
Sandridge Pk, ROY	1171	D2
Scera Pk, OREM	2820	E6
Sertoma Pk, PRVO	2928	C2
Shady Lane Pk, PTVW	998	C5
Shallmar Pk, ANFK	2604	D6
Shannon Pk, PTGV	2712	C3
Sharon Pk, OREM	2820	E3
Shepard Pk, FMTN	1346	B6
Sherwood Pk, SLCY	1857	D4
Slaterville Pk, MTSV	1055	C5
Smith Fields Pk, DRPR	2388	D4
Smoot Pk, CTRV	1448	D7
Snow Pk, BMCY	766	E4
South County Pk, RIVN	2387	E2
South Main Pk, BMCY	766	E7
South Pk, FMTN	1448	C5
South Pk, SNST	1227	D2
Southridge Pk, TYVL	2068	C4
Southwest Pk, ROY	1170	C5
Southwood Pk, MRRY	2070	E7
Springville City Pk, SGVL	3143	C2
Stoker Pk, SRCS	1227	B7
Stone Mountain Pk, OGDN	1173	C3
Storm Mountain Pk, SNDY	2283	A6
Strasburg Pk, HILD	2604	C2
Stratford Pk, SLCY	1965	D3
Sugarhouse Pk, SLCY	1965	C2
Sullivan Hollow Pk, OGDN	1116	A5
Summerhill Pk, RIVN	2281	D7
Sunnyside Pk, SLCY	1859	C5
Sunset Central Pk, SNST	1227	D1
Sunset View Pk, PRVO	2927	E7
Tanner Pk, SLCY	1966	A4
Taylorsville Pk, TYVL	2069	C3
Teton Estates Pk, WJDN	2280	C1
The Pk at Rock Canyon, PRVO	2928	E2
This Is The Place State Pk, SLCY	1860	B5
Thomas Pk, OGDN	1116	D2
Timp Ball Pk, PRVO	2928	B5
Timp Kiwanis Bounous Pk, PRVO	2928	D1
Town Square, PNCY	996	C6
Trail Head Equestrian Pk, NHON	999	D5
Train Watch Pk, CRFD	1227	D4
Uintah Town Pk, UNTH	1173	E7
Uinta National Forest, UthC	2822	C4
Union Pk, MDVL	2176	E3
Utah Lake State Pk, UthC	2926	E6
Vae View Pk, LYTN	1282	B1
Valley Pk, TYVL	2069	A4
Veterans Memorial State Pk, BFDL	2494	D6
Vista Pk, TYVL	2069	C4
Vista West, WJDN	2174	C7
W&M Butterfield Pk, HRMN	2385	C5
Walden Pk, MRRY	2069	E6
Warm Springs, SLCY	1754	B7
Wasatch-Cache National Forest, WbrC	1058	C4
Wasatch Mountain State Pk, WshC	2503	D2
Wasatch Valley Tank Pk, SNDY	2284	A7
Washington Square Pk, SLCY	1858	D4
Water Department Pk, BNFL	1653	D2
Watkins Pk, BMCY	766	D6
West Bountiful Pk, WBNF	1551	C5
West Haven Country Pk, WHVN	1114	A6
West Lakeview, NHON	998	E3
Westmore Pk, OREM	2927	D1
West Ogden Pk, OGDN	1115	B3
West Pk, PRVO	2927	E6
West Pk, ROY	1171	B2
West Pk, SNQN	3567	D1
West Point, SLCY	1753	B6
West Point City Pk, WPT	1226	B3
West Valley City Pk, WVCY	1962	B5
West View Pk, WVCY	2067	C1
Wetlands Pk, DRPR	2283	A7
Wheeler Historic Farm, MRRY	2071	A7
Wildflower Pk, SNDY	2283	D2
Willard Bay State Pk, BxEC	941	B3
Willowcreek Pk, SNDY	2177	E5
Willow Creek Pk, WLRD	885	D5
Willow Pk, LEHI	2602	B6
Willow Pk, LOGN	527	C5
Winchester Pk, MRRY	2069	E7
Windsor Pk, OREM	2820	D1
Wines Pk, LEHI	2603	C5
Woodland Pk, FMTN	1448	D2
Woodledge Pk, WVCY	2067	E1
Wright Pk, WSTR	1172	D4

Schools

FEATURE NAME Address City ZIP Code	MAP#	GRID
Ability School of Utah 1144 W 3300 S, SSLK, 84119	1963	E5
Academy Park Elementary School 4580 Westpoint Dr, WVCY, 84120	2068	B2
Adams Elementary School 530 N 400 E, LOGN, 84321	527	E2
Adams Elementary School 2200 E Sunset Dr, LYTN, 84040	1229	E7
Adelaide Elementary School 731 W 3600 S, DvsC, 84010	1653	B6
Adele C Young Intermediate School 830 Law Dr, BMCY, 84302	827	D1
Albion Middle School 2755 Newcastle Dr, SNDY, 84093	2178	B7
Alpine Elementary School 400 E 300 N, ALPN, 84004	2498	A4
Alta High School 11055 S 1000 E, SNDY, 84094	2283	A5
Altara Elementary School 800 E 11000 S, SNDY, 84094	2283	A5
Alta View Elementary School 10333 Crocus St, SLkC, 84094	2283	A3
Amelia Earhart Elementary 2585 W 200 S, PRVO, 84601	2927	C7
American Fork High School 510 Caveman Blvd, ANFK, 84003	2604	E6
American Fork Junior High School 20 W 1120 N, ANFK, 84003	2604	C5
American Heritage School 736 N 11th E, ANFK, 84003	2605	A6
American Preparatory Academy 12892 Pony Express Rd, DRPR, 84020	2388	C2
Antelope Elementary School 1810 S Main St, CRFD, 84015	1281	D1
Arcadia Elementary School 3461 W 4850 S, TYVL, 84118	2068	E3
Art City Elementary School 121 S 900 E, SGVL, 84663	3143	E2
Aspen Elementary School 945 W 2000 N, OREM, 84057	2713	A7
Backman Elementary School 601 N 1500 W, SLCY, 84116	1857	D1
Barnett Elementary School 333 E 400 N, PYSN, 84651	3355	A4
Barratt Elementary 168 N 900 E, ANFK, 84003	2605	A7
Bates Elementary School 850 E 3100 N, NHON, 84414	999	B4
Beacon Heights Elementary School 1850 S 2500 E, SLCY, 84108	1966	A1
Bear River High School 1350 S Main St, GRLD, 84312	520	E4
Bear River Middle School 300 S Main St, GRLD, 84312	520	E2
Beehive Elementary School 5655 Sarah Jane Dr, SLkC, 84118	2067	E5
Bella Vista Elementary School 2131 Fort Union Blvd, CDHT, 84121	2177	E2
Bellview Elementary School 9800 Sunflower Ln, SLkC, 84094	2283	A2
Benjamin Franklin Academy 425 E 850 S, BMCY, 84302	828	A1
Ben Lomond High School 800 Jackson Av, OGDN, 84404	1057	B6
Bennion Junior High School 6055 S 2700 W, TYVL, 84118	2069	A6
Bennion School 5775 Sierra Grande Dr, TYVL, 84118	2069	A6
Bingham High School 2160 W South Jordan Pkwy, SJDN, 84095	2281	B3
Blessed Sacrament School 1745 E 9800 S, SLkC, 84092	2283	C2
Bluffdale Elementary School 14323 S 2700 W, BFDL, 84065	2387	A6
Bluff Ridge Elementary School S 775 W, SRCS, 84075	1281	C2
Bonneville Elementary School 490 Gramercy Av, OGDN, 84404	1057	A6
Bonneville Elementary School 1245 N 800 W, OREM, 84057	2820	B2
Bonneville Elementary School 1145 S 1900 E, SLCY, 84108	1859	D6
Bonneville High School 251 W Laker Wy, WSTR, 84405	1172	D3
Bonneville Junior High School Gurene Dr, SLkC, 84117	2071	C5
Boulton Elementary School 2611 Orchard Dr, BNFL, 84010	1653	D4
Bountiful Elementary School 1620 S 50 W, BNFL, 84010	1653	D2
Bountiful Junior High School 30 W Willey St, BNFL, 84010	1551	D7
Bountiful Senior High School 695 Orchard Dr, BNFL, 84010	1653	E1
Box Elder High School 380 S 600 Blvd W, BMCY, 84302	766	D6
Box Elder Middle School 18 S 500 E, BMCY, 84302	767	A6
Bridger Elementary School 1261 N 400 W, LOGN, 84341	463	C7
Brighton High School 2220 Bengal Blvd, CDHT, 84093	2177	E3
Brockbank Elementary School 340 W 500 N, SPFK, 84660	3249	C2
Brockbank Junior High School 2935 S 8560 W, SLkC, 84044	1960	B4
Brookside Elementary School 750 E 400 S, SGVL, 84663	3143	D3
Brookwood Elementary School 8640 Snowbird Dr, SNDY, 84093	2178	A6

Salt Lake City Points of Interest Index

Schools

FEATURE NAME Address City ZIP Code	MAP#	GRID
Bryant Intermediate School 40 S 800 E, SLCY, 84102	1859	A3
Bunderson Elementary School 641 E 200 N, BMCY, 84302	767	A5
Burton Elementary School 827 E 200 S, FTHT, 84037	1345	E1
Butler Elementary School 2700 Fort Union Blvd, CDHT, 84121	2178	A2
Butler Middle School 7530 S 2700 E, CDHT, 84121	2178	A3
Cache High School 265 W 1400 N, LOGN, 84341	463	C6
Calvin S Smith Elementary School 2150 Bennion Blvd, TYVL, 84118	2069	B7
Canyon Crest Elementary School 4664 N Canyon Rd, PRVO, 84604	2821	C5
Canyon Elementary School 1492 E 1240 S, SPFK, 84660	3250	A5
Canyon Rim Elementary School 3005 S 2900 E, SLkC, 84109	1966	B4
Canyon View Elementary School 3050 Bengal Blvd, CDHT, 84121	2178	B4
Canyon View Elementary School 1100 Orchard Av, OGDN, 84404	1057	A7
Canyon View Junior High School 655 Eagle Dr, OREM, 84097	2821	A2
Canyon View School 1100 Orchard Av, OGDN, 84404	1057	A7
Carden Memorial School 1452 E 2700 S, SLCY, 84106	1965	C4
Carl H Taylor Elementary School 2130 Taylor Av, OGDN, 84401	1116	C2
Carl Sandberg Elementary School 3900 S 5325 W, WVCY, 84120	1961	E7
Carmen B Pingree School 780 Guardsman Wy, SLCY, 84102	1859	C5
Cascade Elementary School 160 N 800 E, BNFL, 84010	1552	A7
Cedar Ridge Elementary School 4501 W Cedar Hills Dr, CRHL, 84062	2605	A3
Cedar Ridge Middle School 65 N 200 W, HDPK, 84318	399	E7
Centennial Middle School 305 E 2320 N, PRVO, 84604	2928	D2
Centerville Elementary School 350 N 100 E, CTRV, 84014	1551	E3
Centerville Junior High School 625 S Main St, CTRV, 84014	1551	E4
Central Davis Junior High School 663 Church St, LYTN, 84041	1283	A3
Central Elementary School 210 S Main St, BMCY, 84302	766	E6
Central Elementary School 95 N 400 E, PTGV, 84062	2712	E3
Central High School 501 E 3900 S, SSLK, 84106	1964	E7
Central Middle School 2563 Monroe Blvd, OGDN, 84401	1116	A4
Century Elementary School 5820 N 4800 W, BRCY, 84301	645	C5
Challenger School 730 N 300 E, OREM, 84057	2820	E3
Challenger School 10693 S 1000 E, SNDY, 84094	2283	A4
Challenger School Gardner Ln, WJDN, 84088	2175	B6
Challenger Schools 1325 S Main St, SLCY, 84115	1858	C7
Cherry Hill Elementary School 250 E 1650 S, OREM, 84058	2927	E2
Childrens Academy 1821 Moor Dale Ln, SLkC, 84117	2071	D4
Childrens Choice 10750 S 1300 E, SNDY, 84094	2283	B4
Christian Heritage School 5101 S 1050 W, RVDL, 84405	1172	A3
Christ Lutheran School 240 E 5600 S, MRRY, 84107	2070	D5
Church Hill Junior High School 3450 Oakview Dr, SLkC, 84124	2072	C1
City Academy 2416 E 1700 S, SLCY, 84108	1966	A1
Clayton Middle School 1471 Rosecrest Dr, SLCY, 84108	1859	D7
Clearfield High School 931 S 1000 E, CRFD, 84015	1228	A6
Clinton Elementary School 1101 Clinton Rd, CLTN, 84015	1227	B1
Club Heights Elementary School E 4150 S, SOGN, 84403	1173	A1
Columbia Elementary School 378 S 50 W, KYVL, 84037	1345	C2
Columbia Elementary School 3505 W 7800 S, WJDN, 84088	2174	E4
Cook Elementary School 1175 W 1350 S, SRCS, 84075	1227	B7
Copper Canyon Elementary School 8917 Copperwood Dr, WJDN, 84088	2173	E6
Copper Hills Elementary School 7635 Washington Rd, SLkC, 84044	1960	D6
Copper Hills High School 5545 New Bingham Hwy, WJDN, 84088	2173	E6
Copperview Elementary School 8449 Monroe St, MDVL, 84047	2176	C5
Corrine Elementary School 2275 N 3900 W, CRNN, 84307	704	E7
Cottonwood Elementary School 5205 Holladay Blvd, HLDY, 84117	2072	A4
Cottonwood Heights Elementary School 2415 Bengal Blvd, CDHT, 84121	2178	A3
Cottonwood High School 5715 S 1300 E, MRRY, 84121	2071	B6
Country View Elementary School 4650 Grizzly Wy, WHVN, 84315	1170	B3
Creekside Elementary School 275 W Mutton Hollow Rd, KYVL, 84037	1283	C6
Creekside High School 179 E Murray Park Ln, MRRY, 84107	2070	D4
Crescent Elementary School 11100 S 230 E, SNDY, 84070	2282	D5
Crescent View Middle School 11150 S 300 E, SNDY, 84070	2282	D5
Crestview Elementary School 2100 Lincoln Ln, HLDY, 84124	2071	E1
Crestview Elementary School 185 W Golden Av, LYTN, 84041	1282	E3
Cyprus High School 8623 W 3000 S, SLkC, 84044	1960	A5
Dale Young Community High School 230 W 200 S, BMCY, 84302	766	E6
Dan Petersen School 169 N 1100 E, ANFK, 84003	2605	A7
David Gourley Elementary School 4905 S 4300 W, SLkC, 84118	2068	C3
Davis County School 931 S 1000 E, CRFD, 84015	1228	A6
Davis High School 325 S Main St, KYVL, 84037	1345	D2
Davis Junior High School 464 S 500 E, KYVL, 84037	1345	D2
Dee Elementary School 550 22nd St, OGDN, 84401	1115	E3
Deerfield Elementary School 4353 Harvey Blvd, CRHL, 84062	2605	B4
Deseret Academy 3098 Highland Dr, SLkC, 84106	1965	B5
Dilworth Elementary School 1953 S 2100 E, SLCY, 84108	1965	E1
Discovery Academy 197 E 500 S, BNFL, 84010	1653	E1
Discovery Elementary School 820 N 500 W, BMCY, 84302	766	E3
Dixon Junior High School 750 W 200 N, PRVO, 84601	2928	B6
Douglas Orchard Elementary School 6744 W 3800 S, WVCY, 84128	1961	A7
Doxey Elementary School 944 N 250 W, SNST, 84015	1227	D2
Draper Elementary School 1080 E 12660 S, DRPR, 84020	2389	A2
Eagle Bay Elementary School 1933 Clark Ln, FMTN, 84025	1447	D1
Eaglecrest Elementary School 2760 N 300 W, LEHI, 84043	2603	B2
East High School 840 S 1300 E, SLCY, 84102	1859	B5
East Layton Elementary School 2470 E Cherry Ln, LYTN, 84040	1283	E2
East Midvale Elementary 6990 S 300 E, MDVL, 84047	2176	D2
Eastmont Middle School 10100 S 1300 E, SNDY, 84094	2283	B3
East Sandy Elementary School 8295 S 865 E, SNDY, 84094	2177	A5
Eastwood Elementary School 3305 Wasatch Blvd, SLkC, 84109	1966	C5
Ecker Hill Middle School 2465 Kilby Rd, SmtC, 84098	1865	C7
Edgemont Elementary School 566 E 3650 N, PRVO, 84604	2821	D7
Edgemont Elementary School 1085 Galena Dr, SNDY, 84094	2283	B2
Edison Elementary School 935 E 1050 N, OGDN, 84404	1057	B3
Edison Elementary School 466 Cheyenne St, SLCY, 84104	1857	D4
EG King Elementary School 601 E Gordon Av, LYTN, 84041	1283	B3
Eisenhower Junior High School 4351 S Redwood Rd, TYVL, 84123	2069	C2
Elk Meadows Elementary School 3448 W 9800 S, SJDN, 84095	2280	E2
Elk Ridge Middle School 3659 W 9800 S, SJDN, 84095	2280	D2
Ellis Elementary School 348 W 300 N, LOGN, 84321	527	C2
Emerson Elementary School 1017 Harrison Av, SLCY, 84105	1859	A7
Ensign Elementary School 775 12th Av, SLCY, 84103	1859	A1
Ensign Schools 215 N Center St, ANFK, 84003	2604	C7
Escalante Elementary School 1810 W 900 N, SLCY, 84116	1753	C7
Evergreen Junior High School 3401 S 2000 E, SLkC, 84109	1965	D6
Fairfield Junior High School 951 N Fairfield Rd, KYVL, 84037	1283	C6
Faith Baptist Academy 2430 N Fairfield Rd, LYTN, 84040	1229	B7
Farmington Elementary School 50 W 200 S, FMTN, 84025	1448	C2
Farmington Junior High School 150 S 200 W, FMTN, 84025	1448	C2
Farrer Middle School 100 N 600 E, PRVO, 84606	2928	D6
Farr West Elementary School 2190 W 2700 N, FRWT, 84404	997	C6
Foothill Elementary School 820 N 100 E, BMCY, 84302	766	E3
Foothill Elementary School 921 N 1240 E, OREM, 84097	2821	B3
Foothills Elementary School 13717 Shaggy Peak Dr, RIVN, 84065	2386	A5
Forbes Elementary School 281 N 200 E, ANFK, 84003	2604	D7
Fox Hills North Elementary School 3775 Vixen Wy, TYVL, 84118	2068	D6
Franklin Elementary School 350 S 600 W, PRVO, 84601	2928	B7
Franklin Elementary School 1115 W 300 S, SLCY, 84104	1857	E4
Freedom Elementary School N 6800 W, HILD, 84003	2604	A2
Freedom Elementary School 4600 W 5500 S, HOPR, 84315	1170	C4
Freemont Elementary School 2525 N 160 W, SNST, 84015	1171	D6
Fremont High School 1900 N 4700 W, PNCY, 84404	1054	B1
Garfield Alternative School 1838 S 1500 E, SLCY, 84105	1965	C1
Garland Elementary School 250 N Main St, GRLD, 84312	520	E1
Geneva Elementary School 665 W 400 N, OREM, 84057	2820	B4
Glendale Intermediate School 1430 Andrew Av, SLCY, 84104	1857	D7
Grace Lutheran School 1815 E 9800 S, SLkC, 84092	2283	D2
Gramercy Elementary School 1270 N Gramercy Av, OGDN, 84404	1057	A2
Grandview Elementary School 960 39th St, OGDN, 84403	1116	B7
Grandview Elementary School 1591 Jordan Av, PRVO, 84604	2928	A4
Granger Elementary School 2450 W 3800 S, WVCY, 84119	1963	B7
Granger High School 3690 S 3600 W, WVCY, 84120	1962	D6
Granite Elementary School 9760 S 3100 E, SLkC, 84092	2284	B2
Granite High School 3305 Farmer Wy, SSLK, 84106	1964	E5
Granite Park Junior High School 450 E 3700 S, SSLK, 84115	1964	E7
Granite Park Middle School 3031 S 200 E, SSLK, 84115	1964	D5
Grant Elementary School 105 S 400 E, SGVL, 84663	3143	D2
Grant School 662 Bulldog Cir, MRRY, 84123	2070	A7
Green Acres Elementary School 640 E 1900 N, NHON, 84414	999	A7
Greenville Elementary School 2450 N 400 E, NHLN, 84341	463	E4
Greenwood Elementary School 50 E 200 S, ANFK, 84003	2711	C1
Grovecrest Elementary School 200 E 1100 N, PTGV, 84062	2712	E1
Guadalupe Elementary School 340 Goshen St, SLCY, 84104	1857	E4
Harris Intermediate School 515 N 800 W, TMTN, 84337	520	D5
Harry S Truman Elementary School 4639 S 3200 W, WVCY, 84119	2068	E3
Hartvigsen School 350 Baird Cir, SSLK, 84115	1964	D6
Hawthorne Academy 1323 W 7900 S, WJDN, 84088	2175	D4
Hawthorne Elementary School 1675 S 600 E, SLCY, 84105	1964	E1
Hayden Peak Elementary School 5120 Hayden Peak Dr, WJDN, 84088	2174	A4
Heartland Elementary School 1451 W 7000 S, WJDN, 84084	2175	D2
Heber Valley Elementary School 730 S 600 W, HRCY, 84032	2398	C5
Helquist Academy 651 E Antelope Dr, LYTN, 84041	1283	B1
Heritage Elementary School 1354 Weaver Ln, LYTN, 84041	1282	C7
Heritage Foundation School 236 E 800 S, BMCY, 84302	828	A1
Herriman Elementary School 13170 S Pioneer St, HRMN, 84065	2385	C3
H Guy Child Elementary School 655 E 5500 S, SOGN, 84405	1173	A4
Highland Elementary School 10865 N 6000 W, HILD, 84003	2604	C1
Highland High School 2166 Ram Blvd, SLCY, 84106	1965	C2
Highland Middle School 325 Gramercy Av, OGDN, 84404	1057	A5
Highland Park Elementary School 1738 E 2700 S, SLCY, 84106	1965	D4
Hillcrest Elementary School 651 E 1400 S, KYVL, 84037	1345	E4
Hillcrest Elementary School 960 N 1400 E, LOGN, 84321	528	C1
Hillcrest Elementary School 130 N Eccles Av, OGDN, 84404	1057	B5
Hillcrest High School 7350 S 900 E, MDVL, 84047	2177	A3
Hillcrest Junior High School 126 E 5300 S, MRRY, 84107	2070	D4
Hill Feld Elementary School 389 S 1000 E, CRFD, 84015	1228	A5
Hillsdale Elementary School 3275 W 3100 S, WVCY, 84119	1962	E5
Hillside Elementary School 4283 S 6000 W, WVCY, 84128	2067	C1
Hillside High School 243 E 2320 N, PRVO, 84604	2928	C2
Hillside Intermediate School 2375 Garfield Av, SLCY, 84108	1965	E1
Hill View Elementary School 4405 S 1025 E, SLkC, 84124	2071	A2
Hobble Creek Elementary School 1145 E 1200 N, MPTN, 84664	3144	C5
Holbrook Elementary School 1018 E 250 N, BNFL, 84010	1552	A7
Holt Elementary School 448 N 1000 W, CRFD, 84015	1227	B3
Hooper Elementary School 5500 S 5900 W, HOPR, 84315	1169	D4
Horace Mann Elementary School 1300 9th St, OGDN, 84404	1057	C7
Horizon Elementary School 5180 Glendon St, MRRY, 84123	2070	A4
Horizon Elementary School 1220 23rd St, OGDN, 84401	1116	B3
Horizonte High School 1234 S Main St, SLCY, 84101	1858	C6
Howard R Driggs Elementary School 4340 S 2700 E, HLDY, 84124	2072	A1
Hunter Elementary School 4351 S 5400 W, WVCY, 84120	2067	E2
Hunter High School 4200 S 5600 W, WVCY, 84128	2067	D1
Hunter Junior High School 6131 Wending Ln, WVCY, 84128	1961	C7
Independence High School 636 Independence Av, PRVO, 84601	2927	E5
Indian Hills Elementary School 2291 S 2000 E, SLCY, 84106	1965	D2
Indian Hills Elementary School 2496 St. Marys Dr, SLCY, 84108	1860	A7
Indian Hills Middle School 1180 Sanders Rd, SNDY, 84094	2283	B6
Intermountain Christian School 6515 Lion Ln, HLDY, 84121	2178	B1
IQRA Academy of Utah 2887 Fort Union Blvd, CDHT, 84121	2178	B2
Ivy Hall Academy 1598 W 820 N, PRVO, 84604	2927	E5
Jacking Elementary School 3760 Atlas Wy, WVCY, 84120	1962	B7
Jackson Elementary School 750 W 200 N, SLCY, 84116	1858	A2
James E Moss Elementary School 4399 S 500 E, SLkC, 84107	2070	E2
Jean Massieu School 209 E 500 S, SLCY, 84111	1858	D4
Je Cosgriff Memorial School 2335 Redondo Av, SLCY, 84108	1965	E2
Jeremy Ranch Elementary School 5060 Rasmussen Rd, SmtC, 84098	1865	B5
Jim Bridger Elementary School 5368 Cyclamen Wy, WJDN, 84084	2067	E7
Joaquin Elementary School 550 N 600 E, PRVO, 84606	2928	D6
Joel P Jensen Middle School 8105 S 3200 W, WJDN, 84088	2174	E4
John C Fremont Elementary School 4249 Atherton Dr, TYVL, 84123	2069	D1
John F Kennedy Junior High School 4495 S 4800 W, WVCY, 84120	2068	A2
John Hancock Charter School 125 N 100 E, PTGV, 84062	2712	D2
Jordan High School 95 Beetdigger Blvd, SNDY, 84070	2282	D2
Jordan Hills Elementary School 8892 S 4800 W, WJDN, 84088	2174	A7
Jordan Ridge Elementary School 2636 W 9800 S, SJDN, 84095	2281	A2
Jordon Valley School for Handicapped 7501 S 1000 E, MDVL, 84047	2177	A3
Joy School 1025 N 600 E, LOGN, 84341	464	A7
JR Smith Elementary School 235 E 500 N, HRCY, 84032	2398	D3
Juan Diego Catholic High School 300 E 11800 S, DRPR, 84020	2282	D7
Judge Memorial Catholic High School 650 S 1100 E, SLCY, 84102	1859	B5
Kanesville Elementary School 3112 S 3500 W, WbrC, 84401	1113	E5
Kaysville Elementary School 50 N 100 E, KYVL, 84037	1345	D1

Salt Lake City Points of Interest Index

FEATURE NAME Address City ZIP Code	MAP#	GRID
Kaysville Junior High School 100 Davis Blvd, KYVL, 84037	1345	D2
Kearns High School 5525 Cougar Ln, SLkC, 84118	2068	A5
Kearns Junior High School 4040 Sam's Blvd, SLkC, 84118	2068	C4
Kearns St. Ann School 430 E 2100 S, SSLK, 84115	1964	E2
Kensington Middle School 25 Kensington Av, SLCY, 84115	1858	C7
Knowlton Elementary School 801 Shepard Ln, FMTN, 84025	1346	B6
Lake Ridge Elementary School 7400 Gardenia Av, SLkC, 84044	1960	E5
Lakeridge Junior High School 951 S 400 W, OREM, 84058	2820	C7
Lakeside Elementary School 2941 Doxey Rd, WPT, 84015	1226	C3
Lake View Elementary School 851 S 200 W, BMCY, 84302	827	E1
Lakeview Elementary School 2025 W 4975 S, ROY, 84067	1171	D3
Landmark High School 320 S Main St, SPFK, 84660	3249	C3
Larsen Elementary School 1175 Flonnette Ln, SPFK, 84660	3250	A3
Layton Elementary School 369 W Gentile St, LYTN, 84041	1282	E5
Layton High School 440 N Wasatch Dr, LYTN, 84041	1283	A4
Legacy Elementary School 28 E 1340 N, ANFK, 84003	2604	C4
Lehi Elementary School 765 N Center St, LEHI, 84043	2603	C5
Lehi High School 180 N 500 E, LEHI, 84043	2603	D6
Lehi Junior High School 700 Cedar Hollow Rd, LEHI, 84043	2603	D4
Lewis Elementary School 455 28th St, OGDN, 84401	1115	E4
Liberty Elementary School 140 W 6100 S, MRRY, 84107	2070	C7
Lincoln Elementary School 90 S Center St, HYRM, 84319	651	B3
Lincoln Elementary School 591 W Antelope Dr, LYTN, 84041	1282	D1
Lincoln Elementary School 1235 Canfield Dr, OGDN, 84404	1057	B2
Lincoln Elementary School 1090 Roberta St, SLCY, 84111	1858	D6
Lincoln Elementary School 450 E 3700 S, SSLK, 84115	1964	E7
Lindon Elementary School 30 N Main St, LNDN, 84042	2713	B6
Logan District South Campus 325 W 400 S, LOGN, 84321	527	C4
Logan High School 162 W 100 S, LOGN, 84321	527	D3
Lomond View Elementary School 3644 N 900 W, PTVW, 84414	998	B3
Lone Peak Elementary School 11515 High Mesa Dr, SNDY, 84092	2283	E6
Lone Peak High School 10189 N 48th W, HILD, 84003	2605	A2
Longview Elementary School 6240 Longview Dr, MRRY, 84107	2070	E7
Lowell Elementary School 134 D St, SLCY, 84103	1858	E2
Lynn Elementary School 605 Grant Av, OGDN, 84404	1056	E6
Magna Elementary School 8500 W 3100 S, SLkC, 84044	1960	B5
Majestic Elementary School 425 W 2550 N, HARR, 84414	998	C6
Majestic Elementary School 7430 Redwood Rd, WJDN, 84084	2175	C3
Manila Elementary School 1726 N 600 W, PTGV, 84062	2605	C7
Mapleton Elementary School 120 W Maple St, MPTN, 84664	3144	A7
Mar-Lon Hills Elementary School 4400 Madison Av, SOGN, 84403	1173	A2
McMillan Elementary School 315 E 5900 S, MRRY, 84107	2070	D6
McPolin Elementary School 2270 Kearns Blvd, PKCY, 84060	2078	E3
Meadowbrook Elementary School 700 N 325 W, BNFL, 84010	1551	D6
Meadowlark Elementary School 497 N Morton Dr, SLCY, 84116	1857	C1
Meadow Moor Elementary School 1700 E 5315 S, SLkC, 84117	2071	C5
Meadows Elementary School 176 S 500 W, LEHI, 84043	2603	B7
Meridian School 931 E 300 N, PRVO, 84606	2928	E6
Midland Elementary School 3100 W 4800 S, ROY, 84067	1171	A3
Midvale Elementary School 362 W Center St, MDVL, 84047	2176	B4
Midvale Middle School 7852 Pioneer St, MDVL, 84047	2176	B4
Midvalley Elementary School 217 E 7800 S, MDVL, 84047	2176	D4
Midway Elementary School 225 S 100 E, HRCY, 84032	2398	D4
Mill Creek Elementary School 3761 S 1100 E, SLkC, 84106	1965	B7
Millcreek Junior High School 245 E 1000 S, BNFL, 84010	1653	E2
M Lynn Bennion Elementary School 429 S 800 E, SLCY, 84102	1859	A4
Monroe Elementary School 4450 W 3100 S, WVCY, 84120	1962	B5
Montessori School Salt Lake 2806 E 3300 S, SLkC, 84109	1966	B5
Monte Vista Elementary School 11121 S 2700 W, SJDN, 84095	2281	A5
Morgan Elementary School 1065 Thornfield Rd, KYVL, 84037	1283	E6
Morningside Elementary School 4170 Bevwood Cir, SLkC, 84124	2072	B1
Morningside School 220 N 100 E, LOGN, 84321	527	D2
Mound Fort Middle School 1440 Mound Fort Dr, OGDN, 84404	1116	A1
Mountain Crest High School HYRM, 84319	651	D3
Mountain High School 490 S 500 E, KYVL, 84037	1345	D2
Mountain Ridge Junior High School 5525 W 10400 N, HILD, 84003	2604	D2
Mountain Shadows Elementary School 5255 W 7000 S, WJDN, 84084	2173	E2
Mountain View Elementary School 650 E 700 S, BMCY, 84302	828	A1
Mountainview Elementary School 1651 Fort Union Blvd, CDHT, 84121	2177	C2
Mountain View Elementary School 2025 E 3100 N, DvsC, 84040	1229	D6
Mountain View Elementary School 170 15th St, OGDN, 84404	1115	D1
Mountain View Elementary School 1380 Navajo St, SLCY, 84104	1857	D7
Mountain View High School 665 W Center St, OREM, 84058	2820	B5
Mount Jordan Middle School 9360 S 300 E, SNDY, 84070	2282	D1
Mount Loafer Elementary School 1025 S Loafer Canyon Rd, SALM, 84653	3356	A5
Mount Logan Middle School 875 N 200 E, LOGN, 84321	527	D1
Mount Mahogany Elementary School 618 N 1300 W, PTGV, 84062	2712	B2
Mount Ogden Middle School 3260 Harrison Blvd, OGDN, 84403	1116	B6
Mount Vernon Academy 184 E Vine St, MRRY, 84107	2070	D3
Mueller Park Junior High School 955 E 1800 S, BNFL, 84010	1654	A3
Muir Elementary School 2275 S Davis Blvd, BNFL, 84010	1653	E4
Municipal Elementary School 5775 S 2200 W, ROY, 84067	1171	C5
Murray High School 5440 S State St, MRRY, 84107	2070	D5
Newman Elementary School 1269 Colorado St, SLCY, 84116	1753	D6
Nibley County School 2545 S 660 W, NBLY, 84321	591	B2
Nibley Elementary School 2545 S 660 W, NBLY, 84321	591	B2
Nibley Park Elementary School 2785 S 800 E, SLCY, 84106	1965	A4
North Campus Alternative School 83 S 100 W, LOGN, 84321	527	D3
North Davis Junior High School 835 State St, CRFD, 84015	1228	A6
North Davis Preparatory Acad 1765 N Hill Field Rd, LYTN, 84041	1282	E1
Northern Utah Academy Charter School 1815 W 4000 S, ROY, 84067	1171	E1
North Layton Junior High School 1100 W Antelope Dr, LYTN, 84041	1282	C1
North Ogden Elementary School 474 E 2650 N, NHON, 84414	998	E5
North Ogden Junior High 575 E 2900 N, NHON, 84414	999	A5
North Park Elementary School 2800 N 800 E, NHLN, 84341	464	A3
North Pike School 4230 S 2175 W, ROY, 84067	1171	D1
Northridge Elementary School 1660 N 50 E, OREM, 84057	2820	D1
Northridge High School 2430 N Hill Field Rd, LYTN, 84041	1228	E7
North Star Elementary School 1545 Morton Rd, SLCY, 84116	1753	B5
Northwest Intermediate School 1400 Goodwin Av, SLCY, 84116	1753	D6
Oak Canyon Junior High School 111 S 725 E, LNDN, 84042	2713	D6
Oakcrest Elementary School 8462 Hilltop Oak Dr, WJDN, 84088	2173	B5
Oakdale Elementary School 1900 Creek Rd, SLkC, 84093	2177	D4
Oak Hills Elementary School E 600 S, BNFL, 84010	1653	E1
Oak Hollow Elementary School 884 Vestry Rd, DRPR, 84020	2389	A6
Oakridge Elementary School 4325 Jupiter Dr, SLkC, 84124	2072	D1
Oakwood Elementary School 5815 Highland Dr, HLDY, 84121	2071	D6
Odyssey Academy 607 E 200 S, SLCY, 84102	1858	E3
Ogden Deamude SDA School 1765 Wilson Ln, WHVN, 84401	1114	E2
Ogden High School 2828 Harrison Blvd, OGDN, 84403	1116	B4
Ogden Preparatory Chtr Academy 2221 Grant Av, OGDN, 84401	1115	E3
Olympus High School HLDY, 84124	2071	E1
Olympus Junior High School 2217 Murray-Holladay Rd, HLDY, 84117	2071	E3
Oquirrh Elementary School 7165 Paddington Rd, WJDN, 84084	2174	E2
Oquirrh Hills Elementary School 5241 Steele St, SLkC, 84118	2068	C4
Oquirrh Hills Middle School 12949 Silver Wolf Wy, RIVN, 84065	2387	A3
Orchard Elementary School 205 E Center St, NSLK, 84054	1653	B7
Orchard Elementary School 1035 N 800 E, OREM, 84097	2821	A2
Orem Elementary School 450 W 400 S, OREM, 84058	2820	C6
Orem High School 175 E 400 S, OREM, 84058	2820	D6
Orem Junior High School 765 N 600 W, OREM, 84057	2820	B3
Orion Junior High School 270 W 2000 N, WbrC, 84414	998	D7
Our Lady of Lords Elementary 1065 E 700 S, SLCY, 84102	1859	B5
Park City Academy 3120 Pinebrook Rd, SmtC, 84098	1865	B6
Park City High School 1750 Kearns Blvd, PKCY, 84060	2078	E3
Park City Winter School 3000 Bear Hollow Dr, SmtC, 84098	1971	C5
Park Elementary School 90 N 600 E, SPFK, 84660	3249	E3
Park Lane Elementary School 9955 Eastdell Dr, SNDY, 84092	2283	E4
Parkside Elementary School 5175 Parkside Dr, MRRY, 84107	2070	E4
Parkview Elementary School 360 S 100 E, PYSN, 84651	3354	E5
Parkview Elementary School 970 Emery St, SLCY, 84104	1857	E6
Parley's Park Elementary School 4600 Silver Springs Dr, SmtC, 84098	1971	E6
Payson High School 1050 S Main St, PYSN, 84651	3354	E7
Payson Junior High School 1025 State Rd, PYSN, 84651	3354	E6
Payson Middle School 851 W 450 S, PYSN, 84651	3354	D6
Perry Elementary School 2515 Park Dr, PRRY, 84302	827	C5
Peruvian Park Elementary School 1545 E 8425 S, SNDY, 84093	2177	C5
Philo T Farnsworth Elementary School 3751 Sunnyvale Dr, WVCY, 84120	1962	C7
Pioneer Elementary School 250 N 1600 W, MTSV, 84404	1055	E4
Pioneer Elementary School 3860 Bonniewood Dr, WVCY, 84119	1962	E7
Plain City Elementary School 4394 W 2425 N, PNCY, 84404	996	C6
Pleasant Green Elementary School 8201 W 2700 S, SLkC, 84044	1960	C4
Pleasant Grove High School 700 E 200 S, PTGV, 84062	2713	A3
Pleasant Grove Junior School 810 N 100 E, PTGV, 84062	2712	D1
Plymouth Elementary School 5220 Canal St, TYVL, 84123	2069	D4
Polk Elementary School 2615 Polk Av, OGDN, 84401	1116	C4
Providence Elementary School 91 E Center St, PVDN, 84332	528	A6
Provo Canyon School 1350 E 750 N, OREM, 84097	2821	B3
Provo Canyon School-Boys Campus 4501 N University Av, PRVO, 84604	2821	C5
Provo High School 1125 N University Av, PRVO, 84604	2928	C4
Provo Seventh Day Adventist School 255 S 700 E, PRVO, 84606	2928	D7
Provost Elementary School 629 S 900 E, PRVO, 84606	3035	E1
Quail Hollow Elementary School 2625 Newcastle Dr, SNDY, 84093	2178	A7
Rainbow Academy 336 W 1060 S, OREM, 84058	2820	C7
Reading Elementary School 360 W 2025 N, CTRV, 84014	1448	D6
Redeemer Lutheran School 1955 E Stratford Av, SLCY, 84106	1965	D3
Redwood Elementary School 2650 S Redwood Rd, WVCY, 84119	1963	C3
Rees Elementary School 574 N Rees Av, SPFK, 84663	3250	A2
Ridgecrest Elementary School 1800 E 7200 S, CDHT, 84121	2177	D2
Riley Elementary School 1431 S 900 W, SLCY, 84104	1858	A7
Riverdale Elementary School 1160 W 4400 S, RVDL, 84405	1172	A2
River Heights Elementary School 780 E 600 S, RVHT, 84321	528	A4
Riverside Elementary School 8737 S 1220 W, WJDN, 84088	2175	E6
Riverside School 650 S 1000 W, LOGN, 84321	527	A5
Riverton Elementary School 13150 S 1830 W, RIVN, 84065	2387	C3
Riverton High School 12476 Silver Wolf Wy, RIVN, 84065	2387	A2
Riverview Junior High School 751 Tripp Ln, MRRY, 84123	2070	A6
Robert Frost Elementary School 3444 W 4400 S, WVCY, 84119	2068	E2
Rock Canyon Elementary School 2405 Timpview Dr, PRVO, 84604	2928	D2
Rocky Mountain Elementary School 55 S 500 E, LNDN, 84042	2713	C6
Rocky Mountain Junior High School 4350 Grizzly Wy, WHVN, 84315	1170	C3
Rolling Meadows Elementary School 2950 Whitehall Dr, WVCY, 84119	1963	A7
Roosevelt Elementary School 3225 S 800 E, SLkC, 84106	1965	A5
Roosevelt Elementary School 190 W 5100 S, WSTR, 84405	1172	D3
Rosamond Elementary School 12195 S 1975 W, RIVN, 84065	2387	C1
Rose Creek Elementary School 12812 S 3600 W, RIVN, 84065	2386	D2
Rosecrest Elementary School 2420 Fisher Ln, SLkC, 84109	1966	A4
Rose Park Elementary School 1105 W 1000 N, SLCY, 84116	1753	E7
Rowland Hall-St. Mark's School 720 Guardsman Wy, SLCY, 84102	1859	C5
Roy Elementary School 2888 W 5600 S, ROY, 84067	1171	B5
Roy High School 2150 W 4800 S, ROY, 84067	1171	C3
Roy Junior High School 2100 W 5400 S, ROY, 84067	1171	C4
Sage Creek Elementary School 1050 S 700 E, SGVL, 84663	3143	D4
St. Francis Xavier School 4501 W 5215 S, SLkC, 84118	2068	B4
St. John The Baptist Elementary School 300 E 11800 S, DRPR, 84020	2282	D7
St. John The Baptist Middle School 300 E 11800 S, DRPR, 84020	2282	D7
St. Joseph Catholic Elementary School 2980 Quincy Av, OGDN, 84403	1116	A5
St. Joseph High School 1790 Lake St, OGDN, 84401	1116	D4
St. Olaf School 1793 Orchard Dr, BNFL, 84010	1653	E3
St. Paul Lutheran School 3329 Harrison Blvd, OGDN, 84403	1116	B6
St. Sophia School 5335 Highland Dr, HLDY, 84117	2071	D5
St. Vincent School 1385 Spring Ln, SLkC, 84117	2071	B4
Salem Elementary School 140 W 100 S, SALM, 84653	3356	A3
Salt Lake Arts Academy 261 S 900 E, SLCY, 84102	1859	A4
Salt Lake Junior Academy 965 E 3370 S, SLkC, 84106	1965	A5
Salt Lake Lutheran High School 4020 S 900 E, SLkC, 84124	2071	A1
Sand Ridge Junior High School 2075 W 4600 S, ROY, 84067	1171	D2
Sand Springs Elementary School 242 N 3200 W, LYTN, 84041	1281	D4
Sandy Elementary School 8725 S 280 E, SNDY, 84070	2176	D6
Scera Park Elementary School 450 S 400 E, OREM, 84058	2820	E6
Scott Matheson Junior High School 3650 Montclair St, SLkC, 84044	1960	D6
Sego Lily Elementary School 550 E 900 N, LEHI, 84043	2603	D5
Sharon Elementary School 525 N 400 E, OREM, 84057	2820	E3
Shelley Elementary School 602 N 200 W, ANFK, 84003	2604	C6
Silver Hills Elementary School 5100 S 5700 W, WVCY, 84118	2067	D4
Silver Mesa Elementary School 8920 S 1700 E, SNDY, 84093	2177	C7
Skyline High School 3251 Upland Dr, SLkC, 84109	1966	C7
Sky View High School 520 S 250 E, SHFD, 84335	399	E4
Slate Canyon School 1991 S State St, PRVO, 84606	3036	A3
Snow Crest Junior High School WbrC, 84310	1001	D5

Salt Lake City Points of Interest Index

Schools

FEATURE NAME Address City ZIP Code	MAP#	GRID
Soaring Wings Montessori School 1255 Park Av, PKCY, 84060	2078	D5
South Clarfield Elementary School 990 Bernard Fisher Hwy, CRFD, 84015	1228	A6
South Davis Junior High School 298 W 2600 S, BNFL, 84010	1653	D4
South Hills Middle School 13508 S 4000 W, RIVN, 84065	2386	C4
South Jordan Elementary School 11205 S Black Cherry Wy, SJDN, 84095	2281	D5
South Jordan Middle School 10245 S 2700 W, SJDN, 84095	2281	A3
South Kearns Elementary School 4430 W 5570 S, SLkC, 84118	2068	B5
Southland Elementary School 12675 Silver Wolf Wy, RIVN, 84065	2387	A2
South Ogden Junior High School 4300 Madison Av, SOGN, 84403	1173	A2
Southpointe High School 825 E 9085 S, SNDY, 84094	2177	A7
South Weber Elementary School 1285 Lester Dr, SWBR, 84405	1229	B2
Spanish Fork Community School 99 N 300 W, SPFK, 84660	3249	C2
Spanish Fork Junior High School 600 S 820 E, SPFK, 84660	3249	E4
Spanish Fork Middle School 50 N 900 E, SPFK, 84660	3249	E3
Spanish Fork Senior High School 99 N 300 W, SPFK, 84660	3249	C2
Spanish Oaks Elementary School 2701 E Canyon Crest Dr, SPFK, 84660	3250	C6
Spring Creek Elementary School 1740 Nevada Av, PRVO, 84606	3036	A3
Spring Creek Middle School 350 W 100 N, PVDN, 84332	527	E6
Spring Lake Elementary School 1750 S 500 W, PYSN, 84651	3461	D2
Springville High School 1205 E 900 S, SGVL, 84663	3143	E3
Springville Junior High School 165 S 700 E, SGVL, 84663	3143	D2
Springville Middle School 484 S 200 E, SGVL, 84663	3143	C3
Sprucewood Elementary School 12025 S 1000 E, SNDY, 84094	2283	A7
Stansbury Elementary School 3050 Constitution Blvd, WVCY, 84119	1963	A5
Stewart Elementary School 1155 N Main St, CTRV, 84014	1551	D1
Success Charter School 4122 Carriage Sq, TYVL, 84119	2069	C1
Summit Academy Charter School 1285 E 13200 S, DRPR, 84020	2389	B3
Summit Elementary School 80 W Center St, SHFD, 84335	399	D3
Suncrest Elementary School 668 W 150 N, OREM, 84057	2820	B4
Sunrise Elementary School 225 S 455 E, SHFD, 84335	399	E3
Sunrise Elementary School 1520 E 11265 S, SNDY, 84092	2283	C5
Sunset Elementary School 2014 N 250 W, SNST, 84015	1171	D7
Sunset Junior High School 1610 N 250 W, SNST, 84015	1227	D1
Sunset View Elementary School 525 S 1600 W, PRVO, 84601	3034	E1
Syracuse Elementary School 1503 S 2000 W, SRCS, 84075	1226	E7
Syracuse Junior High School 1450 S 2000 W, SRCS, 84075	1226	E7
Taylor Elementary School 293 E Pages Ln, CTRV, 84014	1551	E5
Taylor Elementary School 40 S 500 W, PYSN, 84651	3354	D5
Taylorsville Elementary School 2010 Mantle Av, TYVL, 84119	2069	C1
Taylorsville High School 5225 S Redwood Rd, TYVL, 84123	2069	C4
Terra Linda Elementary School 8400 Old Bingham Hwy, WJDN, 84088	2174	E5
TH Bell Junior High School 165 W 5100 S, WSTR, 84405	1172	D3
The McGillis School 668 S 1300 E, SLCY, 84102	1859	B5
Thomas Edison Charter School 180 E 2600 N, NHLN, 84341	463	D3
Thomas Jefferson Junior High School 5850 S 5600 W, SLkC, 84118	2067	D6
Thomas O Smith Elementary School 3295 Gramercy Av, OGDN, 84403	1116	A6
Thomas W Bacchus School 5925 Copper City Dr, SLkC, 84118	2067	C6
Timberline Middle School 500 W Canyon Crest Dr, ALPN, 84004	2497	D5
Timpanogos Elementary School 449 N 500 W, PRVO, 84601	2928	B6
Timpganogos Academy 55 S 100 E, LNDN, 84042	2713	B6
Timpview High School 3570 Timpview Dr, PRVO, 84604	2821	D7
Tolman Elementary School 300 E 1200 N, BNFL, 84010	1551	E6
Trailside Elementary School 5700 Trailside Dr, SmtC, 84098	1972	D3
Treasure Mountain Middle School 2530 Kearns Blvd, PKCY, 84060	2079	A2
Twin Peaks Elementary School 5325 Revere Dr, MRRY, 84117	2071	A5
Uintah Elementary School 1571 E 1300 S, SLCY, 84105	1859	C7
Uintah Elementary School 6115 S 2225 E, WbrC, 84403	1173	E6
Union Middle School 615 E 8000 S, SNDY, 84070	2176	E4
Upland Terrace Elementary School 3700 Sunnydale Dr, SLkC, 84109	1966	B7
Utah School for Deaf Scera Park 450 S 400 E, OREM, 84058	2820	E6
Vae View Elementary School 1750 W 1600 N, LYTN, 84041	1282	B1
Valley Christian School 3818 W 4700 S, WVCY, 84120	2068	D3
Valley Crest Elementary School 5240 W 3100 S, WVCY, 84120	1961	E5
Valley Elementary School 7436 E 200 S, HTVL, 84317	1061	A5
Valley High School 11020 State St, SNDY, 84070	2282	C5
Valley Junior High School 4195 S 3200 W, WVCY, 84119	2068	E1
Valley View Elementary School 1395 S 600 E, BNFL, 84010	1654	A2
Valley View Elementary School 941 Orchard Dr, PTGV, 84062	2713	A3
Valley View Elementary School 2465 W 4500 S, ROY, 84067	1171	C2
Valley View School 130 S Main St, LOGN, 84321	527	D3
Viewmont High School 120 W 100 N, BNFL, 84010	1551	D7
Viewmont School 745 Anderson Av, MRRY, 84123	2070	A6
Vineyard Elementary School 950 W 800 S, OREM, 84058	2820	B7
Vista Elementary School 4925 S 2200 W, TYVL, 84118	2069	B3
Wahlquist Junior High School 1033 N 1200 W, FRWT, 84404	1056	A3
Wasatch Alternative School 301 S Main St, HRCY, 84032	2398	D4
Wasatch County High School 64 E 600 S, HRCY, 84032	2398	D5
Wasatch Elementary School 270 E Center St, CRFD, 84015	1227	E4
Wasatch Elementary School 3370 Polk Av, OGDN, 84403	1116	C6
Wasatch Elementary School 1080 N 900 E, PRVO, 84604	2928	E5
Wasatch Elementary School 30 R St, SLCY, 84103	1859	B3
Wasatch Junior High School 3750 S 3100 E, SLkC, 84109	1966	B7
Wasatch Mountain Jr High School 200 E 800 S, HRCY, 84032	2398	D5
Washington Elementary School 340 W 650 S, BNFL, 84010	1653	D1
Washington Elementary School 420 N 200 W, SLCY, 84103	1858	C1
Washington High School 956 20th St, OGDN, 84401	1116	B2
Washington Ter Elementary School 20 E 4600 S, WSTR, 84405	1172	D2
Waterford School 1480 E 9400 S, SNDY, 84092	2283	C1
Weber High School 430 Weber High Dr, PTVW, 84414	998	C4
Welby Elementary School 4130 W 9580 S, SJDN, 84095	2280	C1
Wellsville Elementary School 90 E 100 S, WELV, 84339	649	D2
West Bountiful Elementary School 750 W 400 N, WBNF, 84087	1551	B6
Westbrook Elementary School 3451 Bennion Blvd, TYVL, 84084	2068	E7
West Clinton Elementary School 2826 Clinton Rd, CLTN, 84015	1226	C1
Western Hills Elementary School 5190 Heath Av, SLkC, 84118	2068	A4
Westfield Elementary School 380 Long Dr, ALPN, 84004	2497	D5
West Haven Elementary School 4385 S 3900 W, WHVN, 84315	1170	D1
West High School 241 N 300 W, SLCY, 84103	1858	B2
West Hills Middle School 8270 Grizzly Wy, WJDN, 84088	2173	E5
West Jordan Elementary School 7220 S 2370 W, WJDN, 84084	2175	B2
West Jordan High School 8136 Jaguar Dr, WJDN, 84088	2175	A5
West Jordan Middle School 7550 Redwood Rd, WJDN, 84084	2175	C3
West Kearns Elementary School 4900 S 4620 W, SLkC, 84118	2068	B3
West Lake Junior High School 3400 S 3450 W, WVCY, 84119	1962	E5
Westland Elementary School 2925 W 7180 S, WJDN, 84084	2175	A2
Westmore Elementary School 1150 S Main St, OREM, 84058	2927	D1
West Point Elementary School 3788 West Point Rd, WPT, 84015	1226	B4
West Point Junior High School 2775 W 550 N, WPT, 84015	1226	C3
Westridge Elementary School 1720 W 1460 N, PRVO, 84604	2927	E4
Westside Elementary School 740 W Center St, SGVL, 84663	3143	B2
Westvale Elementary School 2300 Gardner Ln, WJDN, 84088	2175	B6
West Valley Elementary School 6049 Brud Dr, WVCY, 84128	1961	C5
West Weber Elementary School 4178 W 900 S, WbrC, 84404	1054	D6
Whitesides Elementary School 233 Colonial Av, LYTN, 84041	1283	B4
Whittier Elementary School 1568 S 300 E, SLCY, 84115	1858	D7
Whittier Elementary School 3585 S 6000 W, WVCY, 84128	1961	C6
Willard Elementary School 40 S Center St, WLRD, 84340	885	C6
William Penn Elementary School 1670 Siggard Dr, SLkC, 84106	1965	C6
Willow Canyon Elementary School 9650 S 1700 E, SNDY, 84092	2283	C1
Willowcreek Middle School 2275 W 8800 N, LEHI, 84043	2602	D6
Willow Valley Middle School 525 N 200 W, WELV, 84339	589	C7
Wilson Elementary School 89 S 500 E, LOGN, 84321	527	E3
Wilson Elementary School 590 W 500 S, PYSN, 84651	3354	D6
Windridge Elementary School 1300 Kadie Ln, KYVL, 84037	1345	E4
Wind River School 470 W 1000 N, OREM, 84057	2820	C2
Windsor Elementary School 1315 N Main St, OREM, 84057	2820	D1
Woodland Hills School 5858 S 900 E, MRRY, 84107	2071	A6
Woodrow Wilson Elementary School 2825 S 200 E, SSLK, 84115	1964	D4
Woodruff Elementary School 650 S 1000 W, LOGN, 84321	527	A5
Woods Cross Elementary School 745 W 1100 S, WDCR, 84087	1653	B2
Woods Cross High School 600 W Porters Ln, WBNF, 84087	1551	C4
Woodstock Elementary School 6015 S 1300 E, MRRY, 84121	2071	B6

Shopping Centers

FEATURE NAME Address City ZIP Code	MAP#	GRID
Brickyard Plaza Brickyard Rd, SLCY, 84106	1965	B5
Cache Valley Mall 1300 N Main St, LOGN, 84341	463	D7
Cottonwood Mall 4835 Highland Dr, HLDY, 84117	2071	D3
Crossroads Plaza 50 S Main St, SLCY, 84101	1858	C3
Fashion Place Mall 6191 S State St, MRRY, 84107	2070	D7
Jordan Landing Shopping Center Bangerter Hwy, WJDN, 84084	2174	D2
Layton Hills Mall 1200 N Hill Field Rd, LYTN, 84041	1282	D2
Newgate Mall 3651 Wall Av, OGDN, 84405	1115	D7
Provo Towne Center 1200 Towne Centre Blvd, PRVO, 84601	3035	B2
South Towne Center 10450 State St, SNDY, 84070	2282	C3
The Family Center at Fort Union Fort Union Blvd, CDHT, 84121	2177	B1
The Family Center at Midvalley S Redwood Rd, TYVL, 84118	2069	C5
The Family Center at Riverdale W Riverdale Rd, RVDL, 84405	1172	A2
The Gateway 400 W 100 S, SLCY, 84101	1858	B3
Trolley Square 602 E 500 S, SLCY, 84102	1858	E4
University Mall 1199 S State St, OREM, 84097	2927	E1
Valley Fair Mall Constitution Blvd, WVCY, 84119	1963	A6
ZCMI Center Mall 36 S State St, SLCY, 84111	1858	C3

Subdivisions & Neighborhoods

FEATURE NAME	MAP#	GRID
Arsenal, SNST	1227	E1
Atwood, MRRY	2176	C1
Becks, SLCY	1753	E3
Belmont Heights, SLkC	2177	B6
Bennion, TYVL	2069	C7
Buena Vista, SLCY	1856	E4
Crescent, SNDY	2282	C5
East Bay, PRVO	3035	D1
Eastwood Hills, SLkC	1966	D6
Evona, OGDN	1115	B3
Foothill, SLCY	1859	D6
Granger, WVCY	1962	E6
Greenville, LOGN	463	C5
Hardy, LNDN	2712	E6
Hunter, WVCY	1961	E6
Madsen, HYVL	586	B5
Park Terrace, SLkC	1966	D5
Peruvian Park, SLkC	2177	B6
Redwood, WVCY	1963	D4
Roper, SSLK	1964	B3
Sherwood Park, SLkC	2177	B5
Sugar House, SLCY	1965	A2
Wilson, WHVN	1114	D2

Transportation

FEATURE NAME	MAP#	GRID
Amtrak, SLCY	1858	A4
Greyhound-Ogden, OGDN	1115	D3
Greyhound-Salt Lake City, SLCY	1858	C3

Visitor Information

FEATURE NAME Address City ZIP Code	MAP#	GRID
Ogden Convention & Visitors Bureau 2501 Wall Av, OGDN, 84401	1115	D4
Salt Lake Convention & Visitors Bureau 90 S West Temple, SLCY, 84101	1858	C3
Utah Valley Convention & Visitors Bureau 111 S University Av, PRVO, 84606	2928	C7

CUT ALONG DOTTED LINE

RAND McNALLY

Thank you for purchasing this Rand McNally Street Guide! We value your comments and suggestions.

Please help us serve you better by completing this postage-paid reply card.
This information is for internal use ONLY and will not be distributed or sold to any external third party.

Missing pages? Maybe not... Please refer to the "Using Your Street Guide" page for further explanation.

Street Guide Title: Salt Lake City **ISBN# 0-528-85559-X** **Edition: 6th** **MKT: SLC**

Today's Date: ____________ Gender: ☐M ☐F Age Group: ☐18-24 ☐25-31 ☐32-40 ☐41-50 ☐51-64 ☐65+

1. What type of industry do you work in?
   ☐Real Estate ☐Trucking ☐Delivery ☐Construction ☐Utilities ☐Government
   ☐Retail ☐Sales ☐Transportation ☐Landscape ☐Service & Repair
   ☐Courier ☐Automotive ☐Insurance ☐Medical ☐Police/Fire/First Response
   ☐Other, please specify: ____________
2. What type of job do you have in this industry? ____________
3. Where did you purchase this Street Guide? (store name & city) ____________
4. Why did you purchase this Street Guide? ____________
5. How often do you purchase an updated Street Guide? ☐Annually ☐2 yrs. ☐3-5 yrs. ☐Other: ____________
6. Where do you use it? ☐Primarily in the car ☐Primarily in the office ☐Primarily at home ☐Other: ____________
7. How do you use it? ☐Exclusively for business ☐Primarily for business but also for personal or leisure use
   ☐Both work and personal evenly ☐Primarily for personal use ☐Exclusively for personal use
8. What do you use your Street Guide for?
   ☐Find Addresses ☐In-route navigation ☐Planning routes ☐Other: ____________
   Find points of interest: ☐Schools ☐Parks ☐Buildings ☐Shopping Centers ☐Other: ____________
9. How often do you use it? ☐Daily ☐Weekly ☐Monthly ☐Other: ____________
10. Do you use the internet for maps and/or directions? ☐Yes ☐No
11. How often do you use the internet for directions? ☐Daily ☐Weekly ☐Monthly ☐Other: ____________
12. Do you use any of the following mapping products in addition to your Street Guide?
    ☐Folded paper maps ☐Folded laminated maps ☐Wall maps ☐GPS ☐PDA ☐In-car navigation ☐Phone maps
13. What features, if any, would you like to see added to your Street Guide? ____________
14. What features or information do you find most useful in your Rand McNally Street Guide? (please specify)
15. Please provide any additional comments or suggestions you have. ____________

We strive to provide you with the most current updated information available if you know of a map correction, please notify us here.

Where is the correction? Map Page #: ________ Grid #: ________ Index Page #: ________

Nature of the correction: ☐Street name missing ☐Street name misspelled ☐Street information incorrect
☐Incorrect location for point of interest ☐Index error ☐Other: ____________

Detail: ____________

I would like to receive information about updated editions and special offers from Rand McNally
☐via e-mail E-mail address: ____________
☐via postal mail
Your Name: ____________ Company (if used for work): ____________
Address: ____________ City/State/ZIP: ____________

Thank you for your time and help. We are working to serve you better.
This information is for internal use ONLY and will not be distributed or sold to any external third party.

CUT ALONG DOTTED LINE

SG-noCD.06

TAPE SHUT

TAPE SHUT

get directions at
randmcnally.com

CUT ALONG DOTTED LINE

2ND FOLD LINE

NO POSTAGE
NECESSARY
IF MAILED
IN THE
UNITED STATES

BUSINESS REPLY MAIL

FIRST-CLASS MAIL PERMIT NO. 388 CHICAGO IL

POSTAGE WILL BE PAID BY ADDRESSEE

RAND MCNALLY
CONSUMER AFFAIRS
PO BOX 7600
CHICAGO IL 60680-9915

1ST FOLD LINE

The most trusted name on the map.

You'll never need to ask for directions again with these Rand McNally products!

- EasyFinder® Laminated Maps
- Folded Maps
- Street Guides
- Wall Maps
- CustomView Wall Maps
- Road Atlases
- Motor Carriers' Road Atlases

CUT ALONG DOTTED LINE

SGTG.06